INVITATION TO PSYCHOLOGY

Sixth Edition

Global Edition

Carole Wade

Dominican University of California

Carol Tavris

Maryanne Garry

Victoria University of Wellington

PEARSON

Boston   Columbus   Indianapolis   New York   San Francisco   Upper Saddle River
Amsterdam   Cape Town   Dubai   London   Madrid   Milan   Munich   Paris   Montréal   Toronto
Delhi   Mexico City   São Paulo   Sydney   Hong Kong   Seoul   Singapore   Taipei   Tokyo

Editor in Chief: *Dickson Musslewhite*
Executive Editor: *Erin Mitchell*
Editorial Assistant: *Sarah Henrich*
Director of Marketing: *Brandy Dawson*
Marketing Assistant: *Frank Alarcon*
Senior Managing Editor: *Linda Behrens*
Procurement Manager: *Mary Fischer*
Senior Procurement Specialist: *Diane Peirano*
Program Manager: *Judy Casillo*
Head of Learning Asset Acquisition, Global Edition: *Laura Dent*
Publishing Administrator and Business Analyst, Global Edition: *Shokhi Shah Khandelwal*

Acquisitions Editor, Global Edition: *Vrinda Malik*
Assitant Project Editor, Global Edition: *Sinjita Basu*
Creative Director: *Blair Brown*
Senior Art Director: *Kathryn Foot*
Media Production Manager: *Peggy Bliss*
Media Project Manager: *Pamela Weldin*
Digital Media Editor: *Lisa Dotson*
Full-Service Project Management: *Integra*
Cover Designer: *Lumina Datamatics*
Cover Photo: *Shutterstock/ Matt Gibson*

Pearson Education Limited
Edinburgh Gate
Harlow
Essex CM20 2JE
England

and Associated Companies throughout the world

Visit us on the World Wide Web at:
www.pearsonglobaleditions.com

© Pearson Education Limited 2015

ISBN 10: 1-292-05656-8
ISBN 13: 978-1-292-05656-2

British Library Cataloguing-in-Publication Data
A catalogue record for this book is available from the British Library

ARP impression 98

Typeset in 10/12 Janson Text LT Std by Integra.

Printed and Bound in Great Britain by Ashford Colour Press Ltd.

Contents at a Glance

About the Authors

Carole Wade earned her Ph.D. in cognitive psychology at Stanford University. She began her academic career at the University of New Mexico, where she taught courses in psycholinguistics and developed the first course at the university on the psychology of gender. She was professor of psychology for 10 years at San Diego Mesa College and then taught at College of Marin and Dominican University of California. Dr. Wade has written and lectured widely on critical thinking and the enhancement of psychology education. In addition to this text, she and Carol Tavris have written *Psychology*; *Psychology in Perspective*; and *The Longest War: Sex Differences in Perspective*.

Carol Tavris earned her Ph.D. in the interdisciplinary program in social psychology at the University of Michigan. Dr. Tavris writes and lectures extensively on diverse topics in psychological science and critical thinking. In addition to working with Carole Wade, she is coauthor with Elliot Aronson of *Mistakes Were Made (But Not by Me): Why We Justify Foolish Beliefs, Bad Decisions, and Hurtful Acts*. She is also author of *The Mismeasure of Woman* and *Anger: The Misunderstood Emotion*. Many of her book reviews and opinion essays have been collected in *Psychobabble and Biobunk: Using Psychology to Think Critically About Issues in the News*.

Maryanne Garry earned her Ph.D. at the University of Connecticut and did postdoctoral training at the University of Washington before moving to Victoria University of Wellington, New Zealand. She is best known for her research on the causes and consequences of false memories, including "imagination inflation" and its dangers as a therapeutic technique. She has served as director of the Innocence Project New Zealand and has acted as an expert witness in trials worldwide on the (un)reliability of human memory. Dr. Garry has received her university's Merit Awards for Excellence in Research and for Excellence in Teaching.

Contents

Preface

An Invitation to *Invitation to Psychology:* Themes and Goals

Invitation to Psychology, 6th Edition, by Carole Wade, Carol Tavris, and Maryanne Garry, shows students why scientific and critical thinking is so important in every aspect of their lives. In clear, lively, warm prose, this edition continues the book's pioneering integration of critical thinking, gender, culture, and ethnicity. By the end, readers will not only have learned the basic content, controversies, and perspectives across many fields of psychology, but they also will have learned how to interpret studies they encounter in the news and on the Internet and how to address and resolve debates about personal, social, and political issues. They will know how to think like a psychologist.

The sixth edition welcomes the addition of Maryanne Garry, professor of psychology at Victoria University of Wellington, New Zealand. Dr. Garry is an internationally recognized expert in the fields of memory, cognition, and learning, and her expertise has enhanced the book's pedagogical focus. This edition introduces the **read-recite-review (3R)** approach, which is grounded in empirical research demonstrating its benefits for learning and memory. In contrast to the usual "read and cram before tests" approach that students often rely on, this method requires students to read a section; close the book and actually recite *out loud* as much as they can about the terms and concepts they have just learned; and then go back, reread, and review that section to make sure they understood it correctly. Students learn about the 3R approach in Chapter 1, along with other important strategies for study that can improve their understanding of what they read and their performance on quizzes and exams.

As always, in every chapter the research has been updated to reflect progress in the field and important new discoveries. Here are just a few highlights:

- The latest findings from the exciting field of epigenetics.
- New findings on how activation of the amygdala is affected by a person's psychological state and core personality traits.
- Evidence that adolescents are more likely than children and adults to be "night owls," which is why school schedules can be hard on them.
- New findings on the consolidation of memories during sleep.
- New research on the drawbacks of multitasking.
- Recent meta-analyses showing that four early interventions can boost IQ scores.

- Important research showing that episodic memories have a "time-travel" function, enabling people to imagine future experiences.
- Real-life research on the consequences of offering students cash rewards for achievement.
- New methods of measuring implicit prejudice, including measures of "microaggressions" (the small insults that members of minority or stigmatized groups endure).
- An updated discussion of gender identity, transgendered and transsexual individuals and intersex conditions, including longitudinal studies of young children who feel they are "the wrong sex."
- A full revision of Chapter 11 (Psychological Disorders) to reflect changes in diagnoses and controversies raised by the *DSM-5*.

Activities and Supplements to Aid Teaching and Learning

As valuable as a good textbook is, it is but one element of a comprehensive learning package. Pearson has made every effort to provide high-quality instructor and student supplements that will save you preparation time and add to the classroom experience.

Supplements for Instructors

The Instructor's Resource Center (**www.pearsonglobal editions.com/Wade**) provides information and the following downloadable supplements:

Test Bank: This test bank, prepared by Alan Swinkels, St. Edward's University, contains more than 3,000 multiple-choice, true/false, matching, short-answer, and essay questions, each referenced to the relevant page in the textbook. An additional feature is the inclusion of *rationales for the conceptual and applied multiple-choice questions*. The rationales help instructors to evaluate the questions they are choosing for their tests and give instructors the option to use the rationales as an answer key

A Total Assessment Guide chapter overview makes creating tests easier by listing all of the test items in an easy-to-reference grid. All multiple-choice questions are categorized as factual, conceptual, or applied; they are correlated to each of the chapter's **learning objectives** and to the new **American Psychological Association Guidelines learning outcomes**. The Test Bank can be downloaded from the Instructor's Resource Center at www.pearsonglobaleditions.com/Wade.

Instructor's Resource Manual, prepared by Alan Swinkels, St. Edward's University, includes a detailed Chapter Lecture Outline, learning objectives for each chapter, chapter summary, and direct links to the instructor resources in *Multimedia Library*. The instructor's manual is available for download from the Instructor's Resource Center at www.pearsonglobaleditions.com/Wade.

Online Options for Instructors and Students

MyPsychLab® for *Invitation to Psychology*, 6th Edition, delivers proven results in helping students succeed, provides engaging experiences that personalize learning, and comes from a trusted partner with educational expertise and a deep commitment to helping students and instructors achieve their goals. MyPsychLab's wealth of instructor and student resources includes the following:

- **MyPsychLab Video Series is a** comprehensive, cutting-edge set of more than 100 original video clips covering the most recent research, science, and applications across the general psychology curriculum, many using the latest film and animation technology. Each 4- to 6-minute video clip has automatically graded assessment questions tied to it.
- **Writing Space** helps students master concepts and develop critical thinking through writing. Writing Space provides a single place within MyPsychLab to create and track writing assignments, access writing resources, and exchange meaningful personalized feedback quickly and easily. Instructors will appreciate the fact that Writing Space has integrated access to Turnitin, the global leader in preventing plagiarism.
- **MyPsychLab Simulations** allow students to participate in online simulations of classic psychology experiments and research-based inventories, thereby reinforcing what they are learning in class and in their book.
- **An audio version** of the textbook increases accessibility of the textbook.
- **A personalized study plan** for each student, to promote better critical thinking skills and help students succeed in the course and beyond.
- **Assessment tied to videos, applications, and the material in every chapter** enables instructors and students to track progress and get immediate feedback. With results feeding into a powerful grade book, the assessment program helps instructors identify student challenges early and find the best resources with which to help them.
- **An assignment calendar** allows instructors to assign graded activities with specific deadlines and measure student progress.

CourseSmart* Textbooks Online is an exciting new option for students looking to save money. Students can subscribe to the same content online and save up to 50 percent off the suggested list price of the print text. The students can search the text, make notes online, print out reading assignments that incorporate lecture notes, and bookmark important passages for later review. For information, or to subscribe to the CourseSmart eTextbook, visit www.coursesmart.co.uk.

For technical support for any of your Pearson products, you and your students can contact http://247.pearsoned .com.

Acknowledgments from the Authors

Like any other cooperative effort, writing a book requires a support team. We are indebted to the following reviewers for their many insightful and substantive suggestions during the development of the new editions of *Psychology* and *Invitation to Psychology* and for their work on supplements.

Pam Ansburg, Metropolitan State College of Denver
Joy Berrenberg, University of Colorado, Denver
Larry Cahill, University of California, Irvine
David Calhoun, Columbia College
Eve Clark, Stanford University
Paul Chance, Tokyo, Japan
Anne Coglianese, Ivy Tech Community College
Katherine Demitrakis, Central New Mexico Community College
William Domhoff, University of California, Santa Cruz
Michael Domjan, University of Texas
Kari Dudley, University of New Hampshire
Bart Ellenbroek, Victoria University of Wellington
Phoebe Ellsworth, University of Michigan
Kathleen Gerbasi, Niagara County Community College
Susan Gray, Barry University
Gina Grimshaw, Victoria University of Wellington
David Harper, Victoria University of Wellington
David Healy, Cardiff University
Diana Hingson, Florida Gateway College
Sheneice Hughes, Eastfield Community College
Fiona Jack, University of Otago
Lisa Jackson, Schoolcraft College
William Kimberlin, Lorain County Community College
Irving Kirsch, University of Plymouth
    and Harvard Medical School
Jennifer Lee, Cabrillo College
Geoff Loftus, University of Washington

---

*This product may not be available in all markets. For more details, please visit www.coursesmart.co.uk or contact your local Pearson representative.

Martha Low, Winston-Salem State University
Steven Jay Lynn, Binghamton University
Dorothy Marsil, Kennesaw State University
David McAllister, Salem State University
Kasey Melvin, Craven Community College
Diana Milillo, Nassau Community College
Bradley Mitchell, Ivy Tech State College
Robert Plomin, Institute of Psychiatry,
  King's College, London
Devon Polaschek, Victoria University of Wellington
Mark Rittman, Cuyahoga Community College
Susan Schenk, Victoria University of Wellington
Suzanne Schultz, Umpqua Community College
Lori Sheppard, Winston-Salem State University
Alan Swinkels, St. Edward's University
Nancy Voorhees, Ivy Tech Community College
David Waxler, Temple University
Eric Weiser, Curry College
Christine Williams, Salem State University
Rachel Zajac, University of Otago

We also thank the dozens of other reviewers, too numerous to list here, who have served as expert reviewers for content and pedagogy on previous editions.

We are indebted to the members of our superb editorial and production teams at Pearson, who have unfailingly come through for us on every edition of this complex project. Our thanks to Jessica Mosher, who was our Editor-in-Chief for many editions, Executive Editor Erin Mitchell, Project Manager Joan Foley, for keeping the project (and us) on track, and Program Manager Judy Casillo, who, as she has done so brilliantly on previous editions, supervised every detail of the revision from start to finish. We are grateful to Executive Marketing Manager Brandy Dawson for her marketing contributions.

Our special thanks go to the excellent production team at Integra compositors, especially production manager Angel Chavez, who supervised copyediting, production, and layout with exceptional efficiency and patience. Our thanks also to Ilze Lemesis for the warm, clean text design. Maryanne Garry also wishes to thank Jeff Foster and Eryn Newman for their research assistance and her graduate students for their many helpful ideas.

We have always loved learning about psychological discoveries and introducing them to students. We hope you will enjoy reading and using this book as much as we have enjoyed writing it.

Carole Wade
Carol Tavris
Maryanne Garry

Pearson wishes to thank and acknowledge the following people for their work on the Global Edition:

Contributor:

Jayanti Banerjee
The Mother's International School, New Delhi

Reviewers:

Dr. Chun-Hsien Kuo
Department of Psychology, Asia University, Taiwan

Dr. Jase Moussa-Inaty
Educational Psychologist and Professor, Zayed University, United Arab Emirates

Dr. S. Jeyavel
School of Social and Behavioural Sciences, Central University of Karnataka

LEARNING OUTCOMES AND ASSESSMENT

GOALS AND STANDARDS

In recent years many psychology departments have been focusing on core competencies and how methods of assessment can better enhance students' learning. In response to this need, in 2008, the American Psychological Association (APA) established ten recommended goals for the undergraduate psychology major. These guidelines were revised in 2013 and currently consist of five goals. Specific learning outcomes have been established for each goal and suggestions are provided on how best to tie assessment practices to these goals. In writing this text, we have used the APA goals and assessment recommendations as guidelines for structuring content and integrating the teaching and homework materials. For details on the APA learning goals and assessment guidelines, please see www.apa.org/.

Based on APA recommendations, each chapter is structured around detailed learning objectives. All of the instructor and student resources are also organized around these objectives, making the text and resources a fully integrated system of study. The flexibility of these resources allows instructors to choose which learning objectives are important in their courses as well as which content they want their students to focus on.

APA UNDERGRADUATE GOALS AND OUTCOMES	WADE CONTENT

GOAL 1. KNOWLEDGE BASE IN PSYCHOLOGY

Demonstrate fundamental knowledge and comprehension of the major concepts, theoretical perspectives, historical trends, and empirical findings to discuss how psychological principles apply to behavioral problems.	
1.1 Describe key concepts, principles, and overarching themes in psychology 1.2 Develop a working knowledge of psychology's content domains 1.3 Describe applications that employ discipline-based problem solving	**Ch 1:** 1.1–1.5 and Taking Psychology With You: Lying with Statistics **Ch 2:** 2.1–2.14, 2.17–2.19 and Taking Psychology With You: How to Avoid the "Barnum Effect" **Ch 3:** 3.1–3.18 and Taking Psychology With You: Bringing Up Baby **Ch 4:** 4.1–4.16 and Taking Psychology With You: Cosmetic Neurology–Tinkering With the Brain **Ch 5:** 5.1–5.13 and Taking Psychology With You: How to Get a Good Night's Sleep **Ch 6:** 6.1–6.28 and Taking Psychology With You: Can Perception be "Extrasensory"? **Ch 7:** 7.1–7.21 and Taking Psychology With You: Becoming More Creative **Ch 8:** 8.1–8.21 and Taking Psychology With You: This Is Your Life **Ch 9:** 9.1–9.16 and Taking Psychology With You: Does Media Violence Make You Violent? **Ch 10:** 10.1–10.18 and Taking Psychology With You: Dealing With Cultural Differences **Ch 11:** 11.1–11.19 and Taking Psychology With You: When a Friend Is Suicidal **Ch 12:** 12.1–12.12 and Taking Psychology With You: Becoming a Smart Consumer of Psychological Treatments

APA UNDERGRADUATE GOALS AND OUTCOMES	WADE CONTENT

GOAL 1. KNOWLEDGE BASE IN PSYCHOLOGY *continued*

	Ch 13: 13.1–13.18 and Taking Psychology With You: The Dilemma of Anger: "Let It Out" or "Bottle It Up"?
	Ch 14: 14.1–14.15 and Taking Psychology With You: How to Attain Your Goals
	Appendix: Statistical Methods
	Major concepts are reinforced with learning tools: Writing Space, Experiment Simulations, MyPsychLab Video Series, Operation ARA, Visual Brain, and instructor's teaching and assessment package.

GOAL 2. SCIENTIFIC INQUIRY AND CRITICAL THINKING

Demonstrate scientific reasoning and problem solving, including effective research methods.	
2.1 Use scientific reasoning to interpret psychological phenomena 2.2 Demonstrate psychology information literacy 2.3 Engage in innovative and integrative thinking and problem solving 2.4 Interpret, design, and conduct basic psychological research 2.5 Incorporate sociocultural factors in scientific inquiry	**Ch 1:** 1.8–1.20 and Taking Psychology With You: Lying With Statistics **Ch 2:** 2.1–2.14, 2.17–2.19 and Taking Psychology With You: How to Avoid the "Barnum Effect" **Ch 3:** 3.1–3.18 and Taking Psychology With You: Bringing Up Baby **Ch 4:** 4.1–4.16 and Taking Psychology With You: Cosmetic Neurology–Tinkering With the Brain **Ch 5:** 5.1–5.11, 5.13 and Taking Psychology With You: How to Get a Good Night's Sleep **Ch 6:** 6.1–6.28 and Taking Psychology With You: Can Perception be "Extrasensory"? **Ch 7:** 7.1–7.21 and Taking Psychology With You: Becoming More Creative **Ch 8:** 8.1–8.21 and Taking Psychology With You: This Is Your Life **Ch 9:** 9.1–9.16 and Taking Psychology With You: Does Media Violence Make You Violent? **Ch 10:** 10.1–10.18 and Taking Psychology With You: Dealing With Cultural Differences **Ch 11:** 11.1–11.19 and Taking Psychology With You: When a Friend Is Suicidal **Ch 12:** 12.1–12.12 and Taking Psychology With You: Becoming a Smart Consumer of Psychological Treatments **Ch 13:** 13.1–13.18 and Taking Psychology With You: The Dilemma of Anger: "Let It Out" or "Bottle It Up"? **Ch 14:** 14.1–14.15 and Taking Psychology With You: How to Attain Your Goals **Appendix:** Statistical Methods
	Scientific methods are reinforced with learning tools: Writing Space, Experiment Simulations, MyPsychLab Video Series, Operation ARA, Visual Brain, and instructor's teaching and assessment package.

APA UNDERGRADUATE GOALS AND OUTCOMES	WADE CONTENT

GOAL 3. ETHICAL AND SOCIAL RESPONSIBILITY

Develop ethically and socially responsible behaviors for professional and personal settings.	
3.1 Apply ethical standards to psychological science and practice **3.2** Build and enhance interpersonal relationships **3.3** Adopt values that build community at local, national, and global levels	**Ch 2:** 2.16, 2.17 **Ch 3:** 3.8, 3.19 **Ch 4:** 4.16 **Ch 8:** 8.4, 8.19 **Ch 10:** 10.14-10.18 and The Many Targets of Prejudice **Ch 11:** 11.2 **Ch 12:** 12.12 **Ch 13:** 13.7,13.8 **Ch 14:** 14.6, 14.10, 14.11
	Ethics and values are reinforced with learning tools: Writing Space, Experiment Simulations, MyPsychLab Video Series, Operation ARA, Visual Brain, and instructor's teaching and assessment package.

GOAL 4. COMMUNICATION

Demonstrate competence in written, in oral, and in interpersonal communication skills.	
4.1 Demonstrate effective writing in multiple formats **4.2** Exhibit effective presentation skills in multiple formats **4.3** Interact effectively with others	**Ch 2:** 2.15, 2.16 **Ch 10:** 10.5, 10.8, 10.14-10.18 and Taking Psychology With You: Dealing With Cultural Differences **Ch 11:** 11.2 **Ch 13:** 13.7,13.8 **Ch 14:** 14.10-14.12, 14.14
	Communication skills are reinforced with learning tools: Writing Space, Experiment Simulations, MyPsychLab Video Series, Operation ARA, Visual Brain, and instructor's teaching and assessment package.

APA UNDERGRADUATE GOALS AND OUTCOMES	WADE CONTENT

GOAL 5. PROFESSIONAL DEVELOPMENT

Develop abilities that sharpen readiness for employment, graduate school, or professional school.	
5.1 Apply psychological content and skills to career goals **5.2** Exhibit self-efficacy and self-regulation **5.3** Refine project management skills **5.4** Enhance teamwork capacity **5.5** Develop meaningful professional direction for life after graduation	**Ch 1:** 1.6, 1.7 **Ch 2:** 2.15, 2.16 **Ch 10:** 10.5, 10.8, 10.14-10.18 and Taking Psychology With You: Dealing With Cultural Differences **Ch 11:** 11.2 **Ch 13:** 13.7, 13.8 **Ch 14:** 14.11-14.14 and Taking Psychology With You: How to Attain Your Goals
	Professional development is reinforced with learning tools: Writing Space, Experiment Simulations, MyPsychLab Video Series, Operation ARA, Visual Brain, and instructor's teaching and assessment package.

EXPLORING PSYCHOLOGY

PSYCHOLOGY IN THE NEWS ///////////////////////////

Zaniness on Parade in Pasadena

PASADENA, CA, April 27, 2013. The 37th Occasional Pasadena Doo Dah Parade, a joyful celebration of wacky weirdness, took place today to the cheers of fans lining the streets. Known as "the other parade" (the more famous one being Pasadena's Rose Parade on January 1), the event encourages marchers to shed their inhibitions and dress as outrageously as they please. The parade's favorites have included the Men of Leisure Synchronized Nap Team, Tequila Mockingbird & the Royal Doo Dah Orchestra, the BBQ & Hibachi Marching Grill Team, and the Clown Doctors from Outer Space.

Devils or dragons: Anything goes at the Doo Dah Parade.

City's Weight Loss Campaign the "Biggest Loser"

BOSTON, January 23, 2013. It seemed like a great idea last April, when the city of Boston challenged residents to collectively shed a million pounds of excess weight in a year, and offered free exercise classes to help them work off their potbellies and love handles. But with only a few months left in the battle of the bulge, the results have been disappointing: a collective loss of only 74,597 pounds. Ironically, the same week that City Hall kicked off its exercise classes, it hosted the annual "Scooper Bowl," the nation's largest all-you-can-eat ice-cream contest. "A little mixed messaging," concedes a spokesman for the Boston Public Health Commission.

Armstrong Admits Doping, Past Lies

NEW YORK, January 18, 2013. In a much-anticipated interview with Oprah Winfrey, former bicycling champion Lance Armstrong has confessed to taking performance-enhancing drugs and lying repeatedly about it to colleagues and fans for many years. Since the scandal broke, he has seen his seven Tour de France titles taken away and has been banned from the sport. "I will spend the rest of my life trying to earn back trust and apologize to people," he told Oprah. But he also said that the doping had been necessary to level the playing field, "like [putting] air in my tires."

In an interview with Oprah Winfrey, former cyclist Lance Armstrong admitted for the first time that he had used banned substances to enhance his performance.

Court Finds No Evidence Linking Vaccine to Autism

WASHINGTON, DC, March 13, 2010. A special federal court, headed by judges called "special masters," has sustained an earlier court ruling against three sets of parents who blamed their children's autism on the MMR vaccine. Administered by injection, this vaccine inoculates children against measles, mumps, and rubella (German measles).

For years, many parents of children with autism have argued that the vaccines trigger the devastating condition, but one of the special masters said that the evidence for this claim is "weak, contradictory, and unpersuasive." Nonetheless, some autism advocacy groups expressed disappointment and said that they still believe a link exists.

Israel-Gaza Cease-fire after Eight Days of War

GAZA, November 21, 2012. Israel and the Gaza-based group Hamas have agreed to a cease-fire after more than a week of fierce fighting involving heavy bombardment by both sides. The violence has caused the deaths of 150 civilians and wounded hundreds of others, most of them Palestinians. The conflict is the latest in ongoing hostilities between the two enemies. In 2008 and 2009, at least 1,400 men, women, and children were killed when Israeli troops invaded Gaza in response to rocket attacks being launched from the Palestinian territory into civilian areas in Israel.

//////////

Every day, the news brings tales of violence and heroism, scandals in sports and politics, triumphs and failures, joyful playfulness and savage terror, human creativity and human folly. What on earth do these stories have to do with psychology?

The answer is simple: Everything.

People usually associate psychology with mental and emotional disorders, personal problems, and psychotherapy. But psychologists take as their subject the entire spectrum of beautiful and brutish things that human beings do—the kinds of things you read and hear about every day. They want to know why some people, like the jovial marchers in the Doo Dah Parade, are extroverts, whereas others prefer to blend in quietly. They investigate the causes of rising obesity rates, and why most diets fail. They ask why some people cheat and lie in the pursuit of success, and how those who do so rationalize their dishonesty to themselves and others. They explore the reasons that nations and ethnic groups so often see the world in terms of "us versus them" and resort to armed conflict to settle their differences. They ask why some parents of autistic children, when given the good news from scientific research that they don't need to beat themselves up for having had their children vaccinated, react with anger rather than relief.

In this book, we will be discussing the psychological issues raised by these opening stories and many others in the news. But psychology is not only about behavior that is

psychology The discipline concerned with behavior and mental processes and how they are affected by an organism's physical state, mental state, and external environment; the term is often represented by ψ, the Greek letter psi (usually pronounced *sy*).

empirical Relying on or derived from observation, experimentation, or measurement.

newsworthy. Psychologists are also interested in how ordinary human beings learn, remember, solve problems, perceive, feel, and get along or fail to get along with friends and family members. They are therefore as likely to study commonplace experiences—rearing children, gossiping, remembering a shopping list, daydreaming, making love, and making a living—as exceptional ones.

If you have ever wondered what makes people tick, or if you want to gain some insight into your own behavior, then you are in the right course. We invite you now to step into the world of psychology, the discipline that dares to explore the most complex topic on earth: you.

You are about to learn . . .

- how "psychobabble" differs from serious psychology.
- what's wrong with psychologists' nonscientific competitors, such as astrologers and psychics.
- the lesson to be learned from phrenology.
- how and when psychology became a formal discipline.
- three early schools of psychology.
- the four major perspectives in modern psychology.

The Science of Psychology

Psychology can be defined generally as *the discipline concerned with behavior and mental processes and how they are affected by an organism's physical state, mental state, and external environment.* This definition, however, is like defining a car as a vehicle for transporting people without explaining how a car differs from a train or a bus, or how a Ford differs from a Ferrari. To get a clear picture of this field, you need to know about its methods, its findings, and its ways of interpreting information.

Explore the *Concept* Do You Know About Psychology? at *MyPsychLab*

Psychology, Pseudoscience, and Common Sense LO 1.1

Let's begin by considering what psychology is *not*. First, the psychology that you are about to study bears little relation to the popular psychology ("pop psych") often found in self-help books or on talk shows. In recent decades, the public's appetite for psychological information has created a huge market for "psychobabble": pseudoscience and quackery covered by a veneer of psychological language. Pseudoscience (*pseudo* means "false") promises quick fixes to life's problems, such as resolving your unhappiness as an adult by "reliving" the supposed trauma of your birth, or becoming more creative on the job by "reprogramming" your brain. Serious psychology is more complex, more informative, and, we think, far more helpful than psychobabble because it is based on rigorous research and **empirical** evidence—evidence gathered by careful observation, experimentation, or measurement.

Second, serious psychology differs radically from such nonscientific competitors as graphology, fortune-telling, numerology, and astrology. Like psychologists, promoters of these systems try to explain people's problems and predict their behavior. If you are having romantic problems, an astrologer may advise you to choose an Aries instead of an Aquarius as your next love, and a "past-lives channeler" may say it's because you were jilted in a former life. Yet whenever the predictions of psychics, astrologers, and the like are put to the test, they turn out to be so vague as to be meaningless (for example, "Spirituality will increase next year") or just plain wrong (Shaffer & Jadwiszczok, 2010). One well-known "psychic to the stars" predicted that in 2012, a giant earthquake would destroy most of Mexico City, Ellen deGeneres would join the army for a week, and an airplane would crash into the White House. Wrong on all counts! Moreover, contrary to what you might think from watching TV shows or going to psychic websites, no psychic has ever found a missing child, identified a serial killer, or helped police solve any other crime by using "psychic powers" (Radford, 2011). Their "help" merely adds to the heartbreak felt by the victim's family.

Third, psychology is not just another name for common sense. Often, psychological research produces findings that directly contradict prevailing beliefs, and throughout this book you will be discovering many of them. Are unhappy memories repressed and then accurately recalled years later, as if they had been recorded in perfect detail in the brain? Do most women suffer from emotional mood swings due to premenstrual syndrome? Do policies of abstinence from alcohol reduce rates of alcoholism? If you play Beethoven to your infant, will your child become smarter? Can hypnosis help you accurately remember your third birthday or allow you to perform feats that would otherwise be impossible? These beliefs are widely held, but as you will learn, they are wrong.

"According to an article in the upcoming issue of 'The New England Journal of Medicine,' all your fears are well founded."

Psychological findings do not have to be surprising or counterintuitive, however, to be important. Sometimes they validate common beliefs and explain or extend them. Like scientists in other fields, psychological researchers strive not only to discover new phenomena and correct mistaken ideas, but also to deepen our understanding of an already familiar world—by identifying the varieties of love, the origins of aggression, or the reasons that a great song can lift our hearts.

 Watch the **Video** The Big Picture: How to Answer Psychological Questions at **MyPsychLab**

The Birth of Modern Psychology
LO 1.2, LO 1.3

Many of the great thinkers of history, from Aristotle to Zoroaster, raised questions that today would be called psychological. They wanted to know how people take in information through their senses, use information to solve problems, and become motivated to act in brave or villainous ways. They wondered about the elusive nature of emotion, and whether it controls us or is something we can control. Like today's psychologists, they wanted to *describe*, *predict*, *understand*, and *modify* behavior to add to human knowledge and increase human happiness. But unlike modern psychologists, scholars of the past did not rely heavily on empirical evidence. Often, their observations were based simply on anecdotes or descriptions of individual cases.

This does not mean that psychology's forerunners were always wrong. Hippocrates (c. 460 B.C.– c. 377 B.C.), the Greek physician known as the founder of modern medicine, observed patients with head injuries and inferred that the brain must be the ultimate source of "our pleasures, joys,

laughter, and jests as well as our sorrows, pains, griefs, and tears." And so it is. In the seventeenth century, the English philosopher John Locke (1643–1704) argued that the mind works by associating ideas arising from experience, and this notion continues to influence many psychologists today.

But without empirical methods, the forerunners of psychology also committed terrible blunders. One was the theory of **phrenology** (Greek for "study of the mind"), which became wildly popular in Europe and the United States in the early 1800s. Phrenologists argued that different brain areas accounted for specific character and personality traits, such as stinginess and religiosity, and that such traits could be read from bumps on the skull. Thieves, for example, supposedly had large bumps above the ears. So how to account for people who had these "stealing bumps" but who were not thieves? Phrenologists explained away this counterevidence by saying that the person's thieving impulses were being held in check by *other* bumps representing positive traits. In the United States, parents, teachers, and employers flocked to phrenologists for advice and self-improvement (Benjamin, 1998). But phrenology was a classic pseudoscience—sheer nonsense.

At about the time that phrenology was peaking in popularity, several pioneering men and women

phrenology The now-discredited theory that different brain areas account for specific character and personality traits, which can be "read" from bumps on the skull.

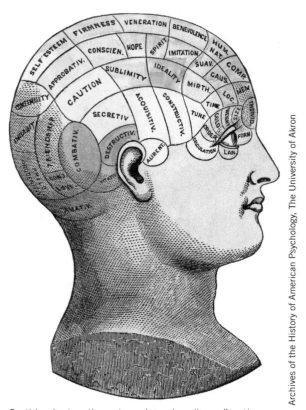

On this nineteenth-century phrenology "map," notice the tiny space allocated to self-esteem and the large one devoted to cautiousness!

functionalism An early psychological approach that emphasized the function or purpose of behavior and consciousness.

psychoanalysis A theory of personality and a method of psychotherapy, originally formulated by Sigmund Freud, that emphasizes unconscious motives and conflicts.

biological perspective A psychological approach that emphasizes bodily events and changes associated with actions, feelings, and thoughts.

evolutionary psychology A field of psychology emphasizing evolutionary mechanisms that may help explain human commonalities in cognition, development, emotion, social practices, and other areas of behavior.

learning perspective A psychological approach that emphasizes how the environment and experience affect a person's or animal's actions; it includes behaviorism and social-cognitive learning theories.

in Europe and the United States were starting to study psychological issues using scientific methods. In 1879, Wilhelm Wundt (VIL-helm Voont) officially established the first psychological laboratory in Leipzig, Germany. Wundt (1832–1920), who was trained in medicine and philosophy, promoted a method called *trained introspection*, in which volunteers were taught to carefully observe, analyze, and describe their own sensations, mental images, and emotional reactions. Wundt's introspectors might take as long as 20 minutes to report their inner experiences during a 1.5-second experiment. The goal was to break down behavior into its most basic elements, much as a chemist might analyze water into hydrogen plus oxygen. Most psychologists eventually rejected trained introspection as too subjective, but Wundt is still usually credited for formally initiating the movement to make psychology a science.

Another early approach to scientific psychology, called **functionalism**, emphasized the function or purpose of behavior, as opposed to its analysis and description. One of its leaders was William James (1842–1910), an American philosopher, physician, and psychologist. Attempting to grasp the nature of the mind through introspection, wrote James (1890/1950), is "like seizing a spinning top to catch its motion, or trying to turn up the gas quickly enough to see how the darkness looks." Inspired in part by the evolutionary theories of British naturalist Charles Darwin (1809–1882), James and other functionalists instead asked how various actions help a person or animal adapt to the environment. This emphasis on the causes and consequences of behavior was to set the course of psychological science.

The nineteenth century also saw the development of psychological therapies. The one that would have the greatest impact for much of the twentieth century had roots in Vienna, Austria. While researchers were at work in their laboratories, struggling to establish psychology as a science, Sigmund Freud (1856–1939), an obscure physician, was in his office listening to his patients' reports of depression, nervousness, and obsessive habits. Freud became convinced that many of these symptoms had mental, not bodily, causes. His patients' distress, he concluded, stemmed from childhood conflicts and traumas that were too threatening to be remembered consciously, such as forbidden sexual feelings for a parent. Freud's ideas eventually evolved into a broad theory of personality, and both his theory and his method of treating people with emotional problems became known as **psychoanalysis**. Today, the majority of empirically oriented psychologists reject most Freudian

concepts, but some schools of psychotherapy still draw on psychoanalytic ideas.

From its early beginnings in philosophy, natural science, and medicine, psychology eventually grew into a complex discipline encompassing many specialties, perspectives, and methods. Today the field is like a large, sprawling family. The members of this family have common great-grandparents, and many of the cousins have formed alliances, but some are quarreling and a few are barely speaking to one another.

Psychology's Present LO 1.4

Today's psychological scientists typically approach their work from one of four different but overlapping theoretical perspectives: biological, learning, cognitive, or sociocultural. These perspectives reflect different questions about human behavior, different assumptions about how the mind works, and most important, different ways of explaining why people do what they do.

1 The **biological perspective** focuses on how bodily events affect behavior, feelings, and thoughts. Electrical impulses shoot along the intricate pathways of the nervous system. Hormones course through the bloodstream, telling internal organs to slow down or speed up. Chemical substances flow across the tiny gaps that separate one microscopic brain cell from another. Psychologists who take a biological perspective study how these physical events interact with events in the external environment to produce perceptions, memories, emotions, and vulnerability to mental disorder. They also investigate the contribution of genes and other biological factors to the development of abilities and personality traits. One popular specialty, **evolutionary psychology**, follows in the footsteps of functionalism by focusing on how genetically influenced behavior that was functional or adaptive during our evolutionary past may be reflected in many of our present behaviors, mental processes, and traits. The message of the biological approach is that we cannot really know ourselves if we do not know our bodies.

> 👁 **Watch** the **Video** Thinking Like a Psychologist: Evolutionary Psychology at **MyPsychLab**

2 The **learning perspective** is concerned with how the environment and experience affect a person's (or a nonhuman animal's) actions. Within this perspective, *behaviorists* focus on the environmental rewards and punishers that maintain or discourage specific behaviors. Behaviorists do not invoke the mind to explain behavior; they prefer to stick to what they can observe and measure

Psychologists study many puzzles of human behavior. What could motivate ordinary individuals to torture and humiliate prisoners, as soldiers did at the notorious Abu Ghraib prison in Iraq? Why do other people bravely come to the aid of their fellow human beings, even when it's not their official duty? How do some people become champion athletes despite having physical disabilities? What causes someone to become anorexic, willing even to starve to death? Psychologists approach these and other questions from four major perspectives: biological, learning, cognitive, and sociocultural.

directly: acts and events taking place in the environment. Do you have trouble sticking to a schedule for studying? A behaviorist would analyze the environmental factors that might account for this common problem, such as the pleasure you get from hanging out with your friends instead of hitting the books. *Social-cognitive learning theorists* combine elements of behaviorism with research on thoughts, values, and intentions. They believe that people learn not only by adapting their behavior to the environment, but also by imitating others and by thinking about the events happening around them.

3 The **cognitive perspective** emphasizes what goes on in people's heads—how people reason, remember, understand language, solve problems, explain experiences, acquire moral standards, and form beliefs. (The word *cognitive* comes from the Latin for "to know.") Using clever methods to infer mental processes from observable behavior, cognitive researchers have been able to study phenomena that were once only the stuff of speculation, such as emotions, motivations, insight, and the kind of "thinking" that goes on without awareness. They are designing computer programs that model how humans perform complex tasks, discovering what goes on in the mind of an infant, and identifying types

of intelligence not measured by conventional IQ tests. The cognitive approach is one of the strongest forces in psychology and has inspired an explosion of research on the intricate workings of the mind.

4 The **sociocultural perspective** focuses on social and cultural forces outside the individual, forces that shape every aspect of behavior, from how we kiss to what and where we eat. Most of us underestimate the impact of other people, the social context, and cultural rules on nearly everything we do: how we perceive the world, express joy or grief, manage our households, and treat our friends and enemies. We are like fish that are unaware they live in water, so obvious is water in their lives. Sociocultural psychologists study the water—the social and cultural environments that people "swim" in every day. Because human beings are social animals who are profoundly affected by their different cultural worlds, the sociocultural perspective has made psychology a more representative and rigorous discipline.

Of course, not all psychologists feel they must swear allegiance to one approach or another; many draw on what they take to be the best features of diverse schools of thought. In addition, many psychologists have been affected

cognitive perspective
A psychological approach that emphasizes mental processes in perception, memory, language, problem solving, and other areas of behavior.

sociocultural perspective A psychological approach that emphasizes social and cultural influences on behavior.

by social movements and intellectual trends, such as humanism and feminism, that do not fit neatly into any of the major perspectives or that cut across all of them. Moreover, despite the diversity of psychological approaches, most psychological scientists agree on basic guidelines about what is and what is not acceptable in their discipline. Nearly all reject supernatural explanations of events—evil spirits, psychic forces, miracles, and so forth. Most believe in the importance of gathering empirical evidence and not relying on hunches or personal belief. This insistence on rigorous standards of proof is what sets psychology apart from nonscientific explanations of human experience.

👁 **Watch** the **Video** The Basics: Diverse Perspectives at **MyPsychLab**

Using Psychology to Study Psychology

We are coming up on a practice quiz. But please don't take it yet! First we want to share four winning strategies that can help you master the material in this book (and any other courses you may be taking). These strategies have been proven to work in scientific laboratories and in schools from junior high to the university level (Dunlosky et al., 2013; McDaniel, Roediger, & McDermott, 2007; Roediger, Putnam, & Smith, 2011).

Strategy #1: Use the 3R technique: Read, Recite, Review. Many students think it's enough to read the textbook and their notes and then read them again, but usually that won't do it (Karpicke, Butler, & Roediger, 2009). What's essential is to test yourself on what you've studied: asking yourself questions, retrieving the answers, going back and restudying what you didn't know—again and again until you learn the material. To help you get in the 3R habit, we will begin each quiz with a reminder to *recite aloud* what you recall about the major concepts in the section you just finished reading. You may feel foolish at first, but it really works. You can recite to yourself, a friend, or your cat, or into your cell phone. Then we will ask you to review the prior section to correct anything you got wrong or find out what you overlooked. After you do that, you can go on to the regular quiz questions.

Strategy #2: Dig Deep. The mind is not a bin or a sponge; you can't just pour information into it and assume it will stay there. Instead, you have to *process* it until you get it. An excellent way to do this is to connect new information to information you already know. These associations will organize the information in your memory, creating new mental pathways that will help you retrieve the material later. For instance, you just read about the four basic perspectives in psychological science. Taking each one, you could think of examples you have read about or that apply to your own life: "Many of my friends take medication to manage their depression or anxiety; that would follow from the biological perspective's approach."

Strategy #3: Once you learn it, don't ignore it. You might be tempted to skip the parts of a chapter that you feel sure you know. Resist that temptation. Instead, take advantage of a powerful research finding: Students who retest themselves by recalling information they could remember previously do twice as well on exams as students who skipped retesting themselves on familiar material (Karpicke & Roediger, 2007).

Strategy #4: Forget about cramming. Like many students, you may believe that studying for exams means staying up all night, guzzling coffee or other stimulants, and rereading your textbook and notes until your eyeballs bleed. Cramming might give you the feeling that you know the material, but if you haven't really *understood* what you've read, it becomes easier to "blank out" when you actually take the test. Rather than cramming all your attempts to test yourself into one giant awful block of time, test yourself regularly throughout the semester, say once a week (Bjork & Bjork, 2011). That way, once you've learned something, it will stay learned.

We also encourage you to give your full attention to lectures and class discussions. (Sorry, but you can't do that while texting or searching the Web; later you will learn why multitasking messes up concentration and learning.) Take good notes in class or when you are watching a recorded lecture. Capture the important points instead of trying to scribble down every word. Later, go over any messy or incomplete notes, organizing and rewriting them.

We are sure these techniques will help you, especially if you remember the ultimate strategy for success: No matter how good they are, no course and no textbook can do your work for you. Now onward!

Recite & Review

 Study and **Review** at **MyPsychLab**

Recite: Say aloud everything you know about how serious psychology differs from psychobabble, pseudoscience, and "common sense"; phrenology; Wilhelm Wundt; functionalism; William James; the role played by Freud and psychoanalysis in early psychology; and the four major perspectives in present-day psychological science.

Review: Next, go back and reread the previous section to see how you did.

Now take this *Quick Quiz;* **you won't be graded!**

1. *True or false?* Psychology is another name for common sense.

2. _____ argued that the mind works by associating ideas arising from experience.

3. Carefully observing, analyzing, and describing one's own sensations, mental images, and emotional reactions is known as _____.

4. Anxiety is a common problem. Which major perspective in psychology is associated with each of these explanations? (a) Anxious people often think about the future in distorted ways. (b) Anxiety symptoms often bring hidden rewards, such as being excused from exams. (c) Excessive anxiety can be caused by a chemical imbalance. (d) A national emphasis on competition and success promotes anxiety about failure.

Answers:

1. false 2. John Locke 3. Trained introspection 4. (a) cognitive (b) learning (c) biological (d) sociocultural

You are about to learn...

- why you can't assume that all therapists are psychologists or that all psychologists are therapists.
- the three major areas of psychologists' professional activities.
- the difference between a clinical psychologist and a psychiatrist.

What Psychologists Do

Now you know the main viewpoints that guide psychologists in their work. But what do psychologists actually do with their time between breakfast and dinner?

The professional activities of psychologists generally fall into three broad categories: (1) teaching and doing research in colleges and universities; (2) providing mental health services, often referred to as *psychological practice*; and (3) conducting research or applying its findings in nonacademic settings such as business, sports, government, law, and the military (see Table 1.1). Some psychologists move flexibly across these areas. A researcher might also provide counseling services in a mental health setting, such as a clinic or a hospital; a university professor might teach, do research, and serve as a consultant in legal cases.

Psychological Research LO 1.5

Most people who do psychological research have doctoral degrees (Ph.D.s or Ed.D.s, doctorates in education). Some, seeking knowledge for its own sake, work in **basic psychology**; others, concerned with the practical uses of knowledge, work in **applied psychology**. A psychologist doing basic research might ask, "How does peer pressure influence people's attitudes and behavior?" An applied psychologist might ask, "How can knowledge about peer pressure be used to reduce binge drinking by college students?"

Psychologists doing basic and applied research have made important scientific contributions in areas as diverse as health, education, child development, testing, conflict resolution, marketing, industrial design, worker productivity, and urban planning. Their findings are the main focus of this book and of your course. Yet scientific research is the aspect of the discipline least recognized and understood by the public (Benjamin, 2003). We hope that by the time you finish this book, you will have a greater understanding of what research psychologists do and of their contributions to human knowledge and welfare.

Psychological Practice LO 1.6

Psychological practitioners, whose goal is to understand and improve people's physical and

basic psychology The study of psychological issues for the sake of knowledge rather than for its practical application.

applied psychology The study of psychological issues that have direct practical significance; also, the application of psychological findings.

TABLE 1.1 What Is a Psychologist?

Not all psychologists do clinical work. Many do research, teach, work in business, or consult. The professional activities of psychologists fall into three general categories.

Academic/Research Psychologists	Clinical Psychologists	Psychologists in Industry, Law, or Other Settings
Specialize in areas of basic or applied research, such as:	*Do psychotherapy and sometimes research; may work in any of these settings:*	*Do research or serve as consultants to institutions on such issues as:*
Human development	Private practice	Sports
Psychometrics (testing)	Mental health clinics	Consumer issues
Health	General hospitals	Advertising
Education	Mental hospitals	Organizational problems
Industrial/organizational psychology	Research laboratories	Environmental issues
Physiological psychology	Colleges and universities	Public policy
Sensation and perception		Opinion polls
Design and use of technology		Military training
		Animal behavior
		Legal issues

mental health, work in mental hospitals, general hospitals, clinics, schools, counseling centers, the criminal justice system, and private practice. Since the late 1970s, the proportion of psychologists who are practitioners has steadily increased; practitioners now account for more than two-thirds of new psychology doctorates and members of the American Psychological Association. (The APA, despite its name, is international).

Some practitioners are *counseling psychologists*, who generally help people deal with problems of everyday life, such as test anxiety, family conflicts, or low job motivation. Others are *school psychologists*, who work with parents, teachers, and students to enhance students' performance and resolve emotional difficulties. The majority, however, are *clinical psychologists* who diagnose, treat, and study mental or emotional problems. Clinical psychologists are trained to do psychotherapy with severely disturbed people, as well as with those who are simply troubled or unhappy and want to learn to handle their problems better.

In almost all states, a license to practice clinical psychology requires a doctorate. Most clinical psychologists have a Ph.D., some have an Ed.D., and a smaller number have a Psy.D. (doctorate in psychology, pronounced *sy-dee*). Clinical psychologists typically do four or five years of graduate work in psychology, plus at least a year's internship under the direction of a licensed psychologist.

Clinical programs leading to a Ph.D. or Ed.D. are usually designed to prepare a person both as a scientist and as a practitioner; they require completion of a *dissertation*, a research project that contributes to knowledge in the field. Programs leading to a Psy.D. do not usually require a dissertation, although they typically require the student to complete an extensive study, theoretical paper, or literature review.

People often confuse *clinical psychologist* with three other terms: *psychotherapist*, *psychoanalyst*, and *psychiatrist*. But these terms mean different things:

- **A *psychotherapist* is simply someone who does any kind of psychotherapy.** The term is not legally regulated; in fact, in most states, anyone can say that he or she is a therapist of one sort or another without having any training at all.

- **A *psychoanalyst* is a person who practices one particular form of therapy, psychoanalysis.** To call yourself a psychoanalyst, you must have an advanced degree, get specialized training at a psychoanalytic institute, and undergo extensive psychoanalysis yourself. At one time, admission to a psychoanalytic institute required an M.D. or a Ph.D., but today, clinical social workers with master's degrees, and even interested laypeople, are often admitted.

• A *psychiatrist* is a medical doctor (M.D.) who has done a three-year residency in psychiatry to learn to diagnose and treat mental disorders. Like some clinical psychologists, some psychiatrists do research on mental problems, such as depression or schizophrenia, instead of, or in addition to, working with patients. Psychiatrists and clinical psychologists do similar work, but psychiatrists, because of their medical training, are more likely to focus on possible biological causes of mental disorders and to treat these problems with medication. Unlike psychiatrists, most clinical psychologists at present cannot write prescriptions.

Other mental health professionals include licensed clinical social workers (LCSWs) and marriage, family, and child counselors (MFCCs). These professionals ordinarily treat general problems in adjustment and family conflicts rather than severe mental disturbance, although their work may bring them into contact with people who have serious problems, such as those with drug addictions or victims of domestic violence. Licensing requirements vary from state to state but usually include a master's degree in psychology or social work and one or two years of supervised experience. (For a summary of the types of psychotherapists and the training they receive, see Table 1.2.)

Many research psychologists, and some practitioners, are worried about an increase in the number of counselors and psychotherapists who are unschooled in research methods and the empirical findings of psychology, and who use untested, outdated, or ineffective therapy techniques (Baker, McFall, & Shoham, 2008; Lilienfeld, Lynn, & Lohr, 2003). Such concerns contributed to the formation of the Association for Psychological Science (APS), an international organization devoted to the needs and interests of psychology as a science, and to recent efforts to mandate scientific training for all clinical psychologists before they can be accredited (Bootzin, 2009). Many practitioners, however, argue that psychotherapy is an art and that research findings are largely irrelevant to the work they do with clients. In Chapter 12, we will discuss the gap in training and attitudes between scientists and many therapists, and the efforts underway to bridge that gap and improve patient care.

Psychology in the Community LO 1.7

During the second half of the twentieth century, psychology expanded so rapidly that the APA now has 54 divisions. Some represent major fields, such as developmental psychology or physiological psychology. Others represent specific research or professional interests, such as the psychology of women, the psychology of men, ethnic minority issues, sports, the arts, environmental concerns, gay and lesbian issues, peace, psychology and the law, and health.

Psychologists contribute to their communities in about as many areas as you can think of. They advise utility companies on how best to promote energy conservation. They consult with companies to improve worker satisfaction and productivity. They establish programs to reduce

TABLE 1.2 Types of Psychotherapists

Just as not all psychologists are psychotherapists, not all psychotherapists are clinical psychologists. Here are the major terms used to refer to mental health professionals:

Psychotherapist	Does any kind of psychotherapy; may have anything from no degree to an advanced professional degree; the term is unregulated.
Clinical psychologist	Diagnoses, treats, and/or studies mental and emotional problems, both mild and severe; has a Ph.D., an Ed.D., or a Psy.D.
Psychoanalyst	Practices psychoanalysis; has specific training in this approach after an advanced degree (usually, but not always, an M.D. or a Ph.D.); may treat any kind of emotional disorder or pathology.
Psychiatrist	Does work similar to that of a clinical psychologist but is likely to take a more biological approach; has a medical degree (M.D.) with a specialty in psychiatry.
Licensed clinical social worker (LCSW); marriage, family, and child counselor (MFCC)	Treats common individual and family problems, but may also deal with more serious problems such as addiction or abuse; generally has at least an M.A. in psychology or social work, though licensing requirements vary.

Psychological researchers and practitioners work in all sorts of settings, from classrooms to courtrooms. On the left, a police psychologist talks to a man threatening to jump from his hotel window. The psychologist succeeded in preventing the man's suicide. On the right, a researcher studies a dolphin's ability to understand an artificial language consisting of hand signals.

ethnic tensions and resolve international conflicts. They advise commissions on how pollution and noise affect mental health. They do rehabilitation training for people who are physically or mentally disabled. They educate judges and juries about eyewitness testimony. They conduct public opinion surveys. They run suicide-prevention hotlines. They advise zoos on the care and training of animals. They help coaches improve the athletic performances of their teams. And those are just for starters. Is it any wonder that people are often a little fuzzy about what a psychologist is?

Recite & Review

✓ Study and Review at MyPsychLab

Recite: Say aloud everything you can recall about the main settings in which psychologists work; basic and applied research; psychological practice; counseling, school, and clinical psychologists; and the terms *psychotherapist, psychoanalyst, and psychiatrist.*

Review: Next, go back and reread this section.

Fortunately, you aren't fuzzy about what a student is—so now try this *Quick Quiz:*

Can you match the specialties on the left with their defining credentials and approaches on the right?

1. psychiatrist

2. psychoanalyst

3. clinical psychologist

4. counseling psychologist

5. organizational psychologist

a. Practices one particular form of therapy known as psychoanalysis

b. Has a medical degree, specializing in psychiatry

c. Helps in team building, motivating, and handling stress

d. Helps people cope with everyday life problems such as test anxiety or family conflicts

e. Diagnoses or treats mental and emotional problems, both mild and severe

Answers:

1.b 2.a 3.e 4.d 5.c

You are about to learn...

- what it means to think critically.
- why not all opinions are created equal.
- eight guidelines for evaluating psychological claims.
- why a psychological theory is unscientific if it explains anything that could conceivably happen.
- what's wrong with drawing conclusions about behavior from a collection of anecdotes.

Critical and Scientific Thinking in Psychology LO 1.8, LO 1.9

One of the greatest benefits of studying psychology is that you learn not only how the brain works in general but also how to use yours in particular—by thinking critically. **Critical thinking** is the ability and willingness to assess claims and make objective judgments on the basis of well-supported reasons and evidence, rather than emotion or anecdote. Critical thinkers look for flaws in arguments and resist claims that have no support. They realize that criticizing an argument is not the same as criticizing the person making it, and they are willing to engage in vigorous debate. Critical thinking, however, is not merely negative thinking. It includes the ability to be creative and constructive—the ability to come up with alternative explanations for events, think of implications of research findings, and apply new knowledge to social and personal problems.

Watch the Video Thinking Like a Psychologist: Thinking Critically at MyPsychLab

Most people know that you have to exercise the body to keep it in shape, but they may not realize that clear thinking also requires effort and practice. All around us we can see examples of flabby thinking. Sometimes people justify their mental laziness by proudly telling you they are open-minded. It's good to be open-minded, scientists have countered, but not so open that your brains fall out! If you prefer the look of a Chevy truck to the look of a Honda Accord, no one can argue with your personal taste. But if you say, "The Chevy truck is better than a Honda and gets better mileage, besides," you have uttered more than a mere opinion. Now you have to support your belief with evidence of the car's reliability, mileage, and safety record (Ruggiero,

2004). And if you say, "Chevy trucks are the best in the world and Hondas do not exist; they are a conspiracy of the Japanese government," you forfeit the right to have your opinion taken seriously. If your opinion ignores reality, it is *not* equal to any other.

Critical thinking is not only indispensable in ordinary life; it is also fundamental to all sciences, including psychological science. By exercising critical thinking, you will be able to distinguish serious psychology from the psychobabble that clutters the airwaves and bookstores. You may also become better at using the Internet. Many college students pride themselves on their skill at using their favorite search engine, but researchers have found that most students are less skilled than they think (Pan et al., 2007; Thompson, 2011). They tend to rely on the material at the top of the results list, without assessing its credibility: Was that hostile profile of Martin Luther King, Jr. written by a scholar or by a racist blogger? Is that article really a paid advertisement for some product? The researchers found that high school and college students are typically unable to detect hidden agendas in what they read; they need, in the words of Internet pioneer and critic Howard Rheingold, a course in "crap detection 101."

Critical thinking requires logical skills, but other skills and dispositions are also important (Anderson, 2005; Halpern, 2002; Levy, 2010; Stanovich, 2010). Here are eight essential critical-thinking guidelines that we will be emphasizing throughout this book.

1 **Ask Questions; Be Willing to Wonder.** What is the one kind of question that most exasperates parents of young children? "Why is the sky blue, Mommy?" "Why doesn't the plane fall?" "Why don't pigs have wings?" Unfortunately, as children grow up, they tend to stop asking "why" questions like these. (Why do you think this is?) But critical and creative thinking begins with wondering why. This educational program isn't working; why not? I want to stop smoking and improve my grades but can't seem to do it; why? Is my way of doing things the best way, or just the most familiar way? Critical thinkers are willing to question received wisdom—"We do it this way because this is the way we have always done things around here"—and ask, in essence, "Oh, yeah? Why?"

In psychological science, knowledge begins with a question. What is the biological basis of consciousness? How are memories stored and retrieved? Why do we sleep and dream? What causes schizophrenia? What are the cultural

critical thinking The ability and willingness to assess claims and make objective judgments on the basis of well-supported reasons and evidence rather than emotion or anecdote.

hypothesis A statement that attempts to predict or to account for a set of phenomena; scientific hypotheses specify relationships among events or variables and are empirically tested.

operational definition A precise definition of a term in a hypothesis, which specifies the operations for observing and measuring the process or phenomenon being defined.

influences on addiction? Critical thinkers are not discouraged by the fact that questions like these have not yet been fully answered; they see them as an exciting challenge.

2 Define Your Terms. Once you have raised a general question, the next step is to frame it in clear and concrete terms. "What makes people happy?" is a fine question for midnight reveries, but it will not lead to answers until you have defined what you mean by "happy." Does it mean enjoying a state of euphoria most of the time? Feeling pleasantly contented with life? Being free of serious problems or pain? Vague or poorly defined terms can lead to misleading or incomplete answers and can even cause terrible misunderstandings. For example, are people becoming less prejudiced? The answer may depend in part on how you define prejudice. Is conscious dislike the same as discomfort with a group of people whose rules and beliefs differ from yours? (We will discuss this issue further in Chapter 10.)

For scientists, defining terms means being precise about just what it is that they're studying. Researchers often start out with a **hypothesis**, a statement that attempts to describe or explain a given behavior. Initially, this hypothesis may be stated quite generally, as in, say, "Misery loves company." But before any research can be done, the hypothesis must be made more precise. "Misery loves company" might be rephrased as "People who are anxious about a threatening situation tend to seek out others facing the same threat."

A hypothesis, in turn, leads to predictions about what will happen in a particular situation. In a prediction, terms such as *anxiety* or *threatening situation* are given **operational definitions**, which specify how the phenomena in question are to be observed and measured. "Anxiety" might be defined operationally as a score on an anxiety questionnaire, and "threatening situation" as the threat of an electric shock. The prediction might be, "If you raise people's anxiety scores by telling them they are going to receive electric shocks, and then you give them the choice of waiting alone or with others in the same situation, they will be more likely to choose to wait with others than they would be if they were not anxious." The prediction can then be tested using systematic methods.

3 Examine the Evidence. Have you ever heard someone in the heat of an argument exclaim, "I just know it's true, no matter what you say"? Have you ever made such a statement yourself? Accepting a claim or conclusion without evidence, or expecting others to do so, is a sure sign of lazy thinking. A critical thinker asks, "What evidence supports or refutes this argument and its opposition? How reliable is the evidence?" Have you ever received some dire warning or funny story that you immediately posted on your Facebook page, only to learn later that it was a hoax or an urban legend? A critical thinker would ask, "Is this story something I'd better check out on snopes.com before I tell my closest 90,000 friends?"

We often hear that all viewpoints should be taught to students in the name of "fairness" and "open-mindedness," but not all viewpoints, theories, and opinions are equally valid or supported by the evidence.

When demonstrating "levitation" and other supposedly magical phenomena, illusionists exploit people's tendency to trust the evidence of their own eyes even when such evidence is misleading. Critical thinkers ask about the nature and reliability of the evidence afor a phenomenon.

In scientific research, an idea may initially generate excitement because it is plausible, imaginative, or appealing, but eventually it must be backed by empirical evidence if it is to be taken seriously. A collection of anecdotes or an appeal to authority will not do. Sometimes, of course, checking the reliability of the evidence directly is not practical. In those cases, critical thinkers consider whether it came from a reliable source. Sources who are reliable exercise critical thinking themselves. They usually have education or experience in the field in which they claim expertise. They do not pressure people to agree with them. They share their evidence openly. They draw on research that has been reviewed by other experts on the subject, rather than merely announced to the public in a press release or blog.

4 **Analyze Assumptions and Biases.** *Assumptions* are beliefs that are taken for granted, and *biases* are assumptions that keep us from considering the evidence fairly or that cause us to ignore the evidence entirely. Critical thinkers try to identify and evaluate the unspoken assumptions on which claims and arguments may rest—in the books they read, the political speeches they hear, and the advertisements that bombard them every day. In science, some of the greatest scientific advances have been made by those who dared to doubt widespread assumptions: that the sun revolves around the earth, that illness can be cured by applying leeches to the skin, that madness is a sign of demonic possession.

Critical thinkers are willing to analyze and test not only other people's assumptions, but also their own, which is much harder. Researchers put their own assumptions to the test by stating a hypothesis in such a way that it can be *refuted*, or disproved by counterevidence. This principle, known as the **principle of falsifiability**, does not mean that the hypothesis *will* be disproved, only that it *could be* if contrary evidence were to be discovered.

Another way of saying this is that a scientist must risk disconfirmation by predicting not only what will happen, but also what will *not* happen if the hypothesis is correct. In the misery-loves-company study, the hypothesis would be supported if most anxious people sought each other out, but disconfirmed if most anxious people went off alone to sulk and worry, or if anxiety had no effect on their behavior (see Figure 1.1 on the next page). A willingness to risk disconfirmation forces scientists to take negative evidence seriously and to abandon mistaken hypotheses.

The principle of falsifiability is often violated in everyday life because all of us are vulnerable to the **confirmation bias**: the tendency to look for and accept evidence that supports our pet theories and assumptions and to ignore or reject evidence that contradicts our beliefs. Thus, if a police interrogator is convinced of a suspect's guilt, he or she may interpret anything the suspect says, even the person's maintenance of innocence, as confirming evidence that the suspect is guilty ("Of course he *says* he's innocent; he's a liar") (Leo, 2008). But what if the suspect *is* innocent? The principle of falsifiability compels scientists, and the rest of us, to resist the confirmation bias and to consider counterevidence.

👁 Watch the Video Confirmation Bias at MyPsychLab

5 **Avoid Emotional Reasoning.** Emotion has a place in critical thinking and in science. Passionate commitment to a view motivates people to think boldly, to defend unpopular ideas, and to seek evidence for creative new theories. But emotional conviction alone cannot settle arguments, and in fact it usually makes them worse. The fact that you *really*, *really* feel strongly that something is true—or want it to be—doesn't make it so.

All of us are apt to feel threatened and get defensive whenever our most cherished beliefs, or commitment to a course of action, are challenged by empirical evidence (Tavris & Aronson, 2007). At such times, it is especially important to separate the data from emotional reasoning. In our opening news story about the ruling that vaccines do not cause autism, one of the judges expressed sympathy for the parents, but added, "I must decide this case not on sentiment, but by analyzing the evidence."

You probably hold strong beliefs about drug use, the causes of crime, the origins of intelligence, gender differences, obesity, and many

principle of falsifiability The principle that a scientific theory must make predictions that are specific enough to expose the theory to the possibility of disconfirmation; that is, the theory must predict not only what will happen but also what will *not* happen.

confirmation bias The tendency to look for or pay attention only to information that confirms one's own belief, and ignore, trivialize, or forget information that disconfirms that belief.

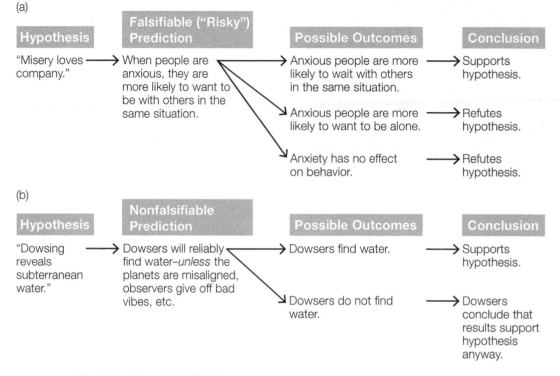

FIGURE 1.1 The Principle of Falsifiability

The scientific method requires researchers to expose their ideas to the possibility of counterevidence, as in row (a). In contrast, people claiming psychic powers, such as dowsers (who say they can find underground water with a "dowsing rod" that bends when water is present), typically interpret all possible outcomes as support for their assertions, as in row (b). Their claims are therefore untestable.

other issues of interest to psychologists. As you read this book, you may find yourself quarreling with findings that you dislike. Disagreement is fine; it means that you are reading actively and are engaged with the material. All we ask is that you think about why you are disagreeing: Is it because the evidence is unpersuasive, or is it because the results make you feel anxious or annoyed?

6 Don't Oversimplify. A critical thinker looks beyond the obvious, resists easy generalizations, and rejects either–or thinking. For instance, is it better to feel you have control over what happens to you, or to accept with tranquility whatever life serves up? Either answer oversimplifies. As we will see in Chapter 13, control has many important benefits, but sometimes it's best to go with the flow.

A common form of oversimplification is *argument by anecdote*, generalizing from a personal experience or a few examples to everyone: One crime committed by a paroled ex-convict means that parole should be abolished; one friend who hates his or her school means that everybody who goes there hates it; one friend who swears that seaweed cured her headaches means that seaweed

is beneficial for everyone. Anecdotes are often the source of stereotyping, as well: One dishonest mother on public assistance means everyone on welfare is dishonest; one encounter with an unconventional Californian means they are all flaky. Critical and scientific thinkers want more evidence than one or two stories before drawing such sweeping conclusions.

7 Consider Other Interpretations. A critical thinker creatively formulates hypotheses that offer reasonable explanations of the topic at hand. In science, the goal is to arrive at a **theory**, an organized system of assumptions and principles that purports to explain a set of observations and how they are related. A scientific theory is not just someone's personal opinion, as in "It's only a theory" or "I have a theory about why he told that lie." It is true that many scientific theories are tentative, pending more research, but others, such as the theory of evolution, are accepted by virtually all scientists. Theories that come to be accepted by the scientific community make as few assumptions as possible and account for many empirical findings.

Before settling on an explanation of some behavior, however, critical thinkers are careful

theory An organized system of assumptions and principles that purports to explain a specified set of observations and their interrelationships.

Hypnosis has traditionally been considered a trance state in which people involuntarily do things they ordinarily could not or would not do. But might there be another interpretation of the surprising things that hypnotized people often do? (We will look at competing explanations in Chapter 5.)

not to shut out alternative possibilities. They generate as many interpretations of the evidence as they can before choosing the most likely one. Suppose a news magazine reports that people who are chronically depressed are more likely than nondepressed people to develop cancer. Before concluding that depression causes cancer, you would need to consider some other possibilities. Perhaps depressed people are more likely to smoke and to drink excessively, and these unhealthful habits increase their cancer risk. Or perhaps early, as-yet-undetected cancers produce biochemical changes that contribute to the physical and emotional symptoms of depression. Alternative explanations such as these must be ruled out by further investigation before we can conclude that depression is a direct cause of cancer. (It's not, by the way.)

8 Tolerate Uncertainty. Ultimately, learning to think critically teaches us one of the hardest lessons of life: how to live with uncertainty. Sometimes there is little or no evidence available to examine. Sometimes the evidence permits only tentative conclusions. Sometimes the evidence seems strong enough to permit strong conclusions until, exasperatingly, new evidence throws

our beliefs into disarray. Critical thinkers are willing to accept this state of uncertainty. They are not afraid to say, "I don't know yet" or "I'm not sure."

In science, tolerating uncertainty means that researchers must avoid drawing firm conclusions until other researchers have repeated, or *replicated*, their studies and verified their findings. Secrecy is a big no-no in science; you must be willing to tell others where you got your ideas and how you tested them so that others can challenge them if they think your findings are wrong. Replication is an essential part of the scientific process because sometimes what seems to be a major discovery turns out to be only a fluke.

The need to accept a certain amount of uncertainty does not mean that we must abandon all assumptions, beliefs, and convictions. That would be impossible, in any case: We all need values and principles to guide our actions. The problem is not that people hold convictions; it is that they so often refuse to give up convictions that have proven to be outdated, dangerous, foolish, or simply wrong.

Critical thinking is a tool to guide us on a lifelong quest for understanding—a tool that we must keep sharpening. No one ever becomes a perfect critical thinker, entirely unaffected by emotional reasoning and wishful thinking. We are all less open-minded than we think; it is far easier to poke holes in another person's argument than to critically examine our own position. Yet we think the journey is well worth the mental effort because the ability to think critically can help you in countless ways, from saving you money to improving your relationships.

As you read this book, we will give you many opportunities to apply the eight guidelines to psychological theories and to personal and social issues that affect us all. From time to time, a tab with a light bulb symbol (like the one shown here) will highlight a discussion where one or more of our critical-thinking guidelines are especially relevant. In Quick Quizzes, the light bulb will identify questions that give you practice in applying the guidelines yourself. Keep in mind, however, that critical thinking is important throughout the book, not only where the light bulb appears. Finally, at

THINKING CRITICALLY

About...

the end of every chapter, a feature called "Taking Psychology With You" will help you apply critical thinking to a topic in the chapter and take its message with you.

Recite & Review

 Study and **Review** at **MyPsychLab**

Recite: Out loud, say as much as you can about theories, hypotheses, operational definitions, the principle of falsifiability, the confirmation bias, and the importance of replication.

Review: Next, go back and reread this section to see what you might have left out.

Now bulk up your thinking muscles by answering these *Quick Quiz* **questions:**

1. Benjamin Rush, an eighteenth-century physician, believed that yellow fever should be treated by blood-letting. Many of his patients died, but Rush did not lose faith in his approach; he attributed each recovery to his treatment and each death to the severity of the disease (Stanovich, 2010). How did his explanations violate critical thinking?

2. Amelia and Harold are arguing about the death penalty. "Look, I just feel strongly that it's barbaric, ineffective, and wrong," says Harold. "You're nuts," says Amelia, "I believe in an eye for an eye, and besides, I'm absolutely sure it's a deterrent to further crime." Which lapses of critical thinking might Amelia and Harold be committing?

Answers:

1. Rush failed to analyze and test his assumptions; he violated the principle of falsifiability, explaining away each death, so there was no possible counterevidence that could refute the theory (which by the way was dead wrong; the treatment was actually as dangerous as the disease). **2.** Harold and Amelia are reasoning emotionally ("I feel strongly about this, so I'm right and you're wrong"). They do not cite evidence that supports or contradicts their arguments. What do studies show about the link between the death penalty and crime? How often are innocent people executed? They have not examined their biases. And they may not be clearly defining the problem: What is the purpose of the death penalty? Is it to deter criminals, to satisfy the public desire for revenge, or to keep criminals from being paroled and returned to the streets?

You are about to learn...

- how participants are selected for psychological studies, and why it matters.
- the methods psychologists use to describe behavior.
- the advantages and disadvantages of each descriptive method.

Descriptive Studies: Establishing the Facts

Psychologists gather evidence to support their hypotheses by using different methods, depending on the kinds of questions they want to answer. These methods are not mutually exclusive, however. Just as a police detective may rely on DNA samples, fingerprints, and interviews of suspects to figure out "who done it," psychological sleuths often draw on different techniques at different stages of an investigation.

No matter what technique is used, one of the first challenges facing any researcher is to select the participants (sometimes called "subjects") for the study. Ideally, the researcher would prefer to get a **representative sample**, a group of randomly chosen participants that accurately represents the larger population that the researcher is interested in.

Suppose you wanted to learn about drug use among first-year college students. Questioning or observing every first-year student in the country would obviously not be practical; instead, you would need to recruit a sample. You could use special selection procedures to ensure that this sample contained the same proportion of women, men, blacks, whites, Asians, Latinos, poor people, rich people, Catholics, Jews, Muslims, atheists, and so on as in the general population of new college students. Even then, a sample drawn just from your own school or town might not produce results applicable to the entire country or even your state.

A sample's size is less critical than its representativeness. A small but representative sample may yield extremely accurate results, whereas a study that fails to use proper sampling methods may yield questionable results, no matter how large the sample. But in practice, psychologists must often settle for a sample of people who happen to be available—a "convenience" sample—and usually this means undergraduate students. Most of the time, that's fine; many psychological processes, such as basic perceptual or memory processes, are likely to be the same in students as in anyone else. But college students, on average, are also younger and tend to have better cognitive skills than nonstudents. Moreover, most research participants, whether

representative sample A group of individuals, selected from a population for study, which matches that population on important characteristics such as age and sex.

students or not, are what one group of researchers calls WEIRDos—from Western, Educated, Industrialized, Rich, and Democratic cultures—and thus are hardly representative of humans as a whole (Henrich, Heine, & Norenzayan, 2010). Scientists are now turning to technology to reduce this problem. Internet sites such as Amazon's Mechanical Turk make it possible to quickly and cheaply recruit a diverse sample of thousands of people from all over the world (Buhrmester, Kwang, & Gosling, 2011).

We turn now to the specific methods used most commonly in psychological research. As you read about these methods, you may want to list their advantages and disadvantages so you will remember them better, and then check your list against the one in Table 1.3 on page 44. We will begin with **descriptive methods**, which allow researchers to describe and predict behavior but not necessarily to choose one explanation over competing ones.

✳ Explore the Concept What Do You Think about Psychological Research? at MyPsychLab

Case Studies LO 1.10

A **case study** (or *case history*) is a detailed description of a particular individual, based on careful observation or on formal psychological testing. It may include information about a person's childhood, dreams, fantasies, experiences, and relationships—anything that will provide insight into the person's behavior. Case studies are most commonly used by clinicians, but sometimes academic researchers use them as well, especially when they are just beginning to study a topic or when practical or ethical considerations prevent them from gathering information in other ways.

Suppose you want to know whether the first few years of life are critical for acquiring a first language. Can children who have missed out on hearing speech (or, in the case of deaf children, seeing signs) catch up later? Obviously, psychologists cannot answer this question by isolating children and seeing what happens. So instead they have studied unusual cases of language deprivation.

One such case involved a 13-year-old girl who had been cruelly locked up in a small room since infancy. Her mother, a battered wife, barely cared for her, and no one in the family spoke a word to her. If she made the slightest sound, her severely disturbed father beat her with a large piece of wood. When she was finally rescued, Genie, as researchers called her, did not know how to chew or to stand erect, and her only sounds were high-pitched whimpers. Eventually, she was able to

learn some rules of social conduct, and she began to understand short sentences and to use words to convey her needs, describe her moods, and even lie. Yet Genie's grammar remained abnormal; for example, she never learned to use pronouns or ask questions correctly (Curtiss, 1977, 1982; Rymer, 1993). This sad case, along with similar ones, suggests that a critical period during childhood exists for language development.

Case studies illustrate psychological principles in a way that abstract generalizations and statistics never can, and they produce a more detailed picture of an individual than other methods do. In biological research, cases of patients with brain damage have yielded important clues to how the brain is organized (see Chapter 4). But in most instances, case studies have serious drawbacks. Information is often missing or is hard to interpret; in Genie's case, no one knows whether she was born with mental deficits or what her language development was like before she was locked up. The observer who writes up the case may have biases that influence which facts are noticed or overlooked. The person who is the focus of the study may have selective or inaccurate memories, making conclusions unreliable. For all these reasons, case studies are usually only sources, rather than tests, of hypotheses.

Be especially wary of compelling case histories of psychotherapy patients reported in the media. Consider the example of "Sybil," whose account of her 16 personalities became a famous

When investigative journalist Debbie Nathan painstakingly reassessed the famous case of "Sybil," she found that Sybil had admitted inventing her "multiple personalities" to please her psychiatrist. Sybil's story, which became hugely popular as a book and film, illustrates the dangers of accepting any sensational case study uncritically.

descriptive methods Methods that yield descriptions of behavior but not necessarily causal explanations.

case study A detailed description of a particular individual being studied or treated.

observational study
A study in which the researcher carefully and systematically observes and records behavior without interfering with the behavior; it may involve either naturalistic or laboratory observation.

psychological tests
Procedures used to measure and evaluate personality traits, emotional states, aptitudes, interests, abilities, and values.

book and TV movie, eventually launching an epidemic of multiple personality disorder (see Chapter 11). Detective work by investigative journalists and other skeptics later revealed that Sybil was not a multiple personality after all; her diagnosis was invented by her psychiatrist, Cornelia Wilbur, who hoped to profit professionally and financially from the story (Nathan, 2011). Wilbur conveniently omitted the fact that she had prescribed addictive drugs to her patient and had threatened to withhold them unless Sybil produced other "personalities."

Observational Studies

In **observational studies**, the researcher systematically and unobtrusively observes, measures, and records behavior while taking care to avoid intruding on the people (or animals) being observed. The purpose of *naturalistic observation* is to find out how people or other animals act in their normal social environments. Psychologists use this method wherever people happen to be: at home, on playgrounds or streets, or in schoolrooms, offices, and bars. But they also do observational studies in the laboratory. In *laboratory observation*, they have more control of the situation: They can use cameras and recording devices, determine how many people will be observed at once, maintain a clear line of vision, and so forth.

Suppose that you wanted to know how infants of different ages respond when left with a stranger. You might have parents and their infants come to your lab, observe them playing together for a while through a one-way window, then have a stranger enter the room and, a few minutes later, have the parent leave. You could record signs of distress, interactions with the stranger, and other behavior. If you did this, you would find that very young infants carry on cheerfully with whatever they are doing when the parent leaves. However, by the age of about 8 months, children will often burst into tears or show other signs of what child psychologists call "separation anxiety" (see Chapter 3).

One shortcoming of laboratory observation is that the presence of researchers and special equipment may cause participants to behave differently than they would in their usual surroundings. Further, observational studies, like other descriptive studies, are more useful for describing behavior than for explaining it. If we observe infants protesting whenever a parent leaves the room, we cannot be sure why they are protesting. Is it because they have become attached to their parents and want them nearby, or have they learned from experience that crying brings an adult with a cookie and a cuddle? Observational studies alone cannot answer such questions.

Tests LO 1.11

Psychological tests are procedures for measuring and evaluating personality traits, emotional states,

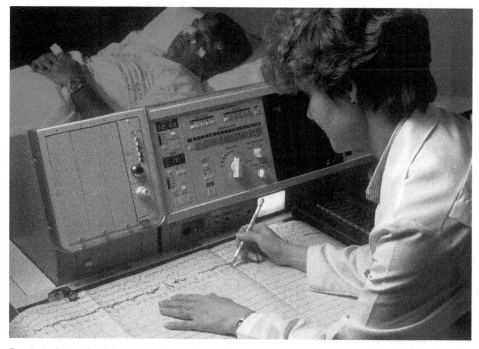

Psychologists using laboratory observation have gathered valuable information about brain and muscle activity during sleep.

Get Involved! A Study of Personal Space

Try a little naturalistic observation of your own. Go to a public place where people seat themselves, such as a movie theater or a cafeteria with large tables. You might recruit some friends to help you; you can divide the area into sections and assign each observer one section to observe. As individuals and groups sit down, note how many seats they leave between themselves and the next person. On average, how far do people tend to sit from strangers? Once you have your results, see how many possible explanations you can come up with.

aptitudes, interests, abilities, and values. Typically, tests require people to answer a series of written or oral questions. The answers may then be totaled to yield a single numerical score, or a set of scores. *Objective tests*, also called *inventories*, measure beliefs, feelings, or behaviors of which an individual is aware; *projective tests* are designed to tap unconscious feelings or motives (see Chapter 11).

At one time or another, you no doubt have taken a personality test, an achievement test, or a vocational-aptitude test. Hundreds of psychological tests are used in industry, education, the military, and the helping professions. Some tests are given to individuals, others to large groups. These measures help clarify differences among individuals, as well as differences in the reactions of the same person on different occasions or at different stages of life. Tests may be used to promote self-understanding, to evaluate treatments and programs, or, in scientific research, to draw generalizations about human behavior. Well-constructed psychological tests are a great improvement over simple self-evaluation because many people have a distorted view of their own abilities and traits. In the workplace, employees tend to overestimate their skills and top executives are overconfident in their judgments; in school and on the job, people are often blissfully unaware of their own lack of competence (Dunning, Heath, & Suls, 2004).

One test of a good test is whether it is **standardized**, that is, whether uniform procedures exist for giving and scoring the test. It would hardly be fair to give some people detailed instructions and plenty of time and others only vague instructions and limited time. Those who administer the test must know exactly how to explain the tasks involved, how much time to allow, and what materials to use. Scoring is usually done by referring to **norms**, or established standards of performance. The usual procedure for developing norms is to give the test to a large group of people who resemble those for whom the test is intended. Norms determine which scores can be considered high, low, or average.

Test construction presents two central challenges. First, the test must have **reliability**, producing the same results from one time and place to the next. A vocational-interest test is not reliable if it tells Tom that he would make a wonderful engineer but a poor journalist, and then gives different results when Tom retakes the test a week later. Nor is it reliable if alternate forms of the test, intended to be comparable, yield different results. Second, the test must have **validity**, measuring what it is designed to measure. A creativity test is not valid if what it actually measures is verbal sophistication. The validity of a test is often measured by its ability to predict other, independent measures, or *criteria*, of the trait in question. The criterion for a scholastic aptitude test might be college grades; the criterion for a test of shyness might be behavior in social situations. Among psychologists and educators, controversy exists about the validity of even some widely used tests, such as the Scholastic Assessment Test (SAT) and standardized IQ tests.

Criticisms and reevaluations of psychological tests keep psychological assessment honest and scientifically rigorous. In contrast, the pop-psych tests frequently found in magazines and

standardize In test construction, to develop uniform procedures for giving and scoring a test.

norms In test construction, established standards of performance.

reliability In test construction, the consistency of test scores from one time and place to another.

validity The ability of a test to measure what it was designed to measure.

Many people attach a lot of importance to their test scores!

Roz Chast/Cartoon Bank.Com

surveys Questionnaires and interviews that ask people directly about their experiences, attitudes, or opinions.

volunteer bias A shortcoming of findings derived from a sample of volunteers instead of a representative sample; the volunteers may differ from those who did not volunteer.

newspapers and on the Internet usually have not been evaluated for either validity or reliability. These questionnaires often have inviting headlines such as "What Breed of Dog Do You Most Resemble?" or "What's Your Love Profile?" but they are merely lists of questions that someone thought sounded good.

Surveys LO 1.12

Psychological tests usually generate information about people indirectly. In contrast, **surveys** are questionnaires and interviews that gather information by asking people *directly* about their experiences, attitudes, or opinions about everything from political preferences to sexual preferences. Most of us are familiar with national opinion surveys, such as the Gallup and Roper polls. And if you eat at a restaurant, get your car serviced, stay at a hotel, or order something online, you're apt to get a satisfaction survey five minutes later. How reliable are all these surveys?

Surveys produce bushels of data, but they are not easy to do well. Sampling problems are often an issue. When a talk-radio host or TV personality invites people to post comments on the Internet about a political matter, the results are unlikely to generalize to the population as a whole, even if thousands of people respond. Why? As a group, people who listen to someone like Rush Limbaugh are more conservative than fans of someone like Jon Stewart.

THINKING CRITICALLY

About Opinion Polls and Surveys

Popular polls and surveys also frequently suffer from a **volunteer bias**: People who are willing to volunteer their opinions may differ from those who decline to take part. When you read about a survey, or any other kind of study, always ask who participated. A nonrepresentative sample does not necessarily mean that a survey is worthless or uninteresting, but it does mean that the results may not hold true for other groups.

Yet another problem with surveys, as with self-reports in general, is that people sometimes lie, especially when the survey is about a touchy or embarrassing topic ("I would never do that disgusting/dishonest/fattening thing!") or asks about an illegal act, such as using banned drugs (Tourangeau & Yan, 2007). The likelihood of lying is reduced when respondents are guaranteed anonymity and allowed to respond in private. Researchers can also check for lying by asking the same question several times with different wording to see whether the answers are consistent.

And again, technology can help, because many people feel more anonymous when they interact with a computer than when they fill out a paper-and-pencil questionnaire, and so are less likely to lie (Turner et al., 1998). If the survey is filled out online, however, it may be hard to know whether participants have understood the questions and have taken them seriously.

When you hear about the results of a survey or opinion poll, you also need to consider which questions were (and were not) asked, and how the questions were phrased. These aspects of a survey's design may nudge responses in a particular direction, as political pollsters well know ("Do you favor raising your property tax to spend millions of dollars to repair your local schools?" is more likely to evoke a *no* than "Do you favor rebuilding schools that are decaying, lack heat, and are infested with rats?"). Many years ago, the famed sex researcher Alfred Kinsey made it his practice always to ask, "*How many times have you* (masturbated, had nonmarital sex, etc.)?" rather than "*Have you ever* (masturbated, had nonmarital sex, etc.)?" The first way of phrasing the question tended to elicit more truthful responses than the second because it removed the respondent's self-consciousness about having done any of those things. The second way of phrasing the question would have permitted embarrassed respondents to reply with a simple but dishonest "No."

As you can see, although surveys can be extremely informative, they must be conducted and interpreted carefully.

"Are you (a) contented, (b) happy, (c) very happy, (d) wildly happy, (e) deliriously happy?"

You are about to learn...

- what it means to say that two things, such as grades and TV watching, are "negatively" correlated.

- whether a positive correlation between TV watching and hyperactivity means that too much TV makes kids hyperactive.

Correlational Studies: Looking for Relationships

In descriptive research, psychologists often want to know whether two phenomena are related and, if so, how strongly. Are students' grade-point averages related to the number of hours they spend watching TV shows, playing video games, or texting? To find out, a psychologist would do a **correlational study**.

Measuring Correlations
LO 1.13, LO 1.14

The word **correlation** is often used as a synonym for "relationship." Technically, however, a correlation is a numerical measure of the *strength* of the relationship between two things. The things may be events, scores, or anything else that can be recorded and tallied. In psychological studies, such things are called **variables** because they can vary in quantifiable ways. Height, weight, age, income, IQ scores, number of items recalled on a memory test, number of smiles in a given time period—anything that can be measured, rated, or scored can serve as a variable.

A **positive correlation** means that high values of one variable are associated with high values of the other, and that low values of one variable are associated with low values of the other:

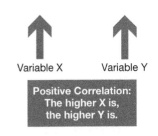

Variable X   Variable Y

Positive Correlation: The higher X is, the higher Y is.

Height and weight are positively correlated; so are IQ scores and school grades. Rarely is a

correlational study A descriptive study that looks for a consistent relationship between two phenomena.

correlation A measure of how strongly two variables are related to each other.

variables Characteristics of behavior or experience that can be measured or described by a numeric scale.

positive correlation An association between increases in one variable and increases in another, or between decreases in one and decreases in the other.

negative correlation
An association between increases in one variable and decreases in another.

coefficient of correlation A measure of correlation that ranges in value from −1.00 to +1.00.

correlation perfect, however. Some tall people weigh less than some short ones; some people with average IQs are superstars in the classroom, and some with high IQs get poor grades. Figure 1.2(a) shows a positive correlation between scores on a psychology exam and the average number of kumquats eaten per month by students who took the exam. (Obviously, we made this up.) Each dot represents a student. You can find each student's score by drawing a horizontal line from the person's dot to the vertical axis. You can find the number of kumquats a student ate by drawing a vertical line from the student's dot to the horizontal axis. In general, the more kumquats eaten, the higher the score.

A **negative correlation** means that high values of one variable are associated with low values of the other:

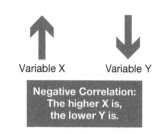

Figure 1.2(b) shows a negative correlation between scores on a psychology exam and number of kumquats eaten per month. This time, the more kumquats eaten, the lower the test score. To take a much more realistic example: How about hours spent watching TV and average grades? They too are negatively correlated: Spending lots of hours in front of the television is associated with lower grades (Potter, 1987; Ridley-Johnson, Cooper, & Chance, 1983). See whether you can think of other variables that are negatively correlated. Remember that a negative correlation means a relationship exists; the more of one thing, the less of another. If there is no relationship between two variables, as in Figure 1.2(c), we say that they are *uncorrelated*. Shoe size and IQ scores are uncorrelated.

The statistic used to express a correlation is called the **coefficient of correlation**. This number conveys both the size of the correlation and its direction. A perfect positive correlation has a coefficient of +1.00, and a perfect negative correlation has a coefficient of −1.00. Suppose you weighed 10 people and listed them in order, from lightest to heaviest, then measured their heights and listed them in order, from shortest to tallest. If the names on the two lists were in exactly the same order, the correlation between weight and height would be +1.00. If the correlation between two variables is +.80, it means that the two are strongly related. If the correlation is −.80, the relationship is just as strong, but it is negative. When there is no association between two variables, the coefficient is zero or close to zero.

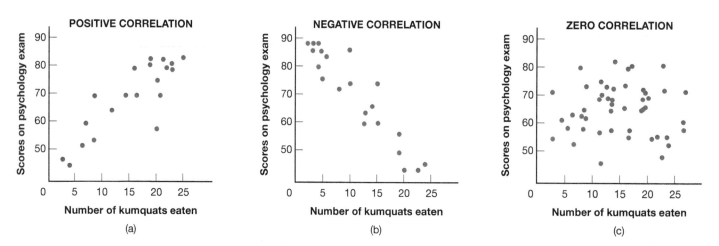

(a)   (b)   (c)

FIGURE 1.2 Correlations

Graph (a) shows a hypothetical positive correlation between scores on a psychology test and number of kumquats eaten per month: In general, test scores rise with the number of kumquats eaten. Graph (b) shows a negative correlation: In general, test scores fall as the number of kumquats eaten rises. Graph (c) shows the reality—no relationship between kumquat eating and test scores.

Cautions About Correlations LO 1.15

Correlational studies are common in psychology and often make the news. But beware; many supposed correlations reported in the media or on the Internet are based on rumor and anecdote instead of reliable evidence. Some are based on mere coincidence and are meaningless, and are therefore called *illusory correlations*.

The alleged link between vaccines and autism is an illusory correlation, probably a result of the fact that most symptoms of childhood autism emerge at about the same time that children are vaccinated. Some parents think the culprit is thimerosal, a preservative that was used in childhood vaccines until 1999 and is now contained in trace amounts in only a few. Yet there is no convincing evidence that thimerosal ever was involved in autism, and after it was removed from most vaccines, the incidence of autism did not decline, as it would have if thimerosal were to blame. Moreover, study after study has failed to find any causal connection whatsoever between vaccination and autism (Mnookin, 2011; Offit, 2008). In one major study of all the children born in Denmark between 1991 and 1998 (more than a half million children), the incidence of autism in vaccinated children was actually a bit *lower* than in unvaccinated children (Madsen et al., 2002). Unfortunately, rates of measles and whooping cough, which can be fatal, are rising in children whose frightened parents have refused to have them vaccinated.

Even when correlations are meaningful, they can be hard to interpret because *a correlation does not establish causation*. It is often tempting to assume that if variable A predicts variable B, then A must be causing B, but that is not necessarily so. A positive correlation has been found between the number of hours that children watch television between ages 1 and 3 and their risk of hyperactivity (impulsivity, attention problems, difficulty concentrating) by age 7 (Christakis et al., 2004). Does this mean that watching TV *causes* hyperactivity? Maybe, but it is also possible that children with a disposition to become hyperactive are more attracted to television than those disposed to being calm. Or perhaps the harried parents of distractible children are more likely than other parents to rely on TV as a babysitter. It is also possible that neither variable causes the other directly: Perhaps parents who allow their young kids to watch a lot of TV have attention problems themselves, and therefore create a home environment that fosters hyperactivity and inattentiveness. Likewise, that negative correlation we mentioned between TV watching and grades might exist because heavy TV watchers have less time to study, or because they have some personality trait that causes an attraction to TV *and* an aversion to studying, or because they use TV as an escape when their grades are low…you get the idea.

The moral: When two variables are associated, one variable may or may not be causing the other.

Explore the *Concept* Correlation vs. Causation at *MyPsychLab*

The number of hours toddlers spend watching TV is correlated with their risk of being hyperactive a few years later. Does that mean TV watching causes hyperactivity problems? What other explanations for this correlation are possible?

Recite & Review

 Study and **Review** at **MyPsychLab**

Recite: Out loud, say everything you can about correlational studies, variables, positive versus negative correlations, illusory correlations, and drawing causal conclusions from correlational findings.

Review: Next, go back and reread this section.

Frequent testing and grades are positively correlated, so now take this *Quick Quiz:*

1. Identify each of the following as a positive or negative correlation:
    a. More the time spent watching television shows or playing video games, lesser the concentration on academic pursuits.
    b. The hotter the weather, the higher the crime rate.
    c. The older people get, the less they are attracted towards partying.

2. Can you also generate two or three possible explanations for each of the preceding findings?

    Answers:

    1. a. positive **b.** positive **c.** negative **2. a.** Lack of time and shifting attention may hinder academic pursuits as the television programs and games are always in progress, and people tend to complete the task or watch the full program. **b.** Hot weather causes intolerance in people. **c.** Elderly people may get attracted to partying to pass their time. (There can be more than one explanation for these correlations. These are not the only possible explanations.)

You are about to learn...

- why psychologists rely so heavily on experiments.
- what control groups control for.
- who is "blind" in single- and double-blind experiments, and what they are not supposed to "see."

The Experiment: Hunting for Causes

Researchers gain plenty of information from descriptive studies, but when they want to actually track down the causes of behavior, they rely heavily on the experimental method. An **experiment** allows them to control and manipulate the situation being studied. Instead of being passive recorders of behavior, researchers actively do something that they believe will affect people's behavior and then observe what happens. These procedures allow experimenters to draw conclusions about cause and effect—about what causes what.

All psychological studies must conform to ethical guidelines, but such guidelines are especially important in experimental research. In colleges and universities, a review committee must approve all studies and be sure they conform to federal regulations. Volunteers in the study must consent to participate and know enough about it to make an intelligent decision, a doctrine known as **informed consent**. Researchers must protect participants from physical and mental harm, and if any risk exists, must warn them and give them an opportunity to withdraw at any time.

Watch the **Video** Special Topics: Ethics and Psychological Research at **MyPsychLab**

Ethical guidelines also require the humane treatment of research animals, which are used in only a small minority of psychological studies but are crucial to progress in some fields, especially biological psychology and behavioral research. Because of increased concern about the rights and welfare of animals, the APA's guidelines for using animals in research have been made more comprehensive, and federal regulations governing the housing and care of animals have been strengthened.

Experimental Variables LO 1.16

Imagine that you are a psychologist whose research interest is multitasking. Everyone seems to multitask these days, and you want to know whether that's a good thing or a bad thing. Specifically, you want to know whether or not using a handheld cell phone while driving is dangerous. Talking on a cell phone while driving is associated with an increase in traffic accidents, but maybe that's just for people who are risk takers or

experiment A controlled test of a hypothesis in which the researcher manipulates one variable to discover its effect on another.

informed consent The doctrine that anyone who participates in human research must do so voluntarily and must know enough about the study to make an intelligent decision about whether to take part.

lousy drivers to begin with. To pin down cause and effect, you decide to do an experiment.

 Watch the **Video** What's In It For Me?: The Myth of Multitasking at **MyPsychLab**

In a laboratory, you ask participants to "drive" using a computerized driving simulator equipped with an automatic transmission, steering wheel, gas pedal, and brake pedal. The object, you tell them, is to maximize the distance covered by driving on a busy highway while avoiding collisions with other cars. Some of the participants talk on the phone for 15 minutes to a research assistant in the next room about a topic that interests them; others just drive. You are going to compare how many collisions the two groups have. The basic design of this experiment is illustrated in Figure 1.3, which you may want to refer to as you read the next few pages.

The aspect of an experimental situation manipulated or varied by the researcher is known as the **independent variable**. The reaction of the subjects—the behavior that the researcher tries to predict—is the **dependent variable**. Every experiment has at least one independent and one dependent variable. In our example, the independent variable is cell phone use (use versus nonuse). The dependent variable is the number of collisions.

Ideally, everything in the experimental situation except the independent variable is held constant—that is, kept the same for all participants. You would not have those in one group use a stick shift and those in the other group drive an automatic, unless shift type were an independent variable. Similarly, you would not have people in one group go through the experiment alone and those in the other group perform in front of an audience. Holding everything but the independent variable constant ensures that whatever happens is the result of the researcher's manipulation and not something else. It allows you to rule out other interpretations.

independent variable
A variable that an experimenter manipulates.

dependent variable A variable that an experimenter predicts will be affected by manipulations of the independent variable.

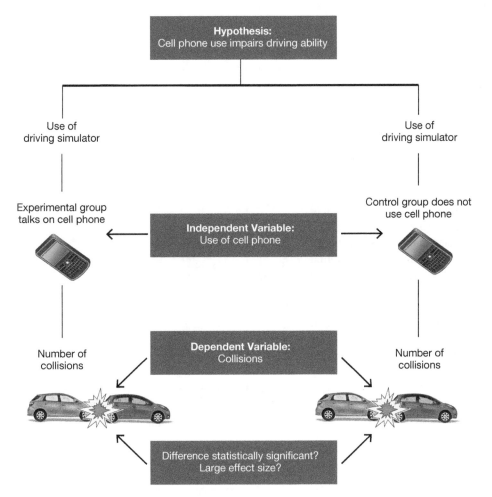

FIGURE 1.3 Do Cell Phone Use and Driving Mix?
The text describes this experimental design to test the hypothesis that talking on a cell phone while driving impairs driving skills and leads to accidents.

control condition In an experiment, a comparison condition in which subjects are not exposed to the same treatment as are those in the experimental condition.

random assignment A procedure for assigning people to experimental and control groups in which each individual has the same probability as any other of being assigned to a given group.

placebo An inactive substance or fake treatment used as a control in an experiment.

You might think of it this way: The dependent variable—the outcome of the study—*depends* on the independent variable. When psychologists set up an experiment, they think, "If I do X, the people in my study will do Y." The "X" represents the independent variable; the "Y" represents the dependent variable:

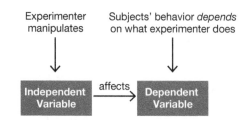

Most variables may be either independent or dependent, depending on what the experimenter wishes to find out. If you want to know whether eating chocolate makes people nervous, then the amount of chocolate eaten is the independent variable. If you want to know whether feeling nervous makes people eat chocolate, then the amount of chocolate eaten is the dependent variable.

Experimental and Control Conditions

Experiments usually require both an experimental condition and a **control condition** for comparison. People in the control condition are treated exactly like those in the experimental condition, except that they are not exposed to the same treatment, or manipulation of the independent variable. Without a control condition, you cannot be sure that the behavior you are interested in would not have occurred anyway, even without your manipulation. In some studies, the same subjects can be used in both the control and the experimental condition; they are said to serve as their own controls. In other studies, people are assigned to either an *experimental group* or a *control group*.

In our cell phone study, we will use two different groups. Participants who talk on the phone while driving make up the experimental group, and those who just drive along silently make up the control group. We want these two groups to be roughly the same in terms of average driving skill. It would not do to start out with a bunch of reckless roadrunners in the experimental group and a bunch of tired tortoises in the control group. We also want the two groups to be similar in age, education, driving history, and other characteristics so that none of these variables will affect our results. One way to accomplish this is to use **random assignment** of

people to one group or another, say by randomly assigning them numbers and putting those with even numbers in one group and those with odd numbers in another. If we have enough participants in our study, individual characteristics that could possibly affect the results are likely to be roughly balanced in the two groups, so we can safely ignore them.

Sometimes researchers use several experimental or control groups. In our study, we might want to examine the effects of short versus long phone conversations, or conversations on different topics—say, work, personal matters, and *very* personal matters. In that case, we would have more than one experimental group to compare with the control group. In our hypothetical example, though, we'll just have one experimental group, and all participants in it will drive for 15 minutes while talking about a topic of their own choice.

This description does not cover all the procedures used by psychological researchers. In some kinds of studies, people in the control group get a **placebo,** a fake treatment or sugar pill that looks, tastes, or smells like a real treatment or medication but is phony. If the placebo produces the same result as the real thing, the reason must be the participants' expectations rather than the treatment itself. Placebos are critical in testing new drugs because of the optimism that a potential cure often generates (see Chapter 12). Medical placebos usually take the form of pills or injections that contain no active ingredients. (To see what placebos revealed in a study of Viagra for women's sexual problems, see Figure 1.4.)

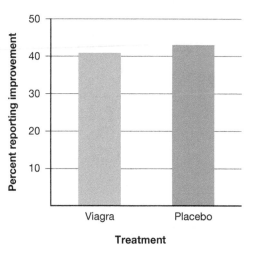

FIGURE 1.4 Does Viagra Work for Women?
Placebos are essential to determine whether people taking a new drug improve because of the drug or because of their expectations about it. In one study, 41 percent of women taking Viagra said their sex lives had improved. That sounds impressive, but so did 43 percent of those taking a placebo pill (Basson et al., 2002).

Control groups can also be crucial in descriptive studies. For example, if you give a self-esteem test only to girls, you can't conclude that they have lower self-esteem than boys do. And if someone reports that divorce has long-term consequences for the children, you will need to know how children in a control group (whose parents are still together) are doing.

Experimenter Effects LO 1.17

Because expectations can influence the results of a study, participants should not know whether they are in an experimental or a control group. When this is so, as it usually is, the experiment is said to be a **single-blind study**. But participants are not the only ones who bring expectations to the laboratory; so do researchers. And researchers' expectations, biases, and hopes for a particular result may cause them to inadvertently influence the participants' responses through facial expressions, posture, tone of voice, or some other cue. Such **experimenter effects** can be powerful; even an experimenter's friendly smile can affect people's responses in a study (Rosenthal, 1994).

One solution to this problem is to do a **double-blind study**. In such a study, the person running the experiment, the one having actual contact with the participants, also does not know who is in which group until the data have been gathered. Double-blind procedures are standard in drug research. Different doses of a drug (and whether it is the active drug or a placebo) are coded in some way, and the person administering the drug is kept in the dark about the code's meaning until after the experiment. To run our cell phone study in a double-blind fashion, we could use a simulator that automatically records collisions and have the experimenter give instructions through an intercom so that he or she will not know which group a participant was in until after the results are tallied.

Advantages and Limitations of Experiments

Because experiments allow conclusions about cause and effect, and because they permit researchers to distinguish real effects from placebo effects, they have long been the method of choice in psychology.

However, like all methods, the experiment has its limitations. Just as in other kinds of studies, the participants are typically college students and may not always be representative of the larger population. Moreover, in an experiment, the researcher sets up what is often a rather artificial situation, and the participants try to do as they are told. In their desire to cooperate, advance scientific knowledge, or present themselves in a positive light, they may act in ways that they ordinarily would not.

single-blind study An experiment in which subjects do not know whether they are in an experimental or a control group.

experimenter effects Unintended changes in subjects' behavior as a result of cues that the experimenter inadvertently conveys.

double-blind study An experiment in which neither the people being studied nor the individuals running the study know who is in the control group and who is in the experimental group until after the results are tallied.

Psychologists doing field research have studied diverse questions, such as whether men and women differ in how much they talk and how people in crowded places modify their gaze and body position to preserve a sense of privacy.

field research

Descriptive or experimental research conducted in a natural setting outside the laboratory.

Thus, experimental psychologists confront a dilemma: The more control they exercise over the situation, the more unlike real life it may be. For this reason, many psychologists have called for more **field research**, the careful study of behavior in natural contexts such as schools and the workplace. Have you ever wondered if women are more "talkative" than men, as the stereotype suggests? A field study of people in their everyday lives would be the best way to answer this question. Indeed, such a study has been done: The participants wore an unobtrusive recording device as they went about their normal lives, talking and chatting. The researchers found no gender differences at all (Mehl et al., 2007).

Every research method has strengths and weaknesses. Did you make a list of each method's advantages and disadvantages, as we suggested earlier? If so, compare it now with the one in Table 1.3.

TABLE 1.3 Research Methods in Psychology: Their Advantages and Disadvantages

Method	Advantages	Disadvantages
Case study	Good source of hypotheses. Provides in-depth information on an individual. Unusual cases can shed light on situations or problems that are unethical or impractical to study in other ways.	Vital information may be missing, making the case hard to interpret. The person's memories or self-reports may be selective or inaccurate. The individual may not be representative or typical.
Naturalistic observation	Allows description of a behavior as it occurs in the natural environment.	Allows the researcher little or no control of the situation. Observations may be biased. Does not allow firm conclusions about cause and effect.
Laboratory observation	Allows more control than naturalistic observation. Allows use of sophisticated equipment.	Allows researcher only limited control of the situation. Observations may be biased. Does not allow firm conclusions about cause and effect. Behavior may differ from behavior in the natural environment.
Test	Yields information on personality traits, emotional states, aptitudes, and abilities.	Difficult to construct tests that are reliable and valid.
Survey	Provides a large amount of information on large numbers of people.	If the sample is nonrepresentative or biased, it may be impossible to generalize from the results. Responses may be inaccurate or untrue.
Correlational study	Shows whether two or more variables are related.	Usually does not permit identification of cause and effect.
Experiment	Allows the researcher to control the situation. Permits the researcher to identify cause and effect and to distinguish placebo effects from treatment effects.	The situation is artificial, and results may not generalize well to the real world. It is sometimes difficult to avoid experimenter effects.

You are about to learn...

- why averages can be misleading.
- how psychologists can tell whether a finding is strong or trivial.
- why some findings are significant statistically yet unimportant in practical terms.
- how psychologists can combine results from many studies of a question to get a better overall answer.

Evaluating the Findings

If you are a psychologist who has just done an observational study, a survey, or an experiment, your work has just begun. Once you have some results in hand, you must do three things with them: (1) describe them, (2) assess how reliable and meaningful they are, and (3) figure out how to explain them.

Descriptive Statistics: Finding Out What's So LO 1.18

Let's say that 30 people in the cell phone experiment talked on the phone and 30 did not. We have recorded the number of collisions for each person on the driving simulator. Now we have 60 numbers. What can we do with them?

The first step is to summarize the data. The world does not want to hear how many collisions each person had. It wants to know what happened in the cell phone group as a whole, compared to what happened in the control group. To provide this information, we need numbers that sum up our data. Such numbers, known as **descriptive statistics**, are often depicted in graphs and charts.

A good way to summarize the data is to compute group averages. The most commonly used type of average is the **arithmetic mean**, which is calculated by adding up all the individual scores and dividing the result by the number of scores. We can compute a mean for the cell phone group by adding up the 30 collision scores and dividing the sum by 30. Then we can do the same for the control group. Now our 60 numbers have been boiled down to 2. For the sake of our example, let's assume that the cell phone group had an average of 10 collisions, whereas the control group's average was only 7.

We must be careful, however, about how we interpret these averages. It is possible that no one in our cell phone group actually had 10 collisions. Perhaps half the people in the group were motoring

descriptive statistics Statistics that organize and summarize research data.

arithmetic mean An average that is calculated by adding up a set of quantities and dividing the sum by the total number of quantities in the set.

Most people assume that "average" means "typical," but sometimes it doesn't. Averages can be misleading if you don't know the extent to which events deviated from the statistical mean and how they were distributed.

maniacs and had 15 collisions, whereas the others were more cautious and had only 5. Perhaps almost all of the participants had 9, 10, or 11 collisions. Perhaps the number of accidents ranged from 0 to 15. The mean does not tell us about such variability in the subjects' responses. For that, we need other descriptive statistics. For example, the **standard deviation** tells us how clustered or spread out the individual scores are around the mean; the more spread out they are, the less typical of everybody the mean is. Unfortunately, when research is reported in the news, you usually hear only about the mean.

Inferential Statistics: Asking "So What?" LO 1.19

At this point in our experiment, we have one group with an average of 10 collisions and another with an average of 7. Should we break out the champagne? Hold a press conference? Call our mothers? Better hold off. Perhaps if one group had an average of 15 collisions and the other an average of 1, we could get excited. But rarely does a psychological study hit you between the eyes with a sensationally clear result. In most cases, there is some possibility that the difference between the two groups was simply the result of chance. Despite all of our precautions, perhaps the people in the cell phone group just happened to be a little more accident-prone, and their extra 3 collisions had nothing to do with talking on the phone.

To find out how impressive the data are, psychologists use **inferential statistics**. These statistics do not merely describe the findings; they permit researchers to draw inferences (conclusions based on evidence) about how meaningful the findings are. Like descriptive statistics, inferential statistics involve the application of mathematical formulas to the data.

Historically, the most commonly used inferential statistics have been **significance tests**, which tell researchers how likely it is that a result occurred by chance. Let's hypothesize that in the real world, people who talk on cell phones have no more

collisions than people who do not. How likely, then, would we be to obtain the difference we found (or an even larger one) between the experimental group and the control group? If that likelihood is quite low, we can reject the hypothesis that there is no difference in the real world, and we can say that the result is *statistically significant*—that the difference we found in our study is probably real.

By convention, psychologists consider a result to be significant if it would be expected to occur by chance 5 or fewer times in 100 repetitions of the study. They would then say that the result is significant at the .05 ("point oh five") level, or $p<.05$, where p stands for probability and .05 is referred to as the p *value*. If, however, the p value is greater than .05, many researchers would have little confidence in the study's result, although they might still want to do further research to confirm their judgment.

Today, a growing number of psychologists and other researchers also report their results by using a statistical formula that creates a **confidence interval**. The mean from a particular sample will almost never be exactly the same as the true mean in the population. A confidence interval specifies, with a particular probability, a range a little higher and lower than the sample mean to help depict where the true population mean probably lies (Fidler & Loftus, 2009). As Figure 1.5 shows, if you repeated your study many times, you would get a somewhat different sample mean and confidence interval each time, but most of the intervals would contain the true population mean (Cumming, 2012).

By the way, many studies similar to our hypothetical one have confirmed the dangers of talking on a cell phone while driving. In one study, cell phone users, whether their phones were handheld or hands-free, were as impaired in their driving ability as intoxicated drivers were (Strayer, Drews, & Crouch, 2006). Because of such research, some states have made it illegal to drive while holding a cell phone to your ear. Others are considering making any cell phone use by a driver illegal. We will revisit this topic, and the general issue of multitasking, in Chapter 7.

standard deviation A commonly used measure of variability that indicates the average difference between scores in a distribution and their mean.

inferential statistics Statistical procedures that allow researchers to draw inferences about how statistically meaningful a study's results are.

significance tests Statistical tests that assess how likely it is that a study's results occurred merely by chance.

Confidence interval A statistical measure that provides, with a specified probability, a range of values within which a population mean is likely to lie.

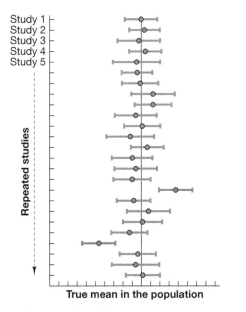

FIGURE 1.5 Confidence Intervals Across Repeated Studies

If you repeat your study over and over, you will get a slightly different sample mean and confidence interval each time. But the vast majority of the confidence intervals would contain the true population mean (the straight vertical line). Occasionally, though, you will get a rogue result (the gray bars). That is why it can be risky to draw strong conclusions on the basis of only one study: It might be the one rogue.

Interpreting the Findings LO 1.20

The last step in any study is to figure out what the findings mean. Trying to understand behavior from uninterpreted findings is like trying to become fluent in Swedish by reading a Swedish–English dictionary. Just as you need the grammar of Swedish to tell you how the words fit together, psychologists need hypotheses and theories to explain how the facts that emerge from research fit together.

Choosing the Best Explanation. Sometimes it is hard to choose between competing explanations. Does cell phone use disrupt driving by impairing coordination, by increasing a driver's vulnerability to distraction, by interfering with the processing of information, by distorting the driver's perception of danger, or by some combination of these or other factors? Several explanations may fit the results equally well, which means that more research will be needed to determine the best one.

Sometimes the best interpretation does not emerge until a hypothesis has been tested in different ways. If the findings of studies using different methods converge, there is greater reason to be confident about them. On the other hand, if they conflict, researchers will know they must modify their hypotheses or do more research.

Here is an example. When psychologists compare the mental-test scores of young people and old people, they usually find that younger people consistently outscore older ones. This type of study, in which different groups are compared at the same time, is called a **cross-sectional study**:

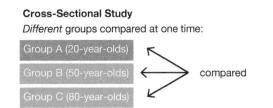

Cross-Sectional Study
Different groups compared at one time:

But **longitudinal studies**, in which the same people are followed over a period of time and reassessed at regular intervals, can also be used to investigate mental abilities across the life span:

Longitudinal Study
Same group compared at different times:

In contrast to cross-sectional studies, longitudinal studies find that as people age, they sometimes continue to perform as well as they ever did on many mental tests. A *general* decline in ability may not occur until people reach their 70s or 80s (see Chapter 3). Why do results from the two types of studies conflict? Probably because cross-sectional studies measure generational differences. Younger generations tend to outperform older ones in part because they are better educated or more familiar with the tests used. Without longitudinal studies, we might falsely conclude that all types of mental ability inevitably decline with advancing age.

Judging the Result's Importance. Sometimes psychologists agree on the reliability and meaning of a finding but not on its ultimate relevance for theory or practical application. Part of the problem is statistical. Traditional tests of significance are widely used in psychology, which is why we have described them here, but these tests have some serious drawbacks (Cumming, 2012; Cumming et al., 2007; Erceg-Hurn & Mirosevich, 2008). A result may be statistically significant at the "point oh-five level,"

yet be small and of little consequence in everyday life because the independent variable does not explain most of the variation in people's behavior.

cross-sectional study
A study in which groups of people (or animals) of different ages are compared at a given time.

longitudinal study A study in which people (or animals) are followed and periodically reassessed over a period of time.

effect size An objective, standardized way of describing the strength of the independent variable's influence on the dependent variable.

meta-analysis A set of techniques for combining and analyzing data from a number of related studies to determine the explanatory strength of a particular independent variable.

Further, *p* values can vary considerably from one replication to another, which is why many findings don't pan out in later studies (Miller, 2011).

To protect against spurious results, many journals now encourage or require the use of alternate methods that yield an **effect size**, which helps us understand how important an effect is. One such measure reveals how much of the variation in the data is accounted for by the independent variable. If it explains 5 percent of the variation, it's not too meaningful, even if the result is statistically significant; if it explains 40 percent, it's impressive.

Another useful set of statistical techniques, called **meta-analysis**, combines and analyzes data from a large number of related studies instead of assessing each study's results separately. Meta-analysis tells the researcher how powerful an independent variable is across all the studies in the analysis.

Suppose we did 10 studies on everybody's favorite subject, gender differences. We might get contradictory results, or some results that were significant and others that were not. Meta-analysis can come to the rescue, providing us with a clearer picture. For example, what is the reason for the

gender gap in math achievement, which persists in some nations but not others? Is it due mainly to a "natural" male superiority in math, or to gender differences in educational and professional opportunities? A meta-analysis of studies across 69 nations, representing nearly 500,000 students ages 14 to 16, found that although boys have more positive attitudes toward math than girls, average effect sizes in actual mathematics achievement are small. However, *national* effect sizes show considerable variability; that is, a male-female math gap is wider in some countries than others. The strongest predictors of that cross-national variation are whether boys and girls are equally likely to be enrolled in school, the percentage of women in research jobs, and women's representation in their nation's government (Else-Quest, Hyde, & Linn, 2010).

Techniques such as meta-analysis are useful because rarely does one study prove anything, in psychology or any other field. That is why you should be suspicious of headlines that announce a sudden major scientific breakthrough based on a single study. Such breakthroughs do occur, but they are rare.

Recite & Review

✓ Study and Review at MyPsychLab

Recite: Major scientific breakthrough: Reciting what you've read really helps! So go ahead and recite everything you know about the arithmetic mean, the standard deviation, statistical significance, confidence intervals, cross-sectional versus longitudinal studies, effect sizes, and meta-analysis.

Review: Next, go back and reread this section.

Now take this *Quick Quiz*—but not while you're driving or multitasking!

A. Check your understanding of the descriptive–inferential distinction by mentally placing a check in the appropriate column for each phrase:

	Descriptive Statistics	Inferential Statistics
1. Summarize the data	_____	_____
2. Give likelihood of data occurring by chance	_____	_____
3. Include the mean	_____	_____
4. Give a measure of statistical significance	_____	_____
5. Tell you whether to call your mother about your results	_____	_____
6. Provide a confidence interval around the sample mean	_____	_____

B. Suppose a researcher wants to know how energy drinks affect memory, but in the 45 studies on this question the results have varied. What method might help determine whether the relationship between energy drinks and memory is strong or weak?

C. On the Internet, you read about a "Fantastic New Finding" about treating shyness. Why should you be cautious about this announcement?

Answers:

A. 1. descriptive **2.** inferential **3.** descriptive **4.** inferential **5.** inferential **6.** inferential **B.** meta-analysis **C.** Scientific progress usually proceeds gradually, not all at once. And besides, anyone can post a claim on the Internet, so you would want to ask: What is the original source of that claim? What was the science supporting it? How was shyness defined, and what was the method of treating it? How was success defined and measured?

PSYCHOLOGY IN THE NEWS REVISITED ///////

Now that you have finished this chapter, you are ready to explore more deeply what psychologists have learned about human behavior.

At the start of each of the remaining chapters, we will present one or more real news stories that raise psychological questions. Then, at the end of the chapter, we will revisit the story to show how the material you have learned can help you answer those questions. For now, if you are ready to share the excitement of studying human behavior; if you love a mystery and want to know not only who did it but also why they did it; if you are willing to reconsider what you think you think...then you are ready to read on.

Taking Psychology With You

Lying With Statistics

We have seen that statistical procedures are indispensible tools for assessing research. But statistics can also be manipulated, misrepresented, and even made up by people hoping to promote a particular political or social agenda. An essential part of critical and scientific thinking is learning not only how to use statistics correctly but also how to identify their misuse.

We don't want you to distrust all statistics. Statistics don't lie; people do—or, more likely, they misinterpret what the numbers mean. When statistics are used correctly, they neither confuse nor mislead. On the contrary, they can expose unwarranted conclusions, promote clarity and precision, and protect us from our biases and blind spots. You need to be careful, though, about statistics in blogs and the media. Here are a few things you can do when you hear that "2 million people do this" or "one out of four people are that":

Ask how the number was computed. Suppose someone on your campus gives a talk about a social problem and cites some big number to show how serious and widespread the problem is. You should ask how the number was calculated. Was it based on government data, such as the census? Did it come from just one small study, several published studies, or a meta-analysis of many studies? Or is it pure conjecture?

Ask about base rates and absolute numbers. Suppose we tell you that the *relative risk* of getting ulcers is increased by 300 percent in college students who eat a bagel every morning (it isn't, of course). That may sound pretty alarming, but it does not tell you much. You would need to know how many students get ulcers in the first place, and then how many bagel-eating students get ulcers. If the "300 percent increased risk" is a jump from 100 students in every thousand to 300 students in every thousand, then you might reasonably be concerned. If the number shifts from one in every thousand to three in every thousand, that is still a 300 percent increase, but the risk is small and could even be a random fluke. Many health findings are presented as an increased relative risk of this or that. But what you want to know before you start to worry is the *absolute risk*—that is, what the increase is in actual, absolute numbers. It may be trivial (Bluming & Tavris, 2009; Gigerenzer et al., 2008).

Ask how terms were defined. If we hear that "one out of every four women" will be raped at some point in her life, we need to ask: How was rape defined? If women are asked if they have ever experienced any act of unwanted sex, the percentages will be higher than if they are asked specifically whether they have been forced or coerced into intercourse. Conversely, although far more women are raped by men they know than by strangers, many women do not define acts of date rape or acquaintance rape as rape, and that fact will lower the percentages.

"I still don't have all the answers, but I'm beginning to ask the right questions."

Always, always look for the control group. If an experiment does not have a control group, then, as they say in New York, "fuhgeddaboutit." Lack of a control group is a frequent problem in "research" promoting a new herbal supplement, treatment, or self-improvement program. As you will learn in Chapter 7, people are motivated to justify any program or treatment in which they have invested time, money, or effort. Further, thanks to the placebo effect, people's expectations of success are often what helps them, not the treatment itself. This is why testimonials don't provide a full or accurate picture of a medication's or treatment's benefits or harms.

Be cautious about correlations. We said this before, but we'll say it again: With correlational findings, you usually cannot be sure what's causing what. A study reported that teenagers who listened to music five or more hours a day were eight times more likely to be depressed than those who didn't listen that much (Primack et al., 2011). Does listening to music make you depressed? Or do depressed teenagers tend to tune out and listen to music because they don't have the mental energy to do much else? "At this point, it is not clear whether depressed people begin to listen to more music to escape, or whether listening to large amounts of music can lead to depression, or both," said the lead researcher.

Unfortunately, bad statistics, repeated again and again, can infiltrate popular culture, spread like a virus on the Internet, and become difficult to eradicate. The information in this chapter will get you started on telling the difference between numbers that are useful and those that mislead or deceive. For entertaining books on this topic, we recommend *Damned Lies and Statistics* by Joel Best (2012) and *Naked Statistics: Stripping the dread from the data* by Charles Wheelan (2013). In future chapters, we will give you additional information to help you think critically and scientifically about popular claims and findings that make the news.

Summary

(((Listen to the Audio File at MyPsychLab

The Science of Psychology

- *Psychology* is the discipline concerned with behavior and mental processes and how they are affected by an organism's external and internal environment. Psychology's methods and reliance on *empirical evidence* distinguish it from pseudoscience and "psychobabble."

- Psychological findings often contradict prevailing beliefs, but a finding does not have to be surprising or counterintuitive to be scientifically important.

- Psychology's forerunners made some valid observations and had some useful insights, but without rigorous empirical methods, they also made serious errors in the description and explanation of behavior, as in the case of *phrenology*.

- The official founder of scientific psychology was Wilhelm Wundt, who established the first psychological laboratory in 1879, in Leipzig, Germany. Wundt emphasized the analysis of experience into basic elements, through *trained introspection*.

- A competing approach, *functionalism*, which was inspired in part by the evolutionary theories of Charles Darwin, emphasized the functions of behavior. One of its leading proponents was William James.

- Psychology as a method of psychotherapy has roots in Sigmund Freud's theory of *psychoanalysis*, which emphasizes unconscious causes of mental and emotional problems.

- Four points of view predominate today in psychological science. The *biological perspective* emphasizes bodily events associated with actions, thoughts, and feelings, as well as genetic contributions to behavior. Within this perspective, a popular specialty, *evolutionary psychology*, emphasizes the purposes and functions of behavior, as functionalism did.

- The *learning perspective* emphasizes how the environment and a person's history affect behavior; within this perspective, *behaviorists* reject mentalistic explanations and *social–cognitive learning theorists* combine elements of behaviorism with the study of thoughts, values, and intentions.

- The *cognitive perspective* emphasizes mental processes in perception, problem solving, belief formation, and other human activities.

- The *sociocultural perspective* explores how social contexts and cultural rules affect an individual's beliefs and behavior.

- Each approach has made important contributions to psychology, but many psychologists draw on more than one school of thought.

What Psychologists Do

- Psychologists do research and teach in colleges and universities, provide mental health services (*psychological practice*), and conduct research and apply findings in a wide variety of nonacademic settings.

- *Applied psychology* is concerned with the practical uses of psychological knowledge. *Basic psychology* is concerned with knowledge for its own sake.

- *Psychotherapist* is an unregulated term for anyone who does therapy, including people who have no credentials or training at all. Licensed therapists differ according to their training and approach. *Clinical psychologists* have a Ph.D., an Ed.D., or a Psy.D.; *psychiatrists* have an M.D.; *psychoanalysts* are trained in psychoanalytic institutes; and licensed clinical social workers (LCSWs) and marriage, family, and child counselors (MFCCs) generally have at least a master's degree in social work or psychology, although licensing requirements vary.

- Many psychologists are concerned about an increase in poorly trained psychotherapists who lack a firm understanding of research methods and findings, or use untested or ineffective techniques.

Critical and Scientific Thinking in Psychology

- One benefit of studying psychology is the development of *critical-thinking* skills and attitudes. Critical thinkers ask questions, define terms clearly, examine the evidence, analyze assumptions and biases, avoid emotional reasoning, avoid oversimplification, consider alternative interpretations, and tolerate uncertainty. These practices are not only useful in ordinary life but are also the basis of the scientific method.

- Scientists are required to state hypotheses and predictions precisely and formulate *operational definitions* ("define your terms"); to gather empirical evidence; to comply with the *principle of falsifiability* ("analyze assumptions") and resist the *confirmation bias*; to be cautious in settling on a theory ("consider other interpretations"); and to resist drawing firm conclusions until results are replicated ("tolerate uncertainty").

Descriptive Studies: Establishing the Facts

- In any study, the researcher would like to use a sample that is representative of the larger population that the researcher wishes to describe. But in practice, researchers must often rely on "convenience samples," which typically means college undergraduates. Most of the time, that does not pose a problem, but in some cases, conclusions about "people in general" must be interpreted with caution.

- *Descriptive methods* allow psychologists to describe and predict behavior but not necessarily to choose one explanation over others. Such methods include case studies, observational studies, psychological tests, and surveys, as well as correlational methods.

- *Case studies* are detailed descriptions of individuals. They are often used by clinicians, and they can also be valuable in exploring new research topics and addressing questions that would otherwise be difficult to study. But because information is often missing or hard to interpret, and because the person under study may not be representative of people in general, case studies are typically sources rather than tests of hypotheses.

- In *observational studies*, researchers systematically observe and record behavior without interfering in any way with the behavior. *Naturalistic observation* is used to find out how people behave in their natural environments. *Laboratory observation* allows more control and the use of special equipment; behavior in the laboratory, however, may differ in certain ways from behavior in natural contexts.

- *Psychological tests* are used to measure and evaluate personality traits, emotional states, aptitudes, interests, abilities, and values. A good test is one that has been *standardized*, is scored using established *norms*, and has both *reliability* and *validity*. Controversy exists about the validity of even some widely used tests.

- *Surveys* are questionnaires or interviews that ask people directly about their experiences, attitudes, and opinions. They are difficult to do well; sampling problems and *volunteer bias* can influence the generalizability of the results. Findings can also be affected by biased questions and by the fact that respondents sometimes lie, misremember their experiences, or misinterpret the questions. Technology and use of the Internet can minimize some of these problems, but people should be cautious about tests posted on the Internet, because not all of them meet scientific standards.

Correlational Studies: Looking for Relationships

- In descriptive research, studies that look for relationships between phenomena are known as *correlational*. A *correlation* is a measure of the strength of a positive or negative relationship between two variables, and is expressed by the *coefficient of correlation*.

- Many correlations reported in the media or on the Internet are based on rumor and anecdote. An *illusory correlation* may occur because of a coincidental link between two variables. Even when a correlation is real, it does not necessarily demonstrate a causal relationship between the variables.

The Experiment: Hunting for Causes

- *Experiments* allow researchers to control the situation being studied, manipulate an *independent variable*, and assess the effects of the manipulation on a *dependent variable*. Because of the element of manipulation, ethical guidelines are especially important in experimental research. These guidelines govern studies with human beings, who must give *informed consent* before participating, and also studies of animals, which must be treated humanely.

- Experimental studies usually require a comparison or *control condition*, and often involve *random assignment* of participants to experimental and control groups. In some studies, those in the control group receive a *placebo*, or fake treatment. *Single-blind* and *double-blind* procedures can be used to prevent the expectations of the participants or the experimenter from affecting the results. Because experiments allow conclusions about cause and effect, they have long been the method of choice in psychology. However, like laboratory observations, experiments create a special situation that may call forth behavior not typical in other environments. Many psychologists, therefore, have called for more *field research*.

Evaluating the Findings

● Psychologists use *descriptive statistics*, such as the *arithmetic mean* and the *standard deviation*, to summarize data. They use *inferential statistics* to find out how impressive the data are.

● *Significance tests* tell researchers how likely it is that the results of a study occurred merely by chance. The results are said to be *statistically significant* if this likelihood is very low. *Confidence intervals* help researchers evaluate where the real population mean is likely to be if the study could be repeated over and over.

● Choosing among competing interpretations of a finding can be difficult, and care must be taken to avoid going beyond the facts. Sometimes the best interpretation does not emerge until a hypothesis has been tested in more than one way, such as by using both *cross-sectional* and *longitudinal methods*.

● Statistical significance does not always imply real-world importance because the amount of variation in the data accounted for by the independent variable may be small. Therefore, many psychologists are now turning to other measures. The *effect size* provides a way of describing the strength of an independent variable's influence on the dependent variable. *Meta-analysis* is a set of techniques for combining data from related studies to determine the overall explanatory strength of an independent variable.

Taking Psychology With You

● Statistics help scientists understand the complexity of behavior, but statistics can also be misrepresented and misused. Critical thinkers should ask how numbers were calculated, consider percentages that reveal *absolute risk* rather than just *relative risk*, ask how terms were defined, look for a control group, and be cautious about inferring causation from a correlation.

Key Terms

Use this list to check your understanding of terms and people in this chapter. If you have trouble with a term, you can find it on the page listed.

The Science of Psychology

↓

Psychology is the discipline concerned with behavior and mental processes and how they are affected by an organism's physical state, mental state, and external environment. Unlike pseudoscientific approaches to behavior, it relies on **empirical** data.

The Birth of Modern Psychology

- Wilhelm Wundt founded the first psychology laboratory in Leipzig, Germany, in 1879, and emphasized the analysis of experience through trained introspection.
- American William James emphasized the adaptive nature of behavior, an approach known as **functionalism**.
- Sigmund Freud developed **psychoanalysis**, an early form of psychotherapy, in Vienna, Austria.

Psychology's Present

The four major perspectives of psychological science:
- The **biological perspective** focuses on how bodily events interact with the external environment to affect behavior, feelings, and thoughts.
- The **learning perspective** emphasizes the environment's effect on behavior.
- The **cognitive perspective** emphasizes mental processes in reasoning, memory, perception, language, problem solving, and beliefs.
- The **sociocultural perspective** focuses on the influence of social and cultural forces on behavior.

What Psychologists Do

↓

Psychologists differ in the work they do. They may:
- conduct research, either in **basic psychology**, to gain knowledge for its own sake; or in **applied psychology**, to find practical uses for knowledge.
- teach.
- provide mental health services (psychological practice).
- consult with business, governmental, and other groups to apply the findings of research.

Psychological practitioners seek to understand and improve people's physical and mental health. There are many kinds, with different qualifications:
- Psychotherapist is an unregulated term.
- Clinical psychologists have Ph.D., Ed.D., or Psy.D. degrees.
- Psychiatrists have M.D. degrees.
- Psychoanalysts have completed training in psychoanalytic institutes.

Critical and Scientific Thinking in Psychology

↓

Critical thinking rests on eight basic guidelines:
- Ask questions.
- Define terms.
- Examine the evidence for a claim.
- Analyze assumptions (beliefs taken for granted) and biases (beliefs that prevent us from considering the evidence fairly).

  — **Principle of falsifiability**, the statement of a **hypothesis** in such a way that it can be disproved by counterevidence.

  — **Confirmation bias**, the tendency to look for and accept evidence that supports our beliefs and ignore evidence that disconfirms them.

- Avoid emotional reasoning.
- Avoid oversimplification.
- Consider alternative explanations.

  — In science, the goal is to develop a **theory**, an organized system of assumptions and principles that explain a set of phenomena and their interrelationships.

- Tolerate uncertainty.

  — Psychological scientists resist drawing firm conclusions until others have **replicated** the study and gotten similar results.

Strategies for Studying

→

- Read, recite, review.
- Dig deep—process the information.
- Retest yourself on previously recalled material.
- Forget about cramming.

Research Methods in Psychology

Representative Samples

A **representative sample** is a group of participants that accurately represents the larger population that the researcher is interested in.

↓

Descriptive Studies: Establishing the Facts

- **Case study**: a detailed description of a particular individual, based on observation or formal psychological testing.
- **Observational study**: careful observation, measurement, and recording of behavior without intruding on the subjects.
- **Psychological tests**: assessment instruments that measure and evaluate personality traits, emotional states, aptitudes, interest, abilities, and values.
- **Surveys**: questionnaires or interviews that ask people directly about their experiences, attitudes, or opinions.

Correlational Studies: Looking for Relationships

A **positive** or **negative correlation** is a measure of the strength of a relationship between two variables.
- A **coefficient of correlation** summarizes the strength and direction of a relationship.
- A correlation does not establish cause and effect.

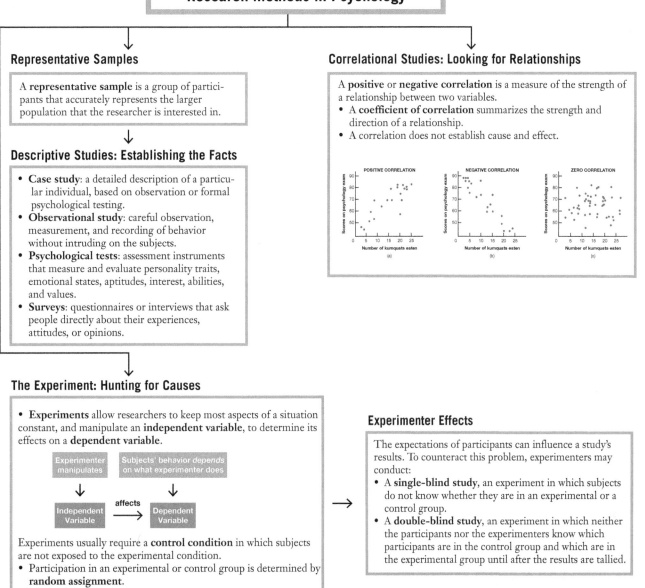

The Experiment: Hunting for Causes

- **Experiments** allow researchers to keep most aspects of a situation constant, and manipulate an **independent variable**, to determine its effects on a **dependent variable**.

Experiments usually require a **control condition** in which subjects are not exposed to the experimental condition.
- Participation in an experimental or control group is determined by **random assignment**.
- Drug experiments typically include the use of a **placebo**, an inactive substance used as a control.

→

Experimenter Effects

The expectations of participants can influence a study's results. To counteract this problem, experimenters may conduct:
- A **single-blind study**, an experiment in which subjects do not know whether they are in an experimental or a control group.
- A **double-blind study**, an experiment in which neither the participants nor the experimenters know which participants are in the control group and which are in the experimental group until after the results are tallied.

Evaluating the Findings

- **Descriptive statistics** (including the **arithmetic mean and standard deviation**) organize and summarize data.
- **Inferential statistics** help to determine how meaningful the findings are.
- **Significance tests** measure the probability that the study's findings could have occurred by chance.
- **Confidence intervals** provide a range of values within which a true population mean is likely to lie.
- Interpretation of findings may need to await studies using different methods. For example, **cross-sectional studies** compare subjects of different ages; **longitudinal** studies follow subjects over many years.

- Statistical procedures can reveal the **effect size**, how powerful the independent variable is.
- **Meta-analysis** combines and analyzes data from many related studies to determine the explanatory strength of a particular independent variable.

CONCEPT MAP CHAPTER 1 Exploring Psychology

UNDERSTANDING PERSONALITY

PSYCHOLOGY IN THE NEWS //////////////////////////

Steve Jobs, "Father of the Digital Revolution," Dead at 56

PALO ALTO, CA, October 5, 2011. Steve Jobs, celebrated worldwide as a visionary, a master of innovation, and "the father of the digital revolution," died today of the pancreatic cancer he fought for eight years. His family announced that there would be only a private memorial service and that Jobs would be buried in an unmarked grave, as was his wish.

The son of a Syrian immigrant and an American mother, Jobs was adopted shortly after his birth by Paul and Clara Jobs, a California couple. His early education was erratic. He dropped out of college after six months, spending the next year and a half taking classes that interested him, including one on calligraphy. Jobs later said that taking that single calligraphy class was the source of his fascination with typefaces and proportionally spaced fonts—a passion he eventually brought to creation of the Mac.

Before long, he went to India, where he roamed ashrams, shaved his head, and wore Indian attire. There he was heavily influenced by Buddhism, which teaches tranquility, lack of ego, compassion for others, and nonattachment to material things. Yet despite these lessons, Jobs later taught himself to stare unblinkingly at others to make them uncomfortable, and frequently yelled at his employees, calling them morons and other insulting names, sometimes screaming that their work "sucked." *Fortune* magazine wrote that he was "considered one of Silicon Valley's leading egomaniacs." According

to colleagues, he took credit for other people's work but went ballistic when he thought other people were taking credit for his. Yet, although he could be remarkably harsh to his employees, Jobs also inspired them, pressuring them to achieve what they never dreamed possible.

With Steve Wozniak, Jobs launched Apple Computers in his father's garage when he was only 21, amassed a net worth of $256 million by age 25, lost control of his company at 30, and was hired back a decade later for

Steve Jobs is remembered as a man of many contradictions.

$1 a year to turn that same company around. And turn it around, he did: He introduced the iMac, the iPod, the iPhone, and the iPad. Yet Jobs made some colossal mistakes because of his stubbornness and arrogance: The man who ran one of the most technologically advanced companies on the planet rejected cancer treatment for months because he didn't want his body to be opened up. Instead, he tried all kinds of unproven alternative diets and cancer "cures" that he found, of all places, on the Internet, including vegan diets, acupuncture, and herbs; he consulted a psychic and a doctor who prescribed juice fasts and bowel cleansings. Finally, in 2004, Jobs had surgery to remove the tumor, but by that time the cancer had spread.

Jobs is survived by his wife Laureen, their three children, a daughter from a previous relationship, and his sister Patty.

/////////

Who was the real Steve Jobs? Peaceful Buddhist or aggressive egomaniac? Introverted loner or dynamic leader? Smart or foolish? What led him to become a legend in the high-tech world? What personality traits best describe him: bold, insecure, kind, cruel, eccentric? Was he cruel to some employees because that was part of his personality or because he thought it was the way to get the job done? The kaleidoscope of qualities that made up Steve Jobs was a source of amazement to almost everyone who knew him.

When you think about your own personality, how would you describe yourself? Do you feel that you are "yourself" pretty consistently, across almost all situations, or do you think you change quite a bit depending on what group you're with, whether you're working on your own or hanging out at a bar, or whether you're with a friend or a romantic partner? Do you feel shy in new situations but outgoing in familiar ones, or that you are consistently a "shy person" everywhere you go?

In this chapter, we will see how psychologists study such questions. In psychology, **personality** refers to a distinctive pattern of behavior, mannerisms, thoughts, motives, and emotions that characterizes an individual over time and across different situations. This pattern consists of many distinctive **traits**, habitual ways of behaving, thinking, and feeling: shy, outgoing, friendly, hostile, gloomy, confident, and so on.

We will begin with the oldest theory of personality, the psychodynamic view, so that you will have a sense of how influential it was, why it still appeals to some, and why many of its ideas have become outdated. Next we will consider evidence for the newest theory, the genetic view. Few scientists today think that babies are little lumps of clay, shaped entirely by their experiences, or that parents alone determine whether their infant becomes an adventurer, a sourpuss, a worrywart, . . . or a Steve Jobs.

Yet, even if some of the human variation in personality traits comes from genetics, what is responsible for the rest? To answer that question, we will then examine leading approaches to personality that are neither psychodynamic nor biological. The environmental approach emphasizes the role of social learning, situations, parents, and peers. It makes us think critically about what we even think "personality" is, given that our behavior often changes quite dramatically across different situations and with different people. The cultural approach emphasizes cultural influences on traits and behavior, and invites us to think about how many behaviors that we think of as personality traits are actually determined by cultural norms and expectations—such as being "on time" or tardy, bathing often or rarely, being quick to anger or accepting of frustrations. Finally, we consider the humanist approach, which emphasizes self-determination and people's own view of themselves. When we are done, we will return to the puzzle of Steve Jobs and the forces that may have contributed to his unique personality.

personality A distinctive and relatively stable pattern of behavior, thoughts, motives, and emotions that characterizes an individual.

trait A characteristic of an individual, describing a habitual way of behaving, thinking, or feeling.

psychoanalysis A theory of personality and a method of psychotherapy developed by Sigmund Freud; it emphasizes unconscious motives and conflicts.

psychodynamic theories Theories that explain behavior and personality in terms of unconscious energy dynamics within the individual.

id In psychoanalysis, the part of personality containing inherited psychic energy, particularly sexual and aggressive instincts.

libido (li-BEE-do) In psychoanalysis, the psychic energy that fuels the life or sexual instincts of the id.

ego In psychoanalysis, the part of personality that represents reason, good sense, and rational self-control.

superego In psychoanalysis, the part of personality that represents conscience, morality, and social standards.

Sigmund Freud
(1856–1939).

You are about to learn...

- Sigmund Freud's theory of the structure and development of personality.
- Carl Jung's theory of the collective unconscious.
- the nature of the "objects" in the object-relations approach to personality.
- why many psychologists reject most psychodynamic ideas.

Psychodynamic Theories of Personality

LO 2.1

A man apologizes for "displacing" his frustrations at work onto his family. A woman suspects that she is "repressing" a childhood trauma. An alcoholic reveals that he is no longer "in denial" about his drinking. A teacher informs a divorcing couple that their 8-year-old child is "regressing" to immature behavior. All of this language about displacing, repressing, denying, and regressing can be traced to the first psychodynamic theory of personality, Sigmund Freud's theory of **psychoanalysis**.

Freud's theory is called **psychodynamic** because it emphasizes the movement of psychological energy within the person, in the form of attachments, conflicts, and motivations. (Freud did not use "dynamic" in today's sense, to mean "powerful" or "energetic." *Dynamics* is a term from physics that refers to the motion and balance of systems under the action of outside or internal forces.) Today's psychodynamic theories differ from Freud's and from one another, but they all share an emphasis on unconscious processes going on within the mind. They also share an assumption that adult personality and ongoing problems are formed primarily by experiences in early childhood. These experiences produce unconscious thoughts and feelings, which later contribute to characteristic habits, conflicts, and often self-defeating behavior.

Freud and Psychoanalysis LO 2.2, LO 2.3, LO 2.4

To enter the world of Freud is to enter a realm of unconscious motives, passions, guilty secrets, unspeakable yearnings, and conflicts between desire and duty. These unseen forces, Freud believed, have far more power over our personalities than our conscious intentions do. The unconscious reveals itself, said Freud, in art, dreams, jokes, apparent accidents, and slips of the tongue (which came to be called "Freudian slips"). According to Freud (1920/1960), the British member of Parliament who referred to the "honourable member from Hell" when he meant to say "from Hull" was revealing his true but unconscious appraisal of his colleague.

The Structure of Personality. In Freud's theory, personality consists of three major systems: the id, the ego, and the superego. Any action we take or problem we have results from the interaction and degree of balance among these systems (Freud, 1905, 1920/1960, 1923/1962).

The **id**, which is present at birth, is the reservoir of unconscious psychological energies and the motives to avoid pain and obtain pleasure. The id contains two competing instincts: the life, or sexual, instinct (fueled by psychic energy called the **libido**) and the death, or aggressive, instinct. As energy builds up in the id, tension results. The id may discharge this tension in the form of reflex actions, physical symptoms, or uncensored mental images and unbidden thoughts.

The **ego**, the second system to emerge, is a referee between the needs of instinct and the demands of society. It bows to the realities of life, putting a rein on the id's desire for sex and aggression until a suitable, socially appropriate outlet for them can be found. The ego, said Freud, is both conscious and unconscious, and it represents "reason and good sense."

The **superego**, the last system of personality to develop, is the voice of conscience, representing morality and parental authority. The superego judges the activities of the id, handing out good feelings of pride and satisfaction when you do something well and handing out miserable feelings of guilt and shame when you break the rules. The superego is partly conscious but largely unconscious.

According to Freud, the healthy personality must keep all three systems in balance. Someone who is too controlled by the id is governed by impulse and selfish desires. Someone who is too controlled by the superego is rigid, moralistic, and bossy. Someone who has a weak ego is unable to balance personal needs and wishes with social duties and realistic limitations.

✸ Explore the Concept Freud: Id, Ego, and Superego at MyPsychLab

If a person feels anxious or threatened when the wishes of the id conflict with social rules, the ego has weapons at its command to relieve the

"VERY WELL, I'LL INTRODUCE YOU. EGO, MEET ID. NOW GET BACK TO WORK."

tension. These unconscious strategies, called **defense mechanisms**, deny or distort reality, but they also protect us from conflict and anxiety. They become unhealthy only when they cause self-defeating behavior and emotional problems. Here are five of the primary defense mechanisms identified by Freud and later analysts (A. Freud, 1967; Vaillant, 1992):

1 **Repression** occurs when a threatening idea, memory, or emotion is blocked from consciousness: for example, a woman who had a frightening childhood experience that she cannot remember is said to be repressing her memory of it. Freud used the term *repression* to mean both unconscious expulsion of disturbing material from awareness and conscious suppression of such material. However, modern analysts tend to think of it only as an unconscious defense mechanism.

2 **Projection** occurs when a person's own unacceptable or threatening feelings are repressed and then attributed to someone else. A person who is embarrassed about having sexual feelings toward members of a different ethnic group may project this discomfort onto them, saying, "Those people are dirty-minded and oversexed."

3 **Displacement** occurs when people direct emotions that make them uncomfortable or conflicted (commonly, anger and sexual desire) toward people, animals, or things that are not the real object of their feelings. A boy who is forbidden to express anger toward his father may "take it out" on his toys or his younger sister. When displacement serves a higher cultural or socially useful purpose, as in the creation of art or inventions, it is called *sublimation*. Freud argued that society has a duty to help people sublimate their unacceptable impulses for the sake of civilization. Sexual passion may be sublimated into the creation of art or literature, and aggressive energy into sports.

4 **Regression** occurs when a person reverts to a previous phase of psychological development. An 8-year-old boy who is anxious about his parents' divorce may regress to earlier habits of thumb sucking or clinging. Adults may regress to immature behavior when they are under pressure, perhaps by having temper tantrums when they don't get their way.

5 **Denial** occurs when people refuse to admit that something unpleasant is happening, such as mistreatment by a partner; that they have a problem, such as drinking too much; or that they are feeling a forbidden emotion, such as anger. Denial protects a person's self-image and preserves the illusion of invulnerability: "It can't happen to me."

The Development of Personality. Freud argued that personality develops in a series of **psychosexual stages**, in which sexual energy takes different forms as the child matures. Each new stage produces a certain amount of frustration, conflict, and anxiety. If these are not resolved properly, normal development may be interrupted, and the child may remain *fixated*, or stuck, at the current stage.

Freud believed that some people remain fixated at the *oral stage*, which occurs during the first year of life, when babies experience the world through their mouths. As adults, they will seek oral gratification in smoking, overeating, nail biting, or chewing on pencils; some may become clingy and dependent, like a nursing child. Others remain fixated at the *anal stage*, at ages 2 to 3, when toilet training and control of bodily wastes are the key issues. They may become "anal retentive," holding everything in, obsessive about neatness and cleanliness. Or they may become just the opposite, "anal expulsive"—messy and disorganized.

For Freud, however, the most crucial stage for the formation of personality was the *phallic (Oedipal) stage*, which lasts roughly from age 3 to age 5 or 6. During this stage, he said, the child unconsciously wishes to possess the parent of the other sex and to get rid of the parent of the same sex. Children often proudly announce, "I'm going

defense mechanisms
Methods used by the ego to prevent unconscious anxiety or threatening thoughts from entering consciousness.

psychosexual stages
In Freud's theory, the idea that sexual energy takes different forms as a child matures; the stages are oral, anal, phallic (Oedipal), latency, and genital.

"I'm sorry, I'm not speaking to anyone tonight. My defense mechanisms seem to be out of order."

to marry Daddy (or Mommy) when I grow up," and they reject the same-sex "rival." Freud labeled this phenomenon the **Oedipus complex**, after the Greek legend of King Oedipus, who unwittingly killed his father and married his mother. (Although Freud was tolerant of homosexuality, he could not have imagined that one day many same-sex couples would be raising children!)

Boys and girls, Freud believed, go through the Oedipal stage differently. Boys are discovering the pleasure and pride of having a penis, so when they see a naked girl for the first time, they are horrified. Their unconscious exclaims (in effect), "Her penis has been cut off! Who could have done such a thing to her? Why, it must have been her powerful father. And if he could do it to her, my father could do it to me!" This realization, said Freud, causes the boy to repress his desire for his mother and identify with his father. He accepts his father's authority and the father's standards of conscience and morality; the superego has emerged.

Freud admitted that he did not quite know what to make of girls, who, lacking a penis, could not go through the same steps. He speculated that a girl, on discovering male anatomy, would panic that she had only a puny clitoris instead of a stately penis and conclude that she already had lost her penis. As a result, Freud said, girls do not have the powerful motivating fear that boys do to give up their Oedipal feelings and develop a strong superego; they have only a lingering sense of "penis envy."

Freud believed that when the Oedipus complex is resolved, at about age 5 or 6, the child's personality is fundamentally formed. Unconscious conflicts with parents, unresolved fixations and guilt, and attitudes toward the same and the other sex will continue to replay themselves throughout

life. The child settles into a supposedly nonsexual *latency* stage, in preparation for the *genital stage*, which begins at puberty and leads to adult sexuality.

In Freud's view, therefore, your adult personality is shaped by how you progressed through the early psychosexual stages, which defense mechanisms you developed to reduce anxiety, and whether your ego is strong enough to balance the

Oedipus complex In psychoanalysis, a conflict occurring in the phallic (Oedipal) stage, in which a child desires the parent of the other sex and views the same-sex parent as a rival.

A Freudian might say that this man's obsessive smoking is a sign he has an oral fixation.

conflict between the id (what you would like to do) and the superego (your conscience).

As you might imagine, Freud's ideas were not exactly received with yawns. Sexual feelings in 5-year-old children! Repressed longings in respectable adults! Unconscious meanings in dreams! Penis envy! This was strong stuff in the early years of the twentieth century, and before long, psychoanalysis had captured the public imagination in Europe and the United States.

But psychoanalysis also produced a sharp rift with the emerging schools of empirical psychology, because so many of Freud's ideas were scientifically untestable or failed to be supported when they were tested. Modern critics have discovered that Freud was not the theoretical genius, impartial scientist, or even successful clinician that he claimed to be. On the contrary, Freud often bullied his patients into accepting his explanations of their symptoms and, committing the greatest sin for anyone claiming to be a scientist, he ignored all evidence disconfirming his ideas (Borch-Jacobsen & Shamdasani, 2012; McNally, 2003; Powell & Boer, 1995).

On the positive side, Freud welcomed women into the profession of psychoanalysis, wrote eloquently about the devastating results for women of society's suppression of their sexuality, and argued, ahead of his time, that homosexuality was neither a sin nor a perversion but a "variation of the sexual function" and "nothing to be ashamed of" (Freud, 1961). Freud was thus a mixture of intellectual vision and blindness, sensitivity and arrogance. His provocative ideas left a powerful legacy to psychology, one that others began to tinker with immediately.

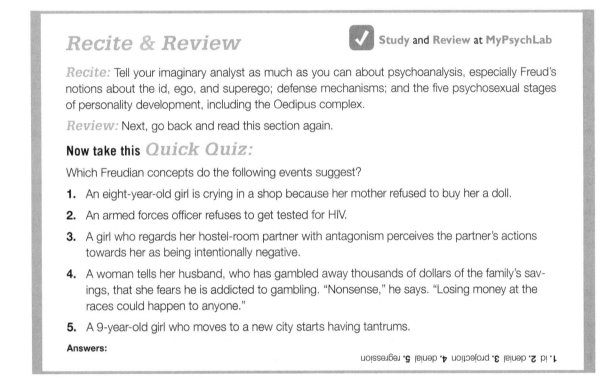

Recite & Review

✓ Study and Review at MyPsychLab

Recite: Tell your imaginary analyst as much as you can about psychoanalysis, especially Freud's notions about the id, ego, and superego; defense mechanisms; and the five psychosexual stages of personality development, including the Oedipus complex.

Review: Next, go back and read this section again.

Now take this *Quick Quiz:*

Which Freudian concepts do the following events suggest?

1. An eight-year-old girl is crying in a shop because her mother refused to buy her a doll.

2. An armed forces officer refuses to get tested for HIV.

3. A girl who regards her hostel-room partner with antagonism perceives the partner's actions towards her as being intentionally negative.

4. A woman tells her husband, who has gambled away thousands of dollars of the family's savings, that she fears he is addicted to gambling. "Nonsense," he says. "Losing money at the races could happen to anyone."

5. A 9-year-old girl who moves to a new city starts having tantrums.

Answers:

1. id 2. denial 3. projection 4. denial 5. regression

Other Psychodynamic Approaches

LO 2.5, LO 2.6

Some of Freud's followers stayed in the psychoanalytic tradition and modified Freud's theories from within. Women, as you might imagine, were not too pleased about "penis envy." Clara Thompson (1943/1973) and Karen Horney [HORN-eye] (1926/1973) argued that it was insulting and unscientific to claim that half the human race is dissatisfied with its anatomy. When women feel inferior to men, they said, we should look for explanations in the disadvantages that women live with and their second-class status. Other psychoanalysts broke away from Freud, or were actively rejected by him, and went off to start their own schools.

Jungian Theory. Carl Jung (1875–1961) was originally one of Freud's closest friends and a member of his inner circle, but the friendship ended with a furious quarrel about the nature of the unconscious. In addition to the individual's own unconscious, said Jung (1967), all human beings share a vast **collective unconscious**, containing universal memories, symbols, and themes, which he called *archetypes*.

collective unconscious In Jungian theory, the universal memories and experiences of humankind, represented in the symbols, stories, and images (*archetypes*) that occur across all cultures.

In the Jungian view, Lord Voldemort is a modern archetype of evil, fighting the wise and kindly Hero archetype, Dumbledore.

An archetype can be an image, such as the "magic circle," called a *mandala* in Eastern religions, which Jung thought symbolizes the unity of life and "the totality of the self." Or it can be a figure found in fairy tales, legends, and popular stories, such as the Hero, the nurturing Earth Mother, the Strong Father, or the Wicked Witch. It can even be an aspect of the self; the *shadow* archetype reflects the prehistoric fear of wild animals and represents the bestial, evil side of human nature. Some archetypes, such as the Hero, Villain, and Earth Mother, do appear in the stories and images of virtually every society (Campbell, 1949/1968; Neher, 1996). Jungians would consider the Joker, Darth Vader, Dracula, the Dark Lord Sauron, and Harry Potter's tormentor Voldemort as expressions of the shadow archetype.

Although Jung shared with Freud a fascination with the darker aspects of the personality, he had more confidence in the positive, forward-moving strengths of the ego than Freud did. He believed that people are motivated not only by past conflicts but also by their future goals and their desire to fulfill themselves. Jung was also among the first to identify extroversion–introversion as a basic dimension of personality. Nonetheless, many of Jung's ideas were more suited to mysticism and philosophy than to empirical psychology, which may be why so many Jungian ideas later became popular with New Age movements.

The Object-Relations School. Freud essentially regarded babies as if they were independent, greedy little organisms ruled by their own instinctive desires; other people were relevant only insofar as they gratified the infant's drives or blocked them. But by the 1950s, increased awareness of the importance of human attachments led to a different view of infancy, put forward by the **object-relations school**,

object-relations school A psychodynamic approach that emphasizes the importance of the first two years of life and an infant's formative relationships, especially with the mother.

which was developed in Great Britain by Melanie Klein, D. W. Winnicott, and others. To object-relations theorists, the central problem in life is to find a balance between the need for independence and the need for others. This balance requires constant adjustment to separations and losses: small ones that occur during quarrels, moderate ones such as leaving home for the first time, and major ones such as divorce or death. The way we react to these separations, according to object-relations analysts, is largely determined by our experiences in the first year or two of life.

The reason for the clunky word *object* in object-relations, instead of the warmer word *human* or *parent*, is that the infant's attachment is not only to a real person (usually the mother) but also to the infant's evolving perception of her. The child creates a mental representation

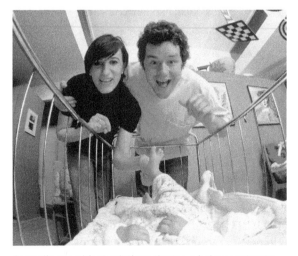

According to object-relations theory, a baby constructs unconscious representations of his or her parents that will influence the child's relations with others throughout life.

of the mother—someone who is kind or fierce, protective or rejecting. The child's representations of important adults, whether realistic or distorted, unconsciously affect personality throughout life, influencing whether the person relates to others with trust or suspicion, acceptance or criticism.

The object-relations school also departs from Freudian theory regarding the nature of male and female development (Sagan, 1988; Winnicott, 1957/1990). In the object-relations view, children of both sexes identify first with the mother. Girls, who are the same sex as the mother, do not need to separate from her; the mother treats a daughter as an extension of herself. But boys must break away from the mother to develop a masculine identity; the mother encourages a son to be independent and separate. Thus, in this view, men develop more rigid boundaries between themselves and other people than women do.

Evaluating Psychodynamic Theories LO 2.7

Although modern psychodynamic theorists differ in many ways, they share a general belief that to understand personality we must explore its unconscious dynamics and origins. And they consider the overall framework of Freud's theory to be timeless and brilliant, even if many of his specific ideas have proved faulty (Westen, 1998). Yet psychodynamic psychology differs radically from empirical approaches in psychology, in its language, methods, and standards of acceptable evidence. That is why the majority of psychological scientists regard most of the assumptions of psychoanalytic theory as literary metaphors

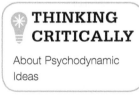

THINKING CRITICALLY

About Psychodynamic Ideas

rather than as scientific explanations (Cioffi, 1998; Crews, 1998). Indeed, most of the cornerstone assumptions in psychoanalytic theory, such as the notion that the mind "represses" traumatic experiences, have not been supported scientifically (McNally, 2003; Rofé, 2008; see Chapter 8).

Psychological scientists have shown that psychodynamic theories are typically guilty of three scientific failings:

1 Violating the principle of falsifiability. As we saw in Chapter 1, a theory that is impossible to disconfirm in principle is not scientific. Many psychodynamic concepts about unconscious

motivations are, in fact, impossible to confirm or disconfirm. Followers often accept an idea because it seems intuitively right or their experience seems to support it. Anyone who doubts the idea or offers disconfirming evidence is then accused of being "defensive" or "in denial."

2 Drawing universal principles from the experiences of a few atypical patients. Freud and most of his followers generalized from a few individuals, often patients in therapy, to all human beings. Of course, sometimes case studies can generate valid insights about human behavior. The problem occurs when observers fail to confirm their observations by studying larger, more representative samples and including appropriate control groups. For example, some psychodynamically oriented therapists, believing in Freud's notion of a childhood latency stage, have assumed that if a child masturbates or enjoys sex play, the child has been sexually molested. But research finds that masturbation and sexual curiosity are normal and common childhood behaviors, hardly unique to abused children (Bancroft, 2006; Friedrich et al., 1998).

3 Basing theories of personality development on the retrospective accounts of adults. Most psychodynamic theorists have not observed random samples of children at different ages, as modern child psychologists do, to construct their theories of development. Instead they have worked backward, creating theories based on themes in adults' recollections of childhood. (In the case of the object-relations school, this means making assumptions about what an infant feels and wants.) The analysis of memories can be an illuminating way to achieve insights about our lives; in fact, it is the only way we can think about our own lives! But memory is often inaccurate, influenced as much by what is going on in our lives now as by what happened in the past. That is why, if you are currently not getting along with your mother, you may remember all the times when she was hard on you and forget the counter-examples of her kindness.

Retrospective analysis has another problem: It creates an *illusion of causality* between events. People often assume that if A came before B, then A must have caused B. If your mother spent three months in the hospital when you were 5 years old and today you feel shy and insecure in college, an object-relations analyst might draw a connection between the two facts. But a lot of other things could be causing your shyness and insecurity, such as being away from home for the first time

Freud claimed, without much empirical evidence, that all little girls suffer from "penis envy." But studies of preschool girls and boys find that young children of *both* sexes are curious about the reproductive abilities of the other sex (Linday, 1994).

at a large and impersonal college. When psychologists conduct longitudinal studies, following people from childhood to adulthood, they often get a different picture of causality from the one that emerges by looking backward.

Despite these serious problems, some psychodynamic concepts have been empirically tested and validated. Researchers have identified unconscious processes in thought, memory, and behavior. They have found evidence for the major defense mechanisms, such as projection, denial, and displacement (Baumeister, Dale, & Sommer, 1998; Cramer, 2000; Marcus-Newhall et al., 2000). One intriguing study suggests that homophobia may sometimes be an attempt to deal with unconscious but threatening homosexual feelings. People were subliminally shown the word *me* or *other* before seeing pictures and words related to heterosexuality or homosexuality and then were asked to sort the pictures and words into the appropriate categories on a computer. Most sorted the words and pictures associated with their own sexual orientation faster when *me* had been the subliminal cue. But a subset of self-identified straight people sorted the discrepant (homosexual) words and images faster when they had been exposed to *me*—and those people were more likely to favor antigay policies (Weinstein et al., 2012).

Most important, research has confirmed the psychodynamic idea that we are often unaware of the motives behind our own puzzling or self-defeating actions.

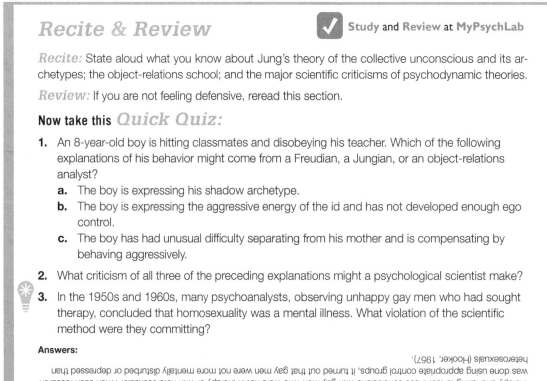

Recite & Review

✓ **Study** and **Review** at **MyPsychLab**

Recite: State aloud what you know about Jung's theory of the collective unconscious and its archetypes; the object-relations school; and the major scientific criticisms of psychodynamic theories.

Review: If you are not feeling defensive, reread this section.

Now take this *Quick Quiz:*

1. An 8-year-old boy is hitting classmates and disobeying his teacher. Which of the following explanations of his behavior might come from a Freudian, a Jungian, or an object-relations analyst?
    a. The boy is expressing his shadow archetype.
    b. The boy is expressing the aggressive energy of the id and has not developed enough ego control.
    c. The boy has had unusual difficulty separating from his mother and is compensating by behaving aggressively.

2. What criticism of all three of the preceding explanations might a psychological scientist make?

3. In the 1950s and 1960s, many psychoanalysts, observing unhappy gay men who had sought therapy, concluded that homosexuality was a mental illness. What violation of the scientific method were they committing?

Answers:

1 **a.** Jung **b.** Freud **c.** object-relations analyst **2.** All three explanations are nonfalsifiable; that is, there is no way to disconfirm them or confirm them. They are just subjective interpretations. **3.** The analysts were drawing conclusions from patients in therapy and failing to test these conclusions with gay men who were not in therapy or with heterosexuals. When such research was done using appropriate control groups, it turned out that gay men were not more mentally disturbed or depressed than heterosexuals (Hooker, 1957).

You are about to learn...

- whether you can trust tests that tell you what "personality type" you are.
- how psychologists can tell which personality traits are more central or important than others.
- the five dimensions of personality that describe people the world over.

The Modern Study of Personality

People love to fit themselves and their friends into "types"; they have been doing it forever. Early Greek philosophers thought our personalities fell into four fundamental categories depending on mixes of body fluids. If you were an angry, irritable sort of person, you supposedly had an excess of choler, and even now the word *choleric* describes a hothead. If you were sluggish and unemotional, you supposedly had an excess of phlegm, making you a "phlegmatic" type.

👁 **Watch** the **Video** The Big Picture: What is Personality at **MyPsychlab**

Popular Personality Tests LO 2.8

That particular theory is long gone, but other unscientific tests of personality types still exist, aimed at predicting how people will do at work, whether they will get along with others, or whether they will succeed as leaders. One such test, the Myers-Briggs Type Indicator, is hugely popular in business, at motivational seminars, and with matchmaking

services; several million Americans take it each year (Gladwell, 2004). The test assigns people to one of 16 different types, depending on how the individual scores on four dimensions (introversion/extroversion, thinking/feeling, judging/perception, and sensing/intuition). Unfortunately, the Myers-Briggs test is not much more reliable than measuring body fluids; one study found that fewer than half of the respondents scored as the same type a mere five weeks later. And there is little evidence that knowledge of a person's type reliably predicts behavior on the job or in relationships (Barbuto, 1997; Paul, 2004; Pittenger, 1993). Equally useless from a scientific point of view are many of the tests that some businesses and government agencies require their employees to take, hoping to predict which "types" are apt to steal, take drugs, or be disloyal on the job (Ehrenreich, 2001).

THINKING CRITICALLY

About Personality Tests

In contrast, many scientifically designed measures of personality traits *are* valid and useful in research. These **objective tests (inventories)** are standardized questionnaires requiring written responses, typically to multiple-choice or true–false items. They provide information about countless aspects of personality, including needs, values, interests, self-esteem, emotional problems, and typical ways of responding to situations. Using well-constructed inventories, psychologists have identified hundreds of traits, ranging from sensation seeking (the enjoyment of risk) to erotophobia (the fear of sex).

👁 **Watch** the **Video** Thinking Like a Psychologist: Measuring Personality at **MyPsychLab**

objective tests (inventories) Standardized questionnaires requiring written responses; they typically include scales on which people are asked to rate themselves.

THE MIXED VEGETABLE PERSONALITY INVENTORY

A.) WELL ADJUSTED; PRAGMATIC, REALISTIC, "TAKES THINGS AS THEY COME."

B.) NEUROTIC; OBSESSED BY NEED FOR ORDER AND CONTROL, "CAN'T LEAVE THINGS ALONE."

C.) IMPULSIVE/CHAOTIC; "WAS ALWAYS SO QUIET."

Bill Long/www.CartoonStock.com

factor analysis A statistical method for analyzing the intercorrelations among various measures or test scores; clusters of measures or scores that are highly correlated are assumed to measure the same underlying trait, ability, or attitude (factor).

Core Personality Traits LO 2.9

Are some personality traits more important or central than others? Do some of them overlap or cluster together? For Gordon Allport, one of the most influential psychologists in the early study of personality, the response to both questions was yes. Allport (1961) recognized that not all traits have equal weight and significance in people's lives. Most of us, he said, have five to 10 *central traits* that reflect a characteristic way of behaving, dealing with others, and reacting to new situations. For instance, some people see the world as a hostile, dangerous place, whereas others see it as a place for fun and frolic. *Secondary traits*, in contrast, are more changeable aspects of personality, such as music preferences, habits, casual opinions, and the like.

Raymond B. Cattell (1973) advanced the study of this issue by applying a statistical method called **factor analysis**. Performing a factor analysis is like adding water to flour: It causes the material to clump up into little balls. When applied to traits, this procedure identifies clusters of correlated items that seem to be measuring some common, underlying factor. Today, hundreds of factor-analytic studies support the existence of a cluster of five central "robust factors," known informally as the *Big Five Personality Factors* (Chang, Connelly, & Geeza, 2012; McCrae & Costa, 2008; McCrae et al., 2005; Paunonen, 2003; Roberts & Mroczek, 2008):

1 **Extroversion versus introversion** describes the extent to which people are outgoing or shy. It includes such traits as being sociable or reclusive, adventurous or cautious, socially dominant or more passive, eager to be in the limelight or inclined to stay in the shadows.

People's personalities are often reflected in how they arrange their work spaces. Some want their environment to be neat and organized; others enjoy clutter and having lots of stuff around.

2 **Neuroticism (negative emotionality) versus emotional stability** describes the extent to which a person suffers from such traits as anxiety, an inability to control impulses, and a tendency to feel negative emotions such as anger, guilt, contempt, and resentment. Neurotic individuals are worriers, complainers, and defeatists, even when they have no major problems. They are always ready to see the sour side of life and none of its sweetness.

3 **Agreeableness versus antagonism** describes the extent to which people are good-natured or irritable, cooperative or abrasive, secure or suspicious and jealous. It reflects the tendency to have friendly relationships or hostile ones.

4 **Conscientiousness versus impulsiveness** describes the degree to which people are responsible or undependable, persevering or quick to give up, steadfast or fickle, tidy or careless, self-disciplined or impulsive.

5 **Openness to experience versus resistance to new experience** describes the extent to which people are curious, imaginative, questioning, and creative or conforming, unimaginative, predictable, and uncomfortable with novelty.

Despite some cultural variations, the Big Five have emerged as distinct, central personality dimensions throughout the world, in countries as diverse as Britain, Canada, the Czech Republic, China, Ethiopia, Turkey, the Netherlands, Japan, Spain, the Philippines, Germany, Portugal, Israel, Korea, Russia, and Australia (Digman & Shmelyov, 1996; Katigbak et al., 2002; McCrae et al., 2005; Somer & Goldberg, 1999). One monumental research venture gathered data from thousands of people across 50 cultures. In this massive project as in many smaller ones, the five personality factors emerged whether people were asked for self-reports or were assessed by others (McCrae et al., 2005; Terracciano & McCrae, 2006).

Simulate the Experiment IPIP Neo Personality Inventory at **MyPsychLab**

Although the Big Five are quite stable over a lifetime, they are influenced by the universal processes of maturation and aging. Data from an enormous cross-sectional sample, involving more than 1.2 million people ages 10 to 65, revealed that whereas adult trends are overwhelmingly in the direction of greater maturity and adjustment, maturity actually plummets between late childhood and adolescence (Soto et al., 2011). Another survey of thousands of people in 10 countries, and a meta-analysis of 92 longitudinal studies, found that young people, ages 16 to 21,

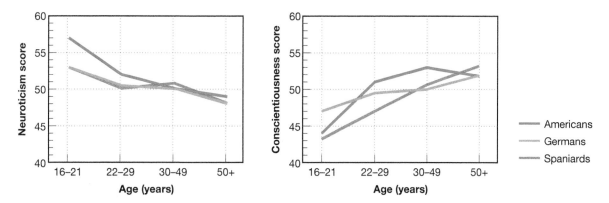

FIGURE 2.1 Consistency and Change in Personality Over the Life Span
Although the Big Five traits are fairly stable, changes do occur over the life span. As you can see, neuroticism (negative emotionality) is highest among young adults and then declines, whereas conscientiousness is lowest among young adults and then steadily increases (Costa et al., 1999).

are the most neurotic (emotionally negative) and the least agreeable and conscientious.

But most of these crabby, irresponsible neurotics do grow up eventually. As you can see in Figure 2.1, people tend to become more agreeable and conscientious and less negative between ages 30 and 40 (Costa et al., 1999; Roberts, Walton, & Viechtbauer, 2006). The slow, steady rise of conscientiousness over the life span, a change that is found in many countries, suggests that this trait is associated with maturation and having adult responsibilities. Finally, in their later years, people tend to become less extroverted and less open to new experiences (Roberts & Mroczek, 2008; Specht, Egloff, & Schmukle, 2011).

Get Involved! Rate Your Traits

For each of the 10 items that follow, write a number from 1 to 7 indicating the extent to which you see that trait as being characteristic of you, where 1 = "I *disagree* strongly that this trait describes me" to 7 = "I *agree* strongly that this trait describes me." Use the midpoint, 4, if you neither agree nor disagree that the trait describes you. (This self-test comes from Gosling, Rentfrow, & Swann, 2003.)

1. _____ Extroverted, enthusiastic
2. _____ Critical, quarrelsome
3. _____ Dependable, self-disciplined
4. _____ Anxious, easily upset
5. _____ Open to new experiences, complex
6. _____ Reserved, quiet
7. _____ Sympathetic, warm
8. _____ Disorganized, careless
9. _____ Calm, emotionally stable
10. _____ Conventional, uncreative

To score yourself on the Big Five traits, use this key:

Extroversion:	High on question 1, low on question 6
Emotional stability:	High on question 9, low on question 4
Agreeableness:	High on question 7, low on question 2
Conscientiousness:	High on question 3, low on question 8
Openness:	High on question 5, low on question 10

Now ask a friend or relative to rate you on each of the 10 items. How closely does that rating match your own? If there is a discrepancy, what might be the reason for it?

Experience, too, shapes personality traits. For example, extroverts obviously seek out certain experiences that shy people might not, but once people are in a situation that brings out qualities they did not know they had, their traits may be modified accordingly (Specht, Egloff, & Schmukle, 2011). Those situations can change with social and economic conditions, such as job shortages.

The Big Five do not provide a complete picture of personality, of course. Clinical psychologists note that important traits involved in mental disorders are missing, such as psychopathy (lack of remorse and empathy), self-absorption, impulsivity, and obsessiveness (Westen & Shedler, 1999). Personality researchers note that other significant traits are missing, such as religiosity, dishonesty, humorousness, independence, and conventionality (Abrahamson, Baker, & Caspi, 2002; Paunonen & Ashton, 2001). But most agree that the Big Five do lie at the core of key personality variations among individuals, and not only human individuals, either, as we are about to see.

 Watch the **Video** In the Real World: Putting Popular Personality Assessments to the Test at **MyPsychLab**

Recite & Review

 Study and **Review** at **MyPsychLab**

Recite: Out loud, say as much as you can about objective tests, factor analysis, and the Big Five personality traits.

Review: Next, show that you have the trait of conscientiousness by rereading this section.

Now take this *Quick Quiz:*

1. Raymond B. Cattell advanced the study of personality by (a) developing case-study analysis, (b) using factor analysis, (c) devising the Myers-Briggs Type Indicator.

2. Which of the following are not among the Big Five personality factors? (a) neuroticism, (b) agreeableness, (c) self-absorption, (d) conscientiousness, (e) introversion

3. Which traits show a characteristic way of behaving, dealing with others, and reacting to new situations?

Answers:

1. b 2. c 3. central traits

You are about to learn . . .

- whether animals have "personalities" just as people do.

- the extent to which temperamental and personality differences among people are influenced by genes.

- why people who have highly heritable personality traits are not necessarily stuck with them forever.

Genetic Influences on Personality

A mother we know was describing her two children: "My daughter has always been difficult, intense, and testy," she said, "but my son is the opposite, placid and good-natured. They came out of the womb that way." Was this mother right? Is it possible to be born touchy or good-natured? What aspects of personality might have an inherited component?

For centuries, efforts to understand why people differ from one another have swung from biological explanations ("It's in their nature; they are born that way") to learning and environmental ones ("It's all a matter of nurture—how they are raised and the experiences they have"). The *nature–nurture* debate has been one of the longest running either–or arguments in philosophy and psychology. Edward L. Thorndike (1903), one of the leading psychologists of the early 1900s, staked out the nature position by claiming that "in the actual race of life…the chief determining factor is heredity." But in stirring words that became famous, his contemporary, behaviorist John B. Watson (1925), insisted that experience

"THERE'S ANOTHER HEREDITARY DISEASE THAT RUNS IN THE ROYAL FAMILY. YOUR GRANDFATHER WAS A STUBBORN FOOL, YOUR FATHER WAS A STUBBORN FOOL, AND _YOU_ ARE A STUBBORN FOOL."

could write virtually any message on the blank slate of human nature: "Give me a dozen healthy infants, well-formed, and my own specified world to bring them up in and I'll guarantee to take any one at random and train him to become any type of specialist I might select—doctor, lawyer, artist, merchant-chief and yes, even beggar-man and thief, regardless of his talents, penchants, tendencies, abilities, vocations, and race of his ancestors."

Today, however, almost all psychologists would say the nature–nurture debate is over. Biology and experience, genes and environment, are interacting influences, each shaping the other over time (Johnson et al., 2009). In this section and the next, we will examine the interlaced influences of nature and nurture on personality.

How can heredity affect personality? **Genes**, the basic units of heredity found in every cell of the body, are made up of elements of _DNA_ (deoxyribonucleic acid). These elements form chemical codes for the synthesis of proteins. Proteins, in turn, affect virtually every aspect of the body, from its structure to the chemicals that keep it running. Genes can affect the traits we call "personality" through their effects on an infant's developing brain and nervous system. They can also affect the functioning of an adult's brain and nervous system, directly and also indirectly, by switching other genes on or off.

People differ in part because they carry different mutations (variant forms of genes) in their genetic code. Mutations may be inherited or may arise before or after birth. Some occur as a result of environmental factors, as when ultraviolet radiation from the sun causes mutations that lead to skin cancer. But individuals also differ for another reason: Stable changes in the expression (activity) of genes, and thus of traits associated with those genes, can occur _without_ any changes in a gene's DNA. One of the most exciting developments in genetics is a specialty called **epigenetics**, which studies the molecular bases and consequences of these changes in genetic activity (Berger et al., 2009). Epigenetic changes affect behavior, learning and memory, and vulnerability to mental disorders (Zhang & Meaney, 2010). Thus, genes do not provide a static blueprint of development.

Watch the Video Special Topics: Epigenetics: A Revolutionary Science at MyPsychLab

Epigenetic changes may help explain why one identical twin might get a disease and the other not get it, and why identical twins and even cloned, genetically identical animals living in exactly the same environment may differ considerably in appearance and behavior (Raser & O'Shea, 2005). Yes, you read that right: Even clones can differ. The study of epigenetics is demonstrating that the timing and pattern of genetic activity are critical not only before birth but also throughout life (Feinberg, 2008). And just like

Genes are not destiny. In part because of epigenetic influences on gene expression, even identical twins and cloned animals can differ. The first cat ever cloned was named CC, for "carbon copy," but she's not really a carbon copy of her genetically identical mother (shown here nuzzling her grown daughter). The two have different coat patterns and different personalities.

genes The functional units of heredity; they are composed of DNA and specify the structure of proteins.

epigenetics The study of stable changes in the expression of a particular gene that occur without changes in DNA; the Greek prefix _epi-_ means "on top of" or "in addition to."

temperaments
Physiological dispositions to respond to the environment in certain ways; they are present in infancy and are assumed to be innate.

mutations, epigenetic changes can be affected by environmental factors throughout life (Plomin, DeFries, & Knopik, 2013; Zhang & Meaney, 2010). In coming years, you will be hearing a lot more about epigenetics, and how your own habits, activities, drug use, and stress level might affect the activity of your genes.

Researchers measure genetic contributions to personality in three ways: by studying personality traits in other species, by studying the temperaments of human infants and children, and by doing heritability studies of twins and adopted individuals. Many people misunderstand the meaning of "genetic contributions," so we want to clarify what these discoveries mean—and don't mean.

Puppies and Personalities

When we think of an individual who has a personality, we usually think of a human being. But bears, dogs, mice, pigs, hyenas, goats, cats, and of course primates also have distinctive, characteristic ways of behaving that make them different from others of their kind (Weinstein, Capitanio, & Gosling, 2008). Two researchers dropped a crab into a tank of octopuses and had independent observers note what happened. Some of the creatures aggressively grabbed that dinner right away; others waited for the crab to swim near them; and some waited and then attacked the crab when no one was watching (Mather & Anderson, 1993). Apparently, you don't have to be a person to have a personality. You don't even have to be a mammal.

Scientists draw on research in physiology, genetics, ecology, and ethology (the study of animals in their natural habitats) to better understand the evolutionary and biological underpinnings of human personality traits. Just as it has been evolutionarily beneficial for human beings to vary in their ways of responding to the world and those around them, so it has been for animals. It is good for a species if some of its members are bold or impulsive enough to risk life and limb to confront a stranger or to experiment with a new food, and if other members are more cautious.

In an imaginative set of studies, Samuel D. Gosling and his colleagues (2003) recruited dog owners and their dogs in a local park. In the first study, the owners provided personality assessments of their dogs and filled out the same personality inventory for themselves. The owners then designated another person who knew them and their dogs, and who could judge the personalities of both. In a second study, the owners brought their dogs to an enclosed section of the park where three independent observers rated the dogs, so the researchers could compare the owners' judgments of their dogs' personalities with the observers' ratings. The dog owners, their friends, and the neutral observers all agreed strongly in their ratings of the dogs' personalities along four of the Big Five dimensions: extroversion, agreeableness, emotional reactivity (neuroticism), and openness to experience.

To date, most of the Big Five factors have been found in 64 different species, including the squishy squid. These findings point to the evolutionary importance of the Big Five and their biological basis. So when you hear your dog- or horse- or cat-crazy friend say, "Pluto is such a shy and nervous guy, whereas Pepper is outgoing and sociable," your friend is probably being a pretty accurate observer.

Heredity and Temperament LO 2.10

Let's turn now to human personalities. Even in the first weeks after birth, human babies differ in activity level, mood, responsiveness, heart rate, and attention span (Fox et al., 2005a). Some are irritable and cranky; others are placid and calm. Some will cuddle up in an adult's arms and snuggle; others squirm and fidget, as if they cannot stand being held. Some smile easily; others fuss and cry. These differences appear even when you control for possible prenatal influences, such as the mother's nutrition, drug use, or problems with the pregnancy.

Thus, babies are born with genetically determined **temperaments**, dispositions to respond to the environment in certain ways (Clark & Watson,

Family portraits of dogs, as of people, often reveal different personalities: Someone is posing nicely, someone isn't paying attention, someone is distracted, and someone is goofing off by biting a neighbor's ear.

Extreme shyness and fear of new situations tend to be biologically based, stable aspects of temperament, both in human beings and in monkeys. On the right, a timid infant rhesus monkey cowers behind a friend in the presence of an outgoing stranger.

2008). Temperaments include *reactivity* (how excitable, arousable, or responsive a baby is), *soothability* (how easily the baby is calmed when upset), and positive and negative emotionality. Temperaments are quite stable over time and are the clay out of which later personality traits are molded (Clark & Watson, 2008; Else-Quest et al., 2006; Rothbart, Ahadi, & Evans, 2000).

Even at 4 months of age, highly reactive infants are excitable, nervous, and fearful; they overreact to any little thing, even a colorful picture placed in front of them. As toddlers, they tend to be wary and fearful of new things—toys that make noise, odd-looking robots—even when their moms are right there. At 5 years, many of these children are still timid and uncomfortable in new situations and with new people (Hill-Soderlund & Braungart-Rieker, 2008). At 7 years, many still have symptoms of anxiety, even if nothing traumatic has ever happened to them. They are afraid of being kidnapped, they need to sleep with the light on, and they are afraid of sleeping in an unfamiliar house. In contrast, nonreactive infants lie there without fussing, babbling happily; they rarely cry. As toddlers, they are outgoing and curious about new toys and events. They continue to be easygoing throughout childhood (Fox et al., 2005b; Kagan, 1997).

Children at these two extremes differ physiologically too. During mildly stressful tasks, reactive children are more likely than nonreactive children to show signs of sympathetic nervous system arousal: increased heart rates, heightened brain activity, and high levels of stress hormones. You can see how these biologically based temperaments might form the basis of the later personality traits we call extroversion, agreeableness, or neuroticism.

Heredity and Traits LO 2.11

A third way to study genetic contributions to personality is to estimate the **heritability** of specific traits within groups of children or adults. This method is central to the interdisciplinary field of **behavioral genetics**, which attempts to identify the genetic bases of individual differences in personality, behavior, and abilities. Within any group, individuals will vary in shyness, cheerfulness, impulsiveness, or any other quality. Heritability gives us a statistical estimate of the *proportion of the total variation in a trait that is attributable to genetic variation within a group*. Because the heritability of a trait is expressed as a proportion (such as .60), the maximum value it can have is 1.00 (equivalent to 100 percent of the variance; all variation in the trait would be due to genetic variation).

We know that heritability is a tough concept to understand at first, so here's an example. Suppose that your entire psychology class takes a test of shyness, and you compute an average shyness score for the group. Some students will have scores close to the average, whereas others will have scores that are much higher or lower than the average. Heritability gives you an estimate of the extent to which your class's variation in shyness is caused by genetic differences among the students who took the test. Note that this estimate applies only to the group as a whole. It does not tell you anything about the impact of genetics on any *particular* individual's shyness or extroversion. You might be shy primarily because of your genes, but your friend might be shy because of an embarrassing experience she had in a school play at the age of 8.

Some traits, such as height, are highly heritable; that is, most of the differences in height

heritability A statistical estimate of the proportion of the total variance in some trait that is attributable to genetic differences among individuals within a group.

behavioral genetics An interdisciplinary field of study concerned with the genetic bases of individual differences in personality, behavior, and abilities.

within a group of equally well-nourished people will be accounted for by their genetic differences. In contrast, table manners have low heritability because most variation among individuals is accounted for by differences in upbringing and cultural rules. Even highly heritable traits, however, can be modified by the environment. If children eat an extremely nutritious diet, they may grow up to be taller than anyone thought they could. North and South Koreans share the same genetic background, yet they currently differ in average height by fully 6 inches (Schwekendiek, 2008).

Computing Heritability.
Scientists currently have no way to estimate the heritability of a trait or behavior directly, so they must infer it by studying people whose degree of genetic similarity is known. You might think that the simplest approach would be to compare biological relatives within families; everyone knows of families that are famous for some talent or trait. But that doesn't tell us much, because close relatives usually share environments as well as genes. If Carlo's parents and siblings all love lasagna, that doesn't mean a taste for lasagna is heritable. The same applies if everyone in Carlo's family is shy, has a high IQ, is mentally ill, or plays the clarinet.

One way to infer heritability is by studying adopted children (e.g., Loehlin, Horn, & Willerman, 1996). Such children share half of their genes with each birth parent, but they grow up in a different environment, apart from their birth parents. They share an environment with their adoptive parents and siblings, but not their genes. Researchers can compare correlations between the children's traits and those of their biological and adoptive relatives and can then use the results to estimate heritability.

Another approach is to compare fraternal twins with identical twins. *Fraternal twins* develop when a woman's ovaries release two eggs instead of one and each egg is fertilized by a different sperm. Fraternal twins are womb-mates, but they are no more alike genetically than any other two siblings (that is, they share, on average, only half their genes), and they may be of different sexes.

In contrast, *identical twins* develop when a fertilized egg divides into two parts that then develop as separate embryos. Because identical twins come from the same fertilized egg, it is usually assumed that they share all their genes. Some surprising evidence, however, suggests that duplicated or missing blocks of DNA can exist in one identical twin but not the other (Bruder et al., 2008). Also, prenatal events, such as the pregnant mother's illness, may modify the genetic expression in only one twin (Plomin, 2011). Still, most identical twins are probably genetically identical.

Behavioral geneticists can estimate the heritability of a trait by comparing groups of same-sex fraternal twins with groups of identical twins. The assumption is that if identical twins are more alike than fraternal twins, then the increased similarity must be due to genetic influences. If you are thinking critically, you might suspect that people do not treat identical and fraternal twins the same way. To avoid this problem, investigators have studied identical twins who were separated early in life and were reared apart. (Decades ago, adoption policies and society's hostility toward unmarried mothers permitted such separations to occur.) In theory, separated identical twins share all their genes but not their environments. Any similarities between them should be primarily genetic and should permit an estimate of heritability.

▶ **Watch** the **Video** Special Topics: Twins and Personality at **MyPsychLab**

There is still another problem, though. Some psychologists argue that the range of environments in adoptive homes, including those of separated twins, is quite narrow, because most people who adopt children are screened to be sure they have a pretty secure income, are psychologically stable, and so forth. But when environments are similar, any differences among individuals must *necessarily* be largely the result of heredity. The fact that the environments of adopted children are similar, these critics maintain, therefore

Separated at birth, the Mallifert twins meet accidentally.

© Charles Addams. With permission Tee and Charles Addams Foundation spuriously inflates the variation attributable to heredity (Nisbett, 2009). When environments differ, the relative influence of genetics may decrease (Johnson et al., 2009).

How Heritable Are Personality Traits?

Nonetheless, findings from adoption and twin studies—representing some 800,000 pairs of twins and more than 50 different study samples—have provided compelling support for a genetic contribution to personality (Johnson et al., 2009). Identical twins reared apart will often have unnerving similarities in gestures, mannerisms, and moods; indeed, their personalities often seem as similar as their physical features. If one twin tends to be optimistic, glum, or excitable, the other will probably be that way too (Braungart et al., 1992; Plomin, DeFries, & Knopik, 2013).

Behavioral-genetic findings have produced remarkably consistent results: For the Big Five and for many other traits, from aggressiveness to overall happiness, heritability is about .50 (Bouchard, 1997a; Jang et al., 1998; Lykken & Tellegen, 1996; Waller et al., 1990; Weiss, Bates, & Luciano, 2008). This means that within a group of people, about half of the variation in such traits is attributable to genetic differences among the individuals in the group. These findings have been replicated in many countries.

Identical twins Gerald Levey (left) and Mark Newman (right) were separated at birth and raised in different cities. When they were reunited at age 31, they discovered some astounding similarities. Both were volunteer firefighters, wore mustaches, and were unmarried. Both liked to hunt, watch old John Wayne movies, and eat Chinese food. They drank the same brand of beer, held the can with the little finger curled around it, and crushed the can when it was empty. It's tempting to conclude that all of these similarities are the result of heredity, but some could result from shared environmental factors such as social class and upbringing, and some could be merely the result of chance. For any given set of twins, we can never know for sure.

Evaluating Genetic Theories

Psychologists hope that one intelligent use of behavioral-genetic findings will be to help people become more accepting of themselves and their children. Although we can all learn to make improvements and modifications to our personalities, most of us probably will never be able to transform our personalities completely because of our genetic dispositions and temperaments.

However, many people oversimplify this information and conclude "It's all in our genes!" A genetic *predisposition* does not necessarily imply genetic *inevitability*. A person might have a genetic predisposition toward anxiety or depression, but without certain environmental stresses or circumstances, the person will probably not develop an emotional disorder. This is why psychological scientists and behavioral geneticists now study *gene-environment interactions* to best understand behavior. When people oversimplify, they also mistakenly assume that personality problems that have a genetic component are permanent—say, that someone is "born to be bad" or to be a miserable grouch forever (Dweck, 2008). And oversimplification can lead people to incorrectly assume that if a problem, such as major depression or extreme shyness, has a genetic contribution, it will respond only to medication, so they need not try other interventions. We discuss this fallacy in Chapter 12.

It seems that nearly every year brings another report about some gene that supposedly explains a human trait. A few years back, newspapers even announced the discovery of a "worry gene." Don't worry about it! Most human traits, even such seemingly straightforward ones as height and eye color, are influenced by more than one gene. Personality traits are especially likely to depend on multiple genes, with each one accounting for just a small part of the variance among people. Conversely, any single gene is apt to influence many different behaviors. That is why you should regard all excited announcements of a "gene for this" or a "gene for that" with extreme caution.

As Robert Plomin (1989), a leading behavioral geneticist, observed, "The wave of acceptance of genetic influence on behavior is growing into a tidal wave that threatens to engulf the second message of this research: These same data provide the best available evidence for the importance of environmental influences." Let us now see what some of those influences might be.

You are about to learn . . .

- how social-cognitive learning theory accounts for apparent changes in personality across situations.
- the extent to which parents can—and can't—influence their children's personalities.
- how your peers shape certain aspects of your personality and suppress others.

Environmental Influences on Personality

The environment may account for much of the variation in people's personalities, but what *is* the environment, exactly? In this section, we will consider the relative influence of three aspects of the environment: the particular situations you find yourself in, how your parents treat you, and who your peers are.

Situations and Social Learning

LO 2.12

The very definition of a trait is that it is consistent across situations. But people often behave one way with their parents and a different way with their friends, one way at work and a different way in other situations. In learning terms, the reason for people's inconsistency is that different behaviors are rewarded, punished, or ignored in different

contexts (see Chapter 9). You are more likely to be extroverted in an audience of screaming, cheering *American Idol* fans than at home with relatives who would regard such noisy displays with alarm and condemnation. This is why some behaviorists think it does not even make sense to talk about "personality."

The **social-cognitive learning theory of personality**, however, holds that people do acquire central traits from their learning history and their resulting expectations and beliefs. A child who studies hard and gets good grades, attention from teachers, admiration from friends, and praise from parents will come to expect that hard work in other situations will also pay off. That child will become, in terms of personality traits, "ambitious" and "industrious." A child who studies hard and gets poor grades, is ignored by teachers and parents, and is rejected by friends for being a grind will come to expect that working hard isn't worth it. That child will become, in terms of personality traits, "unambitious" or "unmotivated."

Today, most personality researchers recognize that people can have a core set of stable traits *and* that their behavior can vary across situations (Fleeson, 2004). Your particular qualities continually interact with the situations you are in. Your temperaments, habits, and beliefs influence how you respond to others, whom you hang out with, and the situations you seek (Bandura, 2001; Cervone & Shoda, 1999; Mischel & Shoda, 1995). In turn, the situation influences your behavior and beliefs, rewarding some and extinguishing others. In social-cognitive learning theory, this process is called **reciprocal determinism**.

social-cognitive learning theory of personality A view that holds that traits result from a person's learning history and his or her expectations, beliefs, perceptions of events, and other cognitions.

reciprocal determinism In social-cognitive learning theory, the two-way interaction between aspects of the environment and aspects of the individual in the shaping of behavior and personality traits.

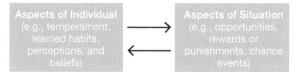

The two-way process of reciprocal determinism (as opposed to the one-way determinism of "genes determine everything" or "everything is learned") helps solve a mystery pondered by everyone who has a sibling: What makes children who grow up in the same family so different, apart from their genes? The answer seems to be an assortment of experiences that affect each child differently, chance events that cannot be predicted, situations that children find themselves in, and peer groups that the children belong to (Harris, 2006; Plomin, 2011; Rutter et al., 2001). Behavioral geneticists refer to these unique experiences that are not shared with other family members as the **nonshared environment**: being in Mrs. Miller's class in the fourth grade (which inspired you to become a scientist), winning the lead in the school play (which pushed you toward an acting career), or being bullied at school (which caused you to see yourself as weak and powerless). All of these experiences work reciprocally with your own interpretation of them, your temperament, and your perceptions (did Mrs. Miller's class excite you or bore you?).

Keeping the concept of reciprocal determinism in mind, let us take a look at two of the most powerful environmental influences in people's lives: their parents and their friends.

Parental Influence—and Its Limits
LO 2.13

There must be 2 zillion parenting books, but despite the different and often contradictory kinds of advice they offer, they reflect one entrenched belief: Parental child-rearing practices are the strongest influence, maybe even the *sole* influence, on children's personality development. For many decades, few psychologists thought to question this assumption, and many still accept it. Yet the belief that personality is primarily determined by how parents treat their children has begun to crumble under the weight of three kinds of evidence (Harris, 2006, 2009; Plomin, 2011):

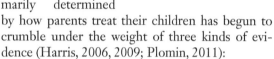

⊛ **THINKING CRITICALLY**

About the Influence of Parents

1 **The shared environment of the home has relatively little influence on most personality traits.** In behavioral-genetic research, the "shared environment" includes the family you grew up with and the experiences and background you shared with your siblings and parents. If these had as strong an influence as commonly assumed, then studies

nonshared environment Unique aspects of a person's environment and experience that are not shared with family members.

Is Susan Boyle, a plain woman who stunned the world with her great voice, a shy, modest introvert or a self-confident performer? Social-cognitive learning theory holds that genetic dispositions, talents, and personality traits, such as Boyle's skill as a singer, cause people to choose some situations over others. But situations, such as Boyle's appearance on *Britain's Got Talent*, in turn influence which aspects of their personalities people express.

would find a strong correlation between the personality traits of adopted children and those of their adoptive parents. In fact, the correlation is weak to nonexistent, indicating that the influence of child-rearing practices and family life is small compared to the influence of genetics (Cohen, 1999; Plomin, 2011). It is only the nonshared environment that has a strong impact.

2 **Few parents have a single child-rearing style that is consistent over time and that they use with all their children.** Developmental psychologists have tried for many years to identify the effects of specific child-rearing practices on children's personality traits. The problem is that parents are inconsistent from day to day and over time. Their child-rearing practices vary, depending on their own stresses, moods, and marital satisfaction (Holden & Miller, 1999). As one child we know said to her exasperated mother, "Why are you so mean to me today, Mommy? I'm this naughty every day." Moreover, parents tend to adjust their methods of child rearing according to the temperament of the child; they are often more lenient with easygoing children and more punitive with difficult ones.

3 **Even when parents try to be consistent in the way they treat their children, what they do often bears little relation to how the children turn out.** Some children of troubled and abusive parents are resilient and do not suffer lasting emotional damage, as we discuss in Chapter 3. Conversely, some children of the kindest and most nurturing parents succumb to drugs, mental illness, or gangs.

Of course, parents do influence their children in lots of ways that are unrelated to the child's personality. They contribute to their children's religious beliefs, intellectual and occupational interests, motivation to succeed, skills, values, and adherence to traditional or modern notions of masculinity and femininity (Beer, Arnold, & Loehlin, 1998; Krueger, Hicks, & McGue, 2001). Above all, what

parents do profoundly affects the quality of their relationship with their children—whether their children feel loved, secure, and valued or humiliated, frightened, and worthless (Harris, 2009).

Parents also have some influence even on traits in their children that are highly heritable. In one longitudinal study that followed children from age 3 to age 21, kids who were impulsive, uncontrollable, and aggressive at age 3 were far more likely than calmer children to grow up to be impulsive, unreliable, and antisocial and were more likely to commit crimes (Caspi, 2000). Early temperament was a strong and consistent predictor of these later personality traits, but not *every* child came out the same way. What protected some of those at risk, and helped them move in a healthier direction? Having parents who made sure they stayed in school, supervised them closely, and gave them consistent discipline.

Nevertheless, it is clear that, in general, parents have less influence on a child's personality than many people think. Because of reciprocal determinism, the relationship runs in both directions, with parents and children continually influencing one another. Moreover, as soon as children leave home, starting in preschool, parental influence on children's behavior *outside* the home begins to wane. The nonshared environment—peers, chance events, and circumstances—takes over.

The Power of Peers LO 2.14

When two psychologists surveyed 275 first-year students at Cornell University, they found that most of them had secret lives and private selves that they never revealed to their parents (Garbarino & Bedard, 2001). The students described having committed crimes, drinking, doing drugs, cheating in school, sexting, and having sex, all without their parents having a clue.

This phenomenon of showing one facet of your personality to your parents and an entirely different one to your peers becomes especially apparent in

Parents may try to keep constant tabs on their children, but how much control do they really have over how their children turn out?

Get Involved!   Situation and Self

Are you a different person when you are alone, with your parents, hanging out with friends, in class, or at a party? If so, in what ways? Do you have a secret self that you do not show to your family? Consider the Big Five factors, or any other personality traits that are important to you, as you think about these questions.

adolescence. At home, children learn how their parents want them to behave and what they can get away with, but as soon as they go to school they conform to the dress, habits, language, and rules of their peers. Most adults can remember how terrible they felt when their classmates laughed at them for pronouncing a word "the wrong way" or doing something "stupid" (that is, not what the rest of the kids were doing), and many recall the pain of being excluded. To avoid being laughed at or rejected, most children will do what they can to conform to the norms and rules of their immediate peer group (Harris, 2009). Children who were law-abiding in the fifth grade may start breaking the law in high school, if that is what it takes—or what they think it takes—to win the respect of their peers.

It can be difficult to tease apart the effects of parents and peers because parents usually try to arrange things so that their children's environments duplicate their own values and customs. To see which has the stronger influence on personality and behavior, therefore, we must look at situations in which the peer group's values clash with the parents' values. For example, when parents value academic achievement and their child's peers think

that success in school is only for sellouts or geeks, whose view wins? The answer, typically, is peers' (Arroyo & Zigler, 1995; Harris, 2009). Conversely, children whose parents gave them no encouragement or motivation to succeed may find themselves with peers who are working like mad to get into college, and start studying hard themselves.

Thus, peers play a tremendous role in shaping our personality traits and behavior, causing us to emphasize some attributes or abilities and downplay others. Of course, as the theory of reciprocal determinism would predict, our temperaments and dispositions also cause us to select particular peer groups (if they are available) instead of others, and our temperaments influence how we behave within the group. But once we are among peers, most of us go along with them, molding facets of our personalities to the pressures of the group.

In sum, core personality traits may stem from genetic dispositions, but they are profoundly shaped by learning, peers, situations, experience, and, as we will see next, the largest environment of all: the culture.

Explore the Concept **What Has Shaped Your Personality?** at MyPsychLab

---

Recite & Review

✓ **Study** and **Review** at MyPsychLab

Recite: Tell one of your peers (even an imaginary one) as much as you can about the social-cognitive learning view of personality, reciprocal determinism, the nonshared environment, and the relative influence of parents and peers.

Review: Even if your peers think you study too much, take the time to reread this section.

Now take this *Quick Quiz:*

1. Why does parental influence on their child's behavior decline outside the home?

2. Which contributes most to the variation among siblings in their personality traits? (a) the unique experiences they have that are not shared with their families, (b) the family environment that all of them share, or (c) the way their parents treat them.

3. Lara comes from a family of doctors and dreams of being one when she grows up too. But after being taught by Mrs. Joel in grade 5, she aspires to be a teacher who can make a difference to her students' lives. What might be the reason for this changed perception?

Answers:

1. Children need to conform to the norms and rules of their immediate peer group. **2.** a **3.** There were positive experiences that worked reciprocally with Lara's own interpretation.

culture A program of shared rules that govern the behavior of members of a community or society and a set of values, beliefs, and attitudes shared by most members of that community.

individualist cultures Cultures in which the self is regarded as autonomous, and individual goals and wishes are prized above duty and relations with others.

collectivist cultures Cultures in which the self is regarded as embedded in relationships, and harmony with one's group is prized above individual goals and wishes.

You are about to learn . . .

- how culture influences your personality, and even whether you think you have a stable one.
- why men in the American South and West are more likely to get angry when insulted than are men from other regions of the country.
- how to appreciate cultural influences on personality without stereotyping.

Cultural Influences on Personality

If you get an invitation to come to a party at 7 P.M., what time are you actually likely to get there? If someone gives you the finger or calls you a rude name, are you more likely to become furious or laugh it off? Most Western psychologists regard conscientiousness about time and quickness to anger as personality traits that result partly from genetic dispositions and partly from experience. But culture also has a profound effect on people's behavior, attitudes, and the traits they value or disdain. A **culture** is a program of shared rules that govern the behavior of members of a community or society, and a set of values and beliefs shared by most members of that community and passed from one generation to another. It provides countless rules that govern our actions and shape our beliefs, as we will see further in Chapter 10. And it is just as powerful an influence on personality and behavior as any biological process.

Culture, Values, and Traits LO 2.15, LO 2.16

Quick! Answer this question: Who are you?

Your answer will be influenced by your cultural background, and particularly by whether your culture emphasizes individualism or community (Hofstede & Bond, 1988; Kanagawa, Cross, & Markus, 2001; Markus & Kitayama, 1991; Triandis, 1996, 2007). In **individualist cultures**, the independence of the individual often takes precedence over the needs of the group, and the self is often defined as a collection of personality traits ("I am outgoing, agreeable, and ambitious") or in occupational terms ("I am a psychologist"). In **collectivist cultures**, group harmony often takes precedence over the wishes of the individual, and the self is defined in the context of relationships and the community ("I am the son of a farmer, descended from three generations of storytellers on my mother's side and five generations of farmers on my father's side."). A study showed how embedded this dimension is in language and how it shapes our thinking: Bicultural individuals born in China but living in the United States tended to reply to "Who am I?" in terms of their own individual attributes when they were writing in English. But they described themselves in terms of their relations to others when they were writing in Chinese (Ross, Xun, & Wilson, 2002).

👁 **Watch** the **Video** Differences Between Collectivistic and Individualistic Cultures at **MyPsychLab**

As Table 2.1 shows, individualist and collectivist ways of defining the "self" influence many aspects of life, including which personality traits we value, how and whether we express our feelings, how much we value having relationships or maintaining freedom, and how freely we express angry or aggressive emotions (Forbes et al., 2009; Oyserman & Lee, 2008). These influences are subtle but powerful. In one study, Chinese and American pairs had to play a communication game that required each partner to be able to take the other's perspective. Eye-gaze

Individualistic Americans exercise by running, walking, bicycling, and skating, all in different directions and wearing different clothes. Collectivist Japanese employees at their hiring ceremony exercise in identical fashion.

TABLE 2.1 Some Average Differences Between Individualist and Collectivist Cultures

Members of Individualist Cultures	Members of Collectivist Cultures
Define the self as autonomous, independent of groups.	Define the self as an interdependent part of groups.
Give priority to individual, personal goals.	Give priority to the needs and goals of the group.
Value independence, leadership, achievement, and self-fulfillment.	Value group harmony, duty, obligation, and security.
Give more weight to an individual's attitudes and preferences than to group norms as explanations of behavior.	Give more weight to group norms than to individual attitudes as explanations of behavior.
Attend to the benefits and costs of relationships; if costs exceed advantages, a person is likely to drop a relationship.	Attend to the needs of group members; if a relationship is beneficial to the group but costly to the individual, the individual is likely to stay in the relationship.

Source: Triandis, 1996.

measures showed that the Chinese players were almost always able to look at the target from their partner's perspective, whereas the American players often completely failed at this task (Wu & Keysar, 2007). Of course, members of both cultures understand the difference between their own view of things and that of another person's, but the collectivist-oriented Chinese pay closer attention to other people's nonverbal expressions, the better to monitor and modify their own responses.

Because people from collectivist cultures are concerned with adjusting their own behavior depending on the social context, they tend to regard personality and the sense of self as being more flexible than people from individualist cultures do. In a study comparing Japanese and Americans, the Americans reported that their sense of self changes only 5 to 10 percent in different situations, whereas the Japanese said that 90 to 99 percent of their sense of self changes (de Rivera, 1989). For the group-oriented Japanese, it is important to enact *tachiba*, to perform social roles correctly so that there will be harmony with others. Americans, in contrast, tend to value "being true to your self" and having a "core identity." Americans often value "self"-enhancement even at the expense of others, but the Japanese way of being a "good self" is through constant self-criticism in the context of maintaining face with others (Hamamura & Heine, 2008).

To further separate universal from culture-specific aspects of personality, a group of cross-cultural psychologists conducted in-depth research with Chinese people and South Africans,

administering Western personality inventories but also developing indigenous measures to capture cultural variations (Cheung, van de Vijver, & Leong, 2011). In China, they found evidence for a personality factor they call "interpersonal relatedness." This trait occurs universally, just as the Big Five do, but Asians, and Asian Americans who are less acculturated to American society, score higher on it than do European Americans or highly acculturated Asian Americans. In South Africa, where a personality inventory has been developed in the nine official Bantu languages, Afrikaans, and English, the researchers found the familiar Big Five, but also a few other central factors, including "relationship harmony," "soft-heartedness," and "facilitating" (providing guidance to others).

Culture and Traits. When people fail to understand the influence of cultural norms on behavior, they often attribute another person's mysterious or annoying actions to individual personality traits. Take cleanliness. How often do you bathe? Once a day, once a week? Do you regard baths as healthy and invigorating or as a disgusting wallow in dirty water? How often, and where, do you wash your hands—or feet? A person who would seem obsessively clean in one culture might seem an appalling slob in another (Fernea & Fernea, 1994).

Or consider helpfulness. Many years ago, in a classic cross-cultural study of children in Kenya, India, Mexico, the Philippines, Okinawa, the United States, and five other societies, researchers measured how often children behaved altruistically (offering help, support, or unselfish suggestions) or egoistically (seeking help and attention or wanting to dominate others) (Whiting & Edwards, 1988; Whiting & Whiting, 1975). American children were the least altruistic on all measures and the most egoistic. The most altruistic children came from societies in which children are assigned many tasks, such as caring for younger children and gathering and preparing food. These children knew that their work made a genuine contribution to the well-being or economic survival of the family. In cultures that value individual achievement and self-advancement, altruism as a personality trait is not cultivated to the same extent.

Or consider tardiness. Individuals differ in whether they try to be places "on time" or are always late, but cultural norms affect how individuals regard time in the first place. In the cultures of northern Europe, Canada, the United States, and most other individualistic cultures, time is organized into linear segments in which people do one thing "at a time" (Hall, 1983; Hall & Hall, 1990; Leonard, 2008). The day is divided into appointments, schedules, and routines, and because time is a precious commodity, people don't like to "waste" time or "spend" too much time on any one activity (hence the popularity

In many cultures, children are expected to contribute to the family's needs, by taking care of their younger siblings or doing important work for the family's income. These experiences encourage helpfulness over independence.

of multitasking). Being on time is taken as a sign of conscientiousness or thoughtfulness and being late as a sign of indifference or intentional disrespect. Therefore, it is considered the height of rudeness (or high status) to keep someone waiting. But in Mexico, southern Europe, the Middle East, South America, and Africa, time is organized along parallel lines. People do many things at once, and the needs of friends and family supersede mere appointments; they think nothing of waiting for hours or days to see someone. The idea of having to be somewhere "on time," as if time were more important than a person, is unthinkable.

Culture and Violence: The Cultivation of Male Aggression

Many people think that men are more violent than women because men have higher levels of testosterone. But if that is so, then why, given that men everywhere have testosterone, do rates of male aggressiveness vary enormously across cultures and throughout history? Why are rates of violence higher in the South and western regions of the United States than in the North and East?

To find out, Richard Nisbett (1993) began by examining the historical record. The South, along with some western regions of the country originally settled by Southerners, has much higher rates of white homicide and other violence than the rest of the country has—but only particular kinds of violence: the use of fists or guns to protect a man's sense of honor, protect his property, or respond to perceived insults. Nisbett considered various explanations, such as poverty or racial tensions. But when he controlled for regional differences in poverty and the percentage of blacks in the population, by county, "Southernness" remained an independent predictor of homicide. Nisbett also ruled out a history of slavery as an explanation: Regions of the South that had the highest concentrations of slaves in the past have the lowest white homicide rates today.

Nisbett hypothesized that the higher rates of violence in the South derive from economic causes: Higher rates occur in cultures that were originally based on herding, in contrast to cultures based on agriculture. Why would this be so? People who depend economically on agriculture tend to develop cooperative strategies for survival. But people who depend on their herds are extremely vulnerable; their livelihoods can be lost in an instant by the theft of their animals. To reduce the likelihood of theft, Nisbett theorized, herders learn to be hyperalert to any threatening act (real or perceived) and respond

Many people assume that men can't help being violent because of their biology. Yet, on average, men in agricultural economies are far more cooperative and nonviolent than men in herding economies. Amish farmers have always had extremely low rates of violence, whereas in the Old West, the cattle-herding cowboy culture was a violent one. (Fortunately, the shoot-out here is a reenactment.)

to it immediately with force. This would explain why cattle rustling and horse thievery were capital crimes in the Old West, and why Mediterranean and Middle Eastern herding cultures even today place a high value on male aggressiveness. And indeed, when Nisbett looked at agricultural practices *within* the South, he found that homicide rates were more than twice as high in the hills and dry plains areas, where herding occurs, as in farming regions.

The emphasis on aggressiveness and vigilance in herding communities, in turn, fosters a *culture of honor*, in which even small disputes and trivial insults (trivial to people from other cultures, that is) put a man's reputation for toughness on the line, requiring him to respond with violence to restore his status (Bosson & Vandello, 2011; Cohen, 1998). Although the herding economy has become much less important in the South and West than it once was, the legacy of its culture of honor remains. These regions have rates of honor-related homicides (such as murder to avenge a perceived insult to one's family) that are *five times higher* than in other regions of the country. Cultures of honor have more school shootings per capita (Brown, Osterman, & Barnes, 2009) and higher rates of domestic violence. Both sexes in such cultures believe it is appropriate for a man to physically assault a woman if he believes she is threatening his honor by being unfaithful or by leaving him (Vandello & Cohen, 2008).

Nisbett and his colleagues also wanted to demonstrate how these external cultural norms literally get under the skin to affect physiology and personality. They brought 173 Northern and Southern male students into their lab and conducted three experiments to measure how these students would respond psychologically and physiologically to being insulted (Cohen et al., 1996). They explained that the experiment would assess the students' performance on various tasks and that the experimenter would be taking saliva samples to measure everyone's blood sugar levels throughout the procedure. Actually, the saliva samples were used to measure levels of cortisol, a hormone associated with high levels of stress, and testosterone, which is associated with dominance and aggression.

At one point in the experiment, a confederate of the experimenter, who seemed to be another student participant, bumped into each man and called him an insulting name (a seven-letter word beginning with "a," if you want to know). As you can see in Figure 2.2 on the next page, Northerners responded calmly to the insult; if anything, they thought it was funny. But many Southerners were immediately inflamed and their levels of cortisol and testosterone shot up. They were more likely to feel that their masculinity had been threatened, and they were more likely to retaliate aggressively than Northerners were. Southerners and Northerners who were not insulted were alike on most measures, with the exception that the Southerners were actually more polite and deferential. It appears that they have more obliging manners than Northerners—until they are insulted. Then, look out.

Evaluating Cultural Approaches

LO 2.17

A woman we know, originally from England, married a Lebanese man. They were happy together but had the usual number of marital misunderstandings

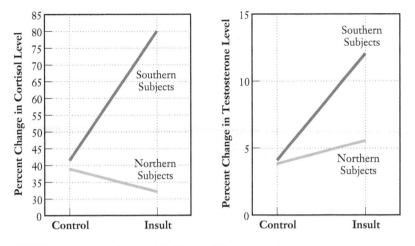

FIGURE 2.2 Aggression and Cultures of Honor
As these two graphs show, when young men from Northern states were insulted in an experiment, they shrugged it off, thinking it was funny or unimportant. But for young Southern men, levels of the stress hormone cortisol and of testosterone shot up, and they were more likely to retaliate aggressively (Cohen et al., 1996).

and squabbles. After a few years, they visited his family home in Lebanon, where she had never been before. "I was stunned," she told us. "All the things I thought he did because of his *personality* turned out to be because he's *Lebanese!* Everyone there was just like him!"

Our friend's reaction illustrates both the contributions and the limitations of cultural studies of personality. She was right in recognizing that some of her husband's behavior was attributable to his culture; his Lebanese notions of time were indeed different from her English notions. But she was wrong to infer that the Lebanese are all "just like him." The challenge in cultural psychology is how to describe cultural influences on personality without oversimplifying or stereotyping (Church & Lonner, 1998). As one student of ours put it, "How come when we students speak of 'the' Japanese or 'the' blacks or 'the' whites or 'the' Latinos, it's called stereotyping, and when you do it, it's called 'cross-cultural psychology'?" This question shows excellent critical thinking! The study of culture does not rest on the assumption that all members of a culture behave the same way or have the same personality traits. As we have seen, people vary according to their temperaments, beliefs, and learning histories, and this variation occurs within every culture.

THINKING CRITICALLY

About Culture and Personality

Moreover, almost every society contains cultural variations. The United States has an individualist culture overall, but the South, with its history of strong regional identity, is more collectivist than the rugged, independent West (Vandello & Cohen, 1999). The collectivist Chinese and the Japanese both value group harmony, but the Chinese are more likely to also promote individual achievement, whereas the Japanese are more likely to strive for group consensus (Dien, 1999; Lu, 2008). Within the United States, African Americans are more likely than white Americans to blend elements of the larger culture's individualism with African collectivism. That fact may help explain why an individualist philosophy predicts grade-point average for white students, but collectivist values are a better predictor for black students (Komarraju & Cokley, 2008). Average cross-cultural differences, even in a dimension as influential as individualist-collectivist, are not rigidly fixed or applicable to everyone within a society (Oyserman & Lee, 2008).

Finally, despite their differences, cultures share many human concerns and the needs for love, attachment, family, work, and religious or communal tradition. Nonetheless, cultural rules are what, *on average*, make Swedes different from Bedouins and Cambodians different from Italians. The traits that we value, our sense of self versus community, and our notions of the right way to behave—all key aspects of personality—begin with the culture in which we are raised.

You are about to learn . . .

- how humanist approaches to personality differ from psychodynamic and genetic ones.

- the contributions of Abraham Maslow, Carl Rogers, and Rollo May to an understanding of our inner lives.

- how psychological scientists evaluate humanist views of personality.

The Inner Experience

A final way to look at personality starts from each person's own point of view, from the inside out. Biology may hand us temperamental dispositions that benefit or limit us, the environment may deal us some tough or fortunate experiences, our parents may treat us as we would or would not have wished. But the sum total of our personality is how we, individually, weave all of these elements together into a *life narrative*, the story that each of us develops to explain ourselves and make meaning of our experiences (Bruner, 1990; McAdams, 2008; McAdams & Pals, 2006; Sarbin, 1997).

Humanist Approaches LO 2.18

One such approach to personality comes from **humanist psychology**, which was launched as a movement in the early 1960s. The movement's chief leaders—Abraham Maslow (1908–1970), Carl Rogers (1902–1987), and Rollo May (1909–1994)—argued that it was time to replace psychoanalysis and behaviorism with a "third force" in psychology, one that would draw a fuller picture of human potential and personality. Psychologists who take a humanist approach to personality emphasize our uniquely human capacity to determine our own actions and futures.

The trouble with psychology, said Abraham Maslow (1970, 1971), was that it had ignored many of the positive aspects of life, such as joy, laughter, love, happiness, and *peak experiences*, rare moments of rapture caused by the attainment of excellence or the experience of beauty. The traits that Maslow thought most important to personality were not the Big Five, but rather the qualities of the *self-actualized person*, someone who strives for a life that is meaningful, challenging, and satisfying.

For Maslow, personality development could be viewed as a gradual progression toward self-actualization. Most psychologists, he argued, had a lopsided view of human nature, a result of their emphasis on studying emotional problems and negative traits such as neuroticism or insecurity. As Maslow (1971) wrote, "When you select out for careful study very fine and healthy people, strong people, creative people…then you get a very different view of mankind. You are asking how tall can people grow, what can a human being become?"

humanist psychology
A psychological approach that emphasizes personal growth, resilience, and the achievement of human potential.

unconditional positive regard To Carl Rogers, love or support given to another person with no conditions attached.

existentialism A philosophical approach that emphasizes the inevitable dilemmas and challenges of human existence.

Carl Rogers (1951, 1961) was interested not only in why some people cannot function well but also in what he called the "fully functioning individual." How you behave, he said, depends on your subjective reality, not on the external reality around you. Fully functioning people experience *congruence*, or harmony, between the image they project to others and their true feelings and wishes. They are trusting, warm, and open, rather than defensive or intolerant. Their beliefs about themselves are realistic.

To become fully functioning people, Rogers maintained, we all need **unconditional positive regard**, love and support for the people we are, without strings (conditions) attached. This doesn't mean that Winifred should be allowed to kick her brother when she is angry with him or that Wilbur may throw his dinner out the window because he doesn't like pot roast. In these cases, a parent can correct the child's behavior without withdrawing love from the child. The child can learn that the behavior, not the child, is what is bad. "House rules are 'no violence,' children," is a different message from "You are horrible children for behaving so badly."

Unfortunately, Rogers observed, many children are raised with *conditional* positive regard: "I will love you if you behave well, and I won't love you if you behave badly." Adults often treat each other this way, too. People treated with conditional positive regard begin to suppress or deny feelings or actions that they believe are unacceptable to those they love. The result, said Rogers, is incongruence, a sense of being out of touch with your feelings, of not being true to your real self, which in turn produces low self-regard, defensiveness, and unhappiness. A person experiencing incongruence scores high on neuroticism, becoming bitter and negative.

👁 **Watch** the **Video** Classic Footage of Carl Rogers on Drive Theory at **MyPsychLab**

Rollo May shared with other humanists a belief in free will, but he also emphasized some of the inherently difficult and tragic aspects of the human condition, including loneliness, anxiety, and alienation. May incorporated elements of the European philosophy of **existentialism**, which emphasizes such inevitable challenges of existence as the search for the meaning of life, the need to confront death, and the necessity of taking responsibility for our actions.

Free will, wrote May, carries a price in anxiety and despair, which is why so many people try to escape from freedom into narrow certainties and

blame others for their misfortunes. For May, our personalities reflect the ways we cope with the struggles to find meaning in existence, to use our freedom wisely, and to face suffering and death bravely. May popularized the humanist idea that we can choose to make the best of ourselves by drawing on inner resources such as love and courage, but he added that we can never escape the harsh realities of life and loss.

Evaluating Humanist Approaches

As with psychodynamic theories, the major scientific criticism of humanist psychology is that many of its assumptions are untestable. Freud looked at humanity and saw destructive drives, selfishness, and lust. Maslow and Rogers looked at humanity and saw cooperation, selflessness, and love. May looked at humanity and saw fear of freedom, loneliness, and the struggle for meaning. These differences, say critics, may tell us more about the observers than about the observed.

Many humanist concepts, although intuitively appealing, are hard to define operationally. How can we know whether a person is self-fulfilled or self-actualized? How can we tell whether a woman's decision to quit her job and become a professional rodeo rider represents an "escape from freedom" or a freely made choice? And what exactly is unconditional positive regard? If it is defined as unquestioned support of a child's efforts at mastering a new skill, or as assurance that the child is loved in spite of his or her mistakes, then it is clearly a good idea. But in the popular culture, it has often been interpreted as an unwillingness ever to say "no" to a child or to offer constructive criticism and set limits, which children need.

✳ **THINKING CRITICALLY**

About Testing Humanist Ideas

Despite such concerns, humanist psychologists have added balance to the study of personality. One direct descendant of humanism, a specialty known as *positive psychology*, investigates the qualities that enable people to be optimistic and resilient in times of stress (Gable & Haidt, 2005; Seligman & Csikszentmihaly, 2000). Influenced in part by the humanists, psychological scientists are studying many

You are never too old for self-actualization. Hulda Crooks, shown here at age 91 climbing Mount Fuji, took up mountain climbing at 54. "It's been a great inspiration for me," she said. "When I come down from the mountain I feel like I can battle in the valley again." She died at the age of 101.

Sidney Harris/ScienceCartoonsPlus.com

constructive traits, such as courage, altruism, the motivation to excel, and self-confidence. Developmental psychologists are studying ways to foster children's empathy and creativity. And some researchers are studying the emotional and behavioral effects of the existential fear of death (Cohen et al., 2009; Pyszczynski, Rothschild, & Abdollahi, 2008).

Humanist views of personality share one central message: We have the power to choose our own destinies, even when fate delivers us into tragedy. Across psychology, this message has fostered an appreciation of resilience in the face of adversity.

Recite & Review

✅ **Study** and **Review** at **MyPsychLab**

Recite: Choose to exercise free will by reciting out loud what you know about humanist psychology, Abraham Maslow and his notions of peak experiences and self-actualization, Carl Rogers and unconditional positive regard, and Rollo May and existentialism.

Review: Next, read this section again.

Now take this *Quick Quiz:*

1. According to Carl Rogers, a man who loves his wife only when she is looking her best is giving her _____ positive regard.

2. The humanist who described the importance of congruence between the public self and private feelings was (a) Abraham Maslow, (b) Rollo May, (c) Carl Rogers.

3. A humanist and a Freudian psychoanalyst are arguing about human nature. What underlying assumptions about psychology and human potential are they likely to bring to their discussion? How can they resolve their differences without either–or thinking?

Answers:

1. conditional 2. c 3. The Freudian assumes that human nature is basically selfish and destructive; the humanist assumes that it is basically loving and cooperative. They can resolve this either–or debate by recognizing that human beings have both capacities, and that the situation and culture often determine which capacity is expressed at a given time.

PSYCHOLOGY IN THE NEWS REVISITED /////////

How are the dimensions of personality woven together in the case of Steve Jobs? How might the approaches to personality described in this chapter help us to understand this fascinating man and his remarkable life?

Some of his traits, such as his openness to new experience and his position at the "antagonistic" end of the "agreeable-antagonistic" dimension of the Big Five, seem likely to have a genetic component. The same applies to his passionate nature: Jobs's biographer wrote that passion—for his work, for excellence, for accomplishment—ran through every project he took on (Isaacson, 2011). As behavioral geneticists would predict, however, his personality was also shaped by unique experiences in his childhood, unshared with his sister. For example, his adoptive father, Paul, who worked as a mechanic and a carpenter, taught Steve how to work with his hands, taking apart and rebuilding radios and televisions in the family garage. As a result, Steve developed a love of tinkering with electronics.

Psychodynamic theorists would emphasize Jobs's early years and unconscious motives, focusing on his abandonment by his birth parents and the anger he apparently felt toward them throughout his life; he refused ever to meet his biological father. They would also suspect that Jobs was, at least at first, "in denial" about the gravity of his cancer diagnosis, and that this defense mechanism led him to delay serious treatment.

Psychologists who take a learning perspective would examine environmental influences on Jobs's personality: notably, his early travels in India and his experiences with psychedelics and the counter-cultural revolution of the 1970s. They would find no inconsistency in the fact that Jobs was both inspiring and infuriating, flexible and stubborn. All of us, they would note, display different parts of ourselves depending on the circumstances and whom we are with. They would also emphasize the role of peers in Jobs's life: In high school, Jobs became friends with a young man who shared his interests, and who in turn introduced Jobs to an older computer whiz kid, Steve Wozniak, who before long invented the Apple I computer. Jobs suggested that they sell it, and the rest is history.

Social-cognitive learning theorists would argue that Jobs's entire life can be seen through the lens of reciprocal determinism: the interaction of his traits with his circumstances and opportunities. When, at age 30, Jobs was fired from Apple, the company he had co-founded, he could have retired for life, perhaps filled with resentment. But in a speech he gave many years later, he said that being fired was the best thing that could have happened to him: "The heaviness of being successful was replaced by the lightness of being a beginner again, less sure about everything. It freed me to enter one of the most creative periods of my life." His *interpretation* of the experience of being fired, not the actual event itself, was what motivated him to change.

Cultural psychologists might observe that American culture values the individual who makes a brilliant comeback after being fired, the creative genius who defeats the odds. Such individuals may even get away with having Jobs's difficult "management style," including his direct expressions of hostility and rudeness. (This management style would not have gone over well in, say, Japan.) A cultural psychologist would also point out that Jobs lived at the perfect time and place to become successful in the computer industry. If he had been born 15 years sooner, or in a collectivist rather than an individualist culture, it might not have happened.

Finally, humanists would observe that Jobs clearly thrived on the "unconditional positive regard" that his adoptive parents gave him; they were enormously supportive of him and his decisions, even when he did poorly in school and dropped out of college. His life shows, humanists might say, how all of us are free to seek self-actualization and to choose the beliefs and values that guide our lives. But this perspective also reminds us that we do not know anything for sure about Jobs's inner, private self. The private man could have been quite different from his public persona.

Although we can only speculate about who the "real" Steve Jobs was, all of us can use the insights of the theorists in this chapter to better understand ourselves and those we care about. Each of us is a mix of genetic factors, learned habits, the influence of peers, new experiences, cultural norms, unconscious fears and conflicts, and our own private visions of possibility. This mix gives each of us the stamp of our personality, the qualities that make us feel uniquely...us.

Watch the **Video** The Basics: Personality Theories at **MyPsychLab**

Taking Psychology With You

How to Avoid the "Barnum Effect"

How well does the following paragraph describe you?

Some of your aspirations tend to be pretty unrealistic. At times you are extroverted, affable, and sociable, while at other times you are introverted, wary, and reserved. You pride yourself on being an independent thinker and do not accept others' opinions without satisfactory proof. You prefer a certain amount of change and variety, and you become dissatisfied when hemmed in by restrictions and limitations. At times you have serious doubts as to whether you have made the right decision or done the right thing.

When people believe that this description was written just for them, as the result of a personalized horoscope or handwriting analysis, they all say the same thing: "It describes me *exactly!*" Everyone thinks this description is accurate because it is vague enough to apply to almost everyone and it is flattering. Don't we all consider ourselves to be "independent thinkers"?

This is why many psychologists worry about the "Barnum effect" (Snyder & Shenkel, 1975). P. T. Barnum was the great circus showman who said, "There's a sucker born every minute." He knew that the formula for success was to "have a little something for everybody," which is just what unscientific personality profiles, horoscopes, and handwriting analysis (graphology) have in common. They have "a little something for everyone."

For example, graphologists claim that they can identify your personality traits from the form and distribution of your handwritten letters. Wide spacing between words means you feel isolated and lonely. If your lines drift upward, you are an "uplifting" optimist, and if your lines droop downward, you are a pessimist who feels you are being "dragged down." If you make large capital I's, you have a large ego (Beyerstein, 1996).

Whenever graphology has been tested empirically, it has failed. A meta-analysis of 200 published studies found no validity or reliability to graphology in predicting work performance, aptitudes, or personality. No school of graphology fared better than any other, and no graphologist was able to perform better than untrained

amateurs making guesses from the same writing samples (Dean, 1992; Klimoski, 1992).

If graphology were just an amusing game, no one would worry about it, but unfortunately it can have harmful consequences. Graphologists have been hired by companies to predict a person's leadership ability, attention to detail, willingness to be a good team player, and more. They pass judgment on people's honesty, generosity, and even supposed criminal tendencies. How would you feel if you were turned down for a job because some graphologist branded you a potential thief on the basis of your alleged "desire-for-possession hooks" on your S's?

If you do not want to be a victim of the Barnum effect, research offers this advice to help you think critically about graphology and its many cousins:

Beware of all-purpose descriptions that could apply to anyone. Sometimes you doubt your decisions; who among us has not? Sometimes you feel outgoing and sometimes

shy; who does not? Do you "have sexual secrets that you are afraid of confessing"? Just about everybody does.

Beware of your own selective perceptions. Most of us are so impressed when an astrologer, psychic, or graphologist gets something right that we overlook all the descriptions that are plain wrong. Be aware of the confirmation bias—the tendency to explain away all the descriptions that don't fit.

Resist flattery and emotional reasoning. This is a hard one! It is easy to reject a profile that describes you as selfish or stupid. Watch out for the ones that make you feel good by telling you how wonderful and smart you are, what a great leader you will be, or how modest you are about your exceptional abilities.

If you keep your ability to think critically with you, you won't end up paying hard cash for soft advice or taking a job you dislike because it fits your "personality type." In other words, you'll have proved Barnum wrong.

Summary

 Listen to the **Audio File** at **MyPsychLab**

- *Personality* refers to an individual's distinctive and relatively stable pattern of behavior, motives, thoughts, and emotions. Personality is made up of many different *traits*, characteristics that describe a person across situations.

Psychodynamic Theories of Personality

- Sigmund Freud was the founder of *psychoanalysis*, which was the first *psychodynamic* theory. Modern psychodynamic theories share an emphasis on unconscious processes and a belief in the formative role of childhood experiences and early unconscious conflicts.

- To Freud, the personality consists of the *id* (the source of sexual energy, which he called the *libido*, and the aggressive instinct); the *ego* (the source of reason); and the *superego* (the source of conscience). *Defense mechanisms* protect the ego from unconscious anxiety. They include, among others, repression, projection, displacement (one form of which is *sublimation*), regression, and denial.

- Freud believed that personality develops in a series of *psychosexual stages*, with the *phallic (Oedipal) stage* most crucial. During this stage, Freud believed, the *Oedipus complex* occurs, in which the child desires the parent of the other sex and feels rivalry with the same-sex parent. When the Oedipus complex is resolved, the child identifies with the same-sex parent, but females retain a lingering sense of inferiority and "penis

envy"—a notion later contested by female psychoanalysts like Clara Thompson and Karen Horney.

- Carl Jung believed that people share a *collective unconscious* that contains universal memories and images, or *archetypes*, such as the *shadow* (evil) and the Earth Mother.

- The *object-relations school* emphasizes the importance of the first two years of life rather than the Oedipal phase; the infant's relationships to important figures, especially the mother, rather than sexual needs and drives; and the problem in male development of breaking away from the mother.

- Psychodynamic approaches have been criticized for violating the principle of falsifiability; for overgeneralizing from atypical patients to everyone; and for basing theories on the unreliable memories and retrospective accounts of adults, which can create an *illusion of causality*. However, some psychodynamic ideas have received empirical support, including the existence of nonconscious processes and defenses.

The Modern Study of Personality

- Most popular tests that divide personality into "types" are not valid or reliable. In research, psychologists typically rely on *objective tests (inventories)* to identify and study personality traits.

- Gordon Allport argued that people have a few *central traits* that are key to their personalities and a greater number of *secondary traits* that are less fundamental. Raymond B. Cattell used *factor analysis* to identify clusters of traits that he considered the basic components of personality.

- Studies around the world provide strong evidence for the *Big Five dimensions of personality*: extroversion versus introversion, neuroticism (negative emotionality) versus emotional stability, agreeableness versus antagonism, conscientiousness versus impulsiveness, and openness to experience versus resistance to new experience. Although these dimensions are quite stable, some of them do change over the life span, reflecting maturational development, societal events, and adult responsibilities.

Genetic Influences on Personality

- The nature–nurture debate is one of the oldest controversies in philosophy and psychology, but it is pretty much over. Today most psychologists recognize that *genes*, the basic units of heredity, account for about half of the variation in human personality traits, but the environment and experience account for the other half. Moreover, the activation of genes can change over time because of mutations that arise before or after birth, and because of *epigenetic changes* that affect the expression of certain genes. Mutations and epigenetic changes are one reason that even identical twins (and cloned offspring and their parent) can differ somewhat.

- One line of evidence for genetic contributions to personality differences comes from studies of other species, which reveal variation in many of the traits that characterize humans.

- In human beings, individual differences in *temperaments*, such as reactivity, soothability, and positive or negative emotionality, emerge early in life and influence subsequent personality development. Temperamental differences in extremely reactive and nonreactive children may result from variations in the responsiveness of the sympathetic nervous system to change and novelty.

- *Behavioral-genetic* data from twin and adoption studies suggest that the *heritability* of many adult personality traits is about .50. Genetic influences create dispositions and set limits on the expression of specific traits. But even traits that are highly heritable are often modified throughout life by circumstances, chance, and learning.

Environmental Influences on Personality

- People often behave inconsistently in different circumstances when behaviors that are rewarded in one situation are punished or ignored in another. According to *social-cognitive learning theory*, personality results from the interaction of the environment and aspects of the individual, in a pattern of *reciprocal determinism*.

- Three lines of evidence challenge the popular assumption that parents have the greatest impact on their children's personalities and behavior: (1) Behavioral-genetic studies find that shared family environment has little influence on variations in most personality traits and that the major environmental influence is from the *nonshared environment*; (2) few parents have a consistent child-rearing style over time and with all their children; and

(3) even when parents try to be consistent, there may be little relation between what they do and how their children turn out. However, parents can modify their children's temperaments, influence many of their children's values and attitudes, and teach them to be kind and helpful. And, of course, parents profoundly affect the quality of their relationship with their children.

- One major environmental influence on personality comes from a person's peer groups, which can be more powerful than parents. Most children and teenagers behave differently with their parents than with their peers.

Cultural Influences on Personality

- Many qualities that Western psychologists treat as individual personality traits are heavily influenced by *culture*. People from *individualist cultures* define themselves in different terms than those from *collectivist cultures*, and they perceive their "selves" as more stable across situations. Cultures vary in their norms for many behaviors, such as cleanliness and notions of time. Altruistic children tend to come from cultures in which their families assign them many tasks that contribute to the family's well-being or economic survival.

- Male aggression is influenced by the economic requirements of the culture a man grows up in, which in turn shape men's beliefs about when violence is necessary. Herding economies foster male aggressiveness more than agricultural economies do. Men in *cultures of honor*, including those in certain regions of the American South and West, are more likely to become angry when they feel insulted and to behave aggressively to restore their sense of honor than are men from other cultures. When they are insulted, their levels of cortisol and testosterone rise quickly, whereas men from other cultures generally do not show this reaction.

- Cultural theories of personality face the problem of describing broad cultural differences and their influences on personality without promoting stereotypes or overlooking universal human needs.

The Inner Experience

- *Humanist psychologists* focus on a person's subjective sense of self, the free will to change, and the *life narrative* each person creates. They emphasize human potential and the strengths of human nature, as in Abraham Maslow's concepts of *peak experiences* and *self-actualization*. Carl Rogers stressed the importance of *unconditional positive regard* in creating a fully functioning person. Rollo May emphasized the philosophy of *existentialism*, which focuses on the inherent challenges of human existence that result from having free will, such as the search for meaning in life.

- Some ideas from humanist psychology are subjective and difficult to measure, but others have fostered research in *positive psychology*, which emphasizes positive aspects of personality such as optimism and resilience under adversity. Other psychologists are studying the consequences of the existential fear of death.

Psychology in the News, Revisited

• Genetic influences, life experiences and learned habits, cultural norms, unconscious fears and conflicts, and our private, inner sense of self all combine in complex ways to create our complex, distinctive personalities.

Taking Psychology With You

• Critical thinkers can learn to avoid the "Barnum effect"—being a sucker for fake inventories, horoscopes, handwriting analysis, and other pseudoscientific "tests" of personality.

Key Terms

personality 57
traits 57
Sigmund Freud 57
psychoanalysis 58
psychodynamic theories 58
id 58
libido 58
ego 58
superego 58
defense mechanisms 59
 repression 59
 projection 59
 displacement and
  sublimation 59
 regression 59
 denial 59

psychosexual stages (oral,
 anal, phallic, latency,
 genital) 59
Oedipus complex 60
Clara Thompson and Karen
 Horney 61
Carl Jung 61
collective unconscious 61
archetypes 61
shadow 62
object-relations school 62
illusion of causality 63
objective tests
 (inventories) 65
Gordon Allport 66
central trait 66

secondary trait 66
Raymond B. Cattell 66
factor analysis 66
the Big Five personality
 factors 66
genes 69
epigenetics 69
temperaments 70
heritability 71
behavioral genetics 71
social-cognitive learning
 theory of personality 74
reciprocal determinism 74
nonshared environment 75
culture 78
individualist cultures 78

collectivist cultures 78
culture of honor 81
life narratives 89
humanist psychology 83
Abraham Maslow 83
peak experiences 83
self-actualization 83
Carl Rogers 84
congruence 84
unconditional positive
 regard 84
Rollo May 70
existentialism 84
positive psychology 84

Personality is a distinctive pattern of behavior, mannerisms, thoughts, and emotions that characterizes an individual over time. **Traits** are habitual ways of behaving, thinking, and feeling.

Psychodynamic Theories of Personality

↓

Psychodynamic theories emphasize unconscious processes, the role of childhood experiences, and unconscious conflicts.

↓   ↓   ↓   ↓

Sigmund Freud

To Freudians, personality consists of three systems, which ideally should be in balance: **id**, **ego**, and **superego**.

Defense mechanisms include *repression*, *projection*, *displacement*, *regression*, and *denial*. They protect the ego from conflict, but can distort reality and cause self-defeating behavior.

Psychosexual stages of personality development:
• *Oral*
• *Anal*
• *Phallic* (Oedipal)
• *Latency*
• *Genital*

Carl Jung

Jung believed that all people share a **collective unconscious**, consisting of universal memories and *archetypes*—symbols, stories, or characters representing good, evil, heroes, villains, and other aspects of human experience.

Object-Relations School

The **object-relations school** emphasizes the importance of the first two years of life and formative relationships, especially with the mother.

Evaluating Psychodynamic Theories

These theories are often guilty of three scientific flaws:
• They violate the principle of falsifiability.
• They draw universal principles from the experiences of a few atypical patients.
• They are based on retrospective accounts and fallible memories of patients.

Some psychodynamic concepts have been empirically supported:
• unconscious processes.
• some defense mechanisms (e.g., denial and projection).

The Modern Study of Personality

↓

Personality Tests and Core Personality Traits

• Many popular personality tests, especially those designed to identify "types," lack reliability and validity.
• **Objective tests** (inventories) are standardized questionnaires about all aspects of personality.
• Raymond B. Cattell used **factor analysis** to identify the core clusters of personality traits.
• Factor-analytic studies support the existence of the *Big Five personality factors*:
  – extroversion versus introversion.
  – neuroticism versus emotional stability.
  – agreeableness versus antagonism.
  – conscientiousness versus impulsiveness.
  – openness to experience versus resistance to new experience.

The Big Five dimensions have been documented around the world. They are remarkably stable over a lifetime, although neuroticism tends to decrease and conscientiousness tends to increase in young adulthood.

Genetic Influences

↓

Genes are the basic units of heredity, accounting for about half of the variation in many human personality traits. The activation of genes can change over time because of mutations that arise before or after birth, and because of **epigenetic** changes that affect the expression of certain genes.

↓   ↓   ↓   ↓

Puppies and Personalities

Some researchers study the biological basis of personality by identifying traits in other species. They have found evidence for some of the Big Five in species as varied as octopuses, bears, and dogs.

Heredity and Temperament

Newborn babies differ in certain key **temperaments**, such as reactivity and soothability, which may form the basis of later personality traits.

Heredity and Traits

• Some researchers investigate genetic contributions to personality by doing **heritability** studies of twins and adopted individuals.
• **Behavioral-genetic** data from these studies show that the heritability of most traits is about 50 percent.

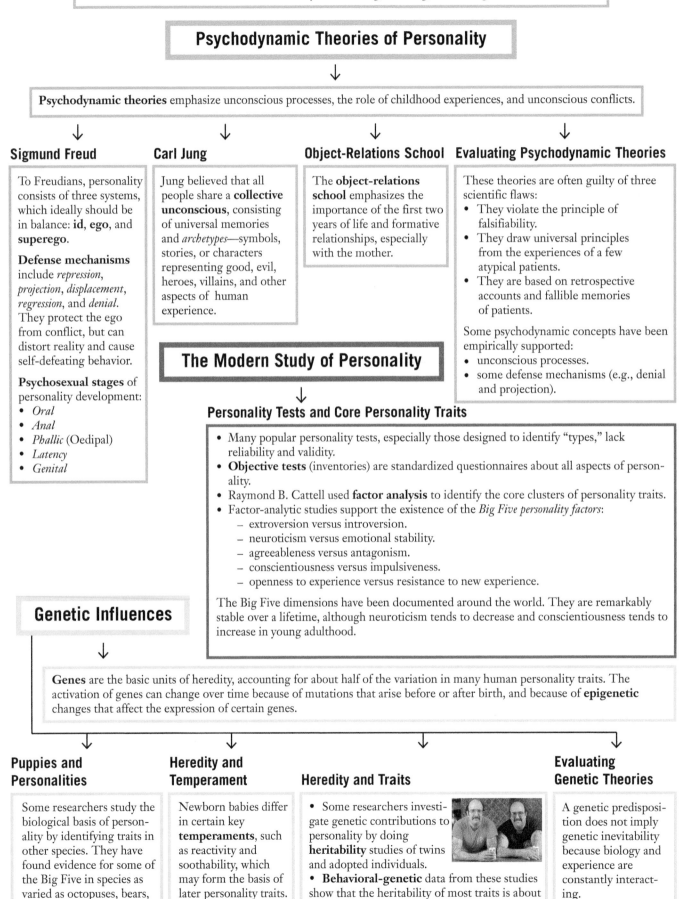

Evaluating Genetic Theories

A genetic predisposition does not imply genetic inevitability because biology and experience are constantly interacting.

Environmental Influences

Situations and Social Learning

The **social-cognitive learning theory of personality:**
- holds that traits result in part from a person's learning history and resulting expectations and beliefs.
- emphasizes **reciprocal determinism**, the two-way interaction between a person's qualities and the specific situation.
- helps explain why siblings who grow up together are often so different, a result of their **nonshared environment**.

Parental Influence—and Its Limits

The widespread belief that parents are the major influence on their children's personalities has been undermined by three lines of evidence:
- The shared environment of the home has relatively little effect on children's personalities; the strongest influences are experiences in the **nonshared environment.**
- Few parents have a single child-rearing style that is consistent over time and that they use with all their children.
- Even when parents try to be consistent, there may be little relation between what they do and how their children turn out.

The Power of Peers

Peer groups' influence can be more powerful than parents' influence on a child's personality development.

Cultural Influences

A **culture** is a program of shared rules or values that govern the behavior of members of a community or society.
- In **individualist cultures**, the independence of the individual often takes precedence over the needs of the group.
- In **collectivist cultures**, group harmony often takes precedence over the wishes of the individual.

Culture, Values, and Traits

- When people fail to understand the influence of culture on behavior, they may misattribute a person's behavior to personality. For example, cultures differ in their rules governing notions of cleanliness, helpfulness, and time.
- Male aggressiveness is often less a matter of testosterone or personality than of cultural norms, determined in turn by a culture's economy and whether men come from a *culture of honor*.

Evaluating Cultural Approaches

- Cultural psychologists seek to describe cultural influences on personality without stereotyping.
- Individuals are affected by their culture, but they vary within it.

The Inner Experience

Humanist psychology emphasizes a person's subjective sense of self.
- Abraham Maslow introduced the concepts of *peak experiences* and *self-actualization*.
- Carl Rogers stressed the importance of **unconditional positive regard**.
- Rollo May's inclusion of **existentialism** emphasized some of the inherent human challenges that result from free will.

Many humanist assumptions are untestable and hard to define operationally, but humanist ideas about positive qualities, such as courage and resilience, have added balance to the study of personality.

CONCEPT MAP   CHAPTER 2 Understanding Personality

3

From Conception Through the First Year

Language Development

Cognitive Development

Moral Development

Gender Development

Adolescence

Adulthood

The Wellsprings of Resilience

Psychology in the News, Revisited

Taking Psychology With You: Bringing Up Baby

HUMAN DEVELOPMENT

PSYCHOLOGY IN THE NEWS ///////////////////////////

Case of Teenager Convicted of Gruesome Murder Goes to Supreme Court

WASHINGTON, DC, March 20, 2012. The U.S. Supreme Court began hearing oral arguments today in the case of Evan Miller, convicted in 2006 of murdering a 52-year-old man by clubbing him repeatedly with a baseball bat, setting his trailer home on fire, and leaving him to die in the blaze. Miller was 14 at the time, and committed the crime with his 16-year-old friend Colby Smith.

Miller was tried as an adult on a charge of capital murder, convicted, and sentenced to life imprisonment without the possibility of parole. Smith, in exchange for his testimony, agreed to plead guilty to felony murder charges and received a life sentence with the possibility of parole.

Miller subsequently filed a motion for a new trial, arguing that the sentence constituted cruel and unusual punishment in violation of the Eighth Amendment. In 2005, the Supreme Court had banned the death penalty for juveniles, and Miller's lawyers argue that life without parole is also excessive and cruel. Developmental psychologists are expected to testify that the brains of teenagers are not fully mature and that Miller was not mentally capable of understanding the meaning and consequences of his actions.

Aubrey Miller, Evan Miller's 19-year-old sister, believes her brother and his friend deserve punishment for their actions. But, she said, neither of the boys are adults and they can't think like adults. That's not an excuse for their crimes, she added, but she feels it is not right for them to be tried as grownups. Especially Evan. When a 14-year-old commits murder, she believes, many people are responsible, starting with their parents, who never supervised Evan, disciplined him, or taught him respect. She and her brother, she added, suffered troubled childhoods of poverty, abuse, and neglect. No wonder he couldn't think clearly the night of the violence.

The hearing will be attended by the family of the victim, Cole Cannon. Cannon's daughter, Candy Cheatham, said she had had no idea that advocacy groups for Evan had filed a motion with the Supreme Court. They make it sound as if her father was at fault, she said, starting the whole confrontation that got out of hand. A ruling by the Court is expected fairly soon.

Colby Smith (left) and Evan Miller (right) at their arraignment.

When does a teenager become capable of thinking like an adult? The case of *Miller v. State of Alabama* shows that this is not just an academic question; it can be a matter of life or death. For that matter, when does a teenager *become* an "adult"? What factors in a person's biology, learning, and environment define adulthood? Why do some 14-year-olds seem "all grown up" and some adults never do?

Throughout history and across cultures, the answers have varied widely. In some societies and eras, even young children were regarded as "little adults"; the idea that childhood is a distinct phase of development was unheard of. (In paintings, children even *looked* like adults—just smaller.) Similarly, for most of human history, the idea that adolescence is a special phase of life would have been considered preposterous. Before the Industrial Revolution, children and teenagers worked alongside adults on farms; in cities, they were sent to work as apprentices or servants, doing whatever job they could get.

Then, during the twentieth century, "age consciousness" emerged. Childhood came to be viewed as a period when powerful formative experiences determined the kind of adult a child would become. Adolescence became a distinctive stage between the physical events of puberty and the social markers of adulthood. Adults, whose lives once had proceeded in a predictable way (school, job, marriage, parenthood, retirement), began to do these things "out of order." Old people were increasingly separated from the rest of society on the grounds that they could not keep up with the fast-moving world—and the definition of "old" began changing, from 60 to 70 to beyond. These changes have made questions about "age-appropriate" behavior and people's responsibility for their actions more complicated.

Developmental psychologists address such issues by studying universal aspects of development across the life span, cultural variations, and differences among individuals. Some focus on children's mental and social development, including **socialization**, the process by which children learn the rules, attitudes, and behaviors expected of them by society. Others specialize in the study of adolescents, adults, or the old. In this chapter, we will explore some of their major findings, starting at the beginning of human development, with the period before birth, and continuing through adulthood into old age. At the end of the chapter, you will find out how the Supreme Court ruled in the case of Evan Miller, what kind of psychological evidence contributed to that decision, and what factors might have caused the teenagers to commit the crime they did.

You are about to learn . . .

- the course of prenatal development and some factors that can harm an embryo or fetus.
- how culture affects a baby's physical maturation.
- why contact comfort and attachment are essential for infants (and adults).
- the varieties of infant attachment.

From Conception Through the First Year
LO 3.1, LO 3.2

A baby's development, before and after birth, is a marvel of *maturation*, the sequential unfolding of genetically influenced behavior and physical characteristics. In only nine months of a mother's pregnancy, a cell grows from a dot this big (.) to a squalling bundle of energy who looks just like Aunt Sarah. In another 15 months, that bundle of energy grows into a babbling toddler who is curious about everything. No other time in human development brings so many changes so fast.

Prenatal Development

Prenatal development begins at fertilization, when the male sperm unites with the female ovum (egg) to form a single-celled egg called a *zygote*. The zygote soon begins to divide, and in 10 to 14 days, it has become a cluster of cells that attaches itself to the wall of the uterus. The outer portion of this cluster will form part of the placenta and umbilical cord, and when implantation is completed, about two weeks after fertilization, the inner portion becomes the *embryo*. The placenta, connected to the embryo by the umbilical cord, serves as the

socialization The processes by which children learn the behaviors, attitudes, and expectations required of them by their society or culture.

Developmental psychologists study people across the life span. They would have a living laboratory with this six-generation family: Sara Knauss, age 118 (center); her daughter, age 95 (right), her grandson, age 73 (center), her great granddaughter, age 49 (standing with her dad), her great-great granddaughter, age 27 (on the floor), and her great-great-great grandson, age 3.

growing embryo's link for food from the mother. It allows nutrients to enter and wastes to exit, and it screens out some, but not all, harmful substances.

At eight weeks after conception, the embryo is only 1 1/2 inches long. During the fourth to eighth weeks, in embryos that are genetically male, rudimentary testes secrete the hormone testosterone; without it, the embryo will develop to be anatomically female. After eight weeks, the organism, now called a *fetus*, further develops the organs and systems that existed in rudimentary form in the embryonic stage.

Although the womb is a fairly sturdy protector of the growing embryo or fetus, the prenatal environment—which is influenced by the mother's own health, allergies, and diet—can affect the course of development, for example by predisposing an infant to later obesity or immune problems (Coe & Lubach, 2008). Most people don't realize it, but fathers, too, play an important role in prenatal development. Because of genetic mutations in sperm, fathers older than 50 have three times the risk of conceiving a child who develops schizophrenia as fathers younger than age 25 do (Malaspina, 2001); teenage fathers have an increased risk that their babies will be born prematurely or have low birth weight; babies of men exposed to solvents and other chemicals in the workplace are more likely to be miscarried or stillborn or to develop cancer later in life; and a child with an older father has an increased probability of having autism or bipolar disorder (Frans et al., 2008; Kong et al., 2012; Reichenberg et al., 2006).

During a woman's pregnancy, some harmful influences can cross the placental barrier (O'Rahilly & Müller, 2001). These influences include the following:

- **Rubella (German measles)**, especially early in the pregnancy, can affect the fetus's eyes, ears, and heart. The most common consequence is deafness. Rubella is preventable if the mother has been vaccinated, which can be done up to 3 months before pregnancy.

- **X-rays or other radiation, pollutants, and toxic substances** can cause fetal deformities and cognitive abnormalities that can last throughout life. Exposure to lead is associated with attention problems and lower IQ scores, as is exposure to mercury (found most commonly in contaminated fish), pesticides, and high air pollution (Newland & Rasmussen, 2003; Perera et al., 2006; Raloff, 2011).

- **Sexually transmitted diseases** can cause mental impairments, blindness, and other physical disorders. Genital herpes affects the fetus only if the mother has an outbreak at the time of delivery, which exposes the newborn to the virus as the baby passes through the birth canal. (This risk can be avoided by having a cesarean section.) HIV, the virus that causes AIDS, can also be transmitted to the fetus, especially if the mother has developed AIDS and has not been treated.

- **Cigarette smoking** during pregnancy increases the likelihood of miscarriage, premature birth, an abnormal fetal heartbeat, and an underweight baby. The negative effects may last long after birth, showing up in increased rates of infant sickness, sudden infant death syndrome (SIDS), and, in later childhood, hyperactivity, learning difficulties, asthma, and even antisocial behavior (Button, Thapar, & McGuffin, 2005).

- **Chronic or severe maternal stress** can affect the fetus, increasing the risk of later cognitive and emotional problems and vulnerability to adult diseases such as hypertension (Talge, Neal, & Glover, 2007; Weinstock, 2005). Babies of mothers who developed posttraumatic stress disorder in the aftermath of the World Trade Center attacks on 9/11 were more likely to have abnormal cortisol levels themselves at 1 year of age and also to weigh less at birth, both indicators of future health problems (Yehuda et al., 2005).

Many parents hope to have an influence on their offspring even before their babies are born.

- **Numerous legal and illegal drugs** can be harmful to the fetus, whether they are illicit ones, such as cocaine and heroin, or legal substances such as antibiotics, antidepressants, antihistamines, tranquilizers, acne medications, prescription opiate painkillers, and diet pills (Healy, 2012; Lester, LaGasse, & Seifer, 1998; Stanwood & Levitt, 2001). Regular consumption of alcohol increases the risk of *fetal alcohol syndrome* (FAS), which is associated with low birth weight, a smaller brain, facial deformities, lack of coordination, and mental impairments (Ikonomidou et al., 2000; Streissguth, 2001).

The lesson is clear. A pregnant woman does well to stop smoking, take prenatal vitamins, get regular prenatal care, and avoid drugs unless they are medically necessary—and then to accept the fact that her child will never be properly grateful for all she has done!

Simulate the Experiment Teratogens and Their Effects at MyPsychLab

The Infant's World LO 3.3

Newborn babies could never survive on their own, but they are far from being passive and inert. Many abilities, tendencies, and characteristics are universal in human beings and are present at birth or develop early, given certain experiences. Newborns begin life with several *motor reflexes*, automatic behaviors that are necessary for survival. They will suck on anything suckable, such as a nipple or finger. They will grasp tightly a finger pressed on their tiny palms. They will turn their heads toward a touch on the cheek or corner of the mouth and search for something to suck on, a handy rooting reflex that allows them to find the breast or bottle. Many of these reflexes eventually disappear, but others—such as the knee-jerk, eye-blink, and sneeze reflexes—remain.

Babies are also equipped with a set of inborn perceptual abilities. They can see, hear, touch, smell, and taste (bananas and sugar water are in, rotten eggs are out). A newborn's visual focus range is only about eight inches, the average distance between the baby and the face of the person holding the baby, but visual ability develops rapidly. Newborns can distinguish contrasts, shadows, and edges. And they can discriminate their mother or other primary caregiver on the basis of smell, sight, or sound almost immediately.

Experience, however, plays a crucial role in shaping an infant's mind, brain, and gene expression right from the get-go. Infants who get little touching will grow more slowly and release less growth hormone than their amply cuddled peers, and throughout their lives, they have stronger reactions to stress and are more prone to depression and its cognitive deficits (Diamond & Amso, 2008; Field, 2009).

Although infants everywhere develop according to the same maturational sequence, many aspects of their development depend on cultural customs that govern how their parents hold, touch, feed, and talk to them (Rogoff, 2003). In the United States, Canada, and Germany and

Infants are born with a grasping reflex; they will cling to any offered finger. And they need the comfort of touch, which their adult caregivers love to provide.

contact comfort In primates, the innate pleasure derived from close physical contact; it is the basis of the infant's first attachment.

most other European countries, babies are expected to sleep for eight uninterrupted hours by the age of 4 or 5 months. This milestone is considered a sign of neurological maturity, although many babies wail when the parent puts them in the crib at night and leaves the room. But among Mayan Indians, rural Italians, African villagers, Indian Rajput villagers, and urban Japanese, this nightly clash of wills rarely occurs because the infant sleeps with the mother for the first few years of life, waking and nursing about every four hours. Mothers in these cultures believe it is important to sleep with the baby so that both will forge a close bond; in contrast, many urban North American and German parents believe it is important to foster the child's independence as soon as possible (Keller et al., 2005; Morelli et al., 1992).

Attachment LO 3.4, LO 3.5

Emotional attachment is a universal capacity of all primates and is essential for health and survival all through life. The mother is usually the first and primary object of attachment for an infant, but in many cultures (and many other species), babies become just as attached to their fathers, siblings, and grandparents (Hrdy, 1999).

Interest in the importance of early attachment began with the work of British psychiatrist John Bowlby (1969, 1973), who observed the devastating effects on babies raised in orphanages without touches or snuggling, and on other children raised in conditions of severe deprivation or neglect. The

babies were physically healthy but emotionally despairing, remote, and listless. By becoming attached to their caregivers, Bowlby said, children gain a secure base from which they can explore the environment and a haven of safety to return to when they are afraid. Ideally, infants will find a balance between feeling securely attached to the caregiver and feeling free to explore and learn in new environments.

Contact Comfort. Attachment begins with physical touching and cuddling between infant and parent. **Contact comfort**, the pleasure of being touched and held, is crucial not only for newborns but also for everyone throughout life because it releases a flood of pleasure-producing and stress-reducing endorphins (see Chapter 14). In hospital settings, even the mildest touch by a nurse or physician on a patient's arm or forehead is reassuring psychologically and lowers blood pressure.

Margaret and Harry Harlow first demonstrated the importance of contact comfort by raising infant rhesus monkeys with two kinds of artificial mothers (Harlow, 1958; Harlow & Harlow, 1966). One, which they called the "wire mother," was a forbidding construction of wires and warming lights, with a milk bottle connected to it. The other, the "cloth mother," was constructed of wire but covered in foam rubber and cuddly terry cloth (see Figure 3.1). At the time, many psychologists thought that babies become attached to their mothers simply because mothers provide food (Blum, 2002). But the Harlows' baby monkeys ran to the terry-cloth mother when they were frightened or startled, and

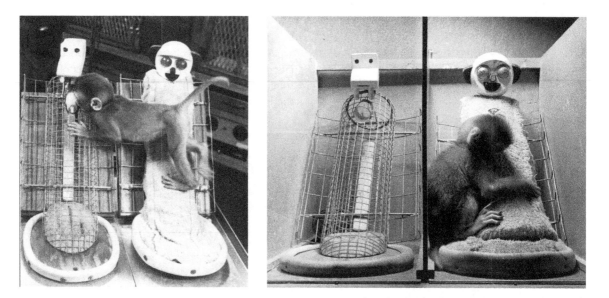

FIGURE 3.1 The Comfort of Contact
Infants need cuddling as much as they need food. In Margaret and Harry Harlow's studies, infant rhesus monkeys were reared with a cuddly terry-cloth "mother" (right) and with a bare-wire "mother" that provided milk (left). The infants would cling to the cuddly mother when they were not being fed. And when an unfamiliar, scary toy was placed in the enclosure, the infant monkey would run to the terry-cloth mother for comfort.

snuggling up to it calmed them down. Human children also seek contact comfort when they are in an unfamiliar situation, are scared by a nightmare, or fall and hurt themselves.

Separation and Security. Once babies are emotionally attached to the mother or other caregiver, separation can be a wrenching experience. Between 6 and 8 months of age, babies become wary or fearful of strangers. They wail if they are put in an unfamiliar setting or are left with an unfamiliar person. And they show **separation anxiety** if the primary caregiver temporarily leaves them. This reaction usually continues until the middle of the second year, but many children show signs of distress until they are about three years old (Hrdy, 1999). All children go through this phase, though cultural child-rearing practices influence how strongly the anxiety is felt and how long it lasts. In cultures where babies are raised with lots of adults and other children, separation anxiety is not as intense or as long-lasting as it can be in countries where babies form attachments primarily or exclusively with the mother (Rothbaum et al., 2000).

To study the nature of the attachment between mothers and babies, Mary Ainsworth (1973, 1979) devised an experimental method called the *Strange Situation*. A mother brings her baby into an unfamiliar room containing lots of toys. After a while, a stranger comes in and attempts to play with the child. The mother leaves the baby with the stranger. She then returns and plays with the child, and the stranger leaves. Finally, the mother leaves the baby alone for three minutes and returns. In each case, observers carefully note how the baby behaves with the mother, with the stranger, and when the baby is alone.

Ainsworth divided children into three categories on the basis of their reactions to the Strange Situation. Some babies were *securely attached*: They cried or protested if the parent left the room; they welcomed her back and then played happily again; they were clearly more attached to the mother than to the stranger. Other babies were *insecurely attached*, and this insecurity took one of two forms. Some children were avoidant, not caring if the mother left the room, making little effort to seek contact with her on her return, and treating the stranger about the same as the mother. Other insecure children were *anxious* or *ambivalent*, resisting contact with the mother at reunion but protesting loudly if she left. Some anxious-ambivalent babies cried to be picked up and then demanded to be put down; others behaved as if they were angry with the mother and resisted her efforts to comfort them.

Simulate the **Experiment** Attachment Classifications in the Strange Situation at **MyPsychLab**

STYLES OF ATTACHMENT

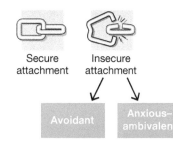

Secure attachment   Insecure attachment

Avoidant   Anxious–ambivalent

What Causes Insecure Attachment? Ainsworth believed that the difference between secure, avoidant, and anxious-ambivalent attachment lies primarily in the way mothers treat their babies during the first year. Mothers who are sensitive and responsive to their babies' needs, she said, create securely attached infants; mothers who are uncomfortable with or insensitive to their babies create insecurely attached infants. To many, the implication was that babies needed exactly the right kind of mothering from the start to become securely attached, and that putting a child in daycare would retard this important development—notions that have caused considerable insecurity among mothers!

Ainsworth's measure of attachment, however, did not take the baby's experience and genetic temperament into account. Babies who become attached to many adults (perhaps because they live in large extended families or have spent a lot of time with adults in daycare) may seem to be avoidant in the Strange Situation because they don't panic when their mothers leave, but perhaps they have simply learned to be comfortable with strangers. Moreover, although there is a modest correlation between a mother's sensitivity to her child and the security of her child's attachment, this doesn't tell us which causes what, or whether something else causes both sensitivity and secure attachment. Programs designed to help new mothers become less anxious and more attuned to their babies do help some moms become more sensitive, but these programs only modestly affect the child's degree of secure attachment (Bakermans-Kranenburg et al., 2008).

The emphasis on maternal sensitivity also overlooks the fact that most children, all over the world, form a secure attachment to their mothers despite wide variations in child-rearing practices (LeVine & Norman, 2008; Mercer, 2006). German babies are frequently left on their own for a few hours at a stretch by mothers who believe that even babies should become self-reliant. And among the Efe of Africa, babies spend about half their time away from their mothers in the care of older children and other adults (Tronick, Morelli, & Ivey, 1992). Yet German and Efe children are not insecure, and they develop as normally as children who spend more time with their

separation anxiety The distress that most children develop, at about 6 to 8 months of age, when their primary caregivers temporarily leave them with strangers.

"Please, Jason. Don't you want to grow up to be an autonomous person?"

mother. Likewise, time spent in daycare—10 hours a week to more than 30—has no effect on the security of a child's attachment (NICHD Early Child Care Research Network, 2006).

What factors, then, do promote insecure attachment?

- **Abandonment and deprivation in the first year or two of life.** Institutionalized babies are more likely than adopted children to have later problems with attachment, whereas babies adopted before age 1 or 2 eventually become as securely attached as their nonadopted peers (Rutter et al., 2004; van den Dries et al., 2009).

- **Parenting that is abusive, neglectful, or erratic because the parent is chronically irresponsible or clinically depressed.** A South African research team observed 147 mothers with their 2-month-old infants and followed up when the babies were 18 months old. Many of the mothers who had suffered from postpartum depression became either too intrusive with

their infants or too remote and insensitive. In turn, their babies were more likely to be insecurely attached at 18 months (Tomlinson, Cooper, & Murray, 2005).

- **The child's own genetically influenced temperament.** Babies who are fearful and prone to crying from birth are more likely to show insecure behavior in the Strange Situation, suggesting that their later insecure attachment may reflect a temperamental predisposition (Gillath et al., 2008; Seifer et al., 1996). However, an infant's temperament interacts with the mother's degree of responsiveness. When infants with a genetic variation that creates high emotional reactivity have particularly responsive mothers, they are more likely to develop secure attachment (Raby et al., 2012).

- **Stressful circumstances in the child's family.** Infants and young children may temporarily shift from secure to insecure attachment, becoming clingy and fearful of being left alone, if their families are undergoing a period of stress, as during parental divorce or a parent's chronic illness (Belsky et al., 1996; Mercer, 2006).

The bottom line, however, is that infants are biologically disposed to become attached to their caregivers. Normal, healthy attachment will occur within a wide range of cultural, family, and individual variations in child-rearing customs. Although, sadly, things can go wrong in prenatal development and in the first year after birth, the plasticity of the brain (see Chapter 4) and human resilience can often overcome early deprivation or even harm. We will return to the issue of resilience at the end of this chapter, and in "Taking Psychology With You," we will discuss other information that might alleviate the anxieties many parents feel about whether they are doing the right thing.

 Watch the **Video** Ross Thompson: Parent-Child Attachments (APS Player) at **MyPsychLab**

Recite & Review

✔ Study and Review at MyPsychLab

Recite: We hope you are feeling secure enough to state out loud what you know about prenatal development, the major kinds of harmful influences on a fetus, infant abilities, contact comfort, separation anxiety, secure and insecure attachment, and factors that promote insecure attachment.

Review: Next, reread this section.

Now take this *Quick Quiz:*

1. Sara is 7 months old and plays happily with her caregivers, but when her aunt visited her and wanted to hold her, she cried loudly. Sara is showing _____.

2. *True or false:* Contact comfort is crucial for the emotional health of all human beings.

3. A baby left in the Strange Situation does not protest when his mother leaves the room, and he seems to ignore her when she returns. According to Ainsworth, what style of attachment does this behavior reflect?

4. In Item 3, what else besides the child's style of attachment could account for the child's reaction?

Answers:

1. separation anxiety 2. True 3. Insecure (avoidant) 4. the child's own temperament and familiarity with being temporarily left alone

Language Development

Try to read this sentence aloud:
Kamaunawezakusomamanenohayawewenimtuwa maanasana.

Can you tell where one word begins and another ends? Unless you know Swahili, the syllables of this sentence will sound like gibberish.[1]

Well, to a baby learning its native tongue, *every* sentence must be gibberish at first. How, then, does an infant pick out discrete syllables and words from the jumble of sounds in the environment, much less figure out what the words mean? And how is it that in only a few years, children not only understand thousands of words but can also produce and understand an endless number of new word combinations? Is there something special about the human brain that allows a baby to discover how language works? Charles Darwin (1874) thought so: Language, he wrote, is an instinctive ability unique to human beings.

To evaluate Darwin's claim, we must first appreciate that a **language** is not just any old communication system; it is a set of rules for combining elements that are inherently meaningless into utterances that convey meaning. The elements are

[1]*Kama unaweza kusoma maneno haya, wewe ni mtu wa maana sana,* in Swahili, means "If you can read these words, you are a remarkable person."

You are about to learn...

- **what a language is—and what it allows us to do that other animals cannot.**
- **innate and learned aspects of acquiring language.**
- **the importance of baby talk in the development of language.**
- **some milestones in the development of language.**

usually sounds, but they can also be the gestures of American Sign Language (ASL) and other manual languages used by deaf or hearing-impaired people. Because of language, we can refer not only to the here and now but also to past and future events and to things or people who are not present. Language, whether spoken or signed, also allows human beings to express and comprehend an infinite number of novel utterances, created on the spot. This ability is critical; except for a few fixed phrases ("How are you?" "Get a life!"), most of the utterances we produce or hear over a lifetime are new. How in the world do we do this?

Language: Built in or Learned?

Many psychological scientists believe that an innate facility for language evolved in human beings because it was extraordinarily beneficial (Pinker, 1994). It permitted our prehistoric ancestors to convey precise information about time, space, and events (as in "Honey, are you going on the mammoth hunt today?") and allowed them to negotiate alliances that were necessary for survival ("If you share your nuts and berries with us, we'll share our mammoth with you"). Language may also have developed because it provides the human equivalent of the mutual grooming that other primates rely on to forge social bonds (Dunbar, 2004). Just as other primates will clean, stroke, and groom one another for hours as a sign of affection and connection, human friends will sit for hours and chat over coffee.

At one time, the leading theory held that children acquired language by imitating adults and paying attention when adults corrected their mistakes. Then along came linguist Noam Chomsky (1957, 1980), who argued that language was far too complex to be learned bit by bit, as one might learn a list of world capitals. Because no one actually teaches a toddler grammar, said Chomsky, the human brain must contain an innate mental module—a *universal grammar*—that allows young children to develop language if they are exposed to an adequate sampling of conversation. Their

language A system that combines meaningless elements such as sounds or gestures to form structured utterances that convey meaning.

The Chomsky school argues that because it's hard for parents to correct their children's syntax (even when they try), grammar must have an innate basis. The culture and learning school argues that parents and other adults play a large role in language acquisition.

brains are sensitive to the core syntactic features common to all languages, such as nouns and verbs, subjects and objects, and negatives. These common features occur even in languages as seemingly different as Mohawk and English, or Okinawan and Bulgarian (Baker, 2001; Cinque, 1999). In English, even 2-year-olds use syntax to help them acquire new verbs in context: They understand that *Jane blicked the baby!* involves two people, but the use of the same verb in *Jane blicked!* involves only Jane (Yuan & Fisher, 2009).

Evidence for Chomsky's theory that humans have an innate mental module for language comes from several directions:

- **Children in many different cultures go through similar stages of linguistic development.** For example, they will often form their first negatives simply by adding *no* or *not* at the beginning or end of a sentence ("No get dirty"), even when their language does not allow such constructions (Klima & Bellugi, 1966; McNeill, 1966.)

- **Children combine words in ways that adults never would.** They reduce a parent's sentences ("Let's go to the store!") to their own two-word versions ("Go store!") and make many charming errors that an adult would not ("The alligator goed kerplunk", "Hey, Horton heared a Who") (Ervin-Tripp, 1964; Marcus et al., 1992).

- **Adults do not consistently correct their children's syntax, yet children learn to speak or sign correctly anyway.** Parents may even reward children for syntactically incorrect or incomplete sentences: The 2-year-old who says "Want milk!" is likely to get it; most parents would not wait for a more grammatical (or polite) request.

- **Deaf children who have never learned a signed or spoken language have made up their own sign languages out of thin air.** These languages often show similarities in sentence structure across cultures as varied as those of the United States, Taiwan, Spain, and Turkey (Goldin-Meadow, 2003). The most astounding case comes from Nicaragua, where a group of deaf children, attending special schools, created a homegrown but grammatically complex sign language that is unrelated to Spanish (Senghas, Kita, & Özyürek, 2004).

However, in the last decade, some psycholinguists have taken aim at Chomsky's view, arguing that the assumption of a universal grammar is

These deaf Nicaraguan children have invented their own grammatically complex sign language, one that is unrelated to Spanish or to any conventional gestural language (Senghas, Kita, & Özyürek, 2004).

wrong (Dunn et al., 2011; Tomasello, 2003; Evans & Levinson, 2009). Despite commonalities in language acquisition around the world, they maintain, the world's 7,000 languages have some major differences that do not seem explainable by a universal grammar (Gopnik, Choi, & Bamberger, 1996). The language spoken by the remote Pirahã in the Amazon and the Wari' language of Brazil apparently lack key grammatical features that occur in other languages (Everett, 2012), though this discovery is hotly debated (Nevins, Pesetsky, & Rodrigues, 2009). One team constructed an evolutionary history for four major language groups and found that each group followed its own structural rules, suggesting that human language is driven by cultural requirements rather than an innate grammar (Dunn et al., 2011). The anti-innate-module school argues that language is a cultural tool, comparable to the physical tools that people have invented in adapting to different physical and cultural environments. Culture, they say, is the primary determinant of a language's linguistic structure, not an innate grammar.

Experience and culture certainly play a large role in language development. Parents may not go around correcting their children's speech all day, but they do recast and expand their children's clumsy or ungrammatical sentences ("Monkey climbing!" "Yes, the monkey is climbing the tree"). Children, in turn, often imitate those recasts and expansions, suggesting that they are learning from them (Bohannon & Symons, 1988).

Some scientists argue that instead of inferring grammatical rules because of an innate disposition to do so, children learn the *probability* that any given word or syllable will follow another, something infants as young as 8 months are able to do (Seidenberg, MacDonald, & Saffran, 2002). Because so many word combinations are used repeatedly ("Pick up your socks!" "Come to dinner!"), little kids seem able to track short word sequences and their frequencies, which in turn plays a role in teaching them not only vocabulary but syntax (Arnon & Clark, 2011). Eventually, children also learn how nonadjacent words co-occur (e.g., *the* and *ducky* in "the yellow ducky"), and are able to generalize their knowledge to learn syntactic categories (Gerken, Wilson, & Lewis, 2005; Lany & Gómez, 2008).

In this view, infants are more like statisticians than grammarians, and their "statistics" are based on experience. Using computers, some theorists have been able to design mathematical models of the brain that can acquire some aspects of language, such as regular and irregular past-tense verbs, without the help of a preexisting mental module or preprogrammed rules. These computer programs simply adjust the connections among hypothetical neurons in response to incoming data, such as repetitions of a word in its past-tense form. The success of these computer models, say their designers, suggests that children, too, may be able to acquire linguistic features without getting a head start from inborn brain modules (Rodriguez, Wiles, & Elman, 1999; Tomasello, 2003).

Although debate about the relative importance of innate factors and learning continues, both sides agree that acquisition of a first language must require both biological readiness and social experience. Children who are not exposed to language during their early years (such as Genie, whom we mentioned in Chapter 1), rarely speak normally or catch up grammatically. Such sad evidence suggests a critical period in language development during the first few years of life or possibly the first decade. During these years, children need exposure to language and opportunities to practice their emerging linguistic skills in conversation with others. Let's see how these skills develop.

From Cooing to Communicating

LO 3.6

The acquisition of language may begin in the womb. Canadian psychologists tested newborn babies' preference for hearing English or Tagalog (a major language of the Philippines) by measuring the number of times the babies sucked on a rubber nipple—a measure of babies' interest in a stimulus—while hearing each language alternating during a 10-minute span. Those whose mothers spoke only English during pregnancy showed a clear preference for English by sucking more during the minutes when English was spoken. Those whose bilingual mothers spoke both languages showed equal preference for both languages (Byers-Heinlein, Burns, & Werker, 2010).

Thus, from birth, infants are already responsive to the pitch, intensity, and sound of language, and they also react to the emotions and rhythms in voices. Adults take advantage of these infant abilities by speaking baby talk, which psycholinguists call *parentese*. When most people speak to babies, their pitch is higher and more varied than usual and their intonation and emphasis on vowels are exaggerated. Parents all over the world do this. Adult members of the Shuar, a nonliterate hunter-gatherer culture in South America, can accurately distinguish American mothers' infant-directed speech from their adult-directed speech just by tone (Bryant & Barrett, 2007). Parentese helps babies learn the melody and rhythm of their native language.

In what has to have been one of the most adorable research projects ever, three investigators compared the way mothers spoke to their babies and to pets, which also tend to evoke baby talk. The mothers exaggerated vowel sounds for their babies but not for Puffy the poodle or Merlin the cat, suggesting that parentese is, indeed, a way of helping infants acquire language (Burnham, Kitamura, & Vollmer-Conna, 2002).

By 4 to 6 months of age, babies can often recognize their own names and other words that are regularly spoken with emotion, such as *mommy* and *daddy*. They also know many of the key consonant and vowel sounds of their native language and can distinguish such sounds from those of other languages (Kuhl et al., 1992). Then, over time, exposure to the baby's native language reduces the child's ability to perceive speech sounds that do not exist in their own. Thus, Japanese infants can hear the difference between the English sounds *la* and *ra*, but older Japanese children cannot. Because this contrast does not exist in their language, they become insensitive to it.

Between 6 months and 1 year, infants become increasingly familiar with the sound structure of their native language. They are able to distinguish words from the flow of speech. They will listen longer to words that violate their expectations of what words should sound like and even to sentences that violate their expectations of how sentences should be structured (Jusczyk, 2002). They start to babble, making many *ba-ba* and *goo-goo* sounds, endlessly repeating sounds and syllables. At 7 months, they begin to remember words they have heard, but because they are also attending to the speaker's intonation, speaking rate, and volume, they can't always recognize the same word when different people speak it (Houston & Jusczyk, 2003). Then, by 10 months, they can suddenly do it—a remarkable leap forward in only three months. And at about 1 year of age, though the timing varies considerably, children take another giant step: They start to name things. They already have some concepts in their minds for familiar people and objects, and their first words represent these concepts (*mama, doggie, truck*).

👁 **Watch the Video** Language Development at **MyPsychLab**

Also at the end of the first year, babies develop a repertoire of symbolic gestures. They gesture to refer to objects (for example, sniffing to indicate *flower*), to request something (smacking the lips for *food*), to describe objects (raising the arms for *big*), and to reply to questions (opening the palms or shrugging the shoulders for *I don't*

Symbolic gestures emerge early!

know). They clap in response to pictures of things they like. Children whose parents encourage them to use gestures acquire larger vocabularies, have better comprehension, are better listeners, and are less frustrated in their efforts to communicate than children who are not encouraged to use gestures (Goodwyn & Acredolo, 1998; Rowe & Goldin-Meadow, 2009). When babies begin to speak, they continue to gesture along with their words, just as adults often gesture when talking. These gestures are not a substitute for language but are deeply related to its development, as well as to the development of thinking and problem solving (Goldin-Meadow, Cook, & Mitchell, 2009). Parents, in turn, use gesture (pointing, touching, tapping) to capture their babies' attention and teach them the meanings of words (Clark & Estigarribia, 2011).

One surprising discovery is that babies who are given infant "brain stimulation" videos to look at do not learn more words than babies in a control group, and often they are actually slower at acquiring words. For every hour a day that 8- to 16-month-old babies watch one of these videos, they acquire six to eight fewer words than other children (DeLoache et al., 2010; Zimmermann, Christakis, & Meltzoff, 2007). But the more that parents read and talk to their babies and infants, the larger the child's vocabulary at age 3 and the faster the child processes familiar words (Marchman & Fernald, 2008).

Between the ages of 18 months and 2 years, toddlers begin to produce words in two- or three-word combinations ("Mama here," "go 'way bug," "my toy").The child's first combinations of words have been described as **telegraphic speech**. When people had to pay for every word in a telegram, they quickly learned to drop unnecessary articles (*a, an,* or *the*) and auxiliary verbs (*is* or *are*). Similarly, the two-word sentences of toddlers omit articles, word endings, auxiliary verbs, and other parts of speech, yet these sentences are remarkably accurate in conveying meaning. Children use two-word sentences to locate things ("there toy"), make demands ("more milk"), negate actions ("no want,"

"all gone milk"), describe events ("Bambi go," "hit ball"), describe objects ("pretty dress"), show possession ("Mama dress"), and ask questions ("where Daddy?"). Pretty good for a little kid, don't you think?

By the age of 6, the average child has a vocabulary of between 8,000 and 14,000 words, meaning that children acquire several new words a day between the ages of 2 and 6. (When did you last learn and use several new words in a day?) They absorb new words as they hear them, inferring their meaning from their knowledge of grammatical contexts and from the social contexts in which they hear the words used (Golinkoff & Hirsh-Pasek, 2006; Rice, 1990).

telegraphic speech A child's first word combinations, which omit (as a telegram did) unnecessary words.

Recite & Review

 Study and **Review** at **MyPsychLab**

Recite: Use your human capacity for language to speak aloud what you have learned about the characteristics of language; the debate between Chomsky and his critics over whether there is an innate universal grammar and the evidence for each side's view; the importance of gestures; and telegraphic speech.

Review: Next, reread this section.

Now take this *Quick Quiz:*

1. The central distinction between human language and other communication systems is that language (a) allows for the generation of an infinite number of new utterances, (b) is spoken, (c) is learned only after explicit training, (d) is only constructed of meaningful elements.

2. Some of Chomsky's critics believe that instead of figuring out grammatical rules when acquiring language, children learn _____.

Answers:

1. a 2. the probability that any given word or syllable will follow another one.

You are about to learn...

- **how Piaget described the stages of cognitive development.**
- **modern approaches to children's mental development.**

Cognitive Development

Children do not think the way adults do. For most of the first year of life, if something is out of sight, it's out of mind: If you cover a baby's favorite rattle with a cloth, the baby thinks the rattle has vanished and stops looking for it. And a 4-year-old may protest that a sibling has more fruit juice when it is only the shapes of the glasses that differ, not the amount of juice.

Yet children are smart in their own way. Like good little scientists, they are always testing

their child-sized theories about how things work (Gopnik, 2009). When your toddler throws her spoon on the floor for the sixth time as you try to feed her, and you say, "That's enough! I will *not* pick up your spoon again!" the child will immediately test your claim. Are you serious? Are you angry? What will happen if she throws the spoon again? She is not doing this to drive you crazy. Rather, she is learning that her desires and yours can differ, and that sometimes those differences are important and sometimes they are not.

How and why does children's thinking change? In the 1920s, Swiss psychologist Jean Piaget [Zhan Pee-ah-ZHAY] (1896–1980) proposed that children's cognitive abilities unfold naturally, like the blooming of a flower, almost independent of what else is happening in their lives. Piaget caused a revolution in thinking about how thinking develops. His great insight was that children's errors are as interesting as their correct

Like a good little scientist, this child is trying to figure out cause and effect: "If I throw this dish, what will happen? Will there be a noise? Will mom come and give it back to me? How many times will she give it back to me?"

responses. Children will say things that seem cute or wildly illogical to adults, but the strategies that children use to think and solve problems are not random or meaningless: They reflect, Piaget said, the child's maturational stage. Although many of Piaget's specific conclusions have been rejected or modified over the years, his ideas inspired thousands of studies by investigators all over the world.

 Watch the **Video** The Basics: How Thinking Develops at **MyPsychLab**

Piaget's Theory of Cognitive Stages LO 3.7

According to Piaget (1929/1960, 1984), as children develop, their minds constantly adapt to new situations and experiences. Sometimes they *assimilate* new information into their existing mental categories; thus a German shepherd and a terrier both fit the category *dogs*. At other times, however, children must change their mental categories to *accommodate* their new experiences; a cat does not belong to the category *dogs* so a new category is required, one for *cats*. Both processes are constantly interacting, Piaget said, as children go through four stages of cognitive development:

From birth to age two, said Piaget, babies are in the *sensorimotor stage*. In this stage, the infant learns through concrete actions: looking, touching, putting things in the mouth, sucking, grasping. "Thinking" consists of coordinating sensory information with bodily movements. Gradually, these movements become more purposeful as the child explores the environment and learns that specific movements will produce specific results. Pulling a cloth away will reveal a hidden toy; letting go of a fuzzy toy duck will cause it to drop out of reach; banging on the table with a spoon will produce dinner (or Mom, taking away the spoon).

A major accomplishment at this stage, said Piaget, is **object permanence**, the understanding that something continues to exist even when you can't see it or touch it. In the first few months, infants will look intently at a little toy, but if you hide it behind a piece of paper, they will not look behind the paper or make an effort to get the toy. By about 6 months of age, however, infants begin to grasp the idea that the toy exists whether or not they can see it. If a baby of this age drops a toy from her playpen, she will look for it; she also will look under a cloth for a toy that is partially hidden. By 1 year of age, most babies have developed an awareness of the permanence of objects; even if a toy is covered by a cloth, it must be under there. This is when they love to play peek-a-boo. Object permanence, said Piaget, represents the beginning of the child's capacity to use mental imagery and symbols. The child becomes able to hold a concept in mind, to learn that the word *fly* represents an annoying, buzzing creature and that Daddy represents a friendly, playful one.

From about ages 2 to 7, the child's use of symbols and language accelerates. Piaget called this the *preoperational stage*, because he believed that children still lack the cognitive abilities necessary for understanding abstract principles and *mental operations*. An operation is a train of thought that can be run backward or forward. Multiplying 2 times 6 to get 12 is an operation; so is the reverse operation, dividing 12 by 6 to get 2. A preoperational child knows that Jessie is his sister, but he may not get the reverse operation, the idea that he is Jessie's brother. Piaget believed (mistakenly, as we will see) that preoperational children cannot take another person's point of view because their thinking is *egocentric*: They see the world only from their own frame of reference and cannot imagine that others see things differently.

Further, said Piaget, preoperational children cannot grasp the concept of **conservation**, the notion that physical properties do not change when their form or appearance changes. Children at this age do not understand that an amount of liquid or a number of blocks remains the same even if you pour the liquid from one glass to another of a different size or if you stack the blocks. If you pour liquid from a short, fat glass into a tall, narrow

object permanence
The understanding, which develops throughout the first year, that an object continues to exist even when you cannot see it or touch it.

conservation The understanding that the physical properties of objects—such as the number of items in a cluster or the amount of liquid in a glass—can remain the same even when their form or appearance changes.

FIGURE 3.2 Piaget's Principle of Conservation
In one test for conservation of size (left), the child must say which is bigger—a round lump of clay or the same amount of clay pressed flat. Preoperational children think that the flattened clay is bigger, because it seems to take up more space. In a test for conservation of quantity (right), the child is shown two short glasses with equal amounts of liquid. Then the contents of one glass are poured into a tall, narrower glass, and the child is asked whether one container now has more. Most preoperational children do not understand that pouring liquid from a short glass into a taller one leaves the amount of liquid unchanged. They judge only by the height of the liquid in the glass.

glass, preoperational children will say there is more liquid in the second glass. They attend to the appearance of the liquid (its height in the glass) to judge its quantity, and so they are misled (see Figure 3.2).

From the ages of 7 to about 12, Piaget said, children increasingly become able to take other people's perspectives and they make fewer logical errors. Piaget called this the *concrete operations stage* because he thought children's mental abilities are tied to information that is concrete, that is, to actual experiences that have happened or concepts that have a tangible meaning to them. Children at this stage make errors of reasoning when they are asked to think about abstract ideas such as "patriotism" or "future education." During these years, nonetheless, children's cognitive abilities expand rapidly. They come to understand the principles of conservation and cause and effect. They learn mental operations, such as basic arithmetic. They are able to categorize things (for example, oaks as trees) and to order things serially from smallest to largest, lightest to darkest, and shortest to tallest.

Finally, said Piaget, beginning at about age 12 or 13 and continuing into adulthood, people become capable of abstract reasoning and enter the *formal operations stage*. They are able to reason about situations they have not experienced firsthand, and they can think about future possibilities. They are able to search systematically for solutions to problems. They are able to draw logical conclusions from premises common to their culture and experience.

✺ Explore the Concept Piaget's Stages of Cognitive Development at MyPsychLab

Current Views of Cognitive Development LO 3.8

Piaget's central idea has been well supported: New reasoning abilities depend on the emergence of previous ones. You cannot learn algebra before you can count, and you cannot learn philosophy before you understand logic. But since Piaget's original work, the field of developmental psychology has undergone an explosion of imaginative research that has allowed investigators to get into the minds of even the youngest infants. The result has been a major modification of Piaget's ideas. Here's why.

Get Involved! A Test of Conservation

If you know any young children, try one of Piaget's conservation experiments. A simple one is to make two rows of seven buttons or pennies, aligned identically. Ask the child whether one row has more. Now simply spread out the buttons in one of the rows, and ask the child again whether one row has more. If the child says, "Yes," ask which one and why. Try to do this experiment with a 3-year-old and a 7- or 8-year-old. You will probably see a big difference in their answers.

1 Cognitive abilities develop in continuous, overlapping waves rather than discrete steps or stages. If you observe children at different ages, as Piaget did, it will seem that they reason differently. But if you study the everyday learning of children at any given age, you will find that a child may use several different strategies to solve a problem, some more complex or accurate than others (Siegler, 2006). Learning occurs gradually, with retreats to former ways of thinking as well as advances to new ones. Children's reasoning ability also depends on the circumstances—who is asking them questions, the specific words used, and what they are reasoning about—and not just on the stage they are in. In short, cognitive development is continuous; new abilities do not simply pop up when a child turns a specific age (Courage & Howe, 2002).

2 Children, even infants, reveal cognitive abilities much earlier than Piaget believed possible. Taking advantage of the fact that infants look longer at novel or surprising stimuli than at familiar ones, psychologists have designed delightfully innovative methods of testing what babies know. These methods reveal that babies may be born with mental modules or core knowledge systems for numbers, spatial relations, the properties of objects, and other features of the physical world (Izard et al., 2009; Kibbe & Leslie, 2011; Spelke & Kinzler, 2007).

Thus, at only 4 months of age, babies will look longer at a ball if it seems to roll through a solid barrier, leap between two platforms, or hang in midair than they do when the ball obeys the laws of physics. This suggests that the unusual event is surprising to them (see Figure 3.3). Infants as young as 2 1/2 to 3 1/2 months are aware that objects continue to exist even when masked by other objects, a form of object permanence that Piaget never imagined possible in babies so young (Baillargeon, 2004). And most devastating to Piaget's notion of infant egocentrism, even 5-month-old infants are able to perceive other people's actions as being intentional; they detect the difference between a person who is actively reaching for a toy with her hand rather than accidentally touching it with a stick (Woodward, 2009). Even some 3-month-old infants can learn this.

3 Preschoolers are not as egocentric as Piaget thought. Most 3- and 4-year-olds *can* take another person's perspective (Flavell, 1999). When 4-year-olds play with 2-year-olds, they modify and simplify their speech so the younger children will understand (Shatz & Gelman, 1973). One preschooler we know showed her teacher a picture she had drawn of a cat and an unidentifiable blob. "The cat is lovely," said the teacher, "but what is this thing here?" "That has nothing to do with you," said the child. "That's what the *cat* is looking at."

By about ages 3 to 4, children also begin to understand that you cannot predict what a person will do just by observing a situation or knowing the facts. You also have to know what the person is feeling and thinking; the person might even be lying. Children also start asking why other people behave as they do ("Why is Johnny so mean?"). In short, they are developing a **theory of mind**, a system of beliefs about how their own and other people's minds work and how people are affected by their beliefs and emotions. They begin to use verbs like *think* and *know*, and by age 4 they understand that what another person thinks might not match their own knowledge. In one typical experiment, a child watched as another child placed a ball in the closet and left the room. An adult then entered and moved the ball into a basket. Three-year-olds predicted that when the other child returned, he would look for the ball in the basket because that is where the 3-year-old knew it was. But 4-year-olds said that the child would look in the closet, where the other child believed it was (Flavell, 1999; Wellman, Cross, & Watson, 2001).

Remarkably, early aspects of a theory of mind are present in infancy: Babies aged 13 to 15 months are surprised when they realize that an adult has a false or pretend belief (Luo & Baillargeon, 2010). The ability to understand that people can have false beliefs is a milestone. It means the child is beginning to question how we know things—the foundation for later higher-order thinking.

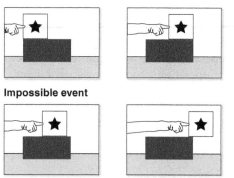

Possible event

Impossible event

FIGURE 3.3 Testing Infants' Knowledge
In this clever procedure, a baby watches as a box is pushed from left to right along a platform. The box is pushed until it reaches the end of the platform (a possible event) or until only a bit of it rests on the platform (an impossible event). Babies look longer at the impossible event, suggesting that it surprises them. Somehow they know that an object needs physical support and can't just float on air (Baillargeon, 1994).

theory of mind A system of beliefs about the way one's own mind and the minds of others work, and about how individuals are affected by their beliefs and feelings.

4 Cognitive development is influenced by a child's culture. Culture—the world of tools, language, rituals, beliefs, games, and social institutions— shapes and structures children's cognitive development, fostering some abilities and not others. Thus, nomadic hunters excel in spatial abilities because this skill helps them find water holes and successful hunting routes. In contrast, children who live in settled agricultural communities, such as the Baoulé of the Ivory Coast, develop rapidly in the ability to quantify but much more slowly in spatial reasoning (Tomasello, 2000; Vygotsky, 1962).

Despite these modifications, Piaget left an enduring legacy: the insight that children are not passive vessels into which education and experience are poured. Children actively interpret their worlds, using their developing abilities to assimilate new information and figure things out.

Experience and culture influence cognitive development. Children who work with clay, wood, and other materials, such as this young potter in India, tend to understand the concept of conservation sooner than children who have not had this kind of experience.

Recite & Review

✓ **Study** and **Review** at **MyPsychLab**

Recite: Use your formal-operations reasoning skills to speak aloud what you have learned about Piaget's stages, object permanence, the principle of conservation, the theory of mind, and the major modifications of Piaget's theory.

Review: Next, reread this section.

Now take this *Quick Quiz:*

1. Understanding that two rows of six pennies are equal in number, even if one row is flat and the other is stacked up, is an example of _____.

2. Understanding that a toy exists even after mom puts it in her purse is an example of _____.

3. A 5-year-old boy who tells his dad that "Sally said she saw a bunny but she was lying" has developed a _____.

Answers:

1. conservation 2. object permanence 3. theory of mind

You are about to learn . . .

- how moral feelings and behavior develop.
- why shouting "Because I say so!" does not get most children to behave well.
- the importance of a child's ability to delay gratification.

Moral Development

LO 3.9, LO 3.10

How do children learn to tell right from wrong, resist the temptation to behave selfishly, and obey the rules of social conduct? Influenced by Piaget's

stage theory of cognitive development, some developmental psychologists once thought the answer lay in children's emerging ability to reason about moral issues (Kohlberg, 1964). Children's verbal responses to moral dilemmas suggested that young children obey because they fear being punished if they disobey, older children come to realize that it is in their best interest to obey, and adults are able to understand the rule of law and the notion of human rights.

It is true that moral-reasoning ability becomes more sophisticated with age, but unfortunately so do cheating, lying, and cruelty. As Thomas Lickona (1983) wryly summarized, "We can reach high levels of moral reasoning, and still behave like

How do children internalize moral rules? How do they learn that cheating, stealing, and grabbing a younger sibling's toy are wrong?

scoundrels." Today, therefore, developmental psychologists place greater emphasis on how children learn to regulate their own emotions and behavior (Mischel & Ayduk, 2004). Most children learn to inhibit their wishes to beat up their younger siblings, steal a classmate's toy, or scream at the top of their lungs if they don't get their way. The child's emerging ability to understand right from wrong, and to behave accordingly, depends on the emergence of conscience and moral emotions such as shame, guilt, and empathy (Kochanska et al., 2005).

As we saw in our discussion of Piaget, even very young children are capable of feeling empathy for others and taking another person's point of view. One-year-olds will point to an object to help an adult find it; by 18 months they show concern for someone who is hurt; early in life, they begin sharing and helping others. Children do these things and obey rules not only because they are afraid of what will happen to them if they do not, but also because they understand right from wrong—they do kind things even if they don't "get credit" for it (Hepach, Vaish, & Tomasello, 2012). By age 5, they know it is wrong to hurt someone even if a teacher tells them to (Turiel, 2002). The capacity for understanding right from wrong seems to be inborn. Evolutionary psychologists argue that this "moral sense" underlies the basic beliefs, judgments, and behavior that are considered moral almost everywhere, and that it originated in cooperative, altruistic strategies that

permitted our forebears to resolve conflicts and get along (Delton et al., 2011; Krebs, 2008).

Can the moral sense and the desire to behave well with others be nurtured or extinguished by specific methods of child rearing? For decades, most developmental psychologists assumed that the answer was "Of course!" and they set about trying to pinpoint which parental techniques create well-behaved, kind, unselfish children. Then came a flood of behavioral-genetic studies that led to a different assumption: The effects of the parents' methods depend (of course!) on the kind of child they have—one who heeds discipline or one who is resistant and hostile?

THINKING CRITICALLY
About Teaching Children Morality

Many researchers are now seeking a middle ground by studying gene-environment interactions (Schmidt et al., 2009). One provocative hypothesis suggests that infants and toddlers who show high levels of distress and irritability are actually more responsive to, and influenced by, styles of parenting than easygoing babies are. Easygoing babies are "dandelions"; they survive in almost any circumstances they encounter because they are, well, easygoing. "Orchid children," in contrast, are highly sensitive to their environments; under adversity, they wither (Ellis & Boyce, 2008). When such babies have impatient, rejecting, or coercive parents, they later tend to become aggressive and even more difficult and defiant. When they have patient, supportive, firm parents, they become better natured and happier—in a word, they bloom (Belsky, Bakermans-Kranenburg, & van IJzendoorn, 2007; Belsky & Pluess, 2009b).

Keeping the complexity of this issue in mind, let's look at how parental discipline methods interact with a child's temperament in the development of conscience and moral behavior.

Getting Children to be Good. When you did something wrong as a child, did the adults in your family spank you, shout at you, threaten you, or explain the error of your ways? One of the most common methods that parents use to enforce moral standards and good behavior is **power assertion**, which includes threats, physical punishment, depriving the child of privileges, and generally taking advantage of being bigger, stronger, and more powerful. Of course, a parent may have no alternative other than "Do it because I say so!" if the child is too young to understand a rule or impishly keeps trying to break it. Moreover, the culture and context in which the discipline occurs makes an enormous

power assertion A method of child rearing in which the parent uses punishment and authority to correct the child's misbehavior.

Power assertion is the use of physical force, threats, insults, or other kinds of power to get the child to obey ("Do it because I say so!" "Stop that right now!"). The child may obey, but only when the parent is present—and the child often feels resentful and ready for the chance to misbehave again.

The parent who uses induction appeals to the child's good nature, empathy, love for the parent, and sense of responsibility to others, while offering explanations of rules ("You're too grown up to behave like that"; "Fighting hurts your little brother"). The child then tends to internalize reasons for good behavior.

difference. Is the parent–child relationship fundamentally loving and trusting or one full of hostility and fighting? Does the child interpret the parents' actions as being fair and caring, or unfair and cruel?

But when power assertion consists of sheer parental bullying, cruel insults ("You are so stupid, I wish you'd never been born"), and frequent physical punishment, it is associated with greater aggressiveness in children and reduced empathy (Alink et al., 2009; Gershoff, 2002; Moore & Pepler, 2006). As we discuss in Chapter 9, physical punishment often backfires, especially when it is used inappropriately or harshly; it spirals out of control, causing the child to become angry and resentful. Moreover, harsh but ineffective discipline methods are often transmitted to the next generation: Aggressive parents teach their children that the way to discipline children is by behaving aggressively (Capaldi et al., 2003).

What is the alternative? In contrast to power assertion, a parent can use **induction**, appealing to the child's own abilities, empathy, helpful nature, affection for others, and sense of responsibility ("You made Doug cry; it's not nice to bite"; "You must never poke anyone's eyes because that could really hurt them"). Or the parent might appeal to the child's own helpful inclinations ("I know you're a person who likes to be nice to others") rather than offering bribes for good behavior ("You'd better be nice or you won't get dessert").

Self-Control and Conscience. One of the most important social-emotional skills that children need to acquire is the ability to control their immediate impulses and wishes. In particular, they need to learn to *delay gratification* to gain later benefits. The original classic study of delayed gratification used a "marshmallow test": Preschoolers were offered a choice between

eating one marshmallow right away or having two marshmallows if they could wait a few minutes while the experimenter stepped out of the room (Mischel, Shoda, & Rodriguez, 1989). Dozens of similar studies have been done since, including follow-ups on what became of the children in the first experiments, and the results are clear: Children who are able to resist the single marshmallow (or other prize) in favor of getting a larger reward later are better able to control negative emotions, pay attention to the task at hand, and do well in school. Indeed, the early ability to postpone gratification has effects on health, success, and well-being that last for *decades* (Casey et al., 2011; Eigsti et al., 2006; Ponitz et al., 2009).

Where does this ability come from? Partly from temperament and personality, because children who can control their emotions and impulses usually do so across situations (de Ridder et al., 2012; Raffaelli, Crockett, & Shen, 2005). Partly from learning: Children and young people can learn to improve their ability to delay gratification by focusing on the later benefits, by distracting themselves from focusing on the appealing prize, and by mentally de-emphasizing the appealing features of the prize (for example, by imagining the marshmallow as a cloud or a little cotton ball, rather than as a sweet treat). And partly from the way their parents treat them.

A longitudinal study of 106 preschool children explored the links between parental discipline, the child's self-control, and the emergence of conscience (Kochanska & Knaack, 2003). The children who were most able to regulate their impulses early in life were the least likely to get in trouble later by fighting or destroying things, and the most likely to have a high conscience score. In turn, their behavior was negatively correlated with

induction A method of child rearing in which the parent appeals to the child's own resources, abilities, sense of responsibility, and feelings for others in correcting the child's misbehavior.

Children's ability to regulate their impulses and delay gratification is a major milestone in the development of conscience and moral behavior.

the mother's use of power assertion, meaning that mothers who ordered their children to "behave" tended to have children who were impulsive and aggressive (see also Alink et al., 2009). However, cause and effect worked in both directions. Some mothers relied on power assertion *because* their children were impulsive, defiant, and aggressive and would not listen to them. This pattern of findings teaches us to avoid oversimplifying, by concluding that "It's all in what the mother does" or that "It's all in the child's personality." Mothers and children, it seems, raise each other.

Recite & Review

✓ **Study** and **Review** at MyPsychLab

Recite: Before going on, exercise self-control by pausing to recite out loud what you know about the development of moral reasoning and its relation to moral emotions and behavior; "orchid" and "dandelion" children; power assertion versus induction; and delay of gratification and its benefits.

Review: Next, reread this material.

Now take this *Quick Quiz:*

1. Which method of disciplining a child who is hitting his younger brother is most likely to teach empathy? (a) induction, (b) indulgence, (c) power assertion, (d) spanking

2. What early ability predicts the development of conscience later on?

Answers:

1. a 2. delay of gratification, the ability to control one's immediate impulses and wishes

---

You are about to learn . . .

- why some people fail to identify themselves as either male or female.

- the biological explanation of why most little boys and girls are "sexist" in their choice of toys, at least for a while.

- when and how children learn that they are male or female.

- learning explanations of some typical sex differences in childhood behavior.

Gender Development

No parent ever excitedly calls a relative to exclaim, "It's a baby! It's a 7 1/2-pound, black-haired baby!" The baby's sex is the first thing everyone notices and announces. How soon do children notice that boys and girls are different sexes and understand which sex they themselves are? How do children learn the rules of masculinity and femininity, the things that boys do that are different from what girls do? Why, as one friend of ours observed, do most preschool children act like the "gender police," insisting, say, on what boys and girls "have to" wear or play with? And why do some children come to feel they don't belong to the sex everyone else thinks they do?

Gender Identity LO 3.11

Gender identity refers to a child's sense of being male or female, of belonging to one sex and not the other. **Gender typing** is the process of socializing children into their gender roles, and thus reflects society's ideas about which abilities, interests, traits, and behaviors are appropriately masculine or feminine. A person can have a strong gender identity and not be gender typed: A man may be confident in his maleness and not feel threatened by doing "unmasculine" things such as needle-pointing a pillow; a woman may be confident in her femaleness and not feel threatened by doing "unfeminine" things such as driving race cars.

The complexity of gender development is especially apparent in the cases of people who do not fit the familiar categories of male and female. Every year, thousands of babies are born with **intersex conditions**, formerly known as hermaphroditism. In these conditions, chromosomal or hormonal anomalies cause the child to be born with ambiguous genitals, or genitals that conflict with the infant's chromosomes. A child who is genetically female might be born with an enlarged clitoris that looks like a penis. A child who is genetically male might be born with androgen insensitivity, a condition that causes the external genitals to appear female.

As adults, many intersexed individuals call themselves *transgender*, a term describing a broad category of people who do not fit comfortably into the usual categories of male and female, masculine and feminine. Some transgender people are comfortable living with the physical attributes of both sexes, considering themselves to be "gender queer" and even refusing to be

gender identity The fundamental sense of being male or female; it is independent of whether the person conforms to the social and cultural rules of gender.

gender typing The process by which children learn the abilities, interests, and behaviors associated with being masculine or feminine in their culture.

intersex conditions Conditions in which chromosomal or hormonal anomalies cause a child to be born with ambiguous genitals, or genitals that conflict with the infant's chromosomes.

Throughout history and across cultures, some people have broken out of conventional gender categories. Some women have lived as men, as did the eighteenth-century pirates Ann Bonny and Mary Read (left). Some men have lived as women: The Muxes (pronounced moo-shays) of southern Mexico are males who consider themselves female, live as females, and are a socially accepted category (center). Some individuals do not wish to identify as traditionally male or female. Thomas Beatie (right) was born a genetic female and later had a sex-change operation. Because he had a womb, he was able to become the world's first "pregnant man."

referred to as he or she. Some feel uncomfortable in their sex of rearing and wish to be considered a member of the other sex. *Transsexuals* are usually not intersexed, yet likewise feel that they are male in a female body or vice versa; their gender identity is at odds with their anatomical sex or appearance. Many transsexuals try to make a full transition to the other sex through surgery or hormones. Intersexed and transsexual people have been found in virtually all cultures throughout history (Denny, 1998; Roughgarden, 2004).

Influences on Gender Identity and Development LO 3.12

To understand the typical course of gender development, as well as the variations, developmental psychologists study the interacting influences of biology, cognition, and learning on gender identity and gender typing.

 Watch the Video The Basics: Sex and Gender Differences at MyPsychLab

Biological Influences. Starting in the preschool years, boys and girls congregate primarily with other children of their sex, and most prefer the toys and games of their own sex. They will play together if required to, but given a choice, they usually choose to play with same-sex friends. The kind of play that young boys and girls enjoy also differs, on average. Little boys, like young males in all primate species, are more likely than females to go in for physical roughhousing, risk taking, and aggressive displays. These sex differences occur all over the world, almost regardless of whether adults encourage boys and girls to play

together or separate them (Lytton & Romney, 1991; Maccoby, 1998, 2002). Many parents lament that although they try to give their children the same toys, it makes no difference; their sons want trucks and guns and their daughters want dolls.

Biological scientists believe that these play and toy preferences have a basis in prenatal hormones, particularly the presence or absence of prenatal androgens (masculinizing hormones). Girls who were exposed to higher-than-normal prenatal androgens in the womb are later more likely than nonexposed girls to prefer "boys' toys" such as cars and fire engines, and they are also more physically aggressive than other girls (Berenbaum & Bailey, 2003). A study of more than 200 healthy children in the general population also found a relationship between fetal testosterone and play styles. (Testosterone is produced in fetuses of both sexes, although it is higher on average in males.) The higher the levels of fetal testosterone, as measured in the amniotic fluid of the children's mothers during pregnancy, the higher the children's later scores on a measure of male-typical play (Auyeung et al., 2009). In studies of rhesus monkeys, who of course are not influenced by their parents' possible gender biases, male monkeys, like human boys, consistently and strongly prefer to play with wheeled toys rather than cuddly plush toys, whereas female monkeys, like human girls, are more varied in their toy preferences (Hassett, Siebert, & Wallen, 2008).

What about the stories in the news of very young boys who not only want to play with girls' toys but want to *be* girls? Or little girls who want to be boys? In 2013, the parents of one such child sued the school system to allow their son—whom they now consider their daughter—for the right to

Look familiar? In a scene typical of many nursery schools and homes, the boy likes to play with trucks and the girl with dolls. Whether or not such behavior is biologically based, the gender rigidity of the early years does not inevitably continue into adulthood unless cultural rules reinforce it.

use the girls' bathroom and otherwise be treated as a girl. Many people infer from individual cases like these that gender identity must be fixed in the brain, possibly even prenatally.

But the reality is more complicated. Researchers at a Canadian clinic have been studying and following the development of nearly 600 children, ages two to 12, who believed they were the "wrong sex." Long-term follow-ups find that only a small percentage—12 to 13 percent—retain their transgender identity as adults (Zucker et al., 2012; see also Zucker, 1999). Other smaller studies find the number to be somewhat higher, but overall, most of these children end up with a gender identity that matches their anatomical sex; they switch back during adolescence or young adulthood (Fausto-Sterling, 2012). Some grow up to be straight, others gay; some become "gender queer," not wishing to choose a permanent gender.

Cognitive Influences. Even before babies can speak, they can distinguish the two sexes. By the age of nine months, most babies can discriminate male from female faces (Fagot & Leinbach, 1993), and they can match female faces with female voices (Poulin-Dubois et al., 1994). By the age of 18 to 20 months, most toddlers have a concept of gender labels; they can accurately identify the gender of people in picture books and begin correctly using the words *boy*, *girl*, and *man* (interestingly, *lady* and *woman* come later) (Zosuls et al., 2009).

Once children can label themselves and others consistently as being a boy or a girl, shortly before age 2, they change their behavior to conform to the category they belong to. Many begin to prefer same-sex playmates and sex-traditional toys without being explicitly taught to do so (Martin, Ruble, & Szkrybalo, 2002; Zosuls et al., 2009).

They become more gender typed in their toy play, games, aggressiveness, and verbal skills than children who still cannot consistently label males and females. Most notably, girls stop behaving aggressively (Fagot, 1993). It is as if they go along behaving like boys until they know they are girls. At that moment, they seem to decide: "Girls don't do this; I'm a girl; I'd better not either."

It's great fun to watch 3- to 5-year-old children struggle to figure out what makes boys and girls different: "The ones with eyelashes are girls; boys don't have eyelashes," said one 4-year-old girl to her aunt in explaining her drawing. After dinner at an Italian restaurant, a 4-year-old boy told his parents that he'd got it. "Men eat pizza and women don't" (Bjorkland, 2000).

By about age 5, most children understand that what boys and girls do does not necessarily indicate what sex they are: A girl remains a girl even if she can climb a tree (or eats pizza!), and a boy remains a boy even if he has long hair. At this age, children consolidate their knowledge, with all of its mistakes and misconceptions, into a **gender schema**, a mental network of beliefs and expectations about what it means to be male or female and about what each sex is supposed to wear, do, feel, and think (Bem, 1993; Martin & Ruble, 2004). Gender schemas are most rigid between ages 5 and 7; at this age, it's really hard to dislodge a child's notion of what boys and girls can do (Martin, Ruble, & Szkrybalo, 2002). A little girl at this stage may tell you stoutly that "girls can't be doctors," even if her own mother is a doctor.

Understanding how cognitive development affects gender identity suggests not only how most children come to think of themselves as boys or girls but also how a boy might decide he is "really" a girl and vice versa. In that long-term Canadian study, one 7-year-old boy, when asked why he wanted to be a girl, said that it was because

gender schema A cognitive schema (mental network) of knowledge, beliefs, metaphors, and expectations about what it means to be male or female.

"Jason, I'd like to let you play, but soccer is a girls' game."

Get Involved! Gender and Generations

Gender norms have been changing rapidly, and one way to see this for yourself is to interview older members of your family or an old person you know. Ask at least one man and one woman these questions: (1) When you were growing up, was there anything your parents did not permit you to do because of your sex? (2) Is there any job you think is unsuitable for a man or a woman to do? (3) Did you ever experience discrimination because of your sex? Now consider how you would answer those questions. Do your answers agree with theirs? Why or why not?

he did not like to sweat and only boys sweat, and because he liked to read and girls read better than boys (Zucker et al., 2012). Such children may not feel like "real" boys or girls because their preferences and interests do not fit the rigidity of early gender schemas. As they grow older, however, and acquire experience and cognitive sophistication, children often become more flexible in their gender schemas, especially if they have friends of the other sex and if their families and cultures encourage such flexibility (Martin & Ruble, 2004). Of course, many people retain inflexible gender schemas throughout their lives, feeling uncomfortable or angry with men or women who break out of traditional roles—let alone with transgendered individuals who don't fit either category or want to change the one they grew up with.

Cultures and religions, too, differ in their schemas for the roles of women and men. In all Western, industrialized nations, it is taken for granted that women and men alike should be educated; indeed, laws mandate a minimum education for both sexes. But in cultures where female education is prohibited in the name of religious law, as in the parts of Afghanistan controlled by the Taliban, many girls who attend school receive death threats and some have had acid thrown on their faces. Gender schemas can be powerful, and events that challenge their legitimacy can be enormously threatening.

Learning Influences. A third influence on gender development is the environment, which is full of subtle and not-so-subtle messages about what girls and boys are supposed to do. Behavioral and social-cognitive learning theorists study how the process of gender socialization instills these messages in children. They find that gender socialization begins at the moment of birth. Parents tend to portray their newborn girls as more feminine and delicate than boys, and boys as stronger and more athletic than girls, although it is hard to know how athletic a newborn boy could be (Karraker, Vogel, & Lake, 1995). Many parents are careful to dress their baby in outfits they consider to be the correct color and pattern for his or her sex. Clothes don't matter to the infant, of course, but they are signals to adults about how to treat the child. Adults often respond to the same baby differently, depending on whether the child is dressed as a boy or a girl.

Parents, teachers, and other adults convey their beliefs and expectations about gender even when they are entirely unaware that they are doing so. When parents believe that boys are naturally better at math or sports and that girls are naturally better at English, they unwittingly communicate those beliefs by how they respond to a child's success or failure. They may tell a son who did well in math, "You're a natural math whiz, Johnny!" But if a daughter gets good grades, they may say, "Wow, you

Startling images or nothing new? The idea of women serving in combat and men teaching preschoolers would once have surprised most people and offended others. As women and men began entering careers that were unusual for their gender—because of changes in the economy, demographics, and gender roles—their job choices lost the power to shock.

really worked hard in math, Joanie, and it shows!" The implication is that girls have to try hard but boys have a natural gift. Messages like these are not lost on children. Both sexes tend to lose interest in activities that are supposedly not natural for them, even when they all start out with equal abilities (Dweck, 2006; Frome & Eccles, 1998).

Gender schemas reflect larger cultural concepts, including metaphors. After age 4, children of both sexes will usually say that rough, spiky, black, or mechanical things are male and that soft, pink, fuzzy, or flowery things are female; that black bears are male and pink poodles are female (Leinbach, Hort, & Fagot, 1997). But the content of these schemas is not innate. A hundred years ago, an article in *The Ladies Home Journal* advised: "The generally accepted rule is pink for the boys, and blue for the girls. The reason is that pink, being a more decided and stronger color, is more suitable for the boy, while blue, which is more delicate and dainty, is prettier for the girl" (Paoletti, 2012). The invention of gender-specific "rules" of clothing for babies and young children, along with a rigid split between "boys' toys" and "girls' toys," was a creation of late twentieth-century marketing. In 1975, few toys were marketed by gender. But as toy companies realized that by segmenting their markets into narrower demographic groups they could sell more versions of the same toy, gender segregation became commonplace—and then normal. And in turn, children began demanding toys considered appropriate for their gender (Sweet, 2012).

In today's fast-moving world, society's messages to men and women, and parents' messages to their children, keep evolving. As a result, gender development has become a lifelong process, in which gender schemas, attitudes, behavior—and even identity—change as people have new experiences and as society itself changes (Fausto-Sterling, 2012; Rosin, 2012). 5-year-old children may behave like sexist piglets while they are trying to figure out what it means to be male or female, but their gender-typed behavior as 5-year-olds often has little to do with how they will behave at 25 or 45. In fact, by early adulthood, men and women show virtually no average differences in cognitive abilities, personality traits, self-esteem or psychological well-being (Hyde, 2007).

That is why children can grow up in an extremely gender-typed family and yet, as adults, find themselves in careers or relationships or identities they would never have imagined for themselves. If 5-year-olds are the gender police, many adults end up breaking the law.

Explore the Concept **How Does Gender Affect You?** at MyPsychLab

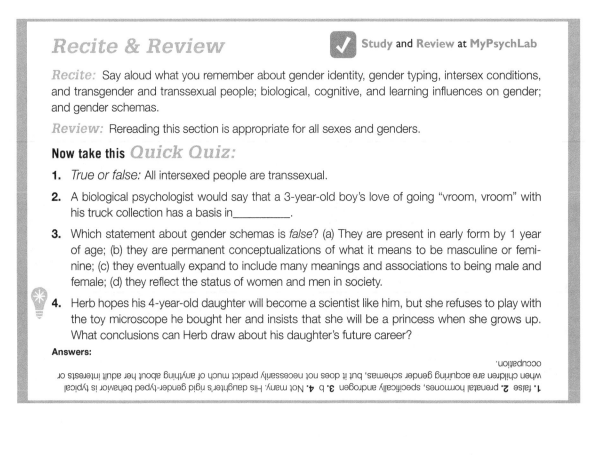

Recite & Review

✓ Study and Review at MyPsychLab

Recite: Say aloud what you remember about gender identity, gender typing, intersex conditions, and transgender and transsexual people; biological, cognitive, and learning influences on gender; and gender schemas.

Review: Rereading this section is appropriate for all sexes and genders.

Now take this *Quick Quiz:*

1. *True or false:* All intersexed people are transsexual.

2. A biological psychologist would say that a 3-year-old boy's love of going "vroom, vroom" with his truck collection has a basis in_____.

3. Which statement about gender schemas is *false*? (a) They are present in early form by 1 year of age; (b) they are permanent conceptualizations of what it means to be masculine or feminine; (c) they eventually expand to include many meanings and associations to being male and female; (d) they reflect the status of women and men in society.

4. Herb hopes his 4-year-old daughter will become a scientist like him, but she refuses to play with the toy microscope he bought her and insists that she will be a princess when she grows up. What conclusions can Herb draw about his daughter's future career?

Answers:

1. false 2. prenatal hormones, specifically androgen 3. b 4. Not many. His daughter's rigid gender-typed behavior is typical when children are acquiring gender schemas, but it does not necessarily predict much of anything about her adult interests or occupation.

You are about to learn . . .

- the physiological changes of adolescence.
- the psychological issues of adolescence.
- findings on brain development in adolescence.

Adolescence

In middle childhood (ages 6 to 12), children go through a period called **adrenarche** (a-DREN-ar-kee), when the adrenal glands begin pumping out hormones that affect brain development, most notably an androgen called DHEA (Campbell, 2011). These hormones divert glucose in the brain to foster the maturation of brain regions vital to interpreting social and emotional cues. Children's brains during these years are at their most flexible and responsive to learning. Children become able to control their impulses, reason better, focus and plan for the future, and understand mortality and death. Their friendships flourish.

All over the world, cultures acknowledge that middle childhood is an important station on the road to adulthood. Adults begin giving children responsibilities—hunting, gardening, care of younger children, chores—though these tasks vary in seriousness (Lancy & Grove, 2011). Ariaal girls in northern Kenya work the hardest, putting in 9.6 hours of farm work daily; but among the Pumé, a foraging group in Venezuela, preadolescent girls do almost nothing. "Pumé girls spend their time socializing, talking and laughing with their friends, beading and resting," observed the researchers who lived among them (Kramer & Greaves, 2011).

And then…adolescence strikes. Adolescence refers to the period of development between **puberty**, the age at which a person becomes capable of sexual reproduction, and adulthood. In some cultures, the time span between puberty and adulthood is only a few months; a sexually mature boy or girl is expected to marry and assume adult tasks. In modern Western societies, however, teenagers are not considered emotionally mature enough to assume the full rights, responsibilities, and roles of adulthood.

The Physiology of Adolescence

LO 3.13

Until puberty, boys and girls produce roughly the same levels of androgens (masculinizing hormones) and estrogens (feminizing hormones). But from puberty on, boys have a higher level of androgens than girls do, and girls have a higher level of estrogens than boys do. In boys, the reproductive glands are the testes (testicles), which produce sperm; in girls, the reproductive glands are the ovaries, which release eggs. During puberty, these organs mature and the individual becomes capable of reproduction. In girls, signs of sexual maturity are the development of breasts and **menarche**, the onset of menstruation. In boys, the signs are the onset of nocturnal emissions and the growth of the testes, scrotum, and penis. Hormones are also responsible for the emergence of *secondary sex characteristics*, such as a deepened voice and facial and chest hair in boys and pubic hair in both sexes.

The onset of puberty is determined by both biological and environmental factors. Menarche depends on a female's having a critical level of body fat, which is necessary to sustain a pregnancy and which triggers the hormonal changes associated with puberty. An increase in body fat among children in developed countries may help explain why the average age of puberty declined in Europe and North America until the mid-twentieth century. The average age of menarche is now about 12 years and 6 months in white girls and a few months earlier in black girls. Other signs of puberty in girls, such as pubic hair and breast buds, are appearing at younger and younger ages. In boys, the average age of puberty (as measured by testicular size) used to be 11 years and 6 months, and a few months earlier in black boys; but boys, too, are entering puberty from seven months to two years sooner than that (Herman-Giddens et al., 2012). Various reasons for the earlier ages for puberty have been suggested—rising obesity rates, environmental pollution, childhood stress—but the answer is still unknown.

The onset and length of puberty vary considerably from one person to another. Some girls go through menarche at 9 or 10, or even earlier, and some boys are still growing in height after age 19. Early-maturing boys generally have a more positive view of their bodies than late-maturing boys do, and their relatively greater size and strength give them a boost in sports and the prestige that being a good athlete brings young men. But they are also more likely to smoke, drink alcohol, use other drugs, and break the law than later-maturing boys (Cota-Robles, Neiss, & Rowe, 2002). Some early-maturing girls have the prestige of being socially popular,

adrenarche [a-DREN-ar-kee] A time in middle childhood when the adrenal glands begin producing the adrenal hormone DHEA and other adrenal hormones that affect cognitive and social development.

puberty The age at which a person becomes capable of sexual reproduction.

menarche [men-ARR-kee] The onset of menstruation during puberty.

but partly because others in their peer group regard them as being sexually precocious, they are also more likely to fight with their parents, drop out of school, have a negative body image, and be angry or depressed (Westling, Andrews, & Peterson, 2012; Westling, 2008). Early menarche itself does not cause these problems; rather, it tends to accentuate existing behavioral problems and family conflicts. Girls who go through puberty relatively late have a more difficult time at first, but by the end of adolescence, many are happier with their appearance and are more popular than their early-maturing classmates (Caspi & Moffitt, 1991; Stattin & Magnusson, 1990).

When people think of physical changes in adolescence, they usually think of hormones and maturing bodies. But the adolescent brain undergoes significant developmental changes, notably a major pruning of synapses (neural connections). This pruning occurs primarily in the prefrontal cortex, which is responsible for impulse control and planning, and in parts of the brain involved in emotional processing (Spear, 2000). Another change involves *myelinization*, which provides a sheath of insulation for neurons and improves the efficiency of neural transmission (see Chapter 4). Myelinization strengthens the connections between the emotional areas of the brain and the reasoning prefrontal cortex. This process continues through the late teens and

early 20s; full neurological and cognitive maturity often does not occur until about age 25, much later than commonly believed (Albert & Steinberg, 2011).

These discoveries would help explain why the strong emotions of the adolescent years often overwhelm rational decision making and self-control, causing some teenagers to behave more impulsively than adults in the heat of the moment (Casey & Caudle, 2013; Steinberg, 2007). It would explain why adolescents are more vulnerable to pressure from peers to try risky, dumb, or dangerous things—why taunts of "I dare you!" and "You're chicken!" have more power over a 15-year-old than a 25-year-old. Even when teenagers know they are doing the wrong thing, many lack the reasoning ability to foresee the consequences of their actions down the line (Reyna & Farley, 2006).

👁 **Watch the Video** Special Topics: Risky Behavior and Brain Development at **MyPsychLab**

The Psychology of Adolescence
LO 3.14

The media love sensational stories about teenagers who are angry, violent, live in emotional turmoil, feel lonely, have low self-esteem, hate their parents, and are running wild sexually. Yet, in reality, most teenagers are doing pretty well. Studies of representative samples of adolescents find that only a small minority is seriously troubled, angry, or unhappy. The rate of violent crimes committed by adolescents has been dropping steadily since 1993. Overall feelings of self-esteem do not suddenly plummet after the age of 13 for either sex (Gentile et al., 2009). And according to the National Youth Risk Behavior Survey, today's high school students are actually more sexually conservative than their parents were at their age: Fewer are having sex, and among those who are, the number of partners has declined (Bogle, 2008; Eaton et al., 2008; Rosin, 2012).

Nevertheless, three kinds of problems are more common during adolescence than during childhood or adulthood: conflict with parents, mood swings and depression, and, as we saw, higher rates of reckless, rule-breaking, and risky behavior (Steinberg, 2007). Rule breaking often occurs because teenagers are developing their own standards and values, often by trying on the styles, actions, and attitudes of their peers, in contrast to those of their parents.

Children typically reach puberty at different times. These girls are all the same age, but they differ considerably in physical maturity.

"So I blame you for everything—whose fault is that?"

Peers become especially important to adolescents because they represent the values and style of the generation that teenagers identify with, the generation that they will share experiences with as adults (Bukowski, 2001; Harris, 2009). Many people report that feeling rejected by their peers when they were teenagers was more devastating than punitive treatment by parents. According to a government-sponsored review of whether and how online technologies affect child safety, the most frequent dangers that teenagers face on the Internet are not pornography or even predatory adults, and definitely not sexting. "Bullying and harassment, most often by peers, are the most frequent threats that minors face, both online and offline," the report found (Berkman Center for Internet & Society, 2008).

Adolescents who are lonely, depressed, worried, or angry tend to express these concerns in ways characteristic of their sex. Boys are more likely than girls to externalize their emotional problems in acts of aggression and other antisocial behavior; the great majority of the mass shootings in schools and other public places have been committed by teenage or young-adult males. Girls are more likely than boys to internalize their feelings and problems by becoming withdrawn, blaming themselves for whatever goes wrong, or developing eating disorders (Wicks-Nelson & Israel, 2003). In general, girls are more dissatisfied than boys with their bodies and general appearance; boys are more dissatisfied than girls with their social behavior at school and with friends (Gentile et al., 2009).

Keep in mind that the "psychology of adolescence" depends profoundly on the larger culture in which teenagers live. During the 1960s and early 1970s, a period of great social upheaval during which many teenagers rebelled against their parents' lives and values, some observers wrote as if teenage rebellion were a universal, biologically driven phase; today, most teenagers remain close to their parents and see no reason to rebel against them.

Recite & Review

✔ **Study** and **Review** at **MyPsychLab**

Recite: State out loud all you remember about adrenarche, puberty, menarche, the psychology of adolescence, the biology of the adolescent brain, and the kinds of problems more common in adolescence than in childhood or adulthood.

Review: Next, reread this section.

Now take this *Quick Quiz:*

1. What does the word *menarche* mean?

2. Often, full neurological and cognitive maturity does not take place until about the age of (a) 14, (b) 25, (c) 18.

3. What changes occur in the brain during adolescence?

Answers:

1. Menarche is the term for the onset of menstruation in girls. 2. b 3. pruning of synapses, myelinization, and strengthening of connections between the emotional parts of the brain and the prefrontal cortex

You are about to learn...

- Erik Erikson's theory of the stages of adult development.
- the typical attitudes and experiences of "emerging adulthood," the years from 18 to 25.
- some common midlife changes in women and men.
- which mental abilities decline in old age and which ones do not.

Adulthood

According to ancient Greek legend, the Sphinx was a monster—half lion, half woman—who terrorized passersby on the road to Thebes. The Sphinx would ask each traveler a question and then murder those who failed to answer correctly. (The Sphinx was a pretty tough grader.) The question was: What animal walks on four feet in the morning, two feet at noon, and three feet in the evening? Only one traveler, Oedipus, knew the solution to the riddle. The animal, he said, is man, who crawls on all fours as a baby, walks upright as an adult, and limps in old age with the aid of a staff.

The Sphinx was the first life span theorist. Since then, many philosophers, writers, and scientists have speculated on the course of adult development. What are the major psychological issues of adult life? Is mental and physical deterioration in old age inevitable?

Stages and Ages LO 3.15

One of the first modern theorists to propose a life span approach to psychological development was psychoanalyst Erik H. Erikson (1902–1994). Erikson (1950/1963, 1982) wrote that all individuals go through eight stages in their lives. Each stage is characterized by what he called a "crisis," a particular psychological challenge that ideally should be resolved before the individual moves on.

- **Trust versus mistrust** is the challenge that occurs during the baby's first year, when the baby depends on others to provide food, comfort, cuddling, and warmth. If these needs are not met, the child may never develop the essential trust of others necessary to get along in the world.
- **Autonomy (independence) versus shame and doubt** is the challenge that occurs when the child is a toddler. The young child is learning to be independent and must do so without feeling too ashamed or uncertain about his or her actions.
- **Initiative versus guilt** is the challenge that occurs as the preschooler develops. The child is acquiring new physical and mental skills, setting goals, and enjoying newfound talents, but must also learn to control impulses. The danger lies in developing too strong a sense of guilt over his or her wishes and fantasies.
- **Competence versus inferiority** is the challenge for school-age children, who are learning to make things, use tools, and acquire the skills for adult life. Children who fail these lessons of mastery and competence may come out of this stage feeling inadequate and inferior.
- **Identity versus role confusion** is the great challenge of adolescence, when teenagers must decide who they are, what they are going to do, and what they hope to make of their lives. Erikson used the term *identity crisis* to describe what he considered to be the primary conflict of this stage. Those who resolve it will emerge with a strong identity, ready to plan for the future. Those who do not will sink into confusion, unable to make decisions.
- **Intimacy versus isolation** is the challenge of young adulthood. Once you have decided who you are, said Erikson, you must share yourself with another and learn to make commitments. No matter how successful you are in your work, you are not complete until you are capable of intimacy.
- **Generativity versus stagnation** is the challenge of the middle years. Now that you know

According to Erik Erikson, children must master the crisis of competence and older adults must resolve the challenge of generativity, as this child and her grandmother are certainly doing. But are the needs for competence and generativity significant at only one stage of life?

who you are and have an intimate relationship, will you sink into complacency and selfishness, or will you experience generativity—creativity and renewal? Parenthood is the most common route to generativity, but people can be productive, creative, and nurturing in other ways, in their work or their relationships with the younger generation.

- **Ego integrity versus despair** is the final challenge of old age. As they age, people strive to reach the ultimate goals of wisdom, spiritual tranquility, and acceptance of their lives. Just as the healthy child will not fear life, said Erikson, the healthy adult will not fear death.

Erikson recognized that cultural and economic factors affect people's progression through these stages. Some societies make the passages relatively easy. If you know you are going to be a farmer like your parents and you have no alternative, you are unlikely to have an adolescent identity crisis (unless you hate farming). If you have many choices, however, as adolescents in urban societies often do, the transition can become prolonged (Schwartz, 2004). Similarly, cultures that place a high premium on independence and individualism will make it difficult for many of their members to resolve Erikson's sixth crisis, that of intimacy versus isolation.

✳ Explore the Concept Stage Theory: Erikson at MyPsychLab

Since Erikson's time, people's lives have become less traditional and predictable, and these psychological issues now often occur in different order or return after having been resolved. Today, for instance, an identity crisis is hardly limited to the teen years. A man who has worked in one job for 20 years, and then is laid off at 45 and must find an entirely new career, may have an identity crisis too. Likewise, competence is not mastered once and for all in childhood. People learn new skills and lose old ones throughout their lives, and their sense of competence rises and falls accordingly. And people who are highly generative, in terms of being committed to helping their communities or the next generation, tend to do volunteer work or choose occupations that allow them to contribute to society throughout their lives (McAdams, 2006).

Erikson's stage theory, therefore, does not adequately describe how adults grow and change, or remain the same, across the life span. Yet Erikson was right to show that development does not stop

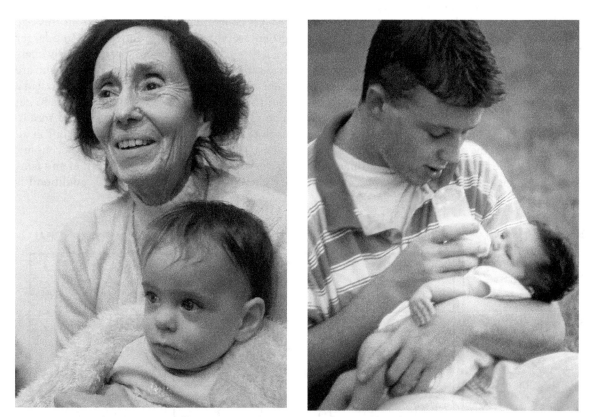

What is your reaction to these two first-time parents? Adriana Iliescu gave birth at age 66; the young man became a father at 15. Many people react negatively to individuals who they feel are "off time" for the transition to parenthood. How young is too young and how old is too old to become a parent?

at adolescence or young adulthood; it is an ongoing process. His ideas were important because he placed adult development in the context of family, work, and society, and he specified many of the timeless and universal concerns of adulthood: trust, competence, identity, generativity, and the ability to enjoy life and accept death (Dunkel & Sefcek, 2009).

The Transitions of Life   LO 3.16

When nearly everyone your age goes through the same experience or enters a new role at the same time—going to school, learning to drive, having a baby, retiring from work—adjusting to these transitions is relatively easy. Conversely, if you aren't doing these things and hardly anyone you know is doing them either, you will not feel out of step.

In addition, however, most people will face unanticipated transitions, events that happen without warning, such as the sudden death of a partner or spouse. And many people have to deal with the fact that changes they expected have not occurred—that they did not get a job right out of college, did not get married when they thought they would, failed to get an expected promotion, cannot afford to retire, or find that they cannot have children (Schlossberg & Robinson, 1996). With this in mind, let's consider some of the major transitions of life.

Emerging Adulthood. In industrialized nations, major demographic changes have postponed the timing of career decisions, marriage or cohabitation, and parenthood until a person's late 20s or even 30s, on the average. Many young people between the ages of 18 and 25 are in college and at least partly dependent financially on their parents. In 2011, because of a difficult economy, nearly 30 percent of adults ages 18 to 34 were living at home with their parents, the highest number in 70 years. This phenomenon has created a phase of life that some call *emerging adulthood* (Arnett, 2004). When emerging adults are asked whether they feel they have reached adulthood, the majority say, "in some ways yes, in some ways no."

Watch the Video What's In It For Me?: Identity at MyPsychLab

In certain respects, emerging adults have moved beyond adolescence into maturity, becoming more emotionally controlled, more confident, less dependent, and less angry and alienated (Azmitia, Syed, & Radmacher, 2008; Roberts, Caspi, & Moffitt, 2001). But they are also the group most likely to live unstable lives and feel unrooted. The Pew Research Group calls them "the boomerang generation," because they don't stay put. Emerging adults move more often than people in other demographic groups do—to college or work and then back to their parents' homes, from one city to another, from living with roommates to living on their own (Parker, 2012.). And their rates of risky behavior (such as binge drinking, having unprotected sex, and driving at high speeds or while drunk) are higher than those of any other age group, including adolescents (Arnett, 2004).

Of course, not all young people in this age group are alike. Some groups within the larger society, such as Mormons, promote early marriage and parenthood. And young people who are poor, who have dropped out of school, who had a child at 16, or who have few opportunities to get a good job will not have the income or leisure to explore many options. But the overall shift in all industrialized nations toward a global economy, increased education, and delayed career and family decisions means that emerging adulthood is

Doonesbury

BY GARRY TRUDEAU

likely to grow in importance as a distinct phase of prolonged exploration and freedom.

The Middle Years. For most women and men, the midlife years between 35 and 65 are the prime of life (MacArthur Foundation, 1999; Mroczek & Sprio, 2005; Newton & Stewart, 2010). These years are typically a time of the greatest well-being, good health, productivity, and community involvement (MacArthur Foundation, 1999; Mroczek & Sprio, 2005; Newton & Stewart, 2010). These midlife years are also often a time of reflection and reassessment People look back on what they have accomplished, take stock of what they regret not having done, and think about what they want to do with their remaining years. When "midlife crises" occur, they are for reasons not related to aging but to specific life-changing events, such as illness, divorce, bereavement, or the loss of a job (Wethington, 2000).

But doesn't menopause make most midlife women depressed, irritable, and irrational? **Menopause**, which usually occurs between ages 45 and 55, is the cessation of menstruation after the ovaries stop producing estrogen and progesterone. Menopause does produce physical symptoms in many women, notably hot flashes, as the vascular system adjusts to the decrease in estrogen. But only about 10 percent of all women have unusually severe physical symptoms.

The negative view of menopause as a syndrome that causes depression and other negative emotional reactions was originally based on women who underwent early menopause following a hysterectomy (removal of the uterus) or who had a lifetime history of depression. But these women were and are not typical. According to many surveys of thousands of healthy, randomly chosen women in the general population, most women view menopause with relief that they no longer have to worry about pregnancy or menstrual periods, or simply don't care one way or the other. The vast majority have only a few physical symptoms (which can be annoying and bothersome but are temporary), and most do not become depressed; only 3 percent even report regret at having reached menopause (McKinlay, McKinlay, & Brambilla, 1987). In one study of 1,000 postmenopausal women, fewer than half reported physical symptoms and only 5 percent of those complained of mood symptoms (Ness, Aronow, & Beck, 2006). Further contrary to stereotype, women in their 40s and 50s often report being most satisfied with the Eriksonian issues of identity, intimacy, and generativity (Newton & Stewart, 2010).

Although women lose their fertility after menopause and men theoretically remain fertile throughout their lives, men have a biological clock too. Testosterone diminishes, although it never drops as sharply in men as estrogen does in women. The sperm count may also gradually drop, and the sperm that remain are more susceptible to genetic mutations that can increase the risk of some diseases in children conceived by older fathers, as we saw earlier (Wyrobek et al., 2006).

The physical changes of midlife do not by themselves predict how people will feel about aging or how they will respond to it. People's views of aging are profoundly influenced by the culture they live in and by the promises of technology to prolong life and health—some realistic, some still science fiction. Is aging something natural and inevitable, to be accepted gracefully? Or is it a process to be fought tooth and nail, with every chemical, surgical, and genetic weapon we can lay our hands on? If we can live to be 100, why not get help from hormones, donated sperm, surrogate mothers, and in vitro fertilization to have a baby at 70, as some women have done? Or father a child in your 80s, as some men have done? To what extent should society pay for life-extending interventions? These issues will be hotly debated in the years to come.

Old Age   LO 3.17, LO 3.18

When does old age start? A few decades ago, you would have been considered old in your 60s, but that has changed. The fastest-growing segment of the population in North America now consists of people older than the age of 85. There were 5.5 million Americans age 85 or older in 2010, and the Census Bureau projects that there may be as many as 19 million by 2050. Close to one million of them will be older than the age of 100. *Gerontologists*, researchers who study aging and the old, have been investigating the likely consequences of this massive demographic change.

Explore the **Concept** Physical Changes in Late Adulthood at MyPsychLab

One is that the life phase of retirement is changing. When people expected to live only until their early 70s, retirement at 65 was associated with loss—a withdrawal from work and fulfilling activities, with not much to look forward to but illness and old age. Today, thanks to the enormous cohort of healthy baby boomers, retirement might last 20 or 30 years. Thus, it is no longer simply a transition from working to not working. People in the phase of what some psychologists are calling "positive retirement" often find a new career, volunteer work, or engrossing activities (Halpern, 2008).

menopause The cessation of menstruation and of the production of ova; it is usually a gradual process lasting up to several years.

The two images of old age: More and more old people are living healthy, active, mentally stimulating lives. But with increasing longevity, many people are also falling victim to degenerative diseases such as Alzheimer's.

fluid intelligence The capacity to reason and use new information to solve problems; it is relatively independent of education and tends to decline in old age.

crystallized intelligence Cognitive skills and specific knowledge acquired over a lifetime; it is heavily dependent on education and tends to remain stable.

Still, various aspects of intelligence, memory, decision making, and several other forms of mental functioning do decline with age. After roughly age 65, adults usually begin to score lower on tests of reasoning, spatial ability, and complex problem solving than do younger adults. It takes them longer to retrieve words and names, dates, and other information; in fact, the speed of cognitive processing in general slows down. However, older people vary considerably in this respect, with some declining significantly and others remaining quite sharp (Lövdén et al., 2010; Salthouse, 2013). Further, generational differences in education and familiarity with tests may help account for some of the cognitive differences between older and younger people (see Chapter 1).

Moreover, not all cognitive abilities worsen with age. **Fluid intelligence** is the capacity to reason and use new information to solve problems. It reflects in part an inherited predisposition, and it parallels other biological capacities in its growth and later decline (Bosworth & Schaie, 1999; Li et al., 2004). **Crystallized intelligence** consists of knowledge and skills built up over a lifetime, the kind of intelligence that gives us the ability to do arithmetic, define words, or take political positions. It depends heavily on education and experience, and it tends to remain stable or even improve over the life span. This is why physicians, lawyers, teachers, farmers,

musicians, insurance agents, politicians, psychologists, and people in many other occupations can continue working well into old age (Halpern, 2008). Also, older adults are often able to compensate for age-related declines by recruiting parts of the brain that are not commonly activated when young people do the same tasks—an example of the brain's impressive flexibility (Huang et al., 2012).

Many of the physical and mental losses that do occur in old age are physiologically and genetically based and are seen in all societies, but others have to do with cultural, behavioral, and psychological factors (Park & Gutchess, 2006). Psychologists have made great strides in separating conditions once thought to be an inevitable part of old age from those that are preventable or treatable:

THINKING CRITICALLY

About Mental Decline in Old Age

- **Malnutrition and medications.** Apparent senility in the elderly is often caused by malnutrition, prescription medications, harmful combinations of medications, and over-the-counter drugs (such as sleeping pills and antihistamines), all of which can be hazardous to old people.

- **Inactivity.** Weakness, frailty, and even many of the diseases associated with old age are often caused by being inactive and sedentary (Booth & Neufer, 2005).

- **Loss of meaningful activities.** Depression, passivity, and memory problems may result from the loss of meaningful activity, intellectual stimulation, goals to pursue, and control over events (Hess, 2005; Schaie & Zuo, 2001).

Older people can profit from aerobic exercise and strength training, which maintain physical strength and flexibility, boost the brain's blood supply, and promote the development of new cells in the hippocampus and other areas of the brain. The result is often improved cognitive functioning in memory, planning, concentration, and making schedules (Colcombe & Kramer, 2003; Erickson et al., 2011; Hertzog et al., 2008). Mental stimulation also fosters the growth of neural connections in the brain, even well into old age. Cognitive enrichment cannot prevent most cases of serious cognitive decline and dementia, which are often strongly influenced or even caused directly by genes, but the declines may be delayed (Gatz, 2007; Hertzog et al., 2008).

Perhaps the best news is that as people get older, most become better able to regulate negative feelings and emphasize the positive. The frequency of intense negative emotions is highest among people aged 18 to 34, then drops sharply to age 65. After 65, it levels off, rising only slightly among old people facing crises of illness and bereavement (Charles & Carstensen, 2004; Urry & Gross, 2010). Apparently, many people do grow wiser, or at least more tranquil, with age.

Some researchers who study aging are therefore optimistic. In their view, people who have challenging occupations and interests, who remain active mentally, who exercise regularly, and who adapt flexibly to change and loss are likely to maintain their cognitive abilities and well-being. "Use it or lose it," they say. They are hopeful that research will one day produce successful interventions to prevent or reverse the most serious forms of cognitive decline (Barnes, 2011; Lövdén et al., 2010). Rates of Alzheimer's and other forms of dementia in England and other countries have dropped by 25 percent in the past two decades, most likely a result of the improved health and higher levels of education of their citizens (Matthews et al., 2013)—more evidence that dementia may not be an inevitable aspect of aging.

Other researchers are less upbeat. "When you've lost it, you can't use it," they reply. They are worried about the growing numbers of people living into their 90s and beyond, when rates of cognitive impairment and dementia rise dramatically (Salthouse, 2006). The challenge for society is to prepare for the many people who will be living into advanced old age, by helping as many as possible to keep using their brains instead of losing them.

Recite & Review

✓ Study and Review at MyPsychLab

Recite: You aren't old enough for cognitive decline, so state aloud what you know about Erikson's eight stages, emerging adulthood, menopause, cognitive functioning in old age, fluid versus crystallized intelligence, and emotional regulation in the later years.

Review: Next, reread this section.

Now take this *Quick Quiz:*

1. Why is identity crisis not limited to the adolescent years?

2. Most women react to menopause by (a) feeling depressed, (b) regretting the loss of femininity, (c) going a little crazy, (d) feeling relieved or neutral.

3. Which of these statements about the decline of mental abilities in old age is *false*? (a) It can often be lessened with regular exercise; (b) it affects all mental abilities equally; (c) it is sometimes a result of malnutrition, medication, or disease rather than aging; (d) it is slowed when people live in stimulating environments.

4. Your 35-year-old sister wants to give up her regular job and get into volunteer service with an NGO. How would you explain the shift in her behavior?

Answers:

1. People's lives have become less traditional and predictable. 2. d 3. b 4. This is a case of positive retirement where retirement is not simply a transition from work to no work, but a change to a more engrossing career.

You are about to learn...

- why terrible childhood experiences do not inevitably affect a person forever.
- what makes most children resilient in the face of adversity.

The Wellsprings of Resilience LO 3.19

Most people take it for granted that the path from childhood to adolescence to adulthood is a fairly straight one. They think of the lasting attitudes, habits, and values their parents taught them. Many carry with them the scars of emotional wounds they suffered as children. Children who have been beaten, neglected, or constantly subjected to verbal or physical abuse by their parents are more likely than other children to have emotional problems, become delinquent and violent, commit crimes, have low IQs, drop out of school, develop mental disorders such as depression, and develop chronic stress-related illnesses (Emery & Laumann-Billings, 1998; Margolin & Gordis, 2004; Repetti, Taylor, & Seeman, 2002).

And yet when researchers examined the assumption that early trauma *always* has long-lasting negative effects and considered the evidence for alternative views, they got quite a different picture. Most children, they discovered, are resilient, eventually overcoming even the effects of

> ☀ **THINKING CRITICALLY**
>
> About the Effects of Childhood Traumas

war, childhood illness, having abusive or alcoholic parents, early deprivation, or being sexually molested (Kaufman & Zigler, 1987; Nelson et al., 2007; Rathbun, DiVirgilio, & Waldfogel, 1958; Rind, Tromovitch, & Bauserman, 1998; Rutter et al., 2004; Werner, 1989; West & Prinz, 1987).

Many of the children who outgrow early deprivation and trauma have easygoing temperaments or personality traits, such as self-efficacy and self-control, that help them roll with even severe punches. They have a secure attachment style, which helps them work through traumatic events in a way that heals their wounds and restores hope and emotional balance (Mikulincer, Shaver, & Horesh, 2006). If children lack secure attachments with their own parents, they may be rescued by love and attention from their siblings, peers, extended family members, or other caring adults. And some have experiences outside the family—in schools, places of worship, or other organizations—that give them a sense of competence, moral support, solace, religious faith, and self-esteem (Cowen et al., 1990; Garmezy, 1991; Masten, 2001).

Perhaps the most powerful reason for the resilience of so many children, and for the changes that all of us make throughout our lives, is that we are all constantly interpreting our experiences. We can decide to repeat the mistakes our parents made or break free of them. We can decide to remain prisoners of childhood or to strike out in new directions at age 20, 50, or 70. As the world changes in unpredictable ways, the territory of adulthood will continue to expand, providing new frontiers as well as fewer signposts and road maps to guide us. Increasingly, age will be what we make of it.

PSYCHOLOGY IN THE NEWS REVISITED ///////

Has this review of events and changes across the life span helped you to think about the case of Evan Miller, who was sentenced to life imprisonment without possibility of parole for the beating and murder of a middle-aged man? The U.S. Supreme Court had previously banned the death penalty for juveniles, partly on the basis of evidence showing that adolescents often get into trouble because of the neurological immaturity of their brains. As we saw, the brain continues to develop throughout the teen years and well into the 20s. Because the teenage

brain is a "work in progress," some researchers have concluded that many teenagers who commit crimes, even murder, should be considered "less guilty by reason of adolescence" (Steinberg & Scott, 2003). In their view, the fact that teenagers are often *neurologically* as well as *psychologically* immature is reason enough to treat them as a separate category under the law. But other researchers observe that teenagers, like any other age group, show plenty of individual variation in maturity, self-control, and the ability to delay gratification, and that stereotyping them as "all gasoline, no brakes" oversimplifies their development (Casey & Caudle, 2013).

In June, 2012, the Supreme Court issued its ruling in the Miller case: laws requiring youths convicted of murder to be sentenced to die in prison, it said, violate the Eighth Amendment's ban on cruel and unusual punishment. Currently in the United States, about 2,500 inmates are serving life sentences for crimes committed when they were juveniles, more than 2,000 of them because of the mandatory sentencing the court has now barred. The problem with mandatory sentences, Justice Elena Kagan wrote in her opinion, is that every teenager receives the same sentence regardless of his or her chronological age (17 is not 14), background (stable home or abusive one), or psychological maturity. Mandatory sentencing means that judges cannot consider the teenager's family environment, no matter how brutal it might be.

However, four members of the court were not persuaded by this argument. Justice Samuel Alito, in a separate dissent, complained that the ruling meant that "[e]ven a 17 1/2-year-old who kills many people in a murderous rampage would have to be given a chance to persuade the courts that he should be released into society in only a few years. The punishment should be up to the courts and the possibility of leniency, he wrote, but the Constitution has nothing to say about it.

Where do you stand on this issue? Should adolescence be a mitigating factor in sentencing decisions? Both sides in this debate realize that teenagers differ in their degree of maturity, competence, and reasoning abilities and the environments in which they were raised. Evan Miller's sister, you'll recall, described their family as having been neglectful and dysfunctional. But they differ on how and whether to weigh such factors in criminal cases. Is the responsibility of teenagers diminished by the fact that adolescence in our culture has grown longer and longer over time? As we saw, cultures differ in the roles and expectations that guide young people's behavior. In cultures that require adolescents to do adult work and take on other adult responsibilities, the idea that teenagers are mentally immature might seem odd.

We also saw that adult development is profoundly shaped by economic opportunities, demographic changes, and sweeping social events—large-scale factors that can cause a marked disconnect between how people are raised and what becomes of them later in life. And we saw that many children are resilient and can be rescued from childhoods like Evan's, childhoods of cruelty and neglect, if they get into better environments and are supported by concerned adults. Given that evidence, is it "cruel and unusual" to assume that all juvenile offenders are a "lost cause," and condemn them to life in prison?

At what point does a person become fully responsible for his or her harmful actions? Is adolescence literally a state of diminished responsibility, and if so, how should the courts treat teenage offenders?

Taking Psychology With You

Bringing Up Baby

Every year or so another best-selling book arrives to tell parents they've been doing it all wrong. Countless books have advised parents to treat their children in specific, if contradictory, ways: Pick them up, don't pick them up; respond when they cry, don't respond when they cry; let them sleep with you, never let them sleep with you; be affectionate, be stern; be highly sensitive to their every need so they will securely attach to you, don't overreact to their every mood or complaint or you will spoil them. Be a Chinese "tiger mother"; no, wait, be a laid-back French mother. A billion-dollar industry has emerged to calm (and inflame) parental worries, offering expensive strollers, toys, "fetal education" techniques, and baby sign-language programs—all to create the perfect child (Paul, 2008).

No need to panic. Critical thinkers can call on two lines of evidence, described in this chapter, to protect themselves from the guilt-mongers and marketers. One is that babies and young children thrive under a wide variety of child-rearing methods. The second is that babies bring their own temperaments and other genetic predispositions to the matter of how best to raise them.

Well, then, how should you treat your children? Should you be strict or lenient, powerful or permissive? Should you require them to stop having tantrums, to clean up their rooms, to be polite? Should you say, "Oh, nothing I do will matter, anyway," or "If I don't get 100 percent compliance on every order, this kid is going to boot camp"? Child development research does suggest general principles that can help parents find that middle way and foster their children's confidence and helpfulness:

Set high expectations that are appropriate to the child's age and temperament, and teach the child how to meet them. Some parents make few demands on their children, either unintentionally or because they believe a parent should not impose standards. Others make many demands, such as requiring children to be polite, help with chores, control their anger, be thoughtful of others, and do well in school. The children of parents who make few demands tend to be aggressive, impulsive, and immature. The children of parents who have high but realistic expectations tend to be helpful and above average in competence and self-confidence (Damon, 1995).

Explain, explain, explain. Induction, telling a child why you have applied a rule, teaches a child to be responsible. Punitive methods ("Do it or I'll spank you") may result in compliance, but the child will tend to disobey as soon as you are out of sight. Explanations also teach children how to reason and understand. While setting standards for your children, you can also allow them to express disagreements and feelings. This does not mean you have to argue with a 4-year-old about the merits of table manners or permit antisocial and destructive behavior. Once you have explained a rule, you need to enforce it consistently.

Encourage empathy. Call the child's attention to the effects of his or her actions on others and appeal to the child's sense of fair play and desire to be good. As we saw, even infants and toddlers are capable of empathy. Vague orders, such as "Don't fight," are less effective than showing the child how fighting disrupts and hurts others.

Notice, approve of, and reward good behavior. Many parents punish the behavior they dislike, a form of attention that may be rewarding to the child. It is much more effective to praise the behavior you do want, which teaches the child what is expected.

Remember the critical-thinking guideline "don't oversimplify." The challenge is to avoid the twin fallacies of "It's all genetic" and "If I just do all the right things, whatever they are, my child will be intelligent, kind, and successful." Even with the best skills and intentions, you cannot control everything that happens to your child or remodel your child's temperamental dispositions. Besides, as children grow up, they are influenced by their peers and generation and by particular experiences that shape their interests and motivation. But you do have the power to make your child's life miserable or secure. You also have the power to profoundly affect the *quality* of the relationship you will have with your child throughout life: one filled with conflict and resentment, or one that is close and loving.

Summary  Listen to the Audio File at MyPsychLab

- *Developmental psychologists* study how people grow and change over the life span. Many study *socialization*, the process by which children learn the rules and behavior society expects of them.

From Conception through the First Year

- *Maturation* is the unfolding of genetically influenced behavior and characteristics. Prenatal development begins at fertilization, when the male sperm unites with the female ovum (egg) to form a single-celled egg called a *zygote*. During the first eight weeks of prenatal development, the organism is called an *embryo*; after that, it is known as a *fetus*.

- Harmful influences that can adversely affect the fetus's development include rubella (German measles), toxic substances, some sexually transmitted diseases, cigarettes, alcohol (which can cause *fetal alcohol syndrome* and cognitive deficits), illegal drugs, some legal prescription drugs and over-the-counter medications, and chronic maternal stress.

- Fathers affect prenatal development too; the sperm of teenage boys and of men older than 50 may have mutations that increase the risk of miscarriage, birth defects, and certain diseases in their offspring.

- Babies are born with *motor reflexes*, perceptual abilities, and rudimentary cognitive skills. Cultural practices affect the timing of physical milestones.

- Babies' innate need for *contact comfort* gives rise to emotional attachment to their caregivers, and by the age of 6 to 8 months,

infants begin to feel *separation anxiety*. Studies of the *Strange Situation* have distinguished *secure* from *insecure* attachment; insecurity can take one of two forms, *avoidant* or *anxious-ambivalent* attachment.

- Styles of attachment are relatively unaffected by the normal range of child-rearing practices and also by whether or not babies spend time in daycare. Insecure attachment is promoted by parents' rejection, mistreatment, or abandonment of their infants; by a mother's postpartum depression, which can affect her ability to care for the baby; by the child's own fearful, insecure temperament; or by stressful family situations.

Language Development

- Human beings are the only species that uses *language* to express and comprehend an infinite number of novel utterances, think about the past and future, and describe things or people who are not present. An innate capacity for language may have evolved in humans because it enhanced the chances of survival and the establishment of social bonds.

- Noam Chomsky argued that the human brain contains a mental module that is sensitive to a universal grammar (features common to all languages). In support of this view, children from many different cultures go through similar stages of language development; children combine words in ways that adults never would; adults do not consistently correct their children's syntax; and groups of children who have never been exposed to adult language often invent their own. However, many psycholinguists no longer believe there is a universal grammar because languages also vary grammatically around the world. Instead, they say, language is a cultural tool, shaped by the world in which children grow up.

- Some models of language acquisition do not assume an innate capacity at all; instead, they assume that children learn the statistical probability that any given word or syllable will follow another. Parental practices, such as recasting a child's incorrect sentence, also aid in language acquisition. It is likely, therefore, that biological readiness and experience interact in the development of language.

- Language acquisition begins in the womb, as even newborns can distinguish the language their mother spoke during pregnancy from an unfamiliar language. Infants are responsive to the pitch, intensity, and sound of language, which may be why adults in many cultures speak to babies in *parentese*, using higher-pitched words and exaggerated intonation of vowels.

- At 4 to 6 months of age, babies begin to recognize the sounds of their own language. They go through a babbling phase from age 6 months to 1 year, and at about 1 year, they start saying single words and using symbolic gestures, which continue to be important for language, thinking, and problem solving. At age 2, children speak in two- or three-word *telegraphic* sentences that convey a variety of messages.

Cognitive Development

- Jean Piaget argued that cognitive development follows predictable stages as the child matures and that children's thinking changes and adapts through *assimilation* and *accommodation*.

- Piaget proposed four stages of cognitive development: *sensorimotor* (birth to age 2), during which the child learns *object permanence*; *preoperational* (ages 2 to 7), during which language and symbolic thought develop, although the child remains *egocentric* in reasoning and has difficulty with some mental *operations*; *concrete operations* (ages 7 to 12), during which the child comes to understand *conservation*; and *formal operations* (age 12 to adulthood), during which abstract reasoning develops.

- Today we know that the changes from one stage to another are not as clear-cut as Piaget implied; development is more continuous and overlapping. Babies and young children have greater cognitive abilities than Piaget thought, perhaps because of the core knowledge they are born with. Young children are not always egocentric in their thinking; by the age of 4 or 5, they have developed a *theory of mind* to account for their own and other people's behavior. And cultural practices affect the pace and content of cognitive development.

Moral Development

- Developmental psychologists study how children learn to internalize standards of right and wrong and to behave accordingly. This ability depends on the emergence of conscience and the moral emotions of guilt, shame, and empathy.

- As a strategy for teaching children to behave, a parent's use of *power assertion* is associated with a child's aggressiveness and lack of empathy. *Induction* is associated with children who develop empathy, internalize moral standards, and can resist temptation. But all methods of discipline interact with the child's own temperament.

- The capacity of preschool children to *delay gratification* and control their impulsive wishes or feelings is associated with the development of internalized moral standards and conscience. This ability is enhanced by mothers who use induction as a primary form of discipline.

Gender Development

- Gender development includes the emerging awareness of *gender identity*, the understanding that people are biologically male or female regardless of what they do or wear, and *gender typing*, the process by which boys and girls learn what it means to be masculine or feminine in their culture.

- Some individuals are born with *intersex* physical conditions, living with the physical attributes of both sexes, and may eventually consider themselves to be *transgender*. *Transsexuals* feel that they are male in a female body or vice versa; their gender identity is at odds with their anatomical sex.

- Universally, young children tend to prefer same-sex toys and playing with other children of their own sex. Biological psychologists account for this phenomenon in terms of genes and prenatal androgens, which appear to provide a basis for gender-typed play.

- Cognitive psychologists study how children develop *gender schemas* for the categories "male" and "female," which in turn shape their gender-typed behavior. Gender schemas tend to be inflexible at first. Later they become more flexible as the child cognitively matures and assimilates new information, if the child's culture promotes flexible gender schemas. Learning theorists study the direct and subtle reinforcers and social messages that foster the contents of gender typing.

- Gender development changes over the life span, depending on people's experiences with work and family life and larger events in society and their culture.

Adolescence

- Middle childhood (ages 6 to 12) is an important phase in which children around the world begin to be assigned various responsibilities. During these years, children go through *adrenarche*, when the adrenal glands begin pumping out hormones that affect brain development.

- *Adolescence* begins with the physical changes of *puberty*. In girls, puberty is signaled by *menarche* and the development of breasts; in boys, it begins with the onset of nocturnal emissions and the development of the testes, scrotum, and penis. Hormones produce *secondary sex characteristics*, such as pubic hair in both sexes and a deeper voice in males.

- The adolescent brain undergoes a major pruning of synapses, along with myelinization, which improves the efficiency of neural transmission and strengthens the connections between the emotional parts of the brain and the reasoning prefrontal cortex. These neurological changes may not be complete until age 25, which would help explain why the strong emotions of the adolescent years sometimes overwhelm rational decision making and why teenagers often behave more impulsively than adults.

- Most American adolescents do not go through extreme emotional turmoil, anger, plummeting of self-esteem, or rebellion. However, conflict with parents, mood swings and depression, and reckless or rule-breaking behavior often increase. The peer group becomes especially influential, which is why peer bullying is often the source of teenagers' greatest unhappiness. Boys tend to externalize their emotional problems in acts of aggression and other antisocial behavior; girls tend to internalize their problems by becoming depressed or developing eating disorders.

Adulthood

- Erik H. Erikson proposed that life consists of eight stages, each with a unique psychological challenge, or crisis, that must be resolved, such as an *identity crisis* in adolescence. Erikson identified many of the essential concerns of adulthood and showed that development is a lifelong process. However, psychological issues or crises are not confined to particular chronological periods or stages.

- When most people in an age group go through the same event at about the same time, transitions are easier than when people feel out of step. In industrialized nations, major demographic changes have caused young adults to postpone the timing of career decisions, marriage or commitment to a partner, and parenthood. Many people between the ages of 18 and 25, especially if they are not financially independent, find themselves in a phase between adolescence and adulthood called *emerging adulthood*.

- The middle years are generally not a time of turmoil or crisis but the prime of most people's lives. In women, menopause begins in the late 40s or early 50s. Many women have temporary physical symptoms, but most do not regret the end of fertility or become depressed and irritable. In middle-aged men, hormone production slows down and sperm counts decline; fertility continues, but with increased risk of fetal abnormalities.

- *Gerontologists* have revised our ideas about old age because so many people are living longer and healthier lives and are entering an extended phase of "positive retirement." During old age, the speed of cognitive processing slows down, and *fluid intelligence* parallels other biological capacities in its eventual decline. *Crystallized intelligence*, in contrast, depends heavily on culture, education, and experience, and it tends to remain stable over the life span.

- Many supposedly inevitable results of aging, such as senility, depression, and physical frailty, are often avoidable. They may result from malnutrition and overmedication, inactivity, and lack of meaningful activities. Exercise and mental stimulation promote cognitive abilities in the human brain, even well into old age, although some mental losses are inevitable.

The Wellsprings of Resilience

- Children who experience violence or neglect are at risk of many problems later in life, but most children are resilient and are able to overcome early adversity. Psychologists now study not only the sad consequences of neglect, poverty, and violence but also the reasons for resilience under adversity.

Psychology in the News, Revisited

- The findings that the adolescent brain does not reach maturity until the 20s raise questions about whether teenagers who commit crimes and other impulsive acts should be considered "less guilty by reason of adolescence."

Taking Psychology With You

- Many child-rearing experts claim to have the one right way to make children smarter, nicer, and more successful. Research in child development can help people think critically about such claims and also offers some general guidelines: Set high but realistic expectations, explain the reasons for your rules, encourage empathy, and reward good behavior.

Key Terms

developmental psychologists 118

socialization 118

maturation 118

zygote 118

embryo 118

fetus 118

fetal alcohol syndrome 95

motor reflexes 118

contact comfort 118

separation anxiety 118

Strange Situation 118

secure, avoidant, and anxious-ambivalent attachment 118

language 118

Noam Chomsky 118

universal grammar 118

parentese 118

telegraphic speech 118

Jean Piaget 118

assimilation 118

accommodation 118

object permanence 118

sensorimotor stage 118

preoperational stage 118

mental operations 118

egocentric thinking 118

conservation 118

concrete operations stage 118

formal operations stage 118

theory of mind 118

power assertion 118

induction 118

delay of gratification 118

gender identity 118

gender typing 118

intersex conditions 118

transgender 118

transsexual 118

gender schema 118

adrenarche 118

puberty 118

menarche 118

secondary sex characteristics 118

myelinization 118

Erik H. Erikson 118

identity crisis 118

emerging adulthood 120

menopause 121

gerontologists 121

fluid intelligence 122

crystallized intelligence 122

Developmental psychologists study people's growth and change over the life span. They begin with **socialization**, the process by which children learn the attitudes and behaviors expected of them by their society.

↓

From Conception Through the First Year

↓

Prenatal Development

Prenatal development begins with a *zygote* (a single-celled egg), which becomes the *embryo*, which becomes the *fetus* at about 8 weeks. Harmful influences that can cross the placental barrier and affect the fetus include:

- rubella (German measles).
- exposure to X-rays, toxic chemicals, or pollution.
- sexually transmitted diseases.
- cigarette smoking.
- chronic or severe maternal stress.
- many drugs, including illegal ones (cocaine and heroin), legal ones (alcohol, which can cause *fetal alcohol syndrome*), prescription drugs, and some over-the-counter medicines.

The Infant's World

- Babies are born with *motor reflexes*, including rooting, sucking, and grasping.
- Newborns also have some innate perceptual and cognitive abilities.
- Cultural influences affect maturational milestones, such as an sleeping through the night.

Attachment

Attachment begins with **contact comfort**, the pleasurable reassurance of being touched and held by the parent or other caregiver.

Between 6 and 8 months of age, babies develop **separation anxiety** if their primary caregiver temporarily leaves them.

Babies may be **securely** or **insecurely attached**. Insecure babies may, in turn, be *avoidant* or *anxious-ambivalent*. These styles of attachment are unaffected by normal child-rearing practices and whether a child goes to daycare. Insecure attachment is promoted by extreme deprivation in infancy; abusive or erratic parenting; stressful family changes; and the child's own fearful temperament.

Language Development

↓

Language is a set of rules for combining elements that are inherently meaningless into utterances that convey meaning.

↓

Language: Built In or Learned?

Noam Chomsky argued that the human brain contains an innate mental module containing a *universal grammar*, which enables young children to acquire language readily. Findings supporting Chomsky's view:

- Children in different cultures go through similar stages of linguistic development.
- Children combine words in ways that adults never would.
- Adults do not consistently correct their children's syntax, yet children learn language anyway.
- Children who are not exposed to adult language may invent a language of their own.

Findings contradicting Chomsky's view:

- The world's 7,000 languages have major differences not explainable by a universal grammar. Culture may be primary determinant of a language's linguistic structure.
- Computer programs can acquire many linguistic features of language.
- Adults do frequently model correct language usage.

Both sides agree that acquisition of a first language must require both biological readiness and social experience. Children who are not exposed to language during their early years rarely speak normally or catch up grammatically.

From Cooing to Communicating

- Acquiring language begins in the womb because newborns recognize the language their mothers spoke during pregnancy.
- First few months: Babies coo and respond to rhythms and emotions in voices.
- 4 to 6 months: Babies begin to recognize key consonant and vowel sounds of their native language.
- 6 months to 1 year: Infants become able to distinguish words from the flow of speech.
- End of first year: Infants start to name things based on familiar concepts and use symbolic gestures to communicate.
- 18 to 24 months: Children begin to speak in two- and three-word phrases (**telegraphic speech**) and understand verbs from the context in which they occur.
- 2 to 6 years: Children rapidly acquire new words, inferring their meaning from the grammatical and social contexts in which they hear them.

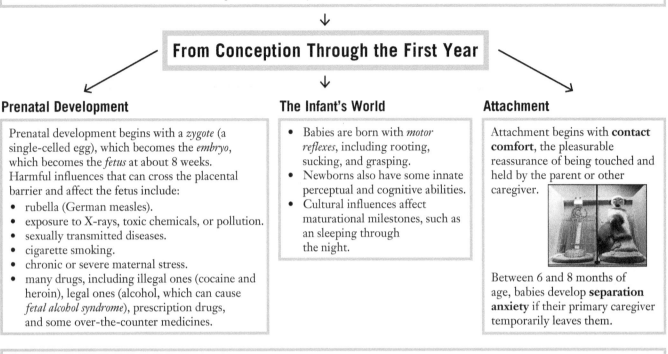

Cognitive Development

↓

Jean Piaget's four stages of cognitive development:
1. *Sensorimotor* (birth to age 2): child learns **object permanence**
2. *Preoperational* (ages 2 to 7): development of language and symbolic thought
3. *Concrete operations* (ages 7 to 12): understanding of **conservation**
4. *Formal operations* (age 12 to adulthood): development of abstract reasoning

Findings challenge many of Piaget's views:
- Cognitive abilities develop in continuous, overlapping waves, rather than in stages.
- Preschoolers are not as egocentric as Piaget thought. As young as 3 to 4 years, children begin developing a **theory of mind**, beliefs about how their own and other people's minds work.
- Children, even infants, reveal cognitive abilities much earlier than Piaget believed possible.
- Cognitive development is influenced by a child's culture.

Moral Development

↓

Children may be born with a "moral sense," which can be nurtured or extinguished. Parental methods of discipline often have different consequences for children's moral behavior, though children's own temperaments may affect how parents treat them and how much attention they require.

- **Power assertion** is associated with children who are aggressive and fail to internalize moral standards.
- **Induction** is associated with children who develop empathy and internalized moral standards and who can resist temptation.
- Young children's ability to delay gratification and regulate their impulses is associated with later internalized moral standards and conscience.

Gender Development

↓

Gender identity: The fundamental sense of being male or female (or transgender).
Gender typing: The process by which boys and girls learn what it means to be masculine or feminine in their culture.
Intersex conditions: Conditions in which children are born with ambiguous genitals or genitals that conflict with their chromosomes; as adults, they may consider themselves *transgender*.
Transsexuals are usually not intersexed, yet feel that they are male in a female body or vice versa; their gender identity is at odds with their anatomical sex or appearance.

- Biological psychologists account for gender differences in behavior in terms of genes and prenatal hormones.
- Cognitive psychologists study how children develop **gender schemas** that shape their gender-typed behavior.
- Learning theorists study the direct and subtle reinforcers and social messages that foster gender typing.
- People's gender schemas, attitudes, and behavior evolve throughout their lives.

Adolescence

↓

- **Adrenarche** occurs in middle childhood (ages 6–12) with increased production of hormones that affect brain development.
- Adolescence begins with the physical changes of **puberty**, including **menarche** in females and genital maturation in males.
- The adolescent brain goes through significant developmental changes, including pruning of synapses and myelinization.
- The stereotype of "adolescent turmoil" is inaccurate for most teens. However, conflicts with parents, mood swings, and rule-breaking behavior are likely to increase.
- The peer group becomes especially important.

The Transitions of Life

- *Emerging adulthood* describes a life phase between 18 and 25, in which young adults accept some responsibilities of adulthood and delay others.
- The middle years are the prime of most people's lives. In women, **menopause** causes some physical symptoms but rarely the emotional distress portrayed in the media. In men, testosterone and sperm production decline.
- People's views of aging are influenced by the culture they live in and by the promises of technology, realistic and unrealistic, to prolong life and health.

Adulthood

↓

Erik Erikson's Stages

- Trust versus mistrust
- Autonomy (independence) versus shame and doubt
- Initiative versus guilt
- Competence versus inferiority
- Identity versus role confusion
- Intimacy versus isolation
- Generativity versus stagnation
- Ego integrity versus despair

Old Age

- Research in *gerontology* shows that **fluid intelligence** parallels other biological capacities in its eventual decline, whereas **crystallized intelligence** tends to remain stable or even improve over the life span.
- Senility, depression, and physical frailty in old age are often the result of poor nutrition, medication (over the counter and prescribed), inactivity, and lack of meaningful activity. Exercise and mental stimulation promote cognitive abilities in the human brain, even into old age, though rates of dementia rise steeply after age 90.
- As people age, most become better able to regulate negative emotions and feel happier than young people do.

4

The Nervous System:
A Basic Blueprint

Communication in the
Nervous System

Mapping the Brain

A Tour Through the Brain

The Two Hemispheres of
the Brain

The Flexible Brain

Psychology in the News,
Revisited

Taking Psychology With
You: Cosmetic Neurology:
Tinkering With the Brain

THE NERVOUS SYSTEM

PSYCHOLOGY IN THE NEWS ////////////////////////

Former Linebacker's Family Sues NFL

SAN DIEGO, January 24, 2013. The family of Junior Seau, the former National Football League linebacker who died of a self-inflicted gunshot wound last May at age 43, has filed a wrongful death suit against the league. The family claims that repeated brain injuries from hits sustained over the course of Seau's 20-season career led to psychological problems and ultimately to the player's suicide. The suit further alleges that the NFL ignored and hid information about the risks associated with brain trauma.

According to Seau's former wife Gina and his 23-year-old son Tyler, during his final years Seau exhibited wild mood swings, irrationality, forgetfulness, and depression. A postmortem study of his brain by the National Institutes of Health earlier this month confirmed that the much-honored athlete suffered from chronic traumatic encephalopathy (CTE), a degenerative brain disease.

Last November, an Associated Press review found that several thousand players have sued the NFL over head injuries. The NFL has consistently denied allegations that it glorifies violence and "big hits," and has provided millions of dollars to support scientific research on player safety. But public concern about football and other violent contact sports, such as hockey and soccer, is increasing. Some coaches and parents of student athletes are requiring players to undergo cognitive and memory testing before the start of the season, then again after suffering a head injury and before they are allowed to return to the field. But there are reports that some student athletes have resumed play while still showing cognitive symptoms.

Concern is also growing among professional football players. Some have quit the sport, citing worries about their long-term health. Several well-known players, such as former

NFL linebacker Junior Seau committed suicide in 2012. His family has filed a wrongful death suit against the league.

linebacker Ted Johnson and former offensive tackle Kyle Turley, have said they will donate their brains to science when they die, to help achieve a better understanding of the risks of the sport.

The brains of several deceased players have already been examined. When safety Dave Duerson killed himself in 2011, he left a note asking that his brain be studied. Like Seau's brain and the brains of a number of other football players who committed suicide, Duerson's brain showed clear evidence of CTE. Some brains have reportedly revealed abnormalities more typically seen in elderly Alzheimer's patients.

Seau's former teammate Tedy Bruschi told ESPN recently that his friend's death "makes me wonder" about the risks. Yet when asked why he continues to play, he replied that football is his life. When you are passionate about a sport, said Bruschi, you will play despite the risks and dangers.

///////////

Cases of brain injury and disease, like those of Junior Seau and other athletes, vividly remind us that the 3-pound organ inside our skulls provides the bedrock for everything we do, feel, and think. When this organ is damaged, life may be forever altered physically, emotionally, or mentally. Sometimes the changes are subtle or even benign, as in the case of a Swiss stroke patient who suddenly became obsessed with, of all things, fine dining. After recovering, he quit his job as a political journalist and became a food columnist (Regard & Landis, 1997). But all too often, the effects are harmful and even tragic.

Scientists are developing revolutionary new methods to help patients with brain disease or injury and are exploring the outer reaches of what is possible for this organ. A few paralyzed patients have learned to control the movement of a robotic arm with *just their thoughts*. Tiny electrodes attached to brain cells that signal arm and hand movements are connected to a computer, which then translates the signals into an electronic command conveyed to a mechanical arm. One woman paralyzed from the neck down was able to use the mechanical arm to feed herself string cheese and chocolates (Collinger et al., 2013). Other patients have succeeded in reaching for and grasping other objects or have controlled a computer cursor solely by thinking of what they want to do (Hochberg et al., 2012).

Neuroscientists in psychology and other disciplines also study the brain and the rest of the nervous system in hopes of gaining a better understanding of healthy brains and everyday behavior. They are concerned with the biological foundations of consciousness, perception, memory, emotion, and stress—of everything, in fact, that human beings feel and do. In this chapter, we will examine the structure of the brain and the rest of the nervous system as background for our later discussions of these and other topics.

At this moment, your own brain, assisted by other parts of your nervous system, is busily taking in these words. Whether you are excited, curious, or bored, your brain is registering some sort of emotional reaction. As you continue reading, your brain will (we hope) store away much of the information in this chapter. Later on, your brain may enable you to smell a flower, climb the stairs, greet a friend, solve a problem, or chuckle at a joke. But the brain's most startling accomplishment is its knowledge that it is doing all these things. This self-awareness makes brain research different from the study of anything else in the universe. Scientists must use the cells, biochemistry, and circuitry of their own brains to understand the cells, biochemistry, and circuitry of brains in general.

William Shakespeare called the brain "the soul's frail dwelling house." Actually, this miraculous organ is more like the main room in a house filled with many alcoves and passageways—the "house" being the nervous system as a whole. Before we can understand the windows, walls, and furniture of this house, we need to become acquainted with the overall floor plan.

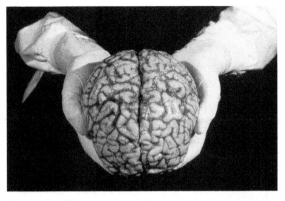

The study of this mysterious 3-pound organ raises many challenging questions. Why can a small glitch in the brain's circuits be devastating to some people, whereas others can function with major damage? How do experiences over the life span alter our brains?

You are about to learn . . .

- why you automatically pull your hand away from something hot, without thinking.
- the major parts of the nervous system and their primary functions.

The Nervous System: A Basic Blueprint LO 4.1

The function of a nervous system is to gather and process information, produce responses to stimuli, and coordinate the workings of different cells. Even the lowly jellyfish and the humble earthworm have the beginnings of such a system. In simple organisms that do little more than move, eat, and eliminate wastes, the "system" may be no more than one or two nerve cells. In human beings, who do such complex things as dance, cook, and take psychology courses, the nervous system contains billions of cells. Scientists divide this intricate network into two main parts: the central nervous system and the peripheral (outlying) nervous system (see Figure 4.1).

The Central Nervous System

The **central nervous system (CNS)** receives, processes, interprets, and stores incoming sensory information—information about tastes, sounds, smells, color, pressure on the skin, the state of internal organs, and so forth. It also sends out messages destined for muscles, glands, and internal organs. The CNS is usually conceptualized as having two components: the brain, which we will consider in detail later, and the **spinal cord**, which is actually an extension of the brain. The spinal

cord runs from the base of the brain down the center of the back, protected by a column of bones (the spinal column), and it acts as a bridge between the brain and the parts of the body below the neck.

The spinal cord produces some behaviors on its own without any help from the brain. These *spinal reflexes* are automatic, requiring no conscious effort. If you accidentally touch a hot iron, you will immediately pull your hand away, even before your brain has had a chance to register what has happened. Nerve impulses bring a message to the spinal cord (hot!), and the spinal cord immediately sends out a command via other nerve impulses, telling muscles in your arm to contract and to pull your hand away from the iron. (Reflexes above the neck, such as sneezing and blinking, involve the lower part of the brain rather than the spinal cord.)

The neural circuits underlying many spinal reflexes are linked to neural pathways that run up and down the spinal cord, to and from the brain. Because of these connections, reflexes can

central nervous system (CNS) The portion of the nervous system consisting of the brain and spinal cord.

spinal cord A collection of neurons and supportive tissue running from the base of the brain down the center of the back, protected by a column of bones (the spinal column).

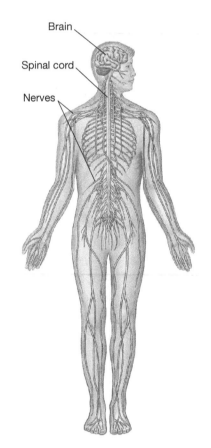

FIGURE 4.1 The Central and Peripheral Nervous Systems
The central nervous system includes the brain and the spinal cord. The peripheral nervous system consists of 43 pairs of nerves that transmit information to and from the central nervous system. 12 pairs of cranial nerves in the head enter the brain directly; 31 pairs of spinal nerves enter the spinal cord at the spaces between the vertebrae.

sometimes be influenced by thoughts and emotions. An example is erection in men, a spinal reflex that can be inhibited by anxiety or distracting thoughts and initiated by erotic thoughts. Moreover, some reflexes can be brought under conscious control. If you concentrate, you may be able to keep your knee from jerking when it is tapped, as it normally would. Similarly, most men can learn to voluntarily delay ejaculation, another spinal reflex. (Yes, they can.)

The Peripheral Nervous System

The **peripheral nervous system (PNS)** handles the central nervous system's input and output. It contains all portions of the nervous system outside the brain and spinal cord, right down to the nerves in the tips of the fingers and toes. If your brain could not collect information about the world by means of a peripheral nervous system, it would be like a radio without a receiver. In the peripheral nervous system, *sensory nerves* carry messages from special receptors in the skin, muscles, and other internal and external sense organs to the spinal cord, which sends them along to the brain. These nerves put us in touch with both the outside world and the activities of our own bodies. *Motor nerves* carry orders from the central nervous system to muscles, glands, and internal organs. They enable us to move, and they cause glands to contract and to secrete substances, including chemical messengers called *hormones*.

Scientists further divide the peripheral nervous system into two parts: the somatic (bodily) nervous system and the autonomic (self-governing) nervous system. The **somatic nervous system**, sometimes called the *skeletal nervous system*, consists of nerves that are connected to sensory receptors—cells that enable you to sense the world—and also to the skeletal muscles that permit voluntary action. When you feel a bug on your arm, or when you turn off a light or write your name, your somatic system is active. The **autonomic nervous system** regulates the functioning of blood vessels, glands, and internal (visceral) organs such as the bladder, stomach, and heart. When you see someone you have a crush on and your heart pounds, your hands get sweaty, and your cheeks feel hot, you can blame your autonomic nervous system.

The autonomic nervous system is itself divided into two parts: the **sympathetic nervous system** and the **parasympathetic nervous system**. These two parts work together, but in opposing ways, to adjust the body to changing circumstances (see Figure 4.2). The sympathetic system acts like the accelerator of a car, mobilizing the body for action and an output of energy. It makes you blush, sweat, and breathe more deeply, and it pushes up your heart rate and blood pressure. As we discuss in Chapter 13, when you are in a situation that requires you to fight, flee, or cope, the sympathetic nervous system whirls into action. The

peripheral nervous system (PNS) All portions of the nervous system outside the brain and spinal cord; it includes sensory and motor nerves.

somatic nervous system The subdivision of the peripheral nervous system that connects to sensory receptors and to skeletal muscles; sometimes called the *skeletal nervous system*.

autonomic nervous system The subdivision of the peripheral nervous system that regulates the internal organs and glands.

sympathetic nervous system The subdivision of the autonomic nervous system that mobilizes bodily resources and increases the output of energy during emotion and stress.

parasympathetic nervous system The subdivision of the autonomic nervous system that operates during relaxed states and that conserves energy.

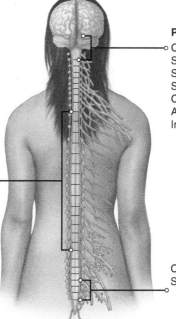

Parasympathetic Division
Constricts pupils
Stimulates tear glands
Strongly stimulates salivation
Slows heartbeat
Constricts bronchial tubes in lungs
Activates digestion
Inhibits glucose release by liver

Sympathetic Division
Dilates pupils
Weakly stimulates salivation
Stimulates sweat glands
Accelerates heartbeat
Dilates bronchial tubes in lungs
Inhibits digestion
Increases epinephrine,
   norepinephrine secretion
   by adrenal glands
Relaxes bladder wall
Decreases urine volume
Stimulates glucose release by liver
Stimulates ejaculation in males

Contracts bladder wall
Stimulates genital erection
   (both sexes) and vaginal
   lubrication (females)

FIGURE 4.2 The Autonomic Nervous System
In general, the sympathetic division of the autonomic nervous system prepares the body to expend energy and the parasympathetic division restores and conserves energy. Sympathetic nerve fibers exit from areas of the spinal cord shown in orange in this illustration; parasympathetic fibers exit from the base of the brain and from spinal cord areas shown in blue.

parasympathetic system is more like a brake: It tends to slow things down and keep them running smoothly, enabling the body to conserve and store energy. In everyday life, the two systems work in harmony. If you have to jump out of the way of a speeding motorcyclist, sympathetic nerves increase your heart rate. Afterward, parasympathetic nerves slow it down again and keep its rhythm regular.

 Watch the **Video** Divisions of the Nervous System at **MyPsychLab**

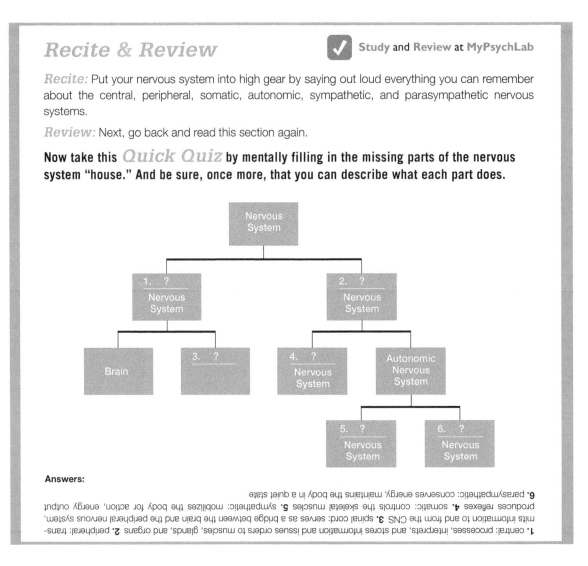

Recite & Review

☑ **Study** and **Review** at **MyPsychLab**

Recite: Put your nervous system into high gear by saying out loud everything you can remember about the central, peripheral, somatic, autonomic, sympathetic, and parasympathetic nervous systems.

Review: Next, go back and read this section again.

Now take this *Quick Quiz* **by mentally filling in the missing parts of the nervous system "house." And be sure, once more, that you can describe what each part does.**

Answers:

1. central: processes, interprets, and stores information and issues orders to muscles, glands, and organs 2. peripheral: transmits information to and from the CNS 3. spinal cord: serves as a bridge between the brain and the peripheral nervous system, produces reflexes 4. somatic: controls the skeletal muscles 5. sympathetic: mobilizes the body for action, energy output 6. parasympathetic: conserves energy, maintains the body in a quiet state

---

neuron A cell that conducts electrochemical signals; the basic unit of the nervous system; also called a *nerve cell.*

glia [GLY-uh or GLEE-uh] Cells that support, nurture, and insulate neurons, remove debris when neurons die, enhance the formation and maintenance of neural connections, and modify neuronal functioning.

You are about to learn . . .

- which cells function as the nervous system's communication specialists, and how they "talk" to each other.

- how cells once thought to be merely "glue" in the brain have other important functions as well.

- why researchers are excited about the discovery of stem cells in the brain.

- what happens when levels of neurotransmitters are too low or too high.

- which hormones are of special interest to psychologists, and why.

- which brain chemicals mimic the effects of morphine by dulling pain and promoting pleasure.

Communication in the Nervous System LO 4.2

The blueprint we just described provides only a general idea of the nervous system's structure. Now let's turn to the details.

Your brain and other parts of the nervous system contain two types of cells. **Neurons**, or *nerve cells*, are the communication specialists, transmitting information to, from, and within the central nervous system. **Glia**, or *glial cells* (from the Greek word for "glue"), hold the neurons in place.

Glial cells used to get much less attention than neurons, but we now know that these cells are much more than just "glue." They provide the neurons

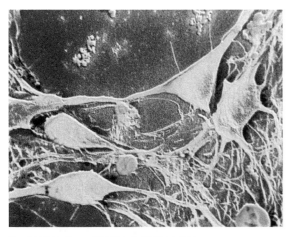

Neurons in the outer layers of the brain.

long! In the human brain, neurons are microscopic. For many years, scientists believed that the brain contained about 100 billion neurons and 10 times as many glia. But recent advances, which allow researchers to count individual cells, indicate that an adult brain contains a total of about 171 billion cells, and that these cells are about evenly divided between neurons and glia (Herculano-Houzel, 2009; Lent et al., 2012).

The Structure of the Neuron LO 4.3

As you can see in Figure 4.4 on the next page, a neuron has three main parts: *dendrites*, a *cell body*, and an *axon*. The **dendrites** look like the branches of a tree; indeed, the word *dendrite* means "little tree" in Greek. Dendrites act like antennas, receiving messages from as many as 10,000 other nerve cells and transmitting these messages toward the cell body. They also do some preliminary processing of those messages. The **cell body** is shaped roughly like a sphere or a pyramid; it includes the cell's *nucleus*, which contains genetic information (DNA) and controls the cell's growth and reproduction. The rest of the cell body contains the biochemical machinery for keeping the neuron alive and for communication with other cells. The **axon** (from the Greek for "axle") transmits messages away from the cell body to other neurons or to muscle or gland cells. Axons commonly divide at the end into branches called *axon terminals*. In adult human beings, axons vary from only four-thousandths of an inch to a few feet in length. Dendrites and axons give each neuron a double role: As one researcher put it, a neuron is first a catcher, then a batter (Gazzaniga, 1988).

Many axons, especially the larger ones, are insulated by a surrounding layer of fatty material

dendrites A neuron's branches that receive information from other neurons and transmit it toward the cell body.

cell body The part of the neuron that keeps it alive and determines whether it will fire.

axon A neuron's extending fiber that conducts impulses away from the cell body and transmits them to other neurons or to muscle or gland cells.

with nutrients, insulate them, help them grow, protect the brain from toxic agents, and remove cellular debris when neurons die. They also communicate chemically with each other and with neurons; without them, neurons could not function effectively. One kind of glial cell appears to give neurons the go-ahead to form connections and to start "talking" to each other (Ullian, Christopherson, & Barres, 2004). Another kind seems to identify and try to repair problems with the nerves' electrical systems (Graeber & Streit, 2010). And over time, glia help determine which neural connections get stronger or weaker, suggesting that they play a vital role in learning and memory (Fields, 2004).

It's neurons, however, that are considered the building blocks of the nervous system, though in structure they are more like snowflakes than blocks, exquisitely delicate and differing from one another greatly in size and shape (see Figure 4.3). In the giraffe, a neuron that runs from the spinal cord down the animal's hind leg may be 9 feet

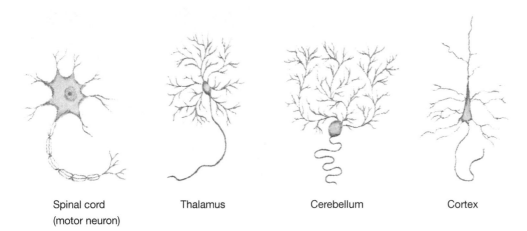

Spinal cord (motor neuron)   Thalamus   Cerebellum   Cortex

FIGURE 4.3 Different Kinds of Neurons
Neurons vary in size and shape, depending on their location and function. More than 200 types of neurons have been identified in mammals.

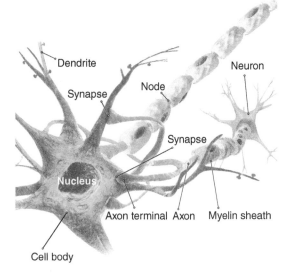

Dendrite

Synapse

Node

Neuron

Synapse

Nucleus

Axon terminal Axon Myelin sheath

Cell body

FIGURE 4.4 The Structure of a Neuron
Incoming neural impulses are received by the dendrites of a neuron and are transmitted to the cell body. Outgoing signals pass along the axon to terminal branches.

myelin sheath A fatty insulation that may surround the axon of a neuron.

nerves Bundles of nerve fibers (axons and sometimes dendrites) in the peripheral nervous system.

neurogenesis The production of new neurons from immature stem cells.

stem cells Immature cells that renew themselves and have the potential to develop into mature cells.

embryonic stem (ES) cells Stem cells from early embryos that can develop into any cell type.

called the **myelin sheath**, which in the central nervous system is made up of glial cells. Constrictions in this covering, called *nodes*, divide it into segments, which make it look a little like a string of link sausages (see Figure 4.4 again). One purpose of the myelin sheath is to prevent signals in adjacent cells from interfering with each other. Another purpose, as we will see shortly, is to speed up the conduction of neural impulses. In individuals with multiple sclerosis, loss of myelin causes erratic nerve signals, leading to loss of sensation, weakness or paralysis, lack of coordination, or vision problems.

In the peripheral nervous system, the fibers of individual neurons (axons and sometimes dendrites) are collected together in bundles called **nerves**, rather like the lines in a telephone cable. The human body has 43 pairs of peripheral nerves; one nerve from each pair is on the left side of the body and the other is on the right. Most of these nerves enter or leave the spinal cord, but 12 pairs in the head, the *cranial nerves*, connect directly to the brain. Cranial nerves are involved in the senses of smell, hearing, and vision.

Neurogenesis: The Birth of Neurons LO 4.4

For most of the twentieth century, scientists assumed that if neurons in the central nervous system were injured or damaged, they could never grow back (regenerate). But then the conventional wisdom got turned upside down. Animal studies showed that severed axons in the spinal cord *can* regrow if you treat them with certain nervous system chemicals (Schnell & Schwab, 1990). Researchers are hopeful that regenerated axons will eventually enable people with spinal cord injuries to use their limbs again.

In the past two decades, scientists have also had to rethink another entrenched assumption: that mammals produce no new CNS cells after infancy. In the early 1990s, Canadian neuroscientists immersed immature cells from mouse brains in a growth-promoting protein and showed that these cells could give birth to new neurons in a process called **neurogenesis**. Even more astonishing, the new neurons continued to divide and multiply (Reynolds & Weiss, 1992). Since then, scientists have discovered that the human brain and other body organs also contain such cells, which are now known as **stem cells**. Many of these cells, including those in brain areas involved in learning and memory, seem to divide and mature throughout adulthood. Animal studies find that physical exercise, effortful mental activity, and an enriched environment promote the production and survival of new cells, whereas aging and stress can inhibit their production and nicotine can kill them (Berger, Gage, & Vijayaraghavan, 1998; Kempermann, 2006; Shors, 2009).

Stem-cell research is one of the hottest areas in biology and neuroscience. **Embryonic stem (ES) cells** are *pluripotent* (the word means "having many powers"); amazingly, they can generate many types of specialist cells, from neurons to kidney cells. Therefore, many scientists believe they will prove useful for treating damaged tissues. ES cells

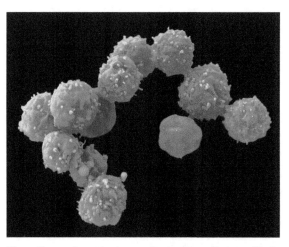

These tiny embryonic stem cells, here greatly magnified, are pluripotent, meaning that they can generate many different kinds of cells in the body.

come from aborted fetuses and from embryos that are a few days old, consisting of just a few cells. (Fertility clinics store many such embryos because several "test tube" fertilizations are created for every patient who hopes to become pregnant; eventually, the extra embryos are destroyed.) In the United States, federal funding for basic stem-cell research has faced resistance by antiabortion activists.

An alternative to the use of ES cells is to reprogram adult cells from certain organs to become stem cells (Takahashi et al., 2007; Yu et al., 2007). In one study, when stem cells derived from human nasal cells were transplanted into mice that had lesions in a part of the brain involved with memory, the mice performed better on learning and memory tasks (Nivet et al., 2011). Like ES cells, **induced pluripotent stem (iPS) cells** derived from adult tissues seem to be capable of giving rise to many kinds of cells. However, they are harder to keep alive than ES cells are, and it is still unclear whether they will prove to be as versatile.

Patient-advocacy groups hope that transplanted stem cells will eventually help people recover from serious diseases of the brain and from damage to the spinal cord and other parts of the body. Scientists have already had some success in animals. For example, mice with recent spinal cord injuries regained much of their ability to walk normally after being injected with stem cells derived from extracted human wisdom teeth (Sakai et al., 2012). Microscopic analysis showed that many of the cells had helped axons regenerate at the site of the injury, by blocking substances that

In an area associated with learning and memory, immature stem cells give rise to new neurons, and physical and mental stimulation promotes the production and survival of these neurons. These mice, who have toys to play with, tunnels to explore, wheels to run on, and other mice to share their cage with, will grow more cells than mice living alone in standard cages.

were inhibiting their growth. Findings like this one hold promise for treatments in humans, but replication has been difficult; perhaps successful approaches will need to be tailored to the unique circumstances of each patient (Noble et al., 2011).

A long road lies ahead, and many daunting technical hurdles remain to be overcome before stem-cell research yields practical benefits for human patients. But exciting developments are on the horizon, including ongoing clinical attempts to restore sight in legally blind people and heal damaged heart tissue. Each year brings more incredible findings about neurons, findings that only a short time ago would have seemed like science fiction.

How Neurons Communicate LO 4.5

Neurons do not directly touch each other, end to end. Instead, they are separated by a minuscule space called the *synaptic cleft*, where the axon terminal of one neuron nearly touches a dendrite or the cell body of another. The entire site—the axon terminal, the cleft, and the covering membrane of the receiving dendrite or cell body—is called a **synapse**. Because a neuron's axon may have hundreds or even thousands of terminals, a single neuron may have synaptic connections with a great many others. As a result, the number of communication links in the nervous system runs into the trillions or perhaps even the quadrillions.

Neurons speak to one another, or in some cases to muscles or glands, in an electrical and chemical language. The inside and outside of a neuron contain positively and negatively charged ions (electrically charged atoms). At rest, the neuron has a negative charge relative to the outside. But when it is stimulated, special "gates" in the cell's membrane open, allowing positively charged sodium ions to move from the outside to the inside, making the neuron less negative. If this change reaches a critical level, it briefly triggers an **action potential**, during which gates in the axon membrane allow even more positively charged sodium into the cell, causing it to become positively charged; as a result, the neuron "fires." Then positively charged potassium ions quickly move from within the axon to the outside, which returns the cell to its negatively charged resting state.

If an axon is unmyelinated, the action potential at each point in the axon gives rise to a new action potential at the next point; thus, the impulse travels down the axon somewhat as fire travels along the fuse of a firecracker. But in myelinated axons, the process is a little different. Conduction of a neural impulse beneath the sheath is impossible, in part because sodium and potassium ions cannot cross the cell's membrane except at the

induced pluripotent stem (iPS) cells Stem cells derived from adult tissues.

synapse The site where transmission of a nerve impulse from one nerve cell to another occurs; it includes the axon terminal, the synaptic cleft, and receptor sites in the membrane of the receiving cell.

action potential A brief change in electrical voltage that occurs between the inside and the outside of an axon when a neuron is stimulated; it serves to produce an electrical impulse.

neurotransmitter A chemical substance that is released by a transmitting neuron at the synapse and that alters the activity of a receiving neuron.

breaks (nodes) between the myelin's "sausages." Instead, the action potential "hops" from one node to the next. (More precisely, the action potential regenerates at each node.) This arrangement allows the impulse to travel faster than it could if the action potential had to be regenerated at every point along the axon. Nerve impulses travel more slowly in babies than in older children and adults because when babies are born, the myelin sheaths on their axons are not yet fully developed.

When a neural impulse reaches the axon terminal's buttonlike tip, it must get its message across the synaptic cleft to another cell. At this point, *synaptic vesicles*, tiny sacs in the tip of the axon terminal, open and release a few thousand molecules of a chemical substance called a **neurotransmitter**. Like sailors carrying a message from one island to another, these molecules then diffuse across the synaptic cleft (see Figure 4.5).

When they reach the other side, the neurotransmitter molecules bind briefly with *receptor sites*, special molecules in the membrane of the receiving neuron's dendrites (or sometimes cell body), fitting these sites much as a key fits a lock. Electrical changes occur in the receiving neuron's membrane, and the ultimate effect is either an *excitatory effect* (a voltage shift in a positive direction) or an *inhibitory effect* (a voltage shift in a negative direction), depending on which receptor sites have been activated. If the effect is excitatory, the probability that the receiving neuron will fire increases; if it is inhibitory, the probability

decreases. Inhibition in the nervous system is vital. Without it, we could not sleep or coordinate our movements. Excitation of the nervous system would be overwhelming, producing convulsions.

What any given neuron does at any given moment depends on the net effect of all the messages being received from other neurons. Only when the cell's voltage reaches a certain threshold will it fire. Thousands of messages, both excitatory and inhibitory, may be coming into the cell, and the receiving neuron must essentially average them. The message that reaches a final destination depends on the rate at which individual neurons are firing, how many are firing, what types of neurons are firing, where the neurons are located, and the degree of synchrony among different neurons. It does *not* depend on how strongly the individual neurons are firing, however, because a neuron always either fires or doesn't. Like the turning on of a light switch, the firing of a neuron is an all-or-none event.

⊚ **Watch** the **Video** The Basics: How the Brain Works, Part I at **MyPsychLab**

Chemical Messengers in the Nervous System LO 4.6, LO 4.7

The nervous system "house" would remain forever dark and lifeless without chemical couriers to carry messages from room to room. These chemicals include neurotransmitters, hormones, and neuromodulators.

Neurotransmitters: Versatile Couriers. As we have seen, neurotransmitters make it possible for one neuron to excite or inhibit another. Neurotransmitters exist not only in the brain but also in the spinal cord, the peripheral nerves, and certain glands. Through their effects on specific nerve circuits, these substances control everything your brain does. The nature of the effect depends on the level of the neurotransmitter, its location, and the type of receptor it binds with. Here we will describe just a few of the better-understood neurotransmitters and some of their known or suspected effects.

Four neurotransmitters travel particular paths through parts of the brain, like buses following a route:

- **Serotonin** affects neurons involved in sleep, appetite, sensory perception, temperature regulation, pain suppression, and mood.

- **Dopamine** affects neurons involved in voluntary movement, learning, memory, emotion, pleasure and reward, and, possibly response to novelty.

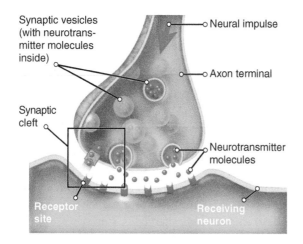

Synaptic vesicles (with neurotransmitter molecules inside)

Neural impulse

Axon terminal

Synaptic cleft

Neurotransmitter molecules

Receptor site

Receiving neuron

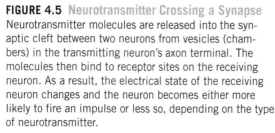

FIGURE 4.5 Neurotransmitter Crossing a Synapse Neurotransmitter molecules are released into the synaptic cleft between two neurons from vesicles (chambers) in the transmitting neuron's axon terminal. The molecules then bind to receptor sites on the receiving neuron. As a result, the electrical state of the receiving neuron changes and the neuron becomes either more likely to fire an impulse or less so, depending on the type of neurotransmitter.

Actor Michael J. Fox has Parkinson's disease, which involves a loss of dopamine-producing cells. He has used his fame to draw public attention to the disorder, and despite noticeable tremors, he continues to act—even launching a television series about a newsman with Parkinson's.

- **Acetylcholine** affects neurons involved in muscle action, arousal, vigilance, memory, and emotion.
- **Norepinephrine** affects neurons involved in increased heart rate, the slowing of intestinal activity during stress, learning, memory, dreaming, waking from sleep, and emotion.

Two other important neurotransmitters are distributed throughout the brain, like taxis that travel in all directions as needed:

- **GABA** (gamma-aminobutyric acid) is the major inhibitory neurotransmitter in the brain.
- **Glutamate** is the major excitatory neurotransmitter in the brain; it is released by about 90 percent of the brain's neurons.

Harmful effects can occur when neurotransmitter levels are too high or too low. Abnormal GABA levels have been implicated in sleep and eating disorders and in convulsive disorders, including epilepsy. People with Alzheimer's disease lose brain cells responsible for producing acetylcholine and other neurotransmitters, and these deficits help account for their devastating memory problems. A loss of cells that produce dopamine accounts for the tremors and rigidity of Parkinson's disease. In multiple sclerosis, immune cells overproduce glutamate, which damages or kills glial cells that normally make myelin.

We want to warn you, however, that pinning down the relationship between neurotransmitter abnormalities and behavioral or physical abnormalities is tricky. Each neurotransmitter plays multiple roles, and the functions of different substances often overlap. Further, it is always possible that something about a disorder leads to abnormal neurotransmitter levels instead of the other way around. (If you have read Chapter 1, you'll recall that correlation does not imply causation.) Although drugs that boost or decrease levels of particular neurotransmitters are sometimes effective in treating severe cases of clinical depression, this fact does not necessarily mean that abnormal neurotransmitter levels *cause* the depression. After all, aspirin can relieve a headache, but headaches are not caused by a lack of aspirin!

Many of us regularly ingest things that affect our own neurotransmitters. For example, serotonin levels decrease after a protein-rich meal and increase after a high-carbohydrate meal. And most recreational drugs produce their effects by blocking or enhancing the actions of neurotransmitters, as do some herbal remedies. St. John's wort, which is often taken for depression, prevents the cells that release serotonin from reabsorbing excess molecules that have remained in the synaptic cleft; as a result, serotonin levels rise. Many people do not realize that such remedies, because they affect the nervous system's biochemistry, can interact with other medications and can be harmful in high doses.

👁 **Watch** the **Video** In the Real World: Neurotransmitters at **MyPsychLab**

Hormones: Long-Distance Messengers. **Hormones**, which make up the second class of chemical messengers, are produced primarily in **endocrine glands**, such as the pancreas, ovaries, testes, and adrenal glands. They are released directly into the bloodstream, which carries them to organs and cells that may be far from their point of origin. Hormones have dozens of jobs, from promoting bodily growth to aiding digestion to regulating metabolism. Neurotransmitters and hormones are not always

hormones Chemical substances, secreted by organs called *glands*, that affect the functioning of other organs.

endocrine glands Internal organs that produce hormones and release them into the bloodstream.

"I'll be a real boy as soon as I'm done with the hormone treatments."

Robert Leighton/The New Yorker Collection/ www.cartoonbank.com

melatonin A hormone, secreted by the pineal gland, that is involved in the regulation of daily biological rhythms.

oxytocin A hormone, secreted by the pituitary gland, that stimulates uterine contractions during childbirth, facilitates the ejection of milk during nursing, and seems to promote, in both sexes, attachment and trust in relationships.

adrenal hormones Hormones that are produced by the adrenal glands and that are involved in emotion and stress.

sex hormones Hormones that regulate the development and functioning of reproductive organs and that stimulate the development of male and female sexual characteristics; they include androgens, estrogens, and progesterone.

Neuromodulators Neurochemicals that modulate the functioning of neurons and neurotransmitters.

endorphins [en-DOR-fins] Chemical substances in the nervous system that are similar in structure and action to opiates; they are involved in pain reduction, pleasure, memory, and other functions, and are known technically as *endogenous opioid peptides*.

chemically distinct because nature has been efficient, giving some substances more than one role. For instance, norepinephrine may be considered either a neurotransmitter or a hormone, depending on where it is located and what function it is performing.

The following hormones, among others, are of particular interest to research psychologists and are discussed further in other chapters:

1 Melatonin, which is secreted by the *pineal gland* deep within the brain, helps to regulate daily biological rhythms and promotes sleep.

2 Oxytocin, which is secreted by another small gland in the brain, the *pituitary gland*, enhances uterine contractions during childbirth and facilitates the ejection of milk during nursing. Along with another hormone called *vasopressin*, oxytocin contributes to relationships in both sexes by promoting attachment and trust.

3 Adrenal hormones, which are produced by the *adrenal glands* (organs that are perched right above the kidneys), are involved in emotion and stress. These hormones also rise in response to other conditions, such as heat, cold, pain, injury, burns, and physical exercise, and in response to some drugs, such as caffeine and nicotine. The outer part of each adrenal gland produces *cortisol*, which increases blood-sugar levels and boosts energy. The inner part produces *epinephrine* (commonly known as adrenaline) and *norepinephrine*. When adrenal hormones are released in your body, activated by the sympathetic nervous system, they increase your arousal level and prepare you for action. Adrenal hormones also enhance memory.

4 Sex hormones, which are secreted by tissue in the gonads (testes in men, ovaries in women) and also by the adrenal glands, include three main types, all occurring in both sexes but in differing amounts and proportions in males and females after puberty. *Androgens* (the most important of which is *testosterone*) are masculinizing hormones produced mainly in the testes but also in the ovaries and the adrenal glands. Androgens set in motion the physical changes males experience at puberty—notably a deepened voice and facial and chest hair—and cause pubic and underarm hair to develop in both sexes. Testosterone also influences sexual arousal in both sexes. *Estrogens* are feminizing hormones that bring on physical changes in females at puberty, such as breast development and the onset of menstruation, and that influence the course of the menstrual cycle. *Progesterone* contributes to the growth and maintenance of the uterine lining

in preparation for a fertilized egg, among other functions. Estrogens and progesterone are produced mainly in the ovaries but also in the testes and the adrenal glands.

Sex hormones are also involved in behavior not linked to sex or reproduction. The body's natural estrogen may enhance learning and memory by promoting the formation of synaptic connections and by indirectly increasing the production of acetylcholine (Gibbs, 2010; Lee & McEwen, 2001; Sherwin, 1998). However, the common belief that fluctuating levels of estrogen and progesterone make most women "emotional" before menstruation has not been borne out by research, as we discuss in Chapter 5.

Neuromodulators: The Brain's Volume Control. The brain is awash in thousands of other chemicals that modulate (vary the strength of) neural functions; they are called **neuromodulators**. One, the *serotonin transporter*, is a protein that acts like a garbage collector, picking up serotonin from the synaptic cleft after it has been released and transporting it back to the sending neuron for recycling. In that way, it controls the amount of serotonin that is available in the brain.

Endorphins are an intriguing group of chemicals known technically as *endogenous opioid peptides*. Some function as neurotransmitters, but most act primarily as neuromodulators, by limiting or prolonging the effects of neurotransmitters. They have consequences similar to those of natural opiates such as heroin, reducing pain and promoting pleasure. Endorphin levels shoot up when an animal or a person is afraid or under stress. This increase has a purpose: By making pain bearable in such situations, endorphins give a species an evolutionary advantage. When an organism is threatened, it needs to do something fast. Pain, however, can interfere with action: A mouse that pauses to lick a wounded paw may become a cat's dinner; a soldier who is overcome by an injury may never get off the battlefield. Of course, the body's built-in system of counteracting pain is only partly successful, especially when painful stimulation is prolonged.

Simulate the **Experiment** Endocrine System at **MyPsychLab**

Endorphins are also thought to play a role in appetite, sexual activity, blood pressure, mood, learning, and memory. And in Chapter 14, we will see that a link exists between endorphins and human attachment: An infant's contact with the mother stimulates the flow of endorphins, which strengthens the baby's bond with her (and the mother's bond with the baby!).

Recite & Review

✅ **Study** and **Review** at **MyPsychLab**

Recite: Fire up your neurons so you can say as much as possible about glia, neurons, nerves, neurogenesis, stem cells, synapses, neural impulses, neurotransmitters, hormones, and neuromodulators.

Review: Next, go back and reread this section. There was a lot in it; what did you miss?

Now get your glutamate going by taking this *Quick Quiz:*

A. Which word in parentheses better fits each of the following definitions?

1. Communication specialists that transmit information to, from, and within the central nervous system (*neurons, glia cells*)

2. Part of a neuron that resembles branches of a tree (*axon, dendrites*)

3. Constrictions dividing the axon into segments (*myelin sheath, nodes*)

4. A chemical substance that alters the activity of a receiving neuron (*synaptic vesicles, neurotransmitters*)

5. A voltage shift in a positive direction (*excitatory effect, inhibitory effect*)

6. Major inhibitory neurotransmitter in the brain (*GABA, glutamate*)

B. Kristen is having a hard time in college and is feeling pretty depressed about it. She starts seeing ads for a new drug that claims it changes the levels of several neurotransmitters thought to be involved in depression. Based on what you have learned, what questions should Kristen ask before deciding whether to ask her doctor to prescribe it for her?

Answers:

A. **1.** glia cells **2.** dendrites **3.** nodes **4.** neurotransmitter **5.** excitatory effect **6.** GABA *B.* Kristen might want to ask, among other things, about side effects (each neurotransmitter has several functions, all of which might be affected by the drug); evidence that the drug not only works, but is also more effective than older drugs; whether there is any reason to believe that her own neurotransmitter levels are abnormal; and whether she should consider ways of coping with her college problems before trying any drug.

You are about to learn...

- ways of peering inside the brain.
- what brain scans can tell us.
- the limitations of brain scans as a way of understanding the brain.

Mapping the Brain LO 4.8

We come now to the main room of the nervous system "house": the brain. A disembodied brain stored in a formaldehyde-filled container is a putty-colored, wrinkled glob of tissue that looks a little like an oversized walnut. It takes an act of imagination to envision this modest-looking organ writing *Hamlet*, discovering radium, or inventing the paper clip.

When researchers work with animals, they sometimes surgically remove or disable a brain structure, and then observe the effects on behavior. This approach is called the *lesion method*, but of course it cannot be used in humans. In a living person, the brain is encased in a thick protective vault of bone. How, then, can scientists study it? One approach is to study patients who have had a part of the brain damaged or removed because of disease or injury. Another is to stimulate the brains of patients having brain surgery to try to identify the functions of various areas. But both of these methods are restricted to brains that have been damaged. Fortunately, neuroscientists have a growing number of other tools for studying healthy human brains.

One general approach is to do something that affects specific brain areas and then observe the consequences for behavior. This approach includes these two methods:

- **Transcranial magnetic stimulation (TMS)** is a relatively new method that stimulates or temporarily disrupts specific neural circuits by delivering a large current through a wire coil placed on a person's head. The current produces a strong magnetic field, which causes neurons under the coil to fire. TMS can be used to produce motor responses (say, a twitch in the thumb or a knee jerk) but researchers also use it to briefly disrupt neural circuits during specific tasks and study the behavioral effects. The drawback of this method is that when neurons fire, they cause many other neurons to become active too, so it can be hard to tell which neurons are critical for a particular task. Still, TMS has been useful for

transcranial magnetic stimulation (TMS)
A method of stimulating brain cells, using a powerful magnetic field produced by a wire coil placed on a person's head; it can be used by researchers to temporarily disrupt neural circuits during specific tasks.

transcranial direct current stimulation (tDCS) A technique that applies a small electric current to stimulate or suppress activity in parts of the cortex; it enables researchers to identify the functions of a particular area.

electroencephalogram (EEG) A recording of neural activity detected by electrodes.

PET scans (positron-emission tomography) A method for analyzing biochemical activity in the brain, for example by using injections of a glucoselike substance containing a radioactive element.

examining the role of various brain regions in everything from vision to emotion to language.

- **Transcranial direct current stimulation (tDCS)** is an even newer way of studying brain function. The researcher applies a small electric current to an area of the cortex, the outer surface of the brain (Nitsche et al., 2008). Depending on the direction of the current, brain activity in that area is temporarily stimulated or suppressed. In one study, applying current in one direction increased activity and improved people's memory for information gained during one task while they focused on doing another. But applying the current in the other direction, which reduced activity, decreased the participants' ability to do this task (Zaehle et al., 2011).

The other general approach to mapping the brain is to do something that affects behavior and then record what happens in the brain:

- **Electroencephalograms (EEGs)** use *electrodes*, devices pasted or taped onto the scalp to detect the electrical activity of millions of neurons in particular regions of the brain. Wires from the electrodes are connected to a machine that translates the electrical energy from the brain into wavy lines on a moving piece of paper or a screen, which is why electrical patterns in the brain are known as "brain waves." A standard EEG is useful but not precise because it reflects the activities of so many cells at once.

"Listening" to the brain with an EEG machine is like standing outside a sports stadium: You know when something is happening, but you can't be sure what it is or who is doing it. Fortunately, computer technology and statistical techniques can be combined with EEG technology to get a clearer picture of brain activity patterns and mental processes associated with specific events, such as seeing a picture or hearing a word.

- **PET (positron-emission tomography) scans** record biochemical changes in the brain as they are happening. One type of PET scan takes advantage of the fact that nerve cells convert glucose, the body's main fuel, into energy. A researcher can inject a person with a glucoselike substance that contains a harmless radioactive element. This substance accumulates in brain areas that are especially active and are therefore consuming glucose rapidly. The substance emits radiation, which is detected by a scanning device, and the result is a computer-processed picture of biochemical activity on a display screen, with different colors indicating different activity levels (see Figure 4.6a). Other kinds of PET scans measure blood flow or oxygen consumption, which also reflect brain activity. PET scans can tell researchers which areas are busiest when a person hears a song, recalls a sad memory, works on a math problem, or shifts attention from one task to another.

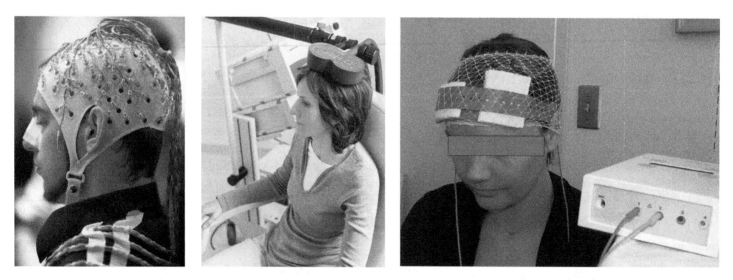

Electrodes on the scalp (left) are used to produce an overall picture of electrical activity in different areas of the brain. Transcranial magnetic stimulation, or TMS (center), delivers a large current through a coil on a person's head, causing neurons under the coil to fire. It can be used to temporarily disrupt specific brain circuits. Transcranial direct current stimulation, or tDCS (right), applies a small electrical current to a specific area of the cortex, which stimulates or suppresses activity in that region depending on the direction of the current.

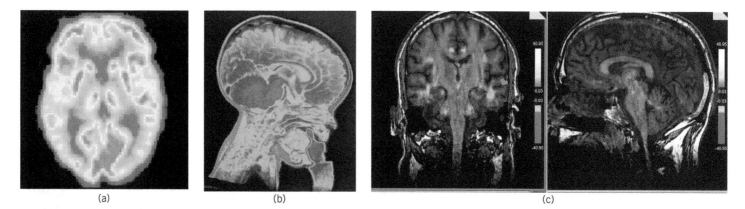

FIGURE 4.6 Scanning the Brain

In the PET scans on the left, arrows and the color red indicate areas of highest activity, and violet indicates areas of lowest activity, as a person does different things. In the center, an MRI shows a child's brain, along with the bottle he was drinking from while the image was obtained. On the right are fMRI images made while a person was listening to music.

- **Magnetic resonance imaging (MRI)** uses powerful magnetic fields and radio frequencies to take highly detailed pictures of bodily organs. The magnets produce vibrations in the nuclei of atoms making up the organ in question. The vibrations are then picked up as signals by special receivers. A computer analyzes the signals, taking into account their strength and duration, and converts them into a high-contrast picture of the organ being studied, such as the brain (see Figure 4.6b).

An ordinary MRI image gives us a terrific picture of what the brain looks like, although not what it does. But an ultrafast version of MRI, called **functional MRI (fMRI)**, allows us to see brain activity associated with specific thoughts or behaviors lasting at least several seconds. It can capture brain changes many times a second as a person performs a task, such as reading a sentence or solving a puzzle (see Figure 4.6c). In fMRI, the receivers detect levels of blood oxygen in different brain areas. Because neurons use oxygen as fuel, active brain areas produce a bigger signal. Scientists are using fMRI to correlate activity in specific brain areas with everything from racial attitudes to moral reasoning to spiritual meditation. Whenever you read about a new specialty with "neuro" in front of it—neuromarketing, neurofinance, neurolaw, even neurocinematics—you can be sure its proponents are using fMRI (though not always wisely).

Controversies and Cautions. Exciting though these developments and technologies are, we need to understand that technology cannot replace critical thinking (Legrenzi & Umiltà, 2011; Tallis, 2011; Wade, 2006). Because brain-scan images seem so "real" and scientific, many people fail to realize

that these images can convey oversimplified and sometimes misleading impressions (see Figure 4.7). Color can be used to either accentuate or minimize contrasts between two brains; small contrasts can be made to look dramatic, larger ones to look insignificant (Dumit, 2004). Combining individual brain scans into one average scan—a common practice—may mask significant variability among people's brains.

MRI (magnetic resonance imaging) A method for studying body and brain tissue, using magnetic fields and special radio receivers.

fMRI (functional magnetic resonance imaging) A fast version of MRI used to study brain activity associated with specific thoughts and behaviors.

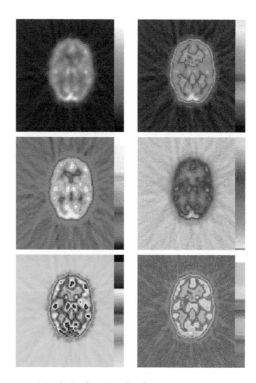

FIGURE 4.7 Coloring the Brain

By altering the colors used in a PET scan, researchers can create the appearance of dramatic brain differences. These scans are actually images of the same brain.

Moreover, research using fMRI has sometimes suffered from questionable statistical procedures that have produced highly inflated correlations between brain activity and measures of personality and emotion (Vul et al., 2009).

Yet the media usually report these findings uncritically, giving the impression that scientists know more about the relationship between the brain and psychological processes than they really do (McCabe & Castell, 2008).

THINKING CRITICALLY

About Brain-Scan Technology

To illustrate this point, a clever group of scientists did an fMRI on a dead salmon (yes, you read that right) while asking it to view emotional images and determine what emotions the person in each photo was feeling (Bennett et al., 2010). You're probably wondering why the fMRI would detect *any* brain activity in a dead salmon, but it did. The scan appeared to show that the salmon was "thinking" about the pictures and the people in them. That was because fMRI produces a mix of signal and noise; picking up the signal is like trying to track a conversation in a crowded bar. Scientists must use sophisticated techniques to filter out the noise and reveal the true signal, and if they don't know what they are doing, they can make errors. In this case, the result is funny, but in real life, too, we may not know if the result is real … or another dead salmon.

The problem is not with technology per se so much as it is with faulty analyses or theories,

poor definitions of the behavior being studied, and inappropriate interpretations of results. For example, the enthusiasm for technology has generated the widespread belief that specific "brain centers" or "critical circuits" explain why you prefer Coke to Pepsi, why you identify as a liberal or conservative, or what your brain is doing when you are in love. These beliefs are appealing because they seem to explain complicated behavior in simple terms (Beck, 2010). But attempts to reduce complex behavior to single locations will almost certainly fail (Gonsalves & Cohen, 2010; Tallis, 2011; Uttal, 2011). At present, technology is better at telling us where things happen than why or how they happen. So if you know that one part of the brain is activated when you are thinking hot thoughts of your beloved, what exactly do you know about love—or your brain? Does that part also light up when you are looking at other things that you love, such as a luscious hot fudge sundae, or thinking about happily riding your horse Horace through the hills? Do other parts become active, too? As neuroscientist Raymond Tallis (2011) noted, love is not a single state, like being cold; it includes many emotions, from desire to jealousy to quiet contentment, and sometimes several conflicting emotions at the same time.

Nonetheless, when used appropriately, these measures do provide an illuminating look at the brain during work and play, and we will be reporting many findings based on brain scan research throughout this book. The brain can no longer hide from researchers behind the fortress of the skull.

Recite & Review

 **Study** and **Review** at **MyPsychLab**

Recite: You know the drill: Tell someone or something everything you can recall about transcranial magnetic stimulation (TMS), transcranial direct current stimulation (tDCS), EEGs, PET scans, MRI, fMRI, and … the dead salmon.

Review: Next, go back and read this section again.

Now take this *Quick Quiz:*

1. What two methods can be used to temporarily disrupt neural activity in an area of the brain?

2. What does fMRI tells us that ordinary MRI does not?

3. A researcher scans the brains of gum-chewing volunteers, finds out which part of their brains is most active, and announces the discovery of the brain's "gum-chewing center." What's wrong with this conclusion?

Answers:

1. TMS and tDCS. **2.** An fMRI allows us to associate brain activity with specific thoughts or behaviors lasting at least several seconds, instead of just picturing the brain at a moment in time. **3.** Many actions and sensations are involved in chewing gum, such as the chewing motion, enjoyment of the flavors, and salivation. A brain scan may tell us where things are happening but not why or how they are happening. The same areas might also become active when you chew a piece of asparagus. Finally, even if there were a gum-chewing center (there isn't!), yours might not be in the same place as someone else's. Brains vary, a fact that may be lost when a researcher averages the results of all the brain scans in his or her study.

Figure 4.8 sho

and that you are wending your way throu "soul's frail dwelling house," starting at the part, just above the spine. Figure 4.8 sho major structures we will encounter along ou you may want to refer to it as we proceed. Bu in mind that any activity—feeling an en having a thought, performing a task—ir many different structures working togethe description, therefore, is a simplification.

You are about to learn...

- the major parts of the brain and some of their major functions.
- why it is a good thing that the outer covering of the human brain is so wrinkled.
- how a bizarre nineteenth-century accident illuminated the role of the frontal lobes.

A Tour Through the Brain

Most modern brain theories assume that different brain parts perform different (though greatly overlapping) tasks. This concept, known as **localization of function**, goes back at least to Joseph Gall (1758–1828), an Austrian anatomist who thought that personality traits were reflected in the development of specific areas of the brain. Gall's theory led to the development of phrenology, which, as we saw in Chapter 1, was completely wrong-headed (so to speak). But his general notion of specialization in the brain had merit.

To learn about what the major brain structures do, let's take an imaginary stroll through the brain. Pretend that you have shrunk to a microscopic size

The Brain Stem LO 4.9

We begin at the base of the skull with the **brain stem,** which began to evolve some 500 million years ago in segmented worms. The brain stem looks like a stalk rising out of the spinal cord. Pathways to and from upper areas of the brain pass through its two main structures: the medulla and the pons. The **pons** is involved in (among other things) sleeping, waking, and dreaming. The **medulla** is responsible for bodily functions that do not have to be consciously willed, such as breathing and heart rate. Hanging has long been used as a method of execution because when it breaks the neck, nerve pathways from the medulla are severed, stopping respiration.

Extending upward from the core of the brain stem is the **reticular activating system (RAS)**. This

brain stem involved in, among other things, sleeping, waking, and dreaming.

medulla [muh-DUL-uh] A structure in the brain stem responsible for certain automatic functions, such as breathing and heart rate.

reticular activating system (RAS) A dense network of neurons found in the core of the brain stem; it arouses the cortex and screens incoming information.

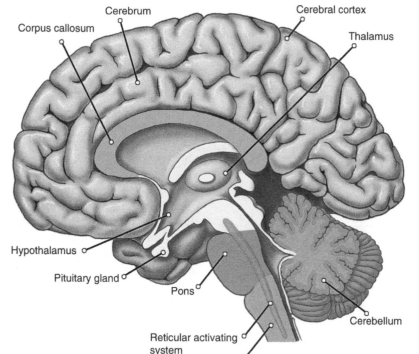

Cerebrum
Corpus callosum
Cerebral cortex
Thalamus
Hypothalamus
Pituitary gland
Pons
Cerebellum
Reticular activating system
Medulla

FIGURE 4.8 Major Structures of the Human Brain
This cross section depicts the brain as if it were split in half, and shows the structures described in the text.

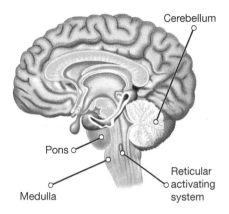

dense network of neurons, which extends above the brain stem into the center of the brain and has connections with areas that are higher up, screens incoming information and arouses the higher centers when something happens that demands their attention. Without the RAS, we could not be alert or perhaps even conscious.

The Cerebellum LO 4.10

Standing atop the brain stem and looking toward the back part of the brain, we see a structure about the size of a small fist. It is the **cerebellum**, or "lesser brain," which contributes to a sense of balance and coordinates the muscles so that movement is smooth and precise. If your cerebellum were damaged, you would probably become exceedingly clumsy and uncoordinated. You might have trouble using a pencil, threading a needle, or even walking. In addition, this structure is involved in remembering simple skills and acquired reflexes. But the cerebellum, which was once considered just a motor center, is not as "lesser" as its name implies: It is also involved in cognitive and emotional learning (Fiez, 1996; Timmann et al., 2010).

The Thalamus LO 4.11

Deep in the brain's interior, roughly at its center, we can see the **thalamus**, the busy traffic officer of the brain. As sensory messages come into the brain—about the sight of a sunset, the sound of a siren, the feel of a fly landing on your arm—the thalamus directs them to higher areas in charge of vision, sound, or touch. The only sense that completely bypasses the thalamus is the sense of smell, which has its own private switching station, the *olfactory bulb*. The olfactory bulb lies near areas involved in emotion. Perhaps that is why odors, such as the smell of fresh laundry or a steaming bowl of chicken soup, sometimes rekindle vivid memories.

The Hypothalamus and the Pituitary Gland

Beneath the thalamus sits a structure called the **hypothalamus** (*hypo* means "under"). It is involved in drives associated with the survival of the individual and the species—hunger, thirst, emotion, sex, and reproduction. It regulates body temperature by triggering sweating or shivering, and it controls the complex operations of the autonomic nervous system. It also contains the biological clock that controls the body's daily rhythms (see Chapter 5).

Hanging down from the hypothalamus, connected to it by a short stalk, is a cherry-sized endocrine gland called the **pituitary gland**, mentioned previously in our discussion of hormones. The pituitary is often called the body's "master gland" because the hormones it secretes affect many other endocrine glands. The master, however, is really only a supervisor. The true boss is the hypothalamus, which sends chemicals to the pituitary that tell it when to "talk" to the other endocrine glands. The pituitary, in turn, sends hormonal messages out to these glands.

The hypothalamus and several other loosely interconnected structures have often been grouped together as the *limbic system*, a term from the Latin for "border": These structures have been thought to form a sort of border between the "higher" and "lower" parts of the brain. Structures in this region are heavily involved in emotions that we share with other animals, such as rage and fear, so the region is also sometimes called "the emotional brain." But researchers now know that these structures also have other functions, and that other parts of the brain are also involved in emotion. As a result, the term *limbic system* has been going out of fashion.

👁 **Watch the Video** Brain Stem and Limbic System at **MyPsychLab**

cerebellum A brain structure that regulates movement and balance and is involved in some cognitive tasks.

thalamus A brain structure that relays sensory messages to the cerebral cortex.

hypothalamus A brain structure involved in emotions and drives vital to survival; it regulates the autonomic nervous system.

pituitary gland A small endocrine gland at the base of the brain that releases many hormones and regulates other endocrine glands.

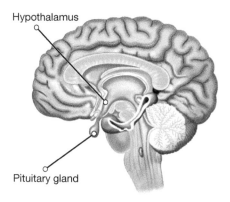

Hypothalamus

Pituitary gland

The Amygdala

The **amygdala** (from the ancient Greek word for "almond") is responsible for evaluating sensory information, quickly determining its emotional importance, and contributing to the initial decision to approach or withdraw from a person or situation (see Chapter 13). Because it assesses danger and threat, it has sometimes been called the brain's "fear center," but it is more than that. Your amygdala rapidly evaluates incoming stimuli for their fit with your current psychological state and even your core personality traits, responding to positive, negative, or even just plain interesting stimuli accordingly. If you're extroverted, your amygdala might respond more actively to photographs of happy people than it would if you were shy; and when you're hungry, your amygdala is likely to respond to food (Cunningham & Brosch, 2012). The amygdala also plays a role in mediating anxiety and depression, and in forming and retrieving emotional memories.

The Hippocampus

The shape of the **hippocampus** must have reminded someone of a sea horse, for in Latin, that is what its name means. This structure compares sensory information with what the brain has learned to expect about the world, and when a match occurs, the hippocampus tells the reticular activating system to "cool it." There's no need for neural alarm bells to go off every time a car goes by, a bird chirps, or you feel your saliva trickling down the back of your throat.

The hippocampus has also been called the "gateway to memory" because it is critical in the formation of long-term memories for facts, events, and spatial relationships. It enables us to take in and combine different components of an experience—sights, sounds, feelings—and bind them together into one "memory," even though the individual components are ultimately stored in the cerebral cortex, which we will be discussing shortly. When you recall meeting someone yesterday, various aspects of the memory—information about the person's greeting, tone of voice, appearance, and location—are probably stored in different locations in the cortex. But without the hippocampus, the information would never get to these destinations. This structure is also involved in the retrieval of information during recall.

The Cerebrum LO 4.12, LO 4.13

At this point in our tour, the largest part of the brain still looms above us. It is the cauliflower-like **cerebrum**, where the higher forms of thinking take place. The complexity of the human brain's circuitry far exceeds that of any computer in existence, and much of its most complicated wiring is packed into this structure. Compared to many other creatures, we humans may be ungainly, feeble, and thin-skinned, but our well-developed cerebrum enables us to overcome these limitations and creatively control our environment (and, some would say, to mess it up).

The cerebrum is divided into two separate halves, or **cerebral hemispheres**, connected by a large band of fibers called the **corpus callosum**. In general, the right hemisphere is in charge of the left side of the body and the left hemisphere is in charge of the right side of the body. The two hemispheres also have somewhat different tasks and talents, a phenomenon known as **lateralization**.

amygdala [uh-MIG-dul-uh] A brain structure involved in the arousal and regulation of emotion and the initial emotional response to sensory information.

hippocampus A brain structure involved in the storage of new information in memory.

cerebrum [suh-REE-brum] The largest brain structure, consisting of the upper part of the brain; divided into two hemispheres, it is in charge of most sensory, motor, and cognitive processes; from the Latin for "brain."

cerebral hemispheres The two halves of the cerebrum.

corpus callosum [CORE-puhs cah-LOW-suhm] The bundle of nerve fibers connecting the two cerebral hemispheres.

lateralization Specialization of the two cerebral hemispheres for particular operations.

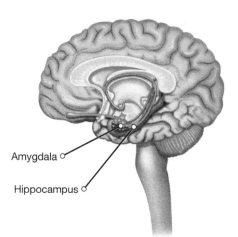

Amygdala

Hippocampus

Explore the Concept The Virtual Brain at MyPsychLab

cerebral cortex A collection of several thin layers of cells covering the cerebrum; it is largely responsible for higher mental functions; *cortex* is Latin for "bark" or "rind."

occipital [ahk-SIP-uh-tuhl] lobes Lobes at the lower back part of the brain's cerebral cortex; they contain areas that receive visual information.

parietal [puh-RYE-uh-tuhl] lobes Lobes at the top of the brain's cerebral cortex; they contain areas that receive information on pressure, pain, touch, and temperature, and that are involved in attention and awareness of spatial relationships.

temporal lobes Lobes at the sides of the brain's cerebral cortex; they contain areas involved in hearing, memory, perception, emotion, and (in the left lobe, typically) language comprehension.

frontal lobes Lobes at the front of the brain's cerebral cortex; they contain areas involved in short-term memory, higher-order thinking, initiative, social judgment, and (in the left lobe, typically) speech production.

The Cerebral Cortex. Working our way right up through the top of the brain, we find that the cerebrum is covered by several thin layers of densely packed cells known collectively as the **cerebral cortex.** Cell bodies in the cortex, as in many other parts of the brain, produce a grayish tissue, hence the term *gray matter.* In other parts of the brain (and in the rest of the nervous system), long, myelin-covered axons prevail, providing the brain's *white matter.* Although the cortex is only about 3 millimeters (1/8 inch) thick, it contains almost three-fourths of all the cells in the human brain. The cortex has many deep crevasses and wrinkles, which enable it to contain its billions of neurons without requiring us to have the heads of giants—heads that would be too big to permit us to be born. In other mammals, which have fewer neurons, the cortex is less crumpled; in rats, it is quite smooth.

Lobes of the Cortex. In each cerebral hemisphere, deep fissures divide the cortex into four distinct regions, or lobes (see Figure 4.9):

- The **occipital lobes** (from the Latin for "in back of the head") are at the lower back part of the brain. Among other things, they contain the *visual cortex,* where visual signals are processed. Damage to the visual cortex can cause impaired visual recognition or blindness.

- The **parietal lobes** (from the Latin for "pertaining to walls") are at the top of the brain. They contain the *somatosensory cortex,* which receives information about pressure, pain, touch, and temperature from all over the body. The areas of the somatosensory cortex that receive signals from the hands and the face are disproportionately large because these body parts

are particularly sensitive. Parts of the parietal lobes are also involved in attention and spatial awareness.

- The **temporal lobes** (from the Latin for "pertaining to the temples") are at the sides of the brain, just above the ears and behind the temples. They are involved in memory, perception, and emotion, and they contain the *auditory cortex,* which processes sounds. An area of the left temporal lobe known as *Wernicke's area* is involved in language comprehension.

- The **frontal lobes,** as their name indicates, are located toward the front of the brain, just under the skull in the area of the forehead. They contain the *motor cortex,* which issues orders to the 600 muscles of the body that produce voluntary movement. In the left frontal lobe, a region known as *Broca's area* handles speech production. During short-term memory tasks, areas in the frontal lobes are especially active. The frontal lobes are also involved in emotion and in the ability to make plans, think creatively, and take initiative.

Because the lobes of the cerebral cortex have different functions, they tend to respond differently when directly stimulated by electrodes during brain surgery. (The brain does not feel touch or pain, so the patient can be awake.) If a surgeon stimulates the somatosensory cortex in the parietal lobes, a patient might feel a tingling in the skin or a sense of being gently touched there. If the visual cortex in the occipital lobes were stimulated, the person might report seeing a flash of light or swirls of color. And, eerily, many areas of the cortex, when stimulated, would produce no obvious response or sensation. These "silent" areas are sometimes called the *association cortex* because they are involved in higher mental processes.

👁 **Watch** the **Video** The Basics: How the Brain Works, Part 2 at **MyPsychLab**

The Prefrontal Cortex. The most forward part of the frontal lobes is the *prefrontal cortex.* This area barely exists in mice and rats and takes up only 3.5 percent of the cerebral cortex in cats and about 7 percent in dogs, but it accounts for approximately one-third of the entire cortex in human beings. It is the most recently evolved part of our brains and is associated with such complex abilities as reasoning, decision making, and planning.

Scientists have long known that the frontal lobes, and the prefrontal cortex in particular, must also have something to do with personality. The first clue appeared in 1848, when a bizarre

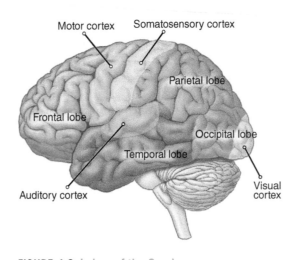

Motor cortex · Somatosensory cortex
Parietal lobe
Frontal lobe
Occipital lobe
Temporal lobe
Auditory cortex
Visual cortex

FIGURE 4.9 Lobes of the Cerebrum
Deep fissures divide the cortex of each cerebral hemisphere into four regions.

"The prefrontal cortex is involved in higher mental functioning, like using a can opener and remembering to feed you."

accident drove an inch-thick, 3 1/2-foot-long iron rod clear through the head of a young railroad worker named Phineas Gage. As you can see in the photos on this page, the rod (which is still on display at Harvard University, along with Gage's skull) entered beneath the left eye and exited through the top of the head, destroying much of the prefrontal cortex (H. Damasio et al., 1994). Miraculously, Gage survived this trauma and, by most accounts, he retained the ability to speak, think, and remember. But his friends complained that he was "no longer Gage." In a sort of Jekyll-and-Hyde transformation, he had changed from a mild-mannered, friendly, efficient worker into a foul-mouthed, ill-tempered, undependable lout who could not hold a steady job or stick to a plan. His employers had to let him go, and he was reduced to exhibiting himself as a circus attraction.

There is some controversy about the details of this sad incident, but many other cases of brain injury, whether from stroke, disease, or trauma, support the conclusion that most scientists draw from the Gage case: Parts of the frontal lobes are involved in social judgment, rational decision making, and the ability to set goals and to make and carry through plans. Like Gage, people with damage in these areas sometimes mismanage their finances, lose their jobs, and abandon their friends. Interestingly, the mental deficits that characterize such damage are accompanied by a flattening out of emotion and feeling, which suggests that normal emotions are necessary for everyday reasoning and the ability to learn from mistakes (H. Damasio et al., 1994; A. Damasio, 2003; Levenson & Miller, 2007).

Watch the **Video** Thinking Like a Psychologist: The Pre-Frontal Cortex: The Good, The Bad, and The Criminal at **MyPsychLab**

The frontal lobes also govern the ability to do a series of tasks in the proper sequence and to stop doing them at the proper time. The pioneering Soviet psychologist Alexander Luria (1980) studied many cases in which damage to the frontal lobes disrupted these abilities. One man Luria observed kept trying to light a match after it was already lit. Another planed a piece of wood in the hospital carpentry shop until it was gone and then went on to plane the workbench.

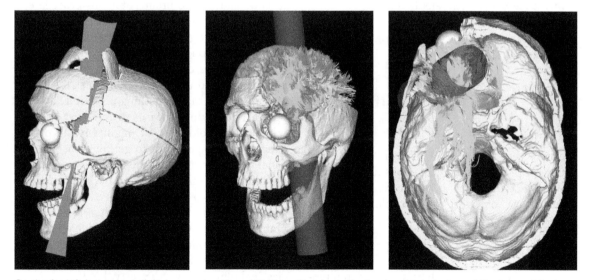

On the far left is a recent digital reconstruction of Phineas Gage's skull, showing the trajectory of the iron rod that penetrated his brain. The photos in the center and on the right show reconstructions of the interior of the skull from the front and from above. The colors indicate the different fiber pathways that were probably affected, including white-matter pathways between the frontal cortex and other brain parts (Van Horn et al., 2012). After the accident, Gage's behavior and personality were altered dramatically, and scientists today understand why: The rod passed through an area of the prefrontal cortex associated with emotional processing and rational decision making.

Recite & Review

 Study and **Review** at **MyPsychLab**

Recite: Using your own brain, say out loud everything you can about localization of function, and the brain stem, RAS, cerebellum, thalamus, hypothalamus, pituitary gland, amygdala, hippocampus, cerebrum, corpus callosum, lateralization, cerebral cortex, lobes of the cortex, and prefrontal cortex.

Review: Next, go back and read this section again. What did you miss?

Now take this *Quick Quiz:*

A. Match each description on the left with a term on the right.

1. Filters out irrelevant information	**a.** reticular activating system
2. Known as the "gateway to memory"	**b.** cerebrum
3. Controls the autonomic nervous system; involved in drives associated with survival	**c.** hippocampus
4. Consists of two hemispheres	**d.** cerebral cortex
5. Wrinkled outer covering of the cerebrum	**e.** frontal lobes
6. Site of the motor cortex; associated with planning and taking initiative	**f.** hypothalamus

B. The aroma of Andy's lunch box made Ronny nostalgic about his hometown. What might be the relation between the aroma and his memory?

Answers:

A. 1. a 2. c 3. f 4. b 5. d 6. e   B. This happens because the olfactory bulb lies near the areas involved in emotion.

You are about to learn...

- what would happen if the two cerebral hemispheres could not communicate with each other.
- why researchers often refer to the left hemisphere as "dominant."
- why "left-brainedness" and "right-brainedness" are exaggerations.

The Two Hemispheres of the Brain LO 4.14

We have seen that the cerebrum is divided into two hemispheres that control opposite sides of the body. Although similar in structure, these hemispheres have somewhat separate talents, or areas of specialization.

Split Brains: A House Divided

In a normal brain, the two hemispheres communicate with one another across the corpus callosum, the bundle of fibers that connects them. Whatever happens in one side of the brain is instantly flashed to the other side. What would happen, though, if the two sides were cut off from one another?

In 1953, Ronald E. Myers and Roger W. Sperry took the first step toward answering this question by severing the corpus callosum in cats. They also cut parts of the nerves leading from the eyes to the brain. Normally, each eye transmits messages to both sides of the brain. After this procedure, a cat's left eye sent information only to the left hemisphere and its right eye sent information only to the right hemisphere.

At first, the cats did not seem to be affected much by this drastic operation. But Myers and Sperry showed that something profound had happened. They trained the cats to perform tasks with one eye blindfolded; a cat might have to push a panel with a square on it to get food but ignore a panel with a circle. Then the researchers switched the blindfold to the cat's other eye and tested the animal again. Now the cats behaved as if they had never learned the trick. Apparently, one side of the brain did not know what the other side was doing; it was as if the animals had two minds in one body. Later studies confirmed this result with other species, including monkeys (Sperry, 1964).

In all of the animal studies, ordinary behavior, such as eating and walking, remained normal. In the early 1960s, a team of surgeons decided to try cutting the corpus callosum in patients with debilitating, uncontrollable epilepsy. In severe forms of

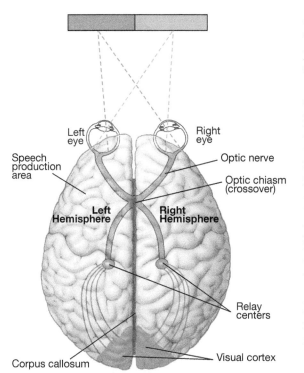

FIGURE 4.10 Visual Pathways
Each cerebral hemisphere receives information from the eyes about the opposite side of the visual field. Thus, if you stare directly at the corner of a room, everything to the left of the juncture is represented in your right hemisphere and vice versa. This is so because half the axons in each optic nerve cross over (at the optic chiasm) to the opposite side of the brain. Normally, each hemisphere immediately shares its information with the other one, but in split-brain patients, severing the corpus callosum prevents such communication.

this disease, disorganized electrical activity spreads from an injured area to other parts of the brain. The surgeons reasoned that cutting the connection between the two halves of the brain might stop the spread of electrical activity from one side to the other. The surgery was done, of course, for the sake of the patients, who were desperate. But there was a bonus for scientists, who would be able to find out what each cerebral hemisphere can do when it is quite literally cut off from the other.

The results of this *split-brain surgery* generally proved successful. Seizures were reduced and sometimes disappeared completely. In their daily lives, split-brain patients did not seem much affected by the fact that the two hemispheres were incommunicado. Their personalities and intelligence remained intact; they could walk, talk, and lead normal lives. Apparently, connections in the undivided deeper parts of the brain kept body movements and other functions normal. But in a series of ingenious studies, Sperry and his

colleagues (and later, other researchers) showed that perception and memory had been affected, just as they had been in the earlier animal research. Sperry won a Nobel Prize for his work.

It had long been known that the two hemispheres are not mirror images of each other. In most people, language is largely handled by the left hemisphere; thus, a person who suffers brain damage because of a stroke—a blockage in or rupture of a blood vessel in the brain—is much more likely to have language problems if the damage is in the left side than if it is in the right. But if the damage is in the right hemisphere, the person may have trouble identifying faces and may get lost easily, even at home. Sperry and his colleagues wanted to know how splitting the brain would affect language and other abilities.

To understand this research, you must know how nerves connect the eyes to the brain. (The human patients, unlike Myers and Sperry's cats, did not have these nerves cut.) When you look straight ahead, everything in the left side of the scene before you—the *visual field*—goes to the right half of your brain, and everything in the right side of the scene goes to the left half of your brain. This is true for both eyes. (See Figure 4.10.)

The procedure was to present information only to one or the other side of the patients' brains. In one early study, the researchers took photographs of different faces, cut them in two, and pasted different halves together (Levy, Trevarthen, & Sperry, 1972). The reconstructed photographs were then presented on slides (see Figure 4.11 on the next page). The person was told to stare at a dot in the middle of the screen, so that half of the image fell to the left of this point and half to the right. Each image was flashed so quickly that the person had no time to move his or her eyes. When the patients were asked to say what they had seen, they named the person in the right part of the image (which would be the little boy in Figure 4.11). But when they were asked to point with their left hands to the face they had seen, they chose the person in the left side of the image (the mustached man in the figure). Further, they claimed they had noticed nothing unusual about the original photographs! Each side of the brain saw a different half-image and automatically filled in the missing part. Neither side knew what the other side had seen.

◉▸ Simulate the Experiment Hemispheric Specialization at MyPsychLab

Why did the patients name one side of the picture but point to the other? When patients responded with speech, it was the left side of the brain, which usually controls speech, doing the talking. And because the left side of the brain had

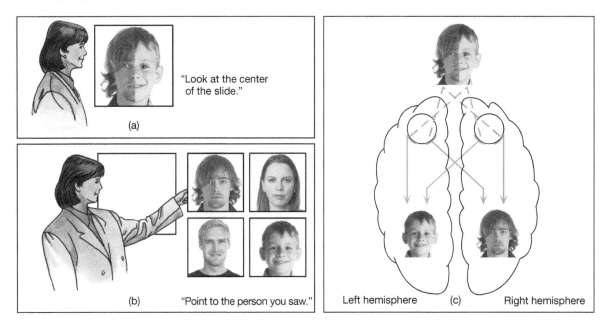

FIGURE 4.11 Divided View
Split-brain patients were shown composite photographs (a) and were then asked to pick out the face they had seen from a series of intact photographs (b). They said they had seen the face on the right side of the composite, yet they pointed with their left hands to the face that had been on the left. Because the two cerebral hemispheres could not communicate, the verbal left hemisphere was aware of only the right half of the picture, and the relatively mute right hemisphere was aware of only the left half (c).

only seen the right side of the image, that was the face it saw and reported. When patients pointed with the left hand, which is controlled by the right side of the brain, the right hemisphere was giving its version of what it had seen.

In another study, the researchers presented slides of ordinary objects and then suddenly flashed a slide of a nude woman. Both sides of the brain were amused, but because only the left side had speech, the two sides responded differently. When the picture was flashed to one woman's left hemisphere, she laughed and identified it as a nude. When it was flashed to her right hemisphere, she said nothing but began to chuckle. Asked what she was laughing at, she said, "I don't know … nothing … oh—that funny machine." The right hemisphere could not describe what it had seen, but it reacted emotionally just the same, and the talking left hemisphere was compelled to come up with a

reasonable explanation for the laughter (Gazzaniga, 1967). Indeed, Michael Gazzaniga (1989), the leading psychological scientist who did this and a lot of other split-brain research, has called the left hemisphere an "interpreter" that is continually providing a reasonable (though not always accurate) story to explain our thoughts, feelings, and behaviors. As another neuroscientist put it, the left hemisphere is the brain's spin doctor (Broks, 2004).

The Two Hemispheres: Allies or Opposites?

The split-brain operation is still being performed, although more rarely, now that better medications are available to treat severe epilepsy. Studies on left–right differences have also been done with people whose brains are intact (Hugdahl & Westerhausen, 2010). Using the technologies

Get Involved!   TAP, TAP, TAP

Have a right-handed friend tap on a paper with a pencil held in the right hand for one minute. Then have the person do the same with the left hand, using a fresh sheet of paper. Finally, repeat the procedure, having the person talk at the same time as tapping. For most people, talking will decrease the rate of tapping—but more for the right hand than for the left, probably because both activities involve the same hemisphere (the left one), and there is competition between them. (Left-handed people vary more in terms of which hemisphere is dominant for language, so the results for them will be less predictable.)

described previously, researchers can find out if one hemisphere has a small "head start" before the corpus callosum transfers information about an image or a sound to the other hemisphere. The results confirm that nearly all right-handed people and a majority of left-handers process language mainly in the left hemisphere. The left side is also more active during some logical, symbolic, and sequential tasks, such as solving math problems and understanding technical material.

In part because of the left hemisphere's linguistic and analytic talents, early researchers often spoke of the left hemisphere as dominant. But today we know that the right hemisphere is far from stupid or passive. It is superior at recognizing facial expressions and also at handling problems requiring spatial-visual abilities, such as reading a map or following a dress pattern. It is active during the creation and appreciation of art and music. It recognizes nonverbal sounds, such as a dog's barking. It also has some language ability. Typically, it can read a word briefly flashed to it and can understand an experimenter's instructions.

Some researchers have also credited the right hemisphere with having a cognitive style that is intuitive and holistic, in contrast to the left hemisphere's more rational and analytic mode. This idea has been oversold by books and programs that promise to make people more creative by making them more "right-brained." In reality, the differences between the two hemispheres are relative, not absolute—a matter of degree. In most

Harley Schwadron/CartoonStock Ltd. CSL

activities, the two sides cooperate naturally, with each making a valuable contribution. In visual perception, the left side generally "sees" the details and the right hemisphere "sees" how they fit together (Robertson, Lamb, & Knight, 1988). In speech perception, the left hemisphere "hears" the individual sounds that make up the words and the right hemisphere "hears" the intonation that tells us if the speaker is happy, sad, or sarcastic. Be cautious, then, about thinking of the two sides as two "minds." As Sperry (1982) himself noted long ago, "The left–right dichotomy ... is an idea with which it is very easy to run wild."

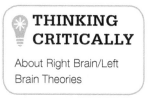

THINKING CRITICALLY

About Right Brain/Left Brain Theories

Recite & Review

✓ Study and Review at MyPsychLab

Recite: Say aloud everything you can about split-brain surgery and the activities of the right and left hemispheres.

Review: Next, go back and read this section again.

Now use as many parts of your brain as necessary to take this *Quick Quiz:*

1. Bearing in mind that both sides of the brain are involved in most activities, identify which of the following is (are) more closely associated with the left hemisphere: (a) enjoying a musical recording, (b) wiggling the left big toe, (c) giving a speech in class, (d) balancing a checkbook, (e) recognizing a long-lost friend.

2. Which hemisphere is called the brain's spin doctor by neurologists?

3. We know that both sides of the brain cooperate with one other normally, but if due to certain interventions, people turned majorly "left-brained," what kind of a world would we be living in?

Answers:

1. c, d 2. left hemisphere 3. People would have a lower emotional quotient with reduced artistic abilities, and a greater focus on logical reasoning. It would not be a very pleasant world to live in because singular rationality devoid of human emotion can be dangerous in many ways.

The Flexible Brain

Many people think of the brain as if it were some fixed and unchanging organ, the same in everyone and essentially the same at birth as at age 8, 18, 28, or 98. It is true that because we are all human and most of us share common early experiences—learning to talk, walk, deal with school and with family members—our brains are fundamentally similar in their basic organization. Yet we also have differing experiences as a result of growing up rich or poor, male or female, nurtured or neglected, and these experiences occur within a particular culture that shapes our values, skills, and opportunities. Such differences can affect the brain's wiring and how it is used.

Experience and the Brain LO 4.15

Our brains are not fully formed at birth. During infancy, synapses proliferate at a great rate (see Figure 4.12). Neurons sprout new dendrites, creating not just new synapses but also more complex connections among the brain's nerve cells (Diamond, 1993; Greenough & Anderson, 1991; Greenough & Black, 1992; Rosenzweig, 1984). New learning and stimulating environments promote this increased complexity. Then, during childhood, synaptic connections that are useful for helping the child respond to the environment are strengthened, whereas those that are not useful wither away, leaving a more efficient neural network. In this way, each brain becomes optimized for its environment. This **plasticity**, the brain's ability to change in response to new experiences, is most pronounced in infancy and early childhood, but it has a resurgence in adolescence and continues throughout life, even into old age.

Many of the experiences that affect us—and our brains—depend on the culture we live in, as children and adults. When two cultures value different skills among their members, when they emphasize different approaches to acquiring common skills, or when they encourage bilingualism, people's brains may reflect those differences. The patterns of brain activity during mathematical processing are different in native Chinese speakers than in native English speakers. Both groups can learn that 2 + 2 = 4, but their brains will take different routes to get there, because of the different ways that the Chinese and English languages process

plasticity The brain's ability to change and adapt in response to experience, by reorganizing or growing new neural connections.

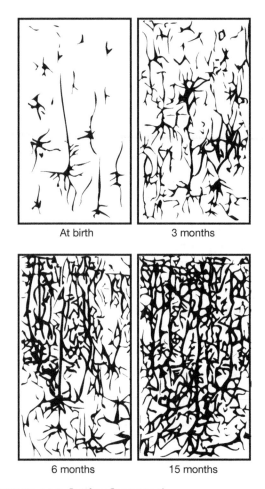

At birth | 3 months

6 months | 15 months

FIGURE 4.12 Getting Connected
Neurons in a newborn's brain are widely spaced, but they immediately begin to form new connections. These drawings show the marked increase in the number of connections from birth to age 15 months.

letters and sounds (Tang et al., 2006). In the words of one researcher, "Much like the changing tide can erode a footprint in the sand, so too can changed experience over time reshape brain activations. In this sense, the brain can be seen as a 'cultural sponge' of sorts, absorbing the regularities of our surrounding physical and social environments" (Ambady, 2011).

Plasticity is especially dramatic in cases of people with brain damage who have experienced remarkable recoveries—such as individuals who cannot recall simple words after a stroke but are speaking normally within months, or who cannot move an arm after a head injury but regain full use of the limb after physical therapy. Their brains have apparently rewired themselves to adapt to the damage (Liepert et al., 2000).

Plasticity is also apparent in some people who have been blind or deaf from birth or early childhood. In the period of rapid development after birth, connections form not only between the eyes and the visual cortex but also between the eyes and the auditory cortex. Likewise, connections form not only between the ears and the auditory cortex but also between the ears and the visual cortex. Typically, experience strengthens the connections between the eyes and the visual cortex, and between the ears and the auditory cortex, and prunes away the other two types (Innocenti & Price, 2005). The intriguing question, therefore, is what happens in the visual cortex of blind people? Is it able to respond to sound because it is not receiving sights?

To answer this question, researchers used PET scans to examine the brains of people as they localized sounds heard through speakers (Gougoux et al., 2005). Some of these people were sighted and others had been blind from their early years. When they heard sounds through both ears, activity in the occipital cortex, an area associated with vision, decreased in the sighted people but *not* in the blind ones. When one ear was plugged, the blind people who did especially well at localizing sounds showed activation in two areas of the occipital cortex; neither sighted people nor blind people with ordinary ability showed that activation. What's more, the degree of activation in these regions was correlated with the blind people's accuracy on the task. The brains of those with the best performance had apparently adapted to blindness by recruiting visual areas to take part in activities involving hearing—a dramatic example of plasticity.

Conversely, when *sighted* people were blindfolded for five days, their brains adapted to their inability to see by temporarily recruiting visual areas for tasks requiring hearing or touch (Pascual-Leone et al., 2005). The visual areas of the brain apparently possess the machinery necessary for processing nonvisual information, but this machinery remains dormant until circumstances require its activation (Amedi et al., 2005). When people have been blind for most of their lives, instead of just five days, new connections may form, permitting lasting structural changes in the brain's wiring.

This research teaches us that the brain is a dynamic organ: Its circuits are continually being modified in response to information, challenges, and changes in the environment. As scientists come to understand this process better, they may be able to apply their knowledge by designing improved rehabilitation programs for people with sensory impairments, developmental disabilities, and brain injuries.

Watch the Video Special Topics: The Plastic Brain at MyPsychLab

Are There "His" and "Hers" Brains? LO 4.16

Many bestselling books have claimed that the "female brain" and the "male brain" are as dissimilar as tomatoes and artichokes. Males and females are said to have hardwired brain differences that explain, among other things, women's allegedly superior intuition and empathy, women's love of talking about feelings and men's love of talking about sports, women's greater verbal ability, men's greater math ability, and why men won't ask for directions when they're lost.

What are we to make of these arguments, which are often presented with lots of fMRI images and other pictures of the brain? Unfortunately, ideology can get in the way of the answer. Some people worry that the research can be used to justify sexist practices and discrimination, a legitimate concern. Others argue, just as legitimately, that ignoring the evidence is antiscientific and an impediment to improving the lives and health of both women and men (Saletan, 2011).

To evaluate this issue intelligently, we need to ask two separate questions: *Do* the brains of males and females differ, on average, in structure or function? And if so, what, if anything, do the differences have to do with men's and women's behavior, abilities, ways of solving problems, or anything else that matters in real life?

The answer to the first question is yes: Many anatomical and biochemical sex differences have been found in animal and human brains (Cahill, 2005; Luders et al., 2004). Some of these differences appear to be universal. An international study combined fMRI data from 24 laboratories and more than 1,000 people in seven countries, from Australia to China to Finland. In every country, men and women showed different patterns of activity across the brain as a whole, even when their brains were not doing mental work. People of all ages, both sexes, and from all cultures showed remarkably similar patterns of connectivity between particular brain regions, but there were also some significant differences between the patterns seen in men and women (Biswal et al., 2010).

In addition, parts of the frontal lobes are larger in women, relative to the overall size of their brains, whereas parts of the parietal cortex and the amygdala are larger in men (Goldstein et al., 2001; Gur et al., 2002). Women also have more cortical folds in the frontal and parietal lobes (Luders et al., 2004). On average, men have more cortical neurons than women do, and some researchers speculate that this difference contributes to a sex difference in spatial abilities, such as skill at mentally rotating objects (Burgaleta et al., 2012). Finally, in men, the right amygdala keeps getting input from the rest of the brain; in women, the left amygdala gets that input. This difference may predispose men and women to encode and remember emotional information differently. In men, better memory is associated with greater

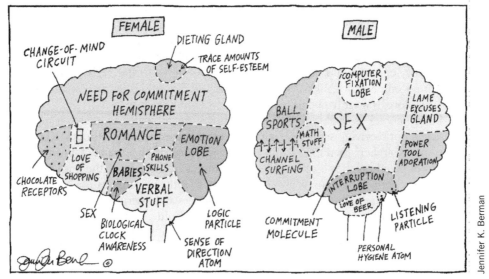

Jennifer K. Berman

Cartoons like this one make most people laugh because men and women do differ, on average, in things like "love of shopping" and "power-tool adoration." But what does the research show about sex differences in the brain? And what do they mean for how people behave in real life?

activity in the right amygdala, but in women, better memory is associated with the left amygdala (Cahill et al., 2004).

Is your own male or female brain spinning yet? The bottom line is that some average sex differences in the brain do exist. But we are still left with our second question: *What do the differences mean for the behavior or personality traits of men and women in ordinary life?* When you hear or read popular accounts of "sex and the brain," keep these cautions in mind:

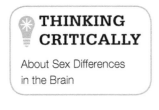

THINKING CRITICALLY

About Sex Differences in the Brain

1 **Many supposed gender differences in intuition, abilities, and traits are stereotypes; they mislead, because the overlap between the sexes is often greater than the difference between them.** Even when gender differences are statistically significant, they are often quite small in practical terms. Some supposed differences, on closer inspection, even disappear. Are women more talkative than men, as many pop-psych books about the sexes assert? To test this assumption, psychologists wired up a sample of men and women with voice recorders that tracked their conversations while they went about their daily lives. The sexes did not differ in the number of words spoken; women and men alike used about 16,000 words per day on average, with large individual differences among the participants (Mehl et al., 2007).

2 **A brain difference does not necessarily produce a difference in behavior.** In many studies, males and females have shown different patterns of brain activity while they were doing something or while an ability was being tested, yet the sexes have not actually differed in the behavior or ability in question (Fine, 2010). If the behavioral difference you are interested in doesn't exist, whatever does it mean if you find a brain difference? One MRI study of men and women with equivalent IQ scores found that women's brains had more white-matter areas related to intelligence, whereas men's had more gray-matter areas related to intelligence (Haier et al., 2005). That's surely an interesting finding for researchers, yet it shouldn't obscure the larger fact that the sexes do not differ in overall intelligence.

3 **Sex differences in the brain do not account for the fact that behavior depends on the situation.** Consider empathy, a skill central to the female stereotype. On self-report questionnaires, women are more likely than men to describe themselves as being high in empathy. But what people say about themselves is often unrelated to how they actually behave in various situations. When we hear that women are hardwired to be empathic, therefore, we need to ask, which women? Under what circumstances? Empathy toward whom? Women are not more empathic than men are toward people they don't like, whether family members they're fighting with or their country's enemies. Over and over, if you watch what people do rather than what they say they would do, and vary the situations in which they do it, gender differences fade (Fine, 2010; Jordan-Young, 2010).

4 **The eternal problem of cause and effect: Some male-female brain differences could be the result rather than the cause of behavioral differences.** We saw that culture and experience are constantly sculpting the circuitry of the brain, affecting the way brains are organized and how they function. Women and men, of course, often have different experiences in childhood and throughout their lives. Thus, when researchers find a sex difference in brain structure or function, they cannot automatically assume that the difference is innate or unchangeable.

5 **The elusive brain difference: Now you see it, now you don't.** Many people tend to think that a brain is a brain; do a study of six brains, and your results should generalize to everyone else's brain. But research on brains, as on anything else, must be replicated, and sometimes the results are surprising.

Researchers once were convinced that men's brains were less lateralized than women's brains, especially in tasks involving language. They thought that women used both sides of the brain when they were doing a task and men primarily one side. But meta-analysis and large scale studies have failed to confirm what "everyone knew" about lateralization (Chiarello et al., 2009; Sommer et al., 2004, 2008).

Scientists differ in their interpretations of the sex-differences research in part because some are focusing on the differences and others are focusing on the similarities. Yet both groups would agree that we all should avoid oversimplifying, jumping to conclusions, and thinking in either–or terms (*either* men and women have "different" brains *or* we are all exactly alike). Critical-thinking skills are something the brains of both sexes can acquire.

Recite & Review

✓ Study and Review at MyPsychLab

Recite: Has your flexible brain absorbed what you've just read? Recite out loud everything you can about plasticity and the effects of experience and maturation on the brain, and what you have learned about sex-related brain differences.

Review: Next, read this section again.

Now take this *Quick Quiz:*

1. During childhood, (a) some synapses are strengthened; (b) some synapses weaken and wither away; (c) both a and b; (d) neither a nor b.

2. A new study reports that in a sample of 11 brains, 4 of the 6 women's brains but only 2 of the 5 men's brains had multiple chocolate receptors. (*Note:* We made this up; there's no such thing as a chocolate receptor—sorry.) The researchers conclude that their findings explain why so many women are addicted to chocolate. What concerns should a critical thinker have about this study?

Answers:

1. c 2. The sample size was small; have the results been replicated? Were the sex differences more impressive than the similarities? Might eating chocolate affect chocolate receptors rather than the other way around? Most important, was the number of receptors actually related to the amount of chocolate eaten by the brains' owners in real life?

PSYCHOLOGY IN THE NEWS REVISITED /////////

Now that you know more about the brain and nervous system, let's return to the opening story about damage to Junior Seau's brain and the brains of other athletes who have played fierce contact sports like football.

Cases like these raise many difficult medical, psychological, and ethical issues. One is the degree of risk that individuals and society should tolerate when damage to this vulnerable organ is a possibility. Of course, many sports carry some risk of serious injury

and even death: skiing, skydiving, horseback riding, motorcycling, and especially bicycling (because so many people don't wear helmets). But contact sports such as football, hockey, and boxing are different, because players may suffer *repeated* blows to the head for years, and the effects, though not dramatic at first, may add up over time.

For any given athlete, it can be difficult to draw firm conclusions about cause and effect, because other factors could also account for a player's subsequent

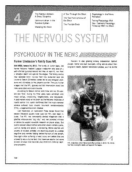

depression, anxiety, and even suicidal tendencies. Many players suffer chronic pain from frequent injuries. Also, as they age, they may feel the sting that comes from being out of the limelight. Some sports fans and commentators are therefore concerned that there has been a rush to judgment about the dangers of repeated "hits." However, a recent study of 85 donated brains from deceased male athletes, veterans, and civilians with histories of repeated traumatic brain injury showed clear evidence of chronic traumatic encephalopathy in 68 of the brains—strong evidence of a link between brain trauma and CTE (McKee et al., 2013). (This study had a control group, and the participants had died of a variety of causes, not just suicide.)

Work on the brains of living athletes is also starting to be done. A small PET scan study of five ex-NFL players who had symptoms of depression, mood swings, and cognitive problems found evidence of chronic traumatic encephalopathy in their brains (Small, et al., 2013). Another study found at least short-term cognitive deficits in high-school soccer players after a single practice session that involved heading the ball (Zhang et al., 2013).

No one knows yet how great the risk of CTE is in contact sports, or whether certain individuals are especially susceptible. However, the evidence to date supports the idea that repeated concussion during sports can cause damage that may have serious psychological consequences, and that such damage is far more prevalent than has previously been realized or acknowledged. What are the implications of this discovery? Should the rules of football, hockey, and other aggressive but wildly popular sports be modified to reduce the risk? Would club owners and fans stand for such changes? Should children and teenagers, whose brains are rapidly developing, be prevented from playing these sports?

The findings you have read about in this chapter teach us that who we are depends in part on well functioning brain cells and nervous-system chemicals—and when they fail to function properly, the consequences can be profound. (Remember Phineas Gage, whose devastating brain injury changed his personality.) The brain's plasticity is an awesome thing, but it does have limits. Each of us is born with just one brain, so we had better treat it with respect! If we do not, there are no brain transplants or prosthetic brains available to help us out.

The study of the brain provides insights into the abilities that those of us with healthy brains take for granted every day. Nearly every week, discoveries by neuroscientists make headlines. Still, their findings should not divert attention from the many other influences that make us who we are: our relationships, our experiences, our place in society, our culture. Keep in your mind (as well as in your brain) that analyzing a human being in terms of physiology alone is like analyzing the Eiffel Tower solely in terms of the materials that were used to build it. Even if we could monitor every cell and circuit of the brain, we would still need to understand the circumstances, thoughts, and cultural rules that affect whether we are gripped by hatred, consumed by grief, lifted by love, or transported by joy.

Taking Psychology With You

Cosmetic Neurology: Tinkering With the Brain

Should healthy people be permitted, even encouraged, to take "brain boosters" or "neuroenhancers," drugs that will sharpen concentration and memory? What about using electrical brain stimulation to rev up a person's mental abilities? If having cosmetic surgery can change parts of your body that you don't like, what's wrong with allowing cosmetic neurology to tinker with parts of your brain that you don't like?

For centuries, people have been seeking ways to stimulate their brains to work more efficiently, with caffeine being an especially popular drug of choice for this purpose. But people who dislike coffee don't complain about the unfair advantage that coffee drinkers have. Likewise, no one has a problem with the finding that omega-3s, found in some kinds of fish, may help protect against age-related mental decline (Beydoun et al., 2007; van Gelder et al., 2007). But when it comes to prescription medications that increase alertness or appear to enhance memory and other cognitive functions, it's another kettle of fish oil, so to speak.

What questions should critical thinkers ask, and what kind of evidence would be needed, to make wise decisions about using such medications? A new interdisciplinary specialty, *neuroethics*, has been formed to address the many legal, ethical, and scientific questions raised by brain research, including those raised by the development of neuroenhancing drugs (Gazzaniga, 2005).

Much of the buzz has focused on Provigil (modafinil), a drug approved for treating narcolepsy and other sleep disorders, and the amphetamines Ritalin and Adderall, approved for attention deficit disorders. Some students, pilots, business people, and jet-lagged travelers are taking one or another of these drugs, either obtaining them illegally from friends or the Internet or getting their own prescriptions. Most of these users claim the drugs help them learn better and stay alert. One review of the literature concluded that Provigil can indeed improve memory for studied material (Smith & Farah, 2011), although the boost that's delivered is less than what most people expect (Repantis et al., 2010).

But the downside to these drugs rarely makes the news. Adderall, like all amphetamines, can cause nervousness, headaches, sleeplessness, allergic rashes, and loss of appetite, and, as the label says, it has "a high potential for abuse." Provigil, too, is habit-forming. Another memory-enhancing drug being studied targets a type of glutamate receptor in the brain. The drug apparently improves short-term memory but at the price of impairing long-term memory (Talbot, 2009).

Even when a drug is benign for most of its users, it may have some surprising and unexpected consequences. For example, the better able people are to focus and concentrate on a task—the reason for taking stimulants in the first place—the less *creative* they often are. Creativity, after all, comes from being able to let our minds roam freely, at leisure. One neurologist therefore worries that the routine use of mind-enhancing drugs among students could create "a generation of very focused accountants" (quoted in Talbot, 2009).

Some bioethicists and neuroscientists feel that the desire for cosmetic neurology is an inevitable part of human nature, because it allows people to adapt to their environments and achieve goals that they could not otherwise achieve (Müller & Schumann, 2011). After all, we use eyeglasses to improve vision and hearing aids to improve hearing; why not use pills to improve our memories and other mental skills? One team of scientists has argued that improving brain function with pills is no more objectionable than eating right or getting a good night's sleep. "In a world in which human

workspans and life spans are increasing," they wrote, cognitive enhancement tools "will be increasingly useful for improved quality of life and extended work productivity, as well as to stave off normal and pathological age-related cognitive declines" (Greely et al., 2008).

Other scientists and social critics, however, consider cosmetic neurology to be a form of cheating that will give those who can

Cosmetic Brain Surgery

afford the drugs an unfair advantage and increase socioeconomic inequalities. They think the issue is no different from the (prohibited) use of performance-enhancing steroids in athletics. Yes, they say, people wear glasses and hearing aids, but glasses and hearing aids do not have side effects or interact negatively with other treatments. Many neuroethicists also worry that ambitious parents will start giving these medications to their children to try to raise the child's

academic performance, despite possible hazards for the child's developing brain. One reporter covering the pros and cons of neuroenhancers concluded that she's not sure she wants to live in a world where people are worked so hard that they have to take drugs simply to keep up (Talbot, 2009).

And what if cognitive enhancement involves not pills but electrical stimulation of your brain? In 2012, neuroscientists in England reported that transcranial direct current stimulation (tDCS) might soon be used with healthy people to improve their math skills, memory, problem-solving, and other mental abilities. One said, "I can see a time when people plug a simple device into an iPad so that their brain is stimulated when they are doing their homework, learning French or taking up the piano." And, he added, tDCS would be a great educational aid for children.

Should you get in line to buy your own tDCS machine? Best to wait. As a critical thinker, you would want to ask how much research on tDCS has been done. (Answer: Most is preliminary laboratory work done only on a small scale.) Has research determined whether there are better or worse ways of using tDCS for different mental abilities? (Not yet.) Has the method been tested on children, whose brains are still developing? (Not yet.) Is it known whether the use of tDCS in the lab can improve people's abilities in everyday life? (Not yet.)

Entrepreneurs may not wait for the answers to these questions before they start trying to market tDCS to parents, patients, and students. But a critical thinker will carefully consider what is to be gained from cosmetic neurology, and what might be lost.

Summary

((Listen to the Audio File at MyPsychLab

- Neuroscientists in psychology and other disciplines study the brain because it is the bedrock of consciousness, perception, memory, and emotion.

The Nervous System: A Basic Blueprint

- The function of the nervous system is to gather and process information, produce responses to stimuli, and coordinate the workings of different cells. Scientists divide it into the *central nervous system* (CNS) and the *peripheral nervous system* (PNS).

The CNS, which includes the brain and *spinal cord*, receives, processes, interprets, and stores information and sends out messages destined for muscles, glands, and organs. The PNS transmits information to and from the CNS by way of *sensory* and *motor nerves*.

- The peripheral nervous system consists of the *somatic nervous system*, which permits sensation and voluntary actions, and the *autonomic nervous system*, which regulates blood vessels, glands, and internal (visceral) organs. The autonomic system usually functions without conscious control, and is further divided into the *sympathetic nervous system*, which mobilizes the body for action, and the *parasympathetic nervous system*, which conserves energy.

Communication in the Nervous System

- Neurons are the basic units of the nervous system. They are held in place by *glial cells*, which also nourish, insulate, protect, and repair them, and thus enable them to function properly. Each neuron consists of *dendrites*, a *cell body*, and an *axon*. In the peripheral nervous system, axons (and sometimes dendrites) are collected together in bundles called *nerves*. Many axons are insulated by a *myelin sheath* that speeds up the conduction of neural impulses and prevents signals in adjacent cells from interfering with one another.

- Research has disproven two old assumptions: that neurons in the human central nervous system cannot be induced to regenerate and that no new neurons form after early infancy. In the laboratory, neurons have been induced to regenerate. Stem cells in various organs, including in brain areas associated with learning and memory, continue to divide and mature throughout adulthood, giving rise to new neurons, and a stimulating environment seems to enhance this process of *neurogenesis. Embryonic stem cells* are pluripotent, meaning that they can generate many different kinds of cells in the body. *Induced pluripotent stem cells*, derived from adult cells, also seem capable of generating different kinds of cells, although it's unclear yet whether they will prove as versatile as embryonic stem cells.

- Communication between two neurons occurs at the *synapse*. When a wave of electrical voltage (*action potential*) reaches the end of a transmitting axon, *neurotransmitter* molecules are released into the *synaptic cleft*. When these molecules bind to *receptor sites* on the receiving neuron, that neuron becomes either more likely to fire or less so. The message that reaches a final destination depends on how frequently particular neurons are firing, how many are firing, what types are firing, their degree of synchrony, and where they are located.

- Neurotransmitters play a critical role in mood, memory, and psychological well-being. *Serotonin, dopamine, acetylcholine*, and *norepinephrine* travel certain paths through the brain; *GABA* and *glutamate* are distributed through the entire brain. Abnormal levels of neurotransmitters have been implicated in several disorders, such as Alzheimer's disease and Parkinson's disease.

- *Hormones*, produced mainly by the *endocrine glands*, affect and are affected by the nervous system. Psychologists are especially interested in *melatonin*, which promotes sleep and helps regulate bodily rhythms; *oxytocin* and *vasopressin*, which play a role in attachment and trust; *adrenal hormones* such as *epinephrine* and *norepinephrine*, which are involved in emotions and stress; and the *sex hormones*, which are involved in the physical changes of puberty, the menstrual cycle (*estrogens* and *progesterone*), sexual arousal (*testosterone*), and some nonreproductive functions.

- *Neuromodulators* modify the strength of neural functions. The *serotonin transporter* helps to recycle serotonin back to the neurons that released it. *Endorphins*, most of which are neuromodulators, reduce pain and promote pleasure. Endorphin levels seem to shoot up when an animal or person is afraid or is under stress.

Mapping the Brain

- Researchers study the brain by using the *lesion method* in animals, and by observing patients with brain damage. In healthy people, they use such techniques as *transcranial magnetic stimulation* (TMS), *transcranial direct current stimulation* (tDCS), *electroencephalograms* (EEGs), *positron emission tomography* (PET scans), *magnetic resonance imaging* (MRI), and *functional MRI* (fMRI).

- These tools reveal which parts of the brain are active during different tasks but do not reveal discrete "centers" for particular functions. Many people fail to realize that brain scans can convey oversimplified and sometimes misleading impressions, and must be interpreted cautiously.

A Tour Through the Brain

- All modern brain theories assume *localization of function*, although many brain areas are likely to be involved in any particular activity.

- In the lower part of the brain, in the *brain stem*, the *medulla* controls automatic functions such as heartbeat and breathing, and the *pons* is involved in sleeping, waking, and dreaming. The *reticular activating system* (RAS) screens incoming information and is responsible for alertness. The *cerebellum* contributes to balance and muscle coordination, and plays a role in cognitive and emotional learning.

- The *thalamus* directs sensory messages to higher centers. The *hypothalamus* is involved in emotion and in drives associated with survival. It also controls the operations of the autonomic nervous system, and sends out chemicals that tell the *pituitary gland* when to "talk" to other endocrine glands.

- The *amygdala* is responsible for evaluating sensory information and quickly determining its emotional importance, and for the initial decision to approach or withdraw from a person or situation; these responses are influenced by your personality traits and current psychological state. It is also involved in forming and retrieving emotional memories.

- The *hippocampus* moderates the reticular activating system, and has been called the "gateway to memory" because it plays a critical role in the formation and retrieval of long-term memories.

- Much of the brain's circuitry is packed into the *cerebrum*, which is divided into two *hemispheres* and is covered by thin layers of cells known collectively as the *cerebral cortex*. The *occipital, parietal, temporal*, and *frontal lobes* of the cortex have specialized (but partially overlapping) functions. The *association cortex* appears to be responsible for higher mental processes. The *frontal lobes*, particularly areas in the *prefrontal cortex*, are involved in social judgment, making and carrying out plans, and decision making.

The Two Hemispheres of the Brain

- Studies of *split-brain* patients, who have had the *corpus callosum* cut, show that the two cerebral hemispheres have somewhat different talents. In most people, language is processed mainly in the left hemisphere, which generally is specialized for logical, symbolic, and sequential tasks. The right hemisphere is associated with spatial-visual tasks, facial recognition, and the creation and appreciation of art and music. In most mental activities, however, the two hemispheres cooperate as partners, with each making a valuable contribution.

The Flexible Brain

• Many synapses have not yet formed at birth. During development, axons and dendrites continue to grow as a result of both physical maturation and experience with the world, and throughout life, new learning results in new synaptic connections in the brain. Thus, the brain's circuits are not fixed and immutable but are continually changing in response to information, challenges, and changes in the environment, a phenomenon known as *plasticity*. In some people who have been blind from an early age, brain regions usually devoted to vision are activated by sound, a dramatic example of plasticity.

• Brain scans and other techniques have revealed some average anatomical and functional differences in the brains of males and females. Controversy exists, however, about what such differences mean in real life. Many behavioral or cognitive "differences" are stereotypes and in reality are small and insignificant,

or even nonexistent. Brain differences do not account for the fact that many behavioral differences depend on the situation. Some findings of brain differences have been widely accepted but then have failed to replicate. Biological differences do not necessarily explain behavioral ones. And sex differences in experience could affect brain organization and function rather than the other way around.

Psychology in the News, Revisited

• The existence of brain damage in some athletes who have suffered repeated concussions raises medical, psychological, and ethical issues. What degree of risk should individuals and society tolerate in aggressive contact sports, and should children and teenagers be prevented from playing them?

Taking Psychology With You

• Scholars in the field of *neuroethics* are addressing the implications of "cosmetic neurology," especially questions raised by the development of drugs that are "neuroenhancers."

Key Terms

central nervous system (CNS) 134
spinal cord 134
spinal reflexes 134
peripheral nervous system (PNS) 135
sensory nerves 135
motor nerves 135
somatic nervous system 135
autonomic nervous system 135
sympathetic nervous system 135
parasympathetic nervous system 135
neuron 136
glia 136
dendrites 137
cell body 137
axon 137
axon terminals 123
myelin sheath 138
nodes 138
nerves 138
neurogenesis 138
stem cells 138

embryonic stem (ES) cells 138
induced pluripotent stem (iPS) cells 139
synaptic cleft 139
synapse 139
action potential 139
synaptic vesicles 140
neurotransmitter 140
receptor sites 140
excitatory and inhibitory effects 140
serotonin 140
dopamine 140
acetylcholine 141
norepinephrine 141
GABA 141
glutamate 141
hormones 141
endocrine glands 141
melatonin 142
pineal gland 142
oxytocin 142
vasopressin 142
adrenal hormones 142
cortisol 142
epinephrine 142
norepinephrine 142

sex hormones (androgens, estrogens, progesterone) 142
neuromodulators 142
serotonin transporter 142
endorphins (endogenous opioid peptides) 142
lesion method 143
transcranial magnetic stimulation (TMS) 143
transcranial direct current stimulation (tDCS) 144
electroencephalogram (EEG) 144
electrode 144
PET scan (positron-emission tomography) 144
MRI (magnetic resonance imaging) 145
functional MRI (fMRI) 145
localization of function 147
brain stem 147
pons 147
medulla 147
reticular activating system (RAS) 147
cerebellum 148
thalamus 148

olfactory bulb 148
hypothalamus 148
pituitary gland 148
amygdala 149
hippocampus 149
cerebrum 149
cerebral hemispheres 149
corpus callosum 149
lateralization 149
cerebral cortex 150
gray and white matter 136
occipital lobes 150
visual cortex 150
parietal lobes 150
somatosensory cortex 150
temporal lobes 150
auditory cortex 150
Wernicke's area 150
frontal lobes 150
motor cortex 150
Broca's area 150
association cortex 150
prefrontal cortex 150
split-brain surgery 153
visual field 153
plasticity 156
neuroethics 160

Neuroscientists study the brain and the rest of the nervous system to gain a better understanding of consciousness, perception, memory, emotion, stress, and mental disorders.

The Nervous System: A Basic Blueprint

↓

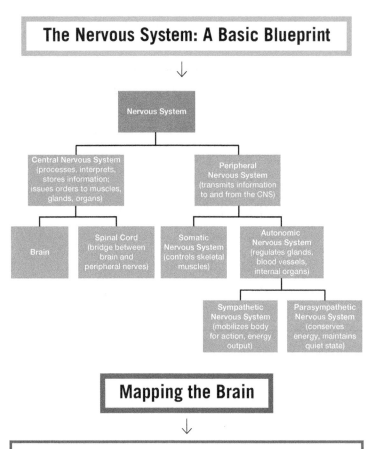

Mapping the Brain

↓

Methods for studying the human brain:

Do something to the brain and observe the consequences:
- **Transcranial magnetic stimulation (TMS):** Briefly inactivates a brain area.
- **Transcranial direct current stimulation (tDCS):** Temporarily stimulates or suppresses cortical activity.

Intervene in behavior and observe the brain:
- **Electroencephalogram (EEG):** brain-wave recording.
- **Positron-emission tomography (PET) scan:** method for analyzing biochemical activity in the brain.
- **Magnetic resonance imaging (MRI):** method for studying body and brain tissue, using magnetic fields and special radio receivers.
- **Functional magnetic resonance imaging (fMRI):** Fast MRI method used to study brain activity associated with specific thoughts and behaviors.

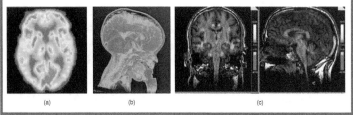

Communication in the Nervous System

↓

- **neurons:** basic units of the nervous system, composed of **dendrites**, a **cell body**, and an **axon**.
- **glial cells:** hold neurons in place as well as nourish, insulate, and protect them.
- **nerves:** bundles of axons and some dendrites in the peripheral nervous system.
- **myelin sheath:** speeds up the conduction of neural impulses and prevents adjacent cells from interfering with one another.
- **stem cells:** give rise to new neurons throughout adulthood (**neurogenesis**).

Communication between neurons occurs at **synapses**, most of which develop after birth:

1. **Action potential** (change in electrical voltage) produces a neutral impulse.
2. **Neurotransmitter** molecules are released into the synaptic cleft and bind to receptor sites on the receiving neuron.

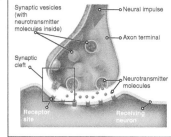

3. Receiving neuron becomes more likely to fire or less likely to fire.

↓

Chemical Messengers in the Nervous System

1. **Neurotransmitters** play a critical role in mood, memory, and psychological well-being. *Serotonin, dopamine, acetylcholine,* and *norepinephrine* travel particular paths through the brain; *GABA* and *glutamate* are distributed throughout the brain.

2. **Hormones,** chemical substances produced primarily by the **endocrine glands,** are released into the bloodstream and affect many organs and cells.
   - **Melatonin** promotes sleep.
   - **Oxytocin** plays a role in attachment and trust.
   - **Adrenal hormones,** such as *epinephrine* and *norepinephrine,* are involved in emotions, memory, and stress.
   - **Sex hormones** are involved in the physical changes of puberty; *estrogens* and *progesterone* are involved in the menstrual cycle, and *testosterone* is involved in sexual arousal.

3. **Neuromodulators** modify the strength of neural functions. Most **endorphins** act as neuromodulators; they reduce pain and promote pleasure.

A Tour Through the Brain

↓

All modern brain theories assume **localization of function**.

- In the **brain stem**, the **medulla** controls automatic functions such as heartbeat and breathing and the **pons** is involved in sleeping, waking, and dreaming. The **reticular activating system (RAS)**, a dense network of neurons, screens incoming information, and is responsible for alertness.
- The **cerebellum** contributes to balance and muscle coordination.
- The **thalamus** directs sensory messages.
- The **hypothalamus** is involved in emotion and drives vital to survival, and controls operations of the autonomic nervous system. It controls the **pituitary gland**, or master gland.
- The **amygdala** evaluates sensory information and determines its emotional importance and helps to make the initial decision to approach or withdraw from a situation.
- The **hippocampus** plays a critical role in forming and retrieving long-term memories.
- The **cerebrum** contains much of the brain's circuitry; it is divided into two **cerebral hemispheres**, connected by a band of fibers called the **corpus callosum**. The cerebrum is covered by thin layers of cells called the **cerebral cortex**.

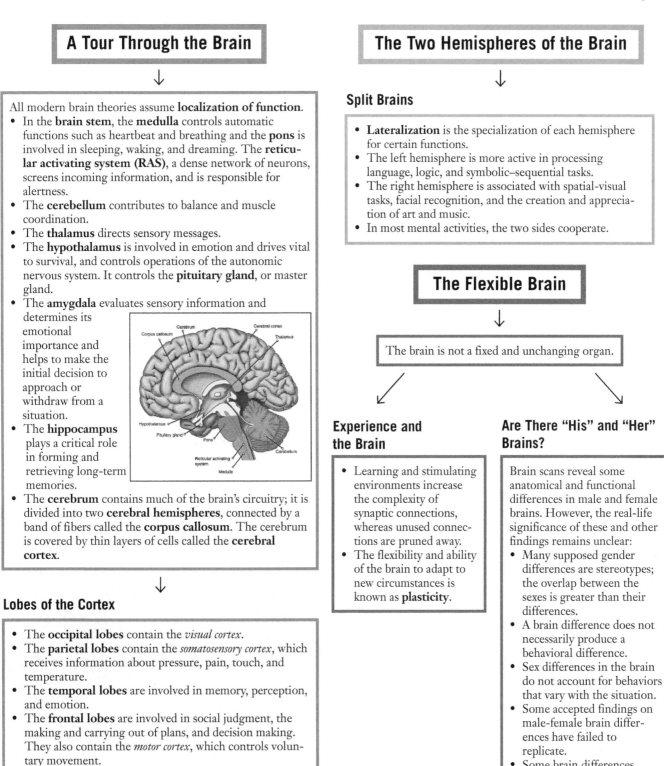

Lobes of the Cortex

- The **occipital lobes** contain the *visual cortex*.
- The **parietal lobes** contain the *somatosensory cortex*, which receives information about pressure, pain, touch, and temperature.
- The **temporal lobes** are involved in memory, perception, and emotion.
- The **frontal lobes** are involved in social judgment, the making and carrying out of plans, and decision making. They also contain the *motor cortex*, which controls voluntary movement.
- The *association cortex* appears to be responsible for higher mental processes.

The Two Hemispheres of the Brain

↓

Split Brains

- **Lateralization** is the specialization of each hemisphere for certain functions.
- The left hemisphere is more active in processing language, logic, and symbolic–sequential tasks.
- The right hemisphere is associated with spatial-visual tasks, facial recognition, and the creation and appreciation of art and music.
- In most mental activities, the two sides cooperate.

The Flexible Brain

↓

The brain is not a fixed and unchanging organ.

Experience and the Brain

- Learning and stimulating environments increase the complexity of synaptic connections, whereas unused connections are pruned away.
- The flexibility and ability of the brain to adapt to new circumstances is known as **plasticity**.

Are There "His" and "Her" Brains?

Brain scans reveal some anatomical and functional differences in male and female brains. However, the real-life significance of these and other findings remains unclear:

- Many supposed gender differences are stereotypes; the overlap between the sexes is greater than their differences.
- A brain difference does not necessarily produce a behavioral difference.
- Sex differences in the brain do not account for behaviors that vary with the situation.
- Some accepted findings on male-female brain differences have failed to replicate.
- Some brain differences could be a result rather than a cause of sex differences in behavior and experience.

CONSCIOUSNESS

PSYCHOLOGY IN THE NEWS /////////////////////////////

Colorado and Washington Legalize Recreational Marijuana

DENVER, November 7, 2012. Last night, Washington and Colorado voters made their states the first to legalize the recreational use of marijuana.

In Colorado, where the state constitution was amended to permit limited use, the tally was 54 percent in favor versus 46 percent against. "The voters have spoken and we have to respect their will," said Governor Hickenlooper, who opposed the amendment. But he added that federal law still bans the drug, "so don't break out the Cheetos or Goldfish too quickly."

In Washington, the vote to legalize small amounts of the drug for people older than 21 and to tax it heavily passed by a similar margin. In contrast, a measure in Oregon went down to defeat, with 55 percent of voters opposed.

Elsewhere, voting on the use of marijuana for medical purposes was mixed. Massachusetts became the 18th state to legalize such use, joining 17 other states and the District of Columbia. But in Arkansas, a measure allowing use for relief of pain by cancer and other patients went down to defeat.

The 50 states currently have a patchwork of laws governing the cultivation, sale, and use of marijuana. As Hickenlooper noted, states that have liberalized their laws are in conflict with federal law, which categorizes the drug as a Schedule 1 controlled substance.

Those states and local jurisdictions that have legalized or decriminalized marijuana are struggling with how to regulate it. In California, the use of less than an ounce for medical purposes has been legal since 1996, and in 2011, a new law changed possession of less than an ounce from a criminal misdemeanor to a civil infraction—like getting a parking ticket. But although some California cities permit pot clubs, others either limit their numbers or prohibit them outright.

Supporters of a constitutional amendment to allow private recreational use of marijuana in Colorado celebrated news of its passage at a gathering in a Denver bar.

In Colorado, a person aged 21 or older may now grow up to six plants privately and may possess more than an ounce of marijuana for recreational use but may not smoke it in public. Commercial sales to recreational users are expected to begin in 2014 and will be taxed, yet many questions remain about whether to limit potency, how to regulate labeling, and how to prevent use by teenagers. Opponents and fans of legalization have hired lobbyists to argue their case, and the new laws are likely to be challenged in the courts.

/////////

Conflicting laws on marijuana show how deeply divided Americans are about this widely used drug. This division is by no means confined to the United States. In March 2013, the president of a United Nations board that monitors narcotic production and use stated that implementation of the Colorado and Washington decisions would violate international laws and treaties. Yet many countries, including Canada, Spain, Italy, Portugal, Israel, Austria, Finland, the Netherlands, and Belgium, have either decriminalized possession of small amounts of marijuana or made it legally available to those who have demonstrated a medical need.

Marijuana is just one of many drugs used throughout the world to alter *consciousness*, the awareness of oneself and of the environment. But consciousness also changes in predictable ways without any help from drugs. Each day we all experience swings in mood, alertness, and efficiency. Each night, we all undergo a dramatic shift in consciousness when the ordinary rules of logic are suspended in the dream world of sleep. Performance and mood may be subject to much longer cycles as well, stretching over a month or even a season.

In this chapter, we will see that fluctuations in subjective experience are accompanied by ups and downs in brain activity, hormone levels, and neurotransmitter levels, and that the mental and physical aspects of consciousness are as intertwined as sunshine and shadow. We will begin with a discussion of the body's natural rhythms, which ebb and flow over time. Next we will zoom in on one fascinating state of consciousness: dreaming. And then we will explore what psychologists have learned about two techniques used to alter consciousness deliberately: hypnosis and the use of recreational drugs. Our goal is to give you a better understanding of the human fascination with altered states of consciousness and why some people use drugs to achieve them.

Are all drugs equally dangerous? Should there be different policies for medical, recreational, and religious use? Are current prohibitions realistic? Does legalization carry dangers? We will return to these issues at the end of the chapter.

You are about to learn ...

- how biological rhythms affect our physiology and performance.
- why you feel out of sync when you fly across time zones or change shifts at work.
- why some people get the winter blues.
- how culture and learning affect reports of "PMS" and estimates of its incidence.

Biological Rhythms: The Tides of Experience

The human body goes through dozens of ups and downs in physiological functioning over the course of a day, a week, and a year, changes that are known as **biological rhythms**. A biological clock

biological rhythms Periodic, more or less regular fluctuations in a biological system; they may or may not have psychological implications.

endogenous Generated from within rather than by external cues.

circadian [sur-CAY-dee-un] rhythms
Biological rhythms with a period (from peak to peak or trough to trough) of about 24 hours; from the Latin *circa*, "about," and *dies*, "a day."

in our brains governs the waxing and waning of hormone levels, urine volume, blood pressure, and even the responsiveness of brain cells to stimulation. Biological rhythms are typically in tune with external time cues, such as changes in clock time, temperature, and daylight, but many rhythms continue to occur even in the absence of such cues; they are **endogenous**, or generated from within.

Circadian rhythms are biological rhythms that occur approximately every 24 hours. The best-known circadian rhythm is the sleep–wake cycle, but hundreds of others affect physiology and performance. For example, body temperature fluctuates about 1 degree centigrade each day, peaking, on average, in the late afternoon and hitting a low point, or trough, in the wee hours of the morning. Other rhythms occur less frequently than once a day—say, once a month, or once a season. In the animal world, seasonal rhythms are common. Birds migrate south in the fall, bears hibernate in the winter, and marine animals become active or inactive, depending on bimonthly changes in the tides. Some seasonal and monthly rhythms also occur in humans. In both men and women, testosterone peaks in the autumn and dips in the spring (Stanton, Mullette-Gillman, & Huettel, 2011); in women, the menstrual cycle occurs roughly every 28 days. Still other rhythms occur more frequently than once a day, many of them on about a 90-minute cycle. In humans, these include physiological changes during sleep and (unless social customs intervene) stomach contractions, hormone levels, susceptibility to visual illusions, verbal and spatial performance, brain-wave responses during cognitive tasks, and daydreaming (Escera, Cilveti, & Grau, 1992; Klein & Armitage, 1979; Kripke, 1974; Lavie, 1976).

With a better understanding of our internal tempos, we may be able to design our days to take better advantage of our bodies' natural tempos.

Circadian Rhythms LO 5.1, LO 5.2

Circadian rhythms evolved in plants, animals, insects, and human beings as an adaptation to the many changes associated with the rotation of the earth on its axis, such as changes in light, air pressure, and temperature.

In most societies, clocks and other external time cues abound, and people's circadian rhythms become tied to them, following a strict 24-hour schedule. Therefore, to identify endogenous rhythms, scientists must isolate volunteers from sunlight, clocks, environmental sounds, and all other cues to time. Some hardy souls have spent weeks isolated in underground caves; usually, however, researchers have had people live in specially designed rooms equipped with audio systems, comfortable furniture, and temperature controls. Free of the tyranny of the timepiece, a few of these people have lived a "day" that is much shorter or longer than 24 hours. If allowed to take daytime naps, however, most people soon settle into a day that averages 5 to 10 minutes longer than 24 hours (Duffy et al., 2011). For many people, alertness, like temperature, peaks in the late afternoon and falls to a low point in the very early morning (Lavie, 2001).

❀ **Explore** the **Concept** Circadian Rhythms at **MyPsychLab**

Stefania Follini (left) spent four months alone in a New Mexico cave, 30 feet underground, as part of an Italian study on biological rhythms. In the absence of clocks, natural light, or changes in temperature, she tended to stay awake for 20 to 25 hours and then sleep for 10. Because her days were longer than usual, when she emerged, she thought she had been in the cave for only two months.

The Body's Clock. Circadian rhythms are controlled by a biological clock, or overall coordinator, located in a tiny cluster of cells in the hypothalamus called the **suprachiasmatic nucleus (SCN)**. Neural pathways from special receptors in the back of the eye transmit information to the SCN and allow it to respond to changes in light and dark. The SCN then sends out messages that cause the brain and body to adapt to these changes. Other clocks also exist, scattered around the body, but for most circadian rhythms the SCN is regarded as the master pacemaker.

The SCN regulates fluctuating levels of hormones and neurotransmitters, and they in turn provide feedback that affects the SCN's functioning. During the dark hours, one hormone regulated by the SCN, **melatonin**, is secreted by the pineal gland, deep within the brain. Melatonin induces sleep. When you go to bed in a darkened room, your melatonin level rises; when light fills your room in the morning, it falls. Melatonin, in turn, appears to help keep the biological clock in phase with the light–dark cycle (Haimov & Lavie, 1996; Lewy et al., 1992).

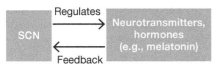

Melatonin treatments have been used to regulate the disturbed sleep–wake cycles of blind people who lack light perception and whose melatonin production does not cycle normally (Sack & Lewy, 1997).

When the Clock Is Out of Sync. Under normal conditions, the rhythms governed by the SCN are in phase with one another. Their peaks may occur at different times, but if you know when one rhythm peaks, you can predict fairly well when another will. It's a little like knowing

Travel can be exhausting, and jet lag makes it worse.

"IF WE EVER INTEND TO TAKE OVER THE WORLD, ONE THING WE'LL HAVE TO DO IS SYNCHRONIZE OUR BIOLOGICAL CLOCKS."

the time in London if you know the time in New York. But when your normal routine changes, your circadian rhythms may be thrown out of phase. Such **internal desynchronization** often occurs when people take airplane flights across several time zones. Sleep and wake patterns usually adjust quickly, but temperature and hormone cycles can take several days to return to normal. The resulting jet lag affects energy level, mental skills, and motor coordination (Sack, 2010).

Internal desynchronization also occurs when workers must adjust to a new shift. Efficiency drops, the person feels tired and irritable, accidents become more likely, and sleep disturbances and digestive disorders may occur. For police officers, first responders, airline pilots, truck drivers, and operators of nuclear power plants, the consequences can be a matter of life and death. Night work itself is not necessarily a problem: With a schedule that always stays the same, even on weekends, people often adapt. However, many swing- and night-shift assignments are made on a rotating basis, so a worker's circadian rhythms never have a chance to resynchronize.

Some scientists hope eventually to help rotating-shift workers adjust more quickly by using melatonin, drugs, or other techniques to "reset the clock," but so far these methods do not seem ready for prime time. Giving shift workers melatonin sometimes helps and sometimes does not; stimulant drugs can improve attention but don't eliminate physical fatigue; and many employers dislike the idea of paying people to take short naps on the job, even though that would make their workers more alert (Kolla & Auger, 2011). When a pilot in Nevada was unable to contact a napping air traffic controller at 2 A.M., scientists butted heads with government officials about who was to

suprachiasmatic [soo-pruh-kye-az-MAT-ick] nucleus (SCN) An area in the hypothalamus of the brain containing a biological clock that governs circadian rhythms.

melatonin A hormone secreted by the pineal gland; it is involved in the regulation of circadian rhythms.

internal desynchronization A state in which biological rhythms are not in phase with one another.

chronotype A person's disposition to be a "morning person" or an "evening person."

seasonal affective disorder (SAD) A disorder in which a person experiences depression during the winter and an improvement of mood in the spring.

blame. "There should be sanctioned on-shift napping. That's the way to handle night-shift work," said one neuroscientist. But the Federal Aviation Administration still bans the practice, while calling for more data.

One reason a simple cure for desynchronization has so far eluded scientists is that circadian rhythms can be affected by illness, stress, exercise, drugs, mealtimes, and many other factors. Also, circadian rhythms can differ greatly from individual to individual. There truly are morning people ("larks") and evening people ("owls"). Scientists call your disposition to be a lark or owl your **chronotype**. Genetic influences may contribute to chronotypes, although attempts to find "chronotype genes" have proven difficult to replicate (Chang et al., 2011; Osland et al., 2011). Your chronotype may change as you age: Adolescents are more likely than children and older adults to be owlish (Biss & Hasher, 2012), which may be why many teenagers have trouble adjusting to school schedules.

You may be able to learn about your own chronotype and biological rhythms through careful self-observation, and you may want to try putting that information to use when planning your daily schedule.

Moods and Long-Term Rhythms

LO 5.3, LO 5.4

According to Ecclesiastes, "To every thing there is a season, and a time for every purpose under heaven." Modern science agrees: Long-term cycles have been observed in everything from the threshold for tooth pain to conception rates. Folklore holds that our moods follow similar rhythms, particularly in response to seasonal changes and, in women, menstrual changes. But do they?

Does the Season Affect Moods? Clinicians report that some people become depressed during particular seasons, typically winter, when periods of daylight are short, a phenomenon that has come

This woman reads and drinks tea for at least 15 minutes a day in front of what she calls her "happy light," which she uses for seasonal depression.

to be known as **seasonal affective disorder (SAD)**. During the winter months, patients report feelings of sadness, lethargy, drowsiness, and a craving for carbohydrates. To counteract the effects of sunless days, physicians and therapists often treat them with phototherapy, having them sit in front of bright fluorescent lights at specific times of the day, usually early in the morning. Some physicians also prescribe antidepressants and other drugs.

Unfortunately, much of the research on the effectiveness of light treatments has been flawed; a review of 173 published studies found that only 20 had used an acceptable design and suitable controls (Golden et al., 2005). But a meta-analysis of the data from those 20 studies did throw some light on the subject, so to speak. When people diagnosed with SAD were exposed to either a brief period (e.g., 30 minutes) of bright light after waking or to light that slowly became brighter, simulating the dawn, their symptoms were in fact reduced. Light therapy even helps people with mild to moderate *non*seasonal depression (Pail et al., 2011).

SAD may occur in people whose circadian rhythms are out of sync; in essence, they have a chronic form of jet lag (Lewy et al., 2006). They may also have some abnormality in the way they

Get Involved! Measuring Your Alertness Cycles

For at least three days, except when you are sleeping, keep an hourly record of your mental alertness level, using this five-point scale: 1 = extremely drowsy or mentally lethargic, 2 = somewhat drowsy or mentally lethargic, 3 = moderately alert, 4 = alert and efficient, 5 = extremely alert and efficient. Does your alertness level appear to follow a circadian rhythm, reaching a high point and a low point once every 24 hours? Or does it follow a shorter rhythm, rising and falling several times during the day? Are your cycles the same on weekends as during the week? Most important, how well does your schedule mesh with your natural fluctuations in alertness?

produce or respond to melatonin: They may produce too much daytime melatonin in the winter, or their morning levels may not fall as quickly as other people's (Wehr et al., 2001). However, it is not clear why light therapy also appears to help some people with nonseasonal depression. True cases of SAD may have a biological basis, but if so, the mechanism remains uncertain. Keep in mind, too, that many people who get the winter blues might do so because they hate cold weather, are physically inactive, do not get outside much, or feel lonely during the winter holidays.

Does the Menstrual Cycle Affect Moods?

Another long-term rhythm, the female menstrual cycle, occurs, on average, every 28 days. During the first half of this cycle, an increase in the hormone estrogen causes the lining of the uterus to thicken in preparation for a possible pregnancy. At mid-cycle, the ovaries release a mature egg, or ovum. Afterward, the ovarian sac that contained the egg begins to produce progesterone, which helps prepare the uterine lining to receive the egg. Then, if conception does not occur, estrogen and progesterone levels fall, the uterine lining sloughs off as the menstrual flow, and the cycle begins again. The interesting question for psychologists is whether these physical changes cause emotional or intellectual changes, as folklore and tradition would have us believe.

Most people nowadays think so. They are often surprised to learn that it was not until the 1970s that a vague cluster of physical and emotional symptoms associated with the days preceding menstruation—including fatigue, headache, irritability, and depression—was packaged together and given a label: *premenstrual syndrome* ("PMS")

Many women say they become more irritable or depressed premenstrually, and PMS remedies line the shelves of drugstores. But what does the evidence show about PMS? How might attitudes and expectations affect reports of emotional symptoms? What happens when women report their daily moods and feelings to researchers without knowing that menstruation is being studied?

(Parlee, 1994). Since then, most laypeople, doctors, and psychiatrists have assumed, uncritically, that many women "suffer" from PMS. What does the evidence actually show?

The answer illustrates the close connection between bodily changes and cultural norms, which help determine how people label and interpret their physical symptoms (Chrisler & Caplan, 2001). PMS symptoms have been reported most often in North America, Western Europe, and Australia. But with the rise of globalization and worldwide drug marketing, reports of such symptoms are increasing in places where they were previously not reported, such as Mexico (Marvan, Diaz-Erosa, & Montesinos, 1998) and Saudi Arabia (Rasheed & Al-Sowielem, 2003). In contrast, in most tribal cultures, PMS is virtually unknown; the concern has been with menstruation itself, which is often considered "unclean." And in some cultures, women report physical symptoms but not emotional ones: In research done in the 1990s, women in China reported fatigue, water retention, pain, and cold (American women rarely report cold), but not depression or irritability (Yu et al., 1996).

In Western societies, many women report physical symptoms associated with menstruation, including cramps, breast tenderness, and water retention. Naturally, these symptoms can make some women feel grumpy, just as pain or discomfort can make men feel grumpy. But emotional symptoms associated with menstruation—notably, irritability and depression—are pretty rare, affecting fewer than 5 percent of women predictably over their cycles (Brooks-Gunn, 1986; Reid, 1991; Walker, 1994).

Then why do so many women think they have a predictable "syndrome," PMS? One possibility is that they tend to notice feelings of depression or irritability when these moods happen to occur premenstrually but overlook times when such moods are *absent* premenstrually. Or, because of cultural attitudes about menstruation, they may label symptoms that occur before a period as PMS ("I am irritable and cranky; I must be getting my period") and attribute the same symptoms at other times of the month to a stressful day or a low grade on an English paper ("No wonder I'm irritable and cranky; I worked really hard on that paper and only got a C"). Some studies have encouraged biases in the reporting of premenstrual and menstrual symptoms by using questionnaires with gloomy titles such as "Menstrual Distress Questionnaire."

To get around these problems, some psychologists have polled women about their psychological and physical well-being without revealing the true purpose of the study (e.g., AuBuchon & Calhoun, 1985; Chrisler, 2000; Gallant et al., 1991; Hardie, 1997; Parlee, 1982; Rapkin, Chang, & Reading, 1988; Slade, 1984; Vila & Beech, 1980; Walker, 1994). Using double-blind procedures, they have had women report symptoms for a single day and have then gone back to see what phase of the menstrual cycle the women were in; or they have had women keep daily records over an extended period of time. Some studies have also included a control group that is usually excluded from research on hormones and moods: men.

In one such study, men and women filled out a symptom questionnaire that made no mention of menstruation (Callaghan et al., 2009). The proportion of men who met the criteria for "premenstrual dysphoric disorder" (PMDD), a presumably more extreme version of PMS, did not differ significantly from the proportion of women who met the criteria! In another study, women and men rated their moods every day for 70 days, for what they thought was a straightforward study of mood and health (McFarlane, Martin, & Williams, 1988). After the 70 days were up, the women then recalled their average moods for each week and phase of their menstrual cycle. In their daily reports, women's moods fluctuated less over the menstrual cycle than over days of the week. (Mondays, it seems, are tough for most of us.) Moreover, women and men reported similar emotional symptoms and number of mood swings at any time of the month, as you can see in Figure 5.1. But in their retrospective reports, women *recalled* feeling angrier, more irritable, and more depressed in the premenstrual and

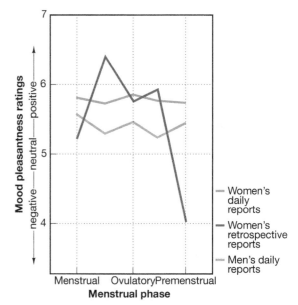

FIGURE 5.1 Mood Changes in Men and Women
In a study that challenged popular stereotypes about PMS, college women and men recorded their moods daily for 70 days without knowing the purpose of the study. At the end of the study, the women thought their moods had been more negative premenstrually than during the rest of the month (purple line), but their daily diaries showed otherwise (orange line). Both sexes experienced only moderate mood changes, and there were no significant differences between women and men at any time of the month (McFarlane, Martin, & Williams, 1988).

menstrual phases than they had reported in their daily journals, showing that their retrospective reports were influenced by their expectations and their belief that PMS is a reliable, recurring set of symptoms.

Other investigations have confirmed that most women do not have typical PMS symptoms even when they firmly believe that they do (Hardie, 1997; McFarlane & Williams, 1994). For example, women often say they cry more premenstrually than at other times, but an interesting Dutch study had women keep "crying diaries" and found no association at all between crying and phase of the menstrual cycle (van Tilburg, Becht, & Vingerhoets, 2003).

The important question is whether the phase of the menstrual cycle a woman is in affects her ability to work, think, study, do brain surgery, run for office, or run a business. In the laboratory, some researchers have found that women tend to be faster on tasks such as reciting words quickly or sorting objects manually before and after ovulation, when their estrogen is high (e.g., Saucier & Kimura, 1998). But empirical research has failed to establish any connection between phase of the menstrual cycle and work efficiency,

"You've been charged with driving under the influence of testosterone."

For both sexes, the hormonal excuse rarely applies.

problem solving, college exam scores, creativity, or any other behavior that matters in real life (Earl-Novell & Jessop, 2005; Golub, 1992; Richardson, 1992). In the workplace, men and women report similar levels of stress, well-being, and ability to do the work required of them—and it doesn't matter whether the women are premenstrual, menstrual, postmenstrual, or nonmenstrual (Hardie, 1997).

In sum, the body only provides the clay for our symptoms and feelings. Learning and culture mold that clay by teaching us which symptoms are important or worrisome, and which are not. Whether we are male or female, the impact of most of the changes associated with our biological rhythms depends on how we interpret and respond to them.

Recite & Review

✅ **Study** and **Review** at MyPsychLab

Recite: It's time to say out loud everything you can about biological rhythms, endogenous rhythms, circadian rhythms, desynchronization, seasonal affective disorder, and PMS.

Review: Next, go back and read this section again.

You have no hormonal excuse for avoiding this *Quick Quiz:*

1. The biological clock controlling the circadian rhythm is located in the _____.

2. Sometimes giving _____ helps people who work in shifts to adjust their body clock.

3. *True or false*: Some people become depressed during particular seasons.

4. A researcher tells male subjects that testosterone usually peaks in the morning and that it probably causes hostility. She then asks them to fill out a "HyperTestosterone Syndrome Hostility Survey" in the morning and again at night. Based on your knowledge of menstrual-cycle findings, what do you think her study will reveal? How could she improve her study?

Answers:

1. hypothalamus 2. melatonin 3. true 4. Because of the expectations that the men now have about testosterone, they may be biased to report more hostility in the morning. It would be better to keep them in the dark about the hypothesis and to measure their actual hormone levels at different points in the day, because individuals vary in their biological rhythms. Also, a control group of women could be added to see whether their hostility levels vary in the same way that men's do. Finally, the title on that questionnaire is pretty biased. A more neutral one, such as "Health and Mood Checklist," would be better.

You are about to learn . . .

- the stages of sleep.
- what happens when we go too long without enough sleep.
- how sleep disorders disrupt normal sleep.
- the mental benefits of sleep.

The Rhythms of Sleep

Perhaps the most perplexing of all our biological rhythms is the one governing sleep and wakefulness. Sleep, after all, puts us at risk: Muscles that are usually ready to respond to danger relax, and senses grow dull. As the British psychologist Christopher Evans (1984) once noted, "The behavior patterns involved in sleep are glaringly, almost insanely, at odds with common sense." Then why is sleep such a profound necessity?

The Realms of Sleep LO 5.5

Let's start with some of the changes that occur in the brain during sleep. Until the early 1950s, little was known about these changes. Then a breakthrough occurred in the laboratory of physiologist Nathaniel Kleitman, who at the time was the only person in the world who had spent his entire career studying sleep. Kleitman had given one of his graduate students, Eugene Aserinsky, the tedious task of finding out whether the slow, rolling eye movements that characterize the onset of sleep continue throughout the night. To both men's surprise, eye movements did occur but they were rapid, not slow (Aserinsky & Kleitman, 1955). Using the electroencephalograph (EEG) to measure the brain's electrical activity (see Chapter 4), these researchers, along with another of Kleitman's students, William Dement, were able to correlate the rapid eye

rapid eye movement (REM) sleep Sleep periods characterized by eye movement, loss of muscle tone, and vivid dreams.

movements with changes in sleepers' brain-wave patterns (Dement, 1992). Adult volunteers were soon spending their nights sleeping in laboratories, while scientists measured changes in their brain activity, muscle tension, breathing, and other physiological responses.

As a result of this research, today we know that during sleep, periods of **rapid eye movement (REM) sleep** alternate with periods of fewer eye movements, or *non-REM sleep*, in a cycle that recurs every 90 minutes or so. The REM periods last from a few minutes to as long as an hour, averaging about 20 minutes in length. Whenever they begin, the pattern of electrical activity from the sleeper's brain changes to resemble that of alert wakefulness. Non-REM periods are themselves divided into distinct stages, each associated with a particular brain-wave pattern (see Figure 5.2).

When you first climb into bed, close your eyes, and relax, your brain emits bursts of *alpha waves*. Compared to brain waves during alert wakefulness, on an EEG recording alpha waves have a somewhat slower rhythm (fewer cycles per second) and a somewhat higher amplitude (height). Gradually, these waves slow down even further, and you drift into the Land of Nod,

passing through four stages, each deeper than the previous one:

Stage 1: Your brain waves become small and irregular, and you feel yourself drifting on the edge of consciousness, in a state of light sleep. If awakened, you may recall fantasies or a few visual images.

Stage 2: Your brain emits occasional short bursts of rapid, high-peaking waves called *sleep spindles*. Minor noises probably won't disturb you.

Stage 3: In addition to the waves that are characteristic of Stage 2, your brain occasionally emits *delta waves*, slow waves with high peaks. Your breathing and pulse have slowed down, your muscles are relaxed, and you are hard to waken.

Stage 4: Delta waves have now largely taken over, and you are in deep sleep. It will probably take vigorous shaking or a loud noise to awaken you. Oddly, though, if you walk in your sleep, this is when you are likely to do so. No one yet knows what causes sleepwalking, which occurs more often in children than adults, but it seems to involve unusual patterns of delta-wave activity (Bassetti et al., 2000).

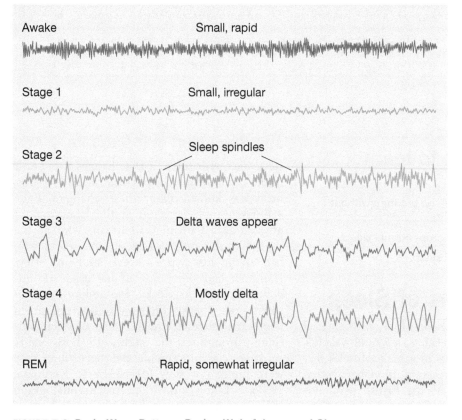

FIGURE 5.2 Brain Wave Patterns During Wakefulness and Sleep
Most types of brain waves are present throughout sleep, but different ones predominate at different stages.

This sequence of stages takes about 30 to 45 minutes. Then you move back up the ladder from Stage 4 to 3 to 2 to 1. At that point, about 70 to 90 minutes after the onset of sleep, something peculiar happens. Stage 1 does not turn into drowsy wakefulness, as one might expect. Instead, your brain begins to emit long bursts of rapid, somewhat irregular waves. Your heart rate increases, your blood pressure rises, and your breathing gets faster and more irregular. Small twitches in your face and fingers may occur. In men, the penis may become somewhat erect as vascular tissue relaxes and blood fills the genital area faster than it exits. In women, the clitoris may enlarge and vaginal lubrication may increase. At the same time, most skeletal muscles go limp, preventing your aroused brain from producing physical movement. You have entered the realm of REM.

Because the brain is extremely active while the body is entirely inactive, REM sleep has also been called "paradoxical sleep." It is during these periods that vivid dreams are most likely to occur. People report dreams when they are awakened from non-REM sleep, too; in one study, dream reports occurred 82 percent of the time when sleepers were awakened during REM sleep, but they also occurred 51 percent of the time when people were awakened during non-REM sleep (Foulkes, 1962). Non-REM dreams, however, tend to be shorter, less vivid, and more realistic than REM dreams, except in the hour or so before a person wakens in the morning.

Explore the Concept Stages of Sleep at MyPsychLab

Occasionally, as the sleeper wakes up, a curious phenomenon occurs. The person emerges from REM sleep before the muscle paralysis characteristic of that stage has entirely disappeared and becomes aware of an inability to move. About 30 percent of the general population has experienced at least one such episode, and about 5 percent have had a "waking dream" in this state. Their eyes are open, but what they "see" are dreamlike hallucinations, most often shadowy figures. They may even "see" a ghost or space alien sitting on their bed or hovering in a hallway, a scary image that they would regard as perfectly normal it if were part of a midnight nightmare. Instead of saying, "Ah! How interesting! I am having a waking dream!" some people interpret this experience literally and come to believe they have been visited by aliens or are being haunted by ghosts (Clancy, 2005; McNally, 2003).

THINKING CRITICALLY

About Waking Dream Images

REM and non-REM sleep continue to alternate throughout the night. As the hours pass, Stages 3 and 4 tend to become shorter or even disappear and REM periods tend to get longer and closer together. This pattern may explain why you are likely to be dreaming when the alarm clock goes off in the morning. But the cycles are far from regular. An individual may bounce directly from Stage 4 back to Stage 2 or go from REM to Stage 2 and then back to REM. Also, the time between REM and non-REM is highly variable, differing from person to person and also within any given individual.

Watch the Video The Basics: Rhythms of Consciousness at MyPsychLab

If you wake people up every time they lapse into REM sleep, nothing dramatic will happen. However, when finally allowed to sleep normally,

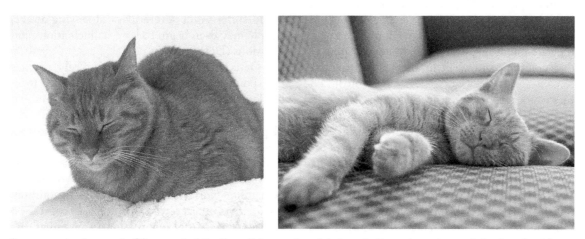

Because cats sleep up to 80 percent of the time, it is easy to catch them in the various stages of slumber. A cat in non-REM sleep remains upright, but during the REM phase its muscles go limp and it flops onto its side.

Whatever your age, sometimes the urge to sleep is irresistible, especially because in fast-paced modern societies, many people of all ages get less sleep than they need. Late hours or inadequate sleep won't do anything for your grade-point average. Daytime drowsiness can interfere with reaction time, concentration, and the ability to learn.

they will spend a longer time than usual in the REM phase, and it will be hard to rouse them. Electrical brain activity associated with REM may burst through into non-REM sleep and even into wakefulness, as if the person is making up for something he or she had been deprived of. Some researchers have proposed that this "something" is connected with dreaming, but that idea has problems. For one thing, in rare cases, brain-damaged patients have lost the capacity to dream, yet they continue to show the normal sleep stages, including REM (Bischof & Bassetti, 2004). Moreover, although nearly all mammals experience REM sleep, it seems unlikely that rats or moles have the cognitive abilities required to construct what we think of as dreams.

✸ Explore the Concept Virtual Brain: Sleep and Dreaming at MyPsychLab

Why We Sleep LO 5.6

A leading sleep scientist, Jerome Siegel (2009), observes that sleep falls along a continuum of states. At one extreme is hibernation, which occurs, for example, in bears, bats, and many rodents. At the other extreme is sleeplessness for significant lengths of time; birds don't sleep while they are migrating, walruses may stop sleeping for days at a time, and whale mothers and their calves remain awake for several weeks after birth. The reason for this variation in sleep patterns, Siegel argues, has to do with which strategy is beneficial for the species. Lions sleep long and deeply, whereas their favorite prey, giraffes, have one of the lowest recorded sleep durations—giraffes had better not sleep deeply if they are going to survive!

In human beings and other species, sleep increases efficiency, in part by decreasing muscle tone and brain and body metabolism during periods of inactivity. This process, says Siegel (2009), is "analogous to turning out the lights when you leave a room." Sleep appears to provide a time-out period, so that the body can eliminate waste products from muscles, repair cells, conserve or replenish energy stores, strengthen the immune system, and recover abilities lost during the day. When we do not get enough sleep, our bodies operate abnormally. Although most people can still get along reasonably well after a day or two of sleeplessness, sleep deprivation that lasts for four days or longer becomes uncomfortable and soon becomes unbearable. This is why forced sleeplessness is a weapon of torture.

The Mental Consequences of Sleeplessness. Sleep is also necessary for normal mental functioning. Chronic sleep deprivation increases levels of the stress hormone cortisol, which may damage or impair brain cells that are necessary for learning and memory (Leproult, Copinschi et al., 1997). Also, new brain cells may either fail to develop or may mature abnormally (Guzman-Marin et al., 2005). Perhaps in part because of such damage, after the loss of even a single night's sleep, mental flexibility, attention, and creativity all suffer. After several days of staying awake, people may even begin to have hallucinations and delusions (Dement, 1978).

Of course, sleep deprivation rarely reaches that point, but people do frequently suffer from milder sleep problems. According to the National Sleep Foundation, about 10 percent of adults are plagued by difficulty in falling or staying asleep. The causes of their insomnia include worry and anxiety, psychological problems, physical problems such as arthritis, and irregular or overly demanding work and study schedules. In addition, many drugs interfere with the normal progression of sleep stages—not just the ones containing caffeine, but also alcohol and some tranquilizers. The result can be grogginess and lethargy the next day.

Another cause of daytime sleepiness is **sleep apnea**, a disorder in which breathing periodically stops for a few moments, causing the person to choke and gasp. Breathing may cease hundreds of times a night, often without the person knowing it. Sleep apnea is seen most often in older males and overweight people but also occurs in others. It has several causes, from blockage of air passages to failure of the brain to control respiration correctly. Over time it can cause high blood pressure and an irregular heartbeat; it may gradually erode a person's health and is associated with a shortened life expectancy (Young et al., 2008).

In **narcolepsy**, an even more serious disorder that often develops in the teenage years, an individual is subject to irresistible and unpredictable daytime attacks of sleepiness lasting from 5 to 30 minutes. When the person lapses into sleep, he or she is likely to fall immediately into the REM stage. Some people experience the paralysis of REM sleep but remain awake; as a result, they may suddenly drop to the ground. This reaction is often triggered by laughing excitedly, but it can also sometimes occur after telling a joke or even having an orgasm (Overeem et al., 2011). The cause of narcolepsy is not well understood, but the disorder has been associated with reduced amounts of a certain brain protein, possibly brought on by an autoimmune problem, a viral infection, or genetic abnormalities (Kornum, Faraco, & Mignot, 2011; Lin, Hungs, & Mignot, 2001; Mieda et al., 2004).

Other disorders also disrupt sleep, including some that cause odd or dangerous behavior. In **REM behavior disorder**, the muscle paralysis associated with REM sleep does not occur, and the sleeper (typically an older male) becomes physically active, often acting out a dream without any awareness of what he is doing (Randall, 2012; Schenck & Mahowald, 2002). If he is dreaming about football, he may try to "tackle" a piece of furniture; if he is dreaming about a kitten, he may try to pet it. Other people may consider this disorder amusing, but it is not at all funny. Sufferers may hurt themselves or others, and they have an increased risk of later developing Parkinson's disease and dementia (Postuma et al., 2009).

Watch the **Video** Special Topics: Sleep Disorders at MyPsychLab

However, the most common cause of daytime sleepiness is the most obvious one—not getting enough sleep. Some people do fine on relatively few hours, but most adults need more than six hours for optimal performance and many adolescents need 10. In the United States, drowsiness is involved in 100,000 vehicle accidents a

"Judith is someone who needs her sleep."

year, causing 1,500 road deaths and 71,000 injuries. Sleep deprivation also leads to accidents and errors in the workplace, a concern especially for first-year doctors doing their medical residency. Although federal law limits work hours for airline pilots, truck drivers, and operators of nuclear plants, in many states medical residents still often work 24- to 30-hour shifts (Landrigan et al., 2008).

Don't doze off as we tell you this, but lack of sleep has also been linked to reduced alertness in school and lower grades. In 1997, a high school in Minneapolis changed its start time from 7:20 A.M. to 8:30 A.M. Teachers watched in surprise as students became more alert and—according to their parents—"easier to live with" (Wahlstrom, 2010). Since then, many other school districts in the United States and other countries have followed suit by starting school later in the morning (Vedaa et al., 2012). Children and teenagers who start school later sleep more, have improved mood, are able to pay more attention in class, and get better test scores; teenage drivers also have fewer car accidents (Fallone et al., 2005; Vorona et al., 2011).

The Mental Benefits of Sleep. Just as sleepiness can interfere with good mental functioning, a good night's sleep can promote it, and not just because you are well rested. In a classic study conducted nearly a century ago, students who slept for eight hours after learning lists of nonsense syllables retained them better than students who went about their usual business (Jenkins & Dallenbach, 1924). For years, researchers attributed this result to the lack of new information coming into the brain during sleep, information that could interfere with already-established memories. Today, however, many scientists believe that sleep is a crucial time for **consolidation**, in which synaptic changes associated with recently stored memories become durable and stable (Racsmány, Conway, & Demeter, 2010).

sleep apnea A disorder in which breathing briefly stops during sleep, causing the person to choke and gasp and momentarily awaken.

narcolepsy A sleep disorder involving sudden and unpredictable daytime attacks of sleepiness or lapses into REM sleep.

REM behavior disorder A disorder in which the muscle paralysis that normally occurs during REM sleep is absent or incomplete, and the sleeper is able to act out his or her dreams.

consolidation The process by which a memory becomes durable and stable.

One theory is that during sleep, the neurons that were activated during the original experience are reactivated, promoting the transfer of memories to long-term storage in the brain and thus making those changes more permanent (Born & Wilhelm, 2012). During sleep, consolidation seems to target important information that we know we might need at a later time. When researchers had people learn new information and then let them sleep, those people who were told before sleeping that they would later be taking a memory test did better on it than those who did not know about the upcoming test (Wilhelm et al., 2011). Sleep strengthens many kinds of memories, including the recollection of events, locations, facts, and emotional experiences, especially negative ones (see Figure 5.3).

Memory consolidation is most closely associated with the slow-wave sleep of Stages 3 and 4 (Rasch et al., 2007). But REM sleep, too, is related to improvements in learning and memory on certain kinds of tasks (Mednick et al., 2011). When people or animals learned a perceptual task and were allowed to get normal REM sleep, their memory for the task was better the next day, even when they had been awakened during non-REM periods. When they were deprived of REM sleep, however, their memories were impaired (Karni et al., 1994). Thus, both periods of sleep, slow-wave and REM, are probably important for consolidation (Born & Wilhelm, 2012).

If sleep enhances memory, then perhaps it also enhances problem solving, which relies on information stored in memory. To find out, German researchers gave volunteers a math test that required them to use two mathematical rules to generate one string of numbers from another and to deduce the final digit in the new sequence as quickly as possible. The volunteers were not told about a hidden shortcut that would enable them to calculate the final digit almost immediately. One group was trained in the evening and then got to snooze for eight hours before returning to the problem. Another group was also trained in the evening but then stayed awake for eight hours before coming back to the problem. A third group was trained in the morning and stayed awake all day, as they normally would, before taking the test. Those people who got the nighttime sleep were nearly three times likelier to discover the hidden shortcut as those in the other two groups (Wagner et al., 2004).

 **Watch** the **Video** In the Real World: Sleep, Memory, and Learning at **MyPsychLab**

Sleep, then, seems essential in memory and problem solving. The underlying biology appears to involve not only the formation of new synaptic connections in the brain but also the weakening of connections that are no longer needed (Donlea, Ramanan, & Shaw, 2009; Gilestro, Tononi, & Cirelli, 2009). In other words, we sleep to

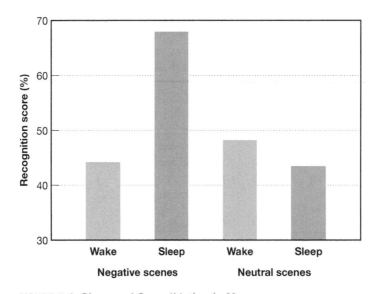

FIGURE 5.3 Sleep and Consolidation in Memory
When college students studied neutral scenes (e.g., an ordinary car) and emotionally negative scenes (e.g., a car totaled in an accident), sleep affected how well they later recognized the objects in the scenes. Students who studied the scenes in the evening and then got a night's sleep before being tested did better at recognizing emotional objects than did those who studied the scenes in the morning and were tested after 12 hours of daytime wakefulness (Payne et al., 2008).

remember, but we also sleep to forget, so that the brain will have space and energy for new learning. Remember that the next time you are tempted to pull an all-nighter. Even a quick nap may help your mental functioning and increase your ability to put together separately learned facts in new ways (Lau, Alger, & Fishbein, 2011; Mednick et al., 2002). Sleep on it.

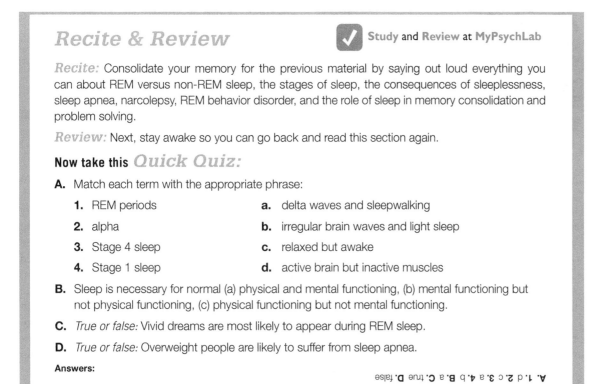

Recite & Review

✓ Study and Review at MyPsychLab

Recite: Consolidate your memory for the previous material by saying out loud everything you can about REM versus non-REM sleep, the stages of sleep, the consequences of sleeplessness, sleep apnea, narcolepsy, REM behavior disorder, and the role of sleep in memory consolidation and problem solving.

Review: Next, stay awake so you can go back and read this section again.

Now take this *Quick Quiz:*

A. Match each term with the appropriate phrase:

1. REM periods   **a.** delta waves and sleepwalking

2. alpha   **b.** irregular brain waves and light sleep

3. Stage 4 sleep   **c.** relaxed but awake

4. Stage 1 sleep   **d.** active brain but inactive muscles

B. Sleep is necessary for normal (a) physical and mental functioning, (b) mental functioning but not physical functioning, (c) physical functioning but not mental functioning.

C. *True or false:* Vivid dreams are most likely to appear during REM sleep.

D. *True or false:* Overweight people are likely to suffer from sleep apnea.

Answers:

A. 1. d 2. c 3. a 4. b B. a C. true D. false

You are about to learn ...

- why Freud called dreams the "royal road to the unconscious."
- how dreams might be related to your current problems and concerns.
- how dreams might be related to ordinary daytime thoughts.
- how dreams might be caused by meaningless brain-stem signals.

Exploring the Dream World LO 5.7

Except in a few rare cases of brain injury, everyone dreams; most people who insist that they never have dreams will report them if they are awakened during REM sleep. In dreaming, the focus of attention is inward, though occasionally an external event, such as a wailing siren, can influence the dream's content. While a dream is in progress, it may be vivid or vague, terrifying or peaceful. It may also make perfect sense—until you wake up and recall it as illogical, bizarre, and disjointed. Although most of us are unaware of our bodies or where we are while we are dreaming, some people say that they occasionally have **lucid dreams**, in which they know they are dreaming and feel as though they are conscious (LaBerge & Levitan, 1995). A few even claim that they can control the action in these dreams, much as a scriptwriter decides what will happen in a movie.

Why do dream images arise at all? Why doesn't the brain just rest, switching off all thoughts and images and launching us into a coma? Why, instead, do we spend our nights taking a chemistry exam, reliving an old love affair, flying through the air, or fleeing from dangerous strangers or animals in the fantasy world of our dreams?

✳ Explore the Concept Are Dreams Meaningful? at MyPsychLab

lucid dreams Dreams in which the dreamer is aware of dreaming.

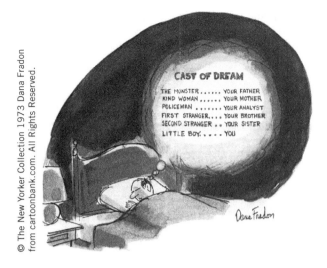

CAST OF DREAM

THE MONSTER . . . . . . YOUR FATHER
KIND WOMAN . . . . . . YOUR MOTHER
POLICEMAN . . . . YOUR ANALYST
FIRST STRANGER . . . . YOUR BROTHER
SECOND STRANGER . . YOUR SISTER
LITTLE BOY. . . . . YOU

In popular culture, many people still hold to psychoanalytic notions of dreaming. Freud (1900/1953) concluded that our nighttime fantasies are "the royal road to the unconscious" because they reflect unconscious conflicts and wishes, which are often sexual or violent in nature. The thoughts and objects in these dreams, he said, are disguised as symbols to make them less threatening: Your father might appear as your brother, a penis might be disguised as a snake or a cigar, or intercourse with a forbidden partner might be expressed as a train entering a tunnel.

Most psychologists today accept Freud's notion that dreams are more than incoherent ramblings of the mind and that they can have psychological meaning. But they also consider psychoanalytic interpretations of dreams to be far-fetched. No reliable rules exist for interpreting the unconscious meaning of a dream, and there is no objective way to know whether a particular interpretation is correct. Nor is there any convincing empirical support for most of Freud's claims. Psychoanalytic interpretations are common in popular books and on the Internet, but they are only the writers' personal hunches. Even Freud warned against simplified "this symbol means that" interpretations; each dream, said Freud, must be analyzed in the context of the dreamer's waking life. Not everything in a dream is symbolic; sometimes, he cautioned, "A cigar is only a cigar."

Dreams as Efforts to Deal With Problems

One modern explanation of dreams holds that they reflect the ongoing *conscious* preoccupations of waking life, such as concerns over relationships, work, sex, or health (Cartwright, 2010; Hall, 1953a, 1953b). In this *problem-focused approach* to dreaming, the symbols and metaphors in a dream do not disguise its true meaning; they convey it. Psychologist Gayle Delaney told of a woman who dreamed she was swimming underwater. The woman's 8-year-old son was on his back, his head above the water. Her husband was supposed to take a picture of them, but for some reason he wasn't doing it, and she was starting to feel as if she were going to drown. To Delaney, the message was obvious: The woman was "drowning" under the responsibilities of child care and her husband wasn't "getting the picture" (in Dolnick, 1990).

The problem-focused explanation of dreaming is supported by findings that dreams are more likely to contain material related to a person's current concerns—such as a breakup or exams—than chance would predict (Domhoff, 1996). Among college students, who are often worried about grades and tests, test-anxiety dreams are common: The dreamer is unprepared for or unable to finish an

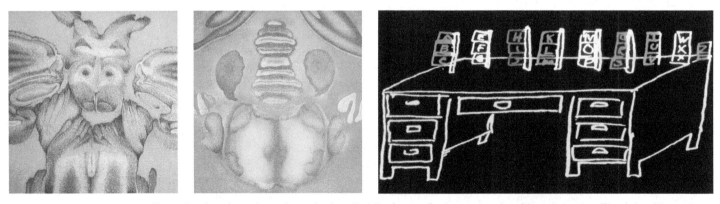

These drawings from dream journals show that the images in dreams can be either abstract or literal. In either case, the dream may reflect a person's concerns, problems, and interests. The two fanciful paintings (left and center) represent the dreams of a person who worked all day long with brain tissue, which the drawings rather resemble. The desk was sketched in 1939 by a scientist to illustrate his dream about a mechanical device for instantly retrieving quotations—a sort of early desktop computer.

exam, or shows up for the wrong exam, or can't find the room where the exam is being given. (Sound familiar?) For their part, instructors sometimes dream that they have left their lecture notes at home or that their PowerPoint slides are blank. Traumatic experiences can also affect people's dreams. In a cross-cultural study in which children kept dream diaries for a week, Palestinian children living in neighborhoods under threat of violence reported more themes of persecution and violence than did Finnish or Palestinian children living in peaceful environments (Punamaeki & Joustie, 1998).

Sleep researcher Rosalind Cartwright (2010) believes that dreams not only reflect our waking concerns but also provide us with an opportunity to resolve them. In people suffering from the grief of divorce, recovery is related to a particular pattern of dreaming: The first dream of the night often comes sooner than it ordinarily would, lasts longer, and is more emotional and story-like. Depressed people's dreams tend to become less negative and more positive as the night wears on, and this pattern, too, predicts recovery (Cartwright et al., 1998). Cartwright concluded that getting through a crisis or a rough period in life takes "time, good friends, good genes, good luck, and a good dream system."

Dreams as Thinking

Like the problem-focused approach, the *cognitive approach* to dreaming emphasizes current concerns, but it makes no claims about problem solving during sleep. In this view, dreaming is simply a modification of the cognitive activity that goes on when we are awake. In dreams, we construct reasonable simulations of the real world, drawing on the same kinds of memories, knowledge, metaphors, and assumptions that we do when we are not sleeping (Antrobus, 1991, 2000; Domhoff, 2003; Foulkes, 1999). Thus, the content of our dreams may include thoughts, concepts, and scenarios that may or may not be related to our daily problems. We are most likely to dream about our families, friends, studies, jobs, worries, or recreational interests—topics that also occupy our waking thoughts.

In the cognitive view, the brain is doing the same kind of work during dreams as it does when we are awake; indeed, parts of the cerebral cortex involved in perceptual and cognitive processing during the waking hours are highly active during dreaming. The difference is that when we are asleep we are cut off from sensory input and feedback from the world and from our bodily movements; the only input to the brain is its own output. Therefore, our dreaming thoughts tend to be less focused and more diffuse than our waking ones—unless we happen to be daydreaming. Our brains show similar patterns of activity when we are night dreaming as when we are daydreaming, a finding that suggests that nighttime dreaming, like daydreaming, might be a mechanism for envisioning events that we think (or hope, or fear) might occur in the future (Domhoff, 2011).

The cognitive view predicts that if a person could be totally cut off from all external stimulation while awake, mental activity would be much like that during dreaming, with the same hallucinatory quality—and this is, in fact, the case (see Chapter 6). The cognitive approach also predicts that as cognitive abilities and brain connections mature during childhood, dreams should change in nature, and they do. Toddlers may not dream at all in the sense that adults do. And although young children may experience visual images during sleep, their cognitive limitations keep them from creating true narratives until age 7 or 8 (Foulkes, 1999). Their dreams are infrequent and tend to be bland and static, often about everyday things ("I saw a dog; I was sitting"). But as they grow older, their dreams gradually become more and more intricate and story-like.

Dreams as Interpreted Brain Activity

A third approach to dreaming, the **activation–synthesis theory**, draws heavily on physiological research, and aims to explain not why you might dream about an upcoming exam, but why you might dream about being a cat that turns into a hippo that plays in a rock band. Often dreams just don't make sense; indeed, most are bizarre, illogical, or both. According to the activation-synthesis explanation, first proposed by psychiatrist J. Allan Hobson (1988, 1990), these dreams are not "children of an idle brain," as Shakespeare called them. They are largely the result of neurons firing spontaneously in the pons (in the lower part of the brain) during REM sleep. These neurons control eye movement, gaze, balance, and posture, and they send messages to sensory and motor areas of the cortex responsible for visual processing and voluntary action during wakefulness.

In this theory, the signals originating in the pons have no psychological meaning in themselves. But the cortex tries to make sense of them by *synthesizing*, or integrating, them with existing knowledge and memories to produce some sort of coherent interpretation. This is just what the cortex does when signals come from sense organs during

activation–synthesis theory The theory that dreaming results from the cortical synthesis and interpretation of neural signals triggered by activity in the lower part of the brain.

ordinary wakefulness. The idea that one part of the brain interprets what has gone on in other parts, whether you are awake or asleep, is consistent with modern theories of how the brain works.

**ACTIVATION–SYNTHESIS
THEORY OF DREAMS**

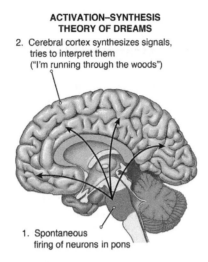

2. Cerebral cortex synthesizes signals, tries to interpret them ("I'm running through the woods")

1. Spontaneous firing of neurons in pons

When neurons fire in the part of the brain that handles balance, for instance, the cortex may generate a dream about falling. When signals occur that would ordinarily produce running, the cortex may manufacture a dream about being chased. Because the signals from the pons occur randomly, the cortex's interpretation—the dream—is likely to be incoherent and confusing. And because the cortical neurons that control the initial storage of new memories are turned off during sleep, we typically forget our dreams on waking unless we write them down or immediately recount them to someone else.

Since Hobson's original formulation, he and his colleagues have added further details and modifications (Hobson, Pace-Schott, & Stickgold, 2000; Hobson et al., 2011). The brain stem, they say, sets off responses in emotional and visual parts of the brain. At the same time, brain regions that handle logical thought and sensations from the external world shut down. These changes could account for the fact that dreams are often emotionally charged, hallucinatory, and illogical.

In sum, wishes do not cause dreams; brain mechanisms do. Dream content, says Hobson (2002), may be "as much dross as gold, as much cognitive trash as treasure, and as much informational noise as a signal of something." But that does not mean dreams are *always* meaningless. Hobson (1988) has argued that the brain "is so inexorably bent upon the quest for meaning that it attributes and even creates meaning when there is little or none to be found in the data it is asked to process." By studying these attributed meanings, you can learn about your unique perceptions, conflicts, and concerns—not by trying to dig below the surface of the dream, as Freud would, but by examining the surface itself. Or you can relax and enjoy the nightly entertainment that dreams provide.

Evaluating Dream Theories LO 5.8

How are we to evaluate these attempts to explain dreaming? All three modern approaches account for some of the evidence, but each one also has its drawbacks.

Are dreams a way to solve problems? It seems pretty clear that some dreams

THINKING CRITICALLY

About Dream Theories

are related to current worries and concerns, but some experts doubt that people can actually solve problems or resolve conflicts while sound asleep (Blagrove, 1996; Squier & Domhoff, 1998). Dreams, they say, merely give expression to our problems. The insights into those problems that people attribute to dreaming could be occurring after they wake up and have a chance to think about what is troubling them.

The activation–synthesis theory has also come in for criticism (Domhoff, 2003). Not all dreams are as disjointed or as bizarre as the theory predicts; in fact, many tell a coherent, if fanciful, story. Moreover, the activation–synthesis

Get Involved! Keep a Dream Diary

It can be fun to record your dreams. Keep a notebook, smartphone, or tablet by your bedside (but if you use a phone or tablet, put it in sleep mode and turn off the sound so you're not awakened by beeps or calls). As soon as you wake up in the morning, or if you awaken during the night while dreaming, record everything you can remember about your dreams, even short fragments. After you have collected several dreams, see which theory or theories discussed in this chapter seem to best explain them. Do your dreams contain any recurring themes? Do you think they provide any clues to your current problems, activities, or concerns? (By the way, if you are curious about other people's dreams, you can find lots of them online at www.dreambank.net.)

approach does not account well for dreaming that goes on outside of REM sleep. Some neuropsychologists emphasize different brain mechanisms involved in dreams, and many believe that dreams do reflect a person's goals and desires.

Finally, the cognitive approach to dreams is promising, but some of its claims remain to be tested against neurological and cognitive evidence. At present, however, it is a leading contender because it incorporates many elements of other theories and fits with what we currently know about waking cognition and cognitive development.

Perhaps it will turn out that different kinds of dreams have different purposes and origins. We all know from experience that some of our dreams are related to daily problems, some are vague and incoherent, and some are anxiety dreams that occur when we are worried or depressed. But whatever the source of the images in our sleeping brains may be, we need to be cautious about interpreting our own dreams or anyone else's. A study of people in India, South Korea, and the United States showed that individuals are biased and self-serving in their dream interpretations, accepting those that fit in with their preexisting beliefs or needs and rejecting those that do not. They will give more weight to a dream in which God commands them to take a year off to travel the world than one in which God commands them to take a year off to work in a leper colony. They are likelier to see meaning in a dream in which a friend protects them from attackers than one in which their romantic partner is caught kissing that same friend (Morewedge & Norton, 2009). Our biased interpretations may tell us more about ourselves than do our actual dreams.

Recite & Review

✔ **Study** and **Review** at MyPsychLab

Recite: No, it's not a dream: It's time to say everything you can remember about lucid dreams, Freud's ideas about dreams, and the three modern theories of dreaming.

Review: Next, read this section again.

Now see if you can dream up the correct answers to this *Quick Quiz:*

In a dream, Andy is a child crawling through a dark tunnel looking for something he has lost. Which theory of dreams would be most receptive to each of the following explanations?

1. Andy recently found a valuable watch he had misplaced.

2. While Andy was sleeping, neurons in his pons that would ordinarily stimulate parts of the brain involved in leg-muscle movements were active.

3. Andy has repressed an early sexual attraction to his mother; the tunnel symbolizes her vagina.

4. Andy has broken up with his lover and is working through the emotional loss.

Answers:

1. the cognitive approach (the dreamer is thinking about a recent experience) 2. the activation–synthesis theory 3. psychoanalytic theory 4. the problem-focused approach

---

You are about to learn...

- common misconceptions about what hypnosis can do.

- the legitimate uses of hypnosis in psychology and medicine.

- two ways of explaining what happens during hypnosis.

The Riddle of Hypnosis

For many years, stage hypnotists, "past-lives channelers," and some psychotherapists have claimed that they can "age regress" hypnotized people to earlier years or even earlier centuries. Some therapists claim that hypnosis helps their patients accurately retrieve long-buried memories, and a few even claim that hypnosis has helped their patients recall alleged abductions by extraterrestrials. What are we to make of all this?

Hypnosis is a procedure in which a practitioner suggests changes in the sensations, perceptions, thoughts, feelings, or behavior of the subject (Kirsch & Lynn, 1995). The hypnotized person, in turn, tries to alter his or her cognitive processes in accordance with the hypnotist's suggestions (Nash & Nadon, 1997). Hypnotic suggestions typically involve performance of an action ("Your arm will slowly rise"), an inability to perform an act ("You

hypnosis A procedure in which the practitioner suggests changes in a subject's sensations, perceptions, thoughts, feelings, or behavior.

will be unable to bend your arm"), or a distortion of normal perception or memory ("You will feel no pain," "You will forget being hypnotized until you hear a bell"). People usually report that their response to a suggestion feels involuntary, as if it happened without their willing it.

To induce hypnosis, the hypnotist typically suggests that the person being hypnotized feels relaxed, is getting sleepy, and feels the eyelids getting heavier and heavier. In a singsong or monotonous voice, the hypnotist may assure the subject that he or she is sinking "deeper and deeper." Sometimes the hypnotist has the person concentrate on a color or a small object. People who have been hypnotized report that the focus of attention turns outward, toward the hypnotist's voice. They sometimes compare the experience to being totally absorbed in a good movie or favorite piece of music. The hypnotized person almost always remains fully aware of what is happening and remembers the experience later unless explicitly instructed to forget it. Even then, the memory can be restored by a prearranged signal.

Because hypnosis has been used for everything from parlor tricks and stage shows to medical and psychological treatments, it is important to understand just what this procedure can and cannot achieve. We will begin with the major findings on hypnosis and then consider two leading explanations of hypnotic effects.

The Nature of Hypnosis LO 5.9

The popular notion of hypnosis—that it is a strange, mystical state of consciousness, a kind of dark art—has interfered with people's understanding of it (Posner & Rothbart, 2011). Since the late 1960s, thousands of scientific articles on hypnosis have appeared, and scientists generally agree on the following points (Kirsch & Lynn, 1995; Nash, 2001; Nash & Nadon, 1997):

1 **Hypnotic responsiveness depends more on the efforts and qualities of the person being hypnotized than on the skill of the hypnotist.** Some people are more responsive to hypnosis than others, but why they are is unknown. Surprisingly, hypnotic susceptibility is unrelated to general personality traits such as gullibility, trust, submissiveness, or conformity (Nash & Nadon, 1997). And it is only weakly related to the ability to become easily absorbed in activities and the world of imagination (Council, Kirsch, & Grant, 1996; Nash & Nadon, 1997).

2 **Hypnotized people cannot be forced to do things against their will.** Like drunkenness, hypnosis can be used to justify letting go of inhibitions ("I know this looks silly, but after all, I'm hypnotized"). Hypnotized individuals may even comply with a suggestion to do something that looks embarrassing or dangerous. But the individual is choosing to turn responsibility over to the hypnotist and to cooperate with the hypnotist's suggestions (Lynn, Rhue, & Weekes, 1990). Hypnotized people will not do anything that actually violates their morals or constitutes a real danger to themselves or others.

3 **Feats performed under hypnosis can be performed by motivated people without hypnosis.** Hypnotized subjects sometimes perform what seem like extraordinary mental or physical feats, but most research finds that hypnosis does not actually enable people to do things that would otherwise be impossible. With proper motivation, support, and encouragement, the same people could do the same things even without being hypnotized (Chaves, 1989; Spanos, Stenstrom, & Johnson, 1988).

4 **Hypnosis does not increase the accuracy of memory.** In rare cases, hypnosis has been used successfully to jog the memories of crime victims, but usually the memories of hypnotized witnesses have been completely mistaken. Although hypnosis does sometimes boost the amount of information recalled, it also increases errors, perhaps because hypnotized people are more willing than others to guess, or because they mistake

Is it hypnosis that enables this woman to stretch out rigidly between two chairs without falling? Audiences at countless demonstrations have assumed so. But research with control groups finds that hypnosis does not confer special abilities that would otherwise be impossible. People can do what this woman is doing when they are not hypnotized and can even balance another person standing or sitting on top of them, without flinching.

vividly imagined possibilities for actual memories (Dinges et al., 1992; Kihlstrom, 1994). Because pseudo memories and errors are so common in hypnotically induced recall, many scientific societies around the world, including the American Psychological Association and the American Medical Association, oppose the use of "hypnotically refreshed" testimony in courts of law

5 **Hypnosis does not produce a literal re-experiencing of long-ago events.** Many people believe that hypnosis can be used to recover memories from as far back as birth. When one clinical psychologist who used hypnosis in his own practice surveyed more than 800 marriage and family therapists, he was dismayed to find that more than half agreed with this common belief (Yapko, 1994). But it is just plain wrong. When people are "regressed" to an early age, their mental and moral performance remains adultlike (Nash, 1987). Their brain wave patterns and reflexes do not become childish; they do not reason as children do or show child-sized IQs. They may use baby talk or report that they feel 4 years old again, but the reason is not that they are actually reliving the experience of being 4; they are just willing to play the role.

6 **Hypnotic suggestions have been used effectively for many medical and psychological purposes.** Although hypnosis is not of much use for finding out what happened in the past, it can be useful in the treatment of psychological and medical problems. Its greatest success is in pain management; some people experience dramatic relief of pain resulting from conditions as diverse as burns, cancer, and childbirth, and others have learned to cope better emotionally with chronic pain. Hypnotic suggestions have also been used in the treatment of stress, anxiety, obesity, asthma, irritable bowel syndrome, chemotherapy-induced nausea, and even skin disorders (Nash & Barnier, 2007; Patterson & Jensen, 2003).

Theories of Hypnosis LO 5.10

Over the years, people have proposed many explanations of what hypnosis is and how it produces its effects. Today, two competing theories predominate.

Dissociation Theories. Years ago, Ernest Hilgard (1977, 1986) argued that hypnosis, like lucid dreaming and even simple distraction, involves **dissociation**, a split in consciousness in which one part of the mind operates independently of the rest of consciousness. In many hypnotized people, said Hilgard, although most of the

mind is subject to hypnotic suggestion, one part is a *hidden observer*, watching but not participating. Unless given special instructions, the hypnotized part remains unaware of the observer.

Hilgard attempted to question the hidden observer directly. In one procedure, hypnotized volunteers had to submerge an arm in ice water for several seconds, an experience that is normally excruciating. They were told that they would feel no pain, but that the unsubmerged hand would be able to signal the level of any hidden pain by pressing a key. In this situation, many people said they felt little or no pain—yet at the same time, their free hand was busily pressing the key. After the session, these people continued to insist that they had felt no pain unless the hypnotist asked the hidden observer to issue a separate report.

The contemporary version of Hilgard's theory holds that during hypnosis, dissociation occurs between two brain systems: the one that processes incoming information about the world and an "executive" system that controls how the information is used. In hypnosis, the executive system turns off and hands its function over to the hypnotist. That leaves the hypnotist able to suggest how the hypnotized person should interpret the world and act in it (Woody & Bowers, 1994; Woody & Sadler, 2012).

DISSOCIATION THEORIES OF HYPNOSIS

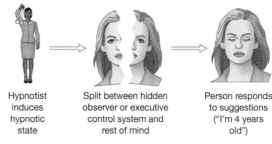

| Hypnotist induces hypnotic state | Split between hidden observer or executive control system and rest of mind | Person responds to suggestions ("I'm 4 years old") |

The Sociocognitive Approach. The *sociocognitive explanation* holds that the effects of hypnosis result from an interaction between the social influence of the hypnotist (the "socio" part) and the abilities, beliefs, and expectations of the subject (the "cognitive" part) (Kirsch, 1997; Sarbin, 1991; Spanos, 1991). The hypnotized person is basically playing a role. This role has analogies in ordinary life, where we willingly submit to the suggestions of parents, teachers, doctors, therapists, and television commercials. In this view, even the "hidden observer" is simply a reaction to the social demands of the situation and the suggestions of the hypnotist (Lynn & Green, 2011).

dissociation A split in consciousness in which one part of the mind operates independently of others.

SOCIOCOGNITIVE THEORIES OF HYPNOSIS

Social influence of hypnotist ("You're going back in time")

Person's own cognitions ("I believe in age regression")

Person conforms to suggestions ("I'm 4 years old")

The hypnotized person is not merely faking or playacting, however. A person who has been instructed to fool an observer by faking a hypnotic state will tend to overplay the role and will stop playing it as soon as the other person leaves the room. In contrast, hypnotized subjects continue to follow the hypnotic suggestions even when they think they are not being watched (Kirsch et al., 1989; Spanos et al., 1993). Like many social roles, the role of "hypnotized person" is so engrossing and involving that actions required by the role may occur without the person's conscious intent.

The sociocognitive view explains why some people under hypnosis have reported apparent "memories" of alien abductions (Clancy, 2005; Spanos, 1996). They go to a therapist or hypnotist seeking an explanation for loneliness, unhappiness, nightmares, puzzling symptoms (such as waking up in the middle of the night in a cold sweat), or the waking dreams we described previously. A therapist who already believes in alien abduction may use hypnosis, along with subtle and not-so-subtle cues about UFOs ("those cold sweats could mean that an alien presence was in your bedroom"), to shape the way the client interprets these symptoms.

The sociocognitive view can also explain apparent cases of past-life regression. In a fascinating program of research, Nicholas Spanos and his colleagues (1991) directed hypnotized Canadian university students to regress past their own births to previous lives.

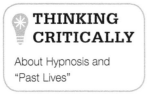

THINKING CRITICALLY

About Hypnosis and "Past Lives"

About a third of the students who already believed in reincarnation reported being able to do so. But when they were asked, while supposedly reliving a past life, to name the leader of their country, say whether the country was at peace or at war, or describe the money used in their community, the students could not do it. (One young man, who thought he was Julius Caesar, said the year was 50 A.D. and he was emperor of Rome.

But Caesar died in 44 B.C. and was never crowned emperor, and dating years as A.D. or B.C. did not begin until several centuries later.) Not knowing anything about the language, customs, and events of their "previous life" did not deter the students from constructing a story about it. They tried to fulfill the requirements of the role by weaving events, places, and people from their *present* lives into their accounts, and by picking up cues from the experimenter.

The researchers concluded that the act of "remembering" another self involves the construction of a fantasy that accords with the rememberer's own beliefs and also the beliefs of others—in this case, those of the authoritative hypnotist.

In an effort to further illuminate the mysteries of hypnosis, psychological scientists are now using functional MRI, PET scans, and other technologies to see if they can find out what is going on in the brain of a hypnotized person. In one PET study, highly hypnotizable people, under hypnosis, were able to visually drain color from a drawing of red, blue, green, and yellow rectangles and, conversely, to see color when the rectangles were shown in gray. When told to see color in the gray drawing, their brains showed activation in areas associated with color perception; when told to see gray in the colored drawing, the same areas showed decreased activation (Kosslyn et al., 2000).

Findings like this one give encouragement to those who believe that hypnosis is a special state, different from elaborate role-playing or extreme concentration. But others feel it's too soon to draw any conclusions about the mechanisms or nature

Sidney Harris/ScienceCartoonsPlus.com

"THE WITNESS HAS BARKED, MEOWED AND GIVEN US FIVE MINUTES OF BABY TALK. I'D SAY HYPNOSIS IS NOT THE ANSWER."

of hypnosis. *Every* experience alters brain activity in some way, and there is no reason to think hypnosis is any exception, however it may work. Moreover, as we've seen, suggestion can often alter people's behavior even without hypnosis. Highly suggestible people can even hallucinate color without being hypnotized (McGeown et al., 2012).

Future work may tell us whether or not hypnosis is a special state of mind—or brain. But whatever the outcome of this debate, all hypnosis researchers agree that hypnosis does not cause memories to become sharper or allow early experiences to be replayed with perfect accuracy. The study of hypnosis is teaching us much about human suggestibility, the power of imagination, and the way we perceive the present and remember the past.

👁 **Watch** the **Video** Thinking Like a Psychologist: The Uses and Limitations of Hypnosis at **MyPsychLab**

Recite & Review

✓ **Study** and **Review** at **MyPsychLab**

Recite: We'd like to plant a suggestion in your mind, that you say aloud what you know about what hypnosis can and cannot achieve, dissociation theories of hypnosis, and the sociocognitive approach to hypnosis.

Review: You are not getting sleepy . . . you are not getting sleepy . . . so reread this section.

Now take this *Quick Quiz:*

A. True or false:

1. A hypnotist tries to alter the cognitive processes of the subject.

2. The memory of the hypnotized person cannot be restored by any method.

3. Hypnosis is dangerous and can violate morals of the subject.

4. Hypnosis confers special abilities to the subjects.

5. According to Nash, when people are "regressed" to an early age, their mental and moral performance remains adultlike.

6. Hypnosis improves and sharpens memory.

B. Some people believe that hypnotic suggestions can bolster the immune system and thus help a person fight disease, but the findings have been mixed and many studies have been flawed (Miller & Cohen, 2001). One therapist dismissed these concerns by saying that a negative result just means that the hypnotist isn't skilled enough. As a critical thinker, can you spot what is wrong with his reasoning? (Think back to Chapter 1 and the way a scientific hypothesis must be stated.)

Answers:

A. 1. true 2. false 3. false 4. false 5. true 6. false **B.** The therapist's argument violates the principle of falsifiability. If a result is positive, he counts it as evidence. But if a result is negative, he refuses to count it as counterevidence ("Maybe the hypnotist just wasn't good enough"). With this kind of reasoning, there is no way to tell whether the hypothesis is right or wrong.

You are about to learn . . .

- the major types of psychoactive drugs.
- how recreational drugs affect the brain.
- how people's prior drug experiences, expectations, and mental sets influence their reactions to drugs.

Consciousness-Altering Drugs

In Jerusalem, hundreds of Hasidic men celebrate the completion of the annual reading of the holy Torah by dancing for hours in the streets. For them, dancing is not a diversion; it is a path to religious ecstasy. In South Dakota, several Lakota (Sioux) adults sit naked in the darkness and crushing heat of the sweat lodge; their goal is euphoria, the transcendence of pain, and connection with the Great Spirit of the Universe. In the Amazon jungle, a young man training to be a shaman, a religious leader, takes a whiff of hallucinogenic snuff made from the bark of the virola tree; his goal is to enter a trance and communicate with animals, spirits, and supernatural forces.

These three rituals, seemingly quite different, are all aimed at release from the confines of ordinary consciousness. Because cultures around the world have devised such practices, some writers believe they reflect a human need, one as

All cultures have found ways to alter consciousness. The Maulavis of Turkey (left), the famous whirling dervishes, spin in an energetic but controlled manner to achieve religious rapture. People in many cultures meditate (center) as a way to quiet the mind and achieve spiritual enlightenment. And in some cultures, psychoactive drugs are used for religious inspiration, as in the case of the Huichol Indians of western Mexico, one of whom is shown here harvesting hallucinogenic mushrooms.

psychoactive drugs
Drugs capable of influencing perception, mood, cognition, or behavior.

stimulants Drugs that speed up activity in the central nervous system.

depressants Drugs that slow activity in the central nervous system.

opiates Drugs, derived from the opium poppy, that relieve pain and commonly produce euphoria.

psychedelic drugs
Consciousness-altering drugs that produce hallucinations, change thought processes, or disrupt the normal perception of time and space.

basic as the need for food and water (Siegel, 1989). William James (1902/1936), who was fascinated by alterations in consciousness, would have agreed. After inhaling nitrous oxide ("laughing gas"), he wrote, "Our normal waking consciousness, rational consciousness as we call it, is but one special type of consciousness, whilst all about it, parted from it by the filmiest of screens, there lie potential forms of consciousness entirely different." But it was not until the 1960s, as millions of people began to seek ways to deliberately alter consciousness, that researchers became interested in the psychology as well as the physiology of psychoactive drugs. The filmy screen described by James finally began to lift.

👁 Watch the Video What's In It For Me?: Altered States of Consciousness at **MyPsychLab**

Classifying Drugs LO 5.11

A **psychoactive drug** is a substance that alters perception, mood, thinking, memory, or behavior by changing the body's biochemistry. Around the world and throughout history, the most common ones have been nicotine, alcohol, marijuana, mescaline, opium, cocaine, peyote—and, of course, caffeine. The reasons for taking psychoactive drugs have varied: to alter consciousness, as part of a religious ritual, for recreation, to decrease physical pain or discomfort, and for psychological escape.

In Western societies, a whole pharmacopeia of recreational drugs exists, and new ones, both natural and synthetic, emerge every few years. Most of these drugs can be classified as **stimulants, depressants, opiates**, or **psychedelics**, depending on their effects on the central nervous system and their impact on behavior and mood (see Table 5.1). Here we describe only their physiological and

psychological effects. Chapter 11 discusses addiction and Chapter 12 covers drugs used in the treatment of mental and emotional disorders.

1 Stimulants speed up activity in the central nervous system. They include nicotine, caffeine, cocaine, amphetamines, methamphetamine (meth), and MDMA (Ecstasy, which also has psychedelic properties). In moderate amounts, stimulants produce feelings of excitement, confidence, and well-being or euphoria. In large amounts, they make a person anxious, jittery, and hyperalert. In very large amounts, they may cause convulsions, heart failure, and death.

Amphetamines are synthetic drugs taken in pill form, injected, smoked, or inhaled. Methamphetamine is structurally similar to amphetamines and is used in the same ways; it comes in two forms, as a powder or in a freebase (purified) form as a crystalline solid. Cocaine is a natural drug, derived from the leaves of the coca plant. Rural workers in Bolivia and Peru chew coca leaf every day without apparent ill effects. In North America, the drug is usually inhaled, injected, or smoked in the highly refined form known as *crack* (because of the cracking sound it makes when smoked). These methods reach the blood and therefore the brain more rapidly, giving the drug a more immediate, powerful, and dangerous effect than when coca leaf is chewed. Amphetamines, methamphetamine, and cocaine make users feel charged up but do not actually increase energy reserves. Fatigue, irritability, and depression may occur when the effects of these drugs wear off.

2 Depressants slow down activity in the central nervous system. They include alcohol, tranquilizers, barbiturates, and most of the common chemicals that some people inhale. Depressants

TABLE 5.1 Some Psychoactive Drugs and Their Effects

Class of Drug	Type	Common Effects	Some Results of Abuse/ Addiction
Amphetamines Methamphetamine MDMA (Ecstasy)*	Stimulants	Wakefulness, alertness, raised metabolism, elevated mood	Nervousness, headaches, loss of appetite, high blood pressure, delusions, psychosis, heart damage, convulsions, death
Cocaine	Stimulant	Euphoria, excitation, feelings of energy, suppressed appetite	Excitability, sleeplessness, sweating, paranoia, anxiety, panic, depression, heart damage, heart failure, injury to nose if sniffed
Nicotine (tobacco)	Stimulant	Varies from alertness to calmness, depending on mental set, setting, and prior arousal; decreases appetite for carbohydrates	*Nicotine:* heart disease, high blood pressure, impaired circulation, erectile problems in men, damage throughout the body due to lowering of a key enzyme *Tar (residue from smoking cigarettes):* lung cancer, emphysema, mouth and throat cancer, many other health risks
Caffeine	Stimulant	Wakefulness, alertness, shortened reaction time	Restlessness, insomnia, muscle tension, heartbeat irregularities, high blood pressure
Alcohol (1–2 drinks)	Depressant	Depends on setting and mental set; tends to act like a stimulant because it reduces inhibitions and anxiety	
Alcohol (several/ many drinks)	Depressant	Slowed reaction time, tension, depression, reduced ability to store new memories or retrieve old ones, poor coordination	Blackouts, cirrhosis of the liver, other organ damage, mental and neurological impairment, psychosis, death with very large amounts
Tranquilizers (e.g., Valium); barbiturates (e.g., phenobarbital)	Depressants	Reduced anxiety and tension, sedation	Increased dosage needed for effects; impaired motor and sensory functions, impaired permanent storage of new information, withdrawal symptoms; possibly convulsions, coma, death (especially when taken with other drugs)
Opium, heroin, morphine, codeine, codone-based pain relievers	Opiates	Euphoria, relief of pain	Loss of appetite, nausea, constipation, withdrawal symptoms, convulsions, coma, possibly death
LSD, psilocybin, mescaline, *Salvia divinorum*	Psychedelics	Depending on the drug: exhilaration, visions and hallucinations, insightful experiences	Psychosis, paranoia, panic reactions
Marijuana	Mild psychedelic (classification controversial)	Relaxation, euphoria, increased appetite, reduced ability to store new memories, other effects depending on mental set and setting	Throat and lung irritation, possible lung damage if smoked heavily

*Ecstasy also has psychedelic properties.

usually make a person feel calm or drowsy, and they may reduce anxiety, guilt, tension, and inhibitions. These drugs enhance the activity of GABA, the neurotransmitter that inhibits the ability of neurons to communicate with each other. In large amounts, depressants may produce insensitivity to pain and other sensations. Like stimulants, in very large doses they can cause irregular heartbeats, convulsions, and death.

People are often surprised to learn that alcohol is a central nervous system depressant. In small amounts, alcohol has some of the effects of a stimulant because it suppresses activity in parts of the brain that normally inhibit impulsive behavior, such as loud laughter and clowning around. In the long run, however, it slows down nervous system activity. Like barbiturates and opiates, alcohol can produce anesthesia, which is why people may pass out when they drink excessively (if they don't throw up first).

Over time, alcohol damages the liver, heart, and brain. Extremely large amounts of alcohol can kill by inhibiting the nerve cells in brain areas that control breathing and heartbeat. Every so often, a news report announces the death of a college student who had large amounts of alcohol "funneled" into him as part of an initiation or drinking competition. On the other hand, *moderate* drinking—a daily drink or two of wine, beer, or liquor—is associated with a variety of health benefits, including antidiabetic effects and a reduced risk of heart attack and stroke (Brand-Miller et al., 2007; Mukamal et al., 2003; Reynolds et al., 2003).

3 Opiates relieve pain. They include opium, derived from the opium poppy; morphine, a derivative of opium; heroin, a derivative of morphine; synthetic drugs such as methadone; and codeine and codone-based pain relievers such as oxycodone and hydrocodone. These drugs work on some of the same brain systems as endorphins do, and some have a powerful effect on the emotions. When injected, opiates can enhance the transmission of dopamine and produce a rush, a sudden feeling of euphoria. They may also decrease anxiety and motivation. Opiates are highly addictive and in large amounts can cause coma and even death.

4 Psychedelic drugs disrupt normal thought processes, such as the perception of time and space. Sometimes they produce hallucinations, especially visual ones. Some psychedelics, such as lysergic acid diethylamide (LSD), are made in the laboratory. Others, such as mescaline (from the peyote cactus), *Salvia divinorum* (from an herb native to Mexico), and psilocybin (from certain species of mushrooms), are natural substances. Emotional reactions to psychedelics vary from

person to person and from one time to another for any individual. A "trip" may be mildly pleasant or unpleasant, a mystical revelation or a nightmare. For decades, research on psychedelics languished because of a lack of funding, but a few clinical researchers are now exploring their potential usefulness in psychotherapy, the relief of psychological distress, the treatment of anxiety disorders, and end-of-life distress (Griffiths et al., 2008). In a pilot study in which moderate doses of psilocybin were administered to 12 patients facing death from advanced-stage cancer, the drug significantly reduced anxiety and despair (Grob et al., 2011).

Some commonly used drugs fall outside these four classifications, combine elements of more than one category, or have uncertain effects. One is marijuana, which is smoked or, less commonly, eaten in foods such as brownies; it is the most widely used illicit drug in North America and Europe. Some researchers classify it as a psychedelic, but others feel that its chemical makeup and its psychological effects place it outside the major classifications. The main active ingredient in marijuana is tetrahydrocannabinol (THC), derived from the hemp plant, *Cannabis sativa*. In some respects, THC appears to be a mild stimulant, increasing heart rate and making tastes, sounds, and colors seem more intense. But users often

Marijuana was once regarded as a mild and harmless sedative, but its image changed in the 1930s, when books and movies began to warn about the dire consequences of the "weed with roots in hell."

report reactions ranging from mild euphoria to relaxation or even sleepiness.

Some researchers believe that heavy smoking of marijuana (which is high in tar) may increase the risk of lung damage (Barsky et al., 1998; Zhu et al., 2000). In moderate doses, the drug can interfere with the transfer of information to long-term memory and impair coordination and reaction times, characteristics it shares with alcohol. In large doses, it can cause hallucinations and a sense of unreality. However, a meta-analysis found only a small impairment in memory and learning among long-term users versus nonusers, less than what typically occurs in long-term users of alcohol and other drugs (Grant et al., 2003). And there have been zero deaths reported from marijuana use.

Cannabis has been used therapeutically for nearly 3,000 years and is one of the fundamental herbs of traditional Chinese medicine. Its benefits have been affirmed in contemporary medicine as well. It reduces the nausea and vomiting that often accompany chemotherapy treatment for cancer and AIDS treatments; it reduces the physical tremors, loss of appetite, and other symptoms caused by multiple sclerosis; it reduces pain; it helps reduce the frequency of seizures in some patients with epilepsy; it helps clear arteries; and it alleviates the retinal swelling caused by glaucoma (Aggarwal et al., 2009; Ben Amar, 2006; Grinspoon & Bakalar, 1993; Steffens et al., 2005).

The Physiology of Drug Effects

LO 5.12

Psychoactive drugs produce their effects by acting on brain neurotransmitters, the chemical substances that carry messages from one nerve cell to another. A drug may increase or decrease the release of neurotransmitters at the synapse; prevent the reuptake (reabsorption) of excess neurotransmitter molecules by the cells that have released them; or interfere with the receptors that a neurotransmitter normally binds to (see Chapter 4). Figure 5.4 shows how one drug, cocaine, increases the amount of norepinephrine and dopamine in the brain by blocking the reuptake of these substances following their release. Cocaine also increases the availability of serotonin (Rocha et al., 1998).

Watch the Video What's In It For Me?: Your Brain on Drugs at MyPsychLab

The biochemical changes associated with drug use affect cognitive and emotional functioning. For example, alcohol activates the receptor for GABA, the inhibitory neurotransmitter found in virtually all parts of the brain. Because GABA is so prevalent

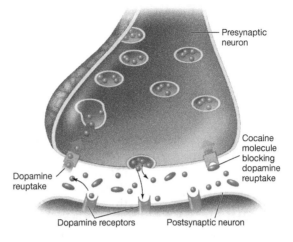

FIGURE 5.4 Cocaine's Effect on the Brain
Cocaine blocks the brain's reuptake of dopamine and norepinephrine, so synaptic levels of these neurotransmitters rise. The result is overstimulation of certain brain receptors and a brief euphoric high. Then, when the drug wears off, a depletion of dopamine may cause the user to crash and become sleepy and depressed.

and modulates the activity of other neurotransmitters, just a couple of drinks can affect perception, response time, coordination, and balance, despite the drinker's own impression of unchanged or even improved performance. As one research team noted, "Alcohol increases mind wandering while simultaneously reducing the likelihood of noticing one's mind wandering" (Sayette, Reichle, & Schooler, 2009). Alcohol also affects memory: Information stored before a drinking session remains intact during the session but is retrieved more slowly (Haut et al., 1989). Consuming small amounts does not seem to affect *sober* mental performance, but binge drinking—usually defined as five or more drinks on a single occasion—can impair later cognitive functioning (Parada et al., 2012). In other words, a Saturday night binge is potentially more dangerous than a daily drink.

As for other recreational drugs, there is little evidence that *light* or *moderate* use can damage the human brain enough to affect cognitive functioning, but nearly all researchers agree that heavy or very frequent use is another matter. In one study, heavy users of methamphetamine had damage to dopamine cells and performed more poorly than other people on tests of memory, attention, and movement, even though they had not used the drug for at least 11 months (Volkow et al., 2001).

Under some conditions, the repeated use of some psychoactive drugs, such as heroin and tranquilizers, can lead to **tolerance**: Over time, more and more of the drug is needed to get the same effect. When habitual heavy users stop taking a drug, they may suffer severe *withdrawal*

tolerance Increased resistance to a drug's effects accompanying continued use.

symptoms, which, depending on the drug, may include nausea, abdominal cramps, sweating, muscle spasms, depression, disturbed sleep, and an intense craving for more of the drug.

The Psychology of Drug Effects

LO 5.13

People often assume that the effects of a drug are automatic, the inevitable result of the drug's chemistry. But reactions to a psychoactive drug involve more than the drug's chemical properties. They also depend on a person's experience with the drug, individual characteristics, environmental setting, and mental set.

THINKING CRITICALLY

About Drug Effects

1 **Experience with the drug refers to the number of times a person has taken it.** When people use a drug—a cigarette, an alcoholic drink, a stimulant—for the first time, their reactions vary markedly, from unpleasant to neutral to enjoyable. But reactions may become increasingly positive once a person has used a drug for a while and has become familiar with its effects.

2 **Individual characteristics include body weight, metabolism, initial state of emotional arousal,** personality characteristics, and physical tolerance for the drug. Women generally get drunker than men on the same amount of alcohol because women are smaller, on average, and their bodies metabolize alcohol differently (Fuchs et al., 1995). Asians are more likely than Anglos to have a genetic variation that prevents alcohol from being metabolized normally. As a result, they may have adverse reactions to even small amounts of alcohol, including severe headaches, facial flushing, and diarrhea (Cloninger, 1990). For any individual, a drug may have one effect after a tiring day and a different one after a rousing quarrel, or the effect may vary with the time of day because of the body's circadian rhythms. And some differences among individuals in their responses to a drug may be due to their personality traits. When people who are prone to anger and irritability wear nicotine patches, dramatic bursts of activity occur in the brain while they are working on competitive or aggressive tasks. These changes do not occur, however, in more relaxed and cheerful people (Fallon et al., 2004).

3 **Environmental setting refers to the context in which a person takes the drug.** A person might have one glass of wine at home alone and feel sleepy but have three glasses of wine at a party and feel full of energy. Someone might feel happy and high drinking with good friends but fearful and nervous drinking with strangers. In an early study of reactions to alcohol, most of

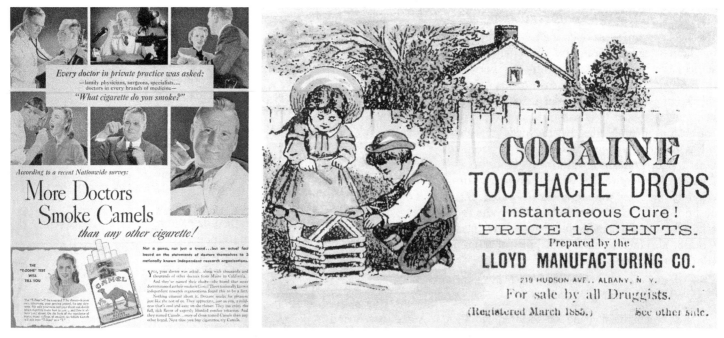

Attitudes about drugs vary with the times. Cigarette smoking was once promoted as healthy and glamorous. And before cocaine was banned in the United States in the 1920s, it was widely touted as a cure for everything from toothaches to timidity. It was used in teas, tonics, throat lozenges, and even soft drinks (including, briefly, Coca-Cola, which derived its name from the coca plant).

the drinkers became depressed, angry, confused, and unfriendly. Then it dawned on the researchers that anyone might become depressed, angry, confused, and unfriendly if asked to drink bourbon at 9:00 A.M. in a bleak hospital room, which was the setting for the experiment (Warren & Raynes, 1972).

4 **Mental set** refers to a person's expectations about the drug's effects and reasons for using it. Some people drink to become more sociable, friendly, or seductive; some drink to try to reduce feelings of anxiety or depression; and some drink to have an excuse for abusiveness or violence. Addicts use drugs to escape from the real world; people living with chronic pain may use the same drugs to function in the real world. The motives for taking a drug greatly influence its effects.

Expectations can sometimes have a more powerful effect than the chemical properties of the drug itself. In several imaginative studies, researchers compared people who were drinking liquor (vodka and tonic) with those who *thought* they were drinking liquor but were actually getting only tonic and lime juice. (Vodka has a subtle taste, and most people could not tell the real and phony drinks apart.) The experimenters found a *"think-drink" effect*: Men behaved more belligerently when

they thought they were drinking vodka than when they thought they were drinking plain tonic water, regardless of the actual content of the drinks. And both sexes reported feeling sexually aroused when they thought they were drinking vodka, whether or not they actually got vodka (Abrams & Wilson, 1983; Marlatt & Rohsenow, 1980).

Expectations and beliefs about drugs are, in turn, shaped by the culture in which you live. The belief that alcohol "releases" anger and aggression, for example, often justifies drunken acts of violence, but alcohol alone doesn't cause them; the link weakens when people believe they will be held responsible for their actions while drunk (Critchlow, 1983). In the nineteenth century, Americans regarded marijuana as a mild sedative. They did not expect it to give them a high, and it didn't; it put them to sleep. Today, motives for using marijuana have changed, and these changes have affected how people respond to it.

None of this means that alcohol and other drugs are merely placebos. Psychoactive drugs, as we have seen, have physiological effects, many of them extremely potent. But by understanding the psychological factors involved in drug use, we can think more critically about the ongoing debate over which drugs, if any, should be legal.

Recite & Review

✔ Study and Review at MyPsychLab

Recite: Say aloud everything you can about psychoactive drugs (stimulants, depressants, opiates, psychedelics, marijuana), the effects of drugs on the brain, withdrawal, tolerance, and psychological influences on drug reactions.

Review: Next, reread this section.

Now take this Quick Quiz:

A. Name the following:
1. A drug that causes impaired permanent storage of new information
2. Any two aftereffects of amphetamines and methamphetamine
3. A central nervous system depressant
4. Drugs that are highly addictive
5. The reaction when a habitual heavy user stops taking a drug

B. A bodybuilder who has been taking anabolic steroids says the drugs make him more aggressive. What are some other possible interpretations?

Answers:

A. 1. tranquilizers (e.g. Valium) 2. irritability; depression 3. alcohol 4. opiates 5. withdrawal symptoms B. The bodybuilder's increased aggressiveness could be due to his expectations (a placebo effect); bodybuilding itself may increase aggressiveness; other influences in his life or other drugs he is taking may be making him more aggressive; or he may only think he is more aggressive, and his behavior may contradict his self-perceptions.

PSYCHOLOGY IN THE NEWS REVISITED /////////

Let's return now to the debate raised by the news story at the beginning of this chapter regarding the legalization of marijuana. What was your reaction to this story?

Because the consequences of drug abuse are so devastating to individuals and to society, people often have trouble thinking critically about drug laws and policies: Which drugs should be legal, which should be illegal, and which should be decriminalized (that is, not made legal, but not used as a reason for arresting and jailing their users)? What if an otherwise illegal drug has medicinal or religious uses? Native Americans are allowed to use peyote in religious rituals, and in 2006, the U.S. Supreme Court ruled unanimously that a small church in New Mexico could use hoasca tea, which contains a prohibited narcotic, in its ceremonies.

At one extreme, some people cannot accept evidence that their favorite drug—be it caffeine, nicotine, alcohol, or marijuana—might have harmful effects. At the other extreme, some cannot accept the evidence that their most hated drug—be it alcohol, morphine, marijuana, or the coca leaf—might not be dangerous in all forms or amounts and might even have some beneficial effects. Both sides often confuse potent drugs with others that have only subtle effects, and confuse light or moderate use with heavy or excessive use.

Once a drug is declared illegal, many people assume it is deadly, even though some legal drugs are more dangerous than illegal ones. Addiction to prescription painkillers and sedatives used for recreational rather than medical purposes has risen dramatically among teenagers and adults. Nicotine, which of course is legal, is as addictive as heroin and cocaine, which are illegal. No one has ever died from smoking marijuana, but according to the Centers for Disease Control and Prevention, tobacco use contributes to between 400,000 and 500,000 deaths in the United States every year, 24 times the number of deaths from all illegal forms of drug use combined, and worldwide it is the largest single cause of preventable deaths. Yet most people have a far more negative view of marijuana, heroin, and cocaine than of nicotine and prescription painkillers.

Emotions run especially high in the debate about marijuana. Heavy use has some physical risks, just as heavy use of any drug does. However, a review of studies done between 1975 and 2003 failed to find any compelling evidence that marijuana causes chronic mental or behavioral problems in teenagers or young adults. The researchers observed that cause and effect could just as well work in the other direction; that is, people with problems could be more likely to abuse the drug (Macleod et al., 2004). Further, as we saw, marijuana has some medical benefits.

In the United States, many people remain committed to the eradication of all currently illegal drugs, whereas others think that all recreational drugs should be legalized or decriminalized. But other strategies are possible. One is to develop programs to reduce or at least delay drug use by young teens (Odgers et al., 2008). Another would legalize narcotics for people who are in chronic pain and marijuana for recreational and medicinal use, but would ban tobacco and most hard drugs. A third approach would regulate where drugs are used (never at work or when driving, for example), provide treatment for addicts, and educate people about the benefits and hazards of particular drugs.

Where, given the research findings, do you stand in this debate? Which illegal psychoactive drugs, if any, do you think should be legalized? Can we create mental sets and environmental settings that promote safe recreational use of some drugs, minimize the likelihood of drug abuse, and permit the medicinal use of beneficial drugs? What do you think?

Taking Psychology With You

How to Get a Good Night's Sleep

You hop into bed, turn out the lights, close your eyes, and wait for slumber. An hour later, you're still waiting. Finally you drop off, but at 3:00 A.M., to your chagrin, you're awake again. By the time the rooster crows, you have put in a hard day's night.

Insomnia affects most people at one time or another, and many people most of the time. No wonder that sleeping pills are a multimillion-dollar business. But many of these pills have side effects, hasten sleep only slightly, or lose their effectiveness over time. Some can actually make matters worse; barbiturates greatly suppress REM sleep, a result that eventually causes wakefulness, and they also suppress Stages 3 and 4, the deeper stages of sleep. Although pills can be helpful on a temporary basis, they do not get at stress and anxiety that may be at the root of your insomnia, and your insomnia is likely to return once you stop taking the pills. Sleep research suggests some alternatives:

Be sure you actually have a sleep problem. Many people only *think* they sleep poorly.

They overestimate how long it takes them to doze off and underestimate how much sleep they are getting. When they are observed in the laboratory, they usually fall asleep in less than 30 minutes and are awake only for short periods during the night (Bonnet, 1990; Carskadon, Mitler, & Dement, 1974). The real test for diagnosing a sleep deficit is not how many hours you sleep—as we saw, people vary in how much they need—but how you feel during the day. Do you doze off without intending to? Do you feel drowsy in class or at meetings?

Get a correct diagnosis of the problem. Do you suffer from sleep apnea? Do you have a physical disorder that is interfering with sleep? Do you live in a noisy place? Are you fighting your biological rhythms by going to bed too early or too late? Do you go to bed early one night and late another? It's better to go to bed at about the same time every night and get up at about the same time every morning.

Avoid excessive use of alcohol or other drugs. Many drugs interfere with sleep, including the caffeine in coffee, tea, cola, "energy drinks," and chocolate. Alcohol suppresses REM sleep; tranquilizers such as Valium and Librium reduce Stage 4 sleep.

Use relaxation techniques. Listening to soft music or meditating at bedtime slows down the heartbeat and breathing, thereby helping you sleep better and longer.

Keep the room dark. Darkness triggers the production of melatonin, which helps bring on sleep. It's best, then, to turn off or put into sleep mode as many light-emitting devices in the room as you can, including smartphones, TVs, and tablets, and to avoid their use if you can before sleeping. When researchers had people play games, watch videos, or read on a tablet for two hours, melatonin levels fell by an average of 22 percent (Wood et al., 2013).

Avoid lying awake for hours waiting for sleep. Your frustration will cause arousal that will keep you awake. If you can't sleep, get up and do something else, preferably something dull and relaxing, in another room. When you feel drowsy, try sleeping again.

When insomnia is related to anxiety and worry, it makes sense to get to the source of your problems, and that may mean a brief round of cognitive-behavior therapy (CBT), which teaches you how to change the negative thoughts that are keeping you awake. (We discuss this form of therapy in Chapter 12.) A placebo-controlled study that compared the effectiveness of a leading sleeping pill and a six-week course of CBT found that both approaches helped alleviate chronic insomnia, but CBT worked better both in the short run and the long run (Jacobs at al., 2004). Other research, too, finds that CBT helps people fall asleep sooner and stay asleep longer (Morin et al., 2006, 2009).

Woody Allen once said, "The lamb and the lion shall lie down together, but the lamb will not be very sleepy." Like a lamb trying to sleep with a lion, you cannot expect to sleep well with stress hormones pouring through your bloodstream and worries crowding your mind. In an evolutionary sense, sleeplessness is an adaptive response to danger and threat. When your anxieties decrease, so may your sleepless nights.

Summary

🔊 Listen to the Audio File at MyPsychLab

Biological Rhythms: The Tides of Experience

- *Consciousness* is the awareness of oneself and the environment. Changing states of consciousness are often associated with *biological rhythms*—periodic fluctuations in physiological functioning. These rhythms are typically tied to external time cues, but many are also *endogenous*, generated from within even in the absence of such cues. *Circadian* fluctuations occur about once a day; other rhythms occur less frequently or more frequently than that.

- When people live in isolation from all time cues, they tend to live a day that is slightly longer than 24 hours. Circadian rhythms are governed by a biological clock in the *suprachiasmatic nucleus* (SCN) of the hypothalamus. The SCN regulates and, in turn, is affected by the hormone *melatonin*, which is responsive to changes in light and dark and which increases during the dark hours. When a person's normal routine changes, the person may experience *internal desynchronization*, in which the usual circadian rhythms are thrown out of phase with one another. The result may be fatigue, mental inefficiency, and an increased risk of accidents.

- Some people experience depression every winter in a pattern that has been labeled *seasonal affective disorder* (SAD), but serious seasonal depression is rare. The causes of SAD are not yet clear. They may involve biological rhythms that are out of phase or an abnormality in the secretion of melatonin, although there can also be other, nonbiological causes. Light treatments can be effective.

- Another long-term rhythm is the menstrual cycle, during which various hormones rise and fall. Well-controlled double-blind studies on PMS do not support claims that emotional symptoms are reliably and universally tied to the menstrual cycle. Overall, women and men do not differ in the emotional symptoms they report or in the number of mood swings they experience over the course of a month. Culture has a major impact on the experience and reporting of PMS symptoms.

- Expectations and learning affect how both sexes interpret bodily and emotional changes. Few people of either sex are likely to undergo dramatic monthly mood swings or personality changes because of hormones.

The Rhythms of Sleep

- During sleep, periods of *rapid eye movement* (REM) alternate with *non-REM sleep* in approximately a 90-minute rhythm. Non-REM sleep is divided into four stages on the basis of characteristic brain wave patterns. During REM sleep, the brain is active, and there are other signs of arousal, yet most of the skeletal muscles are limp; vivid dreams are reported most often during

REM sleep. Some people have had "waking dreams" when they emerge from REM sleep before the paralysis of that stage has subsided, and occasionally, people have misinterpreted the resulting hallucinations as real.

- Sleep is necessary not only for bodily restoration but also for normal mental functioning. Many people get less than the optimal amount of sleep. Some suffer from insomnia, *sleep apnea*, *narcolepsy*, or *REM behavior disorder*, but the most common reason for daytime sleepiness is probably a simple lack of sleep. When schools have delayed their starting time by even an hour, children and teenagers tend to get more sleep, have improved mood, and do better on tests.

- Sleep appears to contribute to the *consolidation* of memories and to subsequent problem solving. These benefits are associated most closely with slow-wave sleep but also with REM sleep, depending on the task.

Exploring the Dream World

- Dreams are sometimes recalled as illogical and disjointed. Some people say they have *lucid dreams* in which they know they are dreaming.

- Freud thought that dreams allow us to express forbidden or unrealistic wishes and desires that have been forced into the unconscious part of the mind and disguised as symbolic images. But there is no objective way to verify psychoanalytic interpretations of dreams and no convincing support for most of Freud's claims.

- Three modern theories of dreaming emphasize the connections between dreams and waking thoughts. The *problem-solving approach to dreams* holds that dreams express current concerns and may even help us solve current problems and work through emotional issues, especially during times of crisis. The *cognitive approach* holds that they are simply a modification of the cognitive activity that goes on when we are awake. The difference is that during sleep we are cut off from sensory input from the world and our bodily movements, so our thoughts tend to be more diffuse and unfocused. The *activation–synthesis theory* holds that dreams occur when the cortex tries to make sense of, or interpret, spontaneous neural firing initiated in the pons. The resulting synthesis of these signals with existing knowledge and memories results in a dream.

- All of the current theories of dreams have some support, and all have weaknesses. Some psychologists doubt that people can solve problems during sleep. The activation–synthesis theory does not seem to explain coherent, story-like dreams or non-REM dreams. The cognitive approach is now a leading contender, although some of its specific claims remain to be tested.

The Riddle of Hypnosis

- *Hypnosis* is a procedure in which the practitioner suggests changes in a person's sensations, perceptions, thoughts, feelings, or behavior, and the person tries to comply. Although hypnosis has been used successfully for many medical and psychological purposes, people hold many misconceptions about what it can accomplish. It cannot force people to do things against their will, confer special abilities that are otherwise impossible, increase the accuracy of memory, or produce a literal re-experiencing of long-ago events.

- A leading explanation of hypnosis is that it involves *dissociation*, a split in consciousness. In one version of this approach, the split is between a part of consciousness that is hypnotized and a *hidden observer* that watches but does not participate. In another version, the split is between an executive-control system in the brain and other brain systems responsible for thinking and acting.

- Another leading approach, the *sociocognitive explanation*, regards hypnosis as a product of normal social and cognitive processes. In this view, hypnosis is a form of role-playing in which the role is so engrossing that the person interprets it as real. Sociocognitive processes can account for the apparent age and past-life "regressions" of people under hypnosis and their reports of alien abductions.

- Brain scans are providing information about what happens in the brain during hypnosis, but to date this research has not resolved the differences between the dissociation and sociocognitive explanations.

Consciousness-Altering Drugs

- In all cultures, people have found ways to produce altered states of consciousness, often by using *psychoactive drugs*, which alter cognition and emotion by acting on neurotransmitters in the brain. Most psychoactive drugs are classified as *stimulants*, *depressants*, *opiates*, or *psychedelics*, depending on their central nervous system effects and their impact on behavior and mood. However, some common drugs, such as marijuana, fall outside these categories.

- When used frequently and in large amounts, some psychoactive drugs can damage neurons in the brain and impair learning and memory. Heavy use of some drugs may lead to *tolerance*, in which increasing dosages are needed for the same effect, and *withdrawal* symptoms if a person tries to quit. Alcohol and marijuana are associated with some health benefits when used in moderation.

- Reactions to a psychoactive drug are influenced not only by its chemical properties but also by the user's prior experience with the drug, individual characteristics, environmental setting, and mental set—the person's expectations and motives for taking the drug. Expectations can be even more powerful than the drug itself, as shown by the *"think–drink" effect*.

Psychology in the News, Revisited

- People often find it difficult to distinguish drug use from drug abuse, heavy use from light or moderate use, and a drug's legality or illegality from its potential dangers and benefits.

Taking Psychology With You

- People who suffer from persistent insomnia should get a correct diagnosis of the sleep problem. Solutions include avoiding heavy use of alcohol or caffeine, keeping the room dark, and meditating. When insomnia is caused by anxiety and worry, cognitive-behavior therapy (CBT) can be helpful.

Key Terms

consciousness 167

biological rhythm 167

endogenous 168

circadian rhythm 168

suprachiasmatic nucleus (SCN) 169

melatonin 169

internal desynchronization 169

chronotypes 170

seasonal affective disorder (SAD) 170

premenstrual syndrome (PMS) 170

rapid eye movement (REM) sleep 174

non-REM sleep 170

alpha waves 170

sleep spindles 174

delta waves 174

sleep apnea 177

narcolepsy 177

REM behavior disorder 177

consolidation 177

lucid dream 179

problem-focused approach to dreaming 180

cognitive approach to dreaming 181

activation–synthesis theory of dreams 181

hypnosis 183

dissociation 185

hidden observer 185

sociocognitive explanation of hypnosis 185

psychoactive drugs 188

stimulants 188

depressants 188

opiates 188

psychedelic drugs 188

tolerance 191

"think–drink" effect 193

Consciousness is the awareness of oneself and the environment.

Biological Rhythms: The Tides of Experience

↓

Biological rhythms are periodic fluctuations in physiological functioning, synchronized to external cues or **endogenous** (generated from within).

Circadian Rhythms

Circadian rhythms occur about once a day.

Circadian rhythms are governed by a biological clock in the **suprachiasmatic nucleus (SCN)** in the hypothalamus.

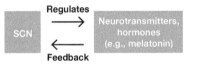

Melatonin, secreted by the pineal gland, helps keep the biological clock in phase with the light-dark cycle.

Internal desynchronization occurs when circadian rhythms are out of phase with one another.

Moods and Long-Term Rhythms

- **Seasonal affective disorder (SAD)** seems to affect some people; light treatments may help.
- Well-controlled double-blind studies of PMS do not support claims that emotional symptoms are tied to the menstrual cycle in most women, or that the menstrual cycle affects the ability to work or study.
- In many studies, when participants have been unaware that the research is about the menstrual cycle, men have reported the same mood changes that women do.
- Expectations and learning affect interpretations of bodily and emotional changes for both sexes.

Why We Sleep

Across species, sleep falls along a continuum from hibernation to sleeplessness for long lengths of time. In humans, sleep is necessary not only for bodily restoration but for normal mental functioning.

The Rhythms of Sleep

↓

Periods of **rapid eye movement (REM)** alternate with *non-REM sleep* in about a 90-minute rhythm.
- The body is limp.
- The brain is active.
- Vivid dreams occur.

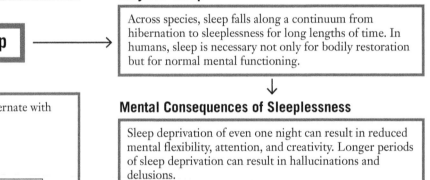

Mental Consequences of Sleeplessness

Sleep deprivation of even one night can result in reduced mental flexibility, attention, and creativity. Longer periods of sleep deprivation can result in hallucinations and delusions.

Sleep disorders include:
- **Sleep apnea**, in which breathing periodically stops for a few moments, causing the person to choke or gasp.
- **Narcolepsy**, in which an individual is subject to irresistible and unpredictable daytime attacks of sleepiness or actual sleep, lasting from five to 30 minutes.
- **REM behavior disorder**, in which the muscle paralysis characteristic of REM sleep does not occur and people become physically active while asleep.

↓

Mental Benefits of Sleep

Evidence shows that sleep:
- Contributes to **consolidation** and retention of memories.
- Enhances problem-solving ability.

Exploring the Dream World

↓

Dreams appear to be out of our control, although some people report having **lucid dreams**, in which they control the action. Freud's psychoanalytic theory held that dreams provide insight into unconscious motives and desires, but no objective method exists for verifying psychoanalytic interpretations of dreams.

There are three leading modern theories of dreams:
1. The *problem-solving approach* holds that dreams reflect the ongoing conscious concerns of waking life and may help us resolve them.
2. The *cognitive approach* holds that dreams are a modification of normal waking cognitive activity.
3. The **activation–synthesis theory** holds that dreams occur when the cortex tries to make sense of spontaneous neural firing initiated in the pons during REM sleep.

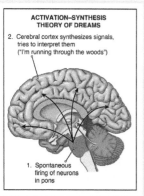

ACTIVATION–SYNTHESIS THEORY OF DREAMS

2. Cerebral cortex synthesizes signals, tries to interpret them ("I'm running through the woods")

1. Spontaneous firing of neurons in pons

The Riddle of Hypnosis

↓

Hypnosis is a procedure in which the practitioner suggests changes in a person's sensations, perceptions, thoughts, feelings, or behavior.
- Hypnotic responsiveness depends more on the efforts and qualities of the person being hypnotized than on the skill of the hypnotist.
- Hypnotized people cannot be forced to do things against their will.
- Feats performed under hypnosis can be performed by motivated people without hypnosis.
- Hypnosis does not increase the accuracy of memory or produce a literal re-experiencing of long-ago events.
- Hypnotic suggestions have been used effectively for many medical and psychological purposes.

→

Theories of Hypnosis

1. The **dissociation** view is that hypnosis is a split in consciousness between a hypnotized part of the mind and a *hidden observer* or an executive control system.

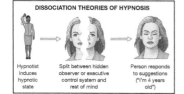

DISSOCIATION THEORIES OF HYPNOSIS

Hypnotist induces hypnotic state

Split between hidden observer or executive control system and rest of mind

Person responds to suggestions ("I'm 4 years old")

2. The **sociocognitive** view regards the hypnotized person as using cognitive strategies, such as imagination, to comply with the hypnotist's suggestions.

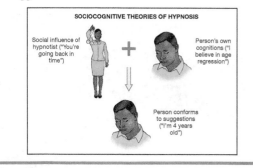

SOCIOCOGNITIVE THEORIES OF HYPNOSIS

Social influence of hypnotist ("You're going back in time")

Person's own cognitions ("I believe in age regression")

Person conforms to suggestions ("I'm 4 years old")

Consciousness-Altering Drugs

↓

Psychoactive drugs alter perception, mood, thinking, memory, or behavior by changing the body's biochemistry.

↙   ↘

Classifying Drugs

Drug classifications, based on their effects on the central nervous system, include:
- **stimulants**.
- **depressants**.
- **opiates**.
- **psychedelics**.

Some drugs, such as marijuana, fall outside of these classifications.

The Physiology and Psychology of Drug Effects

The physiology of drug effects:
- Psychoactive drugs affect neurotransmitters levels in the brain.
- The use of some psychoactive drugs can lead to **tolerance**: increased resistance to a drug's effects.
- When heavy users stop taking a drug, they may suffer severe withdrawal symptoms.

The effects of a drug may vary for psychological reasons, including:
- the person's experience with the drug.
- the person's physical condition.
- the environmental setting.
- the person's mental set, or expectations.

6

Our Sensational Senses

Vision

Hearing

Other Senses

Perceptual Powers: Origins and Influences

Perception Without Awareness

Psychology in the News, Revisited

Taking Psychology With You: Can Perception Be "Extrasensory"?

THE SENSES

PSYCHOLOGY IN THE NEWS /////////////////////////

EDINBURG, TX, March 15, 2013. A new wave of UFO sightings across the world will be discussed this weekend at Edinburg's "Out of This World" conference and festival. Attendees will share their UFO stories, listen to talks by leading UFO researchers, and take part in an alien costume contest. The gathering is expected to attract hundreds of people, both believers and skeptics.

A recent widely publicized report of an unidentified flying object came from actor Russell Crowe, who posted a 23-second video clip on YouTube this month. He tweeted that he and a friend had set up a time-exposure camera to capture fruit bats in Australia's Royal Botanic Gardens, and that the UFO was a big surprise to them. Crowe's video shows two oblong, glowing red or yellow objects, one above the other. They are moving in tandem, with one object appearing to cast a beam of light downward toward the ground.

Other recent sightings have occurred over several parts of Texas. One object that drew particular attention was supposedly caught on camera at a well site near Laredo. The UFO organization that released the photo described the object as saucer-shaped and 60 feet wide, with four lights.

Souvenirs of all kinds (left) are popular at UFO conventions. Many people who view odd objects in the sky (right) are convinced that they have seen alien spacecraft.

UFO sightings seem to be on the increase just about everywhere. In February, a boy on a passenger jet bound for Massachusetts was filming another jet flying some distance away when his camera recorded an unidentified object whizzing by his window. In January, someone posted a video of at least eight objects flying across the sky in Mexico. Sightings have increased off the coast of Cape Town, South Africa, and there have even been reports that a UFO was spotted moving across the sky near the International Space Station, which orbits about 250 miles above the Earth.

One of the earliest UFO accounts occurred in the late 1940s, when a rancher noticed some strange objects strewn about his property near Roswell, New Mexico. When the Air Force quickly blocked off and cleared the site, stories circulated that a spacecraft had crashed and that alien corpses had been recovered. Thousands of believers in UFOs still flock to the International UFO Museum in Roswell.

//////////

Why do some people insist that they have seen UFOs despite the skepticism of others, who scoff and dismiss these objects as planes and planets in the night sky? The answer is that our sensations often deceive us, and not just when we are looking up at mysterious objects in the sky. "I saw it with my own eyes!" people exclaim, as they tell of seeing an image of Jesus on a garage door, Osama bin Laden's face in smoke billowing from the doomed World Trade Center, the Virgin of Guadalupe in a tortilla, or Mother Teresa's face in a cinnamon bun. These illusions seem perfectly real to the people who see them. Why do such reports turn up all over the world, often with specific details?

In this chapter, we will answer these questions by exploring how our senses take in information from the environment and how our brains use this information to construct a model of the world. We will focus on two closely connected sets of processes that enable us to know what is happening both inside our bodies and in the world beyond our own skins. The first, **sensation**, is the detection of physical energy emitted or reflected by physical objects. The cells that do the detecting are located in the *sense organs*—the eyes, ears, tongue, nose, skin, and internal body tissues. Sensory processes produce an immediate awareness of sound, color, form, and other building blocks of consciousness. Without sensation, we would lose touch—literally—with reality.

But to make sense of the world impinging on our senses, we also need **perception**, a set of mental operations that organizes sensory impulses into meaningful patterns. Our sense of vision produces a two-dimensional image on the back of the eye, but we perceive the world in three dimensions. Our sense of hearing brings us the sound of a C, an E, and a G played simultaneously on the piano, but we perceive a C-major chord. Sometimes, a single sensory image produces two alternating perceptions, and the result is an image that keeps changing, as illustrated by the two examples on the next page.

Sensation and perception are the foundation for learning, thinking, and acting. Findings about these processes are often put to practical use, as in the design of industrial robots and in the training of astronauts, who must make crucial decisions based on what they sense and perceive. An understanding of sensation and perception can also help us think more critically about our own experiences and encourages in us a certain humility: Usually we are sure that what we sense and perceive must be true, yet sometimes we are just plain wrong. As you read this chapter, you will

sensation The detection of physical energy emitted or reflected by physical objects; it occurs when energy in the external environment or the body stimulates receptors in the sense organs.

perception The process by which the brain organizes and interprets sensory information.

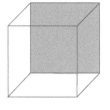

If you stare at the cube, the colored panel will alternate from being at the back to being at the front because your brain can interpret the sensory image in two different ways. The other drawing can also be perceived in two ways. Do you see the word?

learn why people sometimes perceive things that are not there and, conversely, why they sometimes miss things that *are* there—why they can look without seeing, listen without hearing.

You are about to learn...

- why we experience separate sensations even though they all rely on similar neural signals.

- what kind of code in the nervous system helps explain why a pinprick and a kiss feel different.

- how psychologists measure the sensitivity of our senses.

- the bias that influences whether or not you think you hear the phone ringing when you are in the shower.

- what happens when people are deprived of external sensory stimulation.

- why we sometimes fail to see an object that we're looking straight at.

Our Sensational Senses
LO 6.1

At some point, you probably learned that there are five senses: vision, hearing, taste, touch, and smell. Actually, there are more than five senses. The skin, which is the organ of touch or pressure, also senses heat, cold, and pain, not to mention itching and tickling. The ear, which is the organ of hearing, also contains receptors that account for a sense of balance. The skeletal muscles contain receptors responsible for a sense of bodily movement.

 Watch the **Video** The Basics: In Full Appreciation of the Cookie at **MyPsychLab**

All of our senses evolved to help us survive. Even pain, which causes so much human misery, is an indispensable part of our evolutionary heritage because it alerts us to illness and injury. Some people are born with a rare condition that prevents them from feeling the usual hurts and aches of life, but you shouldn't envy them: They are susceptible to burns, bruises, and broken bones, and they often die at an early age because they can't take advantage of pain's warning signals.

The Riddle of Separate Sensations LO 6.2

Sensation begins with the **sense receptors**, cells located in the sense organs. The receptors for smell, pressure, pain, and temperature are extensions

sense receptors
Specialized cells that convert physical energy in the environment or the body to electrical energy that can be transmitted as nerve impulses to the brain.

doctrine of specific nerve energies The principle that different sensory modalities exist because signals received by the sense organs stimulate different nerve pathways leading to different areas of the brain.

(dendrites) of sensory neurons (see Chapter 4). The receptors for vision, hearing, and taste are specialized cells separated from sensory neurons by synapses.

When the sense receptors detect an appropriate stimulus—light, mechanical pressure, or chemical molecules—they convert the energy of the stimulus into electrical impulses that travel along nerves to the brain. Sense receptors are like military scouts who scan the terrain for signs of activity. These scouts cannot make many decisions on their own; they must transmit what they learn to "field officers," sensory neurons in the nerves of the peripheral nervous system. The field officers in turn must report to generals at a command center, the cells of the brain. The generals are responsible for analyzing the reports, combining information brought in by different scouts, and deciding what it all means.

The sensory-neuron "field officers" all use the same form of communication, a neural impulse. It is as if they must all send their messages on a bongo drum and can only go "boom." How, then, are we able to experience so many different kinds of sensations? The answer is that the nervous system *encodes* the messages. One kind of code is *anatomical*, first described in 1826 by the German physiologist Johannes Müller in his **doctrine of specific nerve energies**. According to this doctrine, different sensory modalities (such as vision and hearing) exist because signals received by the sense organs stimulate different nerve pathways leading to different areas of the brain. Signals from the eye cause impulses to travel along the optic nerve to the visual cortex. Signals from the ear cause impulses to travel along the auditory nerve to the auditory cortex. Light and sound waves produce different sensations because of these anatomical differences.

The doctrine of specific nerve energies implies that what we know about the world ultimately reduces to what we know about the state of our own nervous system: We see with the brain, not the eyes, and we hear with the brain, not the ears. It follows that if sound waves could stimulate nerves that end in the visual part of the brain, we would "see" sound. In fact, a similar sort of crossover does occur if you close your right eye and press lightly on the right side of the lid: You will see a flash of light seemingly coming from the left. The pressure produces an impulse that travels up the optic nerve to the visual area in the right side of the brain, where it is interpreted as coming from the left side of the visual field. By taking advantage of such crossover from one sense to another, researchers hope to enable blind people to see by teaching them to interpret impulses from other senses that are then routed to the visual areas of the brain. Neuroscientists have developed a device that translates images from a camera into a pattern of electronic pulses that is sent to electrodes on the tongue, which in turn sends information about the pattern to visual areas of the brain that process images (Chebat et al., 2011; Ptito et al., 2005). Using this device, congenitally blind people have been able to make out shapes, and their visual areas, long quiet, have suddenly become active.

Sensory crossover also occurs in a rare condition called **synesthesia**, in which the stimulation of one sense consistently evokes a sensation in another. A person with synesthesia may say that the color purple smells like a rose, the aroma of cinnamon feels like velvet, or the sound of a note on a clarinet tastes like cherries. Most synesthetes are born with the condition; one leading theory holds that they have a greater number of neural connections between different sensory brain areas than other people do (e.g., Bargary & Mitchell, 2008; Rouw & Scholte, 2007). But in some cases synesthesia may be learned through childhood experiences. In a study of 11 people who experience color when they see written letters or numbers, all reported that they had acquired this ability through playing with colored alphabet blocks—and 10 of them still had those toys! (Witthoft & Winawer, 2013). Synesthesia can also result from damage to the brain. One woman who had recovered from a stroke experienced sounds as a tingling sensation on the left side of her body (Ro et al., 2007).

Synesthesia, however, is an anomaly; for most of us, the senses remain separate. Anatomical encoding does not completely solve the riddle of why this is so, nor does it explain variations of experience *within* a particular sense—the sight of pink versus red, the sound of a piccolo versus the sound of a tuba, or the feel of a pinprick versus the feel of a kiss. An additional kind of code is therefore necessary. This second kind of code has been called *functional* because it has to do with how cells in the nervous system are functioning at any particular time. Functional codes rely on the fact that sensory receptors and neurons fire, or are inhibited from firing, only in the presence of specific sorts of stimuli. At any particular moment, then, some cells in the nervous system are firing and some are not. Information about *which* cells are firing, *how many* cells are firing, the *rate* at which cells are firing, and the *patterning* of each cell's firing forms a functional code. Functional encoding may occur all along a sensory route, starting in the sense organs and ending in the brain.

Measuring the Senses LO 6.3

Just how sensitive are our senses? The answer comes from the field of *psychophysics*, which is concerned with how the physical properties of stimuli are related to our psychological experience of them. Drawing on principles from both physics and psychology, psychophysicists have studied how the strength or intensity of a stimulus affects the strength of sensation in an observer.

Absolute Thresholds.
One way to find out how sensitive the senses are is to show people a series of signals that vary in intensity and ask them to say which signals they can detect. The smallest amount of energy that a person can detect reliably is known as the **absolute threshold**. However, the word *absolute* is a bit misleading because people detect borderline signals on some occasions and miss them on others. Reliable detection is said to occur when a person can detect a signal 50 percent of the time.

If your absolute threshold for brightness were being measured, you might be asked to sit in a

synesthesia A condition in which stimulation of one sense also evokes another.

absolute threshold The smallest quantity of physical energy that can be reliably detected by an observer.

Different species sense the world differently. The flower on the left was photographed under normal light. The one on the right, photographed under ultraviolet light, is what a butterfly might see, because butterflies have ultraviolet receptors. The hundreds of tiny bright spots are sources of nectar.

difference threshold

The smallest difference in stimulation that can be reliably detected by an observer when two stimuli are compared; also called *just noticeable difference* (jnd).

dark room and look at a wall or screen. You would then be shown flashes of light varying in brightness, one flash at a time. Your task would be to say whether you noticed a flash. Some flashes you would never see. Some you would always see. And sometimes you would miss seeing a flash, even though you had noticed one of equal brightness on other trials. Such errors seem to occur in part because of random firing of cells in the nervous system, which produces fluctuating background noise, something like the static in a radio transmission that is slightly out of range.

By studying absolute thresholds, psychologists have found that our senses are sharp indeed. If you have normal sensory abilities, you can see a candle flame on a clear, dark night from 30 miles away. You can taste a teaspoon of sugar diluted in two gallons of water, smell a drop of perfume diffused through a three-room apartment, and feel the wing of a bee falling on your cheek from a height of only one centimeter (Galanter, 1962).

Yet despite these impressive skills, our senses are tuned in to only a narrow band of physical energies. We are visually sensitive to just a tiny fraction of the electromagnetic energy that surrounds us; we do not see radio waves, infrared waves, or microwaves (see Figure 6.1). Many other species can pick up signals that we cannot. Dogs can detect high-frequency sound waves that are beyond our range, and bees can see ultraviolet light, which merely gives human beings a sunburn.

Difference Thresholds. Does an expensive toothpaste really make your teeth noticeably brighter? How about that new laptop you have your eye on; can you really tell that it's lighter than the one you currently lug around? We often need to be able to compare two stimuli and determine whether they are the same or different on some dimension.

Suppose you're in the gym, pressing a barbell loaded with 100 pounds overhead, and one of your practical-joker friends adds weight to it when you are not looking. What is the smallest amount of weight she can add before you think to yourself, "Hey, this bar feels heavier"? If you and your friend tried to answer this question systematically, you would probably determine that the answer is another 2 pounds. In other words, 2 pounds is the smallest difference in the weight of two barbells that you would reliably detect, where again, "reliably" means half of the time. Scientists call this point the **difference threshold** or *just noticeable difference* (jnd).

▶ Simulate the Experiment Weber's Law at MyPsychLab

Now suppose that after you lift a small 1-pound dumbbell overhead, your friend tries the same prank. Would she have to add 2 pounds to that little dumbbell before you would notice? Unlikely—that would triple the weight of the dumbbell. Way back in the nineteenth century, German scientist Ernst Weber determined that for people to detect a difference between two stimuli, such as two weights, those stimuli must differ by a certain fixed proportion (such as 2 percent), *not* a certain amount (such as 2 pounds or 2 ounces). Different properties of stimuli have their own constant percentages: For two weights, it is 2 percent; for the brightness of two lights or the saltiness of two liquids, it is 8 percent; and for the loudness of two noises, it is 5 percent.

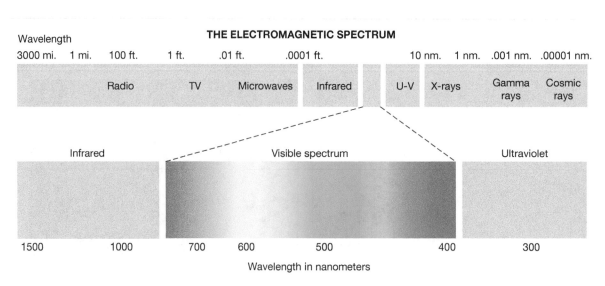

FIGURE 6.1 The Visible Spectrum of Electromagnetic Energy
Our visual system detects only a small fraction of the electromagnetic energy around us.

Signal-Detection Theory. The procedures we have described are useful but have a serious limitation. Measurements for any given individual may be affected by that person's general tendency, when uncertain, to respond, "Yes, I noticed a signal (or a difference)" or "No, I didn't notice anything." Some people are habitual yea-sayers, willing to gamble that the signal was there. Others are habitual naysayers, cautious and conservative. In addition, alertness, motives, and expectations can influence how a person responds on any given occasion. If you are in the shower and you are expecting a call, you may think you heard your cell ring when it did not. In laboratory studies, when observers want to impress the experimenter, they may lean toward a positive response.

Fortunately, these problems of *response bias* are not insurmountable. According to **signal-detection theory**, an observer's response in a detection task can be divided into a *sensory process*, which depends on the intensity of the stimulus, and a *decision process*, which is influenced by the observer's response bias. One way a researcher can separate these two components is by including some trials in which no stimulus is present and others in which a weak stimulus is present. Under these conditions, four kinds of responses are possible: The person (1) detects a signal that was present (a "hit"), (2) says the signal was there when it wasn't (a "false alarm"), (3) fails to detect the signal when it was present (a "miss"), or (4) correctly says that the signal was absent when it was absent (a "correct rejection").

Yea-sayers will have more hits than naysayers because they are quick to say "it was there" when it really was, but they will also have more false alarms because they are also quick to say, "It was there" when it wasn't. Naysayers will have more correct rejections than yea-sayers, but they will also have more misses because they will often say, "Nope, nothing was there" when in fact it was. This information can be fed into a mathematical formula that yields separate estimates of a person's response bias and sensory capacity. The person's true sensitivity to a signal of any particular intensity can then be predicted.

The original method of measuring thresholds assumed that a person's ability to detect a stimulus depended solely on the stimulus. Signal-detection theory assumes that there is no single threshold, because at any given moment a person's sensitivity to a stimulus depends on a decision that he or she actively makes. Signal-detection methods have many real-world applications, from screening applicants for jobs that require keen hearing to training air-traffic controllers, whose decisions about the presence or absence of a blip on a radar screen may mean the difference between life and death.

Sensory Adaptation LO 6.4

Variety, they say, is the spice of life. Variety is also the essence of sensation because our senses are designed to respond to change and contrast in the environment. When a stimulus is unchanging

signal-detection theory A psychophysical theory that divides the detection of a sensory signal into a sensory process and a decision process.

Get Involved! Now You See It, Now You Don't

Sensation depends on change and contrast in the environment. Hold your hand over one eye and stare at the dot in the middle of the circle on the right. You should have no trouble maintaining an image of the circle. However, if you do the same with the circle on the left, the image will fade. The gradual change from light to dark does not provide enough contrast to keep your visual receptors firing at a steady rate. The circle reappears only if you close and reopen your eye or shift your gaze to the *X*.

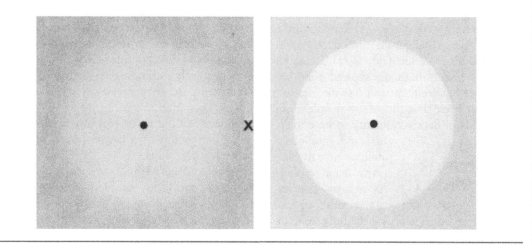

sensory adaptation
The reduction or disappearance of sensory responsiveness when stimulation is unchanging or repetitious.

sensory deprivation
The absence of normal levels of sensory stimulation.

selective attention
The focusing of attention on selected aspects of the environment and the blocking out of others.

inattentional blindness
Failure to consciously perceive something you are looking at because you are not attending to it.

or repetitious, sensation often fades or disappears. Receptors or nerve cells higher up in the sensory system get "tired" and fire less frequently. The resulting decline in sensory responsiveness is called **sensory adaptation**. Usually, such adaptation spares us from having to respond to unnecessary information; most of the time you have no need to feel your watch sitting on your wrist. Sometimes, however, adaptation can be hazardous, as when you no longer smell a gas leak that you thought you noticed when you first entered the kitchen.

We never completely adapt to extremely intense stimuli—a terrible toothache, the odor of ammonia, the heat of the desert sun. And we rarely adapt completely to visual stimuli, whether they are weak or intense. Eye movements, voluntary and involuntary, cause the location of an object's image on the back of the eye to keep changing, so visual receptors do not have a chance to "fatigue."

What would happen if our senses adapted to *most* incoming stimuli? Would we sense nothing, or would the brain substitute its own images for the sensory experiences no longer available by way of the sense organs? In early studies of **sensory deprivation**, researchers studied this question by isolating male volunteers from all patterned sight and sound. Vision was restricted by a translucent visor, hearing by a U-shaped pillow and noise from an air conditioner and fan, and touch by cotton gloves and cardboard cuffs. The volunteers took brief breaks to eat and use the bathroom, but otherwise they lay in bed, doing nothing. The results were dramatic. Within a few hours, many of the men felt edgy. Some were so disoriented that they quit the study the first day. Those who stayed longer became confused, restless, and grouchy. Many reported bizarre and disturbing visions, such as a squadron of squirrels or a procession of marching eyeglasses. It was as though they were having waking nightmares. Few people were willing to remain in the study for more than two or three days (Heron, 1957).

But the notion that sensory deprivation is unpleasant or even dangerous turned out to be an oversimplification (Suedfeld, 1975). Later research, using better methods, showed that hallucinations are less frequent and less disorienting than had first been thought. Many people enjoy limited periods of deprivation, and some perceptual and intellectual abilities actually improve. Your response to sensory deprivation depends on your expectations and interpretations of what

THINKING CRITICALLY

About Sensory Deprivation

Is sensory deprivation pleasant or unpleasant? The answer isn't "either–or"; it depends on the circumstances and how you interpret your situation. Being isolated against your will can be terrifying, but many people have found meditating alone, away from all sights and sounds, to be calming and pleasant.

is happening. Reduced sensation can be scary if you are locked in a room for an indefinite period, but relaxing if you have retreated to that room voluntarily for a little time-out, perhaps at a luxury spa or a monastery.

Nonetheless, the human brain does require a minimum amount of sensory stimulation to function normally. This need may help explain why people who live alone often keep the radio or television on continuously, and why prolonged solitary confinement is used as a form of punishment or even torture.

Sensing Without Perceiving LO 6.5

If sensory deprivation can sometimes be upsetting, so can sensory overload, which can lead to fatigue and mental confusion. Fortunately, our capacity for **selective attention**—the ability to focus on some parts of the environment and block out others—protects us from being overwhelmed by the countless sensory signals that are constantly impinging on our sense receptors. Competing sensory messages do all enter the nervous system, however, and they get some processing, enabling us to pick up anything important, such as our own name spoken by someone several yards away.

Still, our conscious awareness of the environment is much less complete than most people think. We may even fail to consciously register objects that we are looking straight at, a phenomenon known as **inattentional blindness**: We look, but we do not see. When people are shown a video of a ball-passing game and are asked to count up the passes, they may even miss something as seemingly obvious as a woman in a gorilla suit walking slowly among the players, thumping her chest (Most et al., 2001; Simons & Chabris, 1999; Chabris & Simons, 2009). (Most accounts of this research have reported that it was a "man" or "guy" in the gorilla suit. Clearly, many who saw the study were blind to the sentence in the original report saying that it was a woman!)

Inattentional blindness occurs in many circumstances. When radiologists looking for signs of lung cancer examined slides that contained a superimposed image of an arm-waving gorilla, most of them missed the gorilla (Drew, Võ, & Wolfe, 2013). One research team wondered which situation would be most likely to "blind" people to the sight of a colorful clown riding on a unicycle: walking along while talking on a cell phone, walking while listening to music, walking alone, or strolling with one other person. Can you guess? The walkers who were least likely to notice the clown were those who were talking on their cell phones (Hyman et al., 2010).

Selective attention, then, is a mixed blessing. It protects us from overload and allows us to focus

Hard though it is to believe, even a person in a gorilla suit may go unnoticed if people's attention is elsewhere.

on what's important, but it also deprives us of sensory information that we may need. That could be disastrous if you are so focused on texting a friend that you walk right into a pothole or a street full of traffic.

Recite & Review

☑ Study and Review at MyPsychLab

Recite: Say out loud everything you can recall about sensation, perception, sense receptors, the doctrine of specific nerve energies, synesthesia, anatomical and functional codes, absolute and difference thresholds, signal detection theory, sensory adaptation, sensory deprivation, selective attention, and inattentional blindness.

Review: Next, it's time to go back and read this section again, concentrating on what you couldn't remember.

Now take this *Quick Quiz:*

1. A condition in which stimulation of one sense evokes sensation in the other sense is known as _____.

2. On account of _____, your sister might get disturbed if you increase the television volume even though you are both seated at equal distances from the device.

3. _____ will have more false alarms in real-life situations.

4. Being able to see the figures in a dark room after some time is an example of _____.

5. In real-life detection tasks, is it better to be a "naysayer" or a "yea-sayer"?

Answers:

1. synesthesia 2. difference threshold 3. yeasayers 4. sensory adaptation 5. Neither; it depends on the consequences of a "miss," or a "false alarm." Suppose that you are in the shower and you're not sure whether your phone is ringing in the other room. You might want to be a yea-sayer if you are expecting a call about a job interview, but a naysayer if you are not expecting any calls and don't want to get out dripping wet for nothing.

Vision

More information about the external world comes to us through our eyes than through any other sense organ. Because we evolved to be most active in the daytime, we are equipped to take advantage of the sun's illumination. Animals that are active at night tend to rely more heavily on hearing.

What We See LO 6.6

The stimulus for vision is light; even cats, raccoons, and other creatures famous for their ability to get around in the dark need some light to see. Visible light comes from the sun and other stars and from lightbulbs, and it is also reflected off objects. The *physical* characteristics of light affect three *psychological* dimensions of our visual world: hue, brightness, and saturation.

1 **Hue,** the dimension of visual experience specified by color names, is related to the *wavelength* of light—that is, to the distance between the crests of a light wave. Shorter waves tend to be seen as violet and blue, longer ones as orange and red. The sun produces white light, which is a mixture of all the visible wavelengths. Sometimes, drops of moisture in the air act like a prism: They separate the sun's white light into the colors of the visible spectrum, and we are treated to a rainbow.

2 **Brightness** is the dimension of visual experience related to the amount, or *intensity*, of the light an object emits or reflects. Intensity corresponds to the amplitude (maximum height) of the wave. Generally speaking, the more light an object reflects, the brighter it appears. However, brightness is also affected by wavelength: Yellows appear brighter than reds and blues even when their physical intensities are equal.

3 **Saturation** (colorfulness) is the dimension of visual experience related to the *complexity* of light—that is, to how wide or narrow the range of wavelengths is. When light contains only a single wavelength, it is said to be pure, and the resulting color is completely saturated. At the other extreme, white light contains all the wavelengths of visible light (corresponding to all the colors in the visible spectrum) and has zero saturation. Black is a lack of any light at all (it has no color) and so it is also completely unsaturated. In nature, pure light is extremely rare. We usually sense a mixture of wavelengths, and as a result see colors that are duller and paler than completely saturated ones.

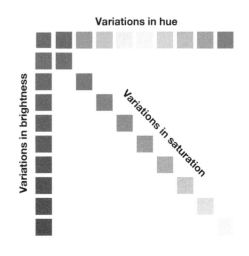

Variations in hue

Variations in brightness

Variations in saturation

An Eye on the World LO 6.7, LO 6.8, LO 6.9

Light enters the visual system through the eye, a wonderfully complex and delicate structure. As you read this section, examine Figure 6.2. Notice that the front part of the eye is covered by the transparent *cornea*. The cornea protects the eye and bends incoming light rays toward a *lens* located behind it. A camera lens focuses incoming light by moving closer to or farther from the shutter opening. However, the lens of the eye works by subtly changing its shape, becoming more or less curved to focus light from objects that are close by or far away. The amount of light that gets into the eye is controlled by muscles in the *iris*, the part of the eye that gives it color. The iris surrounds the round opening, or *pupil*, of the eye. When you enter a dim room, the pupil widens, or dilates, to let more light in. When you emerge into bright sunlight, the pupil gets smaller, contracting to allow in less light.

The visual receptors are located in the back of the eye, or **retina**. (The retina also contains special cells that communicate information about light

hue The dimension of visual experience specified by color names and related to the wavelength of light.

brightness Lightness or luminance; the dimension of visual experience related to the amount (intensity) of light emitted from or reflected by an object.

saturation Vividness or purity of color; the dimension of visual experience related to the complexity of light waves.

retina Neural tissue lining the back of the eyeball's interior, which contains the receptors for vision.

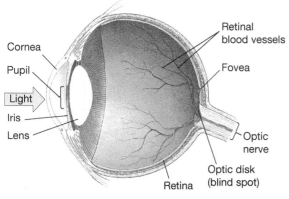

FIGURE 6.2 Major Structures of the Eye
Light passes through the pupil and lens and is focused on the retina at the back of the eye. The point of sharpest vision is at the fovea.

and dark to the brain area that regulates biological rhythms, as discussed in Chapter 5.) In a developing embryo, the retina forms from tissue that projects out from the brain, not from tissue destined to form other parts of the eye; thus, the retina is actually an extension of the brain. As Figure 6.3 shows, when the lens of the eye focuses light on the retina, the result is an upside-down image. Light from the top of the visual field stimulates light-sensitive receptor cells in the bottom part of the retina, and vice versa. The brain interprets this upside-down pattern of stimulation as something that is right side up.

About 120 to 125 million receptors in the retina are long and narrow, and are called **rods**. Another 7 or 8 million receptors are cone-shaped, and are called, appropriately, **cones**. The center of the retina, or *fovea*, where vision is sharpest,

contains only cones, clustered densely together. From the center to the periphery, the ratio of rods to cones increases, and the outer edges contain virtually no cones.

Rods are more sensitive to light than cones are and thus enable us to see even in dim light. (Cats see well in dim light in part because they have a high proportion of rods.) Because rods occupy the outer edges of the retina, they also handle peripheral (side) vision. But rods cannot distinguish different wavelengths of light so they are not sensitive to color, which is why it is often hard to distinguish colors clearly in dim light. To see colors, we need cones, which come in three classes that are sensitive to specific wavelengths of light. Cones need much more light than rods do to respond, so they don't help us much when we are trying to find a seat in a darkened movie theater. (These differences are summarized in Table 6.1.)

We have all noticed that it takes some time for our eyes to adjust fully to dim illumination. This process of **dark adaptation** involves chemical changes in the rods and cones. The cones adapt quickly, within 10 minutes or so, but they never become very sensitive to the dim illumination. The rods adapt more slowly, taking 20 minutes or longer, but are ultimately much more sensitive. After the first phase of adaptation, you can see better but not well; after the second phase, your vision is as good as it ever will get.

Explore the Concept Virtual Brain: The Visual System at MyPsychLab

Rods and cones are connected by synapses to *bipolar cells*, which in turn communicate with neurons called **ganglion cells** (see Figure 6.4). The

rods Visual receptors that respond to dim light.

cones Visual receptors involved in color vision.

dark adaptation A process by which visual receptors become maximally sensitive to dim light.

ganglion cells Neurons in the retina of the eye, which gather information from receptor cells (by way of intermediate bipolar cells); their axons make up the optic nerve.

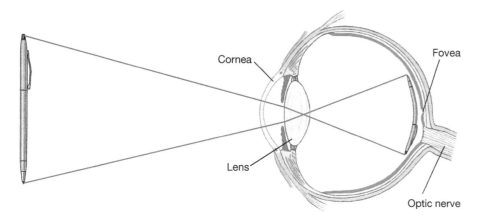

FIGURE 6.3 The Retinal Image
When we look at an object, the light pattern on the retina is upside down. René Descartes (1596–1650) was probably the first person to demonstrate this fact. He cut a piece from the back of an ox's eye and replaced the piece with paper. When he held the eye up to the light, he saw an upside-down image of the room on the paper! You could take any ordinary lens and get the same result.

TABLE 6.1 Differences Between Rods and Cones

	Rods	Cones
How many?	120–125 million	7–8 million
Where most concentrated?	Periphery of retina	Center (fovea) of retina
How sensitive?	High sensitivity	Low sensitivity
Sensitive to color?	No	Yes

axons of the ganglion cells converge to form the *optic nerve*, which carries information out through the back of the eye and on to the brain. Where the optic nerve leaves the eye, at the *optic disk*, there are no rods or cones. The absence of receptors produces a blind spot in the field of vision. Normally, we are unaware of the blind spot because (1) the image projected on the spot is hitting a different, "nonblind" spot in the other eye; (2) our eyes move so fast that we can pick up the complete image; and (3) the brain fills in the gap. You can find your blind spot by doing the Get Involved exercise on the facing page.

feature-detector cells
Cells in the visual cortex that are sensitive to specific features of the environment.

Why the Visual System Is Not a Camera LO 6.10

Although the eye has often been compared with a camera, the visual system, unlike a camera, is not a passive recorder of the external world. Neurons in the visual system actively build up a picture of the world by detecting its meaningful features.

Ganglion cells and neurons in the thalamus of the brain respond to simple features in the environment, such as spots of light and dark. But in mammals, special **feature-detector cells** in the visual cortex respond to more complex features. This

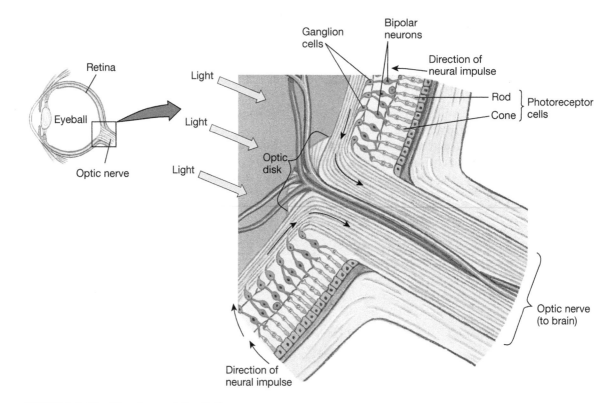

FIGURE 6.4 The Structures of the Retina
For clarity, all cells in this drawing are greatly exaggerated in size. To reach the receptors for vision (the rods and cones), light must pass through the bipolar and ganglion cells as well as the blood vessels that nourish them (not shown). Normally, we do not see the shadow cast by this network of cells and blood vessels because the shadow always falls on the same place on the retina, and such stabilized images are not sensed. But when an eye doctor shines a moving light into your eye, the treelike shadow of the blood vessels falls on different regions of the retina and you may see it—a rather eerie experience.

Get Involved! Find Your Blind Spot

A blind spot exists where the optic nerve leaves the back of your eye. Find the blind spot in your left eye by closing your right eye and looking at the magician. Then slowly move the book toward and away from yourself. The rabbit should disappear when the book is between 9 and 12 inches from your eye.

fact was first demonstrated by David Hubel and Torsten Wiesel (1962, 1968), who painstakingly recorded impulses from individual cells in the brains of cats and monkeys. In 1981, they were awarded a Nobel Prize for their work. Hubel and Wiesel found that different neurons were sensitive to different patterns projected on a screen in front of an animal's eyes. Most cells responded maximally to moving or stationary lines that were oriented in a particular direction and located in a particular part of the visual field. One type of cell might fire most rapidly in response to a horizontal line in the lower right part of the visual field, another to a diagonal line at a specific angle in the upper left part of the visual field. In the real world, such features make up the boundaries and edges of objects.

Since this pioneering work was done, scientists have found that other cells in the visual system have even more specialized roles. A group of cells at the bottom of the cerebral cortex responds much more strongly to faces than to objects—human faces, animal faces, even cartoon faces. Evolutionary scientists note that a facility for deciphering faces makes sense because it would have ensured our ancestors' ability to quickly distinguish friend from foe, or in the case of infants, mothers from strangers. Another area, a part of the cortex near the hippocampus, makes sure you understand your environment. It responds to images of all kinds of places, from your dorm room to an open park, and does so far more strongly than it does to objects or faces. A third region, a part of the occipital cortex, responds selectively to bodies and body parts much more strongly than to faces or objects—and more strongly to other people's bodies than to your own (Kanwisher, 2010).

But there are limits on such specialization. Researchers have studied 20 different classes of objects, from tools to animal predators to chairs, and so far have found no other specialized areas (Downing et al., 2006). This is understandable, because the brain cannot possibly contain a dedicated area for every conceivable object. In general, the brain's job is to take fragmentary

Cases of brain damage support the idea that particular systems of brain cells are highly specialized for identifying important objects or visual patterns, such as faces. One man's injury left him unable to identify ordinary objects, which, he said, often looked like "blobs." Yet he had no trouble with faces, even when they were upside down or incomplete. When shown this painting, he could easily see the face but not the vegetables comprising it (Moscovitch, Winocur, & Behrmann, 1997).

trichromatic theory A theory of color perception that proposes three mechanisms in the visual system, each sensitive to a certain range of wavelengths; their interaction is assumed to produce all the different experiences of hue.

opponent-process theory A theory of color perception that assumes that the visual system treats pairs of colors as opposing or antagonistic.

information about edges, angles, shapes, motion, brightness, texture, and patterns and figure out that a chair is a chair and the thing next to it is a table. The perception of any given object probably depends on the activation of many cells in far-flung parts of the brain and on the overall pattern and rhythm of their activity. Moreover, experiences can modify and shape the brain's circuits. Thus, some of the brain cells that seem especially responsive to faces respond to other things as well, depending on a person's experiences and interests. In one study, "face" cells fired when car buffs examined pictures of classic cars but not when they looked at pictures of exotic birds, whereas the exact opposite was true for birdwatchers (Gauthier et al., 2000). Cars, of course, do not have faces.

How We See Colors LO 6.11

For more than 300 years, scientists have been trying to figure out why we see the world in living color. We now know that different processes explain different stages of color vision.

The Trichromatic Theory. The **trichromatic theory** (also known as the *Young-Helmholtz theory*) applies to the first level of processing, which occurs in the retina of the eye. The retina contains three types of cones. One type responds maximally to blue, another to green, and a third to red. The thousands of colors we see result from the combined activity of these three types of cones.

Total color blindness is usually the result of a genetic variation that causes cones of the retina to be absent or malfunctional. The visual world then consists of black, white, and shades of gray. Many species of animals are totally color-blind, but the condition is extremely rare in human beings. Most

"color-blind" people are actually *color deficient*. Usually they cannot distinguish red and green; the world is painted in shades of blue, yellow, brown, and gray. In rarer instances, they may be blind to blue and yellow and may see only reds, greens, and grays. Color deficiency is found in about 8 percent of white men, 5 percent of Asian men, and 3 percent of black men and Native American men (Sekuler & Blake, 1994). Because of the way the condition is inherited, it is uncommon in women.

The Opponent-Process Theory. The **opponent-process theory** applies to the second stage of color processing, which occurs in ganglion cells in the retina and in neurons in the thalamus and visual cortex of the brain. These cells, known as *opponent-process cells*, either respond to short wavelengths but are inhibited from firing by long wavelengths, or vice versa (DeValois & DeValois, 1975). Some opponent-process cells respond in opposite fashion to red and green, or to blue and yellow; that is, they fire in response to one and turn off in response to the other. (A third system responds in opposite fashion to white and black and thus yields information about brightness.) The net result is a color code that is passed along to the higher visual centers. Because this code treats red and green, and also blue and yellow, as antagonistic, we can describe a color as bluish green or yellowish green but not as reddish green or yellowish blue.

Opponent-process cells that are *inhibited* by a particular color produce a burst of firing when the color is removed, just as they would if the opposing color were present. Similarly, cells that *fire* in response to a color stop firing when the color is removed, just as they would if the opposing color were present. These facts explain why we are

Get Involved! A Change of Heart

Opponent-process cells that switch on or off in response to green send an opposite message— "red"—when the green is removed, producing a negative afterimage. Stare at the black dot in the middle of this heart for at least 20 seconds. Then shift your gaze to a white piece of paper or a white wall. You may get a "change of heart": an image of a red or pinkish heart with a blue border.

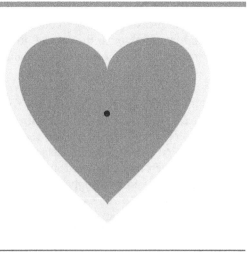

susceptible to *negative afterimages* when we stare at a particular hue—why we see, for instance, red after staring at green. (To see this effect for yourself, do the Get Involved exercise on the previous page.) A sort of neural rebound effect occurs: The cells that switch on or off to signal the presence of "green" send the opposite signal ("red") when the green is removed and vice versa.

Constructing the Visual World
LO 6.12, LO 6.13, LO 6.14, LO 6.15

We do not actually see a retinal image; the mind must actively interpret the image and construct the world from the often-fragmentary data of the senses. In the brain, sensory signals that give rise to vision, hearing, taste, smell, and touch are combined from moment to moment to produce a unified model of the world. This is the process of *perception*.

Form Perception. To make sense of the world, we must know where one thing ends and another begins. In vision, we must separate the teacher from the lectern; in hearing, we must separate the piano solo from the orchestral accompaniment; in taste, we must separate the marshmallow from the hot chocolate. This process of dividing up the world occurs so rapidly and effortlessly that we take it completely for granted, until we must make out objects in a heavy fog or words in the rapid-fire conversation of someone speaking a language we don't know well.

The *Gestalt psychologists*, who belonged to a movement that began in Germany and was influential in the 1920s and 1930s, were among the first to study how people organize the world visually into meaningful units and patterns. In German, *Gestalt* means "form" or "configuration." The Gestalt psychologists' motto was "The whole is more than the sum of its parts." They observed that when we perceive something, properties emerge from the configuration as a whole that are not found in any particular component.

The Gestalt psychologists also noted that people organize the visual field into *figure* and *ground*. The figure stands out from the rest of the environment (see Figure 6.5). Some things stand out as figure by virtue of their intensity or size; it is hard to ignore the bright glare of a flashlight at night or a tidal wave approaching your piece of beach. Unique objects also stand out, such as a banana in a bowl of oranges, and so do moving objects in an otherwise still environment, such as a shooting star. Indeed, it is hard to ignore a sudden change of any kind in the environment because our brains are geared to respond to change and

FIGURE 6.5 Figure and Ground
Which do you notice first in this drawing by M. C. Escher—the fish, geese, or salamanders? It will depend on whether you see the blue, red, or gold sections as figure or ground.

contrast. However, selective attention—the ability to concentrate on some stimuli and to filter out others—gives us some control over what we perceive as figure and ground, and sometimes it blinds us to things we would otherwise interpret as figure, as we saw previously.

Other **Gestalt principles** describe strategies used by the visual system to group sensory building blocks into perceptual units (Köhler, 1929; Wertheimer, 1923/1958). The Gestalt psychologists believed that these strategies were present from birth or emerged early in infancy as a result of maturation. Modern research, however, suggests that at least some of them depend on experience (Quinn & Bhatt, 2005). Here are a few well-known Gestalt principles:

1 **Proximity.** Things that are near each other tend to be grouped together. Thus, you perceive the dots on the left as two groups of dots, not as eight separate, unrelated dots. Similarly, you perceive the pattern on the right as vertical columns of dots, not as horizontal rows:

2 **Closure.** The brain tends to fill in gaps to perceive complete forms. This is fortunate because we often need to decipher less-than-perfect images. The following figures are easily perceived

Gestalt principles
Principles that describe the brain's organization of sensory information into meaningful units and patterns.

as a triangle, a face, and the letter *e*, even though none of the figures is complete:

3 **Similarity.** Things that are alike in some way (as in color, shape, or size) tend to be perceived as belonging together. In the figure on the left, you see the circles as forming an *X*. In the one on the right, you see horizontal bars rather than vertical columns because the horizontally aligned stars are either all red or all outlined in red:

4 **Continuity.** Lines and patterns tend to be perceived as continuing in time or space. You perceive the figure on the left as a single line partially covered by an oval rather than as two separate lines touching an oval. In the figure on the right, you see two lines, one curved and one straight, instead of two curved and two straight lines, touching at one focal point:

Unfortunately, many consumer products and machine controls are designed with little thought for Gestalt principles, which is why it can be a major challenge to, say, operate the correct dials on a new stovetop or see at a glance which lever on a control panel to pull in an emergency. Good design requires, among other things, that crucial distinctions be visually obvious.

Simulate the **Experiment** Gestalt Laws of Perception at **MyPsychLab**

MONOCULAR CUES TO DEPTH

Most cues to depth do not depend on having two eyes. Some monocular (one-eyed) cues are shown here.

LIGHT AND SHADOW

Both of these attributes give objects the appearance of three dimensions.

INTERPOSITION

An object that partly blocks or obscures another one must be in front of the other one, and is therefore seen as closer.

MOTION PARALLAX

When an observer is moving, objects appear to move at different speeds and in different directions. The closer an object, the faster it seems to move. Close objects appear to move backward, whereas distant ones seem to move forward.

Depth and Distance Perception. Ordinarily we need to know not only *what* something is but also *where* it is. Touch gives us this information directly, but vision does not, so we must infer an object's location by estimating its distance or depth.

To perform this remarkable feat, we rely in part on **binocular cues**, cues that require the use of two eyes. One such cue is **convergence**, the turning of the eyes inward, which occurs when they focus on a nearby object. The closer the object, the greater the convergence, as you know if you have ever tried to cross your eyes by looking at your own nose. As the angle of convergence changes, the corresponding muscular changes provide information to the brain about distance.

The two eyes also receive slightly different retinal images of the same object. You can prove this by holding a finger about 12 inches in front of your face and looking at it with only one eye at a time. Its position will appear to shift when you change eyes. Now hold up two fingers, one closer to your nose than the other. Notice that the amount of space between the two fingers appears to change when you switch eyes. The slight difference in lateral (sideways) separation between two objects as seen by the left eye and the right eye is called **retinal disparity**. Because retinal disparity decreases as the distance between two objects increases, the brain can use it to infer depth and calculate distance.

Binocular cues help us estimate distances up to about 50 feet. For objects farther away, we use only **monocular cues**, cues that do not depend on using both eyes. One such cue is *interposition*: When an object is interposed between the viewer and a second object, partly blocking the view of the second object, the first object is perceived as being closer. Another monocular cue is *linear perspective*: When two lines known to be parallel appear to be coming together or converging (say, the edges of a railroad track or a highway stretching for miles ahead of you), they imply the existence of depth. These and other monocular cues are illustrated on these two pages.

binocular cues Visual cues to depth or distance requiring two eyes.

convergence The turning inward of the eyes, which occurs when they focus on a nearby object.

retinal disparity The slight difference in lateral separation between two objects as seen by the left eye and the right eye.

monocular cues Visual cues to depth or distance, which can be used by one eye alone.

RELATIVE SIZE

The smaller an object's image on the retina, the farther away the object appears.

TEXTURE GRADIENTS

Distant parts of a uniform surface appear denser; that is, its elements seem spaced more closely together.

LINEAR PERSPECTIVE

Parallel lines will appear to be converging in the distance; the greater the apparent convergence, the greater the perceived distance. Artists often exaggerate this cue to convey an impression of depth.

RELATIVE CLARITY

Because of particles in the air from dust, fog, or smog, distant objects tend to look hazier, duller, or less detailed.

© 1999 Dan Piraro. Reprinted with special permission of King Features Syndicate.

"I can't go on living with such lousy depth perception!"

perceptual constancy
The accurate perception of objects as stable or unchanged despite changes in the sensory patterns they produce.

Visual Constancies: When Seeing Is Believing. Your perceptual world would be a confusing place without still another perceptual skill. Lighting conditions, viewing angles, and the distances of stationary objects are all continually changing as we move about, yet we rarely confuse these changes with changes in the objects themselves. This ability to perceive objects as stable or unchanging, even though the sensory patterns they produce are constantly shifting, is called **perceptual constancy**. The best-studied constancies are visual and include the following:

1 Size constancy. We see an object as having a constant size even when its retinal image becomes smaller or larger. A friend approaching on the street does not seem to be growing; a car pulling away from the curb does not seem to be shrinking. Size constancy depends in part on familiarity with objects; you know that people and cars do not change size from moment to moment. It also depends on the apparent distance of an object. An object that is close produces a larger retinal image than the same object farther away, and the brain takes this into account. When you move your hand toward your face, your brain registers the fact that the hand is getting closer, and you correctly perceive its unchanging size despite the growing size of its retinal image. There is, then, an intimate relationship between perceived size and perceived distance.

2 Shape constancy. We continue to perceive an object as having a constant shape even though the shape of the retinal image produced by the shape of the retinal image produced by the object changes when our point of view changes. If you hold a Frisbee directly in front of your face, its image on the retina will be round. When you set the Frisbee on a table, its image becomes elliptical, yet you continue to see it as round.

3 Location constancy. We perceive stationary objects as remaining in the same place even though the retinal image moves about as we move our eyes, heads, and body. As you drive along the highway, telephone poles and trees fly by on your retina. But you know that these objects do not move on their own, and you also know that your body is moving, so you perceive the poles and trees as staying put.

4 Brightness constancy. We see objects as having a relatively constant brightness even though the amount of light they reflect changes as the overall level of illumination changes. Snow remains white even on a cloudy day and a black car remains black even on a sunny day. We are not fooled because the brain registers the total illumination in the scene and automatically adjusts for it.

5 Color constancy. Outdoor light is "bluer" than indoor light, and objects outdoors therefore reflect more "blue" light than those indoors. Conversely, indoor light from incandescent lamps is rich in long wavelengths and is therefore "yellower." Yet an apple looks red whether you look at it in your kitchen or outside on the patio; why? Part of the explanation involves sensory adaptation: Outdoors, we quickly adapt to short-wavelength (bluish) light, and indoors, we adapt to long-wavelength light. As a result, our visual responses are similar in the two situations. Also, when computing the color of an object, the brain takes into account *all* the wavelengths in the visual field immediately around it. If an apple is bathed in bluish light, so, usually, is everything else around it. The increase in blue light reflected by the apple is canceled in the visual cortex by the increase in blue light reflected by the apple's surroundings, and so the apple continues to look red. Color constancy is further aided by our knowledge of the world. We know that apples are usually red and bananas are usually yellow, and the brain uses that knowledge to recalibrate the colors in those objects when the lighting changes (Mitterer & de Ruiter, 2008).

Visual Illusions: When Seeing Is Misleading. Perceptual constancies allow us to make sense of the world. Occasionally, however, we can be fooled, and the result is a *perceptual illusion*. For psychologists, illusions are valuable because they are systematic errors that provide us with hints about the perceptual strategies of the mind.

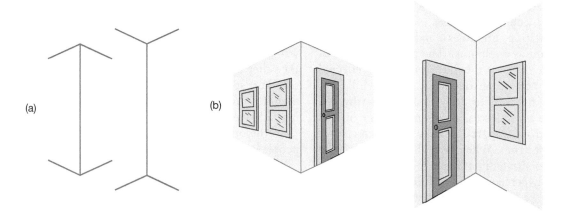

FIGURE 6.6 The Müller-Lyer Illusion
The two lines in (a) are exactly the same length. We are probably fooled into perceiving them as different because the brain interprets the one with the outward-facing branches as farther away, as if it were the far corner of a room, and the one with the inward-facing branches as closer, as if it were the near edge of a building (b).

Although illusions can occur in any sensory modality, visual illusions have been the best studied. Visual illusions sometimes occur when the strategies that normally lead to accurate perception are overextended to situations where they do not apply. Compare the lengths of the two vertical lines in Figure 6.6. You will probably perceive the line on the right as slightly longer than the one on the left, yet they are exactly the same. (Go ahead, measure them; everyone does.) This is the Müller-Lyer illusion, named after the German sociologist who first described it in 1889.

The leading explanation for the Müller-Lyer illusion is that the branches on the lines serve as perspective cues that normally suggest depth (Gregory, 1963). The line on the left is like the near edge of a building; the one on the right is like the far corner of a room (see part b of the figure). Although the two lines produce retinal images of the same size, the one with the outward-facing branches suggests greater distance. We are fooled into perceiving it as longer because we automatically apply a rule about the relationship between size and distance that is normally useful: When two objects produce the same-sized retinal image and one is farther away, the farther one is larger. The problem, in this case, is that the two lines are the same distance away, so the rule is inappropriate. For other illusions that occur when the brain misinterprets sensory information, see Figure 6.7.

Simulate the **Experiment** Müller-Lyer Illusion at **MyPsychLab**

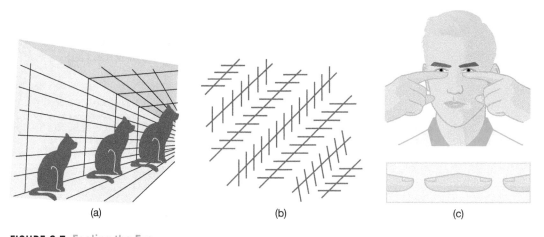

FIGURE 6.7 Fooling the Eye
Although perception is usually accurate, we can be fooled. In (a), the cats as drawn are exactly the same size; in (b), the diagonal lines are all parallel. To see the illusion depicted in (c), hold your index fingers 5 to 10 inches in front of your eyes as shown and then focus straight ahead. Do you see a floating "fingertip frankfurter"? Can you make it shrink or expand?

Just as there are size, shape, location, brightness, and color constancies, so there are size, shape, location, brightness, and color *in*constancies, resulting in illusions. The perceived color of an object depends on the wavelengths reflected by its immediate surroundings, a fact well known to artists and interior designers. That is why you never see a good, strong red unless other objects in the surroundings reflect the blue and green part of the spectrum. When two objects that are the same color have different surroundings, you may mistakenly perceive them as different.

Perhaps the ultimate perceptual illusion occurred when Swedish researchers tricked people into feeling that they were swapping bodies with another person or even a mannequin (Petkova & Ehrsson, 2008). The participants wore virtual-reality goggles connected to a camera on the other person's (or mannequin's) head. This allowed them to see the world from the other body's point of view as an experimenter simultaneously stroked both the participant's body and the other person's (or mannequin's) with a rod. Most people soon had the weird sensation that the other body was actually their own; they even cringed when the other body was poked or threatened. The researchers speculate that some day the body-swapping illusion could be helpful in marital counseling, allowing each partner to *literally* see things from the other's point of view, or in therapy with people who have distorted body images.

In everyday life, most illusions are harmless and entertaining. Occasionally, however, an illusion interferes with the performance of some task or skill, or may even cause an accident. For example, because large objects often appear to move more slowly than small ones, drivers sometimes underestimate the speed of onrushing trains at railroad crossings. They think they can beat the train, with tragic results.

 Watch the **Video** What's In It For Me?: Perceptual Magic in Art at **MyPsychLab**

Recite & Review

✓ **Study** and **Review** at **MyPsychLab**

Recite: This instruction is no illusion: Recite everything you can remember about hue, brightness, saturation, parts of the eye, rods and cones, the optic nerve, feature-detector cells, the trichromatic and opponent process theories of color vision, Gestalt principles, binocular and monocular cues to depth and distance, visual constancies, and visual illusions.

Review: That's a lot of information to learn, so you'd do well to go back and read this section again.

Now take this *Quick Quiz:*

1. Why does a yellow dress look brighter than a blue dress?

2. How can two Gestalt principles help explain why you can make out the Big Dipper on a starry night?

3. *True or false*: The retina can be called an extension of brain.

4. Hold one hand about 12 inches from your face and the other one about 6 inches away. (a) Which hand will cast the smaller retinal image? (b) Why don't you perceive that hand as smaller?

Answers:

1. The color yellow reflects more light in comparison to blue. 2. *Proximity* of certain stars encourages you to see them as clustered together to form a pattern; *closure* allows you to "fill in the gaps" and see the contours of a "dipper." 3. true 4. a. The hand that is 12 inches away will cast a smaller retinal image. b. Your brain takes the differences in distance into account in estimating size; also, you know how large your hands are. The result is size constancy.

You are about to learn . . .

- the basics of how we hear.

- why a note played on a flute sounds different from the same note played on an oboe.

- how we locate the source of a sound.

Hearing

Like vision, the sense of hearing, or *audition*, provides a vital link with the world around us. Because social relationships rely so heavily on hearing, when people lose their hearing they sometimes come to feel socially isolated. That is why many people with hearing impairment feel strongly about teaching deaf children American Sign Language (ASL) or other gestural systems, which allow them to communicate with other signers.

What We Hear LO 6.16

The stimulus for sound is a wave of pressure created when an object vibrates (or when compressed air is released, as in a pipe organ). The vibration (or release of air) causes molecules in a transmitting substance to move together and apart. This movement produces variations in pressure that radiate in all directions. The transmitting substance is usually air, but sound waves can also travel through water and solids, as you know if you have ever put your ear to the wall to hear voices in the next room.

As with vision, *physical* characteristics of the stimulus—in this case, a sound wave—are related in a predictable way to *psychological* aspects of our experience:

1 **Loudness** is the psychological dimension of auditory experience related to the *intensity* of a wave's pressure. Intensity corresponds to the amplitude (maximum height) of the wave. The more energy contained in the wave, the higher it is at its peak. Perceived loudness is also affected by how high or low a sound is. If low and high sounds produce waves with equal amplitudes, the low sound may seem quieter.

Sound intensity is measured in units called *decibels* (dB). A decibel is one-tenth of a *bel*, a unit named for Alexander Graham Bell, the inventor of the telephone. The average absolute threshold of hearing in human beings is zero decibels. Unlike inches on a ruler, decibels are not equally distant; each 10 decibels denotes a 10-fold increase in sound intensity. On the Internet, decibel estimates for various sounds vary from site to site; this is because the intensity of a sound depends on things like how far away it is and the particular person or object producing the sound. What you need to know is that a 60-decibel conversation is not twice as loud as a 30-decibel whisper; it is 1,000 times louder.

2 **Pitch** is the dimension of auditory experience related to the frequency of the sound wave and, to some extent, its intensity. *Frequency* refers to how rapidly the air (or other medium) vibrates—the number of times per second the wave cycles through a peak and a low point. One cycle per second is known as 1 *hertz* (Hz). The healthy ear of a young person normally detects frequencies in the range of 16 Hz (the lowest note on a pipe organ) to 20,000 Hz (the scraping of a grasshopper's legs).

3 **Timbre** is the distinguishing quality of a sound. It is the dimension of auditory experience related to the *complexity* of the sound wave, the relative breadth of the range of frequencies that make up the wave. A pure tone consists of only one frequency, but pure tones in nature are extremely rare. Usually what we hear is a complex wave consisting of several subwaves with different frequencies. Timbre is what makes a note played on a flute, which produces relatively pure tones, sound different from the same note played on an oboe, which produces complex sounds.

When many sound wave frequencies are present but are not in harmony, we hear noise. When all the frequencies of the sound spectrum occur, they produce a hissing sound called *white noise*. Just as white light includes all wavelengths of the visible light spectrum, so white noise includes all frequencies of the audible sound spectrum.

An Ear on the World LO 6.17

As Figure 6.8 shows, the ear has an outer, a middle, and an inner section. The soft, funnel-shaped outer ear is well designed to collect sound waves, but hearing would still be pretty good without it. The essential parts of the ear are hidden from view, inside the head.

A sound wave passes into the outer ear and through an inch-long canal to strike an oval-shaped membrane called the *eardrum*. The eardrum is so sensitive that it can respond to the movement of a single molecule! A sound wave causes it to vibrate with the same frequency and amplitude as the wave itself. This vibration is passed along to three tiny bones in the middle ear, the smallest bones in the human body. These bones, known informally as the hammer, the anvil, and the stirrup, move one after the other, which has the effect of intensifying the force of the vibration. The innermost bone, the stirrup, pushes on a membrane that opens into the inner ear.

The actual organ of hearing, the **organ of Corti**, is a chamber inside the **cochlea**, a snail-shaped structure within the inner ear. The organ of Corti plays the same role in hearing that the retina plays in vision. It contains the crucial receptor cells, which in this case are called *hair cells* and are topped by tiny bristles, or *cilia*. Brief exposure to extremely loud noises, like those from a gunshot or a jet airplane (140 dB), or sustained exposure to more moderate noises, like those from shop tools or truck traffic (90 dB), can damage these fragile cells. The cilia flop over like broken blades of grass, and if the damage affects a critical number, hearing loss occurs. In modern societies, with their rock concerts, crowded bars, leaf blowers,

loudness The dimension of auditory experience related to the intensity of a pressure wave.

pitch The dimension of auditory experience related to the frequency of a pressure wave; the height or depth of a tone.

timbre The distinguishing quality of a sound; the dimension of auditory experience related to the complexity of the pressure wave.

organ of Corti [core-tee] A structure in the cochlea containing hair cells that serve as the receptors for hearing.

cochlea [KOCK-lee-uh] A snail-shaped, fluid-filled organ in the inner ear, containing the organ of Corti, where the receptors for hearing are located.

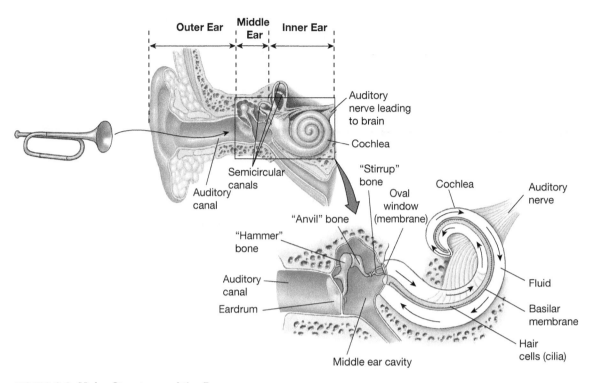

FIGURE 6.8 Major Structures of the Ear
Sound waves collected by the outer ear are channeled down the auditory canal, causing the eardrum to vibrate. These vibrations are then passed along to the tiny bones of the middle ear. Movement of these bones intensifies the force of the vibrations separating the middle and inner ear. The receptor cells for hearing (hair cells), located in the organ of Corti (not shown) within the snail-shaped cochlea, initiate nerve impulses that travel along the auditory nerve to the brain.

jackhammers, and music players turned up to full blast, such damage is increasingly common, even among teenagers and young adults (Agrawal, Platz, & Niparko, 2008). Scientists are looking for ways to grow new, normally functioning hair cells, but hair-cell damage is currently irreversible.

The hair cells of the cochlea are embedded in the rubbery *basilar membrane*, which stretches across the interior of the cochlea. When pressure reaches the cochlea, it causes wavelike motions in fluid within the cochlea's interior. These waves of fluid push on the basilar membrane, causing it to move in a wavelike fashion, too. Just above the hair cells is yet another membrane. As the hair cells rise and fall, their tips brush against it, and they bend. This causes the hair cells to initiate a signal that is passed along to the *auditory nerve*, which then carries the message to the brain. The particular pattern of hair-cell movement is affected by the manner in which the basilar membrane moves. This pattern determines which neurons fire and how rapidly they fire, and the resulting code in turn helps determine the sort of sound we hear. We discriminate high-pitched sounds largely on the basis of where activity occurs along the basilar membrane; activity at different sites leads to different neural codes. We discriminate low-pitched sounds largely on the

basis of the frequency of the basilar membrane's vibration; again, different frequencies lead to different neural codes.

Could you have ever imagined that hearing depends on this complex and odd arrangement of bristles, fluids, and snail shells?

Constructing the Auditory World
LO 6.18

Just as we do not see a retinal image, so we do not hear a chorus of brushlike tufts bending and swaying in the dark recesses of the cochlea. Instead, we use our perceptual powers to organize patterns of sound and to construct a meaningful auditory world.

In your psychology class, your instructor hopes you will perceive his or her voice as *figure* and distant cheers from the athletic field as *ground*. Whether these hopes are realized will depend, of course, on where you choose to direct your attention. Other Gestalt principles also seem to apply to hearing. The *proximity* of notes in a melody tells you which notes go together to form phrases; *continuity* helps you follow a melody on one violin when another violin is playing a different melody; *similarity* in timbre and pitch helps you pick out the soprano voices in a chorus and hear them as a unit; *closure* helps you understand a cell phone

If prolonged, the 120-decibel music at a rock concert can damage or destroy the delicate hair cells of the inner ear and impair the hearing of fans standing close to the speakers. The microphotograph on the right shows minuscule bristles (cilia) projecting from a single hair cell.

caller's words even when interference makes some of the individual sounds unintelligible.

Besides needing to organize sounds, we also need to know where they are coming from. We can estimate the *distance* of a sound's source by using loudness as a cue; we know that a train sounds louder when it is 20 yards away than when it is a mile off. To locate the *direction* a sound is coming from, we depend in part on the fact that we have two ears. A sound arriving from the right reaches the right ear a fraction of a second sooner than it reaches the left ear, and vice versa. The sound may also provide a bit more energy to the right ear (depending on its frequency) because it has to get around the head to reach the left ear. It is hard to localize sounds that are coming from directly behind you or from directly above your head because such sounds reach both ears at the same time. When you turn or cock your head,

you are actively trying to overcome this problem. Horses, dogs, rabbits, deer, and many other animals do not need to do this because the lucky creatures can move their ears independently of their heads.

A few blind people have learned to harness the relationship between distance and sound to navigate their environment in astonishing ways—hiking, mountain biking, even golfing. They use their mouths to make clicking sounds and listen to the tiny echoes bouncing off objects, a process called *echolocation*. It's similar to what bats do when they fly around hunting for food. In blind human echolocators, the visual cortex responds to sounds that produce echoes—that is, sounds that provide information about the size and location of objects—but not to other sounds that don't produce echoes (Thaler, Arnott, & Goodale, 2011).

Recite & Review

✓ **Study** and **Review** at **MyPsychLab**

Recite: Hear this! Recite everything you can recall about loudness, pitch, timbre, the anatomy of the ear, Gestalt principles as applied to hearing, and ways of determining a sound's location.

Review: Next, go back and read this section again.

Now take this *Quick Quiz:*

1. Which psychological dimensions of hearing correspond to the intensity, frequency, and complexity of the sound wave?

2. What is the term used for all sounds of the audible sound spectrum?

3. _____ principles can also be applied to sound.

4. Rahim wonders why he has to turn his head to listen to a distant sound from above while his pet dog, Bunny, doesn't need to do that. How would you explain this?

Answers:

1. loudness, pitch, timbre 2. white noise 3. Gestalt 4. Humans find it difficult to localize a sound coming from directly behind or above them, whereas animals, who can move their ears independently of their heads, can easily hear and identify it.

Other Senses

Psychologists have been particularly interested in vision and audition because of the importance of these senses to human survival. However, research on other senses is growing rapidly, as awareness of how they contribute to our lives increases and new ways are found to study them.

Taste: Savory Sensations
LO 6.19, LO 6.20

Taste, or *gustation*, occurs because chemicals stimulate thousands of receptors in the mouth. These receptors are located primarily on the tongue, but some are also found in the throat, inside the cheeks, on the roof of the mouth, and, incredibly, as we will see, in your gut. If you look at your tongue in a mirror, you will notice many tiny bumps; they are called **papillae** (from the Latin for "pimples"), and they come in several forms. In all but one of these forms, the sides of each papilla are lined with **taste buds**, which up close look a little like segmented oranges (see Figure 6.9). Because of genetic differences, human tongues

papillae [pa-PILL-ee] Knoblike elevations on the tongue, containing the taste buds. (Singular: *papilla*.)

taste buds Nests of taste-receptor cells.

can have as few as 500 or as many as 10,000 taste buds (Miller & Reedy, 1990).

The taste buds are commonly referred to, mistakenly, as the receptors for taste. The actual receptor cells are *inside* the buds, 15 to 50 to a bud. These cells send tiny fibers out through an opening in the bud; the receptor sites are on these fibers. New receptor cells replace old ones about every 10 days. However, after age 40 or so, the total number of taste buds (and therefore receptors) declines. Interestingly, the center of the tongue contains no taste buds. However, as in the case of the eye's blind spot, you will not usually notice the lack of sensation because the brain fills in the gap.

Four tastes are part of our evolutionary heritage: *salty, sour, bitter,* and *sweet,* each produced by a different type of chemical. Their receptors are tuned to molecules that alert us to good or dangerous tastes: Bitter tastes detect poison; sweet tastes attract us to biologically useful sugars, such as those in fruit; salty tastes enable us to identify sodium, a mineral crucial to survival; and sour tastes permit us to avoid acids in concentrations that might injure tissue (Bartoshuk, 2009). Although you may have heard that your tongue has a distinct zone for each of these four tastes, that's a myth. All of the basic tastes can be perceived at any spot on the tongue that has receptors, and differences among the areas are small. When you bite into an egg or a piece of bread or an orange, its unique flavor is composed of some combination of these tastes.

Some researchers believe that there is a fifth basic taste, *umami*, the taste of monosodium glutamate (MSG), which is said to permit the detection of protein-rich foods. Umami was identified by Japanese chemists in the early 1900s as a flavor enhancer. (The word has no exact English translation, but the closest is "delicious" or "savory.") The findings from umami research, which has largely

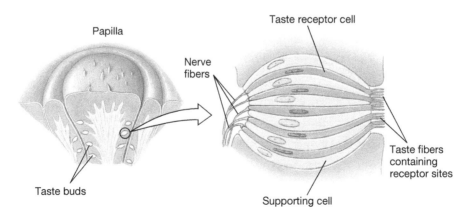

FIGURE 6.9 Taste Receptors
The illustration on the left shows taste buds lining the sides of a papilla on the tongue's surface.
The illustration on the right shows an enlarged view of a single taste bud.

Get Involved! The Smell of Taste

Demonstrate for yourself that smell enhances the sense of taste. While holding your nose, take a bite of a slice of apple, and then do the same with a slice of raw potato. You may find that you can't taste much difference. If you think you do taste a difference, perhaps your expectations are influencing your response. Now try the same thing, but close your eyes and have someone else feed you the slices. Can you tell them apart this time? It's also fun to do this little test with flavored jelly beans. They are still apt to taste sweet, but you may be unable to identify the distinct flavors.

been funded by the MSG industry, are controversial, because in most foods it is not detectable. The attention given to umami, however, has led to the fascinating discovery that taste receptors—for umami, but also sweetness and bitterness—are found throughout the gastrointestinal tract. These receptors send signals to the brain, influencing appetite and possibly conditioned preferences for the sensory properties of certain foods (Trivedi, 2012).

Everyone knows that people live in what psychological scientist Linda Bartoshuk (2000) calls different "taste worlds." Some people love broccoli and others hate it. Some people can eat chili peppers that are burning hot and others cannot tolerate the mildest jalepeño. And perhaps no food divides people more than cilantro (Spanish for coriander). Entire websites are devoted to complaints about those innocent-looking green leaves, whose detractors think taste like soap. What causes these taste differences?

According to Baroshuk's research, about 25 percent of people live in a "neon" taste world. These *supertasters*, who are overrepresented among women, Asians, Hispanics, and blacks, have an unusually large number of small, densely packed papillae (Reedy et al., 1993). For them, bitter foods such as caffeine, quinine (the bitter ingredient in tonic water), and many vegetables are unpleasantly bitter—at least twice as bitter as they are for other people. Supertasters also perceive sweet tastes as sweeter and salty tastes as saltier than other people do, and they feel more "burn" from ginger, pepper, and hot chilies (Bartoshuk et al., 1998; Lucchina et al., 1998).

Taste differences are partly a matter of genetics, but culture and learning also play a role. Many Westerners who enjoy raw oysters or herring are put off by other forms of raw seafood that are popular in Japan, such as sea urchin. Even within a given culture, individuals have different taste preferences, some of which begin in the womb or shortly after birth. Flavors as diverse as vanilla, carrot, garlic, anise, hot spices, and mint can be transmitted to the fetus or newborn through amniotic fluid or breast milk, with long-lasting consequences (Beauchamp & Mennella, 2011; Mennella

et al., 2011). For example, babies fed salty foods are likely to grow into salty-food-loving preschoolers (Stein, Cowart, & Beauchamp, 2012).

The attractiveness of a food can also be affected by its color, temperature, and texture. As Goldilocks found out, a bowl of cold porridge is not nearly as delicious as one that is properly heated. And any peanut butter fan will tell you that chunky and smooth peanut butters just don't taste the same. Even more important for taste is a food's odor. Much of what we call "flavor" is really the smell of gases released by the foods we put in our mouths. Indeed, subtle flavors such as chocolate and vanilla would have little taste if we could not smell them (see Figure 6.10). Smell's influence on flavor explains why you have trouble tasting your food when you have a stuffy nose. Most people who have chronic trouble detecting tastes have a problem with smell, not taste.

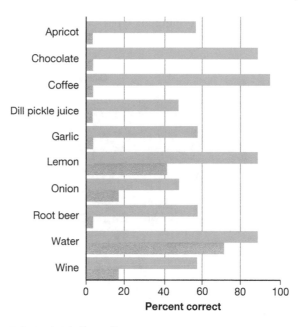

FIGURE 6.10 Taste Test
The green bars show the percentages of people who could identify a substance dropped on the tongue when they were able to smell it. The gold bars show the percentage that could identify the substance when they were prevented from smelling it (Mozell et al., 1969).

Smell: The Sense of Scents LO 6.21

The great author and educator Helen Keller, who became blind and deaf as a toddler, once called smell "the fallen angel of the senses." Yet our sense of smell, or *olfaction*, although seemingly crude when compared to a bloodhound's, is actually quite good; the human nose can detect aromas that sophisticated machines fail to detect.

The receptors for smell are specialized neurons embedded in a tiny patch of mucous membrane in the upper part of the nasal passage, just beneath the eyes (see Figure 6.11). Millions of receptors in each nasal cavity respond to chemical molecules (vapors) in the air. When you inhale, you pull these molecules into the nasal cavity, but they can also enter from the mouth, wafting up the throat like smoke up a chimney. These molecules trigger responses in the receptors that combine to yield the yeasty smell of freshly baked bread or the spicy smell of a curry. Signals from the receptors are carried to the brain's olfactory bulb by the *olfactory nerve*, which is made up of the receptors' axons. From the olfactory bulb, they travel to a higher region of the brain.

Figuring out the neural code for smell has been a real challenge. Of the 10,000 or so smells we detect (rotten, burned, musky, fruity, fishy, spicy, and so on), none seems to be more basic than any other. Moreover, roughly 1,000 kinds of receptors exist, each kind responding to a part of an odor molecule's structure (Axel, 1995; Buck & Axel, 1991). Distinct odors activate unique combinations of receptors, and signals from different types of receptors are combined in individual neurons in the brain.

Some animals have a sense of smell that makes humans seem impaired by comparison. At airports, dogs detect drugs, bombs, and contraband food in people's luggage; in clinics, they detect cancer simply by sniffing a person's breath (Sonoda et al., 2011). In Africa, rats are helping to detect undiagnosed tuberculosis (Mgode et al., 2012). Such olfactory talents evolved because smell is essential to these animals' survival. Although smell is less vital for human survival, we, too, need it in daily life. We sniff out danger by smelling smoke, rotten food, and gas leaks, so a deficit in the sense of smell is nothing to turn up your nose at. Such a loss can result from infection, disease, injury to the olfactory nerve, or smoking. A person who has smoked two packs a day for 10 years must abstain from cigarettes for 10 more years before the sense of smell returns to normal (Frye, Schwartz, & Doty, 1990).

Odors, of course, have psychological effects on us, which is why we buy perfumes and sniff flowers. Perhaps because olfactory centers in the brain are linked to areas that process memories and emotions, specific smells often evoke vivid, emotionally colored memories (Herz & Cupchik, 1995; Vroon, 1997). The smell of hot chocolate may trigger fond memories of cozy winter mornings from your childhood; the smell of rubbing alcohol may remind you of an unpleasant trip to the hospital. Odors can also influence people's everyday behavior, which is why shopping malls and hotels often install aroma diffusers in hopes of putting you in a good mood.

Watch the Video Thinking Like a Psychologist: Can Smells Alter Mood and Behavior? at **MyPsychLab**

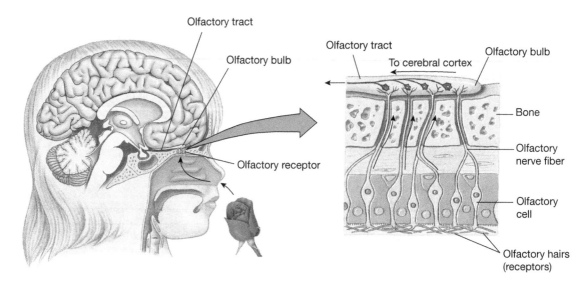

FIGURE 6.11 Receptors for Smell
Airborne chemical molecules (vapors) enter the nose and circulate through the nasal cavity, where the smell receptors are located. The receptors' axons make up the olfactory nerve, which carries signals to the brain. When you sniff, you draw more vapors into the nose and speed their circulation. Vapors can also reach the nasal cavity through the mouth by way of a passageway from the throat.

Smell has not only evolutionary but also cultural significance. These pilgrims in Japan are purifying themselves with holy incense in hopes of gaining good luck and health.

Senses of the Skin LO 6.22

The skin's usefulness is more than just skin deep. Besides protecting our innards, our two square yards of skin help us identify objects and establish intimacy with others. By providing a boundary between ourselves and everything else, the skin also gives us a sense of ourselves as distinct from the environment.

The basic skin senses include *touch* (or pressure), *warmth, cold,* and *pain*. Within these four types are variations such as itch, tickle, and painful burning. Scientists are on the trail of the distinct receptors and nerve fibers that are involved in these skin sensations. One nerve fiber seems responsible for the kind of itching caused by histamines (Schmelz et al., 1997). Other fibers, which detect pain from a punch in the nose or a burn, also seem to detect the kind of pathological itch that is unrelated to histamines (Johanek et al., 2008). A receptor for cold has also been identified (McKemy, Neuhausser, & Julius, 2002; Peier et al., 2002).

But many aspects of touch remain baffling, such as why gently touching adjacent pressure spots in rapid succession produces tickle and why scratching relieves (or sometimes worsens) an itch. Decoding the messages of the skin senses will eventually tell us how we are able to distinguish sandpaper from velvet and glue from grease.

The Mystery of Pain LO 6.23, LO 6.24

Understanding the physiology of pain is an enormous task, for two main reasons. One is that pain, which is both a skin sense and an internal sense, differs from other senses in a terrible way: Even when the stimulus producing it is removed, the sensation may continue, sometimes for years. Chronic pain puts stress on the body and can cause depression and despair. Another reason is that different types of pain (from, say, a thorn, a bruise, or a hot iron) involve different chemical changes and different changes in nerve-cell activity at the site of injury or disease, as well as in the spinal cord and brain. Several chemical substances are involved and so are glial cells, the cells that support nerve cells (see Chapter 4); they release inflammatory substances that can worsen the pain (Watkins & Maier, 2003). Here, however, we will focus on a general theory of pain and on the psychological factors that influence how it is experienced.

The Physiology of Pain. For many years, the most influential theory of pain was the **gate-control theory**, which was first proposed by Canadian psychologist Ronald Melzack and British physiologist Patrick Wall (1965). According to this theory, pain impulses must get past a "gate" in the spinal cord. The gate is not an actual structure, but rather a pattern of neural activity that either blocks pain messages from the skin, muscles, and internal organs or lets those signals through. Normally, the gate is kept shut, either by impulses coming into the spinal cord from large fibers that respond to pressure and other kinds of stimulation or by signals coming down from the brain itself. But when body tissue is injured, the large fibers are damaged and smaller fibers open the gate, allowing pain messages to reach the brain unchecked. The gate-control theory correctly predicts that mild pressure, or other kinds of stimulation, can interfere with severe or protracted pain by closing the spinal gate. When we vigorously rub a banged elbow or apply ice packs, heat, or stimulating ointments to injuries, we are applying this principle.

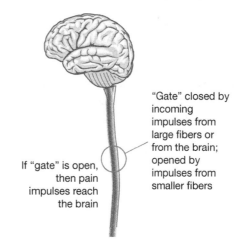

If "gate" is open, then pain impulses reach the brain

"Gate" closed by incoming impulses from large fibers or from the brain; opened by impulses from smaller fibers

In the gate-control theory, the brain not only responds to incoming signals from sensory nerves but is also capable of generating pain entirely on its own (Melzack, 1992, 1993). An extensive *matrix* (network) of neurons in the brain gives us a sense of our own bodies and body parts. When this matrix produces abnormal patterns of activity, the result is pain. The brain's ability to generate

gate-control theory
The theory that the experience of pain depends in part on whether pain impulses get past a neurological "gate" in the spinal cord and thus reach the brain.

pain can help explain the many instances of severe, chronic pain that occur without any sign of injury or disease whatsoever.

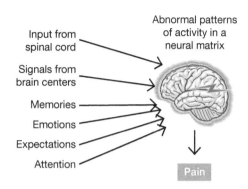

Because technology now allows scientists to study pain at the molecular and cellular level, today we know that the gate-control theory, though still useful, is incomplete. Pain may also be caused by changes to the sensitivity of neurons in the central nervous system (CNS). For example, when bursts of heat are repeatedly applied to an animal's paw, pain receptors in the paw and skin remain sensitive for several hours. During that time, even a light, harmless touch will activate the receptors, and applying anesthetic at the site of injury will not make the receptors return to normal. Such changes can help explain how once-harmless stimuli can end up causing pain (Latremoliere & Woolf, 2009).

An extreme version of pain without injury occurs in **phantom pain**, in which a person continues to feel pain that seemingly comes from an arm or leg that has been amputated, or from a bodily organ that has been surgically removed. Phantom limb pain afflicts up to 90 percent of amputees. The person may feel the same aching, burning, or sharp pain from sores, calf cramps, throbbing toes, or even ingrown toenails that he or she endured before the surgery. Even when the spinal cord has been completely severed, amputees often continue to report phantom pain from areas below the break. There are no nerve impulses for the spinal-cord gate to block or let through, yet the pain can be constant and excruciating; some sufferers have committed suicide.

A leading explanation of phantom pain is that the brain has reorganized itself: An area in the sensory cortex that formerly corresponded to the missing body part has been "invaded" by neurons from another area. Higher brain centers then interpret messages from those neurons as coming from the nonexistent body part (Cruz et al., 2005; Ramachandran & Blakeslee, 1998). Even though the missing limb can no longer send

phantom pain The experience of pain in a missing limb or other body part.

signals through touch and internal sensations, memories of these signals remain in the nervous system, including memories of pain, paralysis, and cramping that occurred prior to amputation. The result is an inaccurate "body map" in the brain and pain signals that cannot be shut off.

Vilayanur Ramachandran, the neurologist who first proposed this explanation of phantom pain, has developed an extraordinarily simple but effective treatment for it. Ramachandran wondered whether he could devise an illusion to trick the brain of an amputee with phantom arm pain into perceiving the missing limb as moving and pain-free. He placed a mirror upright and perpendicular to the sufferer's body, such that the amputee's intact arm was reflected in the mirror. From the amputee's perspective, the result was an illusion of two functioning arms. The amputee was then instructed to move both arms in synchrony while looking into the mirror. With this technique, which has now been used with many people, the brain is fooled into thinking its owner has two healthy arms or legs, resynchronizes the signals—and phantom pain diminishes or even vanishes (Ramachandran & Altschuler, 2009). Neurologists have tested this method with Iraq veterans and are finding it to be more successful than control therapies in which patients just mentally visualize having two intact limbs (Anderson-Barnes et al., 2009; Chan et al., 2007).

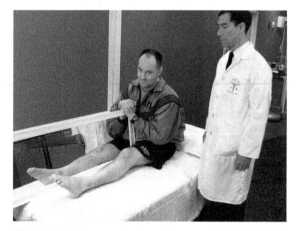

After his right leg was destroyed in an explosion while he was in Iraq, Army Sergeant Nicholas Paupore experienced excruciating phantom limb pain. Even morphine didn't help. Then he underwent a simple daily procedure. A mirror was placed at a strategic angle to reflect his intact leg, tricking his brain into registering two healthy legs that he could move freely. The pain subsided almost immediately. A year after therapy, he had only occasional, milder pain, and needed no medication. In some patients, mirror therapy has eliminated phantom pain entirely.

The Psychology of Pain. Psychological as well as physiological factors affect the severity of chronic pain and a person's reactions to it. When people dwell on their pain and talk about it constantly, or begin to define themselves as a sick, suffering person, their pain typically intensifies (Pincus & Morley, 2001). Conversely, when they are distracted, they may not feel their pain as severely as they usually would.

Expectations also exert a powerful influence. In one study, volunteers were trained to expect jolts of heat applied to their legs after a tone sounded. The longer the delay between the tone and the heat, the stronger the heat. Functional MRI showed that the stronger the pain the volunteers *expected* to feel, the greater the activity in certain brain regions before actual delivery of the pain—and most of these regions overlapped with those that responded to the pain itself. But eventually the delay stopped being predictable. Sometimes a moderate jolt followed a long delay, and sometimes a severe jolt followed a short delay. When the volunteers expected a moderate jolt and instead received a more painful one, their self-reported pain fell by 28 percent, compared with when they expected the most painful heat and actually got it (Koyama et al., 2005; see Figure 6.12). This decrease was equal to what they would have experienced had they received a shot of morphine!

Such findings suggest a mechanism for how placebos reduce pain: When placebos affect expectations ("I'm going to get relief"), they also affect the brain mechanisms underlying pain. Volunteers in another study had an "analgesic cream" (actually a placebo) rubbed on their skin before getting a painful shock to the wrist; MRI scans showed decreased activity in the pain matrix, the pain-sensitive areas of their brains (Wager et al., 2004). And when diabetes patients with painful nerve damage were given either active medication or an inactive placebo and rated their pain before and after treatment, 62 percent of the improvement in the medication group was attributable to the placebo effect (Häuser et al., 2011).

Placebos may also promote the production of endorphins, the body's natural pain-relieving opiates. Researchers gave volunteers a slow, harmless injection of a pain-inducing solution in the jaw and had them rate their pain level (Zubieta et al., 2005). As the injection continued, the researchers told some of the participants (falsely) that a pain-relieving serum had been added and again asked all of the subjects to rank their discomfort. Throughout the procedure, PET scans tracked the activity of endorphins in the subjects' brains. Those who got the placebo produced endorphins in pain-control

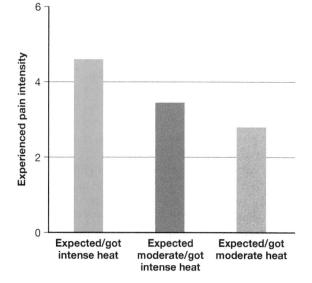

FIGURE 6.12 Expectations and Pain
When people expected moderate heat but got intense heat (blue bar), their self-reported pain was lower than it would have been had they expected the intense heat (green bar).

areas of the brain, which is just what would have happened had they taken a real pain killer.

Expectations about pain are affected not only by placebos but also by your environment (does it make you feel safe or apprehensive?), what your doctor tells you, psychological states such as anxiety or depression, and cultural beliefs about the appropriateness of noticing symptoms and expressing distress. These nonmedical influences contribute to the rise and fall in pain epidemics, such as mysterious outbreaks of back pain, whiplash, and repetitive-motion injuries (Gawande, 1998). People who suffer during such epidemics are not faking it, and their pain is not "just in their heads." But it may be in their brains.

👁 Watch the Video In the Real World: Managing Pain at MyPsychLab

The Environment Within LO 6.25

We usually think of our senses as pipelines to the world around us, but two senses keep us informed about the movements of our own bodies. **Kinesthesis** tells us where our bodily parts are located and lets us know when they move. This information is provided by pain and pressure receptors located in the muscles, joints, and tendons. Without kinesthesis, you would have trouble with any voluntary movement. Think of how hard it is to walk when your leg has fallen asleep or how awkward it feels to chew when a dentist has numbed your jaw.

Equilibrium, or the sense of balance, gives us information about our bodies as a whole. Along

kinesthesis [KIN-es-THEE-sís] The sense of body position and movement of body parts; also called *kinesthesia*.

equilibrium The sense of balance.

semicircular canals
Sense organs in the inner ear that contribute to equilibrium by responding to rotation of the head.

with vision and touch, it lets us know whether we are standing upright or on our heads and tells us when we are falling or rotating. Equilibrium relies primarily on three **semicircular canals** in the inner ear (refer back to Figure 6.8 on page 220). These thin tubes are filled with fluid that moves and presses on hairlike receptors whenever the head rotates. The receptors initiate messages that travel through a part of the auditory nerve that is not involved in hearing.

Normally, kinesthesis and equilibrium work together to give us a sense of our own physical reality, something we take utterly for granted but should not. Oliver Sacks (1985) told the heartbreaking story of Christina, a young British woman who suffered irreversible damage to her kinesthetic nerve fibers because of a mysterious inflammation. At first, Christina was as floppy as a rag doll; she could not sit up, walk, or stand. Then, slowly, she learned to do these things, relying on visual cues and sheer willpower. But her movements remained unnatural; she had to grasp a fork with painful force or she would drop it. Most tragically, despite her remaining sensitivity to light touch on the skin, she said she could no longer experience herself as physically embodied: "It's like something's been scooped right out of me," she told Sacks, "right at the center."

This breakdancer obviously has exceptional kinesthetic talents and equilibrium.

With equilibrium, we come, as it were, to the end of our senses. Every single second, millions of sensory signals reach the brain, which combines and integrates them to produce a model of reality. How does it know how to do this? Are our perceptual abilities inborn, or must we learn them? We turn next to this issue.

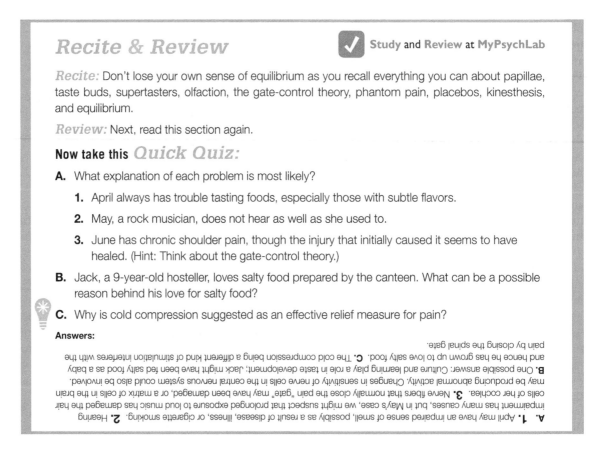

Recite & Review   ✔ **Study** and **Review** at **MyPsychLab**

Recite: Don't lose your own sense of equilibrium as you recall everything you can about papillae, taste buds, supertasters, olfaction, the gate-control theory, phantom pain, placebos, kinesthesis, and equilibrium.

Review: Next, read this section again.

Now take this *Quick Quiz:*

A. What explanation of each problem is most likely?

   1. April always has trouble tasting foods, especially those with subtle flavors.

   2. May, a rock musician, does not hear as well as she used to.

   3. June has chronic shoulder pain, though the injury that initially caused it seems to have healed. (Hint: Think about the gate-control theory.)

B. Jack, a 9-year-old hosteller, loves salty food prepared by the canteen. What can be a possible reason behind his love for salty food?

C. Why is cold compression suggested as an effective relief measure for pain?

Answers:

A. **1.** April may have an impaired sense of smell, possibly as a result of disease, illness, or cigarette smoking. **2.** Hearing impairment has many causes, but in May's case, we might suspect that prolonged exposure to loud music has damaged the hair cells of her cochlea. **3.** Nerve fibers that normally close the pain "gate" may have been damaged, or a matrix of cells in the brain may be producing abnormal activity. Changes in sensitivity of nerve cells in the central nervous system could also be involved. **B.** One possible answer: Culture and learning play a role in taste development; Jack might have been fed salty food as a baby and hence he has grown up to love salty food. **C.** The cold compression being a different kind of stimulation interferes with the pain by closing the spinal gate.

You are about to learn...

- whether babies see the world in the way adults do.
- what happens when people who are born blind or deaf have their sight or hearing restored.
- how psychological and cultural factors affect perception.

FIGURE 6.13 A Cliff-Hanger
Infants as young as 6 months usually hesitate to move past the apparent edge of a visual cliff, which suggests that they are able to perceive depth.

Perceptual Powers: Origins and Influences

What happens when babies first open their eyes? Do they see the same sights, hear the same sounds, and smell the same smells as an adult does? Or is an infant's world, as William James once suggested, only a "blooming, buzzing confusion," waiting to be organized by experience and learning? The truth lies somewhere between these two extremes.

Inborn Abilities LO 6.26

In human beings, most basic sensory abilities and many perceptual skills are inborn or develop soon after birth. Infants can distinguish salty from sweet and can discriminate among odors. They can distinguish a human voice from other sounds. They will startle to a loud noise and turn their heads toward its source, showing that they perceive sound as being localized in space. Many visual skills, too, are present at birth or develop shortly afterward. Human infants can discriminate sizes and colors early, possibly even right away. They distinguish contrasts, shadows, and complex patterns after only a few weeks, and depth perception develops during the first few months.

Testing an infant's perception of depth requires considerable ingenuity. A classic procedure has been to place infants on a device called a *visual cliff* (Gibson & Walk, 1960). The "cliff" is a pane of glass covering a shallow surface and a deep one (see Figure 6.13). Both surfaces are covered by a checkerboard pattern. The infant is placed on a board in the middle, and the child's mother tries to lure the baby across either the shallow side or the deep side. Babies only 6 months of age will crawl across the shallow side but will refuse to crawl out over the "cliff," suggesting that they have depth perception.

Infants younger than 6 months can also be tested on the visual cliff, even though they cannot yet crawl. At only 2 months of age, babies show a drop in heart rate when placed on the deep side but no change when they are placed on the shallow side. A slowed heart rate is usually a sign of increased attention. Thus, although these infants may not be frightened the way an older infant would be, it seems they can perceive the difference between the shallow and deep sides of the cliff (Banks & Salapatek, 1984).

 Watch the **Video** Classic Footage of Eleanor Gibson, Richard Walk, and the Visual Cliff at **MyPsychLab**

Critical Periods

Although many perceptual abilities are inborn, experience also plays a vital role. If an infant misses out on formative experiences during a crucial window of time called a **critical period**, perception will be impaired. Innate abilities may not survive because cells in the nervous system deteriorate, change, or fail to form appropriate neural pathways.

One way to study critical periods is to see what happens when the usual perceptual experiences of early life fail to take place. To do this, researchers have studied animals whose sensory and perceptual systems are similar to our own, such as kittens. Like human infants, kittens are born with the visual ability to detect horizontal and vertical lines and other spatial orientations; at birth, kittens' brains are equipped with the same kinds of feature-detector cells that adult cats have. But if they are deprived of normal visual experience, these cells deteriorate or change and perception suffers (Crair, Gillespie, & Stryker, 1998; Hirsch & Spinelli, 1970).

In one classic study, kittens were reared in darkness for five months after birth, but spent several hours each day in a special cylinder that

critical period A period of time in a person's or animal's life when exposure to certain stimuli or experiences is necessary for the optimal development of a particular skill or ability.

permitted them to see only vertical lines or horizontal ones, and nothing else. Later, cats that were exposed only to vertical lines had trouble perceiving horizontal ones; they would bump into horizontal obstacles. Those exposed only to horizontal lines had trouble perceiving vertical ones; they would run to play with horizontal bars but not vertical ones (Blakemore & Cooper, 1970).

What about human beings? Because of the brain's impressive plasticity (see Chapter 4), some people who are unable to see until middle childhood or even adulthood can regain enough perceptual ability to get along fine in daily life (Ostrovsky, Andalman, & Sinha, 2006). However, their perception is unlikely to fully recover. When adults who have been blind from infancy have their vision restored, most of them do not see well. Areas in the brain normally devoted to vision may have taken on different functions when these individuals were blind. As a result, their depth perception may be poor, causing them to trip constantly. They cannot always make sense of what they see; to identify objects, they may have to touch or smell them. They may have trouble recognizing faces and emotional expressions. They may even lack size constancy and may need to remind themselves that receding objects are not shrinking in size (Fine et al., 2003). Generally, the best recoveries occur when an infant's congenital blindness is corrected early, probably because a critical period for visual development occurs in infancy or early childhood.

Similar findings apply to hearing. When adults who were born deaf, or who lost their hearing before learning to speak, receive cochlear implants (devices that stimulate the auditory nerve and allow auditory signals to travel to the brain), they tend to find sounds confusing. They are unable to learn to speak normally, and sometimes they ask to have the implants removed. But cochlear implants are more successful in children and in adults who became deaf late in life (Bouton, 2013; Rauschecker, 1999). Young children presumably have not yet passed through the critical period for processing sounds, and older adults have already had years of auditory experience.

In sum, our perceptual powers are both inborn and dependent on experience. Because neurological connections in infants' brains and sensory systems are not completely formed, their senses are far less acute than an adult's. It takes time and experience for their sensory abilities to fully develop. But an infant's world is clearly not the blooming, buzzing confusion that William James took it to be.

Psychological and Cultural Influences LO 6.27

A camera doesn't care what it "sees." A digital recorder doesn't ponder what it "hears." But because we human beings care about what we see, hear, taste, smell, and feel, psychological factors can influence what we perceive and how we perceive it. Here are a few of these factors:

1 **Needs and motives.** When we need something, have an interest in it, or want it, we are especially likely to perceive it. That is why hungry people are faster than others at seeing words related to hunger when the words are flashed briefly on a screen (Radel & Clément-Guillotin, 2012; Wispé & Drambarean, 1953). People also tend to perceive objects that they want—a water bottle if they are thirsty, money they can win in a game, a personality test with favorable results—as being physically closer to them than objects they don't want or need. Some psychological scientists call these motivated misperceptions "wishful seeing" (Balcetis & Dunning, 2010).

2 **Beliefs.** What we hold to be true about the world can affect our interpretation of ambiguous sensory signals. Images that remind people of Jesus or Mary have been reported on walls, dishes, tortillas, and plates of spaghetti; the Arabic script for "Allah" has been reported on fish scales, chicken eggs, and beans. Such images cause great excitement among those who believe that divine messages can be found on everyday objects. However, mundane events inevitably

People often see what they want to see. Diana Duyser, a cook at a Florida casino, took a bite out of a grilled cheese sandwich and believed she saw the image of the Virgin Mary in what remained of it. She preserved the sandwich in plastic for 10 years and then decided to sell it. An online casino bought it on eBay for $28,000, even with a bite of it missing!

prove to be the explanation. The image of Jesus on a garage door in California, mentioned at the start of this chapter, attracted crowds until it turned out to be caused by two streetlights that merged the shadows of a bush and a "For Sale" sign in the yard.

3 **Emotions.** Emotions can also influence our interpretation of sensory information, as when a small child afraid of the dark sees a ghost instead of a robe hanging on the bedroom door. Pain, as we noted, is particularly intensified by negative emotions such as anxiety and sadness. Conversely, soldiers who are seriously wounded often deny being in much pain; their relief at being alive may offset the worry and fear that would otherwise make their pain worse (although the body's own pain-fighting mechanisms may also be involved). Interestingly, when people perceive their pain as resulting from another person's malicious intent (e.g., they think the other person intentionally stepped on their toe), they feel the hurt more than they would if they thought it was simply caused by a clumsy accident (Gray & Wegner, 2008).

4 **Expectations.** The tendency to perceive things in a certain way based on our expectations is called a **perceptual set**. Such sets can come in handy, helping us fill in words in spoken sentences when we haven't really heard every one. But perceptaul sets can also cause misperceptions, as you can see in the marginal illustration. Expectations can even reduce our reactions to stimuli that would otherwise be unpleasant, such as the obnoxious sound of fingernails scratching a chalkboard (human ears are highly sensitive to sounds in that frequency range). In one study, people who were told that such sounds were examples of modern "music" found them less unpleasant than did people who knew that the sounds were fingernails

scraping, even though physiological markers of stress were the same in both groups (Reuter & Oehler, 2011).

By the way, did you notice the misspelled word in the preceding paragraph? If not, probably it was because you expected all the words in this book to be spelled correctly.

Simulate the **Experiment** Ambiguous Figures at **MyPsychLab**

Our perceptions and expectations are all affected, in turn, by the culture we live in. In a classic study done in the 1960s, members of some African tribes were much less likely to be fooled by the Müller-Lyer illusion and other geometric illusions than were Westerners. In the West, the researchers observed, people live in a "carpentered" world, full of rectangular structures. Westerners are also used to interpreting two-dimensional photographs and perspective drawings as representations of a three-dimensional world. Therefore, they interpret the kinds of angles used in the Müller-Lyer illusion as right angles extended in space, a habit that increases susceptibility to the illusion. The rural Africans in the study, living in a less carpentered environment and in round huts, seemed more likely to take the lines in the figures literally, as two-dimensional, which could explain why they were less susceptible to the illusion (Segall, Campbell, & Herskovits, 1966; Segall et al., 1999).

Culture also affects perception by telling us what to notice or ignore. Westerners tend to focus mostly on the figure in a scene and much less on the ground. East Asians, in contrast, tend to pay attention to the overall context and the relationship between figure and ground. In a memory experiment, Japanese and Americans were shown animated underwater scenes containing brightly colored fish that were larger and moving faster than other objects in the scene. Afterward, both

perceptual set A habitual way of perceiving, based on expectations.

PARIS
IN THE
THE SPRING

Most people assume that they perceive reality "as it is." But culture has a powerful influence on what we notice and remember. Japanese and other East Asians tend to pay attention to figure and ground equally—in this case, the fish and its surroundings—whereas Americans tend to pay more attention to the moving fish in the foreground.

groups reported the same numbers of details about the fish, but the Japanese remembered more details about everything else in the background (Masuda & Nisbett, 2001). If it doesn't move, one of the researchers concluded, most Americans don't see it.

As you can see... well, what you see partly depends on the culture you live in! When travelers visit another culture and are surprised to find that its members "see things differently," they may be literally correct.

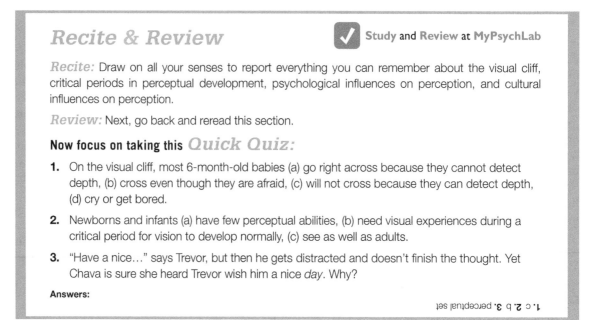

Recite & Review

✓ **Study** and **Review** at **MyPsychLab**

Recite: Draw on all your senses to report everything you can remember about the visual cliff, critical periods in perceptual development, psychological influences on perception, and cultural influences on perception.

Review: Next, go back and reread this section.

Now focus on taking this *Quick Quiz:*

1. On the visual cliff, most 6-month-old babies (a) go right across because they cannot detect depth, (b) cross even though they are afraid, (c) will not cross because they can detect depth, (d) cry or get bored.

2. Newborns and infants (a) have few perceptual abilities, (b) need visual experiences during a critical period for vision to develop normally, (c) see as well as adults.

3. "Have a nice..." says Trevor, but then he gets distracted and doesn't finish the thought. Yet Chava is sure she heard Trevor wish him a nice *day*. Why?

Answers:

1. c 2. b 3. perceptual set

You are about to learn...

- that perception is often unconscious.

- whether "subliminal perception" recordings will help you lose weight or reduce stress.

Perception Without Awareness LO 6.28

Being consciously aware of every single thing we see, hear, touch, or even smell in the course of a day would be impossible. Much of our perception occurs without our conscious awareness yet nonetheless influences our behavior.

Behavior can be affected even by stimuli that are so weak or brief that they are below a person's absolute threshold for detecting them—that is, subliminal. People sometimes correctly sense a change in a scene (say, in the color or location of an object) even though the change took place too quickly to be consciously recognized and identified (Rensink, 2004). And when people are subliminally exposed to a face, they will tend to prefer

that face over one they did not "see" in this way (Bornstein, Leone, & Galley, 1987).

Thus, people often know more than they know they know. In fact, nonconscious processing occurs not only in perception but also in memory, thinking, and decision making, as we discuss in Chapters 7 and 8. However, *subliminal perception* can be hard to demonstrate and replicate. The strongest evidence for its existence comes from studies using simple stimuli (faces or single words such as *bread*) rather than complex stimuli such as sentences ("Eat whole wheat bread, not white bread, if you know what's good for you").

If subliminal exposure to stimuli can affect judgments and preferences in the laboratory, you may be wondering whether it can be used to manipulate people's attitudes and behavior in ordinary life. Subliminal persuasion techniques first became a hot topic way back in the 1950s, when an advertising executive claimed to have increased popcorn and Coke sales at a theater by secretly flashing the words EAT POPCORN and DRINK COKE on the movie screen. The claim turned out to be a hoax, devised to save the man's struggling advertising company.

THINKING CRITICALLY

About Subliminal Persuasion

Ever since then, scientists have been skeptical, but that has not deterred people who market subliminal recordings that promise to help you lose weight, stop smoking, relieve stress, boost your motivation or self-esteem, improve your memory, lower your cholesterol, or stop biting your nails, all without any effort on your part. Ah, if only those claims were true! But they are not. In study after study, placebo recordings, which do not contain the messages that participants think they do, have been just as "effective" as those containing the supposed subliminal messages (Eich & Hyman, 1992; Greenwald et al., 1991; Merikle & Skanes, 1992).

Some efforts at studying subliminal persuasion may have left out an important ingredient: the person's motivation. A team of researchers used subliminal messages—the words *thirst* and *dry*—to make subjects feel thirsty and incline them to drink. Later, when given a chance to drink, they did in fact drink more than control subjects did, though only if they had been moderately thirsty to begin with (Strahan, Spencer, & Zanna, 2002).

But does this mean that advertisers can seduce us into buying soft drinks or voting for political candidates by slipping subliminal slogans and images into what we watch and hear? Given the many studies that have found no evidence of subliminal persuasion in real life and the subtlety of the effects that occur in the laboratory (e.g., you have to already be somewhat thirsty before you can be influenced to drink more), we think there's little cause for worry about subliminal manipulation. It's more appropriate to be worried about the *explicit* manipulation of your buying habits by advertisers tracking your interests on almost every Internet site you visit. And if you want to improve yourself or your life, you'll have to do it the old-fashioned way: by working at it deliberately, with full awareness of what you are doing.

Recite & Review

✓ **Study** and **Review** at **MyPsychLab**

Recite: Tell someone everything you can remember about perception without awareness, especially subliminal persuasion.

Review: Next, read this section again.

Now take this *Quick Quiz:*

A study appears to find evidence of "sleep learning"—the ability to perceive and retain material played on an audio recording while a person sleeps. What would you want to know about this research before deciding to play the audio version of this book by your bedside all night while you slumber on, in hopes of not having to study when you're awake?

Answers:

Was there a control group that listened to, say, a musical selection or white noise? How complicated was the material that was allegedly learned: a few key words, whole sentences, an entire lecture by Professor Arbuckle? Were the results large enough to have practical implications? How did the researchers determine whether the participants really were asleep—by using brain wave measures or just unreliable self-reports?

PSYCHOLOGY IN THE NEWS REVISITED /////////

As we saw throughout this chapter, ordinary perception is not always the best path to knowledge, because we do not passively register the world "out there"; we mentally construct it. All of us, whether gullible or skeptical by nature, have needs, beliefs, and expectations that can fool us into seeing things that we want to see, or lead us to read meanings into sensory experiences that are not inherent in the experience itself. Who has not seen nonexistent water on a hot highway or felt a nonexistent insect on the skin after merely thinking about bugs?

Needs, beliefs, and expectations are all relevant in our opening story about UFO reports. Some people who think they've seen alien spaceships may be habitual yea-sayers who, because of their expectations, are quick to think they saw something that wasn't there. Others are fooled by the normal distortions of perception: When you are looking up at the sky, where you have few points of reference or cues to indicate distance, it is difficult to judge how far away or how big an object is. Still others believe in UFOs and are longing to see one, and that wish can affect their perception of ambiguous objects in the sky.

Whenever impartial investigators have looked into UFO reports, they have found that what people actually saw were weather balloons, rocket launchings, swamp gas, military aircraft, or (in the vast majority of cases) ordinary celestial bodies, such as planets and meteors. Talk of an alien invasion excited some people when four "red fireballs" were spotted in Texas; they turned out to be Chinese lanterns made of lightweight paper lit by candles and sent into the sky by members of a wedding party (Radford, 2013).

As for Russell Crowe's video taken at the Royal Botanical Gardens, a plausible explanation, posted by one commenter on YouTube, is that time-exposure techniques, such as the one he used, often produce unusual looking lighting effects. (Think of time-exposed photographs of busy highways at night, where the cars appear as continuous streaks of light.) Further, the telephoto lens Crowe used probably distorted the perceived distance of objects. The fact that the botanical gardens were near a marina suggests that the "strange" object was probably a sailboat.

The objects in the photo accompanying our news story, which look so much like flying saucers, are really lenticular (lens-shaped) clouds, over Spain, formed by columns of rising air hitting a mountain range. And the "alien bodies" reported in Roswell were simply test dummies made of rubber, which the Air Force was dropping from high-altitude balloons before subjecting human beings to jumps from the same height. But even capable professionals can be fooled. An astronomer who investigates UFO reports told a journalist, "I've been with Air Force pilots who thought they were seeing a UFO. But it was actually the moon. I've seen people look at Venus and say they could see portholes on a spaceship" (quoted in Ratcliffe, 2000).

None of this means that the only real world is the mundane one we see in everyday life. Because our sense organs evolved for particular purposes, our sensory windows on the world are partly shuttered. But we can use reason, ingenuity, and science to pry those shutters open. Ordinary perception tells us that the sun circles the earth, but the great astronomer Copernicus was able to figure out nearly five centuries ago that the opposite is true. Ordinary perception will never let us see ultraviolet and infrared rays directly, but we know they are there, and we can measure them. If science can enable us to overturn the everyday evidence of our senses, who knows what surprises science has in store for us?

Taking Psychology With You

Can Perception Be "Extrasensory"?

Eyes, ears, mouth, nose, skin: We rely on these organs for our experience of the external world. Some people, however, claim they can send and receive messages about the world without relying on the usual sensory channels, by using *extrasensory perception* (ESP). Reported ESP experiences involve things like telepathy, the direct communication of messages from one mind to another without the usual sensory signals, and precognition, the perception of an event that has not yet happened. How should critical thinkers respond to such claims? What questions should they ask, and what kind of evidence should they look for?

Evidence or Coincidence? Much of the supposed evidence for extrasensory perception comes from anecdotal accounts. But people are not always reliable reporters of their own experiences. They often embellish and exaggerate, or they recall only part of what happened. They also tend to forget incidents that do not fit their beliefs, such as "premonitions" of events that fail to occur. Many ESP experiences could merely be unusual coincidences that are memorable because they are dramatic. What passes for telepathy or precognition could also be based on what a person knows or deduces through ordinary means. If Joanne's father has had two recent heart attacks, her premonition that her father will die shortly (followed, in fact, by her father's death) may not be so impressive.

The scientific way to establish a phenomenon is to produce it under controlled conditions. Unfortunately, most attempts to demonstrate ESP in the laboratory have been poorly designed, with inadequate precautions against fraud and improper statistical analysis (Alcock, 2011). As a result, the history of research in this area has been one of initial enthusiasm because of apparently positive results (Bem & Honorton, 1994; Dalton et al., 1996), followed by disappointment when the results cannot be replicated (Galak et al., 2012; Milton & Wiseman, 1999, 2001). One researcher who tried for 30 years to establish the reality of psychic phenomena finally gave up in defeat. "I found no psychic phenomena," she wrote, "only wishful thinking, self-deception, experimental error, and even an occasional fraud. I became a skeptic" (Blackmore, 2001).

The issue has not gone away, however. Many people *really, really* want to believe that ESP exists. James Randi, a famous magician who is dedicated to educating the public about psychic deception, has for years offered a million dollars to anyone who can demonstrate ESP or other paranormal powers in the presence of independent observers and under controlled conditions. Many have taken up the challenge; no one has succeeded. We think Randi's money is safe.

Lessons From a Magician. Despite the lack of evidence for ESP, many people say they believe in it. Perhaps you yourself have had an experience that seemed to involve ESP, or perhaps you have seen a convincing demonstration by someone else. Surely you can trust the evidence of your own eyes. Or can

"What do you mean you didn't know that we were having a pop quiz today?"

you? We will answer this question with a true story, one that contains an important lesson about why it's a good idea to think critically regarding ESP.

During the 1970s, Andrew Weil (now known for his efforts to promote alternative medicine) set out to investigate the claims of a self-proclaimed psychic named Uri Geller (Weil, 1974a, 1974b). Weil, who believed in telepathy, felt that ESP might be explained by principles of modern physics, and he was receptive to Geller's claims. When he met Geller at a private gathering, he was not disappointed. Geller correctly identified a cross and a Star of David sealed inside separate envelopes. He made a stopped watch start running and made a ring sag into an oval shape, apparently without touching them. He made keys change shape. Weil came away a convert. What he had seen with his own eyes seemed impossible to deny... until he went to visit the Amazing Randi.

To Weil's astonishment, Randi was able to duplicate much of what Geller had done. He, too, could bend keys and guess the contents of sealed envelopes. But Randi's feats were tricks, and he was willing to show Weil exactly how they were done. Weil suddenly experienced "a sense of how strongly the mind can impose its own interpretations on perceptions; how it can see what it expects to see, but not see the unexpected."

Weil was dis-illusioned—literally. Even when he knew what to look for in a trick, he could not catch the Amazing Randi doing it. Weil learned that our sense impressions of reality are not the same as reality. Our eyes, our ears, and especially our brains can play tricks on us.

Summary

 Listen to the Audio File at MyPsychLab

- *Sensation* is the detection and direct experience of physical energy as a result of environmental or internal events. *Perception* is the process by which sensory impulses are organized and interpreted.

Our Sensational Senses

- Sensation begins with the sense receptors, which convert the energy of a stimulus into electrical impulses that travel along nerves to the brain. Separate sensations can be accounted for by *anatomical codes* (as set forth by *the doctrine of specific nerve energies*) and *functional codes* in the nervous system. Sensory crossover from one modality to another can sometimes occur, and in *synesthesia*, sensation in one modality consistently evokes a sensation in another, although these experiences are rare.

- Psychologists specializing in psychophysics have studied sensory sensitivity by measuring *absolute* and *difference thresholds*. *Signal-detection theory*, however, holds that responses in a detection task consist of both a sensory process and a decision process and will vary with the person's motivation, alertness, and expectations.

- Our senses are designed to respond to change and contrast in the environment. When stimulation is unchanging, *sensory adaptation* occurs. Too little stimulation can cause *sensory deprivation*. *Selective attention* prevents us from being overwhelmed by the countless stimuli impinging on our senses by allowing us to focus on what is important, but it also deprives us of sensory information we may need, as in *inattentional blindness*.

Vision

- Vision is affected by the wavelength, intensity, and complexity of light, which produce the psychological dimensions of visual experience—*hue*, *brightness*, and *saturation*. The visual receptors, *rods* and *cones*, are located in the *retina* of the eye. They send signals (via other cells) to the *ganglion cells* and ultimately to the *optic nerve*, which carries visual information to the brain. Rods are responsible for vision in dim light; cones are responsible for color vision. *Dark adaptation* occurs in two stages.

- Specific aspects of the visual world, such as lines at various orientations, are detected by *feature-detector cells* in the visual areas of the brain. Some of these cells respond maximally to complex patterns, and separate groups of brain cells help us identify faces, places, and bodies. But the brain must still take in fragmentary information about lines, angles, shapes, motion, brightness, texture, and other features of what we see and come up with a unified view of the world.

- The *trichromatic* and *opponent-process* theories of color vision apply to different stages of processing. In the first stage, three types of cones in the retina respond selectively to different wavelengths of light. In the second, *opponent-process cells* in the retina and the thalamus respond in opposite fashion to short and long wavelengths of light.

- Perception involves the active construction of a model of the world from moment to moment. The *Gestalt principles* (e.g., *figure and ground*, *proximity*, *closure*, *similarity*, and *continuity*) describe visual strategies used by the brain to perceive forms.

- We localize objects in visual space by using both *binocular* and *monocular* cues to depth. Binocular cues include *convergence* and *retinal disparity*. Monocular cues include, among others, interposition and linear perspective. *Perceptual constancies* allow us to perceive objects as stable despite changes in the sensory patterns they produce. *Perceptual illusions* occur when sensory cues are misleading or when we misinterpret cues.

Hearing

- Hearing (*audition*) is affected by the intensity, frequency, and complexity of pressure waves in the air or other transmitting substance, corresponding to the experience of *loudness*, *pitch*, and *timbre* of the sound. The receptors for hearing are *hair cells* (topped by *cilia*) embedded in the *basilar membrane*, located in the *organ of Corti* in the interior of the *cochlea*. These receptors pass signals along to the *auditory nerve*. The sounds we hear are determined by patterns of hair-cell movement, which produce different neural codes. When we localize sounds, we use as cues subtle differences in how pressure waves reach each of our ears. A few blind people are able to use *echolocation* to navigate.

Other Senses

- Taste (*gustation*) is a chemical sense. Elevations on the tongue, called *papillae*, contain many *taste buds*, which in turn contain the taste receptors, but taste receptors also occur in the gastrointestinal tract. The basic tastes include salty, sour, bitter, and sweet. Some researchers believe that *umami* is a fifth basic taste, but this is debatable because in most protein-rich foods, umami is not detectable. Umami and other taste receptors exist in the gastrointestinal tract, however, and may influence conditioned food preferences.

- Responses to a particular taste depend in part on genetic differences among individuals; some people are *supertasters*. Taste preferences are also affected by culture and learning and by the texture, temperature, and smell of food.

- Smell (*olfaction*) is also a chemical sense. No basic odors have been identified, and up to a thousand different receptor types exist. Distinct odors activate unique combinations of receptors, and signals from different types of receptors are combined in individual neurons in the brain. Odors have psychological effects and can sometimes call up emotional memories. Cultural and individual differences affect people's responses to particular odors.

- The skin senses include touch (pressure), warmth, cold, pain, and variations such as itch and tickle. Receptors for some types of itching and a receptor for cold have been identified.

- Pain has proven to be physiologically complicated, involving the release of several different chemicals and changes in both neurons and glial cells. According to the *gate-control theory*, the experience of pain depends on whether neural impulses get past a "gate" in the spinal cord and reach the brain; in addition, a matrix of neurons in the brain can generate pain even in the absence of signals from sensory neurons.

- Pain may also be caused by changes in the sensitivity of central nervous system cells. A leading theory of *phantom pain* holds that it occurs when the brain rewires itself after amputation of a limb or removal of a body organ. Pain is affected by expectations and culture. Placebos affect the subjective experience of pain through their effects on brain activity and endorphin production.

- *Kinesthesis* tells us where our body parts are located and *equilibrium* tells us the orientation of the body as a whole. Together, these two senses provide us with a feeling of physical embodiment.

Perceptual Powers: Origins and Influences

- Many fundamental perceptual skills are inborn or are acquired shortly after birth. The visual cliff studies show that babies have depth perception by the age of 6 months and probably even earlier. But without certain experiences during *critical periods* early in life, cells in the nervous system deteriorate, change, or fail to form appropriate neural pathways, and perception is impaired. This is why efforts to correct congenital blindness or deafness are most successful when they take place early in life.

- Psychological influences on perception include needs, beliefs, emotions, and expectations (which produce *perceptual sets*). Cultures give people practice with different kinds of perceptual experiences and influence what they attend to.

Perception Without Awareness

- In laboratory studies of *subliminal perception*, simple subliminal messages can influence certain behaviors and judgments, depending on a person's motivational state (e.g., thirst). However, in everyday life, there is no evidence that complex behaviors can be altered by commercial subliminal recordings.

Psychology in the News, Revisited

- Human perception does not merely capture objective reality but also reflects our needs, biases, and beliefs. Our eyes and our ears (and especially our brains) can play tricks on us—causing us to "see" things that are not there, such as UFOs, or misinterpret what we see.

Taking Psychology With You

- Years of research have failed to produce convincing evidence for *extrasensory perception* (ESP). What so-called psychics do is no different from what all good magicians do: capitalize on people's beliefs, wishful thinking, and expectations.

Key Terms

sensation 201
perception 201
sense receptors 202
anatomical codes 235
doctrine of specific nerve
  energies 202
synesthesia 203
functional codes 235
psychophysics 203
absolute threshold 203
difference threshold 204
signal-detection theory 205
sensory adaptation 206
sensory deprivation 206
selective attention 206
inattentional blindness 206
hue 208

brightness 208
saturation 208
retina 208
rods 209
cones 209
dark adaptation 209
bipolar cells 209
ganglion cells 209
optic nerve 210
feature-detector cells 210
trichromatic theory 212
opponent-process theory 212
negative afterimage 213
figure and ground 236
Gestalt principles 213
binocular cues 215
convergence 215

retinal disparity 215
monocular cues 215
perceptual constancy 216
perceptual illusion 216
audition 218
loudness 219
pitch 219
frequency (sound wave) 219
timbre 219
organ of Corti 219
cochlea 219
hair cells 219
cilia 219
basilar membrane 220
auditory nerve 220
echolocation 221
gustation 222

papillae 222
taste buds 222
umami 222
supertasters 223
olfaction 224
gate-control theory 225
phantom pain 226
kinesthesis 227
equilibrium 227
semicircular canals 228
visual cliff 228
critical period 229
perceptual set 231
subliminal perception 232
extrasensory perception
  (ESP) 234

Sensation is the detection and direct experience of physical energy as a result of environmental or internal events.
Perception is the process by which sensory impulses are organized and interpreted.

↓

The Senses

↓

- Sensation begins with the **sense receptors**, which convert the energy of a stimulus into electrical impulses that travel along the nerves to the brain.
- *Anatomical codes* (as set forth by the **doctrine of specific nerve energies**) and *functional codes* in the nervous system account for separate sensations. In rare cases, however, sensory crossover results in **synesthesia.**

Measuring the Senses

- Psychologists specializing in psychophysics have studied sensory sensitivity by measuring **absolute** and **difference thresholds**.
- **Signal-detection theory** holds that responses in a detection task consist of both a sensory process and a decision process and vary with the person's motivation, alertness, and expectations.

Sensory Adaptation

- **Sensory adaptation** occurs when sensation is unchanging.
- **Sensory deprivation** occurs with too little stimulation.

Sensing Without Perceiving

- We use **selective attention** to avoid sensory overload.
- **Inattentional blindness** is a failure to consciously perceive something you are looking at because you are not attending to it.

What We See

- Wavelength of light produces the experience of **hue**.
- Intensity of light produces the experience of **brightness**.
- Complexity of light produces the experience of **saturation**.

Color Vision

- The **trichromatic theory** accounts for the first level of color processing, which occurs in the retina, where three types of cones respond to different wavelengths of light.
- The **opponent-process theory** accounts for the second level of color processing, in which opponent-process cells in the retina and thalamus respond in opposite fashion to short and long wavelengths of light.

Visual Receptors

Visual receptors are located in the **retina** of the eye and send signals to the ganglion cells and ultimately to the *optic nerve*.
- **Rods** are responsible for vision in dim light.
- **Cones** are responsible for color vision.
- Rods and cones take time to adjust to dim illumination, a process known as **dark adaptation**.
- Information from rods and cones is processed and communicated by **ganglion cells**, the axons of which converge to form the optic nerve.
- **Feature-detector cells** in the visual areas of the brain detect specific aspects of the environment, such as line orientation.
- Separate groups of brain cells are especially responsive to faces, places, and bodies.

Hearing

↓

The stimulus for hearing (*audition*) is a pressure wave or the release of compressed air.

What We Hear

- Intensity corresponds to the experience of **loudness**.
- Frequency corresponds to the experience of **pitch**.
- Complexity corresponds to the experience of **timbre**.

The receptors for hearing are *hair cells* (topped by *cilia*) embedded in the basilar membrane of the **organ of Corti**, in the interior of the **cochlea**.

Vision

↓

The stimulus for vision is light, which travels in waves.

Depth and Distance Perception

- **Binocular cues** include **convergence** and **retinal disparity**.
- **Monocular cues** include light and shadow; interpostion; motion parallax; relative size; texture gradients; relative clarity; and linear perspective.

Constancies and Illusions

- **Perceptual constancy** is the accurate perception of objects as stable despite changes in size, shape, location, brightness, and color.
- *Perceptual illusions* occur when sensory cues are misleading or we misinterpret them.

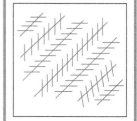

Gestalt Principles

Gestalt principles— such as figure and ground, proximity, closure, similarity, and continuity—describe visual strategies used by the brain to perceive form, distance, and depth.

Other Senses

Taste

Taste (*gustation*) is a chemical sense.
• **Papillae** on the tongue contain **taste buds**, which contain taste receptors.
• The basic tastes are each produced by a different type of chemical: salty, sour, bitter, and sweet. Some consider *umami* to be a fifth basic taste, but this is controversial because in most foods its taste is not perceptible.
• Genetic and cultural differences influence responses to a particular taste.

Smell

Smell (*olfaction*) is also a chemical sense.
• There are up to 1,000 different kinds of receptors.
• Distinct odors activate unique combinations of receptors.
• Cultural and individual differences affect people's responses to odors.

Senses of the Skin

These senses include *touch* (pressure), *warmth*, *cold*, and *pain* and variations such as itch and tickle.

The Environment

Kinesthesis tells us where our body parts are located. **Equilibrium** tells us the orientation of the body as a whole, and relies on three **semicircular canals** in the inner ear.

Pain

Pain is both a skin sense and an internal sense.
• The **gate-control theory** holds that the experience of pain depends on whether neural impulses get past a "gate" in the spinal cord and reach the brain.

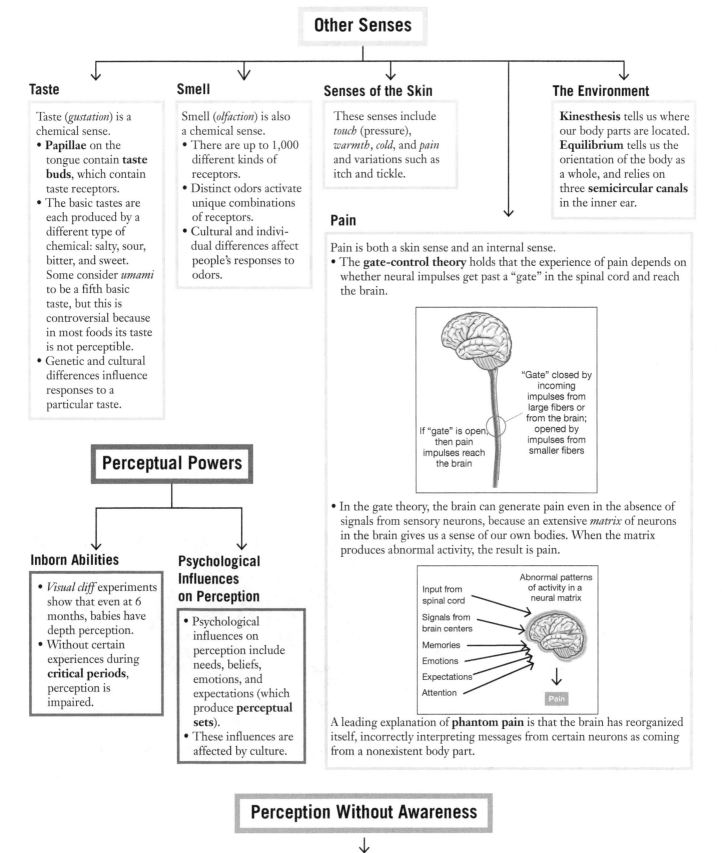

"Gate" closed by incoming impulses from large fibers or from the brain; opened by impulses from smaller fibers

If "gate" is open, then pain impulses reach the brain

• In the gate theory, the brain can generate pain even in the absence of signals from sensory neurons, because an extensive *matrix* of neurons in the brain gives us a sense of our own bodies. When the matrix produces abnormal activity, the result is pain.

Abnormal patterns of activity in a neural matrix

Input from spinal cord
Signals from brain centers
Memories
Emotions
Expectations
Attention

Pain

A leading explanation of **phantom pain** is that the brain has reorganized itself, incorrectly interpreting messages from certain neurons as coming from a nonexistent body part.

Perceptual Powers

Inborn Abilities

• *Visual cliff* experiments show that even at 6 months, babies have depth perception.
• Without certain experiences during **critical periods**, perception is impaired.

Psychological Influences on Perception

• Psychological influences on perception include needs, beliefs, emotions, and expectations (which produce **perceptual sets**).
• These influences are affected by culture.

Perception Without Awareness

• In studies of *subliminal perception*, a person is exposed to explicit or subliminal information and is later tested to see whether the information affects behavior or performance.
• When simple stimuli are used, exposure to subliminal stimuli in the laboratory can influence various behaviors, judgments, and motivational states.
• However, no evidence of subliminal persuasion has been found with commercially marketed subliminal ads and recordings.

7

Thought: Using What We Know

Reasoning Rationally

Barriers to Reasoning Rationally

Measuring Intelligence: The Psychometric Approach

Dissecting Intelligence: The Cognitive Approach

The Origins of Intelligence

Animal Minds

Psychology in the News, Revisited

Taking Psychology With You: Becoming More Creative

COGNITION

PSYCHOLOGY IN THE NEWS ///////////////////////////

Ig Nobel Prize Winners Announced

CAMBRIDGE, MA, September 21, 2012. The twenty-second First Annual Ig Nobel ceremony took place last night at Harvard University's Sanders Theatre, honoring winners of ten Ig Nobel prizes. The event is sponsored by Improbable Research, an organization whose stated goal is to honor achievements that "first make people laugh, then make them think."

Like the real Nobels, the Ig Nobels are awarded in many areas, ranging from public health to peace to biology. The sponsors say that the prizes "are intended to celebrate the unusual, honor the imaginative—and spur people's interest in science, medicine, and technology." This year's winners come from Canada, France, the Netherlands, Japan, Peru, Russia, Rwanda, Sweden, the United Kingdom and the United States:

- **Anatomy:** Frans de Waal and Jennifer Pokorny, for showing that chimpanzees can identify other chimpanzees just by looking at photographs of their fellow apes' rear ends.

- **Psychology:** Anita Eerland, Rolf Zwaan, and Tulio Guadalupe, for discovering that when people lean to the left, they see the Eiffel Tower as being smaller than when they stand upright.

- **Acoustics:** Kazutaka Kurihara and Koji Tsukada, for inventing the SpeechJammer, a handheld machine that disrupts people's speech by playing their words back to them with a slight delay.

- **Peace:** SKN, a Russian company, for converting old ammunition into diamonds (albeit ones so tiny that they're measured in nanometers).

- **Literature:** The U.S. Government General Accountability Office, for issuing a "report about reports about reports that recommends the preparation of a report about the report about reports about reports."

- **Physics:** Joseph Keller, Raymond Goldstein, Patrick Warren, and Robin Ball, for calculating the forces that shape and move hair in a swinging ponytail.

Three scientists spoof the prize-winning "Eiffel Tower" study at the annual Ig Nobel award ceremony, where scientists get to prove they have a sense of humor.

- **Fluid Dynamics:** Rouslan Krechetnikov and Hans Mayer, for studying how liquid sloshes when someone walks while carrying a cup of coffee.
- **Chemistry:** Johan Pettersson, for discovering why the hair of people in certain houses in a Swedish town turned green.
- **Neuroscience:** Craig Bennett, Abigail Baird, Michael Miller, and George Wolford, for showing that brain researchers using complex instruments and inappropriate statistics can turn up seemingly meaningful brain activity anywhere—even in a dead salmon.
- **Medicine:** Emmanuel Ben-Soussan and Michel Antonietti, for helping doctors keep patients' colons from exploding during colonoscopies.

Improbable Research depends on volunteers in many countries and an editorial board of some 50 eminent scientists, including several Nobel (and Ig Nobel) Prize winners. The group publishes a magazine, a newsletter, a newspaper column, books, and a daily blog. But it is best known for the Ig Nobel awards, which the British journal *Nature* calls "arguably the highlight of the scientific calendar."

///////////

The Ig Nobel awards may seem a bit off the wall, but they reflect the human mind's love of wordplay, wit, parody, curiosity, and imagination. You don't even have to be a prizewinner to have an amazing mind. Each day, in the course of ordinary living, we all make countless decisions, construct explanations, draw inferences about other people's behavior, try to understand our own motives, laugh at something that strikes us as funny, and organize and reorganize the contents of our mental world. René Descartes' famous declaration "I think, therefore I am" could just as well have been reversed: "I am, therefore I think." Our powers of thought and intelligence have inspired humans to immodestly call ourselves *Homo sapiens*, Latin for wise or rational man.

Think for a moment about what thinking does for you. It frees you from the confines of the immediate present: You can think about a trip taken three years ago, a party next Saturday, or the War of 1812. It carries you beyond the boundaries of reality: You can imagine unicorns and utopias, Martians and magic. You can make plans far into the future and judge the probability of events, both good and bad. Because you think, you do not need to grope your way blindly through your problems but can apply knowledge and reasoning to solve them intelligently and creatively.

But just how "sapiens" are we, really? In Australia, a 23-year-old man put fireworks between his buttocks and set them off. This trick backfired—literally: He was taken to the hospital with severe burns on his backside and genitals. In Nottingham, England, the mayor distributed flyers telling visitors that Robin Hood and his pals never actually lived in nearby Sherwood Forest, inasmuch as they were fictional characters; tourism plummeted. In Colorado, a woman complained to a local newspaper that the "extra hour of sunlight" during daylight savings time was burning up her lawn.

The human mind, which has managed to come up with poetry, penicillin, and PCs, is certainly a miraculous thing; but the human mind has also managed to come up with traffic jams, spam, and war. To better understand why the same species that figured out how to get to the moon is also capable of breathtaking bumbling here on earth, we will examine in this chapter how people reason, solve problems, and grow in intelligence, as well as some sources of their mental shortcomings. These topics are the focus of *cognitive psychology*, the study of mental processes.

concept A mental category that groups objects, relations, activities, abstractions, or qualities having common properties.

basic concepts Concepts that have a moderate number of instances and that are easier to acquire than those having few or many instances.

You are about to learn . . .

- the basic elements of thought.
- whether the language you speak affects the way you think.
- how conscious and nonconscious thinking help us and can also cause trouble.
- why we must sometimes resort to rules of thumb to solve problems.
- some insights about **insight** and **intuition**.

Thought: Using What We Know

In 2011, when an IBM computer named Watson defeated two incredibly smart human beings on *Jeopardy*, the world was abuzz about whether that meant machines would finally outthink people. Cognitive scientists were quick to point out that the human mind is far more complex than a computer; yes, the machines may be fast, but they have yet to learn to make puns and jokes, acquire an immediate insight into another person's feelings, or write a play or book. Nonetheless, there are also similarities between the mind and the machine: Both of them actively process information by altering it, organizing it, and using it to make decisions. Just as computers internally manipulate representations of 0s and 1s to "think," so we mentally manipulate internal representations of objects, activities, and situations.

The Elements of Cognition LO 7.1

One type of mental representation is the **concept**, a mental category that groups objects, relations, activities, abstractions, or qualities having common properties. The instances of a concept are seen as roughly similar: *Golden retriever, cocker spaniel,* and *border collie* are instances of the concept *dog;* and *anger, joy,* and *sadness* are instances of the concept *emotion.* Concepts simplify and summarize information about the world so that it is manageable and so that we can make decisions quickly and efficiently. You may never have seen a *basenji* or eaten *escargot,* but if you know that the first is an instance of *dog* and the second an instance of *food,* you will know, roughly, how to respond (unless you do not like to eat snails, which is what escargot are).

 Watch the **Video** The Big Picture: I Am, Therefore I Think at **MyPsychLab**

Basic concepts have a moderate number of instances and are easier to acquire than those having either few or many instances (Rosch, 1973). The concept *apple* is more basic than *fruit,* which includes many more instances and is more abstract. It is also more basic than *Braeburn apple,* which is quite specific. Children seem to learn basic-level concepts earlier than others, and adults

Some instances of a concept are more representative or prototypical than others. A bachelor is an unmarried man, but during the years that Robert Pattinson and Kristen Stewart were in a romantic relationship and even shared a home, was he a "bachelor"? Is the Pope a bachelor? What about actor Alan Cumming, who married his long-time male partner in New York in 2012, but whose marriage would not be recognized in most American states?

use them more often than others, because basic concepts convey an optimal amount of information in most situations.

The qualities associated with a concept do not necessarily all apply to every instance: Some apples are not red; some dogs do not bark; some birds do not fly. But all the instances of a concept do share a family resemblance. When we need to decide whether something belongs to a concept, we are likely to compare it to a **prototype**, a representative example of the concept (Rosch, 1973). Which dog is doggier, a golden retriever or a Chihuahua? Which fruit is more fruitlike, an apple or a pineapple? Which activity is more representative of sports, football or weight lifting? Most people within a culture can easily tell you which instances of a concept are most representative, or *prototypical*.

The words used to express concepts may influence or shape how we think about them, an idea originally proposed by Benjamin Lee Whorf in the 1950s. Vocabulary and grammar may affect how we perceive objects, think about time, and remember events (Boroditsky, 2003; Gentner & Goldin-Meadow, 2003). For example, in many languages, speakers must specify whether an object is linguistically masculine or feminine, as in Spanish, where *la cuenta*, the bill, is feminine but *el cuento*, the story, is masculine. Labeling a concept as masculine or feminine affects the attributes that native speakers ascribe to it. Thus, a German speaker will describe a key (masculine in German) as hard, heavy, jagged, serrated, and useful, whereas a Spanish speaker is more likely to describe a key (feminine in Spanish) as golden, intricate, little, lovely, and shiny. German speakers will describe a bridge (feminine in German) as beautiful, elegant, fragile, peaceful, and slender, whereas Spanish speakers are more likely to describe a bridge (masculine in Spanish) as big, dangerous, strong, sturdy, and towering (Boroditsky, Schmidt, & Phillips, 2003).

Concepts are the building blocks of thought, but they would be of limited use if we merely stacked them up mentally. We must also represent their relationships to one another. One way we accomplish this may be by storing and using **propositions**, units of meaning that are made up of concepts and that express a unitary idea. A proposition can express nearly any sort of knowledge ("Emily raises border collies") or belief ("Border collies are smart"). Propositions, in turn, are linked together in complicated networks of knowledge, associations, beliefs, and expectations. These networks, which psychologists call **cognitive schemas**, serve as mental models of aspects of the world. Gender schemas represent a person's beliefs and expectations about what it means to be male or female (see Chapter 3). People also have schemas about cultures, occupations, animals, geographical locations, and many other features of the social and natural environment.

Mental images—especially visual images, pictures in the mind's eye—are also important in thinking and in the construction of cognitive schemas. Although no one can directly see another person's visual images, psychologists can study them indirectly. One method is to measure how long it takes people to rotate an image in their imaginations, scan from one point to another in an image, or read off some detail from an image. The results suggest that visual images are much like images on a computer screen: We can manipulate them, they occur in a mental space of a fixed size, and small ones contain less detail than larger ones (Kosslyn, 1980; Shepard & Metzler, 1971). People often rely on visual images when they solve spatial or mechanical puzzles (Hegarty & Waller, 2005). Most people also report auditory images (such as a song, slogan, or poem you can hear in your "mind's ear"), and many report images in other sensory modalities as well—touch, taste, smell, or pain.

👁 **Watch** the **Video** Special Topics: Mental Imagery: In the Mind's Eye at **MyPsychLab**

Here, then, is a visual summary of the elements of cognition:

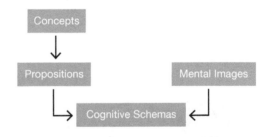

How Conscious Is Thought? LO 7.2

When we think about thinking, we usually have in mind those mental activities that are carried out in a deliberate way with a conscious goal in mind, such as solving a problem, drawing up plans, or making calculated decisions. However, much mental processing is not conscious.

Subconscious Thinking. Some cognitive processes lie outside of awareness but can be brought into consciousness with a little effort when necessary. These **subconscious processes** allow us to handle more information and to perform more complex tasks than if we depended entirely on conscious thought. Indeed, many automatic routines are performed "without thinking," though

prototype An especially representative example of a concept.

proposition A unit of meaning that is made up of concepts and expresses a single idea.

cognitive schema An integrated mental network of knowledge, beliefs, and expectations concerning a particular topic or aspect of the world.

mental image A mental representation that mirrors or resembles the thing it represents; mental images occur in many and perhaps all sensory modalities.

subconscious processes Mental processes occurring outside of conscious awareness but accessible to consciousness when necessary.

**nonconscious pro-
cesses** Mental processes
occurring outside of and
not available to conscious
awareness.

implicit learning
Learning that occurs
when you acquire knowl-
edge about something
without being aware of
how you did so and with-
out being able to state
exactly what it is you
have learned.

they might once have required careful, conscious attention: knitting, typing, driving a car, decoding the letters in a word in order to read it.

Because of the capacity for automatic process- ing, people can eat lunch while reading a book or drive a car while listening to music. In such cases, one of the tasks has become automatic. This does not mean you should go ahead and check your Facebook page or text your friends while reading this paragraph. That's *multitasking*, and it rarely works well. Far from saving time, toggling between two or more tasks that require attention increases the time required to complete them. In addition, stress goes up, errors increase, reac- tion times lengthen, and memory suffers (Lien, Ruthruff, & Johnston, 2006). This is *especially* true for people who consider themselves to be tech- nologically proficient multitaskers. In a series of experiments designed to test the supposed skills of such multitaskers, their performance on each of the tasks was impaired by interference from the other tasks (Ophir, Nass, & Wagner, 2009). "The shocking discovery of this research," said one of the investigators, is that supposedly adept mul- titaskers "are lousy at everything that's necessary for multitasking. They're suckers for irrelevancy. Everything distracts them."

Even overhearing one side of someone else's cell phone conversation siphons your attention away from the task you are doing, possibly because of the effort required to make sense of just one half of a conversation. When people listened to a "halfalogue" while performing a visual task, they made more than six times as many errors on the task as they did when they listened to an ordinary

Some well-learned skills do not require much conscious thought and can be performed while doing other things, but multitasking can also get you into serious trouble. It's definitely not a good idea to talk on your cell phone, eat, and try to drive all at the same time.

two-person conversation (Emberson et al., 2010). And when you are the one doing the talking, mul- titasking can be hazardous to your health. As we saw in Chapter 1, cell phone use greatly impairs a person's ability to drive, whether the phone is hands-free or not (Strayer & Drews, 2007). Other distractions are equally dangerous. A government study caught drivers on camera checking their stocks, fussing with MP3 players, drinking beer, reading e-mails, applying makeup, flossing their teeth, and putting in contact lenses, all while hur- tling down the highway at high speeds (Klauer et al., 2006). Then there's texting: A commuter train's engineer violated company policy by texting while on the job, and never saw an oncoming freight train. The resulting collision killed 25 people, including the engineer himself.

Nonconscious Thinking. Other kinds of think- ing, **nonconscious processes**, remain outside of awareness, even when you try to bring them back. People often find the solution to a problem when it suddenly pops into mind after they have given up trying to figure it out. And sometimes people learn a new skill without being able to explain how they perform it. For instance, they may discover the best strategy for winning a card game without ever being able to consciously identify what they are doing (Bechara et al., 1997). With such **implicit learning**, you learn a rule or an adaptive behavior, either with or without a conscious intention to do so, but you don't know how you learned it and you can't state, either to yourself or to oth- ers, exactly what it is you have learned (Frensch & Rünger, 2003; Lieberman, 2000). Many of our abilities, from speaking our native language prop- erly to walking up a flight of stairs, are the result of implicit learning.

Even when our thinking is conscious, often we are not thinking very *hard*. We may act, speak, and make decisions out of habit, without stopping to analyze what we are doing or why we are doing it. *Mindlessness*—mental inflexibility, inertia, and obliviousness to the present context—keeps peo- ple from recognizing when a change in a situation requires a change in behavior. In a classic study of mindlessness, a researcher approached people as they were about to use a photocopier and made one of three requests: "Excuse me, may I use the Xerox machine?" "Excuse me, may I use the Xerox machine, because I have to make copies?" or "Excuse me, may I use the Xerox machine, because I'm in a rush?" Normally, people will let someone go before them only if the person has a legitimate reason, as in the third request. In this study, however, people also complied when the reason sounded like an authentic explanation

MORE GOOD NEWS FROM MADISON AVENUE!

Jennifer K. Berman

Advertisers sometimes count on mindlessness in consumers.

but was actually meaningless ("because I have to make copies"). They heard the form of the request but they did not hear its content, and they mindlessly stepped aside (Langer, Blank, & Chanowitz, 1978).

Problem Solving and Decision Making LO 7.3

Conscious and nonconscious processes are both involved in solving such everyday problems as finding a missing letter in a crossword puzzle, assembling a cabinet, or increasing a cookie recipe. In well-defined problems, the nature of the problem is clear ("I need more cookies for the party tomorrow"). To solve the problem, you may only need to apply an **algorithm**, a set of procedures guaranteed to produce a solution whether or not you know how it works. To increase a cookie recipe, you can simply multiply the number of cookies you want per person by the number of people you need to feed. If the original recipe produced 10 cookies and you need 40, you can then multiply each ingredient by four. The recipe itself is also an algorithm (add flour, stir lightly, add raisins…), though you probably won't know what chemical changes are involved when you combine the ingredients and cook the batter in an oven.

Other problems are fuzzier. There is no specific goal ("What should I have for dinner tomorrow?") and no clearly correct solution, so no algorithm applies. In such cases, you may resort to a **heuristic**, a rule of thumb that suggests a course of action without guaranteeing an optimal solution ("Maybe I'll browse through some recipes online, or go to the market and see what catches my eye"). Many heuristics, like those used when playing chess, help you limit your options to a manageable number of promising ones, reducing the cognitive effort it takes to arrive at a decision (Galotti, 2007). Heuristics are useful to a student trying to choose a major, an investor trying to predict the stock market, a doctor trying to determine the best treatment for a patient, and a factory owner trying to boost production. All are faced with incomplete information for reaching a solution and may therefore resort to rules of thumb that have proven effective in the past.

Explore the Concept Heuristics at MyPsychLab

As useful as algorithms and heuristics are, sometimes the conscious effort to solve a problem seems to get you nowhere. Then, with insight, you suddenly see how to solve an equation or finish a puzzle without quite knowing how you found the solution. *Insight* probably involves different stages of mental processing (Bowers et al., 1990). First, clues in the problem automatically activate certain memories or knowledge. You begin to see a pattern or structure to the problem, although you cannot yet say what it is; possible solutions percolate in your mind. Although you are not aware of it, considerable mental work is guiding you toward a hypothesis, reflected in your brain as patterns of activity that differ from those associated with ordinary, methodical problem solving (Kounios & Beeman, 2009). Eventually, a solution springs into mind, seemingly from nowhere ("Aha, now I see!").

People also say they sometimes rely on *intuition*—hunches and gut feelings—rather than conscious thought when they make judgments or solve problems. Sometimes, in fact, changes in people's bodies—such as changes in sweating and heart rate—signal that they "know" a winning strategy in a laboratory game long before they can consciously say what it is (Bechara et al., 1997). But that does not necessarily mean you should go with your gut or take your pulse when answering questions on your next exam. In his book *Thinking, Fast and Slow* (2011), Daniel Kahneman explains why: "Fast" thinking applies to rapid, intuitive, emotional, almost automatic

algorithm A problem-solving strategy guaranteed to produce a solution even if the user does not know how it works.

heuristic A rule of thumb that suggests a course of action or guides problem solving but does not guarantee an optimal solution.

decisions; "slow" thinking requires intellectual effort. Naturally, most people rely on fast thinking because it saves time and effort, but it is often wrong. Here is one of his examples: Suppose that a bat and ball together cost $1.10 and that the bat costs one dollar more than the ball. How much does the ball cost? Most people answer with fast thinking and say 10 cents. But the correct answer is 5 cents. Think (slowly) about it.

 Watch the **Video** In the Real World: Changing Your Mind at **MyPsychLab**

Recite & Review

✓ **Study** and **Review** at **MyPsychLab**

Recite: Mindfully, say out loud what you know about concepts, prototypes, propositions, cognitive schemas, mental images, subconscious and nonconscious processes, multitasking, implicit learning, mindlessness, algorithms and heuristics, and insight and intuition.

Review: Next, consciously as well as conscientiously reread this section.

Now take this *Quick Quiz:*

1. Which concept will children find easier to grasp: *apple* or *fruit*?

2. What can Shayne's ability to solve mechanical puzzles be attributed to: *mental images* or *prototypes*?

3. Rivika enjoys listening to rock music while going for long drives, but when she was learning to drive she used to get distracted by it. What can be the reason behind her improved ability?

4. While deciding the ingredients of a cake for a group of ten people, what will be more helpful— an *algorithm* or a *heuristic*?

5. Mina goes to phone her mother and discovers that she has called her boyfriend's number instead. Her error can be attributed to _____.

6. When you solve a long-division problem, which are you using, an algorithm or a heuristic?

Answers:

1. fruit 2. mental images 3. When people indulge in two tasks simultaneously, subconscious processes allow one of them to become automatic upon much practice. 4. algorithm 5. mindlessness 6. an algorithm

---

reasoning The drawing of conclusions or inferences from observations, facts, or assumptions.

dialectical reasoning A process in which opposing facts or ideas are weighed and compared, with a view to determining the best solution or resolving differences.

You are about to learn...

- the importance of dialectical reasoning in solving real-life problems.
- how cognitive development affects how people reason about complex issues.

Reasoning Rationally

LO 7.4

Multitasking, mindlessness, and operating on automatic pilot have their place; life would be impossible if we had to think carefully and consciously about every little thing we do, say, decide, or hear. But automatic processes and unconscious impressions can also lead to errors and mishaps, ranging from the trivial (misplacing your keys) to the serious (walking into traffic because you're texting). Cognitive psychologists have, therefore, devoted a great deal of study to mindful, conscious thought and the capacity to reason.

Reasoning is purposeful mental activity that involves operating on information to reach a conclusion. Unlike impulsive ("fast") or nonconscious responding, reasoning requires us to draw specific inferences from observations, facts, or assumptions. In *formal reasoning* problems—the kind you might find, say, on an intelligence test or a college entrance exam—the information needed for drawing a conclusion or reaching a solution is specified clearly, and there is a single right (or best) answer. In *informal reasoning* problems, there is often no clearly correct solution. Many approaches, viewpoints, or possible solutions may compete, and you may have to decide which one is most "reasonable."

To do this wisely, a person must be able to use **dialectical reasoning**, the process of comparing and evaluating opposing points of view to resolve differences. Philosopher Richard Paul (1984) once described dialectical reasoning as movement "up and back between contradictory lines of reasoning, using each to critically cross-examine the other":

DIALECTAL REASONING

Arguments:

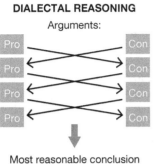

Most reasonable conclusion based on evidence and logic

Dialectical reasoning is what juries are supposed to do to arrive at a verdict: consider arguments for and against the defendant's guilt, point and counterpoint. It is also what voters are supposed to do when thinking about whether the government should raise or lower taxes or about the best way to improve public education. However, many adults have trouble thinking dialectically; they take one position, and that's that. When do people develop the ability to think critically—to question assumptions, evaluate and integrate evidence, consider alternative interpretations, and reach conclusions that can be defended as the most reasonable?

To find out, Patricia King and Karen Kitchener (1994, 2002, 2004) provided a large, diverse sample of adolescents and adults with statements describing opposing viewpoints on various topics. Each person then had to answer several questions, such as "What do you think about these statements?" "On what do you base your position?" and "Why do you suppose disagreement exists about this issue?" From the responses of thousands of participants, King and Kitchener identified seven cognitive stages on the road to what they call *reflective judgment* and we have called critical thinking. At each one, people make different assumptions about how things are known and use different ways of justifying their beliefs.

Most talk-radio shows do not exactly encourage reflective judgment!

In general, people who rely on *prereflective thinking* tend to assume that a correct answer always exists and that it can be obtained directly through the senses ("I know what I've seen") or from authorities ("They said so on the news"; "That's what I was brought up to believe"). If authorities do not yet have the truth, prereflective thinkers tend to reach conclusions on the basis of what "feels right" at the moment. They do not distinguish between knowledge and belief or between belief and evidence, and they see no reason to justify a belief. One respondent at this stage, when asked about evolution, said, "Well, some people believe that we evolved from apes and that's the way they want to believe. But I would never believe that way and nobody could talk me out of the way I believe because I believe the way that it's told in the Bible."

Get Involved! Practice Your Dialectical Reasoning

Choose a controversial topic, such as whether abortion should remain legal or the death penalty should be revoked. First, list all the arguments you can to support your own position. Then list all the arguments you can on the other side of the issue. You do not have to agree with these arguments; just list them. Do you feel a mental block or emotional discomfort while doing this? Can you imagine how opponents of your position would answer your arguments? Having strong opinions is fine; you should have an informed opinion on matters of public interest. But does that opinion get in the way of even imagining a contrary point of view or of altering your view if the evidence warrants a change?

People who are *quasi-reflective thinkers* recognize that some things cannot be known with absolute certainty and that judgments should be supported by reasons, yet they pay attention only to evidence that fits what they already believe. They seem to think that because knowledge is uncertain, any judgment about the evidence is purely subjective. Quasi-reflective thinkers will defend a position by saying, "We all have a right to our own opinion," as if all opinions are created equal. One college student, when asked whether one opinion on the safety of food additives was right and others were wrong, answered, "No. I think it just depends on how you feel personally because people make their decisions based upon how they feel and what research they've seen. So what one person thinks is right, another person might think is wrong. If I feel that chemicals cause cancer and you feel that food is unsafe without it, your opinion might be right to you and my opinion is right to me."

Finally, some people become capable of reflective judgment. They understand that although some things can never be known with certainty, some judgments are more valid than others because of their coherence, their fit with the available evidence, and their usefulness. They are willing to consider evidence from a variety of sources and to reason dialectically. This interview with a graduate student illustrates reflective thinking:

Interviewer: Can you ever say you know for sure that your point of view on chemical additives is correct?

Student: No, I don't think so [but] I think that we can usually be reasonably certain, given the information we have now, and considering our methodologies… [I]t might be that the research wasn't conducted rigorously enough. In other words, we might have flaws in our data or sample, things like that.

Interviewer: How then would you identify the "better opinion"?

Student: One that takes as many factors as possible into consideration. I mean one that uses the higher percentage of the data that we have, and perhaps that uses the methodology that has been most reliable.

Interviewer: And how do you come to a conclusion about what the evidence suggests?

Student: I think you have to take a look at the different opinions and studies that are offered by different groups. Maybe some studies offered by the chemical industry, some studies by the government, some private studies….You have to try to interpret people's motives and that makes it a more complex soup to try to strain out.

Sometimes people are able to think reflectively about some issues even though they think preflectively on other issues that hold deep emotional meaning for them (Haidt, 2012; King & Kitchener, 2004). But most people show no evidence of reflective judgment until their middle or late 20s, if ever. A longitudinal study found that many college students graduate without learning to distinguish fact from opinion, evaluate conflicting reports objectively, or resist emotional statements and political posturing (Arum & Roksa, 2011). Yet there's reason for hope. When students get ample support for thinking reflectively, have opportunities to practice it in their courses, and apply themselves seriously to their studies, their thinking tends to become more complex, sophisticated, and well-grounded (Kitchener et al., 1993). You can see why, in this book, we emphasize thinking about psychological findings and not just memorizing them.

One reason that Auguste Rodin's *The Thinker* became world famous and has been much imitated is that it captures so perfectly the experience of thinking reflectively.

Recite & Review

 Study and **Review** at **MyPsychLab**

Recite: State out loud what you know about formal and informal reasoning problems, dialectical reasoning, and prereflective, quasi-reflective, and reflective judgment.

Review: Next, reread this section.

Now be reasonable and take this *Quick Quiz:*

1. As the country was getting ready to face an election, the political science teacher gave an assignment to her students, which required them to collect data and information on political parties, reading their political manifestos, and rating their achievements. This exercise will help the students in developing their _____.

2. Seymour thinks the media have a liberal political bias, and Sophie thinks they are too conservative. "Well," says Seymour, "I have my truth and you have yours. It's purely subjective." Which of King and Kitchener's types of thinking describes Seymour's statement?

Answers:

1. critical thinking 2. quasi-reflective

You are about to learn...

- some biases in reasoning that impair the ability to think rationally and critically.

- why people worry more about vivid but rare disasters than about dangers that are far more likely.

- how the way a decision is framed affects the choices people make.

- why people often value fairness above rational self-interest.

- why people need to justify the time, money, or effort they invest in an action.

Barriers to Reasoning Rationally

Although most people have the capacity to think logically, reason dialectically, and make judgments reflectively, it is abundantly clear that

THINKING CRITICALLY

About Why We Don't Always Think Critically

they do not always do so. One obstacle is the need to be right; if your self-esteem depends on winning arguments, you will find it hard to listen with an open mind to competing views. Other obstacles include limited information and a lack of time to reflect carefully. But human thought processes are also tripped up by many predictable, systematic biases and errors. Psychologists have studied dozens of them (Kahneman, 2003, 2011). Here we describe just a few.

Exaggerating the Improbable (and Minimizing the Probable) LO 7.5

One common bias is the inclination to exaggerate the probability of rare events. This bias helps explain why so many people enter lotteries and buy disaster insurance, and why some irrational fears persist. As we discuss in Chapter 9, evolution has equipped us to fear certain natural dangers, such as snakes. However, in modern life, many of these dangers are no longer much of a threat; the risk of a renegade rattler sinking its fangs into you in Chicago or Atlanta is pretty low! Yet the fear lingers on, so we overestimate the danger. Evolution has also given us brains that are terrific at responding to an immediate threat, real or imagined. Unfortunately, our brains did not evolve to become alarmed by serious *future* threats that do not pose much danger right now, such as global warming (Gilbert, 2006).

When judging probabilities, people are strongly influenced by the **affect heuristic**: the tendency to consult their emotions (affect) when judging the "goodness" or "badness" of a situation instead of judging it objectively (Slovic & Peters, 2006; Slovic et al., 2002). Emotions can often help us make decisions by narrowing our options or by allowing us to act quickly in an ambiguous or dangerous situation. But emotions can also mislead us by preventing us from accurately assessing risk. One unusual field study looked at how people in France responded to a "mad cow" crisis that occurred several years ago. (Mad cow disease affects the brain and can be contracted by eating meat from contaminated cows.) Whenever newspaper articles reported the dangers of "mad cow disease," beef consumption fell during the following month. But when news articles, reporting

affect heuristic The tendency to consult one's emotions instead of estimating probabilities objectively.

Because of the affect and availability heuristics, many of us overestimate the chances of suffering a shark attack. Such attacks are extremely rare, but they are terrifying and easy to visualize.

availability heuristic The tendency to judge the probability of a type of event by how easy it is to think of examples or instances.

framing effect The tendency for people's choices to be affected by how a choice is presented or framed, such as whether it is worded in terms of potential losses or gains.

fairness bias The bias, in some circumstances, to value cooperation and fair play over rational self-interest.

the same dangers, used the technical names of the disease—Creutzfeldt-Jakob disease, or bovine spongiform encephalopathy—beef consumption remained the same (Sinaceur, Heath, & Cole, 2005). The more alarming labels caused people to reason emotionally and to overestimate the danger. (During the entire period of the supposed crisis, only six people in France were diagnosed with the disease.)

Our judgments about risks are also influenced by the **availability heuristic**, the tendency to judge the probability of an event by how easy it is to think of examples of it (Tversky & Kahneman, 1973). The availability heuristic often works hand in hand with the affect heuristic. Catastrophes and shocking accidents evoke a strong emotional reaction in us, and thus stand out in our minds, becoming more available mentally than other kinds of negative events. (An image of a "mad cow"—that sweet, placid creature running amok!—is highly "available.") This is why people overestimate the frequency of deaths from tornadoes and underestimate the frequency of deaths from asthma, which occur thousands of times more often but do not make headlines.

Avoiding Loss LO 7.6

In general, people try to avoid or minimize the risk of incurring losses when they make decisions. That strategy is rational enough, but people's perceptions of risk are subject to the **framing effect**: the tendency for choices to evoke different responses depending on how they are presented. When a choice is framed in terms of the risk of losing something, people will respond more cautiously than when the identical choice is framed in terms of a potential gain. They

will choose a ticket that has a 1 percent chance of winning a raffle but reject one that has a 99 percent chance of losing. Or they will rate a condom as effective when they are told it has a 95 percent success rate in protecting against the AIDS virus, but not when they are told it has a 5 percent failure rate—which of course is exactly the same thing (Linville, Fischer, & Fischhoff, 1992).

Suppose you had to choose between two health programs to combat a disease expected to kill 600 people. Which would you prefer: a program that will definitely save 200 people, or one with a one-third probability of saving all 600 people and a two-thirds probability of saving none? (Problem 1 in Figure 7.1 illustrates this choice.) When asked this question, most people, including physicians, say they would prefer the first program. In other words, they reject the riskier though potentially more rewarding solution in favor of a sure gain. However, people *will* take a risk if they see it as a way to avoid loss. Suppose now that you have to choose between a program in which 400 people will definitely die and a program in which there is a one-third probability of nobody dying and a two-thirds probability that all 600 will die. If you think about it, you will see that the alternatives are exactly the same as in the first problem; they are merely worded differently (see Problem 2 in Figure 7.1). Yet this time, most people choose the second solution. They reject risk when they think of the outcome in terms of lives saved, but they accept risk when they think of the outcome in terms of lives lost (Tversky & Kahneman, 1981).

Few of us will have to face a decision involving hundreds of lives, but we may have to choose between different medical treatments for ourselves or a relative. Our decision may be affected by whether the doctor frames the choice in terms of chances of surviving or chances of dying.

The Fairness Bias LO 7.7

Interestingly, in some circumstances we do not try to avoid loss altogether, because we are subject to a **fairness bias**. Imagine that you are playing a two-person game called the *Ultimatum Game*, in which your partner gets $20 and must decide how much to share with you. You can choose to accept your partner's offer, in which case you both get to keep your respective portions, or you can reject the offer, in which case neither of you gets a penny. How low an offer would you accept?

Rationally, it makes sense to accept any amount at all, no matter how paltry, because then

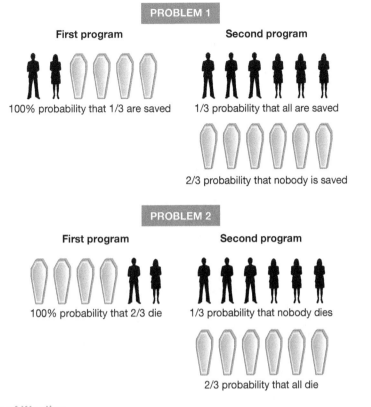

PROBLEM 1

First program

100% probability that 1/3 are saved

Second program

1/3 probability that all are saved

2/3 probability that nobody is saved

PROBLEM 2

First program

100% probability that 2/3 die

Second program

1/3 probability that nobody dies

2/3 probability that all die

FIGURE 7.1 A Matter of Wording
The decisions we make often depend on how the alternatives are framed. When asked to choose between the two programs in Problem 1, which are described in terms of lives saved, most people choose the first program. When asked to choose between the programs in Problem 2, which are described in terms of lives lost, most people choose the second program. Yet the alternatives in the two problems are actually identical.

at least you will get *something*. But that is not how people respond when playing the Ultimatum Game: If the offer is too low, they are likely to reject it. In industrial societies, offers of 50 percent are typical and offers below 20 or 30 percent are commonly rejected, even when the absolute sums are large. In other societies, the amounts offered and accepted may be higher or lower, but there is always some amount that people consider unfair and refuse to accept (Henrich et al., 2001). People may be competitive and love to win, but they are also powerfully motivated to cooperate and to see fairness prevail.

Using the Ultimatum Game and other laboratory games, scientists are exploring how a sense of fairness often takes precedence over rational self-interest when people make economic choices. Their work, which belongs to a field called *behavioral economics*, verifies and extends the pioneering work of Nobel Prize winner Herbert Simon (1955), who first showed that economic decisions are not always rational. Cognitive psychologist Daniel Kahneman also won a Nobel for his work on the irrational processes of decision

making, but because there is (as yet) no Nobel Prize in psychology, he won it in economics. This was a delicious irony, because many economists still have a difficult time accepting the evidence of human irrationality.

Why does a desire for fair play sometimes outweigh the desire for economic gain? Evolutionary theorists believe that cooperative tendencies and a desire for fairness and reciprocity evolved because they enhanced the survival of early human groups (Fehr & Fischbacher, 2003; Trivers, 2004). The idea that the Golden Rule has a basis in biology has gained support from research with nonhuman primates. In one study, capuchin monkeys received a token that they could then exchange for a slice of cucumber. The monkeys regarded this exchange as a pretty good deal—until they saw a neighboring monkey exchanging tokens for an even better reward, a grape. At that point, they began to refuse to exchange their tokens, even though they were then left with no reward at all (Brosnan & de Waal, 2003). Sometimes they even threw the cucumber slice on the ground in apparent disgust!

hindsight bias The tendency to overestimate one's ability to have predicted an event once the outcome is known; the "I knew it all along" phenomenon.

confirmation bias The tendency to look for or pay attention only to information that confirms one's own belief.

Some behavioral economists are using MRI scans to examine brain activity when people play variations of the Ultimatum Game (Camerer, 2003; Sanfey et al., 2003). While a person is deciding whether to accept a low offer, two brain areas are active: a part of the prefrontal cortex linked to rational problem solving and an area that is associated with disgust and other unpleasant feelings. According to economist Colin Camerer, "Basically the brain toggles between 'Yes, money is good' and 'Ugh, this guy is treating me like crap'" (quoted in D'Antonio, 2004). Some people choose the money and others go for respect. Which choice do you think you would make?

The Hindsight Bias

There is a reason for the saying that hindsight is 20/20. When people learn the outcome of an event or the answer to a question, they are often sure that they "knew it all along." Armed with the wisdom of hindsight, they see the outcome that actually occurred as inevitable, and they overestimate their ability to have predicted what happened beforehand (Fischhoff, 1975; Hawkins & Hastie, 1990). This **hindsight bias** shows up all the time in evaluating relationships ("I always knew their marriage wouldn't last"), politics ("I could have told you that candidate would win"), and military opinions ("The generals should have known the other side would attack").

According to Scott Hawkins and Reid Hastie (1990), "Hindsight biases represent the dark side of successful learning and judgment." They are the dark side because when we are sure that we knew something all along, we are also less willing to find out what we need to know to make accurate predictions in the future. For example, in medical conferences, when doctors are told what the postmortem findings were for a patient who died, they tend to think the case was easier to diagnose than it actually was ("I would have known it was a brain tumor"), and so they learn less from the case than they should (Dawson et al., 1988).

Perhaps you feel that we are not telling you anything new because you have always known about the hindsight bias. But you may just have a hindsight bias about the hindsight bias.

The Confirmation Bias

When people want to make the most accurate judgment possible, they usually try to consider all of the relevant information. But as we saw in Chapter 1, when they are thinking about an issue they feel strongly about, they often succumb to the **confirmation bias**, paying attention only to evidence that confirms their belief and finding fault with evidence or arguments that point in a different direction (Edwards & Smith, 1996; Nickerson, 1998). You rarely hear someone say, "Oh, thank you for explaining to me why my lifelong philosophy of child rearing (or politics, or investing, or dieting) is wrong. I'm so grateful for the facts!" The person is more likely to say, "Get lost, and take your crazy ideas with you."

Once you start looking for it, you will see the confirmation bias everywhere. Politicians brag about economic reports that confirm their party's position and dismiss counterevidence as

Get Involved! Confirming the Confirmation Bias

Suppose someone deals out four cards, each with a letter on one side and a number on the other. You can see only one side of each card:

Your task is to find out whether the following rule is true: "If a card has a vowel on one side, then it has an even number on the other side." Which two cards do you need to turn over to find out?

The vast majority of people say they would turn over the E and the 6, but they are wrong. You do need to turn over the E (a vowel), because if the number on the other side is even, it confirms the rule, and if it is odd, the rule is false. However, the card with the 6 tells you nothing. The rule does *not* say that a card with an even number must always have a vowel on the other side. Therefore, it doesn't matter whether the 6 has a vowel or a consonant on the other side. The card you do need to turn over is the 7, because if it has a vowel on the other side, that fact disconfirms the rule.

People do poorly on this problem because they are biased to look for confirming evidence and to ignore the possibility of disconfirming evidence. Don't feel too bad if you missed it. Most judges, lawyers, and people with Ph.D.s do, too.

biased or unimportant. Police officers who are convinced of a suspect's guilt take anything the suspect says or does as evidence that confirms it, including the suspect's claims of innocence (Davis, 2010). Many jury members, instead of weighing possible verdicts against the evidence, quickly construct a story about what happened at the start of the trial and then consider only the evidence that supports it (Kuhn, Weinstock, & Flaton, 1994). We bet you can see the confirmation bias in your own reactions to what you are learning in psychology. In thinking critically, most of us apply a double standard; we think most critically about results we dislike. That is why the scientific method can be so difficult: It forces us to consider evidence that *disconfirms* our beliefs.

Mental Sets

Another barrier to rational thinking is the development of a **mental set**, a tendency to try to solve new problems by using the same heuristics, strategies, and rules that worked in the past on similar problems. Mental sets make human learning and problem solving efficient; because of them, we do not have to keep reinventing the wheel. But mental sets are not helpful when a problem calls for fresh insights and methods. They cause us to cling rigidly to the same old assumptions and approaches, blinding us to better or more rapid solutions.

One general mental set is the tendency to find patterns in events or data ("when it's hot, earthquakes occur"; "I see signs of a conspiracy"). This tendency helps us understand and exert some control over what happens in our lives, and indeed the first step in forensic and scientific investigations of a problem is to find meaningful patterns despite

"noise" in the information. But it also leads us to see meaningful patterns even when they do not exist. For example, many people with arthritis think that their symptoms follow a pattern dictated by the weather. They suffer more, they say, when the barometric pressure changes or when the weather is damp or humid. Yet when researchers followed 18 arthritis patients for 15 months, no association whatsoever emerged between weather conditions and the patients' self-reported pain levels, their ability to function in daily life, or a doctor's evaluation of their joint tenderness (Redelmeier & Tversky, 1996). Of course, because of the confirmation bias, the patients refused to believe the results.

The Need for Cognitive Consistency LO 7.8, LO 7.9, LO 7.10

Mental sets and the confirmation bias cause us to avoid evidence that contradicts our beliefs. But what happens when disconfirming evidence finally smacks us in the face, and we cannot ignore or discount it any longer? Consider doomsday predictions, which have been made throughout history. When these predictions fail, how come we never hear believers say, "Boy, what a fool I was"?

According to the theory of **cognitive dissonance**, people will resolve such conflicts in predictable, though not always obvious, ways (Festinger, 1957; see Chapter 10). *Dissonance*, the opposite of consistency (*consonance*), is a state of tension that occurs when you hold either two cognitions (beliefs, thoughts, attitudes) that are psychologically inconsistent with one another or a belief that is incongruent with your behavior. This tension is psychologically uncomfortable, so you will be motivated to reduce it. You may do this by

mental set A tendency to solve problems using procedures that worked before on similar problems.

cognitive dissonance A state of tension that occurs when a person holds two cognitions that are psychologically inconsistent, or when a person's belief is incongruent with his or her behavior.

Get Involved! Connect the Dots

Copy this figure, and try to connect the dots by using no more than four straight lines without lifting your pencil or pen. A line must pass through each point. Can you do it?

Most people have difficulty with this problem because they have a mental set to interpret the arrangement of dots as a square. They then assume that they can't extend a line beyond the apparent boundaries of the square. Now that you know this, you might try again if you haven't yet solved the puzzle. Some solutions are given at the end of this chapter.

**postdecision disso-
nance** In the theory of
cognitive dissonance,
tension that occurs when
you believe you may have
made a bad decision.

rejecting or modifying one of those inconsistent beliefs, changing your behavior, denying the evidence, or rationalizing:

COGNITIVE DISSONANCE

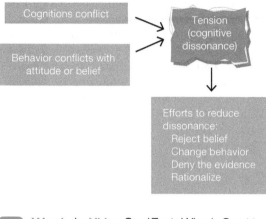

 Watch the **Video** Carol Tavris: What Is Cognitive Dissonance? at **MyPsychLab**

Years ago, in a famous field study, Leon Festinger and two associates infiltrated a group of people who thought the world would end on December 21 (Festinger, Riecken, & Schachter, 1956). The group's leader, whom the researchers called Marian Keech, promised that the faithful would be picked up by a flying saucer and whisked to safety at midnight on December 20. Many of her followers quit their jobs and spent all their savings, waiting for the end to come. What would they do or say, Festinger and his

colleagues wondered, to reduce the dissonance between "The world is still muddling along on the 21st" and "I predicted the end of the world and sold all my worldly possessions"?

Festinger's team predicted that believers who had made no public commitment to the prophecy, who awaited the end of the world by themselves at home, would simply lose their faith. However, those who had acted on their conviction by selling their property and waiting with Keech for the spaceship would be in a state of dissonance. They would have to *increase* their religious belief to avoid the intolerable realization that they had behaved foolishly and others knew it. That is just what happened. At 4:45 a.m., long past the appointed hour of the saucer's arrival, the leader had a new vision. The world had been spared, she said, because of the impressive faith of her little band.

Cognitive dissonance theory predicts that in more ordinary situations as well, people will resist, dismiss, or rationalize information that conflicts with their existing ideas or behavior, just as the people in the arthritis study did. To reduce the dissonance between "I smoke" and "Smoking could kill me," cigarette smokers have two choices: quit smoking, or reject or minimize the evidence that smoking is bad. Those who don't quit tend to persuade themselves that they will quit later on, that smoking helps them relax, or that they don't want a long life, anyhow ("It will be shorter but sweeter").

You are especially likely to reduce dissonance under three conditions (Aronson, 2012):

1　**When you need to justify a choice or decision that you made freely.** All car dealers know about buyer's remorse: The second that people buy a car, they worry that they made the wrong decision or spent too much, a phenomenon called **postdecision dissonance.** You may try to resolve this dissonance by deciding that the car you chose (or the toaster, or house, or spouse) is really, truly the best in the world. *Before* people make a decision, they can be open-minded, seeking information on the pros and cons of the choice at hand. But *after* they make that choice, the confirmation bias will kick in, and they will now notice all the good things about their decision and overlook or ignore evidence that they might have been wrong.

2　**When you need to justify behavior that conflicts with your view of yourself.** If you consider yourself to be honest, shoplifting will put you in a state of dissonance. To avoid feeling like a hypocrite, you will try to reduce the dissonance by justifying your behavior ("Everyone else does it"; "It's just this once"; "The store can afford this loss"). Or if you see yourself as a kind person and you harm someone, you may reduce your dissonance by blaming the person you have victimized ("She brought it on herself"; "It's his fault").

3 **When you need to justify the effort put into a decision or choice.** The harder you work to reach a goal, or the more you suffer for it, the more you will try to convince yourself that you value the goal, even if the goal turns out to be not so great after all (Aronson & Mills, 1959). This explains why hazing, whether in social clubs, on athletic teams, or in the military, turns new recruits into loyal members (see Figure 7.2). The cognition "I went through a lot of awful stuff to join this group" is dissonant with the cognition "only to find I hate the group." Therefore, people must decide either that the hazing was not so bad or that they really like the group. This mental reevaluation is called the **justification of effort**, and it is one of the most popular methods of reducing dissonance.

Some people are secure enough to own up to their mistakes instead of justifying them, and individuals and cultures vary in the kinds of experiences that cause them to feel dissonance. However, the need for cognitive consistency in those beliefs that are most central to our sense of self and our values is universal (Tavris & Aronson, 2007).

Our mental biases have some benefits. The ability to reduce cognitive dissonance helps us preserve our self-confidence and avoid sleepless nights second-guessing ourselves; having a sense of fairness keeps us from behaving like self-centered louts; mental sets and the hindsight bias help us impose order on all the information we have to deal with. But our mental biases can also get us into trouble. The confirmation bias, the justification of effort, and the need to reduce postdecision dissonance permit people to stay stuck with decisions that eventually prove to be self-defeating, harmful, or incorrect. Physicians may continue using outdated methods, district attorneys may overlook evidence that a criminal suspect might be innocent, and managers may refuse to consider better business practices.

To make matters worse, most people have a "bias blind spot": They acknowledge that *other* people have biases that distort reality, but they think that they themselves are free of bias and see the world as it really is (Pronin, Gilovich, & Ross, 2004; Ross, 2010). This blind spot is itself a bias, and it is a dangerous one, because it can prevent individuals, nations, and ethnic or religious groups from resolving conflicts with others. Each side thinks that its own proposals for ending a conflict, or its own analyses of a disagreement, are reasonable and fair but the other side's are biased. Cognitive psychologists, though, don't think the situation is hopeless. They find that once we understand a bias, we may be able to reduce or eliminate it, especially if we make an active, mindful effort to do so and take time to think carefully (Kida, 2006).

Some people, of course, seem to think more rationally than others; we call them "intelligent." Just what is intelligence, and how can we measure and improve it? We take up these questions next.

justification of effort
The tendency of individuals to increase their liking for something that they have worked hard or suffered to attain; a common form of dissonance reduction.

FIGURE 7.2 The Justification of Effort
The more effort you put into reaching a goal, the more highly you are likely to value it. As you can see in the graph on the left, after people listened to a boring group discussion, those who went through a severe initiation to join the group rated it most highly (Aronson & Mills, 1959). In the photo, mud-covered soldiers are undergoing difficult training to join an elite unit. They will probably become extremely devoted members.

Recite & Review

 Study and **Review** at **MyPsychLab**

Recite: Make a rational decision now to say aloud what you know about the affect heuristic, the availability heuristic, the framing effect, the fairness bias, the hindsight bias, the confirmation bias, mental sets, cognitive dissonance reduction, postdecision dissonance, and the justification of effort.

Review: In hindsight, you might feel you knew this material already, but read it again to be sure you do.

Now take this *Quick Quiz:*

1. While selling insurance policies, an agent often says "if I die, my family will not be left uncared for. The coverage will help, and in the case of completing the tenure of the policy, you gain a bonus with your principal amount." By referring to "I" and "you," what strategy is the agent using to convince his client about the deal?

2. *True or false:* Studies have shown that economic decisions are always rational.

3. Yuhan tells his son that smoking is injurious to health. But when he smokes, he reasons with himself that he does so in order to reduce his stress and not for pleasure. How would you justify Yuhan's behavior?

4. In a classic experiment on cognitive dissonance, students did some boring, repetitive tasks and then had to tell another student, who was waiting to participate in the study, that the work was interesting and fun (Festinger & Carlsmith, 1959). Half the students were offered $20 for telling this lie and the others only $1. Based on what you have learned about cognitive dissonance reduction, which students do you think decided later that the tasks had been fun after all? Why?

Answers:

1. framing effect 2. false 3. As the two cognitions are inconsistent, Yuhan rationalizes his behavior to maintain consonance. 4. The students who got only $1 were more likely to say that the task had been fun. They were in a state of dissonance because "The task was as dull as dishwater" is dissonant with "I said I enjoyed it—and for a mere dollar, at that." Those who got $20 could rationalize that the large sum (which really was large in the 1950s) justified the lie.

---

intelligence An inferred characteristic of an individual, usually defined as the ability to profit from experience, acquire knowledge, think abstractly, act purposefully, or adapt to changes in the environment.

psychometrics The measurement of mental abilities, traits, and processes.

factor analysis A statistical method for analyzing the intercorrelations among various measures or test scores; clusters of measures or scores that are highly correlated are assumed to measure the same underlying trait, ability, or aptitude (factor).

g factor A general intellectual ability assumed by many theorists to underlie specific mental abilities and talents.

You are about to learn...

- both sides of the debate about whether a single thing called "intelligence" actually exists.

- how the original purpose of intelligence testing changed when IQ tests came to the United States.

- the difficulties of designing intelligence tests that are free of cultural influence.

Measuring Intelligence: The Psychometric Approach LO 7.11

Intelligent people disagree on just what intelligence is. Some equate it with the ability to reason abstractly, others with the ability to learn and profit from experience in daily life. Some emphasize the ability to think rationally, others the ability to act purposefully. These qualities are all probably part of what most people mean by **intelligence**, but theorists weigh them differently.

Explore the **Concept** What Is Intelligence? at **MyPsychLab**

The traditional approach to intelligence relies on **psychometrics**, the measurement of mental abilities, traits, and processes. It focuses on how well people perform on standardized aptitude tests, which are designed to measure the ability to acquire skills and knowledge. A typical intelligence test asks you to do several things: provide a specific bit of information, notice similarities between objects, solve arithmetic problems, define words, fill in the missing parts of incomplete pictures, arrange pictures in a logical order, arrange blocks to resemble a design, assemble puzzles, use a coding scheme, or judge what behavior would be appropriate in a given situation. A statistical method called **factor analysis** helps to identify clusters of correlated items that seem to be measuring some common ability, or factor (see Chapter 2).

More than a century of research has convinced most psychometric psychologists that a general ability, or **g factor**, underlies the various abilities and talents measured by intelligence tests (Gottfredson, 2002; Jensen, 1998; Lubinski, 2004;

Spearman, 1927; Wechsler, 1955). This general ability has two components. **Crystallized intelligence** refers to knowledge and skills, the kind that allow you to do arithmetic, define words, and make political decisions. **Fluid intelligence** refers to the capacity to reason and use information to solve new problems (Horn & Cattell, 1966). Crystallized *g* depends heavily on education and tends to remain stable or even increase over a lifetime. Fluid *g* is relatively independent of education and tends to decrease in old age.

Tests of *g* do a good job of predicting academic achievement, occupational success, and eminence in many fields (Kuncel, Hezlett, & Ones, 2004; Schmidt & Hunter, 2004; Simonton & Song, 2009). But, as we will see, some scientists dispute the existence of a global quality called "intelligence," observing that a person can be smart in some areas and not in others (Gould, 1994; Guilford, 1988).

The Invention of IQ Tests LO 7.12

The first widely used intelligence test was devised in 1904, when the French Ministry of Education asked psychologist Alfred Binet (1857–1911) to find a way to identify children who were slow learners so they could be given remedial work. The ministry was reluctant to let teachers identify such children because the teachers might have prejudices about poor children or might assume that shy or disruptive children were mentally impaired. The government wanted a more objective approach.

A child taking an intelligence test.

Binet's Brainstorm. Wrestling with the problem, Binet had a great insight: In the classroom, the responses of "dull" children resembled those of ordinary children of younger ages. Bright children, on the other hand, responded like children of older ages. The thing to measure, then, was a child's **mental age (MA)**, or level of intellectual development relative to that of other children. Then instruction could be tailored to the child's capabilities.

The test devised by Binet and his colleague, Théodore Simon, measured memory, vocabulary, and perceptual discrimination. Items ranged from those that most young children could do easily to those that only older children could handle, as determined by the testing of large numbers of children. A scoring system developed later by others used a formula in which the child's mental age was divided by the child's actual age to yield an **intelligence quotient,** or **IQ** (a quotient is the result of division). A child of 8 who performed like the average 10-year-old would have a mental age of 10 and an IQ of 125 (10 divided by 8, times 100).

Unfortunately, this method of computing IQ had serious flaws. At one age, scores might cluster tightly around the average, whereas at another age they might be more dispersed. As a result, the score necessary to be in the top 10 or 20 or 30 percent of your age group varied, depending on your age. Also, the IQ formula did not make sense for adults; a 50-year-old who scores like a 30-year-old does not have low intelligence, though his score would be only 60! Today, therefore, intelligence tests are scored differently. The mean (average) is usually set arbitrarily at 100. Tests are constructed so that about two-thirds of all people score between 85 and 115, and individual scores are computed from tables based on established norms. These scores are still informally referred to as IQs, and they still reflect how a person compares with other people, either children of the same age or adults in general. At all ages, the distribution of scores approximates a normal (bell-shaped) curve, with scores near the average (mean) more common than high or low scores (see Figure 7.3).

The IQ Test Comes to America. In the United States, Stanford psychologist Lewis Terman revised Binet's test and established norms for American children. His version, the *Stanford–Binet Intelligence Scales*, was first published in 1916 and has been updated several times since. It can be given to children as young as 2 or adults as old as 85. The test asks a person to perform a variety of tasks—for example, to fill in missing words in sentences, answer questions requiring general knowledge, predict how a folded paper will look

crystallized intelligence Cognitive skills and specific knowledge acquired over a lifetime; it is heavily dependent on education and tends to remain stable.

fluid intelligence The capacity to reason and use information to solve problems; it is relatively independent of education and tends to decline in old age.

mental age (MA) A measure of mental development expressed in terms of the average mental ability at a given age.

intelligence quotient (IQ) A measure of intelligence originally computed by dividing a person's mental age by his or her chronological age and multiplying the result by 100; it is now derived from norms provided for standardized intelligence tests.

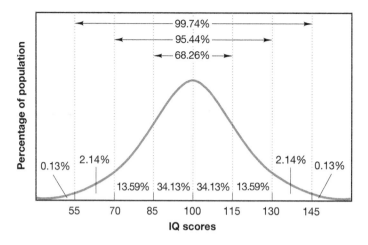

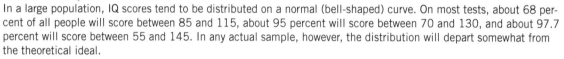

FIGURE 7.3 Expected Distribution of IQ Scores

In a large population, IQ scores tend to be distributed on a normal (bell-shaped) curve. On most tests, about 68 percent of all people will score between 85 and 115, about 95 percent will score between 70 and 130, and about 97.7 percent will score between 55 and 145. In any actual sample, however, the distribution will depart somewhat from the theoretical ideal.

when unfolded, measure a quantity of water using two containers of different sizes, and distinguish concepts that are similar but not exactly the same (such as *vigor* and *energy*). The older the test taker is, the more the test requires in the way of verbal comprehension and fluency, spatial ability, and reasoning.

Two decades later, David Wechsler designed another test expressly for adults, which became the *Wechsler Adult Intelligence Scale* (WAIS); it was followed by the *Wechsler Intelligence Scale for Children* (WISC). These tests, which also have been updated periodically, produce a general IQ score and separate scores for verbal comprehension, perceptual

reasoning, processing speed, and memory. Items measure a range of abilities, including vocabulary, arithmetic skills, recognition of similarities (e.g., "How are books and movies alike?"), general knowledge and comprehension (e.g., "Who was Thomas Jefferson?"; "Why do people who want a divorce have to go to court?"), and a variety of nonverbal skills, such as the ability to identify a part missing from a picture. (See Figure 7.4 for some typical nonverbal items.)

Binet had emphasized that his test merely *sampled* intelligence and did not measure everything covered by that term. A test score, he said, could be useful, along with other information,

Picture arrangement
(Arrange the panels to make a meaningful story.)

Object assembly
(Put together a jigsaw puzzle.)

Digit symbol
(Using the key at the top, fill in the appropriate symbol beneath each number.)

Picture completion
(Supply the missing feature.)

FIGURE 7.4 Nonverbal Tasks on the Wechsler Tests

Items such as these are especially useful for measuring the abilities of those who have poor hearing, are not fluent in the tester's language, have limited education, or resist doing classroom-type problems. A large gap between a person's verbal score and performance on nonverbal tasks sometimes indicates a specific learning problem.

for predicting school performance, but it should not be confused with intelligence itself. The tests were designed to be given individually, so that the test giver could tell when a child was ill or nervous, had poor vision, or was unmotivated. The purpose was to identify children with learning problems, not to rank all children. But when intelligence testing was brought from France to the United States, its original purpose got lost at sea. IQ tests became widely used not to bring slow learners up to the average, but to categorize people in school and in the armed services according to their presumed "natural ability." The testers overlooked the fact that in the United States, with its many ethnic groups, people did not all share the same background and experience (Gould, 1996).

👁 Watch the Video Special Topics: Intelligence Testing, Then and Now at MyPsychLab

Culture and Intelligence Testing.
Intelligence tests developed between World War I and the 1960s for use in schools favored city children over rural ones, middle-class children over poor ones, and white children over nonwhite children. One item asked whether the Emperor Concerto was written by Beethoven, Mozart, Bach, Brahms, or Mahler. (The answer is Beethoven.) Critics complained that the tests did not measure the kinds of knowledge and skills that indicate intelligent behavior in a minority neighborhood or a remote rural community. They feared that because teachers thought IQ scores revealed the limits of a child's potential, low-scoring children would not get the educational attention or encouragement they needed.

Test makers responded by trying to construct tests that were unaffected by culture or that incorporated knowledge and skills common to many different cultures. But these efforts were disappointing, in part because cultures differ in the problem-solving strategies they emphasize (Serpell, 1994). In the West, white, middle-class children typically learn to classify things by category—to say that an apple and a peach are similar because they are both fruits, and that a saw and a rake are similar because they are both tools. But children who are not trained in middle-class ways of sorting things may classify objects according to their sensory qualities or functions; they may say that an apple and a peach are similar because they taste good. That may be a charming and innovative answer, but it is one that test administrators have interpreted as less intelligent (Miller-Jones, 1989).

Testing experts also discovered that cultural values and experiences affect many things besides responses to specific test items. These include a person's general attitude toward exams, motivation, rapport with the test giver, competitiveness, comfort in solving problems independently, and familiarity with the conventions for taking tests (Anastasi & Urbina, 1997; López, 1995; Sternberg, 2004).

Moreover, people's performance on mental-ability tests depends in part on their own expectations about how they will do, and those expectations are affected by cultural stereotypes. Stereotypes that portray women, old people, poor people, or ethnic and racial minorities as unintelligent can actually depress the performance of people in those groups. You might think that a woman would say, "So sexists think women are dumb at math? I'll show them!" or that an African American would say, "So racists believe that blacks aren't as smart as whites? Just give me that exam." But often that is not what happens.

On the contrary, such individuals commonly feel a burden of doubt about their abilities, creating an insecurity known as **stereotype threat** (Steele, 1992, 1997). The threat occurs when people believe that if they do not do well, they will confirm the stereotypes about their group. Negative thoughts intrude and disrupt their concentration ("I hate this test," "I'm no good at math") (Cadinu et al., 2005). The resulting anxiety may then worsen their performance or kill their motivation to even try to do well.

stereotype threat A burden of doubt a person feels about his or her performance, due to negative stereotypes about his or her group's abilities.

STEREOTYPE THREAT

Hundreds of studies have shown that stereotype threat can affect the test performance of many African Americans, Latinos, low-income people, women, and elderly people, all of whom perform better when they are not feeling self-conscious about themselves as members of negatively stereotyped groups (e.g., J. Aronson, 2010; Brown & Josephs, 1999; Inzlicht & Ben-Zeev, 2000; Levy, 1996; Quinn & Spencer, 2001; Steele & Aronson, 1995; Thomas & Dubois, 2011). Anything that increases the salience of group stereotypes can increase stereotype threat and affect performance, including taking the test in a setting where you are the only member from your group, or being asked to state your race, gender, age, or ethnicity before taking the test. The good news is that stereotype threat can be reduced by simply telling people about it, which often inoculates them against its

Whether or not you feel stereotype threat depends on what category you are identifying with at the time. Asian women do worse on math tests when they see themselves as "women" (stereotype = poor at math) rather than as "Asians" (stereotype = good at math) (Shih, Pittinsky, & Ambady, 1999).

effects (Good, Aronson, & Harder, 2008; Johns, Schmader, & Martens, 2005; Schmader, 2010).

Watch the **Video** In the Real World: Intelligence Tests and Stereotypes at **MyPsychLab**

Stereotype threat is thus an important contributing factor in group differences in test performance, but it is not the only one. Group differences remain, and that fact points to a dilemma at the heart of intelligence and mental-ability testing. Intelligence and other mental-ability tests put some groups of people at a disadvantage, yet they also measure skills and knowledge useful in the classroom and on the job. How can psychologists and educators recognize and accept cultural differences and, at the same time, promote the mastery of the skills, knowledge, and attitudes that can help people succeed in school and in the larger society?

Recite & Review

✔️ **Study** and **Review** at **MyPsychLab**

Recite: Check your Quiz Quotient (QQ) by saying aloud everything you can about intelligence, the psychometric approach, factor analysis, the *g* factor, the intelligence quotient, IQ tests, and stereotype threat.

Review: Next, reread this section and make sure you really understand it.

Now act intelligently by taking this *Quick Quiz:*

1. Which method helps to identify clusters of correlated items that seem to be measuring some common ability?

2. Monica is a sensitive girl who is always empathetic in her approach to situations. Instead of shouting or getting angry, she steps back, assesses, and evaluates the situation before responding. What type of intelligence is Monica high on?

3. While preparing for her tests, Amanda is not able to absorb difficult parts of her syllabus, and she keeps on revising the material she already knows. Amanda is weak in her _____.

Answers:

1. factor analysis 2. emotional intelligence 3. metacognition

---

You are about to learn...

- how the ability to control attention enhances intelligence.

- about some proposed kinds of intelligence that are not measured by IQ tests.

- why "emotional intelligence" might be as important as IQ.

Dissecting Intelligence: The Cognitive Approach

Critics of standard intelligence tests point out that such tests tell us little about *how* a person goes about answering questions and solving problems. Nor do the tests explain why people with low scores often do intelligent things in real life, from making smart consumer decisions to devising a winning betting strategy at the racetrack. Therefore, many psychological scientists believe that the psychometric approach yields an incomplete picture of intelligence. They take a *cognitive approach to intelligence*, aiming to identify the cognitive processes and strategies that people use when they are thinking and behaving intelligently.

💡 **THINKING CRITICALLY**

About What It Means to Be Smart

Elements of Intelligence
LO 7.13, LO 7.14

One cognitive ingredient of intelligence is **working memory**, a complex capacity that enables you to manipulate information retrieved from long-term memory and interpret it appropriately while you are working on a given task (see Chapter 8). Working memory permits you to juggle your attention while you are working on a problem, shifting your attention from one piece of information to another while ignoring distracting or irrelevant information. People who do well on tests of working memory tend to be good at many real-life tasks requiring the control of attention, including reading comprehension, writing, and reasoning (Engle, 2002). In contrast, people with less working-memory capacity often have trouble keeping their minds on the job at hand and may not get better on a task, even with practice (Kane et al., 2007).

Another cognitive ingredient of intelligence is **metacognition**, the knowledge or awareness of your own cognitive processes and the ability to monitor and control those processes. Students who are weak in metacognition fail to notice when a passage in a textbook is difficult, and they do not always realize that they haven't understood what they've been reading. As a result, they spend too little time on difficult material and too much time on material they already know. They are overconfident about their comprehension and memory, and then are surprised when they do poorly on exams (Dunlosky & Lipko, 2007). In contrast, students who are strong in metacognition check their comprehension by restating what they have read, testing themselves, backtracking when necessary, and questioning what they are reading. When time is limited, they tackle fairly easy material first (where the payoff will be great), and then move on to more difficult material; as a result, they learn better (Metcalfe, 2009).

It works in the other direction, too: The kind of intelligence that enhances academic performance can help you develop metacognitive skills. Students with poor academic skills typically fail to realize how little they know; they think they're doing fine (Dunning, 2005). The very weaknesses that keep them from doing well in their courses also keep them from realizing their weaknesses. People with strong academic skills tend to be more realistic. Often they even underestimate slightly how their performance compares with the performance of their peers.

The Triarchic Theory.
Some people who have a good working memory and strong metacognitive skills still keep making the same dumb choices in their relationships, and some people who don't seem especially bright are successful in love and work. That is why some psychological scientists reject the idea of a *g* factor as an adequate description of intelligence, and prefer to speak of different kinds of intelligence.

One is Robert Sternberg (1988, 2004, 2012), who has developed the **triarchic theory of intelligence** (1988) (*triarchic* means "three-part"). He defines intelligence as "the skills and knowledge needed for success in life, according to one's own definition of success, within one's sociocultural context." A guitar player, builder, scientist, and farmer can all be called successful if they make the most of their strengths, correct their weaknesses, and adapt to, select, and shape their environments to improve their lives. According to Sternberg, successfully intelligent people balance three kinds of intelligence: analytic, creative, and practical. If they are weak in one, they learn to work around that weakness.

1 Componential or analytical intelligence refers to the information-processing strategies (components) you draw on when you are thinking intelligently about a problem: recognizing and defining the problem, comparing and contrasting alternatives, selecting a strategy for solving it, mastering and carrying out the strategy, and evaluating the result. Such abilities are required in every culture but are applied to different kinds of problems in different cultures. One society may emphasize the use of these components to solve abstract problems, whereas another may emphasize using the same components to maintain smooth relationships. In Western cultures, analytic intelligence is associated with academic work and is the kind most often measured on standardized tests.

2 Experiential or creative intelligence refers to your creativity in transferring skills to new situations. People with experiential intelligence cope well with novelty and learn quickly to make new tasks automatic. Those who are lacking in this area perform well only under a narrow set of circumstances. They may do well in school, where assignments have specific due dates and feedback is immediate, but be less successful after graduation if their jobs require them to set their own deadlines and their supervisors don't provide regular evaluations.

3 Contextual or practical intelligence refers to the practical application of intelligence, which requires you to take into account the different contexts in which you find yourself. If you are strong in contextual intelligence, you know when to adapt

---

working memory A complex type of memory that permits the manipulation of information retrieved from long-term memory and makes it available for working on a given task.

metacognition The knowledge or awareness of one's own cognitive processes and the ability to monitor and control those processes.

triarchic [try-ARE-kick] theory of intelligence A theory of intelligence that emphasizes analytic, creative, and practical abilities.

"You're wise, but you lack tree smarts."

to the environment (you are in a dangerous neighborhood, so you become more vigilant). You know when to change environments (you had planned to be a teacher but discover that you dislike working with kids, so you switch to accounting). And you know when to fix the situation (you and your partner are fighting a lot, so you both go for counseling).

Contextual intelligence allows you to acquire **tacit knowledge**—practical, action-oriented strategies for achieving your goals that usually are not formally taught or even verbalized but must instead be inferred by observing others. College professors, business managers, and salespeople who have tacit knowledge and practical intelligence tend to be better than others at their jobs. Among college students, tacit knowledge about how to be a good student predicts academic success as well as entrance exams do (Sternberg et al., 2000).

Emotional Intelligence. Other psychologists, too, are expanding the definition of intelligence. One of the most important kinds of nonintellectual "smarts" may be **emotional intelligence**, the ability to identify your own and other people's emotions accurately, express your emotions clearly, and manage emotions in yourself and others (Mayer & Salovey, 1997; Salovey & Grewal, 2005). People with high emotional intelligence, popularly known as "EQ," use their emotions to motivate themselves, to spur creative thinking, and to deal empathically with others. People who are lacking in emotional intelligence are often unable to identify their own emotions; they may insist that they are not depressed when a relationship ends, but meanwhile they start drinking too much, become irritable, and stop going out with friends. They express emotions inappropriately, perhaps by acting violently or impulsively when they are angry or worried. They often misread

nonverbal signals from others; they will give a long-winded account of all their problems even when the listener is obviously bored.

Studies of brain-damaged adults suggest a biological basis for emotional intelligence. Neuroscientist Antonio Damasio (1994) has studied patients with prefrontal-lobe damage that makes them incapable of experiencing strong feelings. Although they score in the normal range on conventional mental tests, these patients persistently make "dumb," irrational decisions because they cannot assign values to different options based on their own emotional reactions, and cannot read emotional cues from others.

Not everyone agrees that broadening the definition of intelligence is helpful. Some argue that EQ is a collection of ordinary personality traits, such as empathy and extroversion (Matthews, Zeidener, & Roberts, 2003). And some think that including any variations muddies the fundamental concept of intelligence. Yet this debate has forced us to think more critically about what we mean by intelligence and to consider how different abilities help us function in our everyday lives. It has generated research on tests that provide ongoing feedback to the test taker so that the person can learn from the experience and improve performance. The cognitive approach has also led to a focus on teaching children strategies for improving their reading, writing, homework, and test-taking ability—such as managing their time and studying differently for multiple-choice exams than for essay exams (Sternberg, 2004; Sternberg et al., 1995). Most important, new approaches to intelligence encourage us to overcome the mental set of assuming that the only abilities necessary for a successful life are the kind captured by IQ tests.

People with emotional intelligence are skilled at reading nonverbal emotional cues. Which of these girls is the most confident and relaxed, which one is shyest, and which feels most anxious? What cues are you using to answer?

tacit knowledge
Strategies for success that are not explicitly taught but that instead must be inferred.

emotional intelligence
The ability to identify your own and other people's emotions accurately, express your emotions clearly and appropriately, and regulate emotions in yourself and others.

You are about to learn...

- the extent to which intelligence may be heritable.
- a common error in the argument that one group is genetically smarter than another.
- how the environment nurtures or thwarts mental ability.
- the role of motivation and hard work in intellectual performance.

The Origins of Intelligence

"Intelligence," as we have seen, can mean many things. But however we define or measure it, clearly some people think and behave more intelligently than others. What accounts for these differences?

Genes and Individual Differences

LO 7.15

Behavioral geneticists approach this question by doing heritability studies, focusing mainly on *g*, the kind of intelligence measured by IQ tests. **Heritability** is the proportion of the total variance in a trait within a group that is attributable to genetic variation within the group (see Chapter 2). This proportion can have a maximum value of 1.0, which means that the trait is completely heritable—although most traits, including even height, are not perfectly heritable; genes interact constantly with the environment throughout our lives (Johnson

et al., 2009). (You might review pages 71–73 to refresh your memory about heritability.)

Behavioral-genetic studies show that the kind of intelligence that produces high IQ scores is partly heritable, at least in the middle-class samples usually studied. For children and adolescents, heritability estimates average around .40 or .50; that is, genetic differences explain about half of the variance in IQ scores (Chipuer, Rovine, & Plomin, 1990; Devlin, Daniels, & Roeder, 1997; Plomin, 1989). For adults, most estimates are even higher—in the .60 to .80 range (Bouchard, 1995; McClearn et al., 1997; McGue et al., 1993). These estimates show that the genetic contribution becomes relatively larger and the environmental one relatively smaller with age.

In studies of twins, the scores of identical twins are always much more highly correlated than those of fraternal twins, a difference that reflects the influence of genes. In fact, the scores of identical twins reared *apart* are more highly correlated than those of fraternal twins reared *together*, as you can see in Figure 7.5. In adoption studies, the scores of adopted children are more highly correlated with those of their birth parents than with those of their biologically unrelated adoptive parents; the higher the birth parents' scores, the higher the child's score is likely to be. As adopted children grow into adolescence, the correlation between their IQ scores and those of their biologically unrelated family members diminishes, and in adulthood, the correlation falls to *zero* (Bouchard, 1997b; Scarr, 1993; Scarr & Weinberg, 1994). This does not mean that adoption has no positive effects; as a group, adopted

heritability A statistical estimate of the proportion of the total variance in some trait that is attributable to genetic differences among individuals within a group.

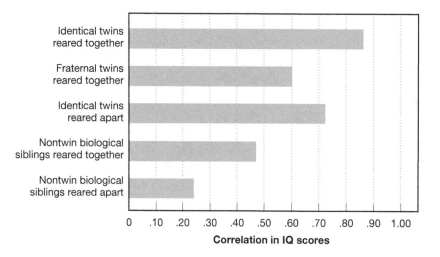

FIGURE 7.5 Correlations in Siblings' IQ Scores
The IQ scores of identical twins are highly correlated, even when they are reared apart. The figures represented in this graph are based on average correlations across many studies. *Source:* Graph based on data from Bouchard & McGue, 1981.

children score higher on IQ tests than do birth siblings who were not adopted, probably because adoptees grow up in a more enriched environment (van IJzendoorn et al., 2005).

Scientists are now looking for specific genes that might influence mental ability, but so far, findings have been elusive and difficult to replicate (Chabris et al., 2012). Any one gene is likely to contribute just a small piece to the puzzle of genetic variation in intelligence (Plomin, DeFries, & Knopik, 2013).

The Question of Group Differences. LO 7.16
If genes influence individual differences in intelligence, do they also help account for differences *between* groups, as many people assume? Unfortunately, the history of this issue has been marred by ethnic and class prejudice. Because this question has enormous political and social importance, we are going to examine it closely.

Most of the focus has been on black–white differences in IQ, because black children score lower, on average, than do white children. (We are talking about *averages*; the distributions of scores for black children and white children overlap considerably.) A few psycholo-

THINKING CRITICALLY

About Group Differences in IQ

gists have proposed a genetic explanation of this difference and conclude that there is little point in spending money on programs that try to raise the IQs of low-scoring children, of whatever race (Murray, 2008; Rushton & Jensen, 2005). Genetic explanations of group differences, however, have a fatal flaw. They use heritability estimates based

mainly on white samples to estimate the role of heredity in group differences, a procedure that is not valid. This problem sounds pretty technical, but it is really not too difficult to understand, so stay with us.

Consider, first, not people but tomatoes. (Figure 7.6 will help you visualize the following "thought experiment.") Suppose you have a bag of tomato seeds that vary genetically; all things being equal, some will produce tomatoes that are puny and tasteless, and some will produce tomatoes that are plump and delicious. Now you take a bunch of

FIGURE 7.6 The Tomato Plant Experiment
In the hypothetical experiment described in the text, even if the differences among plants within each pot resulted entirely from genetics, the average differences between pots could be environmental. The same general principle applies to individual and group differences among human beings.

these seeds in your left hand and another bunch from the same bag in your right hand. Although one seed differs genetically from another, there is no *average* difference between the seeds in your left hand and those in your right. You plant the left hand's seeds in pot A, with some enriched soil that you have doctored with nitrogen and other nutrients, and you plant the right hand's seeds in pot B, with soil from which you have extracted nutrients. You sing to pot A and put it in the sun; you ignore pot B and leave it in a dark corner.

When the tomato plants grow, they will vary *within* each pot in terms of height, the number of tomatoes produced, and the size of the tomatoes, purely because of genetic differences. But there will also be an average difference between the plants in pot A and those in pot B: The plants in pot A will be healthier and bear more tomatoes. This difference *between* pots is due entirely to the different soils and the care that has been given to them, even though the heritability of the *within*-pot differences is 100 percent (Lewontin, 1970, 2000).

The principle is the same for people as it is for tomatoes. Although intellectual differences *within* groups are at least partly genetic in origin, that does not mean differences *between* groups are genetic. Blacks and whites do not grow up, on the average, in the same "pots" (environments). Because of a long legacy of racial discrimination and de facto segregation, black children, as well as Latino and other minority children, often receive far fewer nutrients—literally, in terms of food, and figuratively, in terms of education, encouragement by society, and intellectual opportunities (Nisbett, 2009).

Doing good research on the origins of group differences in IQ is extremely difficult in the United States, where racism has affected the lives of even many affluent, successful African Americans.

However, the few studies that have overcome past methodological problems fail to support a genetic explanation. Children fathered by black and white American soldiers in Germany after World War II and reared in similar German communities by similar families did not differ significantly in IQ (Eyferth, 1961). Contrary to what a genetic theory would predict, degree of African ancestry (which can be roughly estimated from skin color, blood analysis, and genealogy) is not related to measured intelligence (Scarr et al., 1977).

An intelligent reading of the research on intelligence, therefore, does not direct us to conclude that differences among cultural, ethnic, or national groups are permanent, genetically determined, or signs of any group's innate superiority. On the contrary, the research suggests that we should make sure that all children grow up in the best possible soil, with room for the smartest and the slowest to find a place in the sun.

The Environment and Intelligence
LO 7.17

By now you may be wondering what kinds of experiences hinder intellectual development and what kinds of environmental "nutrients" promote it. Here are some of the factors associated with reduced mental ability:

- **Poor prenatal care.** If a pregnant woman is malnourished, contracts infections, smokes, is exposed to secondhand smoke, has insufficient levels of folic acid, or drinks alcohol regularly, her child is at risk of having learning disabilities and a lower IQ.

- **Malnutrition.** The average IQ gap between severely malnourished and well-nourished

The children of migrant workers (left) often spend long hours in backbreaking field work and may miss out on the educational opportunities and intellectual advantages available to middle-class children from the same culture (right).

children can be as high as 20 points (Stoch & Smythe, 1963; Winick, Meyer, & Harris, 1975).

- **Exposure to toxins.** Many children, especially poor and minority children, are exposed to dangerous levels of lead from dust, contaminated soil, lead paint, and old lead pipes, and lead can damage the brain and nervous system. Even children exposed to fairly low, supposedly safe levels develop attention problems, have lower IQ scores, and do worse in school than other children (Hornung, Lanphear, & Dietrich, 2009; Koller et al., 2004). In addition, children exposed in utero to high levels of pesticides (still legal for spraying on farm fields) later have an IQ score that is 7 points lower on average than that of children with the least exposure (Raloff, 2011).

- **Stressful family experiences.** Factors that predict reduced intellectual competence include having a father who does not live with the family; a mother with a history of mental illness; parents with limited work skills; and stressful events, such as domestic violence, early in life (Sameroff et al., 1987). On average, each risk factor reduces a child's IQ score by 4 points.

- **Living in severely disadvantaged and impoverished neighborhoods.** When children grow up in neighborhoods that are falling apart, are unsafe, have high crime rates, and lack opportunities for education and exercise, their IQs decline over time, even after they have moved to better areas; the drop is comparable to that seen when a child misses a year of school (Sampson, 2008).

In contrast, a healthy and stimulating environment can raise children's IQ scores. Meta-analyses of virtually all of the available controlled research show that four interventions are clearly helpful: supplementing the diets of pregnant women and newborns with essential fatty acids; reading interactively with young children; providing intense early education; and sending children to preschool (Protzko, Aronson, & Blair, 2013). In one study, attending quality preschool increased the reading and math skills of children from racial and ethnic minorities, especially if they were not getting much cognitive stimulation elsewhere (Tucker-Drob, 2012). And two important longitudinal studies found that inner-city children who got lots of early mental enrichment at home and in preschool showed significant IQ gains and had much better school achievement than did children in a control group (Campbell & Ramey, 1995; Reynolds et al., 2011).

Perhaps the best evidence for the importance of environmental influences on intelligence is the fact that in developed countries IQ scores have been climbing steadily for several generations (Flynn, 1987, 1999). (See Figure 7.7.) Genes cannot possibly have changed enough to account for these findings. Then what can? One possibility is improvements in the education, health care, diets, and job opportunities of the poorest, lowest-scoring people, which increases the overall mean. If that is so, we would expect to see large and rapid increases in developing countries, and so we do. In Kenya, IQ scores of rural 6- to 8-year-old children jumped about 11 points between 1984 and 1998, the fastest rise in a group's average IQ scores ever reported (Daley et al., 2003).

We see, then, that although heredity may provide the range of a child's intellectual potential—a Homer Simpson can never become an Einstein—many other factors affect where in that range the child will fall.

Motivation, Hard Work, and Intellectual Success LO 7.18

Even with a high IQ, emotional intelligence, and practical know-how, you still might get nowhere at all. Talent, unlike cream, does not inevitably rise to the top; success also depends on drive and determination.

Consider a finding from one of the longest-running psychological studies ever conducted. In 1921, Louis Terman and his associates began following more than 1,500 children with IQ scores in the top one percent of the distribution. These boys and girls, nicknamed Termites after Terman, started out bright, physically healthy, sociable, and well adjusted. As they entered adulthood, most became successful in the traditional ways of the times: men in careers and women as homemakers (Sears & Barbee, 1977; Terman & Oden, 1959). However, some gifted men failed to live up to their early promise, dropping out of school or drifting into low-level work. The 100

Severe poverty, exposure to toxic materials, run-down neighborhoods, and stressful family circumstances can all impede children's cognitive development and lower their IQ.

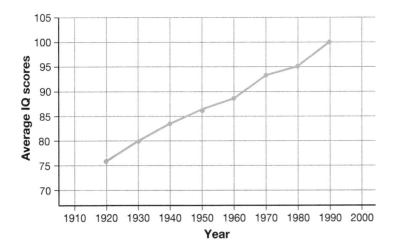

FIGURE 7.7 Climbing IQ Scores
Raw scores on IQ tests have been rising in developed countries for many decades at a rate much too steep to be accounted for by genetic changes. Because test norms are periodically readjusted to set the average score at 100, most people are unaware of the increase. On this graph, average scores are calibrated according to 1989 norms. As you can see, performance was much lower in 1918 than in 1989. *Source:* Data from Horgan, 1995.

most successful men were ambitious, were socially active, had many interests, and had been encouraged by their parents. The 100 least successful drifted casually through life. There was no average difference in IQ between the two groups.

Once you are motivated to succeed intellectually, you need self-discipline to reach your goals. In a longitudinal study of ethnically diverse eighth graders attending a magnet school, students were assigned a self-discipline score based on their self-reports, parents' reports, teachers' reports, and questionnaires. They were also scored on a behavioral measure of self-discipline—their ability to delay gratification. (The teens had to choose between keeping an envelope containing a dollar or returning it in exchange for getting two dollars a week later.) Self-discipline accounted for more than twice as much of the variance in the students' final grades and achievement test scores as IQ did (Duckworth & Seligman, 2005). As you can see in Figure 7.8, correlations between self-discipline and academic performance were much stronger than those between IQ and academic performance.

Self-discipline and motivation to work hard at intellectual tasks depend, in turn, on your attitudes about intelligence and achievement, which are strongly influenced by cultural values. For many years, Harold Stevenson and his colleagues studied attitudes toward achievement in Asia and the United States, comparing large samples of grade school children, parents, and teachers in Minneapolis, Chicago, Sendai (Japan), Taipei (Taiwan), and Beijing (Stevenson, Chen, & Lee, 1993; Stevenson & Stigler, 1992). Their results have much to teach us about the cultivation of intellect.

In 1980, the Asian children far outperformed the American children on a broad battery of mathematical and reading tests. On computation, reading, and word problems, there was virtually no overlap between schools, with the lowest-scoring Beijing schools doing better than the highest-scoring Chicago schools. By 1990, the gulf between the Asian and American children had grown even greater. Only 4 percent of the Chinese children and 10 percent of the Japanese children had math scores as low as those of the *average* American child. Educational resources did not explain these

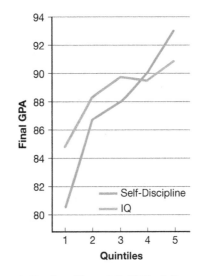

FIGURE 7.8 Grades, IQ, and Self-Discipline
Eighth-grade students were divided into five groups (quintiles) based on their IQ scores and then followed for a year to test their academic achievement. Self-discipline was a stronger predictor of success than IQ was (Duckworth & Seligman, 2005).

differences: The Chinese had worse facilities and larger classes than the Americans, and on average, the Chinese parents were poorer and less educated than parents in the U.S. Nor did it have anything to do with intellectual abilities in general: The American children were just as knowledgeable and capable as the Asian children on tests of general information. But the Asians and Americans were worlds apart in their attitudes and efforts:

- **Beliefs.** American parents, teachers, and children were far more likely than Asians to believe that mathematical ability is innate: If you have this ability you don't have to work hard, and if you don't have it, there's no point in trying. (See Figure 7.9.)

- **Standards.** American parents had far lower standards for their children's performance; they were satisfied with scores barely above average on a 100-point test. In contrast, Chinese and Japanese parents were happy only with very high scores.

- **Values.** American students did not value education as much as Asian students did, and they were more complacent about mediocre work. When asked what they would wish for if a wizard could give them anything they wanted, more than 60 percent of the Chinese fifth graders named something related to their education. Can you guess what the American children wanted? A majority said money or possessions.

When it comes to intellect, then, it's not just what you've got that counts, but what you do with

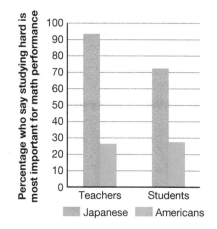

FIGURE 7.9 What's the Secret of Math Success? Japanese schoolteachers and students are much more likely than their American counterparts to believe that the secret to doing well in math is working hard. Americans tend to think that you either have mathematical intelligence or you don't (Stevenson, Chen, & Lee, 1993).

it—and also the value your society places on intellectual accomplishment (Ripley, 2013). A 2012 report from the National Center for Educational Statistics found that educational reforms in some U.S. states have boosted children's performance significantly in recent years, but in others scores remain low. Complacency, fatalism, low standards, inadequate teaching methods, and a cultural emphasis on immediate gratification can all prevent people from recognizing what they don't know and can stifle their ability to learn.

👁 **Watch** the **Video** Thinking Like a Psychologist: Intelligence Tests and Success at **MyPsychLab**

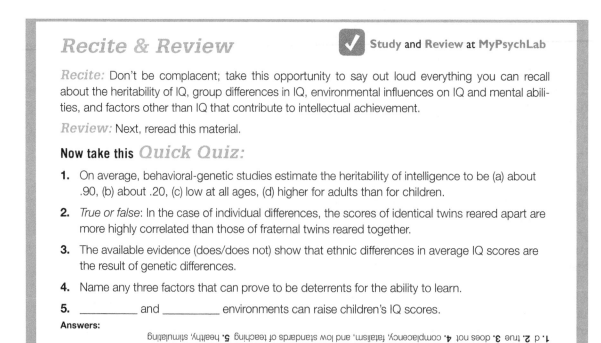

Recite & Review ✓ **Study** and **Review** at **MyPsychLab**

Recite: Don't be complacent; take this opportunity to say out loud everything you can recall about the heritability of IQ, group differences in IQ, environmental influences on IQ and mental abilities, and factors other than IQ that contribute to intellectual achievement.

Review: Next, reread this material.

Now take this *Quick Quiz:*

1. On average, behavioral-genetic studies estimate the heritability of intelligence to be (a) about .90, (b) about .20, (c) low at all ages, (d) higher for adults than for children.

2. *True or false*: In the case of individual differences, the scores of identical twins reared apart are more highly correlated than those of fraternal twins reared together.

3. The available evidence (does/does not) show that ethnic differences in average IQ scores are the result of genetic differences.

4. Name any three factors that can prove to be deterrents for the ability to learn.

5. _____ and _____ environments can raise children's IQ scores.

Answers:

1. d 2. true 3. does not 4. complacency, fatalism, and low standards of teaching 5. healthy, stimulating

Animal Minds

A green heron swipes some bread from a picnicker's table and scatters the crumbs on a nearby stream. When a minnow rises to the bait, the heron strikes, swallowing its prey before you can say "dinner's ready." A sea otter, floating calmly on its back, bangs a mussel shell against a stone that is resting on its stomach. When the shell cracks apart, the otter devours the tasty morsel inside, tucks the stone under its flipper, and dives for another shell, which it will open in the same way. Incidents such as these and scores of others have convinced some biologists, psychologists, and ethologists that we are not the only animals with cognitive abilities—that "dumb beasts" are not so dumb after all. But how smart are they?

Animal Intelligence LO 7.19

For decades, any scientist who claimed that animals could think was likely to be ignored or laughed at. Today the study of animal intelligence is booming, especially in the interdisciplinary field of *cognitive ethology*. (Ethology is the study of animal behavior, especially in natural environments.) Cognitive ethologists argue that some animals can anticipate future events, make plans, and coordinate their activities with those of their comrades (Griffin, 2001).

When we think about animal cognition, we must be careful, because even complex behavior that appears to be purposeful can be genetically

Dodger, a 2-year-old dolphin in Shark Bay, Australia, carries a sea sponge on her sensitive beak as protection against stinging creatures and sharp coral. Dolphin "sponge moms" apparently teach the behavior to their daughters.

prewired and automatic (Wynne, 2004). The assassin bug of South America catches termites by gluing nest material on its back as camouflage, but it is hard to imagine how the bug's tiny dab of brain tissue could enable it to plan this strategy consciously. Yet explanations of animal behavior that leave out any sort of consciousness at all and that attribute animals' actions entirely to instinct do not seem to account for some of the amazing things that animals can do.

Like the otter that uses a stone to crack mussel shells, many animals use objects in the natural environment as rudimentary tools, and some nonhuman primates learn this skill from others of their species. Chimpanzee mothers occasionally show their young how to use stones to open hard nuts (Boesch, 1991). Orangutans in one Sumatran swamp have learned to hold sticks in their mouths to pry insects from holes in tree trunks and to get seeds out of cracks in a bulblike fruit, whereas nearby groups of orangutans use only brute force to get to the delicacies (van Schaik, 2006). Even some nonprimates may have the capacity to learn to use tools, although the evidence remains controversial among ethologists. Female bottlenose dolphins off the coast of Australia attach sea sponges to their beaks while hunting for food, which protects them from sharp coral and stinging stonefish, and they seem to have acquired this unusual skill from their mothers (Krützen et al., 2005). Is this yet another case of mothers telling their daughters what to wear?

In the laboratory, nonhuman primates have accomplished even more surprising things. For example, chimpanzees have demonstrated a rudimentary sense of number. In one study, chimps compared two pairs of food wells containing chocolate chips. One pair might contain, say, 5 chips and 3 chips, the other 4 chips and 3 chips. Allowed

How smart is this otter?

In the 1920s, Wolfgang Köhler (1925) put chimpanzees in situations in which some tempting bananas were just out of reach and watched to see what the apes would do. Most did nothing, but a few turned out to be quite clever. Sultan, shown here, was able to figure out how to reach the bananas by stacking some boxes and climbing on top of them.

to choose which pair they wanted, the chimps almost always chose the one with the higher combined total, showing some sort of summing ability (Rumbaugh, Savage-Rumbaugh, & Pate, 1988). Chimpanzees can even remember over a period of 20 minutes which of two containers holds more bananas (e.g., 5 versus 8, or 6 versus 10), after watching the bananas being placed one at a time into the containers. In fact, they do as well as young children on this task (Beran & Beran, 2004).

One of the most controversial questions about animal cognition is whether any animals besides human beings have a **theory of mind**: a system of beliefs about the way one's own mind and the minds of others work, and an understanding of how thoughts and feelings affect behavior. A theory of mind enables you to draw conclusions about the intentions, feelings, and beliefs of others; empathize with others ("What would I experience if I were in the other person's position?"); deceive others; recognize when someone else is lying; recognize yourself in a mirror; and know when others can or cannot see you. In human beings, a theory of mind starts to develop in the second year and is clearly present by about age 3 or 4 (see Chapter 3).

Some researchers believe that the great apes (chimpanzees, gorillas, and orangutans), dolphins, and elephants have some abilities that reflect a theory of mind (de Waal, 2001; Plotnik, de Waal, & Reiss, 2006; Suddendorf & Whiten, 2001). When looking in a mirror, these animals may try to find marks on their bodies that are not directly visible, suggesting self-recognition, or at least bodily awareness.

In addition, chimpanzees console other chimps who are in distress, use deceptive tactics when competing for food, and point to draw attention to objects, suggesting that they are able to grasp what is going on in another chimp's mind. In the wild, when one male African chimp makes an exaggerated scratching movement on part of its body during social grooming—say, on the forehead—a comrade will then groom the indicated spot, even if he was already grooming some other spot (Pika & Mitani, 2006). Chimps and even monkeys may also be capable of some metacognition. When they are tested on a new task, they will sometimes avoid difficult trials in which they are likely to be wrong. And they will press an icon on a touch screen to request "hints" provided by their human observers when they are unsure of the correct response, even when seeking a hint means getting a lesser reward for a correct answer (Kornell, 2009). These findings suggest that the animals know what they know and don't know.

Animals and Language LO 7.20

A primary ingredient of human cognition is *language*, the ability to combine elements that are themselves meaningless into an infinite number of utterances that convey meaning

theory of mind A system of beliefs about the way one's own mind and the minds of others work, and of how individuals are affected by their beliefs and feelings.

"It's always 'Sit,' 'Stay,' 'Heel'–never 'Think,' 'Innovate,' 'Be Yourself.'"

and that permit communication about objects and events that are not present here and now (see Chapter 3). Do animals have anything comparable?

Animals do communicate, of course, using gestures, body postures, facial expressions, vocalizations, and odors, and some of these signals have highly specific meanings. Vervet monkeys seem to have separate calls to warn each other about leopards versus eagles versus snakes (Cheney & Seyfarth, 1985). But vervets cannot combine these sounds to produce entirely novel utterances, as in "Look out, Harry, that eagle-eyed leopard is a real snake-in-the-grass."

Kanzi, a bonobo who answers questions and makes requests by punching symbols on a specially designed computer keyboard, also understands short English sentences. Kanzi is shown here with researcher Sue Savage-Rumbaugh.

Perhaps, however, some animals could acquire language if they got a little help from their human friends. Because the vocal tract of an ape does not permit speech, most researchers have used innovative approaches that rely on gestures or visual symbols. In one project, chimpanzees learned to use, as words, geometric plastic shapes arranged on a magnetic board (Premack & Premack, 1983). In another, they learned to punch symbols on a keyboard connected to a computer (Rumbaugh, 1977). In yet another, they learned hundreds of signs in American Sign Language (ASL) (Fouts & Rigby, 1977; Gardner & Gardner, 1969).

Animals in these studies learned to follow instructions, answer questions, and make requests. They even seemed to use their newfound skills to apologize for being disobedient, scold their trainers, and talk to themselves. Koko, a lowland gorilla, reportedly used signs to say that she felt happy or sad, to refer to past and future events, to mourn for her dead pet kitten, and to lie when she did something naughty (Patterson & Linden, 1981). Most important, the animals combined individual signs or symbols into longer utterances that they had never seen before.

Unfortunately, in their desire to talk to the animals and their affection for their primate friends, some early researchers overinterpreted the animals' communications, reading all sorts of meanings and intentions into a single sign or symbol, ignoring scrambled word order ("banana eat me"), and unwittingly giving nonverbal cues that might enable the apes to respond correctly.

Watch the Video Classic Footage of Chimpanzees and Sign Language at MyPsychLab

But as researchers have improved their techniques, they have discovered that with careful training, chimps can indeed acquire some aspects of language, including the ability to use symbols to refer to objects. Some animals have also used signs spontaneously to converse with one another, suggesting that they are not merely imitating or trying to get a reward (Van Cantfort & Rimpau, 1982). Bonobos (a type of ape) are especially adept at language. One bonobo named Kanzi has learned to understand English words, short sentences, and keyboard symbols without formal training (Savage-Rumbaugh & Lewin, 1994; Savage-Rumbaugh, Shanker, & Taylor, 1998). Kanzi responds correctly to commands such as "Put the key in the refrigerator" and "Go get the ball that is outdoors," even when he has never heard the words combined in that way before. He picked up language as children do, by observing others using it and through normal social interaction. He has also learned to manipulate keyboard symbols to request favorite foods or activities (games, TV, visits to friends) and to announce his intentions.

Research on animal language and comprehension of symbols is altering our understanding of animal cognition, and not only of primates. Dolphins have learned to respond to requests made in two artificial languages, one consisting of computer-generated whistles and another of hand and arm gestures (Herman, Kuczaj, & Holder, 1993; Herman & Morrel-Samuels, 1996). Taking the meaning of symbols and their order (syntax) into account, they were able to understand the difference between "To left Frisbee, right surfboard take" and "To right surfboard, left Frisbee take."

Some psychologists are calling border collies "the new chimps," ever since researchers discovered that a border collie named Rico and another named Betsy had acquired vocabularies of more than 200 words (Kaminski, Call, & Fisher, 2004; Morell, 2008). Since then, another border collie, Chaser, has stunned the public and psychologists by showing that she knows more than 1,100 words. When Chaser is asked to retrieve an object from another room, she can do it with astonishing accuracy. Even more impressive, when a new toy she had never seen (a Darwin doll) was placed among a dozen of her familiar toys and she was asked to fetch it, she did. She paused and walked among the toys, seemingly making an inference: Because none of the familiar toys matched the request, the new Darwin toy must be the one that was wanted.

Most amazingly, we now know that birds are not as bird-brained as once assumed. Irene Pepperberg (2000, 2002, 2008) has been working since the late 1970s with African gray parrots. Her favorite, named Alex, learned to count, classify, and compare objects by vocalizing English words. When he was shown up to six items and was asked how many there were, he responded with spoken (squawked?) English phrases, such as "two cork(s)" or "four key(s)." He even responded correctly to questions about items specified on two or three dimensions, as in "How many blue key(s)?" or "What matter [material] is orange and three-cornered?" Alex also made requests ("Want pasta") and answered simple questions about objects ("What color [is this]?" "Which is bigger?"). When presented with a blue cork and a blue key and asked "What's the same?" he would correctly respond "color." He

Alex was a remarkably clever bird. His abilities have raised intriguing questions about the intelligence of animals and their capacity for specific aspects of language.

actually scored slightly better with new objects than with familiar ones, suggesting that he was not merely "parroting" a set of stock phrases. He could also sum two small sets of objects, such as nuts or jelly beans, for amounts up to six (Pepperberg, 2006).

Alex was able to say remarkably appropriate things in informal interactions. He would tell Pepperberg, "I love you," "I'm sorry," and, when she was feeling stressed out, "Calm down." One day, Alex asked Pepperberg's accountant, "Wanna nut?" "No," said the accountant. "Want some water?" "No," she said. "A banana?" "No." After making several other suggestions, Alex finally said, "What *do* you want?" (quoted in Talbot, 2008). To the sorrow of thousands of his admirers all over the world, Alex died suddenly in 2007. Pepperberg is continuing her work with other African grays.

Thinking About the Thinking of Animals LO 7.21

These results on animal language and cognition are impressive, but scientists are still divided over just what the animals in

🔆 **THINKING CRITICALLY**

About Animal Cognition

these studies are doing. Do they have true language? Are they thinking, in human terms? How

This old photo shows Clever Hans in action. His story has taught researchers to beware of anthropomorphism when they interpret findings on animal cognition.

intelligent are they? Are Kanzi, Chaser, and Alex unusual, or are they typical of their species? In their efforts to correct the centuries-old underestimation of animal cognition, are modern researchers now reading too much into their data and *over*estimating animals' abilities?

On one side are those who worry about *anthropomorphism*, the tendency to falsely attribute human qualities to nonhuman beings without considering simpler explanations for the animals' behavior (Balter, 2012; Wynne, 2004). They like to tell the story of Clever Hans, a "wonder horse" at the turn of the century who was said to possess mathematical and other abilities (Spitz, 1997). Clever Hans would answer math problems by stamping his hoof

the appropriate number of times. But a little careful experimentation by psychologist Oskar Pfungst (1911/1965) revealed that when Clever Hans was prevented from seeing his questioners, his powers left him. It seems that questioners were staring at the horse's feet and leaning forward expectantly after stating the problem, then lifting their eyes and relaxing as soon as he completed the right number of taps. Clever Hans was indeed clever, but not at math or other human skills. He was merely responding to nonverbal signals that people were inadvertently providing. (Perhaps he had a high EQ.)

On the other side are those who warn against the opposite error—the tendency to think, mistakenly, that human beings have nothing in common with other animals, who are, after all, our evolutionary cousins (de Waal, 2001; Fouts, 1997). The need to see our own species as unique, they say, may keep us from recognizing that other species, too, have cognitive abilities, even if not as sophisticated as our own. Those who take this position point out that most modern researchers have gone to great lengths to avoid the Clever Hans problem.

The outcome of this debate is bound to affect the way we view ourselves and our place among other species. Perhaps we can find a way to study and think about animal abilities and emotions without assuming sentimentally that they are just like our own. There is no disputing, however, that scientific discoveries about the cognitive abilities of our animal relatives are teaching us to have greater respect for animal minds.

Recite & Review

✓ **Study** and **Review** at **MyPsychLab**

Recite: Express aloud to the smartest animal you can find what you know about cognitive ethology, animal intelligence, evidence that some animals have a theory of mind and a degree of metacognition, and animals' capacity for language.

Review: Next, reread this section.

Now take this *Quick Quiz:*

1. Which of the following abilities have primates demonstrated, either in the natural environment or the laboratory? (a) the use of objects as simple tools, (b) the summing of quantities, (c) the use of symbols to make requests, (d) an understanding of short English sentences

2. Barnaby thinks his pet snake Curly is harboring angry thoughts about him because Curly has been standoffish and won't curl around his neck anymore. What error is Barnaby making?

Answers:

1. all of them 2. anthropomorphism

PSYCHOLOGY IN THE NEWS REVISITED //////

Has reading this chapter given you an appreciation of what it takes mentally to concoct the experiments that win Ig Nobel prizes? Many of these awards reflect great intelligence and creativity. Consider Catherine Douglas and Peter Rowlinson's 2009 prize for their finding that cows with names produce more milk than cows without names. That may seem to be a charming but trivial discovery, yet it shows that the quality of the human-animal relationship can affect not just an animal's behavior but also the animal's basic biology. Some Ig Nobel projects also have practical applications. Those tiny diamonds produced by the Russian researchers in our opening story may not be usable in a glittery necklace but they have many industrial and even biomedical uses. And if you ever have a colonoscopy, you'll appreciate that discovery of ways to prevent your bowels from exploding during the procedure—a rare but real occurrence. The Ig Nobel awards are good fun, but they also vividly demonstrate the first, most fundamental step in critical thinking: Ask questions and be willing to wonder.

So it is for good reason that we are used to thinking of ourselves as the smartest species around. Our cognitive abilities allow us to be funny, playful, smart, and creative. A great artist like Rodin can create *The Thinker* and then countless creative imitators will make their own versions in sand, metal, cartoons, ice, or, who knows, ice cream. Human beings not only can think critically, but also can think critically about thinking critically—and understand the reasons that sometimes they don't or can't.

Yet, as the studies in this chapter have shown, we humans also get ourselves into colossal muddles. We think we are better at many skills than we actually are, we have many cognitive biases that distort reality, and we often behave mindlessly. And as if our mental flaws in thinking and reasoning weren't bad enough, many people worry that machines are gaining on us in the mental abilities department—a frequent theme in science fiction. Enormous strides have been made in the field of *artificial intelligence* (AI), the use of computers to simulate human thinking. Avatars already are being designed to diagnose patients' illnesses by long distance, provide psychotherapy, and serve as virtual personal assistants. As speech recognition and other AI technologies improve, ethicists are concerned about the potential for their manipulation and misuse. On a social level, will corporations shield themselves behind robot voices designed to chill out angry consumers? On a personal level, will computers and robots eventually be able to make crucial decisions for us on how to improve public education, choose a life partner, or manage a baseball team?

Computers are impressive, but keep in mind—your own complicated, remarkable, fallible mind!—that real intelligence is more than the capacity to perform computations with lightning speed. As we have seen, it involves the ability to deal with informal reasoning problems, find novel solutions, reason dialectically and reflectively, devise mental shortcuts, read emotions, and acquire tacit knowledge. Robots and computers, of course, are not the least bit troubled by their lack of cleverness, inasmuch as they lack a mind to be troubled. As computer scientist David Gelernter (1997) put it, "How can an object that wants nothing, fears nothing, enjoys nothing, needs nothing, and cares about nothing have a mind?"

So what is the take-away message of this chapter? Should we humans be humbled by our cognitive blunders or encouraged by our cognitive achievements? The answer, of course, is both. Because machines are mindless, they lack the one trait that distinguishes human beings not only from computers but also from other species: We try to understand our own misunderstandings (Gazzaniga, 2008). It is our crowning accomplishment. We want to know what we don't know; we are motivated to overcome our mental shortcomings. This uniquely human capacity for self-examination is probably the best reason to remain optimistic about our cognitive abilities.

Human beings worry that machines will outsmart us, but it's not likely.

Taking Psychology With You

Becoming More Creative

Throughout this book, we have been emphasizing the importance of asking questions, thinking of nonobvious explanations, and examining assumptions and biases. These critical thinking guidelines involve creativity as much as they do reasoning.

Take a few moments to test your own creativity by answering these items based on the Remote Associates Test, a test of the mental flexibility necessary for creativity. Your task is to come up with a fourth word that is associated with each item in a set of three words (Mednick, 1962). For example, an answer for the set *news–clip–wall* is *paper*. Got the idea? Now try these. (The answers are given at the end of this chapter.)

1. piggy—green—lash
2. surprise—political—favor
3. mark—shelf—telephone
4. stick—maker—tennis
5. cream—cottage—cloth

Creative thinking requires you to associate elements of a problem in new ways by finding unexpected connections among them, as on the Remote Associates Test. People who are uncreative rely on *convergent thinking*, following a set of steps that they think will converge on one correct solution. Then, once they have solved a problem, they tend to develop a mental set and approach future problems the same way. Creative people, in contrast, exercise *divergent thinking*; instead of stubbornly sticking to one tried-and-true path, they explore side alleys and generate several possible solutions. They come up with new hypotheses, imagine other interpretations, and look for unexpected connections.

For artists and novelists, of course, creativity is a job requirement, but it also takes creativity to invent a tool, put together a recipe from leftovers, find ways to distribute unsold food to the needy, or decorate your room. Creative people tend to have three central characteristics (Helson, Roberts, & Agronick, 1995; McCrae, 1987; Schank, 1988):

Nonconformity. Creative individuals are not overly concerned about what others think of them. They are willing to risk ridicule by proposing ideas that may initially appear foolish or off the mark. Geneticist Barbara McClintock's research was ignored or belittled by many for nearly 30 years. But she was sure she could show how genes move around and produce sudden changes in heredity. In 1983, when McClintock won the Nobel Prize, the judges called her work the second greatest genetic discovery of our time, after the discovery of the structure of DNA.

For artists, creativity is a job requirement. Using a special 3D technique, a Chinese/Korean artist group created this amazing work. The boy is real; the tiger isn't.

Curiosity. Creative people are open to new experiences; they notice when reality contradicts expectations, and they are curious about the reason. Wilhelm Roentgen, a German physicist, was studying cathode rays when he noticed a strange glow on one of his screens. Other people had seen the glow, but they ignored it because it didn't jibe with their understanding of cathode rays. Roentgen studied the glow, found it to be a new kind of radiation, and thus discovered X-rays.

Persistence. After that imaginary light bulb goes on over your head, you still have to work hard to make the illumination last. Or, as Thomas Edison, who invented the real light bulb, reportedly put it, "Genius is one percent inspiration and ninety-nine percent perspiration." No invention or work of art springs forth full-blown from a person's head. There are many false starts and painful revisions along the way.

If you are thinking critically (and creatively), you may wonder whether these personal qualities are enough. Do you recall the Termites who were the most successful? They were smart, but they also got plenty of encouragement for their efforts. Likewise, some individuals may be more creative than others, but there are also *circumstances* in our work, school, and family environments that foster creative accomplishment:

Encouragement of intrinsic motivation. Creativity flourishes when schools and employers encourage intrinsic motivation (a sense of accomplishment, intellectual curiosity, the sheer love of an activity) and not just extrinsic rewards such as gold stars and money.

Opportunities to work and socialize with different kinds of people. Creativity thrives when you work and hang out with others who have different ideas, perspectives, and occupational training, because they tend to jolt you out of your familiar ways of seeing problems.

Allowing solitude and the time and space to daydream. Individual creativity can also require solitude—having "lazy" time to daydream productively—and the freedom to perform a task or solve a problem independently. "Brainstorming" sessions with others tend to produce more storm than brain (Amabile, 1983; Amabile & Khair, 2008).

Permission to take risks—and occasionally fail. Finally, organizations encourage creativity when they let people take risks, give them plenty of time to think about problems, and welcome innovation.

In sum, if you hope to become more creative, you can do two things. One is to cultivate your own talents and qualities of curiosity, intrinsic motivation, and self-discipline. The other is to seek out the kinds of situations that will permit you to express your abilities and experiment with new ideas.

Summary Listen to the Audio File at MyPsychLab

Thought: Using What We Know

- Thinking is the mental manipulation of information. Our mental representations simplify and summarize information from the environment.

- A *concept* is a mental category that groups objects, relations, activities, abstractions, or qualities that share certain properties. *Basic concepts* have a moderate number of instances and are easier to acquire than concepts with few or many instances. *Prototypical* instances of a concept are more representative than others. The language we use to express concepts may influence how we think about the world.

- *Propositions* are made up of concepts and express a unitary idea. They may be linked together to form *cognitive schemas*, which serve as mental models of aspects of the world. *Mental images* also play a role in thinking.

- *Subconscious processes* lie outside of awareness but can be brought into consciousness when necessary. They allow us to perform two or more actions at once when one of the actions is highly automatic. But multitasking is usually inefficient, introduces errors, and can even be dangerous, as when people attempt to multitask while driving.

- *Nonconscious processes* remain outside of awareness but nonetheless affect behavior; they are involved in *implicit learning*, which occurs when we learn something but aren't able to state exactly what we've learned. Even conscious processing may be carried out in a *mindless* fashion.

- Both conscious and nonconscious processes are involved in problem solving and making decisions. When problems are well defined, they can often be solved with an *algorithm*; fuzzier problems may require application of rules of thumb called *heuristics*. "Fast" thinking refers to rapid, intuitive, emotional, almost automatic decisions; "slow" thinking requires intellectual effort, which is why most people rely on the former—and make mistakes.

Reasoning Rationally

- *Reasoning* is purposeful mental activity that involves drawing inferences and conclusions from observations, facts, or assumptions. *Formal reasoning problems* permit a single correct or best solution. *Informal reasoning problems* often have no clearly correct solution. People may not have all the information they need, or may disagree about basic assumptions. For these reasons, people need practice in *dialectical thinking* about opposing points of view.

- Studies of *reflective judgment* show that many people have trouble thinking dialectically. *Prereflective* thinkers do not distinguish between knowledge and belief or between belief and

evidence. *Quasi-reflective* thinkers believe that because knowledge is sometimes uncertain, any judgment about the evidence is purely subjective. Those who think *reflectively* understand that even when knowledge is uncertain, some judgments are more valid than others, depending on their coherence and fit with the evidence. Many people never learn to think reflectively, but when students get encouragement and ample opportunities to practice this ability, their thinking becomes more complex and sophisticated.

Barriers to Reasoning Rationally

- The ability to reason clearly and rationally is affected by many cognitive biases. People tend to exaggerate the likelihood of improbable events in part because of the *affect* and *availability heuristics*. They are swayed in their choices by the desire to *avoid loss* and by the *framing effect*. They forgo economic gain because of a *fairness bias*. They overestimate their ability to have made accurate predictions (the *hindsight bias*), attend mostly to evidence that confirms what they want to believe (the *confirmation bias*), and are often mentally rigid, forming *mental sets* and seeing patterns where none exist.

- The theory of *cognitive dissonance* holds that people are motivated to reduce the tension that exists when two cognitions, or a cognition and a behavior, conflict. They can reduce dissonance by rejecting or changing a belief, changing their behavior, or rationalizing. Dissonance is uncomfortable, and people are motivated to reduce it after a decision has been made (*postdecision dissonance*), when their actions violate their concept of themselves as honest and kind, and when they have put hard work into an activity (the *justification of effort*).

Measuring Intelligence: The Psychometric Approach

- *Intelligence* is hard to define. The *psychometric approach* focuses on how well people perform on standardized aptitude tests. Most psychometric psychologists believe that a general ability, a *g factor*, underlies this performance. They distinguish between *crystallized intelligence* (which reflects accumulated knowledge) and *fluid intelligence* (which reflects the ability to reason and to use information to solve new problems).

- The *intelligence quotient*, or *IQ*, represents how well a person has done on an intelligence test compared to other people. Alfred Binet designed the first widely used intelligence test to identify children who could benefit from remedial work. But in the United States, people assumed that intelligence tests revealed natural ability and used the tests to categorize people in school and in the armed services.

- IQ tests have been criticized for being biased in favor of white, middle-class people. However, efforts to construct tests that are free of cultural influence have been disappointing. Culture affects nearly everything to do with taking a test, from attitudes to problem-solving strategies. Negative stereotypes about a person's ethnicity, gender, or age may cause the person to feel the effects of *stereotype threat*, which can lead to anxiety that interferes with test performance.

Dissecting Intelligence: The Cognitive Approach

- *Cognitive approaches* to intelligence emphasize several kinds of intelligence and the strategies people use to solve problems. One important cognitive ingredient is *working memory*, which allows you to juggle your attention when thinking or working on a problem and to ignore distractions. Another is *metacognition*, the understanding and monitoring of your own cognitive processes.

- Sternberg's *triarchic theory* proposes three aspects of intelligence: *componential/analytic, experiential/creative,* and *contextual/practical*. Contextual intelligence allows you to acquire *tacit knowledge*, practical strategies that are important for success but are not explicitly taught.

- Another important kind of intelligence, *emotional intelligence*, is the ability to identify your own and other people's emotions accurately, express emotions clearly, and regulate emotions in yourself and others.

The Origins of Intelligence

- *Heritability* estimates for intelligence (as measured by IQ tests) average about .40 to .50 for children and adolescents, and .60 to .80 for adults. Identical twins are more similar in IQ-test performance than fraternal twins, and adopted children's scores correlate more highly with those of their biological parents than with those of their nonbiological relatives. These results do not mean that genes determine intelligence; the remaining variance in IQ scores must largely result from environmental influences. Although many genes may influence IQ performance, any one gene is likely to have just a tiny influence.

- It is a mistake to draw conclusions about *group* differences from heritability estimates based on differences *within* a group. The available evidence fails to support genetic explanations of black–white differences in performance on IQ tests.

- Environmental factors such as poor prenatal care, malnutrition, exposure to toxins, stressful family circumstances, and living in an extremely disadvantaged neighborhood are associated with lower performance on intelligence tests. Conversely, a healthy and stimulating environment can improve performance. IQ scores have been rising in many countries for several generations, most likely because of improved education, health care, diets, and job opportunities for the poorest people.

- Intellectual achievement also depends on motivation, hard work, and self-discipline. Cross-cultural work shows that beliefs about the origins of mental abilities, parental standards, and attitudes toward education play a big role in creating differences in academic performance.

Animal Minds

- Some researchers, especially those in *cognitive ethology*, argue that nonhuman animals have greater cognitive abilities than has previously been thought. Some animals can use objects as simple tools. Chimpanzees have shown evidence of a simple understanding of number. Some researchers believe that the great apes, and possibly other animals, have aspects of a *theory of mind*, an understanding of how their own minds and the minds of others work. In some apes and monkeys, these aspects may include some metacognition.

- In projects using visual symbol systems or American Sign Language (ASL), primates have acquired linguistic skills. Some animals, even nonprimates such as dolphins and African gray parrots, seem able to use simple grammatical ordering rules to convey or comprehend meaning. However, scientists are divided about how to interpret the findings on animal cognition, with some worrying about *anthropomorphism* and others about the opposite error, failure to acknowledge that humans and animals share many cognitive abilities.

Psychology in the News, Revisited

- Our cognitive abilities allow us to be playful, smart, and creative, yet we are also blinded by cognitive biases that distort reality and allow us to behave mindlessly. Although enormous strides have been made in the field of *artificial intelligence*, human intelligence is more than the capacity to perform computations with lightning speed. We remain the only creatures that try to understand our own minds and misunderstandings.

Taking Psychology With You

- Creativity is part of critical thinking. Creative people rely on *divergent* rather than *convergent* thinking when solving problems. They tend to be nonconformist, curious, and persistent. External circumstances also matter: Settings foster creative accomplishment when they promote intrinsic motivation, provide contact with different kinds of people, create opportunities for solitude and daydreaming, and encourage risk-taking and occasional failure.

Key Terms

cognitive psychology 241
concept 242
basic concept 242
prototype 243
proposition 243
cognitive schema 243
mental image 243
subconscious processes 243
nonconscious processes 244
implicit learning 244
mindlessness 244
algorithms 245
heuristics 245
intuition 242
insight 242
reasoning 246
formal reasoning 246
informal reasoning 246

dialectical reasoning 246
reflective judgment 247
prereflective thinking 247
quasi-reflective thinking 248
affect heuristic 249
availability heuristic 250
avoidance of loss 250
framing effect 250
fairness bias 250
Ultimatum Game 250
behavioral economics 251
hindsight bias 252
confirmation bias 252
mental set 253
cognitive dissonance 253
postdecision dissonance 254
justification of effort 255
intelligence 256

psychometrics 256
factor analysis 256
g factor 256
crystallized
    intelligence 257
fluid intelligence 257
mental age (MA) 257
intelligence quotient (IQ) 257
Stanford–Binet Intelligence
    Scales 257
Wechsler Adult Intelligence
    Scale (WAIS) 258
Wechsler Intelligence Scale
    for Children (WISC) 258
stereotype threat 259
cognitive approach to
    intelligence 260
working memory 261
metacognition 261

triarchic theory of
    intelligence 261
componential/analytic
    intelligence 261
experiential/creative
    intelligence 261
contextual/practical
    intelligence 261
tacit knowledge 262
emotional
    intelligence 262
heritability 263
cognitive ethology 269
theory of mind 270
anthropomorphism 273
artificial intelligence 274
convergent versus divergent
    thinking 275

Answers to the creativity test on page 275: back, party, book, match, cheese

Some solutions to the nine-dot problem in the Get Involved exercise on page 253 (from Adams, 2001):

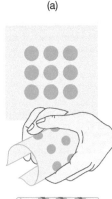

(a)

(b)

Cut the puzzle apart, tape it together
in a different format, and use
one line.

(c)

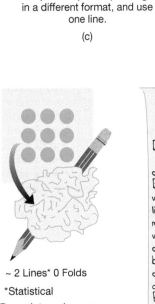

(d)

Roll up the puzzle
and draw a spiral
through the dots.

(e)

1 line 0 Folds

Lay the paper on the
surface of the Earth.
Circumnavigate the
globe twice + a few
inches, displacing a little
each time so as to pass
through the next row
on each circuit as you
"Go West, young man."

(f)

~ 2 Lines* 0 Folds

*Statistical

Draw dots as large as
possible. Wad paper into
a ball. Stab with pencil.
Open up and see if you
did it. If not, try again.
"Nobody loses: play
until you win."

(g)

May 30, 1974
5 FDR   Navasa
Roosevelt Rds. N̶a̶
Celba, PR 00635
Dear Prof. James L. Adams,
    My dad and I were
doing Puzzles from "Conceptual
Blockbusting." We were mostly
working on the dot ones,
like  My dad said a
man found a way to do it
with one line. I tried and
did it. Not with folding,
but I used a fat line. I
does'nt say you can't use
a fat line. Like this➔ ▰
P.S.
acctually you
need a very   Sincerely,
fat writing   Becky Buechel
apparatice.   age: 10

(h)

Thought

The Elements of Cognition

- A **concept** is a mental category that groups objects, relations, activities, abstractions, or qualities that share certain properties.
- **Basic concepts** have a moderate number of instances and are easier to acquire than those having few or many instances.
- **Prototypical** instances of a concept are more representative than others.
- The words and grammatical rules used to express concepts may influence how we think about them.
- **Propositions** are made up of concepts and express a unitary idea. They may be linked together to form **cognitive schemas**, which serve as mental models of aspects of the world.
- **Mental images** also play a role in thinking.

```
Concepts
   │
   ▼
Propositions        Mental Images
   │                    │
   ▼                    │
Cognitive Schemas ◄─────┘
```

How Conscious Is Thought?

- **Subconscious processes** lie outside of awareness but can be brought into consciousness when necessary.
- Because of the capacity for automatic processing, many people think they are good multitaskers, but in reality multitasking increases stress, errors, and reaction times, while impairing memory and attention.
- **Nonconscious processes** remain outside of awareness and can be involved in **implicit learning**, where you can't state exactly what it is you have learned.
- *Mindlessness* keeps people from recognizing the need for a change in behavior.

Problem Solving and Decision Making

- Conscious and unconscious processes are both involved in solving problems.
- Well defined problems can often be solved by using an **algorithm**, but fuzzier problems may require application of a **heuristic**.
- People also rely on intuition and insight to solve problems and make decisions.

Reasoning Rationally

Reasoning

Reasoning is purposeful mental activity that involves drawing inferences and conclusions from observations or propositions.

- *Formal reasoning problems* usually have a correct or best solution.
- *Informal reasoning problems* often have no clearly correct solution and require **dialectical reasoning**, the process of comparing and evaluating opposing points of view.

Reflective judgment is the ability to evaluate and integrate evidence, consider alternative interpretations, and reach a defensible conclusion. Many people never do develop this ability.

Barriers to Reasoning Rationally

Many cognitive biases are obstacles to rational thinking:
- Exaggerating the probability of improbable events, in part because of the **affect** and **availability heuristics**.
- Avoidance of loss, which makes people susceptible to the **framing effect**; in general, people are more cautious when a choice is framed in terms of loss rather than gain.
- the **fairness bias**.
- the **hindsight bias**.
- the **confirmation bias**.
- formation of **mental sets**.
- The need to reduce **cognitive dissonance**, the tension created when two cognitions or a cognition and a behavior conflict. People reduce **postdecision dissonance** in various ways, including the **justification of effort**.

COGNITIVE DISSONANCE

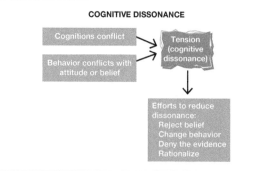

Intelligence

↓

Intelligence is an inferred characteristic, usually defined as the ability to profit from experience, acquire knowledge, think abstractly, act purposefully, or adapt to change.

Measuring Intelligence

The **psychometric approach** to intelligence focuses on performance on standardized aptitude tests.

- The use of **factor analysis** can help identify clusters of correlated items on a test that measure some common ability, such as a *g* **factor** in intelligence.
- Alfred Binet came up with the idea of measuring a person's **mental age**, or level of intellectual development relative to that of others.
- The **intelligence quotient (IQ)** represents a person's score on a particular test, compared to others' scores.
- Efforts to create intelligence tests unaffected by culture have been disappointing.
- **Stereotype threat** can affect the test performance of women, old people, and minority groups.

Dissecting Intelligence

Cognitive approaches to intelligence emphasize problem-solving strategies and several kinds of intelligence, rather than a *g* factor.

- **Working memory** and **metacognition** are important cognitive ingredients of intelligence.
- The **triarchic theory of intelligence** proposes three aspects of intelligence: componential/analytic, experiential/creative, and contextual/practical (which allows acquisition of **tacit knowledge**).
- **Emotional intelligence** is an important type of nonintellectual intelligence.

The Origins of Intelligence

Behavioral-genetic studies show the **heritability** of intelligence (as measured by IQ tests) to be high.

Motivation, Hard Work, and Intellectual Success

- Intellectual performance is strongly influenced by motivation and self-discipline.
- These in turn are affected by cultural expectations, attitudes toward education, and beliefs about the origins of mental abilities.

The Question of Group Differences

- Genetic explanations of black–white differences in IQ have inappropriately used heritability estimates based mainly on white samples.
- Environmental influences on intelligence include:
  – poor prenatal care.
  – malnutrition.
  – exposure to toxins.
  – stressful family circumstances.
  – living in an impoverished, disadvantaged neighborhood.

Animal Minds

Animal Intelligence

Cognitive ethologists study animal intelligence, cognition, and behavior in natural environments.

- Some animals can use rudimentary tools.
- In the laboratory, chimpanzees have learned to use numerals and symbols.
- Whether or not animals possess a **theory of mind** is the subject of much debate. Some theorists argue that the great apes, and even some other animals, have some understanding of their own minds and those of others.

In thinking about animal cognition, we must avoid both *anthropomorphism* and the opposite error, the failure to recognize our commonalities with other animals.

Animals and Language

In several studies, primates and other animals, such as border collies and African grey parrots, have acquired some aspects of human language.

MEMORY

PSYCHOLOGY IN THE NEWS ///////////////////////////////

Wrongly Convicted Man and His Accuser Tell Their Story

NEW YORK, NY, January 5, 2010. St. Martin's Press has announced the release of the paperback edition of *Picking Cotton*, a remarkable true story described by novelist John Grisham as an account of "violence, rage, redemption, and, ultimately, forgiveness."

The story began in 1987, in Burlington, North Carolina, with the rape of a young white college student named Jennifer Thompson. During her ordeal, Thompson swore to herself that she would never forget the face of her rapist, a man who climbed through the window of her apartment and assaulted her brutally. During the attack, she made an effort to memorize every detail of his face, looking for scars, tattoos, or other identifying marks. When the police asked her if she could identify the assailant from a book of mug shots, she picked one that she was sure was correct, and later she identified the same man in a lineup.

Based on her convincing eyewitness testimony, a 22-year-old black man named Ronald Cotton was sentenced to prison for two life terms. Cotton's lawyer appealed the decision, and by the time of the hearing, evidence had come to light suggesting that the real rapist might have been a man who looked very like Cotton, an imprisoned criminal named Bobby Poole. Another trial was held. Jennifer Thompson looked at both men face to face, and once again said that Ronald Cotton was the one who raped her. Cotton was sent back to prison.

Eleven years later, DNA evidence completely exonerated Cotton and just as unequivocally implicated Poole, who confessed to the crime. Thompson was devastated. "The man I was so sure I had never seen in my life was the man who was inches from my throat, who raped me, who hurt me, who took my spirit away, who robbed me of my soul," she wrote. "And the man I had identified so emphatically on so many occasions was absolutely innocent."

Thompson decided to meet Cotton and apologize to him personally. Remarkably, they were both able to put this tragedy behind them and became friends. Eventually they wrote

Ronald Cotton (left) was wrongly convicted of rape solely on the basis of Jennifer Thompson's eyewitness testimony. The real rapist, Bobby Poole (right), was eventually identified by DNA tests.

Picking Cotton, which they subtitled "Our memoir of injustice and redemption."

Nevertheless, Thompson says, she has had to live with the anguish of knowing that her mistake cost Cotton years of liberty. "I cannot begin to imagine what would have happened," she says, "had my mistaken identification occurred in a capital case."

/////////

Eyewitness testimony is an important and necessary part of the legal system, yet Ronald Cotton's case is not terribly unusual. That raises a difficult question: In the absence of corroborating evidence, should a witness's confidence in his or her memory be sufficient for establishing guilt? Much is at stake in our efforts to answer this question: getting justice for crime victims and also avoiding the false conviction of defendants who are innocent.

Memory refers to the capacity to retain and retrieve information and also to the structures that account for this capacity. Human beings are capable of astonishing feats of memory. Most of us can easily remember the tune of our national anthem, how to use an ATM, the most embarrassing experience we ever had, and hundreds of thousands of other bits of information. Memory confers competence; without it, we would be as helpless as newborns, unable to carry out even the most trivial daily tasks. Memory also endows us with a sense of identity; each of us is the sum of our recollections, which is why we can feel threatened when others challenge them. Individuals and cultures alike rely on a remembered history for a sense of coherence and meaning; memory gives us our past and guides our future.

And yet our memories can be distorted, embellished, and even completely false. Have you ever had a conversation with a sibling, parent, or friend about a memory of a shared experience, only to realize you completely differ on what "really" happened? ("I was there and remember that evening perfectly," one of you says. "You think you were *there*?" the other says in astonishment.

"You weren't even in the same city. You didn't even *know* about that evening for three months!")

This chapter will raise some fascinating but troubling questions about memory: When should we trust our memories, and when should we be cautious about doing so? We all forget things that happened; do we also "remember" things that never took place? Are memory malfunctions the exception to the rule or are they commonplace? And if memory is not always reliable, what does that tell us about the story we "remember" so clearly of our own lives. How can we hope to understand the past?

You are about to learn . . .

- why memory does not work like a camera—and how it *does* work.
- why errors can creep into our memories of even surprising or shocking events.
- why having a strong emotional reaction about a remembered event does not mean that the memory is accurate.

Reconstructing the Past

What would life be like if you could never form any new memories? That's what happens to older people who are suffering from dementia and sometimes in younger people who have brain injuries or diseases. The case of one such man, Henry Molaison, is probably the most intensely studied in the annals of medicine (Corkin, 1984, 2013; Corkin et al., 1997; Hilts, 1995; Milner, 1970; Ogden & Corkin, 1991). In 1953, when Henry, known in the scientific literature as H. M., was 27, surgeons removed most of his hippocampus, along with most of his amygdala and a portion of his temporal lobes. The operation was a last-ditch effort to relieve H. M.'s severe and life-threatening epilepsy, which was causing unrelenting, uncontrollable seizures. The operation did achieve its goal: Henry's seizures became milder and could be managed with medication. His memory, however, had been affected profoundly. Although he continued to recall most events that had occurred before the operation, he could no longer remember new experiences for much longer than 15 minutes. Facts, songs, stories, and faces all vanished like water down the drain. He would read the same magazine over and over without realizing it. He could not recall the day of the week, the year, or even his last meal.

H. M. loved to do crossword puzzles and play bingo, skills he had learned before the operation. And he remained cheerful, even though he knew he had memory problems. He would occasionally recall an unusually emotional event, such as the assassination of someone named Kennedy, and he sometimes remembered that both of his parents were dead. But according to Suzanne Corkin, who studied Henry extensively, these "islands of remembering" were the exceptions in a vast sea of forgetfulness. This good-natured man could not recognize a photograph of his own face, and he never remembered the scientists who studied him for decades; he was stuck in a time warp from the past. After Henry died in 2008 at age 82, one neuroscientist observed that he had given science

the ultimate gift: his memory (Ogden, 2012). He taught neuroscientists a great deal about the biology of memory, and we will meet him again at several points in this chapter.

◉ **Watch** the **Video** Special Topics: When Memory Fails at **MyPsychLab**

The Manufacture of Memory LO 8.1

People's descriptions of memory have always been influenced by the technology of their time. Ancient philosophers compared memory to a soft wax tablet that would preserve anything imprinted on it. Later, with the advent of the printing press, people began to think of memory as a gigantic library, storing specific events and facts for later retrieval. Today, many people compare memory to a digital recorder or video camera, automatically capturing every moment of their lives.

Popular and appealing though this belief about memory is, however, it is utterly wrong. Not everything that happens to us or impinges on our senses is tucked away for later use. Memory is selective. If it were not, our minds would be cluttered with mental junk: the temperature at noon on Thursday, the price of milk two years ago, a phone number needed only once. Moreover, remembering is not at all like replaying a recording of an event. It is more like watching a few unconnected clips and then figuring out what the rest of the recording must have been like.

If these happy children remember this birthday party later in life, their constructions may include details picked up from this photograph, videos, and stories. And they will probably be unable to distinguish an actual memory from information they got elsewhere.

One of the first scientists to make this point was the British psychologist Sir Frederic Bartlett (1932). Bartlett asked people to read lengthy, unfamiliar stories from other cultures and then tell the stories back to him. As the volunteers tried to recall the stories, they made interesting errors: They often eliminated or changed some details and added others from their own culture to make the story more sensible to them. Memory, Bartlett concluded, must therefore be largely a *reconstructive* process. We may reproduce some kinds of simple information by rote, said Bartlett, but when we remember complex information, our memories are influenced by previous knowledge and beliefs. Since Bartlett's time, hundreds of studies have supported this idea and have shown it to apply to all sorts of memories—of stories, conversations, personal experiences.

In reconstructing their memories, people often draw on many sources. Suppose that someone asks you to describe one of your early birthday parties. You may have some direct recollection of the event, but you may also incorporate information from family stories, photographs, or home videos, and even from accounts of other people's birthdays and reenactments of birthdays on television. You take all these bits and pieces and build one integrated account. Later, you may not be able to distinguish your actual memory from information you got elsewhere. This phenomenon is known as **source misattribution**, or sometimes *source confusion* (Johnson, Hashtroudi, & Lindsay, 1993; Mitchell & Johnson, 2009).

Of course, some shocking or tragic events—such as earthquakes, accidents, a mass killing, or an assassination—do hold a special place in memory. So do some unusual, exhilaratingly happy events, such as learning that you just won a lottery. Years ago, these vivid recollections of emotional and important events were named *flashbulb memories*, to capture the surprise, illumination, and seemingly photographic detail that characterize them (Brown & Kulik, 1977). Some flashbulb memories can last for years. In a Danish study, older people who had lived through the Nazi occupation of

their country in World War II often retained accurate memories, for decades, of the day that the radio had announced liberation and even what the weather had been like at the time (Berntsen & Thomsen, 2005).

Yet despite their vividness, flashbulb memories are not always complete or accurate. People typically remember the *gist* of a startling, emotional event they experienced or witnessed, such as the destruction of the World Trade Centers in New York in 2001 or the bombing at the Boston Marathon in 2013. But when researchers question them about their memories over time, errors creep into the details, and after a few years, some people even forget the gist (Neisser & Harsch, 1992; Talarico & Rubin, 2003). Even with flashbulb memories, then, facts tend to get mixed with fiction. Remembering is an active process, one that involves not only dredging up stored information but also putting two and two together to reconstruct the past. Sometimes, unfortunately, we put two and two together and get five.

The Conditions of Confabulation
LO 8.2

Because memory is reconstructive, it is subject to **confabulation**—confusing an event that happened to someone else with one that happened to you, or coming to believe that you remember something that never happened. Such confabulations are especially likely under the following circumstances (Garry et al., 1996; Hyman & Pentland, 1996; Mitchell & Johnson, 2009):

1 **You have thought, heard, or told others about the imagined event many times.** Suppose that at family gatherings you keep hearing about the time that Uncle Sam scared everyone at a New Year's party by pounding a hammer into a wall with such force that the wall collapsed. You interpret this to mean Sam was angry, and the story is so colorful that you can practically see it unfold in your mind. The more you think about this event, the more likely you are to believe that you were there, even if you were, in fact, sound asleep in another house. This process has been called *imagination inflation*, because your own active imagination inflates your belief that the event occurred as you assume it did (Garry & Polaschek, 2000). Even merely explaining how a hypothetical childhood experience *could* have happened inflates people's confidence that it *did* happen. Explaining an event makes it seem familiar and thus real (Sharman, Manning, & Garry, 2005).

source misattribution
The inability to distinguish an actual memory of an event from information you learned about the event elsewhere.

confabulation
Confusion of an event that happened to someone else with one that happened to you, or a belief that you remember something when it never actually happened.

In the 1980s, Whitley Strieber published the best seller *Communion*, in which he claimed to have had encounters with nonhuman beings, possibly aliens from outer space. An art director designed this striking image for the cover. Ever since, many people have assumed that this is what an extraterrestrial must look like, and some have imported the image into their own confabulated memories of alien abduction.

NEVER FORGETS   SOMETIMES FORGETS   ALWAYS FORGETS

Sidney Harris/ScienceCartoonsPlus.com

2 **The image of the event contains lots of details.** Ordinarily, we can distinguish an imagined event from an actual one by the amount of detail we recall; memories of real events tend to contain more details. But the longer you think about an imagined event, the more likely you are to embroider those images with details—what your uncle was wearing, the crumbling plaster, the sound of the hammer—and these added details may persuade you that you remember the event and aren't just confusing other people's reports with your own experience (Johnson et al., 2011).

3 **The event is easy to imagine.** If imagining an event takes little effort (as does visualizing a man pounding a wall with a hammer), then we are especially likely to think that a memory is real, not false. In contrast, when we must make an effort to form an image of an experience, a place we have never seen, or an activity that is utterly foreign to us, our cognitive efforts serve as a cue that we are imagining the event or have heard about it from others.

As a result of confabulation, you may end up with a memory that feels emotionally, vividly real to you and yet is false. This means that your feelings about an event, no matter how strong they are, do not guarantee that the event occurred. Consider again our Sam story, which happens to be true. A woman we know believed for years that she had been present as an 11-year-old child when her uncle destroyed the wall. Because the story was so vivid and upsetting to her, she felt angry at him for what she thought was his mean and violent behavior, and she assumed that she must have been angry at the time as well. Then, as an adult, she learned that she was not at the party at all but had merely heard about it repeatedly over the years. Moreover, Sam had not pounded the wall in anger, but as a joke, to inform the assembled guests that he and his wife were about to remodel their home. Nevertheless, our friend's family has had a hard time convincing her that her "memory" of this event is entirely wrong, and they are not sure she believes them yet.

As the Sam story illustrates, and as laboratory research verifies, false memories can be as stable over time as true ones (Roediger & McDermott, 1995). There's just no getting around it: Memory is reconstructive.

Recite & Review

[✓] **Study** and **Review** at **MyPsychLab**

Recite: Reconstruct what you just read so you can say what you can remember about why memory is reconstructive, and about source misattribution, flashbulb memories, and confabulation.

Review: Next, go back and read this section again.

Now take this *Quick Quiz:*

1. Information in the memory is (a) selective, (b) random, (c) none of these.

2. *True or false:* When we collect bits and pieces of information from other sources and integrate it in our memory, we can always distinguish them later.

3. Which of the following confabulated "memories" might a person be most inclined to accept as having happened to them, and why? (a) getting lost in a shopping center at the age of 5, (b) taking a class in astrophysics, (c) visiting a monastery in Tibet as a child, (d) being bullied by another kid in the fourth grade.

Answers:

1. a 2. false 3. a and d, because they are common events that are easy to imagine and that contain a lot of vivid details. It would be harder to induce someone to believe that he or she had studied astrophysics or visited Tibet because these are rare events that take an effort to imagine.

You are about to learn . . .

• how memories of an event can be affected by the way someone is questioned about it.

• why children's memories and testimony about sexual abuse can be unreliable.

Memory and the Power of Suggestion

The reconstructive nature of memory helps the mind work efficiently. Instead of cramming our brains with infinite details, we can store the essentials of an experience and then use our knowledge of the world to figure out the specifics when we need them. But precisely because memory is so often reconstructive, it is also vulnerable to suggestion—to ideas implanted in our minds after the event, which then become associated with it. This fact raises thorny problems in legal cases that involve eyewitness testimony or people's memories of what happened, when, and to whom.

The Eyewitness on Trial LO 8.3

Without the accounts of eyewitnesses, many guilty people would go free. But, as Jennifer Thompson learned to her sorrow, eyewitness testimony is not always reliable. Lineups and photo arrays don't necessarily help because witnesses may simply identify the person who looks most like the perpetrator of the crime (Wells & Olson, 2003). As a result, some convictions based on eyewitness testimony, like that of Ronald Cotton, turn out to be tragic mistakes.

Eyewitnesses are especially likely to make mistaken identifications when the suspect's ethnicity differs from their own. Because of unfamiliarity with other ethnic groups, the eyewitness may focus solely on the ethnicity of the person they see committing a crime ("He's black"; "She's white"; "He's an Arab") and ignore the distinctive features that would later make identification more accurate (Levin, 2000; Meissner & Brigham, 2001).

In a program of research spanning four decades, Elizabeth Loftus and her colleagues have shown that memories are also influenced by the way in which questions are put to the eyewitness and by suggestive comments made during an interrogation or interview. In one study, the researchers showed how even subtle changes in the wording of questions can lead a witness to give different answers. Participants first viewed short films depicting car collisions. Afterward, the researchers asked some of them, "About how fast were the cars going when they hit each other?" Other viewers were asked the same question, but with the verb changed to *smashed, collided, bumped,* or *contacted.* Estimates of how fast the cars were going varied, depending on which word was used. *Smashed* produced the highest average speed estimates (40.8 mph), followed by *collided* (39.3 mph), *bumped* (38.1 mph), *hit* (34.0 mph), and *contacted* (31.8 mph) (Loftus & Palmer, 1974).

Misleading information from other sources also can alter what witnesses report. Consider what happened when students were shown the face of a young man who had straight hair,

On TV crime shows, witnesses often identify a criminal from a lineup or a group of photos. But these methods can mislead witnesses, who may wrongly identify a person because he or she resembles the actual culprit more closely than the other people in the lineup or photos do. Because of psychological research, many law enforcement agencies are now using better methods, such as having witnesses look at photos of suspects one at a time without being able to go back to a previous one.

then heard a description of the face supposedly written by another witness—a description that wrongly said the man had light, curly hair (see Figure 8.1). When the students reconstructed the face using a kit of facial features, a third of their reconstructions contained the misleading detail, whereas only 5 percent contained it when curly hair was not mentioned (Loftus & Greene, 1980).

What if several eyewitnesses are involved? Does that affect a person's susceptibility to misleading information? In a study of this question, people first watched a video of a simulated crime and later read three eyewitness reports about the crime, each report containing the same misleading claim—for example, about the location of objects, the thief's actions, or the name on the side of a van. One group was told that a single person wrote all three reports, whereas another group was told that each report was written by a different person. It made no difference; a single witness's report proved to be as influential as the reports of three different witnesses. Such is the power of a single witness's voice (Foster et al., 2012).

Leading questions, suggestive comments, and misleading information affect people's memories not only for events they have witnessed but also for their own experiences. Researchers have successfully used these techniques to induce people to believe they are recalling complicated events from early in life that never happened, such as getting lost in a shopping mall, being hospitalized for a high fever, being harassed by a bully, getting in trouble for playing a prank on a first grade

FIGURE 8.1 The Influence of Misleading Information
In a study described in the text, students saw the face of a young man with straight hair and then had to reconstruct it from memory. On the left is one student's reconstruction in the absence of misleading information about the man's hair. On the right is another person's reconstruction of the same face after exposure to misleading information that mentioned curly hair (Loftus & Greene, 1980).

teacher, or spilling punch all over the mother of the bride at a wedding (Hyman & Pentland, 1996; Lindsay et al., 2004; Loftus & Pickrell, 1995; Mazzoni et al., 1999). When people were shown a phony Disneyland ad featuring Bugs Bunny, about 16 percent later recalled having met a Bugs character at Disneyland (Braun, Ellis, & Loftus, 2002). Some people even claimed to remember shaking hands with the character, hugging him, or seeing him in a parade. But these memories were impossible, because Bugs Bunny is a Warner Brothers creation and would definitely be rabbit non grata at Disneyland!

Watch the Video Thinking Like a Psychologist: Police Line-Up at MyPsychLab

Children's Testimony LO 8.4

The power of suggestion can affect anyone, but its impact on children who are being questioned regarding possible sexual or physical abuse is especially worrisome.

THINKING CRITICALLY

About Children's Testimony

How can adults find out whether a young child has been sexually molested without influencing or tainting what the child says? The answer is crucial. Throughout the 1980s and 1990s, accusations of child abuse in daycare centers across the United States skyrocketed. After being interviewed by therapists

and police investigators, children were claiming that their teachers had molested them in the most terrible ways: hanging them in trees, raping them, and even forcing them to eat feces. Although in no case had parents actually seen the daycare teachers treating the children badly, although none of the children had complained to their parents, and although none of the parents had noticed any symptoms or problems in their children, the accused teachers were often sentenced to many years in prison.

Thanks largely to research by psychological scientists, the hysteria eventually subsided and people were able to assess more clearly what had gone wrong in the way children had been interviewed in these cases: The interviewers had influenced the children by bombarding them with leading questions, suggestions, and other forms of pressure to say that something happened when it did not (Ceci & Bruck, 1995). In the courtroom, too, the style of questions put to children under cross-examination often leads them to be highly inaccurate (O'Neill & Zajac, 2012). The question to ask, therefore, is not "Can children's memories be trusted?" but "Under what conditions are children apt to be suggestible and to report that something happened to them when in fact it did not?"

The answer, from many experimental studies, is that a child is more likely to give a false report when the interviewer strongly believes that the child has been molested and then uses suggestive techniques to get the child to reveal molestation (Bruck, 2003). Interviewers who are biased in this way seek only confirming evidence and ignore discrepant evidence and other explanations for a child's behavior. They reject a child's denial of having been molested and assume the child is "in denial." They use techniques that encourage imagination inflation ("Let's pretend it happened") and that blur reality and fantasy in the child's mind. They pressure or encourage the child to describe terrible events, badger the child with repeated questions, tell the child that "everyone else" said the events happened, or use bribes and threats (Poole & Lamb, 1998).

A team of researchers analyzed the actual transcripts of interrogations of children in the first highly publicized sexual abuse case, the McMartin preschool case (which ended in a hung jury). Then they applied the same suggestive techniques in an experiment with preschool children (Garven et al., 1998). A young man visited children at their preschool, read them a story, and handed out treats. The man did nothing aggressive, inappropriate, or surprising. A week later, an experimenter questioned the children individually about the man's visit. She asked children in one group leading questions ("Did he bump the teacher? Did he throw a crayon at a kid who was talking?" "Did he tell you a secret and tell you not to tell?"). She asked a second group the same questions but also applied influence techniques used by interrogators in the McMartin and other daycare cases, such as telling the children what "other kids" had supposedly said, expressing disappointment if answers were negative, and praising the children for making allegations.

In the first group, children said "Yes, it happened" to about 17 percent of the false allegations about the man's visit. And in the second group, they said "yes" to the false allegations a whopping 58 percent of the time. As you can see in Figure 8.2, the 3-year-olds in this group, on average, said "yes" to more than 80 percent of the false allegations, and the 4- to 6-year-olds said "yes" to more than half of the allegations. Note that the interviews in this study lasted only 5 to 10 minutes, whereas in actual investigations, interviewers often question children repeatedly over many weeks or months.

Many people believe that children cannot be induced to make up experiences that are ttruly traumatic, but psychologists have shown that this assumption, too, is wrong. When schoolchildren were asked for their recollections of an actual sniper incident at their school, many of those who had been absent from school that day reported memories of hearing shots,

FIGURE 8.2 Social Pressure and Children's False Allegations

When researchers asked 3-year-olds leading questions about events that had not occurred—such as whether a previous visitor to their classroom had committed aggressive acts—nearly 30 percent said that yes, he had. This percentage declined among older children. But when the researchers used influence techniques taken from actual child-abuse investigations, most of the children agreed with the false allegation, regardless of their age (Garven et al., 1998).

seeing someone lying on the ground, and other details they could not possibly have experienced directly. Apparently, they had been influenced by the accounts of the children who had been there (Pynoos & Nader, 1989). Rumor and hearsay play a big role in promoting false beliefs and memories in children, just as they do in adults (Principe et al., 2006).

As a result of such findings, psychologists have been able to develop ways of interviewing children that reduce the chances of false reporting. If the interviewer says, "Tell me the reason you came to talk to me today," and nothing more, most actual victims will disclose what happened to them (Bruck, 2003). The interviewer must not assume that the child was molested, must avoid leading or suggestive questions, and must understand that children do not speak the way adults do. Young children often drift from topic to topic, and their words may not be the words adults use (Poole & Lamb, 1998). One little girl being interviewed thought her "private parts" were her elbows!

In sum, children, like adults, can be accurate in what they report and, also like adults, they can distort, forget, fantasize, and be misled. Their memory processes are only human.

Recite & Review

 Study and **Review** at **MyPsychLab**

Recite: Here's a suggestion: Tell someone—anyone—out loud what you remember about the influence of misleading information on people's reports of an event, and about conditions that increase suggestibility in children.

Review: Next, go back and read this section again.

Now take this *Quick Quiz:*

1. *True or false*: Among children, rumors and hearsay play an important role in promoting false beliefs.

2. Asking leading questions to witnesses can (a) help in remembering the incident, (b) help in procuring correct information, (c) result in misleading information, (d) result in a traumatic experience.

3. Some years back, hundreds of people in psychotherapy began claiming that they could recall long-buried memories of having taken part in satanic rituals involving animal and human torture and sacrifice. Yet the FBI was unable to confirm any of these reports. Based on what you have learned so far, how might you explain such "memories"?

Answers:

1. true 2. c 3. Therapists who uncritically assumed that satanic cults were widespread may have asked leading questions and otherwise influenced their patients. Patients who were susceptible to their therapists' interpretations may then have confabulated and "remembered" experiences that did not happen, borrowing details from fictionalized accounts or from other troubling experiences in their lives. The result was source misattribution and the patients' mistaken conviction that their memories were real.

You are about to learn . . .

- why multiple-choice test items are generally easier than short-answer or essay questions.

- whether you can know something without knowing that you know it.

- why the computer is often used as a metaphor for the mind.

In Pursuit of Memory

Now that we have seen how memory *doesn't* work—namely, like an infallible recording of everything that happens to you—we turn to studies of how it *does* work.

Measuring Memory LO 8.5, LO 8.6

Conscious, intentional recollection of an event or an item of information is called **explicit memory**. It is usually measured using one of two methods. The first method tests for **recall**, the ability to retrieve and reproduce information encountered previously. Essay and fill-in-the-blank exams require recall. The second method tests for **recognition**, the ability to identify information you have previously observed, read, or heard about. The information is given to you, and all you have to do

is say whether it is old or new, or perhaps correct or incorrect, or pick it out of a set of alternatives. The task, in other words, is to compare the information you are given with the information stored in your memory. True–false and multiple-choice tests call for recognition.

Recognition tests can be tricky, especially when false items closely resemble correct ones. Under most circumstances, however, recognition is easier than recall. Recognition for visual images is particularly impressive. If you show people 2,500 slides of faces and places, and later you ask them to identify which ones they saw out of a larger set, they will be able to identify more than 90 percent of the original slides accurately (Haber, 1970).

The superiority of recognition over recall was once demonstrated in a study of people's memories of their high school classmates (Bahrick, Bahrick, & Wittlinger, 1975). The participants, ages 17 to 74, first wrote down the names of as many classmates as they could remember. Recall was poor; even when prompted with yearbook pictures, the youngest people failed to name almost a third of their classmates, and the oldest failed to name most of them. Recognition, however, was far better. When the participants were asked to look at a series of cards, each of which contained a set of five photographs, and were asked to say which picture in each set showed a former classmate, recent graduates were right 90 percent of

explicit memory
Conscious, intentional recollection of an event or of an item of information.

recall The ability to retrieve and reproduce from memory previously encountered material.

recognition The ability to identify previously encountered material.

the time—and so were people who had graduated 35 years earlier. The ability to recognize names was nearly as impressive.

Sometimes, information encountered in the past affects our thoughts and actions even though we do not consciously or intentionally remember it, a phenomenon known as **implicit memory** (Schacter, Chiu, & Ochsner, 1993). To get at this subtle sort of memory, researchers must rely on indirect methods instead of the direct ones used to measure explicit memory. One common method, **priming**, asks you to read or listen to some information and then tests you later to see whether the information affects your performance on another type of task.

Suppose that you had to read a list of words, some of which began with the letters *def* (such as *define*, *defend*, or *deform*). Later, if you were asked to complete word fragments (such as *def-*) with the first word that came to mind, you would be more likely to complete the fragments so they turned into words from the list than if you had never seen the list—even if you could not remember the original words very well (Richardson-Klavehn & Bjork, 1988; Roediger, 1990). That is, the words on the list have "primed" (made more available) your responses on the word-completion task.

Priming isn't limited to words: Priming people to complete sentence fragments by using a particular syntactic construction (as in *Meghan gave Michael a toy* versus *Meghan gave a toy to Michael*) biased them to produce the same construction in another task a week later (Kaschak, Kutta, & Schatschneider, 2011). Fragments of pictures, too, can act as primes. In one study, people briefly saw fragments of drawings depicting objects and animals and were asked to name the object the fragments were part of. Then, *17 years later*, they were mailed the same fragments and also fragments of new drawings, with a request to name what the

fragments depicted. Even when people could not remember having been in the original experiment, they identified the primed objects much better than the new objects (Mitchell, 2006). These studies show that people know more than they think they know—and that they can know it for a very long time.

PRIMING

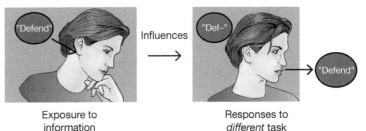

Exposure to information | Influences | Responses to *different* task

Another way to measure implicit memory, the **relearning method**, or *savings method*, was devised by Hermann Ebbinghaus (1885/1913) in the nineteenth century. The relearning method requires you to relearn information or a task that you have already learned. If you master it more quickly the second time around, you must be remembering something from the first experience.

Models of Memory LO 8.7

Although people usually refer to memory as a single faculty, as in "I must be losing my memory" or "He has a memory like an elephant's," the term *memory* covers a complex collection of abilities and processes. If a video camera is not an accurate metaphor for capturing these diverse components of memory, what metaphor would be better?

Many cognitive psychologists liken the mind to an information processor, along the lines of a computer, though more complex. They have constructed *information-processing models* of cognitive processes, liberally borrowing computer-programming terms

implicit memory
Unconscious retention in memory, as evidenced by the effect of a previous experience or previously encountered information on current thoughts or actions.

priming A method for measuring implicit memory in which a person reads or listens to information and is later tested to see whether the information affects performance on another type of task.

relearning method A method for measuring retention that compares the time required to relearn material with the time used in the initial learning of the material.

Get Involved! Recalling Rudolph's Friends

You can try this test of recall if you are familiar with the poem that begins "'Twas the Night Before Christmas" or the song "Rudolph the Red-Nosed Reindeer." Rudolph had eight reindeer friends; name as many of them as you can. After you have done your best, turn to the Get Involved exercise on the next page for a recognition test on the same information.

Get Involved!   Recognizing Rudolph's Friends

If you took the recall test in the Get Involved exercise on page 291, now try a recognition test. From the following list, see whether you can identify the correct names of Rudolph the Red-Nosed Reindeer's eight reindeer friends. The answers are at the end of this chapter, but no fair peeking!

Blitzen	Dander	Dancer	Masher
Cupid	Dasher	Prancer	Comet
Kumquat	Donner	Flasher	Pixie
Bouncer	Blintzes	Trixie	Vixen

Which was easier, recall or recognition? Can you speculate on the reason?

such as *input*, *output*, *accessing*, and *information retrieval*. When you type something on your computer's keyboard, a software program encodes the information into an electronic language, stores it on a hard drive, and retrieves it when you need to use it. Similarly, in information-processing models of memory, we *encode* information (convert it to a form that the brain can process and use), *store* the information (retain it over time), and *retrieve* the information (recover it for use). In storage, the information may be represented as concepts, propositions, images, or *cognitive schemas*, mental networks of knowledge, beliefs, and expectations concerning particular topics or aspects of the world. (If you can't retrieve these terms, see Chapter 7.)

Explore the **Concept** Information-Processing Model of Memory at MyPsychLab

In most information-processing models, storage takes place in three interacting memory systems. A *sensory register* retains incoming sensory information for a second or two, until it can be processed further. *Short-term memory* holds a limited amount of information for a brief period of time, perhaps up to 30 seconds or so, unless a conscious effort is made to keep it there longer. *Long-term memory* accounts for longer storage, from a few minutes to decades (Atkinson & Shiffrin, 1968, 1971). Information can pass from the sensory register to short-term memory and in either direction between short-term and long-term memory, as illustrated in Figure 8.3.

This model, which is known informally as the *three-box model*, has dominated research on memory since the late 1960s. The problem is that the human brain does not operate like your average computer. Most computers process instructions and data sequentially, one item after another, and so the three-box model has emphasized sequential operations. In contrast, the brain performs many operations simultaneously, in parallel. It recognizes patterns all at once rather than as a sequence of information bits, and it perceives new information, produces speech, and searches memory all at the same time. It can do these things because millions of neurons are active at

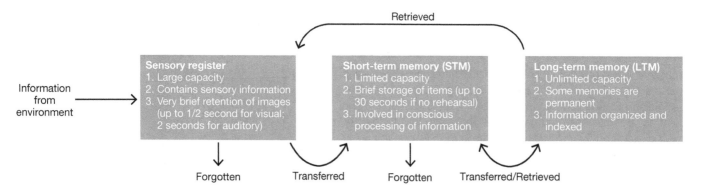

FIGURE 8.3 Three Memory Systems
In the three-box model of memory, information that does not transfer out of the sensory register or short-term memory is assumed to be forgotten forever. Once in long-term memory, information can be retrieved for use in analyzing incoming sensory information or performing mental operations in short-term memory.

once, and each neuron communicates with thousands of others, which in turn communicate with millions more.

Because of these differences between human beings and machines, some cognitive scientists prefer a **parallel distributed processing (PDP)** or *connectionist* model. Instead of representing information as flowing from one system to another, a PDP model represents the contents of memory as connections among a huge number of interacting processing units, distributed in a vast network and all operating in parallel, just like the neurons of the brain (McClelland, 1994, 2011; Rumelhart, McClelland, & the PDP Research Group, 1986). As information enters the system, the ability of these units to excite or inhibit each other is constantly adjusted to reflect new knowledge.

In this chapter, we emphasize the three-box model, but keep in mind that the computer metaphor that inspired it could one day be as outdated as the metaphor of memory as a camera.

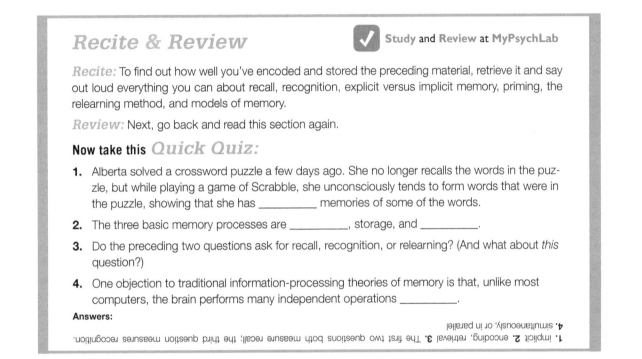

Recite & Review

Study and Review at MyPsychLab

Recite: To find out how well you've encoded and stored the preceding material, retrieve it and say out loud everything you can about recall, recognition, explicit versus implicit memory, priming, the relearning method, and models of memory.

Review: Next, go back and read this section again.

Now take this *Quick Quiz:*

1. Alberta solved a crossword puzzle a few days ago. She no longer recalls the words in the puzzle, but while playing a game of Scrabble, she unconsciously tends to form words that were in the puzzle, showing that she has _____ memories of some of the words.

2. The three basic memory processes are _____, storage, and _____.

3. Do the preceding two questions ask for recall, recognition, or relearning? (And what about *this* question?)

4. One objection to traditional information-processing theories of memory is that, unlike most computers, the brain performs many independent operations _____.

Answers:

1. implicit 2. encoding, retrieval 3. The first two questions both measure recall; the third question measures recognition. 4. simultaneously, or in parallel

You are about to learn...

- how the three "boxes" in the three-box model of memory operate.
- why short-term memory is like a leaky bucket.
- why a word can feel like it's "on the tip of your tongue."
- the difference between "knowing how" and "knowing that."

The Three-Box Model of Memory

The information-processing model of three separate memory systems—sensory, short-term, and long-term—remains a leading approach because it offers a convenient way to organize the major findings on memory, does a good job of accounting for these findings, and is consistent with the biological facts about memory. Let us now peer into each of the "boxes."

The Sensory Register: Fleeting Impressions LO 8.8

In the three-box model, all incoming sensory information must make a brief stop in the **sensory register**, the entryway of memory. The sensory register includes a number of separate memory subsystems, as many as there are senses. Visual images remain in a visual subsystem for a maximum of a half-second. Auditory images remain in an auditory subsystem for a slightly longer time, by most estimates up to two seconds or so.

The sensory register acts as a holding bin, retaining information in a highly accurate form until we can select items for attention from the stream of stimuli bombarding our senses. It gives

parallel distributed processing (PDP) model A model of memory in which knowledge is represented as connections among thousands of interacting processing units, distributed in a vast network, and all operating in parallel. Also called a *connectionist model*.

sensory register A memory system that momentarily preserves extremely accurate images of sensory information.

short-term memory (STM) In the three-box model of memory, a limited-capacity memory system involved in the retention of incoming information for brief periods; it also holds information retrieved from long-term memory for temporary use.

chunk A meaningful unit of information; it may be composed of smaller units.

us a moment to decide whether information is extraneous or important; not everything detected by our senses warrants our attention. And the identification of a stimulus on the basis of information already contained in long-term memory occurs during the transfer of information from the sensory register to short-term memory.

Information that does not quickly go on to short-term memory vanishes forever, like a message written in disappearing ink. That is why people who see an array of 12 letters for just a fraction of a second can report only four or five of them; by the time they answer, their sensory memories are already fading (Sperling, 1960). The fleeting nature of incoming sensations is actually beneficial; it prevents multiple sensory images—"double exposures"—that might interfere with the accurate perception and encoding of information.

Short-Term Memory: Memory's Notepad LO 8.9

Like the sensory register, **short-term memory (STM)** retains information only temporarily—for up to about 30 seconds by many estimates, although some researchers think that the maximum interval may extend to a few minutes for certain tasks. In short-term memory, the material is no longer an exact sensory image but is an encoding of one, such as a word or a phrase. This material either transfers into long-term memory or decays and is lost forever.

Victims of brain injury such as H. M. demonstrate the importance of transferring new information from STM into long-term memory. H. M. was able to store information on a short-term basis; he could hold a conversation and his behavior appeared normal when you first met him. Yet, for the most part, he could not retain explicit information about new facts and events for longer than a few minutes. His terrible memory deficits involved a problem in transferring memories from short-term storage into long-term storage. With a great

deal of repetition and drill, patients like H. M. can learn some new visual information, retain it in long-term memory, and recall it normally (McKee & Squire, 1992). But usually information does not get into long-term memory in the first place.

The Leaky Bucket. H. M. fell at the extreme end on a continuum of forgetfulness, but even those of us with normal memories know from personal experience how frustratingly brief short-term retention can be. We look up a telephone number, and after dialing it we find that the number has vanished from our minds. We meet someone new and two minutes later find ourselves groping for the person's name. Is it any wonder that short-term memory has been called a "leaky bucket"?

According to most memory models, if the bucket did not leak it would quickly overflow, because at any given moment, short-term memory can hold only so many items. Years ago, George Miller (1956) estimated its capacity to be "the magical number 7 plus or minus 2." Conveniently, 5-digit zip codes and 7-digit telephone numbers fall in this range (at least in the United States); 16-digit credit card numbers do not. Since Miller's work, estimates of STM's capacity have ranged from 2 items to 20, with one estimate putting the "magical number" at 4 (Cowan et al., 2008; Cowan, 2010). Everyone agrees, however, that the number of items that STM can handle at any one time is small.

Given the limits on short-term memory, how do we remember the beginning of a spoken sentence until the speaker reaches the end? After all, most sentences are longer than just a few words. According to most information-processing models, we overcome this problem by grouping small bits of information into larger units, or **chunks.** The real capacity of STM, it turns out, is not a few bits of information but a few chunks (Gilchrist & Cowan, 2012). A chunk can be a word, a phrase, a sentence, or even an image, and it depends on previous experience. For most Americans, the

Get Involved! Your Sensory Register at Work

In a dark room or closet, swing a flashlight rapidly in a circle. You will see an unbroken circle of light instead of a series of separate points. The reason: The successive images remain briefly in the sensory register.

If you do not play chess, you probably will not be able to recall the positions of these chess pieces after looking away from the board for a while. But experienced chess players can remember the position of every piece after glancing only briefly at the board. They are able to "chunk" the pieces into a few standard configurations instead of trying to memorize where each piece is located.

number 1776 is one chunk, not four, and the acronym FBI is one chunk, not three. In contrast, the number 7167 is four chunks and IBF is three, unless 7167 is your address (or PIN) or your initials are IBF. Some chunks are visual: If you know football, when you see a play unfolding you may see a single chunk of information—say, a wishbone formation—and be able to remember it. If you do not know football, you will see only a field full of players, and you probably won't be able to remember their positions when you look away.

But even chunking cannot keep short-term memory from eventually filling up. Information that will be needed for longer periods must therefore be transferred to long-term memory or it will be displaced by new information and spill out of the "bucket." Particularly meaningful items may transfer quickly, but other information will usually require processing—unless we do something to keep it in STM for a while, as we will discuss shortly.

 Simulate the **Experiment** Memory Experiment at **MyPsychLab**

Working Memory. In the original three-box model, short-term memory functioned basically as a container for temporarily holding on to new information or information retrieved from long-term memory. But this view did not account for the sense of effort we feel when trying to solve a problem. Does $2 \times (3 + 5)/4 = 4$? Solving that problem requires that we not simply hold on to information but also *work* with it, which is why psychologists today think that STM is part of a **working memory** system. STM keeps its job as a temporary holding bin, but another more active part—an "executive"—controls attention,

focusing it on the information we need for the task at hand and warding off distracting information (Baddeley, 1992, 2007; Engle, 2002). In our math problem, your working memory must contain the numbers and instructions for operating on them, and also carry out those operations and retain the intermediate results from each step.

People who do well on tests of working memory tend to do well on intelligence tests and on tasks requiring complex cognition and the control of attention, such as understanding what you read, following directions, taking notes, playing bridge, learning new words, estimating how much time has elapsed, and many other real-life tasks (Broadway & Engle, 2011). When they are engrossed in challenging activities that require their concentration and effort, they stay on task longer, and their minds are less likely than other people's to wander (Kane et al., 2007).

The ability to bring information from long-term memory into short-term memory or to use working memory is not disrupted in patients like H. M. They can do arithmetic, relate events that occurred before their injury, and do anything else that requires retrieval of information from long-term into short-term memory. Their problem is with the flow of information in the other direction, from short-term to long-term memory.

Long-Term Memory: Final Destination LO 8.10, LO 8.11, LO 8.12

The third box in the three-box model of memory is **long-term memory (LTM)**. The capacity of LTM seems to have no practical limits. The vast amount of information stored there enables us to learn, get around in the environment, and build a sense of identity and a personal history.

Organization in Long-Term Memory. Because long-term memory contains so much information, it must be organized in some way so that we can find the particular items we are looking for. One way to organize words is by the *semantic categories* to which they belong. *Chair*, for example, belongs to the category *furniture*. In a study done many years ago, people had to memorize 60 words that came from four semantic categories: animals, vegetables, names, and professions. The words were presented in random order, but when people were allowed to recall the items in any order they wished, they tended to recall them in clusters corresponding to the four categories (Bousfield, 1953). This finding has been replicated many times.

Evidence on the storage of information by semantic category also comes from cases of people with brain damage. In one such case, a patient

working memory In many models of memory, a cognitively complex form of short-term memory; it involves active mental processes that control retrieval of information from long-term memory and interpret that information appropriately for a given task.

long-term memory (LTM) In the three-box model of memory, the memory system involved in the long-term storage of information.

called M. D. appeared to have made a complete recovery after suffering several strokes, with one odd exception: He had trouble remembering the names of fruits and vegetables. M. D. could easily name a picture of an abacus or a sphinx, but he drew a blank when he saw a picture of an orange or a carrot. He could sort pictures of animals, vehicles, and other objects into their appropriate categories, but did poorly with pictures of fruits and vegetables. On the other hand, when M. D. was *given* the names of fruits and vegetables, he immediately pointed to the corresponding pictures (Hart, Berndt, & Caramazza, 1985). Apparently, M. D. still had information about fruits and vegetables, but his brain lesion prevented him from using their names to get to the information when he needed it, unless someone else provided the names. This evidence suggests that information in memory about a particular concept (such as *orange*) is linked in some way to information about the concept's semantic category (such as *fruit*).

Indeed, many models of long-term memory represent its contents as a vast network of interrelated concepts and propositions (Anderson, 1990; Collins & Loftus, 1975). In these models, a small part of a conceptual network for *animals* might look something like the one in Figure 8.4. The way people use these networks, however, depends

on experience and education. In rural Liberia, the more schooling children have, the more likely they are to use semantic categories in recalling lists of objects (Cole & Scribner, 1974). This makes sense, because in school, children must memorize a lot of information in a short time, and semantic grouping can help. Unschooled children, having less need to memorize lists, do not cluster items and do not remember them as well. But this does not mean that unschooled children have poor memories. When the task is one that is meaningful to them, such as recalling objects that were in a story or a village scene, they remember extremely well (Mistry & Rogoff, 1994).

We organize information in long-term memory not only by semantic groupings but also in terms of the way words sound or look. Have you ever tried to recall some word that was on the "tip of your tongue"? Nearly everyone experiences such *tip-of-the-tongue* (TOT) *states*, which occur across languages and cultures; users of sign language call them "tip-of-the-finger" states (Thompson, Emmorey, & Gollan, 2005). Scientists value them as a sort of slow-motion video of memory processes (A. Brown, 2012). People in a TOT state tend to come up with words that resemble the right one in sound, meaning, or form (e.g., number of syllables) before finally recalling the one they're

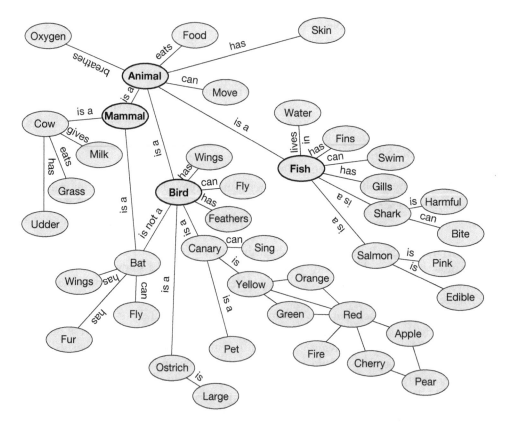

FIGURE 8.4 Part of a Conceptual Grid in Long-Term Memory
Many models of memory represent the contents of long-term semantic memory as an immense network or grid of concepts and the relationships among them. This illustration shows part of a hypothetical grid for *animals*.

Culture affects the encoding, storage, and retrieval of information in long-term memory. Navajo healers, who use stylized, symbolic sand paintings in their rituals, must commit to memory dozens of intricate visual designs, because no exact copies are made and the painting is destroyed after each ceremony.

searching for, which indicates that information in long-term memory is organized in those terms (R. Brown & McNeill, 1966). For the name *Kevin* they might say, "Wait…it starts with a K and has two syllables…Kenny? Kerran?…"

Information in long-term memory may also be organized by its familiarity, relevance, or association with other information. The method used in any given instance probably depends on the nature of the memory; you would no doubt store information about the major cities of Europe differently from information about your first romantic kiss. To understand the organization of LTM, then, we must know what kinds of information can be stored there.

The Contents of Long-Term Memory. Most theories of memory distinguish skills or habits ("knowing how") from abstract or representational knowledge of facts and events ("knowing that"). **Procedural memories** are memories of knowing how to do something—comb your hair, use a pencil, solve a jigsaw puzzle, knit a sweater, or swim. Many researchers consider procedural memories to be implicit, because once skills and habits are learned well, they do not require much conscious processing. **Declarative memories** involve knowing that something is true, as in knowing that Ottawa is the capital of Canada or that you once visited there; they are usually assumed to be explicit.

Declarative memories come in two varieties: semantic memories and episodic memories (Tulving, 1985). **Semantic memories** are internal representations of the world, independent of any particular context. They include facts, rules, and concepts—items of general knowledge. On the basis of your semantic memory of the concept *cat*, you can describe a cat as a small, furry mammal that typically spends its time eating, sleeping, prowling, and staring into space, even though a cat may not be present when you give this description, and you probably won't know how or when you first learned it. **Episodic memories** are internal representations of personally experienced events. When you remember how your cat once surprised you in the middle of the night by pouncing on you as you slept, you are retrieving an episodic memory. Figure 8.5 summarizes these kinds of memories.

procedural memories
Memories for the performance of actions or skills ("knowing how").

declarative memories
Memories of facts, rules, concepts, and events ("knowing that"); they include semantic and episodic memories.

semantic memories
Memories of general knowledge, including facts, rules, concepts, and propositions.

episodic memories
Memories of personally experienced events and the contexts in which they occurred.

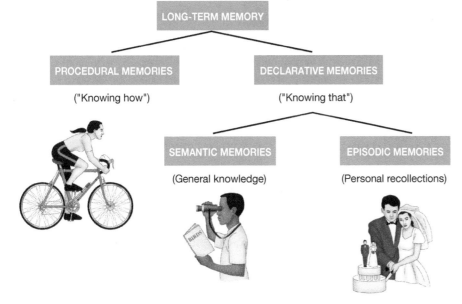

FIGURE 8.5 Types of Long-Term Memories
This diagram summarizes the distinctions among long-term memories. A procedural memory might be of learning how to ride a bike; a declarative memory might be knowing that an eagle is a kind of raptor, or remembering your best friend's wedding last year. Can you come up with your own examples of each memory type?

Episodic memory allows us to mentally travel not only backward in time but also forward, by imagining possible future experiences (Schacter, 2012). We draw on our episodic memories to construct scenarios of what might happen and then rehearse how we might behave. In fact, the same brain regions involved in retrieving personal memories, notably the hippocampus and parts of the prefrontal cortex and temporal lobe, are also activated when we imagine future events (Addis, Wong, & Schacter, 2007). Patients who cannot retrieve episodic memories because of damage to the hippocampus often cannot envision future episodes either, even in response to such simple questions as "what will you do tomorrow?" (Hassabis & Maguire, 2007). The "time-travel" function of episodic memories is often motivating, because unless people are pessimists or depressed, they tend to forget negative episodic memories faster than positive ones, leaving them with a forgiving past and rosy future (Szpunar, Addis, & Schacter 2012).

From Short-Term to Long-Term Memory: A Puzzle.

The three-box model of memory is often invoked to explain an interesting phenomenon called the **serial-position effect**. If you are shown a list of items and are then asked immediately to recall them, your recall will be best for items at the beginning of the list (the *primacy effect*) and at the end of the list (the *recency effect*); the items in the middle will tend to drop away (Bhatarah, Ward, & Tan, 2008; Johnson & Miles, 2009). A serial-position effect occurs when you are introduced to a lot of people at a party and find you can recall the names of the first few and the last few, but almost no one in between.

According to the three-box model, primacy effects happen because the first few items in a list are rehearsed many times and so are likely to make it to long-term memory and remain memorable. Recency effects occur because at the time of recall, they are plucked from short-term memory, where they are still sitting. The items in the middle of a list are not so well retained because by the time they get into short-term memory, it is already crowded with the first few items. As a result, middle items often drop out of short-term memory before they can be stored in long-term memory. The problem with this explanation is that the recency effect sometimes occurs even after a considerable delay, when the items at the end of a list can no longer be in short-term memory (Davelaar et al., 2004). Further, the serial-position effect can also occur with memories of past personal experiences, such as the soccer games you played during the last season. The serial-position curve, therefore, remains something of a puzzle.

 Simulate the Experiment Serial Position Effect at MyPsychLab

serial-position effect
The tendency for recall of the first and last items on a list to surpass recall of items in the middle of the list.

Recite & Review

 Study and Review at MyPsychLab

Recite: To find out whether this section made its way into long-term memory, say out loud everything you can about the sensory register, short-term memory, chunking, working memory, long-term memory, procedural memory, declarative memory (semantic and episodic) and the serial-position effect.

Review: Next, go back and read this section again.

Now take this *Quick Quiz:*

1. _____ images stay for a slightly longer duration in the sensory memory.

2. The estimated capacity of the short-term memory is _____ plus or minus 2.

3. Suppose you must memorize a long list of words that includes *desk, pig, gold, dog, chair, silver, table, rooster, bed, copper,* and *horse.* If you can recall the words in any order you wish, how are you likely to group these items in recall? Why?

4. Which category is helpful in retaining information in the long-term memory?

5. If a child is trying to memorize the alphabet, which sequence should present the greatest difficulty: *abcdefg, klmnopq,* or *tuvwxyz*? Why?

Answers:

1. auditory **2.** 7 **3.** Desk, chair, table, and bed will probably form one cluster; pig, dog, rooster, and horse a second; and gold, silver, and copper a third. Concepts tend to be organized in long-term memory in terms of semantic categories, such as furniture, animals, and metals. **4.** semantic **5.** klmnopq, because of the serial-position effect.

You are about to learn...

- some of the changes that occur in the brain when you store a short-term versus a long-term memory.
- where memories for facts and events are stored in the brain.
- which hormones can improve memory.

The Biology of Memory

We have been discussing memory solely in terms of information processing, but what is happening in the brain while all of that processing is going on?

Changes in Neurons and Synapses LO 8.13

Forming a memory involves chemical and structural changes at the level of synapses, and these changes differ for short-term memory and long-term memory.

In short-term memory, changes within neurons temporarily alter their ability to release neurotransmitters, the chemicals that carry messages from one nerve cell to another (Kandel, 2001). In contrast, long-term memory involves lasting structural changes in the brain. To mimic what they think may happen during the formation of a long-term memory, researchers apply brief, high-frequency electrical stimulation to groups of neurons in the brains of animals or to brain cells in a laboratory culture. In various areas, especially the hippocampus, this stimulation causes receiving neurons at some synapses to become more responsive, making certain synaptic pathways more excitable (Bliss & Collingridge, 1993; Lisman, Yasuda, & Raghavachari, 2012; Whitlock et al., 2006). This increase in the strength of synaptic responsiveness is known as **long-term potentiation**. It is a little like increasing the diameter of a funnel's neck to permit more flow through the funnel. During long-term potentiation, dendrites also grow and branch out, and some types of synapses increase in number (Greenough, 1984). At the same time, in another process, some neurons become *less* responsive than they were previously (Bolshakov & Siegelbaum, 1994).

Most of these changes take time, which probably explains why long-term memories remain vulnerable to disruption for a while after they are stored, and why a blow to the head may disrupt new memories even though old ones are unaffected. Memories must therefore undergo a period of **consolidation**, or stabilization, before they "solidify" (see also Chapter 5). Consolidation can continue for weeks in animals and for several years

Jennifer K. Berman

in human beings. And memories probably never completely solidify, because the very act of remembering previously stored memories can make them unstable again. A new round of consolidation often then sweeps up new information into the old memory, remolding it (Schiller & Phelps, 2011).

Where Memories are Made LO 8.14

Scientists have used electrodes, brain-scan technology, and other techniques to identify the brain structures responsible for the formation and storage of specific types of memories. The amygdala is involved in the formation, consolidation, and retrieval of memories of fearful and other emotional events (Buchanan, 2007; see Chapter 13). Areas in the frontal lobes of the brain are especially active during short-term and working memory tasks (Goldman-Rakic, 1996; Mitchell & Johnson, 2009). The prefrontal cortex and areas adjacent to the hippocampus in the temporal lobe are also important for the efficient encoding of pictures and words.

But it is the hippocampus that has the starring role in many aspects of memory. It is critical to the formation of long-term declarative memories ("knowing that"); as we have seen in the case of H. M., damage to this structure can cause amnesia for new facts and events. The hippocampus is also critical in recalling past experiences (Pastalkova et al., 2008).

long-term potentiation A long-lasting increase in the strength of synaptic responsiveness, thought to be a biological mechanism of long-term memory.

consolidation The process by which a long-term memory becomes durable and stable.

A team of researchers has identified how neurons in the hippocampus may become involved in specific memories. They implanted tiny needle-shaped electrodes into the brains of 13 people about to undergo surgery for severe epilepsy. (This is standard procedure because it enables doctors to pinpoint the location of the brain activity causing the seizures.) As the patients were being prepped, they watched a series of 5- to 10-second film clips of popular shows such as *Seinfeld* or *The Simpsons*, or of animals and landmarks. The researchers recorded which neurons in the hippocampus were firing as the patients watched; for each patient, particular neurons might become highly active during particular videos and respond only weakly to others. After a few minutes, the patients were asked to recall what they had seen. They remembered almost all of the clips, and as they recalled each one, the very neurons that had been active when they first saw it were reignited (Gelbard-Sagiv et al., 2008).

The formation and retention of procedural memories (memory for skills and habits) seem to involve other brain structures and pathways. In work with rabbits, Richard Thompson (1983, 1986) showed that one kind of procedural memory—a simple, classically conditioned response to a stimulus, such as an eye blink in response to a tone—depends on activity in the cerebellum. Human patients with damage in the cerebellum are incapable of this type of conditioning (Daum & Schugens, 1996).

The formation of declarative and procedural memories in different brain areas could explain a curious finding about patients like H. M. Despite their inability to form new declarative memories, with sufficient practice such patients can acquire new procedural memories that enable them to solve a puzzle, read mirror-reversed words, or play tennis—even though they do not recall the training sessions in which they learned these skills. Apparently, the parts of the brain involved in acquiring new procedural memories have remained intact. These patients also retain some implicit memory for verbal material, as measured by priming tasks, suggesting that the brain has separate systems for implicit and explicit tasks. As Figure 8.6 shows, this view has been bolstered by brain scans, which reveal differences in the location of brain activity when people with healthy brains perform explicit versus implicit memory tasks (Reber, Stark, & Squire, 1998; Squire et al., 1992).

The brain circuits that take part in the *formation* and *retrieval* of long-term memories, however, are not the same as those involved in long-term *storage* of those memories. Although the hippocampus is vital for the formation and retrieval of memories, the storage of memories eventually becomes

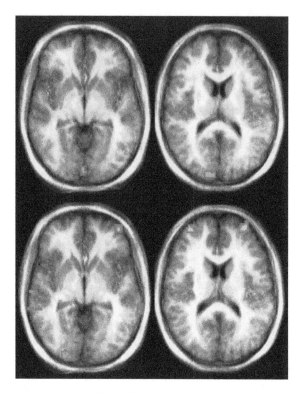

FIGURE 8.6 Brain Activity in Explicit and Implicit Memory

As these composite functional MRI scans show, patterns of brain activity differ depending on the type of memory task involved. When people had an explicit memory for dot patterns they had seen earlier, areas in the visual cortex, temporal lobes, and frontal lobes (indicated by orange in the lower photos) were more active. When people's implicit memories were activated, areas in the visual cortex (blue in the upper photos) were relatively inactive (Reber, Stark, & Squire, 1998).

the responsibility of the cerebral cortex (Battaglia et al., 2011). In fact, memories may be stored in the same cortical areas that were involved in the original perception of the information: When people remember pictures, visual parts of the brain become active; when people remember sounds, auditory areas become active, just as they did when the information was first perceived (Nyberg et al., 2000; Thompson & Kosslyn, 2000).

The typical "memory" is a complex cluster of information. When you recall meeting a man yesterday, you remember his greeting, his tone of voice, how he looked, and where he was. Even a single concept, such as *shovel*, includes a lot of information about its length, what it's made of, and what it's used for. These different pieces of information are probably processed separately and stored at different locations that are distributed across wide areas of the brain, with all the sites participating in the representation of the event or concept as a whole. The hippocampus may somehow bind together the diverse aspects of a memory at the time it is formed, so that even though these aspects are stored in different cortical sites, the memory can later be retrieved as one coherent entity (Squire & Zola-Morgan, 1991).

 Watch the **Video** The Basics: Do You Remember When? at **MyPsychLab**

Hormones, Emotion, and Memory LO 8.15

Have you ever smelled fresh cookies and recalled a tender scene from your childhood? Do you have a vivid memory of seeing a particularly horrifying horror movie? Emotional memories such as these are often especially intense, and the explanation resides partly in our hormones.

Hormones released by the adrenal glands during stress and emotional arousal, including epinephrine (adrenaline) and norepinephrine, can enhance memory. If you give people a drug that prevents their adrenal glands from producing these hormones, they will remember less about emotional stories they heard than a control group will (Cahill et al., 1994). Conversely, if you give animals norepinephrine right after learning, their memories will improve. The link between emotional arousal and memory makes evolutionary sense: Arousal tells the brain that an event or piece of information is important enough to encode and store for future use.

However, extreme arousal is not necessarily a good thing. When animals or people are given very high doses of stress hormones, their memories for learned tasks sometimes suffer instead of improving; a moderate dose may be optimal (Andreano & Cahill, 2006). Two psychologists demonstrated

the perils of high stress and anxiety in a real-life setting: the Horror Labyrinth of the London Dungeon (Valentine & Mesout, 2009). The labyrinth is a maze of disorienting mirrored walls set in Gothic vaults. As visitors walk through it, they hear strange noises and screams, and alarming things suddenly appear, including a "scary person"—an actor dressed in a dark robe, wearing makeup to appear scarred and bleeding. Volunteers wore a wireless heart-rate monitor as they walked through the labyrinth so that their stress and anxiety levels could be recorded. The higher their stress and anxiety, the less able they were to accurately describe the "scary person" later, and the fewer correct identifications they made of him in a lineup.

Such effects on memory do not matter much at an amusement attraction, but they can have serious consequences when crime victims, police officers, and combat soldiers must recall details of a highly stressful experience, such as what happened during a shoot-out or the identity of an enemy interrogator. The unintended effects of misleading suggestions, combined with the effects of extreme stress on memory, mean that we should be especially cautious about how investigators gather intelligence information from captured suspected terrorists (Loftus, 2011).

We have given you just a few small nibbles from the smorgasbord of findings now available about the biology of memory. Neuroscientists hope that someday they will be able to describe the entire stream of events in the brain that occur from the moment you say to yourself "I must remember this" to the moment you actually do remember…or find that you can't.

Recite & Review

✓ **Study** and **Review** at **MyPsychLab**

Recite: Let's see whether your memory for this section has consolidated. Say out loud everything you can about brain changes during short-term versus long-term memory, long-term potentiation, consolidation, the role of the hippocampus, the location of long-term memories in the brain, and hormonal influences on memory.

Review: Next, go back and read this section again.

Now take this *Quick Quiz:*

1. Is long-term potentiation associated with (a) increased responsiveness of certain receiving neurons to signals from transmitting neurons, (b) a decrease in receptors on certain receiving neurons, or (c) reaching your true potential?

2. The cerebellum has been associated with _____ memories; the hippocampus has been associated with _____ memories.

3. *True or false:* Hormone research suggests that if you want to remember well, you should be as relaxed as possible while learning.

Answers:

1. a 2. procedural, declarative 3. false

How We Remember LO 8.16

Mnemonics

mnemonics Strategies and tricks for improving memory, such as the use of a verse or a formula.

In everyday life, people who want to give their powers of memory a boost sometimes use **mnemonics** [neh-MON-iks], formal strategies and tricks for encoding, storing, and retaining information. (Mnemosyne, pronounced neh-MOZ-eh-nee, was the ancient Greek goddess of memory.) Some mnemonics take the form of easily memorized rhymes (e.g., "Thirty days hath September/April, June, and November..."). Others use formulas (e.g., "Every **g**ood **b**oy **d**oes **f**ine" for remembering which notes are on the lines of the treble clef in musical notation). Still others use visual images or word associations. Mnemonics may also reduce the amount of information by chunking it, which is why many companies use words for their phone numbers instead of unmemorable numbers.

Some stage performers with amazing recall rely on far more complicated mnemonics. But for ordinary memory tasks, such tricks are often no more effective than rote repetition, and sometimes they make matters worse (Wang, Thomas, & Ouellette, 1992). Besides, why use a fancy mnemonic to remember a grocery list when you can write down what you need to buy?

"YOU SIMPLY ASSOCIATE EACH NUMBER WITH A WORD, SUCH AS 'TABLE' AND 3,476,029."

Sidney Harris/ScienceCartoonsPlus.com

Well, then, what does work? In Chapter 1, we introduced you to four useful strategies for learning (see page 22). These strategies are based on well-established principles of memory that help us encode and store information so that it sticks in our minds and will be there when we need it. Let's look more closely at those principles.

Effective Encoding

Our memories, as we have seen, are not exact replicas of experience. Sensory information is summarized and encoded as words or images almost as soon as it is detected. When you hear a lecture you may hang on every word (we hope you do), but you do not memorize those words verbatim. You extract the main points and encode them.

To remember information well, you have to encode it accurately in the first place. With some kinds of information, accurate encoding takes place automatically, without effort. Think about where you usually sit in your psychology class. When were you last there? You can probably provide this information easily, even though you never made a deliberate effort to encode it. But many kinds of information require *effortful encoding*: the plot of a novel, the procedures for assembling a cabinet, the arguments for and against a proposed law. To retain such information, you might have to select the main points, label concepts, or associate the information with personal experiences or with material you already know. Experienced students know that most of the information in a college course requires effortful encoding, otherwise known as studying. The mind does not gobble up complex information automatically; you must make the material digestible.

Rehearsal

An important technique for keeping information in short-term memory and increasing the chances of long-term retention is *rehearsal*, the review or practice of material while you are learning it. When people are prevented from rehearsing, the contents of their short-term memories quickly fade (Peterson & Peterson, 1959). You are taking advantage of rehearsal when you look up a phone number and then repeat it over and over to keep it in short-term memory until you no longer need it. And when you can't remember a phone number because you have always used your contact list to

Get Involved Pay Attention!

It seems obvious, but often we fail to remember because we never encoded the information in the first place. Which of these Lincoln pennies is the real one? (The answer is at the end of this chapter.) If you are an American, you have seen zillions of pennies, yet you will probably have trouble recognizing the real one because you have never paid close attention and encoded the details of its design (Nickerson & Adams, 1979). If you are not an American, try drawing the front of one of your most common coins and then check to see how well you did.

> **maintenance rehearsal**
> Rote repetition of material to maintain its availability in memory.
>
> **elaborative rehearsal**
> Association of new information with already stored knowledge and analysis of the new information to make it memorable.

call it, you are learning what happens when you *don't* rehearse.

A poignant demonstration of the power of rehearsal once occurred during a session with H. M. (Ogden & Corkin, 1991). The experimenter gave him five digits to repeat and remember, but then she was unexpectedly called away. When she returned after more than an hour, H. M. was able to repeat the five digits correctly. He had been rehearsing them the entire time.

Short-term memory holds many kinds of information, including visual information and abstract meanings. But most people, or at least most hearing people, seem to favor speech for encoding and rehearsing its contents. The speech may be spoken aloud or to oneself. When people make errors on STM tests that use letters or words, they often confuse items that sound the same or similar, such as *d* and *t*, or *bear* and *bare*. These errors suggest that they have been rehearsing verbally.

Some strategies for rehearsing are more effective than others. **Maintenance rehearsal** merely involves rote repetition of the material. This kind of rehearsal is fine for keeping information in STM, but it will not always lead to long-term retention. A better strategy if you

want to remember for the long haul is **elaborative rehearsal**, also called *elaboration of encoding* (Cermak & Craik, 1979; Craik & Tulving, 1975). Elaboration involves associating new items of information with material that has already been stored or with other new facts. It can also involve analyzing the physical, sensory, or semantic features of an item.

When actors learn a script, they do not rely on maintenance rehearsal alone. They also use elaborative rehearsal and deep processing, analyzing the meaning of their lines and associating their lines with imagined information about the character they are playing.

deep processing In the encoding of information, the processing of meaning rather than simply the physical or sensory features of a stimulus.

Suppose that you are studying the concept of working memory. Simply memorizing the definition is unlikely to help much. But if you can elaborate the concept, you are more likely to remember it. The word *working* should remind you that working memory is involved in tasks that require effort and attention. And effort and attention are related to the ability to concentrate, resist distraction, and therefore solve problems. Many students try to pare down what they are learning to the bare essentials, but knowing more details about something in fact makes it more memorable; that is what elaboration means.

A related strategy for prolonging retention is **deep processing**, or the processing of meaning (Craik & Lockhart, 1972). If you process only the physical or sensory features of a stimulus, such as how the word *hypothalamus* is spelled and how it sounds, your processing will be shallow even if it is elaborated. If you recognize patterns and assign labels to objects or events ("*Hypo* means 'below,' so the *hypo*thalamus must be *below* the thalamus"), your processing will be somewhat deeper. If you fully analyze the meaning of what you are trying to remember (perhaps by encoding the functions and importance of the hypothalamus), your processing will be deeper yet. For some kinds of information, *shallow processing* is useful; when you memorize a poem, you will want to pay attention to (and elaborately encode) the sounds of the words and the patterns of rhythm in the poem and not just the poem's meaning. Usually, though, deep processing is more effective. That is why, if you try to memorize information that has little or no meaning for you, the information may not stick.

Retrieval Practice

Many students think that the way to remember course material for an exam is simply to study it once thoroughly, or maybe twice. Unfortunately, within just a few weeks or months after the exam—or even before it—some of those answers will have vanished like steam on a bathroom mirror. *Retrieval practice*, the repeated retrieval of an item of information from memory, is necessary if a memory is to undergo consolidation and remain available for a long time. After all, that's the goal of learning.

In a college course, a good way to ensure retrieval practice is to take short quizzes after you have learned some material but before the big exam. In a series of experiments in which students learned words in foreign languages, once a student had learned a word it was (a) repeatedly studied but dropped from further testing, (b) repeatedly tested but dropped from further studying, or (c) dropped from studying and testing. To the surprise of the students themselves, studying after learning had no effect on their subsequent ability to recall the foreign words. But repeated *testing*, which caused them to repeatedly retrieve the words from memory, had a large benefit (Karpicke, 2012; Karpicke & Roediger, 2008). So when your professors and your textbook authors want to keep quizzing you, it's only for your own good !

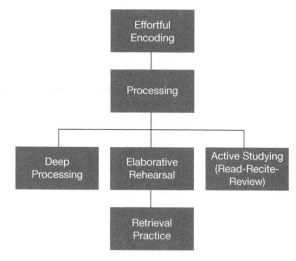

HOW TO REMEMBER BETTER

Remembering the Strategies for Learning

The very first learning strategy we introduced in Chapter 1 was the 3R method—*read, recite, review*—and we have helped you use it by building it into every one of our quizzes in this book. Now might be a good time to go back and—you guessed it—review the other strategies. They work because they encourage you to process deeply, to use your imagination, to use elaborative rehearsal, to test yourself, and to think about what you are hearing or reading. And they all have something important in common: They teach you to be an active rather than a passive learner. Your memory isn't a sponge that simply soaks up whatever is poured on it. Having a good memory requires you to transform new information into something you can understand, use, and retrieve when you most need it.

You are about to learn...

- why remembering everything might not be an advantage.
- the major reasons we forget even when we'd rather not.
- why most researchers are skeptical about claims of repressed and "recovered" memories.

Why We Forget LO 8.17

Have you ever, in the heat of some deliriously happy moment, said to yourself, "I'll never forget this, never, *never*, NEVER"? Do you find that you can more clearly remember saying those words than the deliriously happy moment itself? Sometimes you encode an event, you rehearse it, you analyze its meaning, you tuck it away in long-term storage, and still you forget it. Is it any wonder that most of us have wished, at one time or another, for a "photographic memory"?

Yet having a perfect memory is not the blessing that you might suppose. The Russian psychologist Alexander Luria (1968) once told of a journalist, S., who could reproduce giant grids of numbers both forward and backward, even after the passage of 15 years. To accomplish his astonishing feats, he used mnemonics, especially the formation of visual images. But you should not envy him, for he had a serious problem: He could not forget even when he wanted to. Along with the diamonds of experience, he kept dredging up the pebbles. Images he had formed to aid his memory kept creeping into consciousness, distracting him and interfering with his ability to concentrate. At times he even had trouble holding a conversation because the other person's words would set off a jumble of associations. Eventually, S. took to supporting himself by traveling from place to place, demonstrating his abilities for audiences.

Now consider two modern cases: Brad Williams and Jill Price both have extraordinary memories and have offered scientists the opportunity to study their abilities. When given any date going back for decades, they are able to say instantly what they were doing, what day

WELL, FOR CRYING OUT LOUD! AL TOWBRIDGE! WHAT IS IT, NINE YEARS, SEVEN MONTHS, AND TWELVE DAYS SINCE I LAST RAN INTO YOU? TEN-THIRTY-TWO A.M., A SATURDAY, FELCHER'S HARDWARE STORE. YOU WERE BUYING SEALER FOR YOUR BLACKTOP DRIVEWAY. TELL ME, AL, HOW DID THAT SEALER WORK? DID IT HOLD UP?

MR. TOTAL RECALL

decay theory The theory that information in memory eventually disappears if it is not accessed; it applies better to short-term than to long-term memory.

of the week it was, and whether anything of great importance happened on that date. Mention November 7, 1991, to Williams, and he says (correctly), "Let's see; that would be around when Magic Johnson announced he had HIV. Yes, a Thursday. There was a big snowstorm here the week before." Neither Williams nor Price uses mnemonics or can say where their accurate memories come from. Although Williams and his family regard his abilities as a source of amusement, Price describes her nonstop recollections as a mixed blessing (Parker, Cahill, & McGaugh, 2006). The phenomenon of constant, uncontrollable recall, she wrote, is "totally exhausting. Some have called it a gift, but I call it a burden. I run my entire life through my head every day and it drives me crazy!!!"

👁 **Watch** the **Video** The Big Picture: The Woman Who Cannot Forget at **MyPsychLab**

Paradoxically, then, forgetting is adaptive: We need to forget some things if we wish to remember efficiently. Piling up facts without distinguishing the important from the trivial is just confusing. Nonetheless, most of us forget more than we want to and would like to know why.

In the early days of psychology, in an effort to measure pure memory loss independent of personal experience, Hermann Ebbinghaus (1885/1913) memorized long lists of nonsense syllables, such as *bok*, *waf*, or *ged*, and then tested his retention over a period of several weeks. Most of his forgetting occurred soon after the initial learning and then leveled off. Generations of psychologists adopted Ebbinghaus's method of studying memory, but it did not tell them much about the kinds of memories that people care about most.

A century later, Marigold Linton decided to find out how people forget real events rather than nonsense syllables. Like Ebbinghaus, she used herself as a subject, but she charted the curve of forgetting over years rather than days. Every day for 12 years, she recorded on a 4- × 6-inch card two or more things that had happened to her that day. Eventually, she accumulated a catalogue of thousands of discrete events, both trivial ("I have dinner at the Canton Kitchen: delicious lobster dish") and significant ("I land at Orly Airport in Paris"). Once a month, she took a random sampling of all the cards accumulated to that point, noted whether she could remember the events on them, and tried to date the events. Linton (1978) expected the kind of rapid forgetting reported by Ebbinghaus. Instead, she found that long-term forgetting was slower and proceeded at a more constant pace, as details gradually dropped out of her memories.

Of course, some memories, especially those that mark important transitions, are more memorable than others. But why did Linton, like the rest of us, forget so many details? Psychologists have proposed five mechanisms to account for forgetting: decay, replacement of old memories by new ones, interference, cue-dependent forgetting, and repression.

Decay LO 8.18

One commonsense view, the **decay theory**, holds that memories simply fade with time if they are not accessed now and then. We have already seen that decay occurs in sensory memory and that it occurs in short-term memory as well unless we keep rehearsing the material. However, the mere passage of time does not account so well for forgetting in long-term memory. People commonly forget things that happened only yesterday while remembering events from many years ago. Indeed, some memories, both procedural and declarative, can last a lifetime. If you learned to swim as a child, you will still know how to swim at age 30, even if you have not been in a pool or lake for 22 years. We are also happy to report that some school lessons have great staying power. In one study, people did well on a Spanish test some 50 years after taking Spanish in high school, even though most had hardly

Motor skills, which are stored as procedural memories, can last a lifetime; they rarely decay.

FIGURE 8.7 The Stop Sign Study
When people who saw a car with a yield sign (left) were later asked if they had seen "the stop sign" (a misleading question), many said they had. Similarly, when those shown a stop sign were asked if they had seen "the yield sign," many said yes. These false memories persisted even after the participants were told about the misleading questions, suggesting that misleading information had erased their original mental representations of the signs (Loftus, Miller, & Burns, 1978).

used Spanish at all in the intervening years (Bahrick, 1984). Decay alone cannot entirely explain lapses in long-term memory.

Replacement

Another theory holds that new information entering memory can wipe out old information, just as rerecording on an audiotape or videotape will obliterate the original material. In a study supporting this view, researchers showed people slides of a traffic accident and used leading questions to get them to think that they had seen a stop sign when they had seen a yield sign, or vice versa (see Figure 8.7). People in a control group who were not misled in this way were able to correctly identify the sign they had seen. Later, all the participants were told the purpose of the study and were asked to guess whether they had been misled. Almost all of those who had been misled continued to insist that they had *really, truly* seen the sign whose existence had been planted in their minds (Loftus, Miller, & Burns, 1978). The researchers interpreted this finding to mean that the participants had not just been trying to please them and that people's original perceptions had in fact been erased by the misleading information.

👁 Watch the Video Elizabeth Loftus: Memory at MyPsychLab

Interference

A third theory holds that forgetting occurs because similar items of information interfere with one another in either storage or retrieval; the information may get into memory and stay there, but it becomes confused with other information. Such interference, which occurs in both short- and long-term memory, is especially common

when you have to recall isolated facts such as names, addresses, passwords, and area codes.

Suppose you are at a party and you meet someone named Julie. A little later you meet someone named Judy. You go on to talk to other people, and after an hour, you again bump into Julie, but you call her Judy by mistake. The second name has interfered with the first. This type of interference, in which new information interferes with the ability to remember old information, is called **retroactive interference**:

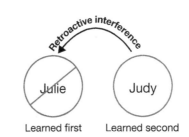

Retroactive interference is illustrated by the story of an absentminded professor of ichthyology (the study of fish) who complained that whenever he learned the name of a new student, he forgot the name of a fish. But whereas with replacement, the new memory erases the old and makes it irretrievable, in retroactive interference the loss of the old memory is sometimes temporary. With a little concentration, that professor could probably recall his new students and his old fish.

Because new information is constantly entering memory, we are all vulnerable to the effects of retroactive interference, or at least most of us are. H. M. was an exception; his memories of childhood and adolescence were unusually detailed, clear, and unchanging. H. M. could remember actors who were famous when he was a child, the films they were in, and who their costars had been. He also

retroactive interference Forgetting that occurs when recently learned material interferes with the ability to remember similar material stored previously.

proactive interference
Forgetting that occurs when previously stored material interferes with the ability to remember similar, more recently learned material.

cue-dependent forgetting The inability to retrieve information stored in memory because of insufficient cues for recall.

state-dependent memory The tendency to remember something when the rememberer is in the same physical or mental state as during the original learning or experience.

mood-congruent memory The tendency to remember experiences that are consistent with one's current mood and overlook or forget experiences that are not.

knew the names of friends from the second grade. Presumably, these early declarative memories were not subject to interference from memories acquired after the operation, for the simple reason that H. M. had not acquired any new memories.

Interference also works in the opposite direction. Old information (such as the foreign language you learned in high school) may interfere with the ability to remember current information (such as the new language you are trying to learn now). This type of interference is called **proactive interference**:

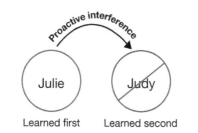

Learned first   Learned second

Over a period of weeks, months, and years, proactive interference may cause more forgetting than retroactive interference does, because we have stored up so much information that can potentially interfere with anything new.

Cue-Dependent Forgetting

Often, when we need to remember, we rely on *retrieval cues*, items of information that can help us find the specific information we're looking for. If you are trying to remember the last name of an actor you saw in an old film, it might help to know the person's first name or another movie the actor starred in.

When we lack retrieval cues, we may feel as if we are lost in the mind's library. In long-term memory, this type of memory failure, called **cue-dependent forgetting**, may be the most common type of all. Willem Wagenaar (1986), who, like Marigold Linton, recorded critical details about events in his life, found that within a year he had forgotten 20 percent of those details and after five years he had forgotten 60 percent. Yet when he gathered cues from witnesses about 10 events that he thought he had forgotten, he was able to recall something about all 10, which suggests that some of his forgetting was cue dependent.

Cues that were present when you learned a new fact or had an experience are apt to be especially useful later as retrieval aids. That may explain why remembering is often easier when you are in the same physical environment as you were when an event occurred: Cues in the present context match those from the past. Ordinarily, this overlap helps us remember the past more

accurately. But it may also help account for the eerie phenomenon of *déjà vu*, the fleeting sense of having been in *exactly* the same situation that you are in now (*déjà vu* means "already seen" in French). Some element in the present situation, familiar from some other context that you cannot identify—even a dream, a novel, or a movie—may make the entire situation seem so familiar that it feels like it happened before (Brown, 2004). In other words, déjà vu may be a kind of mistaken recognition memory. Similar feelings of familiarity can be produced in the laboratory. When something about newly presented words, shapes, or photographs resembles elements of stimuli seen previously, people report that the new words, shapes, or photographs seem familiar even though they can't recall the original ones (Cleary, 2008).

In everyday situations, your mental or physical state may act as a retrieval cue, evoking a **state-dependent memory**. If you were afraid or angry at the time of an event, you may remember that event best when you are once again in the same emotional state (Lang et al., 2001). Your memories can also be biased by whether or not your current mood is consistent with the emotional nature of the material you are trying to remember, a phenomenon known as **mood-congruent memory** (Bower & Forgas, 2000; Buchanan, 2007; Fiedler et al., 2001). You are more likely to remember happy events, and forget or ignore unhappy ones, when you are feeling happy than when you are feeling sad. Likewise, you are apt to remember

FORGETFULNESS— The seven warning signs:

1.

unhappy events better and remember more of them when you are feeling unhappy, which in turn creates a vicious cycle. The more unhappy memories you recall, the more depressed you feel, and the more depressed you feel, the more unhappy memories you recall...so you stay stuck in your depression and make it even worse (Joormann & Gotlib, 2007; Wenzel, 2005).

Explore the Concept What Do You Remember? at MyPsychLab

The Repression Controversy LO 8.19

A final theory of forgetting is concerned with **amnesia**, the loss of memory for important personal information. Amnesia most commonly results from organic conditions such as brain disease or head injury and is usually temporary. In *psychogenic amnesia*, however, the causes of forgetting are psychological, such as a need to escape feelings of embarrassment, guilt, shame, disappointment, or emotional shock. Psychogenic amnesia begins immediately after the precipitating event, involves massive memory loss including loss of personal identity, and usually ends suddenly, after just a few weeks. Despite its frequent portrayal in films and novels, it is quite rare in real life (McNally, 2003).

Psychologists generally accept the notion of psychogenic amnesia. *Traumatic amnesia*, however, is far more controversial. Traumatic amnesia allegedly involves the burying of specific traumatic events for a long period of time, often for many years. When the memory returns, it is supposedly immune to the usual processes of distortion and confabulation and is recalled with perfect accuracy. The notion of traumatic amnesia originated with the psychoanalytic theory of Sigmund Freud, who argued that the mind defends itself from unwelcome and upsetting memories through the mechanism of **repression**, the involuntary pushing of threatening or upsetting information into the unconscious (see Chapter 2).

Most memory researchers reject the argument that a special unconscious mechanism called "repression" is necessary to explain either psychogenic or traumatic amnesia (Rofé, 2008). Richard McNally (2003) reviewed the experimental and clinical evidence and concluded, "The notion that the mind protects itself by repressing or dissociating memories of trauma, rendering them inaccessible to awareness, is a piece of psychiatric folklore devoid of convincing empirical

THINKING CRITICALLY

About Repression and Trauma

support." The problem for most people who have suffered disturbing experiences is not that they cannot remember, but rather that they cannot forget: The memories keep intruding. There is no case on record of anyone who has repressed the memory of being in a concentration camp, being in combat, or being the victim of an earthquake or a terrorist attack, although details of even these horrible experiences are subject to distortion and fading over time, as are all memories.

Further, repression is hard to distinguish from normal forgetting. People who seem to forget disturbing experiences could be intentionally keeping themselves from retrieving their painful memories by distracting themselves whenever such memories are reactivated. Or they may be focusing consciously on positive memories instead. Perhaps, understandably, they are not rehearsing unhappy memories, so those memories fade with time. Perhaps they are simply avoiding the retrieval cues that would evoke the memories. But a reluctance to think about an upsetting experience is not the same as an *inability* to remember it (McNally, 2003).

The debate over traumatic amnesia and repression erupted into the public arena in the 1990s, when claims of recovered memories of sexual abuse began to appear. Many women and some men came to believe, during psychotherapy, that they could recall long-buried memories of having been sexually victimized for many years, often in bizarre ways. For therapists who accepted the notion of repression, such claims were entirely believable (Brown, Scheflin, & Whitfield, 1999; Herman, 1992). But most researchers today believe that almost all of these memories were false, having been evoked by therapists who were unaware of the research we have described on the power of suggestion and the dangers of confabulation (Lindsay & Read, 1994; McNally, 2003; Schacter, 2001). By asking leading questions, and by encouraging clients to construct vivid images of abuse, to revisit those images frequently, and to focus on emotional aspects of the images, such therapists unwittingly set up the very conditions that encourage confabulation and false memories.

Since the 1990s, accusations based on "recovered memories" have steadily declined, and some accusers have reconciled with their families (McHugh et al., 2004). Yet the concept of repression lingers on. Many of its original proponents have turned to the term *dissociation* to account for memory failures in traumatized individuals, the idea being that upsetting memories are split off (dissociated) from everyday consciousness. But

amnesia The partial or complete loss of memory for important personal information.

repression In psychoanalytic theory, the selective, involuntary pushing of threatening or upsetting information into the unconscious.

reviews of the research have found no good evidence that early trauma causes such dissociation (Giesbrecht et al., 2008; Huntjens, Verschuere, & McNally, 2012).

Of course, it is obviously possible for someone to forget a single unhappy or deeply unpleasant experience and not recall it for years, just as going back to your elementary school might trigger a memory of the time that you did something embarrassing in front of your whole class. How then should we respond to an individual's claim to have recovered memories of years of traumatic experiences that were previously "repressed"? How can we distinguish true memories from false ones?

Clearly, a person's recollections are likely to be trustworthy if corroborating evidence is available, such as medical records, police or school reports, or the accounts of other people who had been present at the time. But in the absence of supporting evidence, we may have to tolerate uncertainty, because a person might have a detailed, emotionally rich "memory" that feels completely real but that has been unintentionally confabulated (Bernstein & Loftus,

2009). In such cases, we need to consider the content of the recovered memory and how it was recovered.

Thus, given what we know about memory, we should be skeptical if the person says that he or she has recovered memories from the first year or two of life; as we will see in the next section, this is not possible, physiologically or cognitively. We should be skeptical if, over time, the person's memories become more and more implausible; for instance, the person says that sexual abuse continued day and night for 15 years without ever being remembered and without anyone else in the household ever noticing anything amiss. We should also be skeptical if a person suddenly recovers a traumatic memory as a result of therapy or after hearing about supposed cases of recovered memory in the news or reading about one in a best-selling autobiography. And we should hear alarm bells go off if a therapist used suggestive techniques, such as hypnosis, dream analysis, "age regression," guided imagery, or leading questions, to "recover" the memories. These techniques are all known to increase confabulation.

Recite & Review

✓ **Study** and **Review** at **MyPsychLab**

Recite: Make sure you don't have amnesia for the preceding material by reciting out loud everything you can about the decay theory, replacement of old information, retroactive and proactive interference, cue-dependent forgetting, state-dependent memory, mood-congruent memory, amnesia, and repression.

Review: Next, go back and reread this section.

Now take this *Quick Quiz:*

1. Wilma has been a long-time fan of country singer Tim McGraw. Recently, she met an interesting guy named Tom McGraw, but she keeps calling him Tim. Why?

2. When a man at his 20th high school reunion sees his old friends, he recalls incidents he thought were long forgotten. Why?

3. What mechanisms other than repression could account for a person's psychogenic amnesia?

Answers:

1. proactive interference 2. The sight of his friends provides retrieval cues for the incidents. 3. The person could be intentionally avoiding the memory by using distraction or focusing on positive experiences; failure to rehearse the memory may be causing it to fade; or the person may be avoiding retrieval cues that would evoke the memory.

You are about to learn...

• **why the first few years of life are a mental blank.**

• **why human beings have been called the storytelling animal.**

Autobiographical Memories

For most of us, our memories about our own experiences are by far the most fascinating. We use them to entertain ("Did I ever tell you about the time…?") and to connect with others ("Remember that time we…?"). We analyze them to learn more about who we are. We modify and embellish them to impress others, and some people even publish them.

Childhood Amnesia: The Missing Years LO 8.20

A curious aspect of autobiographical memory is that most adults cannot recall any events from earlier than age 2, and even after that, memories are sketchy at best until about age 6 (Hayne & Jack, 2011). A few people apparently can vaguely recall significant events that occurred when they were as young as 2 years old, such as the birth of a sibling, but not earlier ones (Fivush & Nelson, 2004; Usher & Neisser, 1993). As adults, we cannot remember being fed in infancy, taking our first steps, or uttering our first halting sentences. We are victims of **childhood amnesia** (sometimes called *infantile amnesia*).

Childhood amnesia is disturbing to many people, so disturbing that some people adamantly deny that it exists, claiming to remember events from the second or even the first year of life. But like other false memories, these are reconstructions based on photographs, family stories, and imagination. The "remembered"

THINKING CRITICALLY

About "Memories" from Infancy

event may not even have taken place. Swiss psychologist Jean Piaget (1952) once reported a memory of nearly being kidnapped at the age of 2. Piaget remembered sitting in his pram, watching his nurse as she bravely defended him from the kidnapper. He remembered the scratches she received on her face. He remembered a police officer with a short cloak and white baton who finally chased the kidnapper away. But when Piaget was 15, his nurse wrote to his parents confessing that she had made up the entire story. Piaget noted, "I therefore must have heard, as a child, the account of this story…and projected it into the past in the form of a visual memory, which was a memory of a memory, but false."

Of course, we all retain procedural memories from the toddler stage, when we first learned to use a fork, drink from a cup, and pull a wagon. We also retain semantic memories acquired early in life: the rules of counting, the names of people and things, knowledge about objects in the world, words and meanings. Moreover, toddlers who are only 1 to 2 years old often reveal nonverbally

that they remember past experiences (for example, by imitating something they saw earlier); and some 4-year-olds can remember experiences that occurred before age 2 1/2 (Bauer, 2002; McDonough & Mandler, 1994; Tustin & Hayne, 2010). What young children do not do well is encode and retain their early episodic memories—memories of particular events—and carry them into later childhood or adulthood.

Freud thought that childhood amnesia was a special case of repression, but memory researchers today think that repression has nothing to do with it, and they point to better explanations:

1 **Brain development.** Parts of the brain involved in the formation or storage of events, especially the prefrontal cortex, are not well developed until a few years after birth (McKee & Squire, 1993; Newcombe, Lloyd, & Balcomb, 2012). In addition, the brains of infants and toddlers are busily attending to all the new experiences of life, but this very fact makes it difficult for them to focus on just one event and shut out everything else that's going on—the kind of focus necessary for encoding and remembering (Gopnik, 2009).

2 **Cognitive development.** Before you can carry memories about yourself with you into adulthood, you have to have a self to remember. The

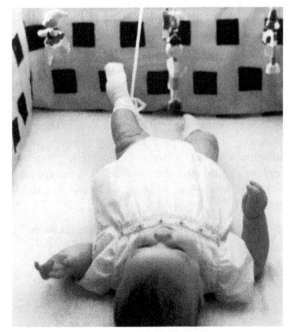

This infant, whose leg is attached by a string to a colorful mobile, will learn within minutes to make the mobile move by kicking it. She may still remember the trick a week later, an example of procedural memory (Rovee-Collier, 1993). However, when she is older, she will not remember the experience itself. She will fall victim to childhood amnesia.

childhood (infantile) amnesia The inability to remember events and experiences that occurred earlier than age 2.

emergence of a self-concept usually does not take place before age 2 (Howe, Courage, & Peterson, 1994). In addition, the cognitive schemas used by preschoolers are very different from those used by older children and adults. Only after acquiring language and starting school do children form schemas that contain the information and cues necessary for recalling earlier experiences (Howe, 2000). Young children's limited vocabularies and language skills also prevent them from narrating some aspects of an experience to themselves or others. Later, after their linguistic abilities have matured, they still cannot use those abilities to recall earlier, preverbal memories, because those memories were not encoded linguistically (Simcock & Hayne, 2002).

3 **Social development.** Preschoolers have not yet mastered the social conventions for reporting events, nor have they learned what is important to others. As a result, they focus on the routine aspects of an experience rather than the distinctive ones that will provide retrieval cues later on, and they encode their experiences far less elaborately than adults do. Instead, they tend to rely on adults' questions to provide retrieval cues ("Where did we go for breakfast?" "Who did you go trick-or-treating with?"). This dependency on adults may prevent them from building up a stable core of remembered material that will be available when they are older (Fivush & Nelson, 2005). But as children mature, their conversations with parents and others help them develop their own autobiographical memories, and thus those conversations play an important role in bringing childhood amnesia to an end (Reese, Jack, & White, 2010).

Nonetheless, our first memories, even when they are vague or inaccurate, may provide useful insights into our personalities, current concerns, ambitions, and attitudes toward life. What are *your* first memories—or, at least, what do you think they are?

 Watch the **Video** Kimberley Cuevas: Learning and Memory in Infants at **MyPsychLab**

Memory and Narrative: The Stories of Our Lives LO 8.21

The communications researcher George Gerbner once observed that human beings are unique because we are the only animal that tells stories—and lives by the stories we tell. This view of human beings as the "storytelling animal" has had a huge impact in cognitive psychology. The *narratives* we compose to simplify and make sense of our lives

have a profound influence on our plans, memories, love affairs, hatreds, ambitions, and dreams.

Thus we say, "I have no academic motivation because I flunked the third grade." We say, "Let me tell you the story of how we fell in love." We say, "When you hear what happened, you'll understand why I felt entitled to take such cold-hearted revenge." These stories are not necessarily fictions; rather, they are attempts to organize and give meaning to the events of our lives. But because these narratives rely heavily on memory, and because memories are reconstructed and are constantly shifting in response to current needs, beliefs, and experiences, our autobiographies are also, to some degree, works of interpretation and imagination. Adult memories can thus reveal as much about the present as they do about the past.

When you construct a narrative about an incident in your life, you have many choices about how to do it. The choice you make will depend on who the audience is; you are apt to put in, leave out, understate, and embellish different things depending on whether you are telling about an event in your life to a therapist, your boss, or friends on Facebook. Your story is also influenced by your purpose in relating it: Is it to convey facts, entertain, or elicit sympathy? As a result of these influences, distortions are apt to creep in, even when you think you are being accurate. And once those distortions have become embedded in your story, they are likely to become part of your memory of the events themselves (Marsh & Tversky, 2004).

Your culture also affects how you encode and tell your story. American college students live in a culture that emphasizes individuality, personal feelings, and self-expression. Their earliest childhood memories reflect that fact: They tend to report lengthy, emotionally elaborate memories of events, memories that focus on—who else?—themselves. In contrast, Chinese students, who live in a culture that emphasizes group harmony, social roles, and

"And here I am at two years of age. Remember? Mom? Pop? No? Or how about this one. My first day of school. Anyone?"

personal humility, tend to report early memories of family or neighborhood activities, conflicts with friends or relatives that were resolved, and emotionally neutral events (Wang, 2008).

Once you have formulated a story's central theme ("My father never liked us"; "My partner was always so competitive with me"), that theme may then serve as a cognitive schema that guides what you remember and what you forget (Mather, Shafir, & Johnson, 2000). Teenagers who have strong and secure attachments to their mothers remember previous quarrels with their moms as being less intense and conflicted than they reported at the time, whereas teenagers who

have more ambivalent and insecure attachments remember such quarrels as being worse than they were (Feeney & Cassidy, 2003).

A story's theme may also influence our judgments of events and people in the present. If you have a fight with your lover, the central theme in your story about the fight might be negative ("He was a jerk") or neutral ("It was a mutual misunderstanding"). This theme may bias you to blame or forgive your partner long after you have forgotten what the conflict was all about or who said what (McGregor & Holmes, 1999). You can see that the spin you give a story is critical, so be careful about the stories you tell!

Recite & Review

 Study and **Review** at **MyPsychLab**

Recite: It's time to say out loud everything you can about childhood amnesia and the role of narratives in autobiographical memory.

Review: Next, go back and read this section again.

Now take this *Quick Quiz:*

1. A friend of yours claims to remember her birth, her first tooth, and her first birthday party. She is most likely to be (a) confabulating, (b) repressing, (c) revealing wishful thinking, (d) accurately remembering.

2. Give three explanations for childhood amnesia (be specific).

3. Why are the themes in our life stories so important?

Answers:

1. a, c 2. the immaturity of certain brain structures, making it difficult for very young children to focus attention, encode, and remember; cognitive factors such as immature cognitive schemas, lack of linguistic skills, and lack of a self-concept; lack of knowledge of social conventions for encoding and reporting events 3. They guide what we remember and forget about our personal pasts, and affect our judgments of events and people.

PSYCHOLOGY IN THE NEWS REVISITED /////////

Psychological research is having a significant impact on people's ability to think critically about memory. Most notably, awareness of the fallibility of memory is growing among police, interrogators, defense attorneys, prosecutors, and judges (Loftus, 2013). Unfortunately, as we saw, the case of Ronald Cotton, described at the start of this chapter, is far from unique. According to the Innocence Project at the Cardozo School of Law, eyewitness mistakes cause more than three-fourths of all wrongful convictions. Of course, not all eyewitness testimony is erroneous. But the potential for errors in identification shows how important it is to gather evidence carefully, ensure adequate legal representation for defendants, conduct police interviews using proper procedures, reduce pressure on witnesses, and obtain a DNA analysis whenever possible.

Inspired by the Innocence Project, grassroots organizations of lawyers and students have been successfully challenging questionable convictions. Since the early 1990s, these efforts have led to the exoneration of more than 300 innocent people in the United States, some of whom had been condemned to death. One man in Illinois, who had been on death row for 16 years, was just hours from execution when a group of Northwestern University journalism students produced evidence that another man had committed the crime. Other investigative projects around the world have produced similar accomplishments.

How would you feel if your testimony resulted in the conviction of an innocent person? Would you, like Jennifer Thompson, be able to admit your mistake, or would you, as most people do, cling more stubbornly than ever to the accuracy of your memory? Thompson

learned from personal experience what you have learned from this chapter: Eyewitnesses can and do make mistakes; ethnic differences can increase these mistakes; even memories for shocking or traumatic experiences are vulnerable to distortion and influence by others; and our confidence in our memories is not a reliable guide to their accuracy. Over the years, Thompson and Cotton have made it their personal goal to educate the public and the criminal justice system, so that the mistake she made will be less likely to be repeated by others (Thompson-Cannino, Cotton, & Torneo, 2009). Their story teaches us to respect the power of memory but at the same time retain humility about our capacity for error, confabulation, and self-deception.

After Ronald Cotton was exonerated of the rape of Jennifer Thompson, the two became friends.

Taking Psychology With You

This Is Your Life

A student once told us how for years she had remembered falling from her bike as a young child and being rushed to the hospital. She remembered the concerned adults hovering around her, the trip in the car, and especially the blood. There was only one problem: The injury, she later learned, had happened to her sister, not to her.

Why had this student made herself the central character in this story? She had her own theory: At the time she had envied all the attention her sister was getting, and so later, as the memory faded, in her imagination she refocused that attention on herself so she could be the star of the drama—a good example of "imagination inflation."

As this story illustrates, we are not merely actors in our personal life stories; we also write the scripts. In this chapter we saw that although our recollections are often accurate, they can also be incomplete or even just plain wrong. Confabulation, source misattribution, poor encoding, interference, inadequate retrieval cues, suggestibility, and biases can all trip us up, even when we are recalling significant events in our own lives.

Here are just a few ways to start exploring your own autobiographical narratives:

Write down your earliest memory. How old do you think you were? Does the memory involve an event or just a sensory impression (the taste of a particular food, the softness of a blanket, the sound of your mother's voice)? There are probably many memories you could have chosen as your "earliest." What does the one you did choose tell you about yourself? Does it reflect your needs or personality traits or family relationships in some way?

Think about how you would relate an embarrassing experience from your past. How would you describe it to a close friend? A parent? A stranger? Would your narrative change depending on the audience? If so, how?

Consider whether your narratives have been consistent over time. For example, if you have ever broken up with a romantic partner, what memories of the relationship did you focus on while you were still together as opposed to after you parted? Did you recall mostly the good aspects of the relationship when you were a happy couple and only the bad ones once you split?

Compare one of your memories with someone else's memory of the same experience. Often people in the same family have different memories of the same event or person. Pick some family event—say a holiday celebration, a visit to a theme park, or a family crisis. Find out if a parent or sibling remembers it the way you do. If there are differences, why do you think that is?

Consider the central "theme" of your life story. If you were writing your life story to date, what would its title be? My Struggles to Overcome Obstacles? My Life as a Victim? Why Success Matters to Me? What does your theme tell you about your sense of who you are, your motivations, needs, and values, or your philosophy of life?

As you grow older, you are likely to remember more from your adolescence and early adulthood than from midlife (Jansari & Parkin, 1996). Perhaps the younger years are especially likely to come to mind later in life when people look back because our early years are full of important transitions—starting and completing college, getting a job, falling in love. As a college student, you will do well to mindfully encode and enjoy the experiences you're having now, for they will be the stuff of memory later on.

Summary   ((Listen to the Audio File at MyPsychLab

Reconstructing the Past

- Unlike a digital recorder or video camera, human memory is highly selective and is *reconstructive*: People add, delete, and change elements in ways that help them make sense of information and events. They often experience *source misattribution*, the inability to distinguish information stored during an event from information added later on. Even vivid *flashbulb memories* tend to become less accurate or complete over time.

- Because memory is so often reconstructive, it is subject to *confabulation*, the confusion of imagined events with actual ones. Confabulation is especially likely when people have thought, heard, or told others about the imagined event many times and are experiencing *imagination inflation;* the image of the event contains many details; or the event is easy to imagine. Confabulated memories can feel vividly real yet be false.

Memory and the Power of Suggestion

- The reconstructive nature of memory makes memory vulnerable to suggestion. Eyewitness testimony is especially vulnerable to error when the suspect's ethnicity differs from that of the witness, when leading questions are put to witnesses, or when witnesses are given misleading information.

- Like adults, children often remember the essential aspects of an event accurately but can also be suggestible, especially when responding to biased interviewing by adults—when they are asked questions that blur the line between fantasy and reality, are asked leading questions, are told what "other kids" supposedly said, and are praised for making false allegations.

In Pursuit of Memory

- The ability to remember depends in part on the type of performance called for. In tests of *explicit memory* (conscious recollection), *recognition* is usually better than *recall*. In tests of *implicit memory*, which is measured by indirect methods such as *priming* and the *relearning method*, past experiences may affect current thoughts or actions even when these experiences are not consciously remembered.

- In *information-processing models*, memory involves the *encoding*, *storage*, and *retrieval* of information. The *three-box model* proposes three interacting systems: the sensory register, short-term memory, and long-term memory. Some cognitive scientists prefer a *parallel distributed processing (PDP)* or *connectionist* model, which represents knowledge as connections among numerous interacting processing units, distributed in a vast network and all operating in parallel. But the three-box model continues to offer a convenient way to organize the major findings on memory.

The Three-Box Model of Memory

- In the three-box model, incoming sensory information makes a brief stop in the *sensory register*, which momentarily retains it in the form of sensory images.

- *Short-term memory* (STM) retains new information for up to 30 seconds by most estimates (unless rehearsal takes place). The capacity of STM is extremely limited but can be extended if information is organized into larger units by *chunking*. Early models of STM portrayed it mainly as a bin for the temporary storage of information, but many models now envision it as a part of a *working memory* system, which includes an "executive" that controls the retrieval of information from long-term memory and focuses attention on information needed for the task being performed. Working memory enables us to resist distraction, and maintain information in an active, accessible state.

- *Long-term memory* (LTM) contains an enormous amount of information that must be organized to make it manageable. Words (or the concepts they represent) are often organized by semantic categories. Many models of LTM represent its contents as a network of interrelated concepts. The way people use these networks depends on experience and education. Research on *tip-of-the-tongue states* shows that words are also indexed in terms of sound and form.

- *Procedural memories* ("knowing how") are memories for how to perform specific actions; *declarative memories* ("knowing that") are memories for abstract or representational knowledge. Declarative memories include *semantic memories* (general knowledge) and *episodic memories* (memories for personally experienced events). Episodic memories allow us to retrieve past events in order to imagine the future.

- The three-box model is often invoked to explain the *serial-position effect* in memory, but although it can explain the *primacy effect*, it cannot explain why a *recency effect* sometimes occurs after a considerable delay.

The Biology of Memory

- Short-term memory involves temporary changes within neurons that alter their ability to release neurotransmitters, whereas long-term memory involves lasting structural changes in neurons and synapses. *Long-term potentiation*, an increase in the strength of synaptic responsiveness, seems to be an important mechanism of long-term memory. Neural changes associated with long-term potentiation take time to develop, which helps explain why long-term memories require a period of *consolidation*.

- The amygdala is involved in the formation, consolidation, and retrieval of fearful and other emotional memories. Areas of the frontal lobes are especially active during short-term and working memory tasks. The prefrontal cortex and parts of the temporal lobes are involved in the efficient encoding of words and pictures. The hippocampus plays a critical role in the formation and retrieval of long-term declarative memories. Other areas, such as the cerebellum, are crucial for the formation of procedural memories. Studies of patients with amnesia suggest that different brain systems are active during explicit and implicit memory tasks. The long-term storage of declarative memories may take place in cortical areas that were active during the original perception of the information or event. The various components of a memory are probably stored at different sites, with all of these sites participating in the representation of the event as a whole.

- Hormones released by the adrenal glands during stress or emotional arousal, including epinephrine and norepinephrine, enhance memory. But very high hormone levels can interfere with the retention of information; a moderate level is optimal for learning new tasks.

How We Remember

- *Mnemonics* can enhance retention, but for ordinary memory tasks, complex memory tricks are often ineffective or even counterproductive.

- To remember material well, we must encode it accurately in the first place. Some kinds of information, such as material in a college course, require *effortful* as opposed to automatic encoding. Rehearsal of information keeps it in short-term memory and increases the chances of long-term retention. *Elaborative rehearsal* is more likely to result in transfer to long-term memory than is *maintenance rehearsal*, and *deep processing* is usually a more effective retention strategy than *shallow processing*. *Retrieval practice* is necessary if a memory is going to be consolidated, and therefore be available for a long time. The *read-recite-review* strategy and other effective study strategies encourage active learning and produce better results than simply reading and rereading material.

Why We Forget

- Forgetting can occur for several reasons. Information in sensory and short-term memory appears to *decay* if it does not receive further processing. New information may erase and replace old information in long-term memory. *Proactive* and *retroactive interference* may take place. *Cue-dependent forgetting* may occur when *retrieval cues* are inadequate. The most effective retrieval cues are those that were present at the time of the initial experience. A person's mental or physical state may also act as a retrieval cue, evoking a *state-dependent memory*. We tend to remember best those events that are congruent with our current mood (*mood-congruent memory*).

- *Amnesia*, the partial or complete forgetting of important personal information, usually occurs because of disease or injury to the brain. *Psychogenic amnesia*, which involves a loss of personal identity and has psychological causes, is rare. *Traumatic amnesia*, which allegedly involves the forgetting of specific traumatic events for long periods of time, is highly controversial, as is *repression*, the psychodynamic explanation of traumatic amnesia. Because these concepts lack good empirical support, psychological scientists are skeptical about their validity and about the accuracy of "recovered memories." Critics argue that many therapists, unaware of the power of suggestion and the dangers of confabulation, have encouraged false memories of victimization.

Autobiographical Memories

- Most people cannot recall any events from earlier than the age of 2. The reasons for such *childhood amnesia* include the immaturity of certain brain structures, making it difficult for very young children to focus attention, encode, and remember; cognitive factors such as immature cognitive schemas, lack of linguistic skills, and lack of a self-concept; and lack of knowledge of social conventions for encoding and reporting events.

- A person's *narrative* "life story" organizes the events of his or her life and gives them meaning.

Psychology in the News, Revisited

- DNA evidence has exonerated many people who were falsely convicted of rape, murder, and other crimes, making the public more aware of the limitations of eyewitness testimony and the fallibility of memory.

Taking Psychology With You

- You can begin exploring your own personal narratives by recalling what you consider to be your earliest memory; considering how you would relate an embarrassing experience to different audiences; thinking about whether your memories have been consistent over time or have changed; comparing a memory of an event with someone else's memory of the same event; and coming up with the "theme" of your life story.

Key Terms

memory 283

reconstructive
  memory 285

source misattribution 285

flashbulb memories 285

confabulation 285

imagination inflation 285

leading questions 287

explicit memory 290

recall 290

recognition 290

implicit memory 291

priming 291

relearning method 291

information-processing
  models 291

encoding, storage, and
  retrieval 315

cognitive schemas 292

three-box model 292

parallel distributed processing
  (PDP) model 293

sensory register 293

short-term memory
  (STM) 294

chunks 294

working memory 295

long-term memory (LTM) 295

semantic categories 295

tip-of-the-tongue (TOT)
  state 296

procedural memories 297

declarative memories 297

semantic memories 297

episodic memories 297

serial-position effect 298

primacy and recency
  effects 298

long-term potentiation 299

consolidation 299

mnemonics 302

effortful versus automatic
  encoding 302

maintenance rehearsal 303

elaborative rehearsal 303

deep processing 304

shallow processing 304

retrieval practice 304

read-recite-review strategy 304

decay theory 306

retroactive interference 307

proactive interference 308

retrieval cues 308

cue-dependent forgetting 308

déjà vu 308

state-dependent memory 308

mood-congruent memory 308

amnesia 309

psychogenic amnesia 309

traumatic amnesia 309

repression 309

childhood (infantile)
  amnesia 311

narratives 312

Answers to the Get Involved exercises on pages 291 and 292: Rudolph's eight friends were Dasher, Dancer, Prancer, Vixen, Comet, Cupid, Donner ("Donder" in some versions), and Blitzen.

Answer to the Get Involved exercise on page 303: The real penny is the left one in the bottom row.

Memory refers to the capacity to retain and retrieve information and also to the structures that account for this capacity.

↓

Reconstructing the Past

↓

The Manufacture of Memory

- Human memory is *reconstructive*: People add, delete, and change elements of many memories.
- **Source misattribution** is the inability to distinguish information stored during an event from information added later.
- Even *flashbulb memories*, though emotionally powerful and vivid, are often embellished or change over time.

↓

The Conditions of Confabulation

Confabulation is the confusion of imagined events with real ones, or confusion of an event that happened to someone else with one that happened to you. Confabulation is especially likely when:
- one has thought, heard, or told others about the imagined event many times.
- the image of the event contains lots of details that make it feel real.
- the event is easy to imagine.

Models of Memory

- In *information-processing models*, memory involves encoding, storage, and retrieval.
- In **parallel distributed processing (PDP)** models, knowledge is represented as connections among thousands of interacting processing units, all operating in parallel.

Memory and the Power of Suggestion

↙   ↘

The Eyewitness on Trial

Eyewitness testimony is especially vulnerable to error when:
- the suspect's ethnicity differs from the witness's.
- leading questions are put to the witness.
- witnesses are exposed to misleading information.

Children's Testimony

Children can be suggestible when:
- interviewers use leading questions or suggestive techniques, or pressure the child to give particular answers.
- the child is affected by rumor and hearsay.

In Pursuit of Memory

↓

Measuring Memory

- In tests of **explicit memory**, or conscious recollection, **recognition** is usually better than **recall**.
- In tests of **implicit memory**, which is measured by indirect methods such as **priming** and the **relearning method**, past experiences may affect current thoughts or actions.

The Three-Box Model of Memory

↓

Sensory Register

Incoming information stops in the **sensory register**, which momentarily retains it in the form of sensory images.

Three Memory Systems

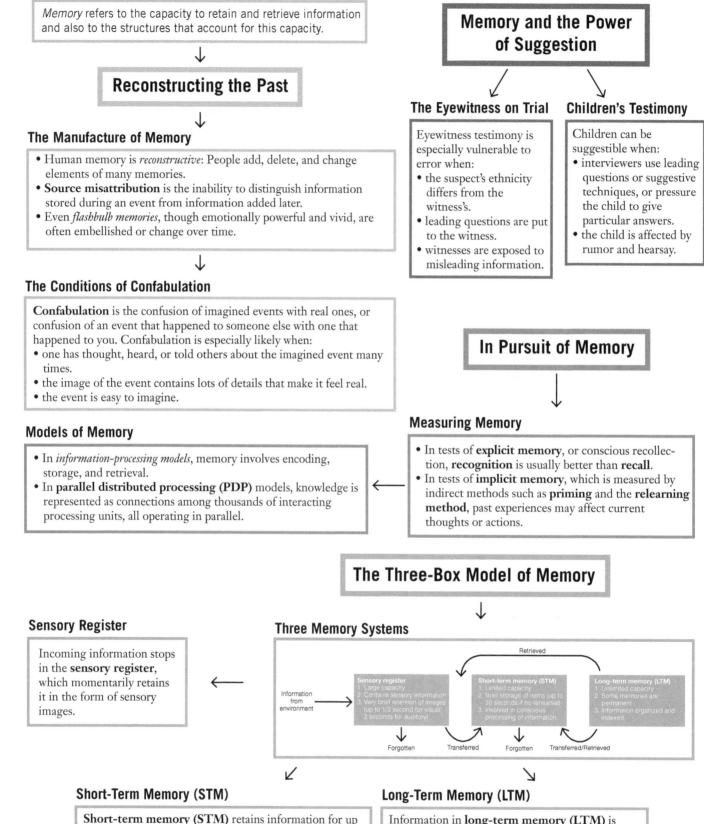

Short-Term Memory (STM)

Short-term memory (STM) retains information for up to 30 seconds, although estimates extend to a few minutes for certain tasks.
- **Chunking** extends the capacity of STM.
- Many models now envision STM as a part of a more general **working memory** system, which includes an "executive" that controls the retrieval of information from long-term memory and focuses attention on information needed for a task.

Long-Term Memory (LTM)

Information in **long-term memory (LTM)** is organized as a network of interrelated concepts and includes:
- **procedural memories**.
- **declarative memories**, which may be **semantic** or **episodic**.

The **serial-position effect** is the tendency to recall the first and last items on a list better than those in the middle.

How We Remember

- **Mnemonics** are strategies or tricks for improving memory.
- Rehearsal of information keeps it in STM longer and increases the chances of retention.
- **Elaborative rehearsal** is more likely to result in transfer to LTM than is **maintenance rehearsal**.
- **Deep processing** is usually more effective than **shallow processing**.
- *Retrieval practice* aids consolidation of memories.
- *Read-recite-review* and other effective study strategies encourage active learning and are more effective than passively reading the material.

Why We Forget

- **Decay theory** holds that a memory eventually disappears if it is not accessed; it applies best to sensory and short-term memory.
- Forgetting may occur when old information is replaced by new information.
- Forgetting may occur because of **proactive** and **retroactive interference** in storage or retrieval.
- **Cue-dependent forgetting** occurs because of inadequate *retrieval cues*. When your physical or mental state acts as a retrieval cue, **state-dependent memory** may result. Similarly, when your mood is consistent with the emotional nature of the material you are trying to remember, **mood-congruent memory** may result.

The Repression Controversy

- **Amnesia** typically occurs as a result of brain disease or head injury and is usually temporary.
- *Psychogenic amnesia* has psychological causes and involves a loss of personal identity.
- *Traumatic amnesia*, which allegedly involves the burying of specific traumatic events for long periods of time, is highly controversial, as is **repression**, the psychodynamic explanation of traumatic amnesia.
- Critics argue that many therapists, unaware of the power of suggestion and the dangers of confabulation, have encouraged false memories of victimization.

The Biology of Memory

Changes in Neurons and Synapses

- In short-term memory, neurons temporarily change in their ability to release neurotransmitters.
- In long-term memory, dendrites grow and branch out, certain synapses increase in number, and some synaptic pathways become more excitable. These neuronal changes are known as **long-term potentiation**. They require some time for completion, during which memories undergo **consolidation**.

Locating Memories

- The amygdala is involved in the formation, consolidation, and retrieval of fearful and other emotional memories.
- The frontal lobes are involved in STM and working memory.
- The hippocampus is critical to the formation and retrieval of long-term declarative memories.
- The cerebellum helps form and retain certain procedural memories.
- The ultimate destinations of declarative memories lie in parts of the cerebral cortex.

Hormones, Emotion, and Memory

- Hormones released by the adrenal glands can enhance memory.
- Extreme arousal, however, often impairs memory.

Autobiographical Memories

Childhood Amnesia

Childhood amnesia may be explained by:
- the immaturity of brain parts involved in memory.
- cognitive factors, such as lack of a self-concept and limited language skills necessary for forming cognitive schemas useful for later recall.
- social factors, such as a lack of mastery of social conventions for reporting events to others.

Memory and Narrative

- A person's *narrative* (life story) organizes remembered life events and gives them meaning.
- Adult memories can reveal as much about the present as they do about the past.

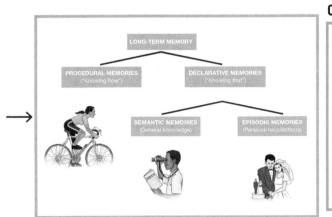

LONG-TERM MEMORY

PROCEDURAL MEMORIES ("Knowing how")

DECLARATIVE MEMORIES ("Knowing that")

SEMANTIC MEMORIES (General knowledge)

EPISODIC MEMORIES (Personal recollections)

LEARNING AND CONDITIONING

PSYCHOLOGY IN THE NEWS //////////////////////////////

High School Student Arrested after Science Experiment

BARTOW, FL, May 1, 2013. A Bartow High School student has been expelled after being arrested last week when a science experiment she performed on the school grounds produced a small explosion. Kiera Wilmont, 16, mixed some toilet bowl cleaner with aluminum foil in a small water bottle, a procedure she saw on YouTube. The bottle's top popped off and there was some smoke, but no one was injured and there was no property damage. Nonetheless, Kiera was handcuffed and taken into custody and charged with two felonies: possession

Across the U.S., children have been suspended or even arrested on felony charges for minor violations of "zero-tolerance" school policies. Zachary Christie, age 6, was briefly suspended for bringing this camping utensil to school.

or discharge of a weapon on school grounds and discharge of a destructive device.

Although the teenager is reportedly a good student who is interested in robotics and science and has never before been in trouble with the law, the school district issued a statement saying that it had an obligation to enforce its code of conduct.

In the aftermath of a horrific school shooting in Columbine, Colorado, in 1999, many schools across the United States instituted zero-tolerance or other inflexible discipline policies. These policies were aimed at reducing drug abuse and violence, but over the years, many school-based arrests have been made for relatively minor infractions, without taking into account the child's age, intent, or character. A 6-year-old who was excited about going on Cub Scout campouts was suspended for bringing a camping utensil with a small fork, knife, and spoon to school. An honor student was expelled for carrying a nail clipper. A third grader was expelled because her grandmother sent a birthday cake to school along with a knife to cut it. A seventh grader was charged with battery for throwing a Tootsie Pop at a friend. A kindergartener was suspended for using a finger as a fake "gun." Older students have been severely disciplined for possessing such "drugs" as cough drops or Midol (used for menstrual cramps).

In 2012, Florida apparently had the largest "school-to-prison pipeline" in the United States. Some 12,000 students were arrested that year, with more than two-thirds of the arrests being for offenses such as fistfights, dress-code violations, and talking back. The number of documented arrests was actually a drop from the 2005 high of 28,000.

Zero-tolerance policies initially gave authorities more leeway in applying them, but critics charged that they were being administered in a discriminatory manner; black children were more likely than white kids to be suspended or expelled for the same offenses, even when their ages and disciplinary histories were similar. As a result, many school districts removed discretion in the application of their policies. But that did not solve the problem. In March, the Justice Department filed a consent degree with a Mississippi school district and private plaintiffs to prevent and address discriminatory enforcement of discipline policies, after an investigation revealed that harsher punishments were being imposed on black students.

//////////

Are zero-tolerance policies justified? Should children who commit minor infractions be punished as severely as those who commit serious ones? If not, how should school administrators treat children who are truly disruptive or violent? Should schools expel them or are there alternatives? In the home, how should parents correct their children's misbehavior? Is "a good spanking" the best recourse for parents, or should there be zero tolerance for parents who use any kind of corporal punishment?

The debate over how to discipline children is an old one, and it is part of a larger issue: How can we change unwanted, self-defeating, or dangerous behavior? Many people want to fix their own bad habits, of course, and they are forever trying to improve or fix other people's behavior as well. We imprison criminals, spank children, and shout at spouses. On the positive side, we give children gold stars for good work, give parents bumper stickers that praise their children's successes, hand out bonuses to employees, and award trophies for top performance. Do any of these efforts get the results we hope for? Well, yes and no. Once you understand the laws of **learning**, you will realize that behavior, whether it's your own or other people's, can change for the better. And you will also understand why often it does not.

Research on learning has been heavily influenced by **behaviorism**, the school of psychology that accounts for behavior in terms of observable acts and events. Unlike the cognitive approach, a behavioral perspective emphasizes the influence of prior experience on current behavior, rather than thoughts or other aspects of the "mind." Behaviorists focus on *conditioning*, which involves relationships between environmental stimuli and behavior. They have shown that two types of conditioning, *classical conditioning* and *operant conditioning*, can explain a great deal of behavior both in animals and in people. But other approaches, including *social-cognitive learning theories*, hold that omitting mental processes from explanations of human learning is like omitting passion from descriptions of sex: You may explain the form, but you miss its essence. To social-cognitive theorists, learning includes not only changes in behavior but also changes in thoughts, expectations, and knowledge, which in turn influence behavior in a reciprocal, or two-way, process.

As you read about the principles of conditioning and learning in this chapter, ask yourself what they can teach us about the use of punishment to control undesirable behavior. What happens when punishment is used inappropriately? What is the best way to modify other people's behavior—and our own?

learning A relatively permanent change in behavior (or behavioral potential) as a result of experience.

behaviorism An approach to psychology that emphasizes the study of observable behavior and the role of the environment and prior experience as determinants of behavior.

You are about to learn...

- how classical conditioning explains why a dog might salivate when it sees a light bulb or hears a buzzer.

- four important features of classical conditioning.

- what is actually learned in classical conditioning.

Classical Conditioning

At the turn of the twentieth century, the great Russian physiologist Ivan Pavlov (1849–1936) was studying salivation in dogs as part of a research program on digestion. One of his procedures was to make a surgical opening in a dog's cheek and insert a tube that conducted saliva away from the animal's salivary gland so that the saliva could be measured. To stimulate the reflexive flow of saliva, Pavlov placed meat powder or other food in the dog's mouth (see Figure 9.1).

Pavlov was a truly dedicated scientific observer. Many years later, as he lay dying, he even dictated his sensations for posterity! And he instilled in his students and assistants the same passion for detail. During his salivation studies, one of the assistants noticed something that most people would have overlooked or dismissed as trivial. After a dog had been brought to the laboratory a few times, it would start to salivate *before* the food was placed in its mouth. The sight or smell of the food, the dish in which the food was kept, and even the sight of the person who delivered the food were enough to start the dog's

mouth watering. These new salivary responses clearly were not inborn, so they must have been acquired through experience.

At first, Pavlov treated the dog's drooling as just an annoying secretion. But he quickly realized that his assistant had stumbled onto an important phenomenon, one that Pavlov came to believe was the basis of most learning in human beings and other animals (Pavlov, 1927). He called that phenomenon a "conditional" reflex because it depended on environmental conditions. Later, an error in the translation of his writings transformed "conditional" into "conditioned," the word most commonly used today.

Pavlov soon dropped what he had been doing and turned to the study of conditioned reflexes, to which he devoted the last three decades of his life. Why were his dogs salivating to things other than food?

New Reflexes from Old   LO 9.1

Pavlov initially speculated about what his dogs might be thinking and feeling when they drooled before getting their food. Was the doggy equivalent of "Oh boy, this means chow time" going through their minds? He soon decided, however, that such speculation was pointless. Instead, he focused on analyzing the environment in which the conditioned reflex arose.

The original salivary reflex, according to Pavlov, consisted of an **unconditioned stimulus (US)**, food in the dog's mouth, and an **unconditioned response (UR)**, salivation. By an unconditioned

unconditioned stimulus (US) The classical-conditioning term for a stimulus that already elicits a certain response without additional learning.

unconditioned response (UR) The classical-conditioning term for a response elicited by an unconditioned stimulus.

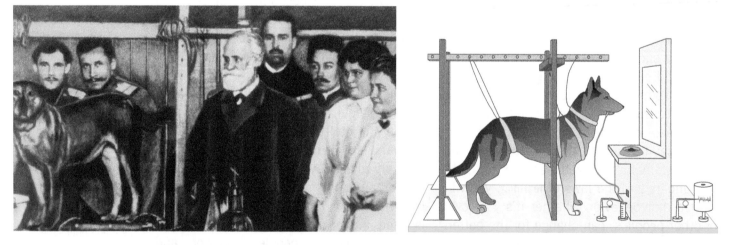

FIGURE 9.1 Pavlov's Method
The photo shows Ivan Pavlov (in the white beard), flanked by his students and a canine subject. The drawing depicts an apparatus similar to the one he used; saliva from a dog's cheek flowed down a tube and was measured by the movement of a needle on a revolving drum.

stimulus, Pavlov meant a thing or event that already produces a certain response without additional learning. By an unconditioned response, he meant the response that is produced:

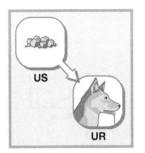

In Pavlov's lab, when some neutral stimulus such as the dish—a stimulus that did not typically cause the dog to salivate—was regularly paired with food, the dog learned to associate the dish and the food. As a result, the dish alone acquired the power to make the dog salivate:

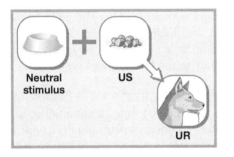

More generally, as a neutral stimulus and US become associated, the neutral stimulus becomes a **conditioned stimulus (CS)**. The CS then has the capacity to elicit a learned or **conditioned response (CR)** that is usually similar or related to the original, unlearned one. In Pavlov's laboratory, the sight of the food dish, which had not previously elicited salivation, became a CS for salivation:

The procedure by which a neutral stimulus becomes a conditioned stimulus eventually became known as **classical conditioning**, and is sometimes also called *Pavlovian* or *respondent* conditioning. Pavlov and his students went on to show that all sorts of things can become conditioned stimuli for salivation if they are paired with food: the ticking of a metronome, the musical tone of a bell, the vibrating sound of a buzzer, a touch on the leg, even a pinprick or an electric shock.

 Watch the **Video** The Basics 1: Classical Conditioning: An Involuntary Response at **MyPsychLab**

Principles of Classical Conditioning LO 9.2

Classical conditioning occurs in all species, from one-celled amoebas to *Homo sapiens*. In the laboratory, many responses besides salivation have been classically conditioned, including heartbeat, stomach secretions, blood pressure, alertness, hunger, and sexual arousal. The optimal interval between the presentation of the neutral stimulus and the presentation of the US is often quite short, sometimes less than a second. Let us look more closely at some of classical conditioning's other important features: extinction, higher-order conditioning, and stimulus generalization and discrimination.

Extinction. Conditioned responses can persist for months or years. But if a conditioned stimulus is repeatedly presented without the unconditioned stimulus, the conditioned response will weaken and may eventually disappear, a process known as **extinction** (see Figure 9.2 on the next page). Suppose that you train your dog Milo to salivate to the sound of a bell, but then you ring the bell every five minutes and do *not* follow it with food. Milo will salivate less and less to the bell and will soon stop salivating altogether; salivation will have been extinguished. Extinction, however, is not the same as unlearning or forgetting. If you come back the next day and ring the bell, Milo may salivate again for a few trials, although the response will probably be weaker. The reappearance of the response, called **spontaneous recovery**, explains why completely eliminating a conditioned response often requires more than one extinction session.

Simulate the **Experiment** Extinction and Spontaneous Recovery at **MyPsychLab**

Higher-Order Conditioning. Sometimes a neutral stimulus can become a CS by being paired with an already established CS, a procedure

conditioned stimulus (CS) The classical-conditioning term for an initially neutral stimulus that comes to elicit a conditioned response after being paired with an unconditioned stimulus.

conditioned response (CR) The classical-conditioning term for a response that is elicited by a conditioned stimulus; it occurs after the conditioned stimulus is paired with an unconditioned stimulus.

classical conditioning The process by which a previously neutral stimulus is paired with a stimulus that already elicits a certain response and, in turn, acquires the capacity to elicit a similar or related response. Also called *Pavlovian* or *respondent* conditioning.

extinction The weakening and eventual disappearance of a learned response; in classical conditioning, it occurs when the conditioned stimulus is no longer paired with the unconditioned stimulus.

spontaneous recovery The reappearance of a learned response after its apparent extinction.

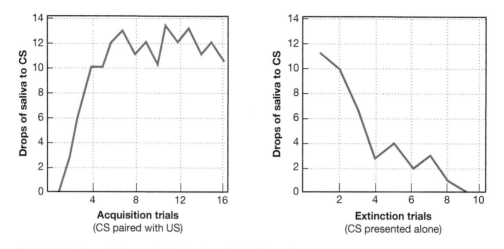

FIGURE 9.2 Acquisition and Extinction of a Salivary Response
A neutral stimulus that is consistently followed by an unconditioned stimulus for salivation will become a conditioned stimulus for salivation (left). But when this conditioned stimulus is then repeatedly presented without the unconditioned stimulus, the conditioned salivary response will weaken and eventually disappear (right); it has been extinguished.

higher-order conditioning In classical conditioning, a procedure in which a neutral stimulus becomes a conditioned stimulus through association with an already established conditioned stimulus.

stimulus generalization After conditioning, the tendency to respond to a stimulus that resembles one involved in the original conditioning; in classical conditioning, it occurs when a stimulus that resembles the CS elicits the CR.

known as **higher-order conditioning**. Say Milo has learned to salivate to the sight of his food dish. Now you flash a bright light before presenting the dish. With repeated pairings of the light and the dish, Milo may learn to salivate to the light. The procedure for higher-order conditioning is illustrated in Figure 9.3.

Higher-order conditioning may explain why some words trigger emotional responses in us—why they can inflame us to anger or evoke warm, sentimental feelings. When words are paired with objects or other words that already elicit some emotional response, they too may come to elicit that response (Staats & Staats, 1957). A child may learn a positive response to the word *birthday* because of its association with gifts and attention. Conversely, the child may learn a negative

response to ethnic or national labels if the labels are paired with words that the child has already learned are disagreeable, such as *dumb* or *dirty*. Higher-order conditioning, in other words, may contribute to the formation of prejudices.

Stimulus Generalization and Discrimination.
After a stimulus becomes a conditioned stimulus for some response, similar stimuli may produce a similar reaction, a phenomenon known as **stimulus generalization**. If you condition your patient pooch Milo to salivate to middle C on the piano, Milo may also salivate to D, which is one tone above C, even though you did not pair D with food. Stimulus generalization is described nicely by an old English proverb: "He who hath been bitten by a snake fears a rope."

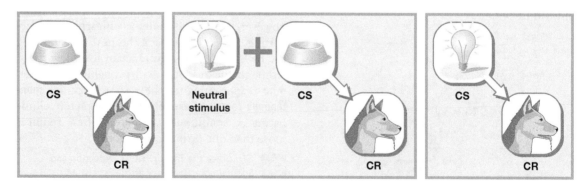

FIGURE 9.3 Higher-Order Conditioning
In this illustration of higher-order conditioning, the food dish is a previously conditioned stimulus for salivation (left). When the light, a neutral stimulus, is paired with the dish (center), the light also becomes a conditioned stimulus for salivation (right).

The mirror image of stimulus generalization is **stimulus discrimination**, in which *different* responses are made to stimuli that resemble the conditioned stimulus in some way. Suppose that you have conditioned Milo to salivate to middle C on the piano by repeatedly pairing the sound with food. Now you play middle C on a guitar, *without* following it by food (but you continue to follow C on the piano by food). Eventually, Milo will learn to salivate to a C on the piano and not to salivate to the same note on the guitar; that is, he will discriminate between the two sounds. If you keep at this long enough, you could train Milo to be a pretty discriminating drooler!

What Is Actually Learned in Classical Conditioning? LO 9.3

A critical feature of classical conditioning is that the animal or person learns to associate stimuli, rather than learning to associate a stimulus with a response. Milo will learn to salivate to the bell because he has learned to associate the bell with food, not (as is commonly thought) because he has learned to associate the bell with salivating. For classical conditioning to be most effective, the stimulus to be conditioned should *precede* the US rather than follow it or occur simultaneously with it. This makes sense, because in classical conditioning, the CS becomes a *signal* for the US.

Classical conditioning is in fact an evolutionary adaptation, one that enables the organism to anticipate and prepare for a biologically important event that is about to happen. In Pavlov's studies, for instance, a bell, buzzer, or other stimulus was a signal that meat was coming, and the dog's salivation was preparation for digesting it. Today, therefore, many psychologists contend that what an animal or person actually learns in classical conditioning is not merely an association between two paired stimuli that occur close together in time, but rather *information* conveyed by one stimulus about another: "If a tone sounds, food is likely to follow."

This view is supported by the research of Robert Rescorla (1988), who showed, in a series of imaginative studies, that the mere pairing of an unconditioned stimulus and a neutral stimulus is not enough to produce learning. To become a conditioned stimulus, the neutral stimulus must reliably signal, or *predict*, the US. If food occurs just as often *without* a preceding tone as with it, the tone is unlikely to become a CS for salivation, because the tone does not provide any information about the probability of getting food. Think of it this way: If every phone call you got brought bad news that made your heart race, your heart might soon start pounding every time the phone rang—a conditioned response. Ordinarily, though, upsetting calls occur randomly among a far greater number of routine ones. The ringtone may sometimes be associated with bad news, but it doesn't always signal disaster, so no conditioned heart-rate response occurs.

Rescorla concluded that "Pavlovian conditioning is not a stupid process by which the organism willy-nilly forms associations between any two stimuli that happen to co-occur. Rather, the organism is better seen as an information seeker using logical and perceptual relations among events, along with its own preconceptions, to form a sophisticated representation of its world." Not all learning theorists agree; traditional behaviorists would say that it is silly to talk about the preconceptions of a rat or about an earthworm's representation of the world—yet rats and earthworms are subject to the laws of classical conditioning. Even in human beings, classical conditioning can occur without any awareness of the link between the CS and the US. Yet for many psychologists, concepts such as "information seeking," "preconceptions," and "representations of the world" open the door to a role for cognition in classical conditioning.

stimulus discrimination The tendency to respond differently to two or more similar stimuli; in classical conditioning, it occurs when a stimulus similar to the CS fails to evoke the CR.

Get Involved! Conditioning an Eye-Blink Response

Try out your behavioral skills by conditioning an eye-blink response in a willing friend, using classical-conditioning procedures. You will need a drinking straw and something to make a ringing sound; a spoon tapped on a water glass works well. Tell your friend that you are going to use the straw to blow air in his or her eye, but do not say why. Immediately before each puff of air, make the ringing sound. Repeat this procedure ten times. Then make the ringing sound but *don't* puff. Your friend will probably blink anyway and may continue to do so for one or two more repetitions of the sound before the response extinguishes. Can you identify the US, the UR, the CS, and the CR in this exercise?

Recite & Review

 Study and **Review** at **MyPsychLab**

Review: When you hear the tone, say as much as you can remember about these concepts (ding!): unconditioned stimulus, conditioned stimulus, unconditioned response, conditioned response, classical conditioning, extinction, higher-order conditioning, stimulus generalization, and stimulus discrimination.

Review: Next, go back and read this section again.

Now take this *Quick Quiz:*

A. Name the unconditioned stimulus, unconditioned response, conditioned stimulus, and conditioned response in these two situations.

1. Five-year-old Samantha is watching a storm from her window. A huge bolt of lightning is followed by a tremendous thunderclap, and Samantha jumps at the noise. This happens several more times. There is a brief lull and then another lightning bolt. Samantha jumps in response to the bolt.

2. Gregory's mouth waters whenever he eats anything with lemon in it. One day, while reading an ad that shows a big glass of lemonade, Gregory finds that his mouth has started to water.

B. Extinction is not the same as _____. A conditioned response needs more than one session for it to be extinct; otherwise there is a chance for _____.

Answers:

A. 1. US = the thunderclap; UR = jumping elicited by the noise; CS = the sight of the lightning; CR = jumping elicited by the lightning 2. US = the taste of lemon; UR = salivation elicited by the taste of lemon; CS = the picture of a glass of lemonade; CR = salivation elicited by the picture B. forgetting; spontaneous recovery

---

You are about to learn . . .

- why advertisers often include pleasant music and gorgeous scenery in ads for their products.

- how classical conditioning might explain your irrational fear of heights or mice.

- how technology is helping researchers study the biological basis of conditioned fears.

- how you might be conditioned to like certain tastes and odors and be turned off by others.

- why sitting in a doctor's office can make you feel sick and placebos can make you feel better.

Classical Conditioning in Real Life

If a dog can learn to salivate to the ringing of a bell, so can you. In fact, you probably have learned to salivate to the sound of a lunch bell, the phrase *hot fudge sundae,* and "mouth-watering" pictures of food. But classical conditioning affects us every day in many other ways.

One of the first psychologists to recognize the real-life implications of Pavlovian theory was John B. Watson, who founded American behaviorism and enthusiastically promoted Pavlov's ideas. Watson believed that the whole rich array of human emotion and behavior could be accounted for by conditioning principles. He even went so far as to claim that we learn to love another person when that person is paired with stroking and cuddling. Most people think Watson was wrong about love, which is a lot more complicated than he thought (see Chapter 14). But he was right about the power of classical conditioning to affect our emotions, preferences, and tastes.

Learning to Like LO 9.4

Classical conditioning plays a big role in our emotional responses to objects, people, symbols, events, and places. It can explain why sentimental feelings sweep over us when we see a school mascot, a national flag, or the logo of the Olympics. These objects have been associated in the past with positive feelings.

Many advertising techniques take advantage of classical conditioning's role in emotional responses. When you see ads, notice how many of them pair a product with music the advertiser thinks you'll like, with good-looking people, with idyllic scenery, or with celebrities you admire or think are funny. In classical-conditioning terms, the music, attractive person, scenery, or celebrity is an unconditioned stimulus for internal responses associated with pleasure, and the advertiser hopes that the product in the ad will become a conditioned stimulus, evoking similar responses in you.

Learning to Fear

Positive emotions are not the only ones that can be classically conditioned; so can dislikes and fears. A person can learn to fear just about anything if it is paired with something that elicits pain, surprise, or embarrassment. Human beings, however, are biologically primed or "prepared" to acquire some kinds of fears more readily than others. It is far easier to establish a conditioned fear of spiders, snakes, and heights than of butterflies, flowers, and toasters. The former can be dangerous to your health, so in the process of evolution, human beings acquired a tendency to learn quickly to be wary of them and to retain this fear (LoBue & DeLoache, 2008; Öhman & Mineka, 2001). Evolution may also have instilled in humans a readiness to learn to fear unfamiliar members of groups other than their own, a tendency that could contribute to the emotional underpinnings of prejudice (Navarrete et al., 2009; Olsson et al., 2005).

Why do most people fear snakes, and why do some even develop a snake phobia?

The Birth of a Phobia. When fear of an object or situation becomes irrational and interferes with normal activities, it qualifies as a *phobia* (see Chapter 11). To demonstrate how a phobia might be learned, John Watson and Rosalie Rayner (1920/2000) deliberately established a rat phobia in an 11-month-old boy named Albert. Their goal was to demonstrate how an inborn reaction of fear could transfer to a wide range of stimuli; today we call this stimulus generalization. They also wanted to demonstrate that adult emotional responses, such as specific fears, could originate in early childhood. The research procedures that Watson and Rayner used had some flaws, and for ethical reasons, no psychologist today would attempt to do such a thing to a child. Nevertheless, the study's main conclusion, that fears can be conditioned, is still well accepted.

"Little Albert" was a placid child who rarely cried. (Watson and Rayner deliberately chose such a child because they thought their demonstration would do him relatively little harm.) When Watson and Rayner gave Albert a live, furry rat to play with, he showed no fear; in fact, he was delighted. The same was true when they showed him a variety of other objects, including a rabbit and some cotton wool. However, like most children, Albert was innately afraid of loud noises. When the researchers made a loud noise behind his head by striking a steel bar with a hammer, he would jump and fall sideways onto the mattress where he was sitting. The noise made by the hammer was an unconditioned stimulus for the unconditioned response of fear.

Having established that Albert liked rats, Watson and Rayner set about teaching him to fear them. Again they offered him a rat, but this time, as he reached for it, one of the researchers struck the steel bar. Startled, Albert fell onto the mattress. A week later, the researchers repeated this procedure several times. Albert began to whimper and tremble. Finally, they held out the rat to him without making the noise. Albert fell over, cried, and crawled away so quickly that he almost reached the edge of the table he was sitting on before an adult caught him; the rat had become a conditioned stimulus for fear (see Figure 9.4). Tests done a few days later showed that Albert's fear had generalized to other hairy or furry objects, including a white rabbit, cotton wool, a Santa Claus mask, and even John Watson's hair.

👁 **Watch** the **Video** Classic Footage of Little Albert at **MyPsychLab**

Unfortunately, Watson and Rayner lost access to Little Albert, so we do not know how long the child's fears lasted. Further, because the study

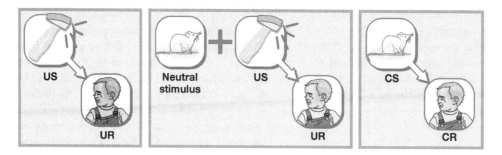

FIGURE 9.4 The Creation of a Fear

In the Little Albert study, noise from a hammer striking a steel bar was an unconditioned stimulus for fear (left). When a white rat, a neutral stimulus, was paired with the noise (center), the rat then became a conditioned stimulus for fear (right).

counterconditioning
In classical conditioning, the process of pairing a conditioned stimulus with a stimulus that elicits a response that is incompatible with an unwanted conditioned response.

ended early, Watson and Rayner had no opportunity to reverse the conditioning. However, Watson and Mary Cover Jones did reverse another child's conditioned fear—one that was, as Watson put it, "home-grown" rather than psychologist-induced (Jones, 1924). A 3-year-old named Peter was deathly afraid of rabbits. To reverse Peter's fear, Watson and Jones used a method called **counterconditioning**, in which a conditioned stimulus is paired with some other stimulus that elicits a response incompatible with the unwanted response (see Figure 9.5). In this case, a rabbit (the CS) was paired with a snack of milk and crackers, and the snack produced pleasant feelings that were incompatible with the CR of fear.

At first, the researchers kept the rabbit some distance from Peter, so that his fear would remain at a low level. Otherwise, Peter might have learned to fear milk and crackers! Then gradually, over several days, they brought the rabbit closer and closer. Eventually Peter learned to like rabbits and was even able to sit with the rabbit in his lap, playing with it with one hand while he ate with the other. A variation of this procedure, called *systematic desensitization*, was later devised for treating phobias in adults (see Chapter 12).

Biology and Conditioned Fears. Back when John Watson was using counterconditioning to help young Peter overcome his fear of rabbits, techniques for understanding the biological basis of classical conditioning were limited. But today, with technology and a better understanding of the brain, scientists can explore methods for helping people overcome debilitating fears in ways that Watson could scarcely have imagined.

The amygdala plays a central role in the conditioning of fear, in part because of a receptor for the neurotransmitter glutamate. Giving rats a drug that blocks this receptor prevents extinction of a conditioned fear, whereas giving a drug that enhances the receptor's activity speeds up extinction (Walker et al., 2002). Inspired by these results, researchers set out to discover whether the receptor-enhancing drug (which is safe in humans) could help people with a conditioned phobic fear of heights (Davis et al., 2005). Using a double-blind procedure, they gave the drug to 15 people with the phobia and a placebo to 15 others. All participants then underwent two therapy sessions in which they donned virtual reality goggles and "rode" a glass elevator to progressively higher floors in a virtual hotel—an incredibly scary thing

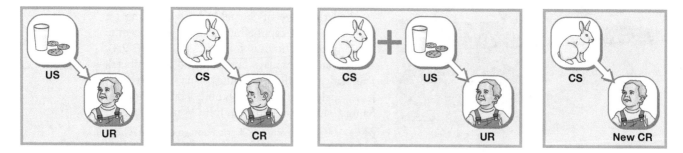

FIGURE 9.5 The Counterconditioning of a Fear

Three-year-old Peter had acquired a conditioned fear of rabbits. To countercondition this fear, the researchers paired a rabbit (the CS) with a snack of milk and crackers (a US), which produced feelings of pleasure that were incompatible with the conditioned response of fear. Eventually, Peter felt as comfortable with the rabbit as with the crackers.

to do if you're terrified of heights. They could also "walk" out on a bridge and look down on a fountain in the hotel lobby. During each session, and again at one-week and three-month follow-up sessions, the participants rated their discomfort at each "floor." Combining the therapy with the drug reduced symptoms far more than combining it with the placebo. Further, in their everyday lives, people who got the drug were less likely than the controls to avoid heights.

Such research helps us to understand the biological mechanisms that underlie our fears, and the principles of behaviorism that may help us control and even overcome them.

Accounting for Taste LO 9.5

Classical conditioning can also explain learned reactions to many foods and odors. In the laboratory, behavioral scientists have taught animals to dislike foods or odors by pairing them with drugs that cause nausea or other unpleasant symptoms. One research team trained slugs to associate the smell of carrots, which slugs normally like, with a bitter-tasting chemical they detest. Soon the slugs were avoiding the smell of carrots. The researchers then demonstrated higher-order conditioning by pairing the smell of carrots with the smell of potato. Sure enough, the slugs began to avoid the smell of potato as well (Sahley, Rudy, & Gelperin, 1981).

Many people have learned to dislike a food after eating it and then falling ill, even when the two events were unrelated. The food, previously a neutral stimulus, becomes a conditioned stimulus for nausea or other symptoms produced by the illness. Psychologist Martin Seligman once told how he himself was conditioned to hate béarnaise sauce. One night, shortly after he and his wife ate a delicious filet mignon with béarnaise sauce, he came down with the flu. Naturally, he felt wretched. His misery had nothing to do with the béarnaise sauce, of course, yet the next time he tried it, he found to his annoyance that he disliked the taste (Seligman & Hager, 1972).

Notice that, unlike conditioning in the laboratory, Seligman's aversion to the sauce occurred after only one pairing of the sauce with illness and with a long delay between the conditioned and unconditioned stimuli. Moreover, Seligman's wife did not become a CS for nausea, and neither did his dinner plate or the waiter, even though they also had been paired with illness. Why? In earlier work with rats, John Garcia and Robert Koelling (1966) had provided the answer: There is a greater biological readiness to associate sickness with taste than with sights or sounds. Like the tendency to acquire certain fears, this biological tendency probably evolved because it enhanced survival. Eating bad food, after all, is more likely to be followed by illness than are particular sights or sounds.

Explore the Concept Taste Aversion at MyPsychLab

Psychologists have taken advantage of this phenomenon to develop humane ways of discouraging predators from preying on livestock, using conditioned taste aversions instead of traps and poisons. In one classic study, researchers laced sheep meat with a nausea-inducing chemical. After eating it just one or two times, coyotes and wolves still ran up to lambs, but instead of attacking, they retreated, hid, and threw up. They had developed a conditioned aversion to sheep (Dingfelder, 2010; Gustavson et al., 1974). Similar techniques have been used to control other predators—for example to deter raccoons from killing chickens, and ravens and crows from eating crane eggs (Garcia & Gustavson, 1997).

Reacting to Medical Treatments

Because of classical conditioning, some medical treatments can create unexpected misery, when unpleasant reactions to a treatment generalize to a range of other stimuli. This is a particular problem for cancer patients. The nausea and vomiting resulting from chemotherapy often generalize to the place where the therapy takes place, the waiting room, the sound of a nurse's voice, or the smell of rubbing alcohol. The drug treatment is an unconditioned stimulus for nausea and vomiting, and through association, the other previously neutral stimuli become conditioned stimuli for these responses. Even *mental images* of the sights and smells of the clinic can become conditioned stimuli for nausea (Dadds et al., 1997; Redd et al., 1993).

Whether we say "yuck" or "yum" to a food may depend on a past experience involving classical conditioning.

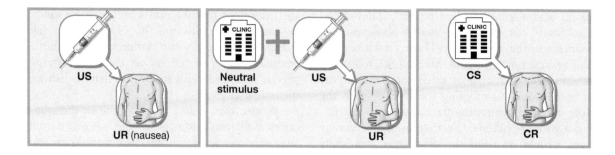

Some cancer patients also acquire a classically conditioned anxiety response to anything associated with their chemotherapy (Jacobsen et al., 1995). Conversely, patients may have *reduced* pain and anxiety when they receive *placebos*, pills and injections that have no active ingredients or treatments that have no direct physical effect on the problem. Placebos can be amazingly powerful, especially when they take the form of an injection, a large pill, or a pill with a brand name (Benedetti & Levi-Montalcini, 2001). Placebos can actually act on the same neural pathways in the brain that real medicines do (Price, Finniss, & Benedetti, 2008; see also Chapter 6).

Why do placebos work? Cognitive psychologists emphasize the role of expectations, at least in humans: Expectations of getting better may reduce anxiety, and that reduction may have a positive effect on the immune system. Such expectations may also cause patients to act in ways that produce the outcome they hope for (Michael, Garry, & Kirsch, 2012). But behaviorists emphasize conditioning: A doctor's white coat, the doctor's office, and pills or injections all become conditioned stimuli for relief from symptoms because these stimuli have been associated in the past with *real* drugs (Ader, 2000). The real drugs are the unconditioned stimuli, and the relief they bring is the unconditioned response. Placebos acquire the ability to elicit similar reactions, thereby becoming conditioned stimuli.

The expectancy explanation of placebo effects and the classical-conditioning explanation are not mutually exclusive (Kirsch, 2004; Stewart-Williams & Podd, 2004). As we saw previously, many researchers now accept the view that classical conditioning itself involves the expectation that the CS will be followed by the US. Thus, at least some classically conditioned placebo effects may involve the patient's expectations. In fact, the patient's previous conditioning history may be what created those expectations to begin with.

Recite & Review

✔ **Study** and **Review** at **MyPsychLab**

Recite: Say aloud everything you know about the classical conditionig of positive emotions, phobias, and tastes; counterconditioning; conditioned reactions to medical treatments; and behavioral explanations of placebo effects.

Review: Next, read this section again and notice anything that you didn't catch the first time.

Now take this *Quick Quiz:*

A. See whether you can supply the correct term to describe the outcome in each of these situations.

1. After Jeff learns to fear spiders, he also responds with fear to ants, beetles, and other crawling bugs.

2. Little Erin is afraid of the bath, so her father puts just a little water in the tub and gives her a lollipop to suck on while she is being washed. Soon Erin loses her fear of the bath.

3. A factory worker's mouth waters whenever a noontime bell signals the beginning of his lunch break. One day, the bell goes haywire and rings every half hour. By the end of the day, the worker has stopped salivating to the bell.

B. A boy who gets weekly allergy shots starts to feel anxious as soon as he enters the doctor's waiting room. What is the behavioral explanation?

Answers:

A. 1. stimulus generalization 2. counterconditioning 3. extinction B. The sight and smells of the waiting room have become conditioned stimuli for the anxiety and discomfort provoked by the shots.

- how the consequences of your actions affect your future behavior.
- what praising a child and quitting your nagging have in common.

Operant Conditioning

At the end of the nineteenth century, in the first known scientific study of anger, G. Stanley Hall (1899) asked people to describe angry episodes they had experienced or observed. One person told of a 3-year-old girl who broke out in seemingly uncontrollable sobs when she was kept home from a ride. In the middle of her outburst, the child suddenly stopped and asked her nanny in a perfectly calm voice if her father was in. Told no, and realizing that he was not around to put a stop to her tantrum, she immediately resumed her sobbing.

Children, of course, cry for many valid reasons—pain, discomfort, fear, illness, fatigue—and these cries deserve an adult's sympathy and attention. The child in Hall's study, however, was crying because she had learned from prior experience that an outburst of sobbing would pay off by bringing her attention and possibly the ride she wanted. Her tantrum illustrates one of the most basic laws of learning: *Behavior becomes more likely or less likely depending on its consequences.*

This principle is at the heart of **operant conditioning** (also called *instrumental conditioning*), the second type of conditioning studied by behaviorists. In classical conditioning, it does not matter whether an animal's or person's behavior has consequences. In Pavlov's procedure, the dog learned an association between two events that were not under its control (e.g., a tone and the delivery of food), and the animal got food whether or not it salivated. But in operant conditioning, the organism's response (such as the little girl's sobbing) *operates* or produces effects on the environment. These effects, in turn, influence whether the response will occur again.

Thus, whereas the central feature of classical conditioning is an association between stimuli (the neutral stimulus and the unconditioned stimulus), in operant conditioning the central feature is an association between a stimulus (i.e., the consequence, such as attention from others) and a response (such as increased crying). Classical and operant conditioning also tend to differ in the types of responses they involve. In

classical conditioning, the response is usually reflexive, an automatic reaction to something happening in the environment, such as the sight of food or the sound of a bell. Generally, responses in operant conditioning are complex and are not reflexive—for instance, riding a bicycle, writing a letter, climbing a mountain,...or throwing a tantrum.

The Birth of Radical Behaviorism LO 9.6 , LO 9.7

Operant conditioning has been studied since the start of the twentieth century, although it was not called that until later. Edward Thorndike (1898), then a young graduate student, set the stage by observing cats as they tried to escape from a "puzzle box" to reach a scrap of fish located just outside the box. At first, the cat would scratch, bite, or swat at parts of the box in an unorganized way. Then, after a few minutes, it would chance on the successful response (loosening a bolt, pulling a string, or hitting a button) and rush out to get the reward. Placed in the box again, the cat now took a little less time to escape, and after several trials, the animal immediately made the correct response. According to Thorndike, this response had been "stamped in" by the satisfying result of getting the food. In contrast, annoying or unsatisfying results "stamped out" behavior. Behavior, said Thorndike, is controlled by its consequences.

This general principle was elaborated and extended to more complex forms of behavior by

operant conditioning
The process by which a response becomes more likely to occur or less so, depending on its consequences.

"YOU GOTTA TRY DIFFERENT THINGS! SOMETIMES A TEMPER TANTRUM WORKS BEST AN' SOMETIMES SULKING AN' SOMETIMES NOT EATING!"

Norman Jung/www.CartoonStock.com

B. F. (Burrhus Frederic) Skinner (1904–1990). Skinner called his approach "radical behaviorism" to distinguish it from the behaviorism of John Watson, who emphasized classical conditioning. Skinner argued that to understand behavior we should focus on the external causes of an action and the action's consequences. He avoided terms that Thorndike used, such as "satisfying" and "annoying," which reflect assumptions about what an organism feels and wants. To explain behavior, he said, we should look outside the individual, not inside.

The Consequences of Behavior
LO 9.8, LO 9.9

In Skinner's analysis, which has inspired an immense body of research, a response ("operant") can be influenced by two types of consequences:

1 **Reinforcement strengthens the response or makes it more likely to recur.** When your dog begs for food at the table, and you give her the lamb chop off your plate, her begging is likely to increase:

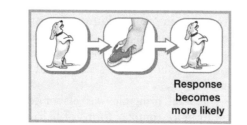

reinforcement The process by which a stimulus or event strengthens or increases the probability of the response that it follows.

punishment The process by which a stimulus or event weakens or reduces the probability of the response that it follows.

primary reinforcer A stimulus that is inherently reinforcing, typically satisfying a biological need; an example is food.

primary punisher A stimulus that is inherently punishing; an example is electric shock.

secondary reinforcer A stimulus that has acquired reinforcing properties through association with other reinforcers.

secondary punisher A stimulus that has acquired punishing properties through association with other punishers.

Reinforcers are roughly equivalent to rewards, and many psychologists use *reward* and *reinforcer* as approximate synonyms. However, strict behaviorists avoid the word *reward* because it implies that something has been earned that results in happiness or satisfaction. To a behaviorist, a stimulus is a reinforcer if it strengthens the preceding behavior, whether or not the organism experiences pleasure or a positive emotion. Conversely, no matter how pleasurable a reward is, it is not a reinforcer if it does not increase the likelihood of a response. It's great to get a paycheck, but if you get paid regardless of the effort you put into your work, the money will not reinforce "hard-work behavior."

2 **Punishment weakens the response or makes it less likely to recur.** Any aversive (unpleasant) stimulus or event may be a *punisher*. If your dog begs for a lamb chop off your plate, and you lightly swat her nose and shout "No," her

begging is likely to decrease—as long as you don't feel guilty and then give her the lamb chop anyway:

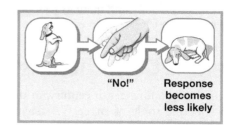

Parents, employers, and governments resort to reinforcers and punishers all the time—to get kids to behave well, employees to work hard, and taxpayers to pay up—but they do not always use them effectively. One mistake they make is waiting too long to deliver the reinforcer or punisher. In general, the sooner a consequence follows a response, the greater its effect; you are likely to respond more reliably when you do not have to wait ages for a grade, a smile, or a compliment. When other responses occur during a delay, it becomes more difficult to learn the connection between the desired or undesired response and the consequence.

Primary and Secondary Reinforcers and Punishers. Food, water, light stroking of the skin, and a comfortable air temperature are naturally reinforcing because they satisfy biological needs. They are therefore known as **primary reinforcers**. Similarly, pain and extreme heat or cold are inherently punishing and are therefore known as **primary punishers**. Primary reinforcers and punishers can be powerful, but they have some drawbacks, both in real life and in research. For one thing, a primary reinforcer may be ineffective if an animal or person is not in a deprived state; a glass of water is not much of a reward if you just drank three glasses. Also, for obvious ethical reasons, psychologists cannot go around using primary punishers (say, by punching their research participants) or taking away primary reinforcers (say, by starving their participants).

Fortunately, behavior can be controlled just as effectively by **secondary reinforcers** and **secondary punishers**, which are learned. Money, praise, applause, good grades, awards, and gold stars are common secondary reinforcers. Criticism, demerits, scolding, fines, and bad grades are common secondary punishers. Most behaviorists believe that secondary reinforcers and punishers acquire their ability to influence behavior by being paired with primary reinforcers and punishers. (If that reminds you of classical conditioning, reinforce your excellent thinking with a pat on the head! Indeed, secondary reinforcers and punishers are often called *conditioned* reinforcers and punishers.) As a secondary reinforcer, money has considerable power over most people's behavior because it can be exchanged for primary reinforcers such as food and shelter. It is also associated with other secondary reinforcers, such as praise and respect.

Positive and Negative Reinforcers and Punishers. In our example of the begging dog, something pleasant (getting the lamb chop) followed the dog's begging response, so the response increased. Similarly, if you get a good grade after studying, your efforts to study are likely to continue or increase. This kind of process, in which a pleasant consequence makes a response more likely, is known as **positive reinforcement**. But there is another type of reinforcement, **negative reinforcement**, which involves the *removal* of something *unpleasant*. Negative reinforcement occurs when you *escape* from something aversive or *avoid* it by preventing it from ever occurring. If someone nags you to study but stops nagging when you comply, your studying is likely to increase because you will then avoid the nagging:

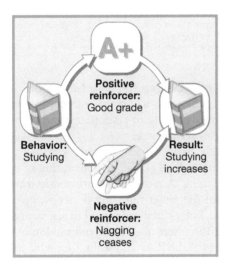

Likewise, negative reinforcement occurs when taking a pill eliminates your pain or when you take a certain route across campus to avoid a rude person.

The positive–negative distinction can also be applied to punishment: Something unpleasant may occur following some behavior (*positive punishment*), or something *pleasant* may be *removed* (*negative punishment*). For example, if your friends tease you for being an egghead (positive punishment) or if studying makes you lose time with your friends (negative punishment), you may stop studying:

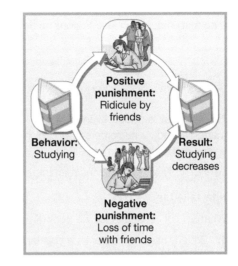

The distinction between positive and negative reinforcement and punishment has been a source of confusion for generations of students, turning many strong minds to mush. You will master these terms more quickly if you understand that "positive" and "negative" have nothing to do with "good" or "bad." They refer to whether something is given or taken away. In the case of reinforcement, think of a positive reinforcer as something that is added or obtained (imagine a plus sign) and a negative reinforcer as avoidance of, or escape from, something unpleasant (imagine a minus sign). *In either case, a response becomes more likely.* Do you recall what happened when Little Albert learned to fear rats through a process of classical conditioning? After he acquired this fear, crawling away was negatively reinforced by escape from the now-fearsome rodent. The negative reinforcement that results from escaping or avoiding something unpleasant explains why so many fears are long-lasting. When you avoid a feared object or situation, you also cut off all opportunities to extinguish your fear.

Understandably, people often confuse negative reinforcement with positive punishment, because both involve an unpleasant stimulus. With punishment, you are subjected to the unpleasant stimulus; with negative reinforcement, you escape from it or avoid it. To keep these terms straight, remember that punishment, whether positive or negative, *decreases* the likelihood of a response; and reinforcement, whether positive or negative, *increases* it. In real life, punishment and negative reinforcement often go hand in hand. If you use a chain collar to teach your dog to heel, a brief

positive reinforcement
A reinforcement procedure in which a response is followed by the presentation of, or increase in intensity of, a reinforcing stimulus; as a result, the response becomes stronger or more likely to occur.

negative reinforcement A reinforcement procedure in which a response is followed by the removal, delay, or decrease in intensity of an unpleasant stimulus; as a result, the response becomes stronger or more likely to occur.

tug on the collar punishes the act of walking; release of the collar negatively reinforces the act of standing by your side.

You can positively reinforce your studying of this material by taking a short break. As you master the material, a decrease in your anxiety will negatively reinforce studying. But we hope you won't punish your efforts by telling yourself "I'll never get it" or "It's too hard"!

 Watch the **Video** The Basics 2: Operant Conditioning: Learning from Consequences at **MyPsychLab**

Recite & Review

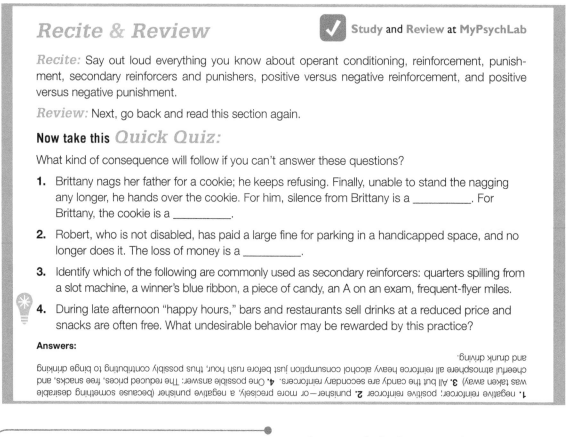

✓ **Study** and **Review** at **MyPsychLab**

Recite: Say out loud everything you know about operant conditioning, reinforcement, punishment, secondary reinforcers and punishers, positive versus negative reinforcement, and positive versus negative punishment.

Review: Next, go back and read this section again.

Now take this *Quick Quiz:*

What kind of consequence will follow if you can't answer these questions?

1. Brittany nags her father for a cookie; he keeps refusing. Finally, unable to stand the nagging any longer, he hands over the cookie. For him, silence from Brittany is a _____. For Brittany, the cookie is a _____.

2. Robert, who is not disabled, has paid a large fine for parking in a handicapped space, and no longer does it. The loss of money is a _____.

3. Identify which of the following are commonly used as secondary reinforcers: quarters spilling from a slot machine, a winner's blue ribbon, a piece of candy, an A on an exam, frequent-flyer miles.

4. During late afternoon "happy hours," bars and restaurants sell drinks at a reduced price and snacks are often free. What undesirable behavior may be rewarded by this practice?

Answers:

1. negative reinforcer; positive reinforcer 2. punisher—or more precisely, a negative punisher (because something desirable was taken away) 3. All but the candy are secondary reinforcers. 4. One possible answer: The reduced prices, free snacks, and cheerful atmosphere all reinforce heavy alcohol consumption just before rush hour, thus possibly contributing to binge drinking and drunk driving.

You are about to learn . . .

- some important features of operant conditioning.
- why it's not always a good idea to reinforce a response every time it occurs.
- how operant principles help explain superstitious behavior.
- what it means to "shape" behavior.
- some biological limits on operant conditioning.

Principles of Operant Conditioning LO 9.10

Thousands of operant conditioning studies have been done, many using animals. A favorite experimental tool is the *Skinner box,* a chamber equipped with a device that delivers a reinforcer, usually food, when an animal makes a desired response, or a punisher, such as a brief shock, when the animal makes an undesired response (see Figure 9.6). In modern versions, a computer records responses and charts the rate of responding and cumulative responses across time.

Early in his career, Skinner (1938) used the Skinner box for a classic demonstration of operant conditioning. A rat that had previously learned to eat from the pellet-releasing device was placed in the box. The animal proceeded to scurry about the box, sniffing here and there, and randomly touching parts of the floor and walls. Quite by accident, it happened to press a lever mounted on one wall, and immediately a pellet of tasty rat food fell into the food dish. The rat continued its movements and again happened to press the bar, causing another pellet to fall into the dish. With additional repetitions of bar pressing followed by food, the animal began to behave less randomly and to press the bar more consistently. Eventually, Skinner had the rat pressing the bar as fast as it could.

 Watch the **Video** Classic Footage of B. F. Skinner and the Skinner Box at **MyPsychLab**

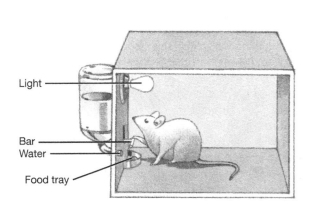

FIGURE 9.6 The Skinner Box
When a rat in a Skinner box presses a bar, a food pellet or drop of water is automatically released. The photo shows Skinner training one of his subjects.

Extinction. In operant conditioning, as in classical conditioning, **extinction** is a procedure that causes a previously learned response to stop. In operant conditioning, however, extinction takes place when the reinforcer that maintained the response is withheld or is no longer available. At first, there may be a spurt of responding, but then the responses gradually taper off and eventually cease. Suppose you put a coin in a vending machine and get nothing back. You may throw in another coin, or perhaps even two, but then you will probably stop trying. The next day, you may put in yet another coin, an example of *spontaneous recovery*. Eventually, however, you will give up on that machine. Your response will have been extinguished.

Stimulus Generalization and Discrimination. In operant conditioning, as in classical, **stimulus generalization** may occur. That is, responses to a stimulus may generalize to other stimuli that were not present during the original learning situation but that resemble the original stimulus in some way. For example, a pigeon that has been trained to peck at a picture of a circle may also peck at a slightly oval figure. But if you wanted to train the bird to discriminate between the two shapes, you would present both the circle and the oval, giving reinforcers whenever the bird pecked at the circle and withholding reinforcers when it pecked at the oval. Eventually, **stimulus discrimination** would occur. Pigeons, in fact, have learned to make some extraordinary discriminations. They have learned to discriminate between two paintings by different artists, such as Vincent Van Gogh and Marc Chagall (Watanabe, 2001). And then, when presented with a new pair of paintings by those same two artists, they have been able to tell the difference between them!

Sometimes an animal or person learns to respond to a stimulus only when some other stimulus, called a **discriminative stimulus**, is present. The discriminative stimulus signals whether a response, if made, will pay off. In a Skinner box containing a pigeon, a light may serve as a discriminative stimulus for pecking at a circle. When the light is on, pecking brings a reward; when it is off, pecking is futile. Human behavior is controlled by many discriminative stimuli, both verbal ("Store hours are 9 to 5") and nonverbal (traffic lights, doorbells, the ring of your cell phone, other people's facial expressions). Learning to respond correctly when such stimuli are present allows us to get through the day efficiently and to get along with others.

Learning on Schedule. LO 9.11 When a response is first acquired, learning is usually most rapid if the response is reinforced each time it occurs; this procedure is called **continuous reinforcement**. However, once a response has become reliable, it will be more resistant to extinction if it is rewarded on an **intermittent (partial) schedule of reinforcement**, which involves reinforcing only some responses, not all of them. Skinner (1956) happened on this fact when he ran short of food pellets for his rats and was forced to deliver reinforcers less often. (Not all scientific discoveries are planned.) On intermittent schedules, a reinforcer is delivered only after a certain number of responses occur or after a certain amount of time has passed since a response was last reinforced; these patterns affect the rate, form, and timing of behavior. (The details are beyond the scope of this book.)

extinction The weakening and eventual disappearance of a learned response; in operant conditioning, it occurs when a response is no longer followed by a reinforcer.

stimulus generalization In operant conditioning, the tendency for a response that has been reinforced (or punished) in the presence of one stimulus to occur (or be suppressed) in the presence of similar stimuli.

stimulus discrimination In operant conditioning, the tendency of a response to occur in the presence of one stimulus but not in the presence of similar stimuli that differ from it on some dimension.

discriminative stimulus A stimulus that signals when a particular response is likely to be followed by a certain type of consequence.

continuous reinforcement A reinforcement schedule in which a particular response is always reinforced.

intermittent (partial) schedule of reinforcement A reinforcement schedule in which a particular response is sometimes but not always reinforced.

shaping An operant-conditioning procedure in which successive approximations of a desired response are reinforced.

successive approximations In the operant-conditioning procedure of shaping, behaviors that are ordered in terms of increasing similarity or closeness to the desired response.

Intermittent reinforcement helps explain why people often get attached to "lucky" hats, charms, and rituals. A batter pulls his earlobe, gets a home run, and from then on always pulls his earlobe before each pitch. A student takes an exam with a purple pen and gets an A, and from then on will not take an exam without a purple pen. Such rituals persist because sometimes they are followed, purely coincidentally, by a reinforcer—a home run, a good grade—and so they become resistant to extinction.

> ✳ **THINKING CRITICALLY**
>
> About Superstitions

Skinner (1948/1976) once demonstrated this phenomenon by creating eight "superstitious" pigeons in his laboratory. He rigged the pigeons' cages so that food was delivered every 15 seconds, even if the birds didn't lift a feather. Pigeons are often in motion, so when the food came, each animal was likely to be doing something. That something was then reinforced by delivery of the food. The behavior, of course, was reinforced entirely by chance, but it still became more likely to occur and thus to be reinforced again. Within a short time, six of the pigeons were practicing some sort of consistent ritual: turning in counterclockwise circles, bobbing their heads up and down, or swinging their heads to and fro. None of these activities had the least effect on the delivery of the reinforcer; the birds were behaving "superstitiously," as if they thought their movements were responsible for bringing the food.

Now listen up, because here comes one of the most useful things to know about operant conditioning: If you want a response to persist after it has been learned, you should reinforce it *intermittently*, not continuously. If you are giving Harry, your hamster, a treat every time he pushes a ball with his nose, and then you suddenly stop the reinforcement, Harry will soon stop pushing that ball. Because the change in reinforcement is large, from continuous to none at all, Harry will easily discern the change. But if you have been reinforcing Harry's behavior only every so often, the change will not be so dramatic, and your hungry hamster will keep responding for quite a while. Pigeons, rats, and people on intermittent schedules of reinforcement have responded in the laboratory thousands of times without reinforcement before throwing in the towel, especially when the timing of the reinforcer has varied. Animals will sometimes work so hard for an unpredictable, infrequent bit of food that the energy they expend is greater than that gained from the reward; theoretically, they could actually work themselves to death.

It follows that if you want to get rid of a response, whether it's your own or someone else's, you should be careful *not* to reinforce it intermittently. If you are going to extinguish undesirable behavior by ignoring it—a child's tantrums, a friend's midnight phone calls, a parent's unwanted advice—you must be absolutely consistent in withholding reinforcement (your attention). Otherwise, the other person will learn that if he or she keeps up the screaming, calling, or advice giving long enough, it will eventually be rewarded. From a behavioral point of view, one of the worst errors people make is to reward intermittently the very responses that they would like to eliminate.

Shaping. **LO 9.12** For a response to be reinforced, it must first occur. But suppose you want to train cows to milk themselves, a child to use a knife and fork properly, or a friend to play terrific tennis. Such behaviors, and most others in everyday life, have almost no probability of appearing spontaneously. You could grow old and gray waiting for them to occur so that you could reinforce them. The operant solution is a procedure called **shaping**.

In shaping, you start by reinforcing a tendency in the right direction, and then you gradually require responses that are more and more similar to the desired final response. The responses that you reinforce on the way to the final one are called **successive approximations**. Take the problem of teaching cows to milk themselves. How can you do it, when cows have no hands? Ah, but cows *can* be trained to use a milking robot, and in several countries psychologists have trained them to do just that (Stiles, Murray, & Kentish-Barnes, 2011). First, they give the cow crushed barley (the cow equivalent of a chocolate treat) for simply standing on a platform connected to the robot. Once that response is established, they give her barley for turning her body toward the spot where the robot attaches the milking cups, then for being in the exact spot

"Maybe you're right, maybe it won't ward off evil spirits, but maybe it will, and these days who wants to take a chance?"

the robot requires, and so on until the cow finally learns to milk herself. The key is that as each approximation is achieved, the next one becomes more likely, making it available for reinforcement. Cows allowed to milk themselves do so three or four times a day instead of the traditional twice a day, and show fewer signs of stress than other cows.

Using shaping and other techniques, Skinner was able to train pigeons to play Ping-Pong with their beaks and to "bowl" in a miniature alley, complete with a wooden ball and tiny bowling pins. (Skinner had a great sense of humor.) Today, animal trainers routinely use shaping to teach animals their parts in movies and TV shows. Animals also act as the "eyes" of the blind and the "limbs" of people with spinal cord injuries, doing such daily tasks as turning on light switches, opening refrigerator doors, and reaching for boxes on shelves.

Biological Limits on Learning. LO 9.13 All principles of operant conditioning, like those of classical conditioning, are limited by an animal's genetic dispositions and physical characteristics. If you try to teach a fish to dance the samba, you're going to get pretty frustrated (and wear out the fish). Operant-conditioning procedures always work best when they capitalize on inborn tendencies.

Years ago, two psychologists who became animal trainers, Keller and Marian Breland (1961), learned what happens when you ignore biological constraints on learning. They found that their animals were having trouble learning tasks that should have been easy. One animal, a pig, was supposed to drop large wooden coins in a box. Instead, the animal would drop the coin, push at it with its snout, throw it in the air, and push at it some more. This odd behavior actually delayed delivery of the reinforcer (food, which is *very* reinforcing to a pig), so it was hard to explain in terms of operant principles. The Brelands finally realized that the pig's rooting instinct—using its snout to uncover and dig up edible roots—was keeping it from learning the task. They called such a reversion to instinctive behavior **instinctive drift**.

In human beings, too, operant learning is affected by genetics, biology, and the evolutionary history of our species. As we discuss in Chapter 3, human children are biologically disposed to learn language and to understand rudimentary numbers, spatial relations, and certain features of the physical world (Izard et al., 2009). Further, temperaments and other inborn dispositions may affect how a person responds to reinforcers and punishers. It

instinctive drift During operant learning, the tendency for an organism to revert to instinctive behavior.

Behavioral techniques such as shaping have many useful applications. Monkeys have been trained to assist their paralyzed owners by opening doors, helping with feeding, and turning the pages of books. Miniature horses have been trained to help blind people navigate everywhere, from crowded subways to rocky, uneven terrain. Note the horse's cool little protective sneakers!

Suppose a filmmaker wants a pigeon, cat, dog, and sheep to pose in a stack for a movie scene. A behaviorist will use shaping to get the animals to agree. But even shaping won't teach the pigeon to purr or the cat to fly.

will be easier to shape belly-dancing behavior if a person is temperamentally disposed to be outgoing and extroverted than if the person is by nature shy.

Skinner: The Man and the Myth

Because of his groundbreaking work on operant conditioning, B. F. Skinner is one of the best known of American psychologists. He is also one of the most misunderstood. Many people (even some psychologists) think that Skinner denied the existence of human consciousness and the value of studying

it. In reality, Skinner (1972, 1990) maintained that private internal events—what we call perceptions, emotions, and thoughts—are as real as any others, and we can study them by examining our own sensory responses, the verbal reports of others, and the conditions under which such events occur. But he insisted that thoughts and feelings cannot *explain* behavior. These components of consciousness, he said, are themselves simply behaviors that occur because of reinforcement and punishment.

Skinner aroused strong passions in both his supporters and his detractors. Perhaps the issue that most provoked and angered people was his insistence that free will is an illusion. In contrast to humanist and some religious doctrines that human beings have the power to shape their own destinies, his philosophy promoted the *determinist view* that our actions are determined by our environments and our genetic heritage.

Because Skinner thought the environment should be manipulated to alter behavior, some critics have portrayed him as cold-blooded. One famous controversy regarding Skinner occurred when he invented an enclosed "living space," the Air Crib, for his younger daughter Deborah when she was an infant. This "baby box," as it came to be known, had temperature and humidity controls to eliminate the usual discomforts that babies suffer: heat, cold, wetness, and confinement by blankets and clothing. Skinner believed that to reduce a baby's cries of discomfort and make infant care easier for the parents, you should fix the environment. But people imagined, incorrectly, that the Skinners were leaving their child in the baby box all the time without cuddling and holding her, and rumors circulated for years (and still do from time to time) that she had sued her father, gone insane, or killed herself. Actually, both of Skinner's daughters were cuddled and doted on, loved their parents deeply, and turned out to be successful, perfectly well-adjusted adults.

Skinner, who was a kind and mild-mannered man, felt that it would be unethical *not* to try to improve human behavior by applying behavioral

Get Involved! Shape Up!

Would you like to improve your study habits? Start exercising? Learn to play a musical instrument? Here are a few guidelines for shaping your own behavior: (1) Set goals that are achievable and specific. "I am going to jog 10 minutes and increase the time by 5 minutes each day" will be far more effective than the vague goal to "get in shape." (2) Track your progress on a graph or in a diary; evidence of progress serves as a secondary reinforcer. (3) Avoid punishing yourself with self-defeating thoughts such as "I'll never be a good student" or "I'm a food addict." (4) Reinforce small improvements (successive approximations) instead of expecting perfection. By the way, a reinforcer does not have to be a thing; it can be something you like to do, like watching a movie. Above all, be patient. Like Rome, new habits are not built in a day.

principles. And he practiced what he preached, proposing many ways to improve society and reduce human suffering. At the height of public criticism of Skinner's supposedly cold and inhumane approach to understanding behavior, the American Humanist Association recognized his efforts on behalf of humanity by honoring him with its Humanist of the Year Award.

Recite & Review

✔ Study and Review at MyPsychLab

Recite: Out loud, say as much as you can about extinction, stimulus generalization and stimulus discrimination in operant conditioning, continuous and intermittent reinforcement, and shaping.

Review: Next, go back and read this section again to check what you recited.

Now take this *Quick Quiz:*

In each of the following situations, choose the best alternative and give your reason for choosing it.

1. You want your 2-year-old to ask for water with a word instead of a grunt. Should you give him water when he says "wa-wa" or wait until his pronunciation improves?

2. Your roommate keeps interrupting your studying even though you have asked her to stop. Should you ignore her completely or occasionally respond for the sake of good manners?

3. Your father, who rarely calls you, has finally left a voice-mail message. Should you reply quickly, or wait a while so he will know how it feels to be ignored?

Answers:

1. You should reinforce "wa-wa," an approximation of water, because complex behaviors need to be shaped. 2. From a behavioral view, you should ignore her completely because intermittent reinforcement (attention) could cause her interruptions to persist. 3. If you want to encourage communication, you should quickly reply because immediate reinforcement is more effective than delayed reinforcement.

You are about to learn . . .

- **when punishment works in real life and why it often does not.**
- **some effective alternatives to punishment.**
- **how reinforcement can be misused.**
- **why paying children for good grades sometimes backfires.**

Operant Conditioning in Real Life

Operant principles can clear up many mysteries about why people behave as they do. They can also explain why people have trouble changing when they want to, despite all the motivational seminars they attend or resolutions they make. If life remains full of the same old reinforcers, punishers, and discriminative stimuli (a grumpy boss, an unresponsive roommate, a refrigerator stocked with junk food), any new responses that have been acquired may fail to generalize.

To help people change unwanted, dangerous, or self-defeating habits, behaviorists have carried operant principles out of the laboratory and into the wider world of the classroom,

athletic field, prison, mental hospital, nursing home, rehabilitation ward, child care center, factory, and office. The use of operant techniques in such real-world settings is called **behavior modification** (also known as *applied behavior analysis*).

Behavior modification has had some enormous successes (Kazdin, 2001; Martin & Pear, 2011). Behaviorists have taught parents how to toilet train their children in only a few sessions. They have trained disturbed and intellectually impaired adults to communicate, dress themselves, mingle socially with others, and earn a living. They have taught patients with brain damage to control inappropriate behavior, focus their attention, and improve their language abilities. They have helped autistic children improve their social and communication skills. And they have helped ordinary folk get rid of unwanted habits, such as smoking and nail biting, or acquire desired ones, such as practicing the piano, exercising more, or studying.

Yet when nonpsychologists try to apply the principles of conditioning to commonplace problems without thoroughly understanding those principles, their efforts sometimes miss the mark, as we are about to see.

behavior modification The application of operant-conditioning techniques to teach new responses or to reduce or eliminate maladaptive or problematic behavior; also called *applied behavior analysis*.

The Pros and Cons of Punishment LO 9.14

In a novel called *Walden Two* (1948/1976), Skinner imagined a utopia in which reinforcers were used so wisely that undesirable behavior was rare. Unfortunately, we do not live in a utopia; bad habits and antisocial acts abound.

Punishment might seem to be an obvious solution. Almost all Western countries have banned the physical punishment of schoolchildren by principals and teachers, but many American states still permit it for disruptiveness, vandalism, and other misbehavior. And, of course, in their relationships, people punish one another frequently by yelling, scolding, and sulking. Does all this punishment work?

When Punishment Works. Sometimes punishment is unquestionably effective. For example, punishment can deter some young criminals from repeating their offenses. A study of the criminal records of all Danish men born between 1944 and 1947 (nearly 29,000 men) examined repeat arrests (recidivism) through age 26 (Brennan & Mednick, 1994). After any given arrest, punishment reduced rates of subsequent arrests for both minor and serious crimes, though recidivism still remained fairly high. Contrary to expectation, however, the *severity* of punishment made no difference; fines and probation were about as effective as jail time. What mattered most was the *consistency* of the punishment. This is understandable in behavioral terms: When lawbreakers sometimes get away with their crimes, their behavior is intermittently reinforced and therefore becomes resistant to extinction.

THINKING CRITICALLY

About Punishment

Unfortunately, that is often the situation in the United States. Young offenders are punished less consistently than in Denmark, in part because prosecutors, juries, and judges do not want to condemn them to mandatory prison terms. This helps to explain why harsh sentencing laws and simplistic efforts to crack down on wrongdoers often fail or even backfire. Because many things influence crime rates—the proportion of young versus older people in the population, poverty levels, drug policies, discriminatory arrest patterns— the relationship between incarceration rates and crime rates in the United States varies from state to state (King, Maurer, & Young, 2005). But international surveys find that overall, the United States has a high rate of violent crime compared to many other industrialized countries, in spite of its extremely high incarceration rates.

When Punishment Fails. What about punishment that occurs every day in families, schools, and workplaces? Laboratory and field studies find that it, too, often fails, for several reasons:

1 **People often administer punishment inappropriately or mindlessly.** They swing in a blind rage or shout things they don't mean, use harsh methods with toddlers, apply punishment so broadly that it covers all sorts of irrelevant behaviors, or misunderstand the proper timing and application of punishment.

2 **The recipient of harsh or frequent punishment often responds with anxiety, fear, or rage.** Through a process of classical conditioning, these emotional side effects may then generalize to the entire situation in which the punishment occurs—the place, the person delivering the punishment, and the circumstances. These negative emotional reactions can create more problems than the punishment solves. A teenager who has been severely punished may strike back or run away. A spouse who is constantly insulted, belittled, and criticized will feel bitter and resentful and is likely to retaliate with small acts of hostility. And extreme punishment—physical abuse—is a risk factor, especially in children, for the development of depression, low self-esteem, violent behavior, and many other problems (Gershoff, 2002; Widom, DuMont, & Czaja, 2007).

3 **The effectiveness of punishment is often temporary, depending heavily on the presence of the punishing person or circumstances.** All of us can probably remember some transgressions of childhood that we never dared commit when our parents were around but that we promptly resumed as soon as they were gone and reinforcers were once again available. All we learned was not to get caught.

4 **Most misbehavior is hard to punish immediately.** Punishment, like reward, works best if it quickly follows a response. But outside the laboratory, rapid punishment is often hard to achieve, and during the delay, the behavior may be reinforced many times. If you punish your dog when you get home for getting into the doggie biscuits and eating them all up, the punishment will not do any good because you are too late. Your pet's misbehavior has already been reinforced by all those delicious treats.

5 **Punishment conveys little information.** It may tell the recipient what *not* to do, but it does not communicate what the person (or animal) *should* do. Spanking a toddler for messing in her pants will not teach her to use the potty chair, and scolding a student for learning slowly will not teach him how to learn more quickly.

6 **An action intended to punish may instead be reinforcing because it brings attention.** Indeed, in some cases, angry attention may be just what the

offender is after. If a mother yells at a child who is throwing a tantrum, the very act of yelling may give him what he wants: a reaction from her. In the schoolroom, teachers who scold children in front of other students, thus putting them in the limelight, may unwittingly reward the very misbehavior they are trying to eliminate.

Because of these drawbacks, most psychologists believe that punishment, especially when it's severe, is a poor way to eliminate unwanted behavior. Consider spanking. A Canadian review of two decades of research found that although spanking may put a halt to a child's annoying or dangerous behavior in the short term, it backfires in the long term, because children who are physically punished tend to become more aggressive and antisocial over time (Durrant & Ensom, 2012). Spanking is also associated with later mental health problems and slower cognitive development. No study has ever established a link between physical discipline and any positive outcome.

In special cases, as when mentally disabled children are in immediate danger of seriously injuring themselves or a school bully is about to beat up a classmate, temporary physical restraint may be necessary. But even in these cases, alternatives are often available. School programs have successfully reduced school violence by teaching kids problem-solving skills, emotional control, and conflict resolution, and by rewarding good behavior (Hahn et al., 2008; Wilson & Lipsey, 2007). And in some situations, the best way to discourage a behavior—a child's pleas for "just one more" video game, a roommate's interruptions when you're studying—is to extinguish it by ignoring it. (Of

Many harried parents habitually resort to physical punishment without being aware of its many negative consequences. Based on your reading of this chapter, what alternatives does this parent have?

course, ignoring a behavior requires patience and is not always feasible. If your dog barks all day and night, telling your neighbors that they should ignore the racket will not go over well, even if you explain that you learned all about the drawbacks of punishment in your psychology class.)

Finally, when punishment must be applied, these guidelines should be kept in mind: (1) It should not involve physical abuse; instead, parents can use time-outs and loss of privileges (negative punishers); (2) it should be consistent; (3) it should be accompanied by information about the kind of behavior that would be appropriate; and (4) it should be followed, whenever possible, by the reinforcement of desirable behavior.

👁 Watch the Video Thinking Like a Psychologist: Physical Punishment - You Decide! at MyPsychLab

As we all know, people often do things they're not supposed to. Have you ever wondered why so many people ignore warnings and threats of punishment?

extrinsic reinforcers
Reinforcers that are not inherently related to the activity being reinforced.

intrinsic reinforcers
Reinforcers that are inherently related to the activity being reinforced.

The Problems With Reward LO 9.15

So far, we have been praising the virtues of praise and other reinforcers. But like punishers, rewards do not always work as expected. Let's look at two complications that arise when people try to use them.

Misuse of Rewards.
For decades, teachers have been handing out lavish praise, happy-face stickers, and high grades, even if students don't deserve them, in hopes that students' performance will improve as they learn to "feel good about

THINKING CRITICALLY

About Rewards

themselves." Scientifically speaking, however, this approach is misguided. Study after study finds that high self-esteem does not improve academic performance (Baumeister et al., 2003). The reason is that academic achievement requires effort and persistence, not self-esteem (Duckworth et al., 2011). It is nurtured not by undeserved rewards but by a teacher's honest appreciation of the content of a student's work, and by specific constructive feedback on how to correct mistakes or fix weaknesses (Damon, 1995). These findings from psychological science have begun to influence some teachers, who are now shifting away from doling out unwarranted "self-esteem boosters" and focusing on helping students appreciate the benefits of diligence and persistence.

One obvious result of the misuse of rewards in schools has been grade inflation at all levels of education. In colleges and universities, grades have risen steadily since the 1970s but graduation rates have not. Moreover, the literacy of graduates has declined, as have scores on entrance exams. At many schools, Cs, which once meant average or satisfactory, are nearly extinct. One study found that a third of college students expected Bs just for showing up to class, and 40 percent felt they were entitled to a B merely for doing the required reading (Greenberger et al., 2008). We have talked to students who feel that hard work should even be enough for an A.

If you yourself have benefited from grade inflation, you may feel it's a good thing—but remember that critical thinking requires us to separate feelings from facts. The problem is that rewards, including grades, serve as effective reinforcers only when they are tied to the behavior one is trying to increase, not when they are dispensed indiscriminately. Getting a good grade for "showing-up-in-class behavior" reinforces going to class, but not necessarily for learning much once you are there. Would you want to be treated by a doctor, represented by a lawyer, or have your taxes done by an accountant who got through school just by

showing up for class? Or who did all the required reading, but without understanding it?

Why Rewards Can Backfire.
Most of our examples of operant conditioning have involved **extrinsic reinforcers**, which come from an outside source and are not inherently related to the activity being reinforced. Money, praise, gold stars, applause, hugs, and thumbs-up signs are all extrinsic reinforcers. But people (and probably some other animals as well) also work for **intrinsic reinforcers**, such as enjoyment of the task and the satisfaction of accomplishment. In real-world settings, extrinsic reinforcement sometimes becomes too much of a good thing because if you focus on it exclusively, it can kill the pleasure of doing something for its own sake.

This downside of extrinsic reinforcement was dramatically revealed in a classic study of how praise affects children's intrinsic motivation (Lepper, Greene, & Nisbett, 1973). Nursery school children were given the chance to draw with felt-tipped pens during free play and observers recorded how long each child spontaneously played with the pens. The children clearly enjoyed this activity. Then the researchers told some of the children that if they would draw with felt-tipped pens they would get a prize, a "Good Player Award," complete with gold seal and red ribbon. After drawing for six minutes, each child got the award as promised. Other children did not expect an award and were not given one. A week later, the researchers again observed the children's free play. Those children who had expected and received an award spent much less time with the pens than they had before the start of the

"That is the correct answer, Billy, but I'm afraid you don't win anything for it."

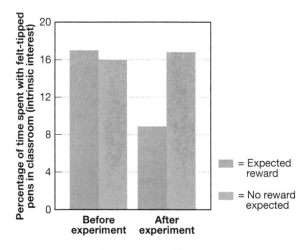

FIGURE 9.7 Turning Play into Work
Extrinsic rewards can sometimes reduce the intrinsic pleasure of an activity. When preschoolers were promised a prize for drawing with felt-tipped pens, the behavior temporarily increased. But after they got their prizes, they spent less time with the pens than they had before the study began (Lepper, Greene, & Nisbett, 1973).

experiment. In contrast, children who had neither expected nor received an award continued to show as much interest in playing with the pens as they had initially, as you can see in Figure 9.7. Similar results have occurred in other studies when children have been offered a reward for doing something they already enjoy.

Why should extrinsic rewards undermine the pleasure of doing something for its own sake? The researchers who did the felt-tipped pen study suggested that when we are paid for an activity, we interpret it as work instead of something we do because of our own interests and skills. It is as if we say to ourselves, "Since I'm being paid, it must be something I wouldn't do if I didn't have to." Then, when the reward is withdrawn, we refuse to "work" any longer. Another possibility is that we tend to regard extrinsic rewards as controlling, so they make us feel pressured and reduce our sense of autonomy and choice ("I guess I have to do what I'm told to do, but *only* what I'm told to do") (Deci et al., 1999). A third, more behavioral explanation is that extrinsic reinforcement sometimes raises the rate of responding above some optimal, enjoyable level, at which point the activity really does become work.

Findings on extrinsic versus intrinsic reinforcements have wide-ranging implications. Economists have shown that financial rewards can undermine the ethical and moral norms of honesty, hard work, and fairness toward others, and can decrease people's willingness to contribute to the common good (e.g., by paying taxes and giving to charity). In other words, an emphasis solely on money encourages selfishness (Bowles, 2008).

We must be careful, however, not to oversimplify this issue. The effects of extrinsic rewards depend on many factors, including a person's initial motivation, the context in which rewards are achieved, and in the case of praise, the sincerity of the praiser (Henderlong & Lepper, 2002). Sometimes extrinsic rewards can help boost achievement. When some American

Get Involved! What's Reinforcing Your Behavior?

For each activity that you do, indicate whether the reinforcers controlling your behavior are primarily extrinsic or intrinsic.

Activity	Reinforcers mostly extrinsic	Reinforcers mostly intrinsic	Reinforcers about equally extrinsic and intrinsic
Studying	_____	_____	_____
Housework	_____	_____	_____
Worship	_____	_____	_____
Grooming	_____	_____	_____
Job	_____	_____	_____
Dating	_____	_____	_____
Attending class	_____	_____	_____
Reading unrelated to school	_____	_____	_____
Sports	_____	_____	_____
Cooking	_____	_____	_____

Is there an area of your life in which you would like intrinsic reinforcement to play a larger role? What can you do to make that happen?

high schools started offering large cash rewards to inner-city students who got high scores on Advanced Placement tests for college, achievement skyrocketed. Suddenly, disadvantaged minority students were taking statistics classes on Saturdays and passing the placement tests in larger numbers. But these effects might be limited to a unique combination of already motivated teachers and students. In a study of more than 27,000 students in Dallas, New York City, and Chicago, students were paid to read books, to complete assignments, or for getting good grades. The financial incentives had no effect. Although the students were excited about getting the money, they did not have the basic study skills they needed to achieve their goals (Fryer, 2011).

As for the relationship between intrinsic and extrinsic reinforcement, in general, if you get praise, money, a high grade, or a trophy for doing a task *well*, for achieving a certain level of performance, or for improving your performance rather than for just doing the task, your intrinsic motivation is not likely to decline; in fact, it may

increase (Cameron, Banko, & Pierce, 2001; Pierce et al., 2003). The rewards are apt to make you feel competent rather than controlled. And if you have always been crazy about reading or about playing the banjo, you will keep reading or playing even when you do not happen to be getting a grade or applause for doing so. In such cases, you will probably attribute your continued involvement in the activity to your own intrinsic interests and motivation rather than to the reward.

So what is the take-home message about extrinsic rewards? First, they are often useful or necessary: Few people would trudge off to work every morning if they never got paid, and in the classroom, teachers may need to offer incentives to some students. But extrinsic rewards should be used carefully and should not be overdone, so that intrinsic pleasure in an activity can blossom. Educators, employers, and policy makers can avoid the trap of either–or thinking by recognizing that most people do their best when they get tangible rewards for real achievement *and* when they have interesting, challenging, and varied kinds of work to do.

Recite & Review

 Study and **Review** at **MyPsychLab**

Recite: You will earn both extrinsic and intrinsic rewards if you say aloud as much as you can about behavior modification, when punishment works and when it fails, and the effects of extrinsic and intrinsic reinforcement.

Review: Next, go back and read this section again.

Now take this *Quick Quiz:*

A. According to behavioral principles, what is happening here?

  1. An adolescent whose parents have hit him for minor transgressions since he was small runs away from home.

  2. A young woman whose parents paid her to clean her room while she was growing up is a slob when she moves to her own apartment.

  3. Two parents scold their young daughter every time they catch her sucking her thumb. The thumb sucking continues anyway.

B. Some school systems are rewarding students for perfect attendance by giving them money, shopping sprees, laptops, and video games. What are the pros and cons of such practices?

Answers:

A. 1. The physical punishment was painful, and through a process of classical conditioning, the situation in which it occurred also became unpleasant. Because escape from an unpleasant stimulus is negatively reinforcing, the boy ran away. **2.** Extrinsic reinforcers are no longer available, and room-cleaning behavior has been extinguished. Also, extrinsic rewards may have displaced the intrinsic satisfaction of having a tidy room. **3.** Punishment has failed, possibly because it rewards thumb sucking with attention or because thumb sucking still brings the child pleasure whenever the parents are not around. **B.** The rewards may improve attendance, and students who attend more regularly may become more interested in their studies and do better in school. But extrinsic rewards can also decrease intrinsic motivation, and when they are withdrawn, attendance may plummet ("If there's no reward, why should I attend?"). Further, students may come to expect bigger and bigger rewards. In some schools, especially those that have de-emphasized penalties for *poor* attendance, the rewards have backfired and attendance has actually fallen. (Bonus question: Some parents pay their children for everything from brushing their teeth to behaving in a restaurant. Given the research in this section, what might be the result of this practice?)

You are about to learn...

- how you can learn something without any obvious reinforcement.
- why two people can learn different lessons from exactly the same experience.
- how we often learn not by doing but by watching.

Learning and the Mind LO 9.16

For half a century, most American learning theories held that learning could be explained by specifying the behavioral "ABCs": *antecedents* (events preceding behavior), *behaviors*, and *consequences*. Behaviorists liked to compare the mind to an engineer's hypothetical "black box," a device whose workings must be inferred because they cannot be observed directly. To them, the box contained irrelevant wiring; it was enough to know that pushing a button on the box would produce a predictable response. But even as early as the 1930s, a few behaviorists could not resist peeking into that black box.

Latent Learning

Behaviorist Edward Tolman (1938) committed virtual heresy at the time by noting that his rats, when pausing at turning points in a maze, seemed to be *deciding* which way to go. Moreover, the animals sometimes seemed to be learning even without any reinforcement. What, he wondered, was going on in their little rat brains that might account for this puzzle?

In a classic experiment, Tolman and C. H. Honzik (1930) placed three groups of rats in mazes and observed their behavior daily for more than two weeks. The rats in Group 1 always found food at the end of the maze and quickly learned to find it without going down blind alleys. The rats in Group 2 never found food and, as you would expect, they followed no particular route. Group 3 was the interesting group. These rats found no food for 10 days and seemed to wander aimlessly, but on the 11th day they received food, and then they quickly learned to run to the end of the maze. By the following day, they were doing as well as Group 1, which had been rewarded from the beginning (see Figure 9.8).

Group 3 had demonstrated **latent learning**, learning that is not immediately expressed in performance. A great deal of human learning also remains latent until circumstances allow or require it to be expressed. A driver gets out of a traffic jam

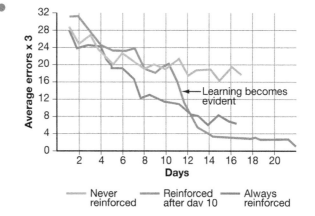

FIGURE 9.8 Latent Learning
In a classic experiment, rats that always found food in a maze made fewer and fewer errors in reaching the food (blue curve). In contrast, rats that received no food showed little improvement (gold curve). But rats that got no food for 10 days and then found food on the 11th day showed rapid improvement from then on (red curve). This result suggests that learning involves cognitive changes that can occur in the absence of reinforcement and that may not be acted on until a reinforcer becomes available (Tolman & Honzik, 1930).

and finds her way to Fourth and Fiddle Streets using a route she has never used before (without GPS!). A little boy observes a parent setting the table or tightening a screw but does not act on this learning for years; then he finds he knows how to do these things.

Latent learning raises questions about what, exactly, is learned during operant learning. In the Tolman and Honzik study, the rats that did not get any food until the 11th day seemed to have acquired a mental representation of the maze. They had been learning the whole time; they simply had no reason to act on that learning until they began to find food. Similarly, the driver taking a new route can do so because she already knows how the city is laid out. What seems to be acquired in latent learning, therefore, is not a specific response, but *knowledge* about responses and their consequences. We learn how the world is organized, which paths lead to which places, and which actions can produce which payoffs. This knowledge permits us to be creative and flexible in reaching our goals.

> **Simulate** the **Experiment** Learning at **MyPsychLab**

Social-Cognitive Learning Theories

During the 1960s and 1970s, many learning theorists concluded that human behavior could not be understood without taking into account the

latent learning A form of learning that is not immediately expressed in an overt response; it occurs without obvious reinforcement.

Social-cognitive theorists emphasize the influence of thoughts and perceptions on behavior (at least in humans).

social-cognitive learning theories Theories that emphasize how behavior is learned and maintained through observation and imitation of others, positive consequences, and cognitive processes such as plans, expectations, and beliefs.

observational learning A process in which an individual learns new responses by observing the behavior of another (a model) rather than through direct experience; sometimes called *vicarious conditioning*.

human capacity for higher-level cognitive processes. They agreed with behaviorists that human beings, along with the rat and the rabbit, are subject to the laws of operant and classical conditioning. But they added that human behavior cannot be fully explained without knowing how people acquire information, make decisions, reason, and solve problems.

We will use the term **social-cognitive learning theories** for all theories that combine behavioral principles with cognitive ones to explain behavior (Bandura, 1986; Mischel, 1973; Mischel & Shoda, 1995). These theories share an emphasis on the importance of beliefs, perceptions, and observations of other peoples' behavior in determining what we learn, what we do at any given moment, and the personality traits we develop (see Chapter 2). To a social-cognitive theorist, differences in beliefs and perceptions help explain why two people who live through the same event may come away with entirely different lessons from it (Bandura, 2001). All siblings know this. One sibling may regard being grounded by their father as evidence of his all-around meanness, whereas another may see the same behavior as evidence of his care and concern for his children. For these siblings, being grounded is likely to affect their behavior very differently.

Learning by Observing. Late one night, a friend living in a rural area was awakened by a loud clattering noise. A raccoon had knocked over a "raccoon-proof" garbage can and seemed to be demonstrating to an assembly of other raccoons how to open it: If you jump up and down on the can's side, the lid will pop off. According to our friend, the observing raccoons learned from this

episode how to open stubborn garbage cans, and the observing humans learned how smart raccoons can be. In short, they all benefited from **observational learning**: learning by watching what others do and what happens to them for doing it.

The behavior learned by the raccoons through observation was an operant one, but observational learning also plays an important role in the acquisition of automatic, reflexive responses, such as fears and phobias (Mineka & Zinbarg, 2006; Olsson & Phelps, 2004). Thus, in addition to learning to be frightened of rats directly through classical conditioning, as Little Albert did, you might also learn to fear rats by observing the emotional expressions of other people when they see or touch one. The perception of someone else's reaction serves as an unconditioned stimulus for your own fear, and the learning that results may be as strong as it would be if you had had a direct encounter with the rat yourself. Children often learn to fear things in this way, say by observing a parent's tense reaction whenever a dog approaches. Adults can acquire fears even by watching suspenseful movies. After seeing the classic horror film *Psycho*, in which a character is knifed to death in a shower, some viewers became nervous about taking a shower.

Behaviorists refer to observational learning as *vicarious conditioning* and believe it can be explained in stimulus–response terms. But social-cognitive theorists maintain that observational learning in human beings cannot be fully understood without taking into account the thought processes of the learner. They emphasize the knowledge that results when a person sees a *model*—another person—behaving in certain ways and experiencing the consequences (Bandura, 1977).

None of us would last long without observational learning. Learning would be both inefficient and dangerous. We would have to learn to avoid oncoming cars by walking into traffic

Line dancers learn their steps through observation.

and suffering the consequences, or learn to swim by jumping into a deep pool and flailing around. Parents and teachers would be busy 24 hours a day shaping children's behavior. Bosses would have to stand over their employees' desks, rewarding every little link in the intricate behavioral chains we call typing, report writing, and accounting. But observational learning has its dark side as well. People often imitate antisocial or unethical actions (they observe a friend cheating and decide they can get away with it too) or self-defeating and harmful ones (they watch a film star smoking and take up the habit in an effort to look just as cool).

Many years ago, Albert Bandura and his colleagues showed just how important observational learning is for children who are learning the rules of social behavior (Bandura, Ross, & Ross, 1963). Nursery school children watched a short film of two men, Rocky and Johnny, playing with toys. (Apparently the children did not think this behavior was the least bit odd.) In the film, Johnny refuses to share his toys, and Rocky responds by clobbering him. Rocky's aggressive actions are rewarded because he winds up with all the toys. Poor Johnny sits dejectedly in the corner, while Rocky marches off with a sack full of loot and a hobbyhorse under his arm. After viewing the film, each child was left alone for 20 minutes in a playroom full of toys, including some of the items shown in the film. Watching through a one-way mirror, the researchers found that the children were much more aggressive in their play than a control group that had not seen the film. Some children imitated Rocky almost exactly. At the end of the session, one little girl even asked the experimenter for a sack!

Watch the Video Classic Footage of Bandura's Bobo Doll Experiment at MyPsychLab

Of course, people imitate positive activities that they observe, too. Matt Groening, the creator of *The Simpsons*, decided it would be funny if the Simpsons' 8-year-old daughter Lisa played the baritone sax. Sure enough, little girls across the country began imitating her. Cynthia Sikes, a saxophone teacher in New York, told *The New York Times*, "When the show started, I got an influx of girls coming up to me saying, 'I want to play the saxophone because Lisa Simpson plays the saxophone.'"

Findings on latent learning, observational learning, and the role of cognition in learning can help us evaluate arguments in the passionate debate about the effects of media violence. Children and teenagers in the United States and many other countries see countless acts of violence on television, in films, and in video games. Does all this depiction of blood and guts affect them? Do you think it has affected *you*? In "Taking Psychology With You," we offer evidence that bears on these questions, and suggest ways of resolving them without oversimplifying the issues.

Watch the Video In the Real World: Learning Aggression at MyPsychLab

Recite & Review

Study and Review at MyPsychLab

Recite: Say everything you know about latent learning, social-cognitive learning theories, and observational learning. Maybe someone will overhear you, realize how smart you are, and adopt the same useful study habit.

Review: Next, go back and read this section again.

Now take this Quick Quiz:

1. A friend asks you to meet her at a new restaurant across town. You have never been to this specific address, but you find your way there anyway because you have experienced _____ learning.

2. To a social-cognitive theorist, the fact that we can learn without being reinforced for any obvious responses shows that we do not learn specific responses but rather _____.

3. After watching her teenage sister put on lipstick, a little girl takes a lipstick and applies it to her own lips. She has acquired this behavior through a process of _____.

Answers:

1. latent 2. knowledge about responses and their consequences 3. observational learning

PSYCHOLOGY IN THE NEWS REVISITED //////

How can the behavioral and social-cognitive learning principles covered in this chapter help us think about the arrest and expulsion of Kiera Wilmot for producing a small explosion in a science experiment?

Findings on learning do not rule out all use of punishment when children misbehave. Certainly, when children or teenagers bring weapons to school or are chronically violent, authorities cannot simply ignore the behavior in hopes of extinguishing it; they have an obligation to protect the other students. But when severe penalties are imposed for minor infractions, as in the cases mentioned in our opening story, punishment can make the recipient feel betrayed and angry at the injustice of it. Social-cognitive theorists remind us that human beings, including children, bring their minds to their experiences, and if they perceive a punishment for breaking a rule as being undeserved or overly harsh, they may continue to break that rule as an act of defiance. Undeserved severe punishment may also bring attention and support from peers, with the same result—defiance and persistence. The humiliation of being barred from school and hauled off in handcuffs may destroy a child's trust in adults and "the system."

After her suspension, Kiera was required to attend an alternative school for students with behavior problems, and her classmates began to make fun of her. But her story quickly went viral and a petition of support on Change.org got almost 200,000 signatures. Several scientists came to her defense and a former astronaut offered Kiera and her twin sister a scholarship to a space camp. The criminal charges were dropped—as they are in most cases—and school district officials decided that she could return to her regular high school the next semester. Kiera Wilmot's story has a happy ending, but she and her family nonetheless say the experience was hard on them.

What about punishment of children at home? Some psychologists believe that occasional, moderate punishment, even spanking, has no long-term detrimental outcomes for most middle-class children, so long as it occurs in an otherwise loving context or as a last resort (Baumrind, Larzelere, & Cowan, 2002).

But, as we saw, punishment does not teach the child *good* behavior, and has all the drawbacks listed in this chapter. And when parents insult, humiliate, or ridicule a child, the results are often devastating. Humiliation and shame can last for years.

What, then, should parents and teachers do when a child's behavior is seriously disruptive or dangerous? First, from a learning perspective, other punishments (time-outs, loss of privileges, and so forth) are preferable to physical punishment, as long as the adult is consistent (no intermittent reinforcement of bad behavior!), applies the punishment as soon as possible after the behavior occurs, and, most important, remembers to reinforce successive approximations toward desirable behavior. It is also important to know *why* a child is misbehaving: Is the child angry, worried, or frightened? Parents and teachers can help children identify their feelings while teaching them how to control their emotions and find nonaggressive, constructive ways to resolve conflicts. In this way, the children can learn that they are being punished not for feeling angry or upset, but for acting inappropriately or harming others: "It is all right to be upset but not to hit or bite."

Finally, a learning theorist would emphasize the role of the environment in causing or maintaining a child's misbehavior. Is the child bored? Does the child have trouble keeping still in the controlled environment of a classroom? From a learning perspective, it may be more effective to change the child's environment than the child, for example by instituting more breaks for physical activities.

Skinner himself never wavered in his determination to apply learning principles to fashion better, healthier environments for everyone. In 1990, just a week before his death, ailing and frail, he addressed an overflow crowd at the annual meeting of the American Psychological Association, making the case one last time for the approach he was convinced could create a better society. When you see the world as the learning theorist views it, Skinner was saying, you see the folly of human behavior, but you also see the possibility of improving it.

Taking Psychology With You

Does Media Violence Make You Violent?

In 2011, the U.S. Supreme Court overturned a California law that banned shops from selling or renting violent video games to anyone under 18. California argued that violence is as obscene as pornography, and if selling or renting porn to young people is illegal, surely selling violent video games should be prohibited as well. The court thought otherwise, ruling that such games are not obscene and noting that many parents consider them to be harmless fun. Just look at what happens to Hansel and Gretel, or Cinderella, said one of the justices; "Grimm's Fairy Tales," he wrote, "are grim indeed." But other countries, such as Australia, New Zealand, and

England, have concluded that violent video games can be dangerous enough to children to justify restrictions or even a complete ban.

Which conclusion is right? Does violence depicted in films, on TV, and in video games lead to real violence?

Psychologists are strongly divided in their answers to this question. One group of researchers concluded, "Research on violent television and films, video games, and music reveals unequivocal evidence that media violence increases the likelihood of aggressive and violent behavior," both in the short term and long term (Anderson et al., 2003). Their meta-analyses have found that the greater the exposure to violence in movies and on television, the stronger the likelihood of a person's behaving aggressively, and this correlation holds for both sexes and across cultures, from Japan to England (Anderson et al., 2010). Video games that directly reward violence, as by awarding points or moving the player to the next level after a "kill," increase feelings of hostility, aggressive thinking, and aggressive behavior (Carnagey & Anderson, 2005). Moreover, when grade-school children cut back on time spent watching TV or playing violent video games, the children's aggressiveness declines (Robinson et al., 2001).

Violent media may also desensitize people to the pain or distress of others. In one field study, people who had just seen a violent movie took longer to come to the aid of a woman struggling to pick up her crutches than did people who had seen a nonviolent movie or people still waiting to see one of the two movies (Bushman & Anderson, 2009).

However, an opposing group of psychologists believes that the effects of video games have been exaggerated and sensationalized (Ferguson & Kilburn, 2010). The correlation between playing violent video games and behaving aggressively is, they maintain, too small to worry about (Ferguson, 2007; Sherry, 2001). Other factors that are correlated with violent criminality are far more powerful; they include genetic influences (.75), perceptions of criminal opportunity (.58), owning a gun (0.35), poverty (.25), and childhood physical abuse (.22). In these researchers' calculations, watching violent video games has a much lower correlation, only .04 (Ferguson, 2009; Ferguson & Kilburn, 2010). Besides, they observe, rates of teenage violence *declined* significantly throughout the 1990s, a period in which the number of violent video games was *increasing* astronomically.

In the social-cognitive view, both conclusions about the relationship of media violence to violent behavior have merit. Repeated acts of aggression in the media *do* model behavior and responses to conflict that a small percentage of people may imitate. However, children and teens watch many different programs and movies and have many models to observe besides those they see in the media, including parents and peers. For every teenager who is obsessed with playing a video game that encourages dark fantasies of blowing up the world, hundreds more think the game is just entertainment and then go off to do their homework.

Moreover, perceptions and interpretations of events, personality dispositions such as aggressiveness and sociability, and the social context in which the violence is viewed can all affect how a person responds (Feshbach & Tangney, 2008). One person may learn from seeing people being blown away in a film that violence is cool and masculine; another may decide that the violent images are ugly and stupid; a third may conclude that they don't mean anything at all, that they are just part of the story.

What should be done, if anything, about media violence? Even if only a small percentage of viewers learn to be aggressive from observing all that violence, the social consequences can be serious, because the total audiences for TV, movies, and video games are immense. But censorship, which some people think is the answer, brings its own set of problems, quite apart from constitutional issues of free speech: Should we ban *Hamlet*? Bloody graphic comics? Films that truthfully depict the realities of war, murder, and torture?

Keep in mind that it's not just video games and other visual media that can increase aggression. In two studies, students read a violent passage from the Bible, with two sentences inserted in which God sanctions the violence. Later, in what they thought was a different study, they played a competitive reaction-time game with a partner. In the game, they were more willing to blast their competitor with a loud noise than were students who had been told the violent passage was from an ancient scroll or students who had read a passage that did not mention God (Bushman et al., 2007). Participants who believed in God were most affected by the passage in which God condones the violence, but many nonbelievers were affected too. Yet few people would be willing to ban the Bible or censure its violent parts.

As you can see, determining a fair and equitable policy regarding media violence will not be easy. It will demand good evidence—and good thinking.

Summary

((Listen to the Audio File at MyPsychLab

- Research on *learning* has been heavily influenced by *behaviorism*, which accounts for behavior in terms of observable events without reference to mental entities such as "mind" or "will." Behaviorists have focused on two types of *conditioning*: classical and operant.

Classical Conditioning

- *Classical conditioning* was first studied by Russian physiologist Ivan Pavlov. In this type of learning, when a neutral stimulus is paired with an *unconditioned stimulus* (US) that elicits a certain *unconditioned response* (UR), the neutral stimulus becomes associated with the US. The neutral stimulus then becomes a *conditioned stimulus* (CS), and has the capacity to elicit a *conditioned response* (CR) that is similar or related to the UR. Nearly any kind of involuntary response can become a CR.

- In *extinction*, the conditioned stimulus is repeatedly presented without the unconditioned stimulus, and the conditioned response eventually disappears, although later it may reappear (*spontaneous recovery*). In *higher-order conditioning*, a neutral stimulus becomes a conditioned stimulus by being paired with an already-established conditioned stimulus. In *stimulus generalization*, after a stimulus becomes a conditioned stimulus for some response, other similar stimuli may produce the same reaction. In *stimulus discrimination*, different responses are made to stimuli that resemble the conditioned stimulus in some way.

• Many theorists believe that what an animal or person learns in classical conditioning is not just an association between the US and CS, but also information conveyed by one stimulus about another. Indeed, classical conditioning appears to be an evolutionary adaptation that allows an organism to prepare for a biologically important event. Considerable evidence exists to show that a neutral stimulus does not become a CS unless it reliably signals or predicts the US.

Classical Conditioning in Real Life

• Classical conditioning helps account for positive emotional responses to particular objects and events, fears and phobias, reactions to particular foods and odors, and reactions to medical treatments and placebos. John Watson showed that after fears are learned they may be unlearned through a process of *counterconditioning*. Work on classical conditioning is now integrating findings on fear, learning, and biology. Using a drug to enhance the activity of a certain receptor in the amygdala speeds up the extinction of a phobia, fear of heights, during virtual-reality treatments. Because of evolutionary adaptations, human beings (and many other species) are biologically primed to acquire some classically conditioned responses easily, such as conditioned taste aversions and certain fears.

Operant Conditioning

• In *operant conditioning*, behavior becomes more likely or less likely to occur depending on its consequences. Responses in operant conditioning are generally not reflexive and are more complex than in classical conditioning. Research in this area is closely associated with B. F. Skinner, who called his approach "radical behaviorism."

• In the Skinnerian analysis, *reinforcement* strengthens or increases the probability of a response, and *punishment* weakens or decreases the probability of a response. Immediate consequences usually have a greater effect on a response than do delayed consequences.

• Reinforcers are called *primary* when they are naturally reinforcing because they satisfy a biological need. They are called *secondary* when they have acquired their ability to strengthen a response through association with other reinforcers. A similar distinction is made for punishers.

• Reinforcement and punishment may be either positive or negative, depending on whether the consequence involves a stimulus that is presented or one that is removed or avoided. In *positive reinforcement*, something pleasant follows a response; in *negative reinforcement*, something unpleasant is removed. In *positive punishment*, something unpleasant follows the response; in *negative punishment*, something pleasant is removed.

• *Extinction*, *stimulus generalization*, and *stimulus discrimination* occur in operant conditioning as well as in classical conditioning. A *discriminative stimulus* signals that a response is likely to be followed by a certain type of consequence.

• *Continuous reinforcement* leads to the most rapid learning. However, *intermittent (partial) reinforcement* makes a response resistant to extinction. In the behavioral view, one of the worst errors people make is to reward intermittently the responses they would like to eliminate.

• *Shaping* is used to train behaviors with a low probability of occurring spontaneously. Reinforcers are given for *successive approximations* to the desired response until the desired response is achieved.

• Biology places limits on what an animal or person can learn through operant conditioning or how easily a behavior is learned. Animals may have trouble learning a task because of *instinctive drift*.

Operant Conditioning in Real Life

• *Behavior modification*, the application of operant conditioning principles, has been used successfully in many settings, but when used inappropriately or incorrectly, reinforcement and punishment both have their pitfalls.

• Punishment, when used properly, can discourage undesirable behavior, including criminal behavior. But it is frequently misused and can have unintended consequences. It is often administered inappropriately because of the emotion of the moment; it may produce rage and fear; its effects are often only temporary; it is hard to administer immediately; it conveys little information about the kind of behavior that is desired; and it may provide attention that is rewarding. Extinction of undesirable behavior, combined with reinforcement of desired behavior, is generally preferable to the use of punishment.

• Reinforcers can also be misused. Rewards that are given out indiscriminately, as in efforts to raise children's self-esteem, do not reinforce desirable behavior. And an exclusive reliance on *extrinsic reinforcement* can sometimes undermine the power of *intrinsic reinforcement*. But money and praise do not usually interfere with intrinsic pleasure when a person is rewarded for succeeding or making progress rather than for merely participating in an activity, or when a person is already highly interested in the activity.

Learning and the Mind

• Even during behaviorism's heyday, some researchers were probing the "black box" of the mind. In the 1930s, Edward Tolman studied *latent learning*, in which no obvious reinforcer is present during learning and a response is not expressed until later on, when reinforcement does become available. What appears to be acquired in latent learning is not a specific response but rather knowledge about responses and their consequences.

• The 1960s and 1970s saw the increased influence of *social-cognitive learning theories*, which focus on *observational learning* and the role played by beliefs, interpretations of events, and other cognitions in determining behavior. Social-cognitive theorists argue that in observational learning as in latent learning, what is acquired is knowledge rather than a specific response. Perceptions, personality traits, and social contexts all influence how people respond to what they see and the different lessons they take away from an experience.

Psychology in the News, Revisited

- Behavioral and social-cognitive learning theories help us understand when punishment might be constructive and appropriate, and also when it backfires, as when harsh discipline is imposed for minor infractions, causing resentment and other undesirable results. The learning perspective offers good alternatives to punishment, and helps us appreciate the role of the environment in promoting "good" or "bad" behavior.

Taking Psychology With You

Psychologists disagree about the effects of depicted violence on real violence. Because people differ in their perceptions and beliefs, they also respond differently to violence in video games and the media. The issue of what restrictions, if any, should be placed on violent media is therefore a difficult one.

Key Terms

learning **321**

behaviorism **321**

conditioning **321**

unconditioned stimulus (US) **322**

unconditioned response (UR) **322**

conditioned stimulus (CS) **323**

conditioned response (CR) **323**

classical conditioning **323**

extinction (in classical conditioning) **323**

spontaneous recovery **323**

higher-order conditioning **324**

stimulus generalization (in classical conditioning) **324**

stimulus discrimination (in classical conditioning) **325**

phobia **327**

counterconditioning **328**

operant conditioning **331**

reinforcement/reinforcers **332**

punishment/punishers **332**

primary reinforcers and punishers **332**

secondary reinforcers and punishers **332**

positive and negative reinforcement and punishment **333**

Skinner box **334**

extinction (in operant conditioning) **335**

stimulus generalization (in operant conditioning) **335**

stimulus discrimination (in operant conditioning) **335**

discriminative stimulus **335**

continuous reinforcement **335**

intermittent (partial) schedule of reinforcement **335**

shaping **336**

successive approximations **336**

instinctive drift **337**

determinist view **338**

behavior modification (applied behavior analysis) **339**

extrinsic reinforcers **342**

intrinsic reinforcers **342**

latent learning **345**

social-cognitive learning theories **346**

observational (vicarious) learning **346**

- **Learning** is any relatively permanent change in behavior resulting from experience.
- **Behaviorism** explains learning as the result of observable acts and events without reference to mental entities, such as "mind" or "will."
- *Conditioning* involves associations between environmental stimuli and behavior.

Classical Conditioning

New Reflexes from Old

↓

Classical conditioning, first studied by Ivan Pavlov, is the process by which a previously neutral stimulus is paired with a stimulus that already elicits a response and, in turn, acquires the capacity to elicit a similar or related response.
- **Unconditioned stimulus (US):** a stimulus that elicits a certain response without additional learning.
- **Unconditioned response (UR):** a response elicited by a stimulus without additional learning.
- **Conditioned stimulus (CS):** an initially neutral stimulus that comes to elicit a conditioned response after being paired with an unconditioned stimulus.
- **Conditioned response (CR):** a response that is elicited by a conditioned stimulus.

Principles of Classical Conditioning

↓

- **Extinction:** the weakening and gradual disappearance of a CR after a CS is repeatedly presented without the US.
- **Counterconditioning:** the gradual disappearance of a CR produced by pairing a CS with another stimulus that elicits an incompatible response.
- **Higher-order conditioning:** a procedure in which a neutral stimulus becomes a CS through association with an already established CS.

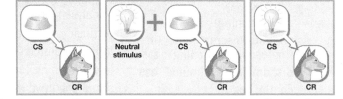

- **Stimulus generalization:** a CR occurs on presentation of a stimulus similar to the CS.
- **Stimulus discrimination:** stimuli similar to the CS produce different responses.

What Is Learned in Classical Conditioning?

↓

- Many psychologists argue that classical conditioning involves information conveyed by one stimulus about another—that the CS becomes a signal for the US.
- Classical conditioning appears to be an evolutionary adaptation that allows an organism to prepare for a biologically important event.

Classical Conditioning in Real Life

↓

Classical conditioning plays an important role in:
- positive emotional responses to particular objects and events.
- learned fears and phobias (as demonstrated in the Little Albert study).
- acquired tastes: likes and dislikes for particular foods and odors.
- unpleasant reactions to stimuli associated with medical treatments and reduced pain or anxiety in response to placebos.

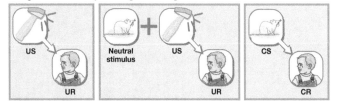

The Consequences of Behavior

- **Reinforcement** strengthens a response or makes it more likely to recur.

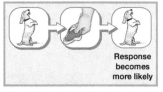

Response becomes more likely

- **Punishment** weakens a response or makes it less likely to recur.

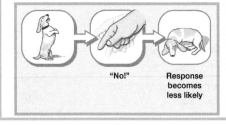

"No!"　Response becomes less likely

↓

Primary and Secondary Reinforcers and Punishers

- A **primary reinforcer** strengthens responses because it satisfies a biological need.
- A **secondary reinforcer** strengthens a response because of its association with other reinforcers.
- A **primary punisher** is a stimulus that is inherently punishing.
- A **secondary punisher** is a stimulus that has acquired punishing properties through association with other punishers.

↓

Positive and Negative Reinforcers and Punishers

- **Positive reinforcement:** a response is followed by the presentation of, or increase in intensity of, a reinforcing stimulus.
- **Negative reinforcement:** a response is followed by the removal, delay, or decrease in intensity of an unpleasant stimulus.
- In *positive punishment*, something unpleasant follows the response; in *negative punishment*, something pleasant is removed.

Operant conditioning is the process by which a response becomes more likely or less likely to occur, depending on its consequences; associated with the work of B. F. Skinner.

Operant Conditioning

Principles of Operant Conditioning

- **Extinction:** occurs when the behavior is no longer followed by the consequence that reinforced it.
- **Stimulus generalization:** a response reinforced (or punished) in the presence of one stimulus occurs (or is suppressed) in the presence of similar stimuli.
- **Stimulus discrimination:** a response occurs in the presence of one stimulus but not in the presence of similar ones that differ from it on some dimension.

- Schedules of reinforcement:
  o **Continuous reinforcement** leads to the fastest learning.
  o **Intermittent (partial) schedule of reinforcement** makes a response resistant to extinction.
- **Shaping:** used to train behaviors through reinforcement of successive approximations until the desired behavior occurs.
- **Instinctive drift:** the tendency for an organism to revert to instinctive behavior.

Operant Conditioning in Real Life

Behavior modification (also known as *applied behavior analysis*): the application of conditioning techniques outside the laboratory to teach new responses or eliminate behavior problems.

The Pros and Cons of Punishment

Punishment can effectively discourage undesirable behavior. However, as a method of correcting behavior, it often fails, for these reasons:
- It is often administered inappropriately or mindlessly.
- Recipients often respond with anxiety, fear, or anger.
- Effectiveness is only temporary, depending on the presence of the punishing person.
- The punishment is often too delayed to be effective.
- It does not convey what the person or animal *should* do.
- Its administration sometimes inadvertently rewards the unwanted behavior because it brings attention.

The Problems With Reward

- Rewards are often misused by being given indiscriminately, unrelated to desired behavior.
- Exclusive reliance on **extrinsic reinforcement** can undermine the power of **intrinsic reinforcement**, such as enjoyment of the task.
- The effects of extrinsic reinforcers depend on many factors, such as a person's initial motivation, the context, and whether improvement at a task is reinforced.

Learning and the Mind

Latent Learning

- **Latent learning** is not immediately expressed in performance.
- It can occur without obvious reinforcers.
- It involves acquiring knowledge about responses and their consequences, which permits flexibility in reaching goals.

Social-Cognitive Learning Theories

- **Social-cognitive learning theories** focus on **observational learning** and the role played by beliefs, interpretations of events, and other cognitions.

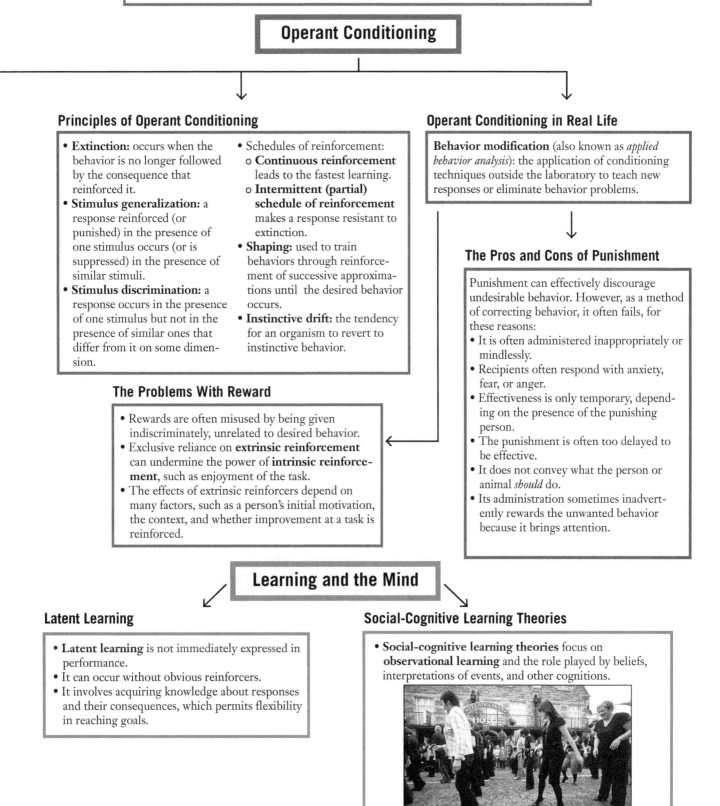

- Social-cognitive theorists argue that because people differ in their perceptions and beliefs, they may learn different lessons from the same situations, as in the case of media violence.

10

Roles and Rules

Social Influences on Beliefs and Behavior

Individuals in Groups

Us Versus Them: Group Identity

Prejudice and Group Conflict

Psychology in the News, Revisited

Taking Psychology With You: Dealing With Cultural Differences

SOCIOCULTURAL INFLUENCES ON HUMAN BEHAVIOR

PSYCHOLOGY IN THE NEWS /////////////////////////////

One Suspect in Boston Marathon Bombing Dead, One Captured

BOSTON, MA, April 19, 2013. Tamerlan Tsarnaev, 26, once hoped to fight on the U.S. Olympic team. His brother Dzhokhar Tsarnaev, 19, had been on his high school wrestling team and was attending the University of Massachusetts at Dartmouth on a city scholarship. The brothers had come to the United States about 10 years ago from Chechnya, a region of Russia. They lived together in Cambridge, and were said to be devout Muslims who did not drink or smoke. Now Tamerlan Tsarnaev is dead and his brother has been captured. Both are suspects in the Boston Marathon bombing last Monday that killed three people and severely injured more than 170 others.

The bombs used were crudely fashioned from ordinary kitchen pressure cookers packed with explosives, nails, and ball bearings designed to inflict maximum harm. The explosions killed an 8-year-old boy and two young women, one a graduate student from China.

Two years ago, Tamerlan told a Boston University student magazine that he did not have a single American friend. "I don't understand them," he said. But Dzhokhar had many American friends and was well liked, though his coach and friends said he was "quiet" and deeply influenced by his older brother. The father of the suspects, reached in Chechyna, described his younger son as "a true angel."

The brothers appeared in a surveillance video released by authorities a few days after the bombing. They were walking down a sidewalk, unnoticed by spectators at the race. Investigators asked for the public's help in identifying the two men, and calls began flooding in. A few hours later, the suspects reportedly carjacked a Mercedes in Cambridge. Police chased the vehicle, and exchanged gunfire with the driver and passenger. Tamerlan Tsarnaev was critically injured and

A surveillance camera captured this image of Dzhokhar Tsarnaev (left, in white cap) and Tamerlan Tsarnaev (in sunglasses), suspects in the Boston marathon bombing. Tamerlan was later killed in a shootout with the police; Dzhokhar was wounded and captured alive.

was soon pronounced dead; his brother fled the scene on foot. After a massive 26-hour manhunt, Dzhokhar was found hiding in a boat behind a suburban house, bleeding.

At a press conference the day after the bombing, Boston mayor Thomas Menino (2013) said, "This is a bad day for Boston but I think that if we pull together we'll get through it. We're a strong city. A lot of people are willing to work together to make this a better place for all the people, and so, as we gather here today with all our officials, let's say Boston will overcome."

/////////

Why would two brothers set off bombs on a beautiful spring day at the Boston Marathon—bombs designed to inflict as much harm and destruction as possible? Were they psychopaths or otherwise mentally ill? Were they unusually brutal and heartless? Even before the young men were identified, people everywhere were speculating on why anyone would commit such a callous act: Was it a random act of madness? Planned terrorism, domestic or foreign?

In an Israeli courtroom in 1961, Adolf Eichmann, who had been a high-ranking officer of the Nazi elite, was sentenced to death for his part in the deportation and killing of millions of Jews during World War II. But he insisted that he was not anti-Semitic. Shortly before his execution, Eichmann said, "I am not the monster I am made out to be. I am the victim of a fallacy" (R. Brown, 1986). The fallacy to which Eichmann referred was the widespread belief that a person who does monstrous deeds must be a monster. There does seem to be so much brutality in the world, and yet so much kindness, sacrifice, and heroism, too. How can we even begin to explain either side of human nature?

The fields of *social psychology* and *cultural psychology* approach this question by examining the powerful influence of the social and cultural environment on the actions of individuals and groups. In this chapter,

we will focus on the foundations of social psychology, basic principles that can help us understand why people who are not "crazy" or "monstrous" nonetheless do unspeakably evil things, and, conversely, why some otherwise ordinary people may reach heights of heroism when the occasion demands. We will look at the influence of roles and attitudes, how people's behavior is affected by the groups and situations they are in, and the conditions under which people conform or dissent. Finally, we will consider some of the social and cultural reasons for prejudice and conflict between groups.

Roles and Rules LO 10.1

"We are all fragile creatures entwined in a cobweb of social constraints," social psychologist Stanley Milgram once said. The constraints he referred to are social **norms**, rules about how we are supposed to act, enforced by threats of punishment if we violate them and promises of reward if we follow them. Norms are the conventions of everyday life that make interactions with other people predictable and orderly; like a cobweb, they are often

norms (social) Rules that regulate social life, including explicit laws and implicit cultural conventions.

role A given social position that is governed by a set of norms for proper behavior.

culture A program of shared rules that govern the behavior of members of a community or society, and a set of values, beliefs, and customs shared by most members of that community.

as invisible as they are strong. Every society has norms for just about everything in human experience: for conducting courtships, for raising children, for making decisions, for behavior in public places. Some norms are enshrined in law, such as "A person may not beat up another person, except in self-defense." Some are unspoken cultural understandings, such as "A man may beat up another man who insults his masculinity." And some are tiny, unspoken regulations that people learn to follow unconsciously, such as "You may not sing at the top of your lungs on a public bus."

When people observe that "everyone else" seems to be violating a social norm, they are more likely to do so too—and this is the mechanism by which entire neighborhoods can deteriorate. In six natural field experiments conducted in the Netherlands, passersby were more likely to litter, to park illegally, and even to steal a five-euro bill from a mailbox if the sidewalks were dirty and unswept, if graffiti marked the walls, or if strangers were setting off illegal fireworks (Keizer, Linderberg, & Steg, 2008). But people's behavior will become more constructive if they think that's the norm. When hotels put notices in guest bathrooms that say "the majority of guests in this room reuse their towels" (in contrast to simply requesting the guest to do the same because it's good for the environment), more than half agree to participate in the reuse program (Goldstein, Cialdini, & Griskevicius, 2008).

In every society, people also fill a variety of social **roles**, positions that are regulated by norms about how people in those positions should behave. Gender roles define the proper behavior for a man and a woman. Occupational roles determine the correct behavior for a manager and an employee, a professor and a student. Family roles set tasks for parent and child. Certain aspects of every role must be carried out or there will be penalties—emotional, financial, or professional. As a student, for instance, you know just what you have to do to pass your psychology course (or you should by now). How do you know what

Many roles in modern life require us to give up our individuality. If one of the members of this colorful marching band suddenly broke into a tango, his career would be brief—and the dazzling effect of the parade would be ruined. But when does adherence to a role go too far?

a role requirement is? You know when you violate it, intentionally or unintentionally, because you will probably feel awfully uncomfortable, or other people will try to make you feel that way.

👁 **Watch** the **Video** The Big Picture: The Social World at **MyPsychLab**

The requirements of a social role are in turn shaped by the culture you live in. **Culture** can be defined as a program of shared rules that govern the behavior of people in a community or society, and a set of values, beliefs, and customs shared by most members of that community and passed from one generation to another (Lonner, 1995). You learn most of your culture's rules and values the way you learn your culture's language: without thinking about it.

One cultural norm governs the rules for *conversational distance*: how close people normally stand to one another when they are speaking (Hall, 1959, 1976). In general, Arabs like to stand close enough to feel your breath, touch your arm, and see your eyes—a distance that makes

Get Involved! Dare to Be Different

Either alone or with a friend, try a mild form of norm violation (nothing alarming, obscene, dangerous, or offensive). You might stand backward in line at the grocery store or cafeteria; sit right next to a stranger in the library or at a movie, even when other seats are available; sing or hum loudly for a couple of minutes in a public place; or stand "too close" to a friend in conversation. Notice the reactions of onlookers, as well as your own feelings, while you violate this norm. If you do this exercise with someone else, one of you can be the "violator" and the other can write down how other people respond; then switch places. Was it easy to do this exercise? Why or why not?

Arabs stand much closer in conversation than Western-ers do. Most Westerners would feel "crowded" standing so close, even when talking to a close friend.

most white Americans, Canadians, and northern Europeans uneasy, unless they are talking inti-mately with a lover. The English and the Swedes stand farthest apart when they converse; southern Europeans stand closer; and Latin Americans and Arabs stand the closest (Keating, 1994; Sommer, 1969).

If you are talking to someone who has differ-ent cultural rules for distance from yours, you are likely to feel very uncomfortable without knowing why. You may feel that the person is crowding you or being strangely cool and distant. A stu-dent from Lebanon told us how relieved he was to understand how cultures differ in their rules for conversational distance. "When Anglo stu-dents moved away from me, I thought they were prejudiced," he said. "Now I see why I was more comfortable talking with Latino students. They like to stand close, too."

Naturally, people bring their own personali-ties and interests to the roles they play. Just as two actors will play the same part differently although they are reading from the same script, they will have their own reading of how to play the role of student, friend, parent, or employee. Nonetheless, the requirements of a social role are strong, so strong that they may even cause you to behave in ways that shatter your fundamental sense of the kind of person you are. We turn now to two classic studies that illuminate the power of social roles in our lives.

The Obedience Study LO 10.2, LO 10.3

In the early 1960s, Stanley Milgram (1963, 1974) designed a study that would become world famous. Milgram wanted to know how many people would obey an authority figure when di-rectly ordered to violate their ethical standards. Participants in the study thought they were part of an experiment on the effects of punishment on learning. Each was assigned, apparently at random, to the role of "teacher." Another person, introduced as a fellow volunteer, was the "learner." Whenever the learner, seated in an adjoining room, made an error in reciting a list of word pairs he was supposed to have memorized, the teacher had to give him an electric shock by depressing a lever on a machine (see Figure 10.1). With each error, the voltage (marked from 0 to 450) was to be increased by another 15 volts. The shock lev-els on the machine were labeled from SLIGHT SHOCK to DANGER—SEVERE SHOCK and, finally, ominously, XXX. In reality, the learners were confederates of Milgram and did not receive

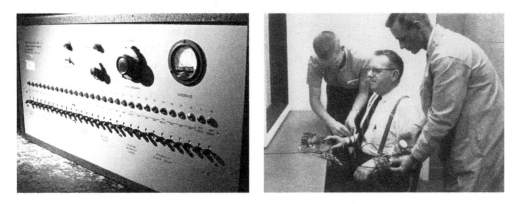

FIGURE 10.1 The Milgram Obedience Experiment
On the left is Milgram's original shock machine; in 1963, it looked pretty ominous. On the right, the "learner" is being strapped into his chair by the experimenter and the "teacher."

any shocks, but none of the teachers ever realized this during the study. The actor-victims played their parts convincingly: As the study continued, they shouted in pain and pleaded to be released, all according to a prearranged script.

 Watch the **Video** Classic Footage of Milgram's Obedience Study at **MyPsychLab**

Before doing this study, Milgram asked a number of psychiatrists, students, and middle-class adults how many people they thought would "go all the way" to XXX on orders from the researcher. The psychiatrists predicted that most people would refuse to go beyond 150 volts, when the learner first demanded to be freed, and that only one person in a thousand, someone who was disturbed and sadistic, would administer the highest voltage. The nonprofessionals agreed with this prediction, and all of them said that they personally would disobey early in the procedure.

That is not, however, the way the results turned out. Every single person administered some shock to the learner, and about two-thirds of the participants, of all ages and from all walks of life, obeyed to the fullest extent. Many protested to the experimenter, but they backed down when he calmly asserted, "The experiment requires that you continue." They obeyed no matter how much the victim shouted for them to stop and no matter how painful the shocks seemed to be. They obeyed even when they themselves were anguished about the pain they believed they were causing. As Milgram (1974) noted, participants would "sweat, tremble, stutter, bite their lips, groan, and dig their fingernails into their flesh"—but still they obeyed.

Over the decades, more than 3,000 people of many different ethnicities have gone through replications of the Milgram study. Most of them, men and women equally, inflicted what they thought were dangerous amounts of shock to another person. High percentages of obedience occur all over the world (Meeus & Raaijmakers, 1995; Smith & Bond, 1994).

Milgram and his team subsequently set up several variations of the study to determine the circumstances under which people might disobey the experimenter. They found that nothing the victim did or said changed the likelihood of compliance, even when the victim said he had a heart condition, screamed in agony, or stopped responding entirely, as if he had collapsed. However, people *were* more likely to disobey under certain conditions:

- **When the experimenter left the room**, many people subverted authority by giving low levels of shock but reporting that they had followed orders.

In Milgram's study, when the "teacher" had to administer shock directly to the learner, most subjects refused, but this one continued to obey.

- **When the victim was right there in the room**, and the teacher had to administer the shock directly to the victim's body, many people refused to go on.

- **When two experimenters issued conflicting demands**, with one telling participants to continue and another saying to stop at once, no one kept inflicting shock.

- **When the person ordering them to continue was an ordinary man**, apparently another volunteer instead of the authoritative experimenter, many participants disobeyed.

- **When the participant worked with peers who refused to go further**, he or she often gained the courage to disobey.

Obedience, Milgram concluded, was more a function of the *situation* than of the personalities of the participants. "The key to [their] behavior," Milgram (1974) summarized, "lies not in pent-up anger or aggression but in the nature of their relationship to authority. They have given themselves to the authority; they see themselves as instruments for the execution of his wishes; once so defined, they are unable to break free."

The Milgram study generated a firestorm of controversy over its ethics, significance, and interpretation, controversy that continues to this day. Some critics considered the experiment unethical because many of the participants suffered emotional pain, believing they might actually have seriously harmed another person, and because of the deception that Milgram relied on to get his results (Baumrind, 1964). Milgram replied that deception was essential because telling people in advance what he was looking for would obviously have invalidated his findings. But his critics were unpersuaded, arguing that telling your participants later the purpose of your research does not justify deceiving them at the outset or making them feel, even temporarily, that they were doing something cruel and injurious to another person.

Milgram's original study could never be repeated in the United States today because of these ethical concerns. However, a "softer" version of the experiment has been done, in which "teachers" were asked to administer shocks only up to 150 volts, when they first heard the learner protest. That amount of shock was a critical choice point in Milgram's study: Nearly 80 percent of those who went past 150 ended up going all the way to the end (Packer, 2008). Overall obedience rates in the "soft" version were only slightly lower than Milgram's, and once again, gender, education, age, and ethnicity had no effect on the likelihood of obeying (Burger, 2009).

Some psychologists have questioned Milgram's conclusions and interpretions, notably that personality traits are almost irrelevant to whether or not people obey an authority. Certain traits, especially hostility, narcissism, and rigidity, do increase obedience and a willingness to inflict pain on others (Blass, 2000; Twenge, 2009). Other critics have objected to the parallel Milgram drew between the behavior of the study's participants and the brutality of the Nazis and others who have committed acts of barbarism in the name of duty (Darley, 1995). The people in Milgram's study typically obeyed only when the experimenter was hovering right there, and many of them felt enormous discomfort and conflict. In contrast, most Nazis acted without direct supervision by authorities, without external pressure, and without feelings of anguish.

Nevertheless, it is clear that Milgram's compelling study has had a tremendous influence on public awareness of the dangers of uncritical obedience. As John Darley (1995) observed, "Milgram shows us the beginning of a path by means of which ordinary people, in the grip of social forces, become the origins of atrocities in the real world."

The Prison Study LO 10.4

Another famous demonstration of the power of roles is known as the Stanford prison study. Its designer, Philip Zimbardo, wanted to know what would happen if ordinary college students were randomly assigned to the roles of prisoners and guards. And so he and his associates set up a serious-looking "prison" in the basement of a Stanford building, complete with individual cells, different uniforms for prisoners and guards, and nightsticks for the guards (Haney, Banks, & Zimbardo, 1973). The students agreed to live there for two weeks.

Within a short time, most of the prisoners became distressed and helpless. They developed emotional symptoms and physical ailments. Some became apathetic; others became rebellious. One panicked and broke down. The guards, however, began to enjoy their new power. Some tried to be nice, helping the prisoners and doing little favors for them. Some were "tough but fair," holding strictly to "the rules." But about a third became punitive and harsh, even when the prisoners were not resisting in any way. One guard became unusually sadistic, smacking his nightstick into his palm as he vowed to "get" the prisoners and instructing two of them to simulate sexual acts (they refused). Zimbardo, who had not expected such a speedy and alarming transformation of ordinary students, ended this study after only six days.

Generations of students and the general public have seen emotionally charged clips from videos of the study made at the time. To Zimbardo and his colleague Craig Haney, the results demonstrated how roles affect behavior: The guards' aggression, they said, was entirely a result of wearing a guard's uniform and having the power conferred by a guard's authority (Haney & Zimbardo, 1998). Some social psychologists, however, have argued that the prison study is really another example of obedience to authority and of how willingly some people obey instructions, in this case from Zimbardo himself (Haslam & Reicher, 2003). Consider the briefing

Prisoners and guards quickly learn their respective roles, which often have more influence on their behavior than their personalities do.

that Zimbardo provided to the guards at the beginning of the study:

> You can create in the prisoners feelings of boredom, a sense of fear to some degree, you can create a notion of arbitrariness that their life is totally controlled by us, by the system, you, me, and they'll have no privacy.... We're going to take away their individuality in various ways. In general what all this leads to is a sense of powerlessness. That is, in this situation we'll have all the power and they'll have none (*The Stanford Prison Study* video, quoted in Haslam & Reicher, 2003).

These are pretty powerful suggestions to the guards about how they would be permitted to behave, and they convey Zimbardo's personal encouragement ("we'll have all the power"), so perhaps it is not surprising that some took Zimbardo at his word and behaved quite brutally. The one sadistic guard later said he was just trying to play the role of the "worst S.O.B. guard" he'd seen in the movies. Even the investigators themselves noted at the time that the data were "subject to possible errors due to selective sampling. The video and audio recordings tended to be focused upon the more interesting, dramatic events which occurred" (Haney, Curtis, & Zimbardo, 1973).

Despite these flaws, the Stanford prison study remains a useful cautionary tale. In real prisons, guards do have the kind of power that was given to these students, and they too may be given instructions that encourage them to treat prisoners harshly. Thus, the prison study provides a good example of how the social situation affects behavior, causing some people to behave in ways that seem out of character.

Watch the **Video** The Stanford Prison Experiment: Phil Zimbardo at **MyPsychLab**

Why People Obey LO 10.5

Of course, obedience to authority or to the norms of a situation is not always harmful or bad. A certain amount of routine compliance with rules is necessary in any group, and obedience to authority has many benefits for individuals and society. A nation could not operate if all its citizens ignored traffic signals, cheated on their taxes, dumped garbage wherever they chose, or assaulted each other. A business organization could not function if its members came to work only when they felt like it. But obedience also has a darker aspect. Throughout history, the plea "I was only following orders" has been offered to excuse actions carried out on behalf of orders that were foolish, destructive, or criminal.

The writer C. P. Snow once observed that "more hideous crimes have been committed in the name of obedience than in the name of rebellion."

Most people follow orders because of the obvious consequences of disobedience: They can be suspended from school, fired from their jobs, or arrested. But they may also obey because they hope to gain advantages or promotions, or expect to learn from the authority's greater knowledge or experience. They obey because they depend on the authority and respect the authority's legitimacy (van der Toorn, Tyler, & Jost, 2011). And, most of all, they obey because they do not want to rock the boat, appear to doubt the experts, or be rude, fearing that they will be disliked or rejected for doing so (Collins & Brief, 1995).

But what about all those people in Milgram's study who felt they were doing wrong and who wished they were free, but who could not untangle themselves from the "cobweb of social constraints"? How do people become morally disengaged from the consequences of their actions?

One answer is **entrapment**, a process in which individuals escalate their commitment to a course of action in order to justify their investment in it (Brockner & Rubin, 1985). The first stages of entrapment pose no difficult choices. But as people take a step, or make a decision to continue, they will justify that action, which allows them to feel that it is the right one. Before long, the person has become committed to a course of action that is increasingly self-defeating, harmful, or foolhardy (Tavris & Aronson, 2007).

Thus, in the Milgram study, once participants had given a 15-volt shock, they had committed themselves to the experiment. The next level was "only" 30 volts. Because each increment was small, before they knew it most people were administering what they believed were dangerously strong shocks. At that point, it was difficult to justify and explain a sudden decision to quit, especially after reaching 150 volts, the point at which the "learner" made his first verbal protests. Those who administered the highest levels of shock justified their actions by adopting the attitude "It's his problem; I'm just following orders," handing over responsibility for their actions to the authority (Kelman & Hamilton, 1989; Modigliani & Rochat, 1995). In contrast, individuals who refused to give high levels of shock took responsibility for their actions. "One of the things I think is very cowardly," said a 32-year-old engineer, "is to try to shove the responsibility onto someone else. See, if I now turned around and said, 'It's your fault... it's not mine,' I would call that cowardly" (Milgram, 1974).

A chilling study of entrapment was conducted with 25 men who had served in the Greek military

entrapment A gradual process in which individuals escalate their commitment to a course of action to justify their investment of time, money, or effort.

In 2003, photos of American guards at Abu Ghraib prison in Iraq, shown abusing and humiliating their prisoners, shocked the world. Lynndie England was convicted of maltreating Iraqi detainees and served half of a three-year sentence. "She was following orders," said England's sister, who said Lynndie was "a kind-hearted, dependable person." Were the Abu Ghraib guards good people who were "just following orders"? Or were they bad people? Social psychologists explain how otherwise good people can do bad things because of the roles they are assigned, the norms of the situation, entrapment, and self-justification.

police during the authoritarian regime that ended in 1974 (Haritos-Fatouros, 1988). A psychologist interviewed the men, identifying the steps used in training them to torture prisoners in the hope of gaining information. First, the men were ordered to stand guard outside the interrogation and torture cells. Then they stood guard inside the detention rooms, where they observed the torture of prisoners. Then they "helped" beat up prisoners. Once they had obediently followed these orders and became actively involved, the torturers found their actions easier to carry out. Similar procedures have been used around the world to train military and police interrogators to torture political opponents and criminal suspects, although torture is forbidden under international law (Conroy, 2000; Huggins, Haritos-Fatouros, & Zimbardo, 2003; Mayer, 2009).

From their standpoint, torturers justify their actions because they see themselves as good guys who are just doing their jobs, especially in wartime. And perhaps they are, but such a justification overlooks entrapment. This prisoner might be a terrorist, but what if this other one is completely innocent? Before long, the torturer has shifted his reasoning from "If this person is guilty, he deserves to be tortured" to "If I am torturing this person, he must be guilty." And so the torture escalates (Tavris & Aronson, 2007).

This is a difficult concept for people who divide the world into "good guys" versus "bad guys" and cannot imagine that good guys might do brutal things; if the good guys are doing it, by definition it's all right to do. Yet in everyday life, as in the Milgram study, people often set out on a path that is morally ambiguous, only to find that they have traveled a long way toward violating their own principles. From Greece's torturers to members of the American military, from Milgram's well-meaning volunteers to the rest of us, people face the difficult task of drawing a line beyond which they will not go. For many, the demands of the role and the social pressures of the situation defeat the inner voice of conscience.

Recite & Review

✓ **Study** and **Review** at **MyPsychLab**

Recite: Step into your role of student and say aloud what you know about norms, roles, conversational distance, the Milgram experiment, the Stanford prison study, and entrapment.

Review: Next, read this section again.

Now take this *Quick Quiz:*

1. In which condition are people likely to disobey the most? (a) when the experimenter physically administers the pain, (b) when the authoritative experimenter continues to give instructions, (c) when the experimenter is present in the room with the subject

2. State any two reasons that result in people behaving obediently.

3. A friend of yours, who is moving, asks you to bring over a few boxes. As long as you are there anyway, he asks you to fill them with books. Before you know it, you have packed up his kitchen, living room, and bedroom. What social-psychological process is at work here?

Answers:

1. a 2. to avoid the consequences of not obeying; on succumbing to group pressure 3. entrapment

You are about to learn...

- two general ways that people explain their own or other people's behavior—and why it matters.

- three self-serving biases in how people think about themselves and the world.

- why most people will believe outright lies and nonsensical statements if they are repeated often enough.

- whether certain fundamental political and religious attitudes have a genetic component.

Social Influences on Beliefs and Behavior

Social psychologists are interested not only in what people do in social situations, but also in what is going on in their heads while they are doing it. Those who study **social cognition** examine how people's perceptions of themselves and others affect their relationships and also how the social environment influences their perceptions, beliefs, and values. Current approaches draw on evolutionary theory, neuroimaging studies, surveys, and experiments to identify universal themes in how human beings perceive and feel about one another. In this section, we will consider two important topics in social cognition: attributions and attitudes.

Attributions LO 10.6, LO 10.7

People read detective stories to find out *who* did the dirty deed, but they also want to know *why* people do bad things. Was it because of a terrible childhood, a mental illness, possession by a demon, or what? According to **attribution theory**, the explanations we make of our behavior and the behavior of others generally fall into two categories. When we make a *situational attribution*, we are identifying the cause of an action as something in the situation or environment: "Joe stole the money because his family is starving." When we make a *dispositional attribution*, we are identifying the cause of an action as something in the person, such as a trait or a motive: "Joe stole the money because he is a born thief."

When people are trying to explain someone else's behavior, they tend to overestimate personality traits and underestimate the influence of the situation (Forgas, 1998; Nisbett & Ross, 1980). In terms of attribution theory, they tend to ignore situational attributions in favor of dispositional ones. This tendency has been called the **fundamental attribution error** (Jones, 1990).

social cognition An area in social psychology concerned with social influences on thought, memory, perception, and beliefs.

attribution theory The theory that people are motivated to explain their own and other people's behavior by attributing causes of that behavior to a situation or a disposition.

fundamental attribution error The tendency, in explaining other people's behavior, to overestimate personality factors and underestimate the influence of the situation.

Were the people who obeyed Milgram's experimenters and the student guards in the prison study sadistic by nature? Were the individuals who pocketed the money from a mailbox on a dirty street "born thieves"? Those who think so are committing the fundamental attribution error. The impulse to explain other people's behavior in terms of their personalities is so strong that we do it even when we know that the other person was *required* to behave in a certain way (Yzerbyt et al., 2001).

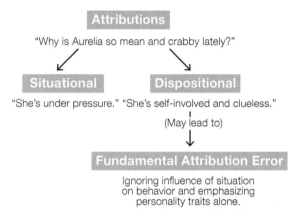

Attributions

"Why is Aurelia so mean and crabby lately?"

Situational   **Dispositional**

"She's under pressure." "She's self-involved and clueless."

(May lead to)

Fundamental Attribution Error

Ignoring influence of situation on behavior and emphasizing personality traits alone.

The fundamental attribution error is especially prevalent in Western nations, where middle-class people tend to believe that individuals are responsible for their own actions and dislike the idea that the situation has much influence over them. They think that *they* would have refused the experimenter's orders to harm another person and *they* would have treated fellow-students-temporarily-called-prisoners fairly. In contrast, in countries such as India, where everyone is embedded in caste and family networks, and in Japan, China, Korea, and Hong Kong, where people are more group oriented than in the West, people are more likely to be aware of situational constraints on behavior, including their own behavior (Balcetis, Dunning, & Miller, 2008; Choi et al., 2003). Thus, if someone is behaving oddly, makes a mistake, or commits an ethical lapse, a person from India or China, unlike a Westerner, is more likely to make a situational attribution of the person's behavior ("He's under pressure") than a dispositional one ("He's incompetent").

A primary reason for the fundamental attribution error is that people rely on different sources of information to judge their own behavior and that of others. We know what we ourselves are thinking and feeling, but we can't always know the same of others. Thus, we assess our own actions by introspecting about our feelings and intentions, but when we observe the actions of others, we have only their behavior to guide our interpretations (Pronin, 2008; Pronin, Gilovich, & Ross, 2004).

 Explore the **Concept** Fundamental Attribution Error at **MyPsychLab**

This basic asymmetry in social perception is further widened by *self-serving biases*, habits of thinking that make us feel good about ourselves, even when we shouldn't. We discuss other cognitive biases in Chapter 7, but here are three self-serving biases that are especially relevant to the attributions that people often make:

1 The bias to choose the most flattering and forgiving attributions of our behavior. People tend to choose attributions that are favorable to them, taking credit for their good actions (a dispositional attribution) but letting the situation account for their failures, embarrassing mistakes, or harmful actions (Mezulis et al., 2004). For instance, most North Americans, when angry, will say, "I am furious for good reason; this situation is intolerable." They are less likely to say, "I am furious because I am an ill-tempered grinch." On the other hand, if they do something admirable, such as donating to charity, they are likely to attribute their motives to a personal disposition ("I'm so generous") instead of the situation ("That guy on the phone pressured me into it").

2 The bias to think that we are better, smarter, and kinder than others. This bias has been called the "self-enhancement" bias or the "better than average" effect. It describes the tendency of most people to think they are much better than their peers on many valued dimensions: more virtuous, honorable, and moral; more competent; better drivers; more compassionate and generous (Balcetis, Dunning, & Miller, 2008; Brown, 2012; Dunning et al., 2003; Loughnan et al., 2011). They overestimate their willingness to do the right thing in a moral dilemma, give to a charity, cooperate with a stranger in trouble, and so on. But when they are actually in a situation that calls for generosity, compassion, or ethical action, most people fail to live up to their own inflated self-image because the demands of the situation have a stronger influence than good intentions. This bias even occurs among people who literally strive to be "holier than thou" and "humbler than thee" because of their religious convictions (Rowatt et al., 2002). In two studies conducted at fundamentalist Christian colleges, the greater the students' intrinsic religiousness and fundamentalism, the greater was their tendency to rate themselves as being more adherent to biblical commandments than other people—and more *humble* than other people, too!

3 The bias to believe that the world is fair. According to the **just-world hypothesis**, attributions are also affected by the need to believe that justice usually prevails, that good people are rewarded and bad ones punished (Lerner, 1980). When this belief is thrown into doubt—especially when bad things happen to "good people" who are just like us—we are motivated to restore it (Aguiar et al., 2008). Unfortunately, one common way of restoring the belief in a just world is to call on a dispositional attribution called *blaming the victim*: Maybe that person wasn't so good after all; he or she must have done something to deserve what happened or to provoke it. Blaming the victim is virtually universal when people are ordered to harm others or find themselves entrapped into harming others (Bandura, 1999). In the Milgram study, some "teachers" made comments such as, "[The learner] was so stupid and stubborn he deserved to get shocked" (Milgram, 1974).

Of course, sometimes dispositional attributions do explain a person's behavior. Just remember that the attributions you make can have huge consequences. Happy couples usually attribute their partners' occasional lapses to something in the situation ("Poor guy is under a lot of stress") and their partners' loving actions to something about them ("He has the sweetest nature"). But unhappy couples do just the reverse. They attribute lapses to their partners' personalities ("He is totally selfish") and good behavior to the situation ("Yeah, he gave me a present, but only because his mother told him to") (Karney & Bradbury, 2000). You can see why the attributions you make about your partner, your parents, and your friends will affect how you get along with them—and how long you will put up with their failings.

just-world hypothesis
The notion that many people need to believe that the world is fair and that justice is served, that bad people are punished and good people rewarded.

"When I was making money, I made the most money, and now that I'm spiritual I'm the most spiritual."

Attitudes LO 10.8

People hold attitudes about all sorts of things—politics, food, children, movies, sports heroes, you name it. An *attitude* is a belief about people, groups, ideas, or activities. Some attitudes are *explicit*: We are aware of them, they shape our conscious decisions and actions, and they can be measured on self-report questionnaires. Others are *implicit*: We are unaware of them, they may influence our behavior in ways we do not recognize, and they are measured in indirect ways (Stanley, Phelps, & Banaji, 2008).

Some of your attitudes change when you have new experiences, and on occasion they change because you rationally decide you were wrong about something. But attitudes also change because of the psychological need for consistency and the mind's normal biases in processing information. In Chapter 7, we discuss **cognitive dissonance**, the uncomfortable feeling that occurs when two attitudes, or an attitude and behavior, are in conflict (are dissonant). To resolve this dissonance, most people will change one of their attitudes. Thus, if a politician or celebrity you admire does something stupid, immoral, or illegal, you can restore consistency either by lowering your opinion of the person or by deciding that the person's behavior wasn't so stupid or immoral after all (Aronson, 2012).

cognitive dissonance
A state of tension that occurs when a person simultaneously holds two cognitions that are psychologically inconsistent or when a person's belief is incongruent with his or her behavior.

👁 **Watch** the **Video** Thinking Like a Psychologist: Changing Attitudes and Behaviors at **MyPsychLab**

Here's an example closer to home: cheating. Let's say two students have the same general attitude toward it: It's not an ideal way to get ahead, but it's not the greatest crime, either. Now they take an important exam and freeze on a crucial question. They have a choice: Read their neighbor's answers (to get a better grade) or refrain from doing so (to maintain feelings of integrity). Impulsively, one cheats; the other doesn't. What happens now? The answer is illustrated in Figure 10.2 on the next page. To reduce dissonance, each one will justify their action to make their beliefs about cheating consonant with their behavior. The one who refrained will begin to think that cheating is serious after all, that it harms everyone, and that cheaters should be punished—expel them! But the one who cheated will need to resolve the dissonance between "I am a fine, honest human being" and "I just cheated." He or she could say, "I guess I'm not an honest person after all," but it is more likely that the person will instead decide that cheating isn't very serious—after all, everyone does it!

Understanding how cognitive dissonance works to keep our beliefs and behavior in harmony is important because the way we reduce dissonance can have major, unexpected consequences. The student who cheated "just this once" will find it easier to cheat again on an assignment, and then again by turning in a term paper written by someone else, sliding down the slippery slope of entrapment. By the time the cheater has slid to the bottom, it will be extremely difficult to go back up because that would mean admitting, "I was wrong; I did a bad thing." That is how a small act of dishonesty, corruption, or error can set a person on a course of action that becomes increasingly self-defeating, cruel, or foolhardy... and difficult to reverse (Tavris & Aronson, 2007).

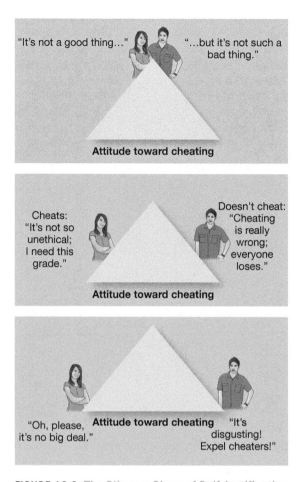

FIGURE 10.2 The Slippery Slope of Self-Justification Imagine two people with the same neutral attitude toward cheating. Given an opportunity, one cheats and the other doesn't. Because of the need to reduce cognitive dissonance, each will then justify the action they took so that their opinion about cheating is consonant with their behavior. Over time, they both will have moved a long way from their original attitude.

Unfortunately for their ability to think critically, people often restore cognitive consistency by dismissing evidence that might otherwise throw their fundamental beliefs into question. In fact, they often become even *more* committed to a discredited belief. In one study, when people were thrown into doubt about the rightness of a belief or their position on some issue that was very important to them—such as being a vegetarian or carnivore, a Mac or PC user—they reduced dissonance by advocating their original position even more strongly (Gal & Rucker, 2010). This mechanism explains why people in religious cults that have invested heavily in failed doomsday predictions rarely say, "What a relief that I was wrong." Instead, many become even more committed proselytizers.

Shifting Opinions and Bedrock Beliefs. All around you, every day, advertisers, politicians, and friends are trying to influence your attitudes. One weapon they use is the drip, drip, drip of a repeated idea. Repeated exposure even to a nonsense syllable such as *zug* is enough to make a person feel more positive toward it (Zajonc, 1968). The **familiarity effect**, the tendency to hold positive attitudes toward familiar people or things, has been demonstrated across cultures, across species, and across states of awareness, from alert to preoccupied. It works even for stimuli you aren't aware of seeing (Monahan, Murphy, & Zajonc, 2000). A related phenomenon is the **validity effect**, the tendency to believe that something is true simply because it has been repeated many times. Repeat something often enough, even the basest lie, and eventually the public will believe it. Hitler's propaganda minister, Joseph Goebbels, called this technique the "Big Lie."

In a series of experiments, Hal Arkes and his associates demonstrated how the validity effect operates (Arkes, 1993; Arkes, Boehm, & Xu, 1991). In a typical study, people read a list of statements, such as "Mercury has a higher boiling point than copper" or "Over 400 Hollywood films were produced in 1948." They had to rate each statement for its validity, on a scale of 1 (definitely false) to 7 (definitely true). A week or two later, they again rated the validity of some of these statements and also rated others that they had not seen previously. The result: Mere repetition increased the perception that the familiar statements were true. The same effect also occurred for other kinds of statements, including unverifiable opinions (e.g., "At least 75 percent of all politicians are basically dishonest"), opinions that subjects initially felt were true, and even opinions they initially felt were false. "Note that no attempt has been made to persuade," said Arkes (1993). "No supporting arguments are offered. We just have subjects rate the statements. Mere repetition seems to increase rated validity. This is scary."

On most everyday topics, such as movies, sports, and the boiling point of mercury, people's attitudes range from casual to committed. If your best friend is neutral about baseball whereas you are an insanely devoted fan, your friendship will probably survive. But when the subject is one involving beliefs that give meaning and purpose to a person's life—most notably, politics and religion—it's another ball game, so to speak. Wars have been fought, and are being fought as you read this, over people's most passionate convictions.

Perhaps the attitude that causes the most controversy and bitterness around the world is the one toward religious diversity: accepting or intolerant. Some people of all religions accept a world of differing religious views and practices; they

familiarity effect The tendency of people to feel more positive toward a person, item, product, or other stimulus the more familiar they are with it.

validity effect The tendency of people to believe that a statement is true or valid simply because it has been repeated many times.

When people hold attitudes that are central to their religious and political philosophies, they often fail to realize that the other side feels just as strongly.

believe that church and state should be separate. But for fundamentalists within any religion, the two domains are inseparable; they believe that one religion should prevail (Jost et al., 2003). You can see, then, why these irreconcilable attitudes cause continuing conflict, and sometimes are used to justify terrorism and war. Why are people so different in these views?

Do Genes Influence Attitudes?   Do you support or disapprove of the death penalty, bans on assault weapons, and tolerant immigration policies? Are you worried about global warming or do you think its dangers have been exaggerated? Where did your attitudes on these issues come from?

Many attitudes result from learning and experience, of course. But some core attitudes stem from personality traits that are heritable. That is, the variation among people in these attitudes is due in part to their genetic differences (see Chapter 2). Two such traits are "openness to experience" and "conscientiousness." We would expect people who are open to new experiences to hold positive attitudes toward novelty and change in general. We would expect people who prefer the familiar and conventional, and who

are conscientious about order and obligations, to be drawn to conservative politics and religious denominations. And that is what research finds. In a study of Protestant Christians, fundamentalists scored much lower than liberals on the dimension of openness to experience (Streyffeler & McNally, 1998). Conversely, conservatives score higher than liberals on conscientiousness (Jost, 2006).

Religious *affiliation*—whether a person is a Methodist, Muslim, Catholic, Jew, Hindu, and so on—is not heritable. Most people choose a religious group because of their parents, ethnicity, culture, and social class, and many switch their religious affiliation at least once in their lives. In the United States, Canada, and Europe, increasing numbers report having no religious affiliation or belief. But, as studies of twins reared apart have found, *religiosity*—a person's depth of religious feeling and adherence to a religion's rules—does have a genetic component. When religiosity combines with conservatism and authoritarianism (an unquestioning trust in authority), the result is a deeply ingrained acceptance of tradition and dislike of those who question it (Olson et al., 2001; Saucier, 2000).

Likewise, political affiliation is not heritable; it is largely related to your upbringing and to the friends you make in early adulthood, the key years for deciding which party you want to join. Nor do the casual political opinions held by many swing voters or people who are politically disengaged have a genetic component. But various political positions on emotionally hot topics that are associated with conservative or liberal views are partly heritable. A team of researchers analyzed two large samples of more than 8,000 sets of twins who had been surveyed about their personality traits, religious beliefs, and political attitudes (Alford, Funk, & Hibbing, 2005). The researchers compared the opinions of fraternal twins (who share, on average, 50 percent of their genes) with those of identical twins (who usually share all of their genes). They calculated how often the identical twins agreed on each issue, subtracted the rate at which fraternal twins agreed, and ended up with a rough measure of heritability. As you can see in Figure 10.3, the attitudes showing the highest heritability were those toward school prayer and property taxes; the attitudes showing the lowest influence of genes included those toward nuclear power, divorce, modern art, and abortion.

As a result of such evidence, some psychological scientists maintain that ideological belief systems may have evolved in human societies to be organized along a left–right dimension, consisting of two core sets of attitudes: (1) whether

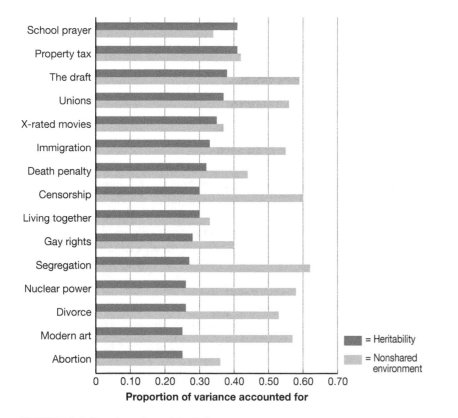

FIGURE 10.3 The Genetics of Belief

A study of thousands of identical and fraternal twins identified the approximate genetic contribution to the variation in attitudes about diverse topics. Heritability was greatest for school prayer and property tax, and lowest for divorce, modern art, and abortion. But notice that, in almost all cases, a person's unique life experiences (the nonshared environment) were far more influential than genes, especially on attitudes toward topics as unrelated as the draft, censorship, and segregation (Alford, Funk, & Hibbing, 2005).

a person advocates social change or supports the system as it is, and (2) whether a person thinks inequality is a result of human policies and can be overcome, or is inevitable and should be accepted as part of the natural order (Graham, Haidt, & Nosek, 2009). Liberals tend to prefer the values of progress, rebelliousness, chaos, flexibility, feminism, and equality, whereas conservatives tend to prefer tradition, conformity, order, stability, traditional values, and hierarchy. In a study of undergraduates, liberal students were more likely than conservative students to have favorable attitudes toward atheists, poetry, Asian food, jazz, street people, tattoos, foreign films, erotica, big cities, recreational drugs, and foreign travel— all examples of "openness to experience" rather than preference for the familiar (Jost, Nosek, & Gosling, 2008).

You can see why liberals and conservatives argue so emotionally over issues such as gun control and gay marriage. They are not only arguing about the specific issue, but also about underlying assumptions and values that emerge from their personality traits. Evolutionary psychologists

point out that both sets of attitudes would have had adaptive benefits over the centuries: Conservatism would have promoted stability, tradition, and order, whereas liberalism would have promoted flexibility and change (Graham, Haidt, & Nosek, 2009; Haidt, 2012).

These findings are provocative, but be careful not to oversimplify—say, by incorrectly assuming that everyone's political opinions are hardwired and unaffected by events. One factor that accounts for even more of the variation in political attitudes than heritability is individual life experiences, or what behavioral geneticists call the *nonshared environment* (Alford, Funk, & Hibbing, 2005; see Chapter 2). Another is generational, reflecting the shared experiences of your age group: Attitudes toward gay marriage, for example, have changed dramatically in a relatively short time; among most people younger than age 30, it's practically a non-issue.

> ⚛ **THINKING CRITICALLY**
>
> About the Genetics of Belief

What do you think might be the personality dispositions that underlie your own ideological commitments? How have experiences you've had, because of your family, gender, ethnicity, social class, or unique history, shaped your own political views?

Persuasion or "Brainwashing"? The Case of Suicide Bombers. LO 10.9

Let's now see how the social-psychological factors discussed thus far might help explain the tragic and disturbing phenomenon of suicide bombers. In many countries, young men and women have wired themselves with explosives and blown up soldiers, civilians, and children, sacrificing their own lives in the process. Although people on two sides of a war dispute the definition of terrorism—one side's "terrorist" is the other side's "freedom fighter"—most social scientists define it as politically motivated violence specifically designed to instill feelings of terror and helplessness in a population (Moghaddam, 2005). Are these perpetrators mentally ill? Have they been "brainwashed"?

"Brainwashing" implies that a person has had a sudden change of mind without being aware of what is happening; it sounds mysterious and strange. On the contrary, the methods used to create a terrorist suicide bomber are neither mysterious nor unusual (Bloom, 2005; Moghaddam, 2005). Some people may be more emotionally vulnerable than others to these methods, but most terrorists are not easily distinguishable from the general population. Indeed, the majority of them—including Mohamed Atta, who led the attack on the World Trade Center—have no psychopathology and are often quite educated and affluent (Krueger, 2007; Sageman, 2008; Silke, 2003). Rather than defining themselves as terrorists, they see themselves as committing "self-sacrificing violence for the greater good"; and far from being seen as crazy loners, most suicide bombers are celebrated and honored by their families and communities for their "martyrdom" (Bloom, 2005). This social support enhances their commitment to the cause (Bloom, 2005; Ginges & Atran, 2011). The methods of indoctrination that lead to that commitment include these elements:

• **The person is subjected to entrapment.** Just as ordinary people do not become torturers overnight, they do not become terrorists overnight either; the process proceeds step by step. At first, the new recruit to the cause agrees only to do small things; gradually the demands increase to spend more time, more money, make more sacrifices. Like other revolutionaries, people who become suicide bombers are idealistic and angry about injustices, real and perceived. But some ultimately take extreme measures because, over time, they have become entrapped in closed groups led by strong or charismatic leaders (Moghaddam, 2005).

The methods used in the indoctrination of suicide bombers are also used to indoctrinate members of some religious and New Age cults, sometimes with tragic results. More than 900 members of the Peoples Temple committed mass suicide at the instigation of their leader, Jim Jones.

- **The person's problems, personal and political, are explained by one simple attribution,** which is repeatedly emphasized: "It's all the fault of those bad people; we have to eliminate them."

- **The person is offered a new identity and is promised salvation.** The recruit is told that he or she is part of the chosen, the elite, or the saved. In 1095, Pope Urban II launched a holy war against Muslims, assuring his forces that killing a Muslim was an act of Christian penance. Any soldier or civilian killed in battle, the pope promised, would bypass thousands of years of torture in purgatory and go directly to heaven. This is what young Muslim terrorists are promised today for killing Western "infidels."

- **The person's access to disconfirming (dissonant) information is severely controlled.** As soon as a person is a committed believer, the leader limits the person's choices, denigrates critical thinking, and suppresses private doubts. Recruits may be physically isolated from the outside world and thus from antidotes

to the leader's ideas. They are separated from their families, are indoctrinated and trained for 18 months or more, and eventually become emotionally bonded to the group and the leader (Atran, 2003).

These methods are similar to those that have been used to entice Americans into religious and other sects (Ofshe & Watters, 1994; Singer, 2003). In the 1970s, the cult leader Jim Jones told the more than 900 members of his "Peoples Temple" that the time had come to die, and they dutifully lined up to drink a Kool-Aid-like drink mixed with cyanide. (The legacy of that massacre is the term "drinking the Kool-Aid," which refers to a person or group's unquestioning belief in an ideology that could lead to their death.) In the 1990s, David Koresh, leader of the Branch Davidian cult in Waco, Texas, led his followers to a fiery death in a shootout with the FBI. In these groups, as in the case of terrorist cells, most recruits started out as ordinary people with no intention of ever committing murder or suicide. Yet, after being subjected to the influence techniques we have described, they ended up doing things that they once would have found unimaginable.

Recite & Review

✔ Study and Review at MyPsychLab

Recite: Speak aloud what you know about implicit and explicit attitudes, cognitive dissonance, the familiarity and validity effects, genetic contributions to certain attitudes, and persuasion techniques used to recruit people into terrorist groups and various sects.

Review: Next, reread this section.

Now, don't make us brainwash you into taking this *Quick Quiz:*

1. Candidate Carson spends $3 million to make sure his name is seen and heard frequently and to repeat unverified charges that his opponent is a thief. What psychological processes is he relying on to win?

2. Which of the following has a significant heritable component? (a) religious affiliation, (b) political affiliation, (c) political conservatism

3. A friend urges you to join a "life-renewal" group called "The Feeling Life." Your friend has been spending increasing amounts of time with her fellow Feelies, and has already contributed more than $2,000 to their cause. You have some doubts about them. What questions would you want to have answered before joining up?

Answers:

1. The familiarity effect and the validity effect 2. c 3. A few things to consider: Is there an autocratic leader who suppresses dissent and criticism, while rationalizing this practice as a benefit for members—for example, by saying to potential skeptics, "Doubt and disbelief are signs that your feeling side is being repressed."? Have long-standing members given up their friends, families, interests, and ambitions for this group? Does the leader offer simple but unrealistic promises to repair your life and all your troubles? Are members required to make sacrifices by donating large amounts of time and money?

You are about to learn...

- why people in groups often go along with the majority even when the majority is dead wrong.
- how "groupthink" can lead to bad decisions.
- how crowds can create "bystander apathy" and unpredictable violence.
- the conditions that increase the likelihood that some people will dissent, take risks to help others, or blow the whistle on wrongdoers.

Individuals in Groups

The need to belong may be the most powerful of all human motivations. That makes good evolutionary sense because, like apes, bees, and elephants, human beings could never have survived without being accepted by their tribe. The need for connection helps explain why sending a prisoner to solitary confinement is everywhere considered a form of torture, more devastating than physical abuse (Gawande, 2009). In fact, the *social* pain of being rejected, humiliated, or excluded activates parts of the brain that are highly diagnostic of *physical* pain (Chen et al., 2008; DeWall & Bushman, 2011; Williams, 2009). Rejection hurts, literally. Accordingly, the most powerful weapon that groups have to ensure their members' cooperation, and to weed out unproductive or disruptive members, is ostracism—rejection or permanent banishment.

Of course, we all belong to many different groups, which vary in their importance to us. But the point to underscore is that as soon as we join a bunch of other people, we act differently than we would on our own. This change occurs regardless of whether the group has convened to solve problems and make decisions, has gathered to have a party, consists of anonymous bystanders or members of an Internet chat room, or is a crowd of spectators or celebrants.

Conformity LO 10.10

The first thing that people in groups do is conform, taking action or adopting attitudes as a result of real or imagined group pressure. Suppose that you are required to appear at a psychology laboratory for an experiment on perception. You join seven other students seated in a room. You are shown a 10-inch line and asked which of three other lines is identical to it. The correct answer, line A, is obvious, so you are amused when the first person in the group chooses line B. "Bad eyesight," you say to yourself. "He's off by 2 whole inches!" The second person also chooses line B. "What a dope," you think. But by the time the fifth person has chosen line B, you are beginning to doubt yourself. The sixth and seventh students also choose line B, and now you are worried about *your* eyesight. The experimenter looks at you. "Your turn," he says. Do you follow the evidence of your own eyes or the collective judgment of the group?

Test line   A   B   C

This was the design for a series of famous studies of conformity conducted by Solomon Asch (1952, 1965), and the seven "nearsighted" students were his confederates. Asch wanted to know what people would do when a group unanimously contradicted an obvious fact. He found that when people made the line comparisons on their own, they were almost always accurate. But in the group, only 20 percent of the students remained completely independent on every trial, and often they apologized for not agreeing with the others. One-third conformed to the group's incorrect decision more than half the time, and the rest conformed at least some of the time. Whether or not they conformed, the students often felt uncertain of their decision. As one participant later said, "I felt disturbed, puzzled, separated, like an outcast from the rest." Asch's experiment has been replicated many times and in many countries (Bond & Smith, 1996).

Two basic motives for conformity appear in many species besides human beings, suggesting that conformity has a highly adaptive function

Sometimes people like to conform to feel part of the group... and sometimes they like to assert their individuality.

(Claidière & Whiten, 2012). One motive is the *need for social acceptance*, which is the reason that people can end up doing all kinds of stupid things (or smart things) simply because their friends are doing them. Taking advantage of this motive, social psychologists have designed interventions that rally people's peer groups to help them stop smoking and binge drinking, stay in school, improve their academic performance, and make many other beneficial changes they might not make on their own (Wilson, 2011).

The second motive for conformity is the *need for information* before deciding on the "right" thing to do (Cialdini, 2009). People often intuitively understand that sometimes the group knows more than they do, and this reliance on group judgment begins in early childhood. When 3- and 4-year-old children were given a choice between relying on information provided by a three-adult majority or a single adult about the name of an unfamiliar object, they sided with the majority (Corriveau, Fusaro, & Harris, 2009). It works the same way with adults: The belief that "everyone else" is doing something must mean it is the wisest choice or course of action.

Like obedience, therefore, conformity has positive aspects. Society runs more smoothly when people feel that they belong, know how to behave in a given situation, and share the same norms. But also like obedience, conformity has negative consequences, notably its power to suppress critical thinking and creativity. In a group, many people will deny their private beliefs, agree with silly notions, and even repudiate their own values—just to be accepted.

Groupthink LO 10.11

Close, friendly groups usually work well together. But they face the problem of getting the best ideas and efforts from their members while avoiding an extreme form of conformity called **groupthink**, the tendency for a group's participants to think alike and suppress dissent. According to Irving Janis (1982, 1989), groupthink occurs when a group's need for total agreement overwhelms its need to make the wisest decision. The symptoms of groupthink include the following:

- **An illusion of invulnerability.** The group believes it can do no wrong and is 100 percent correct in its decisions.

- **Self-censorship.** Dissenters decide to keep quiet rather than make trouble, offend their friends, or risk being ridiculed.

- **Pressure on dissenters to conform.** The leader teases or humiliates dissenters or otherwise pressures them to go along.

- **An illusion of unanimity.** By discouraging dissent and failing to consider alternative courses of action, leaders and group members create an illusion of consensus; they may even explicitly order suspected dissenters to keep quiet.

Throughout history, groupthink has led to disastrous decisions in military and civilian life. In 1961, President John F. Kennedy and his advisers approved a CIA plan to invade Cuba at the Bay of Pigs and try to overthrow the government of Fidel Castro; the invasion was a humiliating defeat. In the mid-1960s, President Lyndon Johnson and his cabinet escalated the war in Vietnam despite obvious signs that further bombing and increased troops were not bringing the war to an end. In 1986, NASA officials insulated themselves from the dissenting objections of engineers who warned them that the space shuttle *Challenger* was unsafe; NASA launched it anyway, and it exploded shortly after takeoff. And when President George W. Bush launched an invasion of Iraq, claiming the country had weapons of mass destruction and was allied with al-Qaeda,

groupthink The tendency for all members of a group to think alike for the sake of harmony and to suppress disagreement.

"All those in favor say 'Aye.'"
"Aye."
"Aye."
"Aye."
"Aye."
"Aye."

he and his team ignored dissenters and evidence from intelligence agencies that neither claim was true (Mayer, 2009). The agencies themselves later accused the Bush administration of "groupthink."

 Watch the **Video** IT Video: Group Thinking at MyPsychLab

Fortunately, groupthink can be minimized if the leader rewards the expression of doubt and dissent, protects and encourages minority views, asks group members to generate as many alternative solutions to a problem as they can think of, and has everyone try to think of the risks and disadvantages of the preferred decision. Resistance to groupthink can also be fostered by creating a group identity that encourages members to think of themselves as open-minded problem solvers rather than invulnerable know-it-alls (Turner, Pratkanis, & Samuels, 2003). When group members identify strongly with the collective enterprise, they are more likely to offer dissenting opinions because they are less willing to support a decision they regard as harmful to the group's goal (Packer, 2009).

Not all leaders want to run their groups this way, of course. For many people in positions of power, from presidents to company executives to movie moguls, the temptation is great to surround themselves with others who agree with what they want to do and to demote or fire those who disagree on the grounds that they are being "disloyal." Perhaps a key quality of great leaders is that they are able to rise above this temptation.

The Wisdom and Madness of Crowds LO 10.12

On the TV quiz show "Who Wants to Be a Millionaire?", contestants are given the chance to ask the audience how it would answer a question. This gimmick comes straight from a phenomenon known as the "wisdom of crowds": the fact that a crowd's judgment is often more accurate than that of most of its individual members (Surowiecki, 2004; Vul & Pashler, 2008). But crowds can create havoc, too. They can spread gossip, rumors, misinformation, and panic as fast as the flu. They can turn from joyful and peaceful to violent and destructive in a flash.

Diffusion of Responsibility. Suppose you were in trouble on a city street or in another public place—say, being mugged or having a sudden appendicitis attack. Do you think you would be more likely to get help if (1) one other person was passing by, (2) several other people were in the area, or (3) dozens of people were in the area? Most people would choose the third answer, but that is not how

Get Involved! Would You Speak Up?

You have been reading in this chapter about why people go along with others, not wanting to be "rude" or disobedient (as in the Milgram experiment), or conforming in order to be liked and accepted. Now imagine that you are hanging out with friends when one makes an ugly remark about "those people," not knowing that you are actually one of "those people." You feel angry and embarrassed, but would you say anything? Why or why not? If you think you would speak up, what would you say? Would you speak up if the ugly remark was not about your own group?

human beings operate. On the contrary, the more people there are around you, the *less* likely that one of them will come to your aid. Why?

The answer has to do with a group process called the **diffusion of responsibility**, in which responsibility for an outcome is diffused, or spread, among many people, reducing each individual's personal sense of accountability. One result is *bystander apathy*: In crowds, when someone is in trouble, individuals often fail to take action or call for help because they assume that someone else will do so (Darley & Latané, 1968; Fischer et al., 2011). This happens all over the world. In Foshan, China, a 2-year-old girl was run over by a van. For the next seven minutes, more than a dozen people, recorded by an impassive security camera, walked or bicycled past her, doing nothing. Eventually, a woman pulled the little girl to the side of the road and she was taken to a hospital, where she died soon thereafter.

A meta-analysis of the many studies done since the first identification of bystander apathy revealed some cause for optimism, though: In truly dangerous, *unambiguous* emergencies—a child is drowning, or people are being shot at by a gunman in a school, movie, or street—people are more likely to rush to help, and in fact are often spurred to do so by the presence of others. One reason is that the person who intervenes counts on getting physical and psychological support from other observers. In addition, dangerous emergencies are most effectively handled by cooperation among observers (Fischer et al., 2011).

 Watch the **Video** The Basics: Under the Influence of Others at MyPsychLab

Deindividuation. The most extreme instances of the diffusion of responsibility occur in large, anonymous mobs or crowds. The crowds may consist of cheerful sports spectators or angry rioters. Either way, people often lose awareness of their individuality and seem to hand themselves over to the mood and actions of the crowd, a state called **deindividuation** (Festinger, Pepitone, & Newcomb, 1952). You are more likely to feel deindividuated in a large city, where no one recognizes you, than in a small town, where it is hard to hide. You are also more likely to feel deindividuated in large classes, where you might—mistakenly—think you are invisible to the teacher, than in small ones. Sometimes organizations actively promote the deindividuation of their members as a way of enhancing conformity and allegiance to the group. This is an important function of uniforms or masks, which eliminate each member's distinctive identity.

Deindividuation has long been considered a prime reason for mob violence. According to

People in crowds, feeling anonymous, may do destructive things they would never do on their own. These soccer hooligans are kicking a fan of the opposition team during a night of violence.

this explanation, because deindividuated people in crowds "forget themselves" and do not feel accountable for their actions, they are more likely to violate social norms and laws—breaking store windows, getting into fights, or rioting at a sports event—than they would be on their own. But deindividuation does not always make people more combative. Sometimes it makes them more friendly; think of all the chatty, anonymous people on buses and planes who reveal things to their seatmates they would never tell anyone they knew.

What really seems to be happening when people are in large crowds or anonymous situations is not that they become mindless or uninhibited. Rather, they become *disinhibited*, just as if they were intoxicated on alcohol. That disinhibition, in turn, makes them more likely to conform to the norms of the *specific situation*, which may be either antisocial or prosocial (Hirsh, Galinsky, & Zhong, 2011; Postmes & Spears, 1998). College students who go on sprees during spring break may be violating local laws and norms not because their aggressiveness has been released but because they are conforming to the "Let's party!" norms of their fellow students. Crowd norms can also foster helpfulness, as they often do in the aftermath of disasters such as the Boston Marathon bombing, when strangers rush to help victims and rescuers with medical aid, food, clothes, and tributes. Sometimes both norms operate at the same time: After a soccer loss to Boston in the World Cup in Vancouver in 2011, many Canucks fans rioted, burning cars, smashing windows, and looting; but other fans did what they could, sometimes at risk

diffusion of responsibility In groups, the tendency of members to avoid taking action because they assume that others will.

deindividuation In groups or crowds, the loss of awareness of one's own individuality.

to themselves, to protect cars and other property and maintain the law.

And so, should the deindividuation excuse, like the "I was only following orders" excuse, exonerate a person of responsibility for looting or even murder? What do you think?

✳ Explore the Concept Could You Be a Hero? at MyPsychLab

Altruism and Dissent LO 10.13

We have seen how roles, norms, and pressures to obey authority and conform to one's group can cause people to behave in ways they might not otherwise. Yet throughout history men and women, as individuals and with allies, have disobeyed orders they believed to be wrong and have gone against prevailing cultural beliefs; their actions have sometimes changed the course of history. In 1955, in Montgomery, Alabama, Rosa Parks refused to give up her bus seat to a white passenger, and she was arrested for breaking the law. Her protest sparked a 381-day bus boycott and helped launch the modern civil rights movement.

So we don't want you to get the impression that social psychology is only about the bleaker side of human nature. Social psychology's study of conformity, obedience, groupthink, and similar processes should not distort the fuller picture: low-status, oppressed groups often challenge authority and fight back even in extreme situations. Some prisoners rebelled in the Stanford prison study, members of underground and resistance groups behaved heroically in Nazi Germany, and blacks and whites in South Africa organized to combat the official policy of apartheid (Haslam & Reicher, 2012).

Nonetheless, the costs of dissent, courage, and rebellion are often high; remember that most groups do not welcome nonconformity and disagreement. Most whistle-blowers, far from being rewarded for their bravery, are punished for it. Three women were named *Time* magazine's Persons of the Year for their courage in exposing wrongdoing in their respective organizations—Enron, WorldCom, and the FBI—yet all paid a steep professional price for doing so. Specialist Joseph Darby was horrified when he observed the abuses going on at Abu Ghraib prison, where guards were tormenting and humiliating detainees. "I had the choice between what I knew was morally right, and my loyalty to other soldiers," he recalled later, articulating his cognitive dissonance. "I couldn't have it both ways." Because the abuse "violated everything I personally believed in and all I'd been taught about the rules of war," he chose to report what he saw to his superiors. For doing this, Darby was shunned by many of his peers and received death threats. Studies of whistle-blowers find that half to two-thirds lose their jobs and have to leave their professions entirely. Many lose their homes and families (Alford, 2001).

Nonconformity, protest, and *altruism*, the willingness to take selfless or dangerous action on behalf of others, are in part a matter of personal convictions and conscience. However, just as there are situational reasons for obedience and conformity, so there are external influences on a person's decision to state an unpopular opinion, choose conscience over conformity, or help a stranger in trouble. Here are some of the situational factors that can overcome bystander apathy and increase the likelihood of helping others or behaving courageously:

1 You perceive the need for intervention or help. It may seem obvious, but before you can take independent action, you must realize that such action is necessary. Sometimes people willfully blind

When we think of "heroes," we tend to think of men, such as firefighters and rescue workers who work hard to save others after a disaster strikes. But heroism comes in many forms, from donating a kidney to save a life to blowing the whistle on your employer's cover-up of wrongdoing, and in most situations both sexes are equally likely to be brave (Rankin & Eagly, 2008). On the right, FBI agent Coleen Rowley is shown testifying to the Senate that the FBI had blocked the investigation of a man involved in planning the terrorist attacks on the World Trade Centers. She was subsequently fired.

themselves to wrongdoing to justify their own inaction ("I'm just minding my business"; "I have no idea what they're doing over there at that concentration camp"). But blindness to the need for action also occurs when a situation imposes too many demands on people's attention, as it often does for residents of densely populated cities.

2 Cultural norms encourage you to take action. Would you spontaneously tell a passerby that he or she had dropped a pen? Offer to help a person with an injured leg who had dropped an armful of magazines? Assist a blind person across the street? An international field study investigated strangers' helpfulness to one another with those three nonemergency acts of kindness, in 23 American cities and 22 cities in other countries. Cultural norms for helping were more important than population density in predicting levels of helpfulness: Pedestrians in busy Copenhagen and Vienna were kinder to strangers than were passersby in busy New York City. Large differences in helping rates emerged, ranging from 93 percent in Rio de Janeiro, Brazil, to 40 percent in Kuala Lumpur, Malaysia (R. Levine, 2003; Levine, Norenzayan, & Philbrick, 2001).

3 You have an ally. In Asch's conformity experiment, the presence of one other person who gave the correct answer was enough to overcome agreement with the majority. In Milgram's experiment, the presence of someone who disobeyed the experimenter's instruction to shock the learner sharply increased the number of people who also disobeyed. One dissenting member of a group may be viewed as a troublemaker, but two or three are a coalition. An ally reassures a person of the rightness of the protest, and their combined efforts may eventually persuade the majority (Wood et al., 1994).

4 You become entrapped. Does this sound familiar by now? Once having taken the initial step of getting involved, most people will increase their commitment. In one study, nearly 9,000 federal employees were asked whether they had observed wrongdoing at work, whether they had told anyone about it, and what happened if they had told. Nearly half of the sample had observed some serious cases of wrongdoing, such as stealing federal funds, accepting bribes, or creating a situation that was dangerous to public safety. Of that half, 72 percent had done nothing at all, but the other 28 percent reported the problem to their immediate supervisors. Once they had taken that step, a majority of the whistle-blowers eventually took the matter to higher authorities (Graham, 1986).

As you can see, certain social and cultural factors make altruism, disobedience, and dissent more likely to occur, just as other external factors suppress them.

Recite & Review

✓ **Study** and **Review** at **MyPsychLab**

Recite: Say aloud what you know about social acceptance and rejection, the motives for conformity, groupthink, the diffusion of responsibility, bystander apathy, deindividuation, and the conditions that foster altruism and dissent.

Review: Next, take responsibility for your learning by rereading this section.

Now take this *Quick Quiz:*

A. Which phenomenon is illustrated in each of the following situations?

   1. The president's closest advisers are afraid to disagree with his views on energy policy.
   2. You are at a costume party wearing a silly gorilla suit. When you see a chance to play a practical joke on the host, you do it.
   3. Walking down a busy street, you see that fire has broken out in a store window. "Someone must already have called the fire department," you say.

B. Imagine you are chief executive officer of a new company that makes electric cars. You want your employees to feel free to offer their suggestions and criticisms to improve productivity and satisfaction. You also want them to inform managers if they find any evidence that the cars are unsafe, even if that means delaying production. What concepts from this chapter could you use in setting company policy?

Answers:

A. 1. groupthink 2. deindividuation 3. bystander apathy brought on by diffusion of responsibility B. Some possibilities: You could encourage, or even require, dissenting views; avoid deindividuation by rewarding innovative suggestions and implementing the best ones; stimulate employees' commitment to the task (building a car that will help solve the world's pollution problem); and establish a written policy to protect whistle-blowers. What else can you think of?

You are about to learn...

- how people in a multicultural society balance ethnic identity and acculturation.
- what causes ethnocentric, us-versus-them thinking and how to decrease it.
- how stereotypes benefit us but also distort reality.

Us Versus Them: Group Identity

social identity The part of a person's self-concept that is based on his or her identification with a nation, religious or political group, occupation, or other social affiliation.

ethnic identity A person's identification with a racial or ethnic group.

acculturation The process by which members of minority groups come to identify with and feel part of the mainstream culture.

Each of us develops a personal identity that is based on our particular traits and unique life history. But we also develop **social identities** based on the groups we belong to, including our national, religious, political, and occupational groups (Brewer & Gardner, 1996; Tajfel & Turner, 1986).

Ethnic Identity LO 10.14

In multicultural societies such as the United States and Canada, different social identities often collide. In particular, people often face the dilemma of balancing an **ethnic identity**, a close identification with a religious or ethnic group, and **acculturation**, identification with the dominant culture (Berry, 2006; Phinney, 1996). The hallmarks of having an ethnic identity are that you identify with the group, feel proud to be a member, feel emotionally attached to the group, and behave in ways that conform to the group's rules, values, and norms.

Interestingly, many North Americans no longer want to be pigeonholed into only one ethnic or racial category. Many have created combined identities, such as Blaxican (African American and Mexican), Negripino (African American and Filipino), Hafu (half-Japanese, half-something else), and Chino-Latino (Chinese and Hispanic). The blurring of traditional ethnic and racial boundaries is likely to continue: In 2010, nearly 15 percent of all new marriages in the United States were interracial, more than double the number in 1980.

Nonetheless, most ethnic minorities remain identified with their culture of origin, while picking and choosing among the values, foods, and customs of the mainstream culture. Yet any observer of the world today knows that acculturation is not always easy, in any nation. Many immigrants arrive in their host country with every intention of becoming part of the mainstream culture. If they encounter discrimination or setbacks, however, they may realize that acculturation is harder than they anticipated and that their original ethnic identity offers greater solace. Indeed, there seems to be a critical period for successful acculturation: People become better able to identify with their host culture the longer they are exposed to it, but, as a study of Chinese immigrants in Canada found, often only if that exposure occurs when they are relatively young (Cheung, Chudek, & Heine, 2011).

Ethnic identities are changing these days, as bicultural North Americans blend aspects of mainstream culture with their own traditions. But many people still like to celebrate their ethnic heritage, as illustrated in these photos of Irish Americans celebrating St. Patrick's Day, Japanese Americans reviving *taiko* (traditional Japanese drumming), and Mexican Americans celebrating Cinco de Mayo.

Get Involved! How Acculturated Are You?

Do you have an ethnic identity? If you are a member of an ethnic minority within your country, city, or college, how acculturated do you feel? Do you feel at ease in more than one culture, or only in your own? Does your comfort level depend on the situation you're in? Now ask five friends, relatives, or acquaintances, ideally from different ethnic groups, how they would answer these questions. If you feel that you do not have an ethnic heritage other than a national identity, why is that? Would your parents and grandparents feel the same as you do?

Ethnocentrism

Social identities give us a sense of place and position in the world. Without them, most of us would feel like loose marbles rolling around in an unconnected universe. It feels good to be part of an "us." But does that mean that we must automatically feel superior to "them"?

Ethnocentrism is the belief that your own culture, nation, or religion is superior to all others. Ethnocentrism is universal, probably because it aids survival by increasing people's attachment to their own group and their willingness to work on its behalf. It is even embedded in some languages: The Chinese word for China means "the center of the world" (consigning the other five billion people to the suburbs?) and the Navajo, the Kiowa, and the Inuit call themselves simply "The People."

Ethnocentrism rests on a fundamental social identity: us. As soon as people have created a category called "us," however, they invariably perceive everybody else as "not us." This in-group solidarity can be manufactured in a minute in the laboratory, as Henri Tajfel and his colleagues (1971) demonstrated in an experiment with British schoolboys. Tajfel showed the boys slides with varying numbers of dots on them and asked the boys to guess how many dots there were. The boys were arbitrarily told that they were "overestimators" or "underestimators" and were then asked to work on another task. In this phase, they had a chance to give points to other boys identified as overestimators or underestimators. Although each boy worked alone in his cubicle, almost every single one assigned far more points to boys he thought were like him, an overestimator or an underestimator. As the boys emerged from their rooms, they were asked, "Which were you?" The answers received either cheers or boos from the others.

Us–them social identities are strengthened when two groups compete with each other. Years ago, Muzafer Sherif and his colleagues used a natural setting, a Boy Scout camp called Robbers Cave, to demonstrate the effects of competition on hostility and conflict between groups (Sherif, 1958; Sherif et al., 1961). Sherif randomly assigned 11- and 12-year-old boys to two groups, the Eagles and the Rattlers. To build a sense of in-group identity and team spirit, he had each group work separately on projects such as making a rope bridge and building a diving board. Sherif then put the Eagles and Rattlers in competition for prizes. During fierce games of football, baseball, and tug-of-war, the boys whipped up a competitive fever that soon spilled off the playing fields. They began to raid each other's cabins, call each other names, and start fistfights. No one dared to have a friend from the rival group. Before long, the Eagles and the Rattlers were as hostile toward each other as any two gangs fighting for turf. Their hostility continued even when they were just sitting around together watching movies.

Then Sherif decided to try to undo the hostility he had created and make peace between the Eagles and Rattlers. He and his associates set up a series of predicaments in which both groups needed to work together to reach a desired goal, such as pooling their resources to get a movie they all wanted to see or pulling a staff truck up a hill on a camping trip. This policy of *interdependence in reaching mutual goals* was highly successful in reducing the boys' ethnocentrism, competitiveness, and hostility; the boys eventually made friends with their former enemies (see Figure 10.4 on the next page). Interdependence has a similar effect in adult groups (Gaertner et al., 1990). The reason, it seems, is that cooperation causes people to think of themselves as members of one big group instead of two opposed groups, us versus them.

Stereotypes LO 10.15

Think of all the ways your friends and family members differ: Jeff is stodgy, Ruth is bossy, and Farah is outgoing. But if you have never met a person from Turkey or Tibet, you are likely to stereotype Turks and Tibetans. A **stereotype** is a summary impression of a group of people in which all members of the group are viewed as sharing a common trait or traits. People have stereotypes of people who drive flashy sports cars or sedate sedans, of engineering students and art students,

ethnocentrism The belief that one's own ethnic group, nation, or religion is superior to all others.

stereotype A summary impression of a group, in which a person believes that all members of the group share a common trait or traits (positive, negative, or neutral).

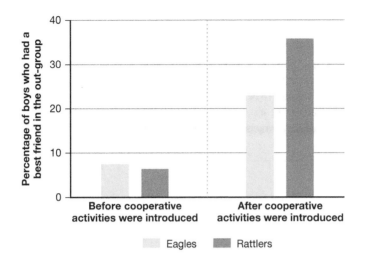

FIGURE 10.4 The Experiment at Robbers Cave
In this study, competitive games fostered hostility between the Rattlers and the Eagles. Few boys had a best friend from the other group (left). But after the teams had to cooperate to solve various problems, the percentage who made friends across "enemy lines" shot up (right) (Sherif et al., 1961).

of feminists and fraternity men. Stereotypes can be positive ("Scots are thrifty and smart with money") or negative ("Scots are miserly and stingy").

Moreover, some stereotypes are statistically accurate; soccer moms *are* more likely than single professionals to drive SUVs, after all (Jussim et al., 2009). Stereotypes therefore are, as some psychologists have called them, useful tools in the mental toolbox—energy-saving devices that allow us to make efficient decisions (Macrae & Bodenhausen, 2000). They help us quickly process new information and retrieve memories. They allow us to organize experience, make sense of differences among individuals and groups, and predict how people will behave. In fact, the brain automatically registers and encodes the basic categories of gender, ethnicity, and age, suggesting that there is a neurological basis for the cognitive efficiency of stereotyping (Ito & Urland, 2003).

However, although stereotypes may reflect real differences among people, they also distort that reality in three ways (Judd et al., 1995). First, *they exaggerate differences between groups*, making the stereotyped group seem odd, unfamiliar, or dangerous, not like "us." Second, *they produce selective perception*; people tend to see only the evidence that fits the stereotype and reject any perceptions that do not fit. Third, *they underestimate differences within the stereotyped group*, creating the impression that all members of that group are the same.

Cultural values affect how people evaluate the actions of another group and whether a stereotype becomes positive or negative. Chinese students in Hong Kong, where communalism and respect for elders are valued, think that a student who comes late to class or argues with a parent about

grades is being selfish and disrespectful of adults. But Australian students, who value individualism, think that the same behavior is perfectly appropriate (Forgas & Bond, 1985). You can see how the Chinese might form negative stereotypes of "disrespectful" Australians, and how the Australians might form negative stereotypes of the "spineless" Chinese. And it is a small step from negative stereotypes to prejudice.

Watch the Video In the Real World: Are Stereotypes and Prejudice Inevitable? at MyPsychLab

What is this woman's occupation? Among non-Muslims in the West, the assumption is that Muslim women who wear the full-length black *niqab* must be repressed sexually as well as politically. But the answer shatters the stereotype. Wedad Lootah, a Muslim living in Dubai, United Arab Emirates, is a marriage counselor and sexual activist, and author of a best-selling Arabic book, *Top Secret: Sexual Guidance for Married Couples.* She wrote it, she says, because of a 52-year-old client who had many children but had never experienced sexual pleasure with her husband. "Finally, she discovered orgasm!" Ms. Lootah reported. "Imagine, all that time she did not know."

Recite & Review

✓ **Study** and **Review** at **MyPsychLab**

Recite: Do you have a positive or a negative stereotype of quizzes yet? Say aloud what you know about social identities, ethnic identity, acculturation, ethnocentrism, and stereotypes.

Review: Next, read this section again.

Now take this *Quick Quiz:*

1. Frank, a black college student, has to decide between living in a dorm with mostly white students who share his interest in science, or living in a dorm with other black students who are studying the history and contributions of African culture. The first choice values _____ whereas the second values_____.

2. John knows and likes the Chicano minority in his town, but he privately believes that Anglo culture is superior to all others. His belief is evidence of his _____.

3. What strategy does the Robbers Cave study suggest for reducing us–them thinking and hostility between groups?

4. What are three ways in which stereotypes can distort reality?

Answers:

1. acculturation, ethnic identity 2. ethnocentrism 3. Interdependence in reaching mutual goals 4. They exaggerate differences between groups; they produce selective perception; and they underestimate differences *within* the stereotyped group.

You are about to learn...

- four primary causes and functions of prejudice.
- four indirect ways of measuring prejudice.
- four conditions necessary for reducing prejudice and conflict.

Prejudice and Group Conflict

A **prejudice** consists of a negative stereotype and a strong, unreasonable dislike or hatred of a group. A central feature of a prejudice is that it remains immune to evidence. In his classic book *The Nature of Prejudice*, Gordon Allport (1954/1979) described the responses characteristic of a prejudiced person when confronted with evidence contradicting his or her beliefs:

Mr. X: The trouble with Jews is that they only take care of their own group.

Mr. Y: But the record of the Community Chest campaign shows that they give more generously, in proportion to their numbers, to the general charities of the community, than do non-Jews.

Mr. X: That shows they are always trying to buy favor and intrude into Christian affairs. They think of nothing but money; that is why there are so many Jewish bankers.

Mr. Y: But a recent study shows that the percentage of Jews in the banking business is negligible, far smaller than the percentage of non-Jews.

Mr. X: That's just it; they don't go in for respectable business; they are only in the movie business or run night clubs.

Notice that Mr. X doesn't even try to respond to Mr. Y's evidence; he just moves along to another reason for his dislike of Jews. That is the slippery nature of prejudice. Indeed, many of the stereotypes underlying anti-Semitism are mutually contradictory and constantly shift across generations and nations. Jews were attacked for being Communists in Nazi Germany and Argentina, and for being greedy capitalists in the Communist Soviet Union. They have been criticized for being too secular and also for being too mystical, for being weak and also for being powerful enough to dominate the world. Although anti-Semitism declined in the 50 years after World War II, it has been on the rise again in the United States, Europe, the Middle East, and around the world (Cohen et al., 2009).

The Origins of Prejudice LO 10.16

Prejudice provides the fuel for ethnocentrism. Its specific targets change, but it persists everywhere in some form because it has so many sources and functions: psychological, social, economic, and cultural.

prejudice A strong, unreasonable dislike or hatred of a group, based on a negative stereotype.

1 **Psychological causes.** Prejudice often serves to ward off feelings of doubt, fear, and insecurity. Around the world, people puff up their low self-esteem or self-worth by disliking or hating groups they see as inferior (Islam & Hewstone, 1993; Stephan et al., 1994). Prejudice also allows people to use the target group as a scapegoat to displace anger and cope with feelings of powerlessness ("Those people are the source of all my troubles").

2 **Social causes.** Not all prejudices have deep-seated psychological roots. Some are acquired because of pressure to conform to the views of friends, relatives, or associates. If you don't agree with your group's prejudices, you may be gently or abruptly asked to leave it. Some prejudices are passed along mindlessly from one generation to another, as when parents communicate to their children, "We don't associate with people like that."

3 **Economic causes.** Prejudice makes official forms of discrimination seem legitimate, by justifying the majority group's dominance, status, competence, knowledge, or other grounds for superiority. It doesn't matter whether the majority consists of whites, blacks, Muslims, Hindus, Japanese, Christians, Jews, or any other category. Wherever a majority group systematically discriminates against a minority to preserve its power, they will claim that their actions are legitimate because the minority is so obviously inferior and incompetent (Islam & Hewstone, 1993; Jost, Nosek, & Gosling, 2008; Morton et al., 2009; Sidanius, Pratto, & Bobo, 1996).

You can see how prejudice rises with changing economic conditions by observing what happens when two groups are suddenly in direct competition for jobs, or when people are worried about their incomes. Consider how white attitudes toward Chinese immigrants in the United States fluctuated during the nineteenth century, as reflected in newspapers of the time (Aronson, 2012). When the Chinese were working in the gold mines and potentially taking jobs from white laborers, the white-run newspapers described them as depraved, vicious, and bloodthirsty. Just a decade later, when the Chinese began working on the transcontinental railroad, doing difficult and dangerous jobs that few white men wanted, prejudice against them declined. Whites described them as hardworking, industrious, and law-abiding. Then, after the railroad was finished and the Chinese had to compete with Civil War veterans for scarce jobs, white attitudes changed again. Whites now thought the Chinese were "criminal," "crafty," "conniving," and "stupid." (The newspapers did not report the attitudes of the Chinese.) Today's Chinese are

Mexican, particularly the migrant workers whose labor is needed in the United States but who are perceived as costing Americans their jobs.

The oldest prejudice in the world may be sexism, and it, too, serves to legitimize existing roles and inequities in power. According to research with 15,000 men and women in 19 nations, *hostile sexism*, which reflects active dislike of women, is different from *benevolent sexism*, which puts women on a pedestal. The latter type of sexism is affectionate but patronizing, conveying the attitude that women are so good, kind, and moral that they should stay at home, away from the rough-and-tumble (and power and income) of public life (Glick et al., 2000; Glick, 2006). Because benevolent sexism lacks a tone of hostility to women, it doesn't seem like a prejudice to many people, and many women find it alluring to think they are better than men. But both forms of sexism, whether someone thinks women are too good for equality or not good enough, legitimize discrimination against women (Christopher & Wojda, 2008).

Perhaps you are thinking: "What about men? There are plenty of prejudices against men, too—that they are sexual predators, emotionally heartless, domineering, and arrogant." In fact, according to a 16-nation study of attitudes toward men, many people do believe that men are aggressive and predatory, and overall just not as warm and wonderful as women (Glick et al., 2004). This attitude seems hostile to men, the researchers found, but it also reflects and supports gender inequality by characterizing men as being designed for leadership, dominance, and high-paying jobs.

4 **Cultural and national causes.** Finally, prejudice bonds people to their own ethnic or national group and its ways; by disliking "them," we feel closer to our own group. That feeling, in turn, justifies whatever we do to "them" to preserve our customs and national policies, and this reaction is especially likely to be aroused during armed conflicts. Although many people assume that prejudice causes war, the reverse is far more often the case: War causes prejudice. When two nations declare war, when one country decides to invade another, or when a weak leader displaces the country's economic problems onto a minority scapegoat, the citizenry's prejudice against that enemy or scapegoat will be inflamed. Of course, sometimes anger at an enemy is justified, but war usually turns legitimate anger into blind prejudice: Those people are not only the enemy; they are less than human and deserve to be exterminated (Keen, 1986; Staub, 1999). That is why enemies are so often described as vermin, rats, mad dogs,

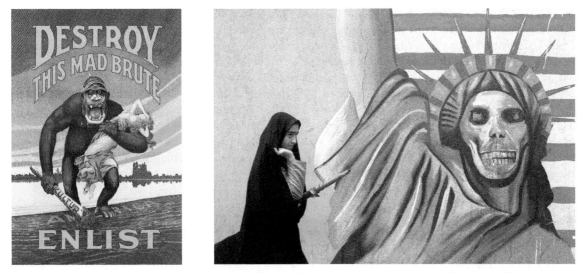

In times of war, most people fall victim to emotional reasoning about the enemy. They start thinking of "them" as aggressors who are less than human, often as monsters, rats, or pigs. All nations do this. Americans depicted the German enemy in World War I as a "mad brute," and anti-U.S. protesters in Iran portrayed the American icon of liberty as a purveyor of war and death.

heathens, baby killers, or monsters—anything but human beings like us.

Defining and Measuring Prejudice LO 10.17

With the historic election in 2008 of Barack Obama as the nation's first black president, and with women serving in high levels of government, many people assumed that the worst forms of racism and sexism in the United States were ending. Indeed, the numbers of people who admit to believing that blacks are inferior to whites, women inferior to men, and gays inferior to straights have been steadily dropping over the past 65 years, especially among young people (Weaver, 2008). But in 2012, white prejudice toward blacks and other minorities began rising significantly again. That is why prejudice is like a weasel, hard to grasp and hold on to. Negative feelings and discriminatory behavior may lie dormant during good times, only to be easily aroused during economic bad times.

Research on prejudice must also take into account that not all prejudiced people are prejudiced in the same way or to the same extent. Suppose that Raymond wishes to be tolerant and open-minded, but he grew up in a small homogeneous community and feels uncomfortable with members of other cultural and religious groups. Should we put Raymond in the same category as Rupert, an outspoken white supremacist? Do good intentions count? What if Raymond knows nothing about Muslims and mindlessly blurts out a remark that reveals his ignorance? Is that prejudice or thoughtlessness?

THINKING CRITICALLY

About Defining Prejudice

Get Involved! Probing Your Prejudices

Are you prejudiced? No? Is there any group of people you dislike because of their gender, ethnicity, sexual orientation, nationality, religion, physical appearance, or political views? How about old people, the one target of prejudice that we all eventually join if we live long enough? Write down your deepest thoughts and feelings about this group. Take as long as you want, and do not censor yourself or say what you think you ought to say. Now reread what you have written. Which of the sources of prejudice discussed in the text might be contributing to your views? Do you feel that your attitudes toward the group are legitimate, or are you uncomfortable about having them?

And what about people who say they are not prejudiced but then make remarks that suggest otherwise? Marilyn Davenport, a member of the Orange County Republican Party Central Committee, sent out a nasty e-mail depicting President Obama and his parents as chimpanzees. She was surprised by the outcry. "Oh, come on! Everybody who knows me knows that I am not a racist. It was a joke. I have friends who are black," she said. When Mel Gibson was arrested for drunk driving, he spewed anti-Semitic insults to the arresting officer ("Jews are responsible for all the wars in the world!"), yet later denied being prejudiced. Should the public have accepted these people's claims that they aren't "really" racist or anti-Semitic?

Gordon Allport (1954/1979) observed that "defeated intellectually, prejudice lingers emotionally." Although many kinds of *explicit*, conscious prejudices have declined and it is no longer fashionable in most circles to admit one's prejudices, some social psychologists are using ingenious measures to see whether *implicit*, unconscious

THE MANY TARGETS OF PREJUDICE

Prejudice has a long and universal history. Why do new prejudices keep emerging, others fade away, and some old ones persist?

Some prejudices rise and fall with historical events such as war or conquest. Anti-Japanese feelings in the United States ran high in the 1920s, and again in the 1940s (World War II) and 1990s (economic competition); Irish immigrants in the nineteenth and early twentieth centuries also endured extensive discrimination; and prejudice against American Indians was widespread for three centuries. Today, prejudices against the Japanese, Irish, and Native Americans have faded. In contrast, some hatreds, notably homophobia and anti-Semitism, reflect people's deeper anxieties and are therefore more persistent.

hostilities between groups have also diminished—or are "lingering emotionally." These researchers maintain that implicit attitudes, being automatic and unintentional, reflect negative feelings that keep prejudice alive below the surface (Dovidio, 2009). They have developed several ways of measuring these feelings (Olson, 2009):

1 **Measures of social distance and "microaggressions."** *Social distance* is a possible behavioral expression of prejudice. Does a straight man stand farther away from a gay man than from another straight man? Does a nondisabled woman move away from a woman in a wheelchair? Some psychologists call these subtle acts "microaggressions": the slights and indignities that many women, minorities, and people with physical disabilities experience (Dovidio, Pagotto, & Hebl, 2011; Nadal et al., 2011). Derald Sue (2010) offers these examples: A white professor compliments an Asian American graduate student on his "excellent English," although the student has lived in the

Prejudices toward blacks and women have long been part of Western history. In the United States, women have been excluded from men's clubs and occupations, and segregation of blacks was legal until the 1950s. Anti-immigrant prejudices always emerge when changing economic conditions create competition for jobs. In the aftermath of 9/11, hostility mounted toward all Middle Easterners and Muslims.

United States his whole life. A white woman leaving work starts to enter an elevator, sees a black man inside, covers her necklace with her hand, and "remembers" she left something at her desk, thereby conveying to her black coworker that she thinks he is a potential thief. Men in a discussion group ignore the contributions of the one female member, talking past her and paying attention only to one another.

2 Measures of unequal treatment. Most forms of explicit discrimination are now illegal in the United States, but prejudices can express themselves in less obvious ways. Consider how blacks and whites are treated unequally in the "war against drugs" (Fellner, 2009). Across the country, blacks are disproportionately arrested, convicted, and incarcerated on drug charges. A study in Seattle, which is 70 percent white, found that the great majority of those who use or sell serious drugs are white, yet almost two-thirds of those who are arrested are black. Whites constitute the majority of those who use or sell methamphetamine, Ecstasy, powder cocaine, and heroin; blacks are the majority of those who use or sell crack. But the police virtually ignore the white market and concentrate on crack arrests. The focus on crack offenders is unrelated to the frequency of crack transactions compared to those for other drugs, public safety or health concerns, crime rates, or citizen complaints. The researchers concluded that the police department's drug law enforcement reflects racial discrimination: the unconscious impact of race on official perceptions of who is causing the city's drug problem (Beckett, Nyrop, & Pfingst, 2006).

3 Measures of what people do when they are stressed or angry. Many people are willing to control their negative feelings under normal conditions, but as soon as they are angry, drunk, or frustrated or get a jolt to their self-esteem, their unexpressed prejudice often reveals itself. In one of the first experiments to demonstrate this phenomenon, white students were asked to administer shock to black or white confederates of the experimenter in what the students believed was a study of biofeedback. In the experimental condition, participants overheard the biofeedback "victim" (who actually received no shock) saying derogatory things about them. In the control condition, participants overheard no such nasty remarks.

Then all the participants had another opportunity to shock the victims; their degree of aggression was defined as the amount of shock they administered. At first, white students showed *less* aggression toward blacks than toward whites. But as soon as the white students were angered by overhearing derogatory remarks about themselves, they showed *more* aggression toward blacks than toward whites (Rogers & Prentice-Dunn, 1981). The same pattern appears in studies of how English-speaking Canadians behave toward French-speaking Canadians (Meindl & Lerner, 1985), straights toward gays, non-Jewish students toward Jews (Fein & Spencer, 1997), and men toward women (Maass et al., 2003).

4 Measures of brain activity. Social neuroscientists have been using fMRI to determine which parts of the brain might be involved in forming stereotypes, holding prejudiced beliefs, and feeling disgust, anger, or anxiety about a stigmatized group, such as addicts or the homeless (Cacioppo et al., 2003; Harris & Fiske, 2006; Stanley, Phelps, & Banaji, 2008). In one study, when blacks and whites saw pictures of each other, activity in the amygdala (the brain structure associated with fear, anxiety, and other negative emotions) was elevated. But it was not elevated when they saw pictures of members of their own group (Hart et al., 2000). Does that mean these participants were "prejudiced" toward members of the other group? In a similar experiment, when participants were registering the faces as individuals or as part of a simple visual test rather than as members of the category "blacks," their amygdalas showed no increased activation. The brain may be designed to register differences, it appears, but any negative associations with those differences depend on context and learning (Wheeler & Fiske, 2005).

5 Measures of implicit attitudes. A final, controversial method of assessing prejudice is the *Implicit Association Test* (IAT), which measures the speed of people's positive and negative associations to a target group (Greenwald, McGhee, & Schwartz, 1998; Greenwald et al., 2009). Its proponents have argued that if white people take longer to respond to black faces associated with positive words (e.g., *triumph, honest*) than to black faces associated with negative words (e.g., *devil, failure*), it must mean that white students have an unconscious, implicit prejudice toward blacks, one that can affect behavior in various ways. Millions of people have taken the test online, and it has also been given to students, business managers, and many other groups to identify their alleged prejudices toward blacks, Asians, women, old people, and other categories (Nosek, Greenwald, & Banaji, 2007).

Some social psychologists, however, believe that the test is not measuring a stable prejudice.

Associations are not necessarily biases: If we associate the words *bread* and *butter*, that doesn't mean we like them or will buy either one (Levitin, 2013). Test–retest reliability on the IAT is low, they maintain, and scores only weakly predict a person's discriminatory *behavior* (Blanton & Mitchell, 2011; De Houwer et al., 2009). One team analyzed data on how people who had taken the IAT acted toward white and black people during a real conversation. They measured 16 behaviors, such as laughing, making eye contact, and fidgeting. Those who received the highest scores for "anti-black bias" on the IAT showed no behavioral bias toward blacks at all. Many who got high "anti-black" scores actually behaved *more* compassionately toward blacks, when given the opportunity, than low scorers (Blanton et al., 2009).

Other critics of the IAT think that the test simply reflects white subjects' unfamiliarity with blacks and the greater salience of white faces to them, rather than an implicit prejudice (Kinoshita & Peek-O'Leary, 2005). Words and images that are unfamiliar take more retrieval and processing time, so naturally people would be slower in responding to them. Moreover, as we saw previously, people find familiar names, products, and even nonsense syllables to be more pleasant than unfamiliar ones. Two experimenters got an IAT effect by matching target faces with nonsense words and neutral words that had no evaluative connotations at all. They concluded that the IAT does not measure emotional evaluations of the target but rather the *salience* of the word associated with it—how much it stands out. Negative words attract more attention in general. When they corrected for these factors, the presumed unconscious prejudice faded away (Rothermund & Wentura, 2004).

> ▶ Simulate the Experiment Implicit Association Test: Cats and Dogs at **MyPsychLab**

As you can see, defining and measuring prejudice are not easy. To understand prejudice, we must distinguish explicit attitudes from unconscious ones, active hostility from simple discomfort, what people say from what they feel, and what people feel from how they actually behave.

Reducing Conflict and Prejudice LO 10.18

The findings that emerge from the study of prejudice show us that efforts to reduce prejudice by appealing to moral or intellectual arguments are not enough. They must also touch people's deeper insecurities, fears, or negative associations with a group. Of course, given the many sources and functions of prejudice, no one method will work in all circumstances or for all prejudices. But just as social psychologists investigate the situations that increase prejudice and animosity between groups, they have also examined the situations that might reduce them. Here are four of them (Allport, 1954/1979; Dovidio & Gaertner, 2010; Pettigrew & Tropp, 2006):

1 Both sides must have equal legal status, economic opportunities, and power. This requirement is the spur behind efforts to change laws that permit discrimination. Integration of public facilities in the American South would never have occurred if civil rights advocates had waited for segregationists to have a change of heart. Women would never have gotten the right to vote, attend college, or do "men's work" (law, medicine, bartending…) without persistent challenges to the laws that barred them from having these rights. But changing the law is not enough if two groups remain in competition for jobs or if one group retains power and dominance over the other.

2 Authorities and community institutions must provide moral, legal, and economic support for both sides. Society must establish norms of equality and support them in the actions of its officials— teachers, employers, the judicial system, government officials, and the police. Where segregation is official government policy or an unofficial but established practice, conflict and prejudice not only will continue but also will seem normal and justified.

3 Both sides must have many opportunities to work and socialize together, formally and informally. According to the *contact hypothesis*, prejudice declines when people have the chance to get used to another group's rules, food, customs, and attitudes, thereby discovering their shared interests and shared humanity and learning that "those people" aren't, in fact, "all alike." The contact hypothesis has been supported by many studies in the laboratory and in the real world: studies of newly integrated housing projects in the American South during the 1950s and 1960s; young people's attitudes toward the elderly; healthy people's attitudes toward the mentally ill; nondisabled children's attitudes toward the disabled; and straight people's prejudices toward gay men and lesbians (Herek & Capitanio, 1996; Pettigrew & Tropp, 2006; Wilner, Walkley, & Cook, 1955). Remarkably, contact actually works best for the most intolerant and mentally rigid people, apparently because it reduces their feelings of threat and anxiety and

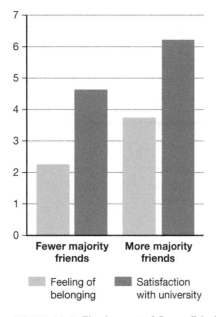

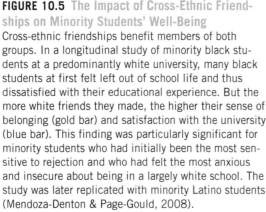

FIGURE 10.5 The Impact of Cross-Ethnic Friendships on Minority Students' Well-Being
Cross-ethnic friendships benefit members of both groups. In a longitudinal study of minority black students at a predominantly white university, many black students at first felt left out of school life and thus dissatisfied with their educational experience. But the more white friends they made, the higher their sense of belonging (gold bar) and satisfaction with the university (blue bar). This finding was particularly significant for minority students who had initially been the most sensitive to rejection and who had felt the most anxious and insecure about being in a largely white school. The study was later replicated with minority Latino students (Mendoza-Denton & Page-Gould, 2008).

increases feelings of empathy and trust (Hodson, 2011).

Multiethnic college campuses are living laboratories for testing the contact hypothesis. White students who have roommates, friends, and romantic relationships across ethnic lines tend to become less prejudiced and find commonalities (Van Laar, Levin, & Sidanius, 2008). Cross-group friendships benefit minorities and reduce their prejudices, too. Minority students who join ethnic student organizations tend to develop, over time, not only an even stronger ethnic identity, but also an increased sense of victimization. Just like white students who live in white fraternities and sororities, many come to feel they have less in common with other ethnic groups (Sidanius et al., 2004). But a longitudinal study of black and Latino students at a predominantly white university found that friendships with whites increased their feelings of belonging and reduced their feelings of dissatisfaction with the school (Mendoza-Denton & Page-Gould, 2008). (See Figure 10.5.)

4 **Both sides must cooperate, working together for a common goal.** Although contact reduces prejudice, it is also true that prejudice reduces contact. And when groups don't like each other, forced contact just makes each side resentful and even more prejudiced, as a longitudinal field survey of students in Germany, Belgium, and England found (Binder et al., 2009). At many multiethnic American high schools, ethnic groups form cliques and gangs, fighting one another and defending their own ways.

To reduce the intergroup tension and competition that exist in many schools, Elliot Aronson and his colleagues developed the "jigsaw" method of building cooperation. Students from different ethnic groups work together on a task that is broken up like a jigsaw puzzle; each person needs to cooperate with the others to put the assignment together. Students in such classes, from elementary school through college, tend to do better, like their classmates better, and become less stereotyped and prejudiced in their thinking than students in traditional classrooms (Aronson, 2000; J. Aronson, 2010; Slavin & Cooper, 1999). Cooperation and interdependence often reduce us–them thinking and prejudice by creating an encompassing social identity—the Eagles and Rattlers solution.

Each of these four approaches to creating greater harmony between groups is important, but none is sufficient on its own. Perhaps one reason that group conflicts and prejudice are so persistent is that all four conditions for reducing them are rarely met at the same time.

When classrooms are structured so that students of different ethnic groups must cooperate in order to do well on a lesson, prejudice decreases.

Recite & Review

 Study and **Review** at **MyPsychLab**

Recite: Try to overcome your prejudice against quizzes by reciting what you know about four major causes of prejudice, hostile and benevolent sexism, explicit versus implicit prejudices, five ways of measuring implicit prejudice, and four conditions necessary for reducing prejudice and conflict.

Review: You have just read a long but important section; you really should reread it.

Now answer this *Quick Quiz* **question:**

Surveys find that blacks, Asian Americans, and Latinos often hold prejudices about other minorities. What are some reasons that people who have themselves been victims of stereotyping and prejudice would hold the same attitudes toward others?

Answer:

Their own ethnocentrism; low self-esteem, anxiety, or feelings of threat; conformity with relatives and friends who share their prejudices; parental lessons; and economic competition for jobs and resources.

PSYCHOLOGY IN THE NEWS REVISITED /////////

Now that you have read about the many external forces and situations that can cause good people to do bad things, what do you think the story of the terrorist bombing at the 2013 Boston Marathon teaches us?

First, it seems clear that the two brothers accused of setting off the bombs were not pathologically disturbed loners or mentally ill. For most of their time in the United States, they had been doing well in school and at work. They had loved participating in their respective sports of wrestling and boxing; they had hopes and ambitions for careers in their adopted country and had every reason to think they would achieve them. The younger brother had become an American citizen, but the older one, it seems, never became fully acculturated into American society and apparently could not find a comfortable resolution between his Muslim identity and American culture. As we saw, there may be a critical period for becoming truly acculturated to a society that is very different from one's culture of origin.

By 2011, Tamerlan had become radicalized and told his mother he was prepared to die for Islam; his younger brother soon shared his beliefs. On March 14, 2012, Dzhokhar tweeted: "a decade in America already, I want out." Why? Perhaps the brothers felt themselves to be victims of prejudice and discrimination, a feeling that would have been inflamed by the jihadist Internet sites that Tamerlan visited and his trip back home to the Russian republic of Dagestan that year. Whatever the process, the young men's decision to set off bombs at the marathon would not have happened overnight, but through steady entrapment, in which they justified each step on the way to committing their final act of terror.

Second, this story shows the power of cognitive dissonance. At a news conference in Dagestan, the young men's parents angrily denied evidence of their sons' guilt and accused the United States of conspiring to kill them. Many observers found their reaction sad or pathetic, but it was predictable. The dissonance between "We are good, devoted parents with kind, loving sons" clashed with "We came back here and left them in America, where they committed a horrible terrorist act." The most tolerable way to reduce this excruciating dissonance was: They didn't do it, but if they did do it, it's all America's fault.

Third, the story highlights the way that people in Boston and the rest of the nation became united in a common cause. Locals reaffirmed their social identity as "Bostonians" and felt increased solidarity and cooperation in working for a shared goal of recovery. As in every disaster, it was not only the first responders who acted heroically to help the wounded but also the countless citizens who did whatever they could: Strangers comforted the wounded and applied tourniquets, sometimes with their belts or their own hands. The need for help was unambiguous, and the sight of others rushing to help quickly created a crowd norm for altruism.

In short, our opening story illustrates a central theme of this chapter: "Human nature" contains the potential for unspeakable acts of cruelty and inspiring acts of goodness.

The philosopher Hannah Arendt (1963), who covered the trial of Adolf Eichmann, used the phrase *the banality of evil* to describe how it was possible for Eichmann and other ordinary people in Nazi Germany to commit the atrocities they did. (*Banal* means "commonplace" or "unoriginal.") The Nazis, of course, systematically exterminated millions of Jews, Gypsies, homosexuals, disabled people, and anyone else who was not a "pure" Aryan. But virtually no country has

These paintings done during wartime poignantly illustrate one child's effort to portray the horror of war and another's dream of peace. Can we learn to design a world in which conflicts and group differences, though inevitable, need not lead to violence?

bloodless hands. Americans and Canadians slaughtered native peoples in North America, Turks slaughtered Armenians, the Khmer Rouge slaughtered millions of fellow Cambodians, the Spanish conquistadors slaughtered native peoples in Mexico and South America, Idi Amin waged a reign of terror against his own people in Uganda, the Japanese slaughtered Koreans and Chinese, Iraqis slaughtered Kurds, despotic political regimes in Argentina and Chile killed thousands of dissidents and rebels, the Hutu in Rwanda murdered thousands of Tutsi, and in the former Yugoslavia, Bosnian Serbs massacred thousands of Bosnian Muslims in the name of "ethnic cleansing."

THINKING CRITICALLY

About "Evil" Cultures

The compelling evidence for the banality of evil is difficult for many people to accept. Clearly, some people do stand out as being unusually heroic or unusually sadistic. But in the social-psychological view, evil does not result from aggressive instincts but from the all-too-normal processes we have discussed in this chapter, including ethnocentrism, obedience to authority, conformity, groupthink, deindividuation, stereotyping, and prejudice.

The good news is that when circumstances within a nation change, societies can also change from being warlike to being peaceful. Ethnocentrism and prejudice, along with compassion, cooperation, and altruism, are part of our human heritage, awaiting the conditions that will awaken them. By identifying the conditions that create the banality of evil, perhaps we can create other conditions that foster the "banality of virtue"—everyday acts of kindness, selflessness, and generosity.

Taking Psychology With You

Dealing With Cultural Differences

A French salesman worked for a company that was bought by Americans. When the new American manager ordered him to step up his sales within the next three months, the employee quit in a huff, taking his customers with him. Why? In France, it takes years to develop customers; in family-owned businesses, relationships with customers may span generations. The American manager wanted instant results, as Americans often do, but the French salesman knew this

was impossible and quit. The American view was, "He wasn't up to the job and disloyal besides, so he stole my customers." The French view was, "There is no point in explaining anything to a person who is so stupid as to think you can acquire loyal customers in three months" (Hall & Hall, 1987).

Both men were committing the fundamental attribution error: assuming that the other person's behavior was due to his personality rather than the situation, in this case one governed by cultural rules. Such rules are not trivial and success in a global economy depends on understanding them. But you don't have to go to another country

to encounter cultural differences; they are right where you live.

If you find yourself getting angry over something a person from another culture is doing, use the skills of critical thinking to find out whether your expectations and perceptions of that person's behavior are appropriate. Take the time to examine your assumptions and biases, consider other explanations of the other person's actions, and avoid emotional reasoning. For example, people who shake hands as a gesture of friendship and courtesy are likely to feel insulted if a person from a non-hand-shaking culture refuses to do the same, unless they have asked themselves the question, "Does everyone have the custom of shaking hands that my culture does?" (No.)

Learning another culture's rules and customs is hard enough, but it is much more difficult to comprehend cultural differences that are deeply embedded in its language. In Iran, the social principle of *taarof* describes the practice of deliberate insincerity, such as giving false praise and making promises you have no intention of keeping. Iranians know that they are supposed to tell you what you want to hear to avoid conflict or to offer room for a compromise. To Iranians, these practices are simply good manners. But members of English-speaking cultures are used to "straight talking," to saying directly what they want. Therefore, they find *taarof* hard to learn, let alone to practice. As

Kian Tajbakhsh, an Iranian social scientist, explained, "Speech has a different function than it does in the West"—in the West, "yes" generally means yes; in Iran, "yes" can mean yes, but it often means maybe or no. "This creates a rich, poetic linguistic culture," he said. "It creates a multidimensional culture where people are adept at picking up on nuances. On the other hand, it makes for bad political discourse" (Slackman, 2006).

You can see why critical thinking can help people avoid the tendency to stereotype and to see cultural differences in communication solely in hostile ways. "Why are the Iranians lying to me?" an American might ask. The answer is that they are not "lying" in Iranian terms; they are speaking in a way that is completely natural for them, according to their cultural rules for communication.

To learn the unspoken rules of a culture, you must look, listen, and observe. What is the pace of life like? Do people regard brash individuality and loud speech as admirable or embarrassing? When customers enter a shop, do they greet and chat with the shopkeeper or ignore the person as they browse? Are people expected to be direct in their speech or evasive? Sociocultural research teaches us to appreciate the many cultural rules that govern people's behavior, values, attitudes, and ways of doing business. Before you write off someone from a culture different from your own as being rude, foolish, stubborn, or devious, consider other interpretations of that person's behavior—just as you would want that person to consider other, more forgiving, interpretations of yours.

Summary

- *Social psychologists* study how social roles, attitudes, relationships, and groups influence individuals; *cultural psychologists* study the influence of culture on human behavior. Many cultural rules, such as those governing correct *conversational distance*, are unspoken but nonetheless powerful.

Roles and Rules

- The environment influences people in countless subtle ways; for example, merely observing that others have broken rules or laws increases the likelihood that a passerby will do the same. Two classic studies illustrate the power of *norms* and *roles* to affect individual actions. In Milgram's obedience study, most people in the role of "teacher" inflicted what they thought was extreme shock on another person because of the authority of the experimenter. In the Stanford prison study, college students tended to behave in accordance with their assigned role of "prisoner" or "guard."

- Obedience to authority contributes to the smooth running of society, but obedience can also lead to actions that are deadly, foolish, or illegal. People obey orders because they can be punished if they do not, out of respect for authority, and to gain advantages. Even when they would rather not obey, they may do so because they have been *entrapped*, justifying each step and decision they make, and handing over responsibility for any harmful actions they commit to the authority.

Social Influences on Beliefs and Behavior

- *Social cognition* is the study of how people's perceptions affect their relationships and how the social environment affects their beliefs and perceptions. According to *attribution theory*, people

are motivated to search for causes to which they can attribute their own and other people's behavior. Their attributions may be *situational* or *dispositional*. The *fundamental attribution error* occurs when people overestimate personality traits as a cause of behavior and underestimate the influence of the situation. A primary reason for the fundamental attribution error is that people rely on introspection to judge their own behavior but only have observation to judge the behavior of others.

- Attributions are further influenced by three *self-serving biases*: the bias to choose the most flattering and forgiving explanations of our own behavior, especially our lapses; the bias that we are better, smarter, and kinder than others; and the bias that the world is fair (the *just-world hypothesis*).

- People hold many *attitudes* about people, things, and ideas. Attitudes may be *explicit* (conscious) or *implicit* (unconscious). Attitudes may change through experience, conscious decision, or as an effort to reduce *cognitive dissonance*. The process of dissonance reduction can cause entrapment, resulting in a "slippery slope" from mild errors to more serious mistakes and ethical transgressions. One powerful way to influence attitudes is by taking advantage of the *familiarity effect* and the *validity effect*: Simply exposing people repeatedly to a name or product makes them like it more, and repeating a statement over and over again makes it seem more believable.

- Many attitudes are acquired through learning and social influence, but some are associated with personality traits that have a genetic component. Religious and political affiliations are not heritable, but religiosity and certain political attitudes do have relatively high heritability. Ideological belief systems may have evolved to be organized along a left–right dimension, consisting of two central sets of attitudes: whether a person advocates or opposes social change, and whether a person thinks inequality is a result of human policies and can be overcome or is an inevitable part of the natural order. Attitudes are also profoundly affected by a person's generation and by the person's *nonshared environment* (unique life experiences).

- Suicide bombers and terrorists have not been "brainwashed" and most are not psychopaths or mentally ill. They have been entrapped into taking increasingly violent actions against real and perceived enemies; encouraged to attribute all problems to that one enemy; offered a new identity and salvation; and cut off from access to dissonant information. These methods have been used to create religious and other cults as well.

Individuals in Groups

- The need to belong is so powerful that the pain of social rejection and exclusion is greater and more memorable than physical pain, which is why groups use the weapon of ostracism or rejection to enforce conformity.

- In groups, individuals often behave differently than they would on their own. Conformity permits the smooth running of society and allows people to feel in harmony with others like them. Two basic motives for conformity are the *need for social acceptance* and the *need for information*. But as the Asch experiment showed, most people will conform to the judgments of others even when the others are plain wrong.

- Close-knit groups are vulnerable to *groupthink*, the tendency of group members to think alike, censor themselves, actively suppress disagreement, and feel that their decisions are invulnerable. Groupthink often produces faulty decisions because group members fail to seek disconfirming evidence for their ideas. However, groups can be structured to counteract groupthink.

- Sometimes a group's collective judgment is better than that of its individual members—the "wisdom of crowds." But crowds can also spread panic, rumor, and misinformation. *Diffusion of responsibility* in a group can lead to inaction on the part of individuals, as in *bystander apathy*. The diffusion of responsibility is likely to occur under conditions that promote *deindividuation*, the loss of awareness of one's individuality. Deindividuation increases when people feel anonymous, as in a large group or crowd or when they are wearing masks or uniforms. In some situations, crowd norms lead deindividuated people to behave aggressively, but in others, crowd norms foster helpfulness.

- The willingness to speak up for an unpopular opinion, blow the whistle on illegal practices, or help a stranger in trouble and perform other acts of *altruism* is partly a matter of personal belief and conscience. But several situational factors are also important: The person perceives that help is needed; cultural norms support taking action; the person has an ally; and the person becomes entrapped in a commitment to help or dissent.

Us Versus Them: Group Identity

- People develop *social identities* based on their ethnicity, nationality, religion, occupation, and other social memberships. In culturally diverse societies, many people face the problem of balancing their *ethnic identity* with *acculturation* into the larger society.

- *Ethnocentrism*, the belief that one's own ethnic group or religion is superior to all others, promotes "us–them" thinking. One effective strategy for reducing us–them thinking and hostility between groups is *interdependence*, having both sides work together to reach a common goal.

- *Stereotypes* help people rapidly process new information, organize experience, and predict how others will behave. But they distort reality by exaggerating differences between groups, underestimating the differences within groups, and producing selective perception.

Prejudice and Group Conflict

- A *prejudice* is an unreasonable negative feeling toward a category of people. Psychologically, prejudice wards off feelings of anxiety and doubt; it bolsters self-esteem when a person feels threatened, by providing a scapegoat. Prejudice also has social causes: People acquire prejudices mindlessly, through conformity and parental lessons. Prejudice serves the cultural and national purpose of bonding people to their social groups and nations, and in extreme cases justifying war. Finally, prejudice also serves to justify a majority group's economic interests and dominance. *Hostile sexism* differs from *benevolent sexism*, but both legitimize gender discrimination. During times of economic insecurity and competition for jobs, prejudice rises.

- Psychologists disagree on whether racism and other prejudices are declining or have merely taken new forms. Some are trying to measure prejudice indirectly, by measuring *social distance* and "microaggressions"; measuring unequal treatment of groups by the police or other institutions; seeing whether people are more likely to behave aggressively toward a target when they are stressed or angry; observing changes in the brain; or assessing unconscious positive or negative associations with a group, as with the *Implicit Association Test* (IAT). Critics of the IAT argue that it is not capturing true prejudice but unfamiliarity and the salience of negative words.

- Efforts to reduce prejudice need to target both the explicit and implicit attitudes that people have. Four conditions help to reduce two groups' mutual prejudices and conflicts: Both sides must have equal legal status, economic standing, and power; both sides must have the legal, moral, and economic support of authorities and cultural institutions; both sides must have opportunities to work and socialize together informally and formally (the *contact hypothesis*); and both sides must work together for a common goal.

Psychology in the News, Revisited

- The bombing at the Boston Marathon illustrates the central theme of this chapter: the human capacity for both cruelty and acts of goodness. Although many people believe that only bad or evil people do bad deeds, the principles of social and cultural psychology show that under certain conditions, good people often can be induced to do bad things too. Everyone is influenced to one degree or another by the social processes of obedience, entrapment, conformity, persuasion, bystander apathy, groupthink, deindividuation, ethnocentrism, stereotyping, and prejudice.

Taking Psychology With You

- Sociocultural research enhances critical thinking by identifying the cultural rules that govern people's behavior, values, communication, and ways of doing business. Understanding these rules can help people examine their assumptions about people in other cultures, and avoid the tendency to jump to conclusions and reason emotionally about group differences.

Key Terms

social psychology **355**
cultural psychology **355**
norms (social) **355**
role **356**
culture **356**
conversational distance **356**
entrapment **360**
social cognition **362**
attribution theory **362**
situational attributions **362**

dispositional attributions **362**
fundamental attribution error **362**
self-serving biases **363**
just-world hypothesis **363**
blaming the victim **363**
attitude **364**
implicit and explicit attitudes **364**
cognitive dissonance **364**

familiarity effect **365**
validity effect **365**
nonshared environment **367**
groupthink **371**
diffusion of responsibility **373**
bystander apathy **373**
deindividuation **373**
altruism **374**
social identity **376**

ethnic identity **376**
acculturation **376**
ethnocentrism **377**
stereotype **377**
prejudice **379**
hostile and benevolent sexism **380**
Implicit Association Test (IAT) **384**
contact hypothesis **385**

- *Social psychologists* study how social roles, attitudes, relationships, and groups influence individuals.
- *Cultural psychologists* study the influence of culture on human behavior.

Roles and Rules

↓

- **Norms** are rules that regulate social life, including explicit laws and implicit cultural conventions.
- **Roles** are social positions that are regulated by norms about how people in those positions should behave.
- Social roles are shaped by **culture**, a set of shared rules and values of a community or society.

Two Classic Studies

- In Milgram's obedience study, most people inflicted what they thought was extreme shock on another person because of the experimenter's authority.
- In the Stanford prison study, students quickly took on the role of "prisoner" or "guard."

Why People Obey

Several factors cause people to obey, including:
- Unpleasant consequences for disobedience and benefits of obedience.
- Respect for and dependence on the authority.
- Wanting to be polite or liked; not wanting to rock the boat.
- **Entrapment:** increasing commitment to a course of action to justify one's investment in it.

Social Influences on Beliefs and Behavior

↓

Social cognition is the study of social influences on thought, memory, perception, and beliefs.

Attributions

Attribution theory holds that people explain their own and other people's behavior by attributing its causes to a *situation* or *disposition*.
- The **fundamental attribution error** is the tendency to ignore situational factors in favor of dispositional ones.

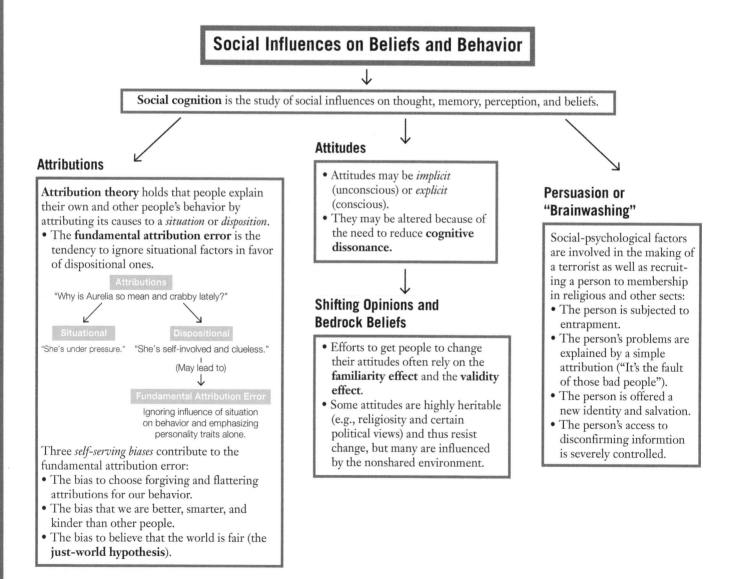

Three *self-serving biases* contribute to the fundamental attribution error:
- The bias to choose forgiving and flattering attributions for our behavior.
- The bias that we are better, smarter, and kinder than other people.
- The bias to believe that the world is fair (the **just-world hypothesis**).

Attitudes

- Attitudes may be *implicit* (unconscious) or *explicit* (conscious).
- They may be altered because of the need to reduce **cognitive dissonance**.

↓

Shifting Opinions and Bedrock Beliefs

- Efforts to get people to change their attitudes often rely on the **familiarity effect** and the **validity effect**.
- Some attitudes are highly heritable (e.g., religiosity and certain political views) and thus resist change, but many are influenced by the nonshared environment.

Persuasion or "Brainwashing"

Social-psychological factors are involved in the making of a terrorist as well as recruiting a person to membership in religious and other sects:
- The person is subjected to entrapment.
- The person's problems are explained by a simple attribution ("It's the fault of those bad people").
- The person is offered a new identity and salvation.
- The person's access to disconfirming informtion is severely controlled.

Individuals in Groups

Conformity

- The Asch experiment shows that most people will conform to others' judgments, even when others are obviously wrong.
- The two main motives for conformity are the need for social acceptance and the need for information.

Groupthink

Groupthink, an extreme form of conformity, leads to faulty decisions because group members are vulnerable to:
- an illusion of invulnerability.
- self-censorship.
- pressure on dissenters to conform.
- an illusion of unanimity.

Altruism and Dissent

Situational factors can influence altruism and dissent, including:
- perceiving that help is needed.
- norms that encourage action.
- having an ally.
- becoming entrapped in a commitment to help or dissent.

The Wisdom and Madness of Crowds

When people are part of large, anonymous groups, two processes may occur:
1. **Diffusion of responsibility**, the spreading out of responsibility among many people. It can lead to *bystander apathy*. When the need for help is unambiguous, bystanders are more likely to help.
2. **Deindividuation**, the loss of awareness of one's own individuality:
   - increases as groups gets larger.
   - increases when group members wear masks or uniforms.
   - may increase helpfulness as well as destructiveness, depending on social norms.

Us Versus Them: Group Identity

Social identities are based on a person's identification with a nation, religion, political group, or other important affiliations.

Ethnic Identity

People often face the dilemma of balancing an **ethnic identity**, a close identification with a religious or ethnic group, and **acculturation**, identification with the dominant culture. Increasing numbers of people are identifying themselves as combinations of ethnicities.

Ethnocentrism

Ethnocentrism, the belief that one's own ethnic group or nation is superior to all others, can create "us–them" thinking and hostile competition.

Stereotypes

Stereotypes can be efficient cognitive summaries of other groups, but they distort reality by:
- exaggerating differences between groups.
- producing selective perception.
- underestimating the differences within other groups.

Prejudice and Group Conflict

A **prejudice** consists of a negative stereotype and a persistent, unreasonable negative feeling toward a category of people.

The Origins of Prejudice

1. *Psychological causes*: Prejudice wards off feelings of anxiety, simplifies problems by providing a scapegoat, and boosts self-esteem.
2. *Social causes*: Prejudice can stem from pressures by friends, relatives, and associates.
3. *Economic causes*: Prejudice justifies a group's economic interests and legitimizes war.
4. *Cultural and national causes*: Prejudice bonds people to their own group and fosters the dehumanization of other groups.

Defining and Measuring Prejudice

Prejudice is a challenge to define and measure; for example, *hostile sexism* is different from *benevolent sexism*, though both legitimize gender discrimination.
- Many *explicit* forms of conscious prejudice have declined, but *implicit*, unconscious prejudice may express itself in new forms.

Some researchers measure prejudice indirectly by:
- studying "microaggressions" and *social distance*, which reveal people's reluctance to get close to another group.
- documenting unequal treatment, for example in arrests for illegal use of drugs.
- seeing whether people are more likely to behave aggressively toward a target when they are stressed or insulted.
- observing changes in the brain.
- assessing unconscious positive or negative associations with a group, as with the *Implicit Association Test* (IAT). However, critics believe that the IAT does not capture true prejudice.

Reducing Conflict and Prejudice

Social psychologists have identified four conditions that decrease prejudice and animosity between groups:
1. Both sides must have equal legal status, economic standing, and power.
2. Both sides must have the moral, legal, and economic support of authorities and institutions.
3. Both sides must have opportuties to work and socialize together (the *contact hypothesis*).
4. Both sides must cooperate in working toward a common goal.

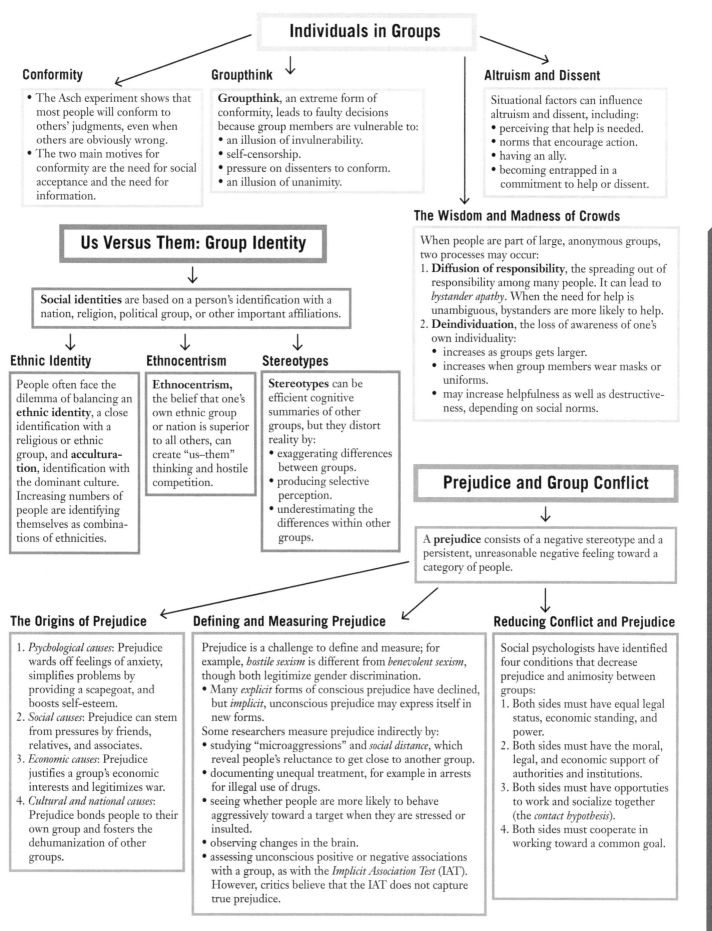

PSYCHOLOGICAL DISORDERS

PSYCHOLOGY IN THE NEWS /////////////////////////////

Celebrity Scandals Revive Sex-Addiction Debate

TUCSON, AZ, March 31, 2010. Motorcycle mogul Jesse James, Sandra Bullock's estranged husband, has reportedly checked himself into an Arizona rehab facility, the Sierra Tucson treatment center. News recently emerged that James has had several extramarital flings, including an 11-month affair with a reputed stripper, Michelle "Bombshell" McGee. The Tucson facility specializes in treating addictions, and because James is not known to have abused drugs or alcohol, speculation has centered on whether he is being treated for a sexual addiction. His representative told *People* magazine only that James had entered rehab "to deal with personal issues," adding that "he realized that this time was crucial to help himself, help his family, and help save his marriage."

A similar scandal erupted earlier this year with the revelation that champion golfer Tiger Woods had had more than a dozen extramarital affairs. Woods promptly checked himself into the Pine Grove clinic in Mississippi for rehabilitation. The details were not made public, but among the courses offered at the clinic are "shame reduction" and "setting sexual boundaries."

These and other high-profile cases of sexual infidelity have provoked controversy about whether people who have serial sexual affairs have a sexual "addiction." Palo Alto sex therapist Marty Klein thinks sex addiction is a bogus term that trivializes the meaning of true addiction, which is a physiological reliance on a substance like drugs or alcohol. "I don't see sex addicts," Klein says. "I see people who use sex in destructive ways." If an addiction is defined as any behavior that

someone repeats despite the risk of serious consequences, almost any sexual affair might qualify, and so might visiting a prostitute or viewing pornography. Because the diagnosis is so vague, many mental health professionals and laypeople alike think it is mostly an excuse for cheating. As comic Jimmy

Jesse James has checked into a rehab facility specializing in addictions, saying he wanted help with his problems.

Kimmel said, "'I'm addicted to sex' is the new, grown-up version of 'the dog ate my homework.'"

Some psychotherapists, however, consider sexual addiction to be a true disorder that involves an escalating preoccupation with sexual activity to cover up past pain or trauma. Therapists may prescribe a 12-step program, group therapy, and sometimes medication to help presumed addicts regulate their cravings. On the Internet, bloggers keep track of "celebrity sex addicts." James himself says he is not a sex addict, the kind of person who can't stop having affairs, though he admitted on "Nightline" that he had done stupid things "to sabotage my life." There is currently much debate about whether the psychiatric reference book, *The Diagnostic and Statistical Manual of Mental Disorders*, will include anything like sex addiction in its forthcoming edition.

/////////

Did Jesse James have a sexual addiction, a mental disorder comparable to alcohol or drug addiction? (Whatever it was, he claims his marriage to a new wife in 2013 cured it.) Or is he simply one of many guys who believe that because they are rich, famous, and successful, they are entitled to all the sex they can get? How broadly should we define the term *addiction*? Should it include compulsive Internet use, shopping more than your budget can afford, or eating too much chocolate?

And how about college student Matthew Small, who had a 4.0 average until he began to immerse himself in the virtual World of Warcraft? He spent at least six hours a day collecting armor, swords, and other cyber-gear for his character. His close friends drifted away, and his grades slipped. One day he realized that in just one semester he had logged more than 1,000 hours playing the game. He decided it was time to turn in his armor.

You don't have to be a psychologist to recognize the most extreme forms of abnormal behavior. When people think of mental illness, they usually think of individuals who have delusions, behave in bizarre ways, or commit random murders and other heartless crimes. But most psychological problems are far less dramatic and far more common than the public's impression of them. Some people go through episodes of complete inability to function, yet get along fine between those episodes. Some people function adequately every day, yet suffer constant melancholy, always feeling below par. And some people cannot control their worries or tempers.

In this chapter, you will learn about some of the psychological problems that cause people unhappiness and anguish, as well as about the severe disorders that make people unable to control their behavior. But be forewarned: One of the most common worries that people have is "Am I normal?" It is normal to fear being abnormal, especially when you are reading about psychological problems! But it is also normal to have problems. All of us on occasion have difficulties that seem too much to handle, and it is often unclear precisely when "normal" problems shade into "abnormal" ones.

You are about to learn . . .

- why insanity is not the same thing as having a mental disorder.
- how mental disorders differ from normal problems.
- why the standard professional guide to the diagnosis of mental disorders is controversial.
- why popular "projective" tests, such as the Rorschach inkblot test, are not reliable.

Diagnosing Mental Disorders LO 11.1

Many people confuse unusual behavior—behavior that deviates from the norm—with mental disorder, but the two are not the same. A person may behave in ways that are statistically rare (collecting ceramic pigs, being a genius at math, committing murder) without having a mental illness. Conversely, some

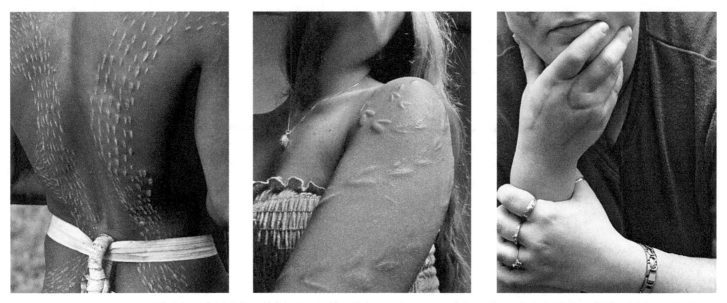

What is a mental disorder? In Papua New Guinea, all young men to go through an initiation rite in which small, deep cuts are made on their backs to create permanent scars that signify a crocodile's scales (left). This common cultural practice would not be defined as a disorder. In contrast, most people would agree that a woman who mutilates herself for the sole purpose of inflicting injury and pain, as the patient on the right has done, has a mental disorder. But what about the scars on the arm of the 23-year-old woman from upstate New York (middle), who had them made by a "body artist"? She also has scars on her leg and her stomach, along with 29 piercings. Does she have a mental disorder?

mental disorders, such as depression and anxiety, are extremely common. People also confuse mental disorder and insanity. In the law, the definition of insanity rests primarily on whether a person is aware of the consequences of his or her actions and can control his or her behavior. But *insanity* is a legal term only; a person may have a mental illness and yet be considered sane by the court.

If frequency of the problem is not a guide, and if insanity reflects only one extreme kind of mental illness, how then should we define a "mental disorder"? Some people do things that depart from current social or cultural notions of what is healthy or acceptable, bothering no one, but that does not mean they have a mental disorder. In contrast, some people think they are just fine, yet do things that cause enormous harm to themselves or others, such as getting pleasure from compulsively setting fires, gambling away the family's savings, or hearing voices telling them to stalk a celebrity day and night.

The central problem for psychiatry and clinical psychology is that diagnosing mental disorder is not as straightforward as diagnosing such medical problems as diabetes or appendicitis. Professionals themselves do not agree on a single definition of mental disorder, although they have tried for decades to settle on one, and there are as yet no reliable biological tests (as there are for, say, pneumonia) for most of the mental problems that

afflict humanity (Frances, 2013). Nonetheless, it is obvious that people suffer from all kinds of emotional and behavioral problems that range from mild to severe, and for which they feel the need to seek help.

In this chapter, therefore, we will use a very broad definition of **mental disorder**: any condition that causes an individual great suffering, does not go away after a reasonable length of time, is self-destructive, seriously impairs the person's ability to work or get along with others, or causes the person to endanger others or the community. By this definition, most people will have some mental health problem in the course of their lives.

◉ **Watch** the **Video** The Big Picture: What Does It Mean to Have a Mental Disorder? at **MyPsychLab**

Dilemmas of Diagnosis LO 11.2

Even armed with that broad definition of mental disorder, psychologists have found that classifying mental disorders into distinct categories is not an easy job. In this section, we will see why this is so.

Classifying Disorders: The DSM. The standard reference manual used to diagnose mental disorders is the *Diagnostic and Statistical Manual of Mental Disorders* (DSM-5), published by the American Psychiatric Association (2013). The DSM's primary aim is *descriptive:* to provide clear diagnostic

mental disorder Any behavior or emotional state that causes an individual great suffering, does not go away after a reasonable length of time, is self-destructive, seriously impairs the person's ability to work or get along with others, or causes the person to endanger others or the community.

categories, so that clinicians and researchers can agree on which disorders they are talking about and then can study and treat these disorders. Its diverse diagnostic categories include, among others, attention deficit disorders, disorders caused by brain damage, eating disorders, problems with sexual identity or behavior, impulse-control disorders (such as violent rages), personality disorders, psychotic disorders such as schizophrenia, and sleep-wake disorders.

The DSM has had an extraordinary impact worldwide. Virtually all textbooks in psychiatry and psychology base their discussions of mental disorders on the DSM. With each new edition of the manual, the number of mental disorders has grown. The first edition, published in 1952, was only 86 pages long and contained about 100 disorders. The fourth edition, published in 1994 and slightly revised in 2000, was 900 pages long and contained nearly 400 mental disorders. The fifth edition, DSM-5, which was published in 2013, is 947 pages long and contains about the same number of disorders.

A primary reason for this explosion of diagnoses is that insurance companies require clinicians to assign their clients an appropriate DSM code number for whatever the client's problem is—from trouble sleeping to trouble giving up coffee, from upsetting conflicts to crippling emotional problems. That means that compilers of the manual are motivated to add more diagnoses so that mental health professionals will be compensated and patients won't have to pay out of pocket (Greenberg, 2013; Zur & Nordmarken, 2008).

The DSM affects you in ways you probably can't imagine. Its influence is reflected in the casual way that people today talk of someone's being "bipolar," having "a touch of Asperger's," "being a borderline," suffering from PTSD, or claiming to have learned they were "ADHD" at the age of 40. As we will see, some of its diagnostic categories, such as childhood bipolar disorder (CBD), became cultural fads that spread like wildfire, causing much harm before the fires were extinguished. Because of the DSM's powerful influence, therefore, we want you to understand its limitations and some of the problems that are built into the effort to classify and label mental disorders.

THINKING CRITICALLY

About Diagnosing Disorders

Watch the Video Special Topics: Diagnosing Mental Disorders at MyPsychLab

1 **The danger of overdiagnosis.** If you give a small boy a hammer, the old saying goes, it will turn out that everything he runs into needs pounding. Likewise, say critics, if you give mental health professionals a new diagnostic label, it will turn out that everyone they run into has the symptoms of the new disorder.

Consider attention deficit/hyperactivity disorder (ADHD), a diagnosis given to children and adults who are impulsive, messy, restless, and easily frustrated and who have trouble concentrating. Since ADHD was added to the third edition of the DSM, the number of cases has skyrocketed in America, where it is diagnosed at least 10 times as often as it is in Europe. Parents, teachers, and mental health professionals are all overdiagnosing this condition, especially in boys, who are labeled ADHD twice as often as girls. The percentage of children given the label increases every year, with rates ranging from 6.2 percent in Utah to 15.6 percent in North Carolina (Centers for Disease Control, 2013). Critics argue that normal boyish behavior—being rambunctious, refusing to nap, being playful, not listening to teachers in school—has been turned into a psychological problem (Cummings & O'Donohue, 2008; Panksepp, 1998). A longitudinal study of more than a hundred 4- to 6-year-olds found that the number of children who met the criteria for ADHD declined as the children got older (Lahey et al., 2005). Those who truly had the disorder remained highly impulsive and unable to concentrate, but others simply matured. Now ADHD is being overdiagnosed in adults as well. Have trouble concentrating? Bored? You could get diagnosed as having ADHD (Frances, 2013).

In children, an alarming example of overdiagnosis involves bipolar disorder, which occurs primarily in adolescents and adults. Childhood bipolar disorder, a diagnosis that was based on small, inconclusive studies, was promoted by one psychiatrist who received multimillion-dollar payments from a pharmaceutical company that makes a powerful, risky antipsychotic drug often prescribed for bipolar children (Greenberg, 2013). As soon as CBD had a name, the number of diagnoses rose from 20,000 to 800,000 in just one year (Moreno et al., 2007; Leibenluft & Rich, 2008). "The CBD fad is the most shameful episode in my forty-five years of observing psychiatry," wrote Allen Frances (2013), an eminent psychiatrist who directed revision of the DSM-IV. The DSM-5 removed this diagnosis.

2 **The power of diagnostic labels.** Once a person has been given a diagnosis, other people begin to see that person primarily in terms of the label and overlook other possible explanations of the person's behavior. Suppose that a rebellious, disobedient teenager is diagnosed as having "oppositional defiant disorder" or that a child who has repeated tantrums is given the new DSM-5 diagnosis of "disruptive mood dysregulation disorder." Having the label suggests that the problem results from some inherent disposition—a "mental" disorder, after all. But perhaps the teenager is defiant because he has been abused or ignored. Perhaps the "dysregulated" child has outbursts only with certain adults or in certain situations, or has parents who have failed to set behavioral limits. Yet once a child or teenager is labeled, observers tend to ignore all the times and situations in which he or she is behaving beautifully.

On the other hand, many people welcome having a diagnostic label applied to them. Being given a diagnosis reassures those who are seeking an explanation for their emotional symptoms or those of their children ("Whew! So *that's* what it is!"). Some people even come to identify themselves according to a diagnosis and make it a central focus of their lives. Many people with Asperger's syndrome have established websites and support groups, and have even adopted a nickname ("Aspies"). What happens, then, when the label vanishes? The DSM-5 has removed Asperger's as a specific diagnosis, enfolding it into the spectrum of autism disorders, over the protests of many people who want the label.

3 The confusion of serious mental disorders with normal problems. The DSM is not called "The Diagnostic and Statistical Manual of Mental Disorders and a Whole Bunch of Everyday Problems." Yet each edition of the DSM has added more everyday problems, including, in DSM-5, "caffeine intoxication" and "parent-child relational problem." Some critics fear that by lumping together everyday difficulties with true mental illnesses such as schizophrenia and major depression, the DSM implies that life's ordinary problems are comparable to serious mental disorders (Houts, 2002).

A related concern is that the DSM-5 has loosened the criteria needed for making a diagnosis, thereby increasing the number of people who can be labeled with a disorder. The DSM-5 has added binge-eating disorder, whose symptoms include "eating until feeling uncomfortably full" or "when not feeling physically hungry." Who would not receive this diagnosis on occasion? One of the most vehement protests regarding the DSM-5 was on just this issue of moving the goalposts for a diagnosis. In the past, people who were grieving over the death of a loved one were not considered to have clinical depression, unless the grief became prolonged or incapacitating. However, the DSM-5 removed the "bereavement exemption" from the diagnosis of major depression. This change outraged many mental health professionals, who objected to the blurring of the symptoms of normal bereavement with those of severe depression (Greenberg, 2013). To the editors of the DSM-5, depression is depression, whatever generates it. To the protesters, this change turns an understandable and universal reason for human sorrow into a mental disorder (Horwitz & Wakefield, 2007).

4 The illusion of objectivity. Finally, critics both inside and outside of psychiatry maintain that the whole enterprise of the DSM is a vain attempt to impose a veneer of science on an inherently subjective process (Frances, 2013; Houts, 2002; Kutchins & Kirk, 1997; Tiefer, 2004). Without objective tests for mental disorder, many decisions about what to include must be based on group consensus—a vote by leading psychiatrists and clinical psychologists. This group consensus reflects prevailing attitudes, which may include cultural prejudices. It is easy to see how prejudice operated in the past. In the early years of the nineteenth century, a physician named Samuel Cartwright argued that many slaves were suffering from *drapetomania*, an urge to escape from slavery (Kutchins & Kirk, 1997; Landrine, 1988). (He made up the word from *drapetes*, the Latin word for "runaway slave," and *mania*, meaning "mad" or "crazy.") Thus, doctors could assure slave owners that a mental illness, not the intolerable condition of slavery, made slaves seek freedom. Today, of course, we recognize that "drapetomania" was foolish and cruel.

👁 Watch the Video Drapetomania: Robert Guthrie at MyPsychLab

Harriet Tubman (left) poses with some of the people she helped to escape from slavery on her "underground railroad." Slaveholders welcomed the idea that Tubman and others who insisted on their freedom had a mental disorder called "drapetomania."

Over the years, psychiatrists have quite properly voted out many other "disorders" that reflected cultural prejudices, such as lack of vaginal orgasm, childhood masturbation disorder, and homosexuality (Wakefield, 1992). But some DSM disorders are still affected by contemporary values, as when clinicians try to decide if wanting to have sex "too often" or not often "enough" is a mental disorder (Wakefield, 2011). Emotional problems allegedly associated with menstruation ("premenstrual dysphoric disorder") are now in the DSM-5, but behavioral problems associated with testosterone have never even been considered for inclusion. In short, critics maintain, many diagnoses still stem from cultural biases about what constitutes normal or appropriate behavior.

Critics of the DSM-5 are also worried about the large number of investigators involved in the revision who have financial ties to pharmaceutical companies that make drugs for the disorders being included. After the fourth edition was criticized because more than half of its researchers had such ties, members of DSM-5 panels responsible for specific revisions had to file financial disclosures. Nonetheless, potential conflicts of interest remained pervasive. For example, 67 percent of the panel on mood disorders, 83 percent of the panel on psychotic disorders, and all seven members of the sleep/wake disorders panel had ties to manufacturers of medications for these disorders or similar conflicts of interest (Cosgrove, 2013). And in a wonderfully ironic touch, the DSM-5 now contains "antidepressant discontinuation syndrome"—symptoms a person might have from trying to withdraw from the antidepressants that psychiatrists are now freer to prescribe for more disorders!

Supporters of the DSM maintain that it is important to help clinicians distinguish among disorders that share certain symptoms, such as anxiety, irritability, or delusions, so they can be diagnosed reliably and treated properly. And they fully acknowledge that the boundaries between "normal problems" and "mental disorders" are fuzzy and often difficult to determine (Helzer et al., 2008; McNally, 2011). That is why the DSM-5 editors decided to classify many disorders along a spectrum of symptoms, and in degrees from mild to severe, rather than as discrete categories.

Moreover, starting with the fourth edition, the DSM has made a concerted effort to recognize the influence of culture on mental disorders and their diagnoses. The DSM-5 discusses three culture-related concepts:

- **Cultural syndrome**, a set of symptoms specific to the culture in which they occur. For

example, Latinos may experience an *ataque de nervios*, an episode of uncontrollable screaming, crying, and agitation. In Japan, *taijin kyofusho* describes an intense fear that the body, its parts, or its functions displease, embarrass, or are offensive to others.

- **Cultural idiom of distress**, a linguistic term for, or way of talking about, suffering among people in a particular cultural group. For example, the Shona of Zimbabwe have *kufungisisa*, "thinking too much"—ruminating on upsetting thoughts and worries.

- **Cultural explanation of symptoms**, something like a culture's own diagnostic system. For example, in Haiti, *maladi moun* ("humanly caused illness") is used to explain various medical and psychological disturbances: Illness is seen as being caused by other people's envy and malice.

By comparing mental and emotional symptoms across different times and places, researchers can distinguish universal disorders from those that are specific to particular cultures. One meta-analysis found that bulimia, involving cycles of binge eating and vomiting to maintain weight, is a cultural syndrome that occurs primarily in the United States and is unknown in most other parts of the world. In contrast, anorexia nervosa, a body image disorder in which the sufferer usually feels too fat even at the point of starving to death, has been found throughout history and across cultures (Keel & Klump, 2003). Likewise, from the Inuit of Alaska to the Pacific Islanders to the Yoruba of Nigeria, some individuals have schizophrenic delusions, are severely depressed, have anxiety disorders, or cannot control their aggressive behavior (Butcher, Lim, & Nezami, 1998; Kleinman, 1988).

Dilemmas of Measurement LO 11.3

Clinical psychologists and psychiatrists usually arrive at a diagnosis by interviewing a patient and observing the person's behavior when he or she arrives at the office, hospital, or clinic. But many also use psychological tests to help them decide on a diagnosis. Such tests are also commonly used in schools (e.g., to determine whether a child has a learning disorder) and in court settings (e.g., to try to determine which parent should have custody in a divorce case, whether a child has been sexually abused, or whether a defendant is mentally competent).

Projective Tests. **Projective tests** consist of ambiguous pictures, sentences, or stories that the

projective tests
Psychological tests used to infer a person's motives, conflicts, and unconscious dynamics on the basis of the person's interpretations of ambiguous stimuli.

test taker interprets or completes. A child or adult may be asked to draw a person, a house, or some other object, or to finish a sentence (such as "My father..." or "Women are..."). The psychodynamic assumption behind all projective tests is that the person's unconscious thoughts and feelings will be "projected" onto the test and revealed in the person's responses. (See Chapter 2 for a discussion of psychodynamic theories.)

Projective tests can help clinicians establish rapport with their clients and can encourage clients to open up about anxieties and conflicts they might be ashamed to discuss. But the evidence is overwhelming that these tests lack reliability and validity, which makes them inappropriate for their most common uses—assessing personality traits or diagnosing mental disorders. They lack reliability because different clinicians often interpret the same person's scores differently, perhaps projecting their own beliefs and assumptions when they decide what a specific response means. The tests have low validity because they fail to measure what they are supposed to measure (Hunsley, Lee, & Wood, 2003). One reason is that responses to a projective test are significantly affected by sleepiness, hunger, medication, worry, verbal ability, the clinician's instructions, the clinician's personality (friendly and warm, or cool and remote), and other events occurring that day.

One of the most popular projectives is the *Rorschach inkblot test*, which was devised by the Swiss psychiatrist Hermann Rorschach in 1921. It consists of 10 cards with symmetrical abstract patterns, originally formed by spilling ink on paper and folding the paper in half. The test taker reports what he or she sees in the inkblots, and the clinician interprets the answers according to the symbolic meanings emphasized by psychodynamic theories. Although the Rorschach is widely used among clinicians, efforts to confirm its reliability and validity have repeatedly failed. The Rorschach does not reliably diagnose depression, posttraumatic stress reactions, personality disorders, or serious mental disorders (Wood et al., 2003).

Many psychotherapists and clinical social workers use projective tests with young children to help them express feelings they cannot reveal verbally. But during the 1980s, some therapists began using projective methods for another purpose: to determine whether a child had been sexually abused. They claimed they could identify a child who had been abused by observing how the child played with "anatomically detailed" dolls (dolls with prominent genitals), and that is how many of them testified in hundreds of court cases (Ceci & Bruck, 1995).

Unfortunately, these therapists had not tested their beliefs by using a fundamental scientific procedure: comparison with a control group. They had not asked, "How do *nonabused* children play with these dolls?" When psychological scientists conducted controlled research to answer this question, they found that large percentages of nonabused children are also fascinated with the doll's genitals. They will poke at them, grab them, pound sticks into a female doll's vagina, and do other things that alarm adults. The crucial conclusion was that you cannot reliably diagnose sexual abuse on the basis of children's doll play (Bruck et al., 1995; Hunsley, Lee, & Wood, 2003; Koocher et al., 1995).

Over the years, clinicians have devised other kinds of "props" and toys that they hope will facilitate children's reporting of having been molested. Unfortunately, props do not improve young children's ability to make accurate reports and actually elevate the risk of false reports of being touched (Poole, Bruck, & Pipe, 2011). You can see how someone who does not understand the problems with projective tests, or who lacks an understanding of children's cognitive limitations, might make inferences about a child's behavior that are dangerously wrong.

Another situation in which projective tests are used widely but often inappropriately is in child custody assessments, where judges long for an objective way to determine which parent is better suited to have custody. When a panel of psychological scientists impartially examined the leading psychological assessment measures, most of which are projective tests, they found that "these measures assess ill-defined constructs, and they do so

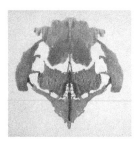

A Rorschach inkblot. What do you see in it?

For years, many therapists used anatomically detailed dolls as props in projective tests to determine whether or not a child had been sexually abused. But the empirical evidence, including studies of nonabused children in a control group, shows that this practice is simply not valid. It can lead to false allegations because it often misidentifies nonabused children who are merely fascinated with the doll's genitals.

PERSONALITY TEST

THIS IS:
(A) A MAN BEING EATEN BY A FISH.
(B) A MAN IN A FISH SUIT.

poorly, leaving no scientific justification for their use in child custody evaluations" (Emery, Otto, & O'Donohue, 2005).

Objective Tests. Many clinicians use **objective tests (inventories)**, standardized questionnaires that ask about the test taker's behavior and feelings. Inventories, such as the Beck Depression Inventory, are generally more reliable and valid than either projective methods or subjective clinical judgments (Dawes, 1994; Meyer et al., 2001). The most widely used diagnostic assessment for personality and emotional disorders is the *Minnesota Multiphasic Personality Inventory* (MMPI). The MMPI is organized into 10 categories, or *scales*, covering such problems as depression, paranoia, schizophrenia, and introversion. Four additional *validity scales* indicate whether a test taker is likely to be lying, defensive, or evasive while answering the items.

Inventories are only as good as their questions and how knowledgeably they are interpreted. Some test items on the MMPI fail to consider differences among cultural, regional, and socioeconomic groups. For example, Mexican, Puerto Rican, and Argentine respondents score differently from non-Hispanic Americans, on average, on the Masculinity–Femininity Scale. This difference does not reflect emotional problems but traditional Latino attitudes toward sex roles (Cabiya et al., 2000). Also, the MMPI sometimes labels a person's responses as evidence of mental disorder when they are a result of understandable stresses, such as during divorce or other legal disputes that usually make participants upset and angry (Guthrie & Mobley, 1994; Leib, 2008). However, testing experts continue to improve the reliability and validity of the MMPI in clinical assessment by restructuring the clinical scales to reflect current research on mental disorders and personality traits (Butcher & Perry, 2008; Sellbom, Ben-Porath, & Bagby, 2008).

We turn now to a closer examination of some of the disorders described in the DSM. We have singled out several that illustrate the range of psychological problems that afflict humanity, from the common to the very rare.

objective tests (inventories) Standardized objective questionnaires requiring written responses; they typically include scales on which people are asked to rate themselves.

Recite & Review

✓ **Study** and **Review** at **MyPsychLab**

Recite: Your mental health will be enhanced if you will say, out loud, what you know about insanity, defining mental disorder, the DSM's uses and limitations, cultural influences on mental disorders, projective tests, objective tests, and the MMPI.

Review: Next, reread this section.

Now take this *Quick Quiz:*

1. The primary purpose of the DSM is to (a) provide descriptive criteria for diagnosing mental disorders, (b) help psychologists assess normal as well as abnormal behavior, (c) describe the causes of common disorders, (d) keep the number of diagnostic categories of mental disorders to a minimum.

2. List four criticisms of the DSM.

3. Which of the following disorders is a cultural syndrome? (a) anorexia nervosa, (b) major depression, (c) bulimia, (d) schizophrenia, (e) panic attacks

4. What is the advantage of inventories, compared with clinical judgments and projective tests, in diagnosing mental disorders?

Answers:

1. a 2. It can foster overdiagnosis; it overlooks the influence of diagnostic labels on the perceptions of others; it often confuses serious mental disorders with everyday problems in living; and it produces an illusion of objectivity. 3. c 4. Inventories have better reliability and validity.

You are about to learn . . .

- the difference between ordinary anxiety and an anxiety disorder.

- why the most disabling of all phobias is known as the "fear of fear."

Anxiety Disorders LO 11.4, LO 11.5

Anyone who is waiting for important news or living in an unpredictable situation quite sensibly feels anxiety, a general state of apprehension or psychological tension. And anyone who is in a dangerous and unfamiliar situation, such as making a first parachute jump or facing a peevish python, quite sensibly feels flat-out fear. In the short run, these emotions are adaptive because they energize us to cope with danger. They ensure that we don't make that first jump without knowing how to operate the parachute, and that we get away from that snake as fast as we can.

But sometimes fear and anxiety become detached from any actual danger, or these feelings continue even when danger and uncertainty are past. The result may be *generalized anxiety disorder*, marked by long-lasting feelings of apprehension and doom; *panic attacks*, short-lived but intense feelings of anxiety; or *phobias*, excessive fears of specific things or situations.

👁 **Watch** the **Video** Anxiety and Worry: Sue Mineka at **MyPsychLab**

Generalized Anxiety Disorder. The hallmark of **generalized anxiety disorder** is excessive, uncontrollable, chronic anxiety or worry—a feeling of foreboding and dread—that is way out of proportion to the actual likelihood of a dreaded event occurring. Physical symptoms often include sweating, diarrhea, and restlessness. The person finds it hard to suppress these worries and to keep them from interfering with everyday activities.

Some people suffer from generalized anxiety disorder without having lived through any specific anxiety-producing event. They may have a genetic predisposition to experience its symptoms—sweaty palms, a racing heart, shortness of breath—when they are in unfamiliar or uncontrollable situations. Genes may also cause abnormalities in the amygdala, the core structure for the acquisition of fear, and in the prefrontal cortex, which is associated with the ability to realize when danger has passed (Lonsdorf et al., 2009). But anxiety disorders may also stem from experience: Some chronically anxious people have a history, starting in childhood, of being unable to control or predict their environments (Barlow, 2000; Mineka & Zinbarg, 2006). Whatever the origin of generalized anxiety disorder, its sufferers have mental biases in the way they attend to and process threatening information. They perceive everything as an opportunity for disaster, a cognitive habit that fuels their worries and keeps their anxiety bubbling along (Mitte, 2008).

Panic Disorder. In **panic disorder**, a person has recurring attacks of intense fear or panic, often with feelings of impending doom or death. Panic attacks may last from a few minutes to (more rarely) several hours. Symptoms include trembling and shaking, dizziness, chest pain or discomfort, rapid heart rate, feelings of unreality, hot and cold flashes, sweating, and—as a result of all these scary physical reactions—a fear of dying, going crazy, or losing control. Many sufferers fear they are having a heart attack.

Although panic attacks seem to come out of nowhere, they in fact usually occur in the aftermath of stress, prolonged emotion, specific worries, or frightening experiences. A friend of ours was on a plane that was a target of a bomb threat while airborne at 33,000 feet. He coped beautifully at the time, but two weeks later, seemingly out of nowhere, he had a panic attack. Such delayed attacks after life-threatening scares are common. The essential difference between people who develop panic disorder and those who do not lies in how they *interpret* their bodily reactions (Barlow, 2000). Healthy people who have occasional panic attacks see them correctly as a result of a passing crisis or period of stress, comparable to another person's migraines. But people who develop panic disorder regard the attack as a sign of illness or impending death, and they begin to live their lives in restrictive ways, trying to avoid future attacks.

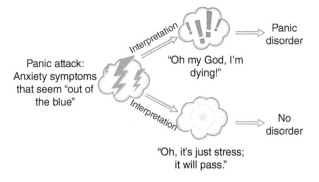

Fears and Phobias. Are you afraid of bugs, snakes, or dogs? Are you vaguely uncomfortable or so afraid that you can't stand to be around one? A **phobia** is an exaggerated fear of a specific situation, activity, or thing. Some common

---

generalized anxiety disorder A continuous state of anxiety marked by feelings of worry and dread, apprehension, difficulties in concentration, and signs of motor tension.

panic disorder An anxiety disorder in which a person experiences recurring panic attacks, periods of intense fear, and feelings of impending doom or death, accompanied by physiological symptoms such as rapid heart rate and dizziness.

phobia An exaggerated, unrealistic fear of a specific situation, activity, or object.

Get Involved! What Scares You?

Everyone fears something. Stop for a moment to think about what you fear most. Is it heights? Snakes? Speaking in public? Ask yourself these questions: (1) How long have you feared this thing or situation? (2) How would you respond if you could not avoid this thing or situation? (3) How much would you be willing to rearrange your life to avoid this feared thing or situation? After considering these questions, would you regard your fear as a full-blown phobia or merely a normal source of apprehension?

phobias—such as fear of snakes (ophidiophobia), insects (entomophobia), heights (acrophobia), thunder (brontophobia), or being trapped in enclosed spaces (claustrophobia)—may have evolved to be easily acquired in human beings because these fears reflected real dangers for the species. Other phobias, such as fear of the number 13 (triskaidekaphobia), may reflect idiosyncratic experiences or cultural traditions. Whatever its source, a true phobia is frightening and often incapacitating for its sufferer. It is not just a tendency to say "ugh" at tarantulas or skip the snake display at the zoo.

People who have a *social phobia* become extremely anxious in situations in which they will be observed by others—eating in a restaurant, speaking in public, or having to perform for an audience. They worry that they will do or say something that will be excruciatingly embarrassing and that other people will laugh at them or reject them. These phobias are more severe forms of the occasional shyness and social anxiety that everyone experiences. For people with a social phobia, the mere thought of being in a new situation with unfamiliar people is scary enough to cause sweating, trembling, nausea, and an overwhelming feeling of inadequacy. So they don't go, increasing their isolation and imagined fears.

By far the most disabling fear disorder is **agoraphobia**. In ancient Greece, the *agora* was the social, political, business, and religious center of town, the public meeting place away from home. The fundamental fear in agoraphobia is panic and its imagined disastrous consequences—being trapped in a public place, where escape might be difficult or where help might be unavailable. Individuals with agoraphobia report many specific fears—of being in a crowded movie theater, driving in traffic or tunnels, or going to parties—but the underlying fear is of being away from a safe place, usually home, or a safe person, usually a parent or partner.

Agoraphobia typically begins with a panic attack that seems to have no cause. The attack is so unexpected and scary that the agoraphobic-to-be begins to avoid situations that he or she thinks may provoke another one. A woman we know had a panic attack while driving on a freeway. This was a perfectly normal posttraumatic response to the suicide of her husband a few weeks earlier. But thereafter she avoided freeways, as if the freeway, and not the suicide, had caused the attack. Because so many of the actions associated with agoraphobia arise as a mistaken effort to avoid a panic attack, psychologists regard agoraphobia as a "fear of fear" rather than simply a fear of places.

👁 **Watch** the **Video** Special Topics: Learning to Overcome Phobias at **MyPsychLab**

agoraphobia A set of phobias, often set off by a panic attack, involving the basic fear of being away from a safe place or person.

Trauma-Related and Obsessive-Compulsive Disorders LO 11.6, LO 11.7

Two other kinds of disorders are related to anxiety but have been given separate categories in the DSM-5.

Posttraumatic Stress Disorder. Stress symptoms, including insomnia and agitation, are entirely normal in the immediate aftermath of any crisis or trauma, such as war, rape, torture, a natural disaster, sudden bereavement, or a terrorist

"I'm not a scaredy-cat—I'm phobic."

Barbara Smaller/The New Yorker Collection/ cartoonbank.com

posttraumatic stress disorder (PTSD) An anxiety disorder in which a person who has experienced a traumatic or life-threatening event has long-lasting symptoms such as recurrent, intrusive thoughts, flashbacks, nightmares, and increased physiological arousal.

obsessive-compulsive disorder (OCD) A disorder in which a person feels trapped in repetitive, persistent thoughts (*obsessions*) and repetitive, ritualized behaviors (*compulsions*).

attack; such symptoms usually subside over time. But in 1980, the third edition of the DSM introduced the diagnosis of **posttraumatic stress disorder (PTSD)** in response to ongoing concerns about the severe psychiatric toll on veterans of the Vietnam War. These soldiers were having symptoms for years after they returned home: recurrent, intrusive thoughts about the trauma; recurrent nightmares; flashbacks; avoidance of anyone or anything that aroused distressing memories; and increased physiological arousal, reflected in insomnia, irritability, and impaired concentration.

As researchers began studying this disorder, they encountered a puzzle: Most people who live through a traumatic experience eventually recover without developing long-lasting PTSD (Bonanno et al., 2010). Why, then, do others continue to have symptoms for years, sometimes for decades? One answer is that many of these individuals have a pre-existing vulnerability. Behavioral-genetic studies of twins in the general population and among combat veterans have found that some people are genetically more vulnerable than others to developing PTSD (Stein et al., 2002; Wilker & Kolassa, 2013; Yehuda et al., 2009). Other studies have found that people who develop PTSD often have a prior history of psychological problems, such as anxiety and impulsive aggression. And some lack the social, psychological, and neurological resources to avoid having preventable traumatic experiences in the first place or to cope with unavoidable ones (Breslau, Lucia, & Alvarado, 2006).

Another preexisting factor is the size of the hippocampus, which is crucially involved in autobiographical memory. In many PTSD sufferers, the hippocampus is smaller than average (McNally, 2003). An abnormally small hippocampus may figure in the difficulty of some trauma survivors to react to their memories as events from their past, causing them to keep reliving those memories in the present (Wilker & Kolassa, 2013). An MRI study of identical twins, only one of whom in each pair had been in combat in Vietnam, showed that the veterans who developed chronic PTSD had served in combat *and* had a smaller hippocampus than normal. Twins who had smaller hippocampi but no military service did not develop PTSD, and neither did the twins who *did* experience combat but who had normal-sized hippocampi (Gilbertson et al., 2002).

In the case of war-related PTSD, however, another contributing factor is experiential, not biological: directly inflicting harm on civilians or prisoners. An in-depth study of 260 male veterans from the National Vietnam Veterans Readjustment study examined the role of three factors: combat exposure, prewar vulnerability, and the vet's personal involvement in harming or killing civilians

This grief-stricken soldier has just learned that the body bag on the flight with him contains the remains of a close friend who was killed in action. Understandably, many soldiers suffer posttraumatic stress symptoms. But why do most eventually recover, whereas others have PTSD for many years?

or prisoners. As in the studies of the hippocampus that we just described, exposure to combat was *necessary* for the onset of PTSD, but not *sufficient*. Among veterans who scored high on all three factors, though, fully 97 percent developed PTSD—and the strongest independent predictor was having inflicted harm on prisoners or civilians (Dohrenwend et al., 2013). Obviously, most soldiers do not feel guilty or remorseful for carrying out orders in war; but those who do, as was the case for many veterans of Vietnam and Iraq, may come home with an added burden of PTSD.

In sum, many cases of persistent PTSD may result from cognitive and neurological vulnerabilities that existed before the trauma took place, combined with undergoing a horrific experience for which one feels responsible or guilty, making it more likely that the trauma will trigger persistent symptoms.

Obsessive-Compulsive and Related Disorders. **Obsessive-compulsive disorder (OCD)** is characterized by recurrent, persistent, unwished-for thoughts or images (*obsessions*) and by repetitive, ritualized behaviors that the person feels must be carried out to avoid disaster (*compulsions*). Of course, many people have trivial compulsions and practice superstitious rituals. Baseball players are famous for them; one won't change his socks and another insists on eating chicken every day while he is on a hitting streak. Obsessions and compulsions become a disorder when they become uncontrollable, time consuming (taking up an hour or more a day), and interfere with a person's life.

People who have obsessive thoughts often find them frightening or repugnant: thoughts of killing a child, of becoming contaminated by a handshake, or of having unknowingly hurt someone in a traffic accident. Obsessive thoughts take many forms, but they are alike in reflecting impaired ways of reasoning and processing information.

As for compulsions, the most common ones are hand washing, counting, touching, and checking. A woman *must* check the furnace, lights, locks, and oven three times before she can sleep; a man *must* run up and down the stairs 60 times in 40 minutes or else start over from the beginning. (The character of Hannah on the TV show *Girls*, like her creator Lena Dunham, has OCD; when Hannah is under particular stress, she starts feeling she must do everything in multiples of eight.) OCD sufferers usually realize that their behavior is senseless, and they are often tormented by their rituals. But if they try to resist the compulsion, they feel mounting anxiety that is relieved only by giving in to it.

In many people with OCD, abnormalities in an area of the prefrontal cortex create a kind of cognitive rigidity, an inability to let go of intrusive thoughts, and behavioral rigidity, an inability to alter compulsive behavior after getting negative feedback (Chamberlain et al., 2008; Clarke et al., 2004). Normally, once danger has passed or a person realizes that there is no cause for fear, the brain's alarm signal turns off. In people with OCD, however, false alarms keep clanging and the emotional networks keep sending out mistaken fear messages (Schwartz et al., 1996). The sufferer feels in a constant state of danger and tries repeatedly to reduce the resulting anxiety.

Simulate the **Experiment** The Obsessive-Compulsive Test at **MyPsychLab**

Extreme hoarding can be hazardous to health. The person who lived here was unable to throw away any papers or magazines. He was buried under this deluge of materials for two days.

The DSM-5 includes *hoarding disorder* in the larger category of obsessive-compulsive and related disorders. Pathological hoarders fill their homes with newspapers, bags of old clothing, used tissue boxes—all kinds of junk. They are tormented by fears of throwing out something they will need later. A PET-scan study compared obsessive hoarders with other people with obsessive symptoms and found that hoarders had less activity in parts of the brain involved in decision making, problem solving, spatial orientation, and memory (Saxena et al., 2004). Perhaps these deficits explain why hoarders keep things and why they often keep decades-old newspapers and junk in the living room, kitchen, or even on the bed. Their inability to decide what to throw away creates a constant worry, and their difficulty in remembering where things are makes them feel the need to have them in sight.

Recite & Review

Study and **Review** at **MyPsychLab**

Recite: Reciting out loud to yourself should not make you anxious, so recite what you know about generalized anxiety disorder, panic disorder, phobias, social phobia, agoraphobia, posttraumatic stress disorder, obsessive-compulsive disorder, and hoarding disorder.

Review: Next, read this section again.

Now take this *Quick Quiz:*

Match each term on the left with a description on the right.

1. social phobia
2. panic disorder
3. posttraumatic stress disorder
4. entomophobia
5. compulsion
6. posttraumatic stress disorder

a. need to perform a ritual
b. fear of insects
c. intense fear of impending doom or death
d. recurrent intrusive thoughts, flashbacks, nightmares, and increased physiological arousal
e. fear of meeting new people
f. nightmares and flashbacks

Answers:

1.e 2.c 3.d, f 4.b 5.a 6.d

You are about to learn . . .

- the difference between major depression and the blues.
- four contributing factors in depression.
- how some people can think themselves into depression.

Depressive and Bipolar Disorders

In the DSM-5, *depressive disorders* include a number of conditions that can cause persistent sad, empty, or irritable moods, accompanied by physical and cognitive changes that affect the person's ability to function in everyday life. People often speak of feeling "depressed," and of course everyone feels sad from time to time. These feelings, however, are a far cry from serious clinical depression.

Major Depression   LO 11.8, LO 11.9

Major depression involves emotional, behavioral, cognitive, and physical changes severe enough to disrupt a person's ordinary functioning. Some episodes can last for months, subside, and later recur. People with major depression feel sad, despairing, and worthless. They feel unable to get up and do things; it takes an enormous effort even to get dressed. They may overeat or stop eating, have difficulty falling asleep or sleeping through the night, have trouble concentrating, and feel tired all the time. They lose interest in activities that usually give them satisfaction and pleasure.

Major depression occurs about twice as often among women as among men (Rohde et al., 2013). However, because women are more likely than men to talk about their feelings and more likely to seek help, depression in males is probably underdiagnosed. Men who are depressed often try to mask their feelings by withdrawing, abusing alcohol or other drugs, driving recklessly, or behaving violently (Canetto, 1992; Kessler et al., 1995). As Susan Nolen-Hoeksema, a leading depression researcher, put it, "Women think and men drink."

One of the great mysteries of depression is that most people who undergo a "depressing" experience do not become clinically depressed, and many people who are clinically depressed have not had objectively "depressing" experiences (Monroe & Reid, 2009). Most researchers thus account for depression in terms of a **vulnerability-stress model**:

major depression
A disorder marked by excessive sadness, loss of interest in usual activities, feelings of worthlessness and hopelessness, thoughts of suicide, and physical symptoms (such as fatigue and loss of appetite).

vulnerability-stress models Approaches that emphasize how individual vulnerabilities interact with external stresses or circumstances to produce mental disorders.

A person's vulnerabilities (in genetic predispositions, personality traits, or habits of thinking) interact with stressful events (such as violence, death of a loved one, or losing a job) to produce most cases of major depression. Let's consider the evidence for four contributing factors:

1 Genetic predispositions or neurotransmitter imbalances. Major depression is a moderately heritable disorder, but the search for specific genes has so far been unsuccessful (Frances, 2013). One focus of investigation has been the genes that regulate serotonin, a neurotransmitter involved in mood. An early theory held that depression results from abnormally low levels of this neurotransmitter; indeed, that theory was the impetus for the development of antidepressants, designed to boost the availability of serotonin in the brain. However, many years of research have failed to support the notion that depression results from a simple neurotransmitter deficiency. Depleting animals of serotonin does not induce depression, nor does increasing brain serotonin necessarily alleviate it. The fact that some antidepressants raise serotonin levels does not mean that low serotonin levels caused the depression—a

Long before she became famous for writing the Harry Potter books, J. K. Rowling suffered incapacitating depression. She contemplated suicide, but the need to remain alive for her infant daughter kept her from killing herself. Later, she told an interviewer that she was never ashamed of having been depressed. On the contrary, she said, she was proud of herself for getting through that difficult time.

common but mistaken inference (Kirsch, 2010; Lacasse & Leo, 2005).

In 2003, a study of New Zealanders seemed to show that a serotonin receptor gene called 5-HTT interacted with experience to cause depression in genetically vulnerable people and prevent depression in others, depending on the form of the gene. But this conclusion turned out to be premature. Meta-analyses of direct replications of the New Zealand study found no links among the 5-HTT gene, life stresses, and depression (Duncan & Keller, 2011; Risch et al., 2009).

Nonetheless, the New Zealand study has stimulated a wave of research into gene-environment interactions in depression. One discovery is that the relative influence of genetic and environmental factors varies over the life span. A review of eight studies of identical twins found that although genetic predispositions predicted the twins' levels of depression and anxiety in childhood and young adulthood, by middle adulthood environmental factors and life experiences had become more powerful influences (Kendler et al., 2011).

2 **Violence, childhood physical abuse, and parental neglect.** One of the most powerful environmental factors associated with major depression is repeated experience with violence. Inner-city adolescents of both sexes who are exposed to high rates of violence in their families or communities report higher levels of depression and more attempts to commit suicide than those who are not subjected to constant violence (Mazza & Reynolds, 1999). The World Health Organization conducted a massive international research project in 21 countries, involving more than 100,000 people older than age 18. In rich and poor countries alike, the strongest predictors of suicide and attempted suicide were repeated experiences of sexual abuse and violence in childhood and adolescence (Stein et al., 2010).

The effects of maltreatment in childhood on later depression are independent of all other childhood and adult risk factors (Brown & Harris, 2008; Widom, DuMont, & Czaja, 2007). One reason is that prolonged stress in childhood puts the body's responses to stress in overdrive, so that it overproduces the stress hormone *cortisol* (Gotlib et al., 2008). People who are depressed tend to have high levels of cortisol, which can affect the hippocampus and amygdala, causing mood and memory abnormalities.

Among adults, domestic violence takes a particular toll on women. A longitudinal study that followed men and women from ages 18 to 26 compared those in physically abusive relationships with those in nonabusive ones. Although depressed women were more likely to enter abusive relationships to begin with, involvement in a violent relationship independently increased their rates of depression and anxiety—but, interestingly, not men's (Ehrensaft, Moffitt, & Caspi, 2006).

3 **Losses of important relationships.** A third line of investigation emphasizes the loss of important relationships in setting off depression in vulnerable individuals. When an infant is separated from a primary attachment figure, as in the Harlow studies of rhesus monkeys described in Chapter 3, the result is not only despair and passivity, but also harm to the immune system, which can later lead to depressive illness (Hennessy, Schiml-Webb, & Deak, 2009). Many people suffering from major depression have a history of separations, losses, rejections, and impaired, insecure attachments (Hammen, 2009; Nolan, Flynn, & Garber, 2003; Weissman, Markowitz, & Klerman, 2000).

4 **Cognitive habits.** Finally, depression involves specific, negative ways of thinking about one's situation (Beck, 2005; Mathews & MacLeod, 2005). Depressed people typically believe that their situation is *permanent* ("Nothing good will ever happen to me") and *uncontrollable* ("I'm depressed because I'm ugly and horrible and I can't do anything about it"). Expecting nothing to get better, they do nothing to improve their lives and therefore remain unhappy. When depressed and nondepressed people are put into a sad mood and given a choice between looking at sad faces or happy faces, depressed people choose the sad faces—a metaphor for how they process the world in general, attending to everything that confirms the gloominess of life rather than any of its joys (Joormann & Gotlib, 2007). When asked to recall happier times, nondepressed people cheer up but depressed people feel even worse, as if the happy memory makes them feel that they will never be happy again (Joormann, Siemer, & Gotlib, 2007).

The cognitive biases associated with depression are not just correlates of the disorder. Longitudinal studies show that they play a causal role, interacting with severe life stresses to generate further depressive episodes (Hallion & Ruscio, 2011; Monroe et al., 2007). Depressed people, especially if they also have low self-esteem, tend to *ruminate*—brooding about everything that is wrong in their lives, persuading themselves that no one cares about them, and dwelling on reasons to feel hopeless. They have trouble preventing these thoughts from entering and remaining in their working memory, which keeps them focused

VULNERABILITY-STRESS MODEL OF DEPRESSION

Stressful, triggering events + Individual vulnerability

Loss of loved one
Loss of job
Failure
Trauma
Violence

Genetic predisposition
History of insecure attachment
Negative ways of thinking
Hopelessness
Brooding rumination

SEVERE DEPRESSION

on negative thoughts and unhappy past events (Joorman, Levens, & Gotlib, 2011; Kuster, Orth, & Meier, 2012). In contrast, nondepressed people who undergo sad and stressful events are usually able to distract themselves, look outward, and seek solutions. Beginning in adolescence, women are much more likely than men to develop a ruminating, introspective style, which contributes both to longer-lasting depressions in women and to the sex difference in reported rates.

The factors we have described—genetics, violence, loss of important relationships, and cognitive habits and biases—combine in different ways to produce any given case of depression. That is why the same sad event, such as flunking a course, being dumped by a lover, or losing a job, can affect two people entirely differently: One rolls with the punch and another is knocked flat.

Bipolar Disorder LO 11.10

At the opposite pole from depression is *mania*, an abnormally high state of exhilaration. Mania is not the normal joy of being in love or winning the Pulitzer Prize. Instead of feeling fatigued and listless, the manic person is excessively wired and often irritable when thwarted. Instead of feeling hopeless and powerless, the person feels powerful and is full of grandiose plans; but these plans are usually based on delusional ideas, such as thinking that he or she has invented something that

bipolar disorder A disorder in which episodes of both depression and mania (excessive euphoria) occur.

will solve the world's energy problems. People in a state of mania often get into terrible trouble by going on extravagant spending sprees or making rash decisions.

When people experience at least one episode of mania, typically alternating with episodes of depression, they are said to have **bipolar disorder** (formerly called *manic-depressive disorder*). The great humorist Mark Twain had bipolar disorder, which he described as "periodical and sudden changes of mood...from deep melancholy to half-insane tempests and cyclones." Other writers, artists, musicians, and scientists have also suffered from this disorder (Jamison, 1992). During the highs, many of these creative people produce their best work, but the price of the lows is disastrous relationships, bankruptcy, and sometimes suicide.

The DSM-5 puts bipolar disorders into their own category, between depressive disorders and schizophrenia. The reason, the manual explains, is that symptoms and causes of bipolar disorder can overlap with those of depression and schizophrenia. Indeed, a study of some 60,000 individuals, compared with matched controls, found several gene variants shared by all three of these disorders, along with ADHD and autism (Cross-Disorder Group of the Psychiatric Genomics Consortium, 2013). Though the variants raise the risk of these disorders only slightly, they suggest that common molecular alterations may underlie different disorders once thought to be unrelated.

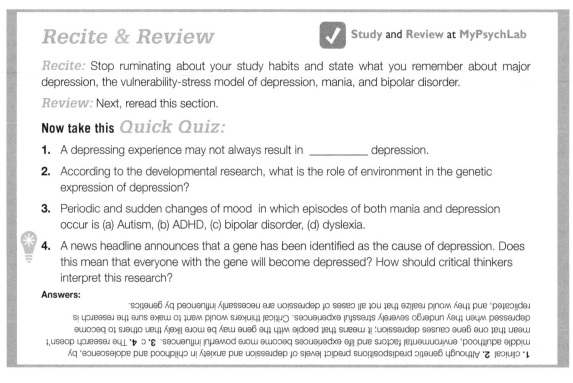

Recite & Review

✓ **Study** and **Review** at **MyPsychLab**

Recite: Stop ruminating about your study habits and state what you remember about major depression, the vulnerability-stress model of depression, mania, and bipolar disorder.

Review: Next, reread this section.

Now take this *Quick Quiz:*

1. A depressing experience may not always result in _____ depression.

2. According to the developmental research, what is the role of environment in the genetic expression of depression?

3. Periodic and sudden changes of mood in which episodes of both mania and depression occur is (a) Autism, (b) ADHD, (c) bipolar disorder, (d) dyslexia.

4. A news headline announces that a gene has been identified as the cause of depression. Does this mean that everyone with the gene will become depressed? How should critical thinkers interpret this research?

Answers:

1. clinical 2. Although genetic predispositions predict levels of depression and anxiety in childhood and adolescence, by middle adulthood, environmental factors and life experiences become more powerful influences. 3. c 4. The research doesn't mean that one gene causes depression; it means that people with the gene may be more likely than others to become depressed when they undergo severely stressful experiences. Critical thinkers would want to make sure the research is replicated, and they would realize that not all cases of depression are necessarily influenced by genetics.

Personality Disorders

Personality disorders involve impairments in personality that cause great distress to an individual or impair his or her ability to get along with others, *and* the presence of pathological traits such as excessive hostility or self-absorption.

Borderline Personality Disorder
LO 11.11

Borderline personality disorder characterizes people who have the personality trait of extremely negative emotionality and who are unable to regulate their emotions. They have a history of intense but unstable relationships in which they alternate between idealizing the partner and then devaluing the partner. They frantically try to avoid real or imagined abandonment by others, even if the "abandonment" is only a friend's brief vacation. They are self-destructive and impulsive, suffer chronic feelings of emptiness, and often threaten to commit suicide, which about 10 percent of them do. They are emotionally volatile, careening from anger to euphoria to anxiety (Crowell, Beauchaine, & Linehan, 2009). They love and hate intensely, sometimes simultaneously. (The term *borderline* comes from the original psychodynamic view of the disorder, as one falling on the border between mild and severe mental illnesses, thereby creating an inconsistent ability to function in the world.)

Many people with borderline disorder deliberately injure themselves in repeated acts of cutting and self-mutilation. This form of "nonsuicidal self-injury" has been known for thousands of years and is found around the world; it is most prevalent among adolescents and young adults. Self-injury has two functions: It reduces stress and arousal within the individual, and it often produces social support or relieves the person of unwanted social obligations (Nock, 2010).

Although there has not been much empirical research on the development of borderline personality disorder, a leading theory is based on a "biosocial" model proposed by Marsha Linehan, who suffers from the disorder herself and has developed one of the most successful treatments for it. In this view, a child is born with a genetic vulnerability that produces abnormalities in the frontal lobes and parts of the brain involved in emotion, along with a disposition toward negative emotionality as a personality trait (see Chapter 2). As a result, the child behaves impulsively and has heightened emotional sensitivity, which in turn is worsened by what Linehan calls an "invalidating environment": The child's parents do not acknowledge or tolerate the child's emotions and their expression, telling the child that those feelings are unjustified and that the child should cope with them alone. At the same time, the parents intermittently reinforce the child's extreme emotional outbursts with their attention. As a result of getting these mixed messages, the child never learns to understand and label what he or she is feeling, or how to regulate those feelings calmly. Instead, the child veers helplessly between trying to inhibit any sign of emotion and giving in to extreme expressions of it (Crowell, Beauchaine, & Linehan, 2009).

 Watch the Video Speaking Out: Liz: Borderline Personality Disorder at **MyPsychLab**

Antisocial Personality Disorder
LO 11.12, LO 11.13

Decades ago, Hervey Cleckley (1976) popularized the term **psychopathy**, which he used to describe individuals who are heartless, utterly lack conscience, and are unable to feel normal emotions. Psychopaths are incapable not only of remorse but also of fear of punishment and of shame, guilt, and empathy for those they hurt. Most psychopaths are not delusional or out of touch with reality. Nor are they unaware of the consequences of their actions; they just don't care about those consequences. If caught in a lie or a crime, psychopaths may seem sincerely sorry and promise to make amends, but it is all an act. Some psychopaths are violent and sadistic, able to kill a pet, a child, or a random adult without a twinge of regret, but many have no criminal records or history of violence. Instead, they are charming and manipulative, able to direct their energies into con games or career advancement, abusing other people emotionally or economically rather than physically (Patrick, Fowles, & Krueger, 2009; Poythress et al., 2010; Skeem et al., 2011). A leading researcher in this field, Robert Hare, calls corporate psychopaths "snakes in suits" (Babiak & Hare, 2007).

Although psychopaths are probably more prevalent in individualistic Western societies, they are believed to exist in all cultures and throughout

borderline personality disorder A disorder characterized by extreme negative emotionality and an inability to regulate emotions; it often results in intense but unstable relationships, impulsiveness, self-mutilating behavior, feelings of emptiness, and a fear of abandonment by others.

psychopathy (sy-KOP-uh-thee) A personality disorder (not in the DSM) characterized by fearlessness; lack of empathy, guilt, and remorse; the use of deceit; and coldheartedness. In the DSM, it is one symptom of antisocial personality disorder.

In the popular imagination, psychopaths are sadistic and violent. Gary L. Ridgway (left), the deadliest convicted serial killer in American history, strangled 48 women, placing their bodies in clusters around the country so he could "keep track of them." But most psychopaths are not murderers; they use charm and elaborate scams to deceive and defraud. Christopher Rocancourt (right, with model Naomi Campbell) conned celebrities and others out of millions of dollars by adopting false identities, including movie producer, Brazilian race car driver, Russian prince, son of Sophia Loren, and financier. He was caught in Canada and spent a year in a correctional center—hosting media interviews and writing his autobiography.

antisocial personality disorder (APD) A personality disorder characterized by a lifelong pattern of irresponsible, antisocial behavior such as lawbreaking, violence, and other impulsive, reckless acts, and lack of remorse for harms inflicted.

history. Even a close-knit culture such as the Yupik in Canada has a word for them: *kunlangeta* (Seabrook, 2008). An anthropologist once asked a member of the tribe what the group would do with a kunlangeta, and he said, "Somebody would have pushed him off the ice when nobody else was looking." Psychopaths are feared and detested everywhere.

Over the objections of many clinical scientists who study psychopathy, the third edition of the DSM replaced that diagnosis with **antisocial personality disorder (APD)**. For several editions, the DSM has described people with APD as having a "pervasive pattern of disregard for and violation of the rights of others," occurring since the age of 15 (although often people with APD have had conduct problems in childhood). This "antisocial" pattern may be expressed in various ways, but to receive the diagnosis, a person needs to meet only three of these criteria: repeatedly breaks the law and violates the rights of others; is deceitful, lying and conning others for profit or pleasure; is impulsive and seeks quick thrills; shows reckless disregard for his or her own safety or anyone else's; gets into physical fights or assaults others; and is chronically irresponsible, failing to hold jobs or meet obligations. The DSM-5 has added one final symptom, the one that is at the heart of psychopathy: lacking remorse for the harms inflicted on others.

As you can see, this definition covers a broad set of behaviors. It includes psychopaths, who are deceitful and lack remorse, but it also includes teenagers who fall in with a bad crowd for a few years and criminals who have been aggressive rule-breakers since early childhood. The latter become what one researcher calls "lifetime persistent offenders," though their offenses take different forms at different ages: "biting and hitting at age 4, shoplifting and truancy at age 10, selling drugs and stealing cars at age 16, robbery and rape at age 22, and fraud and child abuse at age 30" (Moffitt, 1993, 2005). One study found that unusual aggressiveness can be eerily apparent by an infant's first birthday, virtually as soon as a baby has the motor skills to hit or exert force, and seems to be an early predictor of later violence (Hay et al., 2011).

The researchers who study psychopathy believe that something is amiss in the emotional wiring of people who do not feel emotionally connected to others of their kind—who lack the capacity for empathy and remorse (Hare, 1965, 1996; Lykken, 1995; Raine et al., 2000). Most psychopaths do not respond physiologically to the threat of punishment the way other people do, which may be why they can behave fearlessly in situations that would scare others to death. Normally, when a person is anticipating danger, pain, or punishment, the electrical conductance of the skin changes, a classically conditioned response that indicates anxiety or fear. But psychopaths are slow to develop such responses, which suggests that they have difficulty feeling the anxiety necessary for learning that their actions will have unpleasant consequences (Lorber, 2004; see Figure 11.1). Their lack of empathy for others also seems to have a physiological basis. When they are shown pictures of people crying and in distress, their skin conductance barely shifts, in contrast to that of nonpsychopaths, which shoots up (Blair et al., 1997).

Clinical scientists have developed ways of measuring callousness and unemotionality in children, central dispositions that can develop into adult psychopathy (Frick & Viding, 2009). Young children with these traits cannot correctly decode fear expressions in the faces, voices, or gestures of other people. They don't feel fear themselves or "get" fear in others, and as a result they may fail to respond to efforts by their parents and other adults to socialize them—and thus fail to develop a conscience (Sylvers, Brennan, & Lilienfeld, 2011).

As for people with the lifelong violent, antisocial form of APD—who may or may not lack empathy and remorse for their actions, as psychopaths do—many don't do as well as other individuals on neuropsychological tests of frontal lobe functioning, and they have less gray matter in the frontal lobes than other people do (Dinn & Harris, 2000; Raine, 2008). The frontal lobes are responsible for planning and impulse control, and impairments in this area can lead to an inability to control responses to frustration and provocation, to regulate emotions, and to understand the long-term consequences of indulging in immediate gratifications (van Goozen et al., 2007). One PET scan study found that cold-blooded, predatory murderers had less brain activity in the frontal lobes than did men who murdered in the heat of passion or a control group of criminals who had not murdered anybody (Raine et al., 1998).

Frontal lobe damage can result from disease, accident, or physical abuse (Milner & McCanne, 1991), and also from genetic factors. In a longitudinal study of boys who had been physically abused in childhood, those who had a variation in a crucial gene later had far more arrests for violent crimes than did abused boys who had a normal gene (Caspi et al., 2002). Although only 12 percent of the abused boys had this variant, they accounted for nearly half of all later convictions for violent crimes.

Nevertheless, as we keep reminding you, genes are not destiny. The boys who had the genetic variant but whose parents treated them lovingly did not grow up to be violent. Genes may affect the brain in ways that predispose a child to rule-breaking and violent behavior, but many environmental influences can produce the same results, directly or by altering the ways that genes are expressed. One is poor nutrition in the first three years of life, which has been linked with antisocial behavior up through adolescence; others include early separation from the mother and brain damage caused by parental cruelty (Raine, 2008). Likewise, psychopathy can have different origins, and any genetic predispositions or other

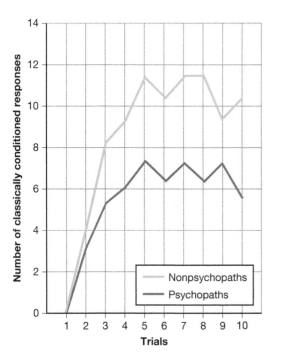

FIGURE 11.1 Emotions and Psychopathy
In several experiments, people diagnosed as psychopaths were slow to develop classically conditioned responses to anticipated danger, pain, or shock—responses that indicate normal anxiety. This deficit may be related to the ability of psychopaths to behave in destructive ways without remorse or regard for the consequences (Hare, 1965, 1993).

biological factors interact with environmental influences. In fact, contrary to popular belief, some children and even adults who score high on measures of psychopathy can change with intensive treatment (Skeem et al., 2011).

Whatever the possible genetic or biological influences on psychopathy and other forms of APD, culture also plays a big role. A culture that rewards ruthless behavior in work and politics will generate many "snakes in suits," and a culture that rewards the slaughter of innocents for purposes of political or religious genocide will generate many cases of heartless violence and lack of empathy.

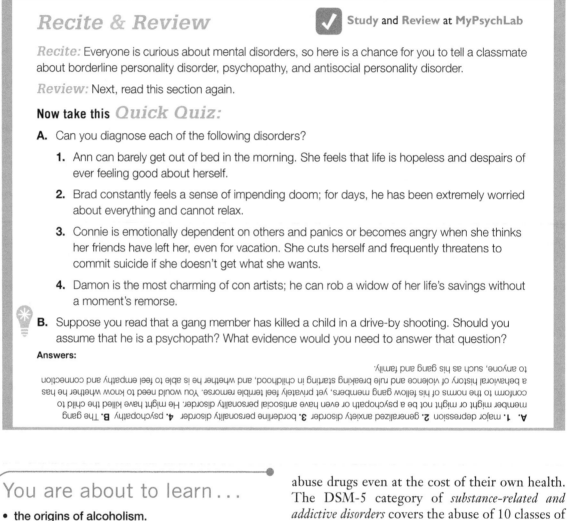

Recite & Review

✓ **Study** and **Review** at **MyPsychLab**

Recite: Everyone is curious about mental disorders, so here is a chance for you to tell a classmate about borderline personality disorder, psychopathy, and antisocial personality disorder.

Review: Next, read this section again.

Now take this *Quick Quiz:*

A. Can you diagnose each of the following disorders?

1. Ann can barely get out of bed in the morning. She feels that life is hopeless and despairs of ever feeling good about herself.

2. Brad constantly feels a sense of impending doom; for days, he has been extremely worried about everything and cannot relax.

3. Connie is emotionally dependent on others and panics or becomes angry when she thinks her friends have left her, even for vacation. She cuts herself and frequently threatens to commit suicide if she doesn't get what she wants.

4. Damon is the most charming of con artists; he can rob a widow of her life's savings without a moment's remorse.

B. Suppose you read that a gang member has killed a child in a drive-by shooting. Should you assume that he is a psychopath? What evidence would you need to answer that question?

Answers:

A. **1.** major depression **2.** generalized anxiety disorder **3.** borderline personality disorder **4.** psychopathy **B.** The gang member might or might not be a psychopath or even have antisocial personality disorder. He might have killed the child to conform to the norms of his fellow gang members, yet privately feel terrible remorse. You would need to know whether he has a behavioral history of violence and rule breaking starting in childhood, and whether he is able to feel empathy and connection to anyone, such as his gang and family.

You are about to learn . . .

- the origins of alcoholism.

- why alcoholism is more common in some cultures than others.

- why social policies of abstinence from alcohol do not reduce problem drinking.

- why narcotics are not usually addictive when people take them for severe pain.

Substance-Related and Addictive Disorders

Most people who use drugs (legal, illegal, or prescription) use them in moderation; but some people depend too much on them, and others abuse drugs even at the cost of their own health. The DSM-5 category of *substance-related and addictive disorders* covers the abuse of 10 classes of drugs, including alcohol, caffeine, hallucinogens, inhalants, cocaine, and tobacco, and adds "other (or unknown) substances," in case as-yet-unidentified ways of getting high turn up. The DSM-5 has also added "gambling disorder" in this category, on the grounds that compulsive gambling activates the brain's reward mechanisms just as drugs do. But it relegated "Internet gaming disorder" to the appendix, as a condition warranting further study, and decided not to include excessive behavioral patterns popularly called "sex addiction," "shopping addiction," or "exercise addiction," because, as the manual explains, there is little evidence that these constitute mental disorders.

The DSM-5 does not use the common term *addiction* as a diagnostic label, preferring "substance use disorder" to reflect the fact that people's misuse of any drug can range in severity from mild impairment to "chronically relapsing, compulsive drug taking" that impairs a person's ability to function and harms the drug-taker or others in his or her life. Thus, symptoms of "*alcohol-use disorder*" include at least two of the following: uncontrollable craving for alcohol; drinking in situations where it is physically hazardous; drinking despite persistent social or personal consequences; inability to cut back or stop; and drinking larger amounts or in greater frequency than intended.

In this section, we will use the term *addiction* to refer to the extreme form of substance misuse, focusing primarily on the example of alcoholism. We will consider the two dominant approaches to understanding addiction and drug abuse—the biological model and the learning model—and then see how they might be reconciled.

Biology and Addiction LO 11.14

The *biological model*, also called the *disease model*, holds that addiction, whether to alcohol or any other drug, primarily stems from a person's neurology and genetic predisposition. The clearest example of the biology of addiction involves nicotine. Although smoking rates have declined over the past 50 years, nicotine addiction remains one of the most serious health problems worldwide. Unlike other addictions, it can begin quickly, within a month after the first cigarette—and for some teenagers, after only one cigarette—because nicotine almost immediately changes neuron receptors in the brain that react chemically to the drug (DiFranza, 2008). Genes produce variation in these nicotine receptors, which is one reason that some people are especially vulnerable to becoming addicted to cigarettes and have tremendous withdrawal symptoms when they try to give them up, whereas other people, even if they have been heavy smokers, can quit cold turkey (Bierut et al., 2008).

For alcoholism, the picture is more complicated. Genes are involved in some kinds of alcoholism but not all. There is a heritable component in the kind of alcoholism that begins in early adolescence and is linked to impulsivity, antisocial behavior, and criminality (Dick, 2007; Dick et al., 2008; Schuckit et al., 2007), but not in the kind of alcoholism that begins in adulthood and is unrelated to other disorders.

Genes also affect alcohol sensitivity: how quickly people respond to alcohol, whether they tolerate it, and how much they need to drink

before feeling high (Hu et al., 2008). In an ongoing longitudinal study of 450 young men, those who at age 20 had to drink more than others to feel any reaction were at increased risk of becoming alcoholic within the decade. This was true regardless of their initial drinking habits or family history of alcoholism (Schuckit, 1998).

In contrast, people who have a high sensitivity to alcohol are less likely to drink to excess, and this may partly account for ethnic differences in alcoholism rates. One genetic factor causes low activity of an enzyme involved in the metabolism of alcohol. People who lack this enzyme respond to alcohol with unpleasant symptoms, such as flushing and nausea. This genetic protection is common among Asians but rare among Europeans, which may be one reason that rates of alcoholism are lower in Asian than in white populations; the Asian sensitivity to alcohol discourages them from drinking a lot (Heath et al., 2003). Not all Asians are the same in this regard, however. Korean-American college students have higher rates of alcohol-use disorders and family histories of alcoholism than do Chinese-American students (Duranceaux et al., 2008). And Native Americans have the same genetic protection that Asians do, yet they have much higher rates of alcoholism.

For years, the usual way of looking at biological factors and addiction was to assume that the first causes the second. However, the relationship also works the other way: *Addictions can result from the abuse of drugs* (Crombag & Robinson, 2004; Lewis, 2011). Many people become addicted not because their brains have led them to abuse drugs, but because the abuse of drugs has changed their brains. Over time, repeated jolts of pleasure-producing dopamine modify brain structures in ways that maximize the appeal of the drug and disrupt cognitive functions such as working memory, self-control, and decision making. Eventually, the addictive behavior comes to feel uncontrollable (Houben, Wiers, & Jansen, 2011; Lewis, 2011).

In addition, heavy use of cocaine, alcohol, and other drugs eventually reduces the number of receptors for dopamine and creates the compulsion to keep using the drug (Volkow et al., 2001; see Figure 11.2). In the case of alcoholism, heavy drinking also reduces the level of painkilling endorphins, produces nerve damage, and shrinks the cerebral cortex. These changes can then create a craving for more liquor, and the person stays intoxicated for longer and longer times, drinking not for pleasure at all but simply to appease the craving (Heilig, 2008).

Explore the Concept Virtual Brain: Drug Addiction and Brain Reward Circuits at MyPsychLab

Robert Downey, Jr., went to prison numerous times for abusing cocaine, heroin, and Valium. He told a judge, "It's like I have a loaded gun in my mouth and my finger's on the trigger, and I like the taste of the gunmetal." Downey's addictions nearly destroyed his acting career.

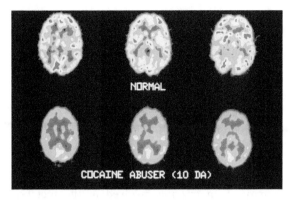

FIGURE 11.2 The Addicted Brain
PET studies show that the brains of cocaine addicts have fewer receptors for dopamine, a neurotransmitter involved in pleasurable sensations. (The more yellow and red in the brain image, the more receptors.) The brains of people addicted to methamphetamine, alcohol, and even food show a similar dopamine deficiency (Volkow et al., 2001).

Thus, drug abuse, which begins as a voluntary action, can turn into drug addiction, a compulsive behavior that addicts find almost impossible to control.

Learning, Culture, and Addiction LO 11.15

Impulsiveness, an inability to control one's immediate craving for something, is one of the defining characteristics of addiction. Yet a surprising discovery emerged when a team of scientists studied the brains of people addicted to stimulants and their biological siblings who had no history of chronic drug abuse (Ersche et al., 2012). The addicts *and* their siblings had abnormalities in the parts of the brain involved in self-control. What enabled the siblings to resist temptation and addiction despite their biological vulnerability? Likely candidates include being in a circle of friends who didn't abuse drugs, a learned ability to manage frustration and adversity, and strong coping skills (Volkow & Baler, 2012).

This finding supports the *learning model* of addiction, which emphasizes the role of the environment, learning, and culture in encouraging or discouraging drug abuse. Four other lines of research support the learning model:

1 **Addiction patterns vary according to cultural practices.** Alcoholism is much more likely to occur in societies that forbid children to drink but condone drunkenness in adults (as in Ireland) than in societies that teach children how to drink responsibly and moderately but condemn adult drunkenness (as in Italy, Greece, and France). In cultures with low rates of alcoholism (except for those committed to a religious rule that forbids use of all psychoactive drugs), adults demonstrate moderate drinking habits to their children, gradually introducing them to alcohol in safe family settings. Alcohol is not used as a rite of passage into adulthood. Abstainers are not sneered at, and drunkenness is not considered charming, comical, sexy, or manly; it is considered stupid and obnoxious (Peele, 2000; Peele & Brodsky, 1991; Vaillant, 1983).

The cultural environment may be especially crucial for the development of alcoholism among young people with a genetic vulnerability to alcohol (Schuckit et al., 2008). In one such group of 401 Native American youths, those who later developed drinking problems lived in a community in which heavy drinking was encouraged and modeled by their parents and peers. But those who felt pride in being Native American and were strongly attached to their religious traditions were less likely to develop drinking problems, even when their parents and peers were encouraging them to drink (Yu & Stiffman, 2007).

Addiction rates can rise or fall rapidly as a culture changes. In colonial America, the average person drank two to three times the amount of liquor consumed today, yet alcoholism was not a serious problem. Drinking was a universally accepted social activity; families drank and ate together. Alcohol was believed to produce pleasant feelings and relaxation, and Puritan ministers endorsed its use (Critchlow, 1986). Then, between 1790 and 1830, when the American frontier was expanding, drinking came to symbolize masculine independence and toughness. The saloon became the place for drinking away from home. As people stopped drinking in moderation with their families, alcoholism rates shot up, as the learning model would predict.

Here's a modern example of how changing cultural norms can affect drinking habits and addiction rates. The cultural norm for American college women was once low to moderate drinking. Today, college women are more likely to abuse alcohol because the culture of many American college campuses encourages drinking games, binge drinking (having at least four to five drinks in a two-hour session), and getting drunk, especially among members of fraternities and sororities (Courtney & Polich, 2009). When everyone around you is downing shots one after another or playing beer pong, it's hard to say, "I'd really rather just have one drink" (or none).

2 **Policies of total abstinence tend to increase rates of addiction rather than reduce them.** In the United States, the temperance movement of the early twentieth century held that drinking inevitably leads to drunkenness, and drunkenness to crime. The solution it won for the Prohibition years (1920–1933) was national abstinence. But

When children learn the rules of social drinking with their families, as at this Jewish family's Passover seder (left), alcoholism rates are much lower than in cultures in which drinking occurs mainly in bars or in privacy. Likewise, when marijuana is used as part of a religious tradition, as it is by members of the Rastafarian church in Jamaica, use of the "wisdom weed" does not lead to addiction or harder drugs.

this victory backfired: Again in accordance with the learning model, Prohibition reduced rates of drinking overall, but it *increased* rates of alcoholism among those who did drink. Because people were denied the opportunity to learn to drink moderately, they drank excessively when given the chance (McCord, 1992). And, of course, when a substance is forbidden, it becomes more attractive to some people. Most schools in America have zero-tolerance policies regarding marijuana and alcohol, but large numbers of students have tried them or use them regularly. In fact, rates of binge drinking have increased the most among underage students, who are legally forbidden to drink until age 21.

3 Not all addicts have withdrawal symptoms when they stop taking a drug. When heavy users of a drug stop taking it, they often suffer such unpleasant symptoms as nausea, abdominal cramps, depression, and sleep problems, depending on the drug. But these symptoms are far from universal. During the Vietnam War, nearly 30 percent of American soldiers were taking heroin in doses far stronger than those available on the streets of their home cities. These men believed themselves to be addicted, and experts predicted a drug-withdrawal disaster among the returning veterans. It never materialized; more than 90 percent of the men simply gave up the drug, without significant withdrawal pain, when they came home to new circumstances (Robins, Davis, & Goodwin, 1974). Subsequent studies have found that this response is the norm among veterans and others once they leave their heavy-drug-use environment (Heyman, 2009, 2011). Similarly, the majority of people who are dependent on cigarettes, tranquilizers, or painkillers are able to stop taking these drugs without outside help and without severe withdrawal symptoms (Prochaska, Norcross, & DiClemente, 1994). Many people find

this information startling, even unbelievable. That is because people who can quit without help aren't entering programs to help them quit, so they are invisible to the general public and to the medical and therapeutic world. But they have been identified in random-sample community surveys.

One reason that many people are able to quit abusing drugs is that the environment in which a drug is used (the setting) and a person's expectations (mental set) have a powerful influence on the drug's *physiological* effects as well as its psychological ones (see Chapter 5). You might think a lethal dose of, say, amphetamines would be the same wherever the drug was taken. But studies of mice have found that the lethal dose varies depending on the mice's environment—whether they are in a large or small test cage, or whether they are alone or with other mice. The physiological response of human addicts to certain drugs also depends on whether the addicts are in a "druggy" environment, such as a crack house, or an unfamiliar one (Crombag & Robinson, 2004; Siegel, 2005). This is the primary reason that addicts need to change environments if they are going to kick their habits. It's not just to get away from a peer group that might be encouraging them, but also to literally change and rewire their brain's response to the drug.

4 Addiction does not depend on properties of the drug alone but also on the reasons for taking it. For decades, doctors were afraid to treat people with chronic pain by giving them narcotics, fearing they would become addicts. As a result of this belief, millions of people were condemned to live with chronic suffering from back pain, arthritis, nerve disorders, and other conditions—and pain impedes healing. But then researchers learned that the great majority of pain sufferers use

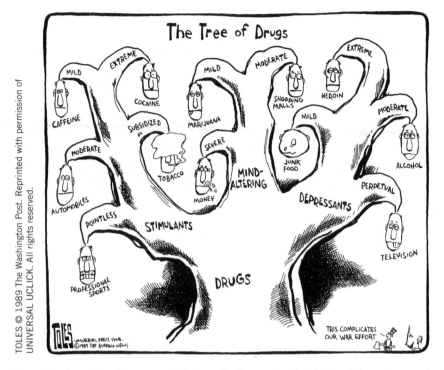

By poking fun at the things people do to make themselves feel better, this cartoon reminds us that a person can become dependent on many things besides alcohol or other drugs.

morphine and other opiates not to escape from the world but to function in the world, and they do not become addicted (Portenoy, 1994; Raja, 2008). In contrast, most of the people who abuse opiates are looking to get high rather than alleviate physical pain.

In the case of alcohol, people who drink simply to be sociable or to relax when they have had a rough day are unlikely to become addicted. *Problem* drinking occurs when people drink to disguise or suppress their anxiety or depression, when they drink alone to drown their sorrows and worries, or when they want an excuse to abandon inhibitions or have casual sex (Cooper et al., 1995; Livingston et al., 2012; Mohr et al., 2001). College students who feel alienated and uninvolved with their studies are more likely than their happier peers to go out drinking with the conscious intention of getting drunk (Flacks & Thomas, 1998).

In many cases, then, the decision to start abusing drugs depends more on people's motives, and on the norms of their peer group and culture, than on the chemical properties of the drug itself.

Get Involved! Test Your Motives for Drinking

If you drink, why do you do so? Check all of the motives that apply to you:

_____	to relax	_____	to cope with depression
_____	to escape from worries	_____	to get drunk and lose control
_____	to enhance a good meal	_____	to rebel against authority
_____	to conform to peers	_____	to relieve boredom
_____	to express anger	_____	to have sex
_____	to be sociable	_____	other (specify)

Do your reasons promote abuse or responsible use? How do you respond physically to alcohol? What have you learned about drinking from your family, your friends, and cultural messages? What do your answers tell you about your own vulnerability to addiction?

Debating the Causes of Addiction LO 11.16

The biological and learning models both contribute to our understanding of substance abuse and addiction. Yet, among many researchers and public health professionals, these views are quite polarized, especially when it comes to thinking about treatment. The result is either–or thinking on a large scale: Either complete abstinence is the solution, or it is the problem.

Those who advocate the biological model say that alcoholics and problem drinkers must abstain completely, and that young people should not be permitted to drink, even at home with their parents, until they are 21. Those who champion the learning model argue that most problem drinkers can learn to drink moderately if they learn safe drinking skills, acquire constructive ways of coping with stress, avoid situations that evoke conditioned responses to using drugs, and avoid friends who pressure them to drink excessively. Besides, they ask, how are young people going to learn to drink moderately if they don't first do so at home or in other safe environments? (Denning, Little, & Glickman, 2004; Rosenberg, 1993).

THINKING CRITICALLY

About Treating Addictions

How can we assess these two positions critically? Because alcoholism and other kinds of substance abuse occur for many reasons, neither model offers the only solution. In the case of alcohol, many problem drinkers may not be able to learn to drink moderately because physiological changes in their brains and bodies have turned them from heavy drinkers into addicts. But many who go through a period of alcohol abuse may indeed be able to learn to drink moderately. They may benefit from programs such as Harm Reduction, which teach people how to drink moderately and keep their drinking under control (Witkiewitz & Marlatt, 2006).

So perhaps the question we should be asking is "What are the factors that make it more or less likely that someone can learn to control problem drinking?" Problem drinkers who are most likely to become moderate drinkers have a history of less severe dependence on the drug. They lead more stable lives and have jobs and families. In contrast, those who are at greater risk of alcoholism (or other drug abuse) have these risk factors: (1) They have a genetic vulnerability to the drug or have been using it long enough for it to have damaged or changed their brains; (2) they believe that they have no control over their drinking or other drug use; (3) they live in a culture or a peer group that promotes and rewards binge drinking or discourages moderate drug use; and (4) they have come to rely on the drug as a way of avoiding problems, suppressing anger or fear, or coping with stress.

After five years in and out of rehab and facing more prison time, Robert Downey, Jr., got serious about getting help. He was able to overcome his addictions and resume a successful acting career. Here he's shown at the 2012 world premiere of *The Avengers*.

Recite & Review

✓ **Study** and **Review** at **MyPsychLab**

Recite: Say aloud what you have learned about substance abuse, the biological model of addiction, the learning model of addiction, and the arguments for and against abstinence-only solutions to addiction.

Review: Next, if you are addicted to passing exams, reread this section.

Now take this *Quick Quiz:*

1. What is the most reasonable conclusion about the role of genes in alcoholism? (a) Without a key gene, a person cannot become alcoholic; (b) the presence of a key gene will almost always cause a person to become alcoholic; (c) genes may increase a person's vulnerability to some kinds of alcoholism.

2. Which cultural practice is associated with low rates of alcoholism? (a) a gradual introduction to social drinking in family settings, (b) infrequent binge drinking, (c) drinking as a rite of passage into adulthood, (d) policies of prohibition.

3. In a national survey, 52 percent of American college students said they drink to get drunk and 42 percent said they usually binge when drinking. To reduce this problem, many schools have instituted zero-tolerance programs. According to the research described in this section, are these programs likely to work? Why or why not?

Answers:

1. c 2. a 3. They are not likely to be successful because zero-tolerance programs do not address the reasons that students binge, do not affect the student culture that fosters binge drinking, and do not teach students how to drink moderately.

You are about to learn . . .

• why most clinicians and researchers are skeptical about multiple personality disorder.

• why the number of "multiple personality" cases jumped from a handful to many thousands.

Dissociative Identity Disorder LO 11.17

One of the most controversial diagnoses ever to arise in psychiatry and psychology is **dissociative identity disorder (DID)**, formerly and still popularly called *multiple personality disorder* (MPD). This label describes the apparent emergence, within one person, of two or more distinct identities, each with its own name, memories, and personality traits. Cases of multiple personality portrayed on TV, in books, and in films such as *The Three Faces of Eve* and *Sybil* have captivated the public for years.

Some psychiatrists and clinical psychologists take DID very seriously, believing that it originates in childhood as a means of coping with sexual abuse or other traumatic experiences (Gleaves, 1996). In their view, the trauma produces a mental "splitting" (*dissociation*): One personality handles everyday experiences, and another personality (called an "alter") emerges to cope with the bad ones. During the 1980s and 1990s, clinicians who believed a client had multiple personalities often used suggestive techniques such as hypnosis, drugs, and even outright coercion to "bring out the alters" (McHugh, 2008; Rieber, 2006; Spanos, 1996). Psychiatrist Richard Kluft (1987) wrote that efforts to determine the presence of alters may require "between 2 1/2 and 4 hours of continuous interviewing. Interviewees must be prevented from taking breaks to regain composure.…In one recent case of singular difficulty, the first sign of dissociation was noted in the 6th hour, and a definitive spontaneous switching of personalities occurred in the 8th hour."

Mercy! After eight hours of "continuous interviewing" without a single break, how many of us wouldn't do what the interviewer wanted? Clinicians who conducted such interrogations argued that they were merely *permitting* other personalities to reveal themselves, but psychological scientists countered that they were actively *creating* other personalities through suggestion and sometimes even intimidation with vulnerable clients who had other psychological problems (Lilienfeld & Lohr, 2003). Researchers have shown that "dissociative amnesia," the mechanism

In the earliest cases, multiple personalities came only in pairs. In the 1886 story of *Dr. Jekyll and Mr. Hyde*, the kindly Dr. Jekyll turned into the murderous Mr. Hyde. But at the height of the MPD epidemic in the 1990s, people were claiming to have dozens of alters, including demons, aliens, and animals.

that supposedly causes traumatized children to repress their ordeal and develop several identities as a result, lacks historical and empirical support (Huntjens, Verschuere, & McNally, 2012; Lynn et al., 2012; see Chapter 8). Truly traumatic experiences are remembered all too long and all too well (McNally, 2003).

So what is this disorder? The evidence suggests that it is a homegrown cultural syndrome (Pope et al., 2007). Only a handful of MPD cases had ever been diagnosed anywhere in the world before 1980, when it first officially appeared in the third edition of the DSM; yet by the mid-1990s, tens of thousands of cases had been reported, mostly in the United States and Canada. MPD became a lucrative business, benefiting hospitals that opened MPD clinics, therapists who had a new disorder to treat, and psychiatrists and patients who wrote bestselling books. Then, in the 1990s, as a result of numerous malpractice cases across the country, courts ruled, on the basis of the testimony of scientific experts in psychiatry and psychology, that MPD was being generated by the clinicians who believed in it. The MPD clinics in hospitals closed, psychiatrists became more wary, and the number of cases dropped sharply almost overnight. But the promoters of the diagnosis have never admitted they were mistaken. They

dissociative identity disorder A controversial disorder marked by the apparent appearance within one person of two or more distinct personalities, each with its own name and traits; formerly known as *multiple personality disorder* (MPD).

continue to treat patients for it, and it remains in the DSM-5 as dissociative identity disorder.

No one disputes that some troubled, highly imaginative individuals can produce many different "personalities" when asked. But the *sociocognitive explanation* of DID holds that this phenomenon is simply an extreme form of the ability we all have to present different aspects of our personalities to others (Lilienfeld et al., 1999; Lynn et al., 2012). The disorder may seem very real to clinicians and their patients who believe in it, but in the sociocognitive view, it results from pressure and suggestion by clinicians, together with acceptance by vulnerable patients who find the idea that they have separate personalities a plausible explanation for their problems. The diagnosis allows patients to account for past sexual or criminal behavior that they now regret or find intolerably embarrassing; they can claim their "other personality did it." In turn, therapists who believe in the disorder reward their patients with attention and praise for revealing more and more personalities—and a culture-bound syndrome is born (Hacking, 1995; Piper & Merskey, 2004). When Canadian psychiatrist Harold Merskey (1992) reviewed the published cases of MPD, he was unable to find a single one in which a patient had not been influenced by the therapist's suggestions or by reports about the disorder in the media.

✳ THINKING CRITICALLY

About the Origins of Multiple Personality Disorder

Even the famous case of "Sybil," a huge hit as a book and television special, was a hoax. Sybil never had a traumatic childhood of sexual abuse, she did not have multiple personality disorder, and her "symptoms" were generated by pressure from her psychiatrist, Cornelia Wilbur, who injected her with heavy-duty drugs to get her to reveal other "personalities" (Borch-Jacobson, 2009; Nathan, 2011). Despite this pressure, even after several years Sybil failed to recall a traumatic childhood memory and was not producing many alters. Finally, she wrote to Wilbur, admitting she was "none of the things I have pretended to be....I do not have any multiple personalities....I do not even have a 'double.'...I am all of them. I have been essentially lying." Wilbur replied that Sybil was merely experiencing massive denial and resistance, and threatened to withhold the drugs that Sybil had become addicted to. Sybil continued with therapy, and the two eventually produced the book that Wilbur hoped would make her famous and wealthy. It did.

The story of MPD/DID offers a good lesson in critical thinking because it teaches us to be cautious about new diagnoses and previously rare disorders that suddenly catch fire in popular culture: to consider other explanations, examine assumptions and biases, and demand good evidence instead of simply accepting unskeptical media coverage.

Recite & Review

✓ **Study** and **Review** at **MyPsychLab**

Recite: Tell what you know about dissociative identity disorder, and the rise and fall of reports on "multiple personalities."

Review: Next, reread this section.

Now, any one of your personalities may answer this *Quick Quiz:*

✳ A woman named Donna Walker was arrested for trying to convince an Indiana couple that she was their long-missing daughter. She claimed that her "bad girl" personality (Allison) was responsible for this deception and also for her long history of perpetrating hoaxes on police, friends, and the media. Her "good girl" personality (Donna), she said, was a victim of childhood sexual abuse who spent years working as an FBI informant. The FBI verified that Walker had worked for them, although some of her reports were fabricated. One agent said that Walker has as many as seven personalities who come and go. As a critical thinker, what questions would you want to ask about Walker and her multiple-personality defense?

Answer:

Some possible questions to ask: Is there corroborating evidence for Walker's claims? (She said she was sexually abused from ages 4 to 13 by a family member and then by the minister of her church, and that she was sent to a psychiatric hospital at age 13; these claims could be checked.) How much of the rest of her life story can be independently corroborated? Did Walker claim to have other personalities only when she was in a jam with the law, or was there evidence of MPD throughout her life? Could she have another mental disorder, such as antisocial personality disorder or major depression?

- the difference between schizophrenia and a "split personality."
- the five key signs of schizophrenia.
- whether schizophrenia is partly heritable.
- why schizophrenia might begin in the womb yet not emerge until adolescence.

Schizophrenia

In 1911, the Swiss psychiatrist Eugen Bleuler coined the term **schizophrenia** to describe cases in which the personality loses its unity. Contrary to popular belief, people with schizophrenia do not have a "split" or "multiple" personality. Rather, schizophrenia is a fragmented condition in which words are split from meaning, actions from motives, perceptions from reality. It is an example of a **psychosis**, a mental condition that involves distorted perceptions of reality, delusions, irrational behavior, and an inability to function in most aspects of life. The DSM-5's category is *schizophrenia spectrum and other psychotic disorders*, which includes conditions that vary in severity and duration.

Symptoms of Schizophrenia LO 11.18

Schizophrenia is the cancer of mental illness: elusive, complex, varied in form, unpredictable to treat. The DSM-5 criteria for the disorder includes five core abnormalities:

1 **Bizarre delusions.** Some people with schizophrenia have delusions of identity, believing that they are Moses, Jesus, or another famous person. Some have paranoid delusions, taking innocent events—a stranger's cough, a helicopter overhead—as evidence that everyone is plotting against them. They may insist that their thoughts have been inserted into their heads by someone controlling them or are being broadcast on television. Some believe that everyday objects or animals are really something else, perhaps extraterrestrials in disguise. Some focus their delusions on other people: Margaret Mary Ray believed with all her heart that talk-show host David Letterman was in love with her. Caught up in this delusion, she stalked Letterman day and night for a decade, writing him letters and repeatedly breaking into his house.

2 **Hallucinations.** People with schizophrenia suffer from false sensory experiences that feel intensely real, such as feeling insects crawling on their bodies or seeing snakes coming through walls. But by far the most common hallucination is hearing voices; it is virtually a hallmark of the disease. Some sufferers are so tormented by these voices that they commit suicide to escape them. One man said he heard as many as 50 voices cursing him, urging him to steal other people's brain cells, or ordering him to kill himself. Once he picked up a ringing telephone and heard them screaming, "You're guilty!" over and over. They yelled "as loud as humans with megaphones," he told a reporter. "It was utter despair. I felt scared. They were always around" (Goode, 2003). (However, hallucinations can also occur in healthy people, for example after bereavement, as part of religious rituals, or in the state between sleep and waking.)

3 **Disorganized, incoherent speech.** People with schizophrenia often speak in an illogical jumble of ideas and symbols, linked by meaningless rhyming words or by remote associations called "*word salads.*" A patient of Bleuler's wrote, "Olive oil is an Arabian liquor-sauce which the Afghans, Moors and Moslems use in ostrich farming. The Indian plantain tree is the whiskey of the Parsees and Arabs. Barley, rice and sugar cane called artichoke, grow remarkably well in India. The Brahmins live as castes in Baluchistan. The Circassians occupy Manchuria and China. China is the Eldorado of the Pawnees" (Bleuler, 1911/1950). Others make only brief, empty replies in conversation, because of diminished thought rather than an unwillingness to speak.

4 **Grossly disorganized or catatonic behavior.** Such behavior may range from childlike silliness to unpredictable and violent agitation. The person may wear three overcoats and gloves on a hot day, start collecting garbage, or hoard scraps of food. Some completely withdraw into a private world, sitting for hours without moving, a condition called *catatonic stupor.* Catatonic states can also produce frenzied, purposeless behavior that goes on for hours.

5 **Negative symptoms.** Many people with schizophrenia lose the motivation and ability to take care of themselves and interact with others; they may stop working or bathing, and become isolated and withdrawn. They lose expressiveness and thus seem emotionally flat; their facial expressions are unresponsive and they make poor eye contact. These symptoms are called "negative" because they involve the absence of normal behaviors or emotions.

Some signs of schizophrenia emerge early, in late childhood or early adolescence (Tarbox &

schizophrenia A psychotic disorder marked by delusions, hallucinations, disorganized and incoherent speech, inappropriate behavior, and negative symptoms such as loss of motivation and emotional flatness.

psychosis An extreme mental disturbance involving distorted perceptions, delusions, and irrational behavior. (Plural: *psychoses.*)

Bryan Charnley painted 17 self-portraits, with comments reflecting his battle with schizophrenia. He painted the one above in March 1991, when his mind was clear. In June, he committed suicide.

April 20: "[I am feeling] paranoid. The person upstairs was reading my mind and speaking back to me to keep me in a sort of ego crucifixion.... I felt this was because I was discharging very strong vibrations."

May 6: "I had no tongue, no real tongue, and could only flatter.... The nail in the mouth expresses this. The people around me cannot understand how I was so stupid and cannot forgive me.... Thus I am a target. The nails in my eyes express that I cannot see whereas other people seem to have extra sensory perception and I am blind in this respect."

May 18: "My mind seemed to be thought broadcasting [and] it was beyond my will to do anything about it. I summed this up by painting my brain as an enormous mouth.... The trouble seemed to stem from a broken heart so I painted a great mass of gore there.... I feel I am giving off strong personality vibrations, hence the wavy lines emanating from my head."

Pogue-Geile, 2008), but the first full-blown psychotic episode typically occurs in late adolescence or early adulthood. In some individuals, the breakdown occurs suddenly; in others, it is more gradual, a slow change in personality. The more breakdowns and relapses the individual has had, the poorer the chances for recovery. Yet, contrary to stereotype, more than 40 percent of people with schizophrenia *do* have one or more periods of recovery and go on to hold good jobs and have successful relationships, especially if they have strong family support

and community programs (Harding, 2005; Hopper et al., 2007; Jobe & Harrow, 2010). What kind of mysterious disease could produce such a variety of symptoms and outcomes?

Simulate the **Experiment** Schizophrenia Overview at **MyPsychLab**

Origins of Schizophrenia LO 11.19

Researchers describe schizophrenia as a brain disease, and indeed people with schizophrenia

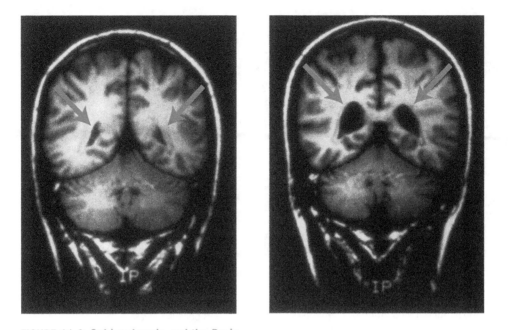

FIGURE 11.3 Schizophrenia and the Brain
People with schizophrenia are more likely to have enlarged ventricles (spaces) in the brain. These MRI scans of 28-year-old male identical twins show the difference in the size of ventricles between the twin without schizophrenia (left) and the one with schizophrenia (right).

tend to have reduced volumes of gray matter in the prefrontal cortex and temporal lobes; abnormalities in the hippocampus; and abnormalities in neurotransmitters, neural activity, and communication between neurons in areas involving cognitive functions such as memory, decision making, and emotional processing (Karlsgodt, Sun, & Cannon, 2010). Most individuals with schizophrenia also show enlargement of the *ventricles*, spaces in the brain that are filled with cerebrospinal fluid (see Figure 11.3) (Heinrichs, 2005). And they are more likely than individuals without schizophrenia to have abnormalities in the thalamus, the traffic-control center that filters sensations and focuses attention (Andreasen et al., 1994; Gur et al., 1998). Many have deficiencies in the auditory cortex and Broca and Wernicke's areas, all involved in speech perception and processing; these might explain the nightmare of voice hallucinations.

Currently, researchers have identified three contributing factors in this disorder:

1 Genetic predispositions. Schizophrenia is highly heritable. A person has a much greater risk of developing the disorder if an identical twin develops it, even if the twins are reared apart (Gottesman, 1991; Gottesman et al., 2010; Heinrichs, 2005). Children with one schizophrenic parent have a lifetime risk of 7 to 12 percent, and children with two schizophrenic parents have a lifetime risk of 27 to 46 percent, compared

to a risk in the general population of only about 1 percent (see Figure 11.4). Researchers all over the world are trying to identify the genes that might be involved in specific symptoms, such as hallucinations, sensitivity to sounds, cognitive impairments, and social withdrawal (Desbonnet, Waddington, & O'Tuathaigh, 2009; Tomppo et al., 2009). However, efforts to find the critical genes in schizophrenia have been difficult because several appear to be involved, and those are linked not only to schizophrenia but also—as we noted previously—to bipolar disorder, depression, and other mental disorders (Walker & Tessner, 2008).

2 Prenatal problems or birth complications. Damage to the fetal brain significantly increases the likelihood of schizophrenia later in life. Such damage may occur if the mother suffers from malnutrition; schizophrenia rates rise during times of famine (St. Clair et al., 2005). Damage may also occur if the mother gets the flu virus during the first four months of prenatal development, which triples the risk of schizophrenia (Brown et al., 2004; Mednick, Huttunen, & Machón, 1994). And it may occur if there are complications during birth that injure the baby's brain or deprive it of oxygen (Cannon et al., 2000). Other nongenetic prenatal factors that increase the child's risk of schizophrenia include maternal diabetes and emotional stress, having a father older than age 55, birth during a

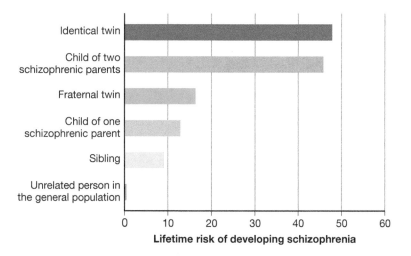

Lifetime risk of developing schizophrenia

FIGURE 11.4 Genetic Vulnerability to Schizophrenia
This graph, based on combined data from 40 European twin and adoption studies conducted over seven decades, shows that the closer the genetic relationship to a person with schizophrenia, the higher the risk of developing the disorder. (Based on Gottesman, 1991; see also Gottesman et al., 2010.)

winter month, and a very low birth weight (King, St-Hilaire, & Heidkamp, 2010).

3 Biological events during adolescence. In adolescence, the brain undergoes a natural pruning away of synapses. Normally, this pruning helps make the brain more efficient in handling the new challenges of adulthood (Walker & Tessner, 2008). But it appears that in schizophrenia, the brain aggressively prunes away too many synapses, which may explain why the first full-blown schizophrenic episode typically occurs in adolescence or early adulthood. Healthy teenagers lose about 1 percent of the brain's gray matter between ages 13 and 18. But as you can see in Figure 11.5, in a study that tracked the loss of gray matter in the brain over 5 years, adolescents with schizophrenia showed much more extensive and rapid tissue loss, primarily in the sensory and motor regions (Thompson et al., 2001). "We were stunned to see a spreading wave of tissue loss that began in a small region of the brain," said Paul Thompson, who headed the study. "It moved across the brain like a forest fire, destroying more tissue as the disease progressed."

Thus, the developmental pathway of schizophrenia is something of a relay. It starts with genetic predispositions, which may combine with prenatal risk factors or birth complications that affect brain development. The resulting vulnerability then awaits the next stage, synaptic pruning within the brain during adolescence. Then, according to the vulnerability-stress model of schizophrenia, these biological changes may interact with

an environmental stressor to trigger the disease. This model explains why one identical twin may develop schizophrenia but not the other: Both may have a genetic susceptibility, but only one may have been exposed to other risk factors in the womb, birth complications, or stressful life events.

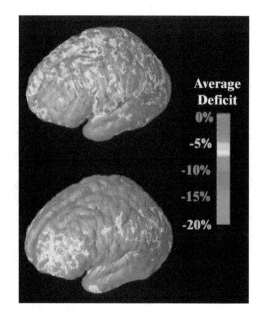

FIGURE 11.5 The Adolescent Brain and Schizophrenia
These dramatic images highlight areas of brain-tissue loss in adolescents with schizophrenia, over a five-year span. The areas of greatest tissue loss (in regions that control memory, hearing, motor functions, and attention) are shown in red and magenta. The brain of a person without schizophrenia (top) looks almost entirely blue (Dr. Arthur W. Toga, Laboratory of Neuro Imaging, UCLA School of Medicine).

Recite & Review

 Study and **Review** at **MyPsychLab**

Recite: Say aloud what you remember about psychosis, the symptoms of schizophrenia, and the origins of schizophrenia.

Review: Next, read the section on schizophrenia again.

Now take this *Quick Quiz:*

1. What are the five major kinds of symptoms in schizophrenia?

2. What are the likely stages in the "relay" that produces schizophrenia?

Answers:

1. delusions, hallucinations, disorganized speech, inappropriate behavior, and negative symptoms including loss of motivation and emotional flatness 2. genetic predispositions, prenatal risk factors or birth complications, and excessive pruning of synapses in the brain during adolescence; these biological changes typically interact with an environmental stressor to trigger onset of the disease.

PSYCHOLOGY IN THE NEWS REVISITED /////////

We have come to the end of a long walk along the spectrum of psychological problems: from those that cause temporary difficulty, such as occasional anxiety, "caffeine intoxication," or a "parent-child relational problem," to others that are severely disabling, such as major depression and schizophrenia. Where on this spectrum would you place "sex addiction," the popular label for the behavior of the many men (and some women) whose sexual behavior has gotten them in trouble?

One of the great questions generated by all diagnoses of mental disorder concerns personal responsibility. In law and in everyday life, many people reach for a psychological reason to exonerate themselves of responsibility for their actions. Romance writer Janet Dailey was once caught having plagiarized whole passages from another writer's work, and in self-defense she said she was suffering from "a psychological problem that I never even suspected I had." We wonder if it was in the DSM! But would it matter if it were? What "psychological problem" would absolve a person of responsibility for cheating?

Similarly, many people nowadays claim they are addicted to some behavior, whether it is having sex, shopping, or eating chocolate, as an excuse for some habit that is unethical, self-defeating, or fattening. Is their behavior really an addiction in the same way that drug addiction is? As we saw in the opening news story, psychologists disagree on the answer, and we also saw later in the chapter that the only behavioral pattern the DSM-5 regards as addictive, besides substance abuse, is pathological gambling. Some think that people who repeatedly engage in sexual fantasies and behaviors in response to stress, anxiety, or depression also have a mental disorder, especially if they lack concern for the physical or emotional harm they

cause themselves or others. But others believe that any behavior can fit this description and that most everyday "addictions" are not disorders (Greenberg, 2013). Rather, they are a way of coping (badly) with stressful problems or a self-justifying way of getting off the hook. Indeed, having many sexual affairs is often considered perfectly normal behavior for rich, powerful celebrities and politicians. It only seems to become a mental disorder when their partner finds out.

Now consider the tragic story of Andrea Yates, a Texas woman who killed her five young children. Yates had suffered from clinical depression and psychotic episodes for years; she had tried to kill herself twice. Her father, two brothers, and a sister had also suffered from mental illness. Yates was overwhelmed by raising and homeschooling all of her children by herself, with no help from her reportedly domineering husband, who permitted her two hours a week of personal time. Although she suffered a postpartum psychotic episode after the birth of their fourth child and a clinical psychologist warned against her having another baby, her husband refused to consider birth control, although not for religious reasons. Yates was convicted of murder and sentenced to life in prison; the jury rejected her claim that she was so psychotic that she thought she was saving the souls of her children by killing them. Four years later, on appeal, another jury found her not guilty by reason of insanity and she was sent to a mental institution.

Does Andrea Yates deserve our condemnation for her horrible acts of murder, or our pity? Before you answer, you might keep this interesting evidence in mind: Many people feel angrier and less sympathetic toward people whose mental illnesses conform to gender stereotypes, such as men who are alcoholic and women who are depressed. They are more sympathetic to people whose illnesses do not conform to the stereotype—alcoholic women and depressed men (Wirth & Bodenhausen, 2009). Apparently, many people think that gender-typical mental disorders are less likely to be "real."

When thinking about the relationship of mental disorder to personal responsibility, therefore, we face a dilemma, one that requires us to tolerate uncertainty. The law recognizes, rightly, that people who are mentally incompetent, delusional, or disturbed should not be judged by the same standards as mentally healthy individuals. At the same time, society has an obligation to protect its citizens from harm and to reject easy excuses for violations of the law. To balance these two positions, we need to find ways to ensure that people who commit crimes or behave reprehensibly face the consequences of their behavior; we also need to ensure that people who are suffering from psychological problems have the compassionate support of society in their search for help. After all, psychological problems of one kind or another are challenges that all of us will face at some time in our lives.

Taking Psychology With You

When a Friend Is Suicidal

Suicide can be frightening to those who find themselves fantasizing about it, and it is devastating to the family and friends of those who go through with it. Every year, more than 1,000 college students commit suicide, and thousands more make an unsuccessful attempt. The group at highest risk of suicide is Native American men, and the group at lowest risk is black women (Goldston et al., 2008). Women are more likely than men to attempt suicide, primarily as a cry for help, whereas men are four times more likely than women to succeed. Moreover, men's efforts to commit suicide are not always obvious: Some men provoke confrontations with the police, hoping to be shot; some intentionally kill themselves in car accidents; and men are more likely than women to destroy themselves with drugs.

Because of the many widespread myths about suicide, it is important to become informed and know what to do in a crisis:

Take all suicide threats seriously. Some people assume they can't do anything when a friend talks about committing suicide. "He'll just do it at another place, another time," they think. In fact, most suicides occur during an acute crisis. Once the person gets through the crisis, the desire to die fades. Others believe that if a friend is talking about committing suicide, he or she won't really do it. This belief also is false. Few people commit suicide without signaling their intentions. Most are ambivalent: "I want to kill myself, but I don't want to be dead—at least not forever." Most suicidal people want relief from the terrible pain of feeling that nobody cares and that life is not worth living. Getting these thoughts and fears out in the open is crucial.

Know the danger signs. One team of psychologists who specialize in the study of suicide looked up the "warning signs of suicide" that can be found on the Internet. The search turned up more than 75 supposed indicators, many of them vague or questionable, such as "perfectionism," "loss of security," and "loss of religious faith." In fact, only a few core factors are crucial in predicting a person's risk of trying to commit suicide: The person feels hopeless, feels alienated and profoundly disconnected from other people, and believes that he or she is a burden to loved ones (Joiner, 2005; Mandrusiak et al., 2006; van Orden et al., 2006).

Get involved: Ask questions and get help. If you believe a friend is suicidal, do not be afraid to ask, "Are you thinking of suicide?" This question does not "put the idea" in anyone's mind. If your friend is contemplating the action, he or she will probably be relieved to talk about it, which in turn will reduce feelings of isolation and despair. Don't try to talk your friend out of it by debating whether suicide is right or wrong, and don't put on phony cheerfulness. If your friend's words scare you, say so. By allowing your friend to unburden his or her grief, you help the person get through the immediate crisis.

Make sure your friend has no access to firearms, the leading means of impulsive suicide, and do not leave your friend alone. If necessary, get the person to a clinic or a hospital emergency room, or call a local suicide hotline. Don't worry about doing the wrong thing. In an emergency, the worst thing you can do is nothing at all.

If you are the one contemplating suicide, remember that you are not alone and that help is a phone call or an e-mail away. You can call the national suicide hotline number, 1-800-273-TALK, or your school's counseling services. For more information, the Centers for Disease Control and Prevention has a website that provides facts about suicide (www.cdc.gov/safeusa/suicide.htm). Many students fear to get help because they think no one will understand, or they fear they will be made fun of by their friends, or they believe they cannot be helped. Wrong, wrong, wrong.

In her book *Night Falls Fast: Understanding Suicide*, Kay Jamison (1999), a psychologist who suffers from bipolar disorder, explored this difficult subject from the standpoint both of a mental health professional and of a person who has been there. In describing the aftermath of her own suicide attempt, she wrote: "I do know...that I should have been dead but was not—and that I was fortunate enough to be given another chance at life, which many others were not."

Summary Listen to the Audio File at MyPsychLab

Diagnosing Mental Disorders LO 11.1

- It is difficult to define *mental disorder*, but in general it describes any condition that causes a person to suffer, is self-destructive, seriously impairs a person's ability to work or get along with others, or endangers others or the community.

- *The Diagnostic and Statistical Manual of Mental Disorders* (DSM) is designed to provide objective criteria and categories for diagnosing mental disorder. Critics argue that the diagnosis of mental disorders, unlike those of medical diseases, is inherently a subjective process that can never be entirely objective. They believe the DSM fosters overdiagnosis; overlooks the negative consequences of being given a diagnostic label; confuses serious mental disorders with everyday problems in living; and creates an illusion of objectivity. Critics are also concerned about the problem of conflicts of interest, because many investigators involved in revising the DSM have financial ties to pharmaceutical companies that make drugs for the disorders being included.

- Supporters of the DSM maintain that it is important to help clinicians distinguish among disorders that share certain symptoms, such as anxiety, irritability, or delusions, so they can be diagnosed reliably and treated properly; and to recognize that symptoms of any disorder can range from mild to severe. The DSM recognizes the influence of culture on mental disorders and diagnoses, and lists various *cultural syndromes, cultural idioms of distress,* and *cultural explanations of symptoms* in addition to universal disorders such as depression, panic attacks, anorexia, and schizophrenia.

- In diagnosing psychological disorders, clinicians often use *projective tests* such as the *Rorschach inkblot test* or, with children, the use of anatomically detailed dolls and other props. These methods have low reliability and validity, creating problems when they are used in the legal arena, as in child abuse cases and custody disputes, or in diagnosing disorders. In general, *objective tests (inventories)*, such as the *MMPI*, are more reliable and valid than projective ones.

Anxiety Disorders

- *Generalized anxiety disorder* involves continuous, chronic anxiety and worry. *Panic disorder* involves sudden, intense attacks of profound fear. *Panic attacks* are common in the aftermath of stress or frightening experiences; those who go on to develop a disorder tend to interpret the attacks as a sign of impending disaster.

- *Phobias* are unrealistic fears of specific situations, activities, or things. Common *social phobias* include fears of speaking in public, eating in a restaurant, or having to perform for an audience. *Agoraphobia*, the fear of being away from a safe place or person, is the most disabling phobia—a "fear of fear." It often begins with a panic attack, which the person tries to avoid in the future by staying close to "safe" places or people.

Trauma-Related and Obsessive-Compulsive Disorders

- Most people who live through a traumatic experience eventually recover, but some develop long-lasting *posttraumatic stress disorder* (PTSD), which involves mentally reliving the trauma in nightmares and flashbacks; emotional detachment; and increased physiological arousal. These sufferers may have a genetic vulnerability, a lack of social and cognitive resources, and a smaller hippocampus than normal. In the case of veterans with prolonged PTSD, an additional contributing factor is having inflicted extreme harm on civilians or prisoners while serving in combat.

- *Obsessive-compulsive disorder* (OCD) involves recurrent, unwished-for thoughts or images (obsessions) and repetitive, ritualized behaviors (compulsions) that a person feels unable to control. Some people with OCD have abnormalities in an area of the prefrontal cortex, which may contribute to their cognitive and behavioral rigidity. Parts of the brain involved in fear and responses to threat are also more active than normal in people with OCD; the "alarm mechanism," once activated, does not turn off when danger is past. *Hoarding disorder* may involve deficiencies in other parts of the brain.

Depressive and Bipolar Disorders

- Symptoms of *major depression* include distorted thinking patterns, feelings of worthlessness and despair, physical ailments such as fatigue and loss of appetite, and loss of interest in once-pleasurable activities. Women are twice as likely as men to suffer from major depression, but depression in men may be underdiagnosed.

- *Vulnerability-stress models* of depression (and other mental disorders) look at interactions between individual vulnerabilities and stressful experiences. The theory that depleted serotonin causes depression has not been supported, but because depression is moderately heritable, the search for specific genes continues. For some vulnerable individuals, repeated losses of important relationships can set off episodes of major depression. Experiences with parental neglect and violence, especially in childhood, increase the risk of developing major depression in adulthood. Cognitive habits also play an important role: believing that the origin of one's unhappiness is permanent and uncontrollable; feeling hopeless and pessimistic; and brooding or ruminating about one's problems.

- In *bipolar disorder*, a person typically experiences episodes of both depression and *mania* (excessive euphoria). It is equally common in both sexes, and may share symptoms and origins with major depression and schizophrenia, and other disorders as well.

Personality Disorders

- Personality disorders are characterized by maladaptive traits that cause distress or an inability to get along with others. One is *borderline personality disorder*, characterized by extreme negative emotionality and an inability to regulate emotions, often resulting in intense but unstable relationships, self-mutilating behavior, feelings of emptiness, and a fear of abandonment by others.

- The term *psychopath* describes people who lack conscience and empathy; who do not feel remorse, shame, guilt, or anxiety over wrongdoing; and who can con others with ease. In *antisocial personality disorder* (APD), symptoms may include the remorselessness of psychopathy but the major criteria involve a lifelong pattern of aggressive, reckless, impulsive, and often criminal behavior (although not necessarily a lack of empathy and other social emotions). Abnormalities in the central nervous system and prefrontal cortex are associated with a lack of emotional responsiveness and with impulsivity in many people with psychopathy and APD. A genetic predisposition also plays a role in these disorders, but it usually must interact with stressful or violent environments to be expressed.

Substance-Related and Addictive Disorders

- The DSM-5 uses the term *substance use disorder* rather than addiction to reflect the fact that people's misuse of any drug can range in severity from mild impairment to compulsive drug taking that impairs a person's ability to function. Symptoms of *alcohol-use disorder* include at least two of these symptoms: uncontrollable craving for alcohol; drinking in situations where it is physically hazardous; drinking despite persistent social or personal consequences; inability to cut back or stop; or drinking larger amounts or in greater frequency than intended.

- According to the *biological (disease) model* of addiction, some people have a genetic vulnerability to the kind of alcoholism that begins in early adolescence and is linked to impulsivity, antisocial behavior, and criminality. Genes also affect sensitivity to alcohol, which varies across ethnic groups as well as among individuals. But cause and effect also runs in the other direction: Heavy drug abuse changes the brain in ways that make addiction more likely.

- Advocates of the *learning model* of addiction point out that addiction patterns vary according to cultural practices and values; policies of total abstinence tend to increase addiction rates and abuse because people who want to drink fail to learn how to drink in moderation; many people can stop taking drugs without experiencing withdrawal symptoms; and drug abuse depends on the reasons for taking a drug.

- The biological and learning models are polarized on many issues, notably that of abstinence versus moderation. People who are most likely to abuse alcohol and other drugs may have a genetic vulnerability; may have damaged brains as a result of prolonged drug abuse; believe that they have no control over the drug; live in a culture or peer group that promotes drug abuse; and rely on the drug to cope with problems.

Dissociative Identity Disorder

- In *dissociative identity disorder* (DID), formerly called *multiple personality disorder* (MPD), two or more distinct personalities and identities appear to split off (*dissociate*) within one person. Some psychiatrists and other clinicians think the disorder is legitimate and originates in childhood trauma. But most psychological scientists hold a *sociocognitive* explanation, namely that DID is an extreme form of the ability to present different aspects of our personalities to others. In this view, the disorder is a cultural syndrome that emerges from pressure and suggestion by clinicians who believe in its prevalence, interacting with vulnerable patients who find the diagnosis a plausible explanation for their problems. Media coverage of sensational alleged cases of multiple personality, including the fraudulent case of "Sybil," greatly contributed to the rise in cases after 1980.

Schizophrenia

- *Schizophrenia* is a psychotic disorder involving delusions, hallucinations, disorganized speech (called *word salads*), inappropriate behavior (including in some cases *catatonic stupor*), and *negative symptoms* such as loss of motivation and emotional flatness. Contrary to stereotype, many people with schizophrenia recover.

- Schizophrenia involves brain abnormalities such as reduced gray matter, abnormalities in the hippocampus, and enlarged ventricles, as well as abnormalities in neurotransmitters and neuronal connections. In the relay that produces the disorder, genetic predispositions interact with prenatal problems (such as the mother's malnutrition or a prenatal viral infection) or birth complications, and excessive pruning of synapses during adolescence, all of which interact with environmental stressors to trigger the disease.

Psychology in the News, Revisited

• The diagnosis of mental disorder raises important questions about personal responsibility in the law and everyday life. When people claim to have a mental disorder, psychologists and others struggle to decide whether the claim is an excuse for illegal, unethical, or destructive behavior, or whether these individuals truly have a disorder that reduces their ability to control their behavior.

Taking Psychology With You

• Suicide is devastating to the family and friends of those who go through with it. If you know someone who you feel is suicidal, take all threats seriously, know the danger signs, ask questions and get help, and do not leave your friend alone or with methods of carrying out their intentions. If you are the one contemplating suicide, help is a phone call away. You will be understood and you will survive.

Key Terms

mental disorder **396**

Diagnostic and Statistical Manual of Mental Disorders (DSM) **396**

cultural syndromes **399**

cultural idioms of distress **399**

cultural explanations of symptoms **399**

projective tests **399**

Rorschach inkblot test **400**

objective tests (inventories) **401**

Minnesota Multiphasic Personality Inventory (MMPI) **401**

generalized anxiety disorder **402**

panic disorder **402**

panic attack **402**

phobia **402**

social phobia **403**

agoraphobia **403**

posttraumatic stress disorder (PTSD) **404**

obsessive-compulsive disorder (OCD) **404**

hoarding disorder **405**

major depression **406**

vulnerability-stress models **406**

mania **408**

bipolar disorder **408**

borderline personality disorder **409**

psychopathy **409**

antisocial personality disorder (APD) **410**

substance-related and addictive disorders **412**

alcohol-use disorder **413**

biological (disease) model of addiction **413**

learning model of addiction **414**

dissociative identity disorder (DID) (multiple personality disorder) **418**

dissociation **418**

sociocognitive explanation of DID **419**

schizophrenia **420**

psychosis **420**

"word salad" **420**

catatonic stupor **420**

negative symptoms (in schizophrenia) **420**

Diagnosing Mental Disorders

↓

Mental disorder generally describes any condition that causes suffering, is self-destructive, seriously impairs a person's ability to function, or endangers the community.

↓

Dilemmas of Diagnosis

The *Diagnostic and Statistical Manual of Mental Disorders* (DSM) is designed to provide criteria and categories for diagnosing mental disorders. Problems with the DSM include:
- The danger of overdiagnosis.
- The influence of diagnostic labels on perceptions and explanations of a person's behavior.
- The confusion of serious mental disorders with everyday problems.
- The illusion of objectivity and universality.

Advantages of the DSM include:
- Ongoing efforts to improve reliability in diagnosis.
- Identification of universal disorders, as well as *cultural syndromes, cultural idioms of distress*, and *cultural explanations of symptoms*.

Measuring Disorders

- **Projective tests,** such as the *Rorschach inkblot test*, have low reliability and validity.
- **Objective tests** (inventories), such as the *Minnesota Multiphasic Personality Inventory* (MMPI), have higher reliability and validity.

Trauma-Related and Obsessive-Compulsive Disorders

↓

- **Posttraumatic stress disorder (PTSD)** involves reliving a trauma in recurrent, intrusive thoughts; a sense of detachment; and increased physiological arousal.
- Most people who undergo a traumatic experience eventually recover. Those who have prolonged symptoms may have preexisting biological or cognitive vulnerabilities and, in the case of war veterans, have inflicted severe harm on civilians or prisoners.
- **Obsessive-compulsive disorder (OCD)** involves recurrent, unwished-for thoughts or images (*obsessions*) and repetitive, ritualized behaviors (*compulsions*).
- People with *hoarding disorder* are unable to get rid of anything, including food wrappers and junk.

Anxiety Disorders

↓

- **Generalized anxiety disorder** involves continuous chronic anxiety.
- **Panic disorder** involves sudden, intense attacks of profound fear.
- **Phobias** are unrealistic fears of specific situations, activities, or things, or, in the case of **agoraphobia**, being away from a safe place.

Depressive and Bipolar Disorders

↓

- **Major depression** involves prolonged grief, hopelessness, and loss of energy, appetite, and interest in activities.
- **Bipolar disorder** involves episodes of both depression and mania and shares symptoms with other major disorders.

Vulnerability-stress models look at interactions between individual vulnerabilities and external sources of stress. Four factors contribute to major depression:
1. Genetic factors, interacting with life experiences.
2. Experiences with violence, childhood abuse, and parental neglect.
3. Loss of important relationships.
4. Cognitive habits, ruminating about problems, and feeling hopeless.

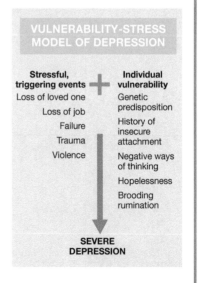

VULNERABILITY-STRESS MODEL OF DEPRESSION

Stressful, triggering events	+	Individual vulnerability
Loss of loved one		Genetic predisposition
Loss of job		
Failure		History of insecure attachment
Trauma		Negative ways of thinking
Violence		Hopelessness
		Brooding rumination

SEVERE DEPRESSION

Personality Disorders

↓

Personality disorders are characterized by rigid, self-destructive traits that cause distress or an inability to get along with others.
- **Borderline personality disorder** is characterized by extreme negative emotionality and an inability to regulate emotions.
- **Psychopathy** is an inability to fear punishment and to feel guilt or remorse for antisocial behavior.
- **Antisocial personality disorder (APD)** describes people who have a lifelong pattern of irresponsible, antisocial behavior such as lawbreaking, violence, and other impulsive, reckless acts.
- Not all people with APD are psychopaths; some lifelong criminals or violent offenders are otherwise capable of normal emotions.
- Factors involved in psychopathy and being a lifelong violent offender:
  - abnormalities in the central nervous system.
  - impaired frontal-lobe functioning.
  - genetic influences.
  - environmental events.

Substance-Related and Addictive Disorders

↓

Substance-abuse disorders range in severity from mild impairment to compulsive drug taking that impairs a person's ability to function and harms the drug-taker or others in his or her life.

↓

Learning, Culture, and Addiction

The *biological (disease) model*: Some people are genetically predisposed to addiction or develop addictions as a result of changes in the brain caused by heavy drug use.

The *learning model*: Most addictions stem from conditions that encourage drug abuse. Evidence for this view:
1. Addiction patterns vary according to cultural practices.
2. Abuse of alcohol increases under policies of total abstinence because people do not learn to drink moderately.
3. Many people stop taking drugs without withdrawal symptoms.
4. Drug abuse depends on the reasons for taking the drug.

Dissociative Identity Disorder

↓

Dissociative identity disorder (DID), formerly called multiple personality disorder, involves two or more identities that appear to split off within one person.
- Some clinicians believe DID is common and originates in childhood trauma.
- Most psychological scientists believe that DID results from suggestion by clinicians themselves.
- Media coverage contributed to the rise in diagnoses of DID after 1980.
- The *sociocognitive explanation* holds that DID is an extreme form of the ability we all have to present different aspects of our personalities to others.

Schizophrenia

↓

Schizophrenia is a form of **psychosis**, a mental condition that involves distortions of reality and inhibits one's ability to function in everyday life.
Symptoms of schizophrenia:
- bizarre delusions.
- hallucinations, sometimes visual but usually auditory.
- disorganized, incoherent speech ("word salads").
- disorganized and inappropriate behavior, including *catatonic stupor*.
- *negative symptoms* such as loss of motivation and emotional flatness.

↓

Causes of Schizophrenia

Schizophrenia involves abnormalities in the brain, including a decrease in the volume of the temporal lobe or hippocampus, reduced numbers of neurons in the prefrontal cortex, and enlarged *ventricles*.

Contributing factors include:
1. Genetic predispositions.
2. Prenatal problems or birth complications.
3. Excessive pruning of synapses in adolescence.
4. Interaction of these biological factors with environmental stressors to trigger the disease.

TREATMENT AND PSYCHOTHERAPY

PSYCHOLOGY IN THE NEWS ////////////////////////

Use of Dogs for Vets With PTSD Is Growing

WASHINGTON, DC, January 4, 2013. Rep. Michael Grimm (R-NY) has officially introduced a bill, H.R. 183, the Veterans Dog Training Therapy Act, which has been referred to the House Veterans' Affairs Committee.

The bill directs the Secretary of Veterans Affairs to implement a pilot program that would evaluate the effectiveness of training and using service dogs to improve the mental health of returning war veterans, with a particular focus on helping vets suffering from posttraumatic stress disorder (PTSD). The bill's 40 cosponsors include Republicans and Democrats, and it is one of the few issues on which they agree.

Many soldiers returning from duty in Afghanistan and Iraq suffer from severe medical and emotional problems. Lt. Col. Kathryn Champion was one of them. She had served 27 years in the Army, but after a particularly horrific tour of duty in Iraq, during which five soldiers under her command died, she began to suffer the symptoms of PTSD. When she returned home, she fell into deep depression: A virus she contracted in Iraq was killing her optic nerves, causing her to go blind; her Army career was finished.

Then Champion found an organization that matched her with a guide dog, a golden retriever mix named Angel. Just two weeks after their training together ended, Angel began helping Champion with her psychological problems as well as her blindness. Champion was terrified of flying and

of having a panic attack in public, but whenever her heart started racing, she would reach down and touch her dog. She was even able to fly across the country to visit her son before his deployment to Afghanistan.

Organizations in many states have begun providing service dogs like Angel to help soldiers recover from PTSD. Their efforts are part of a nationwide trend of animal-assisted therapy, also known as pet therapy, designed to help people

Kathryn Champion, who suffered from posttraumatic stress disorder and anxiety attacks after returning from duty in Iraq, with her dog Angel.

with psychological problems. Pet therapy is used in many hospitals, where volunteers and "certified therapy dogs" offer comfort and companionship to patients. When humans touch and play with dogs, horses, and other social animals, said Dr. Matt Zimmerman, Counseling and Psychological Services psychologist at the University of Virginia, it lowers their blood pressure and makes them less anxious. He added that animal-assisted therapy should generally be used with other forms of psychological treatment or medication.

Zimmerman says there are specific benefits of pet therapy for children with autism. "The animal serves as [a] reinforcement tool for appropriate social behavior," Zimmerman said. "If the child is being gentle and kind to the pet, then [it] stays. If the child is hitting or pulling on the animal, the pet leaves." When it comes to other disorders, however, the effectiveness of the treatment tends to depend more upon the individual in question, he said.

Despite the potential benefits of pet therapy for veterans, political experts give the Grimm bill only a 5 percent chance of getting out of committee and a 2 percent chance of being enacted.

///////////

Have you ever survived a traumatic event—war, assault, violence in your family or neighborhood, the unexpected death of a loved one, or a natural disaster such as an earthquake or hurricane? Have you ever had to move away from the country or ethnic group you grew up in, to find yourself lonely and struggling in a new world? How about the pressures of being in college; do they ever make you feel depressed, worried, or perhaps panicky?

If so, what kind of therapy might help you? For most of the emotional problems that all of us suffer on occasion, the two greatest healers are time and the support of friends—including pet friends. For some people, though, time and friends are not enough, and they continue to be troubled by normal life difficulties, such as family quarrels or fear of public speaking, or by one of the disorders described in the previous chapter: depression, generalized anxiety disorder, phobias, obsessive-compulsive disorder, or schizophrenia. What kind of therapy might help them?

As we saw in Chapter 1, to become a licensed clinical psychologist, a person must have an advanced degree and a period of supervised training. However, the title *psychotherapist* is unregulated; anyone can set up any kind of program and call it "therapy"— and, by the thousands, they do! Across the United States and Canada, people can get credentialed as "experts" in some new fad simply by attending a weekend seminar or a training program lasting a week or two. To get the right treatment for whatever problem concerns you, you need to know what to look for and what to avoid.

In this chapter, we will evaluate (1) biological treatments, which are primarily provided by psychiatrists or other physicians, and which include medications or interventions in brain function; and (2) psychotherapy, specifically these major schools: psychodynamic therapies, cognitive and behavior therapies, humanist therapies, and family or couples therapy. We will assess which kinds of psychotherapy work best for which problems, which ones are not helpful, and which ones might even be harmful.

You are about to learn...

- the types of medications used to treat psychological disorders.
- six cautions about medications for emotional problems.
- ways of electrically stimulating the brain for treatment purposes.

Biological Treatments

For hundreds of years, people have tried to identify the origins of mental illness, attributing the causes at various times to evil spirits, pressure in

Antipsychotic drugs can help some people with schizophrenia live normal lives. At left, Danny Dunn (seated) poses with her mother. Danny was diagnosed as having schizophrenia and bipolar disorder when she was 17, but medication, therapy, and family support help her function. "I still have challenges and problems," Danny says, "but life is so much better than it used to be." The photo on the right shows USC law professor Elyn Saks, who also benefited from medication and therapy, and wrote a memoir of her "journey through madness." She received a MacArthur Foundation "genius grant" for her contributions to mental health law.

the skull, disease, or bad environments. Today, biological explanations and treatments are dominant, partly because of evidence that some disorders have a genetic component or involve a biochemical or neurological abnormality, and partly because physicians and pharmaceutical companies have been aggressively promoting biomedical solutions.

Medications for Mental Disorders LO 12.1

The most commonly used biological treatment is medication that alters the production of or response to neurotransmitters in the brain. Because drugs are so widely advertised and prescribed these days, both for severe disorders such as schizophrenia and for more common problems such as anxiety and depression, consumers need to understand what these drugs are, how they can best be used, and their limitations.

The main classes of drugs used in the treatment of mental and emotional disorders are these:

1 Antipsychotic drugs, also called *neuroleptics*— older ones such as Thorazine and Haldol and second-generation ones such as Clozaril, Risperdal, Zyprexa, and Seroquel—are used primarily in the treatment of schizophrenia and other psychoses. However, antipsychotic drugs are increasingly being prescribed off label for people with nonpsychotic disorders, such as major depression, bipolar disorder, posttraumatic stress disorder (PTSD), autism, attention deficit disorder, and dementia.

Most antipsychotic drugs are designed to block or reduce the sensitivity of brain receptors that respond to dopamine; some also block receptors for serotonin. Antipsychotic drugs can reduce agitation, delusions, and hallucinations, and they can shorten schizophrenic episodes. But they offer little relief from other symptoms of schizophrenia, such as jumbled thoughts, difficulty concentrating, apathy, emotional flatness, or inability to interact with others.

Antipsychotics often cause troubling side effects, especially muscle rigidity, hand tremors, and other involuntary muscle movements that can develop into a neurological disorder. In addition, Zyprexa, Risperdal, and other antipsychotics, which manufacturers have been targeting for children and the elderly, often carry unacceptable risks for these very groups. The immediate side effect is extreme weight gain, anywhere from 24 to 100 extra pounds a year. Other risks include strokes and death from sudden heart failure (Masand, 2000; Ray et al., 2009; Wallace-Wells, 2009).

antipsychotic drugs (neuroleptics) Drugs used primarily in the treatment of schizophrenia and other psychotic disorders; they are often used off label and inappropriately for other disorders such as dementia and impulsive aggressiveness.

Although the newer drugs now comprise 90 percent of the market for antipsychotics, a large federally funded study found that they are not significantly safer or more effective than the older, less expensive medications for schizophrenia, the only disorder for which they were originally approved (Lieberman et al., 2005; Swartz et al., 2007). And although antipsychotics are sometimes used to treat impulsive aggressiveness associated with attention deficit disorder, dementia, and other mental problems, they are actually ineffective for these disorders. One study followed 86 people, ages 18 to 65, who were given Risperdal, Haldol, or a placebo to treat their aggressive outbursts (Tyrer et al., 2008). The placebo group improved the most. Antipsychotics are also ineffective in reducing the symptoms of PTSD, although about one-fifth of combat veterans suffering from PTSD are being given these drugs (Krystal et al., 2011).

2 **Antidepressant drugs** are used primarily in the treatment of depression, but also for anxiety, phobias, and obsessive-compulsive disorder. *Monoamine oxidase inhibitors* (MAOIs), such as Nardil, elevate the levels of norepinephrine and serotonin in the brain by blocking or inhibiting an enzyme that deactivates these neurotransmitters. *Tricyclic antidepressants*, such as Elavil and Tofranil, boost norepinephrine and serotonin levels by preventing the normal reabsorption, or "reuptake," of these substances by the cells that have released them. These older antidepressants are usually more effective for severe depression than the more recent and more popular ones, called *selective serotonin reuptake inhibitors* (SSRIs). SSRIs, such as Prozac, Zoloft, Lexapro, Paxil, and Celexa, work on the same principle as the tricyclics but specifically target serotonin; Cymbalta and Remeron target both serotonin and norepinephrine. Wellbutrin is chemically unrelated to the other antidepressants but is often prescribed for depression and sometimes as an aid to quit smoking.

All antidepressants tend to produce some unpleasant physical reactions, including dry mouth, headaches, constipation, nausea, restlessness, gastrointestinal problems, weight gain, and, in as many as one-third of all patients, decreased sexual desire and blocked or delayed orgasm (Hollon, Thase, & Markowitz, 2002). The specific side effects may vary with the particular drug. MAOIs interact with certain foods (such as cheese) and they can elevate blood pressure in some individuals to dangerously high levels, so they have to be carefully monitored.

Although antidepressants are said to be nonaddictive, all of them, especially the SSRIs, can produce physical dependence (Healy, 2012). These

"*Before Prozac, she loathed company.*"

medications should not be stopped abruptly without supervision by a physician because withdrawal symptoms may occur—including depression and anxiety, which can be mistaken for a relapse, and even mania, which can then cause the sufferer to be misdiagnosed as having bipolar disorder (Kirsch, 2010; Whitaker, 2010).

Antidepressants and most other psychotropic drugs now carry strong warnings about the risks of inducing suicide and violence. Of course, some severely depressed people were suicidal before they began taking medication. But the clinician and the patient need to be aware that a person on these medications may get worse; if that happens, medication should immediately be reassessed (Healy, 2012).

3 **Antianxiety drugs (tranquilizers)**, such as Valium, Xanax, Ativan, and Klonopin, increase the activity of the neurotransmitter gamma-aminobutyric acid (GABA). Tranquilizers may temporarily help individuals who are having an acute anxiety attack, but they are not considered the treatment of choice over time. Symptoms often return if the medication is stopped, and a significant percentage of people who take tranquilizers overuse them and develop problems with withdrawal and tolerance (that is, they need larger and larger doses to get the same effect). *Beta blockers*, a class of drugs primarily used to manage heart irregularities and hypertension, are sometimes prescribed to relieve acute anxiety—for example, caused by stage fright or athletic competition—which they do by slowing the heart rate and lowering blood pressure. But beta blockers are not approved for anxiety disorders.

antidepressant drugs Drugs used primarily in the treatment of mood disorders, especially depression and anxiety.

antianxiety drugs (tranquilizers) Drugs commonly but often inappropriately prescribed for patients who complain of moderate forms of anxiety, worry, or unhappiness.

TABLE 12.1 Drugs Commonly Used in the Treatment of Psychological Disorders

	Antipsychotics (Neuroleptics)	Antidepressants	Antianxiety Drugs (Tranquilizers)	Lithium Carbonate
Examples	Thorazine	Prozac (SSRI)	Valium	
	Haldol	Nardil (MAOI)	Xanax	
	Clozaril	Elavil (tricyclic)	Klonopin	
	Risperdal	Paxil (SSRI)	Beta blockers	
	Seroquel	Wellbutrin (other)		
		Cymbalta (other)		
		Remeron (other)		
Primarily used for	Schizophrenia	Depression	Mild anxiety disorders	Bipolar disorder
	Other psychoses	Severe anxiety disorders	Panic disorder	
	Impulsive anger	Panic disorder	Acute anxiety (e.g., stage fright)	
	Bipolar disorder	Obsessive-compulsive disorder		

4 **Lithium carbonate**, a salt, is a special category of drug often given to people who suffer from bipolar disorder, although the reason it helps is unknown. Lithium must be given in exactly the right dose, and bloodstream levels of the drug must be carefully monitored, because too little will not help and too much is toxic; in some people, lithium produces short-term side effects (tremors) and long-term problems (kidney damage). Other drugs commonly prescribed for people with bipolar disorder include Depakote and Tegretol.

For a review of these drugs and their uses, see Table 12.1.

✳ **Explore** the **Concept** Drugs Commonly Used to Treat Psychiatric Disorders at MyPsychLab

Cautions About Drug Treatments
LO 12.2

Drugs have rescued some people from emotional despair and helped countless others live with chronic problems such as schizophrenia, obsessive-compulsive disorder, and panic attacks. They have enabled people suffering from severe depression or mental disturbances to be released from hospitals, to function in the world, and to respond to psychotherapy. Yet many psychiatrists and drug companies are trumpeting the benefits of medication without informing the public of its limitations.

Most people are unaware of how a *publication bias*—the tendency for journals to publish positive findings but not negative or ambiguous ones—affects what we know. Independent researchers were able to get unpublished data submitted to the U.S. Food and Drug Administration (FDA) on 12 popular antidepressants, and their results were shocking. Of the 38 studies that reported positive results, all but one were published. Of the 36 studies with negative or mixed results, only 14 were published—and most of those 14 were written to imply that the results had been better than they were (Turner et al., 2008). Knowing the results from unpublished studies is crucial: Only after British drug authorities reported that 9 unpublished studies of Paxil found that it tripled the risk of suicidal thoughts and suicide attempts in adolescents who were taking the drug, compared to those given a placebo, did the FDA add a black-box warning against prescribing SSRIs to anyone younger than 18 (Healy, 2012).

Even more worrisome for the prospects of impartial research, the majority of researchers who are studying the effectiveness of medication have financial ties to the pharmaceutical industry, in the form of lucrative consulting fees, funding for their clinical trials, stock investments, and patents. Studies that are independently funded often do not get the positive results that industry-funded drug trials do (Angell, 2004; Healy, 2002; Krimsky, 2003). In this section, therefore, we want to give you an idea of what you are not hearing from the drug companies.

☀ **THINKING CRITICALLY**

About Reported Drug Benefits

lithium carbonate A drug frequently given to people suffering from bipolar disorder.

1 **The placebo effect.** New drugs often promise quick and effective cures. But the **placebo effect** ensures that many people will respond positively to a new drug just because of the enthusiasm surrounding it and because of their own expectations that the drug will make them feel better. After a while, when placebo effects decline, many drugs turn out to be neither as effective as promised nor as widely applicable. This has happened repeatedly with each new generation of tranquilizer and each new "miracle" antipsychotic drug and antidepressant (Healy, 2002; Moncrieff, 2001).

In fact, some investigators maintain that much of the effectiveness of antidepressants, especially for people who are only mildly depressed, can be attributed to a placebo effect (Khan et al., 2003). Overall, only about half of all depressed patients respond positively to any given antidepressant medication, and of those, only about 40 percent are actually responding to the specific biological effects of the drug (Hollon, Thase, & Markowitz, 2002). In a meta-analysis of more than 5,000 patients in 47 clinical trials, investigators found that the placebo effect was "exceptionally large," accounting for more than 80 percent of the alleviation of symptoms. The drugs were most effective for patients with severe depression (Kirsch et al., 2008). We know this result is surprising, so we'll tell you that it was replicated in an even more rigorous study, one that evaluated a 20-year database of meta-analyses and other reviews of the literature (Fournier et al., 2010). The researchers found that the benefits of antidepressants exceed those of a placebo only in patients with very severe depression, and that the benefits are "minimal or nonexistent, on average, in patients with mild or moderate symptoms."

2 **High relapse and dropout rates.** In part because antipsychotic and antidepressant drugs can have unpleasant side effects, anywhere from one-half to two-thirds of patients stop taking them. When they do, they are likely to relapse, especially if they have not learned how to cope with their disorders (Hollon, Thase, & Maskowitz, 2002).

One reason some people may stop taking a drug is that they have been given the wrong dose. The same dose may be metabolized differently in men and women, old people and young people, and Asians, African Americans, and Anglos. For example, Asian patients with schizophrenia require significantly lower doses of antipsychotic medication for optimal treatment than Anglos do (Lin, Poland, & Chien, 1990; Strickland et al., 1995). Groups may differ in the dosages they can tolerate because of variations in metabolic rates, amount of body fat, the number or type of drug receptors in the brain, or cultural differences in smoking and diet.

3 **Disregard for effective nonmedical treatments.** The popularity of drugs has been fueled by pressure from managed-care organizations, which prefer to pay for one patient visit for a prescription rather than 10 visits for psychotherapy, and by drug company marketing and advertising. In 1997, the FDA permitted pharmaceutical companies to advertise directly to the public, a practice still forbidden in Canada and Europe; sales of new drugs skyrocketed as consumers began to request them. Because ads promise wonderful results, medication often seems the best and easiest way to deal with an emotional or behavioral problem. Yet nonmedical treatments may work just as well or better. For example, two psychologists examined data on more than 168,000 children who had been referred to a behavioral care facility to be treated for attention deficit disorder. More than 60 percent of the boys and 23 percent of the girls were on Ritalin or another drug. But after 6 sessions of behavior therapy for the children and 10 sessions for the parent, only 11 percent of the boys and 2 percent of the girls had to remain on medication (Cummings & Wiggins, 2001).

4 **Unknown risks of prolonged use, increased dosages, or drug interactions.** The effects of taking antidepressants indefinitely are still unknown, especially for vulnerable groups such as children, pregnant women, the elderly, and the generation of young adults who have been taking them since childhood or adolescence, when the brain is still developing. Moreover, higher doses of antidepressants do not produce greater reductions in symptoms, only more side effects (Kirsch, 2010). But when the drug isn't working, its manufacturer generally advises the prescribing physician to increase the dose.

The reason we don't know about long-term effects until a drug has been on the market for years is that new drugs are initially tested clinically on only a few hundred people for just a few weeks or months, even when the drug is one that a person might take indefinitely (Angell, 2004; Light, 2010). Nonetheless, many psychiatrists are prescribing "cocktails" of medications—this one for anxiety, plus this one for depression, plus another to manage the side effects. They report anecdotal success in some cases, but to date, there has been virtually no research on the benefits and risks of these combination approaches.

5 **Untested off-label uses.** Most consumers do not realize that once the FDA approves a drug, doctors are permitted to prescribe it for other conditions and for populations other than those

placebo effect The apparent success of a medication or treatment because of the patient's expectations or hopes rather than effects of the drug or treatment itself.

"I think the dosage needs adjusting. I'm not nearly as happy as the people in the ads."

on which it was originally tested. As already noted, antipsychotics such as Risperdal are being used for nonpsychotic disorders. Likewise, antidepressants are being marketed for social phobias; Prozac, when its patent expired, was renamed Sarafem and marketed to women for "premenstrual dysphoric disorder"; Ritalin, originally intended only for school-aged children, was soon being prescribed for 2- and 3-year-olds.

In coming years, you will be hearing about "promising medications" for such common psychological problems as memory loss, eating disorders, smoking, and alcoholism. Every large pharmaceutical company is working on one or more of these.

But we hope you will resist the impulse to jump on any new-drug bandwagon. Critical thinkers must weigh the benefits and limitations of medication for psychological problems, tolerate uncertainty while waiting for the data on safety and effectiveness, and resist the temptation to oversimplify.

Direct Brain Intervention LO 12.3

For most of human history, a person suffering from mental illness often got an extreme form of help. A well-meaning tribal healer or doctor would try to release the "psychic pressures" believed to be causing the symptoms by drilling holes in the victim's skull. It didn't work!

The most famous modern effort to cure mental illness through *psychosurgery*—intervening directly in the brain—was invented in 1935, when a Portuguese neurologist, António Egas Moniz, drilled two holes into the skull of a mental patient and used an instrument to crush nerve fibers running from the prefrontal lobes to other areas. (Later, some doctors just used an ice pick.) This operation, called a *prefrontal lobotomy*, was supposed to reduce the patient's emotional symptoms without impairing intellectual ability. Incredibly, the procedure was never assessed or validated scientifically, yet it was performed on more than 40,000 people in the United States. Tragically, lobotomies left many patients apathetic, withdrawn, and unable to care for themselves (Valenstein, 1986). Yet Moniz won a Nobel Prize for his work.

In contrast to using surgical intervention, some psychiatrists attempt to alter brain function

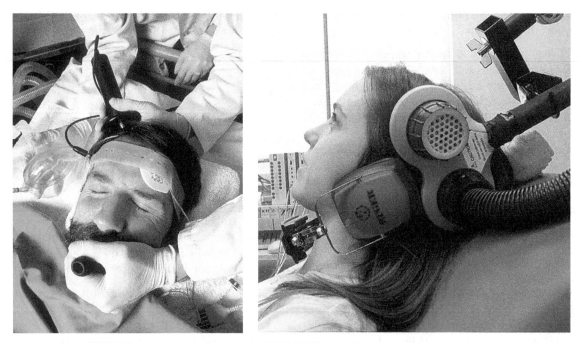

A man receives ECT (left); a researcher demonstrates TMS (right).

by stimulating the brain externally. The oldest method is **electroconvulsive therapy (ECT)**, or "shock therapy," which is used for the treatment of severe depression, although no one knows why it works. An electrode is placed on one side of the head and a brief current is turned on. The current triggers a seizure that typically lasts one minute, causing the body to convulse. In the past, there were many horror stories about the misuse of ECT and its dire effects on memory. Today, patients are given muscle relaxants and anesthesia, so they sleep through the procedure and their convulsions are minimized. The World Psychiatric Association and the FDA have endorsed ECT as safe and effective, especially for people with episodes of crippling depression and suicidal impulses who have not responded to other treatments (Shorter & Healy, 2008). Still, the mood-improving effect of ECT is usually short-lived, and the depression almost always returns within a few weeks or months (U.S. Food and Drug Administration, 2011; Hollon, Thase, & Markowitz, 2002). ECT is occasionally misused for other disorders, such as schizophrenia or alcoholism, even though it is ineffective for these conditions.

Neuroscientists are investigating other ways of electrically stimulating the brains of severely depressed individuals (Nitsche et al., 2009). In Chapter 4 we described two such technologies. One is *transcranial magnetic stimulation* (TMS), in which a magnetic coil is held to a person's skull over the left prefrontal cortex, an area of the brain that is less active in people with depression. The other is *transcranial direct current stimulation* (tDCS), in which two electrodes are placed on the temples, and a mild current (one-400th of the level used in ECT) modulates the resting level of the brain's neurons. As with ECT, the benefits of these two methods are short-lived, but they are effective with some patients and have fewer side effects than ECT (George & Post, 2011). A double-blind controlled trial of tDCS with 120 Brazilian patients suffering from depression found significant improvement after six weeks of almost daily treatment (Brunoni et al., 2013), but no follow-ups have yet been done to determine how long the improvement lasts.

electroconvulsive therapy (ECT) A procedure used in cases of prolonged and severe major depression, in which a brief brain seizure is induced.

Recite & Review

✓ **Study** and **Review** at **MyPsychLab**

Recite: Take a breath, and say out loud everything you can recall about antipsychotic drugs, kinds of antidepressant drugs, tranquilizers, and lithium carbonate; cautions about drug treatments; and psychosurgery, ECT, TMS, and tDCS.

Review: Next, given all the information you need to digest, reread this section.

Now take this *Quick Quiz:*

A. Match these treatments with the problems for which they are typically used.

1. antipsychotic drugs
2. antidepressant drugs
3. lithium carbonate
4. electroconvulsive therapy

a. suicidal depression
b. bipolar disorder
c. schizophrenia
d. depression and anxiety
e. obsessive-compulsive disorder

B. How does the placebo effect influence patients with psychological disorders?

C. Which two electrically stimulating methods are being explored by neuroscientists to help severely depressed people?

Answers:

A. 1. c 2. d, e 3. b 4. a B. Patients respond to new drugs positively because of the enthusiasm linked with it. C. transcranial magnetic stimulation; transcranial direct current stimulation.

You are about to learn...

• the major approaches to psychotherapy.

• how behavior therapists can help you change bad habits and how cognitive therapists can help you get rid of self-defeating thoughts.

• why humanist and existential therapists focus on the "here and now" instead of the "why and how."

• the benefits of treating a whole family instead of only one of its members.

Major Schools of Psychotherapy

All good psychotherapists want to help clients think about their lives in new ways and find solutions to the problems that plague them. In this section, we will consider the major schools of psychotherapy. To illustrate the philosophy and methods of each one, we will focus on a fictional fellow named Murray. Murray is a smart guy whose problem is all too familiar to many students: He procrastinates. He just can't seem to settle down and write his term papers. He keeps getting incompletes, and before long the incompletes turn to Fs. Why does Murray procrastinate, manufacturing his own misery? What kind of therapy might help him?

Psychodynamic Therapy LO 12.4

Sigmund Freud was the father of the "talking cure," as one of his patients called it. In his method of **psychoanalysis**, which required patients to come for treatment several days a week, often for years, patients talked not about their immediate problems but about their dreams and their memories of childhood. Freud believed that intensive analysis of these dreams and memories would give patients insight into the unconscious reasons for their symptoms. With insight and emotional release, he believed, the person's symptoms would disappear.

Freud's psychoanalytic method has since evolved into many different forms of *psychodynamic therapy*, all of which share the goal of exploring the unconscious dynamics of personality, such as defenses and conflicts. Proponents of these therapies often refer to them as "depth" therapies because the purpose is to delve into the deep, unconscious processes believed to be the source of the patient's problems rather than to concentrate on "superficial" symptoms and conscious beliefs. Modern psychodynamic therapies share certain features,

including the discussion of past experience, identification of recurring themes and patterns in the client's life, exploration of fantasies, and a focus on the client's contradictory emotions and feelings (Shedler, 2010).

A central element of most psychodynamic therapies is **transference**, the client's transfer (displacement) of emotional elements of his or her inner life—usually feelings about the client's parents—outward onto the analyst. Have you ever responded to a new acquaintance with unusually quick affection or dislike, and later realized it was because the person reminded you of a relative whom you loved or loathed? That experience is similar to transference. In therapy, a woman might transfer her love for her father to the analyst, believing that she has fallen in love with the analyst. A man who is unconsciously angry at his mother for rejecting him might become furious with his analyst for going on vacation. Through analysis of transference in the therapy setting, psychodynamic therapists believe that clients can see their emotional conflicts in action and work through them (Schafer, 1992; Westen, 1998).

Today, most psychodynamic therapists borrow methods from other forms of therapy. They are more concerned with helping clients solve their problems and ease their emotional symptoms than analysts have traditionally been, and they tend to limit therapy to a specific number of sessions, say 10 or 20. They might help our friend Murray gain the insight that he procrastinates as a way of expressing anger toward his parents. He might realize that he is angry because they insist he study for a career he dislikes. Ideally, Murray will come to this insight by himself. If the analyst suggests it, Murray might feel too defensive to accept it.

Psychodynamic therapists emphasize the clinical importance of transference, the process by which the client transfers emotional feelings toward other important people in his or her life (usually the parents) onto the therapist. They know that "love's arrow" isn't really intended for them!

psychoanalysis A theory of personality and a method of psychotherapy, developed by Sigmund Freud, that emphasizes the exploration of unconscious motives and conflicts; modern *psychodynamic therapies* share this emphasis but differ from Freudian analysis in various ways.

transference In psychodynamic therapies, a critical process in which the client transfers unconscious emotions or reactions, such as emotional feelings about his or her parents, onto the therapist.

Behavior and Cognitive Therapy
LO 12.5, LO 12.6

Clinical psychologists who practice behavior therapy would get right to the problem: What are the reinforcers in Murray's environment that are maintaining his behavior? "Mur," they would say, "forget about insight. You have lousy study habits." Clinicians who practice cognitive therapy would focus on helping Murray understand how his beliefs about studying, writing papers, and success are woefully unrealistic. Often these two approaches are combined.

Behavioral Techniques. **Behavior therapy** is based on principles of classical and operant conditioning that are discussed in Chapter 9. (You may want to review those principles before going on.) Here are some of the main methods that behavior therapists use (Martin & Pear, 2011):

1 Exposure. The most widely used behavioral approach for treating fears and panic is **graduated exposure**. When people are afraid of some situation, object, or upsetting memory, they usually do everything they can to avoid confronting or thinking of it. Unfortunately, this seemingly logical response only makes the fear worse. Exposure treatments, either in the client's imagination or in actual situations, are aimed at reversing this tendency. In graduated exposure, the client controls the degree of confrontation with the source of the fear: Someone who is trying to avoid thinking of a traumatic event might be asked to imagine the event over and over, until it no longer evokes the same degree of panic. A more dramatic form of exposure is **flooding**, in which the therapist takes the client directly into the feared situation and remains there until the client's panic and anxiety decline. Thus, a person suffering from agoraphobia might be taken into a department store or a subway, an action that would normally be terrifying even to contemplate.

2 Systematic desensitization. Systematic desensitization is an older behavioral method, a step-by-step process of breaking down a client's conditioned associations to a feared object or experience (Wolpe, 1958). It is based on the classical-conditioning procedure of *counterconditioning*, in which a stimulus (such as a dog) for an unwanted response (such as fear) is paired with some other stimulus or situation that elicits a response incompatible with the undesirable one (see Chapter 9). In this case, the incompatible response is usually relaxation. The client learns to relax deeply while imagining or looking at a sequence of feared stimuli, arranged in a hierarchy from the least frightening to the most frightening. The hierarchy itself is provided by the client. The sequence for a person who is terrified of spiders might be to read the classic children's story *Charlotte's Web*, then look at pictures of small, cute spiders, then look at pictures of tarantulas, then move on to observing a real spider, and so on. At each step, the person must become relaxed before going on. Eventually, the fear responses are extinguished.

Taking advantage of computer technology, some behavior therapists have developed virtual reality (VR) programs to desensitize clients to anxiety and to various phobias, notably of flying, heights, spiders, and public speaking (Gregg & Tarrier, 2007; Weiderhold & Weiderhold, 2000). Others are experimenting with VR to treat combat veterans who are suffering from intractable posttraumatic stress symptoms. In a program called Virtual Iraq, vets get a combination of exposure and desensitization. They wear a helmet with video goggles and earphones to hear the sounds of war, and then play a version of the VR game *Full Spectrum Warrior* adapted to the Iraq experience (S. Halpern, 2008).

3 Behavioral self-monitoring. Before you can change your behavior, it helps to identify the reinforcers that are supporting your unwanted habits: attention from others, temporary relief from tension or unhappiness, or tangible rewards such as money or a good meal. One way to do this is to keep a record of the behavior that you would like to change.

IN THE BLEACHERS By Steve Moore

Batters overcoming *bonkinogginophobia*, a fear of the ball.

behavior therapy A form of therapy that applies principles of classical and operant conditioning to help people change self-defeating or problematic behaviors.

graduated exposure In behavior therapy, a method in which a person suffering from a phobia or panic attacks is gradually taken into the feared situation or exposed to a traumatic memory until the anxiety subsides.

flooding In behavior therapy, a form of exposure treatment in which the client is taken directly into a feared situation until his or her panic subsides.

systematic desensitization In behavior therapy, a step-by-step process of desensitizing a client to a feared object or experience; it is based on the classical-conditioning procedure of counterconditioning.

behavioral self-monitoring In behavior therapy, a method of keeping careful data on the frequency and consequences of the behavior to be changed.

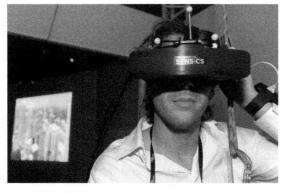

This man is using a virtual reality form of systematic desensitization to overcome his fear of heights.

skills training In behavior therapy, an effort to teach the client skills that he or she may lack, as well as new constructive behaviors to replace self-defeating ones.

cognitive therapy A form of therapy designed to identify and change irrational, unproductive ways of thinking and, hence, to reduce negative emotions and their self-defeating consequences.

Would you like to cut back on eating sweets? You may not be aware of how much you are eating throughout the day to relieve tension, boost your energy, or just to be sociable when you are hanging out; a behavioral record will show how much and when you eat. A mother might complain that her child "always" has temper tantrums; a behavioral record will show when, where, and with whom those tantrums occur. Once the unwanted behavior is identified, along with the reinforcers that have been maintaining it, a treatment program can be designed to change it. For instance, you might find other ways to reduce stress besides eating, and make sure that you are nowhere near junk food in the late afternoon, when your energy is low. The mother can learn to respond to her child's tantrum not with her attention (or a cookie to buy silence) but with a time out: banishing the child to a corner or other place where no positive reinforcers are available.

4 **Skills training.** It is not enough to tell someone "Don't be shy" if the person does not know how to make small talk with others, or "Don't yell!" if the person does not know how to express feelings calmly. Therefore, some behavior therapists use operant-conditioning techniques, modeling, and role-playing to teach the skills a client might lack.

Skills-training programs have been designed for all kinds of behavioral problems: to teach parents how to discipline their children, impulsive adults how to manage anger, shy people how to converse in social situations, autistic children how to behave appropriately, and people with schizophrenia how to hold a job. These skills are also being taught in virtual worlds, such as *Second Life*. After face-to-face sessions with a therapist, the client creates an avatar to explore a virtual environment and experiment with new behaviors; at the same time, the therapist can be monitoring the client's psychological and even physiological reactions.

A behaviorist would treat Murray's procrastination in several ways. Monitoring his own behavior with a diary would let Murray know exactly how he spends his time, and how much time he should realistically allot to a project. Instead of having a vague, impossibly huge goal, such as "I'm going to reorganize my life," Murray would establish specific small goals, such as reading the two books necessary for an English paper and writing one page of an assignment. If Murray does not know how to write clearly, however, even writing one page might feel overwhelming; he might also need some skills training, such as a basic composition class. Most of all, the therapist would change the reinforcers that are maintaining Murray's "procrastination behavior"—perhaps the immediate gratification of partying with friends—and replace them with reinforcers for getting the work done.

Cognitive Techniques. Gloomy thoughts can generate an array of negative emotions and self-defeating behavior. The underlying premise of **cognitive therapy** is that constructive thinking can do the opposite, reducing or dispelling anger, fear, and depression. Cognitive therapists help clients identify the beliefs and expectations that might be unnecessarily prolonging their unhappiness, conflicts, and other problems (Persons, Davidson, & Tompkins,

Get Involved! Cure Your Fears

In Chapter 11, a Get Involved exercise asked you to identify your greatest fear. Now see whether systematic desensitization procedures will help you conquer it. Write down a list of situations that evoke your fear, starting with one that produces little anxiety (e.g., seeing a photo of a tiny spider) and ending with the most frightening one possible (e.g., looking at live tarantulas at a pet store). Then find a quiet room where you will have no distractions or interruptions, sit in a comfortable reclining chair, and relax all the muscles of your body. Breathe slowly and deeply. Imagine the first, easiest scene, remaining as relaxed as possible. Do this until you can confront the image without becoming the least bit anxious. When that happens, go on to the next scene in your hierarchy. Do not try this all at once; space out your sessions over time. Does it work?

2001). They ask clients to examine the evidence for their beliefs that everyone is mean and selfish, that ambition is hopeless, or that love is doomed. Clients learn to consider other explanations for the behavior of people who annoy them: Was my father's strict discipline an attempt to control me, as I have always believed? What if he was really trying to protect and care for me? By requiring people to identify their assumptions and biases, examine the evidence, and consider other interpretations, cognitive therapy, as you can see, teaches critical thinking.

Aaron Beck (1976, 2005), regarded as the father of cognitive therapy, pioneered in its use for treating depression. As we saw in Chapter 11, depression often arises from pessimistic thoughts that the sources of your misery are permanent and that nothing good will ever happen to you again. For Beck, these beliefs are not "irrational"; rather, they are unproductive or based on misinformation. A therapist using Beck's approach would ask you to test your beliefs against the evidence. If you say, "But I *know* no one likes me," the therapist might say, "Oh, yes? How do you know? Do you really not have a single friend? Has anyone in the past year been nice to you?"

Another eminent cognitive therapist was Albert Ellis (1913–2007). Ellis's approach, which he called *rational emotive behavior therapy*, blended existing behavioral techniques with his own brand of cognitive interventions (Ellis, 1993; Ellis & Blau, 1998). Ellis pointed out that people who are emotionally upset often *overgeneralize*: They decide that one annoying act by someone means that person is bad in every way, or that a normal mistake they made is evidence that they are rotten to the core. Many people also *catastrophize*, transforming a small problem into disaster: "I failed this test, and now I'll flunk out of school, and no one will ever like me, and even my cat will hate me, and I'll never get a job." Many people drive themselves crazy with notions of what they "must" do. The

therapist challenges these thoughts, beliefs, and expectations directly, showing the client why they are misguided.

A cognitive therapist might treat Murray's procrastination by having Murray write down his thoughts about work, read the thoughts as if someone else had said them, and then write a rational response to each one. This technique would encourage Murray to examine the validity of his assumptions and beliefs. Many procrastinators are perfectionists; if they cannot do something perfectly, they will not do it at all. Unable to accept their limitations, they set impossible standards and catastrophize:

Negative Thought	Rational Response
If I don't get an A on this paper, my life will be ruined.	My life will be a lot worse if I keep getting incompletes. It's better to get a B or even a C than to do nothing.
My professor is going to think I'm an idiot when she reads this. I'll feel humiliated by her criticism.	She hasn't accused me of being an idiot yet. If she makes some criticisms, I can learn from them and do better next time.

In the past, behavioral and cognitive therapists debated whether it is most helpful to work on changing clients' thoughts or changing their behavior. But today, most of them believe that thoughts and behavior influence each other, which is why *cognitive-behavior therapy* (CBT) is more common than either cognitive or behavior therapy alone.

👁 Watch the Video In the Real World: Cognitive Behavioral Therapy at **MyPsychLab**

Mindfulness and Acceptance Techniques. A new wave of CBT practitioners, inspired by Eastern philosophies such as Buddhism, questions the goal of changing a client's self-defeating

Cognitive therapists encourage clients to emphasize the positive (the early sunny signs of spring) rather than always focusing on the negative (the lingering icy clutch of winter). Poet Michael Casey described the first daffodil that bravely rises through the snow as "a gleam of laughter in a sullen face."

Get Involved! Mind over Mood

See whether the techniques of cognitive therapy can help you control your moods. Think of a time recently when you felt a particularly strong emotion, such as depression, anger, or anxiety. In any form you wish, record (1) the situation—who was there, what happened, and when; (2) the intensity of your feeling at the time, from weak to strong; and (3) the thoughts that were going through your mind (e.g., "She never cares about what I want to do"; "He's going to leave me").

Now examine your thoughts. What is the worst thing that could happen if those thoughts are true? Are your thoughts accurate or are you "mind reading" another person's intentions and motives? Is there another way to think about this situation or the other person's behavior? If you practice this exercise repeatedly, you may learn how your thoughts affect your moods, and find out that you have more control over your feelings than you realized (Greenberger & Padesky, 1995).

humanist therapy A form of psychotherapy based on the philosophy of humanism, which emphasizes the client's free will to change rather than past conflicts.

client-centered therapy A humanist approach, devised by Carl Rogers, which emphasizes the therapist's empathy with the client and the use of unconditional positive regard.

existential therapy A form of therapy designed to help clients explore the meaning of existence and face the great questions of life, such as death, freedom, and loneliness.

thoughts. They argue that it is difficult to completely eliminate unwanted thoughts and feelings, especially when people have been rehearsing them for years. They therefore propose a form of CBT based on "mindfulness" and "acceptance": Clients learn to explicitly identify and accept whatever negative thoughts and feelings arise, without trying to eradicate them or letting them derail healthy behavior (Hayes, Follette, & Linehan, 2004). Instead of trying to persuade a client who is afraid of making public speeches that her fear is irrational, therapists who adopt this approach would encourage her to accept the anxious thoughts and feelings without judging them, or herself, harshly. Then she can focus on coping techniques and ways of giving speeches *despite* her anxiety.

Another version of mindfulness-based cognitive therapy adds the Eastern tradition of "attentional breathing," which a client practices when he or she is in a low mood or embarking on a downward spiral of negative, depressive thoughts (Coelho, Canter, & Ernst, 2007; Segal, Teasdale, & Williams, 2004). By sitting quietly and focusing attention on the present moment, especially on awareness of one's breath, a person can interrupt the negative thinking before it goes too far.

Humanist and Existential Therapy LO 12.7

In the 1960s, *humanist psychologists* rejected the two dominant psychological approaches of the time, psychoanalysis and behaviorism. Humanists regarded psychoanalysis, with its emphasis on dangerous sexual and aggressive impulses, as too pessimistic a view of human nature, one that overlooked human resilience and the capacity for joy. And humanists regarded behaviorism, with its emphasis on observable acts, as too mechanistic and "mindless" a view of human nature, one that ignored what really matters to most people—their hopes and aspirations. In the humanists' view, human behavior is not completely determined by either unconscious conflicts or the environment. Because people have free will, they have the ability to make more of themselves than either psychoanalysts or behaviorists would predict. The goal of humanist psychology was, and still is, to help people express themselves creatively and achieve their full potential.

Humanist therapy therefore starts from the assumption that human nature is basically good and that people behave badly or develop problems when they have been warped by self-imposed limits. Humanist therapists want to know how clients subjectively see their own situations and how they construe the world around them. They

explore what is going on "here and now," not past issues of "why and how."

In **client-centered therapy**, developed by Carl Rogers (1902–1987), one of the most eminent clinical psychologists of the twentieth century, the therapist's role is to listen to the client's needs in an accepting, nonjudgmental way and to offer what Rogers called *unconditional positive regard*. Whatever the client's specific complaint is, the goal is to build the client's self-esteem and self-acceptance and help the client find a more productive way of seeing his or her problems. A Rogerian might assume that Murray's procrastination masks his low self-regard and that Murray is out of touch with his real feelings and wishes. Perhaps he is not passing his courses because he is trying to please his parents by majoring in pre-law when he would secretly rather become an artist.

Rogers (1951, 1961) believed that effective therapists must be warm and genuine. For Rogerians, *empathy*, the therapist's ability to understand what the client says and identify the client's feelings, is the crucial ingredient of successful therapy: "I understand how frustrated you must be feeling, Murray, because no matter how hard you try, you don't succeed." The client will eventually internalize the therapist's support and become more self-accepting.

◉ **Watch** the **Video** Classic Footage of Carl Rogers on the Role of a Therapist at **MyPsychLab**

Existential therapy helps clients face the great questions of existence, such as death, freedom, loneliness, and meaninglessness. Existential therapists, like humanist therapists, believe that our lives are not inevitably determined by our pasts or our circumstances; we have the free will to choose our own destinies. As Irvin Yalom (1989) explained, "The crucial first step in therapy is the patient's assumption of responsibility for his or her life predicament. As long as one believes that

Humanist therapists emphasize the importance of warmth, concern, and empathy in listening to the client.

one's problems are caused by some force or agency outside oneself, there is no leverage in therapy."

Yalom argues that the goal of therapy is to help clients cope with the inescapable realities of life and death and the struggle for meaning. However grim our experiences may be, he believes, "they contain the seeds of wisdom and redemption." Perhaps the most remarkable example of a man able to find seeds of wisdom in a barren landscape was Victor Frankl (1905–1997), who developed a form of existential therapy after surviving a Nazi concentration camp. In that pit of horror, Frankl (1955) observed, some people maintained their sanity because they were able to find meaning in the experience, shattering though it was.

A humanist or existential therapist might teach Murray to think about the significance of his procrastination, what his ultimate goals in life are, and how he might find the strength to reach them.

Family and Couples Therapy LO 12.8

Murray's situation is getting worse. His father has begun to call him Tomorrow Man, which upsets his mother, and his younger brother, the math major, has been calculating how much tuition money Murray's incompletes are costing. His older sister, Isabel, the biochemist who never had an incomplete in her life, now proposes that all of them go to *family therapy*. "Murray's not the only one in this family with complaints," she says.

Family therapists would maintain that Murray's problem developed in the context of his family, that it is sustained by the dynamics of his family, and that any change he makes will affect all members of his family (Nichols & Schwartz, 2008). One of the most famous early family therapists, Salvador Minuchin (1984), compared the family to a kaleidoscope, a changing pattern of mosaics in which the pattern is larger than any one piece. In this view, efforts to isolate and treat one member of the family without the others are doomed. Only if all family members reveal their differing perceptions of each other can mistakes and misperceptions be identified. A teenager may see his mother as crabby and nagging when actually she is tired and worried. A parent may see a child as rebellious when in fact the child is lonely and desperate for attention.

Family members are usually unaware of how they influence one another. By observing the entire family, the family therapist hopes to discover tensions and imbalances in power and communication. A child may have a chronic illness or a psychological problem that affects the workings of the whole family. One parent may become overinvolved with the sick or troubled child while the other parent retreats, and each may start blaming the other. The child, in turn, may cling to the illness or disorder as a way of expressing anger, keeping the parents together, getting the parents' attention, or asserting control (Cummings & Davies, 2011).

Even when it is not possible to treat the whole family, some therapists will treat individuals in a **family-systems perspective**, which recognizes that people's behavior in a family is as interconnected as that of two dancers (Bowen, 1978; Cox & Paley, 2003). Clients learn that if they change in any way, even for the better, their families may protest noisily or may send subtle messages that read, "Change back!" Why? Because when one family member changes, each of the others must change too. But most people do not like change. They are comfortable with old patterns and habits, even those that cause them trouble. They want to keep dancing the same old dance, even if their feet hurt.

When a couple is arguing frequently about issues that never seem to get resolved, they may be helped by going to *couples therapy*, which is designed to help couples manage the inevitable conflicts that occur in all relationships (Christensen & Jacobson, 2000). One of the most common problems that couples complain about is the "demand–withdraw" pattern, in which one partner badgers the other about some perceived failing, demanding that he or she change. The more the badgering partner demands, the more the target withdraws, sulks, or avoids the subject (Baucom et al., 2011; Christensen & Jacobson, 2000). Couples therapists generally insist on seeing both partners, so that they will hear both sides of the story. They cut through the blaming and attacking ("She never listens to me!" "He never does anything!"), and instead focus on helping the couple resolve their differences, get over hurt and blame, and make specific behavioral changes to reduce anger and conflict.

Many couples therapists, like some cognitive therapists, are moving away from the "fix everything" approach. Instead, they are helping couples learn to accept and live with qualities in both partners that aren't going to change much (Baucom et al., 2011; Hayes, 2004). A wife can stop trying to turn her calm, steady husband into a spontaneous adventurer ("After all, that's what I originally loved about him, that he's as steady as a rock"), and a husband can stop trying to make his shy wife more assertive ("I have always loved her serenity").

Family and couples therapists may use psychodynamic, behavioral, cognitive, or humanist approaches in their work; they share only a focus on the family or the couple. In Murray's case, a family therapist would observe how Murray's procrastination fits his family dynamics. Perhaps it allows Murray to get his father's attention and his

family-systems perspective An approach to doing therapy with individuals or families by identifying how each family member forms part of a larger interacting system.

"I've been a cow all my life, honey. Don't ask me to change now."

mother's sympathy. Perhaps it keeps Murray from facing his greatest fear: that if he finishes his work, it will not measure up to his father's impossibly high standards. The therapist will not only help Murray change his work habits, but will also help his family deal with a changed Murray.

The kinds of psychotherapy that we have discussed are all quite different in theory, and so are their techniques (see Table 12.2). Yet in practice, many psychotherapists draw on methods and ideas from various schools, treating clients with whatever methods they feel are most effective. One Internet-based survey of more than 2,400 psychotherapists found that two-thirds said they practice cognitive-behavioral therapy *and* that the single most influential therapist they followed was Carl Rogers *and* that they often incorporate ideas of mindfulness and acceptance (Cook, Biyanova, & Coyne, 2009).

All successful therapies, regardless of their approach, share a key element: They are able to motivate the client into wanting to change, and they replace a client's pessimistic or unrealistic life narrative with one that is more hopeful or attainable (Howard, 1991; Schafer, 1992).

✴ **Explore** the **Concept** Key Components of Psychoanalytic, Humanistic, Behavior, and Cognitive Therapies at MyPsychLab

TABLE 12.2 The Major Schools of Therapy Compared

	Primary Goal	Methods
Psychodynamic	Insight into unconscious motives and feelings that create and prolong symptoms	Probing unconscious motives and fantasies, exploring childhood experiences, examining issues and emotions raised by transference
Cognitive-Behavioral		
Behavioral	Modification of self-defeating behaviors	Graduated exposure and flooding, systematic desensitization, behavioral records, skills training
Cognitive	Modification of irrational or unvalidated beliefs	Prompting the client to test beliefs against evidence; exposing the faulty reasoning in catastrophizing and mind-reading; sometimes helping the client accept unpleasant thoughts and feelings and live with them, instead of trying to eradicate them
Humanist and Existential		
Humanist	Insight; self-acceptance and self-fulfillment; new, more optimistic perceptions of oneself and the world	Providing empathy, unconditional positive regard, and a nonjudgmental setting in which to discuss issues
Existential	Finding meaning in life and accepting inevitable losses	Varies with the therapist; philosophic discussions about the meaning of life, the client's goals, finding the courage to survive loss and suffering
Family and Couples		
Family	Modification of family patterns	May use any of the preceding methods to change family patterns that perpetuate problems and conflicts
Couples	Resolution of conflicts, breaking out of destructive habits	May use any of the preceding methods to help the couple communicate better, resolve conflicts, or accept what cannot be changed

Recite & Review

 Study and **Review** at **MyPsychLab**

Recite: Don't procrastinate, the way Murray would. Recite out loud what you recall about the major schools of psychotherapy and their primary methods: psychoanalysis and psychodynamic therapies, behavior therapy, cognitive therapy, cognitive-behavior therapy, humanist and existential therapies, and family and couples therapy.

Review: Read this section again, to make sure you are clear about the differences among the different approaches.

Now take this *Quick Quiz:*

Match each method or concept with the therapy associated with it:

1. transference	**a.** cognitive therapy
2. systematic desensitization	**b.** psychodynamic therapy
3. facing the fear of death	**c.** humanist therapy
4. reappraisal of thoughts	**d.** behavior therapy
5. unconditional positive regard	**e.** family therapy
6. exposure to feared situation	**f.** existential therapy
7. avoidance of "catastrophizing"	
8. assessment of family patterns	

Answers:

1.b 2.d 3.f 4.a 5.c 6.d 7.a 8.e

You are about to learn...

- **the reasons for the "scientist–practitioner gap" and why it has been widening.**
- **which form of psychotherapy is most likely to help if you are anxious or depressed.**
- **why psychotherapy can sometimes be harmful.**

Evaluating Psychotherapy

Poor Murray! He is getting a little baffled by all these therapies. He wants to make a choice soon; no sense in procrastinating about that, too! Is there any scientific evidence, he wonders, that might help him decide which therapy or therapist will be best for him?

 Watch the **Video** What's In It For Me?: Finding a Therapist if You Need One at **MyPsychLab**

Culture and Psychotherapy
LO 12.9, LO 12.10

Psychotherapy is, first and foremost, a relationship. The first step in treatment, therefore, is for both parties to form an alliance, understanding one another and agreeing on their goals. Sometimes, cultural differences can cause misunderstandings that impede that alliance (Comas-Díaz, 2006; Sue et al., 2007). A lifetime of experience with racism and a general cultural distrust may keep some black clients from revealing feelings that they believe a white therapist would not understand or accept (Whaley & Davis, 2007). Misunderstandings and prejudice may be one reason Asian Americans, Latinos, and African Americans are more likely to stay in therapy when their therapists' ethnicity matches their own. When clients and psychotherapists are culturally matched, they are more likely to share perceptions of what the client's problem is, agree on the best way of coping, and have the same expectations about what therapy can accomplish (Hwang, 2006; Zone et al., 2005).

Understanding a culture's particular traditions can also help clinicians design more effective interventions for individual and community problems. In the Pacific Northwest, where substance abuse among Native Americans has widespread and devastating effects, successful approaches combine bicultural life-skills training with community involvement, which plays an essential role in native life (Hawkins, Cummins, & Marlatt, 2004).

In establishing a bond with clients, therapists must distinguish normal cultural patterns from individual psychological problems. An Irish-American family therapist, Monica McGoldrick

Native Americans in Washington State have been renewing their cultural tradition of canoe journeys. In Seattle, a program designed to prevent drug abuse and other problems among urban Indian adolescents uses canoe journeys as a metaphor for the journey of life. The youths learn the psychological and practical skills, along with the cultural values, that they would need to undertake a canoe journey—and other challenges of life (Hawkins, Cummins, & Marlatt, 2004).

(2005), described some problems that are typical of Irish-American families. These problems arise from Irish history and religious beliefs. "In general, the therapist cannot expect the family to turn into a physically affectionate, emotionally intimate group, or to enjoy being in therapy very much," she observed. "The notion of Original Sin—that you are guilty before you are born—leaves them with a heavy sense of burden. Someone not sensitized to these issues may see this as pathological. It is not. But it is also not likely to change and the therapist should help the family tolerate this inner guilt rather than try to get rid of it." (Did you notice the connection between her observation and acceptance-based forms of cognitive therapy?)

More and more psychotherapists are becoming "sensitized to the issues" caused by cultural differences (Arredondo et al., 2005; Sue et al., 2007). In Latin American cultures, *susto*, or "loss of the soul," is a common response to extreme grief or fright; the person believes that his or her soul has departed along with that of the deceased relative. A psychotherapist unfamiliar with this culturally determined response might conclude that the sufferer was delusional or psychotic. Latino clients are also more likely than Anglos to value harmony in their relationships, which often translates into an unwillingness to express negative emotions or confront family members or friends directly, so therapists need to help such clients find ways to communicate better within that cultural context (Arredondo & Perez, 2003). Latino clinicians, being aware of the stigma associated with psychotherapy in their culture, are also developing ways to help their clients overcome ambivalence about seeking psychological help (Añez et al., 2008).

Being aware of cultural differences, however, does not mean that the therapist should stereotype clients. After all, some Latinos do have psychoses and some Irish do not carry burdens of guilt! It does mean that therapists must ensure that their clients find them to be trustworthy and effective; and it means that clients must be aware of their own prejudices too.

The Scientist–Practitioner Gap

Now suppose that Murray has found a nice psychotherapist who seems smart and friendly. Is that enough? How important is the *kind* of therapy that an individual practices?

These questions have generated a huge debate among clinical practitioners and psychological scientists. Many psychotherapists believe that trying to evaluate psychotherapy using standard empirical methods is an exercise in futility: Numbers and graphs, they say, cannot possibly capture the complex exchange that takes place between a therapist and a client. Psychotherapy, they maintain, is an art that you acquire from clinical experience; it is not a science. That's why almost any method will work for some people (Wampold, 2001). Other clinicians argue that efforts to measure the effectiveness of psychotherapy oversimplify the process, because, among other reasons, many patients have an assortment of emotional problems and need therapy for a longer time than research can reasonably allow (Westen, Novotny, & Thompson-Brenner, 2004).

For their part, psychological scientists agree that therapy is often a complex process. But that is no reason, they argue, that it cannot be scientifically investigated, just like any other complex psychological process such as the development of language or personality (Crits-Christoph, Wilson, & Hollon, 2005; Kazdin, 2008). Moreover, they are concerned that when therapists fail to keep up with empirical findings in the field, their clients may suffer. It is crucial, scientists say, for therapists to be aware of research findings on the most beneficial methods for particular problems, on ineffective or potentially harmful techniques, and on topics relevant to their practice, such as memory, hypnosis, and child development (Lilienfeld, Lynn, & Lohr, 2014).

Over the years, the breach between scientists and therapists has widened, creating what is commonly called the *scientist–practitioner gap* (Lilienfeld et al., 2013). One reason for the growing split has been the rise of professional schools that are not connected to academic psychology departments and that train students solely to do therapy. Graduates of these schools sometimes know little about research methods or even about research assessing different therapy techniques.

The scientist–practitioner gap has also widened because of the proliferation of unvalidated therapies in a crowded market. Some repackage established techniques under a new label; some are based simply on a therapist's name and popularity in the media. A blue-ribbon panel of clinical scientists, convened to assess the problem of the scientist–practitioner gap, reported that the current state of clinical psychology is comparable to that of medicine in the early 1900s, when physicians typically valued personal experience over scientific research. The authors concluded that a new accreditation system is necessary, one "that demands high quality science training as a central feature of doctoral training in clinical psychology" (Baker, McFall, & Shoham, 2008). In 2013, the Psychological Clinical Science Accreditation System, which approves the quality and level of scientific training in clinical programs, was recognized by the Council for Higher Education Accreditation—an important step toward improving clinical education.

Problems in Assessing Therapy

Because so many therapies all claim to be successful, and because of economic pressures on insurers and rising health costs, clinical psychologists are increasingly being called on to provide empirical assessments of therapy. Why can't you just ask people if the therapy helped them? The answer is that no matter what kind of therapy is involved, clients are motivated to tell you it worked. "Dr. Blitznik is a genius!" they will exclaim. "I would *never* have taken that job (or moved to Cincinnati, or found my true love) if it hadn't been for Dr. Blitznik!" Every kind of therapy ever devised

THINKING CRITICALLY

About Evaluating Psychotherapy

produces enthusiastic testimonials from people who feel it saved their lives.

The first problem with testimonials is that none of us can be our own control group. How do people know they wouldn't have taken the job, moved to Cincinnati, or found true love anyway—maybe even sooner, if Dr. Blitznik had not kept them in treatment? Second, Dr. Blitznik's success could be caused by a placebo effect: The client's anticipation of success and the buzz about Dr. B.'s fabulous new method might be the active ingredients, rather than Dr. B.'s therapy itself. Third, notice that you never hear testimonials from the people who dropped out, who weren't helped, or who actually got worse. So researchers cannot be satisfied with testimonials, no matter how glowing. They know that thanks to the *justification of effort* effect (see Chapter 7), people who have put time, money, and effort into something will tell you it was worth it. No one wants to say, "Yeah, I saw Dr. Blitznik for five years, and boy, was it ever a waste of time."

To guard against these problems, some clinical researchers conduct **randomized controlled trials**, in which people with a given problem or disorder are randomly assigned to one or more treatment groups or to a control group. Sometimes the results of randomized controlled trials have been startling. After natural or human-caused disasters, therapists often arrive on the scene to treat survivors for symptoms of trauma. In an intervention called Critical Incident Stress

Two young women comfort each other at a makeshift memorial for the victims of a shooting spree that left 12 dead and 58 wounded at a movie theatre in Aurora, Colorado. It is widely believed that most survivors of any disaster will need the help of therapists to avoid developing posttraumatic stress disorder. What do randomized controlled studies show?

randomized controlled trials Research designed to determine the effectiveness of a new medication or form of therapy, in which people with a given problem or disorder are randomly assigned to one or more treatment groups or to a control group.

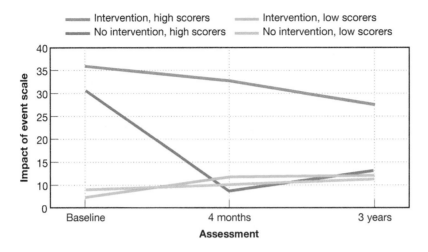

FIGURE 12.1 Do Posttraumatic Interventions Help or Harm?
Victims of serious car accidents were assessed at the time of the event, four months later, and three years later. Half received a form of posttraumatic intervention called Critical Incident Stress Debriefing; half received no treatment. As you can see, most people had recovered within four months, but one group continued to have a lot of stress symptoms even after three years: the people who were the most emotionally distressed right after the accident and who had received CISD. The intervention actually impeded their recovery (Mayou et al., 2000).

Debriefing (CISD), survivors gather in a group for "debriefing," which generally lasts from one to three hours. Participants are expected to disclose their thoughts and emotions about the traumatic experience, and the group leader warns members about traumatic symptoms that might develop.

Yet randomized controlled studies with people who have been through terrible experiences—including burns, accidents, miscarriages, violent crimes, and combat—find that posttraumatic interventions, especially those that require people to focus on their emotions and express them frequently, can actually *delay* recovery in some people (van Emmerik et al., 2002; McNally, Bryant, & Ehlers, 2003). In one study, victims of serious car accidents were followed for three years; some had received CISD and some had not. As you can see in Figure 12.1, almost everyone had recovered in only four months and remained fine after three years. The researchers then divided the survivors into two groups: those who had had a highly emotional reaction to the accident at the outset ("high scorers"), and those who had not. For the latter group, the intervention made no difference; they improved quickly anyway (Mayou et al., 2000).

Now, however, look at what happened to the people who had been the most traumatized by the accident: If they did *not* get CISD, they were fine in four months, too, like most of the others. But for those who *did* get the intervention, CISD actually blocked improvement, and they had higher stress symptoms than all the others in the study even after three years. The researchers concluded that "psychological debriefing is ineffective and has adverse long-term effects. It is not an appropriate

treatment for trauma victims" (Mayou, Ehlers, & Hobbs, 2000). The World Health Organization, which deals with survivors of trauma around the world, has officially endorsed this conclusion (van Ommeren, Saxena, & Saraceno, 2005).

You can see, then, why the scientific assessment of psychotherapeutic claims and methods is important.

👁 Watch the Video Thinking Like a Psychologist: Assessing Treatment Effectiveness at MyPsychLab

When Therapy Helps LO 12.11

We turn now to the evidence on which therapies are most effective (e.g., Chambless & Ollendick, 2001). For many specific problems and most emotional disorders, cognitive and behavior therapies have emerged as the methods of choice:

• **Depression.** Cognitive therapy's greatest success has been in the treatment of mood disorders, especially depression (Beck, 2005), and people in cognitive therapy are less likely than those on drugs to relapse when the treatment is over. The lessons learned in cognitive therapy last a long time after treatment, according to follow-ups done from 15 months to many years later (Hayes et al., 2004; Hollon, Thase, & Markowitz, 2002; Seligman et al., 1999).

• **Suicide attempts.** In a randomized controlled study of 120 adults who had attempted suicide and had been sent to an emergency room, those who were given 10 sessions of cognitive therapy were only about half as likely to attempt suicide again in the next 18 months as those who were simply given referrals for help (Brown et al., 2005).

- **Anxiety disorders.** Exposure techniques are more effective than any other treatment for PTSD, agoraphobia, and specific phobias such as fear of dogs or flying. CBT is often more effective than medication for panic disorder, generalized anxiety disorder, and obsessive-compulsive disorder (Barlow, 2004; Mitte, 2005; Otto et al., 2009; Tolin, 2010).

👁 **Watch** the **Video** Edna Foa: Anxiety Treatment at **MyPsychLab**

- **Anger and impulsive violence.** Cognitive therapy is often successful in reducing chronic anger, abusiveness, and hostility, and it also teaches people how to express anger more calmly and constructively (Deffenbacher et al., 2003).

- **Health problems.** Cognitive and behavior therapies are highly successful in helping people cope with pain, chronic fatigue syndrome, headaches, and irritable bowel syndrome; quit smoking; recover from eating disorders; overcome insomnia and other sleep problems; and manage other health problems (Butler et al., 1991; Crits-Christoph, Wilson, & Hollon, 2005; Skinner et al., 1990; Stepanski & Perlis, 2000).

- **Child and adolescent behavior problems.** Behavior therapy is the most effective treatment for behavior problems that range from bed-wetting to impulsive anger, and even for problems that have biological origins, such as autism (Rogers & Vismara, 2008). Behavior therapy works regardless of the child's age, the therapist's experience, or the specific problem (Weisz et al., 1995).

- **Relapses.** Cognitive-behavioral approaches can reduce the rate of relapse among people with problems such as substance abuse, depression, sexual offending, and even schizophrenia (Hayes et al., 2004; Witkiewitz & Marlatt, 2004).

However, no single type of therapy can help everyone. Despite their many successes, behavior and cognitive therapies have had some failures, especially with people who are unmotivated to carry out a behavioral or cognitive program or who have personality disorders. Also, cognitive-behavior therapies are designed for specific, identifiable problems, but sometimes people seek therapy for less clearly defined reasons, such as wishing to introspect about their feelings or explore moral dilemmas.

There is no simple rule for how long therapy needs to last. Sometimes a single session of treatment is enough to bring improvement, if it is based on sound principles. A therapy called *motivational interviewing*, which focuses specifically on increasing a client's motivation to overcome problems such as drinking, smoking, and binge eating, has been shown to be effective in as few as one or two sessions (Burke et al., 2003; Cassin et al., 2008; Miller & Rollnick, 2002). The therapist essentially puts the client into a state of cognitive dissonance (see Chapter 7): "I want to be healthy and I see myself as a smart, competent person, but here I am doing something stupid and self-defeating. Do I want to feel better or not?" The therapist then offers the client a cognitive and behavioral strategy of improvement (Wagner & Ingersoll, 2008).

Some problems, however, are chronic or particularly difficult to treat and respond better to longer therapy. According to one meta-analysis of eight randomized controlled studies, long-term psychodynamic therapy (lasting a year or more) can be more

THE SEVEN DWARFS AFTER THERAPY

Cognitive-behavior therapy can help people who are grumpy, bashful, and maybe even dopey—as well as people who have far more serious problems.

effective than short-term approaches for complex problems and personality disorders (Leichsenring & Rabung, 2008; see also Shedler, 2010).

Finally, some people and problems require combined approaches. Young adults with bipolar disorder, aggressive disorders, or schizophrenia are best helped by combining medication with family intervention therapies that teach parents behavioral skills for dealing with their troubled children, and that educate the family about how to cope with the illness constructively (Goldstein & Miklowitz, 1995; Miklowitz, 2007).

When Therapy Harms LO 12.12

In a tragic case that made news around the world, two social workers were convicted of recklessly causing the death of 10-year-old Candace Newmaker during a session of "rebirthing" therapy. The procedure supposedly helps adopted children form attachments to their adoptive parents by "reliving" birth. The child was tightly wrapped in a blanket (the "womb") and surrounded with large pillows. The therapists then pressed in on the pillows to simulate contractions and told the girl to push her way out of the blanket over her head. Candace repeatedly said that she could not breathe and felt she was going to die. But instead of unwrapping her, the therapists said, "You've got to push hard if you want to be born—or do you want to stay in there and die?" Candace lost consciousness and was rushed to a local hospital, where she died the next day.

Candace's tragic story is an extreme example, but every treatment and intervention carries some risks, and that includes psychotherapy.

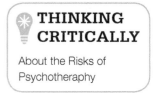

THINKING CRITICALLY

About the Risks of Psychotheraphy

In a small percentage of cases, a person's symptoms may worsen, new symptoms may be created, the client may become too dependent on the therapist, or the client's outside relationships may deteriorate (Dimidjian & Hollon, 2010; Lilienfeld, 2007). The risks to clients increase with any of the following:

1 **The use of empirically unsupported, potentially dangerous techniques.** "Rebirthing" therapy was born (so to speak) in the 1970s, when its founder claimed that, while taking a bath, he had re-experienced his own traumatic birth. But the basic assumptions of this method—that people can recover from trauma, insecure attachment, or other psychological problems by "reliving" their emergence from the womb—are contradicted by the vast research on infancy, attachment, memory, and posttraumatic stress disorder and its treatment.

Rebirthing is one of a variety of practices, collectively referred to as "attachment therapy," that are based on the use of harsh tactics that will allegedly help children bond with their parents. These techniques include withholding food, isolating the children for extended periods, humiliating them, pressing great weights upon them, and requiring them to exercise to exhaustion (Mercer, Sarner, & Rosa, 2003). However, abusive methods not only don't work; they often backfire, making the child angry, resentful, and withdrawn. They are hardly

Some forms of unvalidated psychotherapy can do harm. Candace Newmaker, age 10, was smothered to death during a session of "rebirthing" therapy. The therapists were convicted of reckless child abuse resulting in death. At right, a police officer from a then-new program called Drug Abuse and Resistance Education (DARE) warns young children about the dangers of drugs. Government support for the program was withdrawn when studies found that not only was it ineffective, but also it often boomeranged, increasing rates of drug abuse when the children grew up.

TABLE 12.3 Potentially Harmful Therapies

Intervention	Potential harm
Critical Incident Stress Debriefing	Heightened risk of PTSD
Scared Straight interventions	Worsening of conduct problems
Facilitated communication	False allegations of sexual and child abuse
Attachment therapies	Death and serious injury to children
Recovered memory techniques (e.g., dream analysis)	Induction of false memories of trauma; family breakups
"Multiple personality disorder"-oriented therapy	Induction of "multiple" personalities
Grief counseling for people with normal bereavement reactions	Increased depressive symptoms
Expressive-experiential therapies	Worsening and prolonging of painful emotions
Boot-camp interventions for conduct disorder	Worsening of aggression and conduct problems
Drug Abuse and Resistance Education (DARE)	Increased use of alcohol and other drugs

Source: Based on Lilienfeld (2007).

a way to help an adopted or emotionally troubled child feel more attached to his or her parents.

Table 12.3 lists a number of therapies that have been shown, through randomized controlled trials or meta-analysis, to have a significant risk of harming clients.

2 **Inappropriate or coercive influence by the therapist, which can create new problems for the client.** In any successful therapy, the therapist and client come to agree on an explanation for the client's problems. Of course, the therapist will influence this explanation, according to his or her training and philosophy. Some therapists, however, cross the line from persuasion to coercion. They believe so zealously in the prevalence of certain disorders that they actually induce the client to produce the symptoms they are looking for (Mazzoni, Loftus, & Kirsch, 2001; McHugh, 2008; Nathan, 2011). Therapist coercion is a likely reason for the huge numbers of people who were diagnosed with multiple personality disorder in the 1980s and 1990s (see Chapter 11) and for an epidemic of alleged memories of sexual abuse during this period (see Chapter 8).

3 **Prejudice or cultural ignorance on the part of the therapist.** Some therapists may be consciously or unconsciously prejudiced against some clients because of the client's gender, culture, religion, or sexual orientation, and may express their feelings in nonverbal ways that make the client feel misunderstood or disrespected (Sue et al., 2007). A therapist may also try to induce a client to conform to the therapist's values, even if they are not appropriate for the client. For many years, gay men and lesbians who entered therapy were told that homosexuality was a mental illness that could be cured. Some of the so-called treatments were harsh, such as electric shock for "inappropriate" arousal. Although these methods were discredited decades ago (Davison, 1976), other "reparative" therapies (whose practitioners claim they can turn gay men and lesbians into heterosexuals) still surface from time to time. But there is no reliable empirical evidence supporting these claims, and both the American Psychological Association and the American Psychiatric Association oppose reparative therapies on ethical and scientific grounds.

4 **Sexual intimacies or other unethical behavior on the part of the therapist.** Professional ethical guidelines prohibit clinical psychologists and psychiatrists from having any sexual intimacies with their clients or violating other professional boundaries. Occasionally, some therapists behave like cult leaders, persuading their clients that their mental health depends on staying in therapy and severing their connections to their "toxic" families (Watters & Ofshe, 1999). Such psychotherapy cults are created by the therapist's use of techniques that foster the client's isolation, prevent the client from terminating therapy, and reduce the client's ability to think critically.

To avoid these risks and benefit from what effective psychotherapy has to offer, people looking for the right therapy must become educated consumers, willing to use the critical-thinking skills we have emphasized throughout this book.

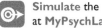 **Simulate** the **Experiment** Ineffective Therapies at **MyPsychLab**

Recite & Review

 Study and **Review** at **MyPsychLab**

Recite: Say aloud whatever you remember about cultural issues in psychotherapy, the scientist–practitioner gap, randomized controlled trials to evaluate therapies, problems for which cognitive or behavior therapy is the treatment of choice, and factors that increase the risk of harm in psychotherapy.

Review: Next, read this section as often as you need to, until you understand what makes psychotherapy successful or can make it harmful.

Now take this *Quick Quiz:*

1. Is the matching of cultures between a therapist and client important? Why?

2. Name any four areas where therapy can be helpful.

3. Ferdie is spending too much time playing softball and not enough time studying, so he signs up for "sportaholic therapy" (ST). The therapist tells him the cure for his "addiction" is to quit softball cold turkey and tap his temples three times whenever he feels the urge to play. After a few months, Ferdie announces that ST isn't helping and he's going to stop coming. The therapist gives him testimonials of clients who swear by ST, adding that Ferdie's doubts are actually a sign that the therapy is working. What is the major scientific flaw in this argument? (Bonus: What kind of therapy might help Ferdie manage his time better?)

Answers:

1. Yes. If the therapist and client share their culture, they are more likely to have a similar perception of the problem, concur on the best way of coping with it, and have the same expectations from the therapy. **2.** health problems; anxiety disorders; anger and impulsive violence; suicide attempts **3.** The therapist has violated the principle of falsifiability (see Chapter 1). If Ferdie is helped by the treatment, that shows it works; if he is not helped, that still shows it works and Ferdie is simply denying its benefits. Also, Ferdie is not hearing testimonials from people who have dropped out of ST and were not helped by it. (Bonus: A good behavioral time-management program might help, so Ferdie can play softball and get other things done, too.)

PSYCHOLOGY IN THE NEWS REVISITED ///////

Now that we have reviewed the major kinds of psychotherapy, along with their successes and risks, let's return to the issues raised by "pet therapy" in our opening story. In late 2012, the Department of Veterans Affairs (VA) announced that it would not pay for animal-assisted therapy for veterans with PTSD, brain injuries, and other mental disabilities, saying it was unclear whether the dogs benefit these veterans.

The VA's decision came as a sad surprise to the many individuals and organizations who are working to train dogs and pair them with veterans, prisoners, patients, and others who might benefit from having a canine companion. They recognize the need for scientific evidence, they say, but are moved by the many personal stories of veterans who say they've recovered from PTSD and other psychological problems, and gotten their lives back, as a result of having a service dog.

Attachment to pets is an emotional subject, and emotional reasoning is generally not the best way to determine the efficacy of a program or a belief. That is why research is important to verify whether pet therapy is effective, and for whom, and why (Lilienfeld & Arkowitz, 2008). Many therapies have

been started on the basis of someone's intuitive idea that "Sure, this will work," only to have the therapy's basic premise turn out to be wrong, as in the case of postcrisis interventions, or to be horribly dangerous, as is the case with rebirthing and other attachment therapies.

Rep. Grimm's bill would only fund a pilot program of research on pet therapy for veterans, but considerable research with other populations has already been done. In a study of nearly 200 people with serious mental illnesses, those with pets were coping and recovering more quickly than those without pets. The pet owners had lower blood pressure and felt more in control of their lives (Wisdom, Saedi, & Green, 2009). Still, there is a big difference between the use of animals as companions (for recreation and attachment) and animals used specifically as psychotherapy. After all, animals cannot help their doting humans solve problems, understand why a relationship is going south, or develop constructive ways of expressing anger. Further, some studies have found that for some people, pets have either no long-term benefits or add to their owners' stress and worry (Herzog, 2011).

Many questions remain. Does the severity of a person's disorder make a difference? What kind of pet is most helpful, for what kind of problem? Horses are being used successfully with people with a variety of mental and physical problems, but are horses and dogs (and cats!) special, or can birds, pigs, reptiles, and fluffy goats also be "animal therapists"? Until we know, two answers seem clear: There's no reason not to provide veterans with canine companions, and, nonetheless, we shouldn't oversimplify the issues involved.

If you ever decide to seek psychotherapy (with a human being), it's wise to be realistic about what it can and cannot do for you. In the hands of an empathic and knowledgeable practitioner, psychotherapy can help you make decisions and clarify your values and goals. It can teach you new skills and new ways of thinking. It can help you get along better with your family and break out of destructive family patterns. It can get you through bad times when no one seems to care or to understand what you are feeling. It can teach you how to manage depression, anxiety, and anger.

However, despite its many benefits, psychotherapy cannot transform you into someone you're not. It cannot turn an introvert into an extrovert. It cannot cure an emotional disorder overnight. It cannot provide a life without problems. And it is not intended to substitute for experience—for work that is satisfying, relationships that are sustaining, activities that are enjoyable. As Socrates knew, the unexamined life is not worth living. But, as we would add, the unlived life is not worth examining.

Taking Psychology With You

Becoming a Smart Consumer of Psychological Treatments

If you have a persistent problem that you do not know how to solve, one that causes you considerable unhappiness and that has lasted six months or more, it may be time to look for help. To take the lessons of this chapter with you, you might want to consider these suggestions:

Take all ads and Internet promotions for prescription drugs with a large grain of salt: Be skeptical! Remember that ads are not about educating you; they are about selling you a product. "New" is not necessarily better; many "me-too" drugs simply tinker with a blockbuster drug's formula in the smallest way, and then the pharmaceutical company is legally entitled to claim it is "new and improved." Check out any drug by going to reliable sources that are not funded by the pharmaceutical industry. The Public Citizen's Health Research Group publishes an excellent consumer guide, its monthly newsletter *Worst Pills, Best Pills*.

Make an informed decision when you choose a therapist. Make sure you are dealing with a reputable individual with appropriate credentials and training. Ask whether the therapist practices one of the empirically supported methods described in this chapter. Your school counseling center is a good place to start. You might also seek out a university psychology clinic, where you can get therapy with a graduate student in training; these students are closely supervised and the fees will be lower.

Choose a therapy most likely to help you. Begin by talking to the psychotherapist about your problem, and ask what intervention might best help you and how long he or she thinks the treatment will last. You should not spend four years in psychodynamic therapy for panic attacks, which can generally be helped in a few sessions of cognitive-behavior therapy. Likewise, if you have a specific emotional problem, such as depression, anger, or anxiety, or if you are coping with chronic health problems, look for a cognitive or behavior therapist. However, if you mostly want to discuss your life with a wise and empathic counselor, the kind of therapy may not matter so much.

Consider, but be wary of, online therapy delivered by apps, video, smartphone, or e-mail. Many people are unwilling or unable to go to a one-on-one therapy session, and online therapy can reach them (Kazdin & Blase, 2011). Some Internet programs work well, such as those that deliver monitored CBT instructions. However, if you start any kind of therapy with a professional therapist via e-mail, smartphone, or video, be sure the therapist is following government guidelines to protect your privacy. As for the many apps that offer to help you monitor and manage your moods and thoughts, they are only as good as the effort you put into them—and the critical thinking you bring to evaluating them.

Consider a self-help group. In the United States, an estimated 7 to 15 million adults belong to self-help groups (online and in person) for every possible problem or life crisis. Self-help groups can be reassuring in ways that family, friends, and psychotherapists sometimes may not be. For example, people with disabilities face unique challenges that involve coping not only with physical problems but also with the condescension and prejudice of many nondisabled people (Linton, 1998). However, self-help groups are not regulated by law or by professional standards, and they vary widely in their philosophies and methods. Some are accepting and tolerant; others are confrontational and coercive.

Choose self-help books that are scientifically based and promote realistic goals. Self-help books are available for every problem, from how to toilet train children to how to find happiness. To distinguish good ones from useless ones, avoid any book that promises the impossible—such as wealth, love, or self-esteem in 30 days. (Sorry.) Look for those based on research, not the author's pseudoscientific theories or personal opinions. People who have survived difficulties can tell inspirational stories, of course, but an author's vague advice to, say, "take charge of your life" won't go far. In contrast, when self-help books propose a step-by-step empirically supported program for readers to follow, they can actually be as effective as treatment administered by a therapist, *if* the reader follows through with the program (Rosen, Glasgow, & Moore, 2003). One such book is *Changing for Good* (Prochaska, Norcross, & DiClemente, 1994), which describes the ingredients of effective change that apply to people in and out of therapy.

It takes knowledge and critical thinking to know how to tell good therapies from potentially harmful ones, the real from the phony, and the phony from the fraudulent. Choose carefully.

Summary   ((Listen to the Audio File at MyPsychLab

Biological Treatments

- Biological treatments for mental disorders are in the ascendance because of research findings on genetic and biological contributions to some disorders and because of economic and social factors. The medications most commonly prescribed for mental disorders include *antipsychotic drugs*, used in treating schizophrenia and other psychotic disorders and, often inappropriately, in treating dementia, PTSD, and aggression disorders; *antidepressants*, used in treating depression, anxiety disorders, and obsessive-compulsive disorder; *antianxiety drugs (tranquilizers)*, often prescribed for anxiety and other emotional problems; and *lithium carbonate*, a salt used to treat bipolar disorder.

- Because of the *publication bias*, studies that find positive results are more likely to be published than those that find no improvement or negative effects. Drawbacks of drug treatment include the *placebo effect*; high dropout and relapse rates among people who take medications without also learning how to cope with their problems or who have been given the incorrect dose (a person's ethnicity, sex, and age can influence a drug's effectiveness); the tendency to overlook nonmedical treatments that may be as effective or even better; unknown risks of prolonged use of medication and from possible drug interactions when several are being taken; and the potential harms of increased doses and untested off-label uses. Medication can be helpful and can even save lives, but in an age in which commercial interests are heavily invested in promoting drugs for psychological problems, the public is largely unaware of drugs' limitations and potential risks.

- When drugs and psychotherapy have failed to help seriously disturbed people, some psychiatrists have intervened directly in the brain (*psychosurgery*). *Prefrontal lobotomy* never had any scientific validation, yet was performed on many thousands of people. Nonsurgical forms of brain intervention include *electroconvulsive therapy* (ECT), in which a brief current is sent through the brain. ECT has been used successfully to treat suicidal depression, although its benefits rarely last. *Transcranial magnetic stimulation* (TMS) and *transcranial direct current stimulation* (tDCS), two newer methods of electrically stimulating the brain, are being studied as ways of treating severe depression.

Major Schools of Psychotherapy

- *Psychodynamic ("depth") therapies* include Freudian *psychoanalysis* and its modern variations. These therapies explore unconscious dynamics and emotions, childhood experiences, and fantasies, and focus on the process of *transference* to break through the patient's defenses.

- *Behavior therapists* draw on classical and operant principles of learning. They use such methods as *graduated exposure* and *flooding*; *systematic desensitization*, based on *counterconditioning*; *behavioral self-monitoring*; and *skills training*. Some behavior therapists use virtual reality techniques for systematic desensitization.

- *Cognitive therapists* aim to change the irrational thoughts that give rise to negative emotions and self-defeating actions. Aaron Beck's cognitive therapy and Albert Ellis's *rational emotive behavior therapy* were pioneering forms of cognitive therapy. Today cognitive and behavioral techniques are commonly combined in the practice of *cognitive-behavior therapy* (CBT). Some cognitive-behavioral therapists teach clients to pay mindful attention to their negative emotions and "irrational" thoughts, learn to accept them, and act despite these feelings rather than constantly fighting to eradicate them.

- *Humanist therapy* holds that human nature is essentially good and attempts to help people feel better about themselves by focusing on here-and-now issues and on their capacity for change. Carl Rogers's *client-centered therapy* emphasizes the importance of the therapist's empathy and ability to provide *unconditional positive regard*. *Existential therapy* helps people cope with the dilemmas of existence, such as the meaning of life and the fear of death.

- *Family therapy is* based on the view that individual problems develop in the context of the whole family. The *family-systems perspective* helps families understand that any one person's behavior in the family affects everyone else. In *couples therapy*, the therapist usually sees both partners in a relationship to help them resolve ongoing disputes or to help them accept and live with qualities of the partner that are unlikely to change.

- In practice, most therapists draw on various methods and ideas. They aim to replace a client's pessimistic or unrealistic life story with one that is more hopeful and attainable.

Evaluating Psychotherapy

- Successful therapy begins with an alliance between the therapist and the client. When the therapist and client are of different ethnicities or cultures, the therapist must be able to distinguish normal cultural patterns from signs of mental illness, and both parties must be aware of potential prejudice and misunderstandings.

- A *scientist–practitioner gap* has developed because of the different assumptions that researchers and many clinicians hold regarding the value of empirical research for doing psychotherapy and for assessing its effectiveness. The gap has led to a proliferation of scientifically unsupported psychotherapies.

- In assessing the effectiveness of psychotherapy, researchers need to control for the placebo effect and the *justification of effort* effect. They rely on *randomized controlled trials* to determine which therapies are empirically supported, which are not, and which may even delay recovery.

- Some psychotherapies are better than others for specific problems. Behavior and cognitive therapies are often the most effective for depression, anxiety disorders, anger problems, certain health problems, and childhood and adolescent behavior problems. Family-systems therapies are especially helpful for children with behavior problems and young adults with schizophrenia.

- The length of time needed for successful therapy depends on the problem and the individual. Some methods, such as *motivational interviewing*, produce benefits in only a session or two; long-term psychodynamic therapy can be helpful for people with severe disorders and personality problems. Some problems and individuals respond best to combined therapeutic approaches.

- In some cases, therapy is harmful. The therapist may use empirically unsupported and potentially harmful techniques, such as "rebirthing"; inadvertently create new disorders in the client through undue influence or coercion; hold a prejudice about the client's gender, ethnicity, religion, or sexual orientation; or behave unethically, for example by permitting a sexual relationship with the client.

Psychology in the News, Revisited

- Animal-assisted therapies are being studied empirically to assess their benefits and limitations, just as all psychotherapies should be.

Taking Psychology With You

- To protect themselves, consumers need to know how to find a therapist and the kind of therapy best suited to their problems. They need to be wary of Internet promotions for medications or fad therapies; choose a therapist who is reputable and well trained; and select an empirically validated therapy. People seeking therapy should also be cautious about online therapy and choose self-help groups or books carefully.

Key Terms

antipsychotic drugs (neuroleptics) 434
antidepressant drugs 435
monoamine oxidase inhibitors (MAOIs) 435
tricyclic antidepressants 435
selective serotonin reuptake inhibitors (SSRIs) 435
antianxiety drugs (tranquilizers) 435
beta blockers 435
lithium carbonate 436
publication bias 436
placebo effect 437
prefrontal lobotomy 438

electroconvulsive therapy (ECT) 439
transcranial magnetic stimulation (TMS) 439
transcranial direct current stimulation (tDCS) 439
psychoanalysis 440
psychodynamic ("depth") therapies 440
transference 440
behavior therapy 441
graduated exposure 441
flooding 441
systematic desensitization 441

counterconditioning 441
behavioral self-monitoring 441
skills training 442
cognitive therapy 442
Aaron Beck 443
Albert Ellis 443
rational emotive behavior therapy 443
cognitive-behavior therapy (CBT) 443
humanist therapy 444
client-centered therapy 444
Carl Rogers 444

unconditional positive regard 444
existential therapy 444
family therapy 445
family-systems perspective 445
couples therapy 445
scientist–practitioner gap 449
justification of effort 449
randomized controlled trials 449
motivational interviewing 451

Biological Treatments

Medications for Mental Disorder

Drugs commonly prescribed for mental disorders include:
- **antipsychotics**, used in treating schizophrenia and other psychotic disorders.
- **antidepressants**, used in treating depression, chronic anxiety disorders, and obsessive-compulsive disorder.
- **antianxiety drugs (tranquilizers)**, often prescribed for acute cases of anxiety.
- **lithium carbonate**, a salt used to treat bipolar disorder.

Cautions About Drug Treatments

Drawbacks of drug treatment include:
- the **placebo effect**.
- high dropout and relapse rates.
- disregard for effective nonmedical treatments.
- unknown risks over time and drug interactions.
- untested off-label uses.

Direct Brain Intervention

- In *psychosurgery*, neurosurgeons intervene directly in the brain.
- *Electroconvulsive therapy* (ECT), in which a brief current is sent through the brain, has been used successfully to treat suicidal depression, but its effects are short-lived and the depression almost always returns. ECT is ineffective for other disorders.
- *Transcranial magnetic stimulation* (TMS) and *transcranial direct current stimulation* (tDCS) are two newer methods of stimulating the brain to treat depression, but long-term efficacy is still unknown.

Major Schools of Psychotherapy

Psychodynamic Therapy

Psychodynamic therapies, including Freudian **psychoanalysis** and its modern variations, explore the unconscious through techniques such as **transference**.

Behavior and Cognitive Therapy

Behavior therapy applies principles of classical and operant conditioning to help change problematic behaviors. It uses such methods as:
- **graduated exposure** and **flooding**.
- **systematic desensitization**.
- **behavioral self-monitoring**.
- **skills training**.

Cognitive therapy identifies ways of thinking that generate negative emotions and self-defeating thoughts; often combined with behavioral methods in *cognitive-behavior therapy* (CBT).
- Aaron Beck was a pioneer in using cognitive therapy for depression.
- Another leading cognitive approach is Albert Ellis's *rational emotive behavior therapy*.
- Many CBT practitioners now emphasize mindfulness and acceptance of unwanted, unpleasant feelings rather than trying to eliminate them.

Humanist and Existential Therapy

Humanist therapy is based on the philosophy of humanism, which stresses the client's free will to change rather than past conflicts.
- Carl Rogers's **client-centered therapy** emphasizes the therapist's role in providing empathy and *unconditional positive regard* for the client.
- **Existential therapy** helps people cope with philosophical issues such as the meaning of life and acceptance of death.

Family and Couples Therapies

- *Family therapy* is based on a **family-systems perspective**, understanding that one person's behavior affects the whole family.
- *Couples therapy* is designed to help couples understand and resolve the inevitable conflicts that occur in relationships.

Evaluating Psychotherapy

The Scientist–Practitioner Gap

A *scientist–practitioner gap* has led to a proliferation of scientifically unsupported therapies, such as Critical Incident Stress Debriefing.

↓

Problems in Assessing Therapy

To determine whether a particular therapeutic approach is beneficial or potentially harmful, clinical scientists conduct **randomized controlled trials**. The evaluation of any therapy must control for:

- the placebo effect.
- the justification of effort.

Therapists and clients must be alert to prejudices and cultural differences between them that might cause misunderstandings.

When Therapy Helps

Cognitive-behavior therapy is most effective for:
- depression.
- suicide attempts.
- anxiety disorders.
- anger and impulsive violence.
- health problems.
- childhood and adolescent behavior problems.
- preventing relapse.

Successful therapy can be brief, as in *motivational interviewing*, or need more time, depending on the individual and problem being treated. Combined methods (such as medication and psychotherapy) may be necessary to help particular individuals or address difficult problems, such asschizophrenia.

When Therapy Harms

Psychotherapy can be risky for clients if the therapist:
- uses empirically unsupported and potentially harmful techniques.
- creates disorders or new symptoms through suggestion or coercion.
- is prejudiced against a client.
- is unethical.

TABLE 12.2 The Major Schools of Therapy Compared

	Primary Goal	Methods
Psychodynamic	Insight into unconscious motives and feelings that create and prolong symptoms	Probing unconscious motives and fantasies, exploring childhood experiences, examining issues and emotions raised by transference
Cognitive-Behavioral		
Behavioral	Modification of self-defeating behaviors	Graduated exposure and flooding, systematic desensitization, behavioral records, skills training
Cognitive	Modification of irrational or unvalidated beliefs	Prompting the client to test beliefs against evidence; exposing the faulty reasoning in catastrophizing and mind-reading; sometimes helping the client accept unpleasant thoughts and feelings and live with them, instead of trying to eradicate them
Humanist and Existential		
Humanist	Insight; self-acceptance and self-fulfillment; new, more optimistic perceptions of oneself and the world	Providing empathy, unconditional positive regard, and a nonjudgmental setting in which to discuss issues
Existential	Finding meaning in life and accepting inevitable losses	Varies with the therapist; philosophic discussions about the meaning of life, the client's goals, finding the courage to survive loss and suffering
Family and Couples		
Family	Modification of family patterns	May use any of the preceding methods to change family patterns that perpetuate problems and conflicts
Couples	Resolution of conflicts, breaking out of destructive habits	May use any of the preceding methods to help the couple communicate better, resolve conflicts, or accept what cannot be changed

13

The Nature of Emotion: Body, Mind, and Culture

The Nature of Stress

Stress and Emotion

Coping With Stress

Psychology in the News, Revisited

Taking Psychology With You: The Dilemma of Anger: "Let It Out" or "Bottle It Up"?

EMOTION, STRESS, AND HEALTH

PSYCHOLOGY IN THE NEWS ///////////////////////////////

Man Crashes Plane Into Austin, Texas, IRS Office

AUSTIN, TX, February 18, 2010. A software engineer who was angry with the Internal Revenue Service launched a suicide attack on the agency Thursday by crashing his small plane into a seven-story office building housing nearly 200 IRS employees, setting off a raging fire that sent workers fleeing for their lives. In addition to the attacker, two employees died in the blaze and two others were seriously burned.

The pilot has been identified as Andrew Joseph (Joe) Stack III, 53, of Austin, who posted a furious, six-page antigovernment farewell note on the Web before getting into his plane for his suicidal flight. Stack cited run-ins with the IRS and ranted about taxes, government bailouts, and corporate America's "thugs and plunderers." "I have had all I can stand," he wrote. "Well, Mr. Big Brother I.R.S. man, let's try something different, take my pound of flesh and sleep well."

Officials almost immediately ruled out the possibility that Stack was connected to terrorist groups. Friends described him as an easygoing man, a talented amateur musician, a husband with marital troubles, and a citizen with a grudge against the tax authorities. Although he was only 53, they said, he felt pushed "over the brink" because financial setbacks had required him to postpone his retirement dreams.

Stack also set fire to his house, which was about six miles from the crash site, before embarking on the suicide flight. His wife and her young daughter had escaped the night before.

Stack married Sheryl Housh about three years ago. He never spoke of his troubles with the IRS to her family, who thought he seemed fine when they gathered at Christmas.

Fire inspectors assess the damage to the office building destroyed by a man who was angry at the IRS and upset about recent financial setbacks. Two workers died in the blaze.

But recently his wife complained to her mother and stepfather, Jack Cook, of an increasingly frightening anger in her husband, which she said was causing terrible problems in the marriage. Worried about her husband's rage, Sheryl Stack took her 12-year-old daughter to a hotel to get away from him. They returned on Thursday morning to find their house ablaze and all of their belongings destroyed. Officials said the house fire was deliberately set, with Stack as the primary suspect.

"This is a shock to me that he would do something like this," Cook said. "But you get your anger up, you do it."

//////////

Almost everyone can understand Joe Stack's feelings of frustration, unhappiness, and anger, if not about their specific target. Fortunately, most people do not act on them the way Stack did. Why do some people give in to their emotions, whereas others are able to keep rage and other unpleasant feelings from turning into violent or self-destructive actions? Why are some people able to cope with the stresses of life—financial worries, broken expectations, marital conflicts, job loss—whereas others are completely overwhelmed and give up?

People often curse their emotions, wishing to be freed from anger, jealousy, shame, guilt, and grief. Yet imagine a life without emotions. You would be unmoved by the magic of music. You would never care about losing someone you love, not only because you would not know sadness but also because you would not know love. You would never laugh because nothing would strike you as funny. And you would be a social isolate because you would not be able to know what other people were feeling.

People often wish for a life without stress, too. Yet try to imagine a life without any stress whatsoever. You would live like a robot. You might have no difficulties, but nothing would surprise, delight, or challenge you either. You would not grow, discover new frontiers, or be required to master skills you never imagined possible.

In this chapter, we will examine the physiology and psychology of emotions and stress. Prolonged anger and other negative emotions can certainly be stressful, and stress can certainly produce negative emotions. Both of these processes, however, are shaped by how we interpret the events that happen to us, by the demands of the situation we are in, and by the rules of our culture.

You are about to learn...

- which facial expressions of emotion are recognized by most people the world over.
- which parts of the brain are involved with different aspects of emotion.
- how mirror neurons generate empathy, mood contagion, and synchrony.
- which two hormones provide the energy and excitement of emotion.
- how thoughts create emotions—and why an infant can't feel shame or guilt.

The Nature of Emotion
LO 13.1

Emotions evolved to help people meet the challenges of life: They bind people together, motivate them to achieve their goals, and help them make decisions and plans (Nesse & Ellsworth, 2009). When you are faced with a decision between two appealing and justifiable career alternatives, your sense of which one "feels right" emotionally may help you make the better choice.

Disgust, though it's not a pleasant emotion, evolved as a mechanism that protects infants and adults from eating tainted or poisonous food (Oaten, Stevenson, & Case, 2009). Embarrassment and blushing, so painful to

emotion A state of arousal involving facial and bodily changes, brain activation, cognitive appraisals, subjective feelings, and tendencies toward action.

facial feedback The process by which the facial muscles send messages to the brain about the basic emotion being expressed.

an individual, also serve important functions: appeasing others when you feel you have made a fool of yourself, broken a moral rule, or violated a social norm (Dijk, de Jong, & Peters, 2009; Feinberg, Willer, & Keltner, 2012). And the positive emotions of joy, love, laughter, and playfulness do not appear to be simply selfish feelings of pleasure; their adaptive function may be to help increase mental flexibility and resilience, build bonds with others, stimulate creativity, and reduce stress (Baas, De Dreu, & Nijstad, 2008; Kok, Catalino, & Frederickson, 2008).

The components of **emotion** are *physiological* changes in the face, brain, and body; *cognitive* processes such as interpretations of events; *action tendencies* that spur us to fight or flee, embrace or withdraw; and subjective feelings. In turn, *culture* and *social context* influence both the inner experience and the outward expression of emotion. If we compare human emotions to a sculpture, the biological capacity for emotion is the clay; thoughts create its size, shape, and details; and culture judges the result, placing some sculptures front and center and relegating others to the attic.

Emotion and the Body LO 13.2

Everywhere on the planet, people feel certain basic emotions, including fear, anger, sadness, joy, surprise, disgust, shame, embarrassment, and contempt (Izard, 2007; Keltner & Buswell, 1997). These emotions have distinctive physiological patterns and corresponding facial expressions, but they and others are also evoked by common human experiences: All over the world, sadness follows perception of loss, fear follows perception of threat and bodily harm, anger follows perception of insult or injustice, and so forth (Scherer, 1997).

Let's begin with some findings from neuroscientists and others who are studying the biological aspects of emotions: facial expressions, brain regions and circuits, and the autonomic nervous system.

The Face of Emotion. The most obvious place to look for emotion is on the face, where emotions are often visibly expressed. In 1872, Charles Darwin argued that human facial expressions—the smile, the frown, the grimace, the glare—are as innate as the wing flutter of a frightened bird, the purr of a contented cat, and the snarl of a threatened wolf. Such expressions evolved, he

said, because they allowed our ancestors to tell at a glance the difference between a friendly stranger and a hostile one, prepared our forbears to respond to challenges in the environment, and enabled them to communicate important information to others.

Modern psychologists have supported Darwin's ideas about the evolutionary functions of emotion (Hess & Thibault, 2009; Shariff & Tracy, 2011). Years ago, Paul Ekman and his colleagues gathered abundant evidence for the universality of the facial expressions of seven emotions: anger, happiness, fear, surprise, disgust, sadness, and contempt (Ekman, 2003; Ekman et al., 1987). In every culture they studied—in Brazil, Chile, Estonia, Germany, Greece, Hong Kong, Italy, Japan, New Guinea, Scotland, Sumatra, Turkey, and the United States—a large majority of people recognized the emotional expressions portrayed by those in other cultures (see Figure 13.1). Even most members of isolated tribes who had never watched a movie or read *People* magazine, such as the Foré of New Guinea or the Minangkabau of West Sumatra, could recognize the emotions expressed in pictures of people who are entirely foreign to them, and Westerners could recognize theirs. Some researchers have added pride to the list, arguing that its adaptive function is to motivate people to achieve and excel, and thereby to increase their attractiveness to others and to their groups (Tracy & Robins, 2008; Williams & DeSteno, 2009).

Simulate the Experiment Recognizing Facial Expressions of Emotions at **MyPsychLab**

Ekman and his associates developed a coding system to analyze and identify each of the nearly 80 muscles of the face, as well as the combinations of muscles associated with each emotion (Ekman, 2003). When people try to hide their feelings and display a false emotion, they generally use different groups of muscles than they do for authentic ones. If they try to pretend that they feel sad, only 15 percent manage to get the eyebrows, eyelids, and forehead wrinkle exactly right, as they would if they were expressing true grief spontaneously. Authentic smiles last only 2 seconds; false smiles may last 10 seconds or more (Ekman, Friesen, & O'Sullivan, 1988).

The Functions of Facial Expressions. Interestingly, facial expressions not only reflect our internal feelings but also *influence* them. In the process of **facial feedback**, the facial muscles send messages to the brain about the basic emotion

FIGURE 13.1 Some Universal Expressions
Most people around the world can readily identify expressions of surprise, disgust, sadness, anger, fear, happiness, and contempt, no matter the age, culture, sex, or historical era of the person conveying the emotion.

being expressed: A smile tells us that we're happy, a frown that we're angry or perplexed (Izard, 1990). When people are told to smile and look pleased or happy, their positive feelings increase. When they are asked to position their mouths in a way that mimics a smile, their stress responses, such as heart rate, decline—even though they don't realize they are smiling (Kraft & Pressman, 2012). Conversely, when people are told to look angry, displeased, or disgusted, positive feelings decrease. If you put on an angry face, your heart rate will rise faster than if you put on a happy face (Kleinke, Peterson, & Rutledge, 1998; Levenson, Ekman, & Friesen, 1990). The next time you are feeling sad, angry, or afraid, try purposely smiling, even if no one is around. Keep smiling. Does facial feedback work for you?

What happens when facial feedback is blocked—say, because of the cosmetic use of botulinum toxin-A, commonly known by the trade name Botox, which paralyzes the facial muscles used in frowning? In a study of 40 women who were tested before and after having Botox injections, researchers found that Botox hindered the women's ability to correctly interpret sentences evoking sadness and anger (Havas et al., 2010). Botoxed women are also significantly less accurate than other women at recognizing both positive and negative emotions in photographs of human eyes (Neal & Chartrand, 2011).

As Darwin suggested, facial expressions also probably evolved to help us communicate our emotional states to others and provoke a response from them—"Come help me!" "Get away!"

Heidi Stetson Mario

Great moms have always understood the importance of facial feedback.

(Fridlund, 1994). This signaling function begins in infancy. A baby's expressions of misery or frustration are apparent to most parents, who respond by soothing an uncomfortable baby or feeding a grumpy one (Izard, 1994b; Stenberg & Campos, 1990). And an infant's happy smile usually melts the heart of the weariest parent, provoking a happy cuddle.

By the age of 6 to 7 months, babies reveal a special sensitivity to adults' fearful expressions (Leppänen & Nelson, 2012) and soon begin to alter their own behavior in reaction to their parents' facial expressions of emotion. This ability, too, has survival value. The visual-cliff studies described in Chapter 6 (page 229) were originally designed to test for depth perception, which emerges early in infancy. But in one experiment, 1-year-old babies were put on a more ambiguous visual cliff that did not drop off sharply and thus did not automatically evoke fear, as the original cliff did. In this case, the babies' behavior depended on their mothers' expressions: 74 percent crossed the cliff when their mothers put on a happy, reassuring expression, but not a single infant crossed when the mother showed an expression of fear (Sorce et al., 1985). If you have ever watched a toddler take a tumble and then look at his or her parent before deciding whether to cry or to forget it,

you will understand the importance of parental facial expressions.

Still, there are cultural, social, and individual limits to the supposedly universal readability of facial expressions. When you perceive another person's expression, you are influenced by what else is happening in the situation, by your own emotional state, and by the cultural context (Barrett, Mesquita, & Gendron, 2011). People are better at identifying emotions expressed by others in their own ethnic, national, or regional group than they are at recognizing the emotions of foreigners (Elfenbein & Ambady, 2003). And people who are habitually angry and aggressive are more likely to interpret other people's neutral facial expressions as being "angry"—which of course maintains their anger and hostility (Penton-Voak et al., 2013).

Moreover, within a culture, facial expressions can have different meanings depending on the situation; a smile can mean "I'm happy!" or "I don't want to make you angry while I tell you this." Likewise, people often interpret identical facial expressions—even of universal emotions such as disgust, sadness, and anger—in different ways, depending on what else they are observing in the immediate situation. For example, almost all adults recognize the expression of disgust, if that's all they see in a picture of a face. But when they see a picture of the same disgusted expression on a man with his arm raised as if to strike, they will say the expression is anger (Aviezer et al., 2008).

Finally, of course, facial expressions are only part of the emotional picture. People can feel sad, anxious, or angry without letting it show—and, conversely, they can use facial expressions to lie about their feelings. In Shakespeare's play *Henry VI*, the villain who will become the evil King Richard III says:

> *Why, I can smile, and murder while I smile;*
> *And cry content to that which grieves my heart;*
> *And wet my cheeks with artificial tears,*
> *And frame my face to all occasions.*

Emotion and the Brain. LO 13.3 Various parts of the brain are involved in the different components of emotional experience: recognizing another person's emotion, feeling a specific emotion, expressing an emotion, and acting on an emotion. People who have a stroke that affects brain areas involved in disgust are often unable to feel disgusted. One young man with stroke damage in these regions had little or no emotional response to images and ideas that would be disgusting to most people, such as feces-shaped chocolate (Calder et al., 2000). Are you making a disgusted expression as you read that? He couldn't.

Most emotions motivate a response (an *action tendency*) of some sort: to embrace or approach the person who instills joy in you, attack a person who makes you angry, withdraw from a food that disgusts you, or flee from a person or situation that frightens you (Frijda, Kuipers, & ter Schure, 1989). The prefrontal regions of the brain are involved in these impulses to approach or withdraw. Regions of the *right* prefrontal region are specialized for the impulse to withdraw or escape, as in disgust and fear. Regions of the *left* prefrontal cortex are specialized for the motivation to approach others, as in happiness (a positive emotion) and anger (a negative one) (Carver & Harmon-Jones, 2009; Harmon-Jones, Peterson, & Harris, 2009). People who have greater-than-average activation of the left areas, compared with the right, have more positive feelings, a quicker ability to recover from negative emotions, and a greater ability to suppress negative emotions (Urry et al., 2004). People with damage to this area often lose the capacity for joy.

Parts of the prefrontal cortex are also involved in the *regulation* of emotion, helping us modify and control our feelings, keeping us on an even keel, and allowing us to respond appropriately to others (Jackson et al., 2003). A degenerative disease that destroys cells in parts of the frontal lobes causes a profound change in personality: Sufferers may become unable to respond to the emotions of others, understand why they and others feel as they do, and adjust their own emotional responses appropriately. A loving mother becomes indifferent to her child's injury; a businessman does embarrassing things and doesn't notice the reaction of others (Levenson & Miller, 2007).

Watch the **Video** James Coan: Emotion Regulation at **MyPsychLab**

The *amygdala* plays a key role in emotion, especially anger and fear (see Chapter 4). It is responsible for evaluating sensory information, determining its emotional importance, and making the initial decision to approach or withdraw from a person or situation (LeDoux, 1996). The amygdala instantly assesses danger or threat, which is a good thing, because otherwise you could be standing in the street asking, "Is it wise to cross now, while that large truck is coming toward me?" The amygdala's initial response may then be overridden by a more accurate appraisal from the cortex. This is why you jump with fear when you suddenly feel a hand on your back in a dark alley, and why your fear evaporates when the cortex registers that the hand belongs to a friend whose lousy idea of humor is to scare you in a dark alley.

Get Involved! Turn on Your Right Hemisphere

These faces have expressions of happiness on one side and sadness on the other. Look at the nose of each face; which face looks happier? Which face looks sadder?

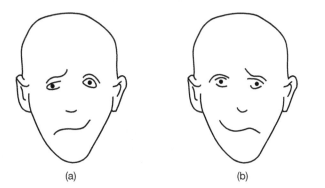

(a)   (b)

You are likely to see face *b* as the happier one and face *a* as the sadder one. The likely reason is that in most people the left side of a picture is processed by the right side of the brain, where recognition of emotional expression primarily occurs (Oatley, Keltner, & Jenkins, 2006).

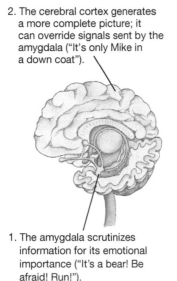

2. The cerebral cortex generates a more complete picture; it can override signals sent by the amygdala ("It's only Mike in a down coat").

1. The amygdala scrutinizes information for its emotional importance ("It's a bear! Be afraid! Run!").

If either the amygdala or critical areas of the cortex are damaged, abnormalities occur in the ability to experience fear or recognize it in others. A patient known as S. M. has a rare disease that destroyed her amygdala, and as a result she cannot feel fear—not toward snakes, not when watching scary movies, not even when she was being attacked in a park by a man with a knife (Feinstein et al., 2011). In a subsequent experiment, she did feel panicky when inhaling carbon monoxide that induced a feeling of suffocation, showing that she can feel fear when the cues are internal; but she does not experience fear when the causes are external (Feinstein et al., 2013). People with damage in the cortex may also have difficulty turning off their own fear responses, causing excessive and chronic anxiety.

Mirror, Mirror, in the Brain: Neurons for Imitation and Empathy. LO 13.4,

Some years ago, a team of Italian neuroscientists accidentally made an astonishing discovery. They had implanted wires in the brains of macaque monkeys, in regions involved in planning and carrying out movement. Every time a monkey moved and grasped an object, the cells fired and the monitor registered the brain activity. Then one day, a graduate student heard the monitor go off when the monkey was simply observing him eating an ice cream cone.

The neuroscientists looked more closely, and found that certain neurons in the monkeys' brains were firing not only when the monkeys were picking up peanuts and eating them but also when the monkeys were merely observing their human caretakers doing exactly the same thing. These neurons responded only to specific actions: A neuron that fired when a monkey grasped a peanut would also fire when

the scientist grasped a peanut but not when the scientist grasped something else (Rizzolatti & Sinigaglia, 2010). The scientists called these cells **mirror neurons**.

Human beings also have mirror neurons that fire when we observe others doing something and when we mimic the action ourselves. The "mirror system," containing millions of neurons, helps us identify what others are feeling, understand other people's intentions, and imitate their actions and gestures (Iacoboni, 2008; Fogassi & Ferrari, 2007). When you see another person in pain, one reason you feel a jolt of empathy is that mirror neurons involved in pain are firing. When you watch a spider crawl up someone's leg, one reason you have a creepy sensation is that your mirror neurons are firing—the same ones that would fire if the spider were crawling up your own leg. And when you see another person's facial expression, your own facial muscles will often subtly mimic it, activating a similar emotional state (Dimberg, Thunberg, & Elmehed, 2000).

The discovery of mirror neurons is exciting, but some popular writers have exaggerated its implications (Gallese et al., 2011). For example, these neurons seem strongly involved in empathy, but empathy has social limits: Mirror neurons go to sleep when people look at individuals they dislike or are prejudiced against. If you like a person, mimicking their facial movements and gestures will increase that liking, but if you dislike the person, trying to perk up your mirror neurons by mimicking won't improve matters at all (Stel et al., 2010; van Baaren et al., 2009).

Among people who do like each other or are in the same social or ethnic group, mirror neurons may be the mechanism responsible for *mood contagion*, the spreading of an emotion from one person to another. Have you ever been in a cheerful mood, had lunch with a depressed friend, and come away

mirror neurons Brain cells that fire when a person or animal observes another carrying out an action; these neurons appear to be involved in empathy, imitation, and reading emotions.

Mirror neurons are surely at work in this conversation.

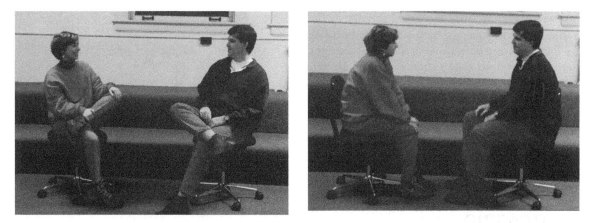

These volunteers, videotaped in a study of conversational synchrony, are obviously in sync with each other, even though they have just met. The degree to which two people's gestures and expressions are synchronized increases the rapport they feel with one another (Grahe & Bernieri, 1999).

feeling vaguely depressed yourself? Have you ever stopped to have a chat with a friend who was nervous about an upcoming exam and ended up feeling edgy yourself? That's mood contagion at work.

Mood contagion also occurs when two people are influenced by one another's *positive* emotions, nonverbal signals, and posture: Their gestures become more synchronized, they behave more cooperatively, and they feel more cheerful (Wiltermuth & Heath, 2009). This phenomenon may be the reason that synchronized human activities—marches, bands, dancing—are socially and emotionally beneficial as well as exciting.

The Energy of Emotion. LO 13.5 Once the brain areas associated with emotion are activated, the next stage is the release of hormones to enable you to respond quickly. When you are under stress or feeling an intense emotion, the sympathetic division of the autonomic nervous system spurs the adrenal glands to send out *epinephrine* and *norepinephrine* (see Chapter 4). These chemical messengers produce arousal and alertness. The pupils dilate, widening to allow in more light; the heart beats faster, blood pressure increases, breathing speeds up, and blood sugar rises. These changes provide the body with the energy needed to take action, whether you are happy and want to get close to someone you love, or are scared and want to escape a person who is frightening you (Löw et al., 2008). All emotions share a neural circuitry that affects the degree of arousal (how intensely you experience an emotion) and subjective ratings of how pleasant or unpleasant the feeling is (Wilson-Mendenhall, Barrett, & Barsalou, 2013).

Epinephrine in particular provides the energy of an emotion, that familiar tingle of excitement. At high levels, it can create the sensation of being "seized" or "flooded" by an emotion that is out of your control. In a sense, you *are* out of control because you cannot consciously alter your heart rate and blood pressure. However, you can learn to control your actions when you are under the sway of an emotion (even intense anger, as we discuss in "Taking Psychology With You"). Eventually, as arousal subsides, anger may pale into annoyance, ecstasy into contentment, fear into suspicion, past emotional whirlwinds into calm breezes.

In sum, the physiology of emotion involves characteristic facial expressions; activity in specific parts of the brain, notably the amygdala, specialized parts of the prefrontal cortex, and mirror neurons; and sympathetic nervous system activity that prepares the body for action.

Biology and Deception: Can Lies Be Detected in the Brain and Body? Social scientists, governments, and police officers yearn to be able to detect liars without falsely accusing truth tellers. Unfortunately, even highly educated and trained individuals have only about a 54 percent chance of detecting a lie (Bond & DePaulo, 2008). For the rest of us, the success rate is 50 percent, no better than flipping a coin. People may speak hesitantly in telling a story, seem stressed in their speech, or avoid looking the interrogator in the eye for many reasons (DePaulo et al., 2003; Leo, 2008; Vrij, Granhag, & Porter, 2010). They may be frightened, not know what answers are expected, have nervous mannerisms, or come from a culture that regards direct eye contact as confrontational or rude.

For centuries, people have tried to determine when a person is lying by detecting physiological responses that cannot be controlled consciously. This is the idea behind the *polygraph machine* (lie detector), which is based on the assumption that a lie generates emotional arousal. A person who is guilty and fearful of being found out will therefore have increased activity in the autonomic nervous system while responding to incriminating questions: a faster heart rate, increased respiration rate, and increased electrical conductance of the skin.

Psychological scientists, however, regard polygraph tests as invalid because no physiological patterns of autonomic arousal are specific to lying (Iacono, 2001; Leo, 2008; Lykken, 1998). Machines cannot tell whether you are feeling guilty, angry, nervous, amused, or revved up from an exciting day. Innocent people may be tense and nervous about the whole procedure. They may react to the word *bank*, not because they robbed a bank but because they recently bounced a check; in either case, the machine will record a lie. The reverse mistake is also common: People who are motivated to escape detection can often beat the machine by tensing muscles or thinking about an exciting experience during neutral questions.

THINKING CRITICALLY

About "Lie Detectors"

The polygraph will correctly catch some liars and guilty people. The main problem is that it also falsely identifies many innocent people as having lied (Saxe, 1994). (See Figure 13.2.) For this reason, polygraph results are inadmissible in most courts. But some government agencies and most police departments continue to use them,

"WE CAN'T DETERMINE IF YOU'RE TELLING THE TRUTH, BUT YOU SHOULD HAVE A DOCTOR CHECK YOUR PRESSURE."

not for their accuracy but because they hope to scare people into telling the truth and induce suspects to confess—by telling them that they failed the test (Leo, 2008).

Because of the unreliability of the polygraph, researchers are trying to find other ways of measuring physiological signs of lying. One approach uses a computer to analyze a person's voice, on the assumption that the human voice contains telltale signals that betray a speaker's emotional state and intent to deceive. But research has mostly yielded negative or inconclusive findings (Harnsberger et al., 2009; Leo, 2008). Like the polygraph, voice analyzers detect physiological changes that may indicate fear, anger, or other signs of stress rather than lying, and they often falsely label true statements as lies.

Other researchers are using bran scans, such as fMRI, to test the hypothesis that when people are lying, they leave "brain fingerprints"—brain activity that reveals guilty knowledge of a crime. Some companies claim that they can predict with better than 90 percent certainty whether someone is telling the truth. Don't buy it. Areas of the brain that light up on an fMRI when people are allegedly lying are also those involved with many other cognitive functions, including memory, self-awareness, and self-monitoring (Greely & Illes, 2007). And because of the normal variability among people in their autonomic and brain reactivity, innocent but highly reactive people are still likely to be mislabeled guilty by these tests (Stix, 2008).

To date, efforts to find physiological markers of lying have produced unreliable results because they rest on a faulty assumption: that there are inevitable, universally identifiable biological signs that reveal with high accuracy when a person is lying. We're telling the truth!

Watch the Video Special Topics: Detecting Lies at MyPsychLab

FIGURE 13.2 Misjudging the Innocent
This graph shows the average percentages across three studies of classifications by lie detectors. Nearly half of the innocent people were classified as guilty, and a significant number of guilty people were classified as innocent. The suspect's guilt or innocence had been independently confirmed by other means, such as by admissions of guilt by the actual perpetrators (Iacono & Lykken, 1997).

Recite & Review

 Study and **Review** at **MyPsychLab**

Recite: A little surge of hormonal energy should help you say aloud what you can about the evolutionary functions of emotion, facial feedback, mirror neurons, mood contagion, brain areas involved in emotion, the role of epinephrine and norepinephrine in emotion, and the polygraph and other methods of "lie detection."

Review: Next, read this section once more.

Now take this *Quick Quiz:*

1. Three-year-old Olivia sees her dad dressed as a gorilla and runs away in fear. What brain structure is probably involved in her emotional reaction?

2. On returning to the city where she had grown up, Nyla visited her school and chanced upon her favorite teacher at the entrance. Elated, she ran to hug her. Which part of the brain motivated this response?

3. Ana Maria is in a surly, grumpy mood but her friends make her come with them to a hilarious Laurel and Hardy film. She can't help laughing, and soon she finds that her grumpy mood is gone. What physiological mechanisms might be the reason?

4. Casey is watching *Horrible Hatchet Homicides in the Haunted House.* What cells in his brain are making him wince when the hero is being attacked?

5. Casey is watching *Horrible Hatchet Homicides in the Haunted House II*. What hormones are causing his heart to pound and his palms to sweat when the murderer is stalking an unsuspecting victim?

Answers:

1. the amygdala 2. the left prefrontal region 3. facial feedback: smiling and laughing communicate to her brain that she is happy. Mood contagion from her friends' happy moods might also be at work. 4. mirror neurons 5. epinephrine and norepinephrine

Emotion and the Mind LO 13.6

Two friends of ours returned from a mountain-climbing trip to Nepal. One said, "I was ecstatic! The crystal-clear skies, the millions of stars, the friendly people, the majestic mountains, the harmony of the universe!" The other said, "I was miserable! The bedbugs and fleas, the lack of toilets, the yak-butter tea, the awful food, the unforgiving mountains!" Same trip, two different emotional reactions to it. Why?

In the first century A.D., the Stoic philosophers suggested an answer: People do not become angry or sad or ecstatic because of actual events, but because of their explanations of those events. Modern psychologists have verified the Stoics' ideas experimentally. Many years ago, Stanley Schachter and Jerome Singer (1962) argued that the experience of emotion depends not only on physiological arousal but also on how you interpret and explain that arousal. Your body may be churning away in high gear, but unless you can explain and label those changes, you will not feel a true emotion. This idea spurred other investigators to study how emotions are created and influenced by **appraisals**: beliefs, perceptions of the situation, expectations, and judgments that people draw on to explain their own and other people's behavior (see Chapter 10) (Moors et al., 2013; Fairholme et al., 2009; Lindquist & Barrett, 2008). Human beings, after all, are the only species that can say, "The more I thought about it, the madder I got." In fact, we often do think ourselves into an emotional state, and sometimes we can think ourselves out of it.

The importance of appraisals in emotion explains why two people can have different emotional reactions to the same situation. Imagine that you get an A on your psychology midterm; how will you feel? Or perhaps you get a D on that midterm; how will you feel then? Most people assume that success brings happiness and failure brings unhappiness, but the emotions you feel will depend more on how you explain your grade than on what you actually get. Do you attribute your grade to your own efforts (or lack of them) or to the teacher, fate, or luck? In a series of experiments, students who believed they did well because of their own efforts tended to feel proud, competent, and satisfied. Those who believed they did well because of a lucky fluke tended to feel gratitude, surprise, or guilt ("I don't deserve this"). Those who believed their failures were their own fault tended to feel regretful, guilty, or resigned. And those who blamed others tended to feel angry (Weiner, 1986).

appraisals The beliefs, perceptions, expectations, and judgments that people draw on to explain their own and other people's behavior, and that influence which emotion a person will feel in a given circumstance.

The appraisals that people make in particular situations depend in part on their culture. Japanese and Americans tend to differ in how they explain their errors and successes, and their emotions differ accordingly. Japanese are more likely to blame themselves when something goes wrong and as a result to experience shame, whereas Americans are more likely to blame others and experience anger. Americans are more likely to take credit for their successes and feel proud, whereas Japanese are more likely to regard a success as the result of the situation and opportunity—and feel lucky (Imada & Ellsworth, 2011).

Cognitions and physiology are inextricably linked in the subjective experience of emotion, and it's a two-way relationship: Thoughts affect emotions, and emotional states influence thoughts (Fairholme et al., 2009; Keltner, Ellsworth, & Edwards, 1993). Blaming others for your woes can make you feel angry, but once you are angry you may be more inclined to think the worst of other people's motives. The complicated mix of emotions that people feel when they have "disappointing wins" (outcomes that were not as good as they had expected) or "relieving losses" (bad outcomes that could have been worse) shows how powerfully thoughts affect emotional responses.

An infant's primitive emotions do not have much mental sophistication: "Hey, I'm mad because no one is feeding me!" As a child's cerebral cortex matures, however, cognitions become

Children need to be old enough to have a sense of self before they can feel the moral emotions of shame, guilt, or remorse.

more complex, and thus so do emotions: "Hey, I'm mad because this situation is entirely unfair!" Some emotions, such as shame, guilt, and remorse, depend completely on the maturation of higher cognitive capacities and do not occur until a child is 2 or 3 years old (and never in some people). These *self*-conscious emotions require the emergence of a sense of self and the ability to perceive that you have behaved badly or let down another person (Baumeister, Stillwell, & Heatherton, 1994; Tangney & Tracy, 2012).

Thoughts affect emotions. Who will be happier: an athlete who wins a second-place silver medal or one who wins a third-place bronze? Won't it be the silver medalist? Nope. Second-place winners usually compare themselves to the gold medalist and see themselves as "losers." But third-place winners compare themselves to those who did worse than they and are happy that they earned a medal at all (Medvec, Madey, & Gilovich, 1995). After a European swimming competition, silver medalist Vitaly Romanovich of Russia (left) clearly felt grumpier than the gold- and bronze-medal winners. He couldn't even bring himself to display his medal!

Appraisals, as you can see, are essential to the creation of most emotions. But when people decide that it is shameful for a man to dance on a table with a lampshade on his head, or for a woman to walk down a street with her arms and legs uncovered, where do their ideas about shame originate? If you are a person who loudly curses others when you are angry, where did you learn that cursing is acceptable? To answer these questions, we turn to the role of culture.

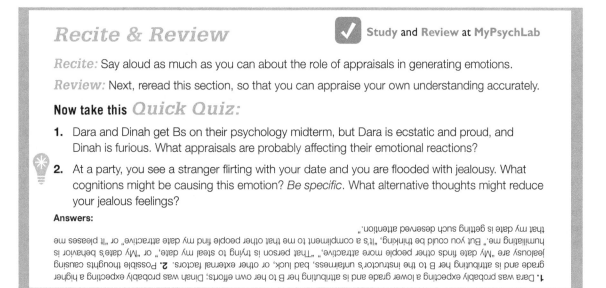

Recite & Review

✓ Study and Review at MyPsychLab

Recite: Say aloud as much as you can about the role of appraisals in generating emotions.

Review: Next, reread this section, so that you can appraise your own understanding accurately.

Now take this *Quick Quiz:*

1. Dara and Dinah get Bs on their psychology midterm, but Dara is ecstatic and proud, and Dinah is furious. What appraisals are probably affecting their emotional reactions?

2. At a party, you see a stranger flirting with your date and you are flooded with jealousy. What cognitions might be causing this emotion? *Be specific*. What alternative thoughts might reduce your jealous feelings?

Answers:

1. Dara was probably expecting a lower grade and is attributing her B to her own efforts; Dinah was probably expecting a higher grade and is attributing her B to the instructor's unfairness, bad luck, or other external factors. 2. Possible thoughts causing jealousy are "My date finds other people more attractive," "That person is trying to steal my date," or "My date's behavior is humiliating me." But you could be thinking, "It's a compliment to me that other people find my date attractive" or "It pleases me that my date is getting such deserved attention."

You are about to learn . . .

- why some emotions may be universal but the reasons people experience them are not.

- how culture shapes emotion prototypes into blends and variations.

- how cultural rules affect the way people display or suppress their emotions.

- why people often do "emotion work" to convey emotions they do not feel.

- whether women are really more "emotional" than men.

Emotion and Culture

A young wife leaves her house one morning to draw water from the local well as her husband watches from the porch. On her way back from the well, a male stranger stops her and asks for some water. She gives him a cupful and then invites him home to dinner. He accepts. The husband, wife, and guest have a pleasant meal together. In a gesture of hospitality, the husband invites the guest to spend the night with his wife. The guest accepts. In the morning, the husband leaves early to bring home breakfast. When he returns, he finds his wife again in bed with the visitor.

At what point in this story will the husband feel angry? The answer depends on his culture (Hupka, 1981, 1991). A North American husband would feel rather angry at a wife who had an extramarital affair, and a wife would feel rather angry at being offered to a guest as if she were a lamb chop. But a Pawnee husband of the nineteenth century would be enraged at any man who dared ask his wife for water. An Ammassalik Inuit husband finds it perfectly honorable to offer his wife to a stranger, but only once; he would be angry to find his wife and the guest having a second encounter. And a century ago, a Toda husband in India would not have been angry at all because the Todas allowed both husband and wife to take lovers. Both spouses might feel angry, though, if one of them had a *sneaky* affair, without announcing it publicly.

All over the world, people feel angry in response to insult and the violation of social rules, but as this story shows, they often disagree about what an insult is or what the correct rule should be. In this section, we will explore how culture influences the emotions we feel and the ways in which we express them.

How Culture Shapes Emotions
LO 13.7

Are some emotions specific to particular cultures and not found in others? What does it mean that some languages have words for subtle emotional states that other languages lack? The Germans have *schadenfreude*, a feeling of joy at another's misfortune. The Japanese speak of *hagaii*, helpless anguish tinged with frustration. Tahitians have *mehameha*, a trembling sensation they experience when ordinary

display rules Social and cultural rules that regulate when, how, and where a person may express (or suppress) emotions.

categories of perception are suspended—at twilight, in the brush, watching fires glow without heat (Levy, 1984). English-speaking people can identify a *bittersweet* experience or feel the mixed emotions of pleasure and regret in *nostalgia*. But English lacks an emotion word that is central to inhabitants of the tiny Micronesian atoll of Ifaluk: *fago*, translated as "compassion/love/sadness," which reflects the sad feeling one has when a loved one is absent or in need, and the pleasurable sense of compassion in being able to care and help (Lutz, 1988).

Do these interesting linguistic differences mean that Germans are more likely than others to actually feel schadenfreude, the Japanese to feel hagaii, Tahitians to feel mehameha, and English speakers to feel nostalgia? Or are they just more willing to give these blended emotions a single name? Most people in all cultures are apparently capable of feeling the emotions that have distinctive physiological hallmarks in the brain, face, and nervous system. But people in different cultures might indeed differ in their ability to experience emotional blends and variations.

In Chapter 7, we noted that a *prototype* is a typical representative of a class of things. People everywhere consider some emotions to be prototypical examples of the concept *emotion*: Most people will say that *anger* and *sadness* are more representative of an emotion than *irritability* and *nostalgia* are. Prototypical emotions are reflected in the emotion words that young children learn first: *happy*, *sad*, *mad*, and *scared*. But as children develop, they begin to draw emotional distinctions that are less prototypical and more specific

to their language and culture, such as *ecstatic*, *depressed*, *hostile*, or *anxious* (Hupka, Lenton, & Hutchison, 1999; Shaver, Wu, & Schwartz, 1992). In this way, they come to experience the nuances of emotional feeling that their cultures emphasize.

Culture also influences the causes of emotion and shapes their expression. Anger may be universal, but the way it is experienced will vary from culture to culture—whether it feels good or bad, useful or destructive. And cultures determine much of what people feel emotional *about*. For example, disgust is universal, but the content of what produces disgust changes as an infant matures, and it varies across cultures (Pole, 2013; Rozin, Lowery, & Ebert, 1994). People in some cultures learn to become disgusted by bugs (which other people find beautiful or tasty), unfamiliar sexual practices, dirt, death, "contamination" by a handshake with a stranger, or particular foods (e.g., meat if they are vegetarian; pork if they are Muslims or Orthodox Jews).

Communicating Emotions

Suppose that someone dear to you died. Would you cry, and if so, would you do it alone or in public? Your answer will depend in part on your culture's **display rules** for emotion (Ekman et al., 1987; Gross, 1998). In some cultures, grief is expressed by weeping; in others, by tearless resignation; and in still others by dance, drink, and song. Once you feel an emotion, how you express it is rarely a matter of "I say what I feel." You may be obliged to disguise what you feel. You may wish you could feel what you say.

Around the world, the cultural rules for expressing emotions differ. The display rule for a formal Japanese wedding portrait is "no direct expressions of emotion," but not every member of this family has learned that rule yet.

Even the smile, which seems a straightforward signal of friendliness, has many meanings and uses that are not universal (LaFrance, 2011). Americans smile more frequently than Germans, not because Americans are inherently friendlier but because they differ in their notions of when a smile is appropriate. After a German–American business meeting, the Americans often complain that the Germans were cold and aloof, and the Germans often complain that the Americans were excessively cheerful, hiding their real feelings under the mask of a smile (Hall & Hall, 1990). The Japanese smile even more than Americans do, to disguise embarrassment, anger, or other negative emotions whose public display is considered rude and incorrect. An American student told us how she learned smile rules when she was visiting Israel. At a social event or bar, she would smile to be nice, even to guys she had no intention of being with. They would get pushy, and then pushier, much to her eventual annoyance. And then she saw how the Israeli women were responding from the get-go: No smiles. No encouragement. They would say to the guy, directly, "I don't want to be with you. Go away." It's a lot harder for "friendly" American women to do that!

Display rules also govern *body language*, nonverbal signals of body movement, posture, gesture, and gaze (Birdwhistell, 1970). Many aspects of body language are specific to particular languages and cultures, which makes even the simplest gesture subject to misunderstanding and offense. The sign of the University of Texas football team, the Longhorns, is to extend the index finger and the pinkie. In Italy and other parts of Europe, it means you're saying a man's wife has been unfaithful to him—a serious insult.

Display rules tell us not only what to do when we are feeling an emotion, but also how and when to show an emotion we do not feel. Most people are expected to demonstrate sadness at funerals, happiness at weddings, and affection toward relatives. What if we don't actually feel sad, happy, or affectionate? Acting out an emotion we do not really feel because we believe it is socially appropriate is called **emotion work**. It is part of an effort to regulate our emotions when we are with others (Gross, 1998). Sometimes emotion work is a job requirement. Flight attendants, waiters, and customer-service representatives must put on a happy face to convey cheerfulness, even if they are privately angry at a rude or drunken customer. Bill collectors must put on a stern face to convey threat, even if they feel sorry for the person they are collecting money from (Hochschild, 2003).

Gender and Emotion LO 13.8

"Women are too emotional," men often complain. "Men are too cool," women often reply. This is a familiar gender stereotype. Generally, when people say that women are "emotional," they are not thinking of the overwhelming evidence that far more men than women "lose their cool" by getting into fistfights or killing each other. What, then, does "too emotional" mean? We need to define our terms and examine our assumptions. And we need to consider the larger culture in which men and women live, which shapes the rules and norms that govern how the sexes are supposed to behave.

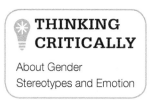

THINKING CRITICALLY

About Gender Stereotypes and Emotion

👁 Watch the Video Lisa Feldman Barrett: What is the Difference in Emotions in Terms of Males and Females? at MyPsychLab

In the United States, women are more likely than men to suffer from clinical depression, but both sexes are equally likely to report feeling the everyday emotions of anger, worry, embarrassment, anxiety, jealousy, love, pride, or grief (Archer, 2004; Deffenbacher et al., 2003; Fischer et al., 1993; Harris, 2003; Kring & Gordon, 1998; Shields, 2005). Where differences do occur, they are generally in a specific domain or subculture: For example, white women are more likely than men to feel guilt and shame about their bodies, sex, and food (Else-Quest et al., 2012). The major differences between the sexes have less to do with whether they feel emotions than with what causes them to feel various emotions, how and when their emotions are expressed, and how others perceive those expressions.

Thus, both sexes unconsciously associate "angry" with male and "happy" with female. When researchers showed students a series of computer-generated, fairly sex-neutral faces with a range of angry to happy expressions, the students consistently rated the angry faces as being masculine and the happy faces as feminine (Becker et al., 2007). This stereotyped link between gender and emotion may help explain why a high-status man who expresses anger in a professional context is considered powerful, but a professional woman who does exactly the same thing loses status. She is considered to be an angry person, someone "out of control" (Brescoll & Uhlmann, 2008). You can see the resulting dilemma: Should a woman express anger when a subordinate or adversary has done something illegal or incompetent (and risk being thought "overemotional—just like a

emotion work
Expression of an emotion, often because of a role requirement, that a person does not really feel.

woman") or behave calmly (and risk being seen as "cold and unemotional—unwomanly")?

Conversely, women who don't smile when others expect them to are often disliked, even if they are actually smiling as often as men would. This may be why North American women, on average, smile more than men do, gaze at their listeners more, have more emotionally expressive faces, use more expressive hand and body movements, and touch others more (DePaulo, 1992; Kring & Gordon, 1998). Women smile more than men not just to convey happiness but also to pacify others, convey deference to someone of higher status, or smooth over conflicts (Hess, Adams, & Kleck, 2005; LaFrance, 2011; Shields, 2005).

Women also talk about their emotions more than men do, even when both sexes feel those emotions. Women are far more likely than men to cry and to acknowledge emotions that reveal vulnerability and weakness, such as "hurt feelings," fear, sadness, loneliness, shame, and guilt, and this sex difference begins in childhood (Chaplin & Aldao, 2012; Grossman & Wood, 1993; Timmers, Fischer, & Manstead, 1998). In contrast, boys and men express only one emotion more freely than women do: anger toward strangers, especially other men. Otherwise, men are expected to control and mask negative feelings. When they are worried or afraid, they are more likely than women to use vague terms, saying that they feel moody, frustrated, or on edge (Fehr et al., 1999).

Despite these average differences, the influence of a particular situation often overrides gender rules. You won't find many gender differences in emotional expressiveness at a football game or the World Series! Further, both sexes do similar emotion work when the situation or job requires it. A male flight attendant has to smile with passengers as much as a female attendant does, and a female FBI agent has to be as emotionally strong and controlled as a male agent.

Perhaps the strongest situational constraint on emotional expression is the status of the participants (Kenny et al., 2010; Snodgrass, 1992). A man is as likely as a woman to control his temper when the target of anger is someone with higher status or power; few people will readily sound off at a professor, police officer, or employer. As for empathy in judging what other people are feeling—supposedly a female skill—a series of experiments found that working-class people of *both* sexes are more skilled than upper-class people at judging emotional expressions in others and reading the emotions of strangers in job interviews. Working-class women *and* men have a greater interest in being able to read the nonverbal cues of those who have higher status and more power than they (Kraus, Côté, & Keltner, 2010).

Finally, keep in mind that even when gender differences exist in one culture, that doesn't mean they are found universally. Italian, French, Spanish, and Middle Eastern men and women can have entire conversations using highly expressive hand gestures and facial expressions. In contrast, in Asian cultures, both sexes are taught to control emotional expression (Matsumoto, 1996; Mesquita & Frijda, 1992). Israeli and Italian men are more likely than women to mask feelings of sadness, but British, Spanish, Swiss, and German men are *less* likely than their female counterparts to inhibit this emotion (Wallbott, Ricci-Bitti, & Bänninger-Huber, 1986).

In sum, the answer to "Which sex is more emotional?" is sometimes men, sometimes women, and sometimes neither, depending on the circumstances and their culture—and how we define "emotional."

Explore the **Concept** How Do You Deal With Your Emotions? at **MyPsychLab**

Both sexes feel emotionally attached to friends, but in many cultures they learn to express their affections differently. A common pattern is that girls tend to prefer "face-to-face" friendships based on shared feelings; boys tend to prefer "side-by-side" friendships based on shared activities.

Recite & Review

 Study and **Review** at **MyPsychLab**

Recite: Say aloud what you know about universal emotions and cultural variations, prototypical emotions, display rules, body language, emotion work, and gender differences and similarities in emotionality.

Review: Please do not display anger at our request that you reread this section.

Now take this *Quick Quiz:*

1. Maureen is working in a fast-food restaurant and is becoming irritated with a customer who isn't ordering fast enough. She is supposed to be pleasant to all customers, but instead she snaps, "Hey, whaddaya want to order, slowpoke?" To keep her job and her temper, Maureen needs practice in _____.

2. In a class discussion, a student says something that embarrasses a student from another culture. The second student smiles to disguise his discomfort; the first student, thinking he is not being taken seriously, gets angry. This misunderstanding reflects the students' different _____ for the expression of embarrassment and anger.

3. *True or false*: Throughout the world, women are more emotionally expressive than men.

Answers:

1. emotion work 2. display rules 3. false

You are about to learn . . .

- **how your body responds to physical, emotional, and environmental stressors.**
- **why being "stressed out" increases the risk of illness in some people but not others.**
- **how psychological factors affect the immune system.**
- **when having a sense of control over events is beneficial and when it is not.**

The Nature of Stress

The factors that shape the experience and expression of emotions involve physiology, cognitive processes, and cultural rules. These same three factors can help us understand those difficult situations in which negative emotions become chronically stressful, and in which chronic stress can create negative emotions.

Stress and the Body LO 13.9

The modern era of stress research began in 1956, when physician Hans Selye published *The Stress of Life*. Environmental stressors such as heat, cold, toxins, and danger, Selye wrote, disrupt the body's equilibrium. The body then mobilizes its resources to attack these stressors and restore normal functioning. Selye described the body's response to stressors of all kinds as a **general adaptation syndrome,** a set of physiological reactions that occur in three phases:

1 **The alarm phase,** in which the body mobilizes the sympathetic nervous system to meet the immediate threat. The threat could be anything from taking a test you haven't studied for to running from a rabid dog. As we saw, the release of adrenal hormones, epinephrine and norepinephrine, occurs with any intense emotion. It boosts energy, tenses muscles, reduces sensitivity to pain, shuts down digestion (so that blood will flow more efficiently to the brain, muscles, and skin), and increases blood pressure. Decades before Selye, psychologist Walter Cannon (1929) described these changes as the *fight-or-flight response*, a phrase still in use.

Stress hormones elevated

Blood flow increases

Heart rate speeds up

Digestion slows

Muscles tense

2 **The resistance phase,** in which your body attempts to resist or cope with a stressor that cannot be avoided. During this phase, the physiological responses of the alarm phase continue, but these very responses make the body more vulnerable to other stressors. That is why, when your body has mobilized to deal with a heat wave or pain from a broken leg, you may find you are more easily annoyed by minor frustrations. In most cases, the body will eventually adapt to the stressor and return to normal.

general adaptation syndrome According to Hans Selye, a series of physiological reactions to stress occurring in three phases: alarm, resistance, and exhaustion.

HPA (hypothalamus–pituitary–adrenal cortex) axis A system activated to energize the body to respond to stressors. The hypothalamus sends chemical messengers to the pituitary gland, which in turn prompts the adrenal cortex to produce cortisol and other hormones.

3 **The exhaustion phase**, in which persistent stress depletes the body of energy, thereby increasing vulnerability to physical problems and illness. The same reactions that allow the body to respond effectively in the alarm and resistance phases are unhealthy as long-range responses. Tense muscles can cause headache and neck pain. Increased blood pressure can become chronic hypertension. If normal digestive processes are interrupted or shut down for too long, digestive disorders may result.

Selye did not believe that people should aim for a stress-free life. Some stress, he said, is positive and productive, even if it also requires the body to produce short-term energy: competing in an athletic event, falling in love, or working hard on a project you enjoy. And some negative stress is simply unavoidable; it's called life.

Explore the Concept Selye's General Adaptation Syndrome at MyPsychLab

Current Approaches. LO 13.10 One of Selye's most important observations was that the biological changes that are adaptive in the short run, because they permit the body to respond quickly to danger, can become hazardous in the long run. Modern researchers are learning how this happens.

When you are under stress, your brain's hypothalamus sends messages to the endocrine glands along two major pathways. One, as Selye observed, activates the sympathetic division of the autonomic nervous system for fight or flight, producing the release of epinephrine and norepinephrine from the inner part (medulla) of the adrenal glands. In addition, the hypothalamus initiates activity along the **HPA axis** (HPA stands for hypothalamus–pituitary–adrenal cortex): The hypothalamus releases chemical messengers that communicate with the pituitary gland, which in turn sends messages to the outer part (cortex) of the adrenal glands. The adrenal cortex then secretes *cortisol* and other hormones that elevate blood sugar and protect the body's tissues from inflammation in case of injury. (See Figure 13.3.)

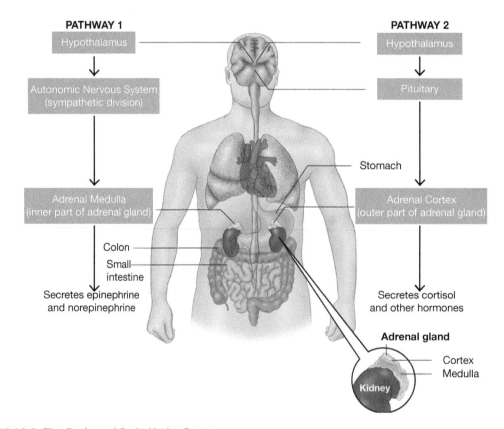

FIGURE 13.3 The Brain and Body Under Stress
When a person is in danger or under stress, the hypothalamus sends messages to the endocrine glands along two major pathways. In one, the hypothalamus activates the sympathetic division of the autonomic nervous system, which stimulates the adrenal medulla to produce epinephrine and norepinephrine. The result is the set of bodily changes associated with fight or flight. In the other pathway, messages travel along the HPA axis to the adrenal cortex, which produces cortisol and other hormones. The result is increased energy and protection from tissue inflammation in case of injury.

Alas, the same stress hormones that help in the short run can have unwanted long-term consequences.

One result of HPA axis activation is increased energy, which is crucial for short-term responses to stress (Kemeny, 2003). But if cortisol and other stress hormones stay high too long, they can lead to hypertension, immune disorders, other physical ailments, and possibly emotional problems. Elevated levels of cortisol also motivate animals (and presumably humans, too) to seek out rich comfort foods and store the extra calories as abdominal fat.

An understanding of the cumulative effects of external sources of stress may partly explain why people at the lower rungs of the socioeconomic ladder have worse health and higher mortality rates for almost every disease and medical condition than do those at the top (Adler & Snibbe, 2003). In addition to their lack of access to good medical care and reliance on diets that lead to obesity and diabetes, people in poverty often live with continuous environmental stressors: higher crime rates, discrimination, fewer community services, run-down housing, and greater exposure to hazards such as chemical contamination (Gallo & Matthews, 2003).

Watch the Video Special Topics: Health Disparities at MyPsychLab

Children are particularly vulnerable to the stressors associated with poverty or parental maltreatment and neglect: The more years they are exposed to family disruption, chaos, and instability, the higher their cortisol levels and the greater the snowballing negative effect on their physical health, mental health, and cognitive abilities in adolescence and adulthood. By the time they are adults, they have an elevated risk of cardiovascular disease, autoimmune disorders, diabetes, and early mortality (Evans & Kim, 2012; Miller, Chen, & Parker, 2011). The harmful effects of these environmental stressors may even begin in infancy. An fMRI study of the brains of 6- to 12-month-old infants, taken *while the babies were sleeping*, found significant neural responses to overhearing parents' enraged quarrels. Babies are extremely sensitive to the emotional tone of the voices they hear, and anger has a particularly powerful and disturbing effect on areas of their developing brains involved in emotion, reactivity to stress, and emotion regulation (Graham, Fisher, & Pfeifer, 2013).

Because work is central in most people's lives, the effects of persistent unemployment can threaten health for people at all income levels, even increasing their vulnerability to the common cold. In one study, heroic volunteers were given either ordinary nose drops or nose drops containing a cold virus, and then were quarantined for five days. The people most likely to get a cold's miserable symptoms were those who had been underemployed or unemployed for at least a month. As you can see in Figure 13.4, the longer the work problems lasted, the greater the likelihood of illness (Cohen et al., 1998).

Nonetheless, people's responses to stress vary according to their learning history, gender, preexisting medical conditions, and genetic predisposition for high blood pressure, heart disease, obesity, diabetes, or other health problems (Belsky & Pluess, 2009a; McEwen, 2000, 2007). This is why some people respond to the same stressor with much greater increases in blood pressure, heart rate, and hormone levels than other individuals do, and why their physical changes take longer to return to normal. These hyperresponsive individuals may be the ones most at risk for eventual illness.

The Immune System: PNI. LO 13.11 Researchers in the growing field of *health psychology* (and its medical relative, behavioral medicine) investigate all aspects of how mind and body affect each other to preserve wellness or cause illness. An interdisciplinary specialty with the cumbersome name **psychoneuroimmunology**, or **PNI** for short, investigates

psychoneuroimmunology (PNI) The study of the relationships among psychology, the nervous and endocrine systems, and the immune system.

FIGURE 13.4 Stress and the Common Cold
Chronic stress lasting a month or more boosts the risk of catching a cold. The risk is increased among people undergoing problems with their friends or loved ones; it is highest among people who are out of work (Cohen et al., 1998).

these interwoven factors. The "psycho" part stands for psychological processes such as emotions and perceptions; "neuro" for the nervous and endocrine systems; and "immunology" for the immune system, which enables the body to combat disease and infection.

PNI researchers are especially interested in the white blood cells of the immune system, which are designed to recognize foreign or harmful

The immune system consists of fighter cells that look more fantastical than any alien creature Hollywood could design. This one is about to engulf and destroy a cigarette-shaped parasite that causes a tropical disease.

substances *(antigens)*, such as flu viruses, bacteria, and tumor cells, and then destroy or deactivate them. The immune system deploys different kinds of white blood cells as weapons, depending on the nature of the enemy. Natural killer cells are important in tumor detection and rejection, and are involved in protection against the spread of cancer cells and viruses. Helper T cells enhance and regulate the immune response; they are the primary target of the HIV virus that causes AIDS. Chemicals produced by the immune cells are sent to the brain, and the brain in turn sends chemical signals to stimulate or restrain the immune system. Anything that disrupts this communication loop, whether drugs, surgery, or chronic stress, can weaken or suppress the immune system (Segerstrom & Miller, 2004).

Some PNI researchers have gotten right down to the level of cell damage to see how stress can lead to illness, aging, and even premature death. At the end of every chromosome is a protein complex called a *telomere* that, in essence, tells the cell how long it has to live. Every time a cell divides, enzymes whittle away a tiny piece of the telomere; when it is reduced to almost nothing, the cell stops dividing and dies. Chronic stress, especially if it begins in childhood, appears to shorten the telomeres (Epel, 2009).

Stress and the Mind LO 13.12, LO 13.13

Before you try to persuade your instructors that the stress of constant studying is bad for your health, consider this mystery: The large majority of individuals who are living with stressors, even serious ones such as loss of a job or the chronic

illness of a loved one, do not get sick (Bonanno, 2004; Taylor, Repetti, & Seeman, 1997). What protects them?

Optimism. When something bad happens to you, what is your first reaction? Do you tell yourself that you will somehow come through it okay, or do you gloomily mutter, "More proof that if something can go wrong for me, it will"? In a fundamental way, optimism—the general expectation that things will go well in spite of occasional setbacks—makes life possible. If people are in a jam but believe things will get better eventually, they will keep striving to make that prediction come true. Even despondent fans of the Chicago Cubs, who have not won the World Series in living memory, maintain a lunatic optimism that "there's always next year."

At first, studies of optimism reported that optimism is also better for health, well-being, and even longevity than pessimism is (Carver & Scheier, 2002; Maruta et al., 2000). You can see why popularizers in the media ran far with this ball, some claiming that having an optimistic outlook would prolong the life of people suffering from serious illnesses. Unfortunately, that hope proved, well, overly optimistic: A team of Australian researchers who followed 179 patients with lung cancer over a period of eight years found that optimism made no difference in who lived or in how long they lived (Schofield et al., 2004). Indeed, for every study showing the benefits of optimism, another shows that in some circumstances it can actually be harmful. Among other things, optimists are more likely to keep gambling even when they lose money, and they can be more vulnerable to depression when the hoped-for outcome does not occur (McNulty & Fincham, 2012). Optimism also backfires when it keeps people from preparing themselves for complications of surgery ("Oh, everything will be fine") or causes them to underestimate risks to their health (Friedman & Martin, 2011; Shepperd et al., 2013).

For optimism to reap any benefits, it must be grounded in reality, spurring people to take better care of themselves and to regard setbacks as challenges rather than as reasons to give up. Realistic optimists are more likely than pessimists to be active problem solvers, get support from friends, and seek information that can help them (Brissette, Scheier, & Carver, 2002; Geers, Wellman, & Lassiter, 2009). They keep their senses of humor, plan for the future, and reinterpret the situation in a positive light. Pessimists, in contrast, often do self-destructive things: They drink too much, smoke, fail to wear seat belts, drive too fast, and refuse to take medication for illness (Peterson et al., 1998). So, however, do unrealistic optimists.

Conscientiousness and Control. Thus, it is not optimism by itself that predicts health and well-being. You can recite "Everything is good! Everything will work out!" 20 times a day, but it won't get you much (except odd glances from your classmates). Optimism needs a behavioral partner.

In one of the longest longitudinal studies ever conducted in psychology—for 90 years!—researchers were able to follow the lives of more than 1,500 children originally studied by Lewis Terman, beginning in 1921 (see Chapter 7). Terman followed these children, affectionately called the "Termites," long into their adulthood, and when he died in 1956, other researchers took up the project. Health psychologists Howard Friedman and Leslie Martin (2011) found that the secret to longevity for the Termites was *conscientiousness*, the ability to persist in pursuit of goals, get a good education, work hard but enjoy the work and its challenges, and be responsible. Conscientious people are optimists, in the sense that they believe their efforts will pay off, and they act in ways to make that expectation come true. The findings on the Termites, who were largely a homogeneous cohort that was white and middle class, have been replicated across more than 20 independent samples that differed in terms of ethnicity and social class (Deary, Weiss, & Batty, 2010).

⊛ **THINKING CRITICALLY**

About the Benefits of Optimism

Who has more stress: corporate managers in highly competitive jobs or assembly-line workers in routine and predictable jobs? People who are bossed usually suffer more from job stress than their bosses do, especially if the employees cannot control many aspects of their work (Karasek & Theorell, 1990).

locus of control A general expectation about whether the results of your actions are under your own control (internal locus) or beyond your control (external locus).

primary control An effort to modify reality by changing other people, the situation, or events; a "fighting back" philosophy.

secondary control An effort to accept reality by changing your own attitudes, goals, or emotions; a "learn to live with it" philosophy.

Conscientiousness is related to another important predictor of health, having an internal locus of control. **Locus of control** refers to your general expectation about whether you can control the things that happen to you (Rotter, 1990). People who have an *internal locus of control* ("internals") tend to believe that they are responsible for what happens to them. Those who have an *external locus of control* ("externals") tend to believe that their lives are controlled by luck, fate, or other people. Having an internal locus of control, especially concerning things you can do right now rather than vague future events, is associated with good health, academic achievement, political activism, and emotional well-being (Frazier et al., 2011; Roepke & Grant, 2011; Strickland, 1989).

Most people can tolerate all kinds of stressors—including pain, crowding, and noise—if they feel able to predict or control them (Evans, Lepore, & Allen, 2000). That is why people who have the greatest control over their work pace and activities, such as executives and managers, have fewer illnesses and stress symptoms than do employees who have little control, who feel trapped doing repetitive tasks (Karasek & Theorell, 1990).

Feeling in control affects the immune system, which may be why it helps to speed up recovery from surgery and some diseases, helps people resist infection by cold viruses, helps people tolerate pain, and offsets even the health-impairing effects of poverty and discrimination (Cohen, Tyrrell, & Smith, 1993; Krieger & Sidney, 1996; Lachman & Weaver, 1998). As with optimism, feeling in control also makes people more likely to take action to improve their health and deal with medical issues. In a group of patients recovering from heart attacks, those who believed the heart attack occurred because they smoked, didn't exercise, or had a stressful job were more likely to change their bad habits and recover quickly. In contrast, those who thought their illness was the result of bad luck or fate—factors outside their control—were less likely to generate plans for recovery and more likely to resume their old unhealthy habits (Ewart, 1995).

Overall, then, a sense of control is a good thing, but critical thinkers might want to ask: Control over what? It is surely not beneficial for people to believe they can control absolutely every aspect of their lives; some things, such as death, taxes, or being a random victim of a crime, are out of anyone's control. Health and well-being are not enhanced by self-blame ("Whatever goes wrong with my health is my fault") or the belief that all disease can be prevented by doing the right thing ("If I take vitamins and hold the right positive attitude, I'll never get sick").

THINKING CRITICALLY

About Control and Health

Culture and Control. Eastern and Western cultures tend to hold different attitudes toward the ability and desirability of controlling one's own life. In general, Western cultures celebrate **primary control**, in which people try to influence events by trying to exert direct control over them: If you are in a bad situation, you change it, fix it, or fight it. The Eastern approach emphasizes **secondary control**, in which people try to accommodate to a bad situation by changing their own aspirations or desires: If you have a problem, you live with it or act in spite of it (Cheng et al., 2012; Rothbaum, Weisz, & Snyder, 1982).

A Japanese psychologist once offered some examples of Japanese proverbs that teach the benefits of yielding to the inevitable (Azuma, 1984): *To lose is to win* (giving in, to protect the harmony of a relationship, demonstrates the superior trait of generosity); *willow trees do not get broken by piled-up snow* (no matter how many problems pile up in your life, flexibility will help you survive them); and *the true tolerance is to tolerate the intolerable* (some "intolerable" situations are facts of life that no amount of protest will change). You can imagine how long "To lose is to win" would survive on an American football field, or how long most Americans would be prepared to tolerate the intolerable! Yet an important part of coping, for any of us, is learning to accept limited resources, irrevocable losses, and circumstances over which we have little or no direct influence—all aspects of secondary control.

People who are ill or under stress can reap the benefits of both Western and Eastern forms of control by avoiding either–or thinking: taking responsibility for future actions while not blaming themselves unduly for past ones. Among first-year college students who are doing poorly, future success depends on maintaining enough primary control to keep working hard and learning to study better, *and* on the ability to come to terms with the fact that success is not going to drop into their laps without effort (Hall et al., 2006). Among women who are recovering from sexual assault or illness, adjustment is related to a woman's belief that she is not to blame for being raped or for getting sick but that she *is* in charge of taking care of herself from now on (Frazier, 2003; Taylor, Lichtman, & Wood, 1984). This way of thinking allows people to avoid guilt and self-blame while retaining a belief that they can take steps to get better.

Many problems require us to decide what we can change and to accept what we cannot; perhaps the secret of healthy control lies in knowing the difference.

Recite & Review

✓ Study and Review at MyPsychLab

Recite: Reduce your stress before the next exam by saying out loud what you know about the general adaptation syndrome, the HPA axis and its role in stress, psychoneuroimmunology and the immune system, and the effects of optimism, conscientiousness, and locus of control.

Review: Next, be conscientious and read this section again.

Now Take this *Quick Quiz*:

1. Steve is unexpectedly called on in class to discuss a question. He hasn't the faintest idea of the answer, and he feels his heart pound and his palms sweat. According to Selye, Steve is in the _____ phase of his stress response.

2. Anika usually takes credit for doing well on her work assignments and blames her failures on lack of effort. Benecia attributes her successes to luck and blames her failures on the fact that she is an indecisive Gemini. Anika has an _____ locus of control whereas Benecia has an _____ locus.

3. Adapting to the reality that you have a chronic medical condition is an example of (primary/secondary) control; joining a protest to make a local company clean up its hazardous wastes is an example of (primary/secondary) control.

4. On television, a self-described health expert explains that "no one gets sick if they don't want to be sick," because we can all control our bodies. As a critical thinker, how should you assess this claim?

Answers:

1. alarm 2. internal; external 3. secondary; primary 4. First, you would want to define your terms: What does "control" mean, and what kind of control is the supposed expert referring to? People can control some things, such as how much they exercise and whether they smoke, and they can control some aspects of treatment once they become ill, but they cannot control everything that happens to them. Second, you would examine the assumption that control is always a good thing; the belief that we have total control over our lives could lead to depression and unwarranted self-blame when illness strikes.

Stress and Emotion

Perhaps you have heard people say things such as "She was so depressed, it's no wonder she got sick" or "He's always so angry, he's going to give himself a heart attack one day." Are negative emotions, especially anger and depression, hazardous to your health?

To answer, we need to separate the effects of negative emotions on healthy people from the effects of such emotions on people who are ill. Once a person is already sick, negative emotions such as anxiety and helplessness can slow recovery (Kiecolt-Glaser et al., 1998). But can anger and depression be causes of illness on their own?

Hostility and Depression

LO 13.14, LO 13.15

One of the first modern efforts to link emotions and illness occurred in the 1970s, with research on the "Type A" personality, a set of qualities thought to be associated with heart disease: ambitiousness, impatience, anger, working hard, and having high standards for oneself. Later work ruled out all of these factors except one: The toxic ingredient in the Type A personality turned out to be hostility (Myrtek, 2007).

By "hostility" we do not mean the irritability or anger that everyone feels on occasion, but *cynical* or *antagonistic hostility*, which characterizes people who are mistrustful of others and always ready to provoke mean, furious arguments. In a classic study of male physicians who had been interviewed as medical students 25 years earlier, those who were chronically angry and resentful were five times as likely as nonhostile men to get heart disease, even when other risk factors such as smoking and a poor diet were taken into account (Ewart & Kolodner, 1994; Williams, Barefoot, & Shekelle, 1985) (see Figure 13.5). These findings have been replicated in other large-scale studies, with women and African Americans as well as white men (Krantz et al., 2006; Williams et al., 2000). Proneness to anger is a significant risk factor all on its own for impairments of the immune system, elevated blood pressure, heart disease, and

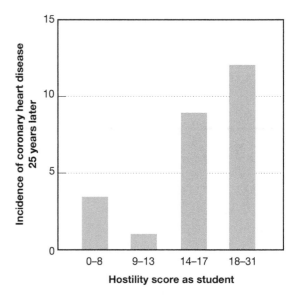

FIGURE 13.5 Hostility and Heart Disease
Anger is more hazardous to health than a heavy workload. Men who had the highest hostility scores as young medical students were the most likely to have coronary heart disease 25 years later (Williams, Barefoot, & Shekelle, 1985).

even a slower healing of wounds (Chida & Hamer, 2008; Gouin et al., 2008; Suinn, 2001).

Clinical depression, too, is linked to at least a doubled risk of later heart attack and cardiovascular disease (Frasure-Smith & Lespérance, 2005; Schulz et al., 2000). The reason seems to be not depression itself, but the lethargy and overeating that depression can produce in some of its sufferers. Depressed people are more likely to accumulate fat in the belly and midriff (perhaps because of the elevated cortisol that often occurs with depression), where it is more likely to increase the risk of diabetes and cardiovascular disease (Vogelzangs et al., 2008).

For some time, researchers thought that depression might also lead to cancer, but now it looks as though the reverse is true: Cancer can cause depression, and not just because the diagnosis is "depressing." Cancerous tumors, as well as the immune system that is combatting them, produce high levels of a chemical that can cause the emotional and behavioral symptoms of depression. A study of cancer in rats, which after all are not aware of having the disease, found that the animals would float passively in water instead of swimming for safety, and show other signs of anxiety and apathy (Pyter et al., 2009). Cancer is also not brought on by some sort of "cancer-prone" personality. Studies of thousands of people around the world, from Japan to Finland, have found no link between cancer and personality traits (Nakaya et al., 2003).

What about positive emotions? Do they promote health and long life? Here it is difficult to separate cause and effect. Finding a group of very old people who are happy does not mean that happiness contributed to their longevity; as people age, they often become less angry and more content (see Chapter 3). Some of them might have been really surly when they were 20 or 40. Nonetheless, positive emotions could be physically beneficial because they soften or counteract the high arousal caused by negative emotions or chronic stressors. They may dispose people to think more creatively about their opportunities and choices and, as with optimism and internal locus of control, motivate people to take action to achieve their goals (Kok, Catalino, & Frederickson, 2008). People who express positive feelings are also more likely to attract friends and supporters than are people who are always bitter and brooding, and, as we will see, social support is one of the most powerful contributors to good health (Friedman & Martin, 2011; Ong, 2010; Pressman & Cohen, 2005).

If you don't feel cheerful and happy all the time, don't worry; everyone feels grumpy, irritable, and unhappy on occasion. But are negative emotions more typical of your life than positive ones? If so, what actions might you take to ensure a better ratio of positive to negative emotions?

👁 **Watch** the **Video** Michael Cohn: Positive Emotions (APS Player) at **MyPsychLab**

Emotional Inhibition and Expression

Many people assume that the healthiest thing to do when they feel angry, depressed, or worried is to try to suppress those feelings. But anyone who has tried to banish an unwelcome thought, a bitter memory, or pangs of longing for an ex-lover knows how hard it can be to do this. When you are trying to avoid a thought, you are in fact processing the thought more frequently; you are rehearsing it. That is why, when you are obsessed with someone you were once romantically involved with, trying not to think of the person actually prolongs your emotional longing (Wegner & Gold, 1995).

Prolonged *emotional inhibition* requires physical effort that can be stressful to the body. People who are able to express matters of great emotional importance to them show elevated levels of disease-fighting white blood cells, whereas people who suppress such feelings tend to have decreased levels (Petrie, Booth, & Pennebaker,

Everyone has secrets and private moments of sad reflection, but when you feel sad or fearful for too long, keeping your feelings to yourself may increase your stress.

1998). Suppressing feelings has a social cost, too. In a study that followed first-year college students as they adjusted to being in a new environment, most of those who expressed their worries and fears openly with other students ended up with better relationships and greater satisfaction with school, compared to those who said they preferred to keep their emotions to themselves (Srivastava et al., 2009).

The Benefits of Confession. Given the findings on the harmful effects of feeling negative emotions and also the difficulty and costs of suppressing them, what is a person supposed to do with them? One way to reduce the wear and tear of negative emotions comes from research on the benefits of confession: divulging (even if only to yourself) private thoughts and feelings that make you ashamed, worried, or sad (Pennebaker, 2002, 2011). First-year college students who wrote about their "deepest thoughts and feelings" in a private journal reported greater short-term homesickness and anxiety, compared to students who wrote about trivial topics. But by the end of the school year, they had had fewer bouts of flu and fewer visits to the infirmary than the control group did (Pennebaker, Colder, & Sharp, 1990).

Get Involved!   **True Confessions**

To see whether the research on confession will benefit you, take a moment to write down your deepest thoughts and feelings about being in college, your past, a secret, your future…anything you have never told anyone. Do this again tomorrow and then again for a few days in a row. Note your feelings after writing. Are you upset, troubled, sad, or relieved? Does your account change over time? Research suggests that if you do this exercise now, you may have fewer colds, headaches, and trips to the doctor over the next few months (Pennebaker, Colder, & Sharp, 1990).

This method is especially powerful when people write about traumatic experiences. When a group of college students was asked to write about a personal, traumatic experience for 20 minutes a day for four days, many told stories of sexual coercion, physical beatings, humiliation, or parental abandonment. Yet most had never discussed these experiences with anyone. The researchers collected data on the students' physical symptoms, white blood cell counts, emotions, and visits to the health center. On every measure, the students who wrote about traumatic experiences were better off than those who wrote only about neutral topics (Pennebaker, Kiecolt-Glaser, & Glaser, 1988).

The benefits of writing occur primarily when the revelation produces insight and understanding, thereby fostering the ability to distance yourself from the bad experience and ending the stressful repetition of obsessive thoughts and unresolved feelings (Kross & Ayduk, 2011; Lepore, Ragan, & Jones, 2000). One young woman, who had been molested at the age of 9 by a boy a year older, at first wrote about her feelings of embarrassment and guilt. By the third day, she was writing about how angry she felt at the boy. By the last day, she had begun to see the whole event differently; he was a child too, after all. When the study was over, she said, "Before, when I thought about it, I'd lie to myself….Now, I don't feel like I even have to think about it because I got it off my chest. I finally admitted that it happened."

The Benefits of Letting Grievances Go. Another way of letting go of negative emotions is to give up the thoughts that produce them and adopt a perspective that might lead to forgiveness. When people rehearse their grievances and hold on to their grudges, their blood pressure, heart rate, and skin conductance rise. Forgiving thoughts, as in the preceding example ("He was a child too"), reduce these signs of physiological arousal and restore feelings of control (Witvliet, Ludwig, & Vander Laan, 2001). (See Figure 13.6.)

Forgiveness, like confession when it works, helps people see events in a new light. It promotes empathy, the ability to see the situation from another person's perspective. It strengthens and repairs ongoing relationships (Fehr, Gelfand, & Nag, 2010).

But let's not oversimplify: Forgiveness is not a cure-all and not always a good thing; it depends on the context in which the conflict or grievance occurs (McNulty & Fincham, 2012). In a study of women at a domestic violence shelter, the women who forgave their abusive partners were more likely to return to them, and thus continue a pattern of psychological and physical violence (McNulty, 2011). Forgiveness does *not* mean that the offended person denies, ignores, or excuses the offense, which might be serious. It does mean that the victim is able, finally, to come to terms with the injustice and let go of obsessive feelings of hurt, rage, and vengefulness. As the Chinese proverb says, "He who pursues revenge should dig two graves."

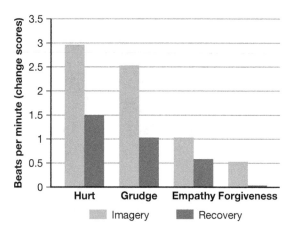

FIGURE 13.6 Heartfelt Forgiveness
Participants in a study were asked to think of someone who they felt had offended or hurt them. Then they were asked to imagine unforgiving reactions (rehearsing the hurt and harboring a grudge) and forgiving reactions (feeling empathy, forgiving). People's heart rates increased much more sharply, and took longer to return to normal, when their thoughts were unforgiving.

Recite & Review

 Study and **Review** at **MyPsychLab**

Recite: You will never forgive yourself if you don't recite aloud what you know about hostility and health, depression and health, the benefits of confessing secrets, and the benefits of forgiveness.

Review: Next, read this section again.

Now Take This *Quick Quiz:*

1. Which aspect of Type A behavior is most hazardous to the heart? (a) working hard, (b) being in a hurry, (c) cynical hostility, (d) irritability in traffic, (e) general grumpiness

2. Amber has many worries about being in college, but she is afraid to tell anyone. What might be the healthiest solution for her? (a) trying not to think about her feelings, (b) writing down her feelings and then rereading and rethinking what she wrote, (c) talking frequently about her worries to anyone who will listen, (d) tweeting her friends about her moods

3. We are giving away an answer to #2, but why might answer *d* not be helpful to Amber?

Answers:

1. c 2. b 3. Sending tweets, or posting her feelings on her Facebook page, might make Amber momentarily feel good, but she probably won't retrieve those messages later to reread and rethink about what she wrote, and rethinking her story is the important element.

You are about to learn . . .

- **ways of calming the body when you are feeling stressed.**
- **the difference between emotion-focused and problem-focused coping.**
- **how to reduce stress by rethinking and reappraising your problems.**
- **the benefits and limitations of social support.**

Coping With Stress

We have noted that most people who are under stress, even those living in difficult situations, do not become ill. In addition to feeling optimistic and in control, being conscientious, and not wallowing around in negative emotions, how do they manage to cope?

These two friends know all about surviving and thriving.

The most immediate way to deal with the physiological tension of stress and negative emotions is to take time out and reduce the body's physical arousal. One beneficial way is through the ancient practice of *meditation*, whether for Eastern purposes of enlightenment or Western purposes of well-being (Sedlmeier et al., 2012). There are various ways of meditating, but they all foster emotional tranquility by helping people accept feelings of anger, sadness, or anxiety without judging those emotions or trying to get rid of them—a form of secondary control (Davidson et al., 2003; Moyer et al., 2011). Another effective buffer between stressors and illness is exercise. People who are physically fit have fewer health problems than people who are less fit even when they are under the same pressures. They also show lower physiological arousal to stressors (Otto & Smits, 2011; Vita et al., 1998). These activities, along with any others that calm your body and focus your mind—including prayer, massage, music, dancing, or baking bread—are all good coping methods. But if your house has burned down or you need a serious operation, other strategies will be necessary.

Watch the **Video** In the Real World: Reducing Stress, Improving Health at **MyPsychLab**

Solving the Problem LO 13.16

Years ago, at the age of 23, a friend of ours named Simi Linton was struck by tragedy. Linton, her new husband, and her best friend were in a horrific car accident. When she awoke in a hospital room, with only a vague memory of the crash, she learned that her husband and friend had been killed and that she herself had permanent injury to the spine and would never walk again.

How in the world does anyone recover from such a devastating event? Some people advise survivors of disaster or tragedy to "get it out of your system" or to "get in touch with your feelings." But survivors know they feel miserable. What should they *do*? This question gets to the heart of the difference between *emotion-focused* and *problem-focused coping* (Lazarus, 2000; Lazarus & Folkman, 1984). Emotion-focused coping concentrates on the emotions the problem has caused, whether anger, anxiety, or grief. For a period of time after any tragedy or disaster, it is normal to give in to these emotions and feel overwhelmed by them. In this stage, people often need to talk constantly about the event, which helps them come to terms with it, make sense of it, and decide what to do about it (Lepore, Ragan, & Jones, 2000).

Eventually, however, most people become ready to concentrate on solving the problem itself. The specific steps in problem-focused coping depend on the nature of the problem: whether it is a pressing but one-time decision; a continuing difficulty, such as living with a disability; or an anticipated event, such as having an operation. Once the problem is identified, the coper can learn as much as possible about it from professionals, friends, books, and others in the same predicament (Clarke & Evans, 1998). Becoming informed increases the feeling of control and can speed recovery (Doering et al., 2000). But be wary of *bad* information, which is as prevalent on the Internet as is the helpful kind.

As for Simi Linton, she learned how to do just about everything in her wheelchair (including dancing!), and she went back to school. She got a Ph.D. in psychology, remarried, and became a highly respected teacher, counselor, writer, and activist committed to improving conditions and opportunities for people with disabilities (Linton, 2006).

Rethinking the Problem LO 13.17

Some problems are unavoidable facts of life, such as developing a chronic illness, losing a job, or having an alcoholic or mentally ill parent. Now what? Health psychologists have identified three effective cognitive coping methods:

1 Reappraising the situation. Although you may not be able to get rid of a stressor, you can choose to think about it differently. We have seen how appraisals can generate emotions and how those emotions can be changed through *reappraisal*. Reappraisal can turn anger into sympathy, worry into determination, and feelings of loss into feelings of opportunity. Maybe that job you lost was dismal but you were too afraid to quit and look for another; now you can. Reappraisal improves well-being and softens negative emotions (Denson, Spanovic, & Miller, 2009; Gross & John, 2003; Moskowitz et al., 2009). You can even reappraise the physiological signals of stress, for example by interpreting that elevated heart rate not as troubling or dangerous or a sign of "nervousness" but as giving you a burst of energy that will help you boost performance (Jamieson, Mendes, & Nock, 2013).

2 Learning from the experience. Some people emerge from adversity with newly acquired skills, having been forced to learn something they had not known before, such as how to cope with the medical system or how to manage a deceased parent's estate. Others discover sources of courage and strength they did not know they had. In fact, having a history of *some* experiences with loss, hardship, illness, or other stressors actually predicts better health outcomes over the years than having a life with *no* adversity (Davis, Nolen-Hoeksema, & Larson, 1998; Seery, 2011). Facing life's stresses head on gives people the skills of mastery and control, which are keys to well-being and knowing how to cope with further problems.

3 Making social comparisons. In a difficult situation, successful copers often compare themselves to others who they feel are less fortunate. Even if they have fatal diseases, they find someone who is worse off (Taylor & Lobel, 1989; Wood, Michela, & Giordano, 2000). Sometimes successful copers also compare themselves to those who are doing better than they are (Collins, 1996). They might say, "She and I have the same kinds of problems; how come she's doing so much better in school than I am? What does she know that I don't?" Such comparisons provide a person with information about ways of coping, managing an illness, or improving a stressful situation (Suls, Martin, & Wheeler, 2002).

Drawing on Social Support LO 13.18

A final way to deal with negative emotions and stress is to reach out to others. Your health depends not only on what is going on in your body and mind but also on what is going on in your relationships—the extent of *social support* that you have. Being involved in social networks and a close community is one of the most powerful predictors of having a long and healthy life (Friedman & Martin, 2011). People who are excessively self-reliant or who have high attachment anxiety—avoiding relationships altogether or being constantly worried about the ones they are in—have a greater risk of stroke, heart attacks, and ulcers (Jaremka et al., 2013). Why?

When Friends Help You Cope. Think of all the ways in which family members, friends, neighbors, and co-workers can help you. They can offer concern and affection. They can help you evaluate problems and plan a course of action. They can offer resources and services such as lending you money or a car, or taking notes in class for you when you are sick. They are sources of attachment and connection. And groups often provide their members with a sense of meaning, purpose, and belonging (Haslam et al., 2009; Uchino, 2009).

Friends can even improve your health. Work-related stress and unemployment may increase a person's vulnerability to the common cold, but having a lot of friends and social contacts reduces that risk (Cohen et al., 2003). Social support is especially important for people who have stressful jobs that require high cardiovascular responsiveness day after day, such as firefighters. Having social support helps the heart rate and stress hormones return to normal more quickly after a stressful episode (Roy, Steptoe, & Kirschbaum, 1998). In contrast, loneliness and lack of support, especially during times of stress, are associated with chronic inflammation, the release by the immune system of white blood cells even when

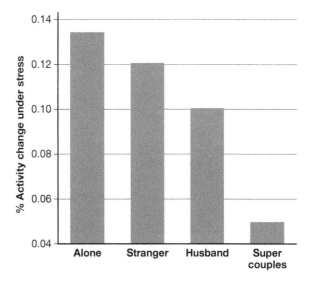

FIGURE 13.7 Hugs and Health

Women had to lie in an MRI machine while receiving mild but stressful shocks on their ankle. Those who went through the test alone showed the highest activation of the hypothalamus and other regions of the brain involved in stress and anxiety. A stranger's calming touch reduced activation somewhat and a husband's touch reduced it even more. The women in "super couples," who felt the closest to their husbands (right bar), showed the lowest signs of stress (Coan, Schaefer, & Davidson, 2006).

there is no injury or disease for them to fight. In turn, chronic inflammation is linked to a variety of illnesses, from cardiovascular problems to herpes (Jaremka et al., 2013).

When social support comes from a loving partner, its benefits are especially dramatic. In a study of 16 couples, the wives had to lie in an MRI machine, periodically receiving a mild but stressful electric shock on the ankle (Coan, Schaefer, & Davidson, 2006). During the procedure, some women received a touch on the hand from a stranger; others held hands with their husbands. The women's brain images showed activation in the hypothalamus and other regions involved with pain, physical arousal, and negative emotions. Yet, as you can see in Figure 13.7, the moment the women felt a husband's reassuring hand, their brain activation subsided in all the regions that had been revved up to cope with threat and fear. Holding hands with a stranger was comforting, but did not produce as great a decrease in brain activation as did a husband's touch.

When a touch is affectionate and welcome, it can actually elevate some "therapeutic" hormones, especially *oxytocin*, the hormone that induces relaxation and is associated with mothering and attachment. In fact, human bodies may be designed not only for a fight-or-flight response to stress and challenge, but also a "tend and befriend"

Friends can be our greatest source of warmth, support, and fun...

response—being friendly and conciliatory, seeking out a friend or loved one, taking care of others (Taylor & Master, 2011). Animal studies find that early nurturing by parents or other adults who care for the young can affect the sensitivity of the HPA axis, making the infants more resilient to later chronic stressors (Young & Francis, 2008). Such findings may help explain why children who lack nurturing become physically more vulnerable to illness, and why a significant minority of children who grow up under adverse conditions do *not* develop health problems: They have been protected by having warm, nurturing mothers (Miller et al., 2011).

However, once again it is important not to oversimplify by concluding that people can defeat any illness if they just have the right amount and kind of social support. Some years ago, a psychiatrist claimed, on the basis of a preliminary study, that women with advanced breast cancer lived longer if they joined support groups, but the study has been discredited and was never replicated (Coyne et al., 2009). (Of course, support groups can be emotionally and socially beneficial to individual members.)

Moreover, not all cultural groups define "social support" the same way or benefit from the same kind. Asians and Asian Americans are more reluctant than white Americans to ask for help explicitly from friends, colleagues, and family and to disclose feelings of distress. Being particularly attuned to the harmony of their relationships, many Asians are concerned about the potentially negative and embarrassing effects of self-disclosure or of seeking help. As a result, they often feel more stressed and have elevated stress hormones when they are required to ask for help or reveal their private feelings (Kim, Sherman, & Taylor, 2008). But Asians do not differ from Anglos in their reliance on, and need for, *implicit* social support—the knowledge that someone will be there to help if they need it.

...And Coping with Friends.

Needless to say, sometimes other people aren't helpful. Sometimes they themselves are the source of unhappiness, stress, and anger. Even social networks like Facebook have a dark side. Because everyone on these sites seems so happy and successful, boasting of accomplishments, babies, promotions, great jobs, adorable new puppies, perfect batches of cookies, and super vacations, many people feel worse about themselves after spending time scrolling through their friends' updates. After all, not many students post that they are lonely or just got dumped; parents don't report the tedium of raising young children or their kids' tantrums. No wonder that many first-year college students consistently underestimate their friends' and peers'

...and friends can also be sources of exasperation, anger, and misery.

bad moods and negative experiences and overestimate how much fun their peers are having. (It's the "no one is as lonely as I am"/ "everyone else is going to parties" syndrome.) Comparing themselves to allegedly happier friends, they feel lonelier and more dejected (Jordan et al., 2011).

In close relationships, the same person who is a source of support can also become a source of stress, especially if the two parties are arguing all the time. Being in a bitter, uncommunicative relationship not only makes the partners depressed and angry, but also affects their health habits, elevates stress hormones, and directly influences their cardiovascular, endocrine, and immune systems (Kiecolt-Glaser & Newton, 2001). Couples who argue in a hostile fashion—criticizing, interrupting, or insulting the other person, and becoming angry and defensive—show significant elevations of cortisol and poorer immune function afterward (Kiecolt-Glaser et al., 2005). Couples who argue in a positive fashion—trying to find common ground, compromising, and using humor to defuse tension—do not show these impairments. As one student of ours observed, "This study gives new meaning to the accusation 'You make me sick!'"

Friends and relatives may also be unsupportive in times of trouble simply out of ignorance or awkwardness. They may abandon you or say something stupid and hurtful. Sometimes they actively block your efforts to change bad health habits, such as binge drinking or smoking, by making fun of you or pressuring you to conform to what "everyone" does. And sometimes, because they have never been in the same situation and do not know what to do to help, they may try to cheer you up, saying, "Everything will be fine," rather than let you talk about your fears or find solutions, or they may try to press you to join a support group "for your own good," even if it wouldn't be.

Finally, we should not forget the benefits of giving support, rather than always being on the receiving end. Julius Segal (1986), a psychologist who worked with Holocaust survivors, hostages, refugees, and other survivors of catastrophe, wrote that a key element in their recovery was compassion for others: "healing through helping." The ability to look outside yourself is related to all of the successful coping mechanisms we have discussed. It encourages you to solve problems instead of blaming others or just venting your emotions; helps you reappraise the situation by seeing it from another person's perspective; fosters forgiveness; and allows you to gain perspective on your own problems (Brown et al., 2003). Healing through helping thus helps everyone to accept difficult situations that are facts of life.

Recite & Review

✓ **Study** and **Review** at **MyPsychLab**

Recite: Find a friend to whom you can describe ways of reducing the physiological arousal of stress, cognitive strategies for coping with stressful problems, and the benefits and potential harms of close relationships.

Review: Next, reappraise any negative attitudes you might have about reviewing this material, and reread it.

Now take this *Quick Quiz:*

1. You accidentally broke your glasses. Which response is an example of reappraisal? (a) "I am such a stupid, clumsy idiot!" (b) "I never do anything right." (c) "What a shame, but I've been wanting new frames anyway." (d) "I'll forget about it in aerobics class."

2. Finding out what your legal and financial resources are when you have been victimized by a crime is an example of (a) problem-focused coping, (b) emotion-focused coping, (c) distraction, (d) reappraisal.

3. "This class drives me crazy, but I'm better off than my friends who aren't in college" is an example of (a) distraction, (b) social comparison, (c) denial, (d) empathy.

4. Your roommate has turned your room into a garbage dump, filled with rotten leftover food and unwashed clothes. Assuming that you don't like living with rotting food and dirty clothes, what coping strategies described in this section might help you?

Answers:

1.c 2.a 3.b 4. You might solve the problem by finding a compromise (e.g., cleaning the room together). You could reappraise the seriousness of the problem ("I only have to live with this person until the end of the term") or compare your roommate to others who are worse ("At least mine is generous and friendly"). And you might mobilize some social support, perhaps by offering your friends a pizza if they help you clean up.

PSYCHOLOGY IN THE NEWS REVISITED ///////

Joe Stack, whose story opened this chapter, burned down his house, with callous disregard for his wife and young stepdaughter, and then killed himself and two IRS employees. In the rant he posted on the Internet, he wrote: "Violence not only is the answer, it is the only answer." Really? What did it accomplish?

As we saw in this chapter, when we are feeling extreme emotions or when major stressors require the body to cope with threat, fear, or danger, the body whirls into action to give us the energy to respond. Just about everyone has had the unpleasant experience of a racing heart, sweaty palms, and other emotional symptoms when we feel betrayed, anxious, or angry. But does that mean we have no control over our emotions, especially those caused by extremely stressful experiences?

As we also saw, biology does not give us the whole picture. It is equally important to understand the role of perceptions, beliefs, and expectations in generating emotions and stress. Stack blamed the IRS for

his financial losses, and his rage resulted from his perception that he was an undeserving victim. But what if he had been able to interpret his problems differently? What if he had been able to evaluate, calmly and perhaps with the help of a financial planner or psychotherapist, the reasons he was in trouble, and had come to understand and accept his own responsibility for his misfortunes? What beliefs made him feel entitled to retire at a relatively young age, when millions of others work hard their whole lives, through hard times as well as boom times?

The findings on the stressful nature of bitter marital relationships may also be relevant to Stack's life. His cruel act of burning down the house certainly suggests he was blaming his wife for his misery as much as he blamed the government. But marital disputes involve two people, and it's rare that one partner is 100 percent to blame. What if he had been able to understand his own role in creating his unhappiness in his marriage?

This chapter also examined the importance of having a sense of control over events, noting the helplessness and panic that can ensue when people lose their feelings of control. Westerners, particularly, tend to have a philosophy of rebelling against unwelcome events rather than of accepting disappointments and

losses. Stack would appear to have been an extreme example of this stance toward the world: feeling helpless and unable to control his life, he did not know what else to do other than end it in a blaze of fury.

Yet there are better ways of coping than by killing your partner or employees of the institution that you think is causing your stress and anger. Stack could have found a way to improve his marriage and his financial situation without committing murder and suicide. These include rethinking the problem, learning from it and resolving the conflict, comparing oneself to others less fortunate, and helping others.

In the final analysis, successful coping does not mean eliminating all sources of stress or all difficult emotions. It does not mean constant happiness or a life without pain and frustration. The healthy person faces problems, deals with them, and gets beyond them, but the problems are necessary if the person is to acquire coping skills that endure. To wish for a life without stress, or a life without emotion, would be like wishing for a life without friends. The result might be calm, but it would be joyless. Daily hassles, difficult decisions, chronic problems, and occasional tragedies are inescapable. How we handle them is the test of our humanity.

Taking Psychology With You

The Dilemma of Anger: "Let It Out" or "Bottle It Up"?

What do you do when you feel angry? Do you tend to brood and sulk, collecting your righteous complaints like acorns for the winter, or do you erupt, hurling your wrath on anyone or anything at hand? Do you discuss your feelings when you have calmed down? Does "letting anger out" get rid of it for you, or does it only make it more intense? The answers are crucial for how you get along with your family, neighbors, employers, and strangers.

Critical thinkers can learn to think carefully about how and when to express anger, and make a calm decision on how to proceed. Inability to control chronic feelings of anger can be as emotionally devastating and unhealthy as chronic problems with depression or anxiety. Yet contrary to much pop-psych advice, expressing anger does

not always get it "out of your system"; often people feel worse, physically and mentally, after an angry confrontation. When people brood and ruminate about their anger, talk to others incessantly about how angry they are, or ventilate their feelings in hostile acts, their blood pressure shoots up, they often feel angrier, and they behave even *more* aggressively later than if they had just let their feelings of anger subside (Bushman et al., 2005; Tavris, 1989). Conversely, when people learn to control their tempers and express anger constructively, they usually feel better, not worse; calmer, not angrier.

When people are feeling angry, they may not be able to control that racing heart and fuming feeling, but they can control what they do next: Take five and cool off, or act impetuously and make matters worse. The Internet is full of impulsively written, venomous comments. Some people scream abuses at their friends or family, send an insulting

text in the heat of the moment, or strike out physically. If a particular action soothes their feelings or gets the desired response from others, they are likely to acquire a habit. Soon that habit feels "natural," as if it could never be changed. But it can be. If you have acquired an abusive or aggressive habit, the research in this chapter offers practical suggestions for learning constructive ways of managing anger:

Don't sound off in the heat of anger; let bodily arousal cool down. Whether your arousal comes from background stresses such as heat, crowds, or loud noise or from conflict with another person, take time to relax and decide whether you are really angry or just tired and tense. This is the reason for the sage old advice to count to 10, count to 100, or sleep on it. Other cooling-off strategies include taking a time-out in the middle of an argument, meditating or relaxing, and calming yourself with a distracting activity.

Don't take it personally. If you feel that you have been insulted, check your perception for its accuracy. Could there be another reason for the behavior you find offensive? People who are quick to feel anger tend to interpret other people's actions as intentional offenses. People who are slow to anger tend to give others the benefit of the doubt, and they are not as focused on their own injured pride. Empathy ("Poor guy, he's feeling rotten") is usually incompatible with anger, so practice seeing the situation from the other person's perspective.

If you decide that expressing anger is appropriate, be sure you use the right verbal and nonverbal language to make yourself understood. Because cultures (and families) have different display rules, make sure the recipient of your anger understands what you are feeling and what complaint you are trying to convey—and find out whether or not the person thinks your anger is *appropriate*. When researchers compared the use of anger by Asian-American and Anglo-American negotiators, expressing anger was effective for the Anglo teams—it got more concessions from the other side—but was much less effective for the Asians (Adam, Shirako, & Maddux, 2010).

Think carefully about how to express anger so that you will get the results you want. What do you want your anger to accomplish? Do you just want to make the other person feel bad, or do you want the other person to understand your concerns and make amends? Shouting "You moron! How *could* you be so stupid!" might accomplish the former goal, but it's not likely to get the person to apologize, let alone to change his or her behavior. If your goal is to improve a bad situation or achieve justice, learning how to express anger so the other person will listen is essential.

Of course, if you just want to blow off steam, go right ahead; but you risk becoming a hothead.

Summary

((• Listen to the Audio File at MyPsychLab

The Nature of Emotion

- Emotions evolved to bind people together, motivate them to achieve their goals, and help them make decisions and plans. The experience of *emotion* involves physiological changes in the face, brain, and autonomic nervous system; cognitive processes such as *appraisal* and interpretation; *action tendencies*; and subjective feelings. In turn, emotions and their expression are influenced and shaped by cultural norms and regulations.

- Some facial expressions—anger, fear, sadness, happiness, disgust, surprise, contempt, and possibly pride—are widely recognized across cultures. They foster communication with others, signal our intentions to others, enhance infant survival, and, as studies of *facial feedback* show, help us to identify our own emotional states. But an accurate reading of others' facial expressions increases among members of the same ethnicity, and depends on the social context. Also, because people can and do disguise their emotions, their expressions do not always communicate accurately.

- Many aspects of emotion are associated with specific parts of the brain. The *amygdala* is responsible for initially evaluating the emotional importance of incoming sensory information and is especially involved in fear. The *cerebral cortex* provides the cognitive ability to override this initial appraisal. Emotions generally involve the motivation to approach or withdraw; regions of the *left* prefrontal cortex appear to be specialized for the motivation to approach others (as with happiness and anger),

whereas regions of the *right* prefrontal region are specialized for withdrawal or escape (as with disgust and fear).

- *Mirror neurons* throughout the brain are activated when people observe others, especially other people of the same group or others they like. These neurons seem to be involved in empathy, imitation, synchrony, and *mood contagion*.

- During the experience of any emotion, the autonomic nervous system spurs production of the hormones *epinephrine* and *norepinephrine*, producing a state of physiological arousal to prepare the body for an output of energy.

- The most popular method of so-called lie detection is the *polygraph machine*, but it has low reliability and validity because no patterns of autonomic nervous system activity are specific to lying. Other methods, such as voice analyzers or brain scans, have similar drawbacks.

- Cognitive approaches to emotion emphasize the *appraisals* that are involved in different emotions. Thoughts and emotions operate reciprocally, each influencing the other. Some emotions, such as shame and guilt, require complex cognitive capacities.

Emotion and Culture

- Many psychologists believe that all human beings share the ability to experience a few basic emotions, a view supported by research on emotion *prototypes*. However, cultural differences in values, norms, and appraisals generate emotion blends and culture-specific emotional variations. Culture affects almost every aspect of emotional experience, including which emotions are considered appropriate or wrong, and what people feel emotional about.

- Culture strongly influences *display rules*, including those governing nonverbal *body language*, that regulate how and whether people express their emotions. *Emotion work* is the effort a person makes to display an emotion he or she does not feel but feels obliged to convey.

- Women and men feel the same range of emotions, but gender rules shape differences in emotional expression. North American women on average are more expressive than men, except when it comes to expressing anger at strangers. But both sexes are less expressive to a person of higher status than they, both sexes will do the emotion work their job requires, and some situations foster expressiveness in everybody. Moreover, gender differences vary across cultures.

The Nature of Stress

- The relationship between emotions and stress is both physiological and psychological. Chronic negative emotions can become chronically stressful, and chronic stress can create negative emotions.

- Hans Selye argued that environmental stressors such as heat, pain, and danger produce a *general adaptation syndrome*, in which the body responds in three stages: *alarm* (during which the body mobilizes a *fight-or-flight response*), *resistance*, and *exhaustion*. If a stressor persists, it may overwhelm the body's ability to cope, and illness may result.

- Modern research has added to Selye's work. When a person is under stress or in danger, the hypothalamus sends messages to the endocrine glands along two major pathways. One activates the sympathetic division of the autonomic nervous system, releasing adrenal hormones from the inner part of the adrenal glands. In the other, the hypothalamus initiates activity along the *HPA axis*. Chemical messengers travel from the hypothalamus to the pituitary, and in turn to the outer part (cortex) of the adrenal glands. The adrenal cortex secretes *cortisol* and other hormones that increase energy. Excess levels of cortisol can become harmful in the long run.

- When the stressors of poverty and unemployment become chronic, they can increase people's stress levels and increase their chances of illness. But responses to stress differ across individuals, depending on the type of stressor and the individual's own genetic predispositions.

- *Health psychologists* and researchers in the interdisciplinary field of *psychoneuroimmunology* (PNI) are studying the interaction among psychological factors, the nervous and endocrine systems, and the immune system (particularly the white blood cells that destroy harmful foreign bodies, called *antigens*). Chronic stress can even shorten *telomeres*, protein complexes at the end of chromosomes that determine cell life.

- Psychological factors affect responses to stress. Realistic optimism, conscientiousness, and having an *internal locus of control*

improve immune function and also increase a person's ability to live with ongoing problems and recover more speedily from illness. Cultures differ in the kind of control they emphasize and value: *primary control*, trying to change a stressful situation, or *secondary control*, learning to accept and accommodate to a stressful situation.

Stress and Emotion

- Researchers have sought links between emotions, stress, and illness. Chronic anger, especially in the form of *cynical* or *antagonistic* hostility, is a strong risk factor in heart disease. Major depression also increases the risk of later heart disease. No link has been found between personality traits and cancer.

- The effort to suppress negative emotions, worries, secrets, and memories of upsetting experiences can become stressful to the body. Two ways of letting go of negative emotions include confession and forgiveness. The goal is to achieve insight and understanding, distance oneself from the bad experience, and let go of grudges. Forgiveness can be harmful, of course, if it keeps people in violent or abusive relationships.

Coping With Stress

- The first step in coping with stress and negative emotions is to reduce their physical effects, such as through *meditation* and exercise. The second is to focus on solving the problem (*problem-focused coping*) rather than on venting the emotions caused by the problem (*emotion-focused coping*). A third approach is to rethink the problem, which involves *reappraisal*, learning from the experience, and comparing oneself to others.

- *Social support* is essential in maintaining physical health and emotional well-being. A touch from a supportive partner calms the alarm circuits of the brain and raises levels of *oxytocin*, which may result in reduced heart rate and blood pressure. However, friends and family can also be sources of stress. Couples who quarrel in a hostile and negative way show impaired immune function. Giving support to others is also associated with health and hastens recovery from traumatic experiences.

Psychology in the News, Revisited

- We may not always be able to control the physiological arousal produced by stress or intense emotions, but we generally are able to decide how to behave when we are upset. Coping with stress does not mean trying to live without pain or problems. It means learning how to live with them.

Taking Psychology With You

- Ventilating anger when you are angry often backfires, making both sides angrier and the problem worse. Constructive alternatives include cooling off before saying or doing anything; not taking a disagreement personally; finding the right verbal and nonverbal ways of making your complaint understood; and thinking about how to express anger to get the results you want.

Key Terms

emotion **462**
action tendencies **462**
facial feedback **462**
amygdala **465**
emotion regulation **465**
mirror neurons **466**
mood contagion **466**
epinephrine **467**
norepinephrine **467**
polygraph machine **467**
appraisals **469**

emotion prototypes **471**
display rules **472**
body language **473**
emotion work **473**
general adaptation syndrome (Selye) **475**
alarm, resistance, and exhaustion phases of stress **475**
fight-or-flight response **476**
HPA axis **476**

cortisol **476**
health psychology **477**
psychoneuroimmunology (PNI) **477**
antigens **478**
telomere **478**
locus of control **480**
internal versus external locus of control **480**
primary versus secondary control **480**

cynical/antagonistic hostility **496**
emotional inhibition **483**
emotion-focused coping **486**
problem-focused coping **486**
reappraisal **486**
social comparison **489**
social support **486**
oxytocin **487**

The Nature of Emotion

↓

Emotion involves physiological changes in the face, brain, and autonomic nervous system; cognitive appraisals of events; tendencies toward action; and subjective feelings, all influenced by cultural norms.

↓   ↓   ↓

Emotion and the Body

Some facial expressions are recognized across cultures and thus seem to reflect key emotions: anger, fear, sadness, happiness, disgust, surprise, contempt, and possibly pride. The functions of facial expressions include:
• identifying our own emotions through **facial feedback**.
• communicating emotion.
• allowing us to lie about our true feelings.

Brain areas associated with emotion:
• The *amygdala* evaluates incoming emotion, especially anger and fear.

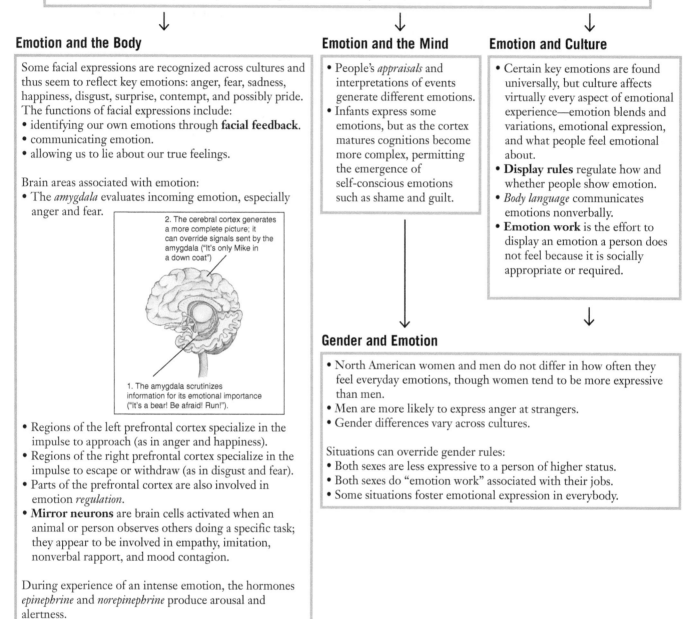

2. The cerebral cortex generates a more complete picture; it can override signals sent by the amygdala ("It's only Mike in a down coat")

1. The amygdala scrutinizes information for its emotional importance ("It's a bear! Be afraid! Run!").

• Regions of the left prefrontal cortex specialize in the impulse to approach (as in anger and happiness).
• Regions of the right prefrontal cortex specialize in the impulse to escape or withdraw (as in disgust and fear).
• Parts of the prefrontal cortex are also involved in emotion *regulation*.
• **Mirror neurons** are brain cells activated when an animal or person observes others doing a specific task; they appear to be involved in empathy, imitation, nonverbal rapport, and mood contagion.

During experience of an intense emotion, the hormones *epinephrine* and *norepinephrine* produce arousal and alertness.

↓

Biology and Deception

• The *polygraph machine* is assumed to detect lies, but it is actually a measure of emotional arousal.
• Polygraphs sometimes identify liars and guilty people, but they have a high rate of falsely accusing innocent people of lying.
• No current technology exists that can directly and reliably determine whether someone is telling a falsehood.

Emotion and the Mind

• People's *appraisals* and interpretations of events generate different emotions.
• Infants express some emotions, but as the cortex matures cognitions become more complex, permitting the emergence of self-conscious emotions such as shame and guilt.

↓

Gender and Emotion

• North American women and men do not differ in how often they feel everyday emotions, though women tend to be more expressive than men.
• Men are more likely to express anger at strangers.
• Gender differences vary across cultures.

Situations can override gender rules:
• Both sexes are less expressive to a person of higher status.
• Both sexes do "emotion work" associated with their jobs.
• Some situations foster emotional expression in everybody.

Emotion and Culture

• Certain key emotions are found universally, but culture affects virtually every aspect of emotional experience—emotion blends and variations, emotional expression, and what people feel emotional about.
• **Display rules** regulate how and whether people show emotion.
• *Body language* communicates emotions nonverbally.
• **Emotion work** is the effort to display an emotion a person does not feel because it is socially appropriate or required.

↓

The Nature of Stress

Stress and the Body

Hans Selye argued that environmental stressors produce a **general adaptation syndrome**, physiological reactions that occur in three phases:
1. Alarm
2. Resistance
3. Exhaustion

The Immune System: PNI

Psychoneuroimmunology (PNI) is the study of the relationships among psychology, the nervous and endocrine systems, and the immune system, interacting to protect health or increase the risk of illness.

Physical Changes

When a person is under stress, the hypothalamus sends messages to the endocrine glands along two major pathways to:
• activate the sympathetic nervous system for a *fight-or-flight response*.
• initiate activity along the **HPA axis**, which spurs production of cortisol and other hormones that increase energy.

Chronic stressors that affect the immune system and increase the risk of illness include:
• unemployment and work-related problems.
• poverty, powerlessness, and low status.

Psychological Factors

Psychological factors that can increase a person's ability to live with ongoing problems and recover from illness include:
• realistic optimism.
• conscientiousness.
• having an internal **locus of control**.

Health and well-being may depend on a combination of:
• **primary control**, trying to change the stressful situation.
• **secondary control**, learning to accept and adapt to the stressful situation.

Stress and Emotion

↓

Emotional factors that increase the risk of heart disease and other illness include:
• cynical or antagonistic hostility.
• chronic depression.
• prolonged inhibition of negative emotions.

Two ways of letting go of negative emotions:
1. confession: revealing private thoughts and feelings.
2. forgiveness: coming to terms with an injustice.

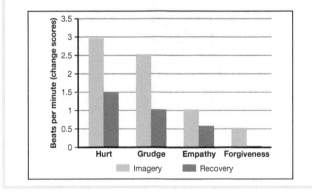

Coping With Stress

↓

Four ways of reducing the physical effects of negative emotions and stress:
1. meditation and exercise.
2. *problem-focused coping* rather than *emotion-focused coping*.
3. rethinking the problem by:
   • reappraising the situation or the symptoms of stress.
   • learning from the experience.
   • comparing yourself to others.
4. drawing on social support or giving it to others, although the wrong kind of social support can be detrimental.

MOTIVATION

PSYCHOLOGY IN THE NEWS //////////////////////////////////

American Teen Wins His Third All-Ireland Dancing Championship

GREENVILLE, OH, March 17, 2012. Drew Lovejoy, 17, has won the all-Ireland dancing championship in Dublin, Ireland, for the third straight year. Lovejoy started dancing at the age of 6, but only when he happened to go to an Irish dance competition in Indianapolis with a friend did he get hooked on this form. Although some people in his farming community bullied him, he persevered. "I was like, 'I want a medal,'" he said. Drew Lovejoy is not only the first American to win three championships, but also the first person of color: Drew's father, from Georgia, is black and his mother, from Iowa, is white. Drew's mother, Andee Goldberg, says "They don't even know he's Jewish. I think it would be too overwhelming."

Hugh Hefner Marries Crystal Harris on New Year's Eve

BEVERLY HILLS, CA, January 1, 2013. Hugh Hefner, 86, married Crystal Harris, 26, at the Playboy Mansion last night. It is his third marriage and, he says, he saved the best for last—he is now a happy, committed, one-woman man. Hefner scoffs when people comment on their 60-year age difference. "It's only people who don't know us, who simply see us as stereotypes in terms of age and beauty," he says. Harris, a Playmate of the Month in 2009, had broken off their previous engagement in 2011, five days before their planned wedding, but the couple reconciled a year later. "He believes in love," Harris told *Esquire* magazine. "Hef loves me more than anybody else in a relationship ever has. It took me time away to realize that."

Hugh Hefner and Crystal Harris at their New Year's Eve wedding.

At Mayor Bloomberg's press conference in New York, a 64-ounce drink with the amount of sugar it contains is displayed with the sugar content of other sizes of soft drinks.

Judge Blocks New York City's Ban on Oversized Sugary Drinks

NEW YORK, NY, March 11, 2013. In a rebuke to Mayor Michael R. Bloomberg's efforts to combat obesity by limiting the size of sugary drinks to 16 ounces at restaurants, theaters, and food carts, a State Supreme Court judge today struck down the ban. The judge agreed with the soft-drink industry that the limits were "arbitrary and capricious." Mayor Bloomberg vowed to appeal. "I've got to defend my children, and yours, and do what's right to save lives," the mayor said. "Obesity kills. There's no question it kills."

Ohio Teenagers Guilty in Rape of 16-Year-Old Girl

STEUBENVILLE, OHIO, March 17, 2013. Two high school football stars have been found guilty of raping a 16-year-old girl last summer. Trent Mays, 17, was sentenced to at least two years in the state juvenile system and Ma'lik Richmond, 16, was sentenced to one year. They had penetrated the girl with their fingers for hours, while she was so drunk she was unable to consent to sex. Mays' sentence was longer because he took pictures of the victim, showing her naked and passed out, and sent them with texts to friends, referring to her as "like a dead body." Other teenagers immediately circulated the photos, eventually calling national attention to the case. After the judge read his decision, both boys sobbed.

///////////

What motivates people like Drew Lovejoy to pursue unlikely dreams, even without role models of their own ethnicity, nationality, or community, when so many others either give up or have no dream to pursue? Can true love withstand a 60-year age difference, and for that matter do you assume that Hefner and Harris were motivated by love or marrying for purely pragmatic reasons? Why would star football players, who presumably could readily have consensual sex, rape and humiliate an unconscious woman? And what actions on the part of governments, organizations, and individuals will help to curb people's appetite for sugary, unhealthy food and halt the epidemic of obesity?

The word *motivation*, like the word *emotion*, comes from the Latin root meaning "to move," and the psychology of motivation is indeed the study of what moves us, why we do what we do. To psychologists, **motivation** refers to a process within a person or animal that causes that organism to move toward a goal or away from an unpleasant situation. The motive may be to satisfy a psychological goal, say, by getting a great job or avoiding loss of the one you have; it may be to satisfy a biological need, say, by eating a sandwich to reduce hunger; or it may be to fulfill a personal ambition, say, by performing in a Broadway musical or being the youngest person to sail around the world.

For many decades, the study of motivation was dominated by a focus on biological *drives*, such as those to acquire food and water, to have sex, to seek novelty, and to avoid cold and pain. But drive theories do not account for the full complexity of human motivation because people are conscious creatures who think and plan ahead, set goals, and plot strategies to reach those goals. People may have a drive to eat, for instance, but that doesn't tell us why some individuals will go on hunger strikes to protest injustice.

motivation An inferred process within a person or animal that causes movement either toward a goal or away from an unpleasant situation.

intrinsic motivation
The pursuit of an activity for its own sake.

extrinsic motivation
The pursuit of an activity for external rewards, such as money or fame.

set point The genetically influenced weight range for an individual; it is maintained by biological mechanisms that regulate food intake, fat reserves, and metabolism.

In this chapter, we will examine four central areas of human motivation: food, love, sex, and achievement. We will see how happiness and well-being are affected by the kinds of goals we set for ourselves, and by whether we are spurred to reach them because of **intrinsic motivation**, the desire to do something for its own sake and the satisfaction it brings, or **extrinsic motivation**, the desire to do something for external rewards.

You are about to learn . . .

- the biological mechanisms that make it difficult for obese people to lose weight and keep it off.
- how notions of the ideal male and female body change over time and across cultures.
- why people all over the world are getting fatter.
- the major forms of eating disorders, and why they are increasing in both sexes.

The Hungry Animal: Motives to Eat

Some people are skinny; others are plump. Some are shaped like string beans; others look more like pears. Some can eat anything they want without gaining an ounce; others struggle unsuccessfully their whole lives to shed pounds. Some hate being fat; others think that fat is fine. How much do genes, psychology, and environment affect our motivation to eat or not to eat?

The Biology of Weight LO 14.1

At one time, most psychologists thought that being overweight was a sign of emotional disturbance. If you were fat, it was because you

THINKING CRITICALLY

About Overeating and Weight

hated your mother, feared intimacy, or were trying to fill an emotional hole in your psyche by loading up on rich desserts. The evidence for psychological theories of overweight, however, came mainly from self-reports and from flawed studies that lacked control groups or objective measures of how much people were actually eating. When researchers did controlled studies, they learned that fat people, on average, are no more and no less emotionally disturbed than average-weight people. Even more surprising, they found that heaviness is not always

caused by overeating (Stunkard, 1980). Many heavy people do eat large quantities of food, but so do some thin people. In one early experiment, in which volunteers gorged themselves for months, it was as hard for slender people to gain weight as it is for most heavy people to lose weight. The minute the study was over, the slender people lost weight as fast as dieters gained it back (Sims, 1974).

Genetic Influences on Weight and Body Shape. The explanation that emerged from such findings was that a biological mechanism keeps your body weight at a genetically influenced **set point**, the weight you stay at—plus or minus 10 percent—when you are not trying to gain or lose (Lissner et al., 1991). Set-point theory generated much research on how the body regulates appetite, eating, and weight. Everyone has a genetically programmed *basal metabolism rate*, the rate at which the body burns calories to maintain vital functions when at rest, and a fixed number of fat cells, which store fat for energy and can change in size. Obese people have about twice the number of fat cells as do adults of normal weight, and their fat cells are bigger (Spalding et al., 2008). When people lose weight, they don't lose the fat cells; the cells just get thinner, and easily plump up again.

A complex interaction of metabolism, fat cells, and hormones keeps people at the weight their bodies are designed to be, much in the way that a thermostat keeps a house at a constant temperature. When a heavy person diets, the body's metabolism slows down to conserve energy and fat reserves (Ravussin et al., 1988). When a thin person overeats, metabolism speeds up, burning energy. In one study, in which 16 slender volunteers ate 1,000 extra calories every day for 8 weeks, their metabolisms sped up to burn the excess calories. They were like hummingbirds, in constant movement: fidgeting, pacing, changing their positions frequently while seated, and so on (Levine, Eberhardt, & Jensen, 1999).

What sets the set point? Genes, to start with. Pairs of adult identical twins who grow up in different families are just as similar in body weight and shape as twins raised together. And when identical twins gain weight, they gain it in the same place: Some pairs store extra pounds around their waists, others on their hips and thighs (Bouchard et al., 1990; Comuzzie & Allison, 1998). Researchers are also identifying gene mutations associated with some cases of human obesity, a variant that causes mice and people to gain a vast amount of weight while eating a normal amount of food (Asai et al., 2013).

Body weight and shape are strongly affected by genetic factors. Set-point theory helps explain why the Pimas of the American Southwest gain weight easily but lose it slowly, whereas the Bororo nomads of Nigeria can eat a lot of food yet remain slender.

Genes also influence how much *brown fat* a person has in addition to the usual white fat. Brown fat is an energy-burning type of fat that seems important in regulating body weight and blood sugar. It is lacking in obese people, and may be one reason that people who have excess fat can't burn all the calories they consume (Cypess et al., 2009). However, production of brown fat is also triggered by cold and exercise, which, in mice at least, turns ordinary white fat brown (Ouellet et al., 2012). Brown fat cells are vampires of the metabolic system: When they run out of their own sources of energy, they suck fat out of other cells where it is stored throughout the body to keep their proprietor warm. No, no, you can't (yet!) order a brown-fat supplement online.

When a mutation occurs in the genes that regulate normal eating and weight control, the result may be obesity. One gene, called *obese*, or *ob* for short, causes fat cells to secrete a protein, which researchers have named *leptin* (from the Greek *leptos*, "slender"). Leptin travels through the blood to the brain's hypothalamus, which is involved in the regulation of appetite. When leptin levels are normal, people eat just enough to maintain their weight. When a mutation of the *ob* gene causes leptin levels to be too low, however, the hypothalamus thinks the body lacks fat reserves and signals the individual to overeat. Injecting leptin into leptin-deficient mice reduces the animals' appetites, speeds up their metabolisms, and makes them more active; as a result, the animals shed weight. For this reason, researchers

initially thought that leptin might be the answer to dieters' prayers: Take leptin, lose weight! For a minority of obese people who have a congenital leptin deficiency, that is true (Farooqi et al., 2007). Alas, for most obese people, and for those who are merely overweight, taking leptin does not produce much weight loss (Comuzzie & Allison, 1998).

Studies of mice suggest that leptin plays its most crucial role during a critical period in infancy, by altering the brain chemistry that influences how much an animal or a person later eats. More specifically, leptin helps regulate body weight by strengthening neural circuits in the hypothalamus that reduce appetite and by weakening circuits that stimulate it (Elmquist & Flier, 2004). Once those neural connections are modified, the set point is, well, set (Bouret, Draper, & Simerly, 2004). Some researchers speculate that because of this early neural plasticity, overfeeding infants while the hypothalamus is developing may later produce childhood obesity.

Numerous other genes and body chemicals are linked to appetite, metabolism, and being overweight or obese (Farooqi & O'Rahilly, 2004; Frayling et al., 2007; Herbert et al., 2006; Stice et al., 2008). You have receptors in your nose and mouth that keep urging you to eat more ("The food is right there! It's good! Eat!"), receptors in your gut telling you to quit ("You've had enough already!"), and leptin and other chemicals telling you that you have stored enough fat or not enough.

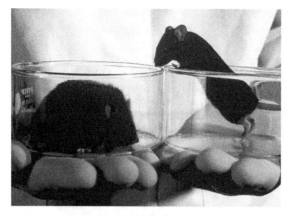

Both of these mice have a mutation in the *ob* gene, which usually makes mice chubby, like the one on the left. But when leptin is injected daily, the mice eat less and burn more calories, becoming slim, like his friendly pal. Unfortunately, leptin injections have not had the same results in most human beings.

The hormone *ghrelin* makes you hungry and eager to eat more, whereas leptin turns off your appetite after a meal, making you eat less. This complex set-point system seems to explain why dieters who lose weight so rarely keep it off. Even a year after their weight loss, their bodies are still leptin deficient, sending out hormonal signals to eat more and re-store the lost pounds (Kissileff et al., 2012).

As if all this weren't enough, your brain will get high on sugary foods even if your tongue can't taste them or enjoy their texture. Sweets increase pleasure-inducing dopamine levels in the brain, making you crave more rich food (de Araujo et al., 2008). (Forget about trying to fool your brain with artificial sweeteners; they just make you want the real thing.) Some obese individuals may have underactive reward circuitry, which leads them to overeat to boost their dopamine levels (Stice et al., 2008). When heavy people lament that they are "addicted" to food, therefore, they may be right. Food manufacturers take advantage of this fact by engineering products that cultivate the craving for sweet, salty, and fat tastes, to ensure that customers will keep coming back for more (Moss, 2013).

✳ Explore the Concept Virtual Brain: Hunger and Eating at MyPsychLab

The complexity of the mechanisms governing appetite and weight explains why appetite-suppressing drugs and diets inevitably fail in the long run: They target only one of the many factors that conspire to keep you the weight you are. Which brings us to an international puzzle: Why are so many people, all over the world, getting fatter? Increases in obesity rates have occurred in both sexes, all social classes, and all age groups,

Until recently, obesity was almost unheard of in many places, such as China; now it is a global problem.

and in many countries, including Mexico, Egypt, North Africa, Canada, Great Britain, Japan, and Australia, and even coastal China and Southeast Asia (Popkin, 2009). What could be responsible?

Environmental Influences on Weight LO 14.2

The leading culprits are four sweeping changes in the "food environment" that affect what we eat and how much (Critser, 2002; Popkin, 2009; Taubes, 2008):

1 **The increased abundance of fast food and processed foods.** These foods are inexpensive, readily available, and high in sugar, starch, and carbohydrates (Taubes, 2008). Human beings are genetically predisposed to gain weight when rich food is abundant because, in our species' evolutionary past, starvation was often a real possibility. Therefore, a tendency to store calories in the form of fat provided a definite survival advantage. Unfortunately, evolution did not produce a comparable mechanism to prevent people who do not have hummingbird metabolisms from gaining weight when food is easily available, tasty, rich, varied, and cheap. That, of course, is precisely the situation today, surrounded as we are by three-quarter-pound burgers, fries, chips, tacos, candy bars, and pizzas.

One research team documented the direct effects of the proximity of fast-food outlets on obesity. They followed thousands of ninth-grade schoolchildren, before and after a new fast-food restaurant opened near their schools. The children whose schools were within a block of a burger or pizza outlet were more likely to become obese in the next year than students whose schools were a quarter of a mile or more away (Currie et al., 2010). Proximity to fast food seems to be a major cause of the "freshman 15" as well. In a study at two different American universities, one in the Midwest and the other in the East, more than 70 percent of all freshmen gained significant amounts of weight in their first year (Lloyd-Richardson et al., 2009).

2 **The widespread consumption of high-sugar, high-calorie soft drinks.** Throughout most of human history, the proportion of calories consumed in beverages (milk, wine, fruit juice, and the like) was low, and thus the human body did not evolve a mechanism that would compensate for fluid intake by lowering food intake. Then, 50 years ago, soft drinks, which are loaded with sugar and calories, began spreading across the globe. Putting sweeteners into drinks has led to a weight gain of up to 14 pounds per person in those who drink two to three sodas a day (Popkin, 2009).

3 **The increased portion sizes of food and drink.** Servings of food and drink have become supersized, double or triple what they were only one generation ago. Even babies and toddlers are being fed as much as 30 percent more calories than they need (Fox et al., 2004). In France, people eat rich food but much less of it than Americans do. Their notion of what a proper portion is—for yogurt, soda, a salad, a sandwich, anything—is way lower than in the United States (Rozin et al., 2003).

4 **The abundance of highly varied foods.** When diets are predictable and routine, people habituate to what they are eating and eat less of it. That is why all diets that restrict people to eating only a few kinds of foods (only watermelon, only protein, only whatever) are successful at first. As soon as food becomes more varied, however, people eat more and gain more weight (Remick, Polivy, & Pliner, 2009). People will even eat more M&Ms when they are available in a bowl containing ten colors than when the same number of candies are in a bowl containing only seven colors (Wansink, 2006).

Other suspects in the mystery of increasing obesity are being investigated. One is sleeplessness. Sleep plays an important role in regulating weight, and many infants, children, and adults are simply not getting enough of it (Bell & Zimmerman, 2010). Another is a woman's excessive weight gain during pregnancy, now known to produce infants of higher-than-normal birth weight. That higher birth weight, in turn, causes metabolic changes that put the infants at greater risk of becoming obese adults (Ludwig & Currie, 2010). A third possibility has to do with the bacterial makeup of the intestines. Research with rats and humans finds that overweight and obesity are linked to the presence of certain gut microbes (Liou et al., 2013). Yet another candidate is exposure to cold viruses: Children exposed to adenovirus-36 are more likely to become obese than children who are not infected, and this link has been found in adults in Korea and Italy as well as the United States (Gabbert et al., 2010). And finally, researchers are investigating environmental pollutants that might be "obesogens," chemicals that disrupt endocrine function and cause animals to store fat (Grün & Blumberg, 2006). These are all intriguing ideas, but we must tolerate some uncertainty until all of the culprits are identified and their relative contributions are known.

Cultural Influences on Weight and the Ideal Body

Eating habits, in turn, are shaped by a culture's customs and standards of what the ideal body should look like: fat or thin, muscular or soft. In many places around the world, especially where famine and crop failures are common, fat is taken as a sign of health, affluence in men, and sexual desirability in women (Stearns, 1997). Among the Calabari of Nigeria, brides are put in special fattening huts where they do nothing but eat, so as to become fat enough to please their husbands.

Cultural influences on obesity can also be observed among white farm families. Farmers originally ate large amounts of food for *intrinsic* reasons: When you do hard, labor-intensive work, you need a lot of calories. But today, many farm families eat for *extrinsic* motives: to be sociable and conform to family tradition. In the farm belt states of the American Midwest, people are expected to eat huge, hearty meals and plenty of

Get Involved! What's Controlling How Much You Eat?

Many people believe that what they eat and how much they eat is regulated by how hungry they feel. But the motivation to eat is complicated, as Brian Wansink (2006) demonstrated in a clever series of experiments. Here are some invisible external influences on your eating habits identified in his research:

- **Package size:** People eat more from a large container (say, of popcorn) than a small one.
- **Plate size:** People eat more when they serve themselves on large plates rather than small ones.
- **Cues to how much has been eaten:** People eat more from a buffet when waiters quickly replace their dirty dishes, thereby eliminating telltale signs of how much food has already been consumed.
- **Kitchen and table layouts:** People eat more when food and snacks are displayed prominently, are varied, and are easily reached.
- **Distraction:** People eat more when they are being distracted by friends and the environment.

The next time you are out with friends, note how much everyone is eating (including yourself), and notice whether any of these influences are at work. If you are trying to lose weight, how can you alter your own "food environment" to correct for these influences?

bulimia nervosa An eating disorder characterized by episodes of excessive eating (bingeing) followed by forced vomiting or use of laxatives (purging).

anorexia nervosa An eating disorder characterized by fear of being fat, a distorted body image, radically reduced consumption of food, and emaciation.

sweet desserts. If you don't join in, you are being antisocial, insulting your hosts and rejecting your kin (Angier, 2000).

Ironically, although people of all ethnicities and social classes have been getting fatter, the cultural ideal for women and men in the United States, Canada, and Europe has been getting thinner. The plump, curvy female body, with ample hips and breasts, was fashionable in eras that celebrated women's role as mothers, such as after World War II, when women were encouraged to give up their wartime jobs and have many children (Stearns, 1997). Today's big-breasted but otherwise skinny female ideal may reflect today's norm: Women are supposed to be both professionally competent *and* maternal. For men too, the ideal body has changed. When most heavily muscled men were laborers and farmers, being physically strong and muscular was considered unattractive, a sign of being working class. Today, having a strong, muscular body is a sign of affluence rather than poverty. It means a man has the money and the time to join a gym and work out (Bordo, 2000).

You can see why many people, especially women, find themselves caught in a battle between their biology and their culture. Evolution has designed women to store fat, which is necessary for the onset of menstruation, for pregnancy and nursing, and, after menopause, for the production of estrogen. In cultures that think women should be very thin, therefore, many women become obsessed with weight and are continually dieting, forever fighting their bodies' need for a little healthy roundness.

The Body as Battleground: Eating Disorders LO 14.3

Some people lose the battle between the body they have and the body they want, developing serious eating disorders that reflect an irrational terror of being fat. In **bulimia nervosa**, the person binges (eats vast quantities of rich food, sometimes everything that is in the kitchen) and then purges by inducing vomiting or abusing laxatives. In **anorexia nervosa**, the person eats hardly anything and therefore becomes dangerously thin; people with anorexia typically have severely distorted body images, thinking they are fat even when they are emaciated. Anorexia has the highest mortality rate of all mental disorders; many of its sufferers die of heart or kidney failure or complications brought on by weakened bones.

👁 **Watch** the **Video** In the Real World: Eating Disorders at **MyPsychLab**

Bulimia and anorexia, which are the best-known eating disorders, occur most often among young white women. But more than 40 percent of

Should a woman be voluptuous and curvy or slim as a reed? Should a man be thin and smooth or strong and buff? What explains cultural changes in attitudes toward the ideal body? During the 1950s, actresses like Jayne Mansfield embodied the postwar ideal: soft, curvy, buxom, and "womanly." Today, when women are expected to work and have families, the ideal is to be thin and have prominent breasts, like actress Megan Fox. Men, too, have been caught up in body-image changes. The ideal in the 1960s and 1970s was to be soft and scrawny, like Mick Jagger; today's ideal man looks like actor Hugh Jackman, tough and muscular.

all cases of eating disorders occur among men, the elderly, ethnic minority groups, young children, and athletes, and do not fit the diagnostic criteria for bulimia or anorexia (Thomas, Vartanian, & Brownell, 2009). People with *binge-eating disorder* binge without purging; others chew whatever food they want but spit it out without swallowing; others are normal weight but take no joy in eating because they worry obsessively about gaining a pound; some develop phobias about eating certain kinds of food. All of these disorders involve an unhealthy attitude toward food, weight, and the body.

Genes play a role in the development of anorexia nervosa, which has been found across cultures and throughout history (Striegel-Moore & Bulik, 2007). But most disorders are generated by psychological factors, including depression and anxiety, low self-esteem, perfectionism, and a distorted body image (Presnell, Bearman, & Stice, 2004; Sherry & Hall, 2009). Cultural factors can also generate dissatisfaction with one's body. Bulimia is rare to nonexistent in non-Western cultures and has only become a significant problem in Western cultures with the rise of the thin ideal for women (Keel & Klump, 2003). A meta-analysis of experimental and correlational studies found that women's exposure to the media ideal of the impossibly thin woman fosters the belief that "thin is beautiful" and increases the risk of disordered eating and body dissatisfaction across all ethnic groups (Grabe, Ward, & Hyde, 2008; Slevec & Tiggemann, 2011). American culture is also rife with relentlessly critical and snide appraisals of other people's bodies that get posted on blogs, YouTube, Facebook, and Twitter, and appear constantly in entertainment magazines and on talk shows.

Eating disorders and body image distortions among boys and men are increasing too, though they take different forms. Just as anorexic women see their gaunt bodies as being too fat, some men have the delusion that their muscular bodies are too puny, so they abuse steroids and exercise or pump iron compulsively (Thompson & Cafri, 2007). Men in cultures that do not think the heavily muscled male body is desirable or attractive, as in Taiwan and Kenya, have fewer body image disorders than American men do (Campbell, Pope, & Filiault, 2005; Yang, Gray, & Pope, 2005).

In sum, within a given environment, genetic predispositions for a certain body weight and metabolism interact with psychological needs, cultural norms, and individual habits to shape, in this case quite literally, who we are.

What is the difference between being slender and being too thin? Does the fashion model on the left look good to you or does she look emaciated? Likewise, what is the difference between being "pleasantly plump" and being too fat? Nikki Blonsky, the exuberant star of the movie *Hairspray*, is overweight but physically fit. Does she look good to you or does she look too heavy?

You are about to learn . . .

- how biology affects attachment and love.
- some key psychological influences on whom and how you love.
- the three basic styles of attachment and how they affect relationships.
- how economic concerns influence love and marriage.

The Social Animal: Motives to Love

In 1875, a teenager named Annie Oakley defeated Frank Butler, the star of the Buffalo Bill Wild West Show, in a sharpshooting competition. "The next day I came back to see the little girl who had beaten me," wrote Butler many years later, "and it was not long until we married." He became her manager, and for the next 50 years, they traveled together across Europe and America, where her skills with a gun made her the toast of both continents. They remained devoted until their deaths in 1926 (Kreps, 1990).

What kept Annie Oakley and Frank Butler in love for 50 years, when so many other romantic passions die in five years, five weeks, or five hours? What *is* love, anyway—the crazy, heart-palpitating feeling of longing for another person, or the steady, stable feeling of deep and abiding attachment?

The Biology of Love LO 14.4

To begin, let's distinguish *passionate (romantic) love*, characterized by a whirlwind of intense emotions and sexual passion, from *companionate love*, characterized by affection and trust. Passionate love is the stuff of crushes, infatuations, "love at first sight," and the early stage of love affairs. It may burn out completely or evolve into companionate love. Passionate love is known in all cultures and has a long and passionate history. Wars and duels have been fought because of it, people have committed suicide because of it, great love affairs have begun, and been torn apart, because of it. Yet, although the experience of romantic love is universal, many cultures have not regarded it as the proper basis for anything serious, such as marriage (Hatfield & Rapson, 2008).

In this era of fMRI, it was inevitable that researchers would seek to explain passionate love by examining the brain. And if you think that what scientists are finding about diet and weight is complicated, their efforts to tease apart the links between romantic passion, sexual yearning, and long-term love make the problem of obesity seem, well, a piece of cake. Olfactory cues in a potential partner's scent can turn you on (or off). Physical cues in a potential partner's voice and body shape, and even in how similar his or her face is to yours, may attract or repel you. You may be exhilarated by the same rewarding dopamine jolt that makes anticipation of a fabulous meal or an addictive drug so pleasurable, and you may be aroused by an increase in adrenaline (Aron et al., 2005; Cozolino, 2006). Eventually, hormones become involved in the longer-lasting phase of attachment and bonding.

The neurological origins of passionate love may begin in infancy, in the baby's attachment to the mother. In the view of evolutionary psychologists, maternal and romantic love, the deepest of human attachments, share a common evolutionary purpose—preserving the species—and so they share common neural mechanisms, the ones that make attachment and pair-bonding feel good. Key neurotransmitters and hormones that are involved in pleasure and reward are activated in the mother–baby pair-bond and again later in the pair-bond of adult lovers (Diamond, 2004).

Two important hormones for social bonding are *oxytocin* and *vasopressin*, which are similar in molecular structure and influence feelings and expressions of love, caring, and trust not only between mothers and babies but also between friends and between lovers (Poulin, Holman, & Buffone, 2012; Walum et al., 2008). In one study, volunteers who inhaled oxytocin in a nasal spray were later more likely than control subjects to trust one another in various risky interactions (Kosfeld et al., 2005). In another study, couples given oxytocin increased their nonverbal expressions of love for one another—gazing, smiling, and touching—compared with couples given a placebo (Gonzaga et al., 2006). Conversely, when prairie voles, a monogamous species, are given a drug that blocks oxytocin, they continue to mate but don't get attached to their partners (Ross et al., 2009).

These findings have inspired some oversimplifiers to call oxytocin the "love" or "cuddle" hormone, or even "liquid trust." Cute, but if it really is such a spur to love and attachment, why are humans fighting so much? It turns out that giving people doses of oxytocin makes them more likely to favor their *own* group over other groups, and increases defensive aggression against outsiders (De Dreu et al., 2011). So perhaps oxytocin is the "cuddle your own kind and the hell with the rest of you" hormone. Moreover, high levels of oxytocin in women and of vasopressin in men are actually biological markers of relationship *distress* (Taylor, Saphire-Bernstein, & Seeman, 2010). Finally, people's love and attachment histories affect how they respond to oxytocin as well as the other way around; this is why giving oxytocin to people with attachment problems often backfires, making them even more distrustful (Miller, 2013). For example, after inhaling oxytocin, men who had had good attachments to their mothers remembered them as being unusually caring and supportive, compared to men with similar attachments who received a placebo. But men who had troubled early home lives remembered their mothers as being much less caring than did similar men who got the placebo (Bartz et al., 2010).

> ### ☀ THINKING CRITICALLY
> About the "Cuddle Hormone"

Some of the characteristic feelings and actions that occur during attachment are mediated by reward circuits in the brain that involve the release of *endorphins*, the brain's natural opiates. When baby mice and other animals are separated from their mothers, they cry out in distress, and the mother's touch (or lick) releases endorphins that soothe the infant. But when puppies, guinea pigs, and chicks are injected with low doses of

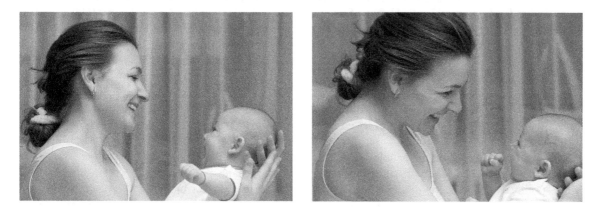

The biology of the baby–mother bond may be the origin of adult romantic love, with its exchange of loving gazes and depth of attachment.

either morphine or endorphins, the animals show much less distress than usual when separated from their mothers; the chemicals seem to be a biological replacement for mom (Panksepp et al., 1980). These findings suggest that endorphin-stimulated euphoria may be a child's initial motive for seeking affection and cuddling—that, in effect, a child attached to a parent is a child addicted to love. The addictive quality of adult passionate love, including the physical and emotional distress that new lovers feel when they are apart, may involve the same biochemistry (Diamond, 2004).

Using fMRI, neuroscientists have found other neurological similarities between infant–mother love and adult romantic love. Certain parts of the brain are activated when people look at images of their sweethearts, and these are the same areas that are activated when mothers see images of their own children as opposed to pictures of other children. In contrast, other brain parts are activated when people look at pictures of friends or furniture (Bartels & Zeki, 2004).

Clearly, then, the bonds of attachment are biologically based. Yet, as we saw with oxytocin, it is important to avoid oversimplifying, by concluding that "love is all in our hormones" or "love occurs in this corner of the brain but not that one." Human love affairs involve many other factors that affect whom we choose, how we get along with that person, and whether we stay with a partner over the years.

The Psychology of Love LO 14.5

Many romantics believe that only one true love awaits them. Considering the presence of 7 billion people on the planet, the odds of finding said person are a bit daunting. What if you're in Omaha or Winnipeg and your true love is in Dubrovnik or Kankakee? You could wander for years and never cross paths.

Fortunately, evolution has made it possible to form deep and lasting attachments without traveling the world. The first major predictor of whom we love is *proximity*: We tend to choose our friends and lovers from the set of people who live, study, or work near us. The second major predictor is *similarity*—in looks, attitudes, beliefs, values, personality, and interests (Berscheid & Reis, 1998). Although it is commonly believed that opposites attract, we tend to choose friends and loved ones who are most like us.

The Internet has made it possible for people to seek their "ideal match" on all kinds of dimensions: political attitudes, religion or secularism, sexual orientation, disabilities, preferences for particular sexual activities, preferences for particular

Internet services capitalize on the fact that like attracts like. How well do these services work?

pets…you name it. Matchmaking services administer lengthy questionnaires and personality inventories, claiming to use scientific principles to pair up potential soul mates (Sprecher et al., 2008).

A review of the research on Internet dating found that these sites often don't deliver the love of your life (or even the love of your month), and they don't do better than old-fashioned methods of meeting people in generating long-term relationships: Online dating profiles, the researchers explained, reduce "three-dimensional people to two-dimensional displays of information," which are often not enough to let participants evaluate true compatibility (Finkel et al., 2012). Besides, many people think they know exactly what they "must have" in a partner, and then they meet someone who has few of those qualities but a whole bunch of others that suddenly become "essential." Yet one underlying premise of most Internet matching sites is basically correct: Like attracts like.

👁 **Watch** the **Video** In the Real World: Speed Dating at **MyPsychLab**

The Attachment Theory of Love. Once you find someone to love, *how* do you love? According to Phillip Shaver and Cindy Hazan (1993), adults, just like babies, can be *secure, anxious,* or *avoidant* in their attachments (see Chapter 3). Securely attached lovers are rarely jealous or worried about being abandoned. They are more compassionate and helpful than insecurely attached people and are quicker to understand and forgive their partners if the partner does something thoughtless or annoying (Mikulincer et al., 2005; Mikulincer & Shaver, 2007).

Avoidant people manage their anxiety and insecurity by distrusting and avoiding intimate attachments. Anxious lovers, however, are always agitated about their relationships; they want to be close but worry that their partners will leave them. Other people often describe them as clingy, which may be why they are more likely than secure lovers to suffer from unrequited love. Their anxiety is physiological as much as psychological: Their levels of cortisol (a stress hormone) spike when they feel the relationship is threatened—for example, when the partner travels somewhere without them—and take longer to calm down (Pietromonaco, DeBuse, & Powers, 2013).

Where do these differences come from? According to the *attachment theory of love*, people's attachment styles as adults derive in large part from how their parents cared for them (Dinero et al., 2008; Mikulincer & Shaver, 2007). Children form internal "working models" of relationships: Can I trust others? Am I worthy of being loved? Will my parents leave me? If a child's parents are cold and rejecting and provide little or no emotional and physical comfort, the child learns to expect other relationships to be the same. If children form secure attachments to trusted parents, they become more trusting of others, expecting to form other secure attachments with friends and lovers in adulthood (Feeney & Cassidy, 2003).

However, a child's own temperament and genetic predispositions could also help account for the consistency of attachment styles from childhood to adulthood, as well as for the working models of relationships that are formed during childhood (Fraley et al., 2011; Gillath et al., 2008). A child who is temperamentally fearful or difficult may reject even the kindest parent's efforts to console and cuddle (see Chapter 3). That child may therefore come to feel anxious or ambivalent in his or her adult relationships.

The Minnesota Longitudinal Study of Risk and Adaptation has followed a large sample of children from birth to adulthood, to see how early attachment styles can create cascading effects on adult relationships. Children who are treated poorly early in life and lack secure attachments may end up on a pathway that makes committed relationships difficult. As children, they have trouble regulating negative emotions; as teenagers, they have trouble dealing with and recovering from conflict with their peers; as adults, they tend to protect themselves by becoming the less-committed partner in their relationships. If these individuals are lucky enough to get into a relationship with a securely attached partner, however, these vulnerabilities in maintaining a stable partnership can be overcome (Oriña et al., 2011; Simpson, Collins, & Salvatore, 2011).

The Ingredients of Love. When people are asked to define the key ingredients of love, most agree that it is a mix of passion, intimacy, and commitment (Lemieux & Hale, 2000). Intimacy is based on deep knowledge of the other person, which accumulates gradually, but passion is based on emotion, which is generated by novelty and change. That is why passion is usually highest at the beginning of a relationship, when two people begin to disclose things about themselves to each other, and lowest when knowledge of the other person's beliefs and habits is at its maximum, when it seems that there is nothing left to learn about the beloved.

Nonetheless, according to an analysis of a large number of adult couples and a meta-analysis of 25 studies of couples in long- and short-term relationships, romantic love can persist for many years and is strongly associated with a couple's happiness. What diminishes among these happy couples is that part of romantic love that can foster obsessiveness, constant thinking and worrying about the loved one and the relationship (Acevedo & Aron, 2009).

Biological factors such as the brain's opiate system may contribute to early passion, as we noted, but most psychologists believe that the ability to sustain a long and intimate love relationship has more to do with a couple's attitudes, values, and balance of power than with genes or hormones. One of the most important psychological predictors of satisfaction in long-term relationships is the perception, by both partners, that the relationship is fair, rewarding, and balanced. Partners who feel over-benefited (getting more than they are giving) tend to feel guilty; those who feel under-benefited (not getting what they feel they deserve) tend to feel resentful and angry (Pillemer, Hatfield, & Sprecher, 2008). A couple may tootle along comfortably until a stressful event—such as the arrival of children, serious

"My preference is for someone who's afraid of closeness, like me."

illness, unemployment, or retirement—evokes simmering displeasure over issues of "what's fair."

Another key psychological factor in a couple's ability to sustain love is the nature of their primary motivation to maintain the relationship: Is it positive (to enjoy affection and intimacy) or negative (to avoid feeling insecure and lonely)? Couples motivated by the former goal tend to report more satisfaction with their partners (Gable & Poore, 2008). We will see that this difference in motivation—positive or negative—affects happiness and satisfaction in many different domains of life.

The critical-thinking guideline "define your terms" may never be more important than in matters of love. The way we define love deeply affects our satisfaction with relationships and whether or not our relationships last. If you believe that the only real love is the kind defined by obsession and sexual passion, then you may decide you are out of love when the initial phase of attraction fades, as it eventually must, and you will be repeatedly disappointed. Robert Solomon (1994) argued that "We conceive of [love] falsely....We expect an explosion at the beginning powerful enough to fuel love through all of its ups and downs instead of viewing love as a process over which we have control, a process that tends to increase with time rather than wane." And in truth, people fall in love in different ways: Some couples do so gradually, after "falling in friendship" first; couples in arranged marriages may come to love each other long after the wedding (Solomon, Robert C., 1994).

THINKING CRITICALLY
About Defining Love

Gender, Culture, and Love LO 14.6

Which sex is more romantic? Which sex truly understands true love? Which sex falls in love but won't commit? Pop-psych books are full of stereotyped answers, but in reality neither sex loves more than the other (Dion & Dion, 1993; Hatfield & Rapson, 1996/2005). Men and women are equally likely to suffer the heart-crushing torments of unrequited love. They are equally likely to be securely or insecurely attached (Feeney & Cassidy, 2003). Both sexes suffer mightily when a love relationship ends, assuming they did not want it to.

However, women and men often differ, on average, in how they *express* the fundamental motives for love and intimacy. Males in many cultures learn early that revelations of emotion can be construed as evidence of vulnerability and weakness, which are considered unmasculine (see Chapter 13). Men in such cultures often develop ways of revealing love that are based on actions rather than words: doing things for and with the partner, supporting the family financially, sharing the same activity, such as watching TV or a football game together, and initiating sex, the most important channel for men's expression of loving feelings. Women tend to express love by tending to the emotional climate of their relationships: offering compliments and kisses, and restraining themselves from complaining and criticizing (Schoenfeld, Bredow, & Huston, 2012; Shields, 2002).

Gender differences in part reflect gender roles, which are in turn shaped by social, economic, and cultural forces. For most of human history, around the world, the idea that two people would marry for love was considered preposterous. ("Love? Please. We have alliances to make, work to do, and kids to produce.") Only in the twentieth century did love come to be seen as the normal motive for marrying (Coontz, 2005). Even then, women remained far more pragmatic than men in choosing a partner until roughly the 1980s (Reis & Aron, 2008). One reason was that a woman did not just marry a man; she married a standard of living. Therefore, many women could not afford to marry someone unsuitable or waste time in a relationship

Passionate love often starts relationships, but companionate love keeps them going.

that was not going anywhere, even if they loved the guy. They married, in short, for extrinsic reasons rather than intrinsic ones. Most men, however, could afford to be sentimental and romantic in their choice of partner.

In the second half of the twentieth century, as women entered the workforce and as two incomes became necessary in most families, the gender difference in romantic love faded, and so did economic motivations to marry, all over the world. People may still fantasize about marrying a zillionaire, but nowadays, most choose a partner to live with for intrinsic motives, for the pleasure of being with the person. Exclusively pragmatic reasons for marriage persist only in countries with high rates of poverty or in which the extended family controls female sexuality and the financial terms of marriage (Coontz, 2005). Yet even in these countries, such as India and Pakistan, the tight rules governing marriage choices are loosening and young people are spurning arranged marriages. The rules forbidding divorce are also weakening, even in once extremely traditional nations such as Japan, China, and South Korea (Rosin, 2012).

As you can see, our motivations to love may start with biology and the workings of the brain, but they are shaped and directed by our early experiences with parents, the culture we live in, the historical era that shapes us, and something as utterly unromantic as economic dependency or self-sufficiency.

Marriage for financial security is still the only option for many women from impoverished nations—like this bride, whose husband chose her from a mail-order catalog.

Recite & Review

✓ **Study** and **Review** at **MyPsychLab**

Recite: Assuming you are passionate about learning, recite aloud what you know about passionate versus companionate love, biological factors in love and attachment, the two major predictors of whom we love, the benefits and problems of online dating, the attachment theory of love, the ingredients and definitions of love, and why motives for marriage have changed in recent history.

Review: Next, reread this section; that shouldn't be a tough assignment.

Now Take This *Quick Quiz:*

1. Why is passion generally found to be high at the beginning of a relationship?

2. Anna and Rehman are a newlywed couple. Rehman is extremely loving but does not share his tensions or anxieties with Anna. She on the other hand, wants to leave her job to give more time to their relationship, while Rehman has persuaded her to continue and focus on her work. Which style of attachment does Rehman have?

3. *True or false*: Proximity is a major determinant in friendship.

4. Stephanie has been texting night and day to a guy she met on an online matching site. The exchanges are fun, but what should she consider before agreeing to go off with him for a hot weekend?

Answers:

1. Passion is an emotion that is based on and generated by novelty and change. 2. avoidant 3. true 4. Quite apart from the safety risks of going away with a stranger, neither of them might have been honest in their self-descriptions, know what they really want in a partner, or be as attracted to the three-dimensional human being as to his or her cyber self.

You are about to learn...

- which part of the anatomy is the "sexiest sex organ."
- why pleasure is only one of many motives for having sex.
- how culture affects sexual practices.
- the puzzling origins of sexual orientation.

The Erotic Animal: Motives for Sex

Most people believe that sex is a biological drive, merely a matter of doing what comes naturally. "What's there to discuss about sexual motivation?" they say. "Isn't it all inborn, inevitable, and inherently pleasurable?"

Desire and sensuality are lifelong pleasures.

It is certainly true that in most other species, sexual behavior is genetically programmed. Without instruction, a male stickleback fish knows exactly what to do with a female stickleback, and a whooping crane knows when to whoop. But as sex researcher Leonore Tiefer (2004) has observed, for human beings "sex is not a natural act." Sex, she argues, is more like dancing than digestion, something you learn and can be motivated to improve rather than a simple physiological process. For one thing, the activities that one culture considers "natural"—such as mouth-to-mouth kissing or oral sex—are often considered unnatural in another culture or historical time. Second, people have to learn from experience and culture what they are supposed to do with their sexual desires and how they are expected to behave. And third,

people's motivations for sexual activity are by no means always and only for intrinsic pleasure. Human sexuality is influenced by a blend of biological, psychological, and cultural factors.

The Biology of Desire LO 14.7, LO 14.8

In the middle of the last century, Alfred Kinsey and his associates (1948, 1953) published two pioneering books on male and female sexuality. Kinsey's team surveyed thousands of Americans about their sexual attitudes and behavior and reviewed the existing research on sexual physiology. At that time, many people believed that women were not as sexually motivated as men and that women cared more about affection than sexual satisfaction, notions soundly refuted by Kinsey's interviews.

Kinsey was attacked not only for his findings, but also for even daring to ask people (especially female people) about their sexual lives. The national hysteria that accompanied the Kinsey Reports seems hard to believe today: "Danger Lurks in Kinsey Book!" screamed one headline. Yet it is still difficult for social scientists to conduct serious, methodologically sound research on the development of human sexuality. As John Bancroft (2006), a leading sexologist, has observed, because many American adults need to believe that young children have no sexual feelings, they interpret any evidence of normal sexual expression in childhood (such as masturbation or "playing doctor") as a symptom of sexual abuse. And because many adults are uncomfortable about sexual activity among teenagers, they try to restrict or eliminate it by promoting abstinence and

The "Kinsey Report on American Women" (though the book was actually titled *Sexual Behavior in the Human Female*) was not exactly greeted with praise and acceptance, let alone clear thinking. Cartoonists made fun of its being a "bombshell," and in this 1953 photo, two famous jazz singers and an actress spoofed women's shock about the book—and their eagerness to read it.

prohibiting sex education—even though research repeatedly finds that these two measures either have no effect or actually increase teens' sexual behavior (Levine, 2003; Santelli et al., 2006).

Following Kinsey, the next wave of sex research began in the 1960s, with the laboratory research of physician William Masters and his associate Virginia Johnson (1966). Masters and Johnson's research helped to sweep away cobwebs of superstition and ignorance about how the body works. In studies of physiological changes during sexual arousal and orgasm, they confirmed that male and female orgasms are indeed remarkably similar and that all orgasms are physiologically the same, regardless of the source of stimulation.

If you have ever taken a sex-ed class, you may have had to memorize Masters and Johnson's description of the "four stages of the sexual response cycle": desire, arousal (excitement), orgasm, and resolution. Unfortunately, the impulse to oversimplify—by treating these four stages as if they were akin to the invariable cycles of a washing machine—led to a mistaken inference of universality. It later turned out that not everyone has an orgasm even following great excitement, and that in many women, desire *follows* arousal (Laan & Both, 2008). People's physiological responses vary according to their age, experience, and culture, and people also vary not only in their propensity for sexual excitation and responsiveness, but also in their ability to inhibit and control that excitement (Bancroft et al., 2009). That is, some people are all accelerator and no brakes, and others are slow to accelerate but quick to brake.

 Watch the **Video** The Big Picture: The Power of Sex at **MyPsychLab**

Hormones and Sexual Response. One biological factor that promotes sexual desire in both sexes is the hormone testosterone, an androgen (masculinizing hormone). This fact has created a market for the legal and illegal use of androgens. The assumption is that if the goal is to reduce sexual desire in sex offenders, testosterone should be lowered, say through chemical castration; if the goal is to increase sexual desire in women and men who complain of low libido, testosterone should be increased, like adding fuel to your gas tank. Yet these efforts often fail to produce the expected results (M. Anderson, 2005; Berlin, 2003). Why?

A primary reason is that in primates, unlike other mammals, sexual motivation requires more than hormones; it is also affected by social experience and context (Wallen, 2001). That is why desire can persist in sex offenders who have lost testosterone, and why desire might remain low in people who have been given testosterone. Indeed,

artificially administered testosterone does not do much more than a placebo to increase sexual satisfaction in healthy people, nor does a drop in testosterone invariably cause a loss of sexual motivation or enjoyment. In studies of women who had had their uteruses or ovaries surgically removed or who were going through menopause, use of a testosterone patch increased their sexual activity to only one more time a month over the placebo group's (Buster et al., 2005).

Sex and the "Sex Drive." The question of whether men and women are alike or different in some underlying, biologically based sex drive continues to provoke lively debate. Men have higher rates of almost every kind of sexual behavior, including masturbation, erotic fantasies, casual sex, and orgasm (Peplau, 2003; Schmitt et al., 2012). These sex differences occur even when men are forbidden by cultural or religious rules to engage in sex at all; Catholic priests have more of these sexual experiences than Catholic nuns do (Baumeister, Catanese, & Vohs, 2001). Biological psychologists argue that these differences occur universally because the hormones and brain circuits involved in sexual behavior differ for men and women (Diamond, 2008).

Other psychologists, however, believe that most human gender differences in sexual behavior reflect women's and men's different roles and experiences and have little or nothing to do with biologically based drives or brain circuits (Eagly & Wood, 1999; Tiefer, 2008). Women may be more reluctant than men to have casual sex not because they have a weaker biological "drive" but because the experience is not as likely to be gratifying to them, because of the greater risk of harm and unwanted pregnancy, and because of the social stigma that may attach to women who have casual sex.

A middle view is that men's sexual behavior is more biologically influenced than is women's, whereas women's sexual desires and responsiveness are more affected by circumstances, the specific relationship, and cultural norms (Baumeister, 2000; Schmitt et al., 2012).

 Watch the **Video** Special Topics: Cultural Norms and Sexual Behavior at **MyPsychLab**

Evolution and Sexual Strategies

Evolutionary psychologists believe that differences between women and men in sex drive and mating practices evolved in response to species' survival needs (Buss, 1994). In this view, it was evolutionarily adaptive for males to compete with other males for access to young and fertile females, and to try to win and then inseminate as many

"It's a guy thing."

females as possible. The more females a male mates with, the more genes he can pass along. The human record in this regard was achieved by a man who fathered 899 children (Daly & Wilson, 1983). What else he did with his time is unknown.

Females, according to many evolutionary psychologists, need to shop for the best genetic deal, as it were, because they can conceive and bear only a limited number of offspring. Having such a large biological investment in each pregnancy, females must choose partners more carefully than males do. Besides, mating with a lot of different males would produce no more offspring than staying with just one. So females try to attach themselves to dominant males who have resources and status and are likely to have superior genes.

In this view, the result of these two opposite sexual strategies is that males generally want sex more often than females do; males are often fickle and promiscuous, whereas females are usually

devoted and faithful; males are drawn to sexual novelty, whereas females want stability and security; males are relatively undiscriminating in their choice of sexual partners, whereas females are cautious and choosy; and males are competitive and concerned about dominance, whereas females are less so.

In human beings, some of these sex differences do appear to be universal or at least very common. In one massive project, 50 scientists studied 10,000 people in 37 cultures located on 6 continents and 5 islands (Buss, 1994; Schmitt, 2003). Around the world, men are more violent and more socially dominant than women. They are more interested in the youth and beauty of their sexual partners, presumably because youth is associated with fertility. According to their responses on questionnaires, they are more sexually jealous and possessive, presumably because if a man's mate had sex with other men, he could never be 100 percent sure that her children were also genetically his. They are quicker than women to have sex with partners they don't know well, presumably so that their sperm will be distributed as widely as possible. Women are more sexually cautious than men; they tend to emphasize the financial resources or prospects of a potential mate, his status, and his willingness to commit to a relationship (Buss & Schmidt, 2011).

Evolutionary views of sex differences in dating and mating have become enormously popular. Many academics and laypeople are persuaded that males have an evolutionary advantage in sowing their seeds far and wide, and females have an evolutionary advantage in finding a man with

THINKING CRITICALLY

About Evolutionary Theories of Sex

high status, a good paycheck, and willingness to commit. But critics, including some evolutionary

This Kenyan man has 40 wives and 349 children. He is unusual even in his own culture, but around the world, it is more common for men than women to have multiple sexual partners. Evolutionary psychologists think the reason is that men have evolved to sow as many wild oats as they can, whereas women have evolved to be happy with just a few grains.

Ah, father love! Evolutionary approaches to sex assume that males across species have only a minimal investment in caring for offspring. But there are many exceptions, including male snow monkeys and lions, who are doting dads.

theorists, have challenged this conclusion on conceptual and methodological grounds:

👁 Watch the Video What's In It For Me? The Dating Game at MyPsychLab

1 **Stereotypes versus actual behavior.** The behavior of humans and other animals often fails to conform to the stereotyped images of sexually promiscuous males and coy, choosy females (Barash & Lipton, 2001; Birkhead, 2001; Fausto-Sterling, 1997; Hrdy, 1994; Roughgarden, 2004). In many species of birds, fish, and mammals, including human beings, females are sexually ardent and often have many male partners. The female's sexual behavior does not seem to depend only on the goal of becoming fertilized by the male, either: Females have sex when they are not ovulating and even when they are already pregnant.

Further, in many species, from penguins to primates to the golden lion tamarind, males do not just mate and run. They stick around, feeding the infants, carrying them on their backs, and protecting them against predators (Hrdy, 1988; Snowdon, 1997). Originally, evolutionary biologists thought that male monogamy evolved among some mammals as a tradeoff: The male gives up the chance to fertilize many females for the increased likelihood of his own offspring's survival. This may be the case in certain species. But it is also possible that male involvement in caring for offspring didn't *cause* monogamy, but *resulted* from it. Two scientists examined 2,545 species of mammals, searching for any factors

that might explain why the males in some of these species evolved from solitary living to monogamy. The found that monogamy emerged in conditions where females live in wide ranges that do not overlap, so females are scarce and males can't prevent other males from mating with them. Therefore, it became a better strategy to stay put and look after their offspring (Lukas & Clutton-Brock, 2013).

Further, contemporary differences in sexual behaviors and attitudes are not as large or universal as the evolutionary stereotype would predict. In Western nations, as gender roles have become more egalitarian, men and women have become more alike (Petersen & Hyde, 2010; Wells & Twenge, 2005). Today, straight women are just as likely as men to say they would accept a sexual offer from a great-looking person (or an unattractive *famous* person, thus explaining the groupie phenomenon). And both sexes are equally likely to say they would accept sex with friends or casual hook-ups who they think will be great lovers and give them a "positive sexual experience" (Conley et al., 2011).

2 **Cultural variation.** Human sexual behavior is amazingly varied and changeable across time and place. Cultures range from those in which women have many children to those in which they have very few, from those in which men are intimately involved in child rearing to those in which they take no part at all, from those in which women may have many lovers to those in which women may be killed for having sex outside of

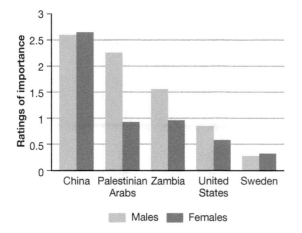

FIGURE 14.1 Attitudes Toward Chastity
In many places, men care more about a partner's chastity than women do, as evolutionary psychologists would predict. But culture has a powerful impact on these attitudes, as this graph shows. In China, at least when this research was done, both sexes preferred a partner who had not yet had intercourse, whereas in Sweden, chastity was and is a nonissue (in Buss, 1995).

marriage. In many places, the chastity of a potential mate is much more important to men than to women, but in other places, it is important to both sexes—or to neither one. (See Figure 14.1.) In some places, just as evolutionary theory predicts, a relatively few men—those with the greatest wealth and power—have a far greater number of offspring than other men do; but in many societies, including some polygamous ones, powerful men do not have more children than men who are poor or who are low in status (Brown, Laland, & Mulder, 2009).

3 **What people say versus what they do.** Evolutionary psychologists have tended to rely on data from questionnaires and interviews, but people's responses can be a poor guide to their actual choices and actions. When people are asked to rank the traits they most value in a sexual partner or someone they'd like to go out with, sex differences appear, just as evolutionary theory would predict: Straight women say they'd like a man who is rich and handsome, and straight men say they'd like a woman who is beautiful and sexy (Kenrick et al., 2001). But people's actual choices about whom to date, love, and marry tell another story, because people who are plain, pudgy, foolish, poor, or goofy all usually manage to find partners. This finding makes good evolutionary sense, because our prehistoric ancestors, unlike undergraduates filling out questionnaires about their ideal mates, did not have 5,000 fellow students to choose from. They lived in small bands, and if they were lucky they might get to choose between Urp and Ork, and that's about it. They could not hold out for someone

more beautiful or a better hunter down the road, even if there had been roads back then (Hazan & Diamond, 2000).

All of this evidence argues against a universal, genetically determined sexual strategy for either sex. What evolution *has* bestowed on us, however, is an amazingly flexible brain. Biology influences sexual behavior but it is only one influence among many, as we shall see next.

The Psychology of Desire LO 14.9

Psychologists are fond of observing that the sexiest sex organ is the brain, where perceptions begin. People's values, fantasies, and beliefs profoundly affect their sexual desire and behavior. That is why a touch on the knee by an exciting potential partner feels terrifically sexy, but the same touch by a creepy stranger on a bus feels disgusting. It is why a worried thought can kill sexual arousal in a second, and why a fantasy can be more erotic than reality.

The Many Reasons for Sex. To most people, the primary motives for sex are pretty obvious: to enjoy the pleasure of it, to express love and intimacy, or to make babies. But there are other motives too, not all of them so positive, including money or perks, duty or feelings of obligation, rebellion, power over the partner, and submission to the partner to avoid his or her anger or rejection.

One survey of nearly 2,000 people yielded 237 motives for having sex, and nearly every one of those motives was rated as the most important one by someone. Most men and women listed the same top 10, including attraction to the partner, love, fun, and physical pleasure. But some said, "I wanted to feel closer to God," "I was drunk," "to get rid of a headache" (that was #173), "to help me fall asleep," "to make my partner feel powerful," "to return a favor," "because someone dared me"; or to hurt an enemy or a rival ("I wanted to make him pay so I slept with his girlfriend"; "I wanted someone else to suffer from herpes as I do"). Men were more likely than women to say they use sex to gain status, enhance their reputation (e.g., because the partner was normally "out of my league"), or get things (such as a promotion) (Meston & Buss, 2007).

Across the many studies of motives for sex, several major categories emerge (Cooper, Shapiro, & Powers, 1998; Meston & Buss, 2007):

- *Pleasure*: the satisfaction and physical pleasure of sex.
- *Intimacy*: emotional closeness with the partner, spiritual transcendence.
- *Insecurity*: reassurance that you are attractive or desirable.

The many motivations for sex range from sex for profit to sex for fun.

- *Partner approval*: the desire to please or appease the partner; the desire to avoid the partner's anger or rejection.
- *Peer approval*: the wish to impress friends, be part of the group, and conform to what everyone else seems to be doing.
- *Attaining a goal*: to get status, money, revenge, or "even the score."

People's motives for having sex affect many aspects of their sexual behavior, including whether they engage in sex in the first place, whether they enjoy it, whether they have unprotected or otherwise risky sex, and whether they have few or many partners (Browning et al., 2000; Impett & Tolman, 2006). Extrinsic motives, such as having sex to gain approval from others or get some tangible benefit, are most strongly associated with risky sexual behavior, including having many partners, not using birth control, and pressuring a partner into sex (Hamby & Koss, 2003). For men, extrinsic motives include peer pressure, inexperience, a desire for popularity, or a fear of seeming unmasculine. Women's extrinsic motives include not wanting to lose the relationship; feeling obligated once the partner has spent time and money on them; feeling guilty about not doing what the partner demands; or wanting to avoid conflict and quarrels (Impett, Gable, & Peplau, 2005).

When one partner is feeling insecure about the relationship, he or she is also more likely to consent to unwanted sex. In a study of 125 college women, one-half to two-thirds of the Asian-American, white, and Latina women had consented to having sex when they didn't really want to, and all of the African-American women said they had. Do you remember the attachment theory of love? Anxiously attached women were the most willing to consent to unwanted sex, especially if they feared their partners were less committed than they were. They reported that they often had sex out of feelings of obligation and to prevent the partner from leaving. Securely attached women also occasionally had unwanted sex, but their reasons were different: to gain sexual experience, to satisfy their curiosity, or to actively please their partners and further the intimacy between them (Impett, Gable, & Peplau, 2005).

Sexual Coercion and Rape. One of the most persistent differences in the sexual experiences of women and men has to do with sexual coercion. A U.S. government survey of rape and domestic violence, based on a nationally representative sample of 16,507 adults, reported that nearly one in five women said they had been raped or experienced attempted rape at least once. (The researchers defined rape as completed or attempted forced penetration, including forced penetration enabled by alcohol or drugs.) Men also reported being victimized, but the numbers were much lower: One in seven said they had been severely beaten at the hands of a partner, and 1 to 2 percent said they had been raped, most when they were younger than 11 (Black et al., 2011).

However, many women who report a sexual assault that meets the legal definition of rape—being forced to engage in sexual acts against their will—do not label it as such (McMullin & White, 2006; Peterson & Muehlenhard, 2011). Most women define "rape" as being forced into intercourse by an acquaintance or stranger, as an act that caused them to fight back, or as having been molested as a child. They are much less likely to call their experience rape if they were sexually assaulted by a boyfriend, had previously had consensual sex with him, were drunk or otherwise drugged, or were forced to have oral or digital sex. Sometimes women are motivated to avoid labeling the experience with such a charged word because they are embarrassed, or simply because they don't want to think of someone they know personally as being a rapist (Koss, 2011; Peterson & Muehlenhard, 2011).

What causes some men to rape? Evolutionary arguments—that rape stems from the male drive to fertilize as many females as possible, the better to distribute their genes—have not been supported (Buss & Schmitt, 2011). Among human beings, rape is often committed by high-status men, including sports heroes and other celebrities, who could easily find consenting sexual partners. All too frequently its victims are children or the elderly, who do not reproduce. And sadistic rapists often injure or kill their victims, hardly a way to perpetuate one's genes. The human motives for rape thus appear to be primarily psychological, and include these:

- **Narcissism and hostility toward women.** Sexually aggressive males often are narcissistic, are unable to empathize with women, and feel entitled to have sexual relations with whatever woman they choose. They misperceive women's behavior in social situations, equate feelings of power with sexuality, and accuse women of provoking them (Bushman et al., 2003; Malamuth et al., 1995; Zurbriggen, 2000).

- **A desire to dominate, humiliate, or punish the victim.** This motive is apparent among soldiers who rape captive women during war and then often kill them (Olujic, 1998). The widespread, systematic harassment and rape of American women soldiers by their own peers and commanding officers also suggest that the rapists' motives are to intimidate and humiliate the women. Aggressive motives also occur in the rape of men by other men, usually by anal penetration (King & Woollett, 1997). This form of rape typically occurs in youth gangs, where the intention is to humiliate rival gang members, and in prison, where again the motive is to conquer and degrade the victim.

- **Sadism.** A minority of rapists are violent criminals who get pleasure out of inflicting pain on their victims and who often murder them in planned, grotesque ways (Turvey, 2008).

You can see that the answer to the question "Why do people have sex?" is not at all obvious. It is not a simple matter of "doing what's natural." In addition to the intrinsic motives of intimacy, pleasure, procreation, and love, extrinsic motives include intimidation, dominance, insecurity, appeasing the partner, approval from peers, and the wish to prove oneself a real man or a desirable woman.

The Culture of Desire LO 14.10

Think about kissing. Westerners like to think about kissing, and to do it, too. But if you think kissing is natural, try to remember your first serious kiss and all you had to learn about noses, breathing, and the position of teeth and tongue. The sexual kiss is so complicated that some cultures have never gotten around to it. They think that kissing another person's mouth—the very place that food enters!—is disgusting (Tiefer, 2004). Others have elevated the sexual kiss to high art; why do you suppose one version is called French kissing?

As the kiss illustrates, having the physical equipment to perform a sexual act is not all there is to sexual motivation. People have to learn what is supposed to turn them on (or off), which parts of the body and what activities are erotic (or repulsive), and even how to have pleasurable sexual relations. In some cultures, oral sex is regarded as a bizarre sexual deviation; in others, it is considered not only normal but also supremely desirable. In many cultures, men believe that women who have experienced sexual pleasure of any kind will become unfaithful, so sexual relations are limited to quick intercourse; in other cultures, men's satisfaction and pride depend on knowing the woman is sexually satisfied too. In some cultures, sex itself is seen as something joyful and beautiful, a skill to be cultivated as one might cultivate the skill of gourmet cooking. In others, it is considered ugly and dirty, something to be gotten through as rapidly as possible.

Sexual Scripts. How do cultures transmit their rules and requirements about sex to their members? During childhood and adolescence, people learn their culture's *gender roles*, collections of rules that determine the proper attitudes and behavior for men and women. Like any actor in a play, a person following a gender role relies on a script, in this case a **sexual script** that provides instructions on how to behave in sexual situations (Gagnon & Simon, 1973; Laumann & Gagnon, 1995). If you are a teenage girl, are you supposed to be sexually adventurous and assertive or sexually modest and passive? What if you are a teenage boy? What if you are an old woman or man? The answers differ from culture to culture because members act in accordance with culturally defined sexual scripts for their gender, age, religion, social status, and peer group.

In many parts of the world, boys acquire their attitudes about sex in a competitive atmosphere where the goal is to impress other males, and they talk and joke with their friends about masturbation and other sexual experiences. Their traditional sexual scripts are encouraging them to value physical sex, whereas traditional scripts are teaching girls to value relationships and make themselves attractive (Matlin, 2012). At an early age, girls learn that the closer they match the cultural ideal of beauty, the greater their power, sexually and in other ways. They learn that they will be scrutinized and evaluated according to their looks, which of course is the meaning of being a "sex object" (Impett et al., 2011). What many girls and women may not realize is that the more sexualized their clothing, the more likely they are to be seen as incompetent and unintelligent (Graff, Murnen, & Smolak, 2012).

When gender roles change because of social and economic shifts in society, so do sexual scripts. Whenever women have needed marriage to ensure their social and financial security, they have regarded sex as a bargaining chip, an asset to be rationed rather than an activity to be enjoyed for its own sake (Hatfield & Rapson, 1996/2005). After all, a woman with no economic resources of her own cannot afford to casually seek sexual pleasure if that means risking an unwanted pregnancy, the security of marriage, her reputation in society, her physical safety, or, in some cultures, her very life. When women become better educated, self-supporting, and able to control their own fertility—three major worldwide changes in recent decades—they are more likely to want sex for pleasure rather than as a means to another goal. When women are not financially dependent on men and have goals of economic self-sufficiency, it is also easier for them to refuse sex and leave an abusive relationship.

What do you think are the sexual scripts that describe appropriate behavior for *your* gender, religion, ethnicity, sexual orientation, social class, and age? Do they differ from those of your friends, male and female?

The Riddle of Sexual Orientation

Why do people become straight, gay, or bisexual? Many psychological explanations for homosexuality have been proposed over the years, but none of them has been supported. Homosexuality is not a result of having a smothering mother, an absent father, or emotional problems. It is not caused by seduction by an older adult (Rind, Tromovich, & Bauserman, 1998). It is not caused by parental practices or role models. Most gay men recall that they rejected the typical boy role and boys' toys and games from an early age, despite enormous pressures from their parents and peers to conform to the traditional male role (Bailey & Zucker, 1995). The overwhelming majority of children of gay parents do not become gay, as a learning explanation would predict, although they are more likely than the children of straight parents to be open-minded about homosexuality and gender roles (Bailey et al., 1995; Patterson, 2006).

Many researchers, therefore, have turned to biological explanations of sexual orientation. One line of supporting evidence is that homosexual behavior—including courtship displays, sexual

sexual scripts Sets of implicit rules that specify proper sexual behavior for a person in a given situation, varying with the person's gender, age, religion, social status, and peer group.

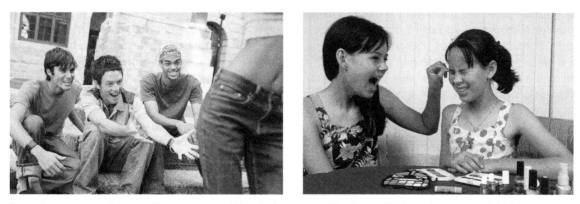

These teenagers are following the sexual scripts for their gender and culture—the boys, by ogling and making sexual remarks about girls to impress their peers, and the girls, by preening and wearing makeup to look good for boys.

activity, and rearing of young by two males or two females—has been documented in more than 450 species, including bottlenose dolphins, penguins, albatrosses, and primates (Bagemihl, 1999). Sexual orientation also seems to be moderately heritable, particularly in men (Bailey, Dunne, & Martin, 2000; Rahman & Wilson, 2003). But the large majority of gay men and lesbians do not have a close gay relative, and their siblings, including twins, are overwhelmingly likely to be heterosexual (Peplau et al., 2000).

Prenatal exposure to androgens might affect brain organization and partner preference (McFadden, 2008; Rahman & Wilson, 2003). Female babies exposed in the womb to unusually high levels of masculinizing hormones are more likely than other girls to become bisexual or lesbian and to prefer typical boys' toys and activities (Collaer & Hines, 1995). However, most androgenized girls do not become lesbians, and most lesbians were not exposed in the womb to atypical prenatal hormones (Peplau et al., 2000).

Other prenatal events might predispose a child toward a same-sex orientation. More than a dozen studies have found that the probability of a man's becoming gay rises significantly according to the number of older brothers he has, gay or not, when these brothers are born of the same mother. (The percentage of males who identify as exclusively gay is nonetheless very low.) A study of 944 gay and straight men suggests that this "brother effect" has nothing to do with family environment, but rather with conditions within the womb before birth (Bogaert, 2006). The only factor that predicted sexual orientation was having older biological brothers; growing up with older stepbrothers or adoptive brothers (or sisters) had no influence at all. The increased chance of homosexuality occurred even when men had older brothers born to the same mother but raised in a different home. No one yet has any idea, however, what prenatal influence might account for these results.

Researchers are investigating other possible biological markers associated with sexual orientation. A team of Swedish scientists exposed people to two odors: a testosterone derivative found in men's sweat and an estrogen-like compound found in women's urine. It appears that when a hormone is from the sex you are *not* turned on by, the olfactory system registers it, but the hypothalamus, which regulates sexual arousal and response, does not. Thus, the brain activity of lesbians in response to the odors was similar to that of straight men, and the brain activity of gay men was similar to that of straight women (Berglund, Lindström, & Savic, 2006; Savic, Berglund, & Lindström,

Same-sex sexual activity occurs in more than 450 nonhuman species. These male penguins, Squawk and Milou, entwine their necks, kiss, call to each other, have sex, and firmly reject females. Another male pair in the same zoo, Silo and Roy, seemed so desperate to incubate an egg together that they put a rock in their nest and sat on it. Their human keeper was so touched that he gave them a fertile egg to hatch. Silo and Roy sat on it for the necessary 34 days until their chick, Tango, was born, and then they raised Tango beautifully. "They did a great job," said the zookeeper.

2005). But the researchers wisely noted that their study could not answer questions of cause and effect: the differences in orientation could have been caused by brain differences, or past sexual experiences could have affected the brains of the gay and straight participants differently.

The basic problem with trying to find a single origin of sexual orientation is that sexual identity and behavior take different forms that don't even correlate strongly (Savin-Williams, 2006). Some people are heterosexual in behavior but have homosexual fantasies and define themselves as gay or lesbian or bisexual or "none of the above." Some men, such as prisoners, are homosexual in behavior because they lack opportunities for heterosexual sex, but they do not define themselves as gay and prefer women as sexual partners. In some cultures, teenage boys go through a homosexual phase that they do not define as homosexual and that does not affect their future relations with women (Herdt, 1984). Similarly, in Lesotho, in South Africa, women have intimate relations with other women, including passionate kissing and oral sex, but they do not define these acts as sexual, as they do when a man is the partner (Kendall, 1999). Some gay men are feminine in interests and manner, but many are not; some lesbians are masculine in interests and manner, but most are not (Singh et al., 1999).

Moreover, although some lesbians have an exclusively same-sex orientation their whole lives,

Phyllis Lyon and Del Martin (left) lived together for 56 years. In 2008, two months after they were finally legally allowed to marry, Del Martin died. Gay men, like the couple on the right, are increasingly likely to adopt children, though in many U.S. states they are still forbidden to do so.

the majority have more fluid sexual orientations. A researcher interviewed 100 lesbian and bisexual women over a 10-year span, and found that only one-third reported consistent attraction only to other women; two-thirds also felt attracted to men. For many of these women, love was truly blind as far as gender was concerned; their sexual behavior depended on whether they loved the partner, not whether the partner was male or female (Diamond, 2008). Similarly, when men and women watch erotic films, men are more influenced than women are by the sex of the people having sex, whereas women are more influenced than men are by the context in which the sex occurs. Thus, most straight men are turned off by watching gay male couples coupling, most gay men are turned off by watching straight couples, and most straight and lesbian women are turned on by watching anyone of either sex, as long as the context is erotic (Rupp & Wallen, 2008).

Biological factors cannot account for this diversity of sexual responses, cultural customs, or experience among gay men and lesbians. At present, therefore, we must tolerate uncertainty about the origins of sexual orientation. Perhaps the origins will turn out to differ, on average, for males and females, and also differ among individuals, whatever their primary orientation.

👁 **Watch** the **Video** Thinking Like a Psychologist: Sexual Orientation at **MyPsychLab**

Recite & Review

✔️ Study and Review at MyPsychLab

Recite: Were you motivated to learn about sexual motivation? Say aloud what you know about biological factors in sexuality; evolutionary approaches to gender differences in sexual behavior; social and cultural criticisms of evolutionary approaches; psychological motives for sex and for rape; sexual scripts and their influence on sexual behavior; and the possible factors involved in sexual orientation.

Review: Next, reread this section.

Now Take This *Quick Quiz:*

1. Biological research finds that (a) homosexual behavior is found in hundreds of animal species, (b) male and female sexual responses are physiologically very different, (c) women have a stronger sex drive than men do, contrary to the stereotype.

2. Which types of motives lead to risky sexual behavior? (a) extrinsic motives, (b) intrinsic motives

3. Which of the following is not true? Women are more reluctant about casual sex because (a) they have a biologically weak sex drive, (b) a casual experience may not be gratifying for them, (c) it puts them at a greater risk of unwanted pregnancy, (d) it would create a social stigma

4. *True or false:* Motivation for sexual activity is only for intrinsic pleasure.

Answers:

1. a 2. a 3. a 4. false

The Competent Animal: Motives to Achieve

Almost every adult works. Students work at studying. Homemakers work at running a household. Artists, poets, and actors work, even if they are paid erratically (or not at all). Most people are motivated to work to meet the needs for food and shelter. Yet survival does not explain why some people want to do their work well and others just want to get it done. And it does not explain why some people work to make a living and then put their passion for achievement into unpaid activities, such as learning to become an accomplished trail rider or traveling to Madagascar to catch sight of a rare bird.

The Effects of Motivation on Work

LO 14.11, LO 14.12

Psychologists, particularly those in the field of *industrial/organizational psychology*, have measured the psychological qualities that spur achievement and success and also the environmental conditions that influence productivity and satisfaction.

The Importance of Goals. To understand the motive to achieve, researchers today emphasize goals rather than inner drives: What you accomplish depends on the goals you set for yourself and the reasons you pursue them (Dweck & Grant, 2008). Not just any old goals will promote achievement, though. A goal is most likely to improve your motivation and performance when three conditions are met (Locke & Latham, 2002, 2006):

- **The goal is specific.** Defining a goal vaguely, such as "doing your best," is as ineffective as having no goal at all. You need to be specific about what you are going to do and when you are going to do it: "I will write four pages of this paper today."

- **The goal is challenging but achievable.** You are apt to work hardest for tough but realistic goals. The highest, most difficult goals produce the highest levels of motivation and performance, unless, of course, you choose impossible goals that you can never attain.

- **The goal is framed in terms of getting what you want rather than avoiding what you do not want.** This means focusing on **approach goals**, positive experiences that you seek directly, such as getting a better grade or learning to scuba dive. **Avoidance goals**, in contrast, involve the effort to avoid unpleasant experiences, such as trying not to make a fool of yourself at parties or trying to avoid being dependent.

All of the motives discussed in this chapter are affected by approach versus avoidance goals. People who frame their goals in specific, achievable approach terms (e.g., "I'm going to lose weight by jogging three times a week") feel better about themselves, feel more competent, are more optimistic, and are less depressed than people who frame the same goals in avoidance terms (e.g., "I'm going to lose weight by cutting out rich foods") (Coats, Janoff-Bulman, & Alpert, 1996; Updegraff, Gable, & Taylor, 2004). Similarly, people who have sex for approach goals—to enjoy their own physical pleasure, to promote a partner's happiness, or to seek intimacy—tend to have happier and less conflicted relationships than those who have sex to avoid a partner's loss of interest or quarrels with the partner (Impett & Tolman, 2006).

Can you guess why approach goals produce better results than avoidance goals? Approach goals allow you to focus on what you can actively do to accomplish them and on the intrinsic pleasure of the activity. Avoidance goals make you focus on what you have to give up.

approach goals Goals framed in terms of desired outcomes or experiences, such as learning to scuba dive.

avoidance goals Goals framed in terms of avoiding unpleasant experiences, such as trying not to look foolish in public.

"Finish it? Why would I want to finish it?"

Get Involved! Reframing Your Goals

As the text discusses, people sometimes frame their goals in vague, unrealistic, or negative ways. Think of two goals you would like to accomplish. You might consider goals related to studying more efficiently, improving communication with a family member, solving problems in a relationship, or becoming more physically fit. Now phrase each of your two goals in a way that makes it (1) specific, (2) challenging but achievable, and (3) something to be approached rather than avoided. How can framing your goals in this way improve your motivation to reach them?

In the case of work, defining your goals will move you along the road to success, but what happens when you hit a pothole? Some people give up when a goal becomes difficult or they are faced with a setback, whereas others become even more determined to succeed. The crucial difference between them is *why* they are working for that goal: to show off in front of others or learn the task for the satisfaction of it.

People who are motivated by **performance goals** are concerned primarily with being judged favorably and avoiding criticism. Those who are motivated by **mastery (learning) goals** are concerned with increasing their competence and skills and finding intrinsic pleasure in what they are learning (Grant & Dweck, 2003; Senko, Durik, & Harackiewicz, 2008). When people who are motivated by performance goals do poorly, they will often decide the fault is theirs and stop trying to improve. Because their goal is to demonstrate their abilities, they set themselves up for grief when they temporarily fail, as all of us must if we are to learn anything new. But people who are motivated to master new skills will generally regard failure and criticism as sources of useful information that will help them improve. They know that learning takes time. They know that failure is essential to eventual success.

Why do some children choose performance goals and others choose mastery goals? In a study of 128 fifth graders, the children worked independently on sets of puzzle problems (Mueller & Dweck, 1998). The experimenter scored their results, told them all they had done well, and gave them one of two additional types of feedback: She praised some of them for their ability ("You must be smart at these problems!") and others for their effort ("You must have worked hard at these problems!"). The children then worked on a more difficult set of problems, but this time the experimenter told them they had done a lot worse. Finally, the children described which goals they preferred to work for: performance (e.g.,

doing "problems that aren't too hard, so I don't get many wrong") or mastery (e.g., doing "problems that I'll learn a lot from, even if I won't look so smart").

The children praised for being smart rather than for working hard tended to lose the pleasure of learning and focused instead on how well they were doing. After these children failed the second set of problems, they tended to give up on subsequent ones, enjoyed them less, and actually performed less well than children who had been praised for their efforts. As you can see in Figure 14.2, nearly 70 percent of fifth graders who were praised for their intelligence later chose performance goals rather than learning goals, compared to fewer than 10 percent

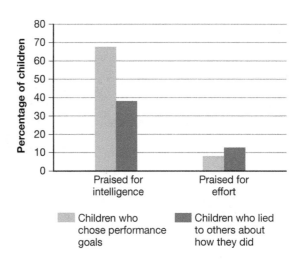

FIGURE 14.2 Mastery and Motivation
Children praised for "being smart" rather than for "working hard" tend to lose the pleasure of learning and focus on how well they are doing. Nearly 70 percent of fifth graders who were praised for intelligence later chose performance goals rather than learning goals, compared to fewer than 10 percent of the children who were praised for their efforts (Mueller & Dweck, 1998). Notice also that the children praised for intelligence were much more likely to lie to others about how well they had done—because their goal was showing off, not learning.

performance goals
Goals framed in terms of performing well in front of others, being judged favorably, and avoiding criticism.

mastery (learning) goals Goals framed in terms of increasing one's competence and skills.

of children who were praised for their efforts. When children realize that all effort is subject to improvement, however, they realize that they can always try again. That is the key to mastery. As one learning-oriented child said to the experimenters, "Mistakes are our friends" (Dweck & Sorich, 1999).

Mastery goals are powerful intrinsic motivators at all levels of education and throughout life. Students who are in college primarily to master new areas of knowledge choose more challenging projects, persist in the face of difficulty, use deeper and more elaborate study strategies, are less likely than other students to cheat, and enjoy learning more than do students who are there only to get a degree and a meal ticket (Elliot &

McGregor, 2001; Grant & Dweck, 2003). As usual, though, we should avoid oversimplifying: World-class athletes, musicians, and others who strive to excel in their fields blend performance and mastery goals.

Expectations and Self-Efficacy. How hard you work for something also depends on your expectations. If you are fairly certain of success, you will work harder to reach your goal than if you are fairly certain of failure.

A classic experiment showed how quickly experience affects these expectations. Young women were asked to solve 15 anagram puzzles. Before working on each one, they had to estimate their chances of solving it. Half of the women started

THE MANY MOTIVES OF ACCOMPLISHMENT

IMMORTALITY
**William Faulkner
(1897–1962)
Novelist**

"Really the writer doesn't want success...He wants to leave a scratch on that wall [of oblivion]—Kilroy was here—that somebody a hundred or a thousand years later will see."

KNOWLEDGE
**Helen Keller
(1880–1968)
Blind/deaf author and lecturer**

"Knowledge is happiness, because to have knowledge—broad, deep knowledge—is to know true ends from false, and lofty things from low."

FREEDOM
**Nelson Mandela
(1918–2013)
Former president of
South Africa**

"For to be free is not merely to cast off one's chains, but to live in a way that respects and enhances the freedom of others."

AUTONOMY
**Georgia O'Keeffe
(1887–1986)
Artist**

"[I] found myself saying to myself—I can't live where I want to, go where I want to, do what I want to...I decided I was a very stupid fool not to at least paint as I wanted to."

off with very easy anagrams, but half began with insoluble ones. Sure enough, those who started with the easy ones increased their estimates of success on later ones. Those who began with the impossible ones decided they would all be impossible. These expectations, in turn, affected the young women's ability to actually solve the last 10 anagrams, which were the same for everyone. The higher the expectation of success, the more anagrams the women solved (Feather, 1966). Once acquired, therefore, expectations can create a **self-fulfilling prophecy** (Merton, 1948): Your expectations make you behave in ways that make the expectation come true. You expect to succeed, so you work hard—and succeed. Or you expect to fail, so you don't do much work—and do poorly.

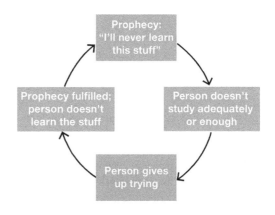

Your expectations are further influenced by your level of confidence in yourself and your abilities (Dweck & Grant, 2008; Judge, 2009).

self-fulfilling prophecy An expectation that becomes reality because of the tendency of the person holding it to act in ways that bring it about.

POWER
Henry Kissinger (b. 1923)
Former Secretary of State

"Power is the ultimate aphrodisiac."

DUTY
Eleanor Roosevelt (1884–1962)
Humanitarian, lecturer, stateswoman

"As for accomplishments, I just did what I had to do as things came along."

EXCELLENCE
Florence Griffith Joyner (1959–1998)
Olympic gold medalist

"When you've been second best for so long, you can either accept it, or try to become the best. I made the decision to try and be the best."

GREED
Ivan Boesky (b. 1937)
Financier, convicted of insider trading violations

"Greed is all right...I think greed is healthy. You can be greedy and still feel good about yourself."

self-efficacy A person's belief that he or she is capable of producing desired results, such as mastering new skills and reaching goals.

No one is born with a feeling of confidence, or **self-efficacy**. You acquire it through experience in mastering new skills (by making mistakes!), overcoming obstacles, and learning from occasional failures. Self-efficacy also comes from having successful role models who teach you that your ambitions are possible and from having people around to give you constructive feedback and encouragement (Bandura, 2006).

People who have a strong sense of self-efficacy are quick to cope with problems rather than stewing and brooding about them. Studies in North America, Europe, and Russia find that self-efficacy has a positive effect on just about every aspect of people's lives: how well they do on a task, the grades they earn, how persistently they pursue their goals, the kind of career choices they make, their ability to solve complex problems, their motivation to work for political and social goals, their health habits, and even their chances of recovery from heart attack. Self-efficacy and the setting of ambitious but achievable goals are the strongest predictors of learning and accomplishment (Lanaj, Chang, & Johnson, 2012; Sitzmann & Ely, 2011).

The Effects of Work on Motivation LO 14.13

Many people think the relationship between work and motivation runs in one direction: You are motivated, so you choose a career and you work hard to get it. But psychological scientists have also studied the reverse direction: How the availability of careers affects motivation. For example, one simple but powerful external factor that affects many people's motivation to work in a particular field is the proportion of men and women in that occupation (Kanter, 2006). When occupations are segregated by gender, many people form gender stereotypes about the requirements of such careers: Female jobs require kindness and nurturance; male jobs require strength and smarts. These stereotypes, in turn, stifle many people's aspirations to enter a nontraditional career and also create self-fulfilling prejudices in employers (Agars, 2004; Cejka & Eagly, 1999; Eccles, 2011).

A natural experiment in India showed the powerful influence of female role models on adolescents' educational and achievement ambitions (Beaman et al., 2012). In 1993, a law was passed reserving leadership positions for women in nearly 500 randomly selected villages. Years later, a survey of 8,453 adolescents (ages 11 to 15) found that in villages with the female leaders, the gender gap in educational aspirations had closed by nearly one-third. What you see, apparently, influences what you want—and what you think you can get.

In the United States, when law, veterinary medicine, pharmacy, and bartending were almost entirely male professions, and nursing, teaching, and child care were almost entirely female, few women aspired to enter the "male" professions. When job segregation became illegal, however, people's career motivations changed. Today, it is common to see a female lawyer, vet, pharmacist, and bartender. And although women are still a minority in engineering, math, and science, their numbers have been rising (Cox & Alm, 2005). In 1960, women earned only 0.4 percent of the doctorates in engineering; in 2010, 43 percent of the younger cohorts of people in engineering were women. As these numbers have increased, the old view that women are not "naturally" suited to engineering, math, and science has been fading fast.

Unhappily, as women attain greater numbers in fields that once were closed to them, today it is men who are more likely to be suffering from dissatisfaction and low motivation to succeed, rejecting college or dropping out of school. Women are far more likely than men to educate themselves for the careers of the future in service industries, health care, and education; men are still reluctant to go into "women's work."

This gender shift is occurring in developing as well as developed nations, a result of changes in the global economy—the slow erosion of traditionally male jobs in construction, manufacturing, and high finance and the expanding need for people who are educated and have good communication and "people" skills. In 2010, young American women had a median income higher than that of their male peers in 1,997 out of 2,000 metropolitan regions. In Brazil, one-third of married women earn more than their husbands. Women are the majorities in colleges and professional schools on every continent except Africa; in Bahrain, Qatar, and Guyana, women are 70 percent of college graduates (Rosin, 2012).

Working Conditions. Imagine that you live in a town that has one famous company, Boopsie's Biscuits & Buns. Everyone in the town is grateful for the 3B company and goes to work there with high hopes. Soon, however, an odd thing starts happening to many employees. They complain of fatigue and irritability. They are taking lots of sick leave. Productivity declines. What's going on at Boopsie's Biscuits & Buns? Is everybody suffering from sheer laziness?

✳ **THINKING CRITICALLY**
About Work Motivation

Most observers would answer that something is wrong with those employees. But what if something is wrong with Boopsie's? Psychologists want to know how conditions at work nurture or crush our motivation to succeed. Once in a job, what motivates people to do well? Why do others lose their motivation altogether?

To begin with, achievement depends on having the *opportunity* to achieve. When someone does not do well at work, others are apt to say it is the individual's own fault because he or she lacks the internal drive to make it. But what the person may really lack is a fair chance to make it, and this is especially true for those who have been subjected to systematic discrimination (Sabattini & Crosby, 2009). Once they have entered a career, people may become more motivated to advance up the ladder or less so, depending on how many rungs they are permitted to climb. Women used to be rare in politics, but it's not news today that they are governors, senators, congresswomen, or presidential candidates.

Several other aspects of the work environment are likely to increase work motivation and satisfaction and reduce the chances of emotional burnout (Bakker, 2011; Maslach, Schaufeli, & Leiter, 2001; Rhoades & Eisenberger, 2002):

- The work feels meaningful and important to employees.
- Employees have control over many aspects of their work, such as setting their own hours and making decisions.
- Tasks are varied rather than repetitive.
- Employees have supportive relationships with their superiors and co-workers.
- Employees receive useful feedback about their work, so they know what they have accomplished and what they need to do to improve.
- The company offers opportunities for its employees to learn and advance.

Companies that foster these conditions tend to have more productive and satisfied employees. Workers become more creative in their thinking, more engaged in their work, and feel better about themselves than they do if they feel stuck in routine jobs that give them no control or flexibility over their daily tasks.

In contrast, when people are put in situations that frustrate their desire and ability to succeed, they often become dissatisfied, their desire to succeed declines, and they may drop out. For example, a study of nearly 2,500 women and men in science, engineering, and technology explored the reasons that many of the women eventually

Like employees, students can have poor working conditions that affect their motivation. In this homeless family rebuilding their lives while living in a two-room shelter, the children may have to study in crowded quarters or may have siblings who interrupt and distract them.

left their jobs, with some abandoning their field altogether. The women who lost their motivation to work in these fields reported feeling isolated (many said they were the only woman in their work group), and two-thirds said they had been sexually harassed (Hewlitt, Luce, & Servon, 2008). Other reasons included being paid less than men for the same work and having working conditions that did not allow them to handle their family obligations. Mothers are still more likely than fathers to reduce their work hours, modify their work schedules, and feel distracted on the job because of child care concerns (Sabattini & Crosby, 2009). What do you think might be the "working conditions" of college today that are causing many men to lose their motivation to enter careers they once dominated, such as pharmacy, and creating the lopsided sex ratio on so many campuses?

In sum, work motivation and satisfaction depend on the right fit between qualities of the individual and conditions of the work.

✴ Explore the Concept Factors in Job Satisfaction at MyPsychLab

Recite & Review

 Study and **Review** at **MyPsychLab**

Recite: To work on your understanding of work motivation, say aloud what you recall about the three conditions under which goals are most effective; approach versus avoidance goals; performance and mastery goals; self-fulfilling prophecies; self-efficacy; and the work conditions that increase motivation.

Review: Next, give your motivation a jolt and reread this material.

Now Take This *Quick Quiz:*

1. Simile wants to lose weight. She decides to exercise twice a week and skip dinner every day. What type of goal has she set for herself? (a) approach goal, (b) avoidance goal

2. Rustom's parents gave him the option of higher studies in a prestigious university, but he refused and appeared for an internship program before appearing for his scholarship exam. He lost one year with this decision, but was happy to pursue his studies after giving his best in these two pursuits. Rustom's decision is an example of a (a) performance goal, (b) mastery goal

3. Which of these will not help in developing self efficacy? (a) failures, (b) successful role models, (c) experiences, (d) genetic makeup

4. An employer is annoyed by the behavior of an employee and is thinking of firing him. His work is competent, but he rarely arrives on time, doesn't seem interested in his job, and has begun to take an unusual number of sick days. The boss has decided the employee is lazy and unmotivated. What guidelines of critical thinking is the boss overlooking, and what information should the boss consider before firing him?

Answers:

1. a 2. b 3. d 4. The boss is jumping to the conclusion that the employee has low work motivation. This may be true, but because his work is competent, the boss should consider other explanations and examine the evidence. Perhaps the work conditions are unsatisfactory; There may be few opportunities for promotion; he may have been getting no feedback that lets him know he is doing well or that could help him improve; perhaps the company does not provide child care, so he is arriving late because, as a single dad, he has child care obligations. What other possible explanations come to mind?

You are about to learn . . .

- why people are poor at predicting what will make them happy or miserable.

- why money can't buy happiness—and what does.

- three basic kinds of motivational conflicts.

Motives, Values, and the Pursuit of Happiness LO 14.14, LO 14.15

When you think about setting goals for yourself, here is a crucial psychological finding to keep in mind: People are really bad at predicting what will make them happy and what will make them miserable, and at estimating how long either of those feelings will last (Wilson & Gilbert, 2005).

In one of the many studies that have demonstrated this, college students were asked how happy or unhappy they imagined they would feel after being randomly assigned to live in a dorm they thought was "desirable" or "undesirable" (Dunn, Wilson, & Gilbert, 2003). The students predicted that their dorm assignments would have a huge impact on their overall level of happiness and that being assigned to an undesirable dorm would essentially wreck their satisfaction for the whole year. But one year later, everyone had nearly identical levels of happiness no matter where they were living, as you can see in Figure 14.3.

Perhaps the undesirable dorms turned out to be unexpectedly pleasant, with cool people living in them? No. The students had focused on the wrong factors when imagining their future feelings of happiness; they had placed far more importance on what the dorm looked like and on its location than on its inhabitants. But it's *people* who make a place fun or unpleasant to live in, and all of the houses had likable people in them. Because the students could not foresee this, or how much

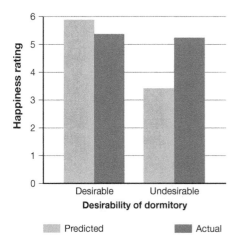

FIGURE 14.3 The Misprediction of Emotion
College students about to be randomly assigned to a
dorm had to predict how happy or unhappy they would
feel about being assigned to a house they had ranked
as "desirable" or "undesirable." Most students thought
that they would be much less happy in an "undesirable"
dorm, but one year later, there was no difference between the two groups (Dunn, Wilson, & Gilbert, 2003).

they would like their new roommates, they mis-
predicted their future happiness.

Across many different contexts, the good is
rarely as good as we imagine it will be, and the bad
is rarely as terrible. The reason is that people adjust
quickly to happy changes—new relationships, a promotion, even winning the lottery—and fail to anticipate that they will handle bad experiences just as
quickly. They will make sense of unexpected events,
cope with tragedies, and make excuses for loved
ones who hurt them. Yet people make many decisions based on false assumptions about how they
will feel in the future. Many spend more money
than they can afford on a car or house because they
think that *this* is what will make them truly happy.

What, then, does make people happy? In all
the domains of human motivation that we have
examined, a key conclusion emerges: People who
are motivated by the intrinsic satisfaction of an
activity are happier and more satisfied than those
motivated solely by extrinsic rewards (Deci &
Ryan, 1985; Kasser & Ryan, 2001).

In the United States, many people are more
motivated to make money than to find activities they enjoy. They imagine that greater wealth
will bring greater happiness, yet once they are at
a level that provides basic comfort and security,
more isn't necessarily better. They adjust quickly
to the greater wealth and then think they need
even more of it to be happier (Gilbert, 2006).
And regardless of whether they live in America
(an affluent nation) or Russia (a struggling nation), people who are primarily motivated to get
rich have poorer psychological adjustment and

lower well-being than do people whose primary
values are self-acceptance, affiliation with others,
or wanting to make the world a better place (Ryan
et al., 1999). This is especially true when the reasons
for striving for money are extrinsic (e.g., you do it
to impress others and show off your possessions)
rather than intrinsic (e.g., you do it so you can afford to do the volunteer work you love) (Carver
& Baird, 1998; Srivastava, Locke, & Bartol, 2001).
Having positive, intrinsically enjoyable *experiences*
makes most people happier than having *things*:
Doing, in other words, is more satisfying than buying (Headey, 2008; Van Boven & Gilovich, 2003).

Simulate the **Experiment** Survey
on Happiness at **MyPsychLab**

Whichever values and goals you choose, if
they are in conflict, the discrepancy can produce
emotional stress and unhappiness. Two motives
conflict when the satisfaction of one leads to the
inability to act on the other—when, that is, you
want to eat your cake and have it, too. There are
three kinds of motivational conflicts (Lewin, 1948):

1 **Approach–approach conflicts** occur when you are
equally attracted to two or more possible activities or goals: You would like to be a veterinarian
and a rock singer; you would like to go out Tuesday
night with friends *and* study like mad for an exam
Wednesday.

2 **Avoidance–avoidance conflicts** require you to
choose between the lesser of two evils because you dislike both alternatives. Novice parachute jumpers, for example, must choose between
the fear of jumping and the fear of losing face if
they don't jump.

"Grab a fork and pitch in if you want to.
Not that it matters. You're damned if you do,
damned if you don't."

A classic avoidance–avoidance conflict.

3 **Approach–avoidance conflicts** occur when a single activity or goal has both a positive and a negative aspect. In culturally diverse nations, differing cultural values produce many approach–avoidance conflicts, as students have told us. A Chicano student says he wants to become a lawyer, but his parents, valuing family closeness, worry that if he goes to graduate school, he will become independent and feel superior to his working-class family. A black student from a poor neighborhood, in college on scholarship, is torn between wanting to leave his background behind him forever and returning to help his home community. And a white student wants to be a marine biologist, but her friends tell her that only nerdy guys and dweebs go into science.

✳ Explore the Concept Types of Conflicts at MyPsychLab

Years ago, humanist psychologist Abraham Maslow (1970) envisioned people's motives as forming a pyramid. At the bottom level were basic survival needs for food, sleep, and water; at the next level were security needs, for shelter and safety; at the third level were social needs, for belonging and affection; at the fourth level were esteem needs, for self-respect and the respect of others; and at the top, when all other needs had been met, were those for self-actualization and self-transcendence.

Maslow's theory became immensely popular, and motivational speakers still often refer to it, using colorful pictures of the pyramid. But the theory, which was based mostly on Maslow's observations of people he personally decided were self-actualized, has had little empirical support (Sheldon et al., 2001; Smither, 1998). The main reason, as we have seen in this chapter, is that people have *simultaneous* needs for comfort and safety and for love, intimacy, and competence. Higher needs may even supersede lower ones. History is full of examples of people who would rather die of torture or starvation than sacrifice their convictions, or who would rather explore, risk, or create new art than be safe and secure at home.

Recite & Review

✓ Study and Review at MyPsychLab

Recite: We hope you don't feel any conflict over the goal of learning this material. Recite what you know about the misprediction of emotion, findings about money and happiness, the three kinds of conflict, and Abraham Maslow's pyramid of needs.

Review: Next, read this section again.

Now Take This *Quick Quiz:*

1. Max has applied for a junior year abroad, but couldn't get into his first choice, a drama school in London. He is feeling so miserable about the rejection that he is thinking of staying home. "Why should I go to a second-rate school somewhere else?" he reasons. What is the matter with his reasoning?

2. A Pakistani student says she desperately wants an education and a career as a pharmacist, but she also does not want to be disobedient to her parents, who have arranged a marriage for her back home. Which kind of conflict does she have?

3. Letitia just got her law degree. She wants to take a job in environmental law, but a corporate firm specializing in real estate contracts has offered her a job with an enormous salary. Why should she think carefully and critically in making a decision?

Answers:

1. Max assumes that how he feels now is how he will feel in the future. He can't imagine the more likely scenario, that he will find things to like about any program he enters. **2.** approach–avoidance **3.** She should think critically because taking a job exclusively for its extrinsic benefits might lower her intrinsic satisfaction in the work. Also, people who are motivated solely to acquire money often have poorer psychological adjustment and lower well-being than people who are motivated by work they enjoy. Of course, money provides material benefits, but psychological needs such as autonomy, competence, self-esteem, and connection to others are also important.

PSYCHOLOGY IN THE NEWS REVISITED //////

Understanding the biological, psychological, and cultural influences on motivation can help us understand the stories that opened this chapter and others that make the news every day.

The item about former Mayor Bloomberg's efforts to ban the sale of supersized soft drinks, which contain enormous amounts of sugar, raises many questions. Would the ban cause people to drink fewer sodas, or would they just double their purchase of smaller-sized drinks? Moreover, if a ban on large containers of soda simply causes people to switch to diet drinks, sugar consumption could actually increase, because artificial sweeteners make people crave more sugar. We saw that the rise in obesity has many causes, including an increase in inexpensive but calorie-laden fast foods and large portion sizes, which means that individuals and health officials will need to think of imaginative interventions—perhaps starting with some of the small but powerful ones that we described in the Get Involved exercise on page 501.

The marriage of Hugh Hefner at age 86 to Crystal Harris, 60 years younger, made many people scoff about their motives. The couple certainly fits the evolutionary prediction that men prefer young, fertile women and women prefer older, rich men! But human love takes many forms and involves many motives, and whether it fades away or lasts for years depends on social, economic, and cognitive factors such as a couple's attitudes, values, and perception of their relationship as being fair or unfair. Maybe Hefner and Harris married each other for pragmatic reasons, but they might also have married for companionship and fun, important aspects of human attachment.

The news item about the rape conviction of the teenage football players demonstrates some of the unpleasant motivations that some people bring to their sexual encounters. As we saw, the causes of rape and sexual assault often have less to do with physical pleasure than with contempt for women; in this case, one young man took pictures of the victim, unconscious and naked, to circulate to friends. Other motives for rape include narcissism, a sense of entitlement, sadism, or a need to prove masculinity. The two young men could easily have attracted consensual partners, which suggests that whatever their motives, their actions were not simply about sexual gratification.

Finally, and on a happier note, the story of Drew Lovejoy, the Jewish, biracial, American Irish-dancing champion, demonstrates the importance of having self-efficacy, setting challenging but achievable goals, and persisting in the pursuit of your dreams. Drew may have been driven in part by performance goals, but we'll bet that he also found intrinsic pleasure in learning to master this difficult dance form.

Abraham Maslow may have been wrong about a universal hierarchy of motives, but perhaps each of us develops our own hierarchy as we grow from childhood to old age. For some people, the needs for love, security, or safety will dominate. For others, the need for achievement or power will rule. Some of us will wrestle with conflicting motives; for others, one consuming ambition will hold sway over all others. The motives and goals that inspire us, and the choices we make in their pursuit, are what give our lives passion, color, and meaning. Choose wisely.

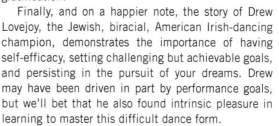

Taking Psychology With You

How to Attain Your Goals

What are your values? What would you most like to achieve and accomplish in your life? Is the answer love, wealth, security, passion, freedom, fame, the opportunity to improve the world, being the best in a sport or other skill? Something else? What are your short-term goals: Would you like to improve your love life? Get better grades? Enjoy school more? Lose weight? Become a better tennis player?

A whole world of motivational speakers, books, and tapes offer inspiration, enthusiasm, and a few magic steps to change your life, but we hope that by now you will apply critical thinking to their promises. Enthusiastic inspiration is fine as far as it goes, but it usually doesn't transfer into helping you make real-life changes. What does help? Think about some of the lessons of motivational research that you have learned in this chapter:

Seek activities that are intrinsically pleasurable. If you really, really want to study Swahili or Italian, even though these languages are

not in your pre-law requirements, try to find a way to do it. As the great writer Ray Bradbury said at age 89, the secret to living to a grand old age is to "do what you love and love what you do." If you are not enjoying your major or your job, consider finding a career that would be more intrinsically pleasurable, or at least make sure you have other projects and activities that you do enjoy for their own sake.

Focus on learning goals, not only on performance goals. In general, you will be better able to cope with setbacks if your goal is to learn rather than to show others how good you are. Regard failure as a chance to learn rather than as a sign of incompetence.

Assess your working conditions. Everyone has working conditions, even students. If your motivation and well-being are starting to wilt, check out your environment. Are you getting support from others? Are you being constantly interrupted? Do you have opportunities to develop ideas and vary your routine? Are there barriers that might limit your advancement in your chosen field?

Take steps to resolve motivational conflicts. Are you torn between competing goals? For instance, are you unhappily stuck between the goal of achieving independence and a desire to be cared for by your parents? The reconciliation of conflicts like these is important for your well-being.

For almost everyone, psychological well-being depends on finding activities and choosing goals that are intrinsically satisfying and on developing the self-efficacy to achieve them. That is why it is important to think critically about the goals you have chosen for yourself: Are they what *you* want to do or what someone else wants you to do? Do they reflect your values? If you are unhappy with your body, your relationships, or your work, why? Think about it.

Summary

((• Listen to the Audio File at MyPsychLab

- *Motivation* refers to a process within a person or animal that causes that organism to move toward a goal—to satisfy a biological need or achieve an ambition—or away from an unpleasant situation.

- A few primary drives are based on physiological needs, but all human motives are affected by psychological, social, and cultural factors. Motivation may be *intrinsic*, for the inherent pleasure of an activity, or *extrinsic*, for external rewards.

The Hungry Animal: Motives to Eat

- Overweight and obesity are not simply a result of failed will-power, emotional disturbance, or overeating. Hunger, weight, and eating are regulated by a set of bodily mechanisms, such as *basal metabolism rate* and number of fat cells; these mechanisms keep people close to their genetically influenced *set point*.

- Genes influence body shape, distribution of fat, number of fat cells, amount of *brown fat*, and whether the body will convert excess calories into fat. Genes may also account for certain types of obesity; the *ob* gene regulates *leptin*, which enables the hypothalamus to regulate appetite and metabolism and may be critical during infancy. The hormone *ghrelin* spurs appetite and leptin reduces it.

- Genetics alone cannot explain why rates of overweight and obesity are rising all over the world among all social classes, ethnicities, and ages. The major environmental reasons are (1) the increased abundance of inexpensive fast food and processed food, because humans have a genetic disposition to gain weight when rich food is plentiful; (2) the increased consumption of high-calorie sugared sodas; (3) increased portion sizes; and (4) the availability of highly varied foods.

- When genetic predispositions clash with cultural standards, physical and mental problems can result. In cultures that foster overeating and regard overweight as a sign of attractiveness and health, obesity is acceptable. In cultures that foster unrealistically thin bodies, eating disorders increase, especially *bulimia nervosa*, *binge-eating disorder*, and *anorexia nervosa*, as do unhealthy attitudes toward food and weight. Bulimia and anorexia are more common in white women than in men, but rates of body image problems and eating disorders among men are increasing.

The Social Animal: Motives to Love

- All human beings have a need for attachment and love. Psychologists distinguish *passionate ("romantic") love* from *companionate love*. Biologically oriented researchers believe that the neurological origins of passionate love begin in the baby's attachment to the mother. Various brain chemicals and hormones, including *vasopressin* and *oxytocin*, are associated with bonding and trust; endorphins and dopamine create the rushes of pleasure and reward associated with romantic passion.

- Two strong predictors of whom people will love are *proximity* and *similarity*. Once in love, people form different kinds of attachments. *Attachment theory* views adult love relationships, like those of infants, as being *secure, avoidant,* or *anxious*. People's attachment styles tend to be stable from childhood to adulthood and affect their close relationships.

- Men and women are equally likely to feel love and need attachment, but they differ, on average, in how they express feelings of love and how they define intimacy. A couple's attitudes, values, and perception that the relationship is fair and balanced are better predictors of long-term love than are genes or hormones.

- As women have entered the workforce in large numbers and pragmatic (extrinsic) reasons for marriage have faded, the two sexes have become more alike in endorsing intrinsic motives such as love and affection as a requirement for marriage.

The Erotic Animal: Motives for Sex

- Human sexuality is not simply a matter of "doing what comes naturally," because what is "natural" for one person or culture may not be so natural for others.

- The Kinsey surveys of male and female sexuality and the laboratory research of Masters and Johnson showed that physiologically, both sexes are capable of sexual arousal and response. However, individuals vary considerably in arousal, response, and inhibition.

- The hormone testosterone promotes sexual desire in both sexes, although hormones do not cause sexual behavior in a simple, direct way.

- Some researchers believe that men have a stronger sex drive than women do, because men have higher rates of almost every kind of sexual behavior. Others believe that gender differences in sexual motivation and behavior are a result of differences in roles, cultural norms, and opportunity. A middle view is that male sexuality is more biologically influenced than is women's, whereas female sexuality is more governed by circumstances, relationships, and cultural norms.

- Evolutionary psychologists argue that males and females have evolved different sexual and courtship strategies in response to survival problems faced in the distant past. In this view, it has been adaptive for males to be promiscuous, to be attracted to young partners, and to want sexual novelty, and for females to be monogamous, to be choosy about partners, and to prefer security to novelty.

- Critics argue that evolutionary explanations of infidelity and monogamy are based on simplistic stereotypes of gender differences; that the variation in human sexual customs across and within cultures argues against a universal, genetically determined sexual strategy; and that evolutionary arguments rely too heavily on answers to questionnaires, which often do not reflect real-life choices. Our ancestors probably did not have a wide range of partners to choose from; what may have evolved is mate selection based on similarity and proximity.

- Men and women have sex to satisfy many different psychological motives, including pleasure, intimacy, security, the partner's approval, peer approval, or to attain a specific goal.

- Extrinsic motives for sex, such as the need for approval, are associated with riskier sexual behavior than intrinsic motives are. Both sexes may agree to intercourse for nonsexual reasons, including revenge, perks, power, to prove oneself, or to preserve the relationship. People's motives for consenting to unwanted sex vary, depending on their feelings of security and commitment in the relationship.

- Men who rape do so for diverse reasons, including narcissism and hostility toward women; a desire to dominate, humiliate, or punish the victim; and sometimes sadism.

- Cultures differ widely in determining which parts of the body people learn are erotic, which sexual acts are considered erotic or repulsive, and whether sex itself is good or bad. Cultures transmit these ideas through *gender roles* and *sexual scripts*, which specify appropriate behavior during courtship and sex, depending on a person's gender, age, ethnicity, religion, social class, and sexual orientation.

- As in the case of love, gender differences and similarities in sexuality are strongly affected by cultural and economic factors. In Western societies, as gender roles have become more alike and women have become more economically independent, the sexual behavior of men and women has become more alike as well, with more women wanting sex for pleasure rather than as a bargaining chip.

- Psychological explanations for homosexuality have not been supported. Genetic and hormonal factors seem to be involved, although the evidence is stronger for gay men than for lesbians. The more older biological brothers a man has, the greater his likelihood of becoming gay, suggesting that prenatal events might be involved.

- Despite evidence of a biological contribution to sexual orientation, the expression of homosexuality varies widely. Women's sexual orientation seems more fluid than men's; that is, their sexual behavior often depends more on whether they love the partner than on whether the partner is male or female.

The Competent Animal: Motives to Achieve

- People achieve more when they have specific, focused goals; when they set high but achievable goals for themselves; and when they have *approach goals* (seeking a positive outcome) rather than *avoidance goals* (avoiding an unpleasant outcome).

- The motivation to achieve also depends on whether people set *mastery (learning) goals*, in which the focus is on learning the task well, or *performance goals*, in which the focus is on performing well for others. Mastery goals lead to persistence in the face of failures and setbacks; performance goals often lead to giving up after failure.

- People's expectations can create *self-fulfilling prophecies* of success or failure. These expectations stem from one's level of *self-efficacy*.

- Work motivation also depends on conditions of the job itself. One factor that strongly influences men's and women's choices of work is the gender ratio of people in an occupation. When jobs are highly gender segregated, people often stereotype the abilities of the women and men working in those fields.

- Working conditions that promote motivation and satisfaction are those that provide workers with a sense of meaningfulness, control, variation in tasks, supportive relationships, feedback, and opportunities for advancement.

Motives, Values, and the Pursuit of Happiness

- People are not good at predicting what will make them happy and what will make them miserable, and at estimating how long those feelings will last, so they often choose goals that do not bring them long-term satisfaction. Well-being increases when people enjoy the intrinsic satisfaction of an activity. Having intrinsically enjoyable experiences makes most people happier than having riches and possessions.

- In an *approach–approach conflict*, a person is equally attracted to two goals. In an *avoidance–avoidance conflict*, a person is equally repelled by two goals. An *approach–avoidance conflict* is the most difficult to resolve because the person is both attracted to and repelled by the same goal.

- Abraham Maslow believed that human motives could be ranked in a pyramid, from basic biological needs for survival to higher psychological needs for self-actualization. This popular theory has not been supported empirically. Rather, psychological well-being depends on finding activities and choosing goals that are intrinsically satisfying and on developing the self-efficacy to achieve them.

Psychology in the News, Revisited

- Psychological research can help us understand the basic motives of our lives, including the enjoyment of food, love and attachment, sex, and the nature and consequences of the goals we set for ourselves. It shows that weight and body shape are affected by more complicated factors than simply diet and will power, and how powerfully culture shapes our notions of the ideal and "healthy" body. It shows that sex is not simply a matter of "doing what comes naturally"; what's "natural" is shaped by learning, culture, and experience. It shows that love may start with the right chemistry and attractions, but it is sustained (or extinguished) by less romantic matters of fairness, income, and power. And it shows that the motivation to work—and work well—is shaped not only by our own personal goals, but by the kind of work we do and whether our work fosters or impedes intrinsic motivation.

Taking Psychology With You

- Motivational research suggests that people are happiest and most fulfilled when they seek intrinsically pleasurable activities, focus on learning, improve their working conditions, resolve conflicts, and choose the goals that reflect their most important values.

Key Terms

motivation **497**

intrinsic motivation **498**

extrinsic motivation **498**

set point **498**

basal metabolism rate **498**

brown fat **499**

ob gene **499**

leptin **499**

ghrelin **500**

bulimia nervosa **502**

anorexia nervosa **502**

binge-eating disorder **503**

passionate and
  companionate love **504**

vasopressin **505**

oxytocin **505**

endorphins **505**

proximity and similarity
  effects **530**

secure, anxious, avoidant
  forms of attachment **506**

attachment theory
  of love **507**

gender roles **502**

sexual scripts **517**

industrial/organizational
  psychology **506**

approach goals **520**

avoidance goals **520**

performance
  goals **521**

mastery (learning) goals **521**

self-fulfilling
  prophecy **523**

self-efficacy **524**

approach-approach
  conflicts **528**

avoidance-avoidance
  conflicts **528**

approach-avoidance
  conflicts **528**

Motivation refers to an inferred process within a person or animal that causes that organism to move toward a goal or away from an unpleasant situation.
• **Intrinsic motivation** is for the inherent pleasure of an activity.
• **Extrinsic motivation** is for external reward, such as money or fame.

The Hungry Animal: Motives to Eat

The Biology of Weight

Hunger, weight, and eating are governed by a genetically influenced **set point**, which regulates food intake, fat reserves, and basal metabolism rate. Genes also influence:
• body shape.
• extent of weight gain.
• percentage and distribution of body fat.
• some forms of obesity.
The obese (*ob*) gene causes fat cells to secrete *leptin*, which helps the hypothalamus to regulate appetite.
Other genes and chemicals such as *ghrelin* are involved in appetite, metabolism, and weight gain.

Environmental Influences on Weight

The primary environmental causes of the worldwide epidemic of overweight and obesity are:
• increased abundance of inexpensive, high-calorie fast food and processed food.
• increased consumption of sugary soft drinks.
• larger portions of food and drink.
• abundance of highly varied foods.

Cultural Influences on Weight

• Eating habits are influenced by cultural standards of the ideal body—fat, thin, soft, muscular.
• These standards vary across cultures and may change within a culture, especially when gender roles change.
• When people believe that their bodies do not match the cultural ideal, eating disorders such as **bulimia, anorexia,** and *binge-eating disorder* may increase
• Eating disorders are more common in women than in men, although body image disorders among men are increasing.

The Erotic Animal: Motives for Sex

The Biology of Desire

• The Kinsey surveys of male and female sexuality and the lab research of Masters and Johnson were pioneering studies of sexual physiology.
• Testosterone influences sexual desire in both sexes but does not directly "cause" sexual behavior.
• On average, males have a higher frequency of many sexual behaviors than females do.

The Riddle of Sexual Orientation

The reasons that some people become gay, lesbian, or bisexual are not fully known.
• Homosexuality is not a result of psychological factors or of having gay parents.
• Same-sex behavior has been documented in more than 450 species.
• There is some evidence for prenatal and genetic contributions to homosexuality.

Evolution and Sex

Evolutionary psychologists argue that men and women have evolved different sexual strategies in response to survival problems faced in the distant past. In this view, it has been adaptive for:
• males to be promiscuous, attracted to young partners, and want sexual novelty.
• females to be monogamous, choosy about partners, and prefer security to novelty.

Critics counter that:
• The assumption that males are promiscuous and females are choosy is a stereotype.
• In some species, males care for their young and females have multiple partners.
• Human sexual behavior is too varied to favor a single evolutionary explanation.
• Human sexual behavior changes with cultural changes.
• What people say is their ideal partner is not necessarily whom they choose.

The Culture of Desire

Cultures differ in determining:
• which body parts are considered erotic.
• which sexual acts are considered erotic.
• whether sex itself is good or bad.
Cultures transmit sexual norms through *gender roles* and **sexual scripts**.

The Psychology of Desire

Psychological approaches to sexual motivation emphasize the influences of values, beliefs, expectations, and fantasies.
• Intrinsic motives for sex include pleasure and intimacy.
• Extrinsic motives for sex include a need for approval from the partner or peers, a need to reduce insecurity about oneself or the relationship, or the wish to attain a goal.
• Extrinsic motives for sex are associated with risky sexual behavior and consenting to unwanted sex.

Sexual Coercion and Rape

Women and men differ in their views of rape and sexual coercion. Motives for rape include:
• narcissism.
• hostility.
• desire to dominate, humiliate, or punish the victim.
• sadism.

The Social Animal: Motives to Love

The Biology of Love

Biological origins of passionate love may begin in infancy. The mother–infant bond involves the release of *vasopressin*, *oxytocin*, and *endorphins*, which are involved in pleasure and reward.

The Psychology of Love

The two major predictors of whom people will love are:
- *proximity*: The people nearest are most likely dearest.
- *similarity*: Like attracts like.

Attachment theory views adults' love relationships, like those of infants, as taking one of three forms:
- secure.
- avoidant.
- anxious-ambivalent.

Gender, Culture, and Love

- In Western societies, the sexes do not differ in their feelings of love but may differ in how they express those feelings.
- Gender differences in love often reflect economic and social forces, such as whether a person can afford to marry for love or must marry for financial reasons.

The Competent Animal: Motives to Achieve

The Effects of Motivation on Work

Industrial/organizational psychologists have measured the psychological qualities that spur achievement and the environmental conditions that influence productivity and satisfaction.

The Importance of Goals

People achieve more and feel better about themselves when goals are:
- specific rather than vaguely defined.
- challenging but achievable.
- framed as **approach goals** rather than as **avoidance goals**.
- **mastery (learning) goals**, learning the task well, rather than **performance goals**, showing off for others.

Expectations of success or failure play an important role in motivation:
- They can create a **self-fulfilling prophecy**.
- Expectations of success stem in part from feelings of **self-efficacy**.

The Effects of Work on Motivation

Working conditions can increase employees' satisfaction and motivation, especially when employees:
- feel their work is meaningful.
- have control over many aspects of their work.
- have varied tasks.
- have supportive relationships.
- get useful feedback.
- have opportunities to learn and advance.

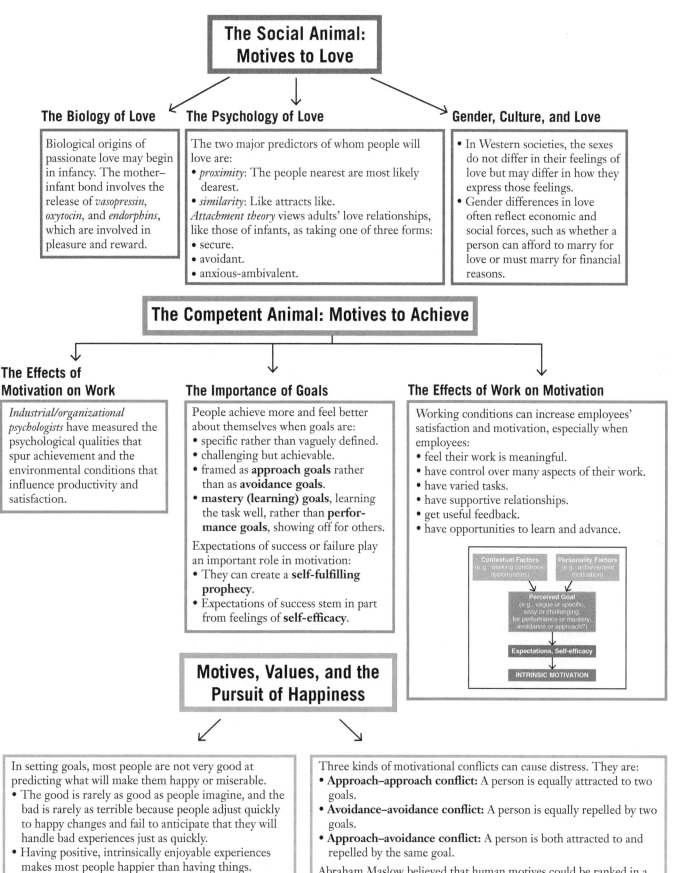

Motives, Values, and the Pursuit of Happiness

In setting goals, most people are not very good at predicting what will make them happy or miserable.
- The good is rarely as good as people imagine, and the bad is rarely as terrible because people adjust quickly to happy changes and fail to anticipate that they will handle bad experiences just as quickly.
- Having positive, intrinsically enjoyable experiences makes most people happier than having things.
- People who are motivated by the intrinsic satisfaction of an activity are happier and more satisfied than those motivated solely by extrinsic rewards.

Three kinds of motivational conflicts can cause distress. They are:
- **Approach–approach conflict:** A person is equally attracted to two goals.
- **Avoidance–avoidance conflict:** A person is equally repelled by two goals.
- **Approach–avoidance conflict:** A person is both attracted to and repelled by the same goal.

Abraham Maslow believed that human motives could be ranked in a hierarchy of needs, from basic safety to personal transcendence, but this theory has had little empirical support.

Glossary

absolute threshold The smallest quantity of physical energy that can be reliably detected by an observer.

acculturation The process by which members of minority groups come to identify with and feel part of the mainstream culture.

action potential A brief change in electrical voltage that occurs between the inside and the outside of an axon when a neuron is stimulated; it serves to produce an electrical impulse.

activation-synthesis theory The theory that dreaming results from the cortical synthesis and interpretation of neural signals triggered by activity in the lower part of the brain.

adrenal hormones Hormones that are produced by the adrenal glands and that are involved in emotion and stress.

adrenarche [a-DREN-ar-kee] A time in middle childhood when the adrenal glands begin producing the adrenal hormone DHEA and other adrenal hormones that affect cognitive and social development.

affect heuristic The tendency to consult one's emotions instead of estimating probabilities objectively.

agoraphobia A set of phobias, often set off by a panic attack, involving the basic fear of being away from a safe place or person.

algorithm A problem-solving strategy guaranteed to produce a solution even if the user does not know how it works.

alternative hypothesis An assertion that the independent variable in a study will have a certain predictable effect on the dependent variable; also called an experimental or research hypothesis.

amnesia The partial or complete loss of memory for important personal information.

amygdala [uh-MIG-dul-uh] A brain structure involved in the arousal and regulation of emotion and the initial emotional response to sensory information.

anorexia nervosa An eating disorder characterized by fear of being fat, a distorted body image, radically reduced consumption of food, and emaciation.

antianxiety drugs (tranquilizers) Drugs commonly but often inappropriately prescribed for patients who complain of moderate forms of anxiety, worry, or unhappiness.

antidepressant drugs Drugs used primarily in the treatment of mood disorders, especially depression and anxiety.

antipsychotic drugs (neuroleptics) Drugs used primarily in the treatment of schizophrenia and other psychotic disorders; they are often used off label and inappropriately for other disorders such as dementia and impulsive aggressiveness.

antisocial personality disorder (APD) A personality disorder characterized by a lifelong pattern of irresponsible, antisocial behavior such as lawbreaking, violence, and other impulsive, reckless acts, and lack of remorse for harms inflicted.

applied psychology The study of psychological issues that have direct practical significance; also, the application of psychological findings.

appraisals The beliefs, perceptions, expectations, and judgments that people draw on to explain their own and other people's behavior, and that influence which emotion a person will feel in a given circumstance.

approach goals Goals framed in terms of desired outcomes or experiences, such as learning to scuba dive.

archetypes [AR-ki-types] Universal, symbolic images that appear in myths, art, stories, and dreams; to Jungians, they reflect the collective unconscious.

arithmetic mean An average that is calculated by adding up a set of quantities and dividing the sum by the total number of quantities in the set.

attribution theory The theory that people are motivated to explain their own and other people's behavior by attributing causes of that behavior to a situation or a disposition.

autonomic nervous system The subdivision of the peripheral nervous system that regulates the internal organs and glands.

availability heuristic The tendency to judge the probability of a type of event by how easy it is to think of examples or instances.

avoidance goals Goals framed in terms of avoiding unpleasant experiences, such as trying not to look foolish in public.

axon A neuron's extending fiber that conducts impulses away from the cell body and transmits them to other neurons or to muscle or gland cells.

basic concepts Concepts that have a moderate number of instances and that are easier to acquire than those having few or many instances.

basic psychology The study of psychological issues for the sake of knowledge rather than for its practical application.

behavior modification The application of operant-conditioning techniques to teach new responses or to reduce or eliminate maladaptive or problematic behavior; also called *applied behavior analysis*.

behavior therapy A form of therapy that applies principles of classical and operant conditioning to help people change self-defeating or problematic behaviors.

behavioral genetics An interdisciplinary field of study concerned with the genetic bases of individual differences in behavior, personality, and abilities.

behavioral self-monitoring In behavior therapy, a method of keeping careful data on the frequency and consequences of the behavior to be changed.

behaviorism An approach to psychology that emphasizes the study of observable behavior and the role of the environment and prior experience as determinants of behavior.

binocular cues Visual cues to depth or distance requiring two eyes.

biological perspective A psychological approach that emphasizes bodily events and changes associated with actions, feelings, and thoughts.

biological rhythm A periodic, more or less regular fluctuation in a biological system; it may or may not have psychological implications.

bipolar disorder A disorder in which a person experiences at least one episode of mania (excessive euphoria) typically alternating with episodes of depression.

borderline personality disorder A disorder characterized by extreme negative emotionality and an inability to regulate emotions; it often results in intense but unstable relationships, impulsiveness, self-mutilating behavior, feelings of emptiness, and a fear of abandonment by others.

brain stem The part of the brain at the top of the spinal cord, consisting of the medulla and the pons.

brightness Lightness or luminance; the dimension of visual experience related to the amount (intensity) of light emitted from or reflected by an object.

bulimia nervosa An eating disorder characterized by episodes of excessive eating (bingeing) followed by forced vomiting or use of laxatives (purging).

case study A detailed description of a particular individual being studied or treated.

cell body The part of the neuron that keeps it alive and determines whether it will fire.

central nervous system (CNS) The portion of the nervous system consisting of the brain and spinal cord.

cerebellum A brain structure that regulates movement and balance and that is involved in some cognitive tasks.

cerebral cortex A collection of several thin layers of cells covering the cerebrum; it is largely responsible for higher mental functions. *Cortex* is Latin for "bark" or "rind."

cerebral hemispheres The two halves of the cerebrum.

cerebrum [suh-REE-brum] The largest brain structure, consisting of the upper part of the brain; divided into two hemispheres, it is in charge of most sensory, motor, and cognitive processes. From the Latin for "brain."

childhood (infantile) amnesia The inability to remember events and experiences that occurred earlier than age 2.

chronotype A person's disposition to be a "morning person" or an "evening person."

chunk A meaningful unit of information; it may be composed of smaller units.

circadian [sur-CAY-dee-un] rhythm A biological rhythm with a period (from peak to peak or trough to trough) of about 24 hours; from the Latin *circa*, "about," and *dies*, "a day."

classical conditioning The process by which a previously neutral stimulus is paired with a stimulus that already elicits a certain response and, in turn, acquires the capacity to elicit a similar or related response. Also called *Pavlovian* or *respondent* conditioning.

client-centered therapy A humanist approach to therapy devised by Carl Rogers, which emphasizes the therapist's empathy with the client and the use of unconditional positive regard.

cochlea [KOCK-lee-uh] A snail-shaped, fluid-filled organ in the inner ear, containing the organ of Corti, where the receptors for hearing are located.

coefficient of correlation A measure of correlation that ranges in value from −1.00 to +1.00.

cognitive dissonance A state of tension that occurs when a person simultaneously holds two cognitions that are psychologically inconsistent or when a person's belief is incongruent with his or her behavior.

cognitive perspective A psychological approach that emphasizes mental processes in perception, memory, language, problem solving, and other areas of behavior.

cognitive schema An integrated mental network of knowledge, beliefs, and expectations concerning a particular topic or aspect of the world.

cognitive therapy A form of therapy designed to identify and change irrational, unproductive ways of thinking and, hence, to reduce negative emotions and their self-defeating consequences.

collective unconscious In Jungian theory, the universal memories and experiences of humankind, represented in the symbols, stories, and images (archetypes) that occur across all cultures.

collectivist cultures Cultures in which the self is regarded as embedded in relationships, and harmony with one's group is prized above individual goals and wishes.

concept A mental category that groups objects, relations, activities, abstractions, or qualities having common properties.

conditioned response (CR) The classical-conditioning term for a response that is elicited by a conditioned stimulus; it occurs after the conditioned stimulus is paired with an unconditioned stimulus.

conditioned stimulus (CS) The classical-conditioning term for an initially neutral stimulus that comes to elicit a conditioned response after being paired with an unconditioned stimulus.

cones Visual receptors involved in color vision.

confabulation Confusion of an event that happened to someone else with one that happened to you, or a belief that you remember something when it never actually happened.

confidence interval A statistical measure that provides, with a specified probability, a range of values within which a population mean is likely to lie.

confirmation bias The tendency to look for or pay attention only to information that confirms one's own belief, and ignore, trivialize, or forget information that disconfirms that belief.

conservation The understanding that the physical properties of objects—such as the number of items in a cluster or the amount of liquid in a glass—can remain the same even when their form or appearance changes.

consolidation The process by which a memory becomes durable and stable.

contact comfort In primates, the innate pleasure derived from close physical contact; it is the basis of an infant's first attachment.

continuous reinforcement A reinforcement schedule in which a particular response is always reinforced.

control condition In an experiment, a comparison condition in which subjects are not exposed to the same treatment as are those in the experimental condition.

convergence The turning inward of the eyes, which occurs when they focus on a nearby object.

corpus callosum [CORE-pus ca-LOW-suhm] The bundle of nerve fibers connecting the two cerebral hemispheres.

correlation A measure of how strongly two variables are related to each other.

correlational study A descriptive study that looks for a consistent relationship between two phenomena.

cortisol A hormone secreted by the adrenal cortex that elevates blood sugar and protects the body's tissues in case of injury; if chronically elevated due to stress, it can lead to hypertension, immune disorders, other illnesses, and possibly depression.

counterconditioning In classical conditioning, the process of pairing a conditioned stimulus with a stimulus that elicits a response that is incompatible with an unwanted conditioned response.

critical period A period of time in a person's or animal's life when exposure to certain stimuli or experiences is necessary for the optimal development of a particular skill or ability.

critical thinking The ability and willingness to assess claims and make objective judgments on the basis of well-supported reasons and evidence rather than emotion or anecdote.

cross-sectional study A study in which individuals of different ages are compared at a given time.

crystallized intelligence Cognitive skills and specific knowledge acquired over a lifetime; it is heavily dependent on education and tends to remain stable.

cue-dependent forgetting The inability to retrieve information stored in memory because of insufficient cues for recall.

culture A program of shared rules that govern the behavior of members of a community or society and a set of values, beliefs, attitudes, and customs shared by most members of that community.

cultural syndromes Symptoms or mental disorders that are specific to particular cultural contexts and practices.

dark adaptation A process by which visual receptors become maximally sensitive to dim light.

decay theory The theory that information in memory eventually disappears if it is not accessed; it applies better to short-term than to long-term memory.

declarative memories Memories of facts, rules, concepts, and events ("knowing that"); they include semantic and episodic memories.

deep processing In the encoding of information, the processing of meaning rather than simply the physical or sensory features of a stimulus.

defense mechanisms Methods used by the ego to prevent unconscious anxiety or threatening thoughts from entering consciousness.

deindividuation In groups or crowds, the loss of awareness of one's own individuality.

dendrites A neuron's branches that receive information from other neurons and transmit it toward the cell body.

dependent variable A variable that an experimenter predicts will be affected by manipulations of the independent variable.

depressants Drugs that slow activity in the central nervous system.

descriptive methods Methods that yield descriptions of behavior but not necessarily causal explanations.

descriptive statistics Statistics that organize and summarize research data.

dialectical reasoning A process in which opposing facts or ideas are weighed and compared, with a view to determining the best solution or to resolving differences.

difference threshold The smallest difference in stimulation that can be reliably detected by an observer when two stimuli are compared; also called *just noticeable difference* (jnd).

diffusion of responsibility In groups, the tendency of members to avoid taking action because they assume that others will.

discriminative stimulus A stimulus that signals when a particular response is likely to be followed by a certain type of consequence.

display rules Social and cultural rules that regulate when, how, and where a person may express (or suppress) emotions.

dissociation A split in consciousness in which one part of the mind operates independently of others.

dissociative identity disorder A controversial disorder marked by the apparent appearance within one person of two or more distinct personalities, each with its own name and traits; formerly known as *multiple personality disorder* (MPD).

doctrine of specific nerve energies The principle that different sensory modalities exist because signals received by the sense organs stimulate different nerve pathways leading to different areas of the brain.

double-blind study An experiment in which neither the participants nor the individuals running the study know which participants are in the control group and which are in the experimental group until after the results are tallied.

effect size An objective, standardized way of describing the strength of the independent variable's influence on the dependent variable.

ego In psychoanalysis, the part of personality that represents reason, good sense, and rational self-control.

elaborative rehearsal Association of new information with already stored knowledge and analysis of the new information to make it memorable.

electroconvulsive therapy (ECT) A procedure used in cases of prolonged and severe major depression, in which a brief brain seizure is induced.

electroencephalogram (EEG) A recording of neural activity detected by electrodes.

embryonic stem (ES) cells Stem cells from early embryos that can develop into any cell type.

emotion A state of arousal involving facial and bodily changes, brain activation, cognitive appraisals, subjective feelings, and tendencies toward action.

emotion work Expression of an emotion, often because of a role requirement, that a person does not really feel.

emotional intelligence The ability to identify your own and other people's emotions accurately, express your emotions clearly and appropriately, and regulate emotions in yourself and others.

empirical Relying on or derived from observation, experimentation, or measurement.

endocrine glands Internal organs that produce hormones and release them into the bloodstream.

endogenous Generated from within rather than by external cues.

endorphins [en-DOR-fins] Chemical substances in the nervous system that are similar in structure and action to opiates; they are involved in pain reduction, pleasure, and memory and are known technically as *endogenous opioid peptides*.

entrapment A gradual process in which individuals escalate their commitment to a course of action to justify their investment of time, money, or effort.

epigenetics The study of stable changes in the expression of a particular gene that occur without changes in DNA; the Greek prefix epi- means "on top of" or "in addition to."

episodic memories Memories of personally experienced events and the contexts in which they occurred.

equilibrium The sense of balance.

ethnic identity A person's identification with a racial or ethnic group.

ethnocentrism The belief that one's own ethnic group, nation, or religion is superior to all others.

evolutionary psychology A field of psychology emphasizing evolutionary mechanisms that may help explain human commonalities in cognition, development, emotion, social practices, and other areas of behavior.

existential therapy A form of therapy designed to help clients explore the meaning of existence and face the great questions of life, such as death, freedom, and loneliness.

existentialism A philosophical approach that emphasizes the inevitable dilemmas and challenges of human existence.

experiment A controlled test of a hypothesis in which the researcher manipulates one variable to discover its effect on another.

experimenter effects Unintended changes in subjects' behavior as a result of cues that the experimenter inadvertently conveys.

explicit memory Conscious, intentional recollection of an event or of an item of information.

extinction The weakening and eventual disappearance of a learned response. In classical conditioning, it occurs when the conditioned stimulus is no longer paired with the unconditioned stimulus; in operant conditioning, it occurs when a response is no longer followed by a reinforcer.

extrinsic motivation The pursuit of an activity for external rewards, such as money or fame.

extrinsic reinforcers Reinforcers that are not inherently related to the activity being reinforced, such as money, prizes, and praise.

facial feedback The process by which the facial muscles send messages to the brain about the basic emotion being expressed.

factor analysis A statistical method for analyzing the intercorrelations among various measures or test scores; clusters of measures or scores that are highly correlated are assumed to measure the same underlying trait, ability, or aptitude (factor).

fairness bias The bias, in some circumstances, to value cooperation and fair play over rational self-interest.

familiarity effect The tendency of people to feel more positive toward a person, item, product, or other stimulus the more familiar they are with it.

family-systems perspective An approach to doing therapy with individuals or families by identifying how each family member forms part of a larger interacting system.

feature-detector cells Cells in the visual cortex that are sensitive to specific features of the environment.

field research Descriptive or experimental research conducted in a natural setting outside the laboratory.

flooding In behavior therapy, a form of exposure treatment in which the client is taken directly into the feared situation until his or her panic subsides.

fluid intelligence The capacity to reason and use new information to solve problems; it is relatively independent of education and tends to decline in old age.

fMRI (functional magnetic resonance imaging) A fast version of MRI used to study brain activity associated with specific thoughts and behaviors.

framing effect The tendency for people's choices to be affected by how a choice is presented or framed; for example, whether it is worded in terms of potential losses or gains.

frequency distribution A summary of how frequently each score in a set occurred.

frequency polygon (line graph) A graph showing a set of points obtained by plotting score values against score frequencies; adjacent points are joined by straight lines.

frontal lobes Lobes at the front of the brain's cerebral cortex; they contain areas involved in short-term memory, higher-order thinking, initiative, social judgment, and (in the left lobe, typically) speech production.

functionalism An early psychological approach that emphasized the function or purpose of behavior and consciousness.

fundamental attribution error The tendency, in explaining other people's behavior, to overestimate personality factors and underestimate the influence of the situation.

g factor A general intellectual ability assumed by many theorists to underlie specific mental abilities and talents.

ganglion cells Neurons in the retina of the eye, which gather information from receptor cells (by way of intermediate bipolar cells); their axons make up the optic nerve.

gate-control theory The theory that the experience of pain depends in part on whether pain impulses get past a neurological "gate" in the spinal cord and thus reach the brain.

gender identity The fundamental sense of being male or female; it is independent of whether the person conforms to the social and cultural rules of gender.

gender schema A cognitive schema (mental network) of knowledge, beliefs, metaphors, and expectations about what it means to be male or female.

gender typing The process by which children learn the abilities, interests, and behaviors associated with being masculine or feminine in their culture.

general adaptation syndrome According to Hans Selye, a series of physiological reactions to stressors occuring in three phases: alarm, resistance, and exhaustion.

generalized anxiety disorder A continuous state of anxiety marked by feelings of worry and dread, apprehension, difficulties in concentration, and signs of motor tension.

genes The functional units of heredity; they are composed of DNA and specify the structure of proteins.

Gestalt principles Principles that describe the brain's organization of sensory information into meaningful units and patterns.

glia [GLY-uh or GLEE-uh] Cells that support, nurture, and insulate neurons, remove debris when neurons die, enhance the formation and maintenance of neural connections, and modify neuronal functioning.

graduated exposure In behavior therapy, a method in which a person suffering from a phobia or panic attacks is gradually taken into the feared situation or exposed to a traumatic memory until the anxiety subsides.

graph A drawing that depicts numerical relationships.

groupthink In close-knit groups, the tendency for all members to think alike for the sake of harmony and to suppress disagreement.

heritability A statistical estimate of the proportion of the total variance in some trait that is attributable to genetic differences among individuals within a group.

heuristic A rule of thumb that suggests a course of action or guides problem solving but does not guarantee an optimal solution.

higher-order conditioning In classical conditioning, a procedure in which a neutral stimulus becomes a conditioned stimulus through association with an already established conditioned stimulus.

hindsight bias The tendency to overestimate one's ability to have predicted an event once the outcome is known; the "I knew it all along" phenomenon.

hippocampus A brain structure involved in the storage of new information in memory and its later retrieval.

histogram (bar graph) A graph in which the heights (or lengths) of bars are proportional to the frequencies of individual scores or classes of scores in a distribution.

hormones Chemical substances, secreted by organs called glands, that affect the functioning of other organs.

HPA (hypothalamus–pituitary–adrenal cortex) axis A system activated to energize the body to respond to stressors. The hypothalamus sends chemical messengers to the pituitary gland, which in turn prompts the adrenal cortex to produce cortisol and other hormones.

hue The dimension of visual experience specified by color names and related to the wavelength of light.

humanist psychology A psychological approach that emphasizes free will, personal growth, resilience, and the achievement of human potential.

humanist therapy A form of psychotherapy based on the philosophy of humanism, which emphasizes the client's free will to change rather than past conflicts.

hypnosis A procedure in which the practitioner suggests changes in a subject's sensations, perceptions, thoughts, feelings, or behavior.

hypothalamus A brain structure involved in emotions and drives vital to survival, such as fear, hunger, thirst, and reproduction; it regulates the autonomic nervous system.

hypothesis A statement that attempts to predict or to account for a set of phenomena; scientific hypotheses specify relationships among events or variables and are empirically tested.

id In psychoanalysis, the part of personality containing inherited psychic energy, particularly sexual and aggressive instincts.

implicit learning Learning that occurs when you acquire knowledge about something without being aware of how you did so and without being able to state exactly what it is you have learned.

implicit memory Unconscious retention in memory, as evidenced by the effect of a previous experience or previously encountered information on current thoughts or actions.

inattentional blindness Failure to consciously perceive something you are looking at because you are not attending to it.

independent variable A variable that an experimenter manipulates.

individualist cultures Cultures in which the self is regarded as autonomous, and individual goals and wishes are prized above duty and relations with others.

induced pluripotent stem (iPS) cells Stem cells derived from adult tissues.

induction A method of child rearing in which the parent appeals to the child's own resources, abilities, sense of responsibility, and feelings for others in correcting the child's misbehavior.

inferential statistics Statistical procedures that allow researchers to draw inferences about how statistically meaningful a study's results are.

informed consent The doctrine that human research subjects must participate voluntarily and must know enough about a study to make an intelligent decision about whether to participate.

instinctive drift During operant learning, the tendency for an organism to revert to instinctive behavior.

intelligence An inferred characteristic of an individual, usually defined as the ability to profit from experience, acquire knowledge, think abstractly, act purposefully, or adapt to changes in the environment.

intelligence quotient (IQ) A measure of intelligence originally computed by dividing a person's mental age by his or her chronological age and multiplying the result by 100; it is now derived from norms provided for standardized intelligence tests.

intermittent (partial) schedule of reinforcement A reinforcement schedule in which a particular response is sometimes but not always reinforced.

internal desynchronization A state in which biological rhythms are not in phase (synchronized) with one another.

intersex conditions Conditions in which chromosomal or hormonal anomalies cause a child to be born with ambiguous genitals, or genitals that conflict with the infant's chromosomes.

intrinsic motivation The pursuit of an activity for its own sake and for the internal pleasure it provides.

intrinsic reinforcers Reinforcers that are inherently related to the activity being reinforced, such as enjoyment of the task and the satisfaction of accomplishment.

justification of effort The tendency of individuals to increase their liking for something that they have worked hard or suffered to attain; a common form of dissonance reduction.

just-world hypothesis The notion that many people need to believe that the world is fair and that justice is served, that bad people are punished and good people rewarded.

kinesthesis [KIN-es-THEE-sis] The sense of body position and movement of body parts; also called *kinesthesia*.

language A system that combines meaningless elements such as sounds or gestures to form structured utterances that convey meaning.

latent learning A form of learning that is not immediately expressed in an overt response; it occurs without obvious reinforcement.

lateralization Specialization of the two cerebral hemispheres for particular operations.

learning A relatively permanent change in behavior (or behavioral potential) due to experience.

learning perspective A psychological approach that emphasizes how the environment and experience affect a person's or animal's actions; it includes behaviorism and social-cognitive learning theories.

libido [li-BEE-do] In psychoanalysis, the psychic energy that fuels the life or sexual instincts of the id.

lithium carbonate A drug frequently given to people suffering from bipolar disorder.

localization of function Specialization of particular brain areas for particular functions.

locus of control A general expectation about whether the results of your actions are under your own control (internal locus) or beyond your control (external locus).

longitudinal study A study in which individuals are followed and periodically reassessed over a period of time.

long-term memory (LTM) In the three-box model of memory, the memory system involved in the long-term storage of information.

long-term potentiation A long-lasting increase in the strength of synaptic responsiveness, thought to be a biological mechanism of long-term memory.

loudness The dimension of auditory experience related to the intensity of a pressure wave.

lucid dreams Dreams in which the dreamer is aware of dreaming.

maintenance rehearsal Rote repetition of material to maintain its availability in memory.

major depression A disorder marked by excessive sadness, loss of interest in usual activities, feelings of worthlessness and hopelessness, thoughts of suicide, and physical symptoms (such as fatigue and loss of appetite).

mastery (learning) goals Goals framed in terms of increasing one's competence and skills.

mean *See* arithmetic mean.

measure of central tendency A number intended to characterize an entire set of data.

measure of variability A number that indicates how dispersed scores are around the mean of the distribution.

median A measure of central tendency; the value at the midpoint of a distribution of scores when the scores are ordered from highest to lowest.

medulla [muh-DUL-uh] A structure in the brain stem responsible for certain automatic functions, such as breathing and heart rate.

melatonin A hormone, secreted by the pineal gland, that is involved in the regulation of daily biological rhythms.

menarche [men-ARR-kee] The onset of menstruation during puberty.

menopause The cessation of menstruation and of the production of ova; it is usually a gradual process lasting up to several years.

mental age (MA) A measure of mental development expressed in terms of the average mental ability at a given age.

mental disorder Any behavior or emotional state that causes an individual great suffering, does not go away after a reasonable length of time, is self-destructive, seriously impairs the person's ability to work or get along with others, or causes the person to endanger others or the community.

mental image A mental representation that mirrors or resembles the thing it represents; mental images can occur in many and perhaps all sensory modalities.

mental set A tendency to solve problems using procedures that worked before on similar problems.

meta-analysis A set of techniques for combining and analyzing data from a number of related studies to determine the explanatory strength of a particular independent variable.

metacognition The knowledge or awareness of one's own cognitive processes and the ability to monitor and control those processes.

mirror neurons Brain cells that fire when a person or animal observes another carrying out an action; these neurons appear to be involved in empathy, imitation, and reading emotions.

mnemonics [neh-MON-iks] Strategies and tricks for improving memory, such as the use of a verse or a formula.

mode A measure of central tendency; the most frequently occurring score in a distribution.

monocular cues Visual cues to depth or distance that can be used by one eye alone.

mood-congruent memory The tendency to remember experiences that are consistent with one's current mood and overlook or forget experiences that are not.

motivation An inferred process within a person or animal that causes movement either toward a goal or away from an unpleasant situation.

MRI (magnetic resonance imaging) A method for studying body and brain tissue, using magnetic fields and special radio receivers. (*See also:* fMRI.)

myelin sheath A fatty insulation that may surround the axon of a neuron.

narcolepsy A sleep disorder involving sudden and unpredictable daytime attacks of sleepiness or lapses into REM sleep.

negative correlation An association between increases in one variable and decreases in another.

negative reinforcement A reinforcement procedure in which a response is followed by the removal, delay, or decrease in intensity of an unpleasant stimulus; as a result, the response becomes stronger or more likely to occur.

nerve A bundle of nerve fibers (axons and sometimes dendrites) in the peripheral nervous system.

neurogenesis The production of new neurons from immature stem cells.

neuromodulators Neurochemicals that modulate the functioning of neurons and neurotransmitters.

neurons Cells that conduct electrochemical signals; the basic unit of the nervous system; also called *nerve cells*.

neurotransmitter A chemical substance that is released by a transmitting neuron at the synapse and that alters the activity of a receiving neuron.

nonconscious processes Mental processes occurring outside of and not available to conscious awareness.

nonshared environment Unique aspects of a person's environment and experience that are not shared with family members.

normal curve A symmetrical, bell-shaped frequency polygon representing a normal distribution.

normal distribution A theoretical frequency distribution having certain special characteristics. For example, the distribution is symmetrical; the mean, mode, and median all have the same value; and the farther a score is from the mean, the less the likelihood of obtaining it.

norms In test construction, established standards of performance.

norms (social) Rules that regulate social life, including explicit laws and implicit cultural conventions.

null hypothesis An assertion that the independent variable in a study will have no effect on the dependent variable.

object permanence The understanding, which develops throughout the first year, that an object continues to exist even when you cannot see it or touch it.

objective tests (inventories) Standardized questionnaires requiring written responses; they typically include scales on which people are asked to rate themselves.

object-relations school A psychodynamic approach that emphasizes the importance of the infant's first two years of life and the baby's formative relationships, especially with the mother.

observational learning A process in which an individual learns new responses by observing the behavior of another (a model) rather than through direct experience; sometimes called *vicarious conditioning*.

observational study A study in which the researcher carefully and systematically observes and records behavior without interfering with the behavior; it may involve either naturalistic or laboratory observation.

obsessive-compulsive disorder (OCD) A disorder in which a person feels trapped in repetitive, persistent thoughts (*obsessions*) and repetitive, ritualized behaviors (*compulsions*) designed to reduce anxiety.

occipital [ahk-SIP-uh-tuhl] lobes Lobes at the lower back part of the brain's cerebral cortex; they contain areas that receive visual information.

Oedipus complex In psychoanalysis, a conflict occurring in the phallic (Oedipal) stage, in which a child desires the parent of the other sex and views the same-sex parent as a rival.

operant conditioning The process by which a response becomes more likely to occur or less so, depending on its consequences.

operational definition A precise definition of a term in a hypothesis, which specifies the operations for observing and measuring the process or phenomenon being defined.

opiates Drugs, derived from the opium poppy, that relieve pain and commonly produce euphoria.

opponent-process theory A theory of color perception that assumes that the visual system treats pairs of colors as opposing or antagonistic.

organ of Corti [CORE-tee] A structure in the cochlea containing hair cells that serve as the receptors for hearing.

oxytocin A hormone, secreted by the pituitary gland, that stimulates uterine contractions during childbirth, facilitates the ejection of milk during nursing, and seems to promote, in both sexes, attachment and trust in relationships.

panic disorder An anxiety disorder in which a person experiences recurring panic attacks, periods of intense fear, and feelings of impending doom or death, accompanied by physiological symptoms such as rapid heart rate and dizziness.

papillae [pa-PILL-ee] Knoblike elevations on the tongue, containing the taste buds. (Singular: *papilla*.)

parallel distributed processing (PDP) model A model of memory in which knowledge is represented as connections among thousands of interact-ing processing units, distributed in a vast network, and all operating in parallel. Also called a *connectionist model*.

parasympathetic nervous system The subdivision of the autonomic nervous system that operates during relaxed states and that conserves energy.

parietal [puh-RYE-uh-tuhl] lobes Lobes at the top of the brain's cerebral cortex; they contain areas that receive information on pressure, pain, touch, and temperature, and that are involved in attention and awareness of spatial relationships.

percentile score A score that indicates the percentage of people who scored at or below a given raw score; also called *centile rank*.

perception The process by which the brain organizes and interprets sensory information.

perceptual constancy The accurate perception of objects as stable or unchanged despite changes in the sensory patterns they produce.

perceptual set A habitual way of perceiving, based on expectations.

performance goals Goals framed in terms of performing well in front of others, being judged favorably, and avoiding criticism.

peripheral nervous system (PNS) All portions of the nervous system outside the brain and spinal cord; it includes sensory and motor nerves.

personality A distinctive and relatively stable pattern of behavior, thoughts, motives, and emotions that characterizes an individual.

PET scan (positron-emission tomography) A method for analyzing biochemical activity in the brain, for example by using injections of a glucoselike substance containing a radioactive element.

phantom pain The experience of pain in a missing limb or other body part.

phobia An exaggerated, unrealistic fear of a specific situation, activity, or object.

phrenology The now discredited theory that different brain areas account for specific character and personality traits, which can be "read" from bumps on the skull.

pitch The dimension of auditory experience related to the frequency of a pressure wave; the height or depth of a tone.

pituitary gland A small endocrine gland at the base of the brain that releases many hormones and regulates other endocrine glands.

placebo An inactive substance or fake treatment used as a control in an experiment.

placebo effect The apparent success of a medication or treatment because of the patient's expectations or hopes rather than to the drug or treatment itself.

plasticity The brain's ability to change and adapt in response to experience, by reorganizing or growing new neural connections.

pons A structure in the brain stem involved in, among other things, sleeping, waking, and dreaming.

positive correlation An association between increases in one variable and increases in another, or between decreases in one and decreases in the other.

positive reinforcement A reinforcement procedure in which a response is followed by the presentation of, or increase in intensity of, a reinforcing stimulus; as a result, the response becomes stronger or more likely to occur.

postdecision dissonance In the theory of cognitive dissonance, tension that occurs when you believe you may have made a bad decision.

posttraumatic stress disorder (PTSD) An anxiety disorder in which a person who has experienced a traumatic or life-threatening event has long-lasting symptoms such as recurrent, intrusive thoughts, flashbacks, nightmares, and increased physiological arousal.

power assertion A method of child rearing in which the parent uses punishment and authority to correct the child's misbehavior.

prejudice A strong, unreasonable dislike or hatred of a group, based on a negative stereotype.

primary control An effort to modify reality by changing other people, the situation, or events; a "fighting back" philosophy.

primary punisher A stimulus that is inherently punishing; an example is electric shock.

primary reinforcer A stimulus that is inherently reinforcing, typically satisfying a physiological need; an example is food.

priming A method for measuring implicit memory in which a person reads or listens to information and is later tested to see whether the information affects performance on another type of task.

principle of falsifiability The principle that a scientific theory must make predictions that are specific enough to expose the theory to the possibility of disconfirmation.

proactive interference Forgetting that occurs when previously stored material interferes with the ability to remember similar, more recently learned material.

procedural memories Memories for the performance of actions or skills ("knowing how").

projective tests Psychological tests used to infer a person's motives, conflicts, and unconscious dynamics on the basis of the person's interpretations of ambiguous stimuli.

proposition A unit of meaning that is made up of concepts and expresses a single idea.

prototype An especially representative example of a concept.

psychedelic drugs Consciousness-altering drugs that produce hallucinations, change thought processes, or disrupt the normal perception of time and space.

psychoactive drugs Drugs capable of influencing perception, mood, cognition, or behavior.

psychoanalysis A theory of personality and a method of psychotherapy, originally formulated by Sigmund Freud, that emphasizes the importance of unconscious motives and conflicts; modern psychodynamic therapies share this emphasis but differ from Freudian analysis in various ways.

psychodynamic theories Theories that explain behavior and personality in terms of unconscious energy dynamics within the individual.

psychological tests Procedures used to measure and evaluate personality traits, emotional states, aptitudes, interests, abilities, and values.

psychology The discipline concerned with behavior and mental processes and how they are affected by an organism's physical state, mental state, and external environment; the term is often represented by Ψ, the Greek letter psi (usually pronounced *sy*).

psychometrics The measurement of mental abilities, traits, and processes.

psychoneuroimmunology (PNI) The study of the relationships among psychology, the nervous and endocrine systems, and the immune system.

psychopathy (sy-KOP-uh-thee) A personality disorder (not in the DSM) characterized by fearlessness; lack of empathy, guilt, and remorse; the use of deceit; and coldheartedness. In the DSM, it is one symptom of antisocial personality disorder.

psychosexual stages In Freud's theory, the idea that sexual energy takes different forms as the child matures; the stages are oral, anal, phallic (Oedipal), latency, and genital.

psychosis An extreme mental disturbance involving distorted perceptions, delusions, and irrational behavior. (Plural: *psychoses*.)

puberty The age at which a person becomes capable of sexual reproduction.

punishment The process by which a stimulus or event weakens or reduces the probability of the response that it follows.

random assignment A procedure for assigning people to experimental and control groups in which each individual has the same probability as any other of being assigned to a given group.

randomized controlled trials Research designed to determine the effectiveness of a new medication or form of therapy, in which people with a given problem or disorder are randomly assigned to one or more treatment groups or to a control group.

range A measure of the spread of scores, calculated by subtracting the lowest score from the highest score.

rapid eye movement (REM) sleep Sleep periods characterized by eye movement, loss of muscle tone, and vivid dreams.

rational emotive behavior therapy A form of cognitive therapy devised by Albert Ellis, designed to challenge the client's unrealistic or irrational thoughts.

reasoning The drawing of conclusions or inferences from observations, facts, or assumptions.

recall The ability to retrieve and reproduce from memory previously encountered material.

reciprocal determinism In social-cognitive learning theories, the two-way interaction between aspects of the environment and aspects of the individual in the shaping of behavior and personality traits.

recognition The ability to identify previously encountered material.

reinforcement The process by which a stimulus or event strengthens or ncreases the probability of the response that it follows.

relearning method A method for measuring retention that compares the time required to relearn material with the time used in the initial learning of the material.

reliability In test construction, the consistency of test scores from one time and place to another.

REM behavior disorder A disorder in which the muscle paralysis that normally occurs during REM sleep is absent or incomplete, and the sleeper is able to act out his or her dreams.

representative sample A group of individuals, selected from a population for study, which matches that population on important characteristics such as age and sex.

repression In psychoanalytic theory, the selective, involuntary pushing of threatening or upsetting information into the unconscious.

reticular activating system (RAS) A dense network of neurons in the core of the brain stem; it arouses the cortex and screens incoming information.

retina Neural tissue lining the back of the eyeball's interior, which contains the receptors for vision.

retinal disparity The slight difference in lateral separation between two objects as seen by the left eye and the right eye.

retroactive interference Forgetting that occurs when recently learned material interferes with the ability to remember similar material stored previously.

rods Visual receptors that respond to dim light.

role A given social position that is governed by a set of norms for proper behavior.

saturation Vividness or purity of color; the dimension of visual experience related to the complexity of light waves.

schizophrenia A psychotic disorder marked by delusions, hallucinations, disorganized and incoherent speech, inappropriate or catatonic behavior, and negative symptoms such as loss of motivation and emotional flatness.

seasonal affective disorder (SAD) A disorder in which a person experiences depression during the winter and an improvement of mood in the spring.

secondary control An effort to accept reality by changing your own attitudes, goals, or emotions; a "learn to live with it" philosophy.

secondary punisher A stimulus that has acquired punishing properties through association with other punishers.

secondary reinforcer A stimulus that has acquired reinforcing properties through association with other reinforcers.

selective attention The focusing of attention on selected aspects of the environment and the blocking out of others.

self-efficacy A person's belief that he or she is capable of producing desired results, such as mastering new skills and reaching goals.

self-fulfilling prophecy An expectation that becomes reality because of the tendency of the person holding it to act in ways that bring it about.

semantic memories Memories of general knowledge, including facts, rules, concepts, and propositions.

semicircular canals Sense organs in the inner ear that contribute to equilibrium by responding to rotation of the head.

sensation The detection of physical energy emitted or reflected by physical objects; it occurs when energy in the external environment or the body stimulates receptors in the sense organs.

sense receptors Specialized cells that convert physical energy in the environment or the body to electrical energy that can be transmitted as nerve impulses to the brain.

sensory adaptation The reduction or disappearance of sensory responsiveness that occurs when stimulation is unchanging or repetitious.

sensory deprivation The absence of normal levels of sensory stimulation.

sensory register A memory system that momentarily preserves extremely accurate sensory information before the information fades or moves into short-term memory.

separation anxiety The distress that most children develop, at about 6 to 8 months of age, when their primary caregivers temporarily leave them with others.

serial-position effect The tendency for recall of the first and last items on a list to surpass recall of items in the middle of the list.

set point The genetically influenced weight range for an individual, maintained by biological mechanisms that regulate food intake, fat reserves, and metabolism.

sex hormones Hormones that regulate the development and functioning of reproductive organs and that stimulate the development of male and female sexual characteristics; they include androgens, estrogens, and progesterone.

sexual scripts Sets of implicit rules that specify proper sexual behavior for a person in a given situation, varying with the person's gender, age, religion, social status, and peer group.

shaping An operant-conditioning procedure in which successive approximations of a desired response are reinforced.

short-term memory (STM) In the three-box model of memory, a limited-capacity memory system involved in the retention of information for brief periods; it is also used to hold information retrieved from long-term memory for temporary use.

signal-detection theory A psychophysical theory that divides the detection of a sensory signal into a sensory process and a decision process.

significance tests Statistical tests that assess how likely it is that a study's results occurred merely by chance.

single-blind study An experiment in which subjects do not know whether they are in an experimental or a control group.

skills training In behavior therapy, an effort to teach the client skills that he or she may lack, as well as new constructive behaviors to replace self-defeating ones.

sleep apnea A disorder in which breathing briefly stops during sleep, causing the person to choke and gasp and momentarily awaken.

social cognition An area in social psychology concerned with social influences on thought, memory, perception, and beliefs.

social identity The part of a person's self-concept that is based on his or her identification with a nation, religious or political group, occupation, or other social affiliation.

social-cognitive learning theories Theories that emphasize how behavior is learned and maintained through observation and imitation of others, positive consequences, and cognitive processes such as plans, expectations, and beliefs.

social-cognitive learning theory of personality A view that holds that traits result from a person's learning history and his or her expectations, beliefs, perceptions of events, and other cognitions.

socialization The process by which children learn the behaviors, attitudes, and expectations required of them by their society or culture.

sociocultural perspective A psychological approach that emphasizes social and cultural influences on behavior.

somatic nervous system The subdivision of the peripheral nervous system that connects to sensory receptors and to skeletal muscles; sometimes called the *skeletal nervous system*.

source misattribution The inability to distinguish an actual memory of an event from information you learned about the event elsewhere.

spinal cord A collection of neurons and supportive tissue running from the base of the brain down the center of the back, protected by a column of bones (the spinal column).

spontaneous recovery The reappearance of a learned response after its apparent extinction.

standard deviation A commonly used measure of variability that indicates the average difference between scores in a distribution and their mean; more precisely, the square root of the average squared deviation from the mean.

standardize In test construction, to develop uniform procedures for giving and scoring a test.

state-dependent memory The tendency to remember something when the rememberer is in the same physical or mental state as during the original learning or experience.

statistically significant A term used to refer to a result that is extremely unlikely to have occurred by chance.

stem cells Immature cells that renew themselves and have the potential to develop into mature cells.

stereotype A summary impression of a group, in which a person believes that all members of the group share a common trait or traits (positive, negative, or neutral).

stereotype threat A burden of doubt a person feels about his or her performance, due to negative stereotypes about his or her group's abilities.

stimulants Drugs that speed up activity in the central nervous system.

stimulus discrimination The tendency to respond differently to two or more similar stimuli. In classical conditioning, it occurs when a stimulus that resembles the conditioned stimulus fails to evoke the conditioned response. In operant conditioning, it occurs when an organism learns to make a response in the presence of one stimulus but not in the presence of other, similar stimuli that differ from it on some dimension.

stimulus generalization After conditioning, the tendency to respond to a stimulus that resembles one involved in the original conditioning. In classical conditioning, it occurs when a stimulus that resembles the conditioned stimulus elicits the conditioned response. In operant conditioning, it occurs when a response that has been reinforced (or punished) in the presence of one stimulus occurs (or is suppressed) in the presence of other, similar stimuli.

subconscious processes Mental processes occurring outside of conscious awareness but accessible to consciousness when necessary.

successive approximations In the operant-conditioning procedure of shaping, behaviors that are ordered in terms of increasing similarity or closeness to the desired response.

superego In psychoanalysis, the part of personality that represents conscience, morality, and social standards.

suprachiasmatic [soo-pruh-kie-az-MAT-ick] nucleus (SCN) An area in the hypothalamus containing a biological clock that governs circadian rhythms.

surveys Questionnaires and interviews that ask people directly about their experiences, attitudes, or opinions.

sympathetic nervous system The subdivision of the autonomic nervous system that mobilizes bodily resources and increases the output of energy during emotion and stress.

synapse The site where transmission of a nerve impulse from one nerve cell to another occurs; it includes the axon terminal, the synaptic cleft, and receptor sites in the membrane of the receiving cell.

synesthesia A condition in which stimulation of one sense also evokes another.

systematic desensitization In behavior therapy, a step-by-step process of desensitizing a client to a feared object or experience; it is based on the classical-conditioning procedure of counterconditioning.

tacit knowledge Strategies for success that are not explicitly taught but that instead must be inferred.

taste buds Nests of taste-receptor cells.

telegraphic speech A child's first word combinations, which omit (as a telegram did) unnecessary words.

temperaments Physiological dispositions to respond to the environment in certain ways; they are present in infancy and are assumed to be innate.

temporal lobes Lobes at the sides of the brain's cerebral cortex; they contain areas involved in hearing, memory, perception, emotion, and (in the left lobe, typically) language comprehension.

thalamus A brain structure that relays sensory messages to the cerebral cortex.

theory An organized system of assumptions and principles that purports to explain a specified set of phenomena and their interrelationships.

theory of mind A system of beliefs about the way one's own mind and the minds of others work, and how individuals are affected by their beliefs and feelings.

timbre The distinguishing quality of a sound; the dimension of auditory experience related to the complexity of the pressure wave.

tolerance Increased resistance to a drug's effects accompanying continued use.

trait A characteristic of an individual, describing a habitual way of behaving, thinking, or feeling.

tranquilizers Drugs commonly but often inappropriately prescribed for patients who complain of unhappiness, anxiety, or worry.

transcranial direct current stimulation (tDCS) A technique that applies a small electric current to stimulate or suppress activity in parts of the cortex; it enables researchers to identify the functions of a particular area.

transcranial magnetic stimulation (TMS) A method of stimulating brain cells, using a powerful magnetic field produced by a wire coil placed on a person's head; it can be used by researchers to temporarily disrupt neural circuits during specific tasks and is also being used therapeutically.

transference In psychodynamic therapies, a critical process in which the client transfers unconscious emotions or reactions, such as emotional feelings about his or her parents, onto the therapist.

triarchic [try-ARE-kick] theory of intelligence A theory of intelligence that emphasizes analytic, creative, and practical abilities.

trichromatic theory A theory of color perception that proposes three mechanisms in the visual system, each sensitive to a certain range of wavelengths; their interaction is assumed to produce all the different experiences of hue.

unconditional positive regard To Carl Rogers, love or support given to another person with no conditions attached.

unconditioned response (UR) The classical-conditioning term for a response elicited by an unconditioned stimulus.

unconditioned stimulus (US) The classical-conditioning term for a stimulus that already elicits a certain response without additional learning.

validity The ability of a test to measure what it was designed to measure.

validity effect The tendency of people to believe that a statement is true or valid simply because it has been repeated many times.

variables Characteristics of behavior or experience that can be measured or described by a numeric scale.

volunteer bias A shortcoming of findings derived from a sample of volunteers instead of a representative sample; the volunteers may differ from those who did not volunteer.

vulnerability-stress models Approaches that emphasize how individual vulnerabilities (e.g., in genes or personality traits) interact with external stresses or circumstances to produce mental disorders.

working memory In many models of memory, a cognitively complex form of short-term memory; it involves active mental processes that control retrieval of information from long-term memory and interpret that information appropriately for a given task.

z-score (standard score) A number that indicates how far a given raw score is above or below the mean, using the standard deviation of the distribution as the unit of measurement.

References

Abrams, David B., & Wilson, G. Terence (1983). Alcohol, sexual arousal, and self-control. *Journal of Personality and Social Psychology, 45,* 188–198.

Abrahamson, Amy C.; Baker, Laura A.; & Caspi, Avshalom (2002). Rebellious teens? Genetic and environmental influences on the social attitudes of adolescents. *Journal of Personality and Social Psychology, 83,* 1392–1408.

Acevedo, Bianca P., & Aron, Arthur (2009). Does a long-term relationship kill romantic love? *Review of General Psychology, 13,* 59–65.

Adam, Hajo; Shirako, Aiwa; & Maddux, William W. (2010). Cultural variance in the interpersonal effects of anger in negotiations. *Psychological Science, 21,* 882–889.

Adams, James L. (2001). *Conceptual blockbusting: A guide to better ideas* (4th ed.). New York: Perseus Books.

Addis, Donna R.; Wong, Alana T; & Schacter, Daniel L. (2007). Remembering the past and imagining the future: Common and distinct neural substrates during event construction and elaboration. *Neuropsychologia, 45,* 1363–1377.

Ader, Robert (2000). True or false: The placebo effect as seen in drug studies is definitive proof that the mind can bring about clinically relevant changes in the body: The placebo effect: If it's all in your head, does that mean you only think you feel better? *Advances in Mind-Body Medicine, 16,* 7–11.

Adler, Nancy E., & Snibbe, Alana C. (2003). The role of psychosocial processes in explaining the gradient between socioeconomic status and health. *Current Directions in Psychological Science, 12,* 119–123.

Agars, Mark D. (2004). Reconsidering the impact of gender stereotypes on the advancement of women in organizations. *Psychology of Women Quarterly, 28,* 103–111.

Agrawal, Yuri; Platz, Elizabeth A.; & Niparko, John K. (2008). Prevalence of hearing loss and differences by demographic characteristics among US adults. *Archives of Internal Medicine, 168,* 1522–1530.

Aggarwal, Sunil K.; Carter Gregory T.; Sullivan Mark D.; et al. (2009). Medicinal use of cannabis in the United States: Historical perspectives, current trends, and future directions. *Journal of Opioid Management, 5,* 153–168.

Aguiar, Patrícia; Vala, Jorge; Correia, Isabel; & Pereira, Cícero (2008). Justice in our world and in that of others: Belief in a just world and reactions to victims. *Social Justice Research, 21,* 50–68.

Ainsworth, Mary D. S. (1973). The development of infant–mother attachment. In B. M. Caldwell & H. N. Ricciuti (Eds.), *Review of child development research* (Vol. 3). Chicago: University of Chicago Press.

Ainsworth, Mary D. S. (1979). Infant–mother attachment. *American Psychologist, 34,* 932–937.

Albert, Dustin, & Steinberg, Laurence (2011). Judgment and decision making in adolescence. *Journal of Research on Adolescence, 21,* 211–224.

Alcock, James E. (2011, March/April). Back from the future: Parapsychology and the Bem affair. *Skeptical Inquirer,* 31–39.

Alford, C. Fred (2001). *Whistleblowers: Broken lives and organizations.* Ithaca, NY: Cornell University Press.

Alford, John R.; Funk, Carolyn L.; & Hibbing, John R. (2005). Are political orientations genetically transmitted? *American Political Science Review, 99,* 153–167.

Allport, Gordon W. (1954/1979). *The nature of prejudice.* Reading, MA: Addison-Wesley.

Alink, Lenneke R. A.; Mesman, Judi; van Zeijl, Jantien; et al. (2009). Maternal sensitivity moderates the relation between negative discipline and aggression in early childhood. *Social Development, 18,* 99–120.

Allport, Gordon W. (1961). *Pattern and growth in personality.* New York: Holt, Rinehart and Winston.

Ambady, Nalini (2011, May/June). The mind in the world: Culture and the brain. *APS Observer, 24.*

Amabile, Teresa M. (1983). *The social psychology of creativity.* New York: Springer-Verlag.

Amabile, Teresa M., & Khaire, Mukti (2008, October). Creativity and the role of the leader. *Harvard Business Review.* http://hbr.org/2008/10/creativity-and-the-role-of-the-leader/ar/1.

Amedi, Amir; Merabet, Lotfi; Bermpohl, Felix; & Pascual-Leone, Alvaro (2005). The occipital cortex in the blind: Lessons about plasticity and vision. *Current Directions in Psychological Science, 14,* 306–311.

American Psychiatric Association (2013). *Diagnostic and statistical manual of mental disorders, fifth edition.* Arlington, VA: American Psychiatric Association.

Anastasi, Anne, & Urbina, Susan (1997). *Psychological testing* (7th ed.). Upper Saddle River, NJ: Prentice Hall.

Anderson, Amanda (2005). *The way we argue now: A study in the cultures of theory.* Princeton, NJ: Princeton University Press.

Anderson, Matthew (2005). Is lack of sexual desire a disease? Is testosterone the cure? *Medscape Ob/Gyn & Women's Health.* www.medscape.com/viewarticle/512218.

Anderson, Cameron; Keltner, Dacher; & John, Oliver P. (2003). Emotional convergence between people over time. *Journal of Personality and Social Psychology, 84,* 1054–1068.

Anderson, Craig A.; Shibuya, Akiko; Ihori, Nobuko; et al. (2010). Violent video game effects on aggression, empathy, and prosocial behavior in Eastern and Western countries: A meta-analytic review. *Psychological Bulletin, 136,* 151–173.

Anderson, John R. (1990). *The adaptive nature of thought.* Hillsdale, NJ: Erlbaum.

Anderson-Barnes, Victoria C.; McAuliffe, Caitlin; Swanberg, Kelly M.; & Tsao, Jack W. (2009). Phantom limb pain: A phenomenon of proprioceptive memory? *Medical Hypotheses, 73,* 555–558.

Andreano, Joseph M., & Cahill, Larry (2006). Glucocorticoid release and memory consolidation in men and women. *Psychological Science, 17,* 466–470.

Andreasen, Nancy C.; Arndt, Stephan; Swayze, Victor, II; et al. (1994). Thalamic abnormalities in schizophrenia visualized through magnetic resonance image averaging. *Science, 266,* 294–298.

Añez, Luis M.; Silva, Michelle A.; Paris Jr., Manuel; Bedregal, Luis E. (2008). Engaging Latinos through the integration of cultural values and motivational interviewing principles. *Professional Psychology: Research and Practice, 39,* 153–159.

Angell, Marcia (2004). *The truth about the drug companies: How they deceive us and what to do about it.* New York: Random House.

Angier, Natalie (2000, November 7). Who is fat? It depends on culture. *New York Times, Science Times,* D1–2.

Antrobus, John (1991). Dreaming: Cognitive processes during cortical activation and high afferent thresholds. *Psychological Review, 98,* 96–121.

Antrobus, John (2000). How does the dreaming brain explain the dreaming mind? *Behavioral and Brain Sciences, 23,* 904–907.

Archer, John (2004). Sex differences in aggression in real-world settings: A meta-analytic review. *Review of General Psychology, 8,* 291–322.

Arendt, Hannah (1963). *Eichmann in Jerusalem: A report on the banality of evil.* New York: Viking.

Arkes, Hal R. (1993). Some practical judgment and decision-making research. In N. J. Castellan, Jr., et al. (Eds.), *Individual and group decision making: Current issues.* Hillsdale, NJ: Erlbaum.

Arkes, Hal R.; Boehm, Lawrence E.; & Xu, Gang (1991). The determinants of judged validity. *Journal of Experimental Social Psychology, 27,* 576–605.

Arnett, Jeffrey J. (2004). *Emerging adulthood: The winding road from the late teens through the twenties.* New York: Oxford University Press.

Arnon, Inbal, & Clark, Eve V. (2011). Why *"on your feet"* is better than *"feet"*: Children's word production is facilitated in familiar sentence-frames. *Language Learning & Development, 7,* 107–129.

Aron, Arthur; Fisher, Helen; Mashek, Debra J.; et al. (2005). Reward, motivation, and emotion systems associated with early-stage intense romantic love. *Journal of Neurophysiology, 94*, 327–337.

Aron, Arthur; Fisher, Helen E.; Strong, Greg; et al. (2008). Falling in love. In S. Sprecher, A. Wenzel, & J. Harvey (Eds.), *Handbook of relationship initiation*. New York: Psychology Press.

Aronson, Elliot (2000). *Nobody left to hate*. New York: Freeman.

Aronson, Elliot (2012). *The social animal* (11th ed.). New York: Worth.

Aronson, Elliot, & Mills, Judson (1959). The effect of severity of initiation on liking for a group. *Journal of Abnormal and Social Psychology, 59*, 177–181.

Aronson, Joshua (2010). Jigsaw and the nurture of human intelligence. In M. H. Gonzales, C. Tavris, & J. Aronson (Eds.), *The scientist and the humanist: A festschrift in honor of Elliot Aronson*. New York: Psychology Press.

Arredondo, Patricia, & Perez, Patricia (2003). Counseling paradigms and Latina/o Americans. In F. Harper & J. McFadden (Eds.), *Culture and counseling: New approaches*. Boston: Allyn & Bacon.

Arredondo, Patricia; Rosen, Daniel C.; Rice, Tiffany; Perez, Patricia; & Tovar-Gamero, Zoila G. (2005). Multicultural counseling: A 10-year content analysis of the Journal of Counseling & Development. *Journal of Counseling and Development, 83*, 155–161.

Arroyo, Carmen G., & Zigler, Edward (1995). Racial identity, academic achievement, and the psychological well-being of economically disadvantaged adolescents. *Journal of Personality and Social Psychology, 69*, 903–914.

Arum, Richard, & Josipa Roksa (2011). *Academically adrift: Limited learning on college campuses*. Chicago: University of Chicago Press.

Asai, Masato; Ramachandrappa, Shwetha; Joachim, Maria; et al. (2013). Loss of function of the melacocortin 2 receptor accessory protein 2 is associated with mammalian obesity. *Science, 341*, 275–278.

Asch, Solomon E. (1952). *Social psychology*. Englewood Cliffs, NJ: Prentice-Hall.

Asch, Solomon E. (1965). Effects of group pressure upon the modification and distortion of judgments. In H. Proshansky & B. Seidenberg (Eds.), *Basic studies in social psychology*. New York: Holt, Rinehart and Winston.

Aserinsky, Eugene, & Kleitman, Nathaniel (1955). Two types of ocular motility occurring in sleep. *Journal of Applied Physiology, 8*, 1–10.

Atkinson, Richard C., & Shiffrin, Richard M. (1968). Human memory: A proposed system and its control processes. In K. W. Spence & J. T. Spence (Eds.), *The psychology of learning and motivation: Vol. 2. Advances in research and theory*. New York: Academic Press.

Atkinson, Richard C., & Shiffrin, Richard M. (1971, August). The control of short-term memory. *Scientific American, 225(2)*, 82–90.

Atran, Scott (2003). Genesis of suicide terrorism. *Science, 299*, 1534–1539.

AuBuchon, Peter G., & Calhoun, Karen S. (1985). Menstrual cycle symptomatology: The role of social expectancy and experimental demand characteristics. *Psychosomatic Medicine, 47*, 35–45.

Auyeung, Bonnie; Baron-Cohen, Simon; Ashwin, Emma; et al. (2009). Fetal testosterone predicts sexually differentiated childhood behavior in girls and in boys. *Psychological Science, 20*, 144–148.

Aviezer, Hillel; Hassin, Ran R.; Ryan, Jennifer; et al. (2008). Angry, disgusted, or afraid? Studies on the malleability of emotion perception. *Psychological Science, 19*, 724–732.

Axel, Richard (1995, October). The molecular logic of smell. *Scientific American*, 154–159.

Azmitia, Margarita; Syed, Moin; & Radmacher, Kimberly (2008). On the intersection of personal and social identities: Introduction and evidence from a longitudinal study of emerging adults. In M. Azmitia, M. Syed, & K. Radmacher (Eds.), *The intersections of personal and social identities*. San Francisco: Jossey-Bass.

Azuma, Hiroshi (1984). Secondary control as a heterogeneous category. *American Psychologist, 39*, 970–971.

Baas, Matthijs; De Dreu, Carsten K. W.; & Nijstad, Bernard A. (2008). A meta-analysis of 25 years of mood-creativity research: Hedonic tone, activation, or regulatory focus? *Psychological Bulletin, 134*, 779–806.

Babiak, Paul, & Hare, Robert (2007). *Snakes in suits*. New York: Collins Business.

Baddeley, Alan D. (1992). Working memory. *Science, 255*, 556–559.

Baddeley, Alan D. (2007). *Working memory, thought, and action*. New York: Oxford.

Bagemihl, Bruce (1999). *Biological exuberance: Animal homosexuality and natural diversity*. New York: St. Martin's Press.

Bahrick, Harry P. (1984). Semantic memory content in permastore: Fifty years of memory for Spanish learned in school. *Journal of Experimental Psychology: General, 113*, 1–29.

Bahrick, Harry P.; Bahrick, Phyllis O.; & Wittlinger, Roy P. (1975). Fifty years of memory for names and faces: A cross-sectional approach. *Journal of Experimental Psychology: General, 104*, 54–75.

Bailey, J. Michael, & Zucker, Kenneth J. (1995). Childhood sex-typed behavior and sexual orientation: A conceptual analysis and quantitative review. *Developmental Psychology, 31*, 43–55.

Bailey, J. Michael; Bobrow, David; Wolfe, Marilyn; & Mikach, Sarah (1995). Sexual orientation of adult sons of gay fathers. *Developmental Psychology, 31*, 124–129.

Bailey, J. Michael; Dunne, Michael P.; & Martin, Nicholas G. (2000). Genetic and environmental influences on sexual orientation and its correlates in an Australian twin sample. *Journal of Personality and Social Psychology, 78*, 524–536.

Baillargeon, Renée (1994). How do infants learn about the physical world? *Current Directions in Psychological Science, 5*, 133–140.

Baillargeon, Renée (2004). Infants' physical world. *Current Directions in Psychological Science, 13*, 89–94.

Baker, Mark C. (2001). *The atoms of language: The mind's hidden rules of grammar*. New York: Basic.

Baker, Timothy B.; McFall, Richard M.; & Shoham, Varda (2008). Current status and future prospects of clinical psychology: Toward a scientifically principled approach to mental and behavioral health care. *Psychological Science in the Public Interest, 9*, entire issue.

Bakermans-Kranenburg, Marian J.; Breddels-van Baardewijk, Philomeen; Juffer, Femmie; et al. (2008). Insecure mothers with temperamentally reactive infants: A chance for intervention. In F. Juffer, M. J. Bakermans-Kranenburg, & M. H. van IJzendoorn (Eds.), *Promoting positive parenting: An attachment-based intervention*. New York: Taylor & Francis.

Bakker, Arnold B. (2011). An evidence-based model of work engagement. *Current Directions in Psychological Science, 20*, 265–269.

Balcetis, Emily, & Dunning, David (2010). Wishful seeing: More desired objects are seen as closer. *Psychological Science, 21*, 147–152.

Balcetis, Emily; Dunning, David; & Miller, Richard L. (2008). Do collectivists know themselves better than individualists? Cross-cultural studies of the holier than thou phenomenon. *Journal of Personality and Social Psychology, 95*, 1252–1267.

Balter, Michael (2012). "Killjoys" challenge claims of clever animals. *Science, 335*, 1036–1037.

Bancroft, John (2006). Normal sexual development. In H. E. Barbaree & W. L. Marshall (Eds.), *The juvenile sex offender* (2nd ed.). New York: Guilford.

Bancroft, John; Graham, Cynthia A.; Janssen, Erick; Sanders, Stephanie A. (2009). The dual control model: Current status and future directions. *Journal of Sex Research, 46*, 121–142.

Bandura, Albert (1977). *Social learning theory*. Englewood Cliffs, NJ: Prentice-Hall.

Bandura, Albert (1986). *Social foundations of thought and action: A social cognitive theory*. Englewood Cliffs, NJ: Prentice-Hall.

Bandura, Albert (1999). Moral disengagement in the perpetration of inhumanities. *Personality and Social Psychology Review, 3*, 193–209.

Bandura, Albert (2001). Social cognitive theory: An agentic perspective. *Annual Review of Psychology, 52*, 1–26. Palo Alto, CA: Annual Reviews.

Bandura, Albert (2006). Toward a psychology of human agency. *Perspectives on Psychological Science, 1*, 164–180.

Bandura, Albert; Ross, Dorothea; & Ross, Sheila A. (1963). Vicarious reinforcement and imitative learning. *Journal of Abnormal and Social Psychology, 67*, 601–607.

Banks, Martin S. (with Philip Salapatek) (1984). Infant visual perception. In P. Mussen (Series Ed.), M. M. Haith & J. J. Campos (Vol. Eds.), *Handbook of child psychology: Vol. II. Infancy and developmental psychobiology* (4th ed.). New York: Wiley.

Barash, David P., & Lipton, Judith Eve (2001). *The myth of monogamy: Fidelity and infidelity in animals and people*. New York: W. H. Freeman.

Barbuto, J. E. (1997). A critique of the Myers-Briggs Type Indicator and its operationalization of Carl Jung's psychological types. *Psychological Reports, 80,* 611–625.

Bargary, Gary, & Mitchell, Kevin J. (2008). Synaesthesia and cortical connectivity. *Trends in Neurosciences, 31,* 335–342.

Barnes, Carol (2011, September 1). Secrets of aging. *The Scientist,* online at http://the-scientist.com/2011/09/01/secrets-of-aging/.

Barrett, Lisa F.; Mesquita, Batja; & Gendron, Maria (2011). Context in emotion perception. *Current Directions in Psychological Science, 20,* 286–290.

Barsky, S. H.; Roth, M. D.; Kleerup, E. C.; Simmons, M.; & Tashkin, D. P. (1998). Histopathologic and molecular alterations in bronchial epithelium in habitual smokers of marijuana, cocaine, and/or tobacco. *Journal of the National Cancer Institute, 90,* 1198–1205.

Bartels, Andreas, & Zeki, Semir (2004). The neural correlates of material and romantic love. *NeuroImage, 21,* 1155–1166.

Bartlett, Frederic C. (1932). *Remembering.* Cambridge, England: Cambridge University Press.

Barlow, David H. (2000). Unraveling the mysteries of anxiety and its disorders from the perspective of emotion theory. *American Psychologist, 55,* 1247–1263.

Barlow, David H. (2004). Psychological treatments. *American Psychologist, 59,* 869–878.

Bartoshuk, Linda M. (2000). Comparing sensory experiences across individuals: Recent psychophysical advances illuminate genetic variation in taste perception. *Chemical Senses, 25,* 447–460.

Bartoshuk, Linda M. (2009). Taste. In J. M. Wolfe, K. R. Kluender, D. M. Levi, et al., *Sensation and perception* (2nd ed.). Sunderland, MA: Sinauer Associates.

Bartoshuk, Linda M.; Duffy, V. B.; Lucchina, L. A.; et al. (1998). PROP (6-npropylthiouracil) supertasters and the saltiness of NaCl. *Annals of the New York Academy of Sciences, 855,* 793–796.

Bartz, Jennifer A.; Zaki, Jamil; Ochsner, Kevin N.; et al. (2010). Effects of oxytocin on recollections of maternal care and closeness. *Proceedings of the National Academy of Sciences, 107,* 21371–21375.

Bassetti, C.; Vella, S.; Donati, F.; et al. (2000). SPECT during sleepwalking. *Lancet, 356,* 484–485.

Basson, Rosemary; McInnis, Rosemary; Smith, Mike D.; et al. (2002). Efficacy and safety of sidenafil citrate in women with sexual dysfunction associated with female sexual arousal disorder. *Journal of Women's Health and Gender-Based Medicine, 11,* 367–377.

Battaglia, Francesco P.; Benchenane, Karim; Sirota, Anton; et al. (2011). The hippocampus: hub of brain network communication for memory. *Trends in Cognitive Sciences, 15,* 310–318.

Baucom, Katherine J. W.; Sevier, Mia; Eldridge, Kathleen A.; et al. (2011). Observed communication in couples two years after integrative and traditional behavioral couple therapy: Outcome and link with five-year follow-up. *Journal of Consulting and Clinical Psychology 79,* 565–576.

Bauer, Patricia (2002). Long-term recall memory: Behavioral and neurodevelopmental changes in the first 2 years of life. *Current Directions in Psychological Science, 11,* 137–141.

Baumeister, Roy F. (2000). Gender differences in erotic plasticity: The female sex drive as socially flexible and responsive. *Psychological Bulletin, 126,* 347–374.

Baumeister, Roy F.; Campbell, Jennifer D.; Krueger, Joachim I.; & Vohs, Kathleen D. (2003). Does high self-esteem cause better performance, interpersonal success, happiness, or healthier lifestyles? *Psychological Science in the Public Interest, 4*(1)[whole issue].

Baumeister, Roy F.; Catanese, Kathleen R.; & Vohs, Kathleen D. (2001). Is there a gender difference in strength of sex drive? Theoretical views, conceptual distinctions, and a review of relevant evidence. *Personality and Social Psychology Review, 5,* 242–273.

Baumeister, Roy F.; Dale, Karen; & Sommer, Kristin L. (1998). Freudian defense mechanisms and empirical findings in modern social psychology: Reaction formation, projection, displacement, undoing, isolation, sublimation, and denial. *Journal of Personality, 66,* 1081–1124.

Baumeister, Roy F.; Stillwell, Arlene M.; & Heatherton, Todd F. (1994). Guilt: An interpersonal approach. *Psychological Bulletin, 115,* 243–267.

Baumrind, Diana (1964). Some thoughts on ethics of research: After reading Milgram's "Behavioral Study of Obedience." *American Psychologist, 19,* 421–423.

Baumrind, Diana; Larzelere, Robert E.; & Cowan, Philip (2002). Ordinary physical punishment—Is it harmful? Commentary on Gershoff's Review. *Psychological Bulletin, 128,* 580–589.

Beaman, Lori; Duflo, Esther; Pande, Rohini; & Topalova, Petia (2012). Female leadership raises aspirations and educational attainment for girls: A policy experiment in India. *Science, 335,* 582–586.

Beauchamp, Gary K., & Mennella, Julie A. (2011). Flavor perception in human infants: Development and functional significance. *Digestion, 83,* 1–6.

Bechara, Antoine; Dermas, Hanna; Tranel, Daniel; & Damasio, Antonio R. (1997). Deciding advantageously before knowing the advantageous strategy. *Science, 275,* 1293–1294.

Beck, Aaron T. (2005). The current state of cognitive therapy: A 40-year retrospective. *Archives of General Psychiatry, 62,* 953–959.

Beck, Diane M. (2010). The appeal of the brain in the popular press. *Perspectives on Psychological Science, 5,* 762–766.

Becker, D. Vaughn; Kenrick, Douglas T.; Neuberg, Steven L.; et al. (2007). The confounded nature of angry men and happy women. *Journal of Personality and Social Psychology, 92,* 179–190.

Beckett, Katherine; Nyrop, Kris; & Pfingst, Lori (2006). Race, drugs, and policing: Understanding disparities in drug delivery arrests. *Criminology, 44,* 105–137.

Beer, Jeremy M.; Arnold, Richard D.; & Loehlin, John C. (1998). Genetic and environmental influences on MMPI factor scales: Joint model fitting to twin and adoption data. *Journal of Personality and Social Psychology, 74,* 818–827.

Bell, Janice F., & Zimmerman, Frederick J. (2010). Shortened nighttime sleep duration in early life and subsequent childhood obesity. *Archives of Pediatric and Adolescent Medicine, 164,* 840–845.

Belsky, Jay, & Pluess, Michael (2009a). Beyond diathesis stress: Differential susceptibility to environmental influences. *Psychological Bulletin, 135,* 885–908.

Belsky, Jay, & Pluess, Michael (2009b). The nature (and nurture?) of plasticity in early human development. *Perspectives on Psychological Science, 4,* 345–351.

Belsky, Jay; Bakermans-Kranenburg, Marian J.; & van IJzendoorn, Marinus H. (2007). For better and for worse: Differential susceptibility to environmental influences. *Current Directions in Psychological Science, 16,* 300–304.

Belsky, Jay; Campbell, Susan B.; Cohn, Jeffrey F.; & Moore, Ginger (1996). Instability of infant-parent attachment security. *Developmental Psychology, 32,* 921–924.

Bem, Daryl J., & Honorton, Charles (1994). Does psi exist? Replicable evidence for an anomalous process of information transfer. *Psychological Bulletin, 115,* 4–18.

Bem, Sandra L. (1993). *The lenses of gender.* New Haven, CT: Yale University Press.

Ben Amar, Mohamed (2006). Cannabinoids in medicine: A review of their therapeutic potential. *Journal of Ethnopharmacology, 105* (1-2), 1–25.

Benedetti, Fabrizio, & Levi-Montalcini, Rita (2001). Opioid and non-opioid mechanisms of placebo analgesia. Paper presented at the annual meeting of the American Psychological Society, Toronto.

Benjamin, Ludy T., Jr. (1998). Why Gorgeous George, and not Wilhelm Wundt, was the founder of psychology: A history of popular psychology in America. Invited address presented at the National Institute on the Teaching of Psychology, St. Petersburg Beach.

Benjamin, Ludy T., Jr. (2003). Why can't psychology get a stamp? *Journal of Applied Psychoanalytic Studies, 5,* 443–454.

Bennett, Craig M.; Baird, Abigail A.; Miller, Michael B.; & Wolford, George L. (2010). Neural correlates of interspecies perspective taking in the post-mortem Atlantic Salmon: An argument for multiple comparisons correction. *Journal of Serendipitous and Unexpected Results. 1,* 1–5.

Beran, Michael J., & Beran, Mary M. (2004). Chimpanzees remember the results of one-by-one addition of food items to sets over extended time periods. *Psychological Science, 15,* 94–99.

Berenbaum, Sheri A., & Bailey, J. Michael (2003). Effects on gender identity of prenatal androgens and genital appearance: Evidence from girls with congenital adrenal hyperplasia. *Journal of Clinical Endocrinology and Metabolism, 88,* 1102–1106.

Berger, F.; Gage, F. H.; & Vijayaraghavan, S. (1998). Nicotinic receptor-induced apoptotic cell death of hippocampal progenitor cells. *Journal of Neuroscience, 18,* 6871–6881.

Berger, Shelley L.; Kouzarides, Tony; Shiekhattar, Ramin; & Shilatifard, Ali (2009). An operational definition of epigenetics. *Genes & Development, 23,* 781–783.

Berglund, Hans; Lindström, Per; & Savic, Ivanka (2006). Brain response to putative pheromones in lesbian women. *Proceedings of the National Academy of Sciences, 103,* 8269–8274.

Berkman Center for Internet & Society (2008, December 31). Enhancing child safety and online technologies: Final report of the Internet Safety Task Force. Final report available at http://cyber.law.harvard.edu/sites/cyber.law.harvard.edu/files/ISTTF_Final_Report.pdf.

Berlin, Fred S. (2003). Sex offender treatment and legislation. *Journal of the American Academy of Psychiatry and the Law, 31,* 510–513.

Bernstein, Daniel M., & Loftus, Elizabeth F. (2009). How to tell if a particular memory is true or false. *Perspectives on Psycholgical Science, 4,* 370–374.

Berntsen, Dorthe, & Thomsen, Dorthe K. (2005). Personal memories for remote historical events: Accuracy and clarity of flashbulb memories related to World War II. *Journal of Experimental Psychology: General, 134,* 242–257.

Berry, John W. (2006). Contexts of acculturation. In D. L. Sam & J. W. Berry (Eds.), *Cambridge handbook of acculturation psychology.* New York: Cambridge University Press.

Berscheid, Ellen, & Reis, Harry T. (1998). Attraction and close relationships. In D. T. Gilbert, S. T. Fiske, & G. Lindzey (Eds.), *The handbook of social psychology,* Vol. 2 (4th ed.). New York: McGraw-Hill.

Best, Joel (2012). *Damned Lies and Statistics: Untangling numbers from the media, politicians, and activists* (Rev. first edition). Berkeley: University of California Press.

Beyerstein, Barry L. (1996). Graphology. In G. Stein (Ed.), *The encyclopedia of the paranormal.* Amherst, NY: Prometheus Books.

Beydoun, M. A.; Kaufman, J. S.; Satia, J. A.; et al. (2007). Plasma n-3 fatty acids and the risk of cognitive decline in older adults: the Atherosclerosis Risk in Communities Study. *American Journal of Clinical Nutrition, 85,* 1103–1111.

Bhatarah, Parveen; Ward, Geoff; & Tan, Lydia (2008). Examining the relationship between free recall and immediate serial recall: The serial nature of recall and the effect of test expectancy. *Memory & Cognition, 36,* 20–34.

Bierut, Laura Jean; Stitzel, Jerry A.; Wang, Jen C.; et al. (2008). Variants in nicotinic receptors and risk for nicotine dependence. *American Journal of Psychiatry, 165,* 1163–1171.

Binder, Jens; Zagefka, Hanna; Brown, Rupert; et al. (2009). Does contact reduce prejudice or does prejudice reduce contact? A longitudinal test of the contact hypothesis among majority and minority groups in three European countries. *Journal of Personality and Social Psychology, 96,* 843–856.

Birdwhistell, Ray L. (1970). *Kinesics and context: Essays on body motion communication.* Philadelphia: University of Pennsylvania Press.

Birkhead, Tim (2001). *Promiscuity: An evolutionary history of sperm competition.* Cambridge, MA: Harvard University Press.

Bischof, Matthias, & Bassetti, Claudio L. (2004). Total dream loss: A distinct neuropsychological dysfunction after bilateral PCA stroke. *Annals of Neurology,* published online Sept. 10, 2004. (DOI: 10.1002/ana.20246.)

Biss, Renée K., & Hasher, Lynn (2012). Happy as a lark: Morning-type younger and older adults are higher in positive affect. *Emotion, 12,* 437–441.

Biswal, Bharat B.; Mennes, Maarten; Zuo, Xi-nian; et al. (2010). Toward discovery science of human brain function. *Proceedings of the National Academy of Sciences of the United States of America, 107,* 4734–4739.

Bjork, Elizabeth L., & Bjork, Robert A. (2011). Making things hard on yourself, but in a good way: Creating desirable difficulties to enhance learning. In M. A. Gernsbacher, R. W. Pew, L. M. Hough, & J. R. Pomerantz (Eds.), *Psychology and the Real World: Essays Illustrating Fundamental Contributions to Society.* New York: Worth.

Bjorkland, D. F. (2000). *Children's thinking: Developmental function and individual differences.* Belmont, CA: Wadsworth.

Black, Michele C.; Basile, Kathleen C.; Breiding, Matthew J.; et al. (2011). *The National Intimate Partner and Sexual Violence Survey: Summary report.* National Center for Injury Prevention and Control, Centers for Disease Control and Prevention, Atlanta, Georgia.

Blackmore, Susan (2001, March/April). Giving up the ghosts: End of a personal quest. *Skeptical Inquirer,* 22–27.

Blagrove, Mark (1996). Problems with the cognitive psychological modeling of dreaming. *Journal of Mind and Behavior, 17,* 99–134.

Blair, R. D. J.; Jones, L.; Clark, F.; & Smith, M. (1997). The psychopathic individual: A lack of responsiveness to distress cues? *Psychophysiology, 45,* 192–198.

Blakemore, Colin, & Cooper, Grahame F. (1970). Development of the brain depends on the visual environment. *Nature, 228,* 477–478.

Blanton, Hart, & Mitchell, Gregory (2011). Reassessing the predictive validity of the IAT II: Reanalysis of Heider & Skowronski (2007). *North American Journal of Psychology, 13,* 99–106.

Blanton, Hart; Jaccard, James; Klick, Jonathan; Mellers, Barbara; Mitchell, Gregory; & Tetlock, Philip E. (2009). Strong claims and weak evidence: Reassessing the predictive validity of the IAT. *Journal of Applied Psychology, 94,* 567–582.

Blass, Thomas (Ed.) (2000). *Obedience to authority: Current perspectives on the Milgram paradigm.* Mahwah, NJ: Erlbaum.

Bleuler, Eugen (1911/1950). *Dementia praecox or the group of schizophrenias.* New York: International Universities Press.

Bliss, T. V., & Collingridge, G. L. (1993). A synaptic model of memory: Long-term potentiation in the hippocampus. *Nature, 361(6407),* 31–39.

Bloom, Mia (2005). *Dying to kill: The allure of suicide terror.* New York: Columbia University Press.

Blum, Deborah (2002). *Love at Goon Park: Harry Harlow and the science of affection.* Cambridge, MA: Perseus Books.

Bluming, Avrum, & Tavris, Carol (2009). Hormone replacement therapy: Real concerns and false alarms. *The Cancer Journal, 15,* 93–104.

Bogaert, Anthony F. (2006). Biological versus nonbiological older brothers and men's sexual orientation. *Proceedings of the National Academy of Sciences,* published online at 10.1073/pnas. 0511152103.

Boesch, Cristophe (1991). Teaching among wild chimpanzees. *Animal Behavior, 41,* 530–532.

Bogle, Kathleen (2008). *Hooking up: Sex, dating, and relationships on campus.* New York: New York University Press.

Bohannon, John N., & Symons, Victoria (1988). Conversational conditions of children's imitation. Paper presented at the biennial Conference on Human Development, Charleston, South Carolina.

Bolshakov, Vadim Y., & Siegelbaum, Steven A. (1994). Postsynaptic induction and presynaptic expression of hippocampal long-term depression. *Science, 264,* 1148–1152.

Bond, Charles F., & DePaulo, Bella M. (2008). Individual differences in judging deception: Accuracy and bias. *Psychological Bulletin, 134,* 477–492.

Bond, Rod, & Smith, Peter B. (1996). Culture and conformity: A meta-analysis of studies using Asch's (1952b, 1956) line judgment task. *Psychological Bulletin, 119,* 111–137.

Bonanno, George A. (2004). Loss, trauma, and human resilience. *American Psychologist, 59,* 20–28.

Bonanno, George A.; Brewin, Chris R.; Kaniasty Krzysztof; & La Greca, Annette M. (2010). Weighing the costs of disaster: Individuals, families, and communities. *Psychological Science in the Public Interest, 11,* 1–49.

Bonnet, Michael H. (1990). The perception of sleep onset in insomniacs and normal sleepers. In R. R. Bootzin, J. F. Kihlstrom, & D. L. Schacter (Eds.), *Sleep and cognition.* Washington, DC: American Psychological Association.

Booth, Frank W., & Neufer, P. Darrell (2005). Exercise controls gene expression. *American Scientist, 93,* 28–35.

Bootzin, Richard R. (2009, March). Update on the psychological science accreditation system. *APS Observer,* 20–21.

Borch-Jacobsen, Mikkel (2009). *Making minds and madness: From hysteria to depression.* Cambridge: Cambridge University Press.

Borch-Jacobsen, Mikkel, & Shamdasani, Sonu (2012). *The Freud files: An inquiry into the history of psychoanalysis.* New York: Cambridge University Press.

Bordo, Susan (2000). *The male body.* New York: Farrar, Straus and Giroux.

Born, Jan, & Wilhelm, Ines (2012). System consolidation of memory during sleep. *Psychological Research, 76,* 192–203.

Bornstein, Robert F.; Leone, Dean R.; & Galley, Donna J. (1987). The generalizability of subliminal mere exposure effects: Influence of stimuli perceived without awareness on social behavior. *Journal of Personality and Social Psychology, 53*, 1070–1079.

Boroditsky, Lera (2003). Linguistic relativity. In L. Nadel (Ed.), *Encyclopedia of cognitive science.* London: Nature Publishing Group.

Boroditsky, Lera; Schmidt, Lauren; & Phillips, Webb (2003). Sex, syntax, and semantics. In D. Gentner & S. Goldin-Meadow (Eds.), *Language in mind: Advances in the study of language and thought.* Cambridge: MIT Press.

Bosson, Jennifer K., & Vandello, Joseph A. (2011). Precarious manhood and its links to action and aggression. *Current Directions in Psychological Science, 20*, 82.

Bosworth, Hayden B., & Schaie, K. Warner (1999). Survival effects in cognitive function, cognitive style, and sociodemographic variables in the Seattle Longitudinal Study. *Experimental Aging Research, 25*, 121–139.

Bouchard, Claude; Tremblay, A.; Despres, J. P.; et al. (1990). The response to long-term overfeeding in identical twins. *New England Journal of Medicine, 322*, 1477–1482.

Bouchard, Thomas J., Jr. (1995). Nature's twice-told tale: Identical twins reared apart—what they tell us about human individuality. Paper presented at the annual meeting of the Western Psychological Association, Los Angeles.

Bouchard, Thomas J., Jr. (1997a). The genetics of personality. In K. Blum & E. P. Noble (Eds.), *Handbook of psychiatric genetics.* Boca Raton, FL: CRC Press.

Bouchard, Thomas J., Jr. (1997b). IQ similarity in twins reared apart: Findings and responses to critics. In R. J. Sternberg & E. Grigorenko (Eds.), *Intelligence: Heredity and environment.* New York: Cambridge University Press.

Bouchard, Thomas J., Jr., & McGue, Matthew (1981). Familial studies of intelligence: A review. *Science, 212*, 1055–1058.

Bouret, Sebastien G.; Draper, Shin J.; & Simerly, Richard B. (2004). Trophic action of leptin on hypothalamic neurons that regulate feeding. *Science, 304*, 108–110.

Bousfield, W. A. (1953). The occurrence of clustering in the recall of randomly arranged associates. *Journal of General Psychology, 49*, 229–240.

Bouton, Katherine (2013). *Shouting won't help.* New York: Sarah Crichton Books/Farrar, Straus, & Giroux.

Bowen, Murray (1978). *Family therapy in clinical practice.* New York: Jason Aronson.

Bower, Gordon H., & Forgas, Joseph P. (2000). Affect, memory, and social cognition. In E. Eich et al. (Eds.), *Cognition and emotion.* New York: Oxford University Press.

Bowers, Kenneth S.; Regehr, Glenn; Balthazard, Claude; & Parker, Kevin (1990). Intuition in the context of discovery. *Cognitive Psychology, 22*, 72–110.

Bowlby, John (1969). *Attachment and loss. Vol. 1. Attachment.* New York: Basic.

Bowlby, John (1973). *Attachment and loss: Vol. 2. Separation.* New York: Basic.

Bowles, Samuel (2008). Policies designed for self-interested citizens may undermine "the moral sentiments": Evidence from economic experiments. *Science, 320*, 1605–1609.

Brand-Miller, Jennie C.; Fatima, Kaniz; Middlemiss, Christopher; et al. (2007). Effect of alcoholic beverages on postprandial glycemia and insulinemia in lean, young, healthy adults. *American Journal of Clinical Nutrition, 85*, 1545–1551.

Braun, Kathryn A.; Ellis, Rhiannon; & Loftus, Elizabeth F. (2002). Make my memory: How advertising can change our memories of the past. *Psychology & Marketing, 19*, 1–23.

Braungart, J. M.; Plomin, Robert; DeFries, J. C.; & Fulker, D. W. (1992). Genetic influence on tester-rated infant temperament as assessed by Bayley's Infant Behavior Record: Nonadoptive and adoptive siblings and twins. *Developmental Psychology, 28*, 40–47.

Breland, Keller, & Breland, Marian (1961). The misbehavior of organisms. *American Psychologist, 16*, 681–684.

Brennan, Patricia A., & Mednick, Sarnoff A. (1994). Learning theory approach to the deterrence of criminal recidivism. *Journal of Abnormal Psychology, 103*, 430–440.

Brescoll, Victoria L., & Uhlmann, Eric L. (2008). Can an angry woman get ahead? Status conferral, gender, and expression of emotion in the workplace. *Psychological Science, 19*, 268–275.

Breslau, Naomi; Lucia, Victoria C.; & Alvarado, German F. (2006). Intelligence and other predisposing factors in exposure to trauma and posttraumatic stress disorder. *Archives of General Psychiatry, 63*, 1238–1245.

Brewer, Marilynn B., & Gardner, Wendi (1996). Who is this "we"? Levels of collective identity and self representations. *Journal of Personality and Social Psychology, 71*, 83–93.

Brissette, Ian; Scheier, Michael F.; & Carver, Charles S. (2002). The role of optimism in social network development, coping, and psychological adjustment during a life transition. *Journal of Personality and Social Psychology, 82*, 102–111.

Broadway, James M., & Engle, Randall W. (2011). Lapsed attention to elapsed time? Individual differences in working memory capacity and temporal reproduction. *Acta Psychologica, 137*, 115–126.

Brockner, Joel, & Rubin, Jeffrey Z. (1985). *Entrapment in escalating conflicts: A social psychological analysis.* New York: Springer-Verlag.

Broks, Paul (2004). *Into the silent land: Travels in neuropsychology.* New York: Grove Press.

Brooks-Gunn, Jeanne (1986). Differentiating premenstrual symptoms and syndromes. *Psychosomatic Medicine, 48*, 385–387.

Brosnan, Sarah F., & de Waal, Frans B. M. (2003). Monkeys reject unequal pay. *Nature, 425*, 297–299.

Brown, Alan S. (2004). *The déjà vu experience: Essays in cognitive psychology.* New York: Psychology Press.

Brown, Alan S. (2012). *The tip of the tongue state.* New York: Psychology Press.

Brown, Alan S.; Begg, M. D.; Gravenstein, S.; et al. (2004). Serologic evidence of prenatal influenza in the etiology of schizophrenia. *Archives of General Psychiatry, 61*, 774–780.

Brown, D.; Scheflin, A. W.; & Whitfield, C. L. (1999). Recovered memories: The current weight of the evidence in science and in the courts. *Journal of Psychiatry and Law, 27*, 5–156.

Brown, G. W. & Harris, T. O. (2008). Depression and the serotonin transporter 5-HTTLPR polymorphism: A review and a hypothesis concerning gene-environment interaction. *Journal of Affective Disorders, 111*, 1–12.

Brown, Gillian R.; Laland, Keven N.; & Mulder, Monique Borgerhoff (2009). Bateman's principles and human sex roles. *Trends in Ecology & Evolution, 24*, 297–304.

Brown, Gregory K.; Ten Have, Thomas; Henriques, Gregg R.; et al. (2005). Cognitive therapy for the prevention of suicide attempts. *Journal of the American Medical Association, 294*, 563–570.

Brown, Jonathon D. (2012). Understanding the better than average effect: Motives (still) matter. *Personality and Social Psychology Bulletin, 38*, 209–219.

Brown, Roger (1986). *Social psychology* (2nd ed.). New York: Free Press.

Brown, Roger, & McNeill, David (1966). The "tip of the tongue" phenomenon. *Journal of Verbal Learning and Verbal Behavior, 5*, 325–337.

Brown, Roger, & Kulik, James (1977). Flashbulb memories. *Cognition, 5*, 73–99.

Brown, Ryan P., & Josephs, Robert A. (1999). A burden of proof: Stereotype relevance and gender differences in math performance. *Journal of Personality and Social Psychology, 76*, 246–257.

Brown, Ryan P.; Osterman, Lindsey L.; & Barnes, Collin D. (2009). School violence and the culture of honor. *Psychological Science, 20*, 1400–1405.

Brown, Stephanie L.; Nesse, Randolph M.; Vinokur, Amiram D.; & Smith, Dylan M. (2003). Providing social support may be more beneficial than receiving it: Results from a prospective study of mortality. *Psychological Science, 14*, 320–327.

Browning, James R.; Hatfield, Elaine; Kessler, Debra; & Levine, Tim (2000). Sexual motives, gender, and sexual behavior. *Archives of Sexual Behavior, 29*, 135–153.

Bruck, Maggie (2003). Effects of suggestion on the reliability and credibility of children's reports. Invited address at the annual meeting of the American Psychological Society, Atlanta.

Bruck, Maggie; Ceci, Stephen J.; Francoeur, E.; & Renick, A. (1995). Anatomically detailed dolls do not facilitate preschoolers' reports of a pediatric examination involving genital touching. *Journal of Experimental Psychology: Applied, 1*, 95–109.

Bruder, Carl E. G. E.; Piotrowski, Arkadjusz; Gijsbers, Antoinet A.; et al. (2008). Phenotypically concordant and discordant monozygotic twins display different DNA copy-number-variation profiles. *American Journal of Human Genetics, 82*, 763–771.

Bruner, Jerome S. (1990). *Acts of meaning.* Cambridge, MA: Harvard University Press.

Brunoni, Andre R.; Valiengo, Leandro; Baccaro, Alessandra; et al. (2013). The sertraline vs electrical current therapy for treating depression clinical study: Results from a factorial, randomized, controlled trial. *Journal of the American Medical Association Psychiatry, 70,* 383–391.

Bryant, Gregory A., & Barrett, H. Clark (2007). Recognizing intentions in infant-directed speech. *Psychological Science, 18,* 746–751.

Buchanan, Tony W. (2007). Retrieval of emotional memories. *Psychological Bulletin, 133,* 761–779.

Buck, Linda, & Axel, Richard (1991). A novel multigene family may encode odorant receptors: A molecular basis for odor recognition. *Cell, 65,* 175–187.

Buhrmester, Michael; Kwang, Tracy; & Gosling, Samuel D. (2011). Amazon's Mechanical Turk: A new source of inexpensive, yet high-quality, data? *Perspectives on Psychological Science.* doi: 10.1177/1745691610393980.

Bukowski, William M. (2001). Friendship and the worlds of childhood. In D. W. Nangle & C. A. Erdley (Eds.), The role of friendship in psychological adjustment. *New directions for child and adolescent development, No. 91.* San Francisco, CA: Jossey-Bass.

Burgaleta, Miguel; Head, Kevin; Álvarez-Linera, Juan; Martínez, Kenia; et al. (2012). Sex differences in brain volume are related to specific skills, not to general intelligence. *Intelligence, 40,* 60–68.

Burger, Jerry M. (2009). Replicating Milgram: Would people still obey today? *American Psychologist, 64,* 1–11.

Burke, Brian L.; Arkowitz, Hal; & Menchola, Marisa (2003). The efficacy of motivational interviewing: A meta-analysis of controlled clinical trials. *Journal of Consulting and Clinical Psychology, 71,* 843–861.

Burnham, Denis; Kitamura, Christine; & Vollmer-Conna, Uté (2002). What's new, pussycat? On talking to babies and animals. *Science, 296,* 1435.

Bushman, Brad J., & Anderson, Craig A. (2009). Comfortably numb: Desensitizing effects of violent media on helping others. *Psychological Science, 20,* 273–277.

Bushman, Brad J.; Bonacci, Angelica M.; Pedersen, William C.; et al. (2005). Chewing on it can chew you up: Effects of rumination on triggered displaced aggression. *Journal of Personality and Social Psychology, 88,* 969–983.

Bushman, Brad; Bonacci, Angelica M.; van Dijk, Mirjam; & Baumeister, Roy F. (2003). Narcissism, sexual refusal, and aggression: Testing a narcissistic reactance model of sexual coercion. *Journal of Personality and Social Psychology, 84,* 1027–1040.

Bushman, Brad J.; Ridge, Robert D.; Das, Enny; et al. (2007). When God sanctions killing. *Psychological Science, 18,* 204–207.

Buss, David M. (1994). *The evolution of desire: Strategies of human mating.* New York: Basic.

Buss, David M. (1995). Evolutionary psychology: A new paradigm for psychological science. *Psychological Inquiry, 6,* 1–30.

Buss, David M., & Schmitt, David P. (2011). Evolutionary psychology and feminism. *Sex Roles, 64,* 768–787.

Buster, J. E.; Kingsberg, S. A.; Aguirre, O.; et al. (2005). Testosterone patch for low sexual desire in surgically menopausal women: a randomized trial. *Obstetrics and Gynecology, 105* (Pt 1), 944–952.

Butcher, James N., & Perry, Julia N. (2008). *Personality assessment in treatment planning: Use of the MMPI-2 and BTPI.* New York: Oxford University Press.

Butcher, James N.; Lim, Jeeyoung; & Nezami, Elahe (1998). Objective study of abnormal personality in cross-cultural settings: The MMPI-2. *Journal of Cross-Cultural Psychology, 29,* 189–211.

Butler, S.; Chalder, T.; Ron, M.; et al. (1991). Cognitive behaviour therapy in chronic fatigue syndrome. *Journal of Neurology, Neurosurgery & Psychiatry, 54,* 153–158.

Button, T. M. M.; Thapar, A.; & McGuffin, P. (2005). Relationship between antisocial behaviour, attention-deficit hyperactivity disorder and maternal prenatal smoking. *British Journal of Psychiatry, 187,* 155–160.

Byers-Heinlein, Krista; Burns, Tracey C.; & Werker, Janet F. (2010). The roots of bilingualism in newborns. *Psychological Science, 21,* 343–348.

Cabiya, Jose J.; Lucio, Emilia; Chavira, Denise A.; et al. (2000). MMPI-2 scores of Puerto Rican, Mexican, and U.S. Latino college students: A research note. *Psychological Reports, 87,* 266–268.

Cacioppo, J. T.; Berntson, G. G.; Lorig, Tyler S.; et al. (2003). Just because you're imaging the brain doesn't mean you can stop using your head: A primer and set of first principles. *Journal of Personality and Social Psychology, 85,* 650–661.

Cadinu, Mara; Maass, Anne; Rosabianca, Alessandra; & Kiesner, Jeff (2005). Why do women underperform under stereotype threat? Evidence for the role of negative thinking. *Psychological Science, 16,* 472–578.

Cahill, Larry (2005, May). His brain, her brain. *Scientific American, 292,* 40–47.

Cahill, Larry; Prins, Bruce; Weber, Michael; & McGaugh, James L. (1994). β-adrenergic activation and memory for emotional events. *Nature, 371,* 702–704.

Cahill, Larry; Uncapher, Melina; Kilpatrick, Lisa; et al. (2004). Sex-Related hemispheric lateralization of amygdala function in emotionally influenced memory: An FMRI investigation. *Learning & Memory, 11,* 261–266.

Callaghan, Glenn M.; Chacon, Cynthia; Coles, Cameron; et al. (2009). An empirical evaluation of the diagnostic criteria for premenstrual dysphoric disorder: Problems with sex specificity and validity. *Women & Therapy, 32,* 1–21.

Calder, A. J.; Keane, J.; Manes, F.; Antoun, N.; & Young, A. W. (2000). Impaired recognition and experience of disgust following brain injury. *Nature Neuroscience, 3,* 1077–1078.

Camerer, Colin F. (2003). Strategizing in the brain. *Science, 300,* 1673–1675.

Cameron, Judy; Banko, Katherine M.; & Pierce, W. David (2001). Pervasive negative effects of rewards on intrinsic motivation: The myth continues. *Behavior Analyst, 24,* 1–44.

Campbell, Benjamin C. (2011). Adrenarche and middle childhood. *Human Nature, 22,* 327–349.

Campbell, Benjamin C.; Pope, Harrison G.; & Filiault, Shaun (2005). Body image among Ariaal men from Northern Kenya. *Journal of Cross-Cultural Psychology, 36,* 371–379.

Campbell, Frances A., & Ramey, Craig T. (1995). Cognitive and school outcomes for high risk students at middle adolescence: Positive effects of early intervention. *American Educational Research Journal, 32,* 743–772.

Campbell, Joseph (1949/1968). *The hero with 1,000 faces* (2nd ed.). Princeton, NJ: Princeton University Press.

Canetto, Silvia S. (1992). Suicide attempts and substance abuse: Similarities and differences. *Journal of Psychology, 125,* 605–620.

Cannon, Tyrone D.; Huttunen, Matti O.; Loennqvist, Jouko; et al. (2000). The inheritance of neuropsychological dysfunction in twins discordant for schizophrenia. *American Journal of Human Genetics, 67,* 369–382.

Cannon, Walter B. (1929). *Bodily changes in pain, hunger, fear and rage* (2nd ed.). New York: Appleton.

Capaldi, Deborah M.; Pears, Katherine C.; Patterson, Gerald R.; & Owen, Lee D. (2003). Continuity of parenting practices across generations in an at-risk sample: A prospective comparison of direct and mediated associations. *Journal of Abnormal Child Psychology, 31,* 127–142.

Carnagey, Nicholas L., & Anderson, Craig A. (2005). The effects of reward and punishment in violent video games on aggressive affect, cognition, and behavior. *Psychological Science, 16,* 882–889.

Carskadon, Mary A.; Mitler, Merrill M.; & Dement, William C. (1974). A comparison of insomniacs and normals: Total sleep time and sleep latency. *Sleep Research, 3,* 130 [Abstract].

Carver, Charles S., & Baird, Eryn (1998). The American dream revisited: Is it what you want or why you want it that matters? *Psychological Science, 9,* 289–292.

Carver, Charles S., & Scheier, M. F. (2002). Optimism. In C. R. Snyder & S. J. Lopes (Eds.), *The handbook of positive psychology.* New York: Oxford University Press.

Cartwright, Rosalind (2010). *The twenty-four hour mind: The role of sleep and dreaming in our emotional lives.* New York: Oxford University Press.

Cartwright, Rosalind D.; Young, Michael A.; Mercer, Patricia; & Bears, Michael (1998). Role of REM sleep and dream variables in the prediction of remission from depression. *Psychiatry Research, 80,* 249–255.

Carver, Charles S., & Harmon-Jones, Eddie (2009). Anger is an approach-related affect: Evidence and implications. *Psychological Bulletin, 135,* 183–204.

Casey, B. J., & Caudle, Kristina (2013). The teenage brain: Self control. *Current Directions in Psychological Science, 22,* 82–87.

Casey, B. J.; Somerville, Leah H.; Gotlib, Ian H.; et al. (2011). Behavioral and neural correlates of delay of gratification 40 years later. *Proceedings of the National Academy of Science, 108,* 14998–15003.

Caspi, Avshalom (2000). The child is father of the man: Personality continuities from childhood to adulthood. *Journal of Personality and Social Psychology, 78,* 158–172.

Caspi, Avshalom, & Moffitt, Terrie E. (1991). Individual differences are accentuated during periods of social change: The sample case of girls at puberty. *Journal of Personality and Social Psychology, 61,* 157–168.

Cassin, Stephanie E.; von Ranson, Kristin M.; Heng, Kenneth; et al. (2008). Adapted motivational interviewing for women with binge eating disorder: A randomized controlled trial. *Psychology of Addictive Behaviors, 22,* 417–425.

Caspi, Avshalom; McClay, Joseph; Moffitt, Terrie E.; et al. (2002). Role of genotype in the cycle of violence in maltreated children. *Science, 297,* 851–857.

Cejka, Mary Ann, & Eagly, Alice H. (1999). Gender-stereotypic images of occupations correspond to the sex segregation of employment. *Personality and Social Psychology Bulletin, 25,* 413–423.

Ceci, Stephen J., & Bruck, Maggie (1995). *Jeopardy in the courtroom: A scientific analysis of children's testimony.* Washington, DC: American Psychological Association.

Centers for Disease Control and Prevention (2013, May 13). Attention deficit/Hyperactivity disorder (ADHD). http://www.cdc.gov/ncbddd/adhd/timeline.html.

Cermak, Laird S., & Craik, Fergus I. M. (Eds.) (1979). *Levels of processing in human memory.* Hillsdale, NJ: Erlbaum.

Cervone, Daniel, & Shoda, Yuichi (1999). Beyond traits in the study of personality coherence. *Current Directions in Psychological Science, 8,* 27–32.

Chabris, Christopher F.; Hebert, Benjamin M.; Benjamin, Daniel J.; et al. (2012). Most reported genetic associations with general intelligence are probably false positives. *Psychological Science, 23,* 1314–1323.

Chambless, Dianne L., & Ollendick, T. H. (2001). Empirically supported psychological interventions: Controversies and evidence. *Annual Review of Psychology, 52,* 685–716.

Chamberlain, Samuel R.; Menzies, Lara; Hampshire, Adam; et al. (2008). Orbitofrontal dysfunction in patients with obsessive-compulsive disorder and their unaffected relatives. *Science, 321,* 421–422.

Chan, Brenda L.; Witt, Richard; Charrow, Alexandra P.; et al. (2007). Mirror therapy for phantom limb pain [correspondence]. *New England Journal of Medicine, 357,* 2206–2207.

Chang, Anne-Marie; Buch, Alison M.; Bradstreet, Dayna S.; et al. (2011). Human diurnal preference and circadian rhythmicity are not associated with the CLOCK 3111C/T gene polymorphism. *Biological Rhythms, 26,* 276–279.

Chang, Luye; Connelly, Brian S.; & Geeza, Alexis A. (2012). Separating method factors and higher order traits of the big five: A meta-analytic multitrait–multimethod approach. *Journal of Personality and Social Psychology, 102,* 408–426.

Chaplin, Tara M., & Aldao, Amelia (2013). Gender differences in emotion expression in children: A meta-analytic review. *Psychological Bulletin, 139,* 735–765.

Charles, Susan T., & Carstensen, Laura L. (2004). A life-span view of emotional functioning in adulthood and old age. In P. Costa (Ed.), *Recent advances in psychology and aging* (Vol. 15). Amsterdam: Elsevier.

Chaves, J. F. (1989). Hypnotic control of clinical pain. In N. P. Spanos & J. F. Chaves (Eds.), *Hypnosis: The cognitive-behavioral perspective.* Buffalo, NY: Prometheus Books.

Chebat, Daniel-Robert; Schneider, Fabian C.; Kupers, Ron; & Ptito, Maurice (2011). Navigation with a sensory substitution device in congenitally blind individuals. *Neuroreport, 22,* 342–347.

Chen, Zhansheng; Williams, Kipling D.; Fitness, Julie; & Newton, Nicola C. (2008). When hurt will not heal. *Psychological Science, 19,* 789–795.

Cheney, Dorothy L., & Seyfarth, Robert M. (1985). Vervet monkey alarm calls: Manipulation through shared information? *Behavior, 94,* 150–166.

Cheng, Cecilia; Cheung, Shu-fai; Chio, Jasmine Hin-man; & Chan, Man-pui Sally (2012). Cultural meaning of perceived control: A meta-analysis of locus of control and psychological symptoms across 18 cultural regions. *Psychological Bulletin, 139,* 152–188.

Cheung, Benjamin Y.; Chudek, Maciej; & Heine, Steven J. (2011). Evidence for a sensitive period for acculturation: Younger immigrants report acculturating at a faster rate. *Psychological Science, 22,* 147–152.

Cheung, Fanny M.; van de Vijver, Fons J. R.; & Leong, Frederick T. L. (2011). Toward a new approach to the study of personality in culture. *American Psychologist, 66,* 593–603.

Cialdini, Robert B. (2009). We have to break up. *Perspectives on Psychological Science, 4,* 5–6.

Chipuer, Heather M.; Rovine, Michael J.; & Plomin, Robert (1990). LISREL modeling: Genetic and environmental influences on IQ revisited. *Intelligence, 14,* 11–29.

Choi, Incheol; Dalal, Reeshad; Kim-Prieto, Chu; & Park, Hyekyung (2003). Culture and judgment of causal relevance. *Journal of Personality and Social Psychology, 84,* 46–59.

Chomsky, Noam (1957). *Syntactic structures.* The Hague, Netherlands: Mouton.

Chomsky, Noam (1980). Initial states and steady states. In M. Piatelli-Palmerini (Ed.), *Language and learning: The debate between Jean Piaget and Noam Chomsky.* Cambridge, MA: Harvard University Press.

Chrisler, Joan C. (2000). PMS as a culture-bound syndrome. In J. C. Chrisler, C. Golden, & P. D. Rozee (Eds.), *Lectures on the psychology of women* (2nd ed.). New York: McGraw-Hill.

Chrisler, Joan C., & Caplan, Paula (2002). The strange case of Dr. Jekyll and Ms. Hyde: How PMS became a cultural phenomenon and psychiatric disorder. *Annual Review of Sex Research, 13,* 274–306.

Christakis, Dimitri A.; Zimmerman, Frederick J.; DiGiuseppe, David L.; & McCarty, Carolyn A. (2004). Early television exposure and subsequent attentional problems in children. *Pediatrics, 113,* 708–713.

Christopher, Andrew N., & Wojda, Mark R. (2008). Social dominance orientation, right-wing authoritarianism, sexism, and prejudice toward women in the workforce. *Psychology of Women Quarterly, 32,* 65–73.

Church, A. Timothy, & Lonner, Walter J. (1998). The cross-cultural perspective in the study of personality: Rationale and current research. *Journal of Cross-Cultural Psychology, 29,* 32–62.

Claidière, Nicolas, & Whiten, Andrew (2012). Integrating the study of conformity and culture in humans and nonhuman animals. *Psychological Bulletin 138,* 126–145.

Clark, Eve V., & Estigarribia, Bruno (2011). Using speech and gesture to inform young children about unfamiliar word meanings. *Gesture, 11,* 1–23.

Clarke, H. F.; Dalley, J. W.; Crofts, H. S.; et al. (2004). Cognitive inflexibility after prefrontal serotonin depletion. *Science, 304,* 878–880.

Chiarello, Christine; Welcome, Suzanne E.; Halderman, Laura K.; et al. (2009). A large-scale investigation of lateralization in cortical anatomy and word reading: Are there sex differences? *Neuropsychology, 23,* 210–222.

Chida, Yoichi, & Hamer, Mark (2008). Chronic psychosocial factors and acute physiological responses to laboratory-induced stress in healthy populations: A quantitative review of 30 years of investigations. *Psychological Bulletin, 134,* 829–885.

Christensen, Andrew, & Jacobson, Neil S. (2000). *Reconcilable differences.* New York: Guilford.

Cinque, Guglielmo (1999). *Adverbs and functional heads: A cross-linguistic approach.* New York: Oxford University Press.

Cioffi, Frank (1998). *Freud and the question of pseudoscience.* Chicago, IL: Open Court.

Clancy, Susan A. (2005). *Abducted: How people come to believe they were kidnapped by aliens.* Cambridge, MA: Harvard University Press.

Clark, Lee Anna, & Watson, David (2008). Temperament: An organizing paradigm for trait psychology. In O. P. John, R.W. Robbins, & L. A. Pervin (Eds.), *Handbook of personality: Theory and research* (3rd ed.). New York: Guilford.

Clarke, Peter, & Evans, Susan H. (1998). *Surviving modern medicine.* Rutgers, NJ: Rutgers University Press.

Cleary, Anne M. (2008). Recognition memory, familiarity, and déjà vu experiences. *Current Directions in Psychological Science, 17,* 353–357.

Cleckley, Hervey (1976). *The mask of sanity* (5th ed.). St. Louis, MO: Mosby.

Cloninger, C. Robert (1990). *The genetics and biology of alcoholism.* Cold Springs Harbor, ME: Cold Springs Harbor Press.

Coan, James A.; Schaefer, Hillary; & Davidson, Richard J. (2006). Lending a hand: Social regulation of the neural response to threat. *Psychological Science, 17,* 1032–1039.

Coats, Erik J.; Janoff-Bulman, Ronnie; & Alpert, Nancy (1996). Approach versus avoidance goals: Differences in self-evaluation and well-being. *Personality and Social Psychology Bulletin, 22*, 1057–1067.

Coe, Christopher L., & Lubach, Gabriele R. (2008). Fetal programming: Prenatal origins of health and illness. *Current Directions in Psychological Science, 17*, 36–41.

Coelho, Helen F.; Canter, Peter H.; & Ernst, Edzard (2007). Mindfulness based cognitive therapy: Evaluating current evidence and informing future research. *Journal of Consulting and Clinical Psychology, 75*, 1000–1005.

Cohen, David B. (1999). *Stranger in the nest: Do parents really shape their child's personality, intelligence, or character?* New York: Wiley.

Cohen, Dov (1998). Culture, social organization, and patterns of violence. *Journal of Personality and Social Psychology, 75*, 408–419.

Cohen, Dov; Nisbett, Richard E.; Bowdle, Brian F.; & Schwarz, Norbert (1996). Insult, aggression, and the Southern culture of honor: An "experimental ethnography." *Journal of Personality and Social Psychology, 70*, 945–960.

Cohen, Florette; Jussim, Lee; Harber, Kent D.; & Bhasin, Gautam (2009). Modern anti-Semitism and anti-Israeli attitudes. *Journal of Personality and Social Psychology, 97*, 290–306.

Cohen Kadosh, Roi; Henik, Avishai; Catena, Andres; et al. (2009). Induced cross-modal synaesthetic experience without abnormal neuronal connections. *Psychological Science, 20*, 258–265.

Cohen, Sheldon; Doyle, William J.; Turner, Ronald; et al. (2003). Sociability and susceptibility to the common cold. *Psychological Science, 14*, 389–395.

Cohen, Sheldon; Frank, Ellen; Doyle, William J.; et al. (1998). Types of stressors that increase susceptibility to the common cold in healthy adults. *Health Psychology, 17*, 214–223.

Cohen, Sheldon; Tyrrell, David A.; & Smith, Andrew P. (1993). Negative life events, perceived stress, negative affect, and susceptibility to the common cold. *Journal of Personality and Social Psychology, 64*, 131–140.

Colcombe, Stanley, & Kramer, Arthur F. (2003). Fitness effects on the cognitive function of older adults: A meta-analytic study. *Psychological Science, 14*, 125–130.

Cole, Michael, & Scribner, Sylvia (1974). *Culture and thought.* New York: Wiley.

Collaer, Marcia L., & Hines, Melissa (1995). Human behavioral sex differences: A role for gonadal hormones during early development? *Psychological Bulletin, 118*, 55–107.

Collinger, Jennifer L.; Wodlinger, Brian; Downey, John E.; et al. (2013). Higher-performance neuroprosthetic control by an individual with tetraplegia. *The Lancet, 381*, 557–564.

Collins, Allan M., & Loftus, Elizabeth F. (1975). A spreading-activation theory of semantic processing. *Psychological Review, 82*, 407–428.

Collins, Barry E., & Brief, Diana E. (1995). Using person-perception vignette methodologies to uncover the symbolic meanings of teacher behaviors in the Milgram paradigm. *Journal of Social Issues, 51*, 89–106.

Collins, Rebecca L. (1996). For better or worse: The impact of upward social comparison on self-evaluations. *Psychological Bulletin, 119*, 51–69.

Comas-Díaz, Lillian (2006). Latino healing: The integration of ethnic psychology into psychotherapy. *Psychotherapy: Theory, Research, Practice, Training, 43*, 436–453

Comuzzie, Anthony G., & Allison, David B. (1998). The search for human obesity genes. *Science, 280*, 1374–1377.

Conley, Terri D.; Moors, Amy C.; Matsick, Jes L.; et al. (2011). Women, men, and the bedroom: Methodological and conceptual insights that narrow, reframe, and eliminate gender differences in sexuality. *Current Directions in Psychological Science, 20*, 296–300.

Conroy, John (2000). *Unspeakable acts, ordinary people: The dynamics of torture.* New York: Knopf.

Cook, Joan M.; Biyanova, Tatyana; & Coyne, James C. (2009). Influential psychotherapy figures, authors, and books: An Internet survey of over 2,000 psychotherapists. *Psychotherapy: Theory, Research, Practice, Training, 46*, 42–51.

Coontz, Stephanie (2005). *Marriage, a history: How love conquered marriage.* New York: Penguin.

Cooper, M. Lynne; Frone, Michael R.; Russell, Marcia; & Mudar, Pamela (1995). Drinking to regulate positive and negative emotions: A motivational model of alcohol use. *Journal of Personality and Social Psychology, 69*, 990–1005.

Cooper, M. Lynne; Shapiro, Cheryl M.; & Powers, Anne M. (1998). Motivations for sex and risky sexual behavior among adolescents and young adults: A functional perspective. *Journal of Personality and Social Psychology, 75*, 1528–1558.

Corkin, Suzanne (1984). Lasting consequences of bilateral medial temporal lobectomy: Clinical course and experimental findings in H. M. *Seminars in Neurology, 4*, 249–259.

Corkin, Suzanne (2013). *Permanent past tense: The unforgettable life of the amnesiac patient, H. M.* New York: Basic.

Corkin, Suzanne; Amaral, David G.; Gonzalez, R. Gilberto; et al. (1997). H. M.'s medial temporal lobe lesion: Findings from magnetic resonance imaging. *Journal of Neuroscience, 17*, 3964–3979.

Corriveau, Kathleen H.; Fusaro, Maria; & Harris, Paul L. (2009). Going with the flow: Preschoolers prefer nondissenters as informants. *Psychological Science, 20*, 372–377.

Cosgrove, Lisa (2013, February 22). On the road to nowhere: Using the framework of institutional corruption to understand bias in diagnostic and treatment guidelines in psychiatry. Invited address at the conference "Selling Sickness," Washington DC.

Costa, Paul T., Jr.; McCrae, Robert R.; Martin, Thomas A.; et al. (1999). Personality development from adolescence through adulthood: Further crosscultural comparisons of age differences. In V. J. Molfese & D. Molfese (Eds.), *Temperament and personality development across the life span.* Hillsdale, NJ: Erlbaum.

Cota-Robles, Sonia; Neiss, Michelle; & Rowe, David C. (2002). The role of puberty in violent and nonviolent delinquency among Anglo American, Mexican American, and African American boys. *Journal of Adolescent Research, 17*, 364–376.

Council, J. R.; Kirsch, Irving; & Grant, D. L. (1996). Imagination, expectancy and hypnotic responding. In R. G. Kunzendorf, N. K. Spanos, & B. J. Wallace (Eds.), *Hypnosis and imagination.* Amityville, NY: Baywood.

Courage, Mary L., & Howe, Mark L. (2002). From infant to child: The dynamics of cognitive change in the second year of life. *Psychological Bulletin, 128*, 250–277.

Courtney, Kelly E., & Polich, John (2009). Binge drinking in young adults: Data, definitions, and determinants. *Psychological Bulletin, 135*, 142–156.

Cowan, Nelson (2010). The magical mystery four: How is working memory capacity limited, and why? *Current Directions in Psychological Science, 19*, 51–57.

Cowan, Nelson; Morey, Candice C.; Chen, Zhijian; et al. (2008). Theory and measurement of working memory capacity limits. In B. H. Ross (Ed.), *The psychology of learning and motivation.* San Diego: Elsevier.

Cowen, Emory L.; Wyman, Peter A.; Work, William C.; & Parker, Gayle R. (1990). The Rochester Child Resilience Project (RCRP): Overview and summary of first year findings. *Development and Psychopathology, 2*, 193–212.

Cox, Martha J., & Paley, Blair (2003). Understanding families as systems. *Current Directions in Psychological Science, 12*, 193–196.

Cox, W. Michael, and Alm, Richard (2005, February 28). Scientists are made, not born. *New York Times*, op-ed page (online).

Coyne, James C.; Thombs, Brett D.; Stefanek, Michael; & Palmer, Steven C. (2009). Time to let go of the illusion that psychotherapy extends the survival of cancer patients. *Psychological Bulletin, 135*, 179–182.

Cozolino, Louis (2006). *The neuroscience of human relationships: Attachment and the developing social brain.* New York: Norton.

Craik, Fergus I. M., & Lockhart, Robert (1972). Levels of processing: A framework for memory research. *Journal of Verbal Learning and Verbal Behavior, 11*, 671–684.

Craik, Fergus I. M., & Tulving, Endel (1975). Depth of processing and the retention of words in episodic memory. *Journal of Experimental Psychology: General, 104*, 268–294.

Crair, Michael C.; Gillespie, Deda C.; & Stryker, Michael P. (1998). The role of visual experience in the development of columns in cat visual cortex. *Science, 279*, 566–570.

Cramer, Phebe (2000). Defense mechanisms in psychology today: Further processes for adaptation. *American Psychologist, 55*, 637–646.

Crews, Frederick (Ed.) (1998). *Unauthorized Freud: Doubters confront a legend.* New York: Viking.

Critchlow, Barbara (1986). The powers of John Barleycorn: Beliefs about the effects of alcohol on social behavior. *American Psychologist, 41*, 751–764.

Crits-Christoph, Paul; Wilson, G. Terence; & Hollon, Steven D. (2005). Empirically supported psychotherapies: Comment on Westen, Novotny, and Thompson-Brenner (2004). *Psychological Bulletin, 131,* 412–417.

Critser, Greg (2002). *Supersize.* New York: Houghton-Mifflin.

Crombag, Hans S., & Robinson, Terry E. (2004). Drugs, environment, brain, and behavior. *Current Directions in Psychological Science, 13,* 107–111.

Cross-Disorder Group of the Psychiatric Genomics Consortium (2013). Identification of risk loci with shared effects on five major psychiatric disorders: a genome-wide analysis. *Lancet, 381,* 1371–1379.

Crowell, Sheila E.; Beauchaine, Theodore P.; & Linehan, Marsha M. (2009). A biosocial developmental model of borderline personality: Elaborating and extending Linehan's theory. *Psychological Bulletin, 135,* 495–510.

Cruz, Vitor Tedim; Nunes, Belina; Reis, Ana Mafalda; & Pereira, Jorge Resende (2005). Cortical remapping in amputees and dysmelic patients: A functional MRI study. *NeuroRehabilitation, 18,* 299–305.

Cumming, Geoff (2012). *Understanding the new statistics: Effect sizes, confidence intervals, and meta-analysis.* New York: Routledge.

Cumming, Geoff; Fidler, Fiona; Leonard, Martine; et al. (2007). Statistical reform in psychology: Is anything changing? *Psychological Science, 18,* 230–232.

Cummings, E. Mark, & Davies, Patrick T. (2011). *Marital conflict and children: An emotional security perspective.* New York: Guilford.

Cunningham, William A., & Brosch, Tobias (2012). Motivational salience: Amygdala tuning from traits, needs, values, and goals. *Current Directions in Psychological Science, 21,* 54–59.

Cummings, Nicholas A., & O'Donohue, William T. (2008). *Eleven blunders that cripple psychotherapy in America.* New York: Routledge/Taylor & Francis.

Currie, Janet; DellaVigna, Stefano; Moretti, Enrico; & Pathania, Vikram (2010). The effect of fast food restaurants on obesity and weight gain. *American Economic Journal: Economic Policy, 2,* 32–63.

Curtiss, Susan (1977). *Genie: A psycholinguistic study of a modern-day "wild child."* New York: Academic Press.

Curtiss, Susan (1982). Developmental dissociations of language and cognition. In L. Obler & D. Fein (Eds.), *Exceptional language and linguistics.* New York: Academic Press.

Cypess, A. M.; Lehman, S.; Williams, G.; et al. (2009). Identification and importance of brown adipose tissue in adult humans. *New England Journal of Medicine, 360,* 1509–1517.

D'Antonio, Michael (2004, May 2). How we think. *Los Angeles Times Magazine,* 18–20, 30–32.

Dadds, Mark R.; Bovbjerg, Dana H.; Redd, William H.; & Cutmore, Tim R. H. (1997). Imagery in human classical conditioning. *Psychological Bulletin, 122,* 89–103.

Daly, Martin, & Wilson, Margo (1983). *Sex, evolution, and behavior* (2nd ed.). Belmont, CA: Wadsworth.

Daley, Tamara C.; Whaley, Shannon E.; Sigman, Marian D.; et al. (2003). IQ on the rise: The Flynn Effect in rural Kenyan children. *Psychological Science, 14,* 215–219.

Dalton, K. S.; Morris, D. L.; Delanoy, D. I.; et al. (1996). Security measures in an automated ganzfeld system. *Journal of Parapsychology, 60,* 129–147.

Damasio, Antonio R. (1994). *Descartes' error: Emotion, reason, and the human brain.* New York: Grosset/Putnam.

Damasio, Antonio R. (2003). *Looking for Spinoza: Joy, sorrow, and the feeling brain.* San Diego: Harcourt.

Damasio, Hanna; Grabowski, Thomas J.; Frank, Randall; et al. (1994). The return of Phineas Gage: Clues about the brain from the skull of a famous patient. *Science, 264,* 1102–1105.

Damon, William, (1995). *Greater expectations.* New York: Free Press.

Darley, John M. (1995). Constructive and destructive obedience: A taxonomy of principal agent relationships. In A. G. Miller, B. E. Collins, & D. E. Brief (Eds.), Perspectives on obedience to authority: The legacy of the Milgram experiments. *Journal of Social Issues, 51(3),* 125–154.

Darley, John M., & Latane, Bibb (1968). Bystander intervention in emergencies: Diffusion of responsibility. *Journal of Personality and Social Psychology, 8,* 377–383.

Darwin, Charles (1874). *The descent of man and selection in relation to sex* (2nd ed.). New York: Hurst.

Daum, Irene, & Schugens, Markus M. (1996). On the cerebellum and classical conditioning. *Psychological Science, 5,* 58–61.

Davelaar, Eddy J.; Goshen-Gottstein, Yonatan; Ashkenazi, Amir; et al. (2004). The demise of short-term memory revisited: Empirical and computational investigations of recency effects. *Psychological Review, 112,* 3–42.

Davis, Christopher G.; Nolen-Hoeksema, Susan; & Larson, Judith (1998). Making sense of loss and benefiting from the experience: Two construals of meaning. *Journal of Personality and Social Psychology, 75,* 561–574.

Davis, Michael; Myers, Karyn M.; Ressler, Kerry J.; & Rothbaum, Barbara O. (2005). Facilitation of extinction of conditioning fear by D-cycloserine. *Current Directions in Psychological Science, 14,* 214–219.

Davison, Gerald C. (1976). Homosexuality: The ethical challenge. *Journal of Consulting and Clinical Psychology, 44,* 157–162.

Dawes, Robyn M. (1994). *House of cards: Psychology and psychotherapy built on myth.* New York: Free Press.

Dawson, Neal V.; Arkes, Hal R.; Siciliano, C.; et al. (1988). Hindsight bias: An impediment to accurate probability estimation in clinicopathologic conferences. *Medical Decision Making, 8(4),* 259–264.

Davidson, Richard J.; Kabat-Zinn, J.; Schumacher, J.; et al. (2003). Alterations in brain and immune function produced by mindfulness meditation. *Psychosomatic Medicine, 65,* 564–570.

Davis, Deborah (2010). Lies, damned lies, and the path from police interrogation to wrongful conviction. In M. H. Gonzales, C. Tavris, & J. Aronson (Eds.), *The scientist and the humanist: A festschrift in honor of Elliot Aronson.* New York: Psychology Press.

Dean, Geoffrey (1992). The bottom line: Effect size. In B. Beyerstein & D. Beyerstein (Eds.), *The write stuff: Evaluations of graphology—The study of handwriting analysis.* Buffalo, NY: Prometheus Books.

de Araujo, Ivan E.; Oliveira-Maia, A.J.; Sotnikova, T.D.; et al. (2008). Food reward in the absence of taste receptor signaling. *Neuron, 57,* 930–941.

Deary, Ian J.; Weiss, Alexander; & Batty, G. David (2010). Intelligence, personality, and health outcomes. *Psychological Science in the Public Interest, 11,* 53–80.

Deci, Edward L., & Ryan, Richard M. (1985). *Intrinsic motivation and self-determination of human behavior.* New York: Plenum.

Deci, Edward L.; Koestner, Richard; & Ryan, Richard M. (1999). A meta-analytic review of experiments examining the effects of extrinsic rewards on intrinsic motivation. *Psychological Bulletin, 125,* 627–668.

De Dreu, Carsten K. W.; Greer, Lindred L.; Van Kleef, Gerben A.; et al. (2011). Oxytocin promotes human ethnocentrism. *Proceedings of the National Academy of Sciences, 108,* 1262–1266.

Deffenbacher, Jerry L.; Deffenbacher, David M.; Lynch, Rebekah S.; & Richards, Tracy L. (2003). Anger, aggression and risky behavior: A comparison of high and low anger drivers. *Behaviour Research and Therapy, 41,* 701–718.

De Houwer, Jan; Teige-Mocigemba, Sarah; Spruyt, Adriaan; & Moors, Agnes (2009). Implicit measures: A normative analysis and review. *Psychological Bulletin, 135,* 347–368.

Delton, Andrew W.; Krasnow, Max M.; Cosmides, Leda; & Tooby, John (2011). Evolution of direct reciprocity under uncertainty can explain human generosity in one-shot encounters. *Proceedings of the National Academy of Sciences, 108,* 13335–13340.

DeLoache, Judy S.; Chiong, Cynthia; Sherman, Kathleen; et al. (2010). Do babies learn from baby media? *Psychological Science, 21,* 1570–1574.

Dement, William (1978). *Some must watch while some must sleep.* New York: Norton.

Dement, William (1992). *The sleepwatchers.* Stanford, CA: Stanford Alumni Association.

Denning, Patt; Little, Jeannie; & Glickman, Adina (2004). *Over the influence: The harm reduction guide for managing drugs and alcohol.* New York: Guilford.

Denny, Dallas (Ed.) (1998). *Current concepts in transgender identity.* New York: Garland Press.

Denson, Thomas F.; Spanovic, Marija; & Miller, Norman (2009). Cognitive appraisals and emotions predict cortisol and immune responses: A meta-analysis of acute laboratory social stressors and emotion inductions. *Psychological Bulletin, 135,* 823–853.

DePaulo, Bella M. (1992). Nonverbal behavior and self-presentation. *Psychological Bulletin, 111,* 203–243.

DePaulo, Bella M.; Lindsay, James J.; Malone, Brian E.; et al. (2003). Cues to deception. *Psychological Bulletin, 129,* 74–118.

de Ridder, Denise T. D.; Lensvelt-Mulders, Gerty; Finkenauer, Catrin; et al. (2012). Taking stock of self-control: A meta-analysis of how trait self-control relates to a wide range of behaviors. *Personality and Social Psychology Review, 16,* 76–99

de Rivera, Joseph (1989). Comparing experiences across cultures: Shame and guilt in America and Japan. *Hiroshima Forum for Psychology, 14,* 13–20.

Desbonnet, L.; Waddington, J. L.; & O'Tuathaigh, C. M. (2009). Mutant models for genes associated with schizophrenia. *Biochemical Society Transactions, 37(Pt 1),* 308–312.

DeValois, Russell L., & DeValois, Karen K. (1975). Neural coding of color. In E. C. Carterette & M. P. Friedman (Eds.), *Handbook of perception* (Vol. 5). New York: Academic Press.

Devlin, B.; Daniels, Michael; & Roeder, Kathryn (1997). The heritability of IQ. *Nature, 388,* 468–471.

de Waal, Frans (2001). *The ape and the sushi master: Cultural reflections by a primatologist.* New York: Basic.

DeWall, C. Nathan, & Bushman, Brad J. (2011). Social acceptance and rejection: The sweet and the bitter. *Current Directions in Psychological Science, 20,* 256–260.

Diamond, Adele, & Amso, Dima (2008). Contributions of neuroscience to our understanding of cognitive development. *Current Directions in Psychological Science, 17,* 136–141.

Diamond, Lisa M. (2004). Emerging perspectives on distinctions between romantic love and sexual desire. *Current Directions in Psychological Science, 13,* 116–119.

Diamond, Lisa (2008). *Sexual fluidity: Understanding women's love and desire.* Cambridge, MA: Harvard University Press.

Diamond, Marian C. (1993, Winter–Spring). An optimistic view of the aging brain. *Generations, 17,* 31–33.

Dick, Danielle M. (2007). Identification of genes influencing a spectrum of externalizing psychopathology. *Current Directions in Psychological Science, 16,* 331–335.

Dick, Danielle M.; Aliev, Fazil; Wang, Jen C.; et al. (2008). A systematic single nucleotide polymorphism screen to fine-map alcohol dependence genes on chromosome 7 identifies association with a novel susceptibility gene ACN9. *Biological Psychiatry, 63,* 1047–1053.

Dien, Dora S. (1999). Chinese authority-directed orientation and Japanese peer-group orientation: Questioning the notion of collectivism. *Review of General Psychology, 3,* 372–385.

DiFranza, Joseph R. (2008, May). Hooked from the first cigarette. *Scientific American,* 82–87.

Digman, John M., & Shmelyov, Alexander G. (1996). The structure of temperament and personality in Russian children. *Journal of Personality and Social Psychology, 71,* 341–351.

Dijk, Corine; de Jong, Peter J.; & Peters, Madelon L. (2009). The remedial value of blushing in the context of transgressions and mishaps. *Emotion, 9,* 287–291.

Dimberg, Ulf; Thunberg, Monika; & Elmehed, Kurt (2000). Unconscious facial reactions to emotional facial expressions. *Psychological Science, 11,* 86–89.

Dimidjian, Sona, & Hollon, Steven D. (2010). How would we know if psychotherapy were harmful? *American Psychologist, 65,* 21–33.

Dinero, Rachel E.; Conger, Rand D.; Shaver, Phillip R.; et al. (2008). Influence of family of origin and adult romantic partners on romantic attachment security. *Journal of Family Psychology, 22,* 622–632.

Dinges, David F.; Whitehouse, Wayne G.; Orne, Emily C.; Powell, John W.; Orne, Martin T.; & Erdelyi, Matthew H. (1992). Evaluating hypnotic memory enhancement (hypermnesia and reminiscence) using multitrial forced recall. *Journal of Experimental Psychology: Learning, Memory, and Cognition, 18,* 1139–1147.

Dingfelder, Sadie F. (2010, November). A second chance for the Mexican wolf. *APA Monitor, 41,* 20.

Dinn, W. M., & Harris, C. L. (2000). Neurocognitive function in antisocial personality disorder. *Psychiatry Research, 97,* 173–190.

Dion, Kenneth L., & Dion, Karen K. (1993). Gender and ethnocultural comparisons in styles of love. *Psychology of Women Quarterly, 17,* 463–474.

Doering, Stephan; Katzlberger, Florian; Rumpold, Gerhard; et al. (2000). Videotape preparation of patients before hip replacement surgery reduces stress. *Psychosomatic Medicine, 62,* 365–373.

Dohrenwend, Bruce; Yager, Thomas J.; Wall, Melanie M.; & Adams, Ben G. (2013). The roles of combat exposure, personal vulnerability, and involvement in harm to civilians or prisoners in Vietnam-War-related posttraumatic stress disorder. *Clinical Psychological Science, 1,* 223–238.

Dolnick, Edward (1990, July). What dreams are (really) made of. *The Atlantic Monthly, 226,* 41–45, 48–53, 56–58, 60–61.

Domhoff, G. William (1996). *Finding meaning in dreams: A quantitative approach.* New York: Plenum.

Domhoff, G. William (2003). *The scientific study of dreams: Neural networks, cognitive development, and content analysis.* Washington, DC: American Psychological Association.

Domhoff, G. William (2011). Dreams are embodied simulations that dramatize conceptions and concerns: the continuity hypothesis in empirical, theoretical, historical context. *International Journal of Dream Research, 4,* 50–62.

Donlea, Jeffrey M.; Ramanan, Narendrakumar; & Shaw, Paul J. (2009). Use-dependent plasticity in clock neurons regulates sleep need in Drosophila. *Science, 324,* 105–108.

Dovidio, J. F.; Pagotto, L.; & Hebl, M. R. (2011). Implicit attitudes and discrimination against people with physical disabilities. In R. L. Wiener & S. L. Willborn (Eds.), *Disability and aging discrimination: Perspectives in law and psychology,* pp. 157–183. New York: Springer Science + Business Media.

Dovidio, John F. (2009). Racial bias, unspoken but heard. *Science, 326,* 1641–1642.

Dovidio, John F., & Gaertner, Samuel L. (2010). Intergroup bias. In Fiske, S. T., Gilbert, D. T., & Lindzey, G. (Eds.), *Handbook of social psychology,* Vol 2 (5th ed.). Hoboken, NJ: Wiley.

Downing, P. E.; Chan, A. W.-Y.; Peelen, M. V.; et al. (2006). Domain specificity in visual cortex. *Cerebral Cortex, 16,* 1453–1461.

Drew, Trafton; Võ, Melissa le-Hoa; & Wolfe, Jeremy M. (2013). The invisible gorilla strikes again: Sustained inattentional blindness in expert observers. *Psychological Science, 24,* 1848–1853.

Duckworth, Angela L., & Seligman, Martin E. P. (2005). Self-discipline outdoes IQ in predicting academic performance of adolescents. *Psychological Science, 16,* 939–944.

Duckworth, Angela Lee; Kirby, Teri A.; Tsukayama, Eli; et al. (2011). Deliberate practice spells success: Why grittier competitors triumph at the national spelling bee. *Social Psychological and Personality Science, 2,* 174–181.

Duffy, Jeanne, F.; Cain, Sean W.; Change, Anne-Marie; et al. (2011). Sex difference in the near-24-hour intrinsic period of the human circadian timing system. *Proceedings of the National Academy of Science, 108,* 15602–15608.

Dunbar, R. I. M. (2004). Gossip in evolutionary perspective. *Review of General Psychology, 8,* 100–110.

Duncan, Laramie E., & Keller, Matthew C. (2011). A critical review of the first 10 years of candidate gene-by-environment interaction research in psychiatry. *American Journal of Psychiatry, 168,* 1041–1049.

Dunkel, Curtis S., & Sefcek, Jon A. (2009). Eriksonian lifespan theory and life history theory: An integration using the example of identity formation. *Review of General Psychology, 13,* 13–23.

Dunlosky, John, & Lipko, Amanda R. (2007). Metacomprehension: A brief history and how to improve its accuracy. *Current Directions in Psychological Science, 16,* 228–232.

Dunlosky, John; Rawson, Katherine A.; Marsh, Elizabeth J.; et al. (2013). Improving students' learning with effective learning techniques: Promising directions from cognitive and educational psychology. *Psychological Science in the Public Interest, 14,* 4–58.

Dunn, Barnaby D.; Stefanovitch, Iolanta; Evans, Davy; et al. (2010). Can you feel the beat? Interoceptive awareness is an interactive function of anxiety- and depression-specific symptom dimensions. *Behaviour Research and Therapy, 48,* 1133–1138.

Dunn, Elizabeth W.; Wilson, Timothy D.; & Gilbert, Daniel T. (2003). Location, location, location: The misprediction of satisfaction in housing lotteries. *Personality and Social Psychology Bulletin, 29,* 1421–1432.

Dunn, Michael; Greenhill, Simon J.; Levinson, Stephen C.; et al. (2011). Evolved structure of language shows lineage-specific trends in word-order universals. *Nature, 473,* 79–92.

Dunning, David (2005). *Self-insight: Roadblocks and detours on the path to knowing thyself.* New York: Psychology Press.

Dunning, David; Heath, Chip; & Suls, Jerry M. (2004). Flawed self-assessment: Implications for health, education, and the workplace. *Psychological Science in the Public Interest, 5,* 69–106.

Dunning, David; Johnson, Kerri; Ehrlinger, Joyce; & Kruger, Justin (2003). Why people fail to recognize their own incompetence. *Current Directions in Psychological Science, 12,* 83–87.

Duranceaux, Nicole C. E.; Schuckit, Marc A.; Luczak, Susan E.; et al. (2008). Ethnic differences in level of response to alcohol between Chinese Americans and Korean Americans. *Journal of Studies on Alcohol and Drugs, 69,* 227–234.

Durrant, Joan, & Ensom, Ron (2012). Physical punishment of children: Lessons from 20 years of research. *Canadian Medical Association Journal, 184,* 1373–1377.

Dweck, Carol S. (2006). *Mindset: The new psychology of success.* New York: Random House.

Dweck, Carol S. (2008). Can personality be changed? *Current Directions in Psychological Science, 17,* 391–394.

Dweck, Carol S., & Grant, Heidi (2008). Self-theories, goals, and meaning. In J. Y. Shah & W. L. Gardner (Eds.), *Handbook of motivation science.* New York: Guilford.

Dweck, Carol S., & Sorich, Lisa A. (1999). Mastery-oriented thinking. In C. R. Snyder (Ed.), *Coping: The psychology of what works.* New York: Oxford University Press.

Eagly, Alice H., & Wood, Wendy (1999). The origins of sex differences in human behavior: Evolved dispositions versus social roles. *American Psychologist, 54,* 408–423.

Earl-Novell, Sarah L., & Jessup, Donna C. (2005). The relationship between perceptions of premenstrual syndrome and degree performance. *Assessment & Evaluation in Higher Education, 30,* 343–352.

Eaton, Danice; Kann, Laura; Kinchen, Steve; et al. (2008, June 6). Youth Risk Behavior Surveillance—United States, 2007. Centers for Disease Control, 57(SS04), 1–131. www.cdc.gov/mmwr/preview/mmwrhtml/ss5704a1 .htm?s_cid=ss5704a1_e.

Ebbinghaus, Hermann M. (1885/1913). *Memory: A contribution to experimental psychology* (H. A. Ruger & C. E. Bussenius, Trans.). New York: Teachers College Press, Columbia University.

Eccles, Jacqueline S. (2011). Understanding women's achievement choices: Looking back and looking forward. *Psychology of Women Quarterly, 35,* 520–516.

Edwards, Kari, & Smith, Edward E. (1996). A disconfirmation bias in the evaluation of arguments. *Journal of Personality and Social Psychology, 71,* 5–24.

Ehrensaft, Miriam K.; Moffitt, Terrie E.; & Caspi, Avshalom (2006). Is domestic violence followed by an increased risk of psychiatric disorders among women but not among men? A longitudinal cohort study. *American Journal of Psychiatry, 163,* 885–892.

Eich, E., & Hyman, R. (1992). Subliminal self-help. In D. Druckman & R. A. Bjork (Eds.), *In the mind's eye: Enhancing human performance.* Washington, DC: National Academy Press.

Eigsti, Inge-Marie; Zayas, Vivian; Mischel, Walter; Shoda, Yuichi; et al. (2006). Predicting cognitive control from preschool to late adolescence and young adulthood. *Psychological Science, 17,* 478–484.

Ekman, Paul (2003). *Emotions revealed.* New York: Times Books.

Ekman, Paul; Friesen, Wallace V.; & O'Sullivan, Maureen (1988). Smiles when lying. *Journal of Personality and Social Psychology, 54,* 414–420.

Ekman, Paul; Friesen, Wallace V.; O'Sullivan, Maureen; et al. (1987). Universals and cultural differences in the judgments of facial expression of emotion. *Journal of Personality and Social Psychology, 53,* 712–717.

Elfenbein, Hillary A., & Ambady, Nalini (2003). When familiarity breeds accuracy: Cultural exposure and facial emotion recognition. *Journal of Personality and Social Psychology, 85,* 276–290.

Elliot, Andrew J., & McGregor, Holly A. (2001). A 2 X 2 achievement goal framework. *Journal of Personality and Social Psychology, 80,* 501–519.

Ellis, Albert (1993). Changing rational-emotive therapy (RET) to rational emotive behavior therapy (REBT). *Behavior Therapist, 16,* 257–258.

Ellis, Albert, & Blau, S. (1998). Rational emotive behavior therapy. *Directions in Clinical and Counseling Psychology, 8,* 41–56.

Ellis, Bruce J., & Boyce, W. Thomas (2008). Biological sensitivity to context. *Current Directions in Psychological Science, 17,* 183–187.

Elmquist, Joel K., & Flier, Jeffrey S. (2004). The fat-brain axis enters a new dimension. *Science, 304,* 63–64.

Else-Quest, Nicole M.; Hyde, Janet S.; Goldsmith, H. Hill; & Can Hulle, Carol A. (2006). Gender differences in temperament: A meta-analysis. *Psychological Bulletin, 132,* 33–72.

Else-Quest, Nicole M.; Hyde, Janet S.; & Linn, Marcia C. (2010). Cross-national patterns of gender differences in mathematics: A meta-analysis. *Psychological Bulletin, 136,* 103–127.

Else-Quest, Nicole M.; Higgins, Ashley; Allison, Carlie; & Morton, Lindsay C. (2012). Gender differences in self-conscious emotional experience: A meta-analysis. *Psychological Bulletin, 138,* 947–981.

Ehrenreich, Barbara (2001, June 4). What are they probing for? [Essay.] *Time,* 86.

Emberson, Lauren L.; Lupyan, Gary; Goldstein, Michael H.; & Spivey, Michael J. (2010). Overheard cell-phone conversations: When less speech is more distracting. *Psychological Science, 21,* 1383–1388.

Emery, Robert E., & Laumann-Billings, Lisa (1998). An overview of the nature, causes, and consequences of abusive family relationships. *American Psychologist, 53,* 121–135.

Emery, Robert E.; Otto, Randy K.; & O'Donohue, William T. (2005). A critical assessment of child custody evaluations: Limited science and a flawed system. *Psychological Science in the Public Interest, 6,* 1–29.

Engle, Randall W. (2002). Working memory capacity as executive attention. *Current Directions in Psychological Science, 11,* 19–23.

Epel, Elissa S. (2009). Telomeres in a life-span perspective: A new "psychobiomarker"? *Current Directions in Psychological Science, 18,* 6–10.

Erceg-Hurn, David M., & Miosevich, Vikki M. (2008). Modern robust statistical methods. *American Psychologist, 63,* 591–601.

Erickson, Kirk I.; Voss, Michelle W.; Prakash, Ruchika S.; et al. (2011). Exercise training increases size of hippocampus and improves memory. *Proceedings of the National Academy of Sciences, 108,* 3017–3022.

Erikson, Erik H. (1950/1963). *Childhood and society* (2nd ed.). New York: Norton.

Erikson, Erik H. (1982). *The life cycle completed.* New York: Norton.

Ersche, Karen D.; Jones, Simon; Williams, Guy B.; et al. (2012). Abnormal brain structure implicated in stimulant drug addiction. *Science, 335,* 601–604.

Ervin-Tripp, Susan (1964). Imitation and structural change in children's language. In E. H. Lenneberg (Ed.), *New directions in the study of language.* Cambridge, MA: MIT Press.

Escera, Carles; Cilveti, Robert; & Grau, Carles (1992). Ultradian rhythms in cognitive operations: Evidence from the P300 component of the event related potentials. *Medical Science Research, 20,* 137–138.

Evans, Christopher (1984). *Landscapes of the night* (edited and completed by Peter Evans). New York: Viking.

Evans, Gary W.; & Kim, Pilyoung (2012). Childhood poverty and young adults' allostatic load: The mediating role of childhood cumulative risk exposure. *Psychological Science, 23,* 979–983.

Evans, Gary W.; Lepore, Stephen J.; & Allen, Karen Mata (2000). Cross-cultural differences in tolerance for crowding: Fact or fiction? *Journal of Personality and Social Psychology, 79,* 204–210.

Evans, Nicholas, & Stephen C. Levinson (2009). The myth of language universals: Language diversity and its importance for cognitive science. *Behavioral and Brain Sciences, 32,* 429–492.

Everett, Daniel L. (2012). *Language: The cultural tool.* New York: Pantheon.

Ewart, Craig K. (1995). Self-efficacy and recovery from heart attack. In J. E. Maddux (Ed.), *Self-efficacy, adaptation, and adjustment: Theory, research, and application.* New York: Plenum.

Ewart, Craig K., & Kolodner, Kenneth B. (1994). Negative affect, gender, and expressive style predict elevated ambulatory blood pressure in adolescents. *Journal of Personality and Social Psychology, 66,* 596–605.

Eyferth, Klaus (1961). [The performance of different groups of the children of occupation forces on the Hamburg-Wechsler Intelligence Test for Children.] *Archiv für die Gesamte Psychologie, 113,* 222–241.

Fagot, Beverly I. (1993, June). Gender role development in early childhood: Environmental input, internal construction. Invited address presented at the annual meeting of the International Academy of Sex Research, Monterey, CA.

Fagot, Beverly I., & Leinbach, Mary D. (1993). Gender-role development in young children: From discrimination to labeling. *Developmental Review, 13,* 205–224.

Fairholme, C. P.; Boisseau, C. L.; Ellard, K. K.; et al. (2009). Emotions, emotion regulation, and psychological treatment: A unified perspective. In A. M. Kring & D. M. Sloan (Eds.), *Emotion regulation and psychopathology.* New York: Guilford.

Fallon, James H.; Keator, David B.; Mbogori, James; et al. (2004). Hostility differentiates the brain metabolic effects of nicotine. *Cognitive Brain Research, 18,* 142–148.

Fallone, Gahan; Acebo, Christine; Seifer, Ronald; & Carskadon, Mary A. (2005). Experimental restriction of sleep opportunity in children: Effects on teacher ratings. *Sleep, 28,* 1280–1286.

Farooqi, I. Sadaf, & O'Rahilly, Stephen (2004). Monogenic human obesity syndromes. *Recent Progress in Hormone Research, 59,* 409–424.

Farooqi, Sadaf; Bullmore, Edward; Keogh, Julia; et al. (2007, Sept. 7). Leptin regulates striatal regions and human eating behavior. *Science, 317,* 1355.

Fausto-Sterling, Anne (2012). The dynamic development of gender variability. *Journal of Homosexuality, 59,* 398–421.

Fausto-Sterling, Anne (1997). Beyond difference: A biologist's perspective. *Journal of Social Issues, 53,* 233–258.

Feather, N. T. (1966). Effects of prior success and failure on expectations of success and subsequent performance. *Journal of Personality and Social Psychology, 3,* 287–298.

Feeney, Brooke C., & Cassidy, Jude (2003). Reconstructive memory related to adolescent-parent conflict interactions. *Journal of Personality and Social Psychology, 85,* 945–955.

Fehr, Beverley; Baldwin, Mark; Collins, Lois; et al. (1999). Anger in close relationships: An interpersonal script analysis. *Personality and Social Psychology Bulletin, 25,* 299–312.

Fehr, Ernest & Fischbacher, Urs (2003). The nature of human altruism. *Nature, 425,* 785–791.

Fehr, Ryan; Gelfand, Michele J.; & Nag, Monisha (2010). The road to forgiveness: A meta-analytic synthesis of its situational and dispositional correlates. *Psychological Bulletin, 136,* 894–914.

Fein, Steven, & Spencer, Steven J. (1997). Prejudice as self-image maintenance: Affirming the self through derogating others. *Journal of Personality and Social Psychology, 73,* 31–44.

Feinberg, Andrew P. (2008). Epigenetics at the epicenter of modern medicine. *Journal of the American Medical Association, 299,* 1345–1350.

Feinberg, Matthew; Willer, Robb; & Keltner, Dacher (2012). Flustered and faithful: Embarrassment as a signal of prosociality. *Journal of Personality and Social Psychology, 102,* 81–97.

Feinstein, Justin S.; Adolphs, Ralph; Damasio, Antonio; & Tranel, Daniel (2011). The human amygdala and the induction and experience of fear. *Current Biology, 21,* 34–38.

Feinstein, Justin; Buzza, Colin; Hurlemann, Rene; et al. (2013). Fear and panic in humans with bilateral amygdala damage. *Nature Neuroscience, 16,* 270–272.

Fellner, Jamie (2009). Race, drugs, and law enforcement in the United States. *Stanford Law and Policy Review, 20,* 257–291.

Ferguson, Christopher J. (2007). The good, the bad and the ugly: A meta-analytic review of positive and negative effects of violent video games. *Psychiatric Quarterly, 78,* 309–316.

Ferguson, Christopher (2009). Media violence effects: Confirmed truth or just another X-file? *Journal of Forensic Psychology Practice, 9,* 103–126.

Ferguson, Christopher J., & Kilburn, John (2010). Much ado about nothing: The misestimation and overinterpretation of violent video game effects in Eastern and Western nations. *Psychological Bulletin, 136,* 174–178.

Fernea, Elizabeth, & Fernea, Robert (1994). Cleanliness and culture. In W. J. Lonner & Malpass (Eds.), *Psychology and culture.* Boston: Allyn & Bacon.

Feshbach, Seymour, & Tangney, June (2008). Television viewing and aggression: Some alternative perspectives. *Perspectives on Psychological Science, 3,* 387–389.

Festinger, Leon (1957). *A theory of cognitive dissonance.* Evanston, IL: Row, Peterson.

Festinger, Leon, & Carlsmith, J. Merrill (1959). Cognitive consequences of forced compliance. *Journal of Abnormal and Social Psychology, 58,* 203–210.

Festinger, Leon; Pepitone, Albert; & Newcomb, Theodore (1952). Some consequences of deindividuation in a group. *Journal of Abnormal and Social Psychology, 47,* 382–389.

Festinger, Leon; Riecken, Henry W.; & Schachter, Stanley (1956). *When prophecy fails.* Minneapolis: University of Minnesota Press.

Fidler, Fiona, & Loftus, Geoffrey R. (2009). Why figures with error bars should replace *p* values: Some conceptual arguments and empirical demonstrations. *Journal of Psychology, 217,* 27–37.

Fiedler, K.; Nickel, S.; Muehlfriedel, T.; & Unkelbach, C. (2001). Is mood congruency an effect of genuine memory or response bias? *Journal of Experimental Social Psychology, 37,* 201–214.

Field, Tiffany (2009). The effects of newborn massage: United States. In T. Field et al. (Eds.), *The newborn as a person: Enabling healthy infant development worldwide.* Hoboken, NJ: Wiley.

Fields, R. Douglas (2004, April). The other half of the brain. *Scientific American,* 54–61.

Fiez, J. A. (1996). Cerebellar contributions to cognition. *Neuron, 16,* 13–15.

Fine, Cordelia (2010). From scanner to sound bite: Issues in interpreting and reporting sex differences in the brain. *Current Directions in Psychological Science, 19,* 280–283.

Fine, Ione; Wade, A. R.; Brewer, A. A.; et al. (2003). Long-term deprivation affects visual perception and cortex. *Nature Neuroscience, 6,* 915–916.

Finkel, Eli J.; Eastwick, Paul W.; Karney, Benjamin R.; et al. (2012). Online dating: A critical analysis from the perspective of psychological science. *Psychological Science in the Public Interest, 13,* 3–66.

Fischer, Pamela C.; Smith, Randy J.; Leonard, Elizabeth; et al. (1993). Sex differences on affective dimensions: Continuing examination. *Journal of Counseling and Development, 71,* 440–443.

Fischer, Peter; Krueger, Joachim I.; Greitemeyer, Tobias; et al. (2011). The bystander-effect: A meta-analytic review on bystander intervention in dangerous and non-dangerous emergencies. *Psychological Bulletin, 137,* 517–537.

Fischhoff, Baruch (1975). Hindsight is not equal to foresight: The effect of outcome knowledge on judgment under uncertainty. *Journal of Experimental Psychology: Human Perception and Performance, 1,* 288–299.

Fivush, Robyn, & Nelson, Katherine (2004). Culture and language in the emergence of autobiographical memory. *Psychological Science, 15,* 573–582.

Fivush, Robyn, & Nelson, Katherine (2005). Parent-child reminiscing locates the self in the past. *British Journal of Developmental Psychology, 24,* 235–251.

Flacks, Richard, & Thomas, Scott L. (1998, November 27). Among affluent students, a culture of disengagement. *Chronicle of Higher Education,* p. A48.

Flavell, John H. (1999). Cognitive development: Children's knowledge about the mind. *Annual Review of Psychology, 50,* 21–45.

Fleeson, William (2004). Moving personality beyond the person-situation debate. *Current Directions in Psychological Science, 13,* 83–87.

Flynn, James R. (1987). Massive IQ gains in 14 nations: What IQ tests really measure. *Psychological Bulletin, 95,* 29–51.

Flynn, James R. (1999). Searching for justice: The discovery of IQ gains over time. *American Psychologist, 54,* 5–20.

Fogassi, Leonardo, & Ferrari, Pier Francesco (2007). Mirror neurons and the evolution of embodied language. *Current Directions in Psychological Science, 16,* 136–141.

Forbes, Gordon; Zhang, Xiaoying; Doroszewicz, Krystyna; & Haas, Kelly (2009). Relationships between individualism-collectivism, gender, and direct or indirect aggression: A study in China, Poland, and the US. *Aggressive Behavior, 35,* 24–30.

Forgas, Joseph P. (1998). On being happy and mistaken: Mood effects on the fundamental attribution error. *Journal of Personality and Social Psychology, 75,* 318–331.

Forgas, Joseph P., & Bond, Michael H. (1985). Cultural influences on the perception of interaction episodes. *Personality and Social Psychology Bulletin, 11,* 75–88

Foster, Jeffrey L.; Huthwaite, Thomas; Yesberg, Julia A.; et al. (2012). Repetition, not number of sources, increases both susceptibility to misinformation and confidence in the accuracy of eyewitnesses. *Acta Psychologica, 139,* 320–326.

Foulkes, D. (1962). Dream reports from different states of sleep. *Journal of Abnormal and Social Psychology, 65,* 14–25.

Foulkes, David (1999). *Children's dreaming and the development of consciousness.* Cambridge, MA: Harvard University Press.

Fournier, J.C.; DeRubeis, R.J.; Hollon, S.D.; et al. (2010). Antidepressant drug effects and depression severity: a patient-level meta-analysis. *Journal of the American Medical Association, 303,* 47–53.

Fouts, Roger S. (with Stephen T. Mills) (1997). *Next of kin: What chimpanzees have taught me about who we are.* New York: Morrow.

Fouts, Roger S., & Rigby, Randall L. (1977). Man–chimpanzee communication. In T. A. Seboek (Ed.), *How animals communicate.* Bloomington: University of Indiana Press.

Fox, Mary Kay; Pac, Susan; Devaney, Barbara; & Jankowski, Linda (2004). Feeding infants and toddlers study: What foods are infants and toddlers eating? *Journal of the American Dietetic Association, 104,* 22–30.

Fox, Nathan A.; Henderson, Heather A.; Marshall, Peter J.; et al. (2005a). Behavioral inhibition: Linking biology and behavior within a developmental framework. *Annual Review of Psychology, 56,* 235–262.

Fox, Nathan A.; Nichols, Kate E.; Henderson, Heather A.; et al. (2005b). Evidence for a gene–environment interaction in predicting behavioral inhibition in middle childhood. *Psychological Science, 16,* 921–926.

Fraley, R. Chris; Vicary, Amanda M.; Brumbaugh, Claudia C.; & Roisman, Glenn I. (2011). Patterns of stability in adult attachment: An empirical test of two models of continuity and change. *Journal of Personality and Social Psychology, 101,* 974–992.

Frances, Allen (2013). *Saving normal: An insider's revolt against out-of-control psychiatric diagnosis, DSM-5, Big Pharma, and the medicalization of ordinary life.* New York: William Morrow.

Frankl, Victor E. (1955). *The doctor and the soul: An introduction to logotherapy.* New York: Knopf.

Frans, Emma M.; Sandin, Sven; Reichenberg, Abraham; et al. (2008). Advancing paternal age and bipolar disorder. *Archives of General Psychiatry, 65,* 1034–1040.

Frasure-Smith, Nancy, & Lespérance, Francois (2005). Depression and coronary heart disease: Complex synergism of mind, body, and environment. *Current Directions in Psychological Science, 14,* 39–43.

Frayling, Timothy M.; Timpson, Nicholas J.; Weedon, Michael N.; et al. (2007). A common variant in the FTO gene is associated with body mass index and predisposes to childhood and adult obesity. *Science, 316,* 889–894.

Frazier, Patricia A. (2003). Perceived control and distress following sexual assault: A longitudinal test of a new model. *Journal of Personality and Social Psychology, 84,* 1257–1269.

Frazier, Patricia; Keenan, Nora; Anders, Samantha; et al. (2011). Perceived past, present, and future control and adjustment to stressful life events. *Journal of Personality and Social Psychology, 100,* 749–765.

Frensch, Peter A., & Rünger, Dennis (2003). Implicit learning. *Current Directions in Psychological Science, 12,* 13–18.

Freud, Anna (1967). *Ego and the mechanisms of defense* (The writings of Anna Freud, Vol. 2) (Rev. ed.). New York: International Universities Press.

Freud, Sigmund (1900/1953). The interpretation of dreams. In J. Strachey (Ed.), The *standard edition of the complete psychological works of Sigmund Freud* (Vols. 4 and 5). London: Hogarth Press.

Freud, Sigmund (1905b). Three essays on the theory of sexuality. In J. Strachey (Ed.), *Standard edition* (Vol. 7).

Freud, Sigmund (1920/1960). *A general introduction to psychoanalysis* (Joan Riviere, trans.). New York: Washington Square Press.

Freud, Sigmund (1923/1962). *The ego and the id* (Joan Riviere, trans.). New York: Norton.

Freud, Sigmund (1961). *Letters of Sigmund Freud, 1873–1939.* Edited by Ernst L. Freud. London: Hogarth Press.

Frick, Paul J., & Viding, Essi (2009). Antisocial behavior from a developmental psychopathology perspective. *Development and Psychopathology, 21,* 1111–1131.

Fridlund, Alan J. (1994). *Human facial expression: An evolutionary view.* San Diego: Academic Press.

Friedman, Howard S., & Martin, Leslie R. (2011). *The longevity project.* New York: Hudson Street Press.

Friedrich, William; Fisher, Jennifer; Broughton, Daniel; et al. (1998). Normative sexual behavior in children: A contemporary sample. *Pediatrics, 101,* 1–8.

Frijda, Nico H.; Kuipers, Peter; & ter Schure, Elisabeth (1989). Relations among emotion, appraisal, and emotional action readiness. *Journal of Personality and Social Psychology, 57,* 212–228.

Frome, Pamela M., & Eccles, Jacquelynne S. (1998). Parents' influence on children's achievement-related perceptions. *Journal of Personality and Social Psychology, 74,* 435–452.

Frye, Richard E.; Schwartz, B. S.; & Doty, Richard L. (1990). Dose-related effects of cigarette smoking on olfactory function. *Journal of the American Medical Association, 263,* 1233–1236.

Fryer, Roland G. (2011). Financial incentives and student achievement: Evidence from randomized trials. *Quarterly Journal of Economics, 126,* 1755–1798.

Fuchs, C. S.; Stampfer, M. J.; Colditz, G. A.; et al. (1995). Alcohol consumption and mortality among women. *New England Journal of Medicine, 332,* 1245–1250.

Gabbert, Charles; Donohue, Michael; Arnold, John; & Schwimmer, Jeffrey B. (2010). Adenovirus 36 and obesity in children and adolescents. *Pediatrics, 126,* 721–726.

Gable, Shelly L., & Haidt, Jonathan (2005). What (and why) is positive psychology? *Review of General Psychology, 9,* 103–110.

Gable, Shelly L., & Poore, Joshua (2008). Which thoughts count? Algorithms for evaluating satisfaction in relationships. *Psychological Science, 19,* 1030–1036.

Gaertner, Samuel L.; Mann, Jeffrey A.; Dovidio, John F.; et al. (1990). How does cooperation reduce intergroup bias? *Journal of Personality and Social Psychology, 59,* 692–704.

Gagnon, John, & Simon, William (1973). *Sexual conduct: The social sources of human sexuality.* Chicago: Aldine.

Gal, David, & Rucker, Derek D. (2010). When in doubt, shout! Paradoxical influences of doubt on proselytizing. *Psychological Science, 21,* 1701–1707.

Galak, Jeff; LeBouef, Robyn A.; Nelson, Leif D.; et al. (2012). Correcting the past: Failures to replicate psi. *Journal of Personality and Social Psychology, 103,* 933–948.

Galanter, Eugene (1962). Contemporary psychophysics. In R. Brown, E. Galanter, H. Hess, & G. Mandler (Eds.), *New directions in psychology.* New York: Holt, Rinehart and Winston.

Gallant, Sheryle J.; Hamilton, Jean A.; Popiel, Debra A.; et al. (1991). Daily moods and symptoms: Effects of awareness of study focus, gender, menstrual-cycle phase, and day of the week. *Health Psychology, 10,* 180–189.

Gallese, Vittorio; Gernsbacher, Morton Ann; Heyes, Cecilia; et al. (2011). Mirror neuron forum. *Perspectives on Psychological Science, 6,* 369–407.

Gallo, Linda C., & Matthews, Karen A. (2003). Understanding the association between socioeconomic status and physical health: Do negative emotions play a role? *Psychological Bulletin, 129,* 10–51.

Galotti, Kathleen (1989). Approaches to studying formal and everyday reasoning. *Psychological Bulletin, 105,* 331–351.

Garbarino, James, & Bedard, Claire (2001). *Parents under siege.* New York: The Free Press.

Garcia, John, & Gustavson, Carl R. (1997, January). Carl R. Gustavson (1946–1996): Pioneering wildlife psychologist. *APS Observer,* 34–35.

Garcia, John, & Koelling, Robert A. (1966). Relation of cue to consequence in avoidance learning. *Psychonomic Science, 4,* 23–124.

Gardner, R. Allen, & Gardner, Beatrice T. (1969). Teaching sign language to a chimpanzee. *Science, 165,* 664–672.

Garmezy, Norman (1991). Resilience and vulnerability to adverse developmental outcomes associated with poverty. *American Behavioral Scientist, 34,* 416–430.

Garry, Maryanne, & Polaschek, Devon L. L. (2000). Imagination and memory. *Current Directions in Psychological Science, 9,* 6–10.

Garry, Maryanne; Manning, Charles G.; & Loftus, Elizabeth F. (1996). Imagination inflation: Imagining a childhood event inflates confidence that it occurred. *Psychonomic Bulletin & Review, 3,* 208–214.

Garven, Sena; Wood, James M.; Malpass, Roy S.; & Shaw, John S., III (1998). More than suggestion: The effect of interviewing techniques from the McMartin Preschool case. *Journal of Applied Psychology, 83,* 347–359.

Gatz, Margaret (2007). Genetics, dementia, and the elderly. *Current Directions in Psychological Science, 16,* 123–127.

Gauthier, Irene; Skudlarksi, P.; Gore, J. C.; & Anderson, A. W. (2000). Expertise for cars and birds recruits brain areas involved in face recognition. *Nature Neuroscience, 3,* 191–197.

Gawande, Atul (2009, March 30). Hellhole. *The New Yorker,* 36–45.

Gazzaniga, Michael S. (1967). The split brain in man. *Scientific American, 217*(2), 24–29.

Gazzaniga, Michael S. (1988). *Mind matters.* Boston: Houghton-Mifflin.

Gazzaniga, Michael S. (1989). Organization of the human brain. *Science, 245,* 947–952.

Gazzaniga, Michael S. (2005). *The ethical brain.* Washington, DC: Dana Press.

Gazzaniga, Michael S. (2008). *Human: The science behind what makes us unique.* New York: Ecco/Harper Collins.

Geers, Andrew L.; Wellman, Justin A.; & Lassiter, G. Daniel (2009). Dispositional optimism and engagement: The moderating influence of goal prioritization. *Journal of Personality and Social Psychology, 96,* 913–932.

Gelbard-Sagiv, H.; Mukamel, R.; Harel, M.; et al. (2008). Internally generated reactivation of single neurons in human hippocampus during free recall. *Science, 322,* 96–101.

Gelernter, David (1997, May 19). How hard is chess? *Time,* 72–73.

Gentile, Brittany; Grabe, Shleey; Dolan-Pascoe, Brenda; et al. (2009). Gender differences in domain-specific self-esteem: A meta-analysis. *Review of General Psychology, 13,* 34–45.

Gentner, Dedre, & Goldin-Meadow, Susan (Eds.) (2003). *Language in mind: Advances in the study of language and thought.* Cambridge: MIT Press.

George, Mark S., & Post, Robert M. (2011). Daily left prefrontal repetitive transcrancial magnetic stimulation for acute treatment of medication-resistant depression. *American Journal of Psychiatry, 168,* 356–364.

Gerken, Louann A.; Wilson, Rachel; & Lewis, William (2005). Infants can use distributional cues to form syntactic categories. *Journal of Child Language, 32,* 249–268.

Gershoff, Elizabeth T. (2002). Parental corporal punishment and associated child behaviors and experiences: A meta-analytic and theoretical review. *Psychological Bulletin, 128,* 539–579.

Gibbs, Robert B. (2010). Estrogen therapy and cognition: A review of the cholinergic hypothesis. *Endocrine Review, 31,* 224–253.

Gibson, Eleanor, & Walk, Richard (1960). The "visual cliff." *Scientific American, 202,* 80–92.

Giesbrecht, Timo; Lynn, Steven Jay; Lilienfeld, Scott O.; & Merckelbach, Harald (2008). Cognitive processes in dissociation: An analysis of core theoretical assumptions. *Psychological Bulletin, 134,* 617–647.

Gilbert, Daniel (2006). *Stumbling on happiness.* New York: Knopf.

Gilbertson, Mark W.; Shenton, Martha E.; Ciszewski, Aleksandra; et al. (2002). Hippocampal volume predicts pathologic vulnerability to psychological trauma. *Nature Neuroscience, 5,* 1242–1247.

Gilchrist, Amanda L., & Cowan, Nelson (2012). Chunking. In V. Ramachandran (Ed.), *Encyclopedia of human behavior* (Vol. 1). San Diego: Academic Press.

Ginges, Jeremy, & Atran, Scott (2011). Psychology out of the laboratory: The challenge of violent extremism. *American Psychologist, 66,* 507–519.

Gladwell, Malcolm (2004, September 20). Personality plus. *The New Yorker,* 42–48.

Gleaves, David H. (1996). The sociocognitive model of dissociative identity disorder: A reexamination of the evidence. *Psychological Bulletin, 120,* 42–59.

Glick, Peter (2006). Ambivalent sexism, power distance, and gender inequality across cultures. In S. Guimond (Ed.), *Social comparison and social psychology: Understanding cognition, intergroup relations, and culture.* New York: Cambridge University Press.

Glick, Peter; Fiske, Susan T.; Mladinic, Antonio; et al. (2000). Beyond prejudice as simple antipathy: Hostile and benevolent sexism across cultures. *Journal of Personality and Social Psychology, 79,* 763–775.

Glick, Peter; Lameiras, Maria; Fiske, Susan T.; et al. (2004). Bad but bold: Ambivalent attitudes toward men predict gender inequality in 16 nations. *Journal of Personality and Social Psychology, 86,* 713–728.

Gigerenzer, Gerd; Gaissmaier, Wolfgang; Kurz-Milcke, Elke; et al. (2008) Helping doctors and patients make sense of health statistics. *Psychological Science in the Public Interest, 8,* 53–96.

Gilestro, Giorgio F.; Tononi, Giulio; & Cirelli, Chiara (2009). Widespread changes in synaptic markers as a function of sleep and wakefulness in Drosophila. *Science, 324,* 109–112.

Gillath, Omri; Shaver, Phillip R.; Baek, Jong-Min; & Chun, David S. (2008). Genetic correlates of adult attachment style. *Personality and Social Psychology Bulletin, 34,* 1396–1405.

Golden, Robert M.; Gaynes, Bradley N.; Ekstrom, R. David; et al. (2005). The efficacy of light therapy in the treatment of mood disorders: A review and meta-analysis of the evidence. *American Journal of Psychiatry, 162,* 656–662.

Goldin-Meadow, Susan (2003). *The resilience of language.* New York: Psychology Press.

Goldin-Meadow, Susan; Cook, Susan W.; & Mitchell, Zachary A. (2009). Gesturing gives children new ideas about math. *Psychological Science, 20,* 267–272.

Goldman-Rakic, Patricia S. (1996). Opening the mind through neurobiology. Invited address at the annual meeting of the American Psychological Association, Toronto, Canada.

Goldstein, Jill M.; Seidman, Larry J.; Horton, Nicholas J.; et al. (2001). Normal sexual dimorphism of the adult human brain assessed by in vivo magnetic resonance imaging. *Cerebral Cortex, 11,* 490–497.

Goldstein, Michael, & Miklowitz, David (1995). The effectiveness of psychoeducational family therapy in the treatment of schizophrenic disorders. *Journal of Marital and Family Therapy, 21,* 361–376.

Goldstein, Noah J.; Cialdini, Robert B.; & Griskevicius, Vladas (2008). A room with a viewpoint: Using social norms to motivate environmental conservation in hotels. *Journal of Consumer Research, 35,* 472–482.

Goldston, David B.; Molock, Sherry D.; Whitbeck, Leslie B.; et al. (2008). Cultural considerations in adolescent suicide prevention and psychosocial treatment. *American Psychologist, 63,* 14–31.

Golinkoff, Roberta M., & Hirsh-Pasek, Kathy (2006). Baby wordsmith: From associationist to social sophisticate. *Current Directions in Psychological Science, 15,* 30–33.

Golub, Sharon (1992). *Periods: From menarche to menopause.* Newbury Park, CA: Sage.

Gonsalves, Brian D., & Cohen, Neal J. (2010) Brain imaging, cognitive processes, and brain networks. *Perspectives on Psychological Science, 5,* 744–752.

Gonzaga, Gian C.; Turner, Rebecca A.; Keltner, Dacher; et al. (2006). Romantic love and sexual desire in close relationships. *Emotion, 6,* 163–179.

Good, Catherine; Aronson, Joshua; & Harder, Jayne A. (2008). Problems in the pipeline: Stereotype threat and women's achievement in high-level math courses. *Journal of Applied Developmental Psychology, 29,* 17–28.

Goode, Erica (2003, May 6). Experts see mind's voices in new light. *New York Times,* Science Times, pp. D1, D4.

Goodwyn, Susan, & Acredolo, Linda (1998). Encouraging symbolic gestures: A new perspective on the relationship between gesture and speech. In J. Iverson & S. Goldin-Meadow (Eds.), *The nature and functions of gesture in children's communication.* San Francisco: Jossey-Bass.

Gopnik, Alison (2009). *The philosophical baby.* New York: Farrar, Straus and Giroux.

Gopnik, Myrna; Choi, Sooja; & Baumberger, Therese (1996). Cross-linguistic differences in early semantic and cognitive development. *Cognitive Development, 11,* 197–227.

Gosling, Samuel D.; Rentfrow, P. J.; & Swann, William B., Jr. (2003). A very brief measure of the Big Five personality domains. *Journal of Research in Personality, 37,* 504–528.

Gosling, Samuel D.; Kwan, Virginia S. Y.; & John, Oliver P. (2003). A dog's got personality: A cross-species comparative approach to personality judgments in dogs and humans. *Journal of Personality and Social Psychology, 85,* 1161–1169.

Gotlib, Ian H.; Joormann, Jutta; Minor, Kelly L.; & Hallmayer, Joachim (2008). HPA axis reactivity: A mechanism underlying the associations among 5-HTTLPR, stress, and depression. *Biological Psychiatry, 63,* 847–851.

Gottesman, Irving I. (1991). *Schizophrenia genesis: The origins of madness.* New York: Freeman.

Gottesman, Irving; Laursen, T. M.; Bertelsen A.; & Mortensen, P. B. (2010). Severe mental disorders in offspring with 2 psychiatrically ill parents. *Archives of General Psychiatry, 67,* 252–257.

Gottfredson, Linda S. (2002). g: Highly general and highly practical. In R. J. Sternberg & E. I. Grigorenko (Eds.), *The general intelligence factor: How general is it?* Mahway, NJ: Erlbaum.

Gougoux, Frederic; Zatorre, Robert J.; Lassonde, Maryse; et al. (2005). A functional neuroimaging study of sound localization: Visual cortex activity predicts performance in early-blind individuals. *PloS Biology, 3,* 324–333.

Gouin, Jean-Philippe; Kiecolt-Glaser, Janice K.; Malarkey, William B.; & Glaser, Ronald (2008). The influence of anger expression on wound healing. *Brain, Behavior, and Immunity, 22,* 699–708.

Gould, Stephen Jay (1994, November 28). Curveball. [Review of The Bell Curve, by Richard J. Herrnstein and Charles Murray.] *The New Yorker,* 139–149.

Gould, Stephen Jay (1996). *The mismeasure of man* (Rev. ed.). New York: Norton.

Grabe, Shelly; Ward, L. Monique; & Hyde, Janet S. (2008). The role of the media in body image concerns among women: A meta-analysis of experimental and correlational studies. *Psychological Bulletin, 134,* 460–476.

Graeber, Manuel B., & Streit, Wolfgang J. (2010). Microglia: Biology and pathology. *Acta Neuropathologica, 119,* 89–105.

Graff, Kaitlin; Murnen, Sarah K.; & Smolak, Linda (2012). Too sexualized to be taken seriously? Perceptions of a girl in childlike vs. sexualizing clothing. *Sex Roles, 66,* 764–775.

Graham, Alice M.; Fisher, Philip A.; & Pfeifer, Jennifer H. (2013). What sleeping babies hear: A functional MRI study of interparental conflict and infants' emotion processing. *Psychological Science, 24,* 782–789.

Graham, Jesse; Haidt, Jonathan; & Nosek, Brian A. (2009). Liberals and conservatives rely on different sets of moral foundations. *Journal of Personality and Social Psychology, 96,* 1029–1046.

Graham, Jill W. (1986). Principled organizational dissent: A theoretical essay. *Research in Organizational Behavior, 8,* 1–52.

Grahe, Jon E., & Bernieri, Frank J. (1999). The importance of nonverbal cues in judging rapport. *Journal of Nonverbal Behavior, 23,* 253–269.

Grant, Heidi, & Dweck, Carol S. (2003). Clarifying achievement goals and their impact. *Journal of Personality and Social Psychology, 85,* 541–553.

Grant, Igor; Gonzalez, Raul; Carey, Catherine L.; et al. (2003). Non-acute (residual) neurocognitive effects of cannabis use: A meta-analytic study. *Journal of the International Neuropsychological Society, 9,* 679–689.

Gray, Kurt, & Wegner, Daniel M. (2008). The sting of intentional pain. *Psychological Science, 19,* 1260–1261.

Greely, Henry T., & Illes, Judy (2007). Neuroscience-based lie detection: The urgent need for regulation. *American Journal of Law & Medicine, 33,* 377.

Greely, Henry T.; Sahakian, Barbara; Harris, John; et al. (2008). Towards responsible use of cognitive-enhancing drugs by the healthy. *Nature, 455,* 702–705.

Greenberg, Gary (2013). *The book of woe: The making of the DSM-5 and the unmaking of psychiatry.* New York: Blue Rider Press.

Greenberger, Dennis, & Padesky, Christine A. (1995). *Mind over mood: A cognitive therapy treatment manual for clients.* New York: Guilford.

Greenberger, Ellen; Lessard, Jared; Chen, Chuansheng; & Farruggia, Susan P. (2008). Self-entitled college students: Contributions of personality, parenting, and motivational factors. *Journal of Youth & Adolescence, 37,* 1193–1204.

Greenough, William T. (1984). Structural correlates of information storage in the mammalian brain: A review and hypothesis. *Trends in Neurosciences, 7,* 229–233.

Greenough, William T., & Anderson, Brenda J. (1991). Cerebellar synaptic plasticity: Relation to learning vs. neural activity. *Annals of the New York Academy of Sciences, 627,* 231–247

Greenough, William T., & Black, James E. (1992). Induction of brain structure by experience: Substrates for cognitive development. In M. Gunnar & C. A. Nelson (Eds.), *Behavioral developmental neuroscience: Vol. 24. Minnesota Symposia on Child Psychology.* Hillsdale, NJ: Erlbaum.

Greenwald, Anthony G.; McGhee, Debbie E.; & Schwartz, Jordan L. K. (1998). Measuring individual differences in implicit cognition: The Implicit Association Test. *Journal of Personality and Social Psychology, 74,* 1464–1480.

Greenwald, Anthony G.; Poehlman, T. Andrew; Uhlmann, Eric L.; & Banaji, Mahzarin R. (2009). Understanding and using the Implicit Association Test: III. Meta-analysis of predictive validity. *Journal of Personality and Social Psychology, 97,* 17–41.

Gregg, L., & Tarrier, N. (2007). Virtual reality in mental health: A review of the literature. *Social Psychiatry and Psychiatric Epidemiology, 42,* 343–54.

Gregory, Richard L. (1963). Distortion of visual space as inappropriate constancy scaling. *Nature, 199,* 678–679.

Griffin, Donald R. (2001). *Animal minds: Beyond cognition to consciousness.* Chicago: University of Chicago Press.

Griffiths, R. R.; Richards, W. A.; Johnson, M. W.; et al. (2008). Mystical-type experiences occasioned by psilocybin mediate the attribution of personal meaning and spiritual significance fourteen months later. *Journal of Psychopharmacology, 22,* 621–632.

Grinspoon, Lester, & Bakalar, James B. (1993). *Marihuana, the forbidden medicine.* New Haven, CT: Yale University Press.

Grob, Charles S.; Danfroth, Alicia L.; Chopra, Gurpreet S.; et al. (2011). Pilot study of psilocybin treatment for anxiety in patients with advanced-stage cancer. *Archives of General Psychiatry, 68,* 71–78.

Gross, James J. (1998). The emerging field of emotion regulation: An integrative review. *Review of General Psychology, 2,* 271–299.

Gross, James J., & John, Oliver, P. (2003). Individual differences in two emotion regulation processes: Implications for affect, relationships, and well-being. *Journal of Personality and Social Psychology, 85,* 348–362.

Grossman, Michele, & Wood, Wendy (1993). Sex differences in intensity of emotional experience: A social role interpretation. *Journal of Personality and Social Psychology, 65,* 1010–1022.

Grün, Felix, & Blumberg, Bruce (2006). Environmental obesogens: Organotins and endocrine disruption via nuclear receptor signaling. *Endocrinology, 147,* (6 Suppl): S50–5.

Guilford, J. P. (1988). Some changes in the structure-of-intellect model. *Educational and Psychological Measurement, 48,* 1–4.

Gur, R. E.; Maany, V.; Mozley, P. D.; et al. (1998). Subcortical MRI volumes in neuroleptic-naive and treated patients with schizophrenia. *American Journal of Psychiatry, 155,* 1711–1717.

Gur, Ruben C.; Gunning-Dixon, Faith; Bilker, Wareen B.; & Gur, Raquel E. (2002). Sex differences in temporo-limbic and frontal brain volumes of healthy adults. *Cerebral Cortex, 12,* 998–1003.

Gustavson, Carl R.; Garcia, John; Hankins, Walter G.; & Rusiniak, Kenneth W. (1974). Coyote predation control by aversive conditioning. *Science, 184,* 581–583.

Guthrie, Paul C., & Mobley, Brenda D. (1994). A comparison of the differential diagnostic efficiency of three personality disorder inventories. *Journal of Clinical Psychology, 50,* 656–665.

Guzman-Marin, Ruben; Suntsova, Natalia; Methippara, Melvi; et al. (2005). Sleep deprivation suppresses neurogenesis in the adult hippocampus of rats. *European Journal of Neuroscience, 22,* 2111–2116.

Haber, Ralph N. (1970, May). How we remember what we see. *Scientific American, 222,* 104–112.

Hacking, Ian (1995). *Rewriting the soul: Multiple personality and the sciences of memory.* Princeton: Princeton University Press.

Hahn, Robert; Fuqua-Whitley, Dawna; Wethington, Holly; et al. (2008). Effectiveness of universal school-based programs to prevent violent and aggressive behaviour: A systematic review. *Child: Care, Health, & Development, 34,* 139.

Haier, Richard J.; Jung, Rex E.; Yeo, Ronald A.; et al. (2005). The neuroanatomy of general intelligence: sex matters. *NeuroImage, 25,* 320–327.

Haidt, Jonathan (2012). *The righteous mind: Why good people are divided by politics and religion.* New York: Pantheon Books.

Haimov, Iris, & Lavie, Peretz (1996). Melatonin—A soporific hormone. *Current Directions in Psychological Science, 5,* 106–111.

Hall, Calvin (1953a). A cognitive theory of dreams. *Journal of General Psychology, 49,* 273–282.

Hall, Calvin (1953b). *The meaning of dreams.* New York: McGraw-Hill.

Hall, Edward T. (1959). *The silent language.* Garden City, NY: Doubleday.

Hall, Edward T. (1976). *Beyond culture.* New York: Anchor.

Hall, Edward T. (1983). *The dance of life: The other dimension of time.* Garden City, NY: Anchor Press/Doubleday.

Hall, Edward T., & Hall, Mildred R. (1987). *Hidden differences: Doing business with the Japanese.* Garden City, NY: Anchor Press/Doubleday.

Hall, Edward T., & Hall, Mildred R. (1990). *Understanding cultural differences.* Yarmouth, ME: Intercultural Press.

Hall, G. Stanley (1899). A study of anger. *American Journal of Psychology, 10,* 516–591.

Hall, Nathan C.; Perry, Raymond P.; Ruthig, Joelle C.; et al. (2006). Primary and secondary control in achievement settings: A longitudinal field study of academic motivation, emotions, and performance. *Journal of Applied Social Psychology, 36,* 1430–1470.

Hallion, Lauren S., & Ruscio, Ayelet M. (2011). A meta-analysis of the effect of cognitive bias modification on anxiety and depression. *Psychological Bulletin, 137,* 940–958.

Halpern, Diane F. (2002). *Thought and knowledge: An introduction to critical thinking* (4th ed.). Hillsdale, NJ: Erlbaum.

Halpern, Diane F. (2008). Psychologists are redefining retirement as a new phase of life. *The General Psychologist, 43,* 22–29.

Halpern, Sue (2008, May 19). Virtual Iraq. *New Yorker,* 32–37.

Hamamura, Takeshi, & Heine, Steven J. (2008). The role of self-criticism in self-improvement and face maintenance among Japanese. In E. C. Chang (Ed.), *Self-criticism and self-enhancement: Theory, research, and clinical implications.* Washington, DC, US: American Psychological Association.

Hammen, Constance (2009). Adolescent depression. *Current Directions in Psychological Science, 18,* 200–204.

Hamby, Sherry L., & Koss, Mary P. (2003). Shades of gray: A qualitative study of terms used in the measurement of sexual victimization. *Psychology of Women Quarterly, 27,* 243–255.

Haney, Craig, & Zimbardo, Philip (1998). The past and future of U.S. prison policy: Twenty-five years after the Stanford Prison Experiment. *American Psychologist, 53,* 709–727.

Haney, Craig; Banks, Curtis; & Zimbardo, Philip (1973). Interpersonal dynamics in a simulated prison. *International Journal of Criminology and Penology, 1,* 69–97.

Hardie, Elizabeth A. (1997). PMS in the workplace: Dispelling the myth of cyclic function. *Journal of Occupational and Organizational Psychology, 70,* 97–102.

Harding, Courtenay M. (2005). Changes in schizophrenia across time: Paradoxes, patterns, and predictors. In L. Davidson, C. Harding, & L. Spaniol (Eds.), *Recovery from severe mental illnesses: Research evidence and implications for practice* (Vol. 1). Boston, MA: Center for Psychiatric Rehabilitation/Boston U.

Hare, Robert D. (1965). Temporal gradient of fear arousal in psychopaths. *Journal of Abnormal Psychology, 70,* 442–445.

Hare, Robert D. (1996). Psychopathy: A clinical construct whose time has come. *Criminal Justice and Behavior, 23,* 24–54.

Haritos-Fatouros, Mika (1988). The official torturer: A learning model for obedience to the authority of violence. *Journal of Applied Social Psychology, 18,* 1107–1120.

Harlow, Harry F. (1958). The nature of love. *American Psychologist, 13,* 673–685.

Harlow, Harry F., & Harlow, Margaret K. (1966). Learning to love. *American Scientist, 54,* 244–272.

Harmon-Jones, Eddie; Peterson, Carly K.; & Harris, Christine R. (2009). Jealousy: Novel methods and neural correlates. *Emotion, 9,* 113–117.

Harnsberger, James D.; Hollien, Harry; Martin Camilo A.; & Hollien, Kevin A. (2009). Stress and deception in speech: Evaluating Layered Voice Analysis. *Journal of Forensic Sciences, 54,* 642–650.

Harris, Gardiner (2003, August 7). Debate resumes on the safety of depression's wonder drugs. *New York Times,* pp. A1, C4.

Harris, Judith R. (2006). *No two alike: Human nature and human individuality.* New York: Norton.

Harris, Judith R. (2009). *The nurture assumption* (2nd ed.). New York: Free Press.

Harris, Lasana T., & Fiske, Susan T. (2006). Dehumanizing the lowest of the low: Neuro-imaging responses to extreme outgroups. *Psychological Science,* 847–853.

Hart, A. J.; Whalen, P. J.; Shin, L. M.; et al. (2000). Differential response in the human amygdala to racial outgroup vs. ingroup face stimuli. *NeuroReport, 11,* 2351–2355.

Hart, John, Jr.; Berndt, Rita S.; & Caramazza, Alfonso (1985). Category-specific naming deficit following cerebral infarction. *Nature, 316,* 339–340.

Haslam, S. Alexander; Jetten, Jolanda; Postmes, Tom; & Haslam, Catherine (2009). Social identity, health and well-being: An emerging agenda for applied psychology. *Applied Psychology: An International Review, 58,* 1–23.

Haslam, S. Alexander, & Reicher, Stephen (2003, Spring). Beyond Stanford: Questioning a role-based explanation of tyranny. *Society for Experimental Social Psychology Dialogue, 18,* 22–25.

Haslam, S. Alexander, & Reicher, Stephen D. (2012). When prisoners take over the prison: A social psychology of resistance. *Personality and Social Psychology Review, 16,* 154–179.

Hassabis, Demis, & Maguire, Eleanor A. (2007). Deconstructing episodic memory with construction. *Trends in Cognitive Sciences, 11,* 299–306.

Hassett, Janice M.; Siebert, Erin R.; Wallen, Kim (2008). Sex differences in rhesus monkey toy preferences parallel those of children. *Hormones and Behavior, 54,* 359–364.

Hatfield, Elaine, & Rapson, Richard L. (1996/2005). *Love and sex: Cross-cultural perspectives.* Boston: Allyn & Bacon.

Hatfield, Elaine, & Rapson, Richard L. (2008). Passionate love and sexual desire: Multidisciplinary perspectives. In J. P. Forgas & J. Fitness (Eds.), *Social relationships: Cognitive, affective, and motivational processes.* New York: Psychology Press.

Häuser, Winfried; Bartram-Wunn, Eva; Bartram, Claas; et al. (2011). Systematic review: Placebo response in drug trials of fibromyalgia syndrome and painful peripheral diabetic neuropathy-magnitude and patient-related predictors. *Pain, 152,* 1709–1717.

Haut, Jennifer S.; Beckwith, Bill E.; Petros, Thomas V.; & Russell, Sue (1989). Gender differences in retrieval from long-term memory following acute intoxication with ethanol. *Physiology and Behavior, 45,* 1161–1165.

Havas, David A.; Glenberg, Arthur M.; Gutowski, Karol A.; et al. (2010). Cosmetic use of botulinum toxin-A affects processing of emotional language. *Psychological Science, 21,* 895–900.

Hawkins, Elizabeth H.; Cummins, Lillian H.; & Marlatt, G. Alan (2004). Preventing substance abuse in American Indian and Alaska Native Youth: Promising strategies for healthier communities. *Psychological Bulletin, 130,* 304–323.

Hawkins, Scott A., & Hastie, Reid (1990). Hindsight: Biased judgments of past events after the outcomes are known. *Psychological Bulletin, 107,* 311–327.

Hay, Dale F.; Mundy, Lisa; Roberts, Siwan; et al. (2011). Known risk factors for violence predict 12-month-old infants' aggressiveness with peers. *Psychological Science, 22,* 1205–1211.

Hayes, Steven C. (2004). Acceptance and commitment therapy and the new behavior therapies: Mindfulness, acceptance, and relationship. In S. C. Hayes, V. M. Follette, & M. M. Linehan (2004), *Mindfulness and acceptance: Expanding the cognitive-behavioral tradition.* New York: Guilford.

Hayes, Steven C.; Follette, Victoria M.; & Linehan, Marsha M. (Eds.) (2004). *Mindfulness and acceptance: Expanding the cognitive-behavioral tradition.* New York: The Guilford.

Hayne, Harlene, & Jack, Fiona (2011). Childhood amnesia. *Cognitive Science, 2,* 136–145.

Hazan, Cindy, & Diamond, Lisa M. (2000). The place of attachment in human mating. *Review of General Psychology, 4,* 186–204.

Headey, Bruce (2008). Life goals matter to happiness: A revision of set-point theory. *Social Indicators Research, 86,* 213–231.

Healy, David (2002). *The creation of psychopharmacology.* Cambridge, MA: Harvard University Press.

Healy, David (2012). *Pharmageddon.* Berkeley, CA: University of California Press.

Heath, A. C.; Madden, P. A. F.; Bucholz, K. K.; et al. (2003). Genetic and genotype x environment interaction effects on risk of dependence on alcohol, tobacco, and other drugs: new research. In R. Plomin et al. (Eds.), *Behavioral genetics in the postgenomic era.* Washington, DC: APA Books.

Hegarty, Mary, & Waller, David (2005). Individual differences in spatial abilities. In P. Shah & A. Miyake (Eds.), *The Cambridge Handbook of Visuospatial Thinking.* New York: Cambridge University Press.

Heilig, Markus (2008, December 1). Triggering addiction. *The Scientist, 22.* www.the-scientist.com/?articles.view/articleNo/26964/title/Triggering-Addiction/.

Helson, Ravenna; Roberts, Brent; & Agronick, Gail (1995). Enduringness and change in creative personality and the prediction of occupational creativity. *Journal of Personality and Social Psychology, 6,* 1173–1183.

Helzer, John E.; Wittchen, Hans-Ulrich; Krueger, Robert F.; & Kraemer, Helena C. (2008). Dimensional options for DSM-V: The way forward. In J. E. Helzer, H. C. Kramer, & R. F. Krueger (Eds.), *Dimensional approaches in diagnostic classification: Refining the research agenda for DSM-V.* Washington, DC: American Psychiatric Association.

Henderlong, Jennifer, & Lepper, Mark R. (2002). The effects of praise on children's intrinsic motivation: A review and synthesis. *Psychological Bulletin, 128,* 774–795.

Hennessy, Michael B.; Schiml-Webb, Patricia A.; & Deak, Terrence (2009). Separation, sickness, and depression. *Current Directions in Psychological Science, 18,* 227–231.

Henrich, Joseph; Boyd, Robert; Bowles, Samuel; et al. (2001). In search of Homo Economicus: Behavioral experiments in 15 small scale societies. *American Economics Review, 91,* 73–78.

Henrich, Joseph; Heine, Steven J.; & Norenzayan, Ara (2010). The weirdest people in the world? *Behavioral and Brain Sciences, 33,* 61–83.

Heinrichs, R. Walter (2005). The primacy of cognition in schizophrenia. *American Psychologist, 60,* 229–242.

Hepach, Robert; Vaish, Amrisha; & Tomasello, Michael (2012). Young children are intrinsically motivated to see others helped. *Psychological Science, 23,* 967–972.

Herbert, Alan; Gerry, Norman P.; McQueen, Matthew B.; et al. (2006). A common genetic variant is associated with adult and childhood obesity. *Science, 312,* 279–283.

Herculano-Houzel, Suzana (2009). The human brain in numbers: A linearly scaled-up primate brain. *Frontiers of Human Neuroscience, 3,* 31.

Herdt, Gilbert (1984). *Ritualized homosexuality in Melanesia.* Berkeley: University of California Press.

Herek, Gregory M., & Capitanio, J. P. (1996). "Some of my best friends": Intergroup contact, concealable stigma, and heterosexuals' attitudes toward gay men and lesbians. *Personality and Social Psychology Bulletin, 22,* 412–424.

Herman, John H. (1992). Transmutative and reproductive properties of dreams: Evidence for cortical modulation of brainstem generators. In J. Antrobus & M. Bertini (Eds.), *The neuropsychology of dreaming.* Hillsdale, NJ: Erlbaum.

Herman, Louis M.; Kuczaj, Stan A.; & Holder, Mark D. (1993). Responses to anomalous gestural sequences by a language-trained dolphin: Evidence for processing of semantic relations and syntactic information. *Journal of Experimental Psychology: General, 122,* 184–194.

Herman, Louis M., & Morrel-Samuels, Palmer (1996). Knowledge acquisition and asymmetry between language comprehension and production: Dolphins and apes as general models for animals. In M. Bekoff & D. Jamieson et al. (Eds.), *Readings in animal cognition.* Cambridge, MA: MIT Press.

Herman-Giddens, Marcia E.; Steffes, Jennifer; Harris, Donna; et al. (2012). Secondary sexual characteristics in boys: Data from the pediatric research in office settings network. *Pediatrics, 130,* 1058–1068.

Heron, Woodburn (1957). The pathology of boredom. *Scientific American, 196(1),* 52–56.

Hertzog, Christopher; Kramer, Arthur F.; Wilson, Robert S.; & Lindenberger, Ulman (2008). Enrichment effects on adult cognitive development: Can the functional capacity of older adults be preserved and enhanced? *Psychological Science in the Public Interest, 9,* 1–65.

Herz, Rachel S., & Cupchik, Gerald C. (1995). The emotional distinctiveness of odor-evoked memories. *Chemical Senses, 20,* 517–528.

Herzog, Harold (2011). The impact of pets on human health and psychological well-being: Fact, fiction, or hypothesis? *Current Directions in Psychological Science, 20,* 236–239.

Hess, Thomas M. (2005). Memory and aging in context. *Psychological Bulletin, 131,* 383–406.

Hess, Ursula, & Thibault, Pascal (2009). Darwin and emotional expression. *American Psychologist, 64,* 120–128.

Hess, Ursula; Adams, Reginald B., Jr.; & Kleck, Robert (2005). Who may frown and who should smile? Dominance, affiliation, and the display of happiness and anger. *Cognition & Emotion, 19,* 515–536.

Hewlitt, Sylvia Ann; Luce, Carolyn B.; & Servon, Lisa J. (2008, June). Stopping the exodus of women in science. *Harvard Business Review,* ePub. http://hbr.org/2008/06/stopping-the-exodus-of-women-in-science/ar/1.

Heyman, Gene M. (2009). *Addiction: A disorder of choice.* Cambridge, MA: Harvard University Press.

Heyman, Gene M. (2011). Received wisdom regarding the roles of craving and dopamine in addiction. *Perspectives on Psychological Science, 6,* 156–160.

Hilgard, Ernest R. (1977). *Divided consciousness: Multiple controls in human thought and action.* New York: Wiley-Interscience.

Hilgard, Ernest R. (1986). *Divided consciousness: Multiple controls in human thought and action* (2nd ed.). New York: Wiley.

Hill-Soderlund, Ashley L., & Braungart-Rieker, Julia M. (2008). Early individual differences in temperamental reactivity and regulation: Implications for effortful control in early childood. *Infant Behavior & Development, 31,* 386–397.

Hilts, Philip J. (1995). *Memory's ghost: The strange tale of Mr. M. and the nature of memory.* New York: Simon & Schuster.

Hirsch, Helmut V. B., & Spinelli, D. N. (1970). Visual experience modifies distribution of horizontally and vertically oriented receptive fields in cats. *Science, 168,* 869–871.

Hirsh, Jacob B.; Galinsky, Adam D.; & Zhong, Chen-Bo (2011). Drunk, powerful, and in the dark: How general processes of disinhibition produce both prosocial and antisocial behavior. *Perspectives on Psychological Science, 6,* 415–427.

Hobson, J. Allan (1988). *The dreaming brain.* New York: Basic.

Hobson, J. Allan (1990). Activation, input source, and modulation: A neurocognitive model of the state of the brain mind. In R. R. Bootzin, J. F. Kihlstrom, & D. L. Schacter (Eds.), *Sleep and cognition.* Washington, DC: American Psychological Association.

Hobson, J. Allan (2002). *Dreaming: An introduction to the science of sleep.* New York: Oxford University Press.

Hobson, J. Allan; Pace-Schott, Edward F.; & Stickgold, Robert (2000). Dreaming and the brain: Toward a cognitive neuroscience of conscious states. *Behavioral and Brain Sciences, 23,* 793–842, 904–1018, 1083–1121.

Hobson, J. Allan; Sangsanguan, Suchada; Arantes, Henry; & Kahn, David (2011). Dream logic: The inferential reasoning paradigm. *Dreaming, 21,* 1–15.

Hochberg, L. R.; Bacher, D.; Jarosiewicz, B.; et al. (2012). Reach and grasp by people with tetraplegia using a neurally controlled robotic arm. *Nature, 485,* 372–375.

Hochschild, Arlie R. (2003). *The Managed Heart: Commercialization of human feeling* (2nd ed.). Berkeley, CA: University of California Press.

Hodson, Gordon (2011). Do ideologically intolerant people benefit from intergroup contact? *Current Directions in Psychological Science, 20,* 154–159.

Hofstede, Geert, & Bond, Michael H. (1988). The Confucius connection: From cultural roots to economic growth. *Organizational Dynamics,* 5–21.

Holden, George W., & Miller, Pamela C. (1999). Enduring and different: A meta-analysis of the similarity in parents' child rearing. *Psychological Bulletin, 125,* 223–254

Hollon, Steven D.; Thase, Michael E.; & Markowitz, John C. (2002). Treatment and prevention of depression. *Psychological Science in the Public Interest, 3,* 39–77.

Hooker, Evelyn (1957). The adjustment of the male overt homosexual. *Journal of Projective Techniques, 21,* 18–31.

Hopper, Kim; Harrison, Glynn; Janca, Aleksandar; & Sartorius, Norman (Eds.) (2007). *Recovery from schizophrenia: An international investigation.* New York: Oxford University Press.

Horgan, John (1995, November). Get smart, take a test: A long-term rise in IQ scores baffles intelligence experts. *Scientific American, 273,* 12–14.

Horn, John L., & Cattell, Raymond B. (1966). Refinement and test of the theory of fluid and crystallized general intelligences. *Journal of Educational Psychology, 57,* 253–270

Horney, Karen (1926/1973). The flight from womanhood. *The International Journal of Psycho-Analysis, 7,* 324–339. Reprinted in J. B. Miller (Ed.), *Psychoanalysis and women.* New York: Brunner/Mazel, 1973.

Hornung, Richard W.; Lanphear, Bruce P.; & Dietrich, Kim N. (2009). Age of greatest susceptibility to childhood lead exposure: A new statistical approach. *Environmental Health Perspectives, 117,* 1309–1312.

Horwitz, Allan V., & Wakefield, Jerome C. (2007). *The loss of sadness: How psychiatry transformed normal misery into depressive disorder.* New York: Oxford University Press.

Houben, Katrijn; Wiers, Reinout W.; & Jansen, Anita (2011). Getting a grip on drinking behavior: Training working memory to reduce alcohol abuse. *Psychological Science, 22,* 968–975.

Houston, Derek M., & Jusczyk, Peter W. (2003). Infants' long-term memory for the sound patterns of words and voices. *Journal of Experimental Psychology: Human Perception & Performance, 29,* 1143–1154.

Houts, Arthur C. (2002). Discovery, invention, and the expansion of the modern Diagnostic and Statistical Manuals of Mental Disorders. In L. E. Beutler & M. L. Malik (Eds.), *Rethinking the DSM: A psychological perspective.* Washington, DC: American Psychological Association.

Howard, George S. (1991). Culture tales: A narrative approach to thinking, cross-cultural psychology, and psychotherapy. *American Psychologist, 46,* 187–197.

Howe, Mark L. (2000). *The fate of early memories: Developmental science and the retention of childhood experiences.* Washington, DC: American Psychological Association.

Howe, Mark L.; Courage, Mary L.; & Peterson, Carole (1994). How can I remember when "I" wasn't there? Long-term retention of traumatic experiences and emergence of the cognitive self. *Consciousness and Cognition, 3,* 327–355.

Hrdy, Sarah B. (1988). Empathy, polyandry, and the myth of the coy female. In R. Bleier (Ed.), *Feminist approaches to science.* New York: Pergamon.

Hrdy, Sarah B. (1994). What do women want? In T. A. Bass (Ed.), *Reinventing the future: Conversations with the world's leading scientists.* Reading, MA: Addison-Wesley.

Hrdy, Sarah B. (1999). *Mother nature.* New York: Pantheon.

Hu, Wei; Saba, Laura; Kechris, Katherina; et al. (2008). Genomic insights into acute alcohol tolerance. *Journal of Pharmacology and Experimental Therapeutics, 326,* 792–800.

Huang, C. M.; Polk, T. A.; Goh, J. O.; & Park, D. C. (2012). Both left and right posterior parietal activations contribute to compensatory processes in normal aging. *Neuropsychologia, 50,* 55–66.

Hubel, David H., & Wiesel, Torsten N. (1962). Receptive fields, binocular interaction and functional architecture in the cat's visual cortex. *Journal of Physiology (London), 160,* 106–154.

Hubel, David H., & Wiesel, Torsten N. (1968). Receptive fields and functional architecture of monkey striate cortex. *Journal of Physiology (London), 195,* 215–243.

Hugdahl, Kenneth, & Westerhausen, René (2010). *The two halves of the brain: Information processing in the cerebral hemispheres.* New York: MIT Press.

Huggins, Martha K.; Haritos-Fatouros, Mika; & Zimbardo, Philip G. (2003). *Violence workers: Police torturers and murderers reconstruct Brazilian atrocities.* Berkeley, CA: University of California Press.

Hunsley, John; Lee, Catherine M.; & Wood, James (2003). Controversial and questionable assessment techniques. In S. O. Lilienfeld, S. J. Lynn, & J. M. Lohn (Eds.), *Science and pseudoscience in clinical psychology.* New York: Guilford.

Huntjens, Rafaële J. C.; Verschuere, Bruno; & McNally, Richard J. (2012). Inter-identity autobiographical amnesia in patients with dissociative identity disorder. *PloS One, 7(7):* e40580.

Hupka, Ralph B. (1981). Cultural determinants of jealousy. *Alternative Lifestyles, 4,* 310–356.

Hupka, Ralph B. (1991). The motive for the arousal of romantic jealousy. In P. Salovey (Ed.), *The psychology of jealousy and envy.* New York: Guilford.

Hupka, Ralph B.; Lenton, Alison P.; & Hutchison, Keith A. (1999). Universal development of emotion categories in natural language. *Journal of Personality and Social Psychology, 77,* 247–278.

Hwang, Wei-Chin (2006). The psychotherapy adaptation and modification framework: Application to Asian Americans. *American Psychologist, 61,* 702–715.

Hyde, Janet S. (2007). New directions in the study of gender similarities and differences. *Current Directions in Psychological Science, 16,* 259–263.

Hyman, Ira E., Jr., & Pentland, Joel (1996). The role of mental imagery in the creation of false childhood memories. *Journal of Memory and Language, 35,* 101–117.

Hyman, Ira E.; Boss, Matthew; Wise, Breanne M.; et al. (2010). Did you see the unicycling clown? Inattentional blindness while walking and talking on a cell phone. *Applied Cognitive Psychology, 24,* 597–607.

Iacoboni, Marco (2008). *Mirroring people: The new science of how we connect with others.* New York: Farrar, Straus and Giroux.

Iacono, William (2001). Forensic "Lie Detection": Procedures without scientific basis. *Journal of Forensic Psychology Practice, 1,* 75–86.

Iacono, William G., & Lykken, David T. (1997). The scientific status of research on polygraph techniques: The case against polygraph tests. In D. L. Faigman, D. Kaye, M. J. Saks, & J. Sanders (Eds.), *Modern scientific evidence: The law and science of expert testimony.* St. Paul, MN: West.

Ikonomidou, Chrysanthy; Bittigau, Petra; Ishimaru, Masahiko J.; et al. (2000). Ethanol-induced apoptotic neurodegeneration and fetal alcohol syndrome. *Science, 287,* 1056–1060.

Imada, Toshie, & Ellsworth, Phoebe C. (2011). Proud Americans and lucky Japanese: Cultural differences in appraisal and corresponding emotion. *Emotion, 11,* 329–345.

Impett, Emily A., & Tolman, Deborah L. (2006). Late adolescent girls' sexual experiences and sexual satisfaction. *Journal of Adolescent Research, 21,* 628–646.

Impett, Emily A.; Gable, Shelly; & Peplau, Letitia A. (2005). Giving up and giving in: The costs and benefits of daily sacrifice in intimate relationships. *Journal of Personality and Social Psychology, 89,* 327–344.

Impett, Emily A.; Henson, James M.; Breines, Juliana G.; et al. (2011). Embodiment feels better: Girls' body objectification and well-being across adolescence. *Psychology of Women Quarterly, 35,* 46–58.

Innocenti, Giorgio M., & Price, David J. (2005). Exuberance in the development of cortical networks. *Nature Reviews Neuroscience, 6,* 955–965.

Inzlicht, Michael, & Ben-Zeev, Talia (2000). A threatening intellectual environment: Why females are susceptible to experiencing problem-solving deficits in the presence of males. *Psychological Science, 11,* 365–371.

Isaacson, Walter (2011). *Steve Jobs.* New York: Simon & Schuster.

Islam, Mir Rabiul, & Hewstone, Miles (1993). Intergroup attributions and affective consequences in majority and minority groups. *Journal of Personality and Social Psychology, 64,* 936–950.

Ito, Tiffany A., & Urland, Geoffrey R. (2003). Race and gender on the brain: Electrocortical measures of attention to the race and gender of multiply categorizable individuals. *Journal of Personality and Social Psychology, 85,* 616–626.

Izard, Carroll E. (1990). Facial expressions and the regulation of emotions. *Journal of Personality and Social Psychology, 58,* 487–498.

Izard, Carroll E. (1994b). Innate and universal facial expressions: Evidence from developmental and cross-cultural research. *Psychological Bulletin, 115,* 288–299.

Izard, Carroll E. (2007). Basic emotions, natural kinds, emotion schemas, and a new paradigm. *Perspectives on Psychological Science, 2,* 260–280.

Izard, Véronique; Sann, Coralie; Spelke, Elizabeth S.; & Streri, Arlette (2009). Newborn infants perceive abstract numbers. *Proceedings of the National Academy of Sciences, 106,* 10382–10385.

Jackson, Daren C.; Mueller, Corrina J.; Dolski, Isa; Dalton, Kim M.; Nitschke, Jack B.; et al. (2003). Now you feel it, now you don't: Frontal brain electrical asymmetry and individual differences in emotion regulation. *Psychological Science, 14,* 612–617.

Jacobs, Gregg D.; Pace-Schott, Edward F.; Stickgold, Robert; & Otto, Michael W. (2004). Cognitive behavior therapy and pharmacotherapy for chronic insomnia: A randomized controlled trial and direct comparison. *Archives of Internal Medicine, 164,* 1888–1896.

Jacobsen, Paul B; Bovbjerg, Dana H.; Schwartz, Marc D.; et al. (1995). Conditioned emotional distress in women receiving chemotherapy for breast cancer. *Journal of Consulting & Clinical Psychology, 63,* 108–114.

James, William (1902/1936). *The varieties of religious experience.* New York: Modern Library.

Jamieson, Jeremy P.; Mendes, Wendy B.; & Nock, Matthew K. (2013). Improving acute stress responses: The power of reappraisal. *Current Directions in Psychological Science, 22,* 51–56.

Jamison, Kay (1992). *Touched with fire: Manic depressive illness and the artistic temperament.* New York: Free Press.

Jamison, Kay (1999). *Night falls fast: Understanding suicide.* New York: Knopf.

Jang, Kerry L.; McCrae, Robert R.; Angleitner, Alois; et al. (1998). Heritability of facet-level traits in a cross-cultural twin sample: Support for a hierarchical model of personality. *Journal of Personality and Social Psychology, 74,* 1556–1565.

Janis, Irving L. (1982). *Groupthink: Psychological studies of policy decisions and fiascoes* (2nd ed.). Boston: Houghton Mifflin.

Janis, Irving L. (1989). *Crucial decisions: Leadership in policymaking and crisis management.* New York: Free Press.

Jansari, Ashok, & Parkin, Alan J. (1996). Things that go bump in your life: Explaining the reminiscence bump in autobiographical memory. *Psychology and Aging, 11,* 85–91.

Jaremka, Lisa M; Fagundes, Christopher P.; Peng, Juan; et al. (2013). Loneliness promotes inflammation during acute stress. *Psychological Science, 24,* 1089–1097.

Jaremka, Lisa M.; Glaser, Ronald; Loving, Timothy J.; et al. (2013). Attachment anxiety is linked to alterations in cortisol production and cellular immunity. *Psychological Science, 24,* 272–279.

Jenkins, John G., & Dallenbach, Karl M. (1924). Obliviscence during sleep and waking. *American Journal of Psychology, 35,* 605–612.

Jensen, Arthur R. (1998). *The g factor: The science of mental ability.* Westport, CT; Praeger/Greenwood.

Jobe, Thomas H., & Harrow, Martin (2010). Schizophrenia course, long-term outcome, recovery, and prognosis. *Current Directions in Psychological Science, 19,* 220–225.

Johanek, Lisa M.; Meyer, Richard A.; Friedman, Robert M.; et al. (2008). A role for polymodal C-fiber afferents in nonhistaminergic itch. *Journal of Neuroscience, 28,* 7659–7669.

Johns, Michael; Schmader, Toni; & Martens, Andy (2005). Knowing is half the battle: Teaching stereotype threat as a means of improving women's math performance. *Psychological Science, 16,* 175–179.

Johnson, Andrew J., & Miles, Christopher (2009). Serial position effects in 2-alternative forced choice recognition: functional equivalence across visual and auditory modalities. *Memory, 17,* 84–91.

Johnson, Marcia K.; Hashtroudi, Shahin; & Lindsay, D. Stephen (1993). Source monitoring. *Psychological Bulletin, 114,* 3–28.

Johnson, Marcia K.; Raye, Carol L.; Mitchell, Karen J.; & Ankudowich, Elizabeth (2011). The cognitive neuroscience of true and false memories. In R. F. Belli (Ed.), *True and false recovered memories: Toward a reconciliation of the debate* (Vol. 58). New York: Springer.

Johnson, Wendy; Turkheimer, Eric; Gottesman, Irving I.; & Bouchard, Thomas J., Jr. (2009). Beyond heritability: Twin studies in behavioral research. *Current Directions in Psychological Science, 18,* 217–221.

Joiner, Thomas (2005). *Myths about suicide.* Cambridge, MA: Harvard University Press.

Jones, Edward E. (1990). *Interpersonal perception.* New York: Macmillan.

Jones, Mary Cover (1924). A laboratory study of fear: The case of Peter. *Pedagogical Seminary, 31,* 308–315.

Joormann, Jutta, & Gotlib, Ian H. (2007). Selective attention to emotional faces following recovery from depression. *Journal of Abnormal Psychology, 116,* 80–85.

Joormann, Jutta; Levens, Sara M.; & Gotlib, Ian H. (2011). Sticky thoughts: Depression and rumination are associated with difficulties manipulating emotional material in working memory. *Psychological Science, 22,* 979–983.

Joormann, Jutta; Siemer, Matthias; & Gotlib, Ian H. (2007). Mood regulation in depression: Differential effects of distraction and recall of happy memories on sad mood. *Journal of Abnormal Psychology, 116,* 484–490.

Jordan, Alexander H.; Monin, Benoît; Dweck, Carol S.; et al. (2011). Misery has more company than people think: Underestimating the prevalence of others' negative emotions. *Personality and Social Psychology Bulletin, 37,* 120–135.

Jordan-Young, Rebecca M. (2010). *Brainstorm: The flaws in the science of sex differences.* Cambridge, Mass.: Harvard University Press.

Jost, John T. (2006). The end of the end of ideology. *American Psychologist, 61,* 651–670.

Jost, John T.; Glaser, Jack; Kruglanski, Arie W.; & Sulloway, Frank J. (2003). Political conservatism as motivated social cognition. *Psychological Bulletin, 129,* 339–375.

Jost, John T.; Nosek, Brian A.; & Gosling, Samuel D. (2008). Ideology: Its resurgence in social, personality, and political psychology. *Perspectives on Psychological Science, 3,* 126–136.

Judd, Charles M.; Park, Bernadette; Ryan, Carey S.; et al. (1995). Stereotypes and ethnocentrism: Diverging interethnic perceptions of African American and white American youth. *Journal of Personality and Social Psychology, 69,* 460–481.

Judge, Timothy A. (2009). Core self-evaluations and work success. *Current Directions in Psychological Science, 18,* 18–22.

Jung, Carl (1967). *Collected works.* Princeton, NJ: Princeton University Press.

Jusczyk, Peter W. (2002). How infants adapt speech-processing capacities to native-language structure. *Current Directions in Psychological Science, 11,* 15–18.

Jussim, Lee; Cain, Thomas R.; Crawford, Jarret T.; et al. (2009). The unbearable accuracy of stereotypes. In T. Nelson (Ed.), *The handbook of prejudice, stereotyping, and discrimination.* New York: Psychology Press.

Kagan, Jerome (1997). Temperament and the reactions to unfamiliarity. *Child Development, 68,* 139–143.

Kahneman, Daniel (2003). A perspective on judgment and choice: Mapping bounded rationality. *American Psychologist, 58,* 697–720.

Kahneman, Daniel (2011). *Thinking, fast and slow.* New York: Farrar, Straus and Giroux.

Kaminski, Juliane; Call, Josep; & Fisher, Julia (2004). Word learning in a domestic dog: Evidence for "fast mapping." *Science, 304,* 1682–1683.

Kanagawa, Chie; Cross, Susan E., & Markus, Hazel R. (2001). "Who am I?" The cultural psychology of the conceptual self. *Personality and Social Psychology Bulletin, 27,* 90–103.

Kandel, Eric R. (2001). The molecular biology of memory storage: A dialogue between genes and synapses. *Science, 294,* 1030–1038.

Kane, Michael J.; Brown, Leslie H.; McVay, Jennifer C.; et al. (2007). For whom the mind wanders, and when: An experience-sampling study of working memory and executive control in daily life. *Psychological Science, 18,* 614–621.

Kanter, Rosabeth M. (2006). Some effects of proportions on group life: Skewed sex ratios and responses to token women. In J. N. Levine & R. L. Moreland (Eds.), *Small groups. Key Readings in Social Psychology.* New York: Psychology Press.

Kanwisher, Nancy (2010). Functional specificity in the human brain: A window into the functional architecture of the mind. *Proceedings of the National Academy of Sciences, 107,* 11163–11170.

Karasek, Robert, & Theorell, Tores (1990). *Healthy work: Stress, productivity, and the reconstruction of working life.* New York: Basic.

Karlsgodt, Katherine H.; Sun, Daqiang; & Cannon, Tyrone D. (2010). Structural and functional brain abnormalities in schizophrenia. *Current Directions in Psychological Science, 19,* 226–231.

Karney, Benjamin, & Bradbury, Thomas N. (2000). Attributions in marriage: State or trait? A growth curve analysis. *Journal of Personality and Social Psychology, 78,* 295–309.

Karni, Avi; Tanne, David; Rubenstein, Barton S.; Askenasy, Jean J. M.; & Sagi, Dov (1994). Dependence on REM sleep of overnight improvement of a perceptual skill. *Science, 265,* 679–682.

Karpicke, Jeffrey D. (2012). Retrieval-based learning: Active retrieval promotes meaningful learning. *Current Directions in Psychological Science, 21,* 157–163.

Karpicke, Jeffrey D., & Roediger, Henry L. III (2007). Repeated retrieval during learning is the key to long-term retention. *Journal of Memory and Language, 57,* 151–162.

Karpicke, Jeffrey D., & Roediger, Henry L. III (2008). The critical importance of retrieval for learning. *Science, 319,* 966–968.

Karpicke, Jeffrey D.; Butler, Andrew C.; & Roediger, Henry L. III (2009). Metacognitive strategies in student learning: Do students practise retrieval when they study on their own? *Memory, 17,* 471–479.

Karraker, Katherine H.; Vogel, Dena A.; & Lake, Margaret A. (1995). Parents' gender-stereotyped perceptions of newborns: The eye of the beholder revisited. *Sex Roles, 33,* 687–701.

Kaschak, Michael P.; Kutta, Timothy J.; & Schatschneider, Christopher (2011). Long-term cumulative structural priming persists for (at least) one week. *Memory & Cognition, 39,* 381–388.

Kasser, Tim, & Ryan, Richard M. (1996). Further examining the American dream: Correlates of financial success as a central life aspiration. *Personality and Social Psychology Bulletin, 22,* 280–287.

Katigbak, Marcia S.; Church, A. Timothy; Guanzon-Lapeña, Ma. Angeles; et al. (2002). Are indigenous personality dimensions culture specific? Philippine inventories and the Five-Factor model. *Journal of Personality and Social Psychology, 82,* 89–101.

Kaufman, Joan, & Zigler, Edward (1987). Do abused children become abusive parents? *American Journal of Orthopsychiatry, 57,* 186–192.

Kazdin, Alan E. (2001). *Behavior modification in applied settings* (6th ed.). Belmont, CA: Wadsworth.

Kazdin, Alan E. (2008). Evidence-based treatment and practice: New opportunities to bridge clinical research and practice, enhance the knowledge base, and improve patient care. *American Psychologist, 63,* 146–150.

Kazdin, Alan E., & Blase, Stacey L. (2011). Rebooting psychotherapy research and practice to reduce the burden of mental illness. *Perspectives on Psychological Science, 6,* 21–37.

Keating, Caroline F. (1994). World without words: Messages from face and body. In W. J. Lonner & R. Malpass (Eds.), *Psychology and culture.* Needham Heights, MA: Allyn & Bacon.

Keel, Pamela K., & Klump, Kelly L. (2003). Are eating disorders culture-bound syndromes? Implications for conceptualizing their etiology. *Psychological Bulletin, 129,* 747–769.

Keen, Sam (1986). *Faces of the enemy: Reflections of the hostile imagination.* San Francisco: Harper & Row.

Keizer, Kees; Lindenberg, Siegwart; & Steg, Linda (2008). The spreading of disorder. *Science, 322,* 1681–1685.

Keller, Heidi; Abels, Monika; Lamm, Bettina; et al. (2005). Ecocultural effects on early infant care: A study in Cameroon, India, and Germany. *Ethos, 33,* 512–541.

Kelman, Herbert C., & Hamilton, V. Lee (1989). *Crimes of obedience: Toward a social psychology of authority and responsibility.* New Haven, CT: Yale University Press.

Keltner, Dacher, & Buswell, Brenda N. (1997). Embarrassment: Its distinct form and appeasement functions. *Psychological Bulletin, 122,* 250–270.

Keltner, Dacher; Ellsworth, Phoebe C.; & Edwards, Kari (1993). Beyond simple pessimism: Effects of sadness and anger on social perception. *Journal of Personality and Social Psychology, 64,* 740–752.

Kemeny, Margaret E. (2003). The psychobiology of stress. *Current Directions in Psychological Science, 12,* 124–129.

Kempermann, Gerd (2006). Adult neurogenesis: Stem cells and neuronal development in the adult brain. New York: Oxford University Press.

Kendall [no other name] (1999). Women in Lesotho and the (Western) construction of homophobia. In E. Blackwood & S. E. Wieringa (Eds.), *Female desires: Same-sex relations and transgender practices across cultures.* New York: Columbia University Press.

Kendler, Kenneth S.; Eaves, Lindon J.; Loken, Erik K.; et al. (2011). The impact of environmental experiences on symptoms of anxiety and depression across the life span. *Psychological Science, 22,* 1343–1352.

Kenny, David A.; Snook, Amanda; Boucher, Eliane; & Hancock, Jeffrey T. (2010). Interpersonal sensitivity, status, and stereotype accuracy. *Psychological Science, 21,* 1735–1739.

Kenrick, Douglas T.; Sundie, Jill M.; Nicastle, Lionel D.; & Stone, Gregory O. (2001). Can one ever be too wealthy or too chaste? Searching for nonlinearities in mate judgment. *Journal of Personality and Social Psychology, 80,* 462–471.

Kessler, Ronald C.; Sonnega, A.; Bromet, E.; et al. (1995). Posttraumatic stress disorder in the National Comorbidity Survey. *Archives of General Psychiatry, 52,* 1048–1060.

Khan, A.; Detke, M.; Khan, S. R.; & Mallinckrodt, C. (2003). Placebo response and antidepressant clinical trial outcome. *Journal of Nervous and Mental Diseases, 191,* 211–218.

Kibbe, Melissa M., & Leslie, Alan M. (2011). What do infants remember when they forget? Location and identity in 6-month-olds' memory for objects. *Psychological Science, 22,* 1500–1505.

Kida, Thomas (2006). *Don't believe everything you think: The 6 basic mistakes we make in thinking.* Amherst, NY: Prometheus Books.

Kiecolt-Glaser, Janice K., & Newton, Tamara L. (2001). Marriage and health: His and hers. *Psychological Bulletin, 127,* 472–503.

Kiecolt-Glaser, Janice K.; Page, Gayle G.; Marucha, Phillip T.; et al. (1998). Psychological influences on surgical recovery: Perspectives from psychoneuroimmunology. *American Psychologist, 53,* 1209–1218.

Kiecolt-Glaser, Janice K.; Loving, Timothy J.; Stowell, Jeffrey R.; et al. (2005). Hostile marital interactions, proinflammatory cytokine production, and wound healing. *Archives of General Psychiatry, 62,* 1377–1384.

Kim, Heejung S.; Sherman, David K.; & Taylor, Shelley E. (2008). Culture and social support. *American Psychologist, 63,* 518–526.

Kihlstrom, John F. (1994). Hypnosis, delayed recall, and the principles of memory. *International Journal of Clinical and Experimental Hypnosis, 40,* 337–345.

King, Michael, & Woollett, Earnest (1997). Sexually assaulted males: 115 men consulting a counseling service. *Archives of Sexual Behavior, 26,* 579–588.

King, Patricia M., & Kitchener, Karen S. (1994). Developing reflective judgment: *Understanding and promoting intellectual growth and critical thinking in adolescents and adults.* San Francisco: Jossey-Bass.

King, Patricia M., & Kitchener, Karen S. (2002). The reflective judgment model: Twenty years of research on epistemic cognition. In B. K. Hofer & P. R. Pintrich (Eds.), *Personal epistemology: The psychology of beliefs about knowledge and knowing.* Mahway, NJ: Erlbaum.

King, Patricia M., & Kitchener, Karen S. (2004). Reflective judgment: Theory and research on the development of epistemic assumptions through adulthood. *Educational Psychologist, 39,* 5–18.

King, Ryan S.; Mauer, Marc; & Young, Malcolm C. (2005). *Incarceration and crime: A complex relationship.* Washington, DC: The Sentencing Project.

King, Suzanne; St-Hilaire, Annie; & Heidkamp, David (2010). Prenatal factors in schizophrenia. *Current Directions in Psychological Science, 19,* 209–213.

Kinoshita, Sachiko, & Peek-O'Leary, Marie (2005). Does the compatibility effect in the race Implicit Association Test reflect familiarity or affect? *Psychonomic Bulletin & Review, 12,* 442–452.

Kinsey, Alfred C.; Pomeroy, Wardell B.; & Martin, Clyde E. (1948). *Sexual behavior in the human male.* Philadelphia: Saunders.

Kinsey, Alfred C.; Pomeroy, Wardell B.; Martin, Clyde E.; & Gebhard, Paul H. (1953). *Sexual behavior in the human female.* Philadelphia: Saunders.

Kirsch, Irving (1997). Response expectancy theory and application: A decennial review. *Applied and Preventive Psychology, 6,* 69–70.

Kirsch, Irving (2004). Conditioning, expectancy, and the placebo effect: Comment on Stewart-Williams and Podd (2004). *Psychological Bulletin, 130,* 341–343.

Kirsch, Irving (2010). *The emperor's new drugs: Exploding the antidepressant myth.* New York: Basic.

Kirsch, Irving, & Lynn, Steven J. (1995). The altered state of hypnosis: Changes in the theoretical landscape. *American Psychologist, 50,* 846–858.

Kirsch, Irving; Deacon, B. J.; Huedo-Medina, T. B.; et al. (2008). Initial severity and antidepressant benefits: A meta-analysis of data submitted to the Food and Drug Administration. *PLoS Medicine, 5,* e45.

Kirsch, Irving; Silva, Christopher E.; Carone, James E.; Johnston, J. Dennis; & Simon, B. (1989). The surreptitious observation design: An experimental paradigm for distinguishing artifact from essence in hypnosis. *Journal of Abnormal Psychology, 98,* 132–136.

Kissileff, H. R.; Thornton, J. C.; Torres M. I.; et al. (2012). Leptin reverses declines in satiation in weight-reduced obese humans. *American Journal of Clinical Nutrition, 95,* 309–317.

Kitchener, Karen S.; Lynch, Cindy L.; Fischer, Kurt W.; & Wood, Phillip K. (1993). Developmental range of reflective judgment: The effect of contextual support and practice on developmental stage. *Developmental Psychology, 29,* 893–906.

Klauer, Sheila G.; Dingus, Thomas A.; Neale, Vicki L.; et al. (2006). The impact of driver inattention on near-crash/crash risk: An analysis using the 100-car naturalistic driving study data. Performed by Virginia Tech Transportation Institute, Blacksburg, VA, sponsored by National Highway Traffic Safety Administration, Washington, DC, DOT HS 810 594.

Klein, Raymond, & Armitage, Roseanne (1979). Rhythms in human performance: 1 1/2-hour oscillations in cognitive style. *Science, 204,* 1326–1328.

Kleinke, Chris L.; Peterson, Thomas R.; & Rutledge, Thomas R. (1998). Effects of self-generated facial expressions on mood. *Journal of Personality and Social Psychology, 74,* 272–279.

Kleinman, Arthur (1988). *Rethinking psychiatry: From cultural category to personal experience.* New York: Free Press.

Klima, Edward S., & Bellugi, Ursula (1966). Syntactic regularities in the speech of children. In J. Lyons & R. J. Wales (Eds.), *Psycholinguistics papers.* Edinburgh, Scotland: Edinburgh University Press.

Klimoski, Richard J. (1992). Graphology and personnel selection. In B. Beyerstein & D. Beyerstein (Eds.), *The write stuff: Evaluations of graphology— The study of handwriting analysis.* Buffalo, NY: Prometheus Books.

Kluft, Richard P. (1987). The simulation and dissimulation of multiple personality disorder. *American Journal of Clinical Hypnosis, 30,* 104–118.

Kochanska, Grazyna, & Knaack, Amy (2003). Effortful control as a personality characteristic of young children: Antecedents, correlates, and consequences. *Journal of Personality, 71,* 1087–1112.

Kochanska, Grazyna; Forman, David R.; Aksan, Nazan; & Dunbar, Stephen B. (2005). Pathways to conscience: Early mother–child mutually responsive orientation and children's moral emotion, conduct, and cognition. *Journal of Child Psychology and Psychiatry, 46,* 19–34.

Kohlberg, Lawrence (1964). Development of moral character and moral ideology. In M. Hoffman & L. W. Hoffman (Eds.), *Review of child development research.* New York: Russell Sage Foundation.

Köhler, Wolfgang (1925). *The mentality of apes.* New York: Harcourt, Brace.

Köhler, Wolfgang (1929). *Gestalt psychology.* New York: Horace Liveright.

Kok, Bethany E.; Catalino, Lahnna I.; & Fredrickson, Barbara L. (2008). The broadening, building, buffering effects of positive emotions. In S. J. Lopez (Ed.), *Positive psychology: Exploring the best in people* (Vol. 2). Westport, CT: Praeger Publishers/Greenwood.

Kolla, Bhanu, P., & Auger, R. Robert (2011). Jet lag and shift work sleep disorders: How to help reset the internal clock. *Cleveland Clinic Journal of Medicine, 78,* 675–684.

Koller, Karin; Brown, Terry; Spurgeon, Anne; & Levy, Len (2004). Recent developments in low-level lead exposure and intellectual impairment in children. *Environmental Health Perspectives, 112,* 987–994.

Komarraju, Meera, & Cokley, Kevin O. (2008). Horizontal and vertical dimensions of individualism-collectivism: A comparison of African Americans and European Americans. *Cultural Diversity and Ethnic Minority Psychology, 14,* 336–343.

Kong, Augustine; Frigge, Michael L.; Masson, Gisli; et al. (2012). Rate of de novo mutations and the importance of father's age to disease risk. *Nature, 48,* 471–475.

Koocher, Gerald P.; Goodman, Gail S.; White, C. Sue; et al. (1995). Psychological science and the use of anatomically detailed dolls in child sexual-abuse assessments. *Psychological Bulletin, 118,* 199–222.

Kornell, Nate (2009). Metacognition in humans and animals. *Current Directions in Psychological Science, 18,* 11–15.

Kornum, Birgitte R.; Faraco, Juliette; & Mignot, Emmanuel (2011). Narcolepsy with hypocretin/orexin deficiency, infections and autoimmunity of the brain. *Current Opinion in Neurobiology, 21,* 897–903.

Kosfeld, Michael; Heinrichs, Markus; Zak, Paul J.; et al. (2005). Oxytocin increases trust in humans. *Nature, 435,* 673–676.

Koss, Mary (2011). Hidden, unacknowledged, acquaintance, and date rape: Looking back, looking forward. *Psychology of Women Quarterly, 35,* 348–354.

Kosslyn, Stephen M. (1980). *Image and mind.* Cambridge, MA: Harvard University Press.

Kosslyn, Stephen M.; Thompson, William L.; Costantini-Ferrando, Maria F.; et al. (2000). Hypnotic visual illusion alters color processing in the brain. *American Journal of Psychiatry, 157,* 1279–1284.

Kounios, John, & Beeman, Mark (2009). The Aha! Moment: The cognitive neuroscience of insight. *Current Directions in Psychological Science, 18,* 210–216.

Koyama, Tetsua; McHaffie, John G.; Laurienti, Paul J.; & Coghill, Robert C. (2005). The subjective experience of pain: Where expectations become reality. *Proceedings of the National Academy of Sciences, 102,* 12950–12955.

Kraft, Tara L., & Pressman, Sarah D. (2012). Grin and bear it: The influence of manipulated facial expression on the stress response. *Psychological Science, 23,* 1372–1378.

Kramer, Karen L., & Greaves, Russell D. (2011). Juvenile subsistence effort, activity levels, and growth patterns: Middle childhood among Pumé foragers. *Human Nature, 22,* 303–326.

Krantz, David S.; Olson, Marian B.; Francis, Jennifer L.; et al. (2006). Anger, hostility, and cardiac symptoms in women with suspected coronary artery disease: The women's ischemia syndrome evaluation (WISE) study. *Journal of Women's Health, 15,* 1214–1223.

Kraus, Michael W.; Côté, Stéphane; & Keltner, Dacher (2010). Social class, contextualism, and empathic accuracy. *Psychological Science, 21,* 1716–1723.

Krebs, Dennis L. (2008). Morality: An evolutionary account. *Perspectives on Psychological Science, 3,* 149–172.

Kreps, Bonnie (1990). *Subversive thoughts, authentic passions.* San Francisco: Harper & Row.

Krieger, Nancy, & Sidney, S. (1996). Racial discrimination and blood pressure: The CARDIA study of young black and white adults. *American Journal of Public Health, 86,* 1370–1378.

Krimsky, Sheldon (2003). *Science in the private interest.* Lanham, MD: Rowman & Littlefield.

Kring, Ann M., & Gordon, Albert H. (1998). Sex differences in emotion: Expression, experience, and physiology. *Journal of Personality and Social Psychology, 74,* 686–703.

Kripke, Daniel F. (1974). Ultradian rhythms in sleep and wakefulness. In E. D. Weitzman (Ed.), *Advances in sleep research* (Vol. 1). Flushing, NY: Spectrum.

Kross, Ethan, & Ayduk, Ozlem (2011). Making meaning out of negative experiences by self-distancing. *Current Directions in Psychological Science, 20,* 187–191.

Krueger, Alan B. (2007). *What makes a terrorist: Economics and the roots of terrorism.* Princeton, NJ: Princeton University Press.

Krueger, Robert F.; Hicks, Brian M.; & McGue, Matt (2001). Altruism and antisocial behavior: Independent tendencies, unique personality correlates, distinct etiologies. *Psychological Science, 12,* 397–402.

Krützen, Michael; Mann, Janet; Heithaus, Michael R.; et al. (2005). Cultural transmission of tool use in bottlenose dolphins. *Proceedings of the National Academy of Sciences, 102,* 8939–8943.

Krystal, J. H.; Rosenheck, Robert A.; Kramer, Joyce A.; et al. (2011). Adjunctive risperidone treatment for antidepressant-resistant symptoms of chronic military service–related PTSD: A randomized trial. *Journal of the American Medical Association, 306,* 493.

Kuhl, Patricia K.; Williams, Karen A.; Lacerda, Francisco; et al. (1992). Linguistic experience alters phonetic perception in infants by 6 months of age. *Science, 255,* 606–608.

Kuhn, Deanna; Weinstock, Michael; & Flaton, Robin (1994). How well do jurors reason? Competence dimensions of individual variation in a juror reasoning task. *Psychological Science, 5,* 289–296.

Kuncel, Nathan R.; Hezlett, Sarah A.; & Ones, Deniz S. (2004). Academic performance, career potential, creativity, and job performance: Can one construct predict them all? *Journal of Personality and Social Psychology, 86,* 148–161.

Kuster, Farah; Orth, Ulrich; & Meier, Laurenz L. (2012). Rumination mediates the prospective effect of low self-esteem on depression: A five-wave longitudinal study. *Personality and Social Psychology Bulletin, 38,* 747–759.

Kutchins, Herb, & Kirk, Stuart A. (1997). *Making us crazy: DSM. The psychiatric bible and the creation of mental disorders.* New York: Free Press.

Laan, Ellen, & Both, Stephanie (2008). What makes women experience desire? In L. Tiefer (Ed.), The New View campaign against the medicalization of sex (Special Issue). *Feminism and Psychology, 18,* 505–514.

LaBerge, Stephen, & Levitan, Lynne (1995). Validity established of DreamLight cues for eliciting lucid dreaming. *Dreaming: Journal of the Association for the Study of Dreams, 5,* 159–168.

Lacasse, Jeffrey R., & Leo, Jonathan (2005). Serotonin and depression: A disconnect between the advertisements and the scientific literature. *PloS Medicine, 2(12)*:e392. doi:10.1371/journal.pmed.0020392.

Lachman, Margie E., & Weaver, Suzanne L. (1998). The sense of control as a moderator of social class differences in health and well-being. *Journal of Personality and Social Psychology, 74,* 763–773.

LaFrance, Marianne (2011). *Lip service.* New York: W.W. Norton.

Lahey, B. B.; Pelham, W. E.; Loney, J.; et al. (2005). Instability of the DSM-IV subtypes of ADHD from preschool through elementary school. *Archives of General Psychiatry, 62,* 896–902.

Lanaj, Klodiana; Chang, Chu-Hsiang; & Johnson, Russell E. (2012). Regulatory focus and work-related outcomes: A review and meta-analysis. *Psychological Bulletin, 138,* 998–1034.

Lancy, David F., & Grove, M. Annette (2011). Getting noticed: Middle childhood in cross-cultural perspective. *Human Nature, 22,* 281–302.

Landrigan, C. P.; Fahrenkopf, A. M.; Lewin, D.; et al. (2008). Effects of the Accreditation Council for Graduate Medical Education duty hour limits on sleep, work hours, and safety. *Pediatrics, 122,* 250–258.

Landrine, Hope (1988). Revising the framework of abnormal psychology. In P. Bronstein & K. Quina (Eds.), *Teaching a psychology of people.* Washington, DC: American Psychological Association.

Lang, Ariel J.; Craske, Michelle G.; Brown, Matt; & Ghaneian, Atousa (2001). Fear-related state dependent memory. *Cognition & Emotion, 15,* 695–703.

Langer, Ellen J.; Blank, Arthur; & Chanowitz, Benzion (1978). The mindlessness of ostensibly thoughtful action: The role of placebic information in interpersonal interaction. *Journal of Personality and Social Psychology, 36,* 635–642.

Lany, Jill, & Gómez, Rebecca L. (2008). Twelve-month-old infants benefit from prior experience in statistical learning. *Psychological Science, 19,* 1247–1252.

Latremoliere, Alban, & Woolf, Clifford J. (2009). Central sensitization: A generator of pain hypersensitivity by central neural plasticity. *The Journal of Pain, 10,* 895–926.

Lau, H.; Alger, S.; & Fishbein, W. (2011). Relational memory: A daytime nap facilitates the extraction of general concepts. PLoS ONE 6(11): e27139. doi:10.1371/journal.pone.0027139.

Laumann, Edward O., & Gagnon John H. (1995). A sociological perspective on sexual action. In R. G. Parker & J. H. Gagnon (Eds.), *Conceiving sexuality: Approaches to sex research in a postmodern world.* New York: Routledge.

Lavie, Peretz (1976). Ultradian rhythms in the perception of two apparent motions. *Chronobiologia, 3,* 21–218.

Lavie, Peretz (2001). Sleep-wake as a biological rhythm. *Annual Review of Psychology, 52,* 277–303.

Lazarus, Richard S. (2000). Toward better research on stress and coping. *American Psychologist, 55,* 665–673.

Lazarus, Richard S., & Folkman, Susan (1984). *Stress, appraisal, and coping.* New York: Springer.

LeDoux, Joseph E. (1996). *The emotional brain.* New York: Simon & Schuster.

Lee, Susan J., & McEwen, Bruce S. (2001). Neurotrophic and neuroprotective actions of estrogens and their therapeutic implications. *Annual Review of Pharmacology & Pharmacological Toxicology, 41,* 569–591.

Legrenzi, Paolo, & Umiltà, Carlo (2011). *Neuromania: On the limits of brain science.* New York: Oxford University Press.

Leib, Rebecca (2008). MMPI-2 family problems scales in child-custody litigants. *Dissertation Abstracts International: Section B: The Sciences and Engineering. 68(7-B),* 4879.

Leibenluft, E., & Rich, B. A. (2008). Pediatric bipolar disorder. *Annual Review of Clinical Psychology, 4,* 163–187.

Leichsenring, Falk, & Rabung, Sven (2008). Effectiveness of longterm psychodynamic therapy: A meta-analysis. *Journal of the American Medical Association, 300,* 1551–1565.

Leinbach, Mary D.; Hort, Barbara E.; & Fagot, Beverly I. (1997). Bears are for boys: Metaphorical associations in young children's gender stereotypes. *Cognitive Development, 12,* 107–130.

Lemieux, Robert, & Hale, Jerold L. (2000). Intimacy, passion, and commitment among married individuals: Further testing of the Triangular Theory of Love. *Psychological Reports, 87,* 941–948.

Lent, Roberto; Azevedo, Frederico A. C.; Andrade-Moraes, Carlos H.; & Pinto, Ana V. O. (2012). How many neurons do you have? Some dogmas of quantitative neuroscience under revision. *The European Journal of Neuroscience, 35,* 1–9.

Leo, Richard A. (2008). *Police interrogation and American justice.* Cambridge, MA: Harvard University Press.

Leonard, Karen M. (2008). A cross-cultural investigation of temporal orientation in work organizations: A differentiation matching approach. *International Journal of Intercultural Relations, 32,* 479–492.

Lepore, Stephen J.; Ragan, Jennifer D.; & Jones, Scott (2000). Talking facilitates cognitive-emotional processes of adaptation to an acute stressor. *Journal of Personality and Social Psychology, 78,* 499–508.

Leppänen, Jukka, & Nelson, Charles A. (2012). Early development of fear processing. *Current Directions in Psychological Science, 21,* 200–204.

Lepper, Mark R.; Greene, David; & Nisbett, Richard E. (1973). Undermining children's intrinsic interest with extrinsic rewards. *Journal of Personality and Social Psychology, 28,* 129–137.

Leproult, Rachel; Copinschi, Georges; Buxton, Orfeu; & Van Cauter, Eve (1997). Sleep loss results in an elevation of cortisol levels the next evening. *Sleep, 20,* 865–870.

Lerner, Melvin J. (1980). *The belief in a just world: A fundamental delusion.* New York: Plenum.

Lester, Barry M.; LaGasse, Linda L.; & Seifer, Ronald (1998). Cocaine exposure and children: The meaning of subtle effects. *Science, 282,* 633–634.

Levenson, Robert W., & Miller, Bruce L. (2007). Loss of cells—loss of self. *Current Directions in Psychological Science, 16,* 289–294.

Levenson, Robert W.; Ekman, Paul; & Friesen, Wallace V. (1990). Voluntary facial action generates emotion-specific autonomic nervous system activity. *Psychophysiology, 27,* 363–384.

Levin, Daniel T. (2000). Race as a visual feature: Using visual search and perceptual discrimination tasks to understand face categories and the cross-race recognition deficit. *Journal of Experimental Psychology: General, 129,* 559–574.

Levine, James A.; Eberhardt, Norman L.; & Jensen, Michael D. (1999). Role of nonexercise activity thermogenesis in resistance to fat gain in humans. *Science, 283,* 212–214.

Levitin, Daniel J. (2013, February 9). What you might be missing. *The Wall Street Journal,* p. C5.

LeVine, Robert A., & Norman, Karin (2008). Attachment in anthropological perspective. In R. A. LeVine & R. S. New (Eds.), *Anthropology and child development: A cross-cultural reader.* Malden: Blackwell.

Levine, Robert V. (2003). The kindness of strangers. *American Scientist, 91,* 227–233.

Levine, Robert V.; Norenzayan, Ara; & Philbrick, Karen (2001). Cross-cultural differences in helping strangers. *Journal of Cross-Cultural Psychology, 32,* 543–560.

Levy, Becca. (1996). Improving memory in old age through implicit self-stereotyping. *Journal of Personality and Social Psychology, 71,* 1092–1107.

Levy, David A. (2010). *Tools of critical thinking: Metathoughts for psychology* (2nd ed.). Long Grove, IL: Waveland.

Levy, Robert I. (1984). The emotions in comparative perspective. In K. R. Scherer & P. Ekman (Eds.), *Approaches to emotion.* Hillsdale, NJ: Erlbaum.

Levy, Jerre; Trevarthen, Colwyn; & Sperry, Roger W. (1972). Perception of bilateral chimeric figures following hemispheric deconnection. *Brain, 95,* 61–78.

Lewin, Kurt (1948). *Resolving social conflicts.* New York: Harper.

Lewis, Marc D. (2011). Dopamine and the neural "now": Essay and review of Addiction: A disorder of choice. *Perspectives on Psychological Science, 6,* 150–155.

Lewontin, Richard C. (1970). Race and intelligence. *Bulletin of the Atomic Scientists, 26(3),* 2–8.

Lewontin, Richard C. (2000). *It Ain't Necessarily So: The dream of the human genome and other illusions.* New York: The New York Review of Books.

Lewy, Alfred J.; Ahmed, Saeeduddin; Jackson, Jeanne L.; & Sack, Robert L. (1992). Melatonin shifts human circadian rhythms according to a phase response curve. *Chronobiology International, 9,* 380–392.

Lewy, Alfred J.; Lefler, Bryan J.; Emens, Jonathan S.; & Bauer, Vance K. (2006). The circadian basis of winter depression. *Proceedings of the National Academy of Sciences, 103,* 7414–7419.

Li, Shu-Chen; Lindenberger, Ulman; Hommel, Bernhard; et al. (2004). Transformations in the couplings among intellectual abilities and constituent cognitive processes across the life span. *Psychological Science, 15,* 155–163.

Lickona, Thomas (1983). *Raising good children.* New York: Bantam.

Lieberman, J. A.; Stroup, T. S.; McEvoy, J. P.; et al. (2005). Effectiveness of antipsychotic drugs in patients with chronic schizophrenia. *New England Journal of Medicine, 353,* 1209–1223.

Lieberman, Matthew (2000). Intuition: A social cognitive neuroscience approach. *Psychological Bulletin, 126,* 109–137.

Lien, Mei-Ching; Ruthruff, Eric; & Johnston, James C. (2006). Attentional limitations in doing two tasks at once: The search for exceptions. *Current Directions in Psychological Science, 16,* 89–93.

Liepert, J.; Bauder, H.; Miltner, W. H.; et al. (2000). Treatment-induced cortical reorganization after stroke in humans. *Stroke, 31,* 1210–1216.

Light, Donald (Ed.) (2010). *The risks of prescription drugs.* New York: Columbia University Press.

Lilienfeld, Scott O. (2007). Psychological treatments that cause harm. *Perspectives on Psychological Science, 2,* 53–70.

Lilienfeld, Scott, & Arkowitz, Hal (2008, June). Is animal-assisted therapy really the cat's meow? *Scientific American.* http://www.scientificamerican.com/article.cfm?id=is-animal-assisted-therapy&offset=2.

Lilienfeld, Scott O.; Gershon, Jonathan; Duke, Marshall; Marino, Lori; & De Waal, Frans B. M. (1999). A preliminary investigation of the construct of psychopathic personality (psychopathy) in chimpanzees (Pan troglodytes). *Journal of Comparative Psychology, 113,* 365–375.

Lilienfeld, Scott O.; Lynn, Steven Jay; & Lohr, Jeffrey M. (Eds.) (2014). *Science and pseudoscience in clinical psychology* (Rev. ed.). New York: Guilford.

Lilienfeld, Scott O.; Ritschel, Lorie A.; Lynn, Steven J.; Cautin, Robin L.; & Latzman, Robert D. (2013). Why many clinical psychologists are resistant to evidence-based practice: Root causes and constructive remedies. *Clinical Psychology Review,* http://dx.doi.org/10.1016/j.cpr.2012.09.008.

Lin, L.; Hungs, M.; & Mignot, E. (2001). Narcolepsy and the HLA region. *Journal of Neuroimmunology, 117,* 9–20.

Lin, Keh-Ming; Poland, Russell E.; & Chien, C. P. (1990). Ethnicity and psychopharmacology: Recent findings and future research directions. In E. Sorel (Ed.), *Family, culture, and psychobiology.* New York: Legas.

Linday, Linda A. (1994). Maternal reports of pregnancy, genital, and related fantasies in preschool and kindergarten children. *Journal of the American Academy of Child and Adolescent Psychiatry, 33,* 416–423.

Lindsay, D. Stephen, & Read, J. Don (1994). Psychotherapy and memories of childhood sexual abuse: A cognitive perspective. *Applied Cognitive Psychology, 8,* 281–338.

Lindsay, D. Stephen; Hagen, Lisa; Read, J. Don; et al. (2004). True photographs and false memories. *Psychological Science, 15,* 149–154.

Lindquist, Kristen A., & Barrett, Lisa F. (2008). Constructing emotion. *Psychological Science, 19,* 898–903.

Linton, Marigold (1978). Real-world memory after six years: An in vivo study of very long-term memory. In M. M. Gruneberg, P. E. Morris, & R. N. Sykes (Eds.), *Practical aspects of memory.* London: Academic Press.

Linton, Simi (1998). *Claiming disability: Knowledge and identity.* New York: New York University Press.

Linton, Simi (2006). *My body politic.* Ann Arbor, MI: University of Michigan Press.

Linville, P. W.; Fischer, G. W.; & Fischhoff, B. (1992). AIDS risk perceptions and decision biases. In J. B. Pryor & G. D. Reeder (Eds.), *The social psychology of HIV infection.* Hillsdale, NJ: Erlbaum.

Liou, Alice P.; Paziuk, Melissa; Jesus-Mario Luevano, Jesus-Mario, Jr.; et al. (2013, March 27). Conserved shifts in the gut microbiota due to gastric bypass reduce host weight and adiposity. *Science Translational Medicine, 5,* 178ra41. DOI:10.1126/scitranslmed.3005687

Lisman, John; Yasuda, Ryohei; & Raghavachari, Stridhar (2012). Mechanisms of CaMKII action in long-term potentiation. *Nature Reviews Neuroscience, 13,* 169–182.

Lissner, L.; Odell, P. M.; D'Agostino, R. B.; et al. (1991). Variability of body weight and health outcomes in the Framingham population. *New England Journal of Medicine, 324,* 1839–1844.

Livingston, Jennifer A.; Bay-Cheng, Laina Y.; Hequembourg, Amy L.; et al. (2012). Mixed drinks and mixed messages: Adolescent girls' perspectives on alcohol and sexuality. *Psychology of Women Quarterly, 37,* 38–50.

Lloyd-Richardson, E. E.; Bailey, S.; Fava, J. L.; Wing, R.; Tobacco Etiology Research Network (TERN) (2009). A prospective study of weight gain during the college freshman and sophomore years. *Preventive Medicine, 48,* 256–261.

LoBue, Vanessa, & DeLoache, Judy S. (2008). Detecting the snake in the grass. *Psychological Science, 19,* 284–289.

Locke, Edwin A., & Latham, Gary P. (2002). Building a practically useful theory of goal setting and task motivation. *American Psychologist, 57,* 705–717.

Locke, Edwin A., & Latham, Gary P. (2006). New directions in goal-setting theory. *Current Directions in Psychological Science, 15,* 265–268.

Loehlin, John C.; Horn, J. M.; & Willerman, L. (1996). Heredity, environment, and IQ in the Texas adoption study. In R. J. Sternberg & E. Grigorenko (Eds.), *Intelligence: Heredity and environment.* New York: Cambridge University Press.

Loftus, Elizabeth F. (2011). Intelligence gathering post-9/11. *American Psychologist, 66,* 532–541.

Loftus, Elizabeth (2013). Psychological memory science and legal reforms. *APS Observer, 26,* 10.

Loftus, Elizabeth F., & Greene, Edith (1980). Warning: Even memory for faces may be contagious. *Law and Human Behavior, 4,* 323–334.

Loftus, Elizabeth F., & Palmer, John C. (1974). Reconstruction of automobile destruction: An example of the interaction between language and memory. *Journal of Verbal Learning and Verbal Behavior, 13,* 585–589.

Loftus, Elizabeth F., & Pickrell, Jacqueline E. (1995). The formation of false memories. *Psychiatric Annals, 25,* 720–725.

Loftus, Elizabeth F.; Miller, David G.; & Burns, Helen J. (1978). Semantic integration of verbal information into a visual memory. *Journal of Experimental Psychology: Human Learning and Memory, 4,* 19–31.

Lonner, Walter J. (1995). Culture and human diversity. In E. Trickett, R. Watts, & D. Birman (Eds.), *Human diversity: Perspectives on people in context.* San Francisco: Jossey-Bass.

Lonsdorf, Tina B.; Weike, Almut I.; Nikamo, Pernilla; et al. (2009). Genetic gating of human fear learning and extinction: Possible implications for gene-environment interaction in anxiety disorder. *Psychological Science, 20,* 198–206.

López, Steven R. (1995). Testing ethnic minority children. In B. B. Wolman (Ed.), *The encyclopedia of psychology, psychiatry, and psychoanalysis.* New York: Holt.

Lorber, Michael F. (2004). Psychophysiology of aggression, psychopathy, and conduct problems: A meta-analysis. *Psychological Bulletin, 130,* 531–552.

Loughnan, Steve; Kuppens, Peter; Allik, Jüri; et al. (2011). Economic inequality is linked to biased self-perception. *Psychological Science, 22,* 1254–1258.

Lövdén, Martin; Bächman, Lars; Lindenberger, Ulman; et al. (2010). A theoretical framework for the study of adult cognitive plasticity. *Psychological Bulletin, 136,* 659–676.

Löw, Andreas; Lang, Peter J.; Smith, J. Carson; & Bradley, Margaret M. (2008). Both predator and prey: Emotional arousal in threat and reward. *Psychological Science, 19,* 865–873.

Lu, Luo (2008). The individual-oriented and social-oriented Chinese bicultural self: Testing the theory. *Journal of Social Psychology, 148,* 347–373.

Lubinski, David (2004). Introduction to the special section on cognitive abilities: 100 years after Spearman's (1904) "'General intelligence,' objectively determined and measured." *Journal of Personality and Social Psychology, 86,* 96–111.

Lucchina, L. A.; Curtis, O. F.; Putnam, P.; et al. (1998). Psychophysical measurement of 6-n-propylthiouracil (PROP) taste perception. *Annals of the New York Academy of Sciences, 855,* 816–819.

Luders, Eileen; Narr, Katherine L.; Thompson, Paul M.; et al. (2004). Gender differences in cortical complexity. *Nature Neuroscience, 7,* 799–800.

Ludwig, David S., & Currie, Janet (2010). The association between pregnancy weight gain and birthweight: A within-family comparison. *Lancet, 376,* 984–990.

Lukas, Dieter, & Clutton-Brock, Tim H. (2013). The evolution of social monogamy in mammals. *Science, 341,* 526–530.

Luria, Alexander R. (1968). *The mind of a mnemonist* (L. Soltaroff, Trans.). New York: Basic.

Luria, Alexander R. (1980). *Higher cortical functions in man* (2nd rev. ed.). New York: Basic.

Lutz, Catherine (1988). *Unnatural emotions.* Chicago: University of Chicago Press.

Lykken, David T. (1995). *The antisocial personalities.* Hillsdale, NJ: Erlbaum.

Lykken, David T. (1998). *A tremor in the blood: Uses and abuses of the lie detector.* New York: Plenum.

Lykken, David T., & Tellegen, Auke (1996). Happiness is a stochastic phenomenon. *Psychological Science, 7,* 186–189.

Lynn, Steven Jay, & Green, Joseph P. (2011). The sociocognitive and dissociation theories of hypnosis: Toward a rapprochement. *Clinical and Experimental Hypnosis, 59,* 277–293

Lynn, Steven Jay; Lilienfeld, Scott O.; Merckelbach, Harald; et al. (2012). Dissociation and dissociative disorders: Challenging conventional wisdom. *Current Directions in Psychological Science, 21,* 48–53.

Lynn, Steven Jay; Rhue, Judith W.; & Weekes, John R. (1990). Hypnotic involuntariness: A social cognitive analysis. *Psychological Review, 97,* 69–184.

Lytton, Hugh, & Romney, David M. (1991). Parents' differential socialization of boys and girls: A meta-analysis. *Psychological Bulletin, 109,* 267–296.

Maass, Anne; Cadinu, Mara; Guarnieri, Gaia; & Grasselli, Annalisa (2003). Sexual harassment under social identity threat: The computer harassment paradigm. *Journal of Personality and Social Psychology, 85,* 853–870.

Maccoby, Eleanor E. (1998). *The two sexes: Growing up apart, coming together.* Cambridge, MA: Belknap Press/Harvard University Press.

MacArthur Foundation Research Network on Successful Midlife Development (1999). Report of latest findings. http://midmac.med.harvard.edu/.

Macleod John; Oakes Rachel; Copello, Alex; et al. (2004). Psychological and social sequelae of cannabis and other illicit drug use by young people: A systematic review of longitudinal, general population studies. *Lancet, 363,* 1568–1569.

Maccoby, Eleanor E. (2002). Gender and group process: A developmental perspective. *Current Directions in Psychological Science, 11,* 54–58.

Macrae, C. Neil, & Bodenhausen, Galen V. (2000). Social cognition: Thinking categorically about others. *Annual Review of Psychology, 51,* 93–120.

Madsen, Kreesten M.; Hviid, Anders; Vestergaard, Mogens; et al. (2002). A population-based study of measles, mumps, and rubella vaccination and autism. *New England Journal of Medicine, 347,* 1477–1482.

Malamuth, Neil M.; Linz, Daniel; Heavey, Christopher L.; et al. (1995). Using the confluence model of sexual aggression to predict men's conflict with women: A 10-year follow-up study. *Journal of Personality and Social Psychology, 69,* 353–369.

Malaspina, Dolores (2001). Paternal factors and schizophrenia risk: De novo mutations and imprinting. *Schizophrenia Bulletin, 27,* 379–393.

Mandrusiak, Michael; Rudd, M. David; Joiner Jr., Thomas E.; et al. (2006). Warning signs for suicide on the Internet: A descriptive study. *Suicide and Life-Threatening Behavior, 36,* 263–271.

Marchman, Virginia A., & Fernald, Anne (2008). Speed of word recognition and vocabulary knowledge in infancy predict cognitive and language outcomes in later childhood. *Developmental Science, 11,* F9–F16.

Marcus, Gary F.; Pinker, Steven; Ullman, Michael; et al. (1992). Overregularization in language acquisition. *Monographs of the Society for Research in Child Development, 57* (Serial No. 228), 1–182.

Marcus-Newhall, Amy; Pedersen, William C.; Carlson, Mike; & Miller, Norman (2000). Displaced aggression is alive and well: A meta-analytic review. *Journal of Personality and Social Psychology, 78,* 670–689.

Margolin, Gayla, & Gordis, Elana B. (2004). Children's exposure to violence in the family and community. *Current Directions in Psychological Science, 13,* 152–155.

Markus, Hazel R., & Kitayama, Shinobu (1991). Culture and the self: Implications for cognition, emotion, and motivation. *Psychological Review, 98,* 224–253.

Marlatt, G. Alan, & Rohsenow, Damaris J. (1980). Cognitive processes in alcohol use: Expectancy and the balanced placebo design. In N. K. Mello (Ed.), *Advances in substance abuse* (Vol. 1). Greenwich, CT: JAI Press.

Marsh, Elizabeth J., & Tversky, Barbara (2004). Spinning the stories of our lives. *Applied Cognitive Psychology, 18,* 491–503.

Martin, Carol Lynn, & Ruble, Diane (2004). Children's search for gender cues. *Current Directions in Psychological Science, 13,* 67–70.

Martin, Carol Lynn; Ruble, Diane N.; & Szkrybalo, Joel (2002). Cognitive theories of early gender development. *Psychological Bulletin, 128,* 903–933.

Martin, Garry, & Pear, Joseph (2007). *Behavior modification: What it is and how to do it* (8th ed.). NY: Prentice Hall.

Martin, Garry, & Pear, Joseph (2011). *Behavior modification: What it is and how to do it* (9th ed.). Upper Saddle River, NJ: Pearson/Prentice Hall.

Maruta, T.; Colligan R. C.; Malinchoc, M.; & Offord, K. P. (2000). Optimists vs.pessimists: Survival rate among medical patients over a 30-year period. *Mayo Clinic Proceedings, 75,* 140–143.

Marvan, M. L.; Diaz-Erosa, M.; & Montesinos, A. (1998). Premenstrual symptoms in Mexican women with different educational levels. *Journal of Psychology, 132,* 517–526.

Masand, P. S. (2000). Side effects of antipsychotics in the elderly. *Journal of Clinical Psychiatry, 61(suppl. 8),* 43–49.

Maslach, Christina; Schaufeli, Wilmar B.; & Leiter, Michael P. (2001). Job burnout. *Annual Review of Psychology, 52,* 397–422.

Maslow, Abraham H. (1970). *Motivation and personality* (2nd ed.). New York: Harper & Row.

Maslow, Abraham H. (1971). *The farther reaches of human nature.* New York: Viking.

Masten, Ann S. (2001). Ordinary magic: Resilience processes in development. *American Psychologist, 56,* 227–238.

Masters, William H., & Johnson, Virginia E. (1966). *Human sexual response.* Boston: Little, Brown.

Matthews, Fiona E.; Arthur, Antony; Barnes, Linda E.; et al. (2013, July 17). A two-decade comparison of prevalence of dementia in individuals aged 65 years and older from three geographical areas of England: results of the Cognitive Function and Ageing Study I and II. *The Lancet,* doi:10.1016/S0140-6736(13)61570-6.

Masuda, Takahiko, & Nisbett, Richard E. (2001). Attending holistically versus analytically: Comparing the context sensitivity of Japanese and Americans. *Journal of Personality and Social Psychology, 81,* 922–934.

Mather, Jennifer A., & Anderson, Roland C. (1993). Personalities of octopuses (Octopus rubescens). *Journal of Comparative Psychology, 197,* 336–340.

Mather, Mara; Shafir, Eldar; & Johnson, Marcia K. (2000). Misremembrance of options past: Source monitoring and choice. *Psychological Science, 11,* 132–138.

Mathews, Andrew, & MacLeod, Colin (2005). Cognitive vulnerability to emotional disorders. *Annual Review of Clinical Psychology, I,* 167–195.

Matlin, Margaret (2012). *The psychology of women* (7th ed.). Belmont, CA: Cengage.

Matthews, Gerald; Zeidner, Moshe; & Roberts, Richard D. (2003). *Emotional intelligence: Science and myth.* Cambridge, MA: MIT Press/ Bradford Books.

Matsumoto, David (1996). *Culture and psychology.* Pacific Grove, CA: Brooks-Cole.

Mayer, Jane (2009). *The dark side: The inside story of how the war on terror turned into a war on American ideals* (reprint edition). New York: Anchor.

Mayer, John D., & Salovey, Peter (1997). What is emotional intelligence? In P. Salovey & D. Sluyter (Eds.), *Emotional development and emotional intelligence: Implications for educators.* New York: Basic.

Mayou, R. A.; Ehlers, A.; & Hobbs, M. (2000). Psychological debriefing for road traffic accident victims. *British Journal of Psychiatry, 176,* 589–593.

Mazza, James J., & Reynolds, William M. (1999). Exposure to violence in young inner-city adolescents: Relationships with suicidal ideation, depression, and PTSD symptomatology. *Journal of Abnormal Child Psychology, 27,* 203–213.

Mazzoni, Giuliana A.; Loftus, Elizabeth F.; Seitz, Aaron; & Lynn, Steven J. (1999). Changing beliefs and memories through dream interpretation. *Applied Cognitive Psychology, 13,* 125–144.

Mazzoni, Giuliana A.; Loftus, Elizabeth F.; & Kirsch, Irving (2001). Changing beliefs about implausible autobiographical events: A little plausibility goes a long way. *Journal of Experimental Psychology: Applied, 7,* 51–59.

McAdams, Dan P. (2006). *The redemptive self: Stories Americans live by.* New York: Oxford University Press.

McAdams, Dan P. (2008). Personal narratives and the life story. In O. P. John, R. W. Robbins, & L. A. Pervin (Eds.), *Handbook of personality: Theory and research.* New York: Guilford.

McAdams, Dan P., & Pals, Jennifer L. (2006). A new Big Five: Fundamental principles for an integrative science of personality. *American Psychologist, 61,* 204–217.

McCabe, David P., & Castel, Alan D. (2008). Seeing is believing: The effect of brain images on judgments of scientific reasoning. *Cognition, 107,* 343–352.

McClelland, James L. (1994). The organization of memory: A parallel distributed processing perspective. *Revue Neurologique, 150,* 570–579.

McClelland, James L. (2011). Memory as a constructive process: The parallel-distributed processing approach. In S. Nalbantian, P. Matthews, & J. L. McClelland (Eds.), *The memory process: Neuroscientific and humanistic perspectives.* Cambridge, MA: MIT Press.

McCord, Joan (1992). Another time, another drug. In M. Glantz & R. Pickens (Eds.), *Vulnerability to drug abuse.* Washington, DC: American Psychological Association.

McCrae, Robert R. (1987). Creativity, divergent thinking, and openness to experience. *Journal of Personality and Social Psychology, 52,* 1258–1265.

McCrae, Robert R., & Costa, Paul T. (2008). The five-factor theory of personality. In O. P. John, R.W. Robbins, & L. A. Pervin (Eds.), *Handbook of personality: Theory and research* (3rd ed.). New York: Guilford.

McCrae, Robert R.; Terracciano, Antonio; & members of the Personality Profiles of Cultures Project (2005). Universal features of personality traits from the observer's perspective: Data from 50 cultures. *Journal of Personality and Social Psychology, 88,* 547–561.

McDaniel, Mark A.; Roediger, Henry L. III; & McDermott, Kathleen B. (2007). Generalizing test-enhanced learning from the laboratory to the classroom. *Psychonomic Bulletin & Review, 14,* 200–206.

McDonough, Laraine, & Mandler, Jean M. (1994). Very long-term recall in infancy. *Memory, 2,* 339–352.

McEwen, Bruce S. (2000). Allostasis and allostatic load: Implications for neuropsychopharmacology. *Neuropsychopharmacology 22,* 108–124.

McEwen, Bruce S. (2007). Physiology and neurobiology of stress and adaptation: Central role of the brain. *Physiological Review, 87,* 873–904.

McFadden, Dennis (2008). What do sex, twins, spotted hyenas, ADHD, and sexual orientation have in common? *Perspectives on Psychological Science, 3,* 309–322.

McFarlane, Jessica; Martin, Carol L.; & Williams, Tannis M. (1988). Mood fluctuations: Women versus men and menstrual versus other cycles. *Psychology of Women Quarterly, 12,* 201–223.

McFarlane, Jessica M., & Williams, Tannis M. (1994). Placing premenstrual syndrome in perspective. *Psychology of Women Quarterly, 18,* 339–373.

McGeown, William J.; Venneri, Annalena; Kirsch, Irving; et al. (2012). Suggested visual hallucination without hypnosis enhances activity in visual areas of the brain. *Consciousness and Cognition, 21,* 100–116.

McGregor, Ian, & Holmes, John G. (1999). How storytelling shapes memory and impressions of relationship events over time. *Journal of Personality and Social Psychology, 76,* 403–419.

McGue, Matt, & Lykken, David T. (1992). Genetic influence on risk of divorce. *Psychological Science, 3,* 368–373.

McGue, Matt; Bouchard, Thomas J., Jr.; Iacono, William G.; & Lykken, David T. (1993). Behavioral genetics of cognitive ability: A life-span perspective. In R. Plomin & G. E. McClearn (Eds.), *Nature, nurture, and psychology.* Washington, DC: American Psychological Association.

McHugh, Paul R. (2008). *Try to remember: Psychiatry's clash over meaning, memory, and mind.* New York: Dana Press.

McKee, Ann C.; Stein, Thor D.; Nowinski, Christopher J.; et al. (2013). The spectrum of disease in chronic traumatic encephalopathy. *Brain, 136(Pt 1),* 43–64.

McKee, Richard D., & Squire, Larry R. (1992). Equivalent forgetting rates in long-term memory for diencephalic and medial temporal lobe amnesia. *Journal of Neuroscience, 12,* 3765–3772.

McKee, Richard D., & Squire, Larry R. (1993). On the development of declarative memory. *Journal of Experimental Psychology: Learning, Memory, and Cognition, 19,* 397–404.

McKemy, D. D.; Neuhausser, W. M.; & Julius, D. (2002). Identification of a cold receptor reveals a general role for TRP channels in thermosensation. *Nature, 416,* 52–58.

McKinlay, John B.; McKinlay, Sonja M.; & Brambilla, Donald (1987). The relative contributions of endocrine changes and social circumstances to depression in mid-aged women. *Journal of Health and Social Behavior, 28,* 345–363.

McClearn, Gerald E.; Johanson, Boo; Berg, Stig; et al. (1997). Substantial genetic influence on cognitive abilities in twins 80 or more years old. *Science, 176,* 1560–1563.

McGoldrick, Monica (2005). Irish families. In M. McGoldrick, J. Giordano, & N. Garcia-Preto (Eds.), *Ethnicity and family therapy* (3rd ed.). New York: Guilford.

McMullin, Darcy, & White, Jacqueline W. (2006). Long-term effects of labeling a rape experience. *Psychology of Women Quarterly, 30,* 96–105.

McNally, Richard J. (2003). *Remembering trauma.* Cambridge, MA: Harvard University Press.

McNally, Richard J. (2011). *What is mental illness?* Cambridge, MA: Harvard University Press.

McNally, Richard J.; Bryant, Richard A.; & Ehlers, Anke (2003). Does early psychological intervention promote recovery from posttraumatic stress? *Psychological Science in the Public Interest, 4,* 45–79.

McNeill, David (1966). Developmental psycholinguistics. In F. L. Smith & G. A. Miller (Eds.), *The genesis of language: A psycholinguistic approach.* Cambridge, MA: MIT Press.

McNulty, James K. (2011). The dark side of forgiveness: The tendency to forgive predicts continued psychological and physical aggression in marriage. *Journal of Family Psychology, 24,* 787–790.

McNulty, James K., & Fincham, Frank D. (2012). Beyond positive psychology? Toward a contextual view of psychological processes and well-being. *American Psychologist, 67,* 101–110.

Mednick, Sara C.; Nakayama, Ken; Cantero, Jose L.; et al. (2002). The restorative effect of naps on perceptual deterioration. *Nature Neuroscience, 5,* 677–681.

Mednick, Sara C.; Cai, Denise J.; Shuman, Tristan; et al. (2011). An opportunistic theory of cellular and systems consolidation. *Trends in Neuroscience, 34,* 504–514.

Mednick, Sarnoff A. (1962). The associative basis of the creative process. *Psychological Review, 69,* 220–232.

Mednick, Sarnoff A.; Huttunen, Matti O.; & Machón, Ricardo (1994). Prenatal influenza infections and adult schizophrenia. *Schizophrenia Bulletin, 20,* 263–267.

Medvec, Victoria H.; Madey, Scott F.; & Gilovich, Thomas (1995). When less is more: Counterfactual thinking and satisfaction among Olympic medalists. *Journal of Personality and Social Psychology, 69,* 603–610.

Meeus, Wim H. J., & Raaijmakers, Quinten A. W. (1995). Obedience in modern society: The Utrecht studies. In A. G. Miller, B. E. Collins, & D. E. Brief (Eds.), Perspectives on obedience to authority: The legacy of the Milgram experiments. *Journal of Social Issues, 51,* 155–175.

Mehl, Matthias R.; Vazire, Simine; Ramírez-Esparza, Nairán; & Pennebacker, James W. (2007). Are women really more talkative than men? *Science, 317,* 82.

Meindl, James R., & Lerner, Melvin J. (1985). Exacerbation of extreme responses to an out-group. *Journal of Personality and Social Psychology, 47,* 71–84.

Meissner, Christian A. & Brigham, John C. (2001). Thirty years of investigating the own-race bias in memory for faces: A meta-analytic review. *Psychology, Public Policy, & Law, 7,* 3–35.

Melzack, Ronald (1992, April). Phantom limbs. *Scientific American, 266,* 120–126.

Melzack, Ronald (1993). Pain: Past, present and future. *Canadian Journal of Experimental Psychology, 47,* 615–629.

Melzack, Ronald, & Wall, Patrick D. (1965). Pain mechanisms: A new theory. *Science, 13,* 971–979.

Mendoza-Denton, Rodolfo, & Page-Gould, Elizabeth (2008). Can cross-group friendships influence minority students' well-being at historically white universities? *Psychological Science, 19,* 933–939.

Mennella, Julie A., Lukasewycz, Laura D., Castor, Sara M., & Beauchamp, Gary K. (2011). The timing and duration of a sensitive period in human flavor learning: A randomized trial. *American Journal of Clinical Nutrition, 93,* 1019–1024.

Mercer, Jean (2006). *Understanding attachment.* Westport, CT: Praeger.

Mercer, Jean; Sarner, Larry; and Rosa, Linda (2003). *Attachment therapy on trial.* Westport, CT: Praeger.

Merikle, Philip M., & Skanes, Heather E. (1992). Subliminal self-help audiotapes: A search for placebo effects. *Journal of Applied Psychology, 77,* 772–776.

Merskey, Harold (1992). The manufacture of personalities: The production of MPD. British *Journal of Psychiatry, 160,* 327–340.

Merton, Robert K. (1948). The self-fulfilling prophecy. *Antioch Review, 8,* 193–210.

Mesquita, Batja, & Frijda, Nico H. (1992). Cultural variations in emotions: A review. *Psychological Bulletin, 112,* 179–204.

Meston, Cindy M., & Buss, David M. (2007). Why humans have sex. *Archives of Sexual Behavior, 36,* 477–507.

Metcalfe, Janet (2009). Metacognitive judgments and control of study. *Current Directions in Psychological Science, 18,* 159–163.

Meyer, Gregory J.; Finn, Stephen E.; Eyde, Lorraine D.; et al. (2001). Psychological testing and psychological assessment. *American Psychologist, 56,* 128–165.

Mezulis, Amy H.; Abramson, Lyn Y.; Hyde, Janet S.; & Hankin, Benjamin L. (2004). Is there a positivity bias in attributions? *Psychological Bulletin, 130,* 711–747.

Mgode, Georgies F.; Wetjens, Bart J.; Nwrath, Thorben; et al. (2012). Diagnosis of tuberculosis by trained African giant pouched rats and confounding impact of pathogens and microflora of the respiratory tract. *Journal of Clinical Microbiology, 50,* 274–280.

Michael, Robert B.; Garry, Maryanne; & Kirsch, Irving (2012). Suggestion, cognition, and behavior. *Current Directions in Psychological Science, 21,* 151–156.

Mieda, Michihiro; Willie, Jon T.; Hara, Junko; et al. (2004). Orexin peptides prevent cataplexy and improve wakefulness in an orexin neuron-ablated model of narcolepsy in mice. *Proceedings of the National Academy of Science, 101,* 4649–4654.

Mikulincer, Mario, & Shaver, Philip R. (2007). *Attachment in adulthood: Structure, dynamics, and change.* New York: Guilford.

Mikulincer, Mario; Shaver, Phillip R.; Gillath, Omri; & Nitzberg, R. E. (2005). Attachment, caregiving, and altruism: Boosting attachment security increases compassion and helping. *Journal of Personality and Social Psychology, 89,* 817–839.

Mikulincer, Mario; Shaver, Phillip R.; & Horesh, Nita (2006). Attachment bases of emotion regulation and posttraumatic adjustment. In D. K. Snyder, J. A. Simpson, & J. N. Hughes (Eds.), *Emotion regulation in couples and families: Pathways to dysfunction and health.* Washington, DC: American Psychological Association.

Milgram, Stanley (1963). Behavioral study of obedience. *Journal of Abnormal and Social Psychology, 67,* 371–378.

Milgram, Stanley (1974). *Obedience to authority: An experimental view.* New York: Harper & Row.

Miklowitz, David J. (2007). The role of the family in the course and treatment of bipolar disorder. *Current Directions in Psychological Science, 16,* 192–196.

Miller, George A. (1956). The magical number seven, plus or minus two: Some limits on our capacity for processing information. *Psychological Review, 63,* 81–97.

Miller, Greg (2011). ESP paper rekindles discussion about statistics. *Science, 331,* 272–273.

Miller, Greg (2013). The promise and perils of oxytocin. *Science, 339,* 267–269.

Miller, Gregory E., & Cohen, Sheldon (2001). Psychological interventions and the immune system: A meta-analytic review and critique. *Health Psychology, 20,* 47–63.

Miller, Gregory E.; Chen, Edith; & Parker, Karen J. (2011). Psychological stress in childhood and susceptibility to the chronic diseases of aging: Moving toward a model of behavioral and biological mechanisms. *Psychological Bulletin, 137,* 959–997.

Miller, Gregory E.; Lachman, Margie E.; Chen, Edith; et al. (2011). Pathways to resilience: Maternal nurturance as a buffer against the effects of childhood poverty on metabolic syndrome. *Psychological Science, 22,* 1591–1599.

Miller, Inglis J., & Reedy, Frank E. (1990). Variations in human taste bud density and taste intensity perception. *Physiology and Behavior, 47,* 1213–1219.

Miller-Jones, Dalton (1989). Culture and testing. *American Psychologist, 44,* 360–366.

Miller, William R., & Rollnick, Stephen (2002). *Motivational interviewing: Preparing people for change* (2nd ed.). New York: Guilford.

Milner, Brenda (1970). Memory and the temporal regions of the brain. In K. H. Pribram & D. E. Broadbent (Eds.), *Biology of memory.* New York: Academic Press.

Milner, J. S., & McCanne, T. R. (1991). Neuropsychological correlates of physical child abuse. In J. S. Milner (Ed.), *Neuropsychology of aggression.* Norwell, MA: Kluwer Academic.

Milton, Julie, & Wiseman, Richard (1999). Does psi exist? Lack of replication of an anomalous process of information transfer. *Psychological Bulletin, 125,* 387–391.

Milton, Julie, & Wiseman, Richard (2001). Does psi exist? Reply to Storm and Ertel (2001). *Psychological Bulletin, 127,* 434–438.

Mineka, Susan, & Zinbarg, Richard (2006). A contemporary learning theory perspective on the etiology of anxiety disorders. *American Psychologist, 61,* 10–26.

Minuchin, Salvador (1984). *Family kaleidoscope.* Cambridge, MA: Harvard University Press.

Mischel, Walter (1973). Toward a cognitive social learning reconceptualization of personality. *Psychological Review, 80,* 252–253.

Mischel, Walter, & Ayduk, Ozlem (2004). Willpower in a cognitive-affective processing system: The dynamics of delay of gratification. In R. F. Baumeister & K. D. Vohs (Eds.), *Handbook of self-regulation: Research, theory, and applications.* New York: Guilford.

Mischel, Walter, & Shoda, Yuichi (1995). A cognitive affective system theory of personality: Reconceptualizing situations, dispositions, dynamics, and invariance in personality structures. *Psychological Review, 102,* 246–268.

Mischel, Walter; Shoda, Yuichi; & Rodriguez, Monica L. (1989). Delay of gratification in children. *Science, 244,* 933–938.

Mistry, Jayanthi, & Rogoff, Barbara (1994). Remembering in cultural context. In W. J. Lonner & R. Malpass (Eds.), *Psychology and culture.* Needham Heights, MA: Allyn & Bacon.

Mitchell, David B. (2006). Nonconscious priming after 17 years: Invulnerable implicit memory? *Psychological Science, 17,* 925–929.

Mitchell, Karen J., & Johnson, Marcia K. (2009). Source monitoring 15 years later: What have we learned from fMRI about the neural mechanisms of source memory? *Psychological Bulletin, 135,* 638–677.

Mitte, Kristin (2005). Meta-analysis of cognitive-behavioral treatments for generalized anxiety disorder: A comparison with pharmacotherapy. *Psychological Bulletin, 131,* 785–795.

Mitte, Kristin (2008). Memory bias for threatening information in anxiety and anxiety disorders: A meta-analytic review. *Psychological Bulletin, 134,* 886–911.

Mitterer, Holger, & de Ruiter, Jan Peter (2008). Recalibrating color categories using world knowledge. *Psychological Science, 19,* 629–634.

Mnookin, Seth (2011). *The panic virus: A true story of medicine, science, and fear.* New York: Simon & Schuster.

Modigliani, Andre, & Rochat, François (1995). The role of interaction sequences and the timing of resistance in shaping obedience and defiance to authority. In A. G. Miller, B. E. Collins, & D. E. Brief (Eds.), Perspectives on obedience to authority: The legacy of the Milgram experiments. *Journal of Social Issues, 51(3),* 107–125.

Moffitt, Terrie E. (1993). Adolescence-limited and life-course-persistent antisocial behavior: A developmental taxonomy. *Psychological Review, 100,* 674–701.

Moffitt, Terrie E. (2005). The new look of behavioral genetics in developmental psychopathology: Gene-environment interplay in antisocial behaviors. *Psychological Bulletin, 131,* 533–554.

Moghaddam, Fathali M. (2005). The staircase to terrorism: A psychological exploration. *American Psychologist, 60,* 161–169.

Mohr, Cynthia; Armeli, Stephen; Tennen, Howard; et al. (2001). Daily interpersonal experiences, context, and alcohol consumption: Crying in your beer and toasting good times. *Journal of Personality and Social Psychology, 80,* 489–500.

Monahan, Jennifer L.; Murphy, Sheila T.; & Zajonc, R. B. (2000). Subliminal mere exposure: Specific, general, and diffuse effects. *Psychological Science, 11,* 462–466.

Moncrieff, Joanna (2001). Are antidepressants overrated? A review of methodological problems in antidepressant trials. *Journal of Nervous and Mental Disease, 189,* 288–295.

Monroe, Scott M., & Reid, Mark W. (2009). Life stress and major depression. *Current Directions in Psychological Science, 18,* 68–72.

Monroe, Scott M.; Slavich, George M.; Torres, Leandro D.; & Gotlib, Ian H. (2007). Severe life events predict specific patterns of change in cognitive biases in major depression. *Psychological Medicine, 37,* 863–871.

Moore, Timothy E., & Pepler, Debra J. (2006). Wounding words: Maternal verbal aggression and children's adjustment. *Journal of Family Violence 21,* 89–93.

Moors, Agnes; Ellsworth, Phoebe C.; Scherer, Klaus; & Frijda, Nico (2013). Appraisal theories of emotion: State of the art and future development. *Emotion Review, 5,* 119–124.

Morell, Virginia (2008, March). Minds of their own. *National Geographic, 213,* 36–61.

Morelli, Gilda A.; Rogoff, Barbara; Oppenheim, David; & Goldsmith, Denise (1992). Cultural variation in infants' sleeping arrangements: Questions of independence. *Developmental Psychology, 28,* 604–613.

Moreno, Carmen; Laje, Gonzalo; Blanco, Carlos; et al. (2007). National trends in the outpatient diagnosis and treatment of bipolar disorder in youth. *Archives of General Psychiatry, 64,* 1032–1039.

Morewedge, Carey K., & Norton, Michael I. (2009). When dreaming is believing: The (motivated) interpretation of dreams. *Journal of Personality and Social Psychology, 96,* 249–264.

Morin, Charles M.; Bootzin, Richard R.; Buysse, Daniel J.; et al. (2006). Psychological and behavioral treatment of insomnia: Update of the recent evidence (1998–2004). *Sleep, 29,* 1398–1414.

Morin, Charles M.; Vallières, Annie; Guay, Bernard; et al. (2009). Cognitive behavioral therapy, singly and combined with medication, for persistent insomnia: A randomized controlled trial. *Journal of the American Medical Association, 301,* 2005–2015.

Morton, Thomas A.; Postmes, Tom; Haslam, S. Alexander; & Hornsey, Matthew J. (2009). Theorizing gender in the face of social change: Is there anything essential about essentialism? *Journal of Personality and Social Psychology, 96,* 653–664.

Moscovitch, Morris; Winocur, Gordon; & Behrmann, Marlene (1997). What is special about face recognition? Nineteen experiments on a person with visual object agnosia and dyslexia but normal face recognition. *Journal of Cognitive Neuroscience, 9,* 555–604.

Moskowitz, Judith T.; Hult, Jen R.; Bussolari, Cori; & Acree, Michael (2009). What works in coping with HIV? A meta-analysis with implications for coping with serious illness. *Psychological Bulletin, 135,* 121–141.

Moss, Michael (2013). *Salt, sugar, fat: How the food giants hooked us.* New York: Random House.

Most, Steven B.; Simons, Daniel J.; Scholl, Brian J.; et al. (2001). How not to be seen: The contribution of similarity and selective ignoring to sustained inattentional blindness. *Psychological Science, 12,* 9–17.

Moyer, Christopher A.; Donnelly, Michael P. W.; Anderson, Jane C.; et al. (2011). Frontal electroencephalographic asymmetry associated with positive emotion is produced by brief meditation training. *Psychological Science, 22,* 1277–1279.

Mozell, Maxwell M.; Smith, Bruce P.; Smith, Paul E.; Sullivan, Richard L.; & Swender, Philip (1969). Nasal chemoreception in flavor identification. *Archives of Otolaryngology, 90,* 367–373.

Mroczek, Daniel K., & Spiro, Avron (2005). Changes in life satisfaction during adulthood: Findings from the veterans affairs normative aging study. *Journal of Personality and Social Psychology, 88,* 189–202.

Mueller, Claudia M., & Dweck, Carol S. (1998). Praise for intelligence can undermine children's motivation and performance. *Journal of Personality and Social Psychology, 75,* 33–52.

Mukamal, Kenneth J.; Conigrove, Katherine M; Mittleman, Murray A.; et al. (2003). Roles of drinking pattern and type of alcohol consumed in coronary heart disease in men. *New England Journal of Medicine, 348,* 109–118.

Müller, Christian P., & Schumann, Gunter (2011). Drugs as instruments: A new framework for non-addictive psychoactive drug use. *Behavioral and Brain Sciences, 34,* 293–310.

Murray, Charles (2008). *Real education: Four simple truths for bringing America's schools back to reality.* New York: Crown Forum.

Myers, Ronald E., & Sperry, R. W. (1953). Interocular transfer of a visual form discrimination habit in cats after section of the optic chiasm and corpus callosum. *Anatomical Record, 115,* 351–352.

Myrtek, Michael (2007). Type A behavior and hostility as independent risk factors for coronary heart disease. In J. Jordan et al. (Eds.), *Contributions toward evidence-based psychocardiology: A systematic review of the literature.* Washington, DC: American Psychological Association.

Nadal, Kevin; Griffin, Katie E.; Vargas, Vivian M.; et al. (2011). Processes and struggles with racial microaggressions from the white American perspective: Recommendations for workplace settings. In M. A. Paludi, C. A. Paludi, & E. R. DeSouza (Eds.), *Praeger handbook on understanding and preventing workplace discrimination.* Santa Barbara, CA: Praeger/ABC-CLIO.

Nakaya, Naoki; Tsubono, Yoshitaka; Hosokawa, Toru; et al. (2003). Personality and the risk of cancer. *Journal of the National Cancer Institute, 95,* 799–805.

Nash, Michael R. (1987). What, if anything, is regressed about hypnotic age regression? A review of the empirical literature. *Psychological Bulletin, 102,* 42–52.

Nash, Michael R. (2001, July). The truth and the hype of hypnosis. *Scientific American, 285,* 46–49, 52–55.

Nash, Michael R., & Barnier, Amanda J. (2007). *The Oxford handbook of hypnosis.* Oxford, UK: Oxford University Press.

Nash, Michael R., & Nadon, Robert (1997). Hypnosis. In D. L. Faigman, D. Kaye, M. J. Saks, & J. Sanders (Eds.), *Modern scientific evidence: The law and science of expert testimony.* St. Paul, MN: West.

Nathan, Debbie (2011). *Sybil exposed: The extraordinary story behind the famous multiple personality case.* New York: Free Press.

Navarrete, Carlos David; Olsson, Andreas; Ho, Arnold K; et al. (2009). Fear extinction to an out-group face: The role of target gender. *Psychological Science, 20,* 155–158.

Neal, David T., & Chartrand, Tanya L. (2011). Embodied emotion perception: Amplifying and dampening facial feedback modulates emotion perception accuracy. *Social Psychological and Personality Science, 2,* 673–678.

Neher, Andrew (1996). Jung's theory of archetypes: A critique. *Journal of Humanistic Psychology, 36,* 61–91.

Neisser, Ulric, & Harsch, Nicole (1992). Phantom flashbulbs: False recollections of hearing the news about Challenger. In E. Winograd & U. Neisser (Eds.), *Affect and accuracy in recall: Studies of "flashbulb memories."* New York: Cambridge University Press.

Nelson, Charles A.; Zeanah, Charles H.; Fox, Nathan A.; et al. (2007). Cognitive recovery in socially deprived young children: The Bucharest early intervention project. *Science, 318,* 1937–1940.

Ness, Jose; Aronow, Wilbert S.; & Beck, Gwen (2006). Menopausal symptoms after cessation of hormone replacement therapy. *Maturitas, 53,* 356–361.

Nesse, Randolph M., & Ellsworth, Phoebe C. (2009). Evolution, emotion, and emotional disorders. *American Psychologist, 64,* 129–139.

Nevins, Andrew; Pesetsky, David; & Rodrigues, Cilene (2009). Pirahã exceptionality: A reassessment. *Language, 85,* 355–404.

Newcombe, Nora S.; Lloyd, Marianne E.; & Balcomb, Frances (2012). Contextualizing the development of recollection: Episodic memory and binding in young children. In S. Ghetti & P. J. Bauer (Eds.), *Origins and development of recollection: Perspectives from psychology and Neuroscience.* New York: Oxford University Press.

Newland, M. Christopher, & Rasmussen, Erin B. (2003). Behavior in adulthood and during aging is affected by contaminant exposure in utero. *Current Directions in Psychological Science, 12,* 212–217.

News.yahoo.com/stories-2-brothers-suspected-bombing-124623274.html

Newton, Nicola, & Stewart, Abigail J. (2010). The middle ages: Change in women's personalities and social roles. *Psychology of Women Quarterly, 34,* 75–84.

Nichols, Michael P., & Schwartz, Richard C. (2008). *Family therapy: Concepts and methods* (8th ed.). Boston, MA: Allyn & Bacon.

Nickerson, Raymond S. (1998). Confirmation bias: A ubiquitous phenomenon in many guises. *Review of General Psychology, 2,* 175–220.

Nickerson, Raymond A., & Adams, Marilyn Jager (1979). Long-term memory for a common object. *Cognitive Psychology, 11,* 287–307.

NICHD Early Child Care Research Network (2006). Infant–mother attachment classification: Risk and protection in relation to changing maternal caregiving quality. *Developmental Psychology, 42,* 38–58.

Nisbett, Richard E. (1993). Violence and U.S. regional culture. *American Psychologist, 48,* 441–449.

Nisbett, Richard E. (2009). *Intelligence and how to get it: Why schools and culture count.* New York: W. W. Norton.

Nisbett, Richard E., & Ross, Lee (1980). *Human inference: Strategies and shortcomings of social judgment.* Englewood Cliffs, NJ: Prentice-Hall.

Nitsche, Michael A.; Cohen, Leonardo G.; Wassermann, Eric M.; et al. (2008). Transcranial direct current stimulation: State of the art 2008. *Brain Stimulation, 1,* 206–223.

Nivet, Emmanuel; Vignes, Michel; Girard, Stéphane D.; et al. (2011). Engraftment of human nasal olfactory stem cells restores neuroplasticity in mice with hippocampal lesions. *Journal of Clinical Investigation, 121,* 2808–2820.

Noble, Mark; Mayer-Pröschel, Margot; Davies, Jeannette E.; et al. (2011). Cell therapies for the central nervous system: How do we identify the best candidates? *Current Opinion in Neurology, 24,* 570–576.

Nock, Matthew K. (2010). Self-injury. *Annual Review of Clinical Psychology, 6,* 339–363.

Nolan, Susan A.; Flynn, Cynthia; & Garber, Judy (2003). Prospective relations between rejection and depression in young adolescents. *Journal of Personality and Social Psychology, 85,* 745–755.

Nosek, Brian A.; Greenwald, Anthony G.; & Banaji, Mahzarin R. (2007). The Implicit Association Test at 7: A methodological and conceptual review. In J. A. Bargh (Ed.), *Social psychology and the unconscious.* New York: Psychology Press.

Nyberg, Lars; Habib, Reza; McIntosh, Anthony R.; & Tulving, Endel (2000). Reactivation of encoding-related brain activity during memory retrieval. *Proceedings of the National Academy of Sciences, 97,* 11120–11124.

Oaten, Megan; Stevenson, Richard J.; & Case, Trevor I. (2009). Disgust as a disease-avoidance mechanism. *Psychological Bulletin, 125,* 303–321.

Oatley, Keith; Keltner, Dacher; & Jenkins, Jennifer M. (2006). *Understanding emotions* (2nd Ed.). Cambridge, MA: Blackwell.

Odgers, Candice L.; Caspi, Avshalom; Nagin, Daniel S.; et al. (2008). Is it important to prevent early exposure to drugs and alcohol among adolescents? *Psychological Science, 19,* 1037–1044.

Offit, Paul A. (2008). *Autism's false prophets: Bad science, risky medicine, and the search for a cure.* NY: Columbia University Press.

Ofshe, Richard J., & Watters, Ethan (1994). *Making monsters: False memory, psychotherapy, and sexual hysteria.* New York: Scribners.

Ogden, Jenni (2012). *Trouble in mind: Stories from a neuropsychologist's casebook.* New York: Oxford University Press.

Ogden, Jenni A., & Corkin, Suzanne (1991). Memories of H. M. In W. C. Abraham, M. C. Corballis, & K. G. White (Eds.), *Memory mechanisms: A tribute to G. V. Goddard.* Hillsdale, NJ: Erlbaum.

Öhman, Arne, & Mineka, Susan (2001). Fears, phobias, and preparedness: Toward an evolved module of fear and fear learning. *Psychological Review, 108,* 483–522.

Olson, James M.; Vernon, Philip A.; Harris, Julie Aitken; & Jang, Kerry L. (2001). The heritability of attitudes: A study of twins. *Journal of Personality and Social Psychology, 80,* 845–850.

Olson, Michael A. (2009). Measures of prejudice. In T. Nelson (Ed.), *The handbook of prejudice, stereotyping, and discrimination.* New York: Psychology Press.

Olsson, Andreas, & Phelps, Elizabeth (2004). Learned fear of "unseen" faces after Pavlovian, observational, and instructed fear. *Psychological Science, 15,* 822–828.

Olsson, Andreas; Ebert, Jeffrey; Banaji, Mahzarin; & Phelps, Elizabeth A. (2005). The role of social groups in the persistence of learned fear. *Science, 309,* 785–787

Olujic, M. B. (1998). Embodiment of terror: Gendered violence in peacetime and wartime in Croatia and Bosnia-Herzegovina. *Medical Anthropology Quarterly, 12,* 31–50.

O'Neill, Sarah, & Zajac, Rachel (2012). The role of repeated interviewing in children's responses to cross-examination-style questioning. *British Journal of Psychology, 104,* 14–38.

Ong, Anthony D. (2010). Pathways linking positive emotion and health in later life. *Current Directions in Psychological Science, 19,* 358–362.

Ophir, Eyal; Nass, Clifford; & Wagner, Anthony D. (2009). Cognitive control in media multitaskers. *Proceedings of the National Academy of Sciences, 106,* 15583–15587.

O'Rahilly, Ronan, & Müller, Fabiola (2001). *Human embryology and teratology.* New York: Wiley.

Oriña, M. Minda; Collins, W. Andrew; Simpson, Jeffry A.; et al. (2011). Developmental and dyadic perspectives on commitment in adult romantic relationships. *Psychological Science, 22,* 908–915.

Osland, Teresa M.; Bjorvatn, Bjørn; Steen, Vidar M.; & Pallesen, Ståle (2011). Association study of a variable-number tandem repeat polymorphism in the clock gene PERIOD3 and chronotype in Norwegian university students. *Chronobiology International, 28,* 764–770.

Ostrovsky, Yuri; Andalman, Aaron; & Sinha, Pawan (2006). Vision following extended congenital blindness. *Psychological Science, 12,* 1009–1014.

Otto, Michael W., & Smits, Jasper A. J. (2011). *Exercise for mood and anxiety.* New York: Oxford University Press.

Otto, Michael W.; Behar, Evelyn; Smits, Jasper A. J.; & Hoffmann, Stefan G. (2009). Combining pharmacological and cognitive behavioral therapy in the treatment of anxiety disorders. In M. M. Antony & M. B. Stein (Eds.), *Oxford handbook of anxiety and related disorders.* New York: Oxford University Press.

Ouellet, Véronique; Labbé, Sébastien M.; Blondin, Denis P.; et al. (2012). Brown adipose tissue oxidative metabolism contributes to energy expenditure during acute cold exposure in humans. *Journal of Clinical Investigation, 122,* 545–552.

Overeem, Sebastiaan; van Nues, Soffie J.; van der Zande, Wendy L.; et al. (2011). The clinical features of cataplexy: A questionnaire study in narcolepsy patients with and without hypocretin-1 deficiency. *Sleep Medicine, 12,* 12–18.

Oyserman, Daphna, & Lee, Spike W. S. (2008). Does culture influence what and how we think? Effects of priming individualism and collectivism. *Psychological Bulletin, 134,* 311–342.

Packer, Dominic J. (2008). Identifying systematic disobedience in Milgram's obedience experiments: A meta-analytic review. *Perspectives on Psychological Science, 3,* 301–304.

Packer, Dominic J. (2009). Avoiding groupthink: Whereas weakly identified members remain silent, strongly identified members dissent about collective problems. *Psychological Science, 20,* 619–626.

Pail, Gerald; Huf, Wolfgang; Pjrek, Edda; et al. (2011). Bright-light therapy in the treatment of mood disorders. *Neuropsychobiology, 64,* 152–162.

Pan, Bing; Hembrooke, Helene; Joachims, Thorsten; et al. (2007). In Google we trust: Users' decisions on rank, position, and relevance. *Journal of Computer-Mediated Communication, 12,* 3.

Panksepp, Jaak (1998). Attention deficit hyperactivity disorders, psychostimulants, and intolerance of childhood playfulness: A tragedy in the making? *Current Directions in Psychological Science, 7,* 91–98.

Panksepp, Jaak; Herman, B. H.; Vilberg, T.; et al. (1980). Endogenous opioids and social behavior. *Neuroscience and Biobehavioral Reviews, 4,* 473–487.

Paoletti, Jo (2012). *Pink and blue: Telling the girls from the boys in America.* Bloomington, IN: University of Indiana Press.

Parada, Maria; Corral, Montserrat; Mota, Nayara; et al. (2012). Executive functioning and alcohol binge drinking in university students. *Addictive Behaviors, 37,* 167–172.

Park, Denise, & Gutchess, Angela (2006). The cognitive neuroscience of aging and culture. *Current Directions in Psychological Science, 15,* 105–108.

Parker, Kim (2012, March 15). The boomerang generation. Pew Research Social and Demographic Trends, on line at www.pewsocialtrends.org.

Parker, Elizabeth S.; Cahill, Larry; & McGaugh, James L. (2006). A case of unusual autobiographical remembering. *Neurocase, 12,* 35–49.

Parlee, Mary B. (1982). Changes in moods and activation levels during the menstrual cycle in experimentally naive subjects. *Psychology of Women Quarterly, 7,* 119–131.

Parlee, Mary B. (1994). The social construction of premenstrual syndrome: A case study of scientific discourse as cultural contestation. In M. G. Winkler & L. B. Cole (Eds.), *The good body: Asceticism in contemporary culture.* New Haven, CT: Yale University Press.

Pascual-Leone, Alvaro; Amedi, Amir; Fregni, Felipe; & Merabet, Lotfe B. (2005). The plastic human brain cortex. *Annual Review of Neuroscience, 28,* 377–401.

Pastalkova, Eva; Itskov, Vladimir; Amarasingham, Asohan; & Buzsáki, György (2008). Internally generated cell assembly sequences in the rat hippocampus. *Science, 321,* 1322–1327.

Patterson, Charlotte J. (2006). Children of lesbian and gay parents. *Current Directions in Psychological Science, 15,* 241–244.

Patterson, David R., & Jensen, Mark P. (2003). Hypnosis and clinical pain. *Psychological Bulletin, 129,* 495–521.

Patterson, Francine, & Linden, Eugene (1981). *The education of Koko.* New York: Holt, Rinehart and Winston.

Patrick, Christopher J.; Fowles, Don C.; & Krueger, Robert F. (2009). Triarchic conceptualization of psychopathy: Developmental origins of disinhibition, boldness, and meanness. *Development and Psychopathology, 21,* 913–938.

Paul, Annie M. (2004). *The cult of personality.* New York: The Free Press.

Paul, Pamela (2008). *Parenting, Inc.: How the billion-dollar baby business has changed the way we raise our children.* New York: Henry Holt.

Paul, Richard W. (1984, September). Critical thinking: Fundamental to education for a free society. *Educational Leadership*, 4–14.

Paunonen, Sampo V. (2003). Big Five factors or personality and replicated predictions of behavior. *Journal of Personality & Social Psychology, 84*, 411–422.

Paunonen, Sampo V., & Ashton, Michael C. (2001). Big Five factors and facets and the prediction of behavior. *Journal of Personality and Social Psychology, 81*, 524–539.

Pavlov, Ivan P. (1927). *Conditioned reflexes* (G. V. Anrep, Trans.). London: Oxford University Press.

Payne, Jessica D.; Stickgold, Robert; Swanberg, Kelley; & Kensinger, Elizabeth. (2008). Sleep preferentially enhances memory for emotional components of scenes. *Psychological Science, 19*, 781–788.

Peele, Stanton (2000). What addiction is and what it is not: The impact of mistaken notions of addiction. *Addiction Research, 8*, 599–607.

Peele, Stanton, & Brodsky, Archie, with Mary Arnold (1991). *The truth about addiction and recovery.* New York: Simon & Schuster.

Peier, A. M.; Moqrich, A.; Hergarden, A. C.; et al. (2002). A TRP channel that senses cold stimuli and menthol. *Cell, 108*, 705–715.

Pennebaker, James W. (2002). Writing, social processes, and psychotherapy: From past to future. In S. J. Lepore & J. M. Smyth (Eds.), *The writing cure: How expressive writing promotes health and emotional well-being.* Washington, DC: American Psychological Association.

Pennebaker, James W. (2011). *The secret life of pronouns: What our words say about us.* New York: Bloomsbury.

Pennebaker, James W.; Colder, Michelle; & Sharp, Lisa K. (1990). Accelerating the coping process. *Journal of Personality and Social Psychology, 58*, 528–537.

Pennebaker, James W.; Kiecolt-Glaser, Janice; & Glaser, Ronald (1988). Disclosure of traumas and immune function: Health implications for psychotherapy. *Journal of Consulting and Clinical Psychology, 56*, 239–245.

Penton-Voak, Ian S.; Thomas, Jamie; Gage, Suzanne H.; et al. (2013). Increasing recognition of happiness in ambiguous facial expressions reduces anger and aggressive behavior. *Psychological Science, 24*, 688–697.

Peplau, Letita Anne (2003). Human sexuality: How do men and women differ? *Current Directions in Psychological Science, 12*, 37–40.

Peplau, Letitia Anne; Spalding, Leah R.; Conley, Terri D.; & Veniegas, Rosemary C. (2000). The development of sexual orientation in women. *Annual Review of Sex Research, 10*, 70–99.

Pepperberg, Irene (2000). *The Alex studies: Cognitive and communicative abilities of grey parrots.* Cambridge, MA: Harvard University Press.

Pepperberg, Irene M. (2002). Cognitive and communicative abilities of grey parrots. *Current Directions in Psychological Science, 11*, 83–87.

Pepperberg, Irene M. (2006). Grey parrot (Psittacus erithacus) numerical abilities: Addition and further experiments on a zero-like concept. *Journal of Comparative Psychology, 120*, 1–11.

Pepperberg, Irene (2008). *Alex and me.* New York: HarperCollins.

Perera, Frederica P.; Rauh, Virginia; Whyatt, Robin M.; et al. (2006). Effect of prenatal exposure to airborne polycyclic aromatic hydrocarbons on neurodevelopment in the first 3 years of life among inner-city children. *Environmental Health Perspectives, 114*, 1287–1292.

Persons, Jacqueline; Davidson, Joan; & Tompkins, Michael A. (2001). *Essential components of cognitive-behavior therapy for depression.* Washington, DC: American Psychological Association.

Peterson, Christopher; Seligman, Martin E. P.; Yurko, Karen H.; et al. (1998). Catastrophizing and untimely death. *Psychological Science, 9*, 127–130.

Petersen, Jennifer L., & Hyde, Janet S. (2010). A meta-analytic review of research on gender differences in sexuality, 1993-2007. *Psychological Bulletin, 136*, 21–38.

Peterson, Lloyd R., & Peterson, Margaret J. (1959). Short-term retention of individual verbal items. *Journal of Experimental Psychology, 58*, 193–198.

Peterson, Zoë D., & Muehlenhard, Charlene L. (2011). A match-and-motivation model of how women label their nonconsensual sexual experiences. *Psychology of Women Quarterly, 35*, 558–570.

Petkova, Valeria I., & Ehrsson, H. Henrik (2008). If I were you: Perceptual illusion of body swapping. *PLoS ONE, 3:* e3832.doi:10.1371/journal.pone.0003832.

Pettigrew, Thomas T., & Tropp, Linda R. (2006). A meta-analytic test of intergroup contact theory. *Journal of Personality and Social Psychology, 90*, 751–783.

Petrie, Keith J.; Booth, Roger J.; & Pennebaker, James W. (1998). The immunological effects of thought suppression. *Journal of Personality and Social Psychology, 75*, 1264–1272.

Pfungst, Oskar (1911/1965). *Clever Hans (The horse of Mr. von Osten): A contribution to experimental animal and human psychology.* New York: Holt, Rinehart and Winston.

Phinney, Jean S. (1996). When we talk about American ethnic groups, what do we mean? *American Psychologist, 51*, 918–927.

Piaget, Jean (1929/1960). *The child's conception of the world.* Paterson, NJ: Littlefield, Adams.

Piaget, Jean (1952). *Play, dreams, and imitation in childhood.* New York: W. W. Norton.

Piaget, Jean (1984). Piaget's theory. In P. Mussen (Series Ed.) & W. Kessen (Vol. Ed.), *Handbook of child psychology: Vol. 1. History, theory, and methods* (4th ed.). New York: Wiley.

Pierce, W. David; Cameron, Judy; Banko, Katherine M.; & So, Sylvia (2003). Positive effects of rewards and performance standards on intrinsic motivation. *Psychological Record, 53*, 561–579.

Pika, Simone, & Mitani, John (2006). Referential gesture communication in wild chimpanzees (Pan troglodytes). *Current Biology, 16*, 191–192.

Pillemer, Jane; Hatfield, Elaine; & Sprecher, Susan (2008). The importance of fairness and equity for the marital satisfaction of older women. *Journal of Women and Aging, 20*, 215–229.

Pincus, Tamar, & Morley, Stephen (2001). Cognitive-processing bias in chronic pain: A review and integration. *Psychological Bulletin, 127*, 599–617.

Pinker, Steven (1994). The language instinct: How the mind creates language. New York: Morrow.

Piper, August, & Merskey, Harold (2004). The persistence of folly: A critical examination of dissociative identity disorder. Part I: The excesses of an improbable concept. *Canadian Journal of Psychiatry, 49*, 592–600.

Pietromonaco, Paula R.; DeBuse, Casey J.; & Powers, Sally I. (2013). Does attachment get under the skin? Adult romantic attachment and cortisol responses to stress. *Current Directions in Psychological Science, 22*, 63–68.

Pittenger, David J. (1993). The utility of the Myers-Briggs Type Indicator. *Review of Educational Research, 63*, 467–488.

Plomin, Robert (1989). Environment and genes: Determinants of behavior. *American Psychologist, 44*, 105–111.

Plomin, Robert (2011). Commentary: Why are children in the same family so different? Non-shared environment three decades later. *International Journal of Epidemiology, 40*, 582–592.

Plomin, Robert; DeFries, John C; & Knopik, Valerie S. (2013). *Behavioral Genetics* (6th ed.). New York: Worth.

Plotnik, Joshua M.; de Waal, Frans B. M.; & Reiss, Diana (2006). Self-recognition in an Asian elephant. *Proceedings of the National Academy of Science, 103*, 17053–17057.

Pole, Nnamdi (2013). Disgust discussed: Introduction to the special section. *Psychological Bulletin, 2013.* Special section on disgust: 269–351.

Ponitz, Claire C.; McClelland, Megan M.; Matthews, J. S.; & Morrison, Frederick J. (2009). A structured observation of behavioral self-regulation and its contribution to kindergarten outcomes. *Developmental Psychology, 45*, 605–619.

Poole, Debra A., & Lamb, Michael E. (1998). *Investigative interviews of children.* Washington, DC: American Psychological Association.

Poole, Debra; Bruck, Maggie; & Pipe, Margaret-Ellen (2011). Forensic interviewing aids: Do props help children answer questions about touching? *Current Directions in Psychological Science, 20*, 11–15.

Pope, Harrison G., Jr.; Poliakoff, Michael B.; Parker, Michael P.; et al. (2007). Is dissociative amnesia a culture-bound syndrome? Findings from a survey of historical literature. *Psychological Medicine, 37*, 22533.

Popkin, Barry M. (2009). *The world is fat: The fads, trends, policies, and products that are fattening the human race.* New York: Avery (Penguin).

Portenoy, Russell K. (1994). Opioid therapy for chronic nonmalignant pain: Current status. In H. L. Fields & J. C. Liebeskind (Eds.), *Progress in pain research and management. Pharmacological approaches to the treatment of chronic pain: Vol. 1.* Seattle: International Association for the Study of Pain.

Posner, Michael I., & Rothbart, Mary K. (2011). Brain states and hypnosis research. *Consciousness & Cognition, 20,* 325–327.

Postmes, Tom, & Spears, Russell (1998). Deindividuation and antinormative behavior: A meta-analysis. *Psychological Bulletin, 123,* 238–259.

Postuma, R. B.; Gagnon, J. F.; Vendette, M.; et al. (2009). Quantifying the risk of neurodegenerative disease in idiopathic REM sleep behavior disorder. *Neurology, 14,* 1296–1300.

Potter, W. James (1987). Does television viewing hinder academic achievement among adolescents? *Human Communication Research, 14,* 27–46.

Poulin, Michael J.; Holman, E. Alison; & Buffone, Anneke (2012). The neurogenetics of nice: Receptor genes for oxytocin and vasopressin interact with threat to produce prosocial behavior. *Psychological Science, 23,* 446–452.

Poulin-Dubois, Diane; Serbin, Lisa A.; Kenyon, Brenda; & Derbyshire, Alison (1994). Infants' intermodal knowledge about gender. *Developmental Psychology, 30,* 436–442.

Powell, Russell A., & Boer, Douglas P. (1995). Did Freud misinterpret reported memories of sexual abuse as fantasies? *Psychological Reports, 77,* 563–570.

Poythress, Norman G.; Edens, John F.; Skeem, Jennifer L.; Lilienfeld, Scott O.; et al. (2010). Identifying subtypes among offenders with antisocial personality disorder: A cluster-analytic study. *Journal of Abnormal Psychology, 119,* 389–400.

Premack, David, & Premack, Ann James (1983). *The mind of an ape.* New York: Norton.

Pressman, Sarah D., & Cohen, Sheldon (2005). Does positive affect influence health? *Psychological Bulletin, 131,* 925–971.

Presnell, Katherine; Bearman, Sarah Kate; & Stice, Eric (2004). Risk factors for body dissatisfaction in adolescent boys and girls: A prospective study. *International Journal of Eating Disorders, 36,* 389–401.

Price, Donald D.; Finniss, Damien G.; & Benedetti, Fabrizio (2008). A comprehensive review of the placebo effect: Recent advances and current thought. *Annual Review of Psychology, 59,* 565–590.

Primack, Brian A.; Silk, Jennifer S.; DeLozier, Christian R.; et al. (2011). Using ecological momentary assessment to determine media use by individuals with and without major depressive disorder. *Archives of Pediatrics & Adolescent Medicine, 165,* 360–365.

Principe, Gabrielle; Kanaya, Tomoe; Ceci, Stephen J.; & Singh, Mona (2006). Believing is seeing: How rumors can engender false memories in preschoolers. *American Psychologist, 17,* 243–248.

Prochaska, James O.; Norcross, John C.; & DiClemente, Carlo C. (1994). *Changing for good.* New York: Morrow.

Pronin, Emily (2008). How we see ourselves and how we see others. *Science, 320,* 1177–1180.

Pronin, Emily; Gilovich, Thomas; & Ross, Lee (2004). Objectivity in the eye of the beholder: Divergent perceptions of bias in self versus others. *Psychological Review, 111,* 781–799.

Protzko, John; Aronson, Joshua; & Blair, Clancy (2013). How to make a young child smarter: Evidence from the database of raising intelligence. *Perspectives on Psychological Science, 8,* 25-40.

Ptito, Maurice; Moesgaard, Solvej M.; Gjedde, Albert; & Kupers, Ron (2005). Cross-modal plasticity revealed by electrotactile stimulation of the tongue in the congenitally blind. *Brain, 128,* 606–614.

Punamaeki, Raija-Leena, & Joustie, Marja (1998). The role of culture, violence, and personal factors affecting dream content. *Journal of Cross-Cultural Psychology, 29,* 320–342.

Pynoos, R. S., & Nader, K. (1989). Children's memory and proximity to violence. *Journal of the American Academy of Child and Adolescent Psychiatry, 28,* 236–241.

Pyszczynski, Tom; Rothschild, Zachary; & Abdollahi, Abdolhossein (2008). Terrorism, violence, and hope for peace: A terror management perspective. *Current Directions in Psychological Science, 17,* 318–322.

Pyter, L.M.; Pineros, V.; Galang, J.A.; et al. (2009). Peripheral tumors induce depressive-like behaviors and cytokine production and alter hypothalamic-pituitary-adrenal axis regulation. *Proceedings of the National Academy of Sciences, 106,* 9069–9074.

Quinn, Diane M., & Spencer, Steven J. (2001). The interference of stereotype threat with women's generation of mathematical problem-solving strategies. *Journal of Social Issues, 57,* 55–71.

Quinn, Paul, & Bhatt, Ramesh (2005). Learning perceptual organization in infancy. *Psychological Science, 16,* 511–515.

Raby, K. Lee; Cicchetti, Dante; Carlson, Elizabeth A.; et al. (2012). Genetic and caregiving-based contributions to infant attachment: Unique associations with distress reactivity and attachment security. *Psychological Science, 23,* 1016–1023.

Racsmány, Mihály; Conway, Martin A.; & Demeter, Gyula (2010). Consolidation of episodic memories during sleep: Long-term effects of retrieval practice. *Psychological Science, 21,* 80–85.

Radel, Rémi, & Clément-Guillotin, Corentin (2012). Evidence of motivational influences in early visual perception: Hunger modulates conscious access. *Psychological Science, 23,* 232–234.

Radford, Benjamin (2013, March 27). UFOs over Texas: Unidentified floating fireballs! LiveScience.com.

Radford, Benjamin (2011, September/October). Holly Bobo still missing: Psychics hurt investigation. *Skeptical Inquirer, 35,* 9.

Raffaelli, Marcela; Crockett, Lisa J.; & Shen, Yuh-ling (2005). Developmental stability and change in self-regulation from childhood to adolescence. *Journal of Genetic Psychology, 166,* 54–75.

Rahman, Qazi, &Wilson, Glenn D. (2003). Born gay? The psychobiology of human sexual orientation. *Personality and Individual Differences, 34,* 1337–1382.

Raine, Adrian (2008). From genes to brain to antisocial behavior. *Current Directions in Psychological Science, 17,* 323–328.

Raine, Adrian; Lencz, Todd; Bihrle, Susan; LaCasse, Lori; & Colletti, Patrick (2000). Reduced prefrontal gray matter volume and reduced autonomic activity in antisocial personality disorder. *Archives of General Psychiatry, 57,* 119–127.

Raine, Adrian; Meloy, J. R.; Bihrle, S.; et al. (1998). Reduced prefrontal and increased subcortical brain functioning assessed using positron emission tomography in predatory and affective murderers. *Behavioral Science and Law, 6,* 319–332.

Raja, Srinivasa (2008, May 8). From poppies to pill-popping: Is there a "middle way?" Paper presented at the annual meeting of the American Pain Society, Tampa, Fl.

Raloff, Janet (2011). Environment: Chemicals linked to kids' lower IQs: Studies identify effects from pesticides still used on farms. *Science News, 179,* 15.

Ramachandran, V. S., & Altschuler, Eric L. (2009). The use of visual feedback, in particular mirror visual feedback, in restoring brain function. *Brain, 132,* 1693–1710.

Ramachandran, V. S., & Blakeslee, Sandra (1998). *Phantoms in the brain.* New York: William Morrow.

Randall, David K. (2012). *Dreamland: Adventures in the strange world of sleep.* New York: Norton.

Rankin, Lindsay E., & Eagly, Alice H. (2008). Is his heroism hailed and hers hidden? Women, men, and the social construction of heroism. *Psychology of Women Quarterly, 32,* 414–422.

Rapkin, Andrea J.; Chang, Li C.; & Reading, Anthony E. (1988). Comparison of retrospective and prospective assessment of premenstrual symptoms. *Psychological Reports, 62,* 55–60.

Rasch, Björn; Büchel, Christian; Gais, Steffen; & Born, Jan (2007). Odor cues during slow-wave sleep prompt declarative memory consolidation. *Science, 315,* 1426–1429.

Raser, Jonathan M., & O'Shea, Erin K. (2005). Noise in gene expression: Origins, consequences, and control. *Science, 309,* 2010–2013.

Rasheed, Parveen, & Al-Sowielem, Latifa S. (2003). Prevalence and predictors of premenstrual syndrome among college-aged women in Saudi Arabia. *Annals of Saudi Medicine, 23,* 381–387.

Ratcliffe, Heather (2000, January 28). Midwest UFO sightings get once-over from scientists. *Detroit News,* Religion Section [online version].

Rathbun, Constance; DiVirgilio, Letitia; & Waldfogel, Samuel (1958). A restitutive process in children following radical separation from family and culture. *American Journal of Orthopsychiatry, 28,* 408–415.

Rauschecker, Josef P. (1999). Making brain circuits listen. *Science, 285,* 1686–1687.

Ravussin, Eric; Lillioja, Stephen; Knowler, William; et al. (1988). Reduced rate of energy expenditure as a risk factor for body-weight gain. *New England Journal of Medicine, 318,* 467–472.

Ray, Wayne A.; Chung, Cecilia P.; Murray, Katherine T.; et al. (2009). Atypical antipsychotic drugs and the risk of sudden cardiac death. *New England Journal of Medicine, 360*, 225–235.

Reber, Paul J.; Stark, Craig E. L.; & Squire, Larry R. (1998). Contrasting cortical activity associated with category memory and recognition memory. *Learning & Memory, 5*, 420–428.

Redd, W. H.; Dadds, M. R.; Futterman, A. D.; Taylor, K.; & Bovbjerg, D. (1993). Nausea induced by mental images of chemotherapy. *Cancer, 72*, 629–636.

Redelmeier, Donald A., & Tversky, Amos (1996). On the belief that arthritis pain is related to the weather. *Proceedings of the National Academy of Sciences, 93*, 2895–2896.

Reedy, F. E.; Bartoshuk, L. M.; Miller, I. J.; et al. (1993). Relationships among papillae, taste pores, and 6-n-propylthiouracil (PROP) suprathreshold taste sensitivity. *Chemical Senses, 18*, 618–619.

Reese, Elaine; Jack, Fiona; & White, Naomi (2010). Origins of adolescents' autobiographical memories. *Cognitive Development, 25*, 352–367.

Regard, Marianne, & Landis, Theodor (1997). "Gourmand syndrome": Eating passion associated with right anterior lesions. *Neurology, 48*, 1185–1190.

Reichenberg, Abraham; Gross, Raz; Weiser, Mark; et al. (2006). Advancing paternal age and autism. *Archives of General Psychiatry, 63*, 1026–1032.

Reid, R. L. (1991). Premenstrual syndrome. *New England Journal of Medicine, 324*, 1208–1210.

Reis, Harry T., & Aron, Arthur (2008). Love: What is it, why does it matter, and how does it operate? *Perspectives on Psychological Science, 3*, 80–86.

Remick, Abigail K.; Polivy, Janet; & Pliner, Patricia (2009). Internal and external moderators of the effect of variety on food intake. *Psychological Bulletin, 135*, 434–451.

Repantis, Dimitris; Schlattmann, Peter; Laisney, Oona; & Heuser, Isabella (2010). Modafinil and methylphenidate for neuroenhancement in healthy individuals: A systematic review. *Pharmacological Research, 62*, 187–206.

Repetti, Rena L.; Taylor, Shelley E.; & Seeman, Teresa E. (2002). Risky families: Family social environments and the mental and physical health of offspring. *Psychological Bulletin, 128*, 330–366.

Rensink, Ronald (2004). Visual sensing without seeing. *Psychological Science, 15*, 27–32.

Rescorla, Robert A. (1988). Pavlovian conditioning: It's not what you think it is. *American Psychologist, 43*, 151–160.

Reuter, Christoph, & Oehler, Michael (2011). Psychoacoustics of chalkboard squeaking. *Journal of the Acoustical Society of America, 130*, 2545.

Reyna, Valerie, & Farley, Frank (2006). Risk and rationality in adolescent decision making. *Psychological Science in the Public Interest, 7*, 1–44.

Reynolds, Arthur J.; Temple, Judy A.; Ou, Suh-Ruu; et al. (2011). School-based early childhood education and age-28 well-being: Effects by timing, dosage, and subgroups. *Science, 333*, 360–364.

Reynolds, Brent A., & Weiss, Samuel (1992). Generation of neurons and astrocytes from isolated cells of the adult mammalian central nervous system. *Science, 255*, 1707–1710.

Reynolds, Kristi; Lewis, L. Brian; Nolen, John David L.; et al. (2003). Alcohol consumption and risk of stroke: A meta-analysis. *Journal of the American Medical Association, 289*, 579–588.

Rhoades, Linda, & Eisenberger, Robert (2002). Perceived organizational support: A review of the literature. *Journal of Applied Psychology, 87*, 698–714.

Rice, Mabel L. (1990). Preschoolers' QUIL: Quick incidental learning of words. In G. Conti-Ramsden & C. E. Snow (Eds.), *Children's language* (Vol. 7). Hillsdale, NJ: Erlbaum.

Richardson, John T. E. (Ed.) (1992). *Cognition and the menstrual cycle.* New York: Springer-Verlag.

Richardson-Klavehn, Alan, & Bjork, Robert A. (1988). Measures of memory. *Annual Review of Psychology, 39*, 475–543.

Ridley-Johnson, Robyn; Cooper, Harris; & Chance, June (1983). The relation of children's television viewing to school achievement and I.Q. *Journal of Educational Research, 76*, 294–297.

Rieber, Robert W. (2006). *The bifurcation of the self.* New York: Springer.

Rind, Bruce; Tromovitch, Philip; & Bauserman, Robert (1998). A meta-analytic examination of assumed properties of child sexual abuse using college samples. *Psychological Bulletin, 124*, 22–53.

Ripley, Amanda (2013). *The smartest kids in the world: And how they got that way.* New York: Simon & Schuster.

Risch, N.; Herrell, R.; Lehner, T.; et al. (2009). Interaction between the serotonin transporter gene (5-HTTLPR), stressful life events, and risk of depression: A meta-analysis. *Journal of the American Medical Association, 301*, 2462–2471.

Rizzolatti, G., & Sinigaglia, C. (2010). The functional role of the parietofrontal mirror circuit: Interpretations and misinterpretations. *Nature Reviews Neuroscience, 11*, 264–274.

Ro, Tony; Farnè, Alessandro; Johnson, Ruth; et al. (2007). Feeling sounds after a thalamic lesion. *Annals of Neurology, 62*, 433–441.

Roberts, Brent W., & Mroczek, Daniel (2008). Personality trait change in adulthood. *Current Directions in Psychological Science, 17*, 31–35.

Roberts, Brent W.; Caspi, Avshalom; & Moffitt, Terrie E. (2001). The kids are alright: Growth and stability in personality development from adolescence to adulthood. *Journal of Personality and Social Psychology, 81*, 670–683.

Roberts, Brent W.; Walton, Kate E.; & Viechtbauer, Wolfgang (2006). Patterns of mean-level change in personality traits across the life course: A meta-analysis of longitudinal studies. *Psychological Bulletin, 132*, 1–25.

Robertson, Lynn C.; Lamb, Marvin R.; & Knight, Robert T. (1988). Effects of lesions of temporal-parietal junction on perceptual and attentional processing in humans. *Journal of Neuroscience, 8*, 3757–3769.

Robins, Lee N.; Davis, Darlene H.; & Goodwin, Donald W. (1974). Drug use by U.S. Army enlisted men in Vietnam: A follow-up on their return home. *American Journal of Epidemiology, 99*, 235–249.

Robinson, Thomas; Wilde, M. L.; Navracruz, L. C.; et al. (2001). Effects of reducing children's television and video game use on aggressive behavior: A randomized controlled trial. *Archives of Pediatric and Adolescent Medicine, 155*, 13–14.

Rocha, Beatriz A.; Scearce-Levie, Kimberly; Lucas, Jose J.; et al. (1998). Increased vulnerability to cocaine in mice lacking the serotonin-1B receptor. *Nature, 393*, 175–178.

Rodriguez, Paul; Wiles, Janet; & Elman, Jeffrey L. (1999). A recurrent neural network that learns to count. *Connection Science, 11*, 5–40.

Roediger, Henry L. (1990). Implicit memory: Retention without remembering. *American Psychologist, 45*, 1043–1056.

Roediger, Henry L., & McDermott, Kathleen B. (1995). Creating false memories: Remembering words not presented in lists. *Journal of Experimental Psychology; Learning, Memory, & Cognition, 21*, 803–814.

Roediger, Henrey L., III; Putnam, Adam L.; & Smith, Megan A. (2011). Ten benefits of testing and their applications to educational practice. In J. Mestre & B. Ross (Eds.), *Psychology of learning and motivation: Cognition in education.* Oxford: Elsevier.

Roepke, Susan K., & Grant, Igor (2011). Toward a more complete understanding of the effects of personal mastery on cardiometabolic health. *Health Psychology, 30*, 615–632.

Rofé, Yacov (2008). Does repression exist? Memory, pathogenic, unconscious and clinical evidence. *Review of General Psychology, 12*, 63–85.

Rogers, Carl (1951). *Client-centered therapy: Its current practice, implications, and theory.* Boston: Houghton-Mifflin.

Rogers, Carl (1961). *On becoming a person.* Boston: Houghton-Mifflin.

Rogers, Ronald W., & Prentice-Dunn, Steven (1981). Deindividuation and anger-mediated interracial aggression: Unmasking regressive racism. *Journal of Personality and Social Psychology, 41*, 63–73.

Rogers, S. J. & Vismara, L. A. (2008). Evidence-based comprehensive treatment for early autism. *Journal of Clinical Child and Adolescent Psychology, 37*, 8–38.

Rogoff, Barbara (2003). *The cultural nature of human development.* New York: Oxford University Press.

Rogge, Ronald D.; Bradbury, Thomas N.; Hahlweg, Kurt; et al. (2006). Predicting marital distress and dissolution: Refining the two-factor hypothesis. *Journal of Family Psychology, 20*, 156–159.

Rohde, Paul; Lewinsohn, Peter M.; Klein, Daniel N.; et al. (2013). Key characteristics of major depressive disorder occurring in childhood, adolescence, emerging adulthood, and adulthood. *Clinical Psychological Science, 1*, 41–53.

Rosch, Eleanor H. (1973). Natural categories. *Cognitive Psychology, 4*, 328–350.

Rosen, Gerald M.; Glasgow, Russell E.; & Moore, Timothy E. (2003). Self-help therapy: The science and business of giving psychology away. In S. O. Lilienfeld, S. J. Lynn, & J. M. Lohr (Eds.), *Science and pseudoscience in clinical psychology.* New York: Guilford.

Rosenberg, Harold (1993). Prediction of controlled drinking by alcoholics and problem drinkers. *Psychological Bulletin, 113,* 129–139.

Rosenthal, Robert (1994). Interpersonal expectancy effects: A 30-year perspective. *Current Directions in Psychological Science, 3,* 176–179.

Rosenzweig, Mark R. (1984). Experience, memory, and the brain. *American Psychologist, 39,* 365–376.

Rosin, Hanna (2012). *The end of men: And the rise of women.* New York: Riverhead Books.

Ross, Heather E.; Freeman, Sara M.; Spiegel, Lauren L.; et al. (2009). Variation in oxytocin receptor density in the nucleus accumbens has differential effects on affiliative behaviors in monogamous and polygamous voles. *Journal of Neuroscience, 29,* 1312–1318.

Ross, Lee (2010). Dealing with conflict: Experiences and experiments. In M. H. Gonzales, C. Tavris, & J. Aronson (Eds.), *The scientist and the humanist: A festschrift in honor of Elliot Aronson.* New York: Psychology Press.

Ross, Michael; Xun, W. Q. Elaine; & Wilson, Anne E. (2002). Language and the bicultural self. *Personality and Social Psychology Bulletin, 28,* 1040–1050.

Rothbart, Mary K.; Ahadi, Stephan A.; & Evans, David E. (2000). Temperament and personality: Origins and outcomes. *Journal of Personality and Social Psychology, 78,* 122–135.

Rothbaum, Fred; Weisz, John; Pott, Martha; et al. (2000). Attachment and culture: Security in the United States and Japan. *American Psychologist, 55,* 1093–1104.

Rothbaum, Fred M.; Weisz, John R.; & Snyder, Samuel S. (1982). Changing the world and changing the self: A two-process model of perceived control. *Journal of Personality and Social Psychology, 42,* 5–37.

Rothermund, Klaus, & Wentura, Dirk (2004). Underlying processes in the Implicit Association Test: Dissociating salience from associations. *Journal of Experimental Psychology: General, 133,* 139–165.

Rotter, Julian B. (1990). Internal versus external control of reinforcement: A case history of a variable. *American Psychologist, 45,* 489–493.

Roughgarden, Joan (2004). *Evolution's rainbow: Diversity, gender, and sexuality in nature and people.* Berkeley: University of California Press.

Rouw, Romke, & Scholte, Steven S. (2007). Increased structural connectivity in grapheme-color synesthesia. *Nature Neuroscience, 10,* 792–797.

Rovee-Collier, Carolyn (1993). The capacity for long-term memory in infancy. *Current Directions in Psychological Science, 2,* 130–135.

Rowatt, Wade C.; Ottenbreit, Alison; Nesselroade Jr., K. Paul; & Cunningham, Paige A. (2002). On being holier-than-thou or humbler-than-thee: A social-psychological perspective on religiousness and humility. *Journal for the Scientific Study of Religion, 41,* 227–237.

Rowe, Meredith L., & Goldin-Meadow, Susan (2009). Differences in early gesture explain SES disparities in child vocabulary size at school entry. *Science, 323,* 951–953.

Roy, Mark P.; Steptoe, Andrew; & Kirschbaum, Clemens (1998). Life events and social support as moderators of individual differences in cardiovascular and cortisol reactivity. *Journal of Personality and Social Psychology, 75,* 1273–1281.

Rozin, Paul; Kabnick, Kimberly; Pete, Erin; et al. (2003). The ecology of eating: Smaller portion sizes in France than in the United States help explain the French paradox. *Psychological Science, 14,* 450–454.

Rozin, Paul; Lowery, Laura; & Ebert, Rhonda (1994). Varieties of disgust faces and the structure of disgust. *Journal of Personality and Social Psychology, 66,* 870–881.

Ruggiero, Vincent R. (2004). *The art of thinking: A guide to critical and creative thought* (7th ed.). Pearson/Longman.

Rumbaugh, Duane M. (1977). *Language learning by a chimpanzee: The Lana project.* New York: Academic Press.

Rumbaugh, Duane M.; Savage-Rumbaugh, E. Sue; & Pate, James L. (1988). Addendum to "Summation in the chimpanzee (Pan troglodytes)." *Journal of Experimental Psychology: Animal Behavior Processes, 14,* 118–120.

Rumelhart, David E.; McClelland, James L.; & the PDP Research Group (1986). *Parallel distributed processing: Explorations in the microstructure of cognition* (Vols. 1 and 2). Cambridge, MA: MIT Press.

Rupp, Heather A., & Wallen, Kim (2008). Sex differences in response to visual sexual stimuli: A review. *Archives of Sexual Behavior, 37,* 206–218.

Rushton, J. Philippe, & Jensen, Arthur R. (2005). Thirty years of research on race differences in cognitive ability. *Psychology, Public Policy, and Law, 11,* 235–294.

Rutter, Michael; Pickles, Andrew; Murray, Robin; & Eaves, Lindon (2001). Testing hypotheses on specific environmental causal effects on behavior. *Psychological Bulletin, 127,* 291–324.

Rutter, Michael; O'Connor, Thomas G.; & the English and Romanian Adoptees (ERA) Study Team (2004). Are there biological programming effects for psychological development? Findings from a study of Romanian adoptees. *Developmental Psychology, 40,* 81–94.

Ryan, Richard M.; Chirkov, Valery I.; Little, Todd D.; et al. (1999). The American dream in Russia: Extrinsic aspirations and well-being in two cultures. *Personality and Social Psychology Bulletin, 25,* 1509–1524.

Sabattini, Laura, & Crosby, Faye (2009). Work ceilings and walls: Work-life and "family-friendly" policies. In M. Barreto, M. Ryan, & M. Schmitt (Eds.), *The glass ceiling in the 21st century: Understanding barriers to gender equality.* Washington, DC: American Psychological Association.

Sack, Robert L. (2010). Jet lag. *New England Journal of Medicine, 362,* 440–447.

Sack, Robert L., & Lewy, Alfred J. (1997). Melatonin as a chronobiotic: Treatment of circadian desynchrony in night workers and the blind. *Journal of Biological Rhythms, 12,* 595–603.

Sacks, Oliver (1985). *The man who mistook his wife for a hat and other clinical tales.* New York: Simon & Schuster.

Sagan, Eli (1988). *Freud, women, and morality: The psychology of good and evil.* New York: Basic.

Sageman, Marc (2008). *Leaderless jihad: Terror networks in the twenty-first century.* Philadelphia: University of Pennsylvania Press.

Sahley, Christie L.; Rudy, Jerry W.; & Gelperin, Alan (1981). An analysis of associative learning in a terrestrial mollusk: 1. Higher-order conditioning, blocking, and a transient US preexposure effect. *Journal of Comparative Physiology, 144,* 1–8.

Sakai, Kiyoshi; Yamamoto, Akihito; Matsubara, Kohki; et al. (2012). Human dental pulp-derived stem cells promote locomotor recovery after complete transection of the rat spinal cord by multiple neuro-regenerative mechanisms. *Journal of Clinical Investigation, 122,* 80–90.

Saletan, William (2011). Sex on the brain: Are boys' brains different from girls' brains? Scientists debate the question. *Slate,* November. www.slate.com/articles/health_and_science/human_nature/2011/11/boys_brains_girls_brains_how_to_think_about_sex_differences_in_psychology_.html.

Salovey, Peter, & Grewal, Daisy (2005). The science of emotional intelligence. *Current Directions in Psychological Science, 14,* 281–285.

Salthouse, Timothy A. (2006). Mental exercise and mental aging: Evaluating the validity of the "use it or lose it" hypothesis. *Perspectives on Psychological Science, 1,* 68–87.

Salthouse, Timothy A. (2013). Within-cohort age-related differences in cognitive functioning. *Psychological Science, 24,* 123–130.

Sameroff, Arnold J.; Seifer, Ronald; Barocas, Ralph; et al. (1987). Intelligence quotient scores of 4-year-old children: Social-environmental risk factors. *Pediatrics, 79,* 343–350.

Sampson, Robert J; Sharkey, Patrick; & Raudenbush, Stephen W. (2008). Durable effects of concentrated disadvantage among verbal ability of African-American children. *Proceedings of the National Academy of Sciences, 105,* 845–853.

Sanfey, Alan G.; Rilling, James K.; Aronson, Jessica K. (2003). The neural basis of economic decision-making in the Ultimatum Game. *Science, 300,* 1755–1758.

Santelli, John; Ott, Mary A.; Lyon, Maureen; et al. (2006). Abstinence and abstinence-only education: A review of U.S. policies and programs. *Journal of Adolescent Health, 38,* 72–81.

Sarbin, Theodore R. (1991). Hypnosis: A fifty year perspective. *Contemporary Hypnosis, 8,* 1–15.

Sarbin, Theodore R. (1997). The power of believed-in imaginings. *Psychological Inquiry, 8,* 322–325.

Saucier, Deborah M., & Kimura, Doreen (1998). Intrapersonal motor but not extrapersonal targeting skill is enhanced during the midluteal phase of the menstrual cycle. *Developmental Neuropsychology, 14,* 385–398.

Saucier, Gerard (2000). Isms and the structure of social attitudes. *Journal of Personality and Social Psychology, 78,* 366–385.

Savage-Rumbaugh, Sue, & Lewin, Roger (1994). *Kanzi: The ape at the brink of the human mind.* New York: Wiley.

Savage-Rumbaugh, Sue; Shanker, Stuart; & Taylor, Talbot (1998). *Apes, language and the human mind.* New York: Oxford University Press.

Savic, Ivanka; Berglund, Hans; & Lindström, Per (2005). Brain response to putative pheromones in homosexual men. *Proceedings of the National Academy of Sciences, 102,* 7356–7361.

Savin-Williams, Ritch C. (2006). Who's gay? Does it matter? *Current Directions in Psychological Science, 15,* 40–44.

Saxe, Leonard (1994). Detection of deception: Polygraph and integrity tests. *Current Directions in Psychological Science, 3,* 69–73.

Saxena, S.; Brody, A. L.; Maidment, K. M.; et al. (2004). Cerebral glucose metabolism in obsessive-compulsive hoarding. *American Journal of Psychiatry, 161,* 1038–1048.

Sayette, Michael; Reichle, Erik; & Schooler, Jonathan (2009). Lost in the sauce: The effects of alcohol on mind wandering. *Psychological Science, 20,* 747–752.

Scarr, Sandra (1993). Biological and cultural diversity: The legacy of Darwin for development. *Child Development, 64,* 1333–1353.

Scarr, Sandra, & Weinberg, Robert A. (1994). Educational and occupational achievement of brothers and sisters in adoptive and biologically related families. *Behavioral Genetics, 24,* 301–325.

Scarr, Sandra; Pakstis, Andrew J.; Katz, Soloman H.; & Barker, William B. (1977). Absence of a relationship between degree of white ancestry and intellectual skill in a black population. *Human Genetics, 39,* 69–86.

Schacter, Daniel L. (2001). *The seven sins of memory: How the mind forgets and remembers.* Boston: Houghton Mifflin.

Schacter, Daniel L. (2012). Constructive memory: Past and future. *Dialogues in Clinical Neuroscience, 14,* 7–18.

Schacter, Daniel L.; Chiu, C. Y. Peter; & Ochsner, Kevin N. (1993). Implicit memory: A selective review. *Annual Review of Neuroscience, 16,* 159–182.

Schachter, Stanley, & Singer, Jerome E. (1962). Cognitive, social, and physiological determinants of emotional state. *Psychological Review, 69,* 379–399.

Schafer, Roy (1992). *Retelling a life: Narration and dialogue in psychoanalysis.* New York: Basic.

Schaie, K. Warner, & Zuo, Yan-Ling (2001). Family environments and cognitive functioning. In R. J. Sternberg & E. Grigorenko (Eds.), *Cognitive development in context.* Hillsdale, NJ: Erlbaum.

Schank, Roger, with Peter Childers (1988). *The creative attitude.* New York: Macmillan.

Schenck Carlos H., & Mahowald, Mark W. (2002). REM sleep behavior disorder: Clinical, developmental, and neuroscience perspectives 16 years after its formal identification in SLEEP. *Sleep, 25,* 120–138.

Scherer, Klaus R. (1997). The role of culture in emotion-antecedent appraisal. *Journal of Personality and Social Psychology, 73,* 902–922.

Schiller, Daniela, & Phelps, Elizabeth A. (2011). Does reconsolidation occur in humans? *Frontiers in Behavioral Neuroscience, 5,* 1–12.

Schlossberg, Nancy K., & Robinson, Susan P. (1996). *Going to plan B.* New York: Simon & Schuster/Fireside.

Schmader, Toni (2010). Stereotype threat deconstructed. *Current Directions in Psychological Science, 19,* 14–18.

Schmelz, M.; Schmidt, R.; Bickel, A.; et al. (1997). Specific C-receptors for itch in human skin. *Journal of Neuroscience, 17,* 8003–8008.

Schmidt, Frank L., & Hunter, John (2004). General mental ability in the world of work: Occupational attainment and job performance. *Journal of Personality and Social Psychology, 86,* 162–173.

Schmidt, Louis A.; Fox, Nathan A.; Perez-Edgar, Koraly; & Hamer, Dean H. (2009). Linking gene, brain, and behavior: DRD4, frontal asymmetry, and temperament. *Psychological Science, 20,* 831–837.

Schmitt, David P. (2003). Universal sex differences in the desire for sexual variety: Tests from 52 nations, 6 continents, and 13 islands. *Journal of Personality and Social Psychology, 85,* 85–104.

Schmitt, David P.; Jonason, Peter K.; Byerley, Garrett J.; et al. (2012). A reexamination of sex differences in sexuality: New studies reveal old truths. *Current Directions in Psychological Science, 21,* 135–139.

Schnell, Lisa, & Schwab, Martin E. (1990). Axonal regeneration in the rat spinal cord produced by an antibody against myelin-associated neurite growth inhibitors. *Nature, 343,* 269–272.

Schoenfeld, Elizabeth A.; Bredow, Carrie A.; & Huston, Ted L. (2012). Do men and women show love differently in marriage? *Personality and Social Psychology Bulletin, 38,* 1396–1409.

Schofield, P.; Ball, D.; Smith, J. G.; et al. (2004). Optimism and survival in lung carcinoma patients. *Cancer, 100,* 1276–1282.

Schuckit, Marc A. (1998). Biological, psychological and environmental predictors of the alcoholism risk: A longitudinal study. *Journal of Studies on Alcohol, 59,* 485–494.

Schuckit, Marc A.; Smith, Tom L.; Pierson, Juliann; et al. (2007). Patterns and correlates of drinking in offspring from the San Diego Prospective Study. *Alcoholism: Clinical and Experimental Research, 31,* 1681–1691.

Schuckit, Marc A.; Smith, Tom L.; Trim, Ryan; et al. (2008). The performance of elements of a "level of response to alcohol"-based model of drinking behaviors in 13-year-olds. *Addiction, 103,* 1786–1792.

Schulz, Richard; Beach, S. R.; Ives, D. G.; et al. (2000). Association between depression and mortality in older adults: The Cardiovascular Health Study. *Archives of Internal Medicine, 160,* 1761–1768.

Schwartz, Barry (2004). *The paradox of choice: Why more is less.* New York: Ecco Press.

Schwartz, Jeffrey; Stoessel, Paula W.; Baxter, Lewis R.; et al. (1996). Systematic changes in cerebral glucose metabolic rate after successful behavior modification treatment of obsessive–compulsive disorder. *Archives of General Psychiatry, 53,* 109–113.

Schwekendiek, D. (2008). Height and weight differences between North and South Korea. *Journal of Biosocial Sciences, 41,* 51–55.

Seabrook, John (2008, November 10). Suffering souls: The search for the roots of psychopathy. *New Yorker,* 64–73.

Sears, Pauline, & Barbee, Ann H. (1977). Career and life satisfactions among Terman's gifted women. In J. C. Stanley, W. C. George, & C. H. Solano (Eds.), *The gifted and the creative: A fifty-year perspective.* Baltimore, MD: Johns Hopkins University Press.

Sedlmeier, Peter; Eberth, Juliane; Schwarz, Marcus; et al. (2012). The psychological effects of meditation: A meta-analysis. *Psychological Bulletin, 138,* 1139–1171.

Seery, Mark D. (2011). Resilience: A silver lining to experiencing adverse life events? *Current Directions in Psychological Science, 20,* 390–394.

Segal, Julius (1986). *Winning life's toughest battles.* New York: McGraw-Hill.

Segal, Zindel V.; Teasdale, John D.; & Williams, J. Mark G. (2004). Mindfulness based cognitive therapy: Theoretical rationale and empirical status. In S. C. Hayes, V. M. Follette, & M. Linehan (Eds.), *Mindfulness and acceptance: Expanding the cognitive-behavioral tradition.* New York: Guilford.

Segall, Marshall H.; Campbell, Donald T.; & Herskovits, Melville J. (1966). *The influence of culture on visual perception.* Indianapolis, IN: Bobbs-Merrill.

Segall, Marshall H.; Dasen, Pierre R.; Berry, John W.; & Poortinga, Ype H. (1999). *Human behavior in global perspective: An introduction to cross-cultural psychology* (2nd ed.). Boston: Allyn & Bacon.

Segerstrom, Suzanne C., & Miller, Gregory E. (2004). Psychological stress and the human immune system: A meta-analytic study of 30 years of inquiry. *Psychological Bulletin, 130,* 601–630.

Sekuler, Robert, & Blake, Randolph (1994). *Perception* (3rd ed.). New York: Knopf.

Sellbom, Martin; Ben-Porath, Yossef S.; & Bagby, R. Michael (2008). Personality and psychopathology: Mapping the MMPI-2 Restructured Clinical (RC) Scales onto the Five Factor Model of Personality. *Journal of Personality Disorders, 22,* 291–312.

Seligman, Martin E. P., & Csikszentmihaly, Mihaly (2000). Positive psychology: An introduction. *American Psychologist, 55,* 5–14.

Seligman, Martin E. P., & Hager, Joanne L. (1972, August). Biological boundaries of learning: The sauce-béarnaise syndrome. *Psychology Today,* 59–61, 84–87.

Seligman, Martin E. P.; Schulman, Peter; DeRubeis, Robert J.; & Hollon, Steven D. (1999). The prevention of depression and anxiety. *Prevention & Treatment, 2,* doi: 10.1037/1522-3736.2.1.28a.

Selye, Hans (1956). *The stress of life.* New York: McGraw-Hill.

Seidenberg, Mark S.; MacDonald, Maryellen C.; & Saffran, Jenny R. (2002). Does grammar start where statistics stop? *Science, 298,* 553–554.

Seifer, Ronald; Schiller, Masha; Sameroff, Arnold; et al. (1996). Attachment, maternal sensitivity, and infant temperament during the first year of life. *Developmental Psychology, 32,* 12–25.

Senghas, Ann; Kita, Sotaro; & Özyürek, Asli (2004). Children creating core properties of language: Evidence from an emerging sign language in Nicaragua. *Science, 305,* 1779–1782.

Senko, Corwin; Durik, Amanda M.; & Harackiewicz, Judith M. (2008). Historical perspectives and new directions in achievement goal theory: Understanding the effects of mastery and performance-approach goals. In J. Y. Shah & W. L. Gardner (Eds.), *Handbook of motivation science.* New York: Guilford.

Serpell, Robert (1994). The cultural construction of intelligence. In W. J. Lonner & R. S. Malpass (Eds.), *Psychology and culture.* Needham Heights, MA: Allyn & Bacon.

Shaffer, Ryan, & Jadwiszczok, Agatha (2010, March/April). Psychic defective: Sylvia Browne's history of failure. *Skeptical Inquirer, 34,* 38–42.

Shariff, Azim F., & Tracy, Jessica L. (2011). What are emotion expressions for? *Current Directions in Psychological Science, 20,* 395–399.

Sharman, Stephanie J.; Manning, Charles G.; & Garry, Maryanne (2005). Explain this: Explaining childhood events inflates confidence for those events. *Applied Cognitive Psychology, 19,* 16–74.

Shatz, Marilyn, & Gelman, Rochel (1973). The development of communication skills: Modifications in the speech of young children as a function of the listener. *Monographs of the Society for Research in Child Development, 38.*

Shaver, Phillip R., & Hazan, Cindy (1993). Adult romantic attachment: Theory and evidence. In D. Perlman & W. H. Jones (Eds.), *Advances in personal relationships* (Vol. 4). London: Kingsley.

Shaver, Phillip R.; Wu, Shelley; & Schwartz, Judith C. (1992). Cross-cultural similarities and differences in emotion and its representation: A prototype approach. In M. S. Clark (Ed.), *Review of Personality and Social Psychology* (Vol. 13). Newbury Park, CA: Sage.

Shedler, Jonathan (2010). The efficacy of psychodynamic therapy. *American Psychologist, 65,* 98–109.

Sheldon, Kennon M.; Elliot, Andrew J.; Kim, Youngmee; & Kasser, Tim (2001). What is satisfying about satisfying events? Testing 10 candidate psychological needs. *Journal of Personality and Social Psychology, 80,* 325–339.

Shepard, Roger N., & Metzler, Jacqueline (1971). Mental rotation of three dimensional objects. *Science, 171,* 701–703.

Shepperd, James A.; Klein, William M. P.; Waters, Erika A.; & Weinstein, Neil D. (2013). Taking stock of unrealistic optimism. *Perspectives on Psychological Science, 8,* 395–411.

Sherif, Muzafer (1958). Superordinate goals in the reduction of intergroup conflicts. *American Journal of Sociology, 63,* 349–356.

Sherif, Muzafer; Harvey, O. J.; White, B. J.; Hood, William; & Sherif, Carolyn (1961). *Intergroup conflict and cooperation: The Robbers Cave experiment.* Norman: University of Oklahoma Institute of Intergroup Relations.

Sherry, John L. (2001). The effects of violent video games on aggression: A meta-analysis. *Human Communication Research, 27,* 409–431.

Sherry, Simon B., & Hall, Peter A. (2009). The perfectionism model of binge eating: Tests of an integrative model. *Journal of Personality and Social Psychology, 96,* 690–709.

Sherwin, Barbara B. (1998). Estrogen and cognitive functioning in women. *Proceedings of the Society for Experimental Biological Medicine, 217,* 17–22.

Shields, Stephanie A. (2002). *Speaking from the heart: Gender and the social meaning of emotion.* New York: Cambridge University Press.

Shields, Stephanie A. (2005). The politics of emotion in everyday life: "Appropriate" emotion and claims on identity. *Review of General Psychology, 9,* 3–15.

Shih, Margaret; Pittinsky, Todd L.; & Ambady, Nalini (1999). Stereotype susceptibility: Identity salience and shifts in quantitative performance. *Psychological Science, 10,* 80–83.

Shors, Tracey J. (2009, March). Saving new brain cells. *Scientific American,* 46–54.

Shorter, Edward, & Healy, David (2008). *Shock therapy: A history of electroconvulsive treatment in mental illness.* New Brunswick, NJ: Rutgers University Press.

Sidanius, Jim; Pratto, Felicia; & Bobo, Lawrence (1996). Racism, conservatism, affirmative action, and intellectual sophistication: A matter of principled conservatism or group dominance? *Journal of Personality and Social Psychology, 70,* 476–490.

Sidanius, Jim; Van Laar, Colette; Levin, Shana; & Sinclair, Stacey (2004). Ethnic enclaves and the dynamics of social identity on the college campus: The good, the bad, and the ugly. *Journal of Personality and Social Psychology, 87,* 96–110

Siegel, Jerome M. (2009). Sleep viewed as a state of adaptive inactivity. *Nature Reviews | Neuroscience, 10,* 747–753.

Siegel, Shepard (2005). Drug tolerance, drug addiction, and drug anticipation. *Current Directions in Psychological Science, 14,* 296–300.

Siegler, Robert S. (2006). Microgenetic analyses of learning. In D. Kuhn & R. S. Siegler (Eds.), *Handbook of child psychology: Vol. 2. Cognition, perception, and language* (6th ed.). New York: Wiley.

Silke, Andrew (Ed.) (2003). *Terrorists, victims, and society: Psychological perspectives on terrorism and its consequences.* New York: Wiley.

Simcock, Gabrielle, & Hayne, Harlene (2002). Breaking the barrier: Children fail to translate their preverbal memories into language. *Psychological Science, 13,* 225–231.

Simon, Herbert A. (1955). A behavioral model of rational choice. *Quarterly Journal of Economics, 69,* 99–118.

Simons, Daniel J., & Chabris, Christopher F. (1999). Gorillas in our midst: Sustained inattentional blindness for dynamic events. *Perception, 28,* 1059–1974.

Simonton, Dean Keith, & Song, Anna (2009). Eminence, IQ, physical and mental health, and achievement domain. *Psychological Science, 20,* 429–434.

Simpson, Jeffry A.; Collins, W. Andrew; & Salvatore, Jessica E. (2011). The impact of early interpersonal experience on adult romantic relationship functioning: Recent findings from the Minnesota Longitudinal Study of Risk and Adaptation. *Current Directions in Psychological Science, 20,* 355–359.

Sims, Ethan A. (1974). Studies in human hyperphagia. In G. Bray & J. Bethune (Eds.), *Treatment and management of obesity.* New York: Harper & Row.

Singer, Margaret T. (2003). *Cults in our midst* (Rev. ed.). New York: Wiley.

Singh, Devendra; Vidaurri, Melody; Zambarano, Robert J.; & Dabbs, James M., Jr. (1999). Lesbian erotic role identification: Behavioral, morphological, and hormonal correlates. *Journal of Personality and Social Psychology, 76,* 1035–1049.

Sitzmann, Traci, & Ely, Katherine (2011). A meta-analysis of self-regulated learning in work-related training and educational attainment: What we know and where we need to go. *Psychological Bulletin, 137,* 421–442.

Skeem, Jennifer L.; Polaschek, Devon L. L.; Patrick, Christopher; & Lilienfeld, Scott O. (2011). Psychopathic personality: Bridging the gap between scientific evidence and public policy. *Psychological Science in the Public Interest, 12,* 95–162.

Skinner, B. F. (1938). *The behavior of organisms: An experimental analysis.* New York: Appleton-Century-Crofts.

Skinner, B. F. (1948/1976). *Walden Two.* New York: Macmillan.

Skinner, B. F. (1956). A case history in the scientific method. *American Psychologist, 11,* 221–233.

Skinner, B. F. (1972). The operational analysis of psychological terms. In B. F. Skinner, *Cumulative record* (3rd ed.). New York: Appleton-Century-Crofts.

Skinner, B. F. (1990). Can psychology be a science of mind? *American Psychologist, 45,* 1206–1210.

Slackman, Michael (2006, August 6). The fine art of hiding what you mean to say. *The New York Times,* Week in Review.

Slade, Pauline (1984). Premenstrual emotional changes in normal women: Fact or fiction? *Journal of Psychosomatic Research, 28,* 1–7.

Slavin, Robert E., & Cooper, Robert (1999). Improving intergroup relations: Lessons learned from cooperative learning programs. *Journal of Social Issues, 55,* 647–663.

Slevec, Julie, & Tiggemann, Marika (2011). Media exposure, body dissatisfaction, and disordered eating in middle-aged women: A test of the sociocultural model of disordered eating. *Psychology of Women Quarterly, 35,* 617–627.

Sinaceur, Marwan; Heath, Chip; & Cole, Steve (2005). Emotional and deliberative reactions to a public crisis: Mad cow disease in France. *Psychological Science, 16,* 247–254.

Slovic, Paul; Finucane, Melissa L.; Peters, Ellen.; & MacGregor, Donald G. (2002). The affect heuristic. In T. Gilovich, D. Griffin, & D. Kahneman (Eds.), *Heuristics and biases: The psychology of intuitive judgment.* New York: Cambridge University Press.

Slovic, Paul, & Peters, Ellen (2006). Risk perception and affect. *Current Directions in Psychological Science, 15,* 322–325.

Small, Gary W.; Kepe, Vladimir; Siddarth, Prabba; et al. (2013). PET scanning of brain tau in retired National Football League players: Preliminary findings. *American Journal of Geriatric Psychiatry, 21,* 138–144.

Smith, M. Elizabeth, & Farah, Martha J. (2011). Are prescription stimulants "smart pills"? The epidemiology and cognitive neuroscience of prescription stimulant use by normal healthy individuals. *Psychological Bulletin, 137,* 717–741.

Smith, Peter B., & Bond, Michael H. (1994). *Social psychology across cultures: Analysis and perspectives.* Boston: Allyn & Bacon.

Smither, Robert D. (1998). *The psychology of work and human performance* (3rd ed.). New York: Longman.

Snyder, C. R., & Shenkel, Randee J. (1975, March). The P. T. Barnum effect. *Psychology Today,* 52–54.

Snodgrass, Sara E. (1992). Further effects of role versus gender on interpersonal sensitivity. *Journal of Personality and Social Psychology, 62,* 154–158.

Snowdon, Charles T. (1997). The "nature" of sex differences: Myths of male and female. In P.A. Gowaty (Ed.), *Feminism and evolutionary biology.* New York: Chapman and Hall.

Solomon, Robert C. (1994). *About love.* Lanham, MD: Littlefield Adams.

Somer, Oya, & Goldberg, Lewis R. (1999). The structure of Turkish trait descriptive adjectives. *Journal of Personality and Social Psychology, 76,* 431–450.

Sommer, Iris E. C.; Aleman, André; Bouma, Anke; & Kahn, René S. (2004). Do women really have more bilateral language representation than men? A meta-analysis of functional imaging studies. *Brain: A Journal of Neurology, 127,* 1845–1852.

Sommer, Iris E. C.; Aleman, André; Somers, Metten; et al. (2008). Sex differences in handedness, asymmetry of the planum temporale and functional language lateralization. *Brain Research, 1206,* 76–88.

Sommer, Robert (1969). *Personal space: The behavioral basis of design.* Englewood Cliffs, NJ: Prentice-Hall.

Sonoda, Hideto; Kohnoe, Shunji; Yamazato, Tetsuro; et al. (2011). Colorectal cancer screening with odour material by canine scent detection. *Gut, 60,* 814–819.

Sorce, James F.; Emde, Robert N.; Campos, Joseph; & Klinnert, Mary D. (1985). Maternal emotional signaling: Its effect on the visual cliff behavior of 1-year-olds. *Developmental Psychology, 21,* 195–200.

Soto, Christopher J.; John, Oliver P.; Gosling, Samuel D.; & Potter, Jeff (2011). Age differences in personality traits from 10 to 65: Big Five domains and facets in a large cross-sectional sample. *Journal of Personality and Social Psychology, 100,* 330–348.

Spalding, K. L.; Arner, E.; Westermark, P. O.; et al. (2008). Dynamics of fat cell turnover in humans. *Nature, 453,* 783–787.

Spanos, Nicholas P. (1991). A sociocognitive approach to hypnosis. In S. J. Lynn & J. W. Rhue (Eds.), *Theories of hypnosis: Current models and perspectives.* New York: Guilford.

Spanos, Nicholas P. (1996). *Multiple identities and false memories: A sociocognitive perspective.* Washington, DC: American Psychological Association.

Spanos, Nicholas P.; Burgess, Cheryl A.; Roncon, Vera; et al. (1993). Surreptitiously observed hypnotic responding in simulators and in skill-trained and untrained high hypnotizables. *Journal of Personality and Social Psychology, 65,* 391–398.

Spanos, Nicholas P.; Stenstrom, Robert J.; & Johnson, Joseph C. (1988). Hypnosis, placebo, and suggestion in the treatment of warts. *Psychosomatic Medicine, 50,* 245–260.

Spear, Linda P. (2000). The adolescent brain and age-related behavioral manifestations. *Neuroscience and Biobehavioral Review, 24,* 417–463.

Spearman, Charles (1927). *The abilities of man.* London: Macmillan.

Specht, Jule; Egloff, Boris; & Schmukle, Stefan C. (2011). Stability and change of personality across the life course. *Journal of Personality and Social Psychology, 101,* 862–882.

Spelke, Elizabeth S., & Kinzler, Katherine D. (2007). Core knowledge. *Developmental Science, 10,* 89–96.

Sperling, George (1960). The information available in brief visual presentations. *Psychological Monographs, 74(498),* 1–29.

Sperry, Roger W. (1964). The great cerebral commissure. *Scientific American, 210*(1), 42–52.

Sperry, Roger W. (1982). Some effects of disconnecting the cerebral hemispheres. *Science, 217,* 1223–1226.

Spitz, Herman H. (1997). *Nonconscious movements: From mystical messages to facilitated communication.* Mahwah, NJ: Erlbaum.

Sprecher, Susan; Schwartz, Pepper; Harvey, John; & Hatfield, Elaine (2008). The businessoflove.com: Relationship initiation at Internet matchmaking services. In S. Sprecher, A. Wenzel, & J. Harvey (Eds.), *The Handbook of Relationship Initiation.* New York: Psychology Press.

Squier, Leslie H., & Domhoff, G. William (1998). The presentation of dreaming and dreams in introductory psychology textbooks: A critical examination with suggestions for textbook authors and course instructors. *Dreaming, 8,* 149–168.

Squire, Larry R., & Zola-Morgan, Stuart (1991). The medial temporal lobe memory system. *Science, 253,* 1380–1386.

Squire, Larry R.; Ojemann, Jeffrey G.; Miezin, Francis M.; et al. (1992). Activation of the hippocampus in normal humans: A functional anatomical study of memory. *Proceedings of the National Academy of Science, 89,* 1837–1841.

Srivastava, Abhishek; Locke, Edwin A.; & Bartol, Kathryn M. (2001). Money and subjective well-being: It's not the money, it's the motives. *Journal of Personality and Social Psychology, 80,* 959–971.

Srivastava, Sanjay; Tamir, Maya; McGonigal, Kelly M.; et al. (2009). The social costs of emotional suppression: A prospective study of the transition to college. *Journal of Personality and Social Psychology, 96,* 883–897.

St. Clair, D.; Xu, M.; Wang, P.; et al. (2005). Rates of adult schizophrenia following prenatal exposure to the Chinese famine of 1959–1961. *Journal of the American Medical Association, 294,* 557–562.

Staats, Carolyn K., & Staats, Arthur W. (1957). Meaning established by classical conditioning. *Journal of Experimental Psychology, 54,* 74–80.

Stanley, Damian; Phelps, Elizabeth; & Banaji, Mahzarin (2008). The neural basis of implicit attitudes. *Current Directions in Psychological Science, 17,* 164–170.

Stanovich, Keith (2010). *How to think straight about psychology* (9th Ed.). Boston: Allyn & Bacon.

Stanton, Stephen J.; Mullette-Gillman, O'Dhaniel A.; & Huettel, Scott A. (2011). Seasonal variation of salivary testosterone in men, normally cycling women, and women using hormonal contraceptives. *Physiology & Behavior, 104,* 804–808.

Stanwood, Gregg D., & Levitt, Pat (2001). *The effects of cocaine on the developing nervous system.* In C. A. Nelson & M. Luciana (Eds.), *Handbook of developmental cognitive neuroscience.* Cambridge, MA: The MIT Press.

Stattin, Haken, & Magnusson, David (1990). *Pubertal maturation in female development.* Hillsdale, NJ: Erlbaum.

Staub, Ervin (1996). Cultural-social roots of violence. *American Psychologist, 51,* 117–132.

Stearns, Peter N. (1997). *Fat history: Bodies and beauty in the modern West.* New York: New York University Press.

Steele, Claude M. (1992, April). Race and the schooling of Black Americans. *Atlantic Monthly,* 68–78.

Steele, Claude M. (1997). A threat in the air: How stereotypes shape intellectual identity and performance. *American Psychologist, 52,* 613–629.

Steele, Claude M., & Aronson, Joshua (1995). Stereotype threat and the intellectual test performance of African-Americans. *Journal of Personality and Social Psychology, 69,* 797–811.

Steffens, Sabine; Veillard, Niels R.; Arnaud Claire; et al. (2005). Low dose oral cannabinoid therapy reduces progression of atherosclerosis in mice. *Nature, 434,* 782–786.

Stein, Dan J.; Chiu, Wai Tat; Hwang, Irving; et al. (2010, May 13). Cross-national analysis of the associations between traumatic events and suicidal behavior: Finding from the WHO World Mental Health surveys. *PLoS One, 5,* Article e10574.

Stein, Leslie J.; Cowart, Beverly J.; & Beauchamp, Gary K. (2012). The development of salty taste acceptance is related to dietary experience in human infants: A perspective study. *American Journal of Clinical Nutrition, 95,* 123–129.

Stein, M. B.; Jang, K. L.; Taylor, S.; Vernon, P. A.; & Livesley, W. J. (2002). Genetic and environmental influences on trauma exposure and posttraumatic stress disorder symptoms: A general population twin study. *American Journal of Psychiatry, 159,* 1675–1681.

Steinberg, Laurence (2007). Risk taking in adolescence. *Current Directions in Psychological Science, 16,* 55–59.

Steinberg, Laurence, & Scott, Elizabeth S. (2003). Less guilty by reason of adolescence. *American Psychologist, 58,* 1009–1018.

Stel, Mariëlle; Blascovich, Jim; McCall, Cade; et al. (2010). Mimicking disliked others: Effects of a priori liking on the mimicry-liking link. *European Journal of Social Psychology, 40,* 867–880.

Stepanski, Edward, & Perlis, Michael (2000). Behavioral sleep medicine: An emerging subspecialty in health psychology. *Journal of Psychosomatic Research, 49,* 343–347.

Stephan, Walter G.; Ageyev, Vladimir; Coates-Shrider, Lisa; et al. (1994). On the relationship between stereotypes and prejudice: An international study. *Personality and Social Psychology Bulletin, 20,* 277–284.

Stenberg, Craig R., & Campos, Joseph (1990). The development of anger expressions in infancy. In N. Stein, B. Leventhal, & T. Trabasso (Eds.), *Psychological and biological approaches to emotion.* Hillsdale, NJ: Erlbaum.

Sternberg, Robert J. (1988). *The triarchic mind: A new theory of human intelligence.* New York: Viking.

Sternberg, Robert J. (2004). Culture and intelligence. *American Psychologist, 59,* 325–338.

Sternberg, Robert J. (2012). The triarchic theory of successful intelligence. In D. P. Flanagan & P. L. Harrison (Eds.), *Contemporary intellectual assessment: Theories, tests, and issues* (3rd Ed.). New York: Guilford.

Sternberg, Robert J.; Forsythe, George B.; Hedlund, Jennifer; et al. (2000). *Practical intelligence in everyday life.* New York: Cambridge University Press.

Sternberg, Robert J.; Wagner, Richard K.; Williams, Wendy M.; & Horvath, Joseph A. (1995). Testing common sense. *American Psychologist, 50,* 912–927.

Stevenson, Harold W., & Stigler, James W. (1992). *The learning gap.* New York: Summit.

Stevenson, Harold W.; Chen, Chuansheng; & Lee, Shin-ying (1993). Mathematics achievement of Chinese, Japanese, and American children: Ten years later. *Science, 259,* 53–58.

Stewart-Williams, Steve, & Podd, John (2004). The placebo effect: Dissolving the expectancy versus conditioning debate. *Psychological Bulletin, 130,* 324–340.

Stice, Eric; Spoor, S.; Bohon, C.; & Small, D.M. (2008). Relation between obesity and blunted striatal response to food is moderated by Taq1A A1 allele. *Science, 322,* 449–452.

Stiles, Carol; Murray, Susan; & Kentish-Barnes, Cosmo (2011, October 28). Udderly Robotic [Radio Broadcast]. *Country Life.* Wellington: Radio New Zealand National.

Stix, Gary (2008, August). Lighting up the lies. *Scientific American,* 18–19.

Stoch, M. B., & Smythe, P. M. (1963). Does undernutrition during infancy inhibit brain growth and subsequent intellectual development? *Archives of Diseases in Childhood, 38,* 546–552.

Strahan, Erin J.; Spencer, Steven J.; & Zanna, Mark P. (2002). Subliminal priming and persuasion: Striking while the iron is hot. *Journal of Experimental Social Psychology, 38,* 556–568.

Strayer, David L., & Drews, Frank A. (2007). Cell-phone-induced driver distraction. *Current Directions in Psychology, 16,* 128–131.

Strayer, David L.; Drews, Frank A.; & Crouch, Dennis J. (2006). A comparison of the cell phone driver and the drunk driver. *Human Factors, 48,* 381–391.

Streissguth, Ann P. (2001). Recent advances in fetal alcohol syndrome and alcohol use in pregnancy. In D. P. Agarwal & H. K. Seitz (Eds.), *Alcohol in health and disease.* New York: Marcel Dekker.

Streyffeler, Lisa L., & McNally, Richard J. (1998). Fundamentalists and liberals: personality characteristics of Protestant Christians. *Personality and Individual Differences, 24,* 579–580.

Strickland, Bonnie R. (1989). Internal–external control expectancies: From contingency to creativity. *American Psychologist, 44,* 1–12.

Strickland, Tony L.; Lin, Keh-Ming; Fu, Paul; et al. (1995). Comparison of lithium ratio between African-American and Caucasian bipolar patients. *Biological Psychiatry, 37,* 325–330.

Striegel-Moore, Ruth H., & Bulik, Cynthia M. (2007). Risk factors for eating disorders. *American Psychologist, 62,* 181–198.

Stunkard, Albert J. (Ed.) (1980). *Obesity.* Philadelphia: Saunders.

Suddendorf, Thomas, & Whiten, Andrew (2001). Mental evolution and development: Evidence for secondary representation in children, great apes, and other animals. *Psychological Bulletin, 127,* 629–650

Sue, D. W. (2010). *Microaggressions in everyday life: Race, gender, and sexual orientation.* Hoboken, NJ: Wiley.

Sue, Derald W.; Capodilupo, Christina M.; Torino, Gina C.; et al. (2007). Racial microaggressions in everyday life: Implications for clinical practice. *American Psychologist, 62,* 271–286.

Suedfeld, Peter (1975). The benefits of boredom: Sensory deprivation reconsidered. *American Scientist, 63(1),* 60–69.

Suinn, Richard M. (2001). The terrible twos—Anger and anxiety. *American Psychologist, 56,* 27–36.

Suls, Jerry; Martin, René; & Wheeler, Ladd (2002). Social comparison: Why, with whom, and with what effect? *Current Directions in Psychological Science, 11,* 159–163.

Surowiecki, James (2004). *The wisdom of crowds.* New York: Doubleday.

Swartz, M. S.; Perkins, D. O.; Stroup, T. S., et al., & CATIE Investigators (2007). Effects of antipsychotic medications on psychosocial functioning in patients with chronic schizophrenia: findings from the NIMH CATIE study. *American Journal of Psychiatry, 164,* 428–36.

Sweet, Elizabeth (2012, Dec. 23). Guys and dolls no more? *New York Times,* op-ed, p. SR-12.

Sylvers, Patrick D.; Brennan, Patricia A.; & Lilienfeld, Scott O. (2011). Psychopathic traits and preattentive threat processing in children: A novel test of the fearlessness hypothesis. *Psychological Science, 22,* 1280–1287.

Szpunar, Karl K.; Addis, Donna R.; & Schacter, Daniel L. (2012). Memory for emotional simulations: Remembering a rosy future. *Psychological Science, 23,* 24–29.

Tangney, June P., & Tracy, Jessica L. (2012). Self-conscious emotions. In M. Leary & J. P. Tangney (Eds.), *Handbook of self and identity* (2nd ed.). New York: Guilford.

Tajfel, Henri, & Turner, John C. (1986). The social identity theory of intergroup behavior. In S. Worchel & W. G. Austin (Eds.), *Psychology of intergroup relations.* Chicago: Nelson-Hall.

Tajfel, Henri; Billig, M. G.; Bundy, R. P.; & Flament, C. (1971). Social categorization and intergroup behavior. *European Journal of Social Psychology, 1,* 149–178

Takahashi, Kazutoshi; Tanabe, Koji; Ohnuki, Mari; et al. (2007). Induction of pluripotent stem cells from adult human fibroblasts by defined factors. *Cell, 131,* 861–872.

Talarico, Jennifer M., & Rubin, David C. (2003). Confidence, not consistency, characterizes flashbulb memories. *Psychological Science, 14,* 455–461.

Talbot, Margaret (2008, May 12). Birdbrain: The woman behind the world's chattiest parrots. *The New Yorker,* on line archive.

Talbot, Margaret (2009, April 27). Brain gain: The underground world of neuroenhancing drugs. *The New Yorker,* pp. 32–43.

Talge, N. M., Neal, C., & Glover, V. (2007). Antenatal maternal stress and longterm effects on child neurodevelopment: how and why? *Journal of Child Psychology and Psychiatry, 48,* 245–261.

Tallis, Raymond (2011). *Aping mankind: Neuromania, Darwinitis, and the misrepresentation of humanity.* Durham, England: Acumen.

Tang, Yiyuan; Zhang, Wutian; Chen, Kewei; et al. (2006). Arithmetic processing in the brain shaped by cultures. *Proceedings of the National Academy of Sciences, 103,* 10775–10780.

Tarbox, Sarah I., & Pogue-Geile, Michael F. (2008). Development of social functioning in preschizophrenia children and adolescents: A systematic review. *Psychological Bulletin, 34,* 561–583.

Taubes, Gary (2008). *Good calories, bad calories: Fats, carbs, and the controversial science of diet and health.* New York: Anchor.

Tavris, Carol (1989). *Anger: The misunderstood emotion* (Rev. ed.). New York: Simon & Schuster/Touchstone.

Tavris, Carol, & Aronson, Elliot (2007). *Mistakes were made (but not by me).* Orlando, FL: Houghton Mifflin Harcourt.

Taylor, Shelley E., & Lobel, Marci (1989). Social comparison activity under threat: Downward evaluation and upward contacts. *Psychological Review, 96*, 569–575.

Taylor, Shelley E., & Master, Sarah L. (2011). Social responses to stress: The tend-and-befriend model. In R. J. Contrada & A. Baum (Eds.). *The handbook of stress science: Biology, psychology, and health.* New York: Springer.

Taylor, Shelley E.; Lichtman, Rosemary R.; & Wood, Joanne V. (1984). Attributions, beliefs about control, and adjustment to breast cancer. *Journal of Personality and Social Psychology, 46*, 489–502.

Taylor, Shelley E.; Repetti, Rena; & Seeman, Teresa (1997). Health psychology: What is an unhealthy environment and how does it get under the skin? *Annual Review of Psychology* (Vol. 48). Palo Alto, CA: Annual Reviews.

Taylor, Shelley E.; Saphire-Bernstein, Shimon; & Seeman, Teresa E. (2010). Are plasma oxytocin in women and plasma vasopressin in men biomarkers of distressed pair-bond relationships? *Psychological Science, 21*, 3–7.

Terman, Lewis M., & Oden, Melita H. (1959). *Genetic studies of genius:* Vol. 5. *The gifted group at mid-life.* Stanford, CA: Stanford University Press.

Terracciano, Antonio, & McCrae, Robert R. (2006). "National character does not reflect mean personality traits levels in 49 cultures": Reply. *Science, 311*, 777–779.

Thaler, Lore; Arnott, Stephen R.; & Goodale, Melvyn A. (2011). Neural correlates of natural human echolocation in early and late blind echolocation experts. *PLoS One, 6*, 1–16.

Thomas, Ayanna K., & Dubois, Stacey J. (2011). Reducing the burden of stereotype threat eliminates age differences in memory distortion. *Psychological Science, 12*, 1515–1517.

Thomas, Jennifer J.; Vartanian, Lenny R.; & Brownell, Kelly D. (2009). The relationship between eating disorder not otherwise specified (EDNOS) and officially recognized eating disorders: Meta-analysis and implications for DSM. *Psychological Bulletin, 135*, 407–433.

Thompson, Clara (1943/1973). Penis envy in women. *Psychiatry, 6*, 123–125. Reprinted in J. B. Miller (Ed.), *Psychoanalysis and women.* New York: Brunner/Mazel, 1973.

Thompson, Clive (2011). Why kids can't search. *Wired*, November 1. www.wired.com/magazine/2011/11/st_thompson_searchresults/.

Thompson, J. Kevin, & Cafri, Guy (Eds.) (2007). *The muscular ideal: Psychological, social, and medical perspectives.* Washington, DC: American Psychological Association.

Thompson, Richard F. (1983). Neuronal substrates of simple associative learning: Classical conditioning. *Trends in Neurosciences, 6*, 270–275.

Thompson, Richard F. (1986). The neurobiology of learning and memory. *Science, 233*, 941–947.

Thompson, Richard F., & Kosslyn, Stephen M. (2000). Neural systems activated during visual mental imagery: A review and meta-analyses. In A. W. Toga & J. C. Mazziotta (Eds.), *Brain mapping: The systems.* San Diego, CA: Academic Press.

Thompson, Robin; Emmorey, Karen; & Gollan, Tamar H. (2005). "Tip of the fingers" experiences by deaf signers. *Psychological Science, 16*, 856–860.

Thompson-Cannino, Jennifer; Cotton, Ronald; & Torneo, Erin (2009). *Picking Cotton: Our memoir of injustice and redemption.* New York: St. Martin's Press.

Thompson, Paul M.; Vidal, Christine N.; Giedd, Jay N.; et al. (2001). Mapping adolescent brain change reveals dynamic wave of accelerated gray matter loss in very early-onset schizophrenia. *Proceedings of the National Academy of Sciences, 98*, 11650–11655.

Thorndike, Edward L. (1898). Animal intelligence: An experimental study of the associative processes in animals. *Psychological Review Monograph Supplement, 2* (Whole No. 8).

Thorndike, Edward L. (1903). *Educational psychology.* New York: Columbia University Teachers College.

Tiefer, Leonore (2004). *Sex is not a natural act, and other essays* (Rev. ed.). Boulder, CO: Westview.

Tiefer, Leonore (Ed.) (2008). The New View campaign against the medicalization of sex. Special issue (12 articles). *Feminism and Psychology, 18.*

Timmann, Dagmar; Drepper, Johannes; Frings, Markus; et al. (2010). The human cerebellum contributes to motor, emotional and cognitive associative learning: A review. *Cortex, 46*, 845–857.

Timmers, Monique; Fischer, Agneta H.; & Manstead, Antony S. R. (1998). Gender differences in motives for regulating emotions. *Personality and Social Psychology Bulletin, 24*, 974–985.

Tolin, D. F. (2010). Is cognitive-behavioral therapy more effective than other therapies? A meta-analytic review. *Clinical Psychology Review, 30*, 710–720.

Tolman, Edward C. (1938). The determiners of behavior at a choice point. *Psychological Review, 45*, 1–35.

Tolman, Edward C., & Honzik, Chase H. (1930). Introduction and removal of reward and maze performance in rats. *University of California Publications in Psychology, 4*, 257–275.

Tomasello, Michael (2000). Culture and cognitive development. *Current Directions in Psychological Science, 9*, 37–40.

Tomasello, Michael (2003). *Constructing a language: A usage-based theory of language acquisition.* Cambridge, MA: Harvard University Press.

Tomlinson, Mark; Cooper, Peter; & Murray, Lynne (2005). The mother–infant relationship and infant attachment in a South African peri-urban settlement. *Child Development, 76*, 1044–1054.

Tomppo, L.; Hennah, W.; Miettunen, J.; et al. (2009). Association of variants in DISC1 with psychosis-related traits in a large population cohort. *Archives of General Psychiatry, 66*, 134–141.

Tourangeau, Roger, & Yan, Ting (2007). Sensitive questions in surveys. *Psychological Bulletin, 133*, 859–883.

Tracy, Jessica L., & Robins, Richard W. (2008). The nonverbal expression of pride: Evidence for cross-cultural recognition. *Journal of Personality and Social Psychology, 94*, 516–530.

Triandis, Harry C. (1996). The psychological measurement of cultural syndromes. *American Psychologist, 51*, 407–415.

Triandis, Harry C. (2007). Culture and psychology: A history of the study of their relationship. In S. Kitayama & D. Cohen (Eds.), *Handbook of cultural psychology.* New York: Guilford.

Trivedi, Bijal P. (2012). Neuroscience: Hardwired for taste. *Nature, 486*, S7–S9.

Trivers, Robert (2004). Mutual benefits at all levels of life. [Book review.] *Science, 304*, 965.

Tronick, Edward Z.; Morelli, Gilda A.; & Ivey, Paula K. (1992). The Efe forager infant and toddler's pattern of social relationships: Multiple and simultaneous. *Developmental Psychology, 28*, 568–577.

Tucker-Drob, Elliot M. (2012). Preschools reduce early academic-achievement gaps: A longitudinal twin approach. *Psychological Science, 23*, 310–319.

Tulving, Endel (1985). How many memory systems are there? *American Psychologist, 40*, 385–398.

Turiel, Elliot (2002). *The culture of morality.* Cambridge, England: Cambridge University Press.

Turner, C. F.; Ku, L.; Rogers, S. M.; et al. (1998). Adolescent sexual behavior, drug use, and violence: Increased reporting with computer survey technology. *Science, 280*, 867–873.

Turner, E. H.; Matthews, A. M.; Linardatos, E.; et al. (2008). Selective publication of antidepressant trials and its influence on apparent efficacy. *New England Journal of Medicine, 358*, 252–260.

Turner, Marlene E.; Pratkanis, Anthony R.; & Samuels, Tara (2003). Identity metamorphosis and groupthink prevention: Examining Intel's departure from the DRAM industry. In A. Haslam, D. van Knippenberg, M. Platow, & N. Ellemers (Eds.), *Social identity at work: Developing theory for organizational practice.* Philadelphia, PA: Psychology Press.

Turvey, Brent E. (2008). Serial crime. In B. E. Turvey (Ed.), *Criminal profiling: An introduction to behavioral evidence analysis* (3rd ed.). San Diego: Elsevier Academic Press.

Tustin, Karen, & Hayne, Harlene (2006). A new method to measure childhood amnesia in children, adolescents, and adults. Poster presented at the annual meeting of the International Society for the Study of Behavioural Development, Melbourne, Australia.

Tversky, Amos, & Kahneman, Daniel (1973). Availability: A heuristic for judging frequency and probability. *Cognitive Psychology, 5*, 207–232.

Tversky, Amos, & Kahneman, Daniel (1981). The framing of decisions and the psychology of choice. *Science, 211*, 453–458.

Twenge, Jean (2009). Change over time in obedience: The jury's still out, but it might be decreasing. *American Psychologist, 64*, 28–31.

Tyrer, P.; Oliver-Africano, P.C.; Ahmed, Z.; et al. (2008). Risperidone, haloperidol, and placebo in the treatment of aggressive challenging behaviour in patients with intellectual disability: A randomised controlled trial. *Lancet, 371*, 57–63.

Uchino, Bert N. (2009). Understanding the links between social support and physical health: A life-span perspective with emphasis on the separability of perceived and received support. *Perspectives on Psychological Science, 4*, 236–255.

Ullian, E. M.; Chrisopherson, K. S.; & Barres, B. A. (2004). Role for glia in synaptogenesis. *Glia, 47*, 209–216.

Updegraff, John A.; Gable, Shelly L.; & Taylor, Shelley E. (2004). What makes experiences satisfying? The interaction of approach-avoidance motivations and emotions in well-being. *Journal of Personality and Social Psychology, 86*, 496–504.

Urry, Heather L., & Gross, James J. (2010). Emotion regulation in older age. *Current Directions in Psychological Science, 19*, 352–357.

Urry, Heather L.; Nitschke, Jack B.; Dolski, Isa; et al. (2004). Making a life worth living: Neural correlates of well-being. *Psychological Science, 15*, 367–372.

Usher, JoNell A., & Neisser, Ulric (1993). Childhood amnesia and the beginnings of memory for four early life events. *Journal of Experimental Psychology: General, 122*, 155–165.

U. S. Food and Drug Administration (2011). Executive Summary prepared for the January 27–28, 2011 meeting of the neurological devices panel to discuss the classification of electroconvulsive therapy devices (ECT). Available online at www.fda.gov/downloads/AdvisoryCommittees/CommitteesMeetingMaterials/MedicalDevicesAdvisoryCommittee/neurologicalDevicesPanel/UCM240933.pdf.

Uttal, William R. (2011). *Mind and brain: A critical appraisal of cognitive neuroscience.* Cambridge, MA: MIT Press.

Vaillant, George E. (1983). *The natural history of alcoholism: Causes, patterns, and paths to recovery.* Cambridge, MA: Harvard University Press.

Vaillant, George E. (Ed.) (1992). *Ego mechanisms of defense.* Washington, DC: American Psychiatric Press.

Valenstein, Elliot (1986). *Great and desperate cures: The rise and decline of psychosurgery and other radical treatments for mental illness.* New York: Basic.

Valentine, Tim, & Mesout, Jan (2009). Eyewitness identification under stress in the London dungeon. *Applied Cognitive Psychology, 23*, 151–161.

Van Baaren, Rick; Janssen, L.; Chartrand, T. L.; & Dijksterhuis, A. (2009). Where is the love? The social aspects of mimicry. *Philosophical Transactions of the Royal Society of London, B: Biological Sciences, 364*, 2381–2389.

Van Boven, Leaf, & Gilovich, Thomas (2003). To do or to have? That is the question. *Journal of Personality and Social Psychology, 85*, 1193–1202.

Van Cantfort, Thomas E., & Rimpau, James B. (1982). Sign language studies with children and chimpanzees. *Sign Language Studies, 34*, 15–72.

van den Dries, Linda; Juffer, Femmie; van IJzendoorn, Marinus H.; & Bakermans-Kranenburg, Marian J. (2009). Fostering security? A meta-analysis of attachment in adopted children. *Children and Youth Services Review, 31*, 410–421.

van der Toorn, Jojanneke; Tyler, Tom R.; & Jost, John T. (2011). More than fair: Outcome dependence, system justification, and the perceived legitimacy of authority figures. *Journal of Experimental Social Psychology, 47*, 127–138.

Vandello, Joseph A., & Cohen, Dov (1999). Patterns of individualism and collectivism across the United States. *Journal of Personality and Social Psychology, 77*, 279–292.

Vandello, Joseph A., & Cohen, Dov (2008). U.S. Southern and Northern differences in perceptions of norms about agression: Mechanisms for the perpetuation of a culture of honor. *Social and Personality Psychology Compass, 2*, 652–667.

Van Emmerik, Arnold A.; Kamphuis, Jan H.; Hulsbosch, Alexander M.; & Emmelkamp, Paul M. G. (2002). Single session debriefing after psychological trauma: A meta-analysis. *Lancet, 360*, 766–771.

Van Gelder, B. M.; Tijhuis, M.; Kalmijn, S.; & Kromhout, D. (2007). Fish consumption, n-3 fatty acids, and subsequent 5-y cognitive decline in elderly men: the Zutphen Elderly Study. *American Journal of Clinical Nutrition, 85*, 1142–1147.

Van Goozen, Stephanie H. M.; Fairchild, Graeme; Snoek, Heddeke; & Harold, Gordon T. (2007). The evidence for a neurobiological model of childhood antisocial behavior. *Psychological Bulletin, 133*, 149–182.

Van Horn, J. D.; Irimia, A.; Torgerson, C. M.; et al. (2012) Mapping connectivity damage in the case of Phineas Gage. *PLoS One, 7*(5): e37454.

van IJzendoorn, Marinus H.; Juffer, Femmie; & Klein Poelhuis, Caroline W. (2005). Adoption and cognitive development: A meta-analytic comparison of adopted and nonadopted children's IQ and school performance. *Psychological Bulletin, 131*, 301–316.

Van Laar, Colette; Levin, Shana; & Sidanius, Jim (2008). Ingroup and outgroup contact: A longitudinal study of the effects of cross-ethnic friendships, dates, roommate relationships and participation in segregated organizations. In U. Wagner, L. R. Tropp, G. Finchilescu, & C. Tredoux (Eds.), *Improving intergroup relations: Building on the legacy of Thomas F. Pettigrew.* Malden: Blackwell.

van Ommeren, Mark; Saxena, Shekhar; & Saraceno, Benedetto (2005). Mental and social health during and after acute emergencies: emerging consensus? *Bulletin of the World Health Organization, 83*, 71–76.

Van Orden, Kimberly A.; Lynam, Meredith E.; Hollar, Daniel; & Joiner Jr., Thomas E. (2006). Perceived burdensomeness as an indicator of suicidal symptoms. *Cognitive Therapy and Research, 30*, 457–467.

van Schaik, Carel (2006, April). Why are some animals so smart? *Scientific American,* 64–71.

van Tilburg, Miranda A. L.; Becht, Marleen C.; & Vingerhoets, Ad J. J. M. (2003). Self-reported crying during the menstrual cycle: Sign of discomfort and emotional turmoil or erroneous beliefs? *Journal of Psychosomatic Obstetrics & Gynecology, 24*, 247–255.

Vedaa, Øystein; West Saxvig, Ingvild; Wilhelmsen-Langeland, Ane; et al. (2012). School start time, sleepiness and functioning in Norwegian adolescents. *Scandinavian Journal of Educational Research, 56*, 55–67.

Vila, J., & Beech, H. R. (1980). Premenstrual symptomatology: An interaction hypothesis. *British Journal of Social and Clinical Psychology, 19*, 73–80.

Vita, A. J.; Terry, R. B.; Hubert, H. B.; & Fries, J. F. (1998). Aging, health risks, and cumulative disability. *New England Journal of Medicine, 338*, 1035–1041.

Vogelzangs, N.; Kritchevsky, S. B.; Beekman, A. T.; et al. (2008). Depressive symptoms and change in abdominal obesity in older persons. *Archives of General Psychiatry, 65*, 1386–1393.

Volkow, Nora D., & Baler, Ruben D. (2012). To stop or not to stop? *Science, 335*, 546–548.

Volkow, Nora D.; Chang, Linda; Wang, Gene-Jack; et al. (2001). Association of dopamine transporter reduction with psychomotor impairment in methamphetamine abusers. *American Journal of Psychiatry, 158*, 377–382.

Vorona, Robert D.; Szklo-Coxe, Mariana; Wu, Andrew; et al. (2011). Dissimilar teen crash rates in two neighboring southeastern Virginia cities with different high school start times. *Journal of Clinical Sleep Medicine, 7*, 145.

Vrij, Aldert; Granhag, Pär Anders; & Porter, Stephen (2010). Pitfalls and opportunities in nonverbal and verbal lie detection. *Psychological Science in the Public Interest, 11*, 89–121.

Vroon, Piet (1997). *Smell: The secret seducer* (Paul Vincent, Trans.). New York: Farrar, Straus & Giroux.

Vul, Edward, & Pashler, Harold (2008). Measuring the crowd within. *Psychological Science, 19*, 645–647.

Vul, Edward; Harris, Christine; Winkielman, Piotr; & Pashler, Harold (2009). Puzzlingly high correlations in fMRI studies of emotion, personality, and social cognition. *Perspectives on Psychological Science, 4*, 274–290.

Vygotsky, Lev (1962). *Thought and language.* Cambridge, MA: MIT Press.

Wade, Carole (2006). Some cautions about jumping on the brain-scan bandwagon. *APS Observer, 19*, 23–24.

Wagenaar, Willem A. (1986). My memory: A study of autobiographical memory over six years. *Cognitive Psychology, 18*, 225–252.

Wager, Tor D.; Rilling, James K.; Smith, Edward E.; et al. (2004). Placebo-induced changes in fMRI in the anticipation and experience of pain. *Science, 303*, 1162–1167.

Wagner, Christopher C., & Ingersoll, Karen S. (2008). Beyond cognition: Broadening the emotional base of motivational interviewing. *Journal of Psychotherapy Integration, 18*, 191–206.

Wagner, Ullrich; Gais, Steffen; Haider, Hilde; et al. (2004). Sleep inspires insight. *Nature, 427*, 304–305.

Wahlstrom, Kyla (2010). School start time and sleepy teens. *Archives of Pediatrics & Adolescent Medicine, 164*, 676–677.

Wakefield, Jerome C. (1992). Disorder as harmful dysfunction: A conceptual critique of DSM-III-R's definition of mental disorder. *Psychological Review, 99*, 232–247.

Wakefield, Jerome (2011). The DSM-5's proposed new categories of sexual disorder: The problem of false positives in sexual diagnosis. *Journal of Clinical Social Work.* doi: 10.1007/s10615-011-0353-2.

Walker, Anne (1994). Mood and well-being in consecutive menstrual cycles: Methodological and theoretical implications. *Psychology of Women Quarterly, 18*, 271–290.

Walker, David L.; Ressler, Kerry J.; Lu, Kwok-Tung; & Davis, Michael (2002). Facilitation of conditioned fear extinction by systemic administration or intraamygdala infusions of D-cycloserine as assessed with fear-potentiated startle in rats. *Journal of Neuroscience, 22*, 2343–2351.

Walker, Elaine, & Tessner, Kevin (2008). Schizophrenia. *Perspectives on Psychological Science, 3*, 30–37.

Wallace-Wells, Ben (2009, February 5). Bitter pill. *Rolling Stone, 56–63*, 74–76.

Wallbott, Harald G.; Ricci-Bitti, Pio; & Bänninger-Huber, Eva (1986). Nonverbal reactions to emotional experiences. In K. R. Scherer, H. G. Wallbott, & A. B. Summerfield (Eds.), *Experiencing emotion: A cross-cultural study.* Cambridge, England: Cambridge University Press.

Wallen, Kim (2001). Sex and context: Hormones and primate sexual motivation. *Hormones and Behavior, 40*, 339–357.

Waller, Niels G.; Kojetin, Brian A.; Bouchard, Thomas J., Jr.; et al. (1990). Genetic and environmental influences on religious interests, attitudes, and values: A study of twins reared apart and together. *Psychological Science, 1*, 138–142.

Walum, Hasse; Westberg, Lars; Henningsson, Susanne; et al. (2008). Genetic variation in the vasopressin receptor 1a gene (AVPR1A) associates with pair-bonding behavior in humans. *Proceedings of the National Academy of Sciences, 105*, 14153–14156.

Wampold, Bruce (2001). *The great psychotherapy debate: Models, methods, and findings.* Mahwah, NJ: Erlbaum.

Wang, Qi (2008). Being American, being Asian: The bicultural self and autobiographical memory in Asian Americans. *Cognition, 107*, 743–751.

Wang, Alvin Y.; Thomas, Margaret H.; & Ouellette, Judith A. (1992). The keyword mnemonic and retention of second-language vocabulary words. *Journal of Educational Psychology, 84*, 520–528.

Wansink, Brian (2006). *Mindless eating.* New York: Bantam.

Watanabe, Shigeru (2001). Van Gogh, Chagall and pigeons: Picture discrimination in pigeons and humans. *Animal Cognition, 4*, 1435–9448.

Warren, Gayle H., & Raynes, Anthony E. (1972). Mood changes during three conditions of alcohol intake. *Quarterly Journal of Studies on Alcohol, 33*, 979–989.

Watkins, Linda R., & Maier, Steven F. (2003). When good pain turns bad. *Current Directions in Psychological Science, 12*, 232–236.

Watson, John B. (1925). *Behaviorism.* New York: Norton.

Watson, John B., & Rayner, Rosalie (1920/2000). Conditioned emotional reactions. *Journal of Experimental Psychology, 3*, 1–14. (Reprinted in *American Psychologist, 55*, 2000, 313–317.)

Watters, Ethan, & Ofshe, Richard (1999). *Therapy's delusions.* New York: Scribner.

Weaver, Charles N. (2008). Social distance as a measure of prejudice among ethnic groups in the United States. *Journal of Applied Social Psychology, 38*, 778–795.

Wegner, Daniel M., & Gold, Daniel B. (1995). Fanning old flames: Emotional and cognitive effects of suppressing thoughts of a past relationship. *Journal of Personality and Social Psychology, 68*, 782–792.

Wehr, Thomas A.; Duncan, Wallace C.; Sher, Leo; et al. (2001). A circadian signal of change of season in patients with seasonal affective disorder. *Archives of General Psychiatry, 58*, 1108–1114.

Weil, Andrew T. (1974a, June). Parapsychology: Andrew Weil's search for the true Geller. *Psychology Today*, 45–50.

Weil, Andrew T. (1974b, July). Parapsychology: Andrew Weil's search for the true Geller: Part II. The letdown. *Psychology Today*, 74–78, 82.

Weiner, Bernard (1986). *An attributional theory of motivation and emotion.* New York: Springer-Verlag.

Weinstein, Netta; Ryan, William S.; DeHaan, Cody R.; et al. (2012). Parental autonomy support and discrepancies between implicit and explicit sexual identities: Dynamics of self-acceptance and defense. *Journal of Personality and Social Psychology, 102*, 815–832.

Weinstein, Tamara A.; Capitanio, John P.; & Gosling, Samuel D. (2008). Personality in animals. In O.P. John, R.W. Robbins, & L.A. Pervin (Eds.), *Handbook of personality: Theory and research.* New York: Guilford.

Weinstock, Marta (2005). The potential influence of maternal stress hormones on development and mental health of the offspring. *Brain, Behavior, and Immunity, 19*, 296–308.

Weiss, Alexander; Bates, Timothy C.; & Luciano, Michelle (2008). Happiness is a personal(ity) thing. *Psychological Science, 19*, 205–210.

Weissman, Myrna M.; Markowitz, John C.; & Klerman, Gerald L. (2000). *Comprehensive guide to interpersonal psychotherapy.* New York: Basic.

Weisz, John R.; Weiss, Bahr; Han, Susan S.; et al. (1995). Effects of psychotherapy with children and adolescents revisited: A meta-analysis of treatment outcome studies. *Psychological Bulletin, 117*, 450–468.

Wellman, Henry M.; Cross, David; & Watson, Julanne (2001). Meta-analysis of theory-of-mind development: The truth about false belief. *Child Development, 72*, 655–684.

Wells, Brooke E., & Twenge, Jean (2005). Changes in young people's sexual behavior and attitudes, 1943–1999: A cross-temporal meta-analysis. *Review of General Psychology, 9*, 249–261.

Wells, Gary L., & Olson, Elisabeth A. (2003). Eyewitness testimony. *Annual Review of Psychology, 54*, 277–295.

Werner, Emmy E. (1989). High-risk children in young adulthood: A longitudinal study from birth to 32 years. *American Journal of Orthopsychiatry, 59*, 72–81.

Wertheimer, Michael (1958/1923). Principles of perceptual organization. In D. C. Beardslee & M. Wertheimer (Eds.), *Readings in perception.* Princeton, NJ: Van Nostrand. [Original work published 1923.]

Wechsler, David (1955). *Manual for the Wechsler Adult Intelligence Scale.* New York: Psychological Corporation.

West, Melissa O., & Prinz, Ronald J. (1987). Parental alcoholism and childhood psychopathology. *Psychological Bulletin, 102*, 204–218.

Westen, Drew (1998). The scientific legacy of Sigmund Freud: Toward a psychodynamically informed psychological science. *Psychological Bulletin, 124*, 333–371.

Westen, Drew, & Shedler, Jonathan (1999). Revising and assessing axis II, Part II: Toward an empirically based and clinically useful classification of personality disorders. *American Journal of Psychiatry, 156*, 273–285.

Westen, Drew; Novotny, Catherine M.; & Thompson-Brenner, Heather (2004). The empirical status of empirically supported psychotherapies: Assumptions, findings, and reporting in controlled clinical trials. *Psychological Bulletin, 130*, 631–663.

Westling, Erika; Andrews, Judy A.; Hampson, Sarah E.; & Peterson, Missy (2008). Pubertal timing and substance use: The effects of gender, parental monitoring and deviant peers. *Journal of Adolescent Health, 42*, 555–563.

Westling, Erika; Andrews, Judy A.; & Peterson, Missy (2012). Gender differences in puberty timing, social competence, and cigarette use: A test of the early maturation hypothesis. *Journal of Adolescent Health, 51*, 150–155.

Wethington, Elaine (2000). Expecting stress: Americans and the "midlife crisis." *Motivation & Emotion, 24*, 85–103.

Whaley, Arthur L., & Davis, King E. (2007). Cultural competence and evidence based practice in mental health services. *American Psychologist, 62*, 563–574.

Wheelan, Charles (2013). *Naked statistics: Stripping the dread from the data.* New York: Norton.

Wheeler, Mary E., & Fiske, Susan T. (2005). Controlling racial prejudice: Social-cognitive goals affect amygdala and stereotype activation. *Psychological Science, 16*, 56–63.

Whitaker, Robert (2010). *Anatomy of an epidemic.* New York: Crown.

Whiting, Beatrice B., & Edwards, Carolyn P. (1988). *Children of different worlds: The formation of social behavior.* Cambridge, MA: Harvard University Press.

Whiting, Beatrice, & Whiting, John (1975). *Children of six cultures.* Cambridge, MA: Harvard University Press.

Whitlock, Jonathan R.; Heynen, Arnold J.; Shuler, Marshall G.; & Bear, Mark F. (2006). Learning induces long-term potentiation in the hippocampus. *Science, 313*, 1093–1098.

Wicks-Nelson, Rita, & Israel, Allen C. (2003). *Behavior disorders of childhood* (5th ed.). Upper Saddle River, NJ: Prentice Hall.

Widom, Cathy Spatz; DuMont, Kimberly; & Czaja, Sally J. (2007). A prospective investigation of major depressive disorder and comorbidity in abused and neglected children grown up. *Archives of General Psychiatry, 64,* 49–56.

Wiederhold, Brenda K., & Wiederhold, Mark D. (2000). Lessons learned from 600 virtual reality sessions. *CyberPsychology & Behavior, 3,* 393–400.

Wilhelm, Ines; Diekelmann, Susanne; Molzow, Ina; et al. (2011). Sleep selectively enhances memory expected to be of future relevance. *The Journal of Neuroscience, 31,* 1563–1569.

Wilker, Sarah, & Kolassa, Iris-Tatjana (2013). The formation of a neural fear network in posttraumatic stress disorder: Insights from molecular genetics. *Clinical Psychological Science, 1,* 452–469.

Williams, Janice E.; Paton, Catherine C.; Siegler, Ilene C.; et al. (2000). Anger proneness predicts coronary heart disease risk. *Circulation, 101,* 2034–2039.

Williams, Kipling D. (2009). Ostracism: Effects of being excluded and ignored. *Advances in Experimental Social Psychology, 41,* 279–314.

Williams, Lisa A., & DeSteno, David (2009). Pride: Adaptive social emotion or seventh sin? *Psychological Science, 20,* 284–288.

Williams, Redford B., Jr.; Barefoot, John C.; & Shekelle, Richard B. (1985). The health consequences of hostility. In M. A. Chesney & R. H. Rosenman (Eds.), *Anger and hostility in cardiovascular and behavioral disorders.* New York: Hemisphere.

Wilner, Daniel; Walkley, Rosabelle; & Cook, Stuart (1955). *Human relations in interracial housing.* Minneapolis: University of Minnesota Press.

Wilson-Mendenhall, Christine D.; Barrett, Lisa F.; & Barsalou, Lawrence W. (2013). Neural evidence that human emotions share core affective properties. *Psychological Science, 24,* 947–956.

Wilson, Sandra Jo, & Lipsey, Mark W. (2007). School-based interventions for aggressive and disruptive behavior: Update of a meta-analysis. *American Journal of Preventive Medicine, 33,* S130–S143.

Wilson, Timothy (2011). *Redirect: The surprising new science of psychological change.* New York: Little, Brown.

Wilson, Timothy D.; & Gilbert, Daniel T. (2005). Affective forecasting: Knowing what to want. *Current Directions in Psychological Science, 14,* 131–134.

Wiltermuth, Scott S., & Heath, Chip (2009). Synchrony and cooperation. *Psychological Science, 20,* 1–5.

Winick, Myron; Meyer, Knarig Katchadurian; & Harris, Ruth C. (1975). Malnutrition and environmental enrichment by early adoption. *Science, 190,* 1173–1175.

Winnicott, D. W. (1957/1990). *Home is where we start from.* New York: Norton.

Wirth, James H., & Bodenhausen, Galen V. (2009). The role of gender in mental illness stigma: A national experiment. *Psychological Science, 20,* 169–173.

Wisdom, Jennifer P.; Saedi, Goal A.; & Green, Carla A. (2009). Another breed of "service" animals: STARS study findings about pet ownership and recovery from serious mental illness. *American Journal of Orthopsychiatry, 79,* 430–436.

Wispé, Lauren G., & Drambarean, Nicholas C. (1953). Physiological need, word frequency, and visual duration thresholds. *Journal of Experimental Psychology, 46,* 25–31.

Witkiewitz, Katie, & Marlatt, G. Alan (2004). Relapse prevention for alcohol and drug problems: That was Zen, this is Tao. *American Psychologist, 59,* 224–235.

Witkiewitz, Katie, & Marlatt, G. Alan (2006). Overview of harm reduction treatments for alcohol problems. *International Journal of Drug Policy, 17,* 285–294.

Witthoft, Nathan, & Winawer, Jonathan (2013). Learning, memory, and synesthesia. *Psychological Science, 24,* 258–265.

Witvliet, Charlotte vanOyen; Ludwig, Thomas E.; & Vander Laan, Kelly L. (2001). Granting forgiveness or harboring grudges: Implications for emotion, physiology, and health. *Psychological Science, 12,* 117–123.

Wolpe, Joseph (1958). *Psychotherapy by reciprocal inhibition.* Palo Alto, CA: Stanford University Press.

Wood, B.; Rea, M.S.; Plitnick, B.; & Figueiro, M.G. (2013). Light level and duration of exposure determine the impact of self-luminous tablets on melatonin suppression. *Applied Ergonomics, 44,* 237–240.

Wood, James M.; Nezworski, M. Teresa; Lilienfeld, Scott O.; & Garb, Howard N. (2003). *What's wrong with the Rorschach?* San Francisco: Jossey-Bass.

Wood, Joanne V.; Michela, John L.; & Giordano, Caterina (2000). Downward comparison in everyday life: Reconciling self-enhancement models with the mood-cognition priming model. *Journal of Personality and Social Psychology, 79,* 563–579.

Wood, Wendy; Lundgren, Sharon; Ouellette, Judith A.; et al. (1994). Minority influence: A meta-analytic review of social influence processes. *Psychological Bulletin, 115,* 323–345.

Woodward, Amanda L. (2009). Infants' grasp of others' intentions. *Current Directions in Psychological Science, 18,* 53–57.

Woody, Erik Z., & Bowers, Kenneth S. (1994). A frontal assault on dissociated control. In S. J. Lynn & J. W. Rhue (Eds.), *Dissociation: Clinical, theoretical and research perspectives.* New York: Guilford.

Woody, Erik Z., & Sadler, Pamela (2012). Dissociation theories of hypnosis. In M. R. Nash, M. Nash, & A. Barnier (Eds.), *The Oxford handbook of hypnosis: Theory, Research, and Practice.* New York: Oxford University Press.

Wu, Shali, & Keysar, Boaz (2007). The effect of culture on perspective taking. *Psychological Science, 18,* 600–606.

Wynne, Clive D. L. (2004). *Do animals think?* Princeton, NJ: Princeton University Press.

Wyrobek, A. J.; Eskenazi, B.; Young, S.; et al. (2006). Advancing age has differential effects on DNA damage, chromatin integrity, gene mutations, and aneuploidies in sperm. *Proceedings of the National Academy of Sciences, 103,* 9601–9606.

Yalom, Irvin D. (1989). *Love's executioner and other tales of psychotherapy.* New York: Basic.

Yang, Chi-Fu Jeffrey; Gray, Peter; & Pope, Harrison G. Jr. (2005). Male body image in Taiwan versus the West: Yanggang Zhiqi meets the Adonis Complex. *American Journal of Psychiatry, 162,* 263–269.

Yapko, Michael (1994). *Suggestions of abuse: True and false memories of childhood sexual trauma.* New York: Simon & Schuster.

Yehuda, Rachel; Cai, Guiqing; Golier, Julia A.; et al. (2009). Gene expression patterns associated with posttraumatic stress disorder following exposure to the World Trade Center attacks. *Biological Psychiatry, 66,* 708–711.

Yehuda, Rachel; Engel, Stephanie M.; Brand, Sarah R.; et al. (2005). Transgenerational effects of posttraumatic stress disorder in babies of mothers exposed to the World Trade Center attacks during pregnancy. *The Journal of Clinical Endocrinology & Metabolism, 90,* 4115–4118.

Young, Larry J., & Francis, Darlene D. (2008). The biochemistry of family commitment and youth competence: Lessons from animal models. In K. Kline (Ed.), *Authoritative communities: The scientific case for nurturing the whole child.* New York: Springer Science + Business Media.

Yu, Junying; Vodyanik, Maxim A.; Smuga-Otto, Kim; et al. (2007). Induced pluripotent stem cell lines derived from human somatic cells. *Science, 318,* 1917–1920.

Yu, M.; Zhu, X.; Li, J.; et al. (1996). Perimenstrual symptoms among Chinese women in an urban area of China. *Health Care for Women International, 17,* 161–172.

Yu, ManSoo, & Stiffman, Arlene R. (2007). Culture and environment as predictors of alcohol abuse/dependence symptoms in American Indian youths. *Addictive Behaviors, 32,* 2253–2259.

Yuan, Sylvia, & Fisher, Cynthia (2009). "Really? She blicked the baby?" Two year-olds learn combinatorial facts about verbs by listening. *Psychological Science, 20,* 619–626.

Yzerbyt, Vincent Y.; Corneille, Olivier; Dumont, Muriel; & Hahn, Kirstin (2001). The dispositional inference strikes back: Situational focus and dispositional suppression in causal attribution. *Journal of Personality and Social Psychology, 81,* 365–376.

Zaehle, Tino; Sandmann, Pascale; Thorne, Jeremy D.; et al. (2011). Transcranial direct current stimulation of the prefrontal cortex modulates working memory performance: Combined behavioural and electrophysiological evidence. *BMC Neuroscience, 12,* 1–11.

Zajonc, R. B. (1968). Attitudinal effects of mere exposure. *Journal of Personality and Social Psychology, 9,* Monograph Supplement 2, 1–27.

Zhang, Marsha R.; Red, Stuart D.; Lin, Angela H.; et al. (2013). Evidence of cognitive dysfunction after soccer playing with ball heading using a novel tablet-based approach. *PLoS ONE*, 8(2): e57364. doi:10.1371/journal .pone.0057364.

Zhang, Tie-Yuan, & Meaney, Michael J. (2010). Epigenetics and the environmental regulation of the genome and its function. *Annual Review of Psychology*, 61, 439–466.

Zhu, L. X.; Sharma, S.; Stolina, M.; et al. (2000). Delta-9-tetrahydrocannabinol inhibits antitumor immunity by a CB2 receptor-mediated, cytokine-dependent pathway. *Journal of Immunology*, 165, 373–380.

Zimmerman, Frederick J.; Christakis, Dimitri A.; & Meltzoff, Andrew N. (2007). Associations between media viewing and language development in children under age 2 years. *Journal of Pediatrics, 151,* 364–368.

Zone, Nolon; Sue, Stanley; Chang, Janer; et al. (2005). Beyond ethnic match: Effects of client–therapist cognitive match in problem perception, coping orientation, and therapy goals on treatment outcomes. *Journal of Community Psychology, 33,* 569–585.

Zosuls, Kristina M.; Ruble, Diane N.; Tamis-LeMonda, Catherine S.; et al. (2009). The acquisition of gender labels in infancy: Implications for gender-typed play. *Developmental Psychology, 45,* 688–701.

Zubieta, Jon-Kar; Bueller, Joshua A.; Jackson, Lisa R.; et al. (2005). Placebo effects mediated by endogenous opioid activity on μ-opioid receptors. *Journal of Neuroscience, 25,* 7754–7762.

Zucker, Kenneth J. (1999). Intersexuality and gender identity differentiation. *Annual Review of Sex Research, 10,* 1–69.

Zucker, Kenneth J.; Wood, Hayley; Singh, Devita; & Bradley, Susan J. (2012). A developmental, biopsychosocial model for the treatment of children with gender identity disorder. *Journal of Homosexuality, 59,* 369–397.

Zur, Ofer, & Nordmarken, M. A. (2008, May/June). DSM: Diagnosing for status and money. *National Psychologist*, 15.

Zurbriggen, Eileen L. (2000). Social motives and cognitive power-sex associations: Predictors of aggressive sexual behavior. *Journal of Personality and Social Psychology, 78,* 559–581.

Credits

Name Index

Subject Index